Let's Eat FRANCE!

Thanks to ...
Laurence Bloch for giving me the chance to speak at France Inter.
Nadia Chougui, Michèle Billoud, and all the contributing writers to *Let's Eat France!*
Rose-Marie Di Domenico, Elisabeth Darets-Chochod, Emmanuel Le Vallois, and to the team at Marabout.
Anne-Julie Bémont, Emmanuelle Roig, and the publishers of Radio France for their complete support of this project.
Thank you to my parents and to my sister Marielle for the long days of proofreading.
Thank you Nathalie Baud for being with me throughout this project.
Thank you also to Alain Cohen, Roland Feuillas, Philippe Val, Philippe Dana, Lydia Bacrie, Jean-Pierre Gabriel, and Stéphane Solier.

And a special thanks to Alexandra.

**FRANÇOIS-RÉGIS GAUDRY
& FRIENDS**
present

ARTISAN | NEW YORK

Why Let's Eat France?

There are many possible answers to this question . . .

For patriotic reasons: because French cuisine is the best in the world!

For nostalgic reasons: because my grandmother's *fiadone* from Bastia and my mother's cheese soufflé deserve to leave their mark.

For reasons of vanity: it was time to introduce into the vast world of gastronomic literature a comprehensive reference devoted just to the cuisine of France.

For reasons of responding to current trends: the Beuchelle Tourangelle, the Savoyard Fondue, and the Saint-Honoré are simply more fun to eat than the dishes consumed by our vegan friends.

But what if the motivation behind this book was simply epicurean? Or, dare I say, just for cultural reasons as a means to simply compile—for gourmandise, good humor, and a certain erudition—all that has shaped the world of food and drink in France? For more than two years, I have solicited the palates and expertise of dozens of friends, journalists, food artisans, cooks, confectioners, academics, sommeliers, illustrators, photographers, comic strip creators, and family members, to create an eclectic, comprehensive, and unique inventory of France's edible heritage.

The result is this copious *mille-feuille* of foods—one that nourishes us both physically and spiritually.

This book is heavy: 6 pounds (3.1 kilos)! But it is also portable enough to easily grab from your shelf as a reference for everything: from breeds of cows, chickens, and pigs, such as the Basque pig and the Nantaise cow, to the recipes for Alain Passard's salt-crusted beetroot and Philippe-Conticini's Paris-Brest, to the language of Rabelais and the jokes of Carambar.

Welcome to this enticing collection of curiosities specific to my country, France, and its insatiable fascination with all things gastronomic.

Bon appétit!

François-Régis Gaudry

Let's start with an *amuse-bouche*...

Who said:

"These are the famous *doubitchous* of Sofia....

Bruno Moynot in *le Père Noël est une ordure*
(*Santa Claus Is a Stinker*, 1982)

They are made of only good things: synthetic cocoa with margarine and sucrose ... handcrafted, rolled by hand under the armpits!"

"Eating tripe without cider is like going to Dieppe without seeing the sea."

Jean Gabin in *Le Tatoué* (*The Tattooed One*, 1968)

"You will make, with stuffed turkey, the worst meal of your life and with exemplary regularity. It's absolutely disgusting every day, except Sunday, closing day!"

Louis de Funès in *L'Aile ou la Cuisse* (*The Wing or the Thigh*, 1976)

"Listen, ma'am, for now, there's only one thing that makes us hard: it's Beaujolais, there you have it, and blanquette de veau!"

Jean-Pierre Marielle in *Calmos* (1976)

"From containers, his bouillabaisse? Maybe you mean canned? Attention, sir, to what you say, you insult him!"

Fernandel in *La Cuisine au Beurre* (1963)

"It's Monday—it's ravioli!"

Hélène Vincent in *La Vie est un long fleuve tranquille*
(*Life Is a Long Quiet River*, 1988)

"You have **a nice, good wine and you're barely drunk**. Essentially, you do not deserve to drink. Do you wonder why he's boozing it up with the Spaniard? It's to try to forget knuckleheads like you."

Jean Gabin in *Un singe en hiver* (*A Monkey in Winter*, 1962)

"**50** potatoes, a bag of sawdust, he threw out 25 liters of 3-star stuff from the still; a real magician, Jo. And that's why I allow myself to intimate the order of some tidy memory; they would do better to shut down their shit!"

Francis Blanche in *Les Tontons flingueurs* (*Monsieur Gangster*, 1963)

'Do you have some batter?

You have some sugar? With batter, you make a crêpe and you put some sugar on it!"

Bruno Moynot in *Les Bronzés font du ski* (*French Fried Vacation 2*, 1979)

"Where is the veal, the roasts, the sausages? Where are the beans, the venison pâté? We feast until our bellies are full to forget this injustice! Isn't there some soissons with good souavre [a spicy sauce], a piglet, a roasted goat, several well-peppered white swans? These appetizers have made me hungry!"

Jean Reno in *Les Visiteurs* (*The Visitors*, 1993)

"Well, this stew is just disgusting! The sauce is watery. . . . Why didn't you reduce it. . . . I told you twenty times: when the meat is cooked, you keep it warm, and the sauce you reduce separately, in a saucepan, other than a saucepan I said it or I did not?"

Jean Yanne in *Que la bête meure* (*The Beast Must Die*, 1969)

A Gastronomic CHRONOLOGY of FRANCE

Loïc Bienassis

MIDDLE AGES

Sauerkraut appears in Alsace and in the Germanic world.

Grated cabbage is placed in barrels, alternating with layers of salt, and seasoned with juniper berries, dill, sage, fennel, chervil, and horseradish.

1393

A crêpe recipe appears in *Le Mesnagier de Paris* made with wheat flour, eggs, water, salt, and wine, cooked in a mixture of lard and butter.

1552

Rabelais, in *Quart Livre*, uses the word "macaron," borrowed from the Italian, without giving more details on how it's made.

Distillation of eau-de-vie begins in the Cognac region.

1620s

AUGUST 31, 1666

The Parliament of Toulouse forbids selling "as real Roquefort cheese" any cheese that does not come from Roquefort.

13th CENTURY

Brie cheese has already become popular in Paris.

14th CENTURY

The reputation of mustard from Dijon is already well established.

16th CENTURY

The plate replaces the medieval butcher's block.

The fork and separate utensils appear within the high nobility of France.

The book *Cuisinier françois*, by François Pierre de la Varenne. This book breaks with the traditional approach to cooking practiced since the Middle Ages. It covers the use of roux liaisons, gives attention to the flavor of the food, uses butter and cream, uses local herbs and spices, and gives a stronger presence to vegetables.

LAST 30 YEARS OF THE 17th CENTURY

Appearance of sparkling Champagne wines.

1650 1700

Emergence of French "grands crus" wines. The English elite distinguish the wines of Haut-Brion, Château Margaux, Château-Latour, Château-Lafite . . . And in Burgundy, thanks to their wide popularity among the French: Montrachet, Volnay, Chambertin, Vougeot . . .

1320s

First versions appear of *Viandier* by Taillevent, the oldest French cookbook.

1542

Appearance of *Livre fort excellent de cuisine* (anonymous) from Lyon, edited by Olivier Arnoullet, a unique French cookbook of the Renaissance.

1653

Publication of *Pastisser françois* (anonymous). The first body of work exclusively devoted to pastry, such as macarons, puff pastry gâteaux, marzipan, and little cream puffs.

2nd half of the 17th Century

The haricot, coming from the Americas, becomes a food product in the south of France. It replaces traditional legumes used in the local dish "cassolo," the distant cousin of the dish cassoulet.

1702

THOMAS CORNEILLE

His universal *Dictionnaire universel géographique et historique* (published in 1708) mentions "the excellent cheeses of the region of Camembert."

18th CENTURY

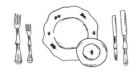

Table settings appear on the tables of the high aristocracy.

1746

The *Cuisinière bourgeoise* by Menon appears. The culinary bestseller of the eighteenth century, it appears in 122 editions up until 1866.

2nd HALF OF THE 18th CENTURY

From the use of a basic pot for cooking emerges the term "pot-au-feu," which means "the amount of meat that should be put in the pot" (*Dictionnaire de l'Académie*, 1798).

Birth of the modern restaurant is attributed to Boulanger. "The purpose of these houses . . . is not to serve food with the host but to serve food any time of the day, per dish, and at a fixed price," according to an almanac of the time. The tables are for individuals and a wide variety of dishes are chosen from a menu where prices are displayed.

1733

Vincent La Chapelle publishes *The Modern Cook* (London), translated into French two years later (*Le cuisinier moderne*, La Haye). Here, the first recipe for "blanquette de veau" (veal in white sauce) appears.

1755

Les Soupers de la cour by Menon is the first French cookbook to contain a recipe with a base of potatoes: "cooked with water, we remove the skin and then put them in a seasoned white sauce or in a mustard sauce."

PALAIS ROYAL

The Palais-Royal becomes the center of Parisian gastronomy: Antoine Beauvilliers is the first restaurateur, followed by the Frères Provençaux, Méot, Véry, and others.

1778

Jean-Pierre Clause, chef of Marshal Contades, creates the foie gras in a pastry crust that becomes a famous dish of Strasbourg.

1790s

The beginnings of truffle farming. Popular since ancient times, *Tuber melanosporum* was exploited only later. The first person to develop its harvesting is the miller Pierre Mauléon, in Poitou.

AROUND 1800

Marie-Antoine Carême (1784–1833) is hired by a famous pastry chef, Sylvain Bailly, located on rue Vivienne. These are the beginnings of this future top chef in the world of haute cuisine.

1801

Publication of the poem *La Gastronomie*, and *L'Homme des champs à table* by Joseph de Berchoux, introduce the word "gastronomy" into the French language.

1803

First edition of *L'Almanach des gourmands* by Alexandre Balthazar Laurent Grimod de la Reynière. Seven other editions will follow, from 1804 to 1812.

Marie-Antoine Carême

1804

In his *Souvenirs de Paris*, the writer August von Kotzebue speaks of a *mayonnaise de poulet* (mayonnaise with chicken). This is the first known occurrence of this term.

1804

AU ROCHER DE CANCALE

In Paris, Alexis Balaine inaugurates his restaurant Le Rocher de Cancale, which becomes famous as a place to eat oysters, next to Les Halles.

1806

Alexandre Viard, *Le Cuisinier impérial*: The first French cookbook to integrate tomato in the form of a sauce.

1809

The *Cours gastronomique*, by Charles-Louis of Cadet de Gassicourt, appears with the first "Gastronomic Map" of France.

1826

Jean-Anthelme Brillat-Savarin publishes *Physiologie du goût, ou Méditations de gastronomie transcendente*, the first book to make good food the subject of philosophical reflection.

1811

Oberrheinisches Kochbuch by Marguerite Spoerlin is published in Mulhouse. The first part is translated into French in 1829 under the title *La Cuisinière du Haut-Rhin*.

1830

LE CUISINIER DURAND
cuisine du midi

First recipe of "bouil-abaïsse à la marseillaise" is published in *Le cuisinier Durand*.

1830s

The hub of Parisian haute cuisine migrates from the Palais Royal to along the boulevards: Boulevard du Temple with Le Cadran Bleu and Boulevard des Italiens with Café Hardy, Café Anglais, Café Riche, and Café de Paris.

GRANDS CRUS CLASSÉS
1855

During the World's Fair in Paris, the Chamber of Commerce of Bordeaux asks several brokers to establish a classification of Bordeaux wines.

The birth of modern oyster farming under the leadership of Victor Coste, inspector general of River and Coastal Fishing. Until then, oysters were simply fished from the waters.

1850   1860

1853

First recipe for small rolls called "croissants," without butter, by Anselme Payen: 2¼ pounds (1 kg) of flour, 1 or 2 eggs, beaten, 1⅛ pounds (500 g) of water and yeast.

1856

Urbain Dubois and Émile Bernard publish *La Cuisine classique, études pratiques, raisonnées et démonstratives de l'école française appliqué au service à la russe.*

18 63

In France, phylloxera is observed for the first time on the plateau of Pujaut, in the Gard region. The crisis will last nearly thirty years.

1866

Baron Brisse is the first culinary columnist to have a column in *La Liberté*. He provides a new menu every day and details the recipes.

The *Grand Dictionnaire universel* by Pierre Larousse (volume II) indicates that the adjective "bourguignon" qualifies as "several dishes prepared with wine" and gives as an example "beef bourguignon."

1867

1873

Jules Gouffé's *Livre de pâtisserie* gives a recipe for "Saint-Honoré: a cream cooked with vanilla," which corresponds almost exactly to the current recipe for the Saint-Honoré pastry. The invention of this cake is credited to Chiboust, a pastry chef on rue Saint-Honoré in the 1840s. Chiboust cream is used as a filling for this pastry.

End of the 19th–Beginning of the 20th Century

New establishments appear that occupy the forefront of the Parisian culinary scene on Place de la Madeleine and rue Royale: Maxim's, Weber, and Lucas (future Lucas-Carton). From the Champs-Élysées to the Bois de Boulogne: Ledoyen, Pavillon de l'Élysée, Laurent, Fouquet's, Grande Cascade, Pré Catelan. On the Left Bank: La Tour d'Argent and Lapérouse.

1884

Chef Auguste Escoffier takes the helm of the Grand Hôtel kitchens in Monte Carlo, run by César Ritz. The birth of modern luxury hotels such as the Savoy Hotel in London, the Ritz in Paris, and the Carlton in London.

December 18, 1889

A newspaper article mentions "Miss Tatin's tart." Stéphanie Marie Tatin (1838–1917) and her sister Geneviève Caroline (1847–1911) run a hotel in Lamotte-Beuvron in Sologne.

1903

Auguste Escoffier publishes *Le Guide culinaire*, a reference text of French haute cuisine for the twentieth century.

August 1, 1905

A law against fraud and falsification of products or services is enacted. It is aimed at the widespread cheating that affects the world of wine, and it creates the *appellations d'origine contrôlée* (AOC).

1st decades of the 20th Century

The term "quiche lorraine" becomes synonymous with a cake made of egg, cream, and bacon. There is use of the word "quiche" in the Lorraine region as early as the sixteenth century.

1912

A decree creates the École pratique d'industrie hôtelière in Thonon-les-Bains. This is the first public school to teach hotel management.

May 6, 1919

A new law is enacted related to protection under *appellations d'origine contrôlée* (AOC), stipulating that "any person who considers that he may have suffered damages directly or indirectly due to protection under an appellation . . . may bring a legal action to prohibit the use by others of this appellation."

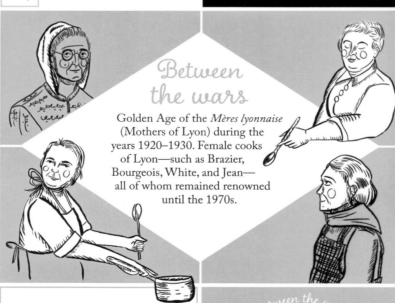

Between the wars

Golden Age of the *Mères lyonnaise* (Mothers of Lyon) during the years 1920–1930. Female cooks of Lyon—such as Brazier, Bourgeois, White, and Jean—all of whom remained renowned until the 1970s.

1921

Curnonsky and Marcel Rouff launch their *La France gastronomique: guide des merveilles culinaires et des bonnes auberges françaises.* There are twenty-six volumes published up until 1928, showcasing the different provinces of France.

JULY 26, 1925

An act is passed to guarantee the *appellation d'origine contrôlée* (AOC) of Roquefort cheese.

1920s

The term "baguette" enters the French vocabulary, describing long white Parisian loaves of bread.

The reputation of France as a country for excellent cheese begins to be established. In 1920, Élisabeth de Gramont, in her almanac of the good things of France, says that "the best cheeses in the whole world are French cheeses."

Between the wars

OCTOBER 1st 1930 A culinary school that prepares students for the trades of baker, butcher, charcutier, cook, grocer, pastry chef, and confectioner opens its doors on rue du Terrage in Paris.

Publication of Ginette Mathiot's *Je sais cuisiner*.

1932

Edward de Pomiane presents the first known radio cooking show on Radio Paris.

1932

 1933

The *Guide Michelin* inaugurates the classification system that we know today: ***Worth a special journey, ** Worth a detour, *A very good restaurant in the area. Twenty-three establishments receive three stars, both in Paris and in the provinces.

1934

The Confrérie des Chevaliers du Tastevin, first of the modern era, is founded in Nuits-Saint-Georges.

1935

Creation of the Comité National des Appellations d'Origine (CNAO), which will eventually become the Institut National des Appellations (INAO) in 1947.

1953
LES RECETTES de M.X

Les Recettes de M. X. is the first cooking show on French television. Raymond Oliver and Catherine Langeais take over with *Les Recettes du chef*, renamed *Art et Magie de la cuisine* in 1955. The program lasts until 1966.

1965

Paul Bocuse gets his 3rd Michelin star for his restaurant L'Auberge du Pont de Collonges.

1965

Publication of Françoise Bernard's *Les Recettes faciles*, by Hachette.

1969

Creation of recipe cards in *Elle* magazine. Madeleine Peter is the first in charge.

1960

The restaurant Les Frères Troisgros adopts *service à l'assiette*, where the plates are prepared in the kitchen before bringing them to the customers. This innovation will be adopted by all the great restaurants.

OCTOBER 1973

The magazine *Gault & Millau* creates the ten commandments of Nouvelle Cuisine: "Thou shalt not overcook; thou shalt use fresh, quality products; thou shalt lighten thy menu; thou shalt not be systematically modernist; thou shalt, however, seek out what new techniques can bring you; thou shalt avoid pickles, cured game meats, fermentations, etc.; thou shalt eliminate rich sauces; thou shalt not ignore dietetics; thou shalt not overdo your presentations; thou shalt be inventive."

Michel Guérard publishes *La Grande Cuisine minceur* (Robert Laffont).

1976

- 1992 -

Yves Camdeborde opens the bistro La Régalade in Paris, marking the beginning of bistro dining (aka "bistronomy").

2·0·0·1

Alain Passard stops cooking red meat at Arpège.

November 16, 2010

The gastronomic meal of the French is added to the UNESCO List of Intangible Cultural Heritage. It is defined as "a customary social practice designed to celebrate the most important moments in the lives of individuals and groups for births, weddings, anniversaries, celebrations, and reunions."

2014

Paul Bocuse celebrates the 50th anniversary of his 3rd Michelin star.

Paul Bocuse

JULY 4, 2015

UNESCO inscribes "The hillsides, maisons, and caves of Champagne" and "The climate of the wine-growing region of Burgundy" on the World Heritage List as cultural landscapes.

The Cornichon (or Gherkin)

The little cornichon commands respect! Far from being insignificant, the minuscule cornichon is an important part of *gribiche* and *ravigote* sauces, an indispensable companion to French terrines, and the paramour of the classic ham and butter sandwich. Here we explore this tiny, but important, condiment.

François-Régis Gaudry

An herbaceous and creeping plant
Name: *Cucumis sativus*
Family: Cucurbitaceae
Origin: western Asia
Season: summer
Calories: 11 calories per 3½ ounces (100 grams)

THE FRENCH CORNICHON COMPARED TO OTHER PICKLES
The French
Small, crunchy, vinegary, spicy. Known worldwide.
The Malossol
In Slavic culture, *malossol* refers to a brine-based fermentation. They are large sour and sweet cornichons (*ogurtsi*), prepared in a brine with spices, garlic, dill, fennel, and sugar.
The Kosher Dill
Prepared with dill, it is widely consumed in Jewish communities in the United States and Canada. It is served particularly with hamburgers.

CUCUMBER AND CORNICHON: THEY ARE THE SAME!
These two cucurbits (plants of the gourd family) belong to the same species, *Cucumis sativus*. Historically, it was the same plant, but the cucumber is grown to maturity while the cornichon is picked while still young. Crossword puzzle fans know that the definition of "old cornichon" is a cucumber.

skip to
Sandwich: The Art of Breaking Bread, p. 297

A word with multiple meanings

"Cornichon" is a diminutive word for *corne* ("**horn**").
In 1547, it denotes a game: *cornichon va devant* ("the cornichon goes first").
In 1549, the meaning of *petite corne* ("**little horn**") has an **erotic connotation**.
In 1808, a "cornichon" is **a fool**.
It is the nickname that is given to the cadets at the school of Saint-Cyr. In the twentieth century, it also refers to **the telephone**, as a reference to its form.
The writer Auguste Le Breton uses it in this sense in his novel *Razzia sur la chnouf* (1954).

HURRAY FOR LA MAISON MARC!
More than 95 percent of the cornichons eaten in France are made in Asia. Cornichons made in France no longer exist, but fortunately one French company is resisting this trend: La Maison Marc, founded in 1952 in Chemilly-sur-Yonne, in the Yonne region. Their cornichons are grown in the ground, without herbicides or insecticides, and have an unmatched flavor and crunch.

★

Brillat-Savarin

Brillat-Savarin is not just the name of a cheese. It is the name of a man who is, above all else, a gastronome and gastronomic writer whose work is still a worldwide success today.
Pascal Ory

WHO WAS HE?
Brillat-Savarin was born neither a cook, like Carême, nor a culinary critic, like Grimod de La Reynière, his two contemporaries. He is the third pillar in this founding trio of French gastronomic culture: *the dinner guest*—and one with enough money to be demanding, enough gourmandise to be tirelessly curious about new experiences, enough intellectual authority to theorize without seeming ridiculous, enough wit to know how to make fun of his professorial tone, and enough writing talent to dazzle Balzac and delight Roland Barthes.

A HEDONIST
Jean-Anthelme Brillat-Savarin was born in 1755 in the heart of Bugey at the southern end of the Jura, where he loved landscapes, tradition, and, mostly, food. He was a cousin by marriage to Madame Juliette Récamier. Elected to the Estates General in 1789, three years later he became a revolutionary, too moderate for radicals. He was exiled for almost four years in the Swiss cantons, then in the United States. When this turmoil had passed, he returned to France in 1796. As a magistrate, he entered, under Bonaparte, into the Court of Cassation where he remained until his death in 1826, meticulously serving during five successive political regimes.

Brillat-Savarin
(1755–1826)

THE MASTER OF BALZAC
Balzac constantly aligned himself with Brillat-Savarin, to the point of adopting the argumentative tone of his book in writing *Physiologie du mariage* (*The Physiology of Marriage*). He went so far as to write the biographical record "Brillat-Savarin," published in 1843, in what was considered the universal biographical reference book of the time. As the author of *La Comédie humaine* (*The Human Comedy*), Balzac's taste for good food is well known, but first and foremost as a writer he was a stylist: "Since the sixteenth century, apart from La Bruyère and La Rochefoucauld, no prose writer has given the French language such a vigorous relief. . . . In his style, all sparkles—everything is as ruby as a blackthorn, like the crimson red lips of the gourmand."

THE BESTSELLER OF GOURMET LITERATURE
Brillat-Savarin's book was a success from the start, which launched the trend of "physiologies," small essays on everyday life. His book has been continually printed for two centuries, with a preface by Balzac and an afterword by Barthes, and was brilliantly translated and annotated in English by the amazing M. F. K. Fisher—a great lover of France and above all its cooking, of whom the English writer W. H. Auden said, that he knew of no one in the United States "who writes better prose."

BRILLAT-SAVARIN IN AMERICA
During his stay in the United States (1794–1796), he makes a living giving lessons in French and violin, then playing in an orchestra in New York. He claims to have introduced scrambled eggs with cheese to America; the dish was placed on the menu of the first French restaurant in Boston. Today in the United States, there is the Académie de Gastronomie Brillat-Savarin.

BRILLAT-SAVARIN, THE PREMIER REGIONAL PERSPECTIVE?
A regional perspective is a foreign concept to the cookbooks of France's Ancien Régime. Brillat-Savarin innovates by repeatedly honoring the delights of his "little homeland," the Bugey, even quoting texts in local dialect. In 1892, the first great book of regional French cuisine by Lucien Tendret, another Bugist, is dedicated as "*La Table au pays de Brillat-Savarin.*"

BRILLAT-SAVARIN EVERYWHERE
Brillat-Savarin's fame is such that, in 1856, a baker gave his name to a cake, which quickly became the name of a particular shape of cake mold. In the period between the world wars, the cheesemaker Androuët named his creamy soft cheese Brillat-Savarin. The most successful gastronomic novel, *La Vie et la passion de Dodin-Bouffant, gourmet*, by Marcel Rouff, is clearly inspired by the life and work of Brillat-Savarin.

A UNIQUE BOOK

La Physiologie du goût (*The Physiology of Taste*), jokingly subtitled *Méditations de gastronomie transcendente* (*Meditations of Transcendent Gastronomy*), appears in December 1825, just over one month before the death of its author Brillat-Savarin. It's a book that combines personal memories, gastronomic theories, and recipes. Some of his quotes from the series *Aphorismes du Professeur* have remained famous:

"Tell me what you eat, **I'll tell you what you are**."

"One can become a **cook** but one must be born a **roaster**."

"**A dessert without cheese** is **like a beautiful woman with only one eye.**"

"**The discovery of a new dish confers more** happiness on humanity

than the discovery of a new star."

France's Little Pralines

From its finest version, those of Montargis, to its least-delicate rendition, the *chouchou*, this French delicacy never goes out of style.

Loïc Bienassis

French definition
Grilled almonds coated with coarse sugar, candied, lending it a rough texture.

Belgian definition
Bonbons made with chocolate, most often filled (with cream, liquor, etc.).

Louisiana definition
Treats made with pecans, cane sugar, milk, and butter. When the French settlers moved to New Orleans in the eighteenth century, they applied their recipe for almonds to pecans.

WHERE DOES THE NAME COME FROM?

The *Dictionnaire françois* (1694) by Pierre Richelet: "For some years we have been calling unskinned almonds cooked in sugar 'almonds à la Prasline,' or simply 'praslines'; they are so called after a sommelier of Marshal Plessis Praslin, who was the first to prepare them in this way." The marshal in question is Caesar de Choiseul-Praslin (1598–1675). The identity of the sommelier, however, is unknown.

THE FIRST RECIPES— PRALINES WITH FLOWERS AND FRUITS

In 1659, the book *Le Maistre d'Hostel qui apprend l'ordre de bien servir sur table* offers recipes for "almond praline" and "violette praline," which are violet flowers placed with almonds in cooked sugar. The flowers attach to the pralines and "will be very beautiful and very good." And it continues with pralines of rose, broom shrub (*genet absolute*), orange, and lemon—the latter two using zests cooked in the sugar.

THE PRALULINE
by François Pralus

Recipe provided by his father Auguste Pralus, Best Craftsman of France (MOF) in pastry, who created it in Roanne in 1955.

SERVES 8 TO 10

2½ cups (250 g) all-purpose flour or Type 55 flour
1 teaspoon (5 g) salt
3 fresh eggs
⅓ ounce (10 g) fresh compressed yeast, crumbled
2½ teaspoons (10 g) sugar
3 tablespoons plus 1 teaspoon (50 mL) water
10½ tablespoons (125 g) high-quality butter, cut into small cubes, slightly softened
11¼ ounces (320 g) good-quality pralines

Equipment
Stand mixer

Prepare the dough the day before: Place the flour in the bowl of a stand mixer fitted with the dough hook. Add the salt, eggs, yeast, sugar, and water. Mix for 4 minutes. Add the butter. Knead for 4 to 5 additional minutes, or until a smooth, supple dough is achieved; wrap the dough in a clean tea towel and refrigerate overnight. The next day, crush the pralines using a mortar and pestle, making sure to leave small pieces for added crunch. Set aside. Roll out the dough onto a floured work surface to a square about ½ inch (1½ cm) thick. ❶ Pour the crushed pralines in the center of the dough, and fold in the sides to enclose the pralines in the center of the dough. ❷ ❸ Roll the dough out thinly again in the shape of a rectangle. ❹ Fold one side and then the other side over into the center. Repeat these steps, flouring the work surface again. Gather the corners of the dough in toward the center and seal them by pressing them down against each other. Gather the four corners again in the same way, turn the dough over, and spread it out by hand ❺ (this step involves turning the dough over onto the floured work surface while keeping it in the palms of the hands). Place the ball of dough on a baking sheet lined with parchment paper. Place in a proofer (or oven) at 113°F (45°C) for 45 minutes. Remove from the proofer or oven and bake in a preheated oven at 300°F (150°C). Leave the door half open and bake for 45 minutes. ❻ Wait a little before enjoying this Praluline. Some prefer to enjoy them warm, but they are usually enjoyed cold, accompanied by strawberries for dessert or with a good breakfast or afternoon tea.

SOME WELL-KNOWN AREAS IN FRANCE FOR PRALINES

1
Aigueperse (Puy-de-Dôme): Famous since the nineteenth century.

2
Montargis (Loiret): Maison Mazet, custodian of the Praslines de Montargis brand, founded by Léon Mazet in 1903.

3
Rhône-Alpes: Pink pralines have become somewhat accepted thanks to several pastries, including brioche from Saint-Genix (Savoie, around 1850), brioche from Bourgoin (early twentieth century), or Praluline by Auguste Pralus, pastry chef in Roanne (1955). As for the praline tart, Alain Chapel borrowed the idea from the cook of one of his friends and popularized it in 1980 in his book *La Cuisine, c'est beaucoup plus que des recettes*. Since then, this tart has adorned the windows of the pastry shops of Lyon.

PINK PRALINES

These are not a result of modern chemistry. In 1692, in the book *Nouvelle instruction pour les confitures, les liqueurs, et les fruits*, François Massialot explains how to make pralines gray, red, white, or gold. Red pralines get their color from cochineal dye: "water in which is boiled cochineal with alum and cream of tartar."

skip to
A Sweet Tour of the Candies of France, p. 164

Praline Production in Roanne

Valencia almonds and Roman and Piedmont hazelnuts are first roasted in the coating machines. Meanwhile, the pastry chef brings the sugar to temperature, then adds coloring and glucose. The last step, the coating, is performed patiently with a ladle. This step is repeated for one hour for each batch of approximately 44 pounds (20 kilos) of pralines. Every day, more than 1,300 pounds (600 kilos) of pralines are made in the Pralus coating machines in Roanne. Most will then be crushed to garnish Pralulines made in Pralus shops.

The Making of Pralulines

The Art of Ti' Punch

Visiting the French West Indies without having ti' punch is a bit like taking a trip to Japan without drinking sake: unthinkable! A vehicle of sociability, this Creole cocktail evokes a joyous intoxication!

François-Régis Gaudry

TI' PUNCH DURING THE COURSE OF A DAY

The "take-off": the first ti' punch of the day, which you drink in the morning and on an empty stomach.

The "ti-lagoutte": the eleven o'clock ti' punch, heralding the noon ti' punch.

The "broken foot": the version that one drinks as a shot at the end of the workday, at the risk of breaking a foot because it might become difficult to walk straight.

The "LRS": the evening's ti' punch (made with lemon, rum, and sugar). The Creole proverb says: *Kote kip a ni wonm, pa ni plei* (Where there is no rum, there is no pleasure).

Clear rum or aged (gold) rum?
Clear rum for purists, but aged rum (preferably around 40 proof) will make you pass as an esthete.

Ice cube or no ice cube?
The authentic ti' punch is simply rum and never "on the rocks." It's the *punch-gendarme*. When it is diluted by adding ice, its nickname is *punch-fillette* (wimp's punch), so called because it is lightened.

Variations?
Substitute the sugar with flavored syrups for a caramel or licorice taste. Add just a few drops of Angostura bitters for extra bitterness. Or grate in a little nutmeg.

skip to
Cuisine of the West Indies p. 350; Rum, p. 393

THE (AUTHENTIC) RECIPE
by Christian de Montaguère*
SERVES 4
1 part cane sugar or simple syrup
4 wedges of lime (very small wedges or ⅛ of a lemon)
4 parts clear rum (*rhum agricole*) from Martinique or Guadeloupe at 50 or 55 proof

Divide the cane sugar (or syrup) among four ti' punch glasses. Squeeze the lime wedges into each glass, then drop in the wedges. Stir with a small spoon to dissolve the sugar; do not muddle the lime too much to avoid adding bitterness. Pour in the rum and stir again. Toast and drink!

One of the world's best rum specialists. A rum cave and delicatessen dedicated to the flavors of the Caribbean, 20, rue de l'Abbé-Grégoire, Paris 5th.

Gastronomy or French Decadence?

In this joyful celebration of French cuisine, this large book, or *grand mille-feuille*, that you hold in your hands, we needed to hear from a contrarian. French-speaking Romanian philosopher and writer Emil Cioran sees gastronomy as nothing more than the swan song of his adopted country. What nourishes the French reflection on food?

"Tearing away values and instinctive nihilism forces the individual to worship sensation. When one believes in nothing, the senses become his religion. And the stomach its finality. The phenomenon of decadence is inseparable from gastronomy. A certain Roman, Gabius Apicius, who roamed the shores of Africa in search of the most beautiful lobsters and who, finding them nowhere to his liking, could not settle in any place, is the symbol of culinary follies that are established in the absence of beliefs. Since France has renounced its vocation, communion has risen to the rank of ritual. What is revealing is not the act of eating, but of meditating, speculating, and talking about it for hours. The awareness of this necessity, the replacement of need by culture—as with love—is a sign of weakening of instinct and of attachment to values. Everyone has had this experience: when we go through a period of doubt in our lives, when everything disgusts, a simple lunch then becomes a party. Food replaces ideas. The French have known for more than a century that they eat. From the lowly peasant to the most refined intellectual, mealtime is the daily liturgy of spiritual emptiness. The transformation of an immediate need into a phenomenon of civilization is a dangerous step and a serious symptom. The belly became the tomb for the Roman Empire, it will be inevitably be that for French Intelligence."

Extracted from *De la France* (1941), *Carnets of L'Herne*.

skip to
A Lesson in French—The "G," p. 27

The Croque-Monsieur

An icon of Parisian brasseries and a loyal companion to the TV tray, the *croque-monsieur* is a true classic—but everyone has his own idea of it. Here is the proof, in three versions.

Mina Soundiram

ITS CREATION

This Parisian sandwich made its appearance in 1910 at Bel Âge, a café on the boulevard des Capucines. According to historian René Girard, bistro owner Michel Lunarca one day made a sandwich using *pain de mie* (white sandwich bread). A customer questioned the meat being used. The owner replied jokingly, "It's the meat of Monsieur!" alluding to the rumor that circulated about cannibalism in his establishment.

THE CROQUE-MADAME

As a companion to the croque-monsieur, restaurateurs created the *croque-madame*: a croque-monsieur topped with a fried egg.

PROUST AND THE CROQUE-MONSIEUR

In 1919, in his book *À l'ombre des jeunes filles en fleur* (*In the Shadow of Young Girls in Flower*), Proust attests the word *croque-monsieur* for the first time. "And when we came out of the concert, as if on the way back to the hotel, we stopped, my grandmother and I, to exchange a few words with Madame de Villeparisis, who told us that she had ordered for us at the hotel 'des croque-monsieur' and eggs cooked in cream." Let us note that Madame de Villeparisis does not use the word in plural—not "croque-messieurs," certainly!

Béchamel or No Béchamel?

Spread béchamel on top if you like your croque-monsieur with a soft layer of this white sauce made from butter, flour, and milk (or cream).

In a Skillet or in the Oven?

Fry the croque-monsieur in a skillet with butter for a beautiful golden color and an unmatched crispness. Bake it in the oven if you do not want the added fat.

White Sandwich Bread or Country-Style Bread?

Use regular white sandwich bread for the classic recipe, but there are several variations using country-style (rustic) bread. The Poilâne bread recipe is so popular in Paris that it has been called a "Croque-Poilâne" (even if it's more of an open-faced sandwich than a croque-monsieur).

---

❶ THE CLASSIC
by Cyril Lignac
Chef of Quinzième (Paris 15th)

PREPARATION TIME: 20 MINUTES
COOKING TIME: 10 MINUTES
SERVES 4

⅔ cup (15 cl) crème fraîche
⅓ cup plus 1 tablespoon (100 mL) heavy cream
5¼ ounces (150 g) grated Comté cheese
1¾ ounces (50 g) grated Parmesan cheese
8 slices sandwich bread
8 thin slices young Cantal cheese
4 slices pressed ham
Grated nutmeg
Freshly ground black pepper

Stir together the crème fraîche and heavy cream. Set aside 2 tablespoons (30 mL) and combine the remaining with the grated Comté and Parmesan. Let stand for 10 minutes. Preheat the oven to 450°F (240°C). Spread the 2 tablespoons (30 mL) of reserved cream mixture in a thin layer on one side of each of four slices of bread. Place a slice of the Cantal on top, then a slice of ham, then a second slice of Cantal. Close with a second slice of bread. Cover the top of the sandwich with the grated-cheese–cream mixture, season with pepper, then sprinkle a little nutmeg on top. Bake for 7 minutes. Set the oven on broil, raise the oven rack so that the sandwiches are close to the heat, and bake for 3 more minutes, or until the cheese on top is browned.

❷ THE POLENTA, HAM, AND CHEESE
by Éric Fréchon
Chef at the Bristol Hotel (Paris 8th)

PREPARATION TIME: 30 MINUTES
COOKING TIME: 35 MINUTES
SERVES 4

4 slices *jambon de Paris* (lightly salted, cooked pressed ham)
4 slices white sandwich bread
3 cups plus 2 tablespoons (750 mL) whole milk
5¼ ounces (150 g) coarse yellow polenta cornmeal
1⅔ cups (400 mL) heavy cream
7 ounces (200 g) Emmental cheese
4 pats (about 1 teaspoon each) unsalted butter
Salt and freshly ground black pepper

Cut out eight square pieces of ham 4 by 4 inches (10 by 10 cm) wide and ⅛ inch (3 mm) thick. Remove the crust from the bread, then process it in a food processor to fine crumbs. Preheat the oven to 325°F (160°C). In a saucepan, bring the milk to a boil, then slowly sprinkle in the cornmeal and cook for 20 minutes over low heat, stirring, while adding the cream little by little and seasoning with salt and pepper. When the polenta is cooked, spread it on a baking sheet in a ⅓-inch- (1 cm) thick layer and refrigerate for 10 minutes to cool. When it is firm, cut the polenta into twelve 4 by 4-inch (10 by 10 cm) squares. Place four squares of polenta side by side on a baking sheet and top each with a slice of Emmental, then a square of ham. Top with another square of polenta and repeat. Sprinkle the bread crumbs over the top, then place a pat of butter on top. Bake for 15 minutes then place under the broiler for 30 seconds. For a smaller portion, create only one layer per sandwich and invite friends to join you!

❸ THE LAUGHING CROQUE
by Yves Camdeborde
Chef of Le Comptoir du Relais Saint-Germain (Paris 6th)

PREPARATION TIME: 5 MINUTES
COOKING TIME: 5 MINUTES
SERVES 4

8 slices sandwich bread
The Laughing Cow cheese
Several slices of ham per sandwich

Spread two slices of sandwich bread with Laughing Cow cheese, top with slices of ham, close, and cook in a skillet over low heat with a little butter. Repeat with the remaining bread, cheese, and ham.

skip to
Cheeses for Melting, p. 114

Pâte de Fruits

It was during the seventeenth century that this cubed confection became the delight of the tables of the bourgeoisie.

Gilbert Pytel

A LITTLE HISTORY
The Egyptians already consumed a kind of pâte de fruits made with honey and flavored with blackberry or quince. The first precisely written recipes appeared in the second century thanks to Greek and Arab doctors who thought the product cured certain ailments.

DELICIOUS PÂTES DE FRUITS FROM FRANCE'S PROVINCES
Guignolettes d'Auvergne: filled with a kirsch-soaked cherry.
Pavés d'Anjou: flavored with Cointreau liqueur.
Pâte de framboise (raspberry) from Colmar: in the shape of raspberries and filled with raspberry liqueur.
Pâte de marron (chestnut) from Tarbes: made with chestnuts from the Pyrénées, lightly flavored with rum and coated in chocolate.

DID YOU KNOW?
→ The fruit pulp must represent 50 percent of the finished product according to the French pâte de fruit *Code d'Usage* (Code of Use), dated September 28, 1999.
→ The name *pâte de framboise* means that only one fruit, the raspberry, has been used, while the name *pâte de fruit à la framboise* indicates that the confection contains a mixture of different fruit pulps along with raspberry.
→ Quince is the most popular, and therefore widely used, fruit for pâte de fruits.

— RASPBERRY — PÂTE
by Jacques Genin*

MAKES ABOUT 2¼ POUNDS (1 KG)

For the pectin mixture
¼ cup (50 g) granulated sugar
½ ounce (15 g) pectin

1⅛ pounds (500 g) raspberry purée**
3 ounces (85 g) glucose syrup
1 pound (450 g) superfine sugar
⅛ ounce (4 g) tartaric acid
A candy thermometer

In a small bowl, combine the granulated sugar and pectin. In a skillet, combine the purée, glucose syrup, and superfine sugar and heat to 176°F (80°C) while stirring. Sprinkle in the pectin-sugar mixture. Increase the heat to 221°F (105°C) while stirring. Turn off the heat and add the tartaric acid; stir well to combine. Pour the mixture into a 15¾ by 2-inch (40 by 60 cm) confectionary frame. Let cool, then slice to the desired size using a guitar slicer (or cut with a knife wiped clean between each slice). This recipe can serve as a base for other flavors.

**Found in specialty grocery stores or online (contains 90 percent raspberry pulp and 10 percent sugar); preferably use frozen brands. Make it yourself using fresh fruit sweetened in the ratio of 10 percent sugar to 90 percent fruit.

skip to
Candied Fruit, p. 43

And Jacques Genin created his pâte de fruits . . .
Pastry chef-chocolatier Jacques Genin states: "A few years ago, while strolling along the banks of the Seine in Paris, I came across a book by Nostradamus called *Traité des confitures*. I used the base recipe from this book. . . . I spent several years and many sleepless nights before coming up with a satisfactory recipe."
*Jacques Genin, 133, rue de Turenne, Paris 3rd

Who Are France's Holy Saints of Foods?

Stéphane Solier

★
GOURMANDS AND GASTRONOMES
Saint Venance Fortunat (December 14)

★
COOKS
Saint Marthe (July 29)
Saint Laurent (August 10), also patron saint of roasters
Saint Euphrosyne (September 11)
Saint Diego d'Alcala (November 12)

★
PORK AND PORK BREEDERS
Saint Antoine le Grand (January 17), also patron saint of truffle farmers

★
CATTLE AND SHEEP BREEDERS
Saint Blaise (February 3)
Saint Marc (April 25)

★
BUTCHERS
Saint Aurélian (May 10)
Saint Barthélemy (August 24)
Saint Luc (October 18)
Saint Nicolas (December 6)

★
HUNTERS
Saint Hubert (November 3)

★
FISHERMEN
Saint Erasme (June 2)
Saint Pierre (June 29)
Saint Gulstan or Goustan (November 27)
Saint André (November 30)

★
SHEPHERDS
Saint Geneviève (January 3)
Saint Germaine Cousin (June 15)
Saint Druon (April 16)
Saint Loup or Leu (July 29)

★
DAIRY FARMERS
Saint Brigide (February 1)

★
CHEESE MAKERS
Saint Uguzon (July 12)

★

★
BAKERS AND PASTRY CHEFS
Saint Honoré (May 16)
Saint Fiacre (August 30)
Saint Michael archangel (September 29)
Saint Macaire (December 8)
Saint Aubert d'Cambrai (December 13)

★
MILLERS
Saint Catherine (November 25)

★
GARDENERS
Saint Agnès (January 21)
Saint Dorothée (February 6)

★
BEEKEEPERS
Saint Maidoc of Fiddown (March 23)
Saint Bernard (August 20)
Saint Ambrose (December 7)

★
TRUCK FARMERS
Saint Fiacre (August 30)
Saint Phocas (September 22)

★
FARMERS
Saint Médard (June 8)
Saint Benoit de Nursie (July 11)
Saint Margaret d'Antioch (July 20)

★
LABORERS
Saint Isidore (May 15)
Saint Guy (September 12)

★
WINE AND VINEGAR MAKERS
Saint Vincent (January 22)
Saint Werner or Verny or Vernier (April 19)

★
BREWERS
Saint Amand de Maastricht (February 7)
Saint Boniface (June 5)
Saint Arnould (August 14)
Saint Venceslas (September 28)

★

skip to
The Gourmet Abbey, p. 77

Oh, Mashed Potatoes!

What's the point of enjoying a Sunday roast at grandma's house without a nice mound of mashed potatoes in which you can dig a well, pour in the gravy, and watch it run out onto your plate? But beware! Making a simple comfort dish such as mashed potatoes isn't as easy as it seems! It takes a little finesse.

Jill Cousin

WHAT A HISTORY!

The destiny of puréed (mashed) potatoes is closely linked to that of puréed soup, for which potatoes can serve as a thickener. It was not until the eighteenth century, with the domestication of the potato in France after the French Revolution, that vegetable purées gave way to those made from potatoes, and the dish became a separate component of a meal.

WHAT VARIETIES OF POTATO SHOULD YOU USE?

Forget the potatoes with a firm flesh that do not mash well. Choose varieties with starchy or soft flesh.

WHEN SHOULD YOU PEEL THEM?

Preferably you peel the potatoes, cut them into equal-size pieces, then wash them to remove any starch *before* cooking them. The purée will be tasty but will also produce more water: remove excess moisture by cooking it over low heat at the end of the cooking time. If you peel the potatoes after cooking them, the purée may be sticky because of the additional starch.

HOW DO YOU COOK THEM?

You can't do without water! Fill your nicest stainless steel pot nearly to the brim! The potatoes must be completely submerged in water. There is no exact science when it comes to the cooking time; the best approach is to regularly pierce a potato with the tip of a knife to check if it is tender, a sign the potatoes are done. If you plan to use salted butter in the potatoes, do not add salt to the water.

HOW SHOULD YOU PURÉE THEM?

Step away from the electric mixer! When using a mixer, the potatoes will be reduced to nearly nothing and will release all their starch, making them gooey. A food mill is most suitable for those who love a smooth purée. Mashing with a fork is best for those who love theirs with small bits of potato. The potato masher guarantees a thick and creamy mashed mixture without requiring too much elbow grease.

HOW DO YOU ACHIEVE A CREAMY TEXTURE?

What's the point of a creamy mixture without the addition of some fat? Purists insist on using cold, diced butter with raw milk that has been warmed, but you can also use olive oil. You will have a hard time achieving a smooth mixture if you add too much of anything . . .

GRANDMA'S MASHED POTATOES

PREPARATION TIME: 20 MINUTES
COOKING TIME: 25 MINUTES
SERVES 6

3⅓ pounds (1.5 kg) Samba potatoes
½ cup minus 1 tablespoon (100 g) salted butter (preferably with sea salt), diced and chilled
⅓ cup plus 1 tablespoon (100 mL) whole milk, warmed
Freshly ground black pepper

Peel and quarter the potatoes. In a large pot filled with cold water, boil the potatoes until tender when pierced with the tip of a knife (about 25 minutes). Drain, then mash them with a potato masher. Add the diced cold butter and the warmed milk. Stir well to thoroughly combine. Season generously with pepper and serve immediately.

skip to
Cooking Vegetables, p. 282; Gratin Dauphinois, p. 197

POTATO PURÉE
by Joël Robuchon

In 1986, Joël Robuchon created this potato purée prepared with La Ratte potatoes, a small potato with a firm flesh, propelling this dish to new gastronomic heights.

PREPARATION TIME: 10 MINUTES
COOKING TIME: 45 MINUTES
SERVES 6

2¼ pounds (1 kg) La Ratte potatoes
Coarse salt
1 cup plus 1 tablespoon (250 g) unsalted butter, chilled
1 cup (250 mL) whole milk

Wash the potatoes but do not peel them. In a saucepan filled with 2 quarts (2 L) of cold water and 1 tablespoon (18 g) of coarse salt, cook the potatoes, covered, until tender when pierced with the tip of a knife (about 25 minutes). Dice the butter and set it aside in the refrigerator. As soon as the potatoes are cooked, drain them. Peel the potatoes when cool enough to handle. Process them over a large saucepan through a food mill fitted with a blade with the smallest holes. Heat the saucepan over medium heat just long enough to slightly dry out the purée, stirring vigorously with a wooden spoon (about 5 minutes). Rinse a small saucepan briefly under running water, then empty it of any water but do not wipe it out. Add the milk to the saucepan and bring it to a boil; set aside. Over low heat, gradually stir the cold butter into the potatoes. Stir vigorously until the mixture is smooth and creamy. Over low heat, slowly drizzle in the milk (which should still be very hot), stirring vigorously until the milk is fully absorbed. Adjust the seasoning as needed. Transfer to a serving dish and serve hot.

Variations

Pomme Duchesse

In a saucepan over low heat, cook 1⅓ pounds (600 g) of mashed potatoes and 3 tablespoons plus 1¾ teaspoons (50 g) of salted butter until any excess moisture is cooked out. Off the heat, vigorously stir in 3 egg yolks. Fill a piping bag fitted with a large fluted pastry tube. Pipe small rosettes onto a greased baking sheet. Bake for several minutes at 350°F (180°C). The potatoes should just turn golden.

Pomme Croquettes

Follow the steps for the Pomme Duchesse recipe, but after adding the egg yolks, pipe a cylinder of potatoes onto a lined baking sheet using a piping bag without a piping tube. Cut the cylinders into even sections measuring 2¼ inches (6 cm) in length. Roll them in flour, dip them in egg yolk, and cover with bread crumbs. Fry them for several minutes in a deep fryer.

Pomme Dauphine

In a saucepan over low heat, cook 10½ ounces (300 g) of mashed potatoes until any excess moisture is cooked out. Off the heat, combine the mashed potatoes with 10½ ounces (300 g) of *pâte à choux* (recipe on page 120). Using two teaspoons, form the mixture into small balls. Fry in a deep fryer.

SERVED AS PART OF A MAIN DISH . . .

Cod Brandade: this is a Languedoc and Provençal specialty made from cod meat emulsified with olive oil and milk. Although not a traditional approach, it is often combined, for reasons of economy, with puréed potatoes.
Hachis Parmentier: a gratin preparation made with puréed potatoes and ground beef.
Aligot: a purée that is stirred together with fresh tomme cheese until a ropelike texture is achieved. For a successful *aligot*, it is necessary to perfectly incorporate the cheese with the potatoes until the mixture "runs."

A Tour de France—Onions

Big, small, peeled, chopped, minced, fried, sliced, confit, glazed, stuffed, puréed, white, yellow, rosé, or red—in any shape, color, or preparation—onions can enliven, or soften, the flavor of any recipe. What would French cuisine be without the onion?

Valentine Oudard

Native to Central Asia, *Allium cepa* is a cousin of garlic and leeks and is probably the most ancient known food crop. Consumed in ancient times by the Egyptians (the workers of the pyramid of Cheops were paid in garlic and onions!), the Greeks, the Etruscans, and the Romans, the onion was the first to be planted in medieval gardens, and one of the most-used ingredients in the kitchen and pharmacopoeia of the time. Starting in the seventeenth century, it was used to accompany and flavor all kinds of dishes, taking the place of many spices. By the nineteenth century, it was considered an essential ingredient in French cuisine.

Brittany

The Pink Onion of Roscoff
History: grown from a seed brought back from Lisbon in 1647 by a monk who planted it at the convent at Roscoff, this onion was eventually cultivated to supply ships, to help prevent scurvy among the sailors. Starting in 1828, "Johnnies," peasants from the region of Léon (now Finistère), sold their onion crops in the ports of England and made a fortune. The AOC (*appellation d'origine contrôlée*, 2009) and the AOP (*appellation d'origine protégée*, 2013) protect its ancestral farming methods, which had been significantly weakened by the competition from hybrid varieties.
Description: an onion that is very sweet and mellow in flavor, with a delicate pink or copperlike peel and white flesh. Does not tolerate refrigeration.
Annual production: 730 metric tons.

Poitou-Charentes

The Sweet Onion of Saint-Trojan , also known as Saint-Turjan or "Rosé des Sables"
History: during the Belle Époque, this onion experienced great popularity. When it was nearing extinction at the end of the twentieth century with the arrival of oyster farming and the development of seaside resorts, a handful of enthusiasts formed the Association of the Onion of Saint-Turjan, which helped revive its production.
Description: a pink onion shaped like a spinning top. Sweet, it could be eaten like an apple.
Annual production: 6 metric tons (5,000 during the Belle Époque).

The Pale Red Onion from Niort
History: a red onion known since the nineteenth century for its pronounced taste and attractive appearance.
Description: a broad and flat bulb, red to coppery pink. Pink flesh; drier than a yellow onion.
Annual production: unknown.

Occitanie

The Sweet Onion of Cévennes or of Saint-André
History: mentioned as early as 1409, it is grown on the southern slopes of the Cévennes. Even if documents provide evidence of its presence in the markets of Nîmes and Montpellier at the end of the nineteenth century, it was really only sold in any significant quantities starting in 1950. It developed thanks to the decline of the cultivation of the mulberry tree from the increase in silkworms that fed on the tree's leaves. It was grown on terraces surrounded by dry-stone walls built in the Middle Ages by the monks to retain cultivable land. It has maintained an AOC (*appellation d'origine contrôlée*) since 2003 and an AOP (*appellation d'origine protégée*) since 2008.
Description: pearly white onion with a slightly elongated and rounded shape.
Annual production: about 2,200 metric tons.

The Onion of Citou
History: the village situated at the foot of the Black Mountain has lent its name to this onion variety, whose seeds have been passed down from generation to generation. The decline of chestnut orchards and viticulture in this area allowed for the farming and commercial growth of this onion, which became a regional specialty beginning in the nineteenth century.
Description: a yellow onion variety with a flattened circular bulb, pearly pink skin, white flesh, and a particularly sweet taste. Renowned for being melt-in-the-mouth sweet and more tender than the sweet onion of Cévennes.
Annual production: about 120 metric tons.

The Cèbe of Lézignan
History: of unknown origin. In the seventeenth century, the town of Lézignan became Lézignan-la-Cèbe (*céba* means "onion" in Catalan), proof of the importance this onion holds as a local product. Today, the *cébières*, the onion-growing lands, have spread to the peripheral communes. The growers created an association with the goal of creating a label for the onion known as "Cèbe de Lézignan."
Description: a circular and flat onion with white skin and flesh, known to be very sweet and juicy. A large onion that can weigh up to 4½ pounds (2 kg).
Annual production: about 250 metric tons.

The Red Onion of Villemagne
History: of unknown origin, but local rumor suggests that its cultivation is very old. However, during the 1970s, young people were no longer taking over their family farms and as a consequence, the onion's production experienced a decline. Its production recovered only after two farmers found the seeds and began production again in 2006!
Description: a very sweet, pink, and flat onion that does not cause burning on the palate and can therefore be eaten like an apple!
Annual production: 1,100 pounds (500 kg).

The Onion of Toulouges
History: a very old crop from the Pyrénées-Orientales. Archives from this department in France mention the throwing of onions between inhabitants of the village in the year XIII of the Republic, a practice that would eventually be prohibited by a town law! Cultivated southwest of Perpignan, it became important in trade during the interwar period, sold by families who, from their carts, would shout, "*Le céba de Toulouges*" ("the onion of Toulouges").
Description: a flattened onion with a ruby-red color and white flesh, renowned for its sweetness. A large, soft onion.
Annual production: not measured.
Use: baked in sweet and savory onion tarts, served every year at the Toulouges Onion Festival.

The Onion of Trébons
History: originally from Bigorre, between the Pyrénées and the upper valley of the Adour, it is mentioned in writings as early as the eighteenth century. The inhabitants of Trébons cultivated it for their personal consumption and sold their surplus in the markets. It was abandoned in favor of corn, and its production declined sharply after 1980. Some small farmers revived their crops in 2000, creating both a committee and a co-op for its production.
Description: an ancient, off-white, elongated bulb–shaped variety with an iridescent green stem. Tender and sweet, it causes little tearing and is easy to digest.
Annual production: not measured.
Use: minced in the dish Chicken with Trébons Onions. The *cébars*, the sweet sprouts of the dried onion, are used in the making of boudin and the Easter omelet.

Corsica

The Onion of Sisco
History: of unknown origin, probably present for several centuries. Discovered one day on the Corsican Cape thanks to a passionate producer who found the seeds in the family attic, leading to the revival of the crop.
Description: a slightly iridescent pink color with white flesh. A tender onion, very similar to the sweet onion of Cévennes. Harvested by hand, it can be kept long term by hanging it in braids or clusters in the attic for consumption the following year.
Annual production: about 50 metric tons, and growing.

Burgundy

The Onion of Auxonne
History: Napoléon, who stayed at the Auxonne artillery around 1790, urged soldiers to eat onions to give them strength and vigor. This onion was therefore widely grown in the Val de Saône region starting in the early nineteenth century. This Mulhouse variety of onion adapted to the sandy soils of the region. Its commercialization developed as a result of mechanized production.
Description: a round bulb, slightly flattened, with coppery skin and yellow flesh. Tender and slightly sweet flavor.
Annual production: about 400 metric tons.
Use: in the famous *oignonade auxonnaise*, an onion confit served with eggs in a *meurette* (red wine) sauce with steamed potatoes.

Auvergne-Rhône-Alpes

The Onion of Tournon
History: it's difficult to date the cultivation of this onion variety, which is similar to the pale red onion of Tournon and the yellow onion of Como. The onion of Tournon, and the onion of Roanne, now extinct, made it possible to mitigate the ravages caused from phylloxera and the silkworm. The elderly population of the area claim that the truck farmers gathered the marc from grapes and the sand from construction sites of dams along the Rhône to grow the onions.
Description: small, round, and flat in shape. Golden in color with a tender and sweet flavor, it is famous for not causing tears when peeled.
Annual production: about 10 metric tons.
Use: traditionally, when the vintners pressed their last vat of the day, they prepared a snack of a salad with onions of Tournon and anchovies.

Alsace

The Onion of Mulhouse and Sélestat
History: an essential product in the daily diet of the poor during the Middle Ages, the onion became a specialty in Alsace during the fifteenth century. In Sélestat, to prevent the wind from carrying away seeds, farmers would press onion seeds into the soil with planks riveted under their trucks, hence the nickname *piétineurs d'oignons* ("onion stompers").
Description: small and golden yellow.
Annual production: no longer commercially produced.

continued →

WHY DOES AN ONION MAKE YOU CRY?

The onion picks up the sulfur from the soil and stores it in its cells in a molecule (1-propenyl-L-cysteine-sulfoxide), which, when the onion is cut, comes into contact with enzymes, causing a chemical reaction that produces an irritating gas. When this gas makes contact with the fluid found in the tear ducts, it becomes a sulfuric acid, causing a person to cry . . .

Tearless techniques for peeling and cutting onions, from the most practical to the craziest

1. Use a blender.
2. Wear a mask or swimming goggles.
3. Soak the onion in vinegar water.
4. Peel the onion outdoors.
5. Peel the onion under water.
6. Wet the knife blade before cutting through the onion.
7. Put the onion in the freezer before peeling it.
8. Light several candles around the cutting board.
9. Place a half-burned match between your teeth while peeling the onion.
10. Clench a metal spoon in your mouth while peeling the onion.
11. Ask someone to do it for you.

2 recipes from Jaïs Mimoun
Chef of Jaïs (Paris 7th)

LA GRATINÉE À L'OIGNON (ONION SOUP)

PREPARATION TIME: 30 MINUTES
COOKING TIME: 20 MINUTES
SERVES 6

¼ cup plus 1 tablespoon (75 g) salted butter
1⅛ pounds (500 g) sweet onions of Cévennes, finely chopped
1 teaspoon (2 g) all-purpose flour
⅓ cup plus 1 tablespoon (100 mL) dry white wine
Several sprigs thyme
1 bay leaf
2 quarts (2 L) chicken broth
Salt and freshly ground black pepper
Freshly grated nutmeg
1 tablespoon (13 g) sugar
6 large slices rustic bread
7 ounces (200 g) grated Comté cheese

Melt the butter in a large saucepan, then add the onions. Cook the onions until lightly browned; add a little water to the pan if they begin to brown too much. Add the flour, wine, thyme, and bay leaf. Stir to combine, then add the broth. Season with salt, pepper, nutmeg, and the sugar and let simmer, uncovered, for about 1 hour.

Preheat the broiler. Prepare six ovenproof soup bowls. Arrange a few scrap pieces of the bread in the bottom of each bowl. Ladle the soup on top, cover the surface of the liquid completely with a slice of bread, then sprinkle with the grated Comté. Place the bowls just under the broiler. When the cheese has browned, the soup is ready!

skip to
Garlic, p. 80

RED ONION AND WALNUT GRATIN

PREPARATION TIME: 20 MINUTES
COOKING TIME: 30 MINUTES
SERVES 6

1⅓ pounds (600 g) red onions
¼ cup plus 1 tablespoon (80 g) unsalted butter
⅓ ounce (10 g) red wine
Salt and freshly ground black pepper
3½ ounces (100 g) grated Parmesan cheese
1¾ ounces (50 g) walnuts, coarsely chopped
½ lemon

Finely mince the onions. Melt the butter in a saucepan, add the wine and onions, then cover. Cook for about 30 minutes; the onions should be very soft and slightly browned. Remove from the heat, season with salt and pepper, and stir in the Parmesan. Preheat the broiler. Transfer the mixture to ovenproof gratin dishes and place them under the broiler until browned. Sprinkle with the walnuts and a squeeze of lemon. Serve hot.

Cheese *and* Dessert

Whether in tarts, brioche, or beignets, cheese has always been an important ingredient in the history of pastry throughout all of France's regions. Here are the cheese-based cakes and pastries of our regions that you must get to know!

Estérelle Payany

LA FLAUNE (Cheese Flan)

A relation to the *fiadone* (a Corsican cheesecake).

Region: Aveyron.

Its appearance: a beautifully golden and refined custard sitting atop a *pâte brisée* (flaky pastry).

Its cheese: the *la recuècha* (meaning "twice cooked")—fresh cheese made of sheep's whey resulting from the production of Roquefort cheese.

Its taste: sweet, flavored with orange blossom—very simple and very good.

Special characteristic: slightly lumpy when cut.

★ ★ ★

LA TARTE AU FROMAGE BLANC (Fromage Blanc Tart)

Also known as *kasküche* in Alsace, *tarte au me'gin* in Lorraine, *tarte au quemeu* in Haute-Marne, and *tarte bourbonnaise* since the Middle Ages. This is the most widespread cheese-based dessert in France!

Regions: Grand Est and Centre.

Its appearance: mostly a tart, but a little like a custard—and always adored.

Its cheese: smooth *fromage blanc*, very drained, sometimes enriched with cream.

Its taste: unctuous, sometimes with vanilla, but just a hint; the quality of the cheese makes the difference.

Special characteristic: Homemade is always best.

★ ★ ★

LA TOURTE AUX BLETTES (Swiss Chard Tart)

As the name suggests, this dessert is vegetable based, but it also contains cheese!

Region: Nice.

Its appearance: a beautifully green tart served as part of the thirteen desserts of Christmas in the region of Nice.

Its cheese: Parmesan, acts as binding agent. Imported from nearby Italy, the Parmesan was sometimes replaced by dry goat cheese.

Its taste: unique, indefinable—and darn tasty to those who set aside their prejudices!

Special characteristic: a must-have at least once in your life!

LA BRIOCHE DE TOMME (Tomme Cheese Brioche)

Lightly sweet, it is the fresh tomme cheese that gives it a faint acidulous taste, an original characteristic of this cake, which is a brioche only in its appearance.

Regions: Cantal, Auvergne.

Its appearance: round and golden, with a soft crumb. Sometimes cooked in a savarin or tube pan.

Its cheese: fresh tomme, the same as is used in *aligot*.

Its taste: surprisingly sweet, delicious with coffee.

Special characteristic: has benefited since 2005 from the brand Parc des volcans d'Auvergne.

LE TOURTEAU FROMAGÉ

One of the few desserts that use goat cheese.

Region: Poitou-Charentes (Deux-Sèvres).

Its appearance: dome shaped; brûléed . . . actually, blackened. This is the only cake that is consumed burned in such a way! Below the burned surface is a soft and melting crumb.

Its cheese: originally goat *faisselle*. Today cow's-milk *faisselle* is most often used.

A tip: the cheese must be very well drained.

Its taste: There is an interesting contrast between the blackened crust and the velvety, slightly sweet crumb.

Special characteristic: usually reserved for important holidays, Easter, Pentecost, or weddings, but it can now be found available year-round.

★ ★ ★

THE RECIPE
by Julie Andrieu

PREPARATION TIME: 20 MINUTES
COOKING TIME: 45 MINUTES
MAKES 1 LARGE BRIOCHE

1 tablespoon (14 g) butter, for greasing the mold

1⅛ pounds (500 g) fresh tomme cheese from Aveyron

3 eggs

1 cup (200 g) sugar

2½ cups (250 g) all-purpose flour

2½ teaspoons (10 g) baking powder (organic)

Preheat the oven to 350°F (170°C). Grease a tube pan with the butter. Crumble the cheese into a large bowl. Add the eggs and sugar; mix well with a fork. Stir the flour and baking powder in a bowl, then combine with the cheese-egg mixture until a sticky paste forms (add up to 1 ounce/30 g of additional flour depending on how runny the tomme cheese is). Scrape the batter into the prepared pan. Bake for 45 minutes, or until the tip of a knife inserted into the cake comes out dry. Serve warm or cold.

The Cheesecake— Is It Norman?

We always talk about "cream cheese" in cheesecake recipes from the United States. These are, however, largely derived from the typical cheesecakes from Eastern Europe (*kaseküchen* in German or *semik* in Polish), which migrants carried in their suitcases when arriving in the United States. And Philadelphia Cream Cheese, created in 1872 and used in most cases, was initially intended to mimic Neufchâtel, a cheese from Normandy! At Frenchie (20, rue du Nil, Paris 2nd), chef Grégory Marchand prepares his using Brillat-Savarin cheese.

skip to
Brocciu, and the Art of Whey, p. 260; At the Dairy, p. 316

Sidonie-Gabrielle Colette

Novelist, journalist, and newspaper food columnist, this endearing woman of letters has always proclaimed her love for the pleasures of the table, from her native Burgundy to her adopted Provence.

Estelle Lenartowicz

HER NATIVE BURGUNDY

It is in her family home in Saint-Sauveur-en-Puisaye that her love of finer things takes root.

Her mother, Sido: having a sweet tooth, Colette's scholarly and refined mother Sido created simple recipes for her daughter yet served them in crystal and porcelain dishes. Some days, she would take her daughter to the large grocery store in the village (to fill up with chocolate, vanilla, and cinnamon), stopping by the butcher shop, where Léonore, the owner, sliced "a ribbon of salted bacon" that little Colette would eat as a treat.

Nighttime cravings: Sido taught Colette her love for animals, plants, and the different seasons. A bit of a wild child, the insatiable Colette would tromp through fields and forests foraging for foods offered by the land, such as water chestnuts or wild strawberries. She would even ask to be awakened at three o'clock in the morning to go "eat to her fill" of strawberries, black currants, and gooseberries.

✦

"**A wonderful time.** We put all the kids together on the beach to cook. Some were roasting on **dry sand**, others were simmering in a bain-marie of **hot puddles**."

Les Vrilles de la vigne, 1908

✦

Woman of letters and culinary columnist
(1873–1954)

✦

"**The pork chop**, whose flavor the cornichon arouses, I do not need to see, because **I sense it**."

Journalist Collette: chronicles and reports

✦

"COLETTE'S PAULINE"

She knows Colette's tastes better than anyone else. Beginning her service for Madame Colette at the tender age of fourteen, Pauline worked all her life (from 1916 to 1954) for the writer as a maid, cook, and companion. Faithful and discreet, Pauline Tissandier knew that "Madame writes better when she eats well." She recalls that at the end of Colette's life, bedridden by her osteoarthritis, Colette began each day with a passionate cry: "Pauliiiiiine, what are we eating today?"

LA FLOGNARDE
Colette's Original Recipe

"Only two eggs, a glass of flour, some cold water or skim milk, a good pinch of salt, three spoonfuls of sugar. In a terrine, you make a well in the flour and sugar and you gradually incorporate the liquid and the whole eggs. You then beat the mixture to a crêpe batter: pour it into a greased tart tin and warm it just on a corner of the stovetop or a hot plate for a quarter of an hour so that the heat from the oven doesn't overwhelm it. After around twenty minutes of cooking, the *flognarde* becomes a huge blister that fills the stove, begins to brown and turns darker, collapses here, swells there. . . . When it's reached its most beautiful state of these various eruptions, remove it, lightly sprinkle it with sugar, then divide it while it's bubbling hot. *Flognarde* loves a sparkling drink: cider, sparkling wine, or a not-too-bitter beer." Colette, *De ma fenêtre*, 1942

PREPARATION TIME:
10 MINUTES
COOKING TIME: 20 MINUTES
SERVES 8

1½ cups (150 g) flour
¼ cup plus 2 tablespoons (75 g) superfine sugar
4 eggs
1 pinch salt
⅔ cup (150 mL) whole milk
1 pinch cinnamon
4 apples, thinly sliced

Thoroughly combine the flour, sugar, eggs, salt, milk, and cinnamon. Line the bottom of a greased tart pan with apple slices and pour the batter over the top. Bake at 400°F (200°C) for 20 minutes.

Her Three Guilty Pleasures

Wine: she takes her first taste as an adolescent. At tea time, her mother-in-law opens aged bottles to introduce her young palate to Château-Lafite and Aux Chambertin. As an adult, she devotes several writings to them (including "La vigne et le vin") and becomes friends with great winemakers and wine traders. A great lover of Château-yquem (a "cure" for her other excesses), she passes away in Paris on rue du Beaujolais, a street whose name befits her.

Garlic: she devours it with *fromage blanc* or even eats the cloves raw "as if they were almonds." A meal is not a meal without a crust of bread bathed in olive oil, rubbed

with garlic, and sprinkled with coarse salt. "When this is all you eat, it makes you feel as if you've escaped to the countryside," she explains in her almanac.

Fish: she discovers the joys of salty flavors while in Brittany at her house in Rozven. On this "rocky perch between the sky and water," the young journalist develops her love for fishing. She catches "bright blue lobsters," "agate-colored shrimp," and "crabs with backs like velvety wool" in her nets. In Provence, her favorite dishes would become scorpion fish (stuffed) and *favouilles* (tiny Provençal crabs) on a plate of rice.

✦

"All is mysterious, **magical**, **spellbinding**, that which is accomplished between the moment of placing a pan or cooking pot and its contents over the fire, and **that sweet moment, full of anxiety** and sensuous hope, when you uncover, on the table, **that steaming dish**."

Prisons et Paradis, 1932

Fried Sea Anemones

Any self-respecting drinker knows the Corsican winemaker Antoine Arena. But who has had the privilege of tasting the beignets prepared by his wife, Marie, with the *bilorbi* (sea anemones) caught by his son Antoine-Marie? This is a rare treat!

Jean-Antoine Ottavi

Scientific name: *Anemonia viridis*

Species: the common anemone is a marine animal, consisting of a contractile fleshy mass crowned at its top by a large number of light green tentacles (200 to 300) with tips that are sometimes purple. Its size varies between 2 inches (5 cm) in height and a diameter of about 4 inches (10 cm). Its stinging venom earned it the nickname "the sea nettle."

Habitat: it is very well distributed throughout the shorelines of France, where it is found in the Mediterranean, the Atlantic from the Canary Islands to Scotland, the English Channel, and the beginning of the North Sea. It is commonly found on well-lit, calm, submerged rocky bottoms just below the surface of the water or in sand up to 65½ feet (20 m) deep, where it attaches to the bottom.

Consumption: sea anemone is rarely eaten. This habit seems to be limited to Corsica, Marseille, and some small areas on the Côte d'Azur.

Season and fishing method: all year. Collected using a fork whose tines have been bent or collected using diving gloves. As a precaution, avoid contact with the eyes before washing your hands.

Taste/texture: a subtle flavor of the sea, becoming chewier in the section closest to the brain.

A little background: in the book *Twenty Thousand Leagues under the Sea* by Jules Vernes, Captain Nemo offers Professor Aronax—a distinguished oceanographer who is both his host and his prisoner—sea anemone jam. In *Finding Nemo*, a Pixar Studios' film, the symbiotic relationship between the clownfish and the sea anemone is depicted.

SEA ANEMONE BEIGNETS
by Marie Arena

PREPARATION TIME: I HOUR
COOKING TIME: 10 SECONDS
SERVES 6

Between 6 to 10 anemones per person
Vegetable oil, for frying
2½ cups (250 g) all-purpose wheat flour
Fleur de sel sea salt
Freshly ground white pepper
Lemon

Thoroughly clean the anemones under water to remove any sand. Drain them, then carefully wipe them dry. Heat the oil in a deep fryer or a skillet to between 325°F (170°C) and 350°F (180°C). Roll the anemones in the flour, tap to remove any excess, then immediately lower them into the hot oil and fry for a good 10 seconds, or just until crisped. Transfer to a paper towel–lined plate to drain. Season lightly with salt and pepper, add a spritz of lemon juice, and serve immediately.

skip to ....
Wild Mollusks, p. 84

CARAMBAR
I thought Mozart was dead
but MOZZAR-et-là.)

Carambar— Laughter in a Bar

This soft caramel, and its legendary wrapper, leaves you not only with a sweet experience to remember it by but with a laugh as well. Created in 1969, Carambar gave its inventors a way to serve up fun along with the extra calories.

Delphine Le Feuvre

AT THE RESTAURANT

Monsieur Dupont exclaims:
"Boy, there's a fly swimming in my soup."
"Oh, it's the chef who added too much soup. Usually, they can touch the bottom!"

The waiter asks the customer:
"How did you find the steak?"
"Oh, quite by chance, by looking under a French fry!"

THE PEOPLE

A customer goes to an art dealer and says:
"I would like something for my dining room. It must be in good taste, not too expensive, and preferably in oil."
"I see," replied the merchant.
"Would you like a can of sardines?"

IN THE KITCHEN

Two eggs meet:
"You look beaten."
"No, I'm totally deflated."

What is a carrot in the middle of a puddle?
A snowman . . . in spring!

A bunch of eggs are lined up together in the fridge. One egg asks the egg next to him:
"Why do you have hair?"
"Because I'm a kiwi!"

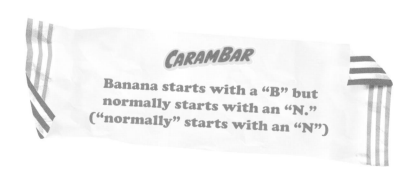

CARAMBAR
Banana starts with a "B" but normally starts with an "N."
("normally" starts with an "N")

skip to ....
Caramel: The Alchemy of Sugar, p. 392

Cardoon—Not What You Think!

The cardoon—cousin of the artichoke—is enjoyed from Lyonnais to Provence.

Camille Pierrard

IT'S NOT CHARD

Recognizable by its long leaves and cut from a blue-green Argenté cultivar, the cardoon is known for its woody stems that resemble those of chard. But the comparison stops there: the chard belongs to the Amaranthaceae family, while the cardoon is part of the Asteraceae family, like the artichoke, which is closer in taste. There are several varieties: completely white and smooth (no thorns); thorny; green-stemmed; and red-stemmed. It is eaten in Lyonnais, Dauphine, Savoie, and Provence. It is harvested in fall and winter, making it a part of holiday meals.

HOW IS IT PREPARED?

To prepare cardoons, cut the stems crosswise into sections measuring 2¾ to 4 inches (7 to 10 cm) in length, then strip off any fibrous strands. We also like to remove the outer membrane that covers the hollow side. Rub the sections with lemon juice to prevent them from turning brown too quickly. To avoid the tedious task of peeling them, you can also purchase them in jars. Cook them in butter, cream, cooking juices from meats, au gratin, or even in a tian—cardoons are a wonderful vegetable to serve as a side dish.

A THORNY SUBJECT

Belonging to the *Cynara* genus, the cardoon (*Cynara cardunculus* var. *altilis*) and the artichoke (*C. cardunculus* var. *scolymus*) belong to the same botanical group: *Cynara cardunculus*. The exact link between them has long been debated. In the middle of the nineteenth century, botanist de Candolle claimed for the first time that cultivated artichokes were actually derived from the wild cardoon (*C. cardunculus* var. *sylvestris*), the primitive form of the cultivated cardoon. Scientific literature has since confirmed this theory: the two plants possess the same common ancestor, the wild cardoon.

THE SHORT HISTORY

Native to the Mediterranean region in its wild form, the cardoon has been cultivated since ancient times by the Greeks and Romans, who probably introduced it to the south of France. It was very popular during the Middle Ages. Its use spread in France along the Rhône corridor to the Alps. After the Edict of Nantes was revoked in 1685, cardoon was exported to Switzerland following the emigration of Protestant farmers, who developed their own variety, the thorny cardoon of Plainpalais, which became very popular among gastronomes.

THE 2 SCHOOLS
Cardoons Gratin

Should you cook them in béchamel sauce or beef bone marrow? Whether you prefer the creaminess of the béchamel or the delectable meaty flavor offered by bone marrow, these two emblematic regional specialties will make everyone agree: the cardoon is delicious!

À LA BÉCHAMEL

PREPARATION TIME: 20 MINUTES
COOKING TIME: I HOUR 20 MINUTES
SERVES 4 TO 6

I bunch cardoons (about 3⅓ lb/1.5 kg)
I lemon
I cup (100 g) all-purpose flour
4 tablespoons plus ¾ teaspoon (60 g) butter
2 cups plus 2 tablespoons (500 mL) cold milk
Salt and freshly ground black pepper
Grated nutmeg
3½ ounces (100 g) grated Emmental cheese (or any good cheese for melting)

Strip the fibrous strands from the cardoon stems, then cut the stems crosswise into sections. Place them in a pot with a mixture of about 2⅛ quarts (2 L) of boiling salted water, the juice of the lemon, ½ cup (50 g) of the flour, and 1 tablespoon (14 g) of the butter. Cook for at least 1 hour (the blade of a knife should easily pierce the cooked cardoons). Preheat the oven to 400°F (200°C). About 25 minutes before the end of the cooking time, prepare the béchamel sauce: melt the remaining butter in a small saucepan and stir in the remaining flour; cook without letting it brown. Add a few spoonfuls of the cold milk, stirring until smooth, then add the remaining milk. Season with salt and pepper and nutmeg. Reduce the heat and cook for 15 to 20 minutes. Drain the cardoons, then dry them with a cloth. Arrange in a baking dish. Top with the béchamel sauce and Emmental. Bake for 15 to 20 minutes, or until the cheese is browned.

À LA BEEF BONE MARROW

PREPARATION TIME: 20 MINUTES
COOKING TIME: I HOUR 30 MINUTES
SERVES 4 TO 6

I bunch cardoons (about 3⅓ lb/1.5 kg)
I lemon
I cup minus I tablespoon (90 g) all-purpose flour
3 tablespoons plus 1¾ teaspoons (50 g) butter
2 or 3 pieces marrow bones
Salt and freshly ground black pepper
3½ ounces (100 g) grated cheese, such as Gruyère

Strip the fibrous strands from the cardoon stems, then cut the stems crosswise into sections. Place them in a pot with a mixture of about 2⅛ quarts (2 L) of boiling salted water, the juice of the lemon, ½ cup (50 g) of the flour, and 1 tablespoon (14 g) of the butter. Cook for at least 1 hour (the blade of a knife should easily pierce the cooked cardoons). About 15 minutes before the end of the cooking time, immerse the marrow bones in a small saucepan of salted water. Bring to a boil and simmer for 10 minutes. Take out the bones and reserve the broth. Preheat the oven to 350°F (180°C). Meanwhile, melt the remaining butter in a separate saucepan. Add ⅓ cup plus 1 tablespoon (40 g) of the flour and make a roux over low heat, stirring constantly. Add the marrow broth (between 1⅔ cups/400 mL and 2 cups/500 mL), stirring until a velvety sauce is achieved. Season with salt and pepper, if needed. Drain the cardoons, then dry them with a cloth. Arrange in a baking dish. Add the marrow bones, sprinkle with the grated cheese, and cover with the sauce. Bake for 30 minutes.

skip to
Artichokes à la Barigoule, p. 224

A LESSON IN FRENCH— THE "G"

The letter **g** in French can be pronounced as a hard sound made with the throat. It is for this reason that it is the letter of many words and ideas relating to the throat and its natural guttural sounds.

The **g** often reflects, in our language, our relation to food and eating.

Aurore Vincenti

A letter whose sounds comes from the throat

For the letter *g*'s origins, we can look as far back as the Indo-European roots of **gwel-** and **gwer-** meaning "to swallow," from which French words such as **gorge** (throat), **gueule** (mouth), and **goulus** (glutton) are derived. The base **gaba** or **gava** also refers to the throat, and thus we see the derivative of such words as **gavage** (force-feeding), as well as the onomatopoeic roots **glut-**, for **glouton** (glutton), and **garg**, associated with **gosier** (throat). Finally, the Gallo roman **gob** (mouth or beak) gave us **gober** (swallow), **goblet**, and **dégobiller** (to throw up). To arrive at the word **gastronomie** (gastronomy), you must begin digestion by going down to the stomach, or the **gaster**.

Manger à grand bruit (To eat loudly)

When at the table, it is strongly discouraged to make noises with your mouth or your throat. However, the root word **garg-** comes from an onomatopoeia. This root suggests a sound from the throat or from a liquid that gurgles and bubbles. This root can be found in English in **gargle**, in German in **gurgeln**, and in Italian in **gargarizzare**.

Gueule (mouth)

➻ **Gueuleton:** this word once evoked the greed and refinement of a feast but, starting in the nineteenth century, the definition changed to describe the convivial and **generous simplicity of a meal** with no conventions. Nothing to be finicky about!

➻ **Goulu:** the adjective *goulu* is used to describe an **eager appetite**, and its root is used in the same sense in the words *ingurgitate* (guzzle) and *regurgitate* (throw up), both without regard for the process of digestion! Gluttons do not care about manners when it comes to cramming things down their throats!

➻ **Gouleyant:** this word, appearing by 1931, is borrowed from the regional French of the West: *Est gouleyant* **le vin qui se coule dans la gorge** ("a lively wine is one that flows easily down the throat"). The sounds made from the linking in French of the **l** and the **y** reinforce the sensation of the silky warmth of a liquid that goes down like velvet.

Gourmand

This word has been subject of many etymological discussions since the sixteenth century, and although the origins of the word *gourmand* remain uncertain, we find the base, **gourm-** ("throat"), common in the words *gourmand, gourme,* and *gourmet*. We have long associated *gourmandise* with **greed** and, therefore, the word *gourmand* with **glouton** (glutton). But in the eighteenth century, the French connotation of the word *glouton* evolved to be closer to that of the word **gourmet**. The word *gourmand*, relieved of its suggested excesses, gracefully switched to the side of **refinement** because the meaning of the word *gourmet* enjoys a refined reputation. Indeed, starting in the fifteenth century, the gourmet became an **expert in wine tasting**. Today, the accepted meaning of the word *gourmand* marries **finesse and fork**.

A "ragoût" for "goûter"?

Goûter in French is a light snack between lunch and dinner, when one avoids something as heavy as, say, a *ragoût* (stew), a dish certainly not intended to simply curb hunger between two large meals! In contrast, the word *goûter* in the seventeenth century meant a dish that was intended to "excite" and "arouse" the appetite." From there is derived the word **ragoûtant** (appetizing), as well as its polar opposite, the word **dégoutant** (disgusting), which, in turn, would come to explain the adjective **ragougnasse** (food that is barely appetizing).

"Gorgeon" (a drink containing alcohol)

This expression dates from the first half of the nineteenth century and refers to enjoying a small libation. The alcohol glides down the throat, where its lingering flavor invites us to take a second drink.

The "Gargouillou"

Chef Michel Bras imagined a dish made of young vegetables, sprouts, leaves, flowers, and other seeds and roots. His name for this dish, *gargouillou*, evokes the sweet symphony of bountiful nature and the gurgling of a small stream. But at the same time, it alludes to the inner workings of digestion! It's the joyful meeting of what is both poetic and natural!

"Le goût"—an exception!

The word *goût* comes from an Indo-European root **geus**, which means "to experience" or "to taste." The ideas of choice *and* discernment are the principal ideas behind "taste." Taste is, therefore, both a flavor and an ability to discern beauty using all the senses: one can have good or bad taste whether one is tasting or not.

★

IS IT "GOÛTEUX" OR "GOÛTU"? It's either, my friend! Using the word **goûteux** would be adhering more to convention than the variant **goûtu**, a word hailing from Normandy and Brittany that spread in the 2000s thanks to **food critics** and is now used around every French table.

★

Gargantua:
this giant found in French literature (François Rabelais, 1534), has the reputation of ingesting astronomical quantities of food and drink. He is, indeed, well named since the word in Old French **gargante** designates the throat. This great character comes from a couple equally well talented since his father, **Grandgousier**, has a large throat and his mother, **Gargamelle**, has a deep throat. **Gargamella**, in Provençal language, refers to the throat. Their pantagruelian appetite gave rise to gargantuan feasts!

Skip to: Michel Bras, p. 175; Rabelais on the Menu, p. 40

Vanilla—The Pleasant Pod

Its universally recognized aroma quickly takes us back to childhood. France has played a key role in the dissemination of vanilla thanks to its many culinary uses, and it is France's overseas territories that are home to some of the best varietals in the world.

Jordan Moilim

A FABULOUS DESTINY

Edmond Albius: this name is known to only a few specialists, but we owe him credit for the global growth of vanilla. In 1841, barely twelve years old, this young slave from Réunion was the first to experiment with manually pollinating the tropical orchid from which vanilla pods grow. Legend has it that one day, when angry at his master, the boy crumpled the flowers of a vanilla orchid in his hands. Thus, a simple fit of rage became a stroke of genius that inspired the famous artificial pollination still used today.

After the abolition of slavery in 1848, Edmond was given the name of Albius, in reference to the white ("alba") color of the flower of the orchid that sealed his fate.

VANILLA'S JOURNEY

Vanilla originated in Mexico. In the sixteenth century, the spice was introduced into Spain before arriving in England in the seventeenth century. France began to pick up on its aroma in the seventeenth century and imported it into Bourbon Island (Madagascar). From present-day Réunion, vanilla was transported to Madagascar in the nineteenth century, and it is also from this same island that the initial plans to bring vanilla to the island of Tahiti began. Finally, it was England that imported vanilla into New Caledonia during the nineteenth century.

PURCHASING VANILLA

To recognize a high-quality vanilla bean, simply roll it between your fingers: it must stick slightly. If the pod gives a little, it means it has a good level of moisture.

Some vanilla beans are marked with a stamp: the grower sometimes marks the pod with his initials as a deterrent against theft.

If the pod has a crystalline coating, or "frost," do not panic; it does not mean it's frostbitten! On the contrary, it is the sign of an exceptional variety called the *vanille givrée* ("givre"). This frost (absent on Tahitian vanilla) is crystallized vanillin. It is important not to remove these crystals, which are the source of vanilla's aromas.

A Botanical Perspective

Vanilla is a climbing orchid that can reach heights of up to 49 feet (15 m). This climber, which clings to its support thanks to its aerial roots, produces white, greenish, or pale yellow flowers grouped in small bunches. After fertilization, the stem at the base of the flower is transformed into capsules commonly called vanilla bean "pods." To proliferate, vanilla must be grown in a tropical climate with significant shade, as the sun can be fatal to the very fragile fruit. After pollination, which occurs artificially on France's island territories—harvest takes place after nine months of maturation.

HANDLING VANILLA: THE RÉUNION APPROACH

Before being sold on the market, the vanilla pod must undergo a "shock" treatment to develop its aromas and to preserve it.

Scalding
To stop their maturation and to allow the development of vanillin, the pods are immersed in water at 149°F (65°C) for 3 minutes.

Steaming
To soften them and to give them their brown color, they are stored—still warm—in wooden crates padded with blankets for one or two days.

Sun drying
For ten days, the pods are exposed to the sun for one to two hours a day, then wrapped in cotton sheets.

Drying in the shade
For a period of two to three months, the pods are left exposed in a shaded and ventilated area.

Calibration
The pods are sorted according to their size in order to prepare them for sale. Those already split are removed.

A World Tour of Vanilla from France

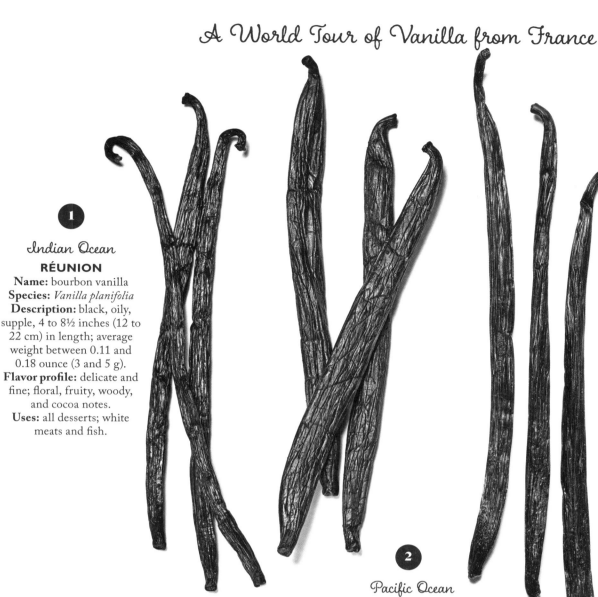

1

Indian Ocean

RÉUNION

Name: bourbon vanilla
Species: *Vanilla planifolia*
Description: black, oily, supple, 4 to 8½ inches (12 to 22 cm) in length; average weight between 0.11 and 0.18 ounce (3 and 5 g).
Flavor profile: delicate and fine; floral, fruity, woody, and cocoa notes.
Uses: all desserts; white meats and fish.

2

Pacific Ocean

FRENCH POLYNESIA

Names: Tahitian vanilla; Taha'a vanilla
Species: *Vanilla tahitensis*
Description: not split; thick, oily, shiny and dark brown surface; 5 to 8½ inches (13 to 22 cm) in length. From 0.18 ounce (5 g) for short ones to ¼ to ½ ounce (12 to 15 g) for larger ones.
Flavor profile: very pronounced vanilla, hints of caramel, licorice, anise, prunes; slight bitterness.
Uses: pastry, ice cream, cocktails, fruit salad, fish.

3

Pacific Ocean

NEW CALEDONIA

Name: "frosted" or givre vanilla
Species: *Vanilla planifolia*
Description: brown to black, fleshy and plump, more than 7¾ inches (20 cm) in length, with a frosted appearance.
Flavor profile: very persistent, round, notes of candied fruit, caramel, and cocoa.
Uses: an excellent varietal that lends itself to all sweet and savory preparations.

ANOTHER REMARKABLE VANILLA

Caribbean

MARTINIQUE, GUADELOUPE, FRENCH GUIANA

Names: vanilla-banana, *vanillon*
Species: *Vanilla pompona*
Description: dark, small, 2¾ to 6 inches (7 to 15 cm), with a characteristic banana shape.
Flavor profile: floral, buttery, tobacco and leather notes.
Uses: cakes, punch, jams, and bananas flambé.

Our Tips on Vanilla

Vanilla milk: split and scrape the beans from a ¾-inch (2 cm) strip of vanilla bean into 1 cup (250 mL) of whole milk and gently bring it to a boil. Steep for 15 minutes off the heat, covered, then reheat it to the desired temperature. This was a childhood treat of Olivier Roellinger!

Vanilla vinaigrette: split and scrape a ¼-inch (0.5 cm) strip of vanilla bean into any salad dressing.

Vanilla sugar: place empty vanilla bean pods in a jar with sugar. Use after a few weeks.

Vanilla veal blanquette: split and scrape the beans from half a vanilla bean into your veal blanquette. This is great for bringing a well-rounded and spicy touch to the dish!

THE CLASSIC CRÈME ANGLAISE

*by Emmanuel Ryon**

This is the perfect recipe for about 1⅛ pounds (500 g) of crème anglaise. But note: a digital scale is a must for precisely measuring each ingredient!

¾ cup plus 3¼ teaspoons (190 g) heavy cream

¾ cup plus 1¾ teaspoons (190 g) milk

½ vanilla bean

2⅔ ounces (76 g) egg yolks (4 to 5 eggs)

3 tablespoons (38 g) superfine sugar

⅛ ounce (5 g) rice flour

In a saucepan, bring the cream, milk, and split and scraped vanilla bean and its seeds to a boil. Vigorously whisk together the egg yolks, sugar, and flour in a bowl until light and frothy. Stir this mixture into the hot cream mixture. Cook over low heat (ideally to 185°F/85°C) while stirring constantly with a spatula. Remove from the heat when the cream coats the back of the spatula. Cool quickly by placing the pan on top of a bowl of ice cubes. Keep refrigerated.

Tip: Infuse the vanilla bean in the cold milk and cream for 24 hours prior to making the crème anglaise.

Meilleur Ouvrier de France (MOF) in ice cream; Une glace à Paris, Paris 4th

The Belgian Endive

This is the story of a wild and bitter chicory, a cousin of escarole and curly endive, which was domesticated by truck farmers, giving birth to the Belgian endive. This is a vegetable that we choose with pleasure!

Marie-Laure Fréchet

Wild chicory

Wild chicory or bitter chicory (*Cichorium intybus*) grows along roadsides, in ditches, or on the edge of the woods. Its starry blue flowers open during the day and wither at night, which earns it the nickname *fiancée du soleil* ("the sun's fiancée").

Cultivated chicory

During the Middle Ages, chicory is cultivated for its medicinal properties. Reference to it is found in the Capitulare Villis of Charlemagne, indicating which plants to grow.

The capuchin beard

In 1630, a Montreuillois cultivated roots of bitter chicory in caves and obtained long, pale leaves. The process became widely popular, and in the nineteenth century, the commune of Montreuil supplied the Parisian markets with fresh lettuce. In 1848, the capuchin beard variety was introduced in Lille by a restaurateur from Lille. Its farming developed in the north of France before declining in the 1950s. Production is now almost gone.

Belgian endive

By adapting the farming methods of the capuchin beard, the Belgians created Belgian endive in 1850. In 1893, Henri de Vilmorin brought back seeds to France and its cultivation flourished in the North.

Hydroponic endive

In 1974, the INRA (Institut National de la Recherche Agronomique, or National Institute of Agricultural Research) marketed the first variety of hybrid endive, allowing out-of-season production and hydroponic farming (currently 95 percent of national production). This Belgian endive takes 20 to 21 days to grow. It is available all year round and also has a less bitter taste, since the new varieties have been modified to be milder and more palatable to consumers.

Coffee Chicory

This industrial chicory developed as a substitute for coffee in the seventeenth century in the Netherlands and then in northern Europe. It owes its growth to the continental blockade under Napoléon, who prohibited the importation of products from England and its colonies, including coffee. The root is cut into cossette (chips), dried, then roasted. Chicory is used in cooking or in pastry in either granular or liquid form. A major food brand has made it a staple of breakfast in France.

GROWING BELGIAN ENDIVE

Only small farms still raise it. This Belgian endive is appreciated for its flavor, its crunchiness, and its performance when cooked.

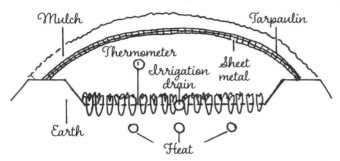

From April to May, a seedling in the open field produces rosettes of leaves connected by a large root. In autumn, the roots are pulled up and the leaves removed. The roots are then protected from the light and "forced" in the ground or in beds covered with a black plastic tarpaulin and a thick bed of straw for insulation. Heat is then applied to the surrounding ground. Belgian endives take four to six weeks to develop new, fleshy, interlocked white leaves. It is harvested starting in January.

ENDIVE, CHICORY . . . A SACRED SALAD!

When the Belgians developed this new kind of vegetable, they named it *chicon*, from the botanical name of the chicory from which it is derived: *Cichorium intybus*. When the vegetable arrived in 1879 at the market at Les Halles de Paris, people searched for a French name for it. Because it was confused with another closely related species, *Cichorium endivia*, it was christened the "Endive of Brussels."

— BELGIAN ENDIVES AND HAM AU GRATIN —

PREPARATION TIME: 45 MINUTES
COOKING TIME: 30 MINUTES
SERVES 4

8 Belgian endives
3 tablespoons plus 2 teaspoons (54 g) unsalted butter
1 teaspoon (4 g) sugar
Salt and freshly ground black pepper
⅓ cup plus 1 tablespoon (40 g) all-purpose flour
2 cups plus 2 tablespoons (500 mL) milk
Freshly ground nutmeg
3½ ounces (100 g) grated Emmental cheese (or any good cheese for melting)
8 slices *jambon de Paris* (slightly salted, cooked pressed ham)

Halve the endives and cut out and discard the hard core. In a skillet, melt 1 tablespoon (14 g) of the butter. Add the endives, sprinkle with the sugar, then season with salt. Add a few tablespoons of water and cook for 20 minutes, turning the endives after 10 minutes. Meanwhile, preheat the oven to 350°F (180°C), and make the béchamel. Melt the remaining butter in a separate saucepan. Add the flour and stir to combine. Cook for 2 minutes, then slowly add the milk while stirring. Let thicken over low heat. Season with salt, pepper, and nutmeg, then stir in half the Emmental. Remove the endives from the skillet, allowing them to drain slightly, then wrap each one tightly with a slice of ham and place it in a baking dish. Cover the endives with the béchamel and sprinkle the remaining Emmental over the top. Bake for 20 to 30 minutes, or until the cheese is golden brown.

IN WHAT OTHER WAYS CAN I PREPARE THEM?

Enjoy them raw in a salad with walnuts or hazelnuts, apples, diced hard cheese, or parsley. Use the leaves **with dips** for an appetizer. **Braise them**, or cook them au gratin or in a tart. **Confit** them to make a chutney.

skip to ....
Let's Talk Salad!, p. 106

Gastronomy Museums

Walking in a museum dedicated to chocolate or randomly stumbling upon a museum of saffron, barley sugar, strawberries, or Camembert cheese? Touring such a museum is an intelligent and delightful way to discover the *terroirs* of France.

Jean-Paul Branlard

THE SAFFRON MUSEUM
Boynes (Loiret)
Since 1988, this museum has been an educational course on the rural heritage of Boynes, tracing the cultivation of saffron, the "red gold" of Gâtinais. Do not miss the "this is too much!" exhibit on the tedious process of weeding the plots of "autumn saffron."

THE CAMEMBERT MUSEUM
Vimoutiers (Orne)
Opened in 1986, this museum bears witness to the traditions of the Pays d'Auge. It includes posters, postcards, a rennet basin, and an iron ladle for scooping curd, among other items. The materials used in a farm from the early nineteenth century are arranged in an authentic setting. About 1,400 Camembert boxes will delight all the *tyrosemitophiles*—cheese-label collectors!

THE STRAWBERRY AND FRENCH HERITAGE MUSEUM
Plougastel-Daoulas (Finistère)
Since opening in 1995, this museum has included nine rooms that present the heritage of Plougastel and its strawberries. The must-see item: the original book of Amédée-François Frézier, recounting his saga of bringing the *Fragaria chiloensis* (white strawberry) from Chile to Brittany in 1714.

THE MUSEUM OF THE ART OF COGNAC
Cognac (Charente)
Opened in 2004 on the ramparts, this museum presents the production of cognac from "viticulture to packaging design," including farming of the Ugni Blanc (Trebbanio) grape, distillation, oak barrels, aromatics (for smelling), and bottling. There is a rich collection of old tools, glassware, labels, and other items.

ARMAGNAC MUSEUM
Condom (Gers)
From a dependency on the former diocese of Condom where Bossuet was a bishop, this museum, which opened in 1954, presents the production cycle of this brandy, which dates back more than 700 years. Stills, old bottles, and an eighteen-ton wooden press delight visitors.

ABSINTHE MUSEUM
Auvers-sur-Oise (Val d'Oise)
This museum, which opened in 1994, re-creates the atmosphere of the cafés of the Belle Époque where the "green fairy" was the chosen drink of the artists. Posters, engravings, glasses, and perforated spoons retrace its role in the life of the nineteenth century before it was declared that this "fairy," or "witch," would drive men insane!

BEER MUSEUM
Stenay (Meuse)
Between the fortified castle of Sedan and the sites of Mémoires de Verdun, the Beer Museum traces, starting from 1986, the history of brewing practices and traditions. The museum includes a reconstruction of a brewery, a café, and a tavern.

THE MUSEUM OF THE VINEYARDS AND WINES OF ALSACE
Kientzheim (Haut-Rhin)
Opened in 1980, this museum features a harvesting car, a mobile press, a mobile still, barrels, vats, and beautiful pieces dedicated to the work of the winemaker and his related trades (barrel and glassmaking). Among the prominent featured pieces are two screw presses from 1716 and 1640.

BARLEY SUGAR MUSEUM
Moret-sur-Loing (Seine-et-Marne)
Barley sugar candy was created in 1638 under Louis XIV by Benedictine sisters. The Barley Sugar Museum has been open since 1994. This museum contains a beautiful staging of a nun in her workshop.

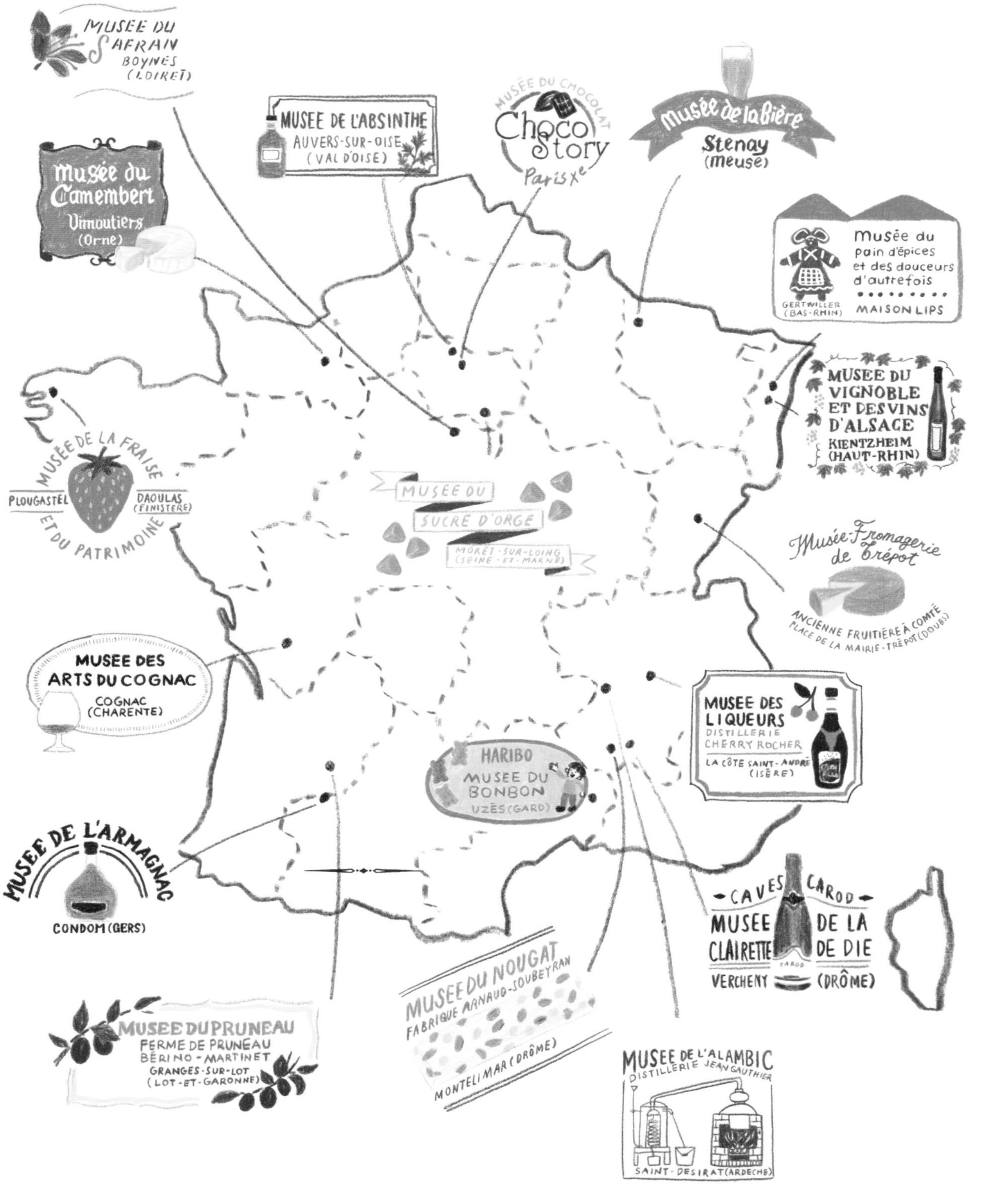

AND ALSO

CHOCO-STORY CHOCOLATE MUSEUM Paris 10th

MUSEUM OF GINGERBREAD AND THE SWEETS OF YESTERYEAR
Maison Lips Gertwiller (Bas-Rhin)

NOUGAT MUSEUM
Arnaud-Soubeyran factory
Montélimar (Drôme)

MUSEUM-FROMAGERIE OF TRÉPOT
In an old fruit store in the comté of Trépot (Doubs)

MUSEUM OF THE STILL
Jean Gauthier Distillery
Saint-Désirat (Ardèche)

LIQUOR MUSEUM
Cherry Rocher Distillery
The Côte Saint-André (Isère)

CLAIRETTE DE DIE MUSEUM
Carod Vercheny wine cellars (Drôme)

PRUNE MUSEUM
Bérino-Martinet prune farm
Granges-sur-Lot (Lot-et-Garonne)

CANDY MUSEUM
St Haribo Uzès (Gard)

skip to
The Brotherhood of French Gastronomy, p. 126

The (Thierry) Far Breton Cake

The Far Breton cake is really intended to just be eggs, sugar, milk, and flour. But then it can get complicated. Should you use buckwheat or wheat flour? Make it with or without prunes? And why not use pork blood? Here, we shed light on this delightful cake from Brittany.

Delphine Le Feuvre

Do You Speak Breton?

Each Celtic territory in Brittany has—or had— its recipe for Far Breton slightly modified!

The farz gwad

A specialty of Ushant Island in which a glass of pork blood is added to the dough! Because in Breton, *gwad* means "blood."

The farz oaled of Ushant

This salty version of the Far is a classic dough filled with smoked bacon, potatoes, raisins, and prunes.

The farz al leue bihan

Nicknamed "the little calf's Far" because it is prepared with the colostrum of the cow; that is to say, the first few days of milk produced by the cow after the birth of the calf.

The farz buan

This means "quick Far" because this recipe involves pouring the batter, a fairly thick crêpe batter, into a crêpe pan or a skillet. The mixture is stirred with a wooden spoon, as if scrambling eggs, while adding sugar and butter. The goal is to create golden, caramelized chunks.

The farz pouloud

An old Léon recipe (northwestern tip of Finistère) similar to the "farz buan." The term *pouloud* means "lump" in Breton.

The billig farz

A Far cooked in a skillet, or rather a thick crêpe that is caramelized with butter and sugar.

THE FAR BATTLE

Prunes or no **prunes**? The debate rages on in the **villages of Brittany**. Some even dare to use **raisins** and caramelized **apples**.

Yet originally, Far Breton used very **few** ingredients. **Thierry Breton**, chef at La Pointe du Grouin (Paris 10th), explains that this **rustic** custard was in the beginning only a wheat **porridge**. It was the privateers of Saint-Malo who added **rum**, **vanilla**, and the **famous prunes** plundered from the **boats of sailors** who landed in Brittany.

skip to
Let's Make a Flan, p. 313

— PEASANT'S FAR —
*by Thierry Breton**

PREPARATION TIME: 10 MINUTES
COOKING TIME: 50 MINUTES
SERVES 4

2¼ cups (220 g) all-purpose wheat flour
¾ cup plus 2 tablespoons (175 g) superfine sugar
1 teaspoon (6 g) *sel de Guérande* sea salt
5 eggs
4¼ cups (1 L) whole milk
1 cup plus 1 tablespoon (250 g) heavy cream
1 tablespoon plus 2 teaspoons (25 g) butter, for greasing the pan
Flour, for flouring the pan

Preheat the oven to 475°F (250°C). In a large bowl, combine the flour, sugar, salt, eggs, milk, and cream. Grease and flour a cake pan with sides; scrape the batter into the pan. Bake for 20 minutes, turn the oven off, then let rest in the oven for another 30 minutes. Let cool before serving.

The PRIVATEER'S
(with prunes)

To the batter add 1 tablespoon (15 mL) rum and 1 vanilla bean (split and its seeds scraped into the batter). Place 35 soft prunes (with the pits) on the bottom of the pan before scraping in the batter.

*Chef at Chez Michel, Casimir, and La Pointe du Grouin, Paris 10th

Pierre Gagnaire

The perennial chef Pierre-Galmier Gagnaire has sowed his inventive and astounding cuisine across the world.
Charles Patin O'Coohoon

"Cooking is not measured in terms of tradition or modernity. What needs to be discerned is the tenderness of the cook."

Pierre Gagnaire

A SIGN

When the chef moved to Saint-Étienne in 1981, the Danish designer Per Arnoldi, who had partnered with the architect Norman Foster, designed a table that has become the chef's emblem.

THE *SURCOUF*

For his military service between 1971 and 1972, he was the admiral-chef on board the *Surcouf*. On June 6, 1971, off the coast of Cartagena, the Soviet oil tanker *General Boucharov* crashed into the French ship. Lives were lost. Pierre Gagnaire just barely escaped.

WHO'S THE BEST?

Pierre Gagnaire has Green Team blood coursing through his veins. In 1963–1964, Saint-Étienne's soccer players would regularly come have lunch at his father's restaurant in Saint-Priest-en-Jarez before games. He was twelve years old and his idols were there in front of him in person. But the most memorable moment remains Saint-Étienne's epic winning streak in the 1970s. The stadium was full and his restaurant, nearby, was empty on game nights. The evening of October 21, 1976, was eventful for him: As Saint-Étienne was going head-to-head against PSV Einghoven in the Coupe d'Europe championship, François Mitterrand dined at his restaurant and his eldest son was about to be born.

Genius of instinct and spontaneity
(born in 1950)

── LOBSTER BISQUE ──

SERVES 4
2 European lobsters (1⅛ lb/500 g to 1⅓ lb/600 g each)
Butter, for sautéing
1 leek, white part only, thinly sliced crosswise
1 onion, peeled and minced
Cognac (2 to 3 tablespoons/30 to 45 mL)
2 fresh tomatoes, chopped
2 cloves garlic, crushed
1 small bouquet garni, with tarragon
1 cup (250 mL) dry white wine
4¼ cups (1 L) fish stock
1 cup (250 mL) crème fraîche
Salt
Ground Espelette pepper

Lower the live lobsters into boiling water for 5 minutes, then remove them and submerge in ice water to cool. Break off the tails and the pincers and remove and reserve the meat. Crush the heads and shells, then sauté them in butter in a saucepan.

Add the leek and onion and stir briefly to combine. Pour in the cognac, then ignite it using a long match. Add the tomatoes, garlic, and bouquet garni. Add the wine and let reduce to three-fourths its original volume, then add the stock. Simmer for 20 to 30 minutes. Add the crème fraîche and cook for 15 minutes over low heat. Drain through a fine-mesh sieve into a bowl, pressing down to release as much of the liquid as possible; reserve the liquid. Add salt and Espelette pepper to taste.

To serve, chop the lobster meat and warm it in a skillet with butter. Divide the meat among four soup bowls. Using an immersion blender, blend the reserved liquid briefly, then pour it over the lobster pieces in the bowls.

THE MENU: THE EMOTION OF WORDS SET TO MUSIC

In 2002, Astonvilla released "Slowfood" from the album *Strange*. A menu by Pierre Gagnaire served as lyrics that were recited by . . .

Jean-Louis Aubert
"A *pascaline* [a traditional Easter dish] of arctic char; a fine escalope poached in an infusion of fresh herbs with Madagascar pepper, straw wine gelée; a bouquet of crayfish in a citron sabayon."

Alain Bashung
"Crispy *mille-feuille* with a 1995 Château Climens; pressed cabbage, beef heart, and crabmeat with melted butter, chervil, and arbutus honey; a variation of green and white asparagus."

Jacques Lanzmann
"Blue fish: steak of bonito tuna cooked in a casserole dish, finished in mackerel vadouvan broth; sardine-eggplant escabèche; fried bluefin tuna bound with a sand shrimp sauce; fresh anchovy pissaladière with cabbage sprouts."

Jean-Pierre Coffe
"Lobster, three ways: small blue lobster poached just before serving then drizzled in browned butter, ginger, and bergamot; a medley of bocconcini, beans, tail and claw meat; consommé glacée with mint, focaccia with roe."

Elise Larnicol
"Sea bass: a fillet of sea bass en papillote with Menton lemon, jus from Jodhpur pearled barley, green-apple glacée, fresh coriander, and grated coconut."

Laurent Muller (called "Doc")
"Soft cookies with Chartreuse, the green liquor made by the Carthusian monks, drops of Yellow Chartreuse; three little heavenly pastries: a *sacristan*, a *religieuse*, a *capucin*." Amen.

skip to
Food That Rhymes, p. 92

France Loves Pasta

From vermicelli to shells, here is a panorama of pasta à la française.
Marie-Laure Fréchet

ITS HISTORY

→ Pasta arrived in France from Italy by way of Provence. **Since the Middle Ages,** the Provençaux have made pastas, served with spices and cheese.

→ Ravioli ❶ arrived from the north, following the conquest of Sicily by the Anglo-Normans. During the **seventeenth century,** ravioli were known as *rafioules* or *raphioules*.

→ **In 1749,** the Corporation des Vermicelliers was created, distinguishing the pasta makers from the bread makers.

→ **In 1767,** the production of pasta was explained by the French doctor Paul-Jacques Malouin in his *Description et détails des arts du meunier, du vermicellier et du boulenger* (Description and Details of the Arts of the Miller, Vermicelli Maker, and Baker).

→ In the **nineteenth century,** there were about twenty pasta factories in France.

PASTA AND FRENCH COOKS

Before the nineteenth century, French cooks took little interest in pasta.

Marie-Antoine Carême (1784–1833) creates recipes for soups including vermicelli, noodles, or macaroni, as well as the dish *timbale à la Mantoue*, filled with lasagna, truffles, and foie gras, topped with a skewer of rooster's comb.

Jules Gouffé devotes a chapter to pasta and timbales in his *Livre de cuisine* (1867). There are recipes for macaroni au gratin, noodles with ham, and a Milanese timbale.

Auguste Escoffier dedicates a section to pasta in his *Guide culinaire* (1903). Pasta is served "Italian," "Milanese," or "Sicilian" style. The book also provides a truffle pasta recipe: 3½ ounces (100 g) raw truffle shavings for every 9 ounces (250 g) of pasta.

Raymond Oliver signs a *Célébration de la nouille* (Celebration of the Noodle) in 1965.

Éric Frechon, chef at the Bristol in Paris, creates pasta stuffed with truffles in 1999.

Alsatian pasta

Pasta appeared in Alsace around the fifteenth century and was rich in eggs: seven eggs per 2¼ pounds (1 kg) of durum wheat flour.

Wasser Striebele consists of a wet dough: **Spätzle** ❷ and **Knepfle** ❸ are included. To make the Spätzle, thin strips of pasta are dropped into boiling water using a special board or a large grater. They are served immediately after being made. Knepfle are a shorter and thicker variety, similar to gnocchi.

The Nüdle ❹ are wide strips cut from pasta that has been rolled out. They are usually formed in the shape of a nest.

Auvergne-Rhône-Alpes
The pasta of the Savoie

Crozets ❺ more than likely originated from *crozetos*, a small round Italian pasta flattened with the finger, similar to *orechiette*. They took on their characteristic square shape starting in the seventeenth century in the Savoie. Today's *crozets* are ¼-inch (5 mm) squares of ⅒ inch (2 mm) thickness. They are made of either hard or soft wheat flour or buckwheat flour.

Taillerins ❻ are ribbon pasta with porcini and bolete mushrooms, chestnuts, *trompettes-des-morts* (horn of plenty), or blueberries.

The pasta of Isère

The ravioli of Dauphiné ❼ (also known under the commercial name *ravioli de Romans* or *du Royans*). Protected by an AOC (*appellation d'origine contrôlée*) and a PGI (Protected Geographical Indication), these are small squares of wheat flour, egg, and water, filled with a mixture of Comté cheese or French Emmental, cottage cheese, and parsley sautéed in butter. Very popular during the nineteenth century, ravioli were handmade by *ravioleuses* who would travel to people's homes to sell their ravioli.

The pasta of Auvergne

Lozans were traditional pasta, cut into small lozenge shapes, consumed as a soup.

The pasta of Provence-Alpes-Côte d'Azur (PACA) and Corsica

The area including Nice claims a tradition of making fresh pasta, as continued today by Maison Brale, an artisan vermicelli maker in Nice since 1892, and the maker of specialties such as gnocchi ❽ or ravioli stuffed with *daube niçoise* and Swiss chard greens. Corsica also continues this tradition with recipes such as **pastacuitta** (spaghetti, beef, tomato, and olive) or **stufatu** (beef stew with fresh pasta).

The pasta of the West Indies

In the West Indies, the **dombrés** ❾ are small balls made from flour and water and boiled in water, similar to gnocchi, served in a sauce. They are an ingredient of *bébélé*, a dish by Marie-Galante made with tripe.

NOODLES FOR ONE
by Raymond Oliver*

3 tablespoons plus 1¾ teaspoons (50 g) unsalted butter
4 tablespoons (60 mL) olive oil
4½ ounces (125 g) very fresh and attractive white button mushrooms
4½ ounces (125 g) blanched noodles, kept warm
Salt
Cayenne pepper
Paprika
3 or 4 eggs

In a skillet, heat half the butter and oil, then add the mushrooms and sauté them until nicely browned. Add about three-fourths of the noodles and give them several turns to coat them well; season with salt, cayenne, and paprika.

Transfer the noodles to a baking dish. Make three or four cavities in the noodles, then break an egg into each of them. Place in the oven. In the same skillet, heat the remaining butter and oil and fry the remaining noodles until crunchy. Once out of the oven, top the baking dish with the crunchy noodles. Relax and enjoy this dish with this year's Beaujolais or a young and fruity Bordeaux. It's a great dish for a hungry person!

*Former chef of Le Grand Véfour, Paris 1st

TIMBALE MILANESE
A modern version (each grandmother has her own recipe)

MAKES I TIMBALE

1⅛ pounds (500 g) long macaroni noodles
1 onion
7 ounces (200 g) mushrooms
4½ ounces (125 g) *jambon de Paris* (slightly salted, cooked pressed ham)
3 eggs
Salt and freshly ground black pepper
2 teaspoons (10 g) butter, plus more for greasing the pan
1 small can (2½ oz/70 g) tomato paste
9 ounces (250 g) grated Emmental cheese (or any good cheese for melting)

Cook the noodles in boiling salted water until al dente. Drain, reserving 1 cup of the pasta water. Peel and slice the onion. Clean and slice the mushrooms. Dice the ham. Lightly beat the eggs together in a bowl with a fork, then season them with salt and pepper. Heat the 2 teaspoons (10 g) of butter in a skillet and sauté the onion, mushrooms, and ham over high heat for a few minutes, while stirring. Add the tomato paste and a little bit of the reserved pasta water, just enough to smooth out the mixture. Preheat the oven to 350°F (180°C). Grease a cake pan with butter. Place a layer of the noodles on the bottom of the pan, arranging them in a spiral. Stack the noodles against the sides of the pan to about 1⅛ inches (3 cm) high. Fill the center with the cooked ham mixture, then sprinkle with some of the grated cheese. Repeat this step until the pan is full, then pour the beaten eggs over the top. Top with a layer of noodles arranged in a spiral. Place an empty shallow plate on top and weigh it down to keep the contents of the pan gently pressed. Cook in a bain-marie for 1 hour.

skip to
Raymond Oliver, p. 359

PASTAS THE FRENCH ADORE

These are pastas that have become available in recent years and are now part of French culinary heritage.

Les coquillettes (elbow pasta) ⑩
Cooked in butter, au gratin with ham, or in risotto.

Noodles (short)
These got their name from an architectural style called Art Nouveau, renamed *noodle style* by its detractors.

Macaroni ⑪
These come from Italy but the French have adopted them in recipes such as macaroni au gratin, timbale Milanese, or *sétoise macaronade* (from Sète)

Alphabet pasta ⑫
Spaghetti alphabetti in Italy, *alphabet pasta* in the United States, these letter-shaped pasta have enabled several generations of children to learn to write from their plates . . . and to eat their soup!

PASTA COMMERCIALS

Rivoire et Carré (founded 1860). In 1975, this pasta brand chooses Pierre Desproges and Daniel Prévost to advertise their product.

Lustucru (founded 1911). In 1994, the slogan "There are no cracked eggs at Lustucru" and the character Germaine are launched.

Panzani (founded 1929). In the 1970s, it is the character of Don Patillo, portrayed by Fernandel, who exclaims: "Pasta, yes, but Panzani!"

The Ideal Way to Cook Pasta

Start with a big pot and a lot of water! **4¼ cups (1 L) per 3½ ounces (100 g)** of pasta. The cooking time begins when the water returns to boiling after the pasta has been added to it. **Salt the water:** add 1 teaspoon (7 g) of salt per 3½ ounces (100 g) pasta when the water begins to boil. There is no need to add oil to the water.

MACARONI AU GRATIN

by Auguste Escoffier

Cook 9 ounces (250 g) of pasta in boiling salted water, drain completely, then add 2 tablespoons (30 g) of butter and 3½ ounces (100 g) of grated cheese (half Gruyère/half Parmesan). Season with salt, pepper, and a little nutmeg, then add about 3 spoonfuls of béchamel sauce, just enough to lightly coat the pasta. Arrange the pasta in a baking dish. Sprinkle the top with more grated cheese and some bread crumbs, drizzle with melted butter, and bake until golden on top.

The Basque Cake That Captures Hearts

From Saint-Jean-de-Luz to Bayonne by way of Biarritz, the cake *etxeko biskotxa* ("house cake") is served at every table in the Basque country of France.

Delphine Le Feuvre

THE ORIGINS

The cake was created in the thermal bath resort of Cambo-les-Bains (Pyrénées-Atlantiques) around 1830 by pastry chef Marianne Hirigoyen. She entrusted her secret recipe to her granddaughters, Elisabeth and Anne Dibar, nicknamed "the sisters Biskotx" (the name of the cake at the time).

THE TWO OFFICIAL VERSIONS

Pastry cream
Soft and moist, flavored with vanilla

Black cherry jam (from the village of Itxassou)
Fruity and gooey filling

These are the only two versions of the cake that are recognized by the Eguzkia Association of Basque Pastry Chefs (*Eguzkia* means "sun" in the local Basque language, in reference to the shape of the cake).

— GÂTEAU BASQUE WITH PASTRY CREAM —
by the Eguzkia Association

PREPARATION TIME: 30 MINUTES
COOKING TIME: 40 MINUTES
SERVES 6

For the dough
8½ tablespoons (120 g) unsalted butter, softened
1 cup (200 g) granulated sugar
3 cups (300 g) all-purpose flour
2½ teaspoons (10 g) baking powder
2 eggs
3 pinches salt
2 tablespoons (30 mL) rum or vanilla extract

For the pastry cream
3 eggs
½ cup plus 2 tablespoons (125 g) superfine sugar
⅓ cup plus 1 tablespoon (40 g) flour
2⅛ cups (½ L) whole milk
2 tablespoons (30 mL) rum or vanilla extract

Make the dough. In a mixing bowl, combine the butter with the granulated sugar, then incorporate the flour, baking powder, eggs, salt, and rum until a ball of dough is formed. Wrap the dough in plastic wrap, flatten it to a 6-inch (15 cm) disk, then refrigerate until firm.

Make the pastry cream. In a bowl, whisk together the eggs and superfine sugar, then add the flour and stir to combine. In a saucepan, bring the milk to a boil, then slowly pour half the hot milk into the bowl over the egg-sugar mixture while whisking continuously. Pour this mixture back into the saucepan with the remaining milk and bring to a boil while stirring for 3 to 4 minutes (the cream must be very thick). Add the rum off the heat and let cool to room temperature.

Assembly

Grease an 8½-inch (22 cm) round cake pan, and dust with flour. Divide the dough in half and gently roll one half to a thickness of ¼ inch (5 mm). Line the bottom and sides of the pan with the dough. Once the pastry cream is chilled, scrape it into the pan. Roll out the second dough half to ¼ inch (5 mm) to make the dough "lid." Brush the entire surface of the dough with an egg wash (1 beaten egg mixed with a little water), then score the dough using a fork. Bake at 325°F (160°C) for about 40 minutes, or until the pastry is golden. Enjoy once cooled.

The Best Pastry Cream–Filled Gâteaux Basques

→ Maison Pariès; 1, Place Bellevue, Biarritz
→ Maison Adam; 27, place Georges-Clemenceau, Biarritz
→ Moulin de Bassilour, Bidart

Salt Is Not Lacking!

Whether just on the table, in cured meats, or in bread, salt is an important ingredient in France! Here is a *tour de France* of our sources for salt.

Estérelle Payany

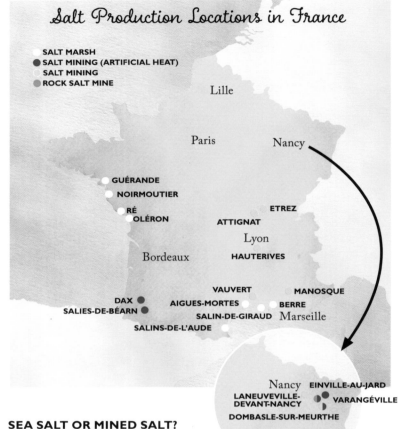

Salt Production Locations in France

- ○ SALT MARSH
- ● SALT MINING (ARTIFICIAL HEAT)
- ● SALT MINING
- ● ROCK SALT MINE

Lille
Paris
Nancy
GUÉRANDE
NOIRMOUTIER
RÉ
OLÉRON
ETREZ
ATTIGNAT
Lyon
Bordeaux
HAUTERIVES
VAUVERT
MANOSQUE
DAX
AIGUES-MORTES
BERRE
SALIES-DE-BÉARN
SALIN-DE-GIRAUD
Marseille
SALINS-DE-L'AUDE

Nancy   EINVILLE-AU-JARD
LANEUVEVILLE-
DEVANT-NANCY   VARANGÉVILLE
DOMBASLE-SUR-MEURTHE

SEA SALT OR MINED SALT?

Sea salt is produced in salt marshes, where the sun and the wind help to crystallize the natural salt contained in seawater along the Mediterranean and on the Atlantic coast. Mined salt is extracted from underground deposits concentrated on the Rhine-Rhône axis and along the Pyrénées.

FLEUR DE SEL OR COARSE SALT?

Fleur de sel sea salt is formed only in salt marshes. This delicate crust of fine salt crystals is harvested by hand at the end of the day or in the morning and has a crunchy texture and delicate aroma. It is typically used to finish a dish.

Coarse salt, which is used primarily for cooking, can be harvested from the sea or from underground salt deposits. This type of salt from along the Atlantic coast is slightly gray and wet, while the type harvested from the Mediterranean is naturally white and drier.

WHAT ABOUT THE FRENCH WORDS SALIN VS. SALINE?

Salt marshes (*salins*) are found in the south of France, but those found along the Atlantic are called *salines*. Furthermore, the term *saline* also refers to the industrial exploitation of natural salt deposits!

WHAT IS A PALUDIER OR SAUNIER?

These terms refer to the same job, but in two different places: the *saunier*, or "salt worker," in the Mediterranean; and the *paludier*, or "saltmonger," on the Atlantic coast who maintains the salt marshes and harvests the salt.

WHAT IS SALT MINING?

Salt can be formed naturally when the sun and wind dry the salt, as is the case with salt marshes, or the seawater can be pumped into the ground, then heated by artificial means so that the salt can be collected and refined, as is done with salt mining.

skip to
Salt—Crust for Crust!, p. 320

The Guide to Glassware

Whether used for wine, water, cocktails, or brandy, the type of glass ("*verre*" in French) is important in the process of tasting. The role that a glass takes in our perception of taste can be very surprising.

Cerval Gwilherm

White Wine Glass
11.5 fl ounces (340 mL)

Bordeaux Wineglass
19 fl ounces (560 mL)

Burgundy Wineglass
23.6 fl ounces (700 mL)

Cognac/Armagnac Glass
20.6 fl ounces (610 mL)

Champagne Flute
7.7 fl ounces (230 mL)

Beer Mug
16.9 fl ounces (500 mL)

Collins Glass
12.1 fl ounces (360 mL)

Cocktail (Martini) Glass
8.4 fl ounces (250 mL)

Cordial Glass
5 fl ounces (150 mL)

Coupe
7.7 fl ounces (230 mL)

Rocks (Old-Fashioned) Glass
9.9 fl ounces (295 mL)

Water Glass
7.4 fl ounces (220 mL)

Shot Glass
1.3 to 1.6 fl ounces (40 to 50 mL)

INAO glass*
7.2 fl ounces (215 mL)

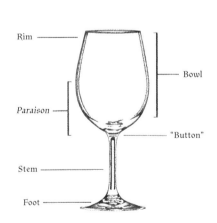

THE WEIGHT
The weight of the glass plays a significant role in our feeling toward the wine. Thus, a heavy wine glass will leave us with the sense that the wine is a little "rough around the edges," while a very thin and light wineglass will create a sense of elegance and finesse in the wine being tasted.

THE THICKNESS
The thinner the edge of the glass, the less contact there is between what you drink and your lips. This allows you to better detect the texture of your beverage.

THE SHAPE
The more **narrow** the glass, the more concentrated the aromas of the beverage. Requiring the drinker to tip his head back to drink from the glass guides the liquid directly to the back of the tongue, which is the part of the tongue that detects acidity and bitterness. A **wide** glass creates more contact with the air and develops the beverage's aromas. Such a glass requires the drinker to bend the head down, directing the liquid to the tip of the tongue where sweet and salty tastes are detected.

THE MATERIAL
A glass is the result of the fusion of three elements: silica (crystals) + soda (dissolving) + lime (fortifying). Imagine being at home and making a caramel from sugar (crystals) and water (dissolving), both heated to a certain temperature—it's the same recipe!

TRANSPARENCY
It is crucial to be able to clearly see the wine in a wineglass: the color, the clarity, any particles, the vibrancy, the level of alcohol, etc.

Created in 1970 by the Institut National des Appellations d'Origine for official tastings.

DID YOU KNOW?
Restaurants usually offer **smaller white wine glasses** than red wine glasses to maintain the lower temperature of the white wine.

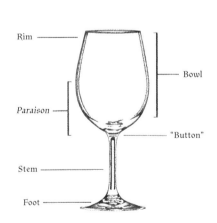

skip to
Happiness in Bottles, p. 225

Alternative Cooking Methods

Cooking over gas—how boring! Simmering on induction—how sad! Roasting in the oven—not interesting!
Cooks are creative people, so they love to invent unorthodox methods for cooking—methods that are a
combination of fantasy, facetious craftsmanship, and improvisation born from necessity.

Baptiste Piegay

Electric Kettle Egg

Inventor: Jean-Philippe Derenne, from *Cuisiner en tous temps en tous lieux* (*Cooking Anytime and Anywhere*), Fayard, 2010.
Method: fed up with the mediocre meals served to his wife while in the hospital, the former head of the pulmonology department of Pitié-Salpêtrière made do with what was available, including an electric kettle. Place an extra-fresh egg at the bottom of the kettle and fill the kettle with water. After the water comes to a boil, turn it off and wait 4 minutes. Remove the egg carefully.
Success rate: 100 percent. It never fails if you don't mind making an omelet with any underdone egg!

Dishwasher Salmon

Inventor: Hervé This, physicist-chemist of the Institut national de la recherche alimentaire (National Institute of Food Research), inspired by Oxford physicist Nicholas Kurti in the early 1980s. Frédérick e. Grasser Hermé (seeker of all things delicious and cookbook author) and journalist Julie Andrieu love this technique.
Method: a classic, born from a spirit of general laziness and curiosity. Hervé This praised the merits of this method in *Ouest-France* (October 21, 2015, edition): "The dishwasher is a very good alternative because it cooks at a low temperature, and constantly, without any waste of energy. It's ecological, delicious, and economical." And to justify this perfect process: "The low cooking temperature is ideal for cooking fish or tender cuts of meats, especially those that contain collagenous tissue—these are foods that do not need to be tenderized by cooking." (Forget the idea of putting a pot-au-feu in the dishwasher!) After seasoning to your tastes—such as with pink peppercorn, dill, or olive oil, for example—seal the salmon airtight (such as in a container or in a freezer bag) and start the dishwasher on a cycle of about 149°F (65°C) for 1 hour 15 minutes.
Success rate: 100 percent (excluding power failures).

Car-Engine Chicken

Inventor: François Simon in his book *Chairs de poule, 200 façons de cuire le Poulet* (Agnès Vienot Éditions, 2000).
Method: a technique bringing together those who love to drive with those concerned about ecology, and which combines a necessary task (taking a long trip) with what is enjoyable: cooking a chicken—and one that will be cooked to perfection upon arrival. The journalist François Simon and the website Autoblog (specializing in mechanics, not in poultry) both share their passion for this technique, and they both have the same technique and process: create any marinade to your liking, massage the bird well with it, then let it marinate for a while before its long journey. Wrap the chicken carefully in aluminum foil, then work it snugly into the car engine. Planning a trip that will take about four hours (perhaps relying on a few traffic jams along the way) with the engine running at about 200°F (90°C) will ensure the chicken is ready upon arrival!
Success rate: 100 percent if the circumstances—traffic, condition of your vehicle, passengers that don't need too much attention—are favorable.

Tarred Leg of Lamb

Inventor: unknown author; turn of the twentieth century.
Method: also known by the name "asphalt lamb," this classic worksite dish, whose appearance coincides with that of major construction projects, has its advantages and disadvantages, starting with the disadvantage of needing access to a major construction site. Start by tightly wrapping—smothering actually, with multiple layers, for obvious reasons—a well-seasoned leg of lamb in aluminum foil, then secure it in a wire net. Submerge the entire thing in a barrel of hot tar (up to 536°F/280°C to 572°F/300°C) to cook for 1 hour, or at a rate of 20 minutes per each 2¼ pounds (1 kg), to which it might be necessary to add 2 hours to get the barrel of tar hot and bubbling. The delectable result has consecrated this as an essential ritual at the end of some construction projects.
Success rate: 60 percent. Most of the work is done ahead of time, but it's necessary to get the permission of the site supervisor, as we generally do not show up uninvited to construction zones. Alternatively, you can prepare your own barrel of tar at home.

skip to
My Little Lambs, p. 181

SARDINES: THE LITTLE DELICACY IN A TIN

Eight thousand metric tons are canned each year in France among sixteen canneries. Among them are a few artisan producers. Here is an overview of some of the best.

Charles Patin O'Coohoon

La Quiberonnaise
La Quiberonnaise Cannery
Quiberon, Morbihan
Founded: 1921
For three generations, this cannery has employed exceptional artisanal methods performed entirely by hand.

La Perle des Dieux
Cannery La Perle des Dieux
Saint-Gilles-Croix-de-Vie, Vendée
Founded: 2004
This is the only artisanal cannery in Vendée. From its beginnings, it has placed special emphasis on vintage sardines.

La Compagnie Bretonne du poisson
Cannery Furic
Saint-Guénolé, Finistère
Founded: 1920
This company was one of the first to can sardines in organic olive oils.

La Belle-Iloise Les Royans Saint-Georges
Cannery La Belle-Iloise
Quiberon, Morbihan
Founded: 1932
This producer, which enjoys a cultlike following, is one of the most important in France. It has launched numerous varieties of canned sardines that supply its sixty-six stores.

Les Mouettes d'Arvor La Molènaise
Cannery Gonidec
Concarneau, Finistère
Founded: 1959
This was the first cannery to start producing limited-edition tins. Today, some of the tins are considered works of art.

La Pointe de Penmarc'h
Cannery Chancerelle
Douarnenez, Finistère
Founded: 1920
This is the upscale brand of Maison Chancerelle (Connétable), the oldest cannery in the world.

THE SARDINE CANNING PROCESS

Between May and October, sardines are fresh caught, then dipped in a brine. They are then cleaned, patted dry, and fried in sunflower oil. Finally, the necks and tails are removed, and they are dried before being placed head-to-tail in the tins.

One tin of sardines contains:
4 ounces (115 g) of meat and oil
1 ounce (25 g) of protein
½ ounce (15 g) of fat
250 calories

SARDINE PÂTÉ
à la Desprogienne

"With this recipe, I scored a hit. I look down on this dish a little because I find it rather commonplace, but it tastes delicious and has some class." —Pierre Desproges

2 tins of sardines, preferably from Dieux de Saint-Gilles-Croix-de-Vie
10 tablespoons (150 g) salted butter, preferably from Vendée
1 heaping tablespoon tomato paste
1 heaping tablespoon ketchup
Juice and zest of 1 lemon
10 tarragon leaves
A little salt
Freshly ground black pepper
Chile paste

Some crushed fennel seeds
1 teaspoon pastis
A few chives

Crush the sardines and combine them with all the remaining ingredients. Place them in a serving bowl and refrigerate.

Amazing, don't you think?

BROILED SARDINES
by Mitsuko Zahar

The Japanese Cordon Bleu chef Mitsuko Zahar gave us this quick recipe to transform simple canned sardines into grilled fish bursting with flavor!

Preheat the oven broiler. Open a tin of sardines and replace their oil with a high-quality olive oil and a few drops of soy sauce. Add a few slices of fresh garlic on top, then broil the sardines for 5 minutes. After removing from the oven, squeeze a lemon over them and add a little grated lemon zest.

skip to
More Noodles!, p. 318

Thanks to the puxisardinophile Alain Boutin, head of La Petite Chaloupe (7, Boulevard de Port-Royal, Paris 13th), the best sardine counter in the city

❧ RABELAIS ❧ ON·THE·MENU

Stéphane Solier

How can you give taste to words? In the sixteenth century, Rabelais was a master of the matter.
Here, in four particularly delicious excerpts from his abundant writings, are some of the stylistic ingredients
with which our chef sprinkles his literary grub, making his readers salivate and smell the scent of his words.

Recine in Style

Brown the words until the outside juices are caramelized: they'll crackle in the writing! Make the sentence sing; draw on every resource available from *alliteration* to *assonance*. Listen to the snap of bones, the joyful sucking, and the pleasure of he or she delighting in a favorite dish.

Don't be shy about adding a bit of *metaphor* to your pot: with the aroma of that garnish, the words to relish will be all the better!

Most noble and illustrious drinkers, and you thrice precious pockified blades (for to you, and none else, do I dedicate my writings) . . .

Or, did you ever see a dog with a marrowbone in his mouth,—the beast of all other, says Plato, lib. 2, de Republica, the most philosophical? If you have seen him, you might have remarked with what devotion and circumspectness he wards and watcheth it: with what care he keeps it: how fervently he holds it: how prudently he gobbets it: with what affection he breaks it: and with what diligence he sucks it. To what end all this? What moveth him to take all these pains? What are the hopes of his labour? What doth he expect to reap thereby? Nothing but a little marrow. True it is, that this little is more savoury and delicious than the great quantities of other sorts of meat, because the marrow (as Galen testifieth, 5. facult. nat. & 11. de usu partium) is a nourishment most perfectly elaboured by nature . . In imitation of this dog, it becomes you to be wise, to smell, feel and have in estimation these fair goodly books, stuffed with high conceptions, which, though seemingly easy in the pursuit, are in the cope and encounter somewhat difficult. And then, like him, you must, by a sedulous lecture, and frequent meditation, break the bone, and suck out the marrow.

Rabelais, Prologue of *Gargantua*

Of the ridiculous statue Manduce; and how and what the Gastrolaters sacrifice to their ventripotent god.

Coming near the Gastrolaters I saw they were followed by a great number of fat waiters and tenders, laden with baskets, dossers, hampers, dishes, wallets, pots, and kettles. Then, under the conduct of Manduce, and singing I do not know what dithyrambics, crepalocomes, and epenons, opening their baskets and pots, they offered their god: white hippocras, with dry toasts, white bread, brown bread. Corbonadoes, six sorts. Brawn. Sweatbreads. Fricassées, nine sorts. Monastical brewis. Gravy soup. Hotch-pots. Soft bread. Household bread. Capirotadoes. Cold loins of veal, with spice. Zinziberine. Beatille pies. Brewis. Marrowbones, toast and cabbage. Hashes. . . . Chitterlings, garnished with mustard. Sausages. Neats' tongues. Hung beef. Chines and peas. Hog's haslets. Scotch collops. Puddings. Cervelats. Bologna sausages. Hams. Brawn heads. Powdered venison, with turnips. Pickled olives. . . . Legs of mutton, with shallots. Olias, Lumber pies with hot sauce. Partridges and young partridges. Dwarf herons. Teals. Duckers. Bitterns. Shovellers. Curlews. Wood-hens. Coots, with leeks. Fat kids. Shoulders of mutton, with capers. Sirloins of beef. Breasts of veal. Pheasants and pheasant poots. Peacocks. Storks. Woodcocks. Snipes. Ortolans. Turkey cockes, hen turkeys, and turkey poots. Stock-doves, and wood culvers. Pigs, with wine sauce. Blackbrids, ouzels, and rails. Moor hens. Bustards and bustard boots. Fig peckekers. Young Guinea hens. . . .

Rabelais, *Chapter 4*, LIX

Vigorously whip your text into *enumeration* until it forms a mousse: the accumulation of dishes will invade the page and the reader's imagination alike.

Flavor your description with phonic spices: the *repetition* of sounds will draw attention to the gustative properties of the dishes.

Do not forget to line your dishes with expressive *alliteration* that your reader will savor for their sonority. Are not La Provence and Gascony in beautiful bloom?

Carefully slice pretty and sweet sounds to reveal the fecundity of the world: your reader's insatiable appetite will be evident in every minced morsel of each word and its variant he digests and also in his voracity for the stuff of words itself.

Finally, fatten your text with *regionalisms*! Fill your menu with the local language of Province (*anchoy*, *tonnine* and *boutargue*) or Arabic (*coscossons*—let's couscous) and make your tongue sing!

How Pantagruel and his company were weary in eating still salt meats; and how Carpalin went a-hunting to have some venison.

•

Eusthenes did help to flay . . . making their prisoner to be their cook, they roasted their venison by the fire wherein the horsemen were burnt; and making great cheer with a good deal of vinegar, the devil a one of them did forbear from his victuals—it was a triumphant and incomparable spectacle to see how they ravened and devoured. Then said Pantagruel, Would to God every one of you had two pairs of little anthem or sacring bells hanging at your chin, and that I had at mine the great clocks of Rennes, of Poictiers, of Tours, and of Cambray, to see what a peal they would ring with the wagging of our chaps.

Rabelais, *Pantagruel*, chap. 26

Shell a few conjunctions and seed a few this way and that: you'll obtain a fine *growing rhythm* that will readily reflect your zeal . . .

——◦——

Thin out the gravy with a filet of *adynaton*: by using this form of impossible hyperbole you'll make palpable Pantagruel's wholehearted and chewy delight.

——◦——

Gently finish cooking by chiseling out a little *neologism* of your own: by forging "chaps" on your tongue and "oinking" you'll give voice to those who ingurgitate with great pleasure.

——◦——

Feel free to flambé with *synesthesia*: it'll bring out all the complex subtleties of the dish. The concert of jaw and lip will become a visual spectacle and the play of sounds will restore the movement of the gulp and the consistency of the dish.

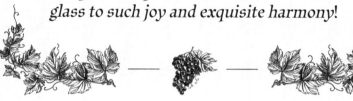

From Rabelais' first page to his last, "the taste of wine recalls the taste of the word and Rabelais' poetry can undoubtedly only be defined by seizing the very tang of words. For example, in the episode when Alcofribas explores his hero's buccal universe, language becomes the drawbridge to entering the imagination." (François Rigolot, *Les Langages de Rabelais*). His string of succulent words, his tasty circumlocutions in which wine transforms into "septembral puree," his lists of dishes seasoned with sound effects in which cooking terms draw their material heft from the food they designate are all an invitation to euphoric, joyful, liberating and iconoclastic excess filled with every lesson about humanity's wisdom and proportion.

•

Most noble and illustrious drinkers, and you thrice precious pockified blades, let us raise a glass to such joy and exquisite harmony!

Spice up your meal with a pinch of *anadiplosis*: By voraciously repeating the word at the end of one sentence at the beginning of the next – in this case, the names of dishes – you'll entice your guests!

——◦——

Fine-tune your seasoning with a good dose of *hyperbole*: by exaggerating numbers and making plurals plentiful, you'll invoke the joy of the eating to come as well as the delicious profusion of the world of giants. Don't be afraid of losing all touch with reality: it's all the more scrumptious.

——◦——

Separately, fry up a few well-chosen *proverbial expressions*: there's nothing like gourmand hyperbolism and the everyday personality of a proverbial saying! "Bite off more than you can chew." can you not feel the eater's wondrous pleasure?

——◦——

Let sit. Stew a few *personifications* so as to add flavor to your approach: make your drinking vessels sing so that the atmosphere of your joyous picnic is festive!

How Gargamelle, being great with Gargantua, did eat a huge deal of tripes.

•

The occasion and manner how Gargamelle was brought to bed, and delivered of her child, was thus: and, if you do not believe it, I wish your bum-gut fall out and make an escapade. Her bum-gut, indeed, or fundament escaped her in an afternoon, on the third day of February, with having eaten at dinner too many godebillios. Godebillios are the fat tripes of coiros. Coiros are beeves fattened at the cratch in ox-stalls, or in the fresh guimo meadows. Guimo meadows are those that for their fruitfulness may be mowed twice a year. Of those fat beeves they had killed three hundred sixty-seven thousand and fourteen, to be salted at Shrovetide, that in the entering of the spring they might have plenty of powdered beef, wherewith to season their mouths at the beginning of their meals, and to taste their wine the better.

They had abundance of tripes, as you have heard, and they were so delicious, that everyone licked his fingers. . . .

The good man Grangousier took great pleasure in their company, and commanded there should be no want nor pinching for anything. . . . Then did they fall upon the chat of victuals and some belly furniture to be snatched at in the very same place. Which purpose was no sooner mentioned, but forthwith began flagons to go, gammons to trot, goblets to fly, great bowls to ting, glasses to ring. . . . So, my friend, so, whip me off this glass neatly, bring me hither some claret, a full weeping glass till it run over. A cessation and truce with thirst.

Rabelais, *Gargantua*, chap. 4

The Art of Tartare

While fashionable food trends today focus on vegetarian or vegan options, a tartare remains a staple of bistro cuisine, and not only in France but around the world. Attention, lovers of fresh meat!

Delphine Le Feuvre

THE ORIGINS

According to legend, tartare was a recipe prepared by the Tatars, a nomadic people whose habit was to consume horse meat, placing pieces of the meat under their saddles to tenderize them while they were riding. In 1876, steak tartare appeared on the menu in a play based on Jules Verne's novel *Michel Strogoff*. In act 2, scene 5, an English journalist trades with a Tatar hotelier who offers him a "*kulbat*—a pie made with ground meat and eggs." During this same time, in Belgium and in the north of France, a similar recipe was served under the name *filet américain* of horse meat chopped by knife and seasoned with mayonnaise. Today, tartare is most often made with ground beef.

★ ★ ★

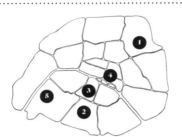

THE BEST TARTARES IN PARIS

1. La Table d'Hugo Desnoyer: a tartare made with thin strips of rump steak. 9 ounces (250 g) minimum! Paris 19th

2. Le Severo: a 12-ounce (350 g) tartar, cut with a knife, seasoned with whole capers. Paris 14th

3. La Rotonde: a tartare prepared with a chilled meat grinder. Three levels of spice are offered: moderate, powerful, and intense. Paris 6th

4. Le Beef Club: 6⅓ ounces (180 g) knife-cut beef, marinated in a preparation of white miso and whiskey. Paris 1st

5. Le Grand Bistro de la Muette: knife-cut Aubrac beef, "Italian style." Paris 16th

1938

A standardized recipe for "steak à la tartare" appears in the first edition of *Larousse Gastronomique* by Prosper Montagné. "'À la tartare' was steak taken from the filet or from the faux filet (tenderloin), chopped, seasoned with salt and pepper, shaped, and served raw with a raw egg yolk on top. Capers and chopped onion and parsley were served on the side."

The recipe

THE MEAT

The tip of the tenderloin—between 5¼ ounces and 6⅓ ounces (150 g and 180 g) per person—cut up using a knife to maintain its texture.

THE SEASONING

An egg yolk, a few drops of Tabasco, Worcestershire, finely chopped parsley, cornichons, capers, mustard, shallots, and a drizzle of olive oil.

THE PRESENTATION

It can be presented with everything already prepared (the meat already seasoned and mixed with the condiments) or with all the condiments and seasonings arranged around the beef, available for the diner to mix to his liking.

THE ACCOMPANIMENT

French fries and/or a green salad.

TARTARE FAUX PAS

Serving the egg yolk in its shell on top of the meat: The shell can carry bacteria.

Preparing the tartare in advance: Chop or grind the meat at the last moment before serving, otherwise it could oxidize.

Grinding the meat too finely: Select a grinder plate with large holes.

TARTARE BY TROISGROS

Michel Troisgros, chef at Le Central in Roanne, mixes chopped rump steak with mayonnaise and "sauce d'enfer" (tomatoes, peppers, coriander, curry, caraway, cardamom, and orange) and mayonnaise. He then adds capers, cornichons, parsley, and chopped shallots.

skip to
Hippophagy, p. 48

Candied Fruit

La Clémentine Corse

La Fraise de Carpentras

L'Abricot du Barroux

La Figue de Cotignac

As a confection to eat on its own, as an ingredient, or as decoration, candied (*glacé*) fruit is a special treat. But as you might expect, its preparation is long and meticulous.
Marie-Laure Fréchet

ITS HISTORY

In existence since ancient times, candied fruits were served as part of the *épices de chambre* as an *issue de table* (spices and candied fruits served after dinner in a special "ceremonial" room to aid with digestion) during the Middle Ages. During the Renaissance, they became widespread as confections due to concerns about consuming fresh fruits. Nostradamus taught the art of "dry jams" in his book *Traité des fardements et confitures*. Even nuts and vegetables were candied.

During the nineteenth century, the inhabitants of Paris couldn't get enough of these sweets, and some streets became devoted entirely to confectionary arts.

THE TECHNIQUE

After blanching, fruits (along with the stems, flowers, and roots) are cooked in a simmering solution of sugar and water (sugar syrup). They are transferred from one batch to the next of hot sugar syrups, each one more concentrated with sugar than the previous one so that the syrup eventually replaces the fruit's natural water. Almost all fruits can be candied in this way.

MARRONS GLACÉES

A specialty of Ardèche, the making of whole candied chestnuts (*marrons glacées*) developed during the late nineteenth century. It requires a great deal of expertise to prevent breaking the chestnuts. *Crème de marrons* (a sweet chestnut purée) was invented as a way to use the broken pieces.

CRYSTALLIZED FLOWERS

Candiflor, created in 1818, is the last Toulousian confectioner to employ traditional methods for crystallizing flowers. Its flagship product, the violets of Toulouse, is a confection made from fresh flowers.

Ice Cream *Plombières*: Its Origins Are a Mystery

○○○○○○○○○○

There are differing opinions on the origin of this ice cream, whose name originates from the lead ("*plomb*") mold in which it was set. It's documented that in 1858 Napoléon III stayed in the spa town of Plombièresles-Bains, in the Vosges, and that a local pastry chef served him a "set" custard studded with candied fruit. But thirty years prior to this time, a *glace plombière* (spelled without the "*s*") was mentioned in documents and served by a Parisian ice cream maker, Tortoni, who used such a mold. This product is not to be confused with *crème plombière*, which was a flavored cream used to fill meringues.

THE RECIPE

PREPARATION TIME: 20 MINUTES
COOKING TIME: 5 MINUTES
SERVES 6

9 ounces (250 g) candied fruits, diced
⅓ cup plus 1 tablespoon (100 mL) high-quality kirsch
6 egg yolks
4¼ cups (1 L) whole milk
1¾ cups (300 g) superfine sugar

Soak the fruit in the kirsch for 45 minutes. Meanwhile, whisk together the egg yolks and sugar, but without lightening the mixture. Bring the milk to a boil in a saucepan, then slowly pour it into the egg-sugar mixture while whisking continuously. Pour the mixture back into the saucepan. Stir continuously over low heat until the cream thickens and coats the back of a spoon; remove from the heat. Remove the fruit from the kirsch, let drain, then stir it into the cream. Transfer the cooled mixture to an ice cream maker.

Apt, the Capital of Candied Fruits

Rich with orchards, the south of France became the center for candied fruits. The city of Apt developed these as its specialty, dating back to the fourteenth century. Since the nineteenth century, Apt's candied fruits have dominated England's markets, and are now exported all over the world. Until the 1980s, the local confectioner employed half the inhabitants of Apt. There are now three artisan confectioners and three large candy manufacturers.

Cake aux fruits confits: inspired by the English plum cake and filled with raisins and a medley of rum-soaked candied fruits.
Orangettes: candied orange peel (previously known as *orangeat*) enrobed in chocolate.
Fruits déguisés: candied (or dried) fruits, sometimes filled with almond paste, coated with a layer of sugar.
Gâteau de semoule: a cake made with semolina cooked in sweetened milk; filled with candied fruits.
Diplomate: a cake made with ladyfinger cookies, sponge cake, or brioche, filled with candied fruits and a stabilized cream filling. Served with crème anglaise.
Polonaise: Parisian brioche soaked in a rum or kirsch syrup, filled in the center with a pastry cream, covered in Italian meringue, and sprinkled with sliced almonds.
Petits-fours: candied fruits presented as "petits-fours" ("small ovens"), so called because they are baked in the oven after the larger cakes are completed and the oven temperature is cooler.
Calissons d'Aix: almond flour–based candy, such as candied melons, in a marquis shape and lightly flavored with orange blossom.

skip to ....
Confitures, p. 368

RESTAURANTS ROUTIERS

Have you ever seen this red and blue logo along the major highways of France? It is the logo of the *restaurants routiers*, or "truck stop restaurants"—atypical eateries where every day one can find professional truck drivers enjoying a good meal. Served up here is food worth the detour: simple, good, and affordable—food that warms both the heart and stomach.

by Estelle Lenartowicz

➡ A ROUTIER RESTAURANT? WHAT IS IT? ⬅

3 QUALIFICATIONS

Not every restaurant can qualify as a *restaurant routier*! To have the right to display the famous tricolor logo, every *restaurant routier* must meet three nonnegotiable qualifications: ❶ be open for lunch and dinner, ❷ have a parking lot that accommodates trucks, ❸ provide showers for its customers.

1 · 0 · 0 · 0

THE NUMBER OF FRANCHISED RESTAURANTS IN FRANCE

AQP The regulatory system that qualifies a good *restaurant routier*. AQP (the letters stand for "welcoming," "irreproachable quality," and "good prices") with square meals and, occasionally, self-service lunch or dinner buffets.

A SHORT HISTORY

→ **IN 1934,** François de Saulieu Chomonerie launches the restaurant chain Les Relais Routiers, which, in the spirit of solidarity and companionship, groups under the same logo those restaurants that serve simple, hearty meals at moderate prices. These places are soon listed in *Le Guide des Relais Routiers*, which becomes known as the "Red Guide" to diners.

→ **IN THE 1970S,** the golden age, *restaurants routiers* start to welcome famous guests: Brigitte Bardot, Jeanne Moreau, Michel Sardou, and the comedian Pierre Brasseur, who donated 50,000 francs to the cause after these restaurants experienced a dark history of watered-down meals, broken dishware, and threats of filing official complaints.

→ **IN 1974,** the first *relais* (truck stop) opens "along the highway," as roadway infrastructure in France progresses.

→ **IN 2014,** for its 80th anniversary, the *Guide des Relais Routiers* publishes a special edition for the general public. Among the one thousand establishments presented, the best receive a "saucepan," a kind of rating badge. The guide contains a wealth of other information, such as maps and a glossary of mechanical terms in eight languages.

• THE INSPECTIONS •

Volunteer inspectors crisscross France, ensuring adherence to the rules and rewarding the most deserving establishments. Their objective is to protect the gastronomical achievements of *restaurants routiers* and to honor their motto: "To properly feed drivers, and to love them."

SAUTEED ARTICHOKES

A recipe by Kerisnel*

PREPARATION TIME: 20 MINUTES
COOKING TIME: 35 TO 45 MINUTES
SERVES 4

4 artichokes, preferably from Brittany
1 drizzle of olive oil
3 tablespoons plus 1¾ teaspoons (50 g) unsalted butter
Salt and freshly ground black pepper
1 spring onion
1 tomato

Cook the artichokes in a pressure cooker or steamer. Quarter them and remove the choke from each one. Heat the oil and butter in a pan. Sauté the artichokes over high heat for 5 minutes. Season with salt and pepper. Peel and mince the onion and large dice the tomato; combine them in a bowl. Serve the artichokes with the onion-tomato mixture.

*Saint-Pol-de-Léon (Finistère)

ÎLE FLOTTANTE (FLOATING ISLAND)

Recipe from the Relais de Saint-Sauveur*

PREPARATION TIME: 25 MINUTES
COOKING TIME: 20 MINUTES
SERVES 4 TO 6

For the crème anglaise
3 egg yolks
2 tablespoons plus 1¼ teaspoons (30 g) superfine sugar
1 vanilla bean
1¼ cups (30 cl) whole milk
½ teaspoon cornstarch
For the meringue
4 egg whites
1 teaspoon superfine sugar
3½ ounces (100 g) pourable caramel

Prepare the crème anglaise. In a large bowl, whisk together the egg yolks and sugar. Split the vanilla bean lengthwise in half and scrape out and reserve the seeds. In a small bowl place a few tablespoons of the milk and whisk in the cornstarch until combined. Pour the mixture into a saucepan, then add the remaining milk along with the vanilla bean pod and seeds. Heat the milk, but do not boil it. Pour the hot milk over the yolk-sugar mixture while whisking constantly. Gently heat the mixture for 20 minutes over a bain-marie while stirring constantly with a spatula; the custard is ready when it coats the back of the spatula. Place the bowl into a separate large bowl containing ice water to stop the cooking. When cooled, cover and refrigerate.

Preheat the oven to 325°F (160°C). Prepare the meringue. Beat the egg whites to stiff peaks with the sugar. Pour the caramel into the bottom of a small baking dish. Scrape the egg whites into the dish and bake for 10 minutes. Slice the meringue into servings and float each piece in a serving bowl on top of some of the crème anglaise.

*Saint-Sauveur-d'Emalleville (Seine-Maritime)

Recipes from Les routiers, *by Isabel Lepage, Tana Éditions*

N7, the Road of Taste, p. 386

PICOLAT MEATBALLS

France certainly does not consider meatballs among its culinary wonders. In Alsace, however, we do come across several *Lewerknepfle* of Jewish origin, but we must travel to the foothills of the Pyrénées to celebrate a real meatball tradition.

Pierre-Brice Lebrun

Picolat meatballs are Catalan meatballs (*picolat* in Catalan means "ground meat"), served in spicy tomato sauce with white beans, porcini mushrooms, pine nuts, and green olives. There are as many recipes for this popular dish as there are families in this region, but everyone agrees on the importance of using a ground meat mixture that is half pork, half beef.

— THE RECIPE —

PREPARATION TIME: 2 HOURS 30 MINUTES
COOKING TIME: 2 HOURS 30 MINUTES
SERVES 5 OR 6

1¾ pounds (800 g) white kidney beans
1 bouquet garni
7 ounces (200 g) dried cèpe (porcini) mushrooms
Milk, for soaking the mushrooms, warmed
1 thick slice stale bread
12 ounces (350 g) ground beef
12 ounces (350 g) ground pork
2 eggs
4 cloves garlic, peeled and chopped
1 bunch parsley, chopped
Salt and freshly ground black pepper
2 or 3 large onions, peeled and chopped
Olive oil, for sautéing
4½ ounces (125 g) bacon, diced
6 cups (1.5 L) fresh tomatoes, peeled and seeded
1 or 2 bay leaves
7 ounces (200 g) pitted green olives (rinsed well if from a jar)
1 pinch chile powder or cinnamon

The day before, soak the beans in water (a little baking soda added to the water will make them more digestible). The next day, add the beans to a large pot with just enough salted water to cover them. Add the bouquet garni, bring to a boil and cook the beans, covered, for 1 hour 30 minutes. Soften the mushrooms in a bowl with the milk; remove them and set aside. Add the bread to the bowl of milk. Next, by hand, mix together the meat, soaked bread (torn into pieces), eggs, half the garlic, and parsley. Season with salt and pepper. In a skillet, lightly sauté the onions in the oil just until translucent. Remove them with a spatula. In the skillet, with a drizzle of olive oil, brown the remaining garlic and the bacon. Quarter the tomatoes and add to the skillet, then add the soaked mushrooms and the cooked onions; cook until the liquid is slightly reduced. Using wet hands, roll the meat mixture into balls measuring 2 to 2¼ inches (5 to 6 cm) in diameter. In a skillet with olive oil, sear the meatballs on all sides. Transfer them to the skillet with the tomato mixture and bring to a boil. Add the soaked beans, bay leaves, olives, and the pinch of chile powder. Let cook for 1 hour, covered, over low heat. It is said that ⅓ cup plus 1 tablespoon (100 mL) of cognac poured into the sauce cannot hurt!

skip to
Porcini, p. 347

The Judgment of Paris

In 1976, for the first time in a blind tasting, French wines were beaten by their Californian rivals. Let's visit the details from this real coup d'état in the world of wine!

Cerval Gwilherm

Date: May 24, 1976
Location: InterContinental Hotel, Paris
The Subject: blind tasting of ten white Chardonnay wines and ten red Cabernet Sauvignon wines (including four French and six Californian in each category); the wines are selected by the two organizers according to the criterion that each wine is a "good representation of each of the vineyards."

ORGANIZERS:
Steven Spurrier, English wine merchant and owner of Caves de la Madeleine in Paris.
Patricia Gallagher, director, at that time, of the Wine Academy.

TASTERS:
Claude Dubois-Millot, commercial director of Gault & Millau.
Odette Kahn, editor-in-chief of the *Revue du Vin de France*.
Raymond Oliver, chef and owner of Le Grand Véfour.
Pierre Tari, proprietor of Château Giscours.
Christian Vannequé, head sommelier of La Tour d'Argent in Paris.
Aubert de Villaine, coproprietor of Domaine de la Romanée Conti.
Jean-Claude Vrinat, owner of Taillevent restaurant.
Pierre Bréjoux, inspector general of the INAO.
Michel Dovaz, from the Institute of Wine.

THE AWARDS

Top 3 white wines

① United States
Château Montelena
1973

② France
Roulot-Meursault
1er cru Charmes
1973

③ United States
Chalone Vineyard
1974

Top 3 red wines

① United States
Stag's Leap Wine Cellars
1973

② France
Château Mouton-Rothschild
1970

③ France
Château Montrose
1970

Conclusion: American wines were recognized as best on that day.
The snag: it was later realized that the vintages of the early 1970s in France had been particularly difficult.
To tell the story: Randall Miller's film *Bottle Shock* and George M. Taber's book *Judgement of Paris* were both released in 2008.

skip to
The Bordeaux and Burgundy Match-Up, p. 272

Sea Urchin—A Prickly Subject!

Present along all of France's coastlines, this funny marine hedgehog hides a heart of gold under its armored shell. Many have grown to love its subtle flavor.

Marie-Amal Bizalion

A NECTAR THAT DIVIDES

There are those who would kill for a taste and those whom it disgusts at first glance—*and that's unfortunate for the latter*! Few dishes, indeed, offer such a complex palette of flavors: a brininess that is at the same time sweet, and one that chef Pierre Gagnaire describes as slightly smoky with notes of hazelnut, honey, and even blood: "An extreme sensation, almost sexual," he says. Today, France consumes three species of sea urchin.

TASTES AND COLORS

Sea urchin from the Atlantic is said to be sweet, while those from the Mediterranean are said to have a briny flavor. In reality, the same species can develop differing flavors according to the algae and plants on which it feeds. The color of its gonads (aka roe or "tongues") is linked to its sex. Those of the female will range from bright orange to dark red, and those of the male are paler, sometimes veiled in a white milt.

METHOD

Selecting it: select those that are alive! Its spines should still be moving.
Opening it: use work gloves and a pair of sharp scissors. Push the blade into the soft hole (the mouth). Cut out a small circle, then open it further by cutting a circular opening about two-thirds of the shell's diameter, making sure to save the roe attached to the bottom.
Cleaning it: clean it over a container, turning the shell upside down and shaking it to empty out any water and the entrails. Be sure to collect any of the roe that might fall out.
Removing the flesh: gently remove the roe using a spoon. The rest of the impurities will release naturally.
Storing it: within just minutes of being extracted from the shell, the roe will release its juices. Sea urchin, therefore, should only be prepared immediately before serving or, in the worst case, frozen immediately.

● PURPLE SEA URCHIN

Official name: *Paracentrotus lividus*
Where is it found? On the Atlantic coast of Ireland, southern Morocco, and the Mediterranean.
How do you recognize it? This variety does not exceed 3 inches (8 cm) in diameter, including its spines, which are long, thin, and tousled. They range in color from olive green to bronze and from deep pink to purple.
How does it taste? Either an iodized or sweet flavor, but always fragrant. The plump roe may fill the interior. For gourmets, this one's the best.

● VIOLET SEA URCHIN

Official name: *Sphaerechinus granularis*
Where is it found? From the English Channel to Cape Verde, in the Mediterranean.
How do you recognize it? Its size reaches 5 inches (13 cm) in diameter. Its short, transparent spines have a white point, which allows them to reflect the color of the shell, ranging from white to violet.
How does it taste? The roe are small for their size. They are tasty when prepared the same day, but they can quickly turn bitter.

● GREEN SEA URCHIN

Official name: *Strongylocentrotus droebachiensis*
Where is it found? In cold water from Brittany to Greenland. In the fish markets of France, it's sold under the name "sea urchin of Iceland."
How do you recognize it?: It can reach up to 3 inches (8 cm) without its spines, which are short, blunt, and pale green to dark.
How does it taste? Less subtle than the violet sea urchin, a little earthy. Plump roe may mean it has been fed pellets after it was caught. Stores well.

PREPARING

Forget using lemon, which ruins the delicate flavor. And cook it only minimally, if at all.

Raw: eating it like this is the ideal way! Just out of the water, placed raw on a buttered baguette, accompanied with a bottle of white wine kept cool in the waters while you sit on the rocks in your diving suit.
In scrambled eggs: with several sea urchin roe as garnish, and the rest beaten with cream, salt, pepper, and eggs, cooked gently over a bain-marie, stirring until creamy, and served in the cleaned shells.
In pasta: using raw roe, a little water, and olive oil mixed together and tossed with hot tagliatelle.
As an appetizer: mixed in softened butter, spread with a hint of salt on grilled rustic bread.
Baked: with the roe cleaned and served in the empty shell, with a quail egg broken over the top then placed under the broiler just until the egg white sets.

skip to ....
Caviar and France, p. 254

ECHINI *WHAT*? ECHINICULTURE

The term *echiniculture* refers to the artificial breeding of sea urchins, developed in 1982 by Pierre Le Gall to mitigate the scarcity of those in the wild. Between 2006 and 2016, on the island of Ré, his son Yvan became the only echinist in the world to raise sea urchins, the violet sea urchins in particular. There are currently no echinists in France, so perhaps this is a great business idea!

SEA URCHIN TERMS TO KNOW—FOR MAKING A GOOD IMPRESSION

Also known as: chestnut; sea hedgehog.
Test: the shell without the spines.
Roe: the gonads, also called the "coral" or "tongues."
Peristome: the fleshy part surrounding the mouth, through which one cuts the sea urchin open.
"Aristotle's lantern": the sea urchin's jaw with five teeth, as described around 345 AD by the philosopher Aristotle, who was fascinated by the sea urchin's anatomy.

PUTTING THE BRAKES ON SEA URCHIN CONSUMPTION

From 1960 to 2011, the sea urchin was part of a celebration that took place on the docks of the Côte Bleue in the Bouches-du-Rhône. Every Sunday in winter, thousands of gourmets would consume tons of sea urchins on large outdoor tables. Renamed the *Fêtes de la Mer*, only those of Carry-le-Rouet and Sausset-les-Pins are currently still taking place as we wait for the replenishment of the sea urchin supply.

PROVIDED IT CONTINUES . . .

Between Marseille and Martigues, ten sea urchin fishing sites have been meticulously scrutinized since 1994. In 2007, there were only 4 violet sea urchins per 10 square feet (1 square meter). In 2010, there were no more than 1.5 sea urchins on average in this same area. By 2015, the rate went back to 3.7 per 10 square feet (1 square meter).* But another threat is looming: the accelerated acidification of the world's waters, which destroys the calcareous particles necessary for the sea urchin larvae to create their shells.
*Source: Syndicat mixte parc marin de la Côte bleue (Joint Marine Park Syndicate of Côte Bleue)

AMATEUR FISHING— A RISKY SPORT

Quotas: Per person and per day: ranging from twelve in Brittany to forty-eight in the Mediterranean. There is a €1,500 ($1,800) fine for being too greedy.

Catching them in season? Depending on the region, opening from September 2 (in Aude) to December 15 (in Corsica). General closure between the 1st and 30th of April.

Catching them out of season? A possible €22,500 ($26,000) fine!* Let them reproduce in peace!

Source: ministère de l'Environnement, de l'Énergie et de la Mer, article L. 945-4 3° du Code rural et de la pêche maritime. (Ministry of Environment, Energy, and Sea, Article L. 945-4 3° of the Rural Code and of Sea Fisheries).

A FUNNY GROUP

In the echinoderm family, there are eight hundred species of sea urchins (echinoids), and four cousins, including starfish (asterias) and sea cucumbers (holothuries). In common among these is a symmetrical skeleton divided into five sections, a unique circumstance in the animal kingdom!

SUPERSTITIONS AND BELIEFS

It brings good luck. The sea urchin was considered a divine seed of survival by the Druids and a symbol of death and resurrection in ancient Freemasonry (fossilized remains of sea urchins were found in many Gallo-Roman burial grounds). It is today a symbol of protection in Auvergne and in the north of France.

It's an aphrodisiac. If iodine is a sexual stimulant, then eating a ton of sea urchin could surely cause excitement. More surprisingly, the sea urchin contains anandamide in large quantities, a molecule with euphoric effects comparable to the THC of cannabis!

Its color indicates its sex. Not true! The ink-black sea urchin found in the Mediterranean Sea is not the male purple sea urchin. It's its cousin *Arbacia lixula*, which is very bitter to eat.

It can be toxic. On France's shores, there is no risk of poisoning, even if some of them are spoiled. The danger comes from its spines, which can be painful if touched.

HURRAY?

Although it ranks far behind Japan, France is second in the world for the highest consumption of sea urchins. However, this is nothing to brag about. Japan has exhausted its supply, and France must import them from Iceland.

AN ANATOMY LESSON

Its shell is made of limestone covered in spines that hide retractable tube feet and pincers used for cleaning; inside is a simple tube connecting a toothed mouth to the anus, and five "tongues" (gonads) arranged in a star pattern. It is these reproductive organs of the male and female sea urchins that we take delight in eating.

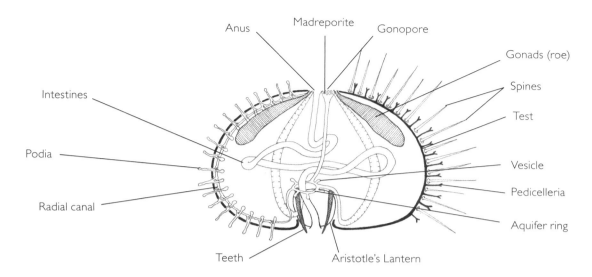

SCRAMBLED EGGS WITH SEA URCHINS

by Nicolas Stromboni

PREPARATION TIME: 20 MINUTES
COOKING TIME: 12 MINUTES
SERVES 12

16 sea urchins
7 tablespoons (100 g) unsalted butter
12 extra-fresh eggs
Salt
3 tablespoons plus 1 teaspoon (50 mL) cream
Freshly ground black pepper

Cut open the sea urchins using a pair of scissors and remove the orange "tongues" (roe); set them aside in the refrigerator. Rinse the shells with water and set aside twelve of the most attractive. In a saucepan, melt half the butter. Beat the eggs with a fork to thoroughly combine them, season with salt, then pour them into the saucepan. Cook the eggs over low heat or over a bain-marie. Using a whisk, stir the eggs, starting from the center of the pan and moving out to the sides. As soon as the eggs start to thicken, remove the pan from the heat; they will finish cooking in the hot pan. Slowly whisk in the remaining butter and cream. Carefully stir the sea urchin roe into the eggs. Transfer the mixture to the empty shells, season with a little pepper, and serve immediately.

Hippophagy

At times hated and at times praised for its virtues, hippophagy (the consumption of horse meat) has its followers. However, eating horse meat is still, today, one of the rare food taboos that exists in France. Here we break it down for you.

Camille Pierrard

The Story of a Taboo

The consumption of horse meat in France started in the second half of the nineteenth century. Veterinary authorities organized a promotional campaign to deal with the shortage of meat, which was particularly prevalent among the working class. But the objective was also a commercial one: to ensure free trade of meat by initiating privileges granted by the associations of traditional butchers.

It's a sausage of horse
A sausage only of horse
That I just made while riding a horse
This is a song of mating

Bobby Lapointe, translated from *Saucisson de cheval N°1* (*Horse Sausage No. 1*)

December 1855

The first hippophagist banquet, to which doctors and journalists are invited to demonstrate to them the nutritional and culinary qualities of horse meat, the only item on the menu. This promotional campaign receives severe criticism and inspires caricature artists such as Honoré Daumier.

1866

Napoléon III legalizes the sale of horse meat and the first French horse butcher is inaugurated in Nancy.

1870

War and food shortages put an end to the reluctance toward eating horse meat.

1911

Peak consumption of horse meat in France.

1914–1920, 1939–1947

The scarcity of food during and after the wars sheds a favorable light on the consumption of horse meat, which is less expensive than other meats.

Starting in 1966

Thanks to economic prosperity, there is a rapid decline in hippophagy.

From 1970

Horse meat by this time represents only 2 percent of the volume of consumed animal flesh. This figure drops to 0.4 percent in 2013.

skip to
Carnivores during the Siege of Paris, p. 256

THE HORSE MEAT INDUSTRY: A PARADOX

Although the people in France who love horse meat consume mostly red meat from mature horses, the majority of what the country produces is meat from foals (those that would have otherwise been used as work horses), intended for export to Italy and Spain.

Since the 1950s, 50 percent of the demand for horse meat in France has been satisfied by imports, either live animals imported from Europe (Belgium and Poland), or meat imported from the Americas (Canada, Argentina, and Mexico).

PRODUCTION IN FRANCE

In 2014, the slaughter of 17,100 equines included:

Riding horses: 32%
Race horses: 52%
Work horses*: 10%
Ponies: 5%
Donkeys: 1%

*Heavy, stocky horses used for pulling.
- FranceAgriMer - IFCE - SIRE, 2015
- Most of the French equine industry 2015, Interbev (livestock and meat inter-branch)

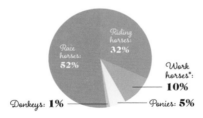

A Few Regional Specialties

Historically, hippophagy developed mostly in urban areas where there was a higher concentration of laborers, particularly in Paris and Nord-Pas-de-Calais. As a result, many specialties using horse meat originate from these regions.

La carbonade flamande: a specialty of Flanders, French or Belgian, the *carbonade* is a stew made with horse meat (or sometimes beef) in beer.

Steak tartar: invented in the brasseries of Paris, this preparation of raw horse or beef chopped with a knife was called *tartare* in reference to the Cossack and Tatar riders, who, according to legend, tenderized raw, salted horse meat fillets by placing them between their saddles and the sides of their horses.

L'entrecôte Bercy: originally a piece of grilled horse meat with parsley and watercress accompanied by a sauce made of white wine, shallots, and lemon. It was served to wine merchants of the Bercy district in Paris, which during the nineteenth century and until the beginning of the twentieth century was one of the largest wine and spirits markets in Europe.

Le rossbif: This has nothing to do with what is called "roast beef" across the English Channel! *Le rossbif*—from the word *ross* ("horse") in old Alsatian—is a horse sauce–based dish that has been marinated for three to four days.

Le saucisson de cheval: This sausage is typical of the foods found in Pas-de-Calais: casing filled with ground horse meat, sometimes smoked, and whose seasoning varies according to its locality. Red in color, it is used as a filling in dough or brioche, or served cold on bread.

What Part of the Horse Is Eaten in France?

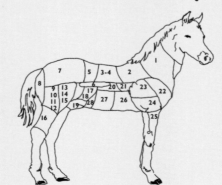

1: Neck (plow steak)
2: Lower chop
3-4: Rib steak
5: Sirloin
6: Filet
7: Rump steak
8: Top round
9-10-11-12: Inside thigh, thigh tip, rounds
13-14-15: Thigh cuts (*Plat de tranche, rond de tranche* and *mouvant*)
16: Hock
17: Bavette (sirloin)
18: Bavette (flank)
19: Spider
20: Skirt
21: Prime cut
22-23-24-25-26-27-28: Blade roast, shoulder, chuck, clavicle, breast tip, breast, and flank

SO LONG AS THERE IS INEBRIATION

The delight of inebriation draws us out of quiet sobriety and lifts our spirits. The exaltation of our senses plunges us into a state of euphoria that inebriates us with love before we become dead drunk!
Aurore Vincenti

A little

It starts gently, there's a slow euphoric rise, a release. The adjective **pompette** (tipsy) undoubtedly refers to the **roundness** of its former homonym from the fifteenth century meaning a **ribbon knot or a pom-pom**. It's a formal shift that occurred, from the **pom-pom to the nose**, that readily becomes round and purplish in a state of drunkenness. The French expression "**nez à pompettes**" (pom-pom nose) can be found in Rabelais. But a person still has a **certain amount of dignity** when tipsy, there's a balanced inhibition, the kind that that comes with Champagne bubbles and the early hours of a night out. Not far off from the pom-pom of being "pompette," the **merry in merriment** is gentle dizziness. The French verb *émécher* sometimes means "to make locks of hair." That unusual use of the French verb nevertheless explains the tousled drunkenness of the merry.

A lot

The French term "**se bourrer la gueule**" (to gorge) doesn't necessarily entail alcohol because one can also gorge on a nonnegligible quantity of food. Nevertheless, in contemporary French, the expression in no way suggests ingesting anything solid. That's because when we wet our whistle, we end up gorging or filling our bellies (*gorge* is also the contents of the stomach). Although the body might not necessarily betray this liquid indulging, the stomach can bloat and become **completely round** (bombed, blasted). To be "soûl" in French is to have eaten and drunk to one's fill. The word comes from the Latin *satullus*, which means "enough, somewhat satisfied." The adjective in French gradually only came to apply to drinking. In French, you can be as "soûl" as a donkey, pig or a Polish person. Drunk as a skunk, in English.

With gusto

The French in the seventeenth century were already using the term "**cuit**" (cooked) to describe someone who had been drinking excessively. The term comes from the kitchen and plays on the image of **alcohol warming you up . . . to the point that you're cooked**. Moreover, in French slang, when you drink, you're "heating your oven." It comes as no surprise that excess leads to "**la grosse cuite**" (being heavily cooked). The French expression "prendre une biture" (get plastered) could have two origins. The first is slang, and has roots in seafaring ("bittes d'amarrage," mooring bollards). After long weeks at sea, docking often entailed celebrating with booze and women. The other is more classical and is related to the evolution of the French word "**boiture**" (from the Latin *bibere*, to drink), which in the fifteenth century designated a "drink or drinking debauch." In French, the expression "prendre une biture" doesn't mean drinking in moderation. If you want another, try the French expression "**se mettre une race**" (get racy)!

Old-fashioned charm. There are a few old-fashioned

French words that make you want to use them just **for how charming they sound**: "Hier soir, nous avons fait ribote comme des petits fous" (Last night, we had merry repast like little fools). One pictures a Sunday afternoon, a spontaneous gathering of friends, a leg of lamb with lots of wine and a few good bottles from the cellar. "***Faire ribote***" means to **feast and be drunk** at a table with lace tablecloths. It's a word related to "***ribaud***," which is much more mischievous and tips the Sunday gathering toward lust and debauchery. "***Ribauder***" means to **rub oneself, become vulgar**. Don't mix up the two terms, but you never know how the night will end . . .

Skip to: **City Beers, Country Beers, p. 210**

Feel free to use

→ *Prendre une chicorée* (Take a chicory)

→ *Prendre une maculature* (Take a maculature, to use a printing term)

→ *Prendre une ronflée* (Take a snore)

→ *S'arsouiller* (Become a roughneck)

★
BERCY AND THE RUE ALPHONSE-MURGE

In the eighteenth century, under Louis XIV, **the first wine warehouses were built in Bercy**. A flourishing market even emerged after the French Revolution. The neighborhood then became **the largest wine market in the world** and its consumption exploded. That's where these French expressions come from: "être né sur les coteaux de Bercy" (**to be born in the hills of Bercy**), "avoir la maladie de Bercy" (**to have Bercy sickness**) and also "tenir une bonne bersillée" (**to have a good Bercy**)! Less commonly known is that the French verb "se murger" (literally to stone wall) is a term from the area as well. The rue Alphonse-Murge, **near the Bercy warehouses**, engendered the expression "**to walk along the walls of the rue Murge**" after getting wasted in the neighborhood cabarets. Those walls must have witnessed countless individuals "faire place à un verre de vin" (literally "**make room for a glass of wine**," meaning to urinate), "piquer un renard" ("**nab a fox**," meaning to vomit) and "batter les murailles" ("**hit the walls**," or walk in zigzags).
★

Herring— A High-Ranking Fish

A common cold-water fish, herring has been of paramount importance in the history of food. It's excellent when marinated or grilled; sublime when salty and smoked.

Marie-Laure Fréchet

FRESH HERRING

Herring, a fish of the family Clupeidae and a cousin of the sardine, travels only in schools. It lives in cold, very salty seas, notably in the Baltic. From October to January, the herring are "full": the males of their milt and the females of their eggs. During this time its flesh is fattier. When it is "empty" (after breeding), from January to March, herring flesh is drier and therefore less tasty. When prepared fresh, it is mainly marinated or grilled.

THE "KING FISH"

Because of herring's significance as a source of food for nearly a millennium, it has the nickname "king fish." Its fishing gave rise to the first maritime laws established in Europe and, for several centuries, its trade played a role as important as that of spices. It was used for bartering, and in times of war, truces were declared to allow fisherman to continue their work. To feed the population year-round, the fish was salted and smoked to preserve it. The entire Côte d'Opale lived to the rhythm of the great herring expeditions through the beginning of the twentieth century, before its supply declined in the 1970s. The establishment of quotas to manage the herring supply and the preservation of the *saurisseries* (fish smokehouses) helped save the salting and smoking traditions.

IN THE FAMILY

In French, *herang saur* is the generic name for salted and smoked herring. *Saur* comes from the Dutch *soor* ("withered"). *Hareng saur* is also called *sauret*. Or, in slang, a *gendarme* ("police officer") because of its rigidity. **Depending on the time of salting and smoking, the different types of herring include:**
Pec: fresh herring placed in a brine as soon as it reaches the smokehouse
Doux **("mild"):** a lightly salted and smoked fillet
Traditionnel **("traditional"):** a coastal herring fillet, pickled and smoked
Bouffi **("swollen") or** *craquelot* **("bloaters"):** whole salted and smoked herring, with its milt
Kipper: a gutted herring, split and butterflied from head to tail, salted and smoked
Rollmops: fillets marinated in vinegar (pickled)

Coastal herring: for connoisseurs!

Coastal herring is caught **once a year in November**, between Boulogne-sur-Mer and Dover, when the herring comes to spawn near the coast. **The fish is salted whole with dry salt**, then stored for a **year in tanks** called *caques* until the next herring season. **It is desalinated** five times a day for two days before being smoked and having the bones removed. **Its taste is intense and well matured**. It is also known as *filet de saur* or *filet demi-sel.*

HERRING AND POTATOES IN OIL

PREPARATION TIME: 20 MINUTES
RESTING TIME: 1 NIGHT
COOKING TIME: 20 MINUTES
SERVES 4

4 herring *doux* (see left)
1 onion
1 carrot
A few sprigs thyme
A few bay leaves
Black peppercorns
Flavorless cooking oil, for marinating
6 potatoes (firm flesh)
⅓ cup plus 1 tablespoon (100 mL) dry white wine
Vinegar, for drizzling

Rinse the herring fillets under cold water. Dry them thoroughly. Peel and thinly slice the onion and carrot. Lay the herring fillets in a terrine, alternating in layers with the onion, carrot, thyme, bay leaves, and peppercorns. Cover with the oil. Set aside to marinate, covered, in a cool place overnight. The next day, cook the potatoes in boiling salted water. Slice them into thick rounds while still hot. Drizzle with wine, a little oil from the terrine, and vinegar, according to your taste. Serve with the herring, and the marinated onion and carrot.

skip to ....
Anchoiade, p. 232

Founded in 1973 in Boulogne-sur-Mer, the JC David herring smokehouse continues the traditional methods for salting and smoking. It takes five days for the salt and smoke to slowly penetrate the herrings' flesh. JC David is also a historic landmark in French heritage: with forty almost-one-hundred-year-old wood-burning ovens and six eight-ton herring pits classified as living heritage equipment, the smokehouse is the oldest salting facility in Europe. Its fillets of herring *doux*, which carry the Label Rouge, are considered an exceptional product.

Smoked Herring—From Boat to Plate

1 Fished off the coast of Iceland, the herring's head is removed, its body is cleaned and butterflied, then it is frozen on the fishing trawler before reaching the smokehouse.

2 The "men of white" (a reference to the color of the fish's flesh before it is smoked) hand salt each herring individually.

3 The herrings are skewered on spits on carts before being rolled into the ovens. Each batch of fish is traced, as a guarantee of quality.

4 The herring is smoked using oak wood for between twenty-four and forty-eight hours under the watchful eye of the master smoker, who constantly monitors the fire and is always adjusting it according to the weather conditions to maintain a constant temperature of 86°F (30°C).

5 The herring are deboned using the tip of a knife.

6 The finished fillets are then packaged and ready.

Cakes of Yesteryear Rise Once Again

These cakes experienced their fifteen minutes of fame before retreating into obscurity. Here, however, they are modernized by some of the kings of pastry.

Gilbert Pytel

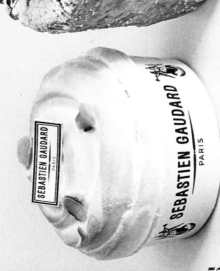

La Polonaise
by Sébastien Gaudard

The history: we find the first traces of this cake in nineteenth-century France, England, and the United States, with different cakes that have similar recipes (Charlotte Polonaise or Polonaise Timbale, for example). **The flavors:** pastry chef Sébastien Gaudard took over the traditional version of this cake as made by his father in Pont-à-Mousson (Meurthe-Moselle); a brioche soaked in rum, covered with an Italian meringue, filled with candied fruit and pastry cream, then decorated with sliced almonds. The entire cake is then briefly placed in the oven to brown.
Addresses: 22, rue des Martyrs, Paris 9th; 1, rue des Pyramides, Paris 1st
www.sebastiengaudard.com

Le Gâteau Napoléon
by Café Pouchkine

The history: the exact origin of this cake is difficult to identify; but legend says it was created in tribute to Napoléon during the Russian campaign of 1812. More likely, this dessert was created in Russia at the end of the nineteenth century, then reimagined by the pastry chef of Café Pouchkine.
The flavors: this cake is the distant cousin of the *mille-feuille*, composed of puff pastry flavored with orange, topped with a piped cream flavored with Bourbon Madagascar vanilla, then coated with delicate flakes of caramel. An ultimate treat.
Addresses: 2, rue des Francs-Bourgeois, Paris 3rd; 64, boulevard Haussman, Paris 8th
www.cafe-pouchkine.fr

Le Puits d'Amour
by Pâtisserie Stohrer

The history: the first recipe of the *puits d'amour* ("fount of love") dates back to 1735. At the time, it was a large vol-au-vent of puff pastry filled with red currant jelly and topped with a gold-leaved handle to represent the bucket of a well. According to legend, Louis XV offered his many mistresses this cake as proof of his love.
The flavors: Pâtisserie Stohrer decided to re-create the original recipe by filling the cake with a vanilla pastry cream and covering the top with a thick caramelized layer, made using a hot iron. As much as we love the little cake made for one, the larger one made to share is even more fun.
Address: 51, rue Montorgueil, Paris 2nd
www.stohrer.fr

La Tarte à la Crème
by Pâtisserie Benoît Castel

The history: it is the Italians that we owe for the creation of the *tarte à la crème* ("cream tart") during the eighteenth century. It first appeared in the countryside north of Botte, where it was served at weddings and baptisms. **The flavors:** the signature dessert of the boulangeries and pâtisseries of Benoît Castel, this tart is rather simple: a sablé crust filled with pastry cream flavored with Bourbon Madagascar vanilla, then topped with light whipped cream from Isigny Saint-Mère. A superbly simple pleasure.
Addresses: 150, rue Ménilmontant, Paris 20th; 40, boulevard Haussman, Paris 9th

Le Bostock aux Amandes
by Lenôtre

The story: with its name of English origin, the *bostock* does not appear in France until the mid-1930s. This pastry was initially a sophisticated variation of *pain perdu* (a very common preparation in Anglo-Saxon countries called "French toast"). It is much more uncommon in mainland France.
The flavors: once you have taken your first bite of this pastry, it is difficult not to finish all of it. It must be said that this brioche mousseline—soaked in almond syrup and orange flower water and filled with almond cream and slivered almonds—is particularly addictive.
Address: www.lenotre.com

skip to

The Tarte Bourdaloue, p. 172

The Story of Garlic

Under the ground, it is merely a rounded bulb composed of several pods destined for use as
a condiment and sometimes as a medicine, but garlic makes a grand impression on our plates!

Blandine Boyer

Wild garlic, or *Allium ursinum*
In a trend started by chefs, foodies scramble to pick the young leaves of this plant to enjoy. The fad may continue, but beware! The leaves are necessary for the plant to flourish: development from seed to matured bulb takes seven to ten years. A bulb cannot develop without its young leaves, so plucking them sparingly is vital to the entire plant's survival. In spring, wild garlic's appearance is ephemeral; its leaves turn yellow and disappear after just a few weeks. To preserve the leaves, you can freeze them, but they will eventually disintegrate.
In the kitchen: the leaves of wild garlic can be used in place of basil for a unique pesto: add a little parsley to temper its pungency, then use a dry goat cheese (which stands up well to its flavor), pumpkin seeds, and a sunflower or a rapeseed oil for balance.

Three-cornered leek, or *Allium triquetrum*
This plant is confined to the coast and is endemic to Brittany, but also very prevalent on the Côte d'Azur and in Corsica. The leaves are collected almost all year long. If you take a handful of wild bulbs and plant them in the shade in your garden, it is as if you were growing both parsley and garlic. To contain it, tear off the leaves in handfuls.
In the kitchen: chop and sprinkle it over omelets, tomatoes, or steamed potatoes. Add it to salads and *fromage frais.*

Many-flowered garlic, or *Allium polyanthum*
This plant doesn't know if it's garlic or a leek. When eaten raw, it is bitter, but its flavor becomes pungent and slightly sweet when cooked. It is perennial, so you only harvest what grows above the ground.
In the kitchen: it is delicious when incorporated into beignet batter, especially one lightened with beer and chickpea flour: (1½ cups/150 g chickpea flour, 1¾ oz/50 g all-purpose flour, ⅔ cup/150 mL water, and 5 tablespoons/75 mL beer).

Branded Cheeses

Some cheeses are sold under brand names and are part of our heritage. Here is the proof in four industrial brands.

Jean-Paul Branlard

A branded cheese product can certainly be considered a cheese. A brand is a "graphical representation used to distinguish a product." Quality cheeses that meet certain standards (such as PDO or PGI) are usually marketed under a brand name (such as Papillon brand Roquefort cheese), as are many "small" artisanal and farmhouse cheeses.

BUT WHAT IS "BRANDED CHEESE"?
This description, which is vague and rather unofficial, evokes industrial or semi-industrial products. Queyras Blue is the trademark of a Dauphinoise industrial-grade cow's-milk cheese; Caprice des Dieux, created in 1956, is a soft pasteurized cow's-milk cheese made by Bongrain, which has been able to carve out a significant portion of the cheese market with its oval box. France also has Saint-Albray, Saint-Môret, Chaussée aux moines, Chavroux, Tartare, Vieux Pané, Bleu de Bresse, Bleu de Laqueuille, Bellocq, and so on. And who among us has never peeled the foil wrapper from a wedge of Vache qui rit (Laughing Cow), created by Léon Bel in 1921, straight out of its famous round box?

BOURSAULT
In Saint-Cyr-sur-Morin, Henri Boursault produced small cheeses made from cow's milk. From having to skim the cream, he was left with a surplus of cream. In 1951, he tried an experiment: by using his surplus of cream, he invented a triple-cream cheese, which was left to mature in its microperforated paper packaging. The brand was launched into mass distribution in 1969.

BOURSIN
On October 11, 1968, at 7:55 p.m. on channel one of the ORTF (the national public radio and television agency in France), the first national TV ad for an industrial cheese was broadcast: Boursin, a cheese made with "garlic and herbs," which would eventually become available in several other flavors. In 1963, François Boursin, its creator, christened the product with his name. The cheese was created thanks to a misprint. In 1961, a newspaper announced the release of a "garlic Boursin," but it was actually a "Boursault," a cheese of its competitor. François Boursin quickly jumped on the idea, however, and invented a new cheese recipe with garlic. The product's success was immediate, and a second major campaign from 1972 featured the famous slogan "Bread, wine, Boursin."

CURÉ NANTAIS
In Saint-Julien-de-Concelles (Loire-Atlantique) around 1880, Pierre Hivert, a farmer, invented a cheese on the advice from a pastor. His product was first called "Régal des gourmets" but was eventually renamed Curé Nantais, in homage to the holy man. Its production remained a family business until it was purchased in 1980 by a creamery, which relocated its production to Pornic and later to Rennes, but the product's artisanal production remained unchanged.

PORT-SALUT
In the 1850s near Laval, the Trappists of Port-Ringeard Abbey, later renamed Port-du-Salut, began making cheese. In 1875, the prior proposed to a Parisian shopkeeper located on rue du Cardinal-Lemoine that he establish a warehouse for the sale of this uncooked, pressed cheese with its orange rind. Its success was immediate. The product adopted the name Port-de-Salut under a registered trademark beginning in 1870, and was later shortened to Port-Salut. In 1959, the monks ceded the brand to an agricultural group, who took it into industrial production and have since been the brand's producers.

At the Table with Claude Sautet

Eating is one of the favorite activities of the characters created by author and filmmaker Claude Sautet. As a great admirer of the filmmaker, the three-star Michelin chef Pierre Gagnaire selected three dishes from three of his films, which he reinterprets here.

François-Régis Gaudry and Delphine Le Feuvre

CÉSAR ET ROSALIE
(1972)

The scene

The last scene of the film marks the return of Rosalie (Romy Schneider), who abandoned César (Yves Montand) and David (Sami Frey). Her two former lovers now live together in a house where they are enjoying a meal together in front of the window when the love of their life suddenly reappears.

The reaction

While enjoying **rock lobster** (which has been changed to American lobster in the following recipe), César asks David: "Do you know what's inside? **Cider**."

SERVED AT SAUTET'S TABLES
A slice of cauliflower marinated in coriander, with crème caramel in *Quelques jours avec moi* (*A Few Days with Me*)
Langoustines and red mullet in *César et Rosalie* (*César and Rosalie*)
A peasant salad *in Nelly et Monsieur Arnaud* (*Nelly and Mr. Arnaud*)
A gratin Dauphinois in *Garçon!* (*Waiter!*)
Sauerkraut in *Max et les ferrailleurs* (Max and the Junkmen)
A Pont-l'Evêque cheese in *Mado*

SERVED IN SAUTET'S GLASSES
A 1961 Sauternes and cognac in *Nelly et Monsieur Arnaud* (*Nelly and Mr. Arnaud*)
A Pouilly and a glass of Champagne "at 5.5°C [42°F]" in *Garçon!* (*Waiter!*)

skip to
The Fishmonger's Stall, p. 218

The recipe

—— **LOBSTER IN CIDER** ——

PREPARATION TIME: 30 MINUTES
COOKING TIME: 10 MINUTES
SERVES 6
½ head cauliflower
1 bottle (750 mL) hard cider
Salt
1 whole 4½-pound (2 kg) lobster, or 3 whole lobsters weighing 1½ pounds (700 g) each
Just over ¾ cup (200 mL) cider-vinegar mayonnaise
2 tablespoons chopped parsley
5½ tablespoons (80 g) unsalted butter
⅓ ounce (10 g) cracked black peppercorns
7 ounces (200 g) string beans, cooked in boiling, salted water
Olive oil

Very thinly slice the cauliflower (ideally use a mandoline slicer). Place the cauliflower slices on a baking sheet, sprinkle them with a little water, and bake for 3 minutes at 400°F (200°C). Heat the cider in a saucepan over medium heat, stirring frequently, until reduced to a syrup. In a large saucepan of boiling salted water, cook the whole lobster(s) for 5 minutes, cool, then peel while still warm. Crush the pincers, remove and chop the meat, then stir the meat into the mayonnaise, add the parsley, and stir to thoroughly combine until

you have a texture similar to that of rillettes (a coarse pâté; see page 365). Melt the butter over medium heat until lightly browned. Remove from the heat and add the peppercorns. Cut the lobster tail meat into large pieces and coat them, while still warm, with the reduced cider, then the browned-butter mixture. Place the meat in a large, warmed serving dish, then arrange the cauliflower in the dish. Serve the mayonnaise mixture on the side in a shallow bowl. Season the string beans with a little olive oil and serve on the plate with the lobster.

VINCENT, FRANÇOIS, PAUL ET LES AUTRES
(1974)

The scene

A meal with friends in the countryside. There are eleven people seated around François (Michel Piccoli), who is slicing a leg of lamb. The debate of the day is about the suburbs, or "urban evolution."

The reaction

"Fuck all of you, and your Sundays with your lousy damn **leg of lamb**. Shit!"

The recipe

—— BONE-IN LEG OF LAMB ——

PREPARATION TIME: 30 MINUTES
RESTING TIME: 48 HOURS
COOKING TIME: 50 MINUTES
SERVES 4 TO 6

1 small container low-fat yogurt
1 teaspoon paprika
½ teaspoon mild curry
½ teaspoon chopped fresh rosemary
4 crushed juniper berries
1 pinch ground star anise
1 pinch ras el hanout
Olive oil
1 splash dry white wine
1 leg of lamb (3⅓ lb/1.5 kg to 4 lb/1.8 kg), prepared by your butcher
Fine salt
9 tablespoons (100 g) unsalted butter
12 cloves garlic, peeled and germs removed

In a small bowl, stir together the yogurt and all the spices. Add 3 tablespoons (45 mL) olive oil and the splash of wine. Brush the meat with this mixture, wrap it in plastic wrap, and let it marinate for 48 hours in the refrigerator. After this time, carefully brown the leg in olive oil in a cast-iron pot. After about 10 minutes, season with salt, then remove the leg from the pot. Preheat the oven to 350°F (180°C). Add the butter and garlic to the pot, then add back the leg of lamb. Bake for about 40 minutes, or until the lamb is cooked to the desired temperature. Be careful, as the butter must not burn. Add a few tablespoons of water during the cooking time to prevent this, if necessary. Turn the meat over from time to time, if needed.

Once out of the oven, let the lamb rest for half an hour before serving with the garlic cloves. Serve with a *caviar d'aubergine* (cold, puréed eggplant) in white miso.

GARÇON!
(1983)

The scene

Alex (Yves Montand), in his sixties, is a waiter in a Parisian brasserie. We see him throughout the movie serving guests. He is listing off the à la carte dishes to two regular customers, who appear twice in the film. The woman is indecisive about her choice.

The reaction

"Today we have **brill fillets in pesto**. It's steamed with pesto, **it's very very very light**."

The recipe

—— POACHED BRILL FILLETS WITH PESTO ——

PREPARATION TIME: 30 MINUTES
COOKING TIME: 20 MINUTES
SERVES 6

2⅛ cups (½ L) olive oil, plus more for drizzling
1 bunch fresh basil, leaves removed
3 cloves garlic, peeled and minced
1 bay leaf
1 sprig silver thyme
2 skinned brill fillets (about 1⅓ lb/600 g total)
3 ounces (80 g) roasted pine nuts
4¼ ounces (120 g) freshly grated Parmesan cheese
3 large ripe tomatoes (or canned)
Fleur de sel sea salt
Ground Espelette pepper

Preheat the oven to very low, about 140°F (60°C). Pour the oil into a large baking dish. Add the basil leaves, garlic, bay leaf, and thyme. Add the brill fillets, then place the dish in the oven for about 20 minutes, or until heated through. Remove the fillets, let them drain, then set them aside and keep warm. Strain and reserve the oil. In a food processor, process the basil leaves, garlic, pine nuts, and Parmesan to obtain a coarse mixture (the "pesto"). Peel the tomatoes, then cut them into large dice. Drizzle them with a little oil, then season them with sea salt and Espelette pepper. Place the chopped tomatoes in a warm, shallow serving dish, place the fillets on top, and top with the pesto. Serve with warm potatoes seasoned with a dash of dry white wine.

Newfound Love for the Chickpea

Snubbed for many years, the chickpea, filled with many virtues, makes a strong comeback to our plates.
And its cultivation is booming once again.

Marie-Amal Bizalion

A SUCCESS STORY

Originally from the Middle East, the chickpea (*Cicerum italicum*) has been grown in French gardens since at least the year 812 AD. It loves dry climates and flourished in southeast France until the middle of the twentieth century, when its cultivation was abandoned.

Today, its cultivation in France has exploded . . . from 2,627 acres (1,063 hectares) dedicated to its cultivation in 2000 to 23,458 acres (9,493 hectares) in 2016. The Occitanie region leads the way, followed by the Provence-Alpes-Côte d'Azur and Nouvelle Aquitaine regions. The cultivation of new crops, such as the black Desi variety, is being tested in the Southwest.

A POWERFUL MIXTURE

Each chickpea is made up of
16 percent protein,
17 percent iron,
17 percent magnesium,
and vitamins B_1, B_2, B_3, B_5, B_6 and B_9. By combining 65 percent durum wheat flour with 35 percent chickpea flour, one finds the **9 amino acids** essential to mankind.*
To avoid uncomfortable gas, add a little **baking soda** to the soaking water.

*Source: Gérard Laurens, known as "the chickpea papi," consultant specializing in seeds.

Purchase in cans, a jar, or in bulk?

Between the first two choices, the jar has the advantage of not leaving behind a taste of iron. Purchasing them dried and, if possible, from local growers, is ideal.

Socca niçoise

Combine 9 ounces (250 g) chickpea flour with 2 cups (500 mL) water, 1 teaspoon (6 g) salt, and 3 tablespoons (45 mL) olive oil. Spread in a thin layer onto an oiled baking sheet, bake in a very hot preheated oven (approximately 450°F/232°C), then immediately set the oven to broil. As soon as the top is browned, remove from the oven, cut into strips, and season with pepper.
For an afternoon snack: enjoy them on the go or at a local bar in the heart of old Nice. To be eaten warm, with the fingers.

Cade Toulonnaise

These are made with the same batter used for *socca* (a thin, unleavened crêpe made from chickpeas; see above right), but spread in a thicker layer. Place them in a hot oven for 10 minutes, then place them on a grill or under the broiler just until golden yet soft. Season with pepper and sprinkle with chopped scallions.
For an afternoon snack: watch for the blue "Cade-Man" scooter with a wood-burning oven on rue Paul-Lendrin at the Toulon market from Tuesday to Sunday—he's an ex-chef serving this snack up plain, with goat cheese, or with basil . . . and it's all organic!

Panisse Marseillaise

Bring 4¼ cups (1 L) salted water and 2 tablespoons (30 mL) olive oil to a boil. Off the heat, pour in 9 ounces (250 g) chickpea flour. Stir to thoroughly combine (using a whisk or an immersion blender), then lower the heat while stirring for several minutes. Spread the batter out to a ⅓-inch- (1 cm) thick layer at the bottom of one or more smooth-bottom pans. Refrigerate for 30 minutes, then stamp out rounds using a cookie cutter or slice into sticks. Fry on both sides in hot oil.
For an afternoon snack: search for them in southern France in front of the kiosks in L'Estaque.

BEST FLAVOR PAIRINGS

Cumin, lemon, saffron, sesame seeds, olive oil, argan oil, garlic, parsley, scallions, lamb, mutton

POICHICHADE

Served as an appetizer with bread or crudités, this purée has been the signature of Chef Armand Arnal* since his arrival in the Camargue in 2006.

SOAKING TIME: 12 HOURS
COOKING TIME: 45 MINUTES, MINIMUM
SERVES 8

7 ounces (200 g) dried chickpeas
1 onion
1 clove
1 clove garlic
1 bouquet garni
1 preserved lemon
1 teaspoon ground turmeric
1 teaspoon Chinese five-spice seasoning
Just over ¾ cup (200 mL) olive oil, plus more for drizzling
Salt and freshly ground black pepper

Soak the chickpeas for 12 hours in cold water. Drain, then transfer them to a large saucepan and cover with water. Quarter the onion and stick the clove into one of the quarters. Add the onion quarters, garlic clove, and bouquet garni to the saucepan. Bring to a boil, then let simmer until the chickpeas are tender (at least 45 minutes). Drain, reserving the cooking liquid. In a blender or food processor, blend together the hot chickpeas, lemon (quartered), turmeric, and five-spice seasoning, then slowly blend in the oil. Add a little of the reserved cooking liquid if the mixture seems too thick. Season with salt and pepper. Drizzle with olive oil to prevent from drying out.

*The Michelin-starred chef at La Chassagnette restaurant uses chickpeas from his own garden. Route du Sambuc, Arles (Bouches-du-Rhône).

PURCHASING THEM LOCALLY

→ **Rougiers (Var)**
In 1999, on volcanic soils, the cultivation of the chickpea was revived, and with great fanfare under the auspices of the Confrérie du pois chiche de Rougiers (Brotherhood of the Chickpeas of Rougiers), which holds a festival each September to celebrate the chickpea seed.

→ **Carlancas (Hérault)**
Grown on basaltic plateaus, this small golden *chichourle* (the name given to the chickpea in Carlancas) melts in the mouth after 25 minutes of cooking. Its farming was revived in 1975 by the Jeanjean family, although it was not exported but instead used for trade as it was during World War II, for items such as shoes and eggs.

skip to
Hungry for Haricots, p. 242

Wild Boar, a Bristly Beast

Despised by farmers, loved by hunters, known as the mammal *Sus scrofa* to those intimately familiar with it:
the wild boar is better known in France for its appearance on plates than in its forests.
Here are a few points to know about France's most-hunted big game.

Marie-Amal Bizalion

Head (hure) · Ear (écoute) · Hide (armure)
Peepers (mirettes)
Superior canines (gres)
Snout (boutoir)
Inferior canines (défense)
Tail (vrille)
Testicles (suites)
Paw (pince)
Bristly fur (pinceau)

A FEW FACTS

The boar can ravage a cornfield in just one night. France is the country with the largest wild boar population in western Europe, so the boar is high on its hunting list, especially since its meat is so highly prized. This champion of biodiversity is able to disperse a considerable amount of plant seeds that stick to its thick fur.

Sow tooth (dent de laie)

IN THE WILD BOAR FAMILY . . .

The boar: this is the male and can reach up to 440 pounds (200 kg). As the boar ages, its lower tusks curve to provide better defense.
The sow: this is the female, which rarely exceeds 220 pounds (100 kg); it has no teeth developed specifically for defense.
The piglet: the baby is born with a striped beige and brown coat. It becomes fully red between four and eight months old, and is referred to as the "redheaded beast."
Close cousins: the pig—a domesticated boar; the *sanglichon*—a cross between a male boar and a female pig; the *cochonglier*—a cross between a pig and a female boar.
Distant cousins: the peccary (America), the warthog and the bush pig (Africa), and the babirusa (Asia). All of these are part of the Suidae family.

BY THE NUMBERS

In France, the total number of slaughtered boars over the last twenty-five years has gone from 130,000 to 666,933. In 2016, the number increased by 13.9 percent compared to 2015, which is to say 1,827 per day!

skip to
Asterix's Gastronomic Tour of Gaul, p. 310

BEFORE COOKING IT

It's important to know: the boar can be infested with trichina, a parasite dangerous to humans. To avoid the parasite when cooking boar, there are two options: cook the meat for a long time or freeze it for 3 weeks at -4°F (-20°C). The meat sold in butcher shops is inspected by veterinary services to avoid the presence of the parasite.

DAUBE À LA PROVENÇALE

PREPARATION TIME: 15 MINUTES
COOKING TIME: 4 HOURS
SERVES 6

For the marinade
3⅓ pounds (1.5 kg) leg or fillet of boar, cut into pieces
4¼ cups (1 L) full-bodied red wine
Scant ¼ cup (50 mL) cognac
1 dash vinegar
3 carrots, sliced into rounds
1 onion
3 cloves, pierced into the onion
3 cloves garlic, unpeeled
Thyme
Bay leaf
10 peppercorns
2 thick strips unwaxed orange peel
For cooking
2 onions, chopped
Olive oil
2 tablespoons (12 g) all-purpose flour
1 to 1½ cups (250 to 375 mL) water
20 pitted black olives
Coarse salt

Make the marinade. The day before, combine all the ingredients in a large bowl, cover, and refrigerate overnight. The next day, remove the meat from the marinade. Strain the marinade liquid and reserve it and the marinated vegetables. Carefully dab the meat pieces dry. In a flameproof casserole dish, cook the onions in a drizzle of olive oil just until translucent; remove them from the casserole dish and set aside. Add a drizzle of olive oil to the casserole dish, then add the meat pieces in small quantities, lightly browning each batch before adding more. Sprinkle the meat with the flour and stir well to coat. Add the marinade liquid and just enough water to cover the meat. Simmer for 1 hour, covered. Add the marinated carrots and the pitted olives, and season with salt. Continue cooking over low heat for at least 3 hours. When the meat is tender, it's ready for the table!

Funny terms for its anatomy

Écoutes: ears
Mirettes: eyes
Boutoir: snout
Hure: head
Vrille: tail

No holds barred—anything goes when hunting wild boar

The boar is cunning: his sense of smell and hearing are very sharp. He can swim, or crouch down in heavy thickets. Nine times out of ten he evades his hunter.
The corral: some hunters follow its prints. The size and spacing of the toes in the prints are an indicator of the weight of the beast. Dogs and "beaters" then chase and corral the boar toward the hunters.
The lookout: this is the favorite method for bow hunters. Hidden up in a tree or in a watchtower, the immobile hunter watches and waits for the boar to simply pass by.
The approach: the hunter simply advances in silence toward his prey.
The straight hunt: A pack of trained dogs pursues and encircles the boar. If it's still living when riders on horseback arrive, they finish it off with a dagger.
The straight shot: in cases when the boar has inflicted major damage to crops, the animal is considered "harmful." For specific periods of time, a licensed hunter can shoot without restrictions or quotas. Only sows that are followed by piglets are spared.

The Gallic banquet—debunking a myth

Contrary to beliefs introduced by the writings of Camille Jullian,* the wild boar was, at the time of her writing, rare prey and hunting it was very dangerous. In the famous cartoon strip *Astérix and Obélix*, the characters were raising pigs, which is what you see depicted on spits.

*Author of Histoire de la Gaule *in eight volumes (from 1907 to 1927)*

① COMMENCEZ PAR LA PÂTE ; SUR VOTRE PLAN DE TRAVAIL, FAITES UNE FONTAINE AVEC LA FARINE. VERSEZ AU CENTRE L'OEUF, L'HUILE D'OLIVE, L'EAU TIÈDE AINSI QU'UNE BONNE PINCÉE DE SEL :

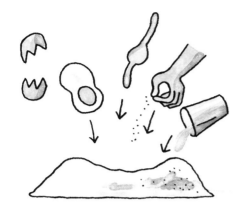

② PÉTRISSEZ LA PÂTE QUELQUES MINUTES EN AJOUTANT UN PEU DE FARINE OU D'EAU AU BESOIN, AFIN D'OBTENIR UNE CONSISTANCE FERME ET LISSE :

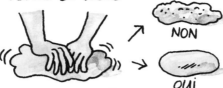

NON

OUI

ENVELOPPEZ LA PÂTE DANS DU FILM ALIMENTAIRE ET LAISSEZ-LA REPOSER AU FRAIS DEUX BONNES HEURES...

③ CONTINUEZ AVEC LA FARCE ; PRÉLEVEZ LA PARTIE VERTE DES BLETTES ET JETEZ LES CÔTES À LA POUBELLE EN PRENANT BIEN SOIN DE VOUS DÉSINFECTER LES MAINS APRÈS :

FAITES-LES BLANCHIR QUELQUES MINU-TES DANS DE L'EAU BOUILLANTE SALÉE PUIS ÉGOUTTEZ-LES ET LAISSEZ-LES REFROIDIR :

④ PRESSEZ FORTEMENT ENTRE VOS MAINS LES FEUILLES DE BLETTES POUR ÉLIMINER L'EXCÉDENT D'EAU, PUIS HACHEZ-LES :

DANS UNE POÊLE, FAITES REVENIR L'AIL ET L'OIGNON ÉMINCÉS DANS UN FILET D'HUILE D'OLIVE, PUIS AJOUTEZ LE RIZ :

⑤ FAITES CUIRE LE RIZ COMME UN RISOTTO, EN AJOUTANT AU FUR ET À MESURE DE L'EAU (ENVIRON 203ML)

TSHH   TSHH

QUAND IL EST PRÊT, RETIREZ LA POÊLE DU FEU ET AJOUTEZ LES BLETTES HACHÉES, LE PARMESAN RÂPÉ, LES OEUFS ET ÉVENTUELLEMENT LE FRO-MAGE DE CHÈVRE ÉMIETTÉ :

C'EST PRÊT!

SALÉPOIVREZ

⑥ CONFECTIONNEZ LES BARBAJUANS AINSI : FARINEZ VOTRE PLAN DE TRAVAIL ET ÉTALEZ UN MORCEAU DE PÂTE AU ROULEAU EN UNE LOOONGUE BANDE RECTANGULAIRE D'ENVIRON 13,7 CM DE LARGE ET 2 À 3 MM D'ÉPAISSEUR :

À L'AIDE DE DEUX PETITES CUILLÈRES, DÉPOSEZ DES NOIX DE FARCE SUR LA PARTIE INFÉRIEURE DE LA BANDE, EN LES ESPAÇANT TOUS LES 5,2 CM :

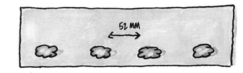

52 MM

⑦ À L'AIDE D'UN PINCEAU, HUMIDIFIEZ LA PARTIE SUPÉRIEURE DU RECTANGLE DE PÂTE ET RABATTEZ-LA SUR LA FARCE :

APPUYEZ BIEN AUTOUR DE CHAQUE TAS DE FARCE POUR SOUDER LES DEUX ÉPAISSEURS DE PÂTE ; AVEC UNE ROU-LETTE À PÂTISSERIE, DÉCOUPEZ CHA-QUE RAVIOLO ET RÉSERVEZ-LES SUR UNE PLANCHE FARINÉE :

⑧ ENFIN, FAITES FRIRE VOS BARBA-JUANS DANS UN BAIN D'HUILE NEUTRE BIEN CHAUDE (180°C) JUSQU'À CE QU'ILS SOIENT BIEN DORÉS :

HUILE NEUTRE

YODELAAIIOOO

ÉGOUTTEZ-LES ET DÉPOSEZ-LES SUR DU PAPIER ABSORBANT :

TO KISSS ME FOREVER ♪ ÉCRIT AU LIPSTICK ♪

BIEN DORÉ

ALOORS? C'EST BON LES BLETTE

OUI OH ÇA VA ON A COMPRIS!

JE SUIS SÛR QU'IL Y A MOYEN D'AMÉLIORER LA RECETTE AVEC DE L'ÉPINARD À LA PLACE.

Guillaume Long is a comic strip artist who handles a drawing pencil equally as well as a fork and who depicts, with biting humor, his gourmet (mis)adventures in his collection *À boire et à manger* (*To Drink and to Eat*, Éditions Gallimard). Here he recounts a recipe of the Barbajuans exclusively for *Let's Eat France*.

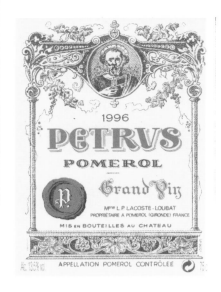

A "Fantasy" in the Glass

For enlightened amateurs and for collectors, some wines are becoming increasingly rare and thus have become, over time, real legends. Here are some prestigious wine estates illustrating the influence of France throughout the world.

Cerval Gwilherm

Bordeaux

In the twelfth century, thanks to the union of Eleanor of Aquitaine and Henry II Plantagenet, then king of England, the first French wines began to be exported from Bordeaux to Great Britain. English, German, Russian, Flemish, and Irish traders (Boyd-Cantenac, Lynch-Bages, Kirwan, and so on) settled in Bordeaux in the seventeeth century. With 323,493 acres (130,913 hectares) of vines, Bordeaux alone represents 17 percent of the vineyards of France.

PÉTRUS

Founding of the estate: in the nineteenth century
Region: Bordeaux
Appellation: Pomerol
Type: red wine
Viticulture: conventional
The birth of the legend: Pétrus built its reputation in the 1950s thanks to the obstinacy and dynamism of one woman: Mme Edmond Loubat ("Aunt Lou" to those close to her)
Particulars: does not use the notion of "château" and is not a cru classé
Classic vintages: 1990
Price per bottle: €2,500 ($2,900) (source: Idealwine)
Price by the glass: €416.60 ($490)
With whom should you drink it? Queen Elizabeth II (who served it for her engagement)

CHÂTEAU LAFITE ROTHSCHILD

Founding of the estate: in the seventeenth century
Region: Bordeaux
Appellation: Pauillac
Type: red wine
Viticulture: conventional
The birth of the legend: this wine was served at the court of Versailles and across the Channel in the eighteenth century
Particulars: became 1er Grand Cru Classé in 1855
Classic vintages: 1959
Price per bottle: €2,652 ($3,085) (source: Finestwine)
Price by the glass: €442 ($514)
With whom should you drink it? the Duke of Richelieu (who was already drinking it around 1760)

CHÂTEAU LATOUR

Founding of the estate: around 1680
Region: Bordeaux
Appellation: Pauillac
Type: red wine
Viticulture: organic
The birth of the legend: its former owner, Alexandre de Ségur, was nicknamed the "Prince of Vines" by Louis XV
Particulars: became 1er Grand Cru Classé in 1855
Classic vintages: 1961
Price per bottle: €3,699 ($4,300) (source: Wine-Searcher)
Price by the glass: €616.50 ($717)
With whom should you drink it? François Pinault (who has owned it since 1993 via the Kering group)

CHÂTEAU MOUTON-ROTHSCHILD

Founding of the estate: 1853
Region: Bordeaux
Appellation: Pauillac
Type: red wine
Viticulture: conventional
The birth of the legend: the baron Nathaniel de Rothschild restricted bottling to the château; until 1924 the wine had been delivered to merchants in barrels
Particulars: 1er Grand Cru Classé since only 1973; its labels are designed by a different artist each year
Classic vintages: 1945
Price per bottle: €10,950 ($12,740) (source: SoDivin)
Price by the glass: €1,825 ($2,120)
With whom should you drink it? Jeff Koons (who designed the label for the 2010 vintage)

CHÂTEAU MARGAUX

Founding of the estate: in the sixteenth century
Region: Bordeaux
Appellation: Margaux
Type: red wine
Viticulture: noncertified organic
The birth of the legend: in 1771, Château Margaux was the first "claret" to appear in a Christie's catalog
Particulars: became 1er Grand Cru Classé in 1855
Classic vintages: 1990
Price per bottle: €1,036 ($1,200) (source: Wine-Searcher)
Price by the glass: €172.60 ($200)
With whom should you drink it? Ernest Hemingway (who loved this wine so much that he named his daughter Margot)

CHÂTEAU HAUT-BRION

Founding of the estate: 1553
Region: Bordeaux
Appellation: Pessac-Léognan
Type: red wine
Viticulture: conventional
The birth of the legend: Talleyrand, then Minister of Foreign Relations for Napoléon Bonaparte (future Napoléon I) and owner of the château, welcomed at his table, with the assistance of his cook Antonin Carême, princes, sovereigns, and other world leaders
Particulars: the unique Graves was named 1er Grand Cru Classé of 1855
Classic vintages: 1989
Price per bottle: €2,112 ($2,450) (source: Finestwine)
Price by the glass: €352 ($409)
With whom should you drink it? Prince Robert of Luxembourg (current owner thanks to the 1935 acquisition by his great-grandfather Clarence Dillon)

CHÂTEAU D'YQUEM

Founding of the estate: 1593
Region: Bordeaux
Appellation: Sauternes
Type: sweet white wine
Viticulture: conventional
The birth of the legend: Thomas Jefferson, then US ambassador to Louis XVI, distributed it in America, with the support of President George Washington
Particulars: became 1er Cru Supérieur in 1855 and was not produced during the poor years (1910, 1915, 1930, 1951, 1952, 1964, 1972, 1974, 1992, 2012)
Classic vintages: 1921
Price per bottle: €8,670 ($10,086) (source: Finestwine)
Price by the glass: €1,445 ($1,681)
With whom should you drink it? Claude Chabrol (who places it in most of his films)

The wines' prices may vary. Prices shown were from December 2016.

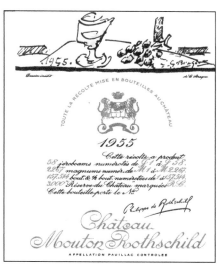

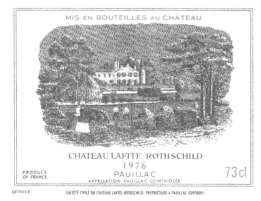

Burgundy

Two thousand years ago, France was already producing wine in Côte de Nuits and Côte de Beaune. These wines aroused enthusiasm in the Romans and Gallo-Romans. With 70,015 acres (28,334 hectares), Burgundy wine represents 3.6 percent of French vineyards and only 0.5 percent of world production. What's more, the Grands Crus represent barely 1 percent of Burgundy production and the average area per wine grower is 16 acres (6.5 hectares). It is often said that "what is rare is expensive." This holds true in Burgundy!

DOMAINE HENRI JAYER
Founding of the estate: early 1950s
Region: Burgundy
Appellation: Richebourg Grand Cru
Type: red wine
Viticulture: noncertified organic
The birth of the legend: an outstanding botanist, philosopher, and wine taster, Henri Jayer worked as hard in his vineyard as he did in his caves for wines that would rival the finesse of the famous Romanée-Conti
Particulars: Prices soared in 2006 after the death of Henri Jayer in Dijon at the age of eighty-four
Classic vintages: 1985
Price per bottle: €18,618 ($21,700) (source: Wine-Searcher)
Price by the glass: €3,103 ($3,610)
With whom should you drink it? Bernard Pivot (journalist and writer friend of Henri Jayer)

DOMAINE ROMANÉE-CONTI
Founding of the estate: 1760
Region: Burgundy
Appellation: Romanée-Conti Grand Cru
Type: red wine
Viticulture: biodynamic
The birth of the legend: Louis-François de Bourbon, prince of Conti, then diplomatic adviser of Louis XV, acquired La Romanée, which would eventually become La Romanée-Conti
Particulars: The Romanée-Conti Grand Cru is a monopoly of 4.03 acres (1.63 hectares)
Classic vintages: 1978
Price per bottle: €5,992 ($6,970) (source: Wine-Searcher)
Price by the glass: €2,665.30 ($3,100)
With whom should you drink it? Jean-Jacques Rousseau (writer, philosopher, musician, and friend of Louis-François de Bourbon)

DOMAINE LEFLAIVE
Founding of the estate: 1717
Region: Burgundy
Appellation: Montrachet Grand Cru
Type: white wine
Viticulture: biodynamic
The birth of the legend: Anne-Claude Leflaive was one of the pioneers of biodynamics in the Burgundy vineyards
Particulars: its perception of scarcity increased after the death of Anne-Claude in 2015 at the age of fifty-nine
Classic vintages: 1996
Price per bottle: €5,980 ($6,957) (source: Finestwine)
Price by the glass: €996.60 ($1,159)
With whom should you drink it? Alexandre Dumas (who said of Montrachet that it should be "drunk on bended knee with head bared")

DOMAINE LEROY
Founding of the estate: 1868
Region: Burgundy
Appellation: Musigny Grand Cru
Type: red wine
Viticulture: noncertified organic
The birth of the legend: in 1942, Henri Leroy became a shareholder of the Domaine de la Romanée-Conti and thus benefited from its network and expertise
Particulars: Lalou Bize-Leroy comanaged Domaine de la Romanée-Conti and strictly enforced biodynamics
Classic vintages: 1949
Price per bottle: €3,794 ($4,414) (source: Wine-Searcher)
Price by the glass: €632.30 ($735)
With whom should you drink it? Gérard Lanvin (who promotes Burgundy wines in the film *Premiers Crus*)

DOMAINE J.-F. COCHE DURY
Founding of the estate: 1964
Region: Burgundy
Appellation: Corton-Charlemagne Grand Cru
Type: white wine
Viticulture: conventional
The birth of the legend: the estate began marketing its wines in bottles in 1964 and developed its reputation thanks to Jean-François starting in 1972
Particulars: maintains a very wise price policy for its direct clientele
Classic vintages: 1989
Price per bottle: €5,561 ($6,470) (source: Wine-Searcher)
Price by the glass: €926.80 ($1,078)
With whom should you drink it? Charlemagne (annoyed from always staining his beard with red wine, he planted Chardonnay grapes on the mountain of Corton)

DOMAINE D'AUVENAY
Founding of the estate: 1989
Region: Burgundy
Appellation: Mazis-Chambertin Grand Cru
Type: red wine
Viticulture: noncertified organic
The birth of the legend: niche vineyard of 9.6 acres (3.9 hectares) established by Lalou Bize-Leroy
Particulars: the estate was an old farmhouse that served as a simple dwelling
Classic vintages: 2009
Price per bottle: €2,695 ($3,135) (source: Wine-Searcher)
Price by the glass: €449.10 ($522)
With whom should you drink it? Stop everything! It would be a tragedy to open this bottle!

DOMAINE ARMAND ROUSSEAU
Founding of the estate: around 1900
Region: Burgundy
Appellation: Chambertin Grand Cru
Type: red wine
Viticulture: noncertified organic
The birth of the legend: the estate began to market its wines in the United States after the end of Prohibition in the late 1930s
Particulars: the estate, which was passed from father to son for several generations, should pass down to Eric's daughter, Cyrielle Rousseau
Classic vintages: 2005
Price per bottle: €1,780 ($2,070) (source: Finestwine)
Price by the glass: €296.60 ($345)
With whom should you drink it? Napoléon I (this was his daily wine and the one that accompanied him during every military campaign)

DOMAINE G & C ROUMIER
Founding of the estate: 1924
Region: Burgundy
Appellation: Musigny Grand Cru
Type: red wine
Viticulture: noncertified organic
The birth of the legend: Georges Roumier initiated its bottling at the estate and implemented a commercial strategy aimed at foreign markets
Particulars: on the 29.33 acres (11.87 hectares) of the estate, only 0.49 acre (0.2 hectare) is for the production of white wine
Classic vintages: 2005
Price per bottle: €8,194 ($9,532) (source: Wine-Searcher)
Price by the glass: €1,365.60 ($1,588)
With whom should you drink it? Cédric Klapisch (filmmaker, great lover of wine, and director of the Burgundy-focused film *Ce qui nous lie* [*Back to Burgundy*])

continued ➡

Champagne

Listed as a World Heritage Site by UNESCO, Champagne earned distinction in the seventeenth century with its famous winemaking advancements refined by Dom Pierre Pérignon. In the nineteenth century, Champagne experienced an international boom thanks to the arrival of the German labels (Bollinger, Krug, and Deutz), which prospered in France. With 309 million bottles produced in 2015 on an area of around 84,016 acres (34,000 hectares), Champagne spearheads the dissemination of French culture overseas.

KRUG
Founding of the estate: 1843
Region and appellation: Champagne
Cuvée: Clos du Mesnil
Type: Champagne blanc
Viticulture: conventional
The birth of the legend: the estate was the first to ferment its Champagnes in small oak barrels and maintain an aging stock of six to eight years minimum, a practice that brings complexity and longevity to its wines
Particulars: produces only prestigious wines
Classic vintages: 1988
Price per bottle: €1,770 ($2,060) (source: Finestwine)
Price by the glass: €295 ($343)
With whom should you drink it? Bernard Arnault (he became owner in 1999 via the LVMH group)

CHAMPAGNE SALON
Founding of the estate: 1911
Region and appellation: Champagne
Cuvée: "S" of Salon
Type: Champagne blanc
Viticulture: conventional
The birth of the legend: the wines are kept in the caves for ten years on average and the vintage is produced only if the quality is considered perfect
Particulars: only vintages that are blanc de blancs (Chardonnay)
Classic vintages: 1959
Price per bottle: €5,812 ($6,760) (source: Wine-Searcher)
Price by the glass: €968.60 ($1,126)
With whom should you drink it? Louis XV (who declared this Champagne the official drink of his private festivals)

CHAMPAGNE DOM PÉRIGNON
Creation of the cuvée: 1936
Region and appellation: Champagne
Cuvée: vintage
Type: Champagne blanc
Viticulture: conventional
The birth of the legend: the friendship between Napoléon I and Jean-Rémy Chandon (founder of Moët & Chandon) marked the beginning of its worldwide success
Particulars: produces only vintages and only during the best years
Classic vintages: 1955
Price per bottle: €1,132 ($1,317) (source: Evinité)
Price by the glass: €188.60 ($219)
With whom should you drink it? Marilyn Monroe (it was her favorite Champagne)

Rhône Valley

Serving as a "hobby" to workers who were tasked with the reconstruction of postwar France, the wines of the Rhône Valley have long been considered "cheap." Now covering more than 108,726 acres (44,000 hectares), these vines were in existence during the time of the Romans (125 BCE) and the popes who fled Avignon in the fourteenth century to settle in the town of Châteauneuf-du-Pape. The estate Châteauneuf-du-Pape experienced a surge in media exposure and commercialization toward the end of the 1990s when a certain wine critic, Robert Parker, succumbed to the charms of these sun-drenched wines.

skip to
Phylloxera: Wine Enemy No. 1, p. 232

CHÂTEAU RAYAS
Founding of the estate: early 1920s
Region: Rhône Valley
Appellation: Châteauneuf-du-Pape
Type: red wine
Viticulture: noncertified organic
The birth of the legend: low yields, aging in old barrels, and very sandy soil allow for the creation of wines with a lot of finesse for the appellation
Particulars: while the appellation allows up to thirteen grape varieties, Château Rayas only uses Grenache
Classic vintages: 1990
Price per bottle: €1,023 ($1,190) (source: Wine-Searcher)
Price by the glass: €170.50 ($198)
With whom should you drink it? Pope John XXII (who built the first château for the Pope in Châteauneuf-du-Pape)

DOMAINE HENRI BONNEAU & FILS
Founding of the estate: 1956
Region: Rhône Valley
Appellation: Châteauneuf-du-Pape
Cuvée: Réserve des Célestins
Type: red wine
Viticulture: noncertified organic
The birth of the legend: long fermentations in concrete vats and the barrel aging of several of its wines for a minimum of six years have contributed to the success of the estate
Particulars: the prices rose in 2016 with the death of Henri Bonneau at age seventy-eight
Classic vintages: 1990
Price per bottle: €2,975 ($3,461) (source: Wine-Searcher)
Price by the glass: €495.80 ($576)
With whom should you drink it? With whomever you want! This opportunity will not appear twice in your lifetime!

· THE SAGA · OF THE CROISSANT

Marie-Laure Fréchet

Like the baguette, the croissant is a national symbol. But the croissant experienced considerable adventures before arriving in Paris. From East to the West, here is the (turbulent) journey of the croissant.

ANTIQUITY	16TH CENTURY	17TH CENTURY	18TH/19TH CENTURY

The Ancient Version

During ancient times, the crescent (from the Latin *crescere*, "to grow") had religious significance. It symbolized the moon and its phases and was an object of superstition and veneration. The Egyptians offered crescent-shaped breads to their goddesses, the Assyrians made them part of their holy meals, and the Persians included them in their worship of the dead. You can also find crescent-shaped breads in the representations of communion by the first Christians.

The Eastern Version

The crescent symbol reached Asia Minor, where the Ottoman Empire adopted it as its emblem. In 1536, Francis I signed an alliance with Sultan Suleiman the Magnificent. This undoubtedly inspired *gâteaux en croissant* (crescent-shaped cakes), which were notably served for a banquet commissioned by Catherine de Médicis. Crescent-shaped pastries then developed throughout the Mediterranean.

The Viennese Version

Is it legend or truth? In 1683, Vienna was besieged by the Turks, who decided to enter the city at night by a subterranean route. But the *boulangers* (bakers) kept watch while busy kneading their doughs. They sounded the alert, which helped avert the assault. In gratitude, Leopold I, archduke of Austria, granted the *boulangers* special privileges. And to commemorate the event, the *boulangers* are said to have invented a pastry in the shape of the Ottoman crescent, called the *Hörnchen* ("little horn").

The Parisian Version

Marie Antoinette is often credited with the arrival of the Viennese croissant in Paris after her marriage in 1770 to Louis XVI. But it is more than likely thanks to a former Viennese officer and entrepreneur, August Zang, who opened a Viennese bakery in Paris in 1838. The success of the pastry was such that within two years, people were rushing to buy his "viennoiseries." The croissant at this time was not yet flaky, but more like a Viennese brioche bread.

EARLY 20TH CENTURY	1970	1977	TODAY

The French Version

In the 1920s, French pastry chefs took hold of the Viennese croissant. It was at this time that it gained its buttery flakiness, as we know it today.

The Butter or Ordinary Version

In the 1970s, the so-called ordinary croissant appeared. It was made with margarine, was less fatty, and was considered more diet-conscious—and above all, less expensive. Purists prefer the butter croissant. The butter croissant and ordinary croissant are differentiated by their shapes: the ordinary is curved, the butter is straight.

The Commercialized Version

In 1977, the La Croissanterie logo was created. At the same time, Danone launched "Danerolles," the croissant that could be baked at home. Food manufacturers delivered frozen pallets of croissants to local bakeries. The result: today, 80 percent of croissants in France are made in factories.

The Real Croissant

It is plump, golden, shiny, and very flaky. Its crumb is lightly layered and buttery, without feeling greasy. It is made by an artisan baker or pastry chef who uses quality ingredients. There is currently no legislation in France that protects its production.

Almond CROISSANTS

6 day-old croissants

For the almond cream
4 tablespoons plus 1¾ teaspoons (65 g) unsalted butter
1 egg
¼ cup plus 3½ teaspoons (65 g) superfine sugar
2½ ounces (75 g) almond flour

For the syrup
1 cup (250 mL) water
3 tablespoons plus 1 teaspoon (50 mL) rum
½ cup (100 g) granulated sugar

For the glaze
1¾ ounces (50 g) sliced almonds
1¾ ounces (50 g) confectioners' sugar

This recipe allows for the use of day-old croissants. A classic in bakeries.

Cooking time: 20 minutes ◆ **Resting time:** 30 minutes ◆ **Serves 6**

Cut the croissants in half lengthwise and arrange on a plate.
   Make the almond cream: melt the butter in a saucepan over low heat. Whisk together the egg and superfine sugar until lightened, then whisk in the melted butter and the almond flour. Set aside for 30 minutes to cool. Make the syrup: stir together the water, rum, and granulated sugar in a saucepan, then bring the contents to a boil and let boil for 10 minutes.
   Brush the cut surfaces of the croissants with the syrup, then fill them with the almond cream. Arrange the croissants on a baking sheet, sprinkle with the sliced almonds, and bake for 15 minutes at 350°F (180°C). Once cool, dust them with confectioners' sugar.

Pot-au-Feu

A dish for Sundays and for meals with family, the pot-au-feu is such a popular tradition that it has risen to the stature of a national dish. Here are recipes and golden rules for successfully executing this sensational stew, which has inspired cooks and writers for centuries.

Camille Pierrard

The Golden Rules

1
The proportion of water added to a pot-au-feu is 12⅔ cups (3 L) of water per 2¼ pounds (1 kg) of meat.

2
Cold water is not a requirement. Lukewarm water reduces the amount of time needed to reach cooking temperature.

3
Rinsing the meat beforehand prevents too much foam from developing at the start of cooking.

4
Salt halfway through the cooking time. Although salt tends to accelerate the loss of juices of the meat into the water, it helps maintain the flavor of the meat while also creating a tasty broth.

5
Choose a large cast-iron or stainless-steel pot. Avoid aluminum, which does not retain heat as well.

6
Cook the potatoes separately as they tend to spoil the broth.

7
If a person says that pot-au-feu is better when it's rewarmed, it's because rewarming causes a change in the meat's collagen. Cook your pot-au-feu for a long time and at a low temperature.

8
Pot-au-feu should always be cooked uncovered.

POT-AU-FEU
by Éric Trochon*

PREPARATION TIME: 45 MINUTES
COOKING TIME: 4 HOURS
SERVES 6

1⅛ pounds (500 g) top rib of beef
1⅓ pounds (600 g) top round or chuck
1⅛ pounds (500 g) beef shoulder
1 bouquet garni (thyme, bay leaves, and parsley, tied together with a green from a leek)
1 onion
Several cloves, pierced into the onion
Coarse salt
1 teaspoon black peppercorns
6 leek whites
6 large carrots
6 round and equal-size turnips
1 small celery root
An assortment of vegetables, depending on the season: Jerusalem artichokes, rutabagas, celery stalks, green cabbage, and the like
4 marrow bones
12 small potatoes (firm flesh)
Rustic bread, sliced and grilled

PREPARATION
Place the meats in a large pot, cover with about 5¼ quarts (5 L) of lukewarm water, then bring the contents to a boil; skim off any foam that forms on the top. Add the bouquet garni, then the clove-studded onion. After 2 hours, season with a pinch of salt, add the peppercorns, and cook for another 30 minutes. Add the vegetables and marrow bones and continue cooking for 1 hour. If necessary, top with a little water during the cooking time. Cook the potatoes separately in a little broth from the pot-au-feu.

TO SERVE
Remove the bouquet garni and the onion. Pour the broth into a soup tureen, taste for seasoning, then lightly skim off any fat remaining on the surface. Drain the meat, remove any twine, and arrange the meat in a large serving bowl. Surround the meat with the cooked vegetables. Scoop the marrow from the bones and use it to spread onto the slices of grilled bread. Serve the pot-au-feu with mustard, cornichons, and coarse salt on the side.

*Chef of Semilla, Paris 6th, and MOF chef 2011

The pot-au-feu in literature: selected pieces

AT TIMES REPRESENTING FRENCH PRIDE . . .
"A pot-au-feu is sometimes described as a piece of beef destined to be treated with lightly salted boiling water to extract the soluble parts. . . . Vegetables or roots are added to the broth to enhance the taste, and bread or pasta is added to make it more nourishing: this is called a *potage*. . . . We agree that we do not eat soup anywhere as good as what is found in France. . . . *Potage* is the foundation of the national French diet, and centuries of experience have raised it to a level of perfection." —*Physiologie du goût* (*The Physiology of Taste*), 1825, by Jean-Anthelme Brillat-Savarin

. . . AT TIMES A DISH OF THE POOR
"She sat down to dine, at the round table which had been covered with a three-day-old tablecloth, opposite her husband who was delighting in the soup from the tureen and who declared, with an enchanted air, 'Ah! A good pot-au-feu! I know nothing better than this.' She thought of fine dinners, shiny silverware, and tapestries covering walls, depicting ancient peoples and strange birds in the middle of a forest of fairies. . . ."
—"La Parure" ("The Necklace"), 1884, by Guy de Maupassant

A RELIGIOUS PLEASURE
"The beef itself, rubbed with saltpeter and salt, was sliced, and the flesh so tender that the lips could sense, in advance, its deliciously fragile quality. The aroma emanating from it came not only from the beef juices steaming up from it like incense, but from the lively scent of tarragon which impregnated it, and from a few, but just a few in fact, perfectly translucent cubes of pork." —*La Vie et la Passion de Dodin-Bouffant* (*The Life and Passion of Dodin-Bouffant*), 1924, by Marcel Rouff

A POETIC METAPHOR
"His **imagination** is always **bubbling** and his ideas dance like **turnips** and **potatoes** in a **pot-au-feu**."
—*L'Endormie* (1887) by Paul Claudel

skip to . . . .
A *Tour de France*: Buckwheat, p. 308

Syrups

Originating from medieval Arabic pharmacopoeia, fruit and plant syrups are simple pleasures that have become indispensable ingredients for some cocktails. Here is an overview of some of France's most iconic mixtures.

Camille Pierrard

Grenadine
Origin: throughout France.
The undisputed star of syrups, grenadine takes its name from its original base, which was made from pomegranate (*grenade* in French). Today, it is a red-fruit syrup flavored with lemon and vanilla.
Uses: in a glass of milk or lemonade, or in a cocktail.

Angelica
Origin: Niort and the Marais Poitevin.
Known for its medicinal properties since the fourteenth century, angelica is a plant with broad stems and white flowers. Since the eighteenth century, it has been grown in the Niort region and used in the production of liquors and candies. To make this syrup, the petioles (stems) are boiled; the boiled stems are also excellent to eat when candied.
Uses: satisfyingly thirst-quenching when added to water or lemonade!

A LITTLE HISTORY
→ In the twelfth century, syrups were created as part of medieval Arabic medicine, and were called "sharab." Arabic pharmacological science soon spread in the Latin world and the word *sharab* gave rise to *siruppus*, the origin of the word *syrup*.
→ The 1920s marked the beginning of industrial manufacturing of syrups in France. Many distilleries, like Teisseire or Monin, makers of liquors, began marketing syrups without alcohol.
→ Today, industrial syrups generally have very low fruit content (sometimes only 30 percent). To find flavorful artisanal and natural syrups, it is best to stock up on those by small producers or to simply make one yourself!

Green mint
Origin: throughout France.
Known for its analgesic and digestive properties, mint is best picked in the morning before the sun adversely impacts its aromas. And don't be fooled by the emerald-green color of a mint syrup; real mint syrups are very pale in color.
Uses: in a glass of ice water on summer days or in a Perroquet cocktail.

Elderberry
Origin: throughout France.
Its delicate white flowers result in a syrup with a slightly acidic and floral taste. The dark red berries, inedible when raw, have a mild taste, making it necessary to add a large amount of berries when making the syrup.
Uses: in water or, in the case of elderflower syrup, in desserts (such as rice pudding or flan).

Orgeat
Origin: in the *midi* (the south of France). This is a southern syrup par excellence. Orgeat was initially composed of a concentration of barley and almonds. Today, this syrup is made with almond milk and orange blossom water.
Uses: dilute it with water or pastis for a Mauresque aperitif.

Violet
Origin: Toulouse, Hyères, Grasse, southern Paris.
Cultivated from the mid-nineteenth century in Toulouse (which adopted the flower as its emblem), in Hyères, and in areas south of Paris for use in perfume, the violet results in a syrup with a very sweet taste.
Uses: provides an aromatic sweetness in pastry creams, ice creams, and fruit salads.

Cassis
Origin: Burgundy.
Many medicinal properties were attributed to cassis (black currant) as early as the eighteenth century: it was known to cure gout, fevers, and rheumatism. Starting from 1840, its cultivation developed in Burgundy to meet the growing demand for liqueurs. Its berries create a very aromatic syrup.
Uses: add to white wine (as a "Kir"), to Champagne (as a "Kir royal"), or to still water (as a "virgin Kir" for children).

Roselle
Origin: Martinique.
Common to the West Indies, roselle is a species of hibiscus, used to make bissap. The Martinican tradition is to consume the syrup during the Christmas season when the roselle shrub is in bloom. The syrup has a sour taste from the buds of its flower.
Uses: diluted in water or used in punch instead of cane sugar.

Syrups & Pastaga: The Saga

Because they are delicious when combined, pastis and syrups make legendary cocktails!

- pastis + **orgeat** = Mauresque
- pastis + **peach** = pelican
- pastis + **grenadine** = tomato
- pastis + **mint** = parrot
- pastis + **mint** + **grenadine** = dead leaf
- pastis + **strawberry** = rourou
- pastis + **grapefruit** = salt miner
- pastis + **banana** = cornichon
- pastis + **lemon** = Indian or canary

MINT SYRUP
by Véronique Verderet*

PREPARATION TIME: 2 DAYS
COOKING TIME: 3 MINUTES

1¾ ounces (50 g) mint leaves
Juice of 1 lemon
1 teaspoon (6 g) coarse salt
1¼ cups (250 g) sugar
2½ cups (600 mL) boiling water

Chop the mint leaves and place in a large jar. Add the lemon juice and muddle with the mint leaves using a wooden spoon. Add the salt and sugar while continuing to muddle the mixture. Let it macerate overnight. The next day, pour the boiling water into the jar and let it rest again overnight. Strain the liquid and boil it for 2 to 3 minutes, then pour it into a bottle with a tight-fitting lid. To increase the shelf life of the syrup, sterilize the jars and bottles before storing the syrup. Once opened, it can be refrigerated for up to 1 month.

English-flower truck farmer in Eulmont (Meurthe-et-Moselle)

CASSIS SYRUP

PREPARATION TIME: 10 MINUTES
COOKING TIME: 20 MINUTES
MAKES 3½ QUARTS (3½ L)

2¼ pounds (1 kg) sugar
4¼ cups (1 L) water
2¼ pounds (1 kg) black currants, seeded

Slowly bring the sugar and water to a boil in a saucepan and let it boil gently for 10 minutes while stirring. Wash and dry the black currants, then add them to the saucepan; let boil for another 10 minutes. Line the inside of a colander with a thin cloth (such as cheesecloth) and strain the hot mixture, crushing the fruit with a pestle or the back of a wooden spoon to extract all the juice. Pour the syrup into a glass bottle with an airtight seal. Store away from light.

skip to
Home-Crafted Liqueurs, p. 296

The Art of the Accident

"Serendipity": the art of making an accidental discovery from a combination of circumstances. Believe it or not, many of France's delicacies were born this way—by accident! From a pinch of creative luck, a large handful of happy mistakes, and a good ladle of storytelling come some of the country's most delectable delights.

Camille Pierrard

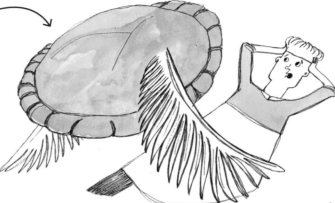

The Vol-au-vent

Created: in the first half of the nineteenth century in Paris.

Once upon a time: a baker's assistant under Marie-Antoine Carême, upon seeing the "king of chefs and the chef of kings" in person, forgot to prick his puff pastry before baking it. Consequently, the pastry doubled in volume in the oven and he shouted, "It's flying in the wind!" The result: a *vol-au-vent* ("flies in the wind"), which is now a dish in which a sauce is served inside a hollow, extremely light case of puff pastry.

Believability factor? 70 percent truth, 30 percent popular culinary myth.

Roquefort

Created: exact date unknown, but first mentioned in a document around 1070.

Once upon a time: while trying to seduce a shepherdess, a shepherd forgot his bread and his sheep's-cheese curds in a cave in Combalou (Aveyron). Returning to the cave after a few months, he noticed the development of a blue mold on the cheese.

Believability factor? 10 percent truth, 40 percent romance novel, 50 local gift of gab.

The Tarte Tatin

Created: end of the nineteenth century at Lamotte-Beuvron.

Once upon a time: sisters Caroline and Stephanie Tatin ran a hotel-restaurant in Sologne. It is said that one day the youngest forgot to put the dough in her pan for her apple tart, so she placed it on top after cooking the apples, creating an upside-down tart. Gastronome and writer Maurice Edmond Sailland, known as Curnonsky, helped popularize the dessert under the name *tarte des demoiselles Tatin* ("the Tatin damsels' tart")

Believability factor? 50 percent truth, 30 percent culinary genius, 20 percent fiction.

The Kouign-amann

Created: in 1860 in Douarnenez.

Once upon a time: in order to quickly replenish his bake shop on a busy day, baker Yves-René Scordia improvised making a cake with ingredients he had on hand: bread dough, butter, and sugar. Using the technique of working with puff pastry, which he had mastered, he produced a caramelized cake oozing with butter. In the language of Breton, *kouign-amann* also means *gâteau* ("cake") or *brioche au beurre* ("brioche with butter").

Believability factor? 90 percent truth, 10 percent Breton pride.

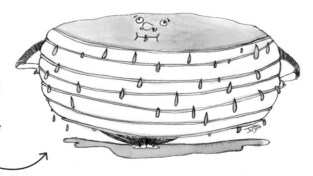

Milk Jam

Created: in the nineteenth century, during one of the Napoléonic battles.

Once upon a time: the Argentineans may claim to have invented *dulce de leche*, but according to French legend, milk jam was discovered by a chef of the Napoléonic army who left a ration of sweetened milk, intended for the soldiers, on the fire to cook too long.

Believability factor? 25 percent truth, 75 percent national pride.

The Gâteau Manqué ("Failed" Cake)

Created: in 1842 in Paris.

Once upon a time: a pastry cook from Maison Félix botched his egg whites while making a *biscuit de Savoie* (a type of sponge cake). To avoid wasting the batter, he added butter instead, then covered the cake with a layer of praline (or crushed almonds, depending on the version of the story).

Believability factor? 40 percent truth, 60 percent old wives' tale.

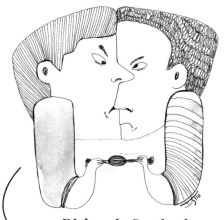

Bêtises de Cambrai (Cambrai "Mistakes")

Created: sometime during the nineteenth century in Cambrai.

Once upon a time: an apprentice confectioner made a mistake in preparing these famous mint candies. Although he was reprimanded, the delicacies he created were very successful with customers. Two candy makers, Afchain and Despinoy, still dispute which of them can lay claim to the creation.

Believability factor? 50 percent truth, 20 percent legend, 30 percent storytelling.

Pineau des Charentes

Created: end of the sixteenth century in Saintonge.

Once upon a time: a winemaker from Charentes mistakenly poured grape must into a barrel containing eau-de-vie from cognac. A few years later when he opened the barrel, he discovered a clear, sweet wine inside. In the 1920s, it became one of the first *mistelles* ("wine juice mixed with a spirit") to be marketed.

Believability factor? 10 percent truth, 60 percent traditional know-how, 30 percent sales pitch.

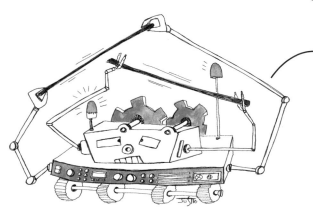

The Carambar

Created: in 1954 in Marcq-en-Baroeul.

Once upon a time: a malfunctioning machine in the candy factory Delespaul contributed the elongated shape to this iconic sweet, which is a bar made of caramel and cocoa. Since that time, it has been repeatedly admitted that it was an intentional invention and not an accident, but it seems the legend sticks as much as the candy!

Believability factor? 0 percent truth, 100 percent fun legend.

Sauternes

Created: depending on which version of the story you hear, either in 1836 in Bommes or in 1847 in Yquem.

Once upon a time: due to a long period of rain, the wine merchant Focke was forced to harvest his grapes late on his estate, Château La Tour Blanche, despite the appearance of rot on the grapes—thus was born sweet wine. According to the other legend, the Marquis de Lur-Saluces, owner of Château d'Yquem, forbade that any harvesting take place in his absence. His extended stay during a hunt in Russia allowed rot to develop on his grapes.

Believability factor? in both cases, 60 percent truth, 40 percent regional embellishment.

Bayonne Ham

Created: sometime during the fourteenth century.

Once upon a time: while hunting, Gaston Phoebus, count of Foix and a hero from Béarn, wounded a wild boar, which wasn't found until four months later, lying perfectly preserved in a salty spring in Salies-de-Béarn. As a result, the practice of salting pork developed around the Adour basin.

Believability factor? 50 percent truth, 50 percent chivalrous fiction.

Nantes Beurre Blanc Sauce

Created: end of the nineteenth century, at La Chapelle-sur-Erdre.

Once upon a time: while preparing a béarnaise sauce, Clémence Lefeuvre of the Marquis de Goulaine forgot to add the eggs. But according to statements by her descendants, the creation of this sauce owes nothing to chance. Listening to her customers' opinions, she had the idea of adding shallots to a sauce of melted butter and vinegar, and gradually adjusted the proportions until it was perfected.

Believability factor? 1 percent truth, 99 percent legend—totaling 100 percent talent.

LA TARTE DES DEMOISELLES TATIN (TARTE TATIN)
from the Lichonneux Brotherhood of Tarte Tatin*

PEPARATION TIME: 2 HOURS
COOKING TIME: 1 HOUR
SERVES 6

For the pâte brisée (flaky pastry)
5 tablespoons (70 g) unsalted butter, softened
1⅓ cups (170 g) all-purpose flour
1 tablespoon plus 1¾ teaspoons (20 g) granulated sugar
1 pinch salt
2 tablespoons (30 mL) water
1 egg yolk (optional)

5½ tablespoons (80 g) unsalted butter, melted
½ cup plus 2 tablespoons plus 1¼ teaspoons (130 g) coarse sugar
3½ pounds (1.6 kg) apples (such as Gala or Jonagold), peeled, cored, and quartered

Make the pâte brisée. In a bain-marie, combine the softened butter with the flour, granulated sugar, and salt. Knead the mixture together using your hands until a sandy mixture is achieved. Add the water and egg yolk, if using, and incorporate them into the mixture to form a dough; smear the dough on a work surface with the palm of your hand three or four times to thoroughly incorporate the butter. Flatten the dough into a disk, wrap it in plastic wrap, and refrigerate it for 1 hour. Preheat the oven to 400°F (200°C). In a 9½-inch- (24 cm) flameproof pan, stir the 5½ tablespoons (80 g) of melted butter and the coarse sugar to combine. Place a layer of the apple wedges

in the bottom of the pan with the sugar-butter mixture, ensuring the thick side of the apple is against the bottom of the pan. Cover this layer with a second layer of apples with the thicker sides pointed up. Bake for 30 minutes.

Roll out the dough to about ⅒ inch (2 mm) thick. Remove the pan from the oven (keep the oven heated) and place it on the stove over medium heat for about 25 minutes. Swirl the pan to prevent the apples from sticking. When the apples in the bottom of the pan are caramelized and have shriveled to about 1 inch (3 cm) in diameter (to check, lift up part of the apple wedges from the top layer), remove the pan from the heat.

Carefully lift the dough circle and place it on top of the cooked apples in the pan. Prick the top of the dough with a fork to make a few holes. Bake for 25 minutes, or until the dough is golden. Let cool overnight. Run a knife around the edges of the pan to release the tart, then reheat it briefly. Place a serving dish on top and quickly invert it, being careful of any hot caramel that might flow out. Serve!

The Lichonneux Brotherhood of Tarte Tatin is an association created in 1979 whose purpose is to preserve the traditional Tarte Tatin recipe.

skip to
Camembert, p. 89;
Carambar—Laughter in a Bar, p. 25

Wild Mushrooms

Keep your eyes peeled and your basket ready! The forest is full of delicious surprises,
provided of course that you know where to look!

Jill Cousin

LET'S TAKE A WALK IN THE WOODS (LEGALLY)

In France, the foraging of wild mushrooms is controlled by the provisions of forest code and environmental code. Whether foraged by individuals or by commercial entities, harvesting wild mushrooms is prohibited without the authorization of the landowner. In wooded areas and forests, under the jurisdiction of the foresting governing body, collecting wild mushrooms is allowed as long as the volume does not exceed 5¼ quarts/5 L (up to 11 lb/5 kg) per person per day. Persons in violation of these limits can incur a fine of between €750 to €45,000 ($874 to $52,400) and three years imprisonment, depending on the amount collected

A GOOD HARVEST

The proliferation of carpophores (mushrooms) depends on the level of precipitation, as well as temperatures and the amount of sunshine.

CAUTION: DANGER OF DEATH!

Rule number one: only collect mushrooms you are certain are edible. Be especially **cautious of those mushrooms that resemble each other!** Each year in France, there are between six and ten deaths due to the ingestion of toxic mushrooms. If in doubt, consult a mycologist or **pharmacist**.

The months of September and October are ideal provided it is not too hot and has rained a few days before collecting is to begin. Finding a spot where mushrooms are proliferating is not a matter of chance. The best ones are hiding in the sandy terrain on slopes. You should avoid roadsides and any place close to a source of pollution. Leave the plastic bags at home and choose a wicker basket, which will allow your collected mushrooms to breathe.

Mushrooms Do Not Like Water!

To preserve their aromas, do not wash or peel your mushrooms; rather, wipe them with a damp cloth or paper towel. You can also use a brush. If they are very dirty, wash them very briefly under running water, but never soak them.

A WORD TO KNOW

dessiccation

This is the process of removing water (dehydration). Desiccation is suitable for mushroom species whose flesh is already poorly hydrated and relatively firm, such as chanterelles, faux mousseron (fairy-ring mushroom), morel, or porcini. Once sliced, these mushrooms can be air-dried or baked.

★ ★ ★

What Should You Do with Wild Mushrooms?

Make a fricassee: in a skillet, melt a good-size pat of butter and cook some peeled and chopped garlic and shallots until browned. Add the sliced mushrooms and cook for several minutes, or until the mushrooms are cooked as desired. Serve with a few sprigs of flat-leaf parsley.

Make a risotto: in a saucepan, cook some peeled and minced shallots until translucent. Add carnaroli rice, then deglaze the pan with a little white wine. Cook the rice by adding chicken broth a little at a time until it is absorbed. Panfry the mushrooms, then add them to the risotto. Off the heat, add a little butter and Parmesan; serve immediately.

Make a velouté: brown the mushrooms with some peeled and sliced shallots in a little butter. Add a little chicken broth and simmer for 15 minutes. Stir the mixture while gradually incorporating a little heavy cream. Serve sprinkled with a handful of parsley.

skip to

The Truffle, p. 276; Porcini, p. 347

MUSHROOM BEIGNETS
by Philippe Emanuelli*

PREPARATION TIME: 10 MINUTES
RESTING TIME: 1 HOUR
COOKING TIME: 2 MINUTES

An assortment of fresh mushrooms (such as agaricus, blue-foot, and oyster mushrooms)
Flour
1 egg
Bread crumbs (from white bread, or use panko)
Oil, for frying
Parsley
Salt
1 lemon

Une initiation à la cuisine du champignon, Marabout, 2013.

Cut off the stems of the mushrooms, if necessary, and cut any large ones in half, then sprinkle with flour. Beat the egg with a fork, then dredge the mushrooms in the egg. Roll the mushrooms in the bread crumbs, then place them on a rack and refrigerate. In a heavy-bottom pot, heat the oil to 350°F (180°C). Drop the mushrooms in the oil in small quantities, and fry until golden on all sides. Remove and let drain on a cloth or paper towel. Serve with parsley, salt, and a fresh squeeze of lemon.

CHANTERELLES À LA POUTARGUE
by Philippe Emanuelli

PREPARATION TIME: 20 MINUTES
COOKING TIME: 10 MINUTES
SERVES 4

14 ounces (400 g) gray chanterelles (their aromas blend particularly well with this dish)
Olive oil
1¾ ounces (50 g) *poutargue* (dried, pressed roe), ground or cut into thin strips
1 lemon

Carefully sort and clean the chanterelles by opening and brushing the large ones. Sauté the chanterelles in a little oil until they have released all their water. Add an additional drizzle of oil, if necessary, then sprinkle the mushrooms with the *poutarge*. Serve with lemon.

France's 10 Most-Foraged Mushrooms

Hedgehog Mushroom
(Pied-de-Mouton)

Hydnum repandum
Availability: August to November
Hiding place: in the undergrowth at the foot of hardwoods and conifers
Taste: sweet, or a bit bitter as it ages
Use: for cooking

Black Morel
(Morille conique)

Morchella conica
Availability: February to April
Hiding place: in the mountains, at the foot of hardwoods and conifers
Taste: very delicate, reminiscent of hazelnut
Use: must be cooked; when raw, it is toxic

Porcini
(Cèpe de Bordeaux)

Boletus edulis
Availability: August to November
Hiding place: in acidic soils, at the foot of hardwoods and conifers
Taste: sweet and nutty
Use: raw, cooked, or dried

Bronze Bolete
(Cèpe bronzé)

Boletus aereus
Availability: May to October
Hiding place: at the foot of oaks and chestnuts
Taste: a bit bitter
Use: suitable for all preparations, but desiccation (dehydration) enhances its flavor

Golden Chanterelles
(Girolles)

Cantharellus cibarius
Availability: May to November
Hiding place: in siliceous soils; in the plains, in the undergrowth of wooded areas; in the mountains, at the foot of conifers
Taste: peppery
Use: raw or cooked

Trumpet Chanterelles
(Chanterelle en tube)

Cantharellus tubaeformis
Availability: end of July to beginning of December
Hiding place: prefers moss and acidic soils
Taste: creamy and woody
Use: cooked or dried; when eaten raw, it causes serious gastric problems

Horn of Plenty
(Trompette-des-morts)

Cantharellus cornucopioides
Availability: August to November
Hiding place: in dark wooded areas at the foot of hardwoods
Taste: spicy and peppery
Use: cooked or dried; consumed in excess, it causes bowel obstruction

St. George's Mushroom
(Mousseron)

Calocybe gambosa
Availability: April to June
Hiding place: in meadows, especially mountain meadows
Taste: flourlike
Use: cooked or dried

Sparassis
(Sparassis crépu)

Sparassis crispa
Availability: September to November
Hiding place: at the foot of pines
Taste: cinnamon and nuts
Use: well cooked; when eaten raw, it is toxic

Black Truffle
(Truffe noire)

Tuber melanosporum
Availability: November to February
Hiding place: between 1,600 and 3,200 feet (500 and 1000 m) in altitude; grows in symbiosis with oaks, ash trees, or hornbeams
Taste: vanilla, humus
Use: raw, finely grated

MUSHROOM CANAPÉS
by Michelle Baud*

PREPARATION TIME: 10 MINUTES
COOKING TIME: 10 MINUTES
SERVES 6

10½ ounces (300 g) button mushrooms
20 morel mushrooms (fresh or dried)
10½ tablespoons (125 g) unsalted butter
Juice of 1 lemon
2 tablespoons plus 1½ teaspoons (15 g) all-purpose flour
⅓ cup plus 1 tablespoon (100 mL) dry white wine
2 egg yolks
Salt and freshly ground black pepper
6 slices bread

Sauté all the mushrooms for 5 minutes in 5 tablespoons (75 g) of the butter. Add the lemon juice, then slowly sprinkle in the flour. Add the wine. Stir to combine and cook for 5 minutes. Remove from the heat and stir in the egg yolks. Season with salt and pepper. Fry the slices of bread in the remaining butter. Spread some of the mushroom mixture on the fried slices of bread and serve immediately.

Michelle Baud, an excellent Italian-Polish saucier, revisits a famous recipe by Ginette Mathiot.

THE GOOD TUBES OF THE ALEMBIC STILL

Many liquors are distilled in France, from Armagnac to vodka. How do you make spirits? Answer: with spirit.

Charles Patin O'Coohoon

NAME OF LIQUOR	MADE WITH WHAT?	MADE WHERE?	TYPE OF DISTILLATION
Armagnac	White grapes	Gers, Landes, Lot-et-Garonne	Double
Cognac	White grapes	Charente, Charente-Maritime, Dordogne, Deux-Sèvres	Double
Calvados	Apple	Calvados, Orne, Seine-Maritime	Double
Chartreuse	130 plants	Isère	Single
Fruit eau-de-vie	Fruit	Anywhere there's an albemic still	Double
Whiskey	Malted barley	From the Côtes-d'Armor to Corsica	Single
Gin	Jenever	From Calvados to Paris	Single
Vodka	Potato, Wheat, Barley	From Aisne to Charente	Double, at least
Rum	Sugarcane	Guadeloupe, French Guiana, Réunion, Martinique	Double, generally
Triple sec	Orange peel	Maine and Loire	Triple

A DISTILLERY IN PARIS!

Founded in 2015, the Distillerie de Paris is the first of its kind in the capital. It was founded by the brothers Nicolas and Sébastien Julhès. From gin to vodka, the company has distilled in its custom-made alembic some forty different eaux-de-vie and infused liquors. Its registration number is 751301. The last two numbers correspond to the quantity in the department. So it's in fact the first alembic in Paris in a hundred years.

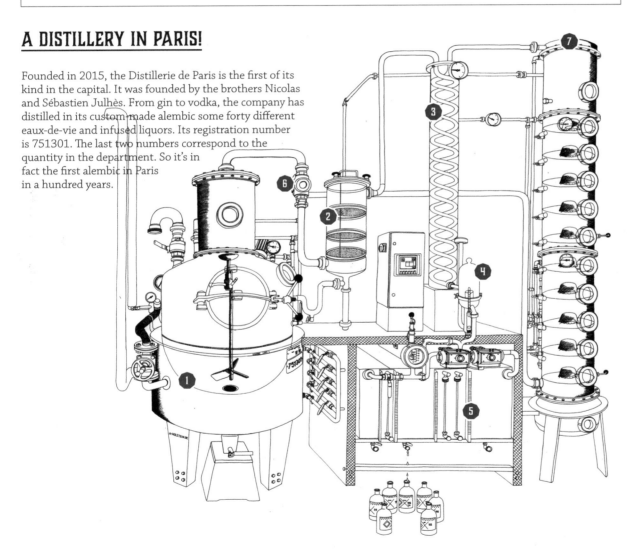

CRAFT DISTILLERIES

There are distilleries throughout France. Take this short tour through the country's craft companies.

CRÈME DE CASSIS
Lejay-Lagoute in Dijon (Côte-d'Or) founded in 1841

MIRABELLE DE LORRAINE
Distillerie de Mélanie in Marieulles-Vezon (Mozelle), known as Maucourt before 2009

PEAR
Manguin in Avignon (Vaucluse) founded in 1957

STRAWBERRY
Distillerie Meyer in Hohwarth (Bas-Rhin) founded in 1958

PLUM
Brana in Saint-Jean-de-Pied-de-Port (Pyrénées-Atlantique) founded in 1974

VINE PEACH
Distillerie Bellet in Brive-la-Gaillarde (Corrèze) founded in 1922

APRICOT
Joseph Cartron in Nuits-Saint-Georges (Côte-d'Or) founded in 1882

AN ALEMBIC LEXICON

A spirit is an alcoholic beverage that is obtained through distillation, sometimes followed by infusion or maceration.

Distillation is a way of separating alcohol from other compounds in a liquid through boiling. The process happens in an alembic, and can be single for Chartreuse, double (twice) for calvados, or triple (three times) for whiskeys.

Fermentation is the stage when yeast transforms the sugar in alcohol and creates a fermented residue. It precedes distillation. For example, fermented grains yield beer; if it's distilled, it becomes whiskey.

Eau-de-vie is the extraction obtained by distilling a beverage with low alcohol content.

Brandy is what eau-de-vie is called in English.

HOW DOES IT WORK?

1 CUCURBIT: lower part of the alembic's boiling chamber, where what is being distilled is stored before it is heated in a bain-marie. The higher the temperature, the more the elements separate as per their evaporation temperature.

2 BOTANICAL BASKET: it only comes into play for plant infusions. Berries are placed inside.

3 CONDENSER: return to a liquid state. The alcohol vapors move through a serpentine coil immersed in cold water. Upon contact, the vapors become liquid. It is what is known as the distillate.

4 THE ALCOHOLMETER is used to verify the alcohol percentage in the distillate.

5 THE TANKS are the separation center. Volatile compounds like methanol go in a first tank known as the "head." The second, the "receiver," is richer in ethanol: that is what will be used to develop the liquor.

6 THE SELECTOR is the switch. It sends alcohol vapors from the first distillation to the column for rectification (a second distillation), which is necessary for making whiskey, for one.

7 THE COLUMN consists of nine plates and serves as a second alembic. It makes the vapors richer in ethanol during the second distillation.

Flemish Carbonade

This is the *boeuf bourguignon* of northern France, composed of stewed meat and
a rich broth with caramel notes. Why wait to go to Flanders to enjoy it?
Kéda Black

THE PERFECT RECIPE

PREPARATION TIME: 30 MINUTES
COOKING TIME: 4 HOURS
SERVES 4

2¼ pounds (1 kg) beef stew meat (cut into large thin slices rather than pieces)
1 tablespoon (15 mL) neutral oil (such as sunflower or grapeseed)
1 tablespoon (6 g) all-purpose flour
4 onions
1 tablespoon (15 g) butter
1 bunch mixed herbs (parsley, chives, chervil, and 1 sprig tarragon)
1 bouquet garni (thyme, bay leaf, parsley sprigs, celery stalk)
1 slice pain d'épices (or soft gingerbread)
1 tablespoon (15 mL) red wine vinegar
1 tablespoon (13 g) demerara sugar
1⅔ cups (400 mL) red ale
Salt and freshly ground black pepper
Boiling water
1 teaspoon capers

In an ovenproof skillet or flameproof casserole dish over high heat, brown the beef slices in the oil on both sides; do not overfill the pan. Cook the meat in several batches. Once all the meat is browned, put all the pieces back in the pan, sprinkle them with the flour, stir well to coat, and set aside. Preheat the oven to 300°F (140°C).

Peel the onions and very thinly slice them. Cook them in the pan in the butter over low heat for about 10 minutes. Wash, dry, and finely chop the herbs. In a baking dish, place a layer of the cooked meat, top with a layer of cooked onions, then a layer of the chopped herbs, and repeat. Place the bouquet garni on top, crumble the pain d'épices over the top, then sprinkle with the vinegar, then the sugar. Add the red ale, and season with salt and pepper. Fill the dish with boiling water to the level of the ingredients. Cover, then place the dish in the oven and cook for 3 to 4 hours; the meat should be tender enough to pull apart with a fork. Distribute the capers over the top before serving.

COOKING WITH BEER—What to Prepare . . .

With a dark beer?
Make a Welsh: this Welsh specialty has spread throughout northern France. In a saucepan, melt a high-quality Cantal cheese with two spoonfuls of dark beer, some mustard, some Worcestershire sauce, and ground Espelette pepper. Spread this mixture onto a thick slice of rustic bread and bake it until browned.

With a blond beer?
Make crêpes: added to crêpe batter (or even waffle or beignet batter), a blond beer with its herbaceous and exotic notes offers a contrasting flavor while lightening the texture of the crêpes.

With a red ale?
Cook mussels: in northern France, a dish of French fries and mussels (*moules frites*) is a perfect pairing with beer. Served with a sauce of shallots cooked in melted butter, a few good splashes of red ale added to the cooking liquid brings pleasingly tart notes to your mussels.

skip to
Light Up the Mussels!, p. 137;
City Beers, Country Beers, p. 210

Turning the Table

What if the small potter's wheel in your garage or an old record player found at the flea market ended up as a tool in your kitchen? This is the idea behind the brilliant invention of pastry chef Yann Brys. This spiraling technique using a turntable has spread throughout the world.

Delphine Le Feuvre

Instructions for Using a Turntable

The mixture: this method adapts to all cream fillings with a soft and creamy texture that have a certain thickness to hold their shape, such as whipped cream, Italian meringue, *crémeux*, or whipped ganache.

The machine: Yann Brys uses a real potter's wheel weighing about 17½ pounds (8 kg). For home use, it's easier to use an old record player made for 78s.

The method: once the cake you want to decorate is placed on the machine, all you have to do is start the machine and carefully apply the cream using a piping bag, a paper cone, or a palette knife, starting from the center of the cake and moving your hand slowly out toward the edge.

The movement: on a stadium running track, runners in the outermost lane must run faster than those on the inside lanes. This same idea must be applied to the speed at which you move your hand out from the center. Be careful not to turn the cake itself while it's rotating; the cake must rotate only under the power of the machine.

THE HISTORY

In 2004, **Yann Brys, Best Craftsman of France (MOF) in pastry**, was reflecting on a way to create a new shape for the *galette des rois* (kings' cake) for caterer Dalloyau's end-of-year offerings. He used a revolving stand to **manually score the top of a galette** with the tip of a knife, starting from the center of the galette and moving to the outside. As a result, the spiral method was born.

He experimented with the technique on other creations: in 2009, he used it for a cherry dessert for Mother's Day, and in 2010 for his selections for the MOF competition for a lemon tart.

THE TURNTABLE TECHNIQUE SPREADS AROUND THE GLOBE

Ten years after its creation, this phenomenon has **become viral on social media networks**, including Instagram. The turntable has been **adopted by many pastry chefs throughout the world**. Among the finest chefs in Paris using this technique are Yann Menguy (Pâtisserie La Goutte d'Or); the star chef of the Meurice, Cédric Grolet; and Nicolas Bacheyre (Pâtisserie Un Dimanche à Paris). But this method has taken hold far outside the perimeter of Paris. Yann Brys has taken his invention to other countries for demonstrations, and other experts **have adopted this approach to create their own designs**. The late Laurent Jeannin (deceased in 2017), pastry chef at Hôtel Le Bristol in Paris, for example, was inspired to design a base for desserts using melted chocolate striped to resemble a vinyl record. And there is no doubt that Yann Brys has not yet finished turning heads with his magical method!

Lesson 1

PIPING CREAM

Using a piping bag fitted with a ribbon piping tube, hold the tip perpendicular to the work surface. Use your other hand to help maintain stability.

Lesson 2

MAKING CHOCOLATE DECORATIONS

Use tempered chocolate, melted first at 113°F (45°C), then cooled to 81°F (27°C), then raised to 84°F (29°C). Once tempered, pour the chocolate into a paper cone, place a square piece of parchment paper on a record player, and turn it on. Place a small drop of chocolate in the center and form the desired spiral shape. Once the chocolate has set at room temperature, it will create a coiled effect when placed on a curve-shaped dessert.

Lesson 3

SCORING A *GALETTE DES ROIS*

A sharp blade will do wonders for creating a spiral decoration. With the hand held at a 75-degree angle, gently press the tip of a knife into the puff pastry, but without piercing it. Use your other hand to help maintain stability. The faster the hand moves outward, the larger the spacing of the spiral will be.

BASIL-LIME SPIRAL

PREPARATION TIME: 30 MINUTES
COOKING TIME: 5 MINUTES
MAKES 6 INDIVIDUAL CAKES

For the crunchy base
3 ounces (80 g) cornflakes
2½ ounces (70 g) ground almonds
1 ounce (25 g) pine nuts
2½ ounces (70 g) white chocolate couverture (preferably Valrhona Opalys or Ivoire)
1½ ounces (45 g) almond praline
1 pinch fleur de sel sea salt

For the lime cream
3 tablespoons (45 g) whole milk
Zest of ½ lime
A few fresh basil leaves
2⅓ ounces (65 g) whole egg (about 1 large egg)
¼ cup plus 1 tablespoon plus 1¾ teaspoons (70 g) superfine sugar
2⅓ ounces (65 g) lemon juice
⅔ teaspoon (2 g) powdered gelatin (preferably fish gelatin)
7 tablespoons (100 g) unsalted butter

For the ganache
3 tablespoons plus 1 teaspoon (50 g) whole milk
Zest of ½ lime
1¼ ounces (35 g) coconut purée
½ vanilla bean
⅓ teaspoon (1 g) powdered gelatin
4½ ounces (130 g) white chocolate couverture (preferably Valrhona Opalys or Ivoire)
½ cup plus 1 tablespoon plus 1 teaspoon (135 g) heavy cream, chilled

Equipment
2 Flexipan silicone mats with six cavities measuring 3 inches (8 cm) in diameter and about ½ inch (12 mm) in height

Make the crunchy base. Crush the cornflakes, then toast them in the oven at 325°F (170°C) with the almonds and pine nuts, stirring frequently to prevent them from burning. Melt the chocolate, add the praline, and stir to combine. ❶ Stir in the toasted cornflakes, almonds, pine nuts, and the sea salt. ❷ Spread the mixture with the back of a fork into the cavities of the silicone mat.

Make the lime cream. In a saucepan, heat the milk with the lime zest. Add the basil leaves and let infuse for 5 minutes. In a bowl, whisk the egg and sugar together until lightened. Strain the hot milk into the egg-sugar mixture, pressing down with a spatula to capture all the liquid absorbed by the basil. ❸ Heat the lemon juice in the saucepan, add the milk mixture to the pan, and bring it to a boil. Add the gelatin (softened for 5 minutes in 1 tablespoon/15 g of water) and stir until it is melted; let the mixture cool to 113°F (45°C). ❹ Add the butter in pieces and blend with an immersion blender. ❺ Pour the cream into the cavities of the second silicone mat. Place the mat in the refrigerator.

Make the ganache. ❻ Heat the milk with the lime zest and set the mixture aside to infuse for 4 minutes. Strain the mixture into the coconut purée. Split the vanilla bean lengthwise in half and scrape the seeds into the mixture. Heat the mixture without boiling it. ❼ Add the gelatin (softened for 5 minutes in 2 teaspoons/10 g of water) and stir until it is melted, then pour the mixture over the chocolate. ❽ Blend using an immersion blender, then blend in the chilled cream. Refrigerate for 4 hours. Briefly whip the ganache to lighten it, then scrape it into a piping bag.

Assembly. ❾ Pipe a small dab of ganache onto each crunchy base, then place a chilled disk of lime cream on top. ❿ Position one of the cakes on a turntable. ⓫ Start the turntable and pipe the ganache on top, starting from the center and moving to the outside edge. Decorate with lime zest and a ribbon of tempered white chocolate. Store refrigerated.

skip to ....
The Macaron, Squared, p. 277

Marcel Pagnol

Packed with allusions to gastronomy, the books and films of Marcel Pagnol, a *galavard*,* speak like the south of France and smell just like Provence . . .

Estelle Lenartowicz

PITCHOU: A LOCAL LAD'S LOVE OF FOOD

Le bar de la Marine
On the menu: pastis, of course, but also absinthe, Picon, eau-de-vie . . . all recommended for their medicinal benefits . . . "The liqueur has to blossom on your tongue. It pinches the tip a bit, and then it fans open and caresses your gums; and then zip!—it goes down the throat as smooth as velvet." —*Les Lettres de mon moulin* (*Letters from My Windmill*; film adapted from the book by Alphonse Daudet, 1954)

Le Vieux-Port
Straight from the fisherman's net, a cascade of fish and shellfish: oysters, mussels, clams, cod, anglerfish . . .
Aubagne, the taste of childhood, bathed in the memory of the pheasants his father hunted, and his mother's almond paste tarts.
La Garrigue and Les Calanques, *herbes de Provence* flowering in the shade of the hillside: thyme, rosemary, genepi, marjoram, sage, mint, lavender, savory (called *pèbre d'ail*).

THE LEGENDARY RECIPE OF 4/3 OR LE PICON-CITRON-CURAÇAO

Dialogue from the film Marius (1931)

César: *But it's not hard, look. Put one-third curaçao. Be careful, OK, it's just a very small third! Then one-third lemon. See? Then a hearty third of Picon. See? And then, a big third of water. There you have it.*
Marius: *And that makes four thirds.*
César: *So what?*
Marius: *In a glass, there's three thirds.*
César: *But, you idiot, it depends on how big the thirds are!*
Marius: *Well, no, it doesn't depend. It's arithmetic.*

Writer, filmmaker, and gourmet from the Bouches-du-Rhône
(1895–1974)

LA RATATOUILLE À LA PAGNOL

PREPARATION TIME: 45 MINUTES
COOKING TIME: 1 HOUR 15 MINUTES
SERVES 6 TO 8 DISGRUNTLED CLASSMATES
4 Goldrush zucchini
2 white zucchini
2 eggplants
3 bell peppers (1 green, 1 yellow, 1 red)
5 fresh tomatoes
Olive oil
Fresh thyme
1 bay leaf
2 bunches basil, plus a few leaves
5 fresh sage leaves
10 mint leaves
1 teaspoon dried marjoram
2 large white onions, sliced
4 cloves purple garlic, peeled and finely chopped
2 tablespoons (30 mL) tomato paste
1 sprig tarragon
1 sprig rosemary
Salt and freshly ground black pepper

Wash, dry, and seed all the vegetables. Rinse the herbs. Halve the zucchini lengthwise, then slice them crosswise. Cube the eggplants and bell peppers. Cut the tomatoes into wedges. Cook the eggplants for 5 minutes in boiling salted water, then drain them. Sauté the vegetables separately in the following combinations, in olive oil and a little of the minced garlic: the onions with the thyme and bay leaf; the bell peppers with the marjoram and sage leaves; the zucchini with the basil; and the eggplants with the mint leaves. Season each with salt and pepper. In a saucepan, cook the remaining garlic in hot olive oil just until softened (do not brown it), then stir in the tomato paste and cook until thickened, while stirring. Add the tomatoes, rosemary, and tarragon. Adjust the seasoning as needed. Let the cooked vegetables cool separately, then carefully combine all the mixtures together and transfer to a serving dish. Refrigerate for 24 to 48 hours before serving, chilled, with chopped basil sprinkled on top.

Recipe taken from the book À table avec Marcel Pagnol: 65 recettes du pays des collines, *Frédérique Jacquemin, Agnès Viénot Éditions.*

Compendium of cooking sayings

About cocktails: **"Even too much water can kill you!—You can drown, for example!"** —Ulysse and Frère Joachim, *Les Lettres de mon moulin* (*Letters from My Windmill*; film adapted from the book by Alphonse Daudet, 1954)

•

"Saint-Émillon, Saint-Galmier, Saint-Marcellin . . . They're drinkable and edible, but they're saints nonetheless." —Uncle Baptiste, *Le Schpountz* (*Heartbeat*, 1938)

•

"Madame Fenuze, saucisson is the best and cheapest meat because it's the only meat without a bone." —Uncle Baptiste, *Le Schpountz* (*Heartbeat*, 1938)

•

"There's bread and then there's bread." —The butcher, *La Femme du boulanger* (*The Baker's Wife*, 1938)

•

"The sin of gluttony only begins when we're not hungry anymore." —Father Abbé, *Les Lettres de mon moulin* (*Letters from My Windmill*)

•

"Seems like it's from vineyards in the North Pole." —César, about very chilled white wine, *Marius* (1931)

•

"No business is possible if you always have to tell your customers the truth." —*César* (1936)

Oeuf Mayonnaise

A star at lunch counters, a household dish, and a popular high-protein food, the *oeuf mayonnaise* (mayonnaise egg) is a world-renowned Parisian legend. So legendary, in fact, that it has strict methods for preparation, famous recipes, and even its own organization dedicated to its preservation!

François-Régis Gaudry

TO THE RESCUE OF THE OEUF MAYONNAISE

In the mid-1990s, as popular bistros struggled, food critic Claude Lebey and his friend Jacques Pessis created the ASOM, or l'Association de sauvegarde de l'oeuf mayo (the Mayonnaise Egg Preservation Association) to revive this iconic specialty. Their approach? Create guidelines for its creation and award a certificate each year to a Parisian establishment that makes this special dish. The ASOM presented its last prize in 2013. Currently, it is La République populaire de l'oeuf mayo (the People's Republic of the Mayonnaise Egg), founded by Fred Fenouil, the owner of the Parisian restaurant Le Petit Choiseul.

THE 4 CRITERIA FOR THE OEUF MAYONNAISE, ACCORDING TO THE ASOM

❶ It must be an appetizing and generous serving.

❷ It must use a high-quality egg, categorized as either "**very large**" or "**large**."

❸ It must use a mayonnaise-**mustard** that is well seasoned and covers the egg well.

❹ In the absence of **fresh vegetables**, serve it sitting atop a lettuce leaf.

*"The oeuf mayonnaise **cannot be explained**, it must be savored."*
Claude Lebey

skip to
Mayonnaise, p. 100;
Endangered Hors d'Oeuvre, p. 124

THE CLASSIC OEUF MAYONNAISE RECIPE

1½ eggs per person
3 lettuce leaves per person

For the mayonnaise
1 egg yolk
Peanut oil (or sunflower oil)
Dijon mustard
Salt and freshly ground black pepper

Cook the eggs for 9 minutes (no more) in simmering water. Cool them under cold running water. Peel them and slice them lengthwise in half. A homemade mayonnaise will have the best consistency: one that is not too firm so that it coats the egg perfectly. For a mayonnaise made using an electric mixer, add a little cream at the end to make it less thick. Do not forget that the mustard flavor should be quite pronounced.

Remove and discard the stems of the lettuce leaves and arrange the leaves on the bottom of a plate. Arrange the three halves of hard-boiled egg (flat side down) on the plate and spoon plenty of the mayonnaise on top so that the eggs are completely covered. You can decorate by adding a leaf of flat-leaf parsley or chervil on top of each egg.

And why not a mimosa version?

What does the oeuf mayonnaise have in common with the yellow flower of the Mediterranean mimosa tree? Just crumble the boiled yolk and you'll see! The *oeuf mimosa* is an oeuf mayonnaise all dressed up. Cook the eggs for 9 minutes, cool them under running water, peel them, then cut them lengthwise in half. Remove the yolks and press them through a colander or a chinois to crumble them finely; set aside one-third. Mix the remaining crumbled yolk with mayonnaise and chopped fresh herbs (such as parsley, chervil, chives, or tarragon). Fill each empty egg half with this mixture, then sprinkle on the reserved crumbled yolk.

The Oeuf James of Le Voltaire

The historic Le Voltaire bistro, which sits on the banks of the Seine in Paris, can boast about serving one of the best oeufs mayonnaise in the city. And the cheapest: only one Euro! A totally anachronistic price. And the Picot family, owners of the bistro for three generations and fierce protectors of this popular recipe, have no intentions of making it an elitist dish! For this minuscule price, the bistro serves an egg cut in two and topped with a generous homemade mayonnaise, accompanied by crudités. To pass for a bistro regular, be sure to order an "*oeuf* James." Le Voltaire's oeuf mayonnaise was renamed in honor of James Lord, the art critic and American biographer, who settled in Paris in the 1950s. He frequently visited artists like Picasso, Giacometti, and Balthus, and was a lover of oeuf mayonnaise.

WHERE CAN YOU ENJOY A GOOD OEUF MAYONNAISE IN PARIS?

→ **Le Voltaire**, Paris 7th
→ **Flottes**, Paris 1st
→ **Le Petit Choiseul**, Paris 2nd
→ **Le Fontaine de Mars**, Paris 7th
→ **Le Closerie des Lilas**, Paris 6th

Is That Algae on Our Plates?

These marine plants come to the table with briny flavors, unique appearances, and uncommon textures.

Pierrick Jégu

Dulse

Sea spaghetti

Royal kombu

Nori

ROYAL KOMBU
Family: *Algues brunes*
Size: up to 19½ feet (6 m)
Harvest season: from February to April. Present in the wild, royal kombu is also cultivated, especially on the coast of Saint-Malo.
Taste: salty and sweet!
Cooking: blanching is highly recommended to tenderize this fleshy laminar. Julienned, it is delicious in salad. A flavor enhancer, it can also be used to wrap white meat or fish, or to form a spectacular papillote. It is also good cooked with legumes, and can help to promote their digestion.
History: royal kombu—and its "cousin" Breton kombu—are the seaweeds richest in iodine. Kombu is the staple ingredient of "dashi," or Japanese broth, and according to some, it is the origin of umami, the fifth flavor (in addition to salty, sweet, sour, and bitter) noted in many Japanese dishes.

WAKAME
Family: *Algues brunes*
Size: 3 to 6 feet (1 to 2 m)
Harvest season: from February to March. It is cultivated in channels on some algae farms in Brittany.
Taste: very briny; reminiscent of oyster.
Cooking: this seaweed, sometimes called "sea fern" and characterized by its soft blade and its crisp central vein, combines well with a multitude of ingredients. It goes perfectly in a miso soup or zucchini soup, marries well with oysters, tuna, poultry, or spinach, and provides an amazing touch to Far Breton!
History: wakame was accidentally introduced in France in the late 1970s as a stowaway attached to Japanese oysters. It was eventually imported to Brittany for cultivation.

NORI
Family: *Algues rouges.* Naturally violet and purple, nori turns dark and green when cooked
Size: up to 2 feet (60 cm)
Harvest season: from April to June and from September to November.
Taste: fresh, its briny flavor is very subtle. Dried, it offers distinct notes of smoked tea and dried mushroom.
Cooking: used as thin dried leaves for making maki. Or use it raw or cooked, like a spice or an aromatic herb, to flavor a broth, fish, white meats, quiche, bread, and pain d'épices. Minced and lightly panfried, nori can also be eaten as a vegetable.
History: consumed for at least two thousand years in Japan, nori was first harvested in the wild. Starting from the Edo period (1600–1868), it was the first seaweed to be cultivated in Tokyo Bay.

SEA LETTUCE
Family: *Algues vertes*
Size: between 6 and 15¾ inches (15 and 40 cm)
Harvest season: from April to October, in Brittany.
Taste: offers a soft and elastic texture. It is distinguished by a slightly bitter vegetable taste, which some claim is similar to parsley while others claim it is similar to sorrel.
Cooking: its leaves are perfect for making papillotes. The freshness and liveliness of sea lettuce, which can be enjoyed raw, cooked, or dried, also excels in salads, pestos, and for seasoning fish and seafood, and, surprisingly, in dessert to replace matcha tea.
History: sea lettuce is without a doubt one of the most widespread macroalgae in the world, present on every shore on the planet.

DULSE
Family: *Algues rouges*
Size: 4 to 12 inches (10 to 30 cm)
Harvest season: on the shores of Brittany along the English Channel and the Atlantic, at low tide, between April and December.
Taste: both sweet and briny, with nutty notes.
Cooking: naturally crunchy, it wilts when cooked at high temperatures. Dulse can also be consumed dried, chopped, crushed, or minced to make a seaweed-and-fish tartare, in salads, to accompany scallops, to enliven sauces, and so on.
History: the Celts and Vikings, and other sailors who followed after, appreciated dulse, which alleviated scurvy thanks to its being rich in vitamin C. Evidence also points to the fact that in the eighteenth century, the Irish would chew it!

SEA SPAGHETTI OR *HARICOT DE MER*
Family: *Algues brunes*
Size: long and slender, 3 to 10 feet (1 to 3 m), approximately
Harvest season: March to May.
Taste: briny, but not too strong.
Cooking: after blanching it to make it softer and greener than in its natural state, it can be prepared in many ways: sautéed in a pan as a vegetable to accompany a fish or seafood, or more surprisingly, fried like calamari, preserved in vinegar, or candied in sugar, or (and why not?) coated with chocolate.
History: this seaweed has its seasons, like any fruit or vegetable. It can be collected outside of the months from March to May, but it is between March and May that it is the most tender and delicate.

THE CASE OF SALICORNIA

Because it grows in a marine environment, salicornia is often considered an algae, but this is incorrect because it is actually a seasonal halophyte, present in coastal areas along tidal flats and in salt marshes. Young shoots are harvested between May and August. It is very low in calories and rich in iodine, magnesium, calcium, and vitamins A, C, and D. It is also very easy to cook, and can be served cold or hot and plain or pickled like cornichons.

skip to Land and Sea Pairings, p. 117

WAYS TO PROCURE SEAWEED
Harvest it yourself? It is better to let professionals who recognize the varieties and who have the expertise harvest seaweeds during the best seasons and tide levels to ensure they are the freshest.
Buy it? Fine groceries, shops, and organic markets sell dried seaweeds and preparations made from seaweed, or fresh seaweed.
Order it? Order them directly from certain harvesting and processing suppliers, such as Algue Service (Finistère), which carries products like Bord à bord (bord-a-bord.fr).

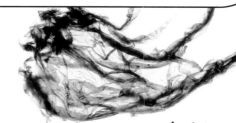

Sea lettuce

Wakame

THE GOURMET ABBEY

Even if gluttony is considered a cardinal sin, the Church nevertheless seems an inexhaustible source of inspiration in French gastronomy. Here is a handbook of gastronomic liturgy.

Stéphane Solier

À LA BÉNÉDICTINE

À LA BÉNÉDICTINE. A preparation of either puréed salt cod and mashed potatoes or a brandade—salt cod is traditionally a fish served for Lent. The French enjoy many dishes with cod, or à la *Bénédictine*.

À LA CARMÉLITE. A preparation of chicken breasts topped with a *chaud-froid* sauce, decorated with truffle shavings, and prepared with a crayfish mousseline; the name is in reference to the color of the white and black habits of nuns of the Carmelite order.

À LA CHANOINESSE. Designates different preparations consisting of either covering chicken breasts with a crayfish sauce, or garnishing sweetbreads or eggs with carrots and truffles in cream, covered with a sauce made from a base of veal stock and sherry. The name comes from the legendary refined dining of the canons under the Ancien Régime, as evidenced by the expression "a life of canon."

À LA DIABLE. Typically a preparation of certain types of chopped meats, seasoned, grilled, and served with a hot sauce. Chicken is particularly suitable for this preparation, but herring and even artichokes can also be used.

À LA MAZARINE. A preparation made with pieces of meat, white button mushrooms, artichoke bottoms, and an assortment of vegetables.

ALLÉLUIAS (HALLELUJAHS). Small citron treats from Castelnaudary. Their name comes from the gratitude expressed in Latin by Pope Pius VII to the pastry chef who offered him these treats.

ANGE DE MER (ANGEL SHARK). A fish related to the ray, but whose meat is considered less tasty.

ANGÉLIQUE (ANGELICA). An aromatic plant long cultivated by the monks, candied and used in pastry or liqueurs.

ANGELOT (CHERUB). Old name for various cheeses from Normandy, including Pont-l'Évêque and Livarot. The word is a derivative of "augeron," meaning from Pays d'Auge (in Normandy).

ANGÉLUS. A famous beer from the brasserie Lepers brewed à *l'ancienne* (in the old-fashioned way) since 1978 and used in the kitchens of chefs in northern France. Its label is based on Millet's famous painting from 1858.

AUMÔNIÈRE (ALMS PURSE). A pocket made of very thin dough containing a salty or sweet mixture, whose name is derived from the purse attached to one's belt used to distribute alms.

BALTHAZAR. A bottle of Champagne with a capacity of sixteen regular wine bottles, referring to the last king of Babylon, known in the Old Testament for a sumptuous banquet during which he had wine served in sacred vases stolen from the temple of Jerusalem by his father.

BARBE-DE-CAPUCIN (CAPUCHIN'S BEARD). A close relative of the endive. Legend has it that in the eighteenth century, a Capuchin monk lost a root of this chicory plant in a *catiche* (limestone quarry) and that it grew into white, serrated leaves that were slightly hairy, reminiscent of the Capuchin's beard.

BATON DE JACOB (JACOB'S STAFF). A small éclair filled with pastry cream and glazed, an allusion to the stick used by Isaac's son to cross the river Jordan.

BÉNÉDICTINE. A plant liqueur whose recipe is attributed to an Italian Benedictine monk and whose label bears the motto of the Benedictines, DOM (*Deo Optimo Maximo*).

BÉNITIER (FONT). A very large bivalve whose meat is consumed in some parts of the world and whose shell is used by some churches as a beautiful container in which to hold baptismal water, hence its name.

BERNIS. A preparation of eggs, especially soft-boiled, including asparagus. This recipe is a tribute to Cardinal de Bernis (1715–1794), who, during his posts as ambassador (Venice and Rome), defended French cuisine and distinguished himself by his refinement for dining.

BONNET D'ÉVÊQUE (BISHOP'S HAT). Nickname for the tail of some poultry, turkey more specifically, due to the miter-headdress shape that it exhibits when raised.

CAMPANILE (OR CACAVELLU). A sort of brioche common in Corsica, which displays whole eggs in their shells in an ornamental fashion during Lent when eggs are traditionally not consumed. *Campanile* means "bell tower"; the name is a reference to the bells of Easter.

CAPUCHIN. A savory tartlet garnished with choux dough made with Gruyère cheese. This has no relationship with the Italian cappuccino, the coffee served in a large cup with milk foam that owes its name to its color, which evokes the color of the robes of the Capuchin monks.

CAPUCINE (NASTURTIUM). An ornamental plant whose flowers are used in salads and whose flower buds can be substituted for capers. Held in high regard in the gardens of monasteries during the Middle Ages, its name is derived from its seedpod's resemblance to the hood of a Capuchin monk's habit.

CARDINAL. 1) A preparation with saltwater fish filled with thin slices of lobster and truffle shavings and topped with a white sauce and lobster coulis, lending the dish a color similar to that of a cardinal's robe. It can be prepared with brill or lobster. 2) A frozen red-fruits dessert (*bombe cardinal*) or a fruit dessert topped with a strawberry, raspberry, or black currant coulis (*poires cardinal*), in reference to the color of a cardinal's robe.

CARDINAL DES MERS (CARDINAL OF THE SEAS). A poetic name for the lobster because of the bright red color of its shell after cooking.

CÉLESTINE. 1) A dish of sautéed chicken (young hen) with mushrooms and truffles, flambéed with cognac, moistened with white wine, and sprinkled with garlic and parsley. 2) Poultry consommé thickened with tapioca and garnished with a julienne of savory herbed crêpes, poached chicken breast, and chervil, perhaps alluding to the clothing of the Celestines, the religious order of Benedictines who wear a white robe with a black scapular.

CHARTREUSE. 1) A large dish made of vegetables (braised cabbage) and meat or game, dome-shaped and arranged in layers of alternating colors. Originally composed only of vegetables, the Chartreuse took its name from the vegetarian diet of the Carthusian monks. 2) A liqueur of various plants produced only in Voiron by the Carthusian monks.

CHATEAUNEUF-DU-PAPE. An AOC (*appellation d'origine contrôlée*) red or white wine from the southern Rhône Valley, produced on the scrublands close to the summer residence of the popes of Avignon.

CHÉRUBIN (CHERUB). A dish prepared with brill surrounded by small mounds of cooked tomatoes, diced truffle, and a julienne of red bell pepper cooked in butter, and covered in hollandaise sauce.

CHEVEUX D'ANGE (ANGEL'S HAIR). Hair-thin strands of sugar used in pastry; or long, very thin strands of pasta used in soups and broths.

CLÉMENTINE (CLEMENTINE ORANGE). This citrus fruit is from a natural cross of a mandarin and a bitter orange tree. It was discovered in Algeria in 1902 by Father Clément, from whom it takes its name.

COQUILLE SAINT-JACQUES (SCALLOP). This famous bivalve owes its name to the fact that its shell served as a symbol for pilgrims who had reached Saint-Jacques-de-Compostela.

CURÉ NANTAIS (NANTAIS PARISH PRIEST). A raw cow's-milk cheese from Vendée with a washed rind. It is said that a priest created this cheese during the Chouannerie uprising of 1794.

DIABLOTINS (LITTLE DEVILS). Thin slices of bread, with or without béchamel sauce on top, covered with grated cheese and baked, to accompany soups and stews. Served in this way, it's said the bread slices remain "hidden," like little mischievous demons in Germanic or Slavic folklore.

ESAÜ. A soup made from lentil purée with a white stock or consommé base, in reference to the biblical episode where Esau, son of Isaac, gives his birthright to his brother Jacob for a dish of lentils.

ÉTOUFFE-CHRÉTIEN (STIFLING CHRISTIAN). Described as a very filling dish, filling to the point of being nearly impossible to digest. To die by one's sin is indeed to go out in style!

FRUIT DE LA PASSION (PASSION FRUIT). A tropical fruit whose reproductive parts are shaped in a way that resembles the different instruments of the Passion of Christ: the crown of thorns, hammer, and nails.

GLORIA. Coffee, or sometimes tea, sweetened with eau-de-vie or rum, a parody reference to the Gloria of Psalms.

JÉSUITE (JESUIT). A triangle of puff pastry filled with frangipane and covered with *glace royale*. The ic-

ing was previously made with praline and chocolate, evoking a Jesuit's hat with its turned-up brim.

JÉSUS (JESUS). A dry sausage with a large diameter from Lyon and all throughout eastern France. Named as such because it is made at Christmas to celebrate the birth of Christ and to enjoy with family.

MAGNIFICAT. An orange, lettuce, and leek soup, but also the name of filled caramels that are both tender and crisp, made by a famous confectionery company. The name refers to the hymn sung by the Virgin during the Visitation of Elizabeth, when her soul exalts—*magnificat*—the Lord.

MAZARIN. Primarily known as a very thick génoise sponge hollowed out in the center, shaped into a cone, and filled with candied fruit, but the name also refers to a cake composed of two disks of dacquoise separated by a layer of praline mousse. The name is in tribute to Cardinal Mazarin, a religious man of high power.

MENDIANTS (BEGGARS). An assortment of four dried fruits and nuts—almonds, figs, hazelnuts, and Malaga raisins—that make up the thirteen desserts of Christmas in Provence and whose colors evoke the robes of the mendicant orders: Dominicans in white, Franciscans in gray, Carmelites in brown, and Augustines in dark purple.

NABUCHODONOSOR (NEBUCHADNEZZAR). A large bottle of Champagne with a capacity of twenty regular Champagne bottles, referring to the king of Babylon, known in the Old Testament for stealing sacred vases from the temple of Jerusalem to use for serving during royal banquets.

NEMROD (NIMROD). A stuffing for wild game (furry game) that consists of a cranberry compote, apple croquettes, and large mushroom caps topped with chestnut purée, a tribute to Nimrod, the "mighty hunter before the Lord" of Genesis.

NONNETTE (YOUNG NUN). Small, moist cakes of *pain d'épices*, round or oval, and frosted, which were once prepared in the convents by nuns.

OREILLE DE JUDAS (EAR OF JUDAS). Another name for the *Auricularia* mushroom, the famous black lobe-shaped mushroom, which is the mainstay of Chinese cuisine. Its "love" of the elderberry tree (on which it can be found growing) explains its name, referring to the legend that after his betrayal of Jesus, Judas, in shame, hanged himself from one of these trees.

PASCALINE. A roast lamb dish that was once reserved for Easter. A whole lamb is stuffed with ground lamb meat, hard-boiled egg yolks, bread crumbs, and herbs and spices, served with a green sauce or with a stew of truffles and ham. The dish was described by Alexandre Dumas in his *Grand Dictionnaire de cuisine* (*Great Dictionary of Cuisine*), from 1872.

PÉCHÉ MIGNON (LITTLE SIN). 1) A cocktail made with cream and peach nectar topped with sparkling wine, rum, or vodka. 2) A sin to which one abandons oneself willingly. Examining the term more closely, it concerns only the harmless aspect of food preferences; it is not considered an act of gluttony but instead an irrepressible tendency to be indulgent with oneself and to accept having a weakness—*a guilty pleasure*.

PET-DE-NUN (NUN'S FART). A small beignet of cream puff pastry (choux dough) that is served either with confectioners' sugar or filled with cream or jam and whose air escapes only discreetly while it's consumed, hence its amusingly irreverent name.

PONT-L'ÉVÊQUE. An AOC (*appellation d'origine contrôlée*) soft cow's-milk cheese from Normandy with a washed rind whose name comes from the eponymous town of Calvados, where it has been produced since the Middle Ages; its recipe was created by Cistercian monks in the twelfth century.

REINE DE SABA (QUEEN OF SHEBA). A chocolate sponge cake lightened with beaten egg whites and served with crème anglaise. Its name evokes the famous dark-skinned queen whom King Solomon met in Jerusalem.

RÉLIGIEUSE (NUN). A Parisian pastry consisting of a large cream puff filled with pastry cream or a coffee or chocolate chiboust cream, topped with a smaller cream puff also filled in the same way. The entire pastry is glazed with fondant. It is so called because the color of its frosting is reminiscent of that of nuns' robes, and because the shape of the pastry forms the silhouette of a woman.

RICHELIEU. 1) A dish made of sole, with a fillet lifted and laid open to one side, breaded, and garnished with maître d'hôtel butter and truffle shavings. 2) A sauce composed of a white roux made from the cooking juices of meat, with mushrooms and minced truffles. 3) A filling for large pieces of meat consisting of tomatoes, stuffed mushrooms, braised lettuces, and fried potatoes. 4) A large piece of pastry made up of several pastry layers, rolled out with almond paste flavored with maraschino and spread with apricot marmalade and frangipane, then overlaid and glazed with fondant and decorated with candied fruit. These recipes were invented by the chef of the Duke of Richelieu, grand-nephew of the cardinal known for his refinements in dining.

SACRISTAIN. A small twisted pastry with no filling made of puff pastry, often sprinkled with sliced almonds or nuts and pearl sugar. Its name refers to the twisted cane that accompanied the sacristans as they opened processions.

SAINT. 1) Many saints have lent their names to many French cheeses. Could it be because of their white interiors, suggesting a white, virginal quality? Examples include fresh cheeses such as Saint-Florentin from Auerroise; creamy cheeses with bloomy rinds such as Saint-Félicien and Saint-Marcellin from Dauphiné; and pressed, uncooked cheeses such as Saint-Nectaire from Auvergne or Saint-Pauline from Brittany. 2) Numerous wines: Saint-Amour (AOC Beaujolais), Saint-Aubin (AOC Côte de Beaune), Saint-Croix-du-Mont (AOC Garonne), Saint-Émilion (AOC Bordeaux), Saint-Estèphe (AOC Médoc), Saint-Joseph (AOC Ardèche), Saint-Julien (AOC Haut-Médoc), Saint-Péray (AOC Rhône), Saint-Raphaël (a flavored wine), Saint-Romain (AOC Côte de Beaune), and Saint-Veran (AOC Mâconnais).

SAINT-FLORENTIN. A génoise sponge cake moistened with kirsch and filled with a cream made from Italian meringue, melted butter, kirsch, and candied cherries.

SAINT-HONORÉ. A Parisian pastry consisting of puff pastry or flaky pastry topped with a ring of cream puff pastry (choux dough) and then with caramelized cream puffs. Its center is filled with chiboust cream, also known as *cream à Saint-Honoré*, or simply *Saint-Honoré*. Named in honor of Saint Honoré, the patron saint of *boulangers* (bread bakers).

SAINT-HUBERT. 1) A game-based dish or a dish made to accompany a game dish. In one version, small game birds are cooked in a casserole dish with a piece of truffle inserted inside each one and served with a deglaze of Madeira and game stock. 2) A purée made of game meat for stuffing mushrooms, tartlets, and small appetizers. The name refers to Hubert de Liège, patron saint of hunters and foresters.

SAINT-MALO. A sauce for serving with grilled fish, made of a fish velouté, shallots, and white wine reduction with a little mustard; or an anchovy sauce. Its name may be a tribute to the saint who evangelized Brittany at the end of a long journey.

SAINT-PIERRE. A fish with succulent flesh. The spots that adorn each side of the fish are, according to legend, the print of the thumb and forefinger of the apostle Peter.

STORZAPRETI. Literally "priest choker," a quenelle with brocciu cheese, chard, and marjoram poached in water and served in meat sauce. A specialty of Haute-Corse.

TRAPPIST. 1) The generic name of various disk-shaped cow's-milk cheeses made by Trappist monks whose provenance is specified in the title using "trappiste de ...": Trappiste de Belval (Picardy), de Briquebec (Manche), de Cîteaux (Burgundy), d'Echourgnac (Périgord), de Entrammes (Mayenne), and so on. 2) A type of high-alcohol-content beer brewed only by Trappist monks from Belgium and the Netherlands.

VISITANDINE. A small cake, either round or boat-shaped (*barquette*), made with a batter rich in wheat flour and almond flour, sometimes glazed with a kirsch fondant, invented by nuns of the Order of the Visitation (nicknamed "Visitandines") in the seventeenth century to overcome the lack of meat (the consumption of meat was forbidden in the convents); its high egg white content provides a significant amount of protein.

France's Iconic Bûche

A log has long been associated with Christmas celebrations in France, and the ancestral traditions surrounding it vary from one place to the next: lighting it with a blessed candle, pouring wine over it, or repeating a prayer upon lighting it. Today, the occasion associated with these traditions is often marked with the classic *bûche de Noël*, or yule log cake.

Loïc Bienassis

THE OLDEST DETAILED RECIPE AVAILABLE

From Pierre Lacam's book *Mémorial historique et géographique de la pâtisserie* (1890): "It is made as a *biscuit* (ladyfinger) if piped from a bag or as a génoise if spread on a plaque. . . . For the génoise, you cut out a dozen equal circles, thereabout, and stick them together with mocha or chocolate cream. You cover the cake entirely and smooth it. You place it on an elongated base that is covered with toasted almonds. You decorate the cake from one end to the other using a Breton icing tip, evenly applied, imitating the bark of the tree, and after, you place on it four or five knots of *biscuit* cut out with a cookie cutter to imitate the knots of branches, and you ice them and decorate them from bottom to top with the same tip, then cover the two ends of the log in the same way but without decoration. There are some who decorate by pressing green almond paste through a strainer and others who instead use very finely chopped pistachios. We make it with Italian meringue, but one that is firm."

Prepared in this way, the cake is not rolled but instead is made up of sponge cake circles held together with cream.

AND THE FROZEN BÛCHE . . .

The frozen version, which is probably almost as old as its nonfrozen cousin, is made similarly.

Le Glacier classique et artistique en France et en Italie (1893), coauthored by Lacam and Charabot, contains a recipe for it, consisting of alternating layers of hazelnut praline or chocolate ice cream with rounds of *biscuit* cake. The bark is made using a fluted tip. It is decorated by "imitating some leaves of pistachio ice cream and some flowers of currant or strawberry ice cream."

skip to

The French Love Galette des Rois, p. 360; 13 Desserts for a Provençal Christmas, p. 132

But Who Invented the Yule Log?

- ☐ **A)** A pastry chef from Saint-Germain-des-Prés in the mid-1830s
- ☐ **B)** It originated in Lyon and dates back to the 1860s
- ☐ **C)** Antoine Charabot, Parisian pastry chef from 1874 to 1879
- ☐ **D)** Pierre Lacam, the pastry chef–ice cream maker of Prince Charles III of Monaco

The correct answer is: C) Antoine Charabot.

It is his colleague, Pierre Lacam, who explains it in *Le Glacier classique et artistique en France et en Italie* (1893): "We never knew who created the bûche de Noël. It was a tradition of all pastry houses and, from research, I found it associated with Antoine Charabot, chef at M. Sanson, 14, rue de Buci, who created the tree branch in 1879. The recipe remained unchanged for several years. Several pastry houses began making it, however, and since 1886 its popularity has not diminished."

CHESTNUT CREAM AND PEAR BÛCHE DE NOËL
by Sébastien Gaudard*

SERVES 6 TO 8

Pears poached with vanilla
Almond génoise (sponge cake)
Chestnut cream filling
1 marron glacé (candied chestnut)

For the pears poached with vanilla

3 red Williams pears (half reserved for decor)
Juice of 1 lemon
1⅔ cups (400 g) water
½ cup plus 2 tablespoons (125 g)
superfine sugar
1 Tahitian vanilla bean

The day before, peel the pears and drizzle them with some of the lemon juice. Bring the water and sugar to a boil in a saucepan. Split the vanilla bean lengthwise in half and scrape out and reserve the seeds. Add the empty vanilla pod and the scraped seeds to the saucepan and bring the contents to a boil. Dunk the pears in the boiling syrup, reduce the heat, and simmer for 5 minutes. The pears are done when they offer only slight resistance when pierced with the tip of a sharp knife. Remove from the heat, transfer the pears and their syrup to a container, and let cool to room temperature.

For the almond génoise

1¼ cups (125 g) all-purpose flour
2 tablespoons plus 2 teaspoons (40 g) unsalted butter
4 eggs
½ cup plus 2 tablespoons (125 g) superfine sugar
1¾ ounces (50 g) almond flour

Preheat the oven to 425°F (220°C). Sift the all-purpose flour. Melt the butter. Break the eggs into a stainless steel bowl, then add the sugar. Prepare a bain-marie, place the bowl over it, and whisk vigorously until the egg-sugar mixture reaches a temperature between 140°F (60°C) and 149°F (65°C). Remove from the bain-marie and beat the mixture until it has cooled completely. Stir 2 tablespoons (30 mL) of this mixture into the butter.

Fold the all-purpose and almond flours into the remaining egg foam, then carefully fold in the butter mixture using a wooden spoon or paddle. Spread the génoise out using a stainless steel spatula onto a sheet of parchment paper measuring 9¾ by 15¾ inches (25 by 40 cm). Slide the paper into the oven and bake for 10 to 12 minutes.

For the chestnut cream filling

1⅛ pounds (500 g) chestnut paste
8⅛ ounces (230 g) crème de marrons (chestnut cream)
14 tablespoons (200 g) unsalted butter, softened

Stir together the chestnut paste and crème de marrons. Add the butter and whisk until the mixture is lightened and pale in color. Set aside 10½ ounces (300 g) in the refrigerator for the decor.

Assembly

Drain the pears, reserving the syrup. Cut the pears into ⅓-inch (1 cm) cubes (you should have about 10½ oz/300 g). Using a pastry brush, lightly soak the génoise cake with the pear syrup. Spread the chestnut cream filling over the génoise, then distribute the diced pear pieces over the top. Roll up the cake; it should be about 9¾ inches (25 cm) in length. Refrigerate it for 2 hours. Ice the cake with the reserved chestnut cream and use the back of a spoon or a spatula to make markings in the icing to simulate the bark of a tree. Halve the remaining pears and cut them into wedges. Sprinkle with lemon juice. Place the pear wedges on top of the yule log, next to the candied chestnut.

Tips from Sébastien Gaudard

"To enhance the aromatic notes of this dessert, add a little pear eau-de-vie to the syrup before using it to soak the génoise."

*Parisian pastry chef (1st and 9th)

Several Regional Specialties, Prior to the Yule Log

In the countryside, delicacies made to honor the Nativity consisted mainly of rich or enhanced breads, although many details about these recipes are missing:

☞ **In Provence**, during the fourteenth century, some consumed **fougasses**. However, we do not know exactly what these consisted of.

☞ **In Savoie**, after returning from midnight mass, some ate **rissoles**, which were small, filled *chaussons* (turnovers). They were attested as early as the fifteenth century.

☞ **In Alsace**, **berewecke**, composed of dried fruits, candied fruits, and spices in a bread dough, is still very popular. Ancient versions of this bread were served centuries before.

Jim Harrison, Francophile Writer

A ruthless hunter with an insatiable appetite, the American writer (1937–2016) enjoyed international success and traveled to France on several occasions—to drink and to eat.
François-Régis Gaudry

His gargantuan travels . . .

TO NORMANDY

"Two old men I hadn't seen laughed beneath a tree. . . . They were gardeners and it was their lunch hour, and on a flat stone they had made a small circle of hot coals. They had cored a half-dozen big red tomatoes, stuffed them with softened cloves of garlic, and added a sprig of thyme, a basil leaf, and a couple of tablespoons of soft cheese. They roasted the tomatoes until they softened and the cheese melted. I ate one with a chunk of bread and healthy-sized swigs of a jug of red wine. When we finished eating, and since this was Normandy, we had a sip or two of Calvados from a flask. A simple snack but indescribably delicious." *The Raw and the Cooked: Adventures of a Roving Gourmand*, 2002

IN PARIS

". . . we went to Gourmet Ternes, owned and operated by the former head of the butchers' union in Paris and reputed to have the best beef. In consideration of the heat I skipped the *rilletes* I desperately wanted and had a lentil salad and an enormous chunk of fillet. So much for American beef pride—this was as good if not better than the Palm or Bruno's Pen & Pencil. We delayed dinner until late waiting, waiting for the heat to subside. . . . During the next day's dawn walk my whole system seemed to be backing up, as it were. A wise man would have fasted and communed with pigeons, but at lunch at Fouquet's I started simply with an eggplant flan and coulis, letting down my guard with a confit of goose thigh accompanied by potatoes fried in goose fat. The saving grace is that these restaurants are not of the 'all you want to eat' variety. Dinner at Bellecour moved gracefully into the top ten of a lifetime category, which is no mean thing. . . . I had a salad of poached ray on a bed of *pass-pierre*, a kind of wild seaside string bean, followed by the roast pigeon I should have communed with, followed by a grand fresh fig tart." *The Raw and the Cooked: Adventures of a Roving Gourmand*, 2002

IN LYON

"At Lyon I had dinner at La Mère Brazier, which included a couple of *crêpe aux truffles* and a *volaille de Bresse demi-deuil* with slices of truffle stuffed up under the thigh skin, cheeses, fruit and lot of Côte de Beaune. Now, this was not an elaborate meal, but it left all but a few others in my life filtering down further toward the bottom. Frankly it was a mystery why it was so superb." *The Raw and the Cooked: Adventures of a Roving Gourmand*, 2002

IN SAINT-GEORGES-MOTEL

"We finally arrived in the little village of Saint-Georges-Motel after driving at breakneck speed from Paris. . . . I ordered *pâté de bécasse*, an omelet with generous amounts of truffle and an enormous piece of wild boar meat, and then there were cheeses, fruit, a few bottles of wine and a sampling of various liqueurs." *The Raw and the Cooked: Adventures of a Roving Gourmand*, 2002

skip to
So Long as There Is Inebriation, p. 49

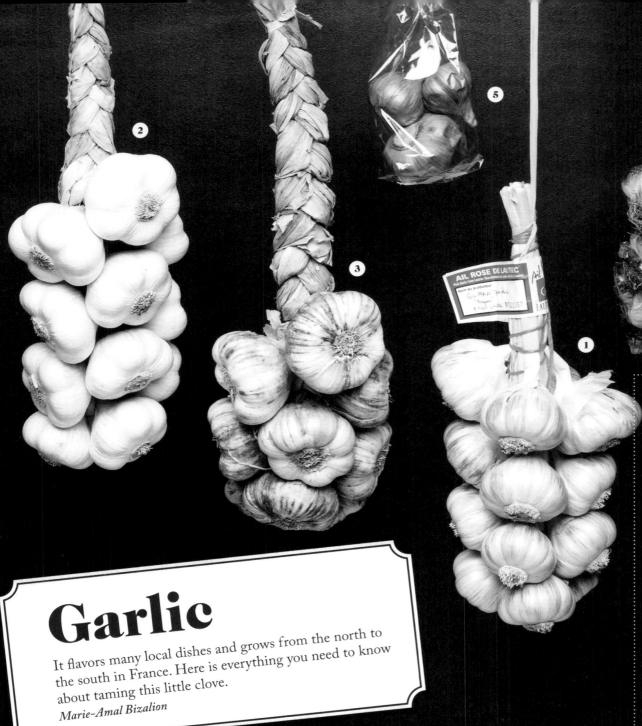

Garlic

It flavors many local dishes and grows from the north to the south in France. Here is everything you need to know about taming this little clove.

Marie-Amal Bizalion

SOME NUMBERS

World production of garlic is **23 million metric tons**, of which **19 million** originates from China. Europe harvests 2 percent, or 300,000 metric tons, per year, and only **18,000 to 20,000 metric tons** are grown **in France**, as compared to **145,000 in Spain**, which inundates France with garlic grown by aggressive farming methods and of questionable quality. The good news is that consumption throughout the world has been growing steadily for 10 years.

A Tour of PGI, AOC, and Other Remarkable Garlics

① PINK GARLIC OF LAUTREC
This has been the only Label Rouge garlic since 1966; PGI (protected geographical indication) since 1996.
Origin: According to legend, it first appeared during the Middle Ages.
Production: Sensitive to harsh climates, from 400 to 800 metric tons more than 160 growers.
Characteristics: Cloves with bright pink marbled skin. Can be stored up to 1 year. Mild flavor, slightly sweet.

② WHITE GARLIC OF LOMAGNE
PGI since 2008.
Origin: Appears in 1265 on a list of royalties in Gariès (Tarn-et-Garonne).
Production: 1,200 metric tons across 75 growers on 358 acres (145 hectares) of clay and limestone.
Characteristics: Large bulb, iridescent pod, round and dense, ideal when cooked still in its peel. Pungent.

③ VIOLET GARLIC OF CADOURS
AOP (*appellation d'origine protégée*) since June 2017.
Origin: Attested in 1750.
Production: 350 metric tons over 86 growers on 296 acres (120 hectares) of clay soil (hence its color).
Characteristics: Large bulb with violet streaks. Peaks early in the season, stops producing in July, can be stored for 6 months. Very intense and pungent.

PINK GARLIC OF AUVERGNE
Registered trademark, applied for PGI in 2016.
Origin: Present since 1850. In 1960, the rich plains of Limagne were the largest producing region.
Production: Today, 140 metric tons over 25 growers on 49 acres (20 hectares) between Billom and Aigueperse. Its cultivation is endangered.
Characteristics: Very long storage (hence its past success), white head, pink-skinned cloves. Fresh flavor of chives.

④ SMOKED GARLIC OF ARLEUX
PGI since 2013.
Origin: Certified in 1804, smoked with peat to ensure drying.
Production: 90 metric tons over 8 growers covering 37 acres (15 hectares).
Characteristics: Small, pink garlic; braided and smoked 10 days over peat, straw, or shaved wood. Can be stored up to 1 year. Layers of golden skin, smoked-wood scent that is barely noticeable when eaten.

GARLIC OF LA DRÔME
PGI since 2008.
Origin: Cited in 1600 by the agronomist Olivier de Serres in his treatise.
Production: 100 metric tons across 15 growers on 148 acres (60 hectares).
Characteristics: Large heads of which two-thirds are white and one-third is purple. Smooth texture, fresh taste, slightly sweet.

We Also Like . . .

⑤ Black Confit Garlic of Billom, Auvergne
For its very secret recipe, Laurent Girard only uses organic pink garlic from Billom. The cloves are of an intense black color and have a caramelized texture evoking flavors of licorice, truffle, and prune.
www.ailnoirdebillom.fr

Sand Garlic of Cherrueix, Brittany
Cultivated between Cancale and Mont-Saint-Michel, this pink or purple garlic does not yet have a PGI, but the proximity to the sea gives it an intense flavor and a saline note.

Garlic of Provence
Interestingly, the biggest region of consumers of garlic in France has no appellation despite the fact that it produces 2,000 metric tons of white, pink, and red garlic. Its advantage? Three-fourths of the garlic production of Provence is abundant with fresh (green) garlic as early as April.

A BIG AND SMALL HISTORY

Garlic has been cultivated since ancient times in Asia and around the Mediterranean. In France, it was recognized by a royal act by Charlemagne, who ordered its cultivation on his lands. Popular in the Middle Ages, it achieved recognition in 1553: the lips of a very young Henry IV were rubbed with garlic by his grandfather to protect him from diseases.

A FAMILY DIVIDED

Known as *Allium sativum* to those who study it closely, garlic has many cousins that resemble it, including onion, leek, chive, and shallot. More surprising, however, are its cousins tulip, lily, hyacinth, lily of the valley, and even aloe, which includes nearly eight hundred varieties.

GARLIC'S ACCEPTED BENEFITS

It's good for the heart
Scientifically proven to fight cardiovascular disease.
And good for the intestines
The prebiotics that garlic contains promote the growth of intestinal flora. But overconsuming garlic can also cause gastric burning!
A health miracle
Researchers have touted its anti-cancer properties and its benefits for HIV (not less than 750 articles in the journal *Nature* have addressed it); the results, however, remain disputed.

WHY DOES IT CREATE SUCH INTENSE BREATH?

As soon as garlic is cut or crushed, enzymes convert its alline (which is odorless) into an allicine, which emits powerful odors and breaks down into four molecules with sulfur compounds. The bad-breath effect of the first three molecules dissipates quickly. But the terrible aroma from the fourth, allyl methyl sulfide, concentrates and increases after ingestion. This compound infiltrates the blood and organs and contaminates sweat and urine. This cycle can last for up to three days, and the more finely the garlic is chopped, the longer the body retains it!

★

INSIDER'S GUIDE TO THE LANGUAGE OF GARLIC

"Aulx": the French plural of garlic (*ail*).
"Bulbe" (Bulb): the other name for a head of garlic, which can contain up to twenty cloves.
"Caïeu" or "bulbille": synonyms in French for the *gousse* (clove).
"Manouille": some garlics have a very rigid stalk. These are bundled and tied tightly together in a special *manouille*, which is stronger than a braid.
"Tresse" (Braid): varieties of garlic with thin, soft stalks are intertwined to form a long, braided garland for hanging.
"Tunique" (Tunic): the external skin that envelopes the entire head.

A few methods

In cream: peeled cloves cooked in milk and seasoned with salt and pepper, then blended and spread on grilled foods or toast.
Unpeeled: the unpeeled clove is cooked in the juices of meat or fish. It's ready when its interior is creamy.
Puréed: crushing it raw with coarse salt facilitates mashing it. This approach is much better than chopping or puréeing it using a blender or food processor; use it for rouille sauce, aïoli, or pesto, or in eggplant or chickpea purées.

Jarred: fresh, peeled garlic covered with a cold brine (made from 1 oz/30 g of gray salt without preservatives diluted in 4¼ cups/1 L of spring water). Fermentation in a sealed jar at room temperature starts around 1 week, then continues when stored at cool room temperature, such as in a cellar (about 3 weeks more) or in the refrigerator (a little longer). It can be refrigerated for a long time after opening and eaten like candy.

Garlic or not with the lamb?

"Oh, never garlic in the lamb, ouh là . . ." From this infamous reply by Jean Yanne in *Le Boucher* (1970), director Claude Chabrol affirms his phobia of adding garlic to leg of lamb, which could spoil the delicate flavor of the meat. One thing is certain: injecting garlic directly into the meat is not a good idea. Not only does the act of piercing the meat harm it, but the garlic remains raw and its flavor remains too pronounced. However, placing whole garlic cloves in the pan with the lamb to cook in the meat's juices is a definite thumbs-up! Since the meat and garlic are not in direct contact, this approach satisfies both those for and against garlic with leg of lamb! Here is a gourmet recipe:

LEG OF LAMB WITH GARLIC
by Julien Duboué*

PREPARATION TIME: 5 MINUTES
COOKING TIME: 2 HOURS
SERVES 4

1 lamb shoulder
Salt
Ground Espelette pepper
1 bouquet garni (thyme, rosemary, bay leaf)
¾ cup plus 1 tablespoon (200 mL) duck fat
¾ cup plus 1 tablespoon (200 mL) olive oil
¾ cup plus 1 tablespoon (200 mL) sunflower oil
20 cloves garlic, unpeeled

The day before, in a baking dish, season the lamb shoulder with salt and Espelette pepper, then add the bouquet garni. Refrigerate overnight. The next day, place the shoulder in a large flameproof casserole dish and add the duck fat and oils to cover. Blanch the whole garlic cloves for 5 minutes in boiling water, then distribute them, with the bouquet garni, around the lamb. Place the casserole dish in a cold oven, then heat it to 350°F (180°C). Cook for 2 hours, or until the lamb is cooked to the desired temperature.

Chef of the restaurant A Noste, Paris 2nd

skip to
A *Tour de France*—Onions, p. 20

Tips for . . .

→ **Selecting it:** select a bulging head, heavy and firm to the touch, with cloves that do not have exposed green sprouts.
→ **Peeling it:** crush the clove under the flat side of the blade of a knife, then cut off the ends: the peel will remove easily.
→ **Storing it:** kept in a cool and dry place, the whole bulb will keep for months. Keep away from potatoes!
→ **Controlling its pungency:** blanch it for a few moments in boiling water before using it raw.
→ **Eliminating its odor on the skin:** rub your fingers with a stainless steel spoon under running water.

GOOD YEAR-ROUND

YOUNG GARLIC

This is garlic harvested before it divides into cloves. It has the appearance of a tiny leek with tender leaves.
When to find it? March to April; store it refrigerated for several days.
Where to find it? In food market stalls in the south, in Aquitaine.
What does it taste like? With a subtle flavor, it's ideal for those who are not fans of the flavor of garlic.
How should you prepare it? Raw and salted; chopped in salad or an omelet; panfried, salted, and eaten on toasted bread.

FRESH GARLIC

Picked before it's fully matured, with only small cloves, and protected by a soft and fleshy peel.
When to find it? From the end of April to July, depending on the region; store for ten days at the bottom of the refrigerator.
Where to find it? Almost everywhere. Choose local varieties.
What does it taste like? Subtle yet intense; a crunchy texture.
How should you prepare it? Raw, or sautéed in a wok with fresh vegetables; sliced and browned in olive oil with chile pepper; on spaghetti.

DRIED GARLIC

Fully formed cloves with thin, brittle skin, peeled at the end of its growing season and dried in the sun.
When to find it? From late June in the south, in August farther north. Store at least until the following spring in a dry environment.
Where to find it? All over.
What does it taste like? Noticeably stronger since it's harvested at maturity.
How should you prepare it? Simmered in tomato sauce, in soups and stews, rubbed inside the baking dish for gratins and fondues, baked in its peel.

Words & Foods

PIG TALK

A mascot of France's culinary repertoire, the pig has been a good friend of the French, both on the plate and page. Here are some juicy bits of pure pork.

Aurore Vincenti

ETYMOLOGY

OINK
A donkey goes **hee-haw**, a cow goes **mooo**, and a pig goes **oink**. In French it's "**kos-kos**," which might be Greek onomatopoeia.

DOLPHIN
Did you know that the dolphin is considered to be the piglet of the sea? The Greek **delphax (-akos)** means "sow, pig"! In Latin, the **porcus marinus**, sea pig, is a porpoise.

PORCELAIN
The Italian word **porcellana**, at the origin of the French word *porcelaine* (porcelain), once meant "fine and hard ceramic" but also "a mollusk sheltered in a univalve shell." It so happens that the shell was shaped like a sow's vulva. That's why the word *porcelaine* is derived from **porcella** (female pig).

★

BIBLIOGRAPHY

Raymond Buren, Michel Pastoureau, and Jacques Verroust,
Le Cochon, histoire symbolique et cuisine du porc
(Sang de la terre, 1987)

Michel Pastoureau,
Histoire d'un cousin mal aimé
(Gallimard, 2003)

Orlando De Rudder,
Aux Petits Oignons
(Larousse, 2006)

Alain Rey,
Dictionnaire historique de la langue française
(Le Robert, 2011)

Christian Etchebest,
Éric Ospital,
Tout est bon dans le cochon
(First, 2015)

★

Three pig bads

❧ Dirty as a pig
You'd say that a person stuffing his face is eating like a pig. The animal not only has the reputation of wallowing in mud but also of feeding on it. Excrement and rotting carcasses: it's all good!

❧ "The rich are like pigs: the older they get, the dumber they become . . ."
Jacques Brel, *Les Bourgeois*, 1962
Pliny the Elder was already giving pigs a bad name in his *Natural History* (77–79 AD). He described them as stupid animals without proper judgment.

❧ Pigs do piggy things
Their reputation as being lewd is relatively recent. In the past, dogs were the symbols of lust. Around the end of the Middle Ages, dogs became man's best friend and pigs took on the vices that once characterized canines.

And yet, everything's good in a pig!

While lust is a vice, opulence is seen more and more as an asset, although it's **sometimes tinged with guilt**... There's guilty pleasure in pigging out on junk food and also in talking dirty. The sexually transgressive insinuation becomes more positive when it has to do with intimacy: with friends and family, you can be **as friendly as pigs**.

To have a pig is a **sign of wealth**. As early as the second half of the eighteenth century, **piggy banks** flourished. It should be noted that the sow is very fertile and so the proverb holds true: "In a good pig, everything's good, even the hair." Pigs eat everything, which means that everything is delectable or at least usable: **from its blood to its bristles**.

"Of all the quadrupeds, the pig seems to be the crudest of animals: the imperfections of its shape seem to influence what's natural; all its habits are unrefined, all its tastes are foul, all its feelings boil down to furious lust and brute greed, which make it indiscriminately devour anything it sees, even its offspring after birth." Buffon, *Histoire naturelle*, second edition, volume 6, 1769. Buffon's words are not the fruit of scientific observation but rather a **symbolic vision**. If the naturalist disregards truth in his passionate words, it's because the pig gives rise to **both disgust and fascination** in the minds of men. The French language and its idioms encapsulate that ambivalence. The historian Michel Pastoureau provides an explanation for the attitude: the **biological similarity** that connects man to pig. Both are omnivores and have the same digestive system. And the pig is considered to be an exceptionally intelligent and sensitive animal. **Different but the same.**

Pork, Lard, or Pig?
"Lard" comes from the Latin **laridum**, which means the **fat** between the skin and flesh of mammals. When someone asks in French if it's lard or pig, it means the person is wondering whether **fat is being passed off as meat**. "Pig" is a common term used in domestic contexts—it's informal—whereas "pork" has a more proper tone. In a formal context, business for example, one might refer to raising pork rather than pigs. The word *pork* commonly describes the meat of the animal, but in French gastronomy, it has become **more chic** to write "côte de cochon" (chop of pig) rather than "côte de porc" (pork chop).

Nevertheless, in the French language, it has not been a good thing to be a pig for ages . . . Insults are redundant but obstinate: **"Old pig! Dirty pig! Lard face!"**

Skip to: On the Butcher's Board, p. 166

George Sand

Although it doesn't appear much in her writing, gastronomy was everywhere in her life. Especially at her small chateau in Nohant, in the heart of the Berry countryside, where the very gourmet author of *La Mare du diable* (*The Devil's Pool*) welcomed family and friends.
Estelle Lenartowicz

GOURMAND PROFILE
Close to seven hundred recipes collected in her notebooks.
Land, my beautiful land: cherishing the Berry of her childhood, her menus drew on the region's rustic riches, including vegetable soups and game.
Heading abroad: from her time at an English boarding school, she took away an Anglo-Saxon sensibility (scones, pudding, *homard à l'américaine* [lobster with wine, tomatoes, and garlic]), and a penchant for exotic tastes (Brazilian beef tenderloin, tea soufflé, and tapioca). So chic!
Guilty pleasures: sugar, in all its forms: candied fruits, chocolate bars with vanilla, brioche cake, meringues . . .

Writer, epicurean, and excellent hostess
(1804–1876)

All around the table

Writers, musicians, painters . . . the greatest artists of the time gathered around the baroness' table.

The poet **Théophile Gautier**, visiting in the summer of 1863, deemed the food "very good" but deplored the unreasonable quantity of game and chicken.

Gustave Flaubert visited the chateau twice, in 1869 and then in 1873.

The playwright **Ivan Turgenev** impressed guests with caviar and reindeer tongue from Lapland brought from his native Russia.

Alexandre Dumas, fils, was often there in the summer; he spent hours swimming in the river and entertained guests with his legendary puns that George Sand "only understood after everyone else."

It is through **Franz Liszt** and his mistress, the writer Marie d'Agoult, that Sand would meet Chopin.

Frédéric Chopin, "Chopinet," as he was nicknamed, became the star of dinners at Nohant by drawing on his unrivaled talents as an imitator.

Honoré de Balzac, began a rich exchange of letters with the mistress of the house after his visit in 1838.

Eugène Delacroix taught painting to her young son Maurice as a way to thank the hostess for her hospitality.

SABLÉS

ESTATE IN NOHANT
Paris–Nohant: 182 miles (293 km), or three days by stagecoach, or ten hours by train (starting in 1868).
A complete garden, consisting of a park (perfect for picnics), a kitchen garden, an orchard, and a greenhouse, where the mistress of the house grew sweet potatoes and pineapple.
A fully equipped kitchen with a professional oven, a slew of saucepans, kettles, and copper skillets.
A luxurious dining room, in which the large dining table was set with stoneware dishes, crystal glasses, and napkins embroidered with the hostess' initials: GS.

PREPARATION TIME: 15 MINUTES
COOKING TIME: 20 MINUTES
RESTING TIME: 12 HOURS
MAKES ABOUT 20 SABLÉS
2½ cups (250 g) all-purpose flour
10½ tablespoons (125 g) butter, cubed and chilled
½ cup (100 g) superfine sugar
2 egg yolks
Flavorings: vanilla, orange blossom water, rose water, and the like

The day before, pour the flour into a mound on a work surface and make a well in the center using your fingers. Add the chilled butter, sugar, egg yolks, and any flavoring to the well. Knead the mixture with the palm of your hand until a firm dough is formed. Roll the dough into a ball, wrap it in a towel, and refrigerate it overnight. The next day, roll out the dough to a thickness of a little less than ¼ inch (0.5 cm). Preheat the oven to 350°F (180°C). Use a cookie cutter to cut shapes, and place them on a greased baking sheet. Place the baking sheet in the oven, rotating it from time to time so that the sablés bake evenly. As soon as the sablés turn a pale golden, take them out of the oven and let cool. Store them in a tin for a few days.

Wild Mollusks

There is an infinite collection of bivalve mollusks and other gastropods on French shores. Here is a detailed review of these funny animals, some of which are very well known while others are more rare, but all of which offer a delicious way to enjoy any day.

Pierrick Jegu

Sea scallop
Bivalve mollusk of the Pectinidae family.
Description: a small version of the great scallop, but more domed. The black sea scallop has two asymmetrical "ears."
Fishing: in the English Channel and in the Atlantic. Beginners fish for it on foot; the professionals use a boat and a net.
Taste/texture: briny and hazelnut-like; delicate flesh.
Preparing: raw, as a carpaccio; seared in a pan; or baked in its shell.
Tip: select wild sea scallops.

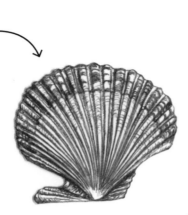

Limpet
Marine gastropod of the Patellidae family.
Description: about 1½ to 2¼ inches (4 to 6 cm) in diameter. Characteristic conical shell.
Fishing: on foot, with a knife to detach its strong, muscular foot, which is usually firmly attached to a rock.
Taste/texture: briny and primitive; chewy.
Preparing: in stews, rillettes, or chopped and sautéed in a pan.
Tip: some people beat the flesh to soften it.

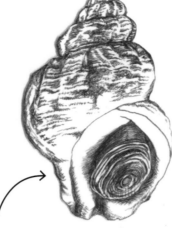

Whelk
Marine gastropod of the Buccinidae family.
Description: its brown, yellow, green, or ocher shell ranges in size from 1½ to 4 inches (4 to 10 cm) long and appears sculpted in a point and a spiral.
Fishing: using pots; found especially in the Normandy–Brittany gulf.
Taste/texture: whelk and mayonnaise make an excellent duo, but whelk is also a delicious addition to salads or prepared as a tartare.
Tip: after draining them, add a dash of vinegar or white wine to the cooking water to remove any sliminess.

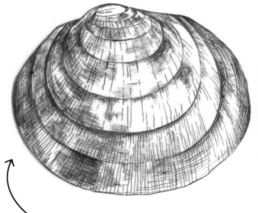

Surf clam
Bivalve mollusk of the Mactridae family, known on île d'Yeu.
Description: smooth shell, white to ivory.
Fishing: only a few islanders are allowed to fish them, from spring to autumn.
Taste/texture: a generous flesh with a briny taste.
Preparing: the islanders cook them with onions, white wine, cream, and parsley.
Tip: only the ones from île d'Yeu are worth eating!

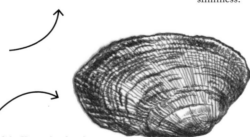

Venus clam
Bivalve mollusk of the Veneridae family.
Description: gray to light brown shell, concentric streaks. Can reach 4¾ inches (12 cm) in diameter.
Fishing: on the coast of Brittany or Vendée. It can be located by looking for small holes in the sand . . . then you dig!
Taste/texture: very pronounced brininess.
Preparing: raw, on a seafood tower; or cooked in the same manner as a dog cockle or a littleneck clam.
Tip: use it in a clam chowder (a soup garnished with potatoes and bacon).

Prairie clam
Bivalve mollusk of the Veneridae family.
Description: 1⅓ to 2 inches (3.5 to 5 cm) in diameter with a domed whitish to brown shell with deep ridges.
Fishing: a few inches under the sand. "Hunted" by fishermen on foot, or in the Norman–Breton Gulf by professionals.
Taste/texture: subtle and briny.
Preparing: plain or stuffed, in a risotto or a shellfish soup.
Tip: use a very short cooking time to avoid a chewing gum–like texture.

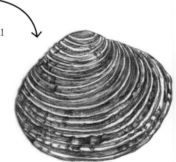

Soft-shell clam
Bivalve mollusk of the Myidae family.
Description: oval and elongated shell, up to 8 inches (20 cm) long, whitish or gray.
Fishing: lives in sand up to 15¾ inches (40 cm) deep. Locate a hole in the sand at least ¼ inch (5 mm) in diameter, then dig!
Taste/texture: briny, primitive.
Preparing: chop the flesh and sauté it with butter.
Tip: in north Finistère it is called *kouillou kezeg*, which translates to "horse balls" in the local dialect.

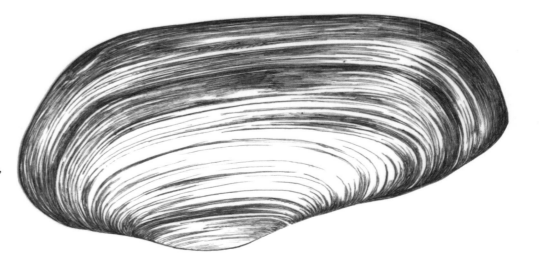

Palourde clam
Bivalve mollusk of the Veneridae family.
Description: a finely ridged shell, slightly convex and up to 2 inches (5 cm) in diameter. Lives buried in sand or mudflats.
Fishing: on all coasts of France. Fished on foot, by rake, or by a net pulled by hand or by boat. Its breeding is called *vénériculture* (the "raising of clams").
Taste/texture: delicately briny.
Preparing: raw on a seafood tower; gratin; or added to pasta, as in *pasta alle vongole*.
Tip: cook it minimally, to maintain its natural flavors and textures.

Abalone
Gastropod of the Haliotididae family.
Description: ear-shaped shell, pearly and iridescent interior.
Fishing: very controlled; walking at lowest tides; some farming.
Taste/texture: very delicate, briny, sweet, and nutty.
Preparing: seared in browned butter, sliced in a salad, or in tartare.
Tip: to tenderize the meat, refrigerate it overnight wrapped in a cloth and placed under a weight.

Fishing Clams on Foot

In France, fishing on foot is not just a leisurely Sunday activity but also a real profession. Those who hold official licenses to fish clams are professionals who are bound by regulations regarding quotas, fishing seasons, sizes, and the like—all of which promote sustainable fishing that respects the clams' "merroir" (coastal *terroir*). If the use of coastal territory were an acquired right for everyone, some amateur fishermen might take advantage and plunder its resources. So before you begin fishing for mollusks on your own, research local regulations, then fish sparingly. Follow a few simple steps before starting, such as placing a pebble at a spot, then returning back to it to note the level of the tide and avoid any unfortunate mishaps.

Common periwinkle
Sea gastropod of the Littorinidae family, present on all France's coasts.
Description: about ¾ to 1⅛ inches (2 to 3 cm) in diameter with a spiral-shaped brown shell.
Fishing: on foot in pools or under the rocks, where it moves to feed on algae and micro-algae.
Taste/texture: briny and tender.
Preparing: serve cold, on a slice of toast with salted butter.
Tip: beware of overcooking, which can make the meat rubbery.

Dog cockle
Bivalve mollusk of the Glycymerididae family, found in the English Channel, Atlantic, and Mediterranean.
Description: up to 3 inches (8 cm) in diameter. Thick, convex shell, light-colored with red spots and sometimes brown markings.
Fishing: on foot, using a trowel to extract it from the sand.
Taste/texture: briny and slightly bitter.
Preparing: raw, baked, poached in a reduced broth, or even à la marinière—cooked in white wine with onions and shallots.
Tip: delicious when the shells are stuffed.

Wedge clam
Bivalve mollusk of the Donacidae family.
Description: 1⅓ inches (3.5 cm) in diameter maximum; pastel colors, soft curves, and a "butterfly" shape when both shells are open.
Fishing: on all France's coasts, buried in the wet sand. Experienced collectors fish it on foot, pulling a small, wheeled dredger.
Taste/texture: briny and delicate.
Preparing: go for simplicity! Cook it on a griddle or in a drizzle of olive oil with a little garlic and cream.
Tip: it's very fragile, so it should be consumed quickly after purchase.

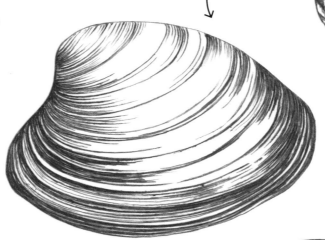

Common cockle
Bivalve mollusk of the Cardiidae family.
Description: small white convex shell with vertical streaks.
Fishing: a "star" for collecting by foot on all of France's coasts. They are also raised in *cérastoculteurs* (cockle fisheries) for farming.
Taste/texture: delicate and briny.
Preparing: enjoy them cold or hot; the flavor lends itself well to meat-seafood combinations: they are very tasty mixed with pork.
Tip: do not discard the cooking liquid; it is delicious and very briny.

Razor clam
Bivalve mollusk of the Solenidae family, present from the North Sea to the Mediterranean.
Description: from 4 to 8 inches (10 to 20 cm), elongated and "sharpened" shape.
Fishing: find small holes in the sand that form a figure eight or a keyhole shape and pour a salt solution into it to flush them out.
Taste/texture: briny and tender.
Preparing: steamed. Pleasant with an herbed butter, Espelette pepper, or citrus zest.
Tip: if its foot retracts when touched, it's alive!

Smooth clam
Bivalve mollusk of the Veneridae family.
Description: thick oval shell, red-brown, smooth and shiny.
Fishing: on foot or by boats equipped with dredges in the Atlantic.
Taste/texture: briny and crunchy.
Preparing: raw, with a drizzle of fresh lemon juice and a glass of white wine.
Tip: given its imposing size, up to 4 inches (10 cm) in diameter, stuffing it is a good option.

skip to
Whelk Stands Out!, p. 373

Natural Wine

Often confused with organic wine, natural wine has no requirements. Whether it's a boho trend or a true awakening, here's a look at a way of winemaking that's at the center of much debate . . .

Cerval Gwilherm

RAW, NATURAL, ALIVE?

Because they feel it adheres to common sense, these wine producers don't use any chemical products in their vineyards, not even baking soda in their storerooms. Sulfites are generally frowned upon and letting the wine be free is favored instead, so the wine is often said to be alive! When it's properly domesticated, it produces a stirringly pure juice. That's how the wine becomes even easier to drink and digest.

SULFITES: ENEMY OR FRIEND?

Sulfur dioxide (or SO_2) is the most controversial of chemical additives and also the most common one used in the winemaking world. It has antioxidant and antiseptic properties, but used in excess, it can block certain aromas and give the drink a standardized taste. On the other hand, because wine is naturally unstable, without sulfites, certain bacteria and other yeasts can prosper and transform the liquid into vinegar. Certain winemakers have found a good compromise: adding SO_2 only before bottling as a way to preserve the most fruit and using only very small amounts to protect it from potential parasites.

CRAZY LABELS

Our top freestyle labels. Watch out for bad puns . . .

"Grololo" (Big boob): for this Grolleau grape wine, Jo Pithon even provides a drawing . . . va voom!

"Tout bu or not tout bu" (To be or not to be all gone): a cross between Shakespeare and Loïc Roure from the Domaine du Possible.

"La vie on y est" (This is life): vintage from the Domaine Gramenon. When pronounced quickly in French, it sounds like the name of the grape variety used to make it: the *viognier*.

"L'aimé chai" (Bombed): a vintage from the Domaine Mouthes Le Bihan, in Côtes du Duras, that's strong enough to blow up a breath test.

"Attention chenin méchant" (Beware of the mean dog): despite winemaker Nicolas Reau's warning, his vintage is something to bark about.

TASTES . . .

Some natural wines try to pass off their unusual tastes as regional traits. Here are natural pitfalls to avoid if you want to properly quench your thirst.

Sweaty smell: spoilage yeast, also known as "brett," which might be due to unhygienic conditions in the wine storeroom.

Rotten egg smell: reduced wine. Lack of air, which often happens after bottling.

Nutty smell: oxidation, which can be harmful in various degrees. When controlled, it can add much-sought-after complexity, especially in Jura vineyards.

Rancid smell: uncontrolled lactic bacteria.

Dank smell: reduced wine.

Vinegar smell: volatile acidity in the wine.

Nail polish smell: related to unhygienic conditions in the wine cave.

Charge!

Today, there's only one natural winemaker association in France: the **Association des vins naturels (AVN).**

A LEXICON OF NATURAL WINE

Glou-glou: describes a delicious wine that's easy to drink.

Rock 'n' roll: describes a wine in which alcohol, acidity, and fruit are imbalanced.

Blocked: describes a wine that generally lacks aromatic definition.

Pet' Nat': French abbreviation for "pétillant naturel" (natural sparkling).

Coup de JaJa: another French expression for a li'l drink.

Perlant: a soft fizz due to a small amount of carbon dioxide.

Reduced: the opposite of oxidized. A wine that has limited exposure to oxygen in the bottle.

Free wine: describes a wine that does not contain any wine product.

Natural wine at home

Storage: store at a temperature below 57°F (14°C) so that it doesn't begin to ferment again in the bottle.

Consumption: drink it chilled and in a carafe. That will eliminate the gas, which is common in this kind of *jaja* ("glass of wine").

The 5 commandments of natural wine

★

You shall boycott chemical products.

★

You shall plow using horses.

★

You shall harvest grapes by hand.

★

You shall censure artificial yeast.

★

You shall not use any sulfites.

"Wine is life"
Horace (65 BC)

10 NATURAL CELEBRITIES

→ **Pierre Overnoy** from the Maison Overnoy-Houillon in Pupillin

→ **Philippe and Michèle Laurent** from the Domaine Gramenon in the Rhône Valley

→ **Henry Frédéric Roch** from the Domaine Prieuré Roch in the Côte de Nuits

→ **Didier Barral** from the Domaine Léon Barral in Faugères

→ **Stéphane Tissot** from the Domaine André and Mireille Tissot in Arbois

→ **Marcel Lapierre** from the eponymous Domaine in Beaujolais

→ **Éric Pfifferling** from the Domaine de l'Anglore in Tavel

→ **Mark Angeli** from the Domaine La Ferme de la Sansonnière in Anjou

→ **Antoine Arena** from the Domaine Antoine Arena in Corsica

→ **Robert and Bernard Plageoles** from the Domaine Plageoles in Gaillac

skip to ....

It Smells like Sulfur!, p. 103;
A Horse in the Vineyard?, p. 133

Crêpes

Hats off to Brittany! With its *bigoudens* (tall lace hats), bawdy songs, and crêpes, this region in northwest France is certainly steeped in folklore. But its specialties, such as crêpes, can also be considered art. To keep your crêpes from falling flat, follow this lesson.

Jill Cousin

EQUIPMENT

Any respectable Breton (a person from Brittany) must have a *bilig*—a large round rimless cast-iron griddle for making crêpes, placed over gas or electricity. And also a *rozell,* a small rakelike tool used to spread the batter on the griddle, and a wooden spatula to flip the crêpes. The commoner, however, must be satisfied with a nonstick cast-iron skillet for making them.

THE RIGHT SKILLS

Do you use a *bilig*? Then you must use a *rozell,* the small wooden rake, to spread the batter. A thin, consistent result is dependent upon the rotation of the wrist. It takes practice . . .

FLIPPING THE CRÊPES

A consolation prize will be awarded to all those who are equipped with only a Teflon-coated pan. Once the crêpe is browned underneath, lift up the edges all around with a small spatula to detach it from the pan, or shake the pan so that it slides around, then, with a confident snap of the wrist, flip the crêpe in the air and over in the pan by quickly moving the pan forward then up. Don't forget to catch the crêpe on its way back down!

THE STAR OF CANDLEMAS

With their round shape and their golden color reminiscent of the solar disk, and with the imminent return, at Candlemas, of the sun in the spring, crêpes became the logical gastronomic symbol of this Christian festival held in February to commemorate the presentation of Christ at the Temple.

WHEAT FLOUR CRÊPE BATTER*
by Bertrand Larcher

PREPARATION TIME: 15 MINUTES
RESTING TIME: 1 HOUR
MAKES ABOUT 25 CRÊPES

12 organic eggs (separate 3 of the eggs, setting aside their whites)
10½ ounces (300 g) granulated sugar or demerara sugar
8½ cups (2 L) whole milk
2¼ pounds (1 kg) organic wheat flour
Option 1: 1 ounce (30 g) browned butter
Option 2: ½ vanilla bean steeped in 1 cup (250 mL) hot milk (important: cool the milk before adding it to the batter)
Option 3: Zest of 1 orange
Option 4: 1 tablespoon (15 mL) gold rum

Thoroughly whisk together all the whole eggs (including the 3 egg yolks) and sugar. Whisk in 6 cups (1.5 L) of the milk. Gently stir in the flour using a wooden spoon (do not use an electric mixer). Add the ingredients from one of the four options. Strain the batter through a sieve, then refrigerate for 1 hour. Before making the crêpes, add the remaining milk to the batter with a ladle and stir it in gently. Beat the 3 egg whites to stiff peaks, then fold them gently into the batter. The batter is now ready to be spread in the pan or on the griddle.

*Both recipes taken from Breizh Café *by Bertrand Larcher, Éditions La Martinière*

LEMON AND HONEY CRÊPE*

PREPARATION TIME: 5 MINUTES
COOKING TIME: 2 MINUTES PER CRÊPE
MAKES 1 CRÊPE

3 ounces (80 g) crêpe batter
½ ounce (12 g) honey
1 squeeze lemon juice
1 slice lemon

Spread the crêpe batter onto the heated *bilig.* When the crêpe is done, fold it into a triangle and place it on a plate. Spread the honey over the crêpe, then add a squeeze of lemon juice over the top.

CRÊPES SUZETTE
by Auguste Escoffier*

MAKES ABOUT 20 CRÊPES

6 eggs
½ cup (100 g) superfine sugar
3 cups (750 mL) milk
2½ cups (250 g) sifted flour
1 pinch salt
Flavoring of your choice (vanilla sugar, kirsch, rum, or cognac)
Juice of 1 candied mandarin orange
2 tablespoons (30 mL) melted butter

For the sauce
7 tablespoons (100 g) unsalted butter, slightly softened

1 tablespoon (15 mL) curaçao liqueur
Zest of 1 candied mandarin orange (from above)
½ cup (100 g) granulated sugar

Prepare the batter as instructed in the Wheat Flour Crêpe Batter recipe, adding the flavoring of your choice, the orange juice, and the melted butter to the batter. Cook the crêpes, then make the sauce. Work the butter into a creamy consistency, then combine the curaçao and the orange zest with the butter. Spread the sauce over the crêpes, then fold each of them over four times on a warm metal sheet pan. Serve them warm on a warmed plate. Sprinkle them with granulated sugar, then sprinkle them with curaçao in front of the guests.

*Recipe from La Cuisine d'Auguste Escoffier *by Christian Constant and Yves Camdeborde, Éditions Lafon*

skip to
Galettes, p. 241

Camembert

It's the king of French cheeses! But it is also one of the most threatened … This is a stirring portrait of France's beloved bloomy-rind cheese.

Laurent Seminel

MARIE HAREL, THE MOTHER OF CAMEMBERT

1791: a refractory priest from Brie took refuge on the Beaumoncel farm, overlooking the small village of Camembert. There he taught the young Marie Harel the secrets of his region's cheese. Thus was born Camembert, sold at the markets of Vimoutiers and Argentan. The five children of Marie's daughter all became cheesemakers …

THE AOP CAMEMBERT DE NORMANDIE

The AOP (*appellation d'origine protégée*) Camembert de Normandie protects authentic Normandy Camembert, which makes up 5 percent of French Camembert production. The requirements of this raw cow's-milk cheese, which is in the bloomy-rind family, are **defined precisely**:

● Milk production, cheese production, and aging must take place in a **defined geographical area, within one of four French departments**: Calvados, Manche, Orne, and Eure. The conditions under which the cheese is sold are also regulated.

● The raw milk must be collected from a herd made up of a **minimum of 50 percent Normande cows**, which must be allowed to graze for at least six months out of the year.

● Certain manufacturing steps (molding, salting, aging, etc.) must meet **very strict criteria**. For example, the curd, which is obtained in large basins, "must be deposited into the molds at a minimum of five batches and waiting at least 40 minutes between each batch."

1 wheel of Camembert

=

5 ladles of curds
2⅓ quarts (2.2 L) of milk
13 to 15 days of aging in the aging room, so that the cheese develops its white "bloomy" rind
9 ounces (250 g) minimum weight after aging

What does it mean to be molded using ladles?

The Camembert de Normandie AOP must be molded either manually "using hemispherical spoons mounted at the end of a handle," or automatically "using articulated molding heads" (the first method, manually, is the method for the majority of Camembert de Normandie AOP cheeses).

THE RAW MILK BATTLE

2007: dairy companies Lactalis and Isigny Sainte-Mère (which produce 90 percent of AOP Camembert) decided to give up the use of raw milk in their cheeses, for fear of health hazards. They called for a relaxation of the regulations of the AOP in order to be allowed to heat treat the raw milk. However, defenders of raw-milk Camembert—the companies Graindorge, Réot, and Gillot—cried foul.
2008: the French Ministry of Agriculture decided in favor of untreated raw milk. Lactalis's response: it informed the country's General Directorate of Food about traces of pathogenic bacteria in Graindorge's Camembert cheeses!
2016: Lactalis bought its former rival company Graindorge. There was gnashing of teeth throughout the countryside.

OTHER CAMEMBERTS

Camembert made in Normandy is different from Camembert de Normandie (Normandy Camembert). Camembert made in Normandy can be made using raw milk, heated milk, microfiltered milk, or pasteurized milk. The milk must come, however, from one of the four departments of Normandy. Camembert, like Cheddar, Brie, and Gruyère, can be made all over the world.

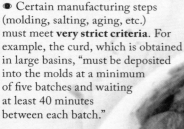

Making Camembert

Ladling

Draining

Unmolding

Salting

Aging

An Exemplary Producer
The only Camembert de Normandie whose milk is both **organic and direct from farms** is produced by **Patrick Mercier of Ferme du Champ Secret**, in the Orne, made from raw milk from 100 percent grass-fed Normande cows.

skip to
Camembert Packages That Tell the History of France, p. 322

APPLE-CAMEMBERT TATIN

SERVES 6

4 apples
2 tablespoons plus 2 teaspoons (40 g) unsalted butter
1 tablespoon demerara sugar
1 wheel (9 oz/250 g) Camembert cheese, sliced
14 ounces (400 g) puff pastry dough

Preheat the oven to 350°F (180°C).
Peel the apples and cut them into thick slices, then lightly sauté them in the butter and sugar. Arrange parchment paper in the bottom of a cake pan or a baking dish. Spread the apples over the top of the parchment, then distribute the slices of Camembert on top. Roll out the puff pastry dough and cover the top of the pan with it, tucking the edges into the pan to make a border. Bake for 20 minutes, or until golden. Serve warm with a green salad and a hard craft cider.

The Omelet

What's simpler and more French than an omelet? Here is a detailed look into this dish, which can be both a home-style dish and a great gastronomic art.

Frédéric Laly-Baraglioli

> *"Eggs scrambled in a certain way and enclosed in a cooked envelope of eggs, and nothing else."*
>
> —Auguste Escoffier

DID YOU SAY OMELET?

The word *omelet* appears in English, German, Dutch, Portuguese, Russian, and even Italian! Its etymology? It comes from *âmelette* (meaning "a small soul," referring to the precious commodity that protects and delivers the egg) or *alumella*, the diminutive of the word *blade* (from the oblong shape of the omelet).

AN INVENTORY OF FRENCH OMELETS

Omelet with vegetables

It's made with onions, young garlic (in Aquitaine), leeks, sorrel and/or dandelions (in Auvergne and Champagne), asparagus, artichokes (in Provence), tomato (in Provence and Corsica), zucchini, peas (in the old-fashioned omelet from Clamart), arugula or purslane (in Nice), Swiss chard (in the *trouchia niçoise* omelet), avocado (in Guadeloupe), and onions-tomatoes-peppers-ginger (in the Creole omelet of Réunion). And in many regions it is made using porcini, truffles, chanterelles, horn of plenty, and oranges.

Omelet with seafood . . . and freshwater fish

Salt cod (the Basque omelet for Good Friday), young eel (Gascony), poutine (Nice), sea urchins (Corsica), herring (salted and smoked herring from Boulogne-sur-Mer), or *hénons* (cockles from the Bay of Somme) . . .

Omelet with cheese

Swiss Emmental (Savoie), Comté (Jura), Brocciu and mint (Corsica), Chaource (Champagne and Burgundy), or Roquefort (Aveyron) . . .

Omelet with cured meats

With pressed cooked ham (Paris), bacon or lardons (eastern France), or blood sausage (Catalonia) . . .

Sweet omelet

With caramelized apples, strawberries, blueberries, raspberries, cherries, chocolate, rum soufflé, and omelet dauphinoise (with ladyfingers soaked in milk then baked until puffed and golden) . . .

THE OMELET WITH LANDAIS PEPPERS

Recipe by Josette Darjo, farmer and ex-livestock breeder from Landes, queen of *gavage* (force-feeding practices to make foie gras), soup pots, and preserved foods—a woman of many talents on the banks of the Adour!

PREPARATION TIME: 10 TO 15 MINUTES
COOKING TIME: 10 TO 20 MINUTES
SERVES 2

A good plate of Landaise peppers (long, green sweet chile peppers)
Duck fat, for frying
5 eggs
Salt and freshly ground black pepper

Halve the peppers, cut off and remove the stems, and remove the seeds. Coarsely chop the peppers, then fry them in a skillet in a little duck fat for about 10 minutes, or until browned (or slightly charred; that is how they will best release all their aromas). Quickly beat the eggs, season them with salt and pepper, and add the cooked peppers to them. Pour the eggs into the skillet and cook them in the duck fat for 5 to 10 minutes, folding them over to form an omelet and ensuring that the center stays moist.

3 tips

1
Use a wooden spatula and a good, flat pan that is nonstick and well greased.

2
Beat the eggs (two or three per person) with a fork, but only lightly (to prevent dry eggs when cooked).

3
Fold the omelet like a wallet, roll it up, or flip it with the aid of a plate—whichever approach you like best and find easiest.

RUNNY OR NOT?

Mastering how the eggs are cooked is the trademark of a French omelet. But eggs cooked just until they are runny does not mean they are raw! When the omelet is folded or rolled at the end, the eggs should be just set on the outside and soft and moist on the inside. When you opt for an omelet that is flipped and cooked on both sides, cook the first side well, then finish the other side over medium heat until it's just set.

★ ★ ★

CRESPEOU

This is a dish from the **region of Avignon**, traditionally enjoyed at harvesttime: an **omelet "cake"** with a Harlequin design! Overlay a thin green omelet (with chard and/or parsley, sage, and other herbs), a red omelet (with bell pepper and/or tomato), a yellow omelet (with zucchini, bell pepper, grated cheese, or onions), a dark omelet (with olive tapenade), a light omelet (with garlic), an orange omelet (with carrot), and perhaps even a pink omelet (with ham or tuna). The omelets are **stacked hot in a mold** and eaten cold, accompanied by a tomato coulis.

★ ★ ★

A LIGHT AND FLUFFY OMELET

by Mapie de Toulouse-Lautrec

SERVES 4

Separate 8 eggs. Beat 4 of the egg whites to stiff peaks. Beat the remaining eggs and egg yolks with a fork. Add 3 tablespoons plus 1 teaspoon (50 g) of cream, some salt, and a generous dose of freshly ground black pepper to the eggs, then beat briefly and carefully to combine. Heat 5 tablespoons (75 g) of butter in a large skillet until melted. Meanwhile, fold the egg whites into the egg mixture, as you would into a chocolate mousse: lift the mixture to fold them in, do not stir it. Pour the mixture into the hot pan, fold the omelet over when the eggs are half cooked, and serve.

THE SECRETS OF MOTHER POULARD'S FAMOUS OMELET

This is an omelet known around the world and created in Mont-Saint-Michel in the kitchen of Annette Boutiaut (married name Poulard). It is hearty yet light because it is puffed. Mother Poulard claimed that the secret to her supple texture lay simply in the quality and quantity of the eggs and butter used. Curnonsky, considered the prince of gastronomes, says she was inspired by Balzac's novel *La Rabouilleuse*:

"He discovered that the omelet was much more delicate when you did not beat the whites and yolks together with the brutality that cooks normally apply to them. According to him, it was necessary to make the whites achieve the state of mousse, then to slowly introduce into the yolks into them . . ."

The Paschal omelet

Why is the omelet traditionally associated with the celebration of Easter (or *Pâques* in French), to the point that it has taken on the names *pâquette* or *pascade*? Because the eating of eggs (which have been symbols of eternity and resurrection since ancient Egypt) celebrates the eternal life of Christ, but also perhaps because it was a clever way to not waste all the eggs that had accumulated (because it was forbidden to eat them) during the forty days of Lent!

THE BROCCIU AND MINT OMELET
by Josette Baraglioli, granddaughter of Bastelicais shepherds and shepherdesses of yesteryear

The secret to this very hearty recipe: add more Brocciu cheese than eggs! Brocciu is both the filling and the essential ingredient of the omelet itself: it replaces all the butter, milk, and cream that are combined with eggs in traditional omelets.

PREPARATION TIME: 5 MINUTES
COOKING TIME: 10 MINUTES
SERVES 4

5 or 6 eggs
1⅛ pounds (500 g) Brocciu cheese (a Corsican cheese)
Salt and freshly ground black pepper
½ bunch finely chopped mint
Olive oil (and possibly butter) for cooking

Beat the eggs with a fork with two-thirds of the Brocciu, cut into very small pieces; season with salt and pepper and incorporate two-thirds of the chopped mint. Heat the oil in a skillet, then pour in the egg mixture. Once the eggs start to set, add the remaining Brocciu on top in chunks, then the remaining mint. Flip the omelet over or, to maintain a softer texture, simply fold it over.

LA TROUCHIA
by Sophie Agrofoglio*

PREPARATION TIME: 10 TO 15 MINUTES
COOKING TIME: 30 MINUTES
SERVES 4 TO 6

2 onions, peeled and chopped
Olive oil
2 bunches small Swiss chard (or 1 bunch large Swiss chard)
6 eggs
1 handful (about ½ cup) grated Parmesan cheese
1 bunch chervil, chopped
1 bunch parsley, chopped
1 pinch nutmeg
1 clove garlic, peeled and crushed
Salt and freshly ground black pepper

Fry the onions in a little olive oil. Wash and dry the chard leaves, remove the stems, then slice the leaves into very thin strips. In a large bowl, beat the eggs and Parmesan together, then add the chard, onions, chervil, parsley, nutmeg, and garlic; season with salt and pepper; beat gently to combine. Heat a little oil in a skillet, pour in the mixture, and press it down; the omelet should be about 1⅛ inch (3 cm) thick. Cook over low heat for 15 minutes, covered. Then remove the omelet from the pan: first detach it from the sides and ensure that it's not stuck to the bottom of the pan, then invert it onto a plate. Add a little oil to the skillet, then slide the omelet back into the skillet and continue cooking for 15 more minutes over low heat. Important: make sure you cook the omelet slowly over low heat because the vegetables are raw and need time to cook!

Cook at À Buteghinna, a small restaurant in Old Nice

skip to
Go Suck an Egg, p. 325;
Brocciu, the Art of Whey, p. 260

Charles Baudelaire, *Les Fleurs du Mal*, "L'Âme du vin," 1857

CIV

L'ÂME DU VIN

Un soir, l'âme du vin chantait dans les bouteilles :
« Homme, vers toi je pousse, ô cher déshérité,
Sous ma prison de verre et mes cires vermeilles,
Un chant plein de lumière et de fraternité !

Je sais combien il faut, sur la colline en flamme,
De peine, de sueur et de soleil cuisant
Pour engendrer ma vie et pour me donner l'âme ;
Mais je ne serai point ingrat ni malfaisant,

Car j'éprouve une joie immense quand je tombe
Dans le gosier d'un homme usé par ses travaux,
Et sa chaude poitrine est une douce tombe
Où je me plais bien mieux que dans mes froids caveaux.

Entends-tu retentir les refrains des dimanches
Et l'espoir qui gazouille en mon sein palpitant ?
Les coudes sur la table et retroussant tes manches,
Tu me glorifieras et tu seras content ;

Le vin

J'allumerai les yeux de ta femme ravie ;
A ton fils je rendrai sa force et ses couleurs
Et serai pour ce frêle athlète de la vie
L'huile qui raffermit les muscles des lutteurs.

En toi je tomberai, végétale ambroisie,
Grain précieux jeté par l'éternel Semeur,
Pour que de notre amour naisse la poésie
Qui jaillira vers Dieu comme une rare fleur ! »

Rabelais, *Fifth Book*, Chapter XLIV, Prière de Panurge à la Dive Bouteille, 1564

O Bouteille
Plaine toute
De misteres,
D'vne aureille
Iet'escoute
Ne differes,
Et le mot proferes,
Auquel pend mon cœur.
En la tant diuine liqueur,
Baccus qui fut d'Inde vainqueur,
Tient toute verité enclose.
Vint ant diuin loin de toy est forclose
Toute mensonge, & toute tromperie.
En ioye soit l'Aire de Noach close,
Lequel de toy nous fist la temperie.
Somme le beau mot, ie t'en prie,
Qui me doit oster de misere.
Ainsi ne se perde vne goutte.
De toy, soit blanche ou soit vermeille.
O Bouteille
Plaine toute
De mysteres
D'vne aureille
Iet'escoute
Ne differes.

870.

Saint-Amant, "Le Melon," 163-

Le Melon

[...] Ô manger précieux ! Délices de la bouche !
Ô doux reptile herbu, rampant sur une couche !
Ô beaucoup mieux que l'or, chef-d'œuvre d'Apollon !
Ô fleur de tous les fruits ! Ô ravissant Melon !
Les hommes de la cour seront gens de paroles,
Les bordels de Rouen seront francs de vérole,
Sans vermine et sans gale on verra les pédants,
Les preneurs de pétun[1] auront de belles dents,
Les femmes des badauds ne seront plus coquettes,
Les corps pleins de santé se plairont aux cliquettes[2],
Les amoureux transis ne seront plus jaloux,
Les paisibles bourgeois hanteront[3] les filous,
Les meilleurs cabarets deviendront solitaires,
Les chantres du Pont-Neuf[4] diront de hauts mystères,
Les pauvres Quinze-Vingts[5] vaudront trois cents
    Argus[6],
Les esprits doux du temps paraîtront fort aigus,
Maillet[7] fera des vers aussi bien que Malherbe,
Je haïrai Faret[8], qui se rendra superbe,

Arthur Rimbaud, "Les Effarés," 1870

LES EFFARÉS[1]

Noirs dans la neige et dans la brume,
Au grand soupirail qui s'allume,
    Leurs culs en rond,

A genoux, cinq petits[2], — misère ! —
Regardent le Boulanger faire
    Le lourd pain blond.

Ils voient le fort bras blanc qui tourne
La pâte grise et qui l'enfourne
    Dans un trou clair.

Ils écoutent le bon pain cuire.
Le Boulanger au gras sourire
    Grogne un vieil air[a].

Ils sont blottis, pas un ne bouge,
Au souffle du soupirail rouge
    Chaud comme un sein[3].

Quand pour quelque médianoche[4],
Façonné comme une brioche[b]
    On sort le pain,

Texte de la copie de Verlaine (fac-similés Messein).
Variantes du recueil Demeny :
    Chante un vieil air.
Et quand pendant que minuit sonne,
    Façonné, pétillant et jaune,
un 3e manuscrit, que Darzens a eu entre les mains, portait : Et quand
que médianoche, corrigé par la suite quand Rimbaud s'est avi

Francis Ponge, *Pièces*, "Plat de poisons frits," 1961

PLAT DE POISSONS FRITS

Goût, vue, ouïe, odorat... c'est instantané :
    Lorsque le poisson de mer cuit à l'huile s'entr'ouvre,
un jour de soleil sur la nappe, et que les grandes épées
qu'il comporte sont prêtes à joncher le sol, que la peau
se détache comme la pellicule impressionnable parfois
de la plaque exagérément révélée (mais tout ici est
beaucoup plus savoureux), ou (comment pourrions-
nous dire encore ?)... Non, c'est trop bon ! Ça fait comme
une boulette élastique, un caramel de peau de poisson
bien grillée au fond de la poêle...

Goût, vue, ouïes, odaurades : cet instant safrané...
    C'est alors, au moment qu'on s'apprête à déguster
les filets encore vierges, oui ! Sète alors que la haute
fenêtre s'ouvre, que la voilure claque et que le pont du
petit navire penche vertigineusement sur les flots,
    Tandis qu'un petit phare de vin doré — qui se tient
bien vertical sur la nappe — luit à notre portée.

Food That Rhymes

◆——◆

A small anthology of poems combining
the tastiest words with the tastiest dishes.
Stéphane Solier

Apollinaire, *Quelconqueries*, "Le Repas," 1915

LE REPAS

Il n'y a que la mère et les deux fils
    Tout est ensoleillé
    La table est ronde
Derrière la chaise où s'assied la mère
    Il y a la fenêtre
    Briller sous le soleil
Les caps aux feuillages sombres des pins et des
    oliviers
Et plus près les villas aux toits rouges
Aux toits rouges où fument les cheminées
    Car c'est l'heure du repas
    Tout est ensoleillé
    Et sur la nappe glacée
    La bonne affairée
    Dépose un plat fumant
    Le repas n'est pas une action vile
Et tous les hommes devraient avoir du pain
La mère et les deux fils mangent et parlent
Et des chants de gaîté accompagnent le repas
Les bruits joyeux des fourchettes et des assiettes
Et le son clair du cristal des verres
Par la fenêtre ouverte viennent les chants des oiseaux
    Dans les citronniers
    Et de la cuisine arrive
La chanson vive du beurre sur le feu
Un rayon traverse un verre presque plein de vin mélangé
    d'eau
Oh ! le beau rubis que font du vin rouge et du
    soleil

    Quand la faim est calmée
    Les fruits gais et parfumés
    Terminent le repas

Ronsard, *Odes*, "III, 24" (À Gaspar d'Auvergne), 1550–1552

...peau vermeille
D'un beau sang ... voir,

Le marchant hardiment vire
    Par la mer, de sa navire
[51] La proue et la poupe encor :
    Je ne suis bruslé d'envie
    Aux chers despens de ma vie
[54] De gaigner des lingots d'or.

Tous ces biens je ne quiers point,
    Et mon courage n'est poinct[2]
[57] De telle gloire excessive.
    Manger ô[3] mon compaignon,
    Ou la figue d'Avignon,
[60] Ou la Provençale olive.

L'artichot, et la salade,
    L'asperge, et la pastenade,
[63] Et les pepons Tourangeaux
Me sont herbes plus friandes
    Que les royales viandes
[66] Qui se servent à monceaux.

Puis qu'il faut si tost mourir,
    Que me vaudroit d'acquerir
Un bien qui ne dure guieres,
Qu'un heritier qui viendroit
Apres mon trepas, vendroit

Jacques Prévert, *Paroles*, "La grasse matinée," 1946

LA GRASSE MATINÉE

Il est terrible
le petit bruit de l'œuf dur cassé sur un comptoir d'étain
il est terrible ce bruit
quand il remue dans la mémoire de l'homme qui a faim
elle est terrible aussi la tête de l'homme
la tête de l'homme qui a faim
quand il se regarde à six heures du matin
dans la glace du grand magasin
une tête couleur de poussière
ce n'est pas sa tête pourtant qu'il regarde
dans la vitrine de chez Potin
il s'en fout de sa tête l'homme
il n'y pense pas
il songe
il imagine une autre tête
une tête de veau par exemple
avec une sauce de vinaigre
ou une tête de n'importe quoi qui se mange
et il remue doucement la mâchoire
doucement
et il grince des dents doucement
car le monde se paye sa tête
et il ne peut rien contre ce monde

92

Pastry Cream

Without it, there would be no éclair, no *réligieuse*, and no *mille-feuille*. Pastry cream provides the filling for small cream puffs, doughs, and various cakes. Dessert and pastry maven Mercotte examines this creamy creation!
Mercotte*

THE ORIGINS OF PASTRY CREAM

A recipe for *Cresme de pâtissier* appeared in the sixteenth century: at the time, it was a cream thickened with flour. Pastry cream was then perfected by François Massialot, who provided the recipe in 1691 in his work *Cuisinier royal et bourgeois*. Among the ingredients used are a dozen whole eggs, a "good" half pound of flour, another dozen eggs, and two and a half pints of boiled milk. Everything is placed in a saucepan and cooked with a pinch of salt and a half pound of butter.

Tips and Tricks for Pastry Cream

☞ For a **thicker pastry cream**, use a coarse-grain flour (such as oatmeal flour), or, as is common, a wheat flour, such as pastry flour (or Type 45).

☞ For people with gluten intolerances, use only potato or cornstarch.

☞ It is best to use **raw milk** or, if raw is not available, whole microfiltered milk.

☞ For a **creamier** pastry cream, you can replace half the milk with cream that is at least 35 percent fat.

☞ It is better to start by simply mixing the yolks and the sugar **without trying to lighten them**: this will facilitate the cooking of the cream.

☞ To avoid lumps, the trick is to dilute the yolk-sugar-flour mixture little by little with a good part of the milk to obtain a consistency that is liquid and therefore not pasty—a consistency similar to the thickness of the milk.

☞ **Cooking slowly** is preferred, while stirring continuously in a figure eight, to prevent the cream from sticking to the bottom of the pan.

☞ Before applying **plastic wrap** to the surface of the cream while cooling it, run a **piece of butter** over the surface of the hot cream to help prevent the formation of a skin.

☞ To cool the pastry cream rapidly, scrape it out onto a sheet pan rather than into a deep bowl; the thinner the layer, the faster it will cool.

THE NEVER-FAIL RECIPE

PREPARATION TIME: 10 MINUTES
COOKING TIME: 5 MINUTES
SERVES 4

½ vanilla bean
3 or 4 egg yolks
¼ cup (50 g) superfine sugar
1 tablespoon plus 2 teaspoons (10 g) all-purpose flour
1 tablespoon (10 g) cornstarch
1 cup (250 mL) fresh whole milk

In a mixing bowl, split the vanilla bean and scrape its seeds into the egg yolks. Add the sugar and whisk thoroughly to combine. Carefully incorporate the flour and cornstarch without overworking the mixture. In a saucepan, bring the milk and vanilla bean pod to a boil. Add three-fourths of the milk to the yolk-sugar mixture, whisking, then pour back into the saucepan. Bring to a boil, then let it cook for 1 minute to thicken while stirring. Scrape the finished cream into a container, cover the surface with plastic wrap, and let cool.

Variations
3½ ounces (100 g) pastry cream . . .

+

3 tablespoons plus 1¾ teaspoons (50 g) slightly softened butter
=
Crème mousseline

½ sheet gelatin added to the hot cream + 3 tablespoons plus 1 teaspoon (50 g) cream, whipped and folded in
=
Diplomat cream

3 tablespoons plus 1 teaspoon (50 g) heavy cream, whipped and folded in
=
Crème Madame or crème Princesse

1 sheet of gelatin, softened in cold water and squeezed to remove excess water, heated until melted, and mixed into the hot pastry cream + Italian meringue (1 large egg white [1 oz/25 g] beaten to stiff peaks with 1¼ teaspoons/5 g of sugar, then beaten with hot syrup made from 2 tablespoons plus 2½ teaspoons/35 g of sugar cooked to 239°F/115°C) folded into the hot gelatin-pastry cream mixture
=
Chiboust cream

8 ounces (225 g) almond cream (made with 3¾ oz/110 g almond flour, 3¾ oz/110 g confectioners' sugar, and 1 tablespoon/10 g cornstarch, mixed with 9½ tablespoons/130 g softened butter, 1 tablespoon/15 mL agricultural rum, and 2 eggs, incorporated one at a time)
=
Frangipane

Hot pastry cream + ¾ ounce (20 g) dark chocolate couverture
=
Chocolate cream

Queen of the macaron, dessert goddess, and judge who provided great advice on Le Meilleur Pâtissier (The Best Pastry Chef) *on channel M6, alongside Cyril Lignac. Mercotte has been enlightening her readers on her blog since 2005. Suggested reading:* Le Meilleur de Mercotte (The Best of Mercotte), *Éditions Altal.*

Meats without Taboo

From Louis XV to Alain Chapel (Michelin three-star chef), even the most discerning of gourmets have delighted in the testicles of all kinds of animals. In addition to nourishing the body, these "taboo meats" are known as a potent aphrodisiac . . .

Hadrien Gonzales

From the Sheep

WEIGHT
FROM 3½ TO 5¼ OUNCES (100 TO 150 G)

LIMOUSIN
A little history: which animal is the emblem of the Millevaches plateau in central France? The sheep! In this region, the ovine reigns. In the town of Bénévent-l'Abbaye (Creuse), the event Moutonnades de la Saint-Barthélemy occurs every August 24 to celebrate the importance of sheep to this region. Since everything from the sheep is considered delicious, the *animelles* (testicles) of sheep have always been a local favorite. But it was the Association of Connoisseurs and Tasters of *Couilla d'Mautou* ("mutton testicles" in the local vernacular) who fifteen years ago brought this dish to the status of a great classic.
In the pan: at local festivals, fans usually eat them fried, generously sprinkled with lemon and parsley.

Aphrodisiac Power Level: 2/5

LYON
A little history: at the beginning of the 1980s, Alain Chapel was one of the founders of the Brotherhood of the Joyeuses. After completing their shopping at the local markets, the group of four or five friends would meet regularly in a bistro on rue La Martinière to enjoy sheep's testicles (so-called *rognons blancs*, or literally "white kidneys"). Now with almost thirty members, the group gathers on the last Saturday of November. Members dress in red robes and wear a cord around their neck from which hangs an egg slicer.
In the pan: the brotherhood has established as their mission the goal of experiencing this delicacy in all its forms: poached, in beignets, drizzled with snail butter, in wine sauce, and so on.

Aphrodisiac Power Level: 1/5

PARIS
A little history: until the closure of the slaughterhouses in 1974, young male butchers' assistants and warehousemen from Les Halles in the northern part of the capital had the custom of savoring so-called "frivolities of La Villette" (aka testicles) as their morning snack.
In the pan: sheep's testicles are sliced into cutlets, coated with beaten egg, then bread crumbs, and sautéed and served with lemon wedges.

Aphrodisiac Power Level: 2/5

From the Rooster

WEIGHT
LIGHT AS A FEATHER

LORRAINE
A little history: it is Marie Leszczyńska, wife of Louis XV, to whom the French owe these aptly named *bouchées à la reine* ("queen's bites"). Unhappy with the sexual performance of her husband, she created, with the complicity of the pastry chefs of Versailles, pastries whose original recipe consisted of a sauce *financère* (a truffle and Madeira wine sauce), with a base of rooster comb and rooster testicles.
In the pan: no one knows how this aphrodisiac dish became a staple on Alsatian tables. Since the 2000s, it has been the subject of an annual competition at the European Fair in Strasbourg in September. But the testicles are often replaced with sweetbreads.

Aphrodisiac Power Level: 5/5

From the Bull

WEIGHT:
9 TO 10½ OUNCES (250 TO 300 G)

LANDES
A little history: during bullfights, few aficionados had the privilege of tasting the *criadillas* (testicles) of the bull killed in the arena. In the late 1980s, chef Michel Carrère had the idea to capitalize on the opportunity. On the night of the bullfight in Floirac, locals gathered in the cellar of his Michelin-starred restaurant La Chamade, in Bordeaux, to savor a dozen *roupettes* (testicles) *du jour*.
In the pan: for twenty years in Saint-Justin in the Landes, the chef has continued to serve, during the fair of Mont-de-Marsan, "things of life," cooked à la plancha (on a griddle), with grilled eggplant and stewed zucchini with garlic and parsley.

Aphrodisiac Power Level: 4/5

MY FRIEND ROGER'S "JOYEUSES"
by Alain Chapel

SERVES 3

6 "joyeuses" of sheep (sheep's testicles)
1 sprig thyme
1 bay leaf
2 lemons
Salt and freshly ground black pepper
14 tablespoons (200 g) fresh butter, melted

Remove the surrounding membrane from the "joyeuses" or, better yet, ask the butcher to do it for you. Blanch the "joyeuses" for 1 minute in simmering water, then let cool. In a saucepan filled with salted water, add the thyme, bay leaf, and slices from 1 of the lemons. Gently poach the "joyeuses" for about 15 minutes, checking their doneness from time to time. Drain, then drizzle the butter over them. When serving, squeeze the juice of the second lemon over them. They can also be sprinkled with parsley or served with capers, or any seasoning to your liking.

PARTY TALK
True gourmets never use the word "testicles." Perhaps it's simply for the love of being poetic, or maybe it is to avoid any confusion, with their own private parts, which would likely be a sensitive topic? The French have many words that are a more appropriate substitute, such as the word *animelles* from the Latin word *anima* ("soul"), which designates the genitals of all animals (for which *animelle* is also the root). When describing those of sheep, the term *rognons blancs* ("white kidneys") is preferred. Because of the term *corrida* (bullfighting), bulls' testicles are referred to in the Spanish: *criadillas* (or "truffles," if the beast is black). Wild boar hunters have the word *suites* in mind (and on their plates), while those of rams are the "honors." *For reading: Blandine Vié*, Testicules, *Éditions de L'Épure*, 2005.

skip to
The Brotherhoods of French Gastronomy, p. 126

In Search of Corsican Soup

Corsican soup can be found on the menus of all traditional inns and restaurants in Corsica as well as in mainland France, but each Corsican keeps with him the memory and flavors of a family recipe—and everyone claims the recipe of his mother or grandmother to be the best.

Frédéric Laly-Baraglioli

Jacqueline Bonci

THE SECRETS OF A "SOUP FROM THE LANDS"

For a long time, mothers had to manage with what they had on hand in the pantry to put together this hearty and tasty dish that was often made in a single vessel. Its ingredients varied according to the seasons, but also to the region in which it was prepared. Hence the current disagreements over which ingredients make up the soup!

THE PARTS THAT NEVER CHANGE

→ **A base of legumes** (an assortment of dried or fresh beans).
→ **A piece of cured Corsican pork,** an essential for adding fat and flavor.
→ **A mixture of starchy and seasonal vegetables,** coarsely chopped to provide tenderness but also some "bite."
→ **A taste of fresh herbs,** such as *nepita* (a Corsican herb), mint, or basil.

THE PARTS THAT CAN CHANGE

Adding different vegetables or other starchy foods, according to the season and one's tastes:
→ The "bean soup" version
→ The "cabbage soup" version
→ The "herb soup" version

TWO DISHES IN ONE

In the past, in some mountain villages, to create the illusion of offering other dishes besides this one for the poor, a portion of the cooked legumes were seasoned and enjoyed in a warm salad.

WHAT DOES IT HAVE TO DO WITH CORSICA? THE ORIGIN OF A NAME . . .

There is no evidence of the term "Corsican soup" before the end of the 1960s, and after this time there is reference only to a "peasant soup" or ***suppa di fasgioli*** ("bean soup"). The soup doesn't become known as a national dish, much like many other dishes in Corsican cooking, until the 1970s and 1980s. If you think about it, there is nothing specifically Corsican about the soup's basic ingredients. It is simply a way to **sublimate the local ingredients** that make this dish the magical and simplistic "***cucina povera***" that it is. Perhaps it is the presence of *panzetta* or *prisuttu*, or the addition of herbs such as mint or *nepita*, that "typify" the dish. In reality, because of the variations in its preparations, *suppa* defines Corsica . . . Corsican soup can thus represent the mountains, the plains, the villages, or the cities, and can be considered **peasant or bourgeois**! Preparing or ordering it has even become a little "snobbish" today and it is often a sought-after dish—one that is **chic, understated, and always in good taste**!

CORSICAN SOUP

by Jacqueline Bonci, Bastian grandmother and cook of enchanting foods

SOAKING TIME: FROM 1 TO 6 HOURS
PREPARATION TIME: 20 MINUTES
COOKING TIME: 30 TO 40 MINUTES
SERVES 8

1 pound (0.45 kg) dried red beans
1 slice of *panzetta* (pancetta)
1 or 2 celery stalks
2 leeks, root ends removed, leaves split and washed of any sand
½ head cabbage
1 red onion, peeled
2 carrots
3 or 4 potatoes
2 zucchini (preferably white)
½ pound (0.25 kg) flat green beans
Olive oil
1 bay leaf
A bunch basil and/or mint
3 to 4 cloves garlic
Spaghetti (3½ to 7 oz/100 to 200 g, depending on desired consistency)
Salt and freshly ground black pepper

Soak the dried beans in cold water for at least 1 hour if they are less than 3 months old, for at least 3 hours if they are between 3 and 6 months old, and for at least 6 hours if they are more than 6 months old (changing the water every 6 hours to avoid fermentation). Parboil the soaked beans for 5 to 10 minutes (discard the cooking liquid) and, in a separate saucepan, boil the slice of *panzetta* and discard the cooking liquid (this will rid it of the foam that it creates when cooked). Meanwhile, thinly slice the celery, leeks (keep a good portion of the green), and cabbage. Coarsely chop the onion, carrots, potatoes, and zucchini, then cut the flat beans in half. Sauté the onion and the boiled slice of *panzetta* in a pressure cooker or on the stovetop with olive oil and salt. Add all the

vegetables and the bay leaf to the pressure cooker. Cover the contents with water and bring to a boil. Slice open several of the parboiled beans (doing so will contribute a thicker consistency to the soup), then add all the beans to the pressure cooker. Remove and discard the bay leaf, cover the pot, and let cook for 20 minutes, starting from when the valve begins to whistle. Remove the lid from the pressure cooker and let the soup cook, uncovered, over low to medium heat, frequently checking the doneness of the vegetables, especially the potatoes and beans, which should be tender. If the consistency of the soup is too watery, mash a few pieces of potato to help thicken it. Coarsely chop the basil and mint, if using, and chop the garlic. Break the spaghetti in half or in thirds. Add the basil,

garlic, and spaghetti near the end of the cooking time. Turn off the heat 5 minutes after adding the spaghetti (it will continue to cook). Pour a good drizzle of olive oil over the surface of the soup. When the soup has cooled, season it with salt and pepper.

Royal Couscous

Preparing couscous in this way is considered heresy according to friends in the Maghreb countries! Yet this is how couscous is enjoyed in France. It even happens to be one of the country's favorite dishes.

Marielle Gaudry

FRENCH-STYLE COUSCOUS

There is no "royal" couscous in North Africa! This dish is a purely Parisian invention, popularized by restaurant Chez Bébert in the Montparnasse district of the city. It is called "royal" because it includes several meats cooked separately and served with the couscous—chicken, lamb, meatballs, and merguez sausage—an approach that is considered the height of vulgarity in the Maghreb because the traditional preparation of couscous does not allow grilled meats to be cooked separately from the couscous. Instead, meat and vegetables are cooked in the broth that is used to cook the couscous.

. . . AND WHAT IF COUSCOUS ORIGINATES IN AUVERGNE?

According to professor and journalist Raymond Dumay, there is no doubt that couscous finds its origins in Auvergne! *"The main dish of Auvergne, one whose radiance will one day extend across the entire planet, is the couchi-coucha. Wheat from Limagne, highly prized by the Romans, supplies the semolina. Included are peas, zucchini, and turnips, grown in the Brive Basin, and fresh vegetables. Everything is accompanied by mutton, chicken, and other delicious meats, including ones more delicate, such as a side of rognons blancs* [sheep's testicles]. *All accompanied by its tangy sauce called 'arrizat.'"*

De Silex au barbecue, guide géogastronomique de la France (*Julliard, 1971*)

THE RECIPE

*by Andrée Zana-Murat**

The ideal recipe for beginners, which can be enhanced with even more meats, as it is when ordered in restaurants.

PREPARATION TIME: 30 MINUTES
COOKING TIME: 1 HOUR 55 MINUTES + 1 HOUR
30 MINUTES (THE COUSCOUS)
SERVES 6

2¼ pounds (1 kg) of lamb (shoulder and neck)
Salt and freshly ground black pepper
5 tablespoons (75 mL) olive oil
12 merguez sausages
½ green bell pepper
½ red bell pepper
3 tomatoes
3 zucchini
3 medium stalks celery
1⅛ pounds (500 g) small turnips
1⅛ pounds (500 g) carrots
4 large onions
1 tablespoon paprika
1 tablespoon (15 mL) tomato paste
3 cloves garlic, peeled and crushed
1 small can (8 oz/227 g) chickpeas
2 bouillon cubes (chicken or vegetable)
1⅛ pounds (500 g) couscous
Drizzle of peanut oil
4 tablespoons (57 g) butter

The meat

Rinse the lamb meat, season it with salt and black pepper, and set it aside in a bowl. In a very large pot, sauté the meat in the olive oil. Start sautéing it over high heat for several minutes, then continue cooking it over medium heat. Remove the meat when it is browned on all sides and set it aside in a shallow dish. Set the pot aside for cooking the vegetables. Cook the merguez sausages in a dry skillet, then set them aside; they can be warmed just before serving.

The vegetables

Wash all the vegetables and peel the onions. Thinly slice the onions, bell peppers, and celery. Dunk the tomatoes in boiling water for 15 seconds, then peel, seed, and crush them. Using a vegetable peeler, remove alternating strips of the zucchini peel, then cut the zucchini lengthwise in half, then slice it crosswise into thick pieces. Perform this same step with the turnips and carrots, but peel them completely. In the oil that was used for searing the meat, fry the chopped onions. When they have browned, remove the pot from the heat, then add the paprika and tomato paste. Return the pot to the heat and add the garlic, bell peppers, celery, carrots, and turnips. Cook for 5 minutes, stirring, then add the tomatoes.

The meat-vegetable-bouillon mixture

Add the meat to the pot with the vegetables, then add the chickpeas. Dissolve the bouillon cubes in just enough hot water to cover the vegetables, then pour the bouillon into the pot. Bring to a boil, then let cook for 1 hour over low heat. After the 1 hour cooking time, add the zucchini to the pot, and let cook for 20 minutes over low heat, covered. Adjust the seasoning as needed throughout the cooking time. Meanwhile, prepare the couscous.

The couscous

Pour the couscous into a large bowl. Cover it with cold water. Stir it by hand (the water will turn cloudy). Wait a few seconds for the grains to fall to the bottom of the bowl, then drain and discard the soaking liquid. Repeat this step, then drain the couscous through a fine-mesh sieve (it does not have to be completely drained). Pour the couscous back into the bowl. Drizzle the couscous with peanut oil, season with salt, then stir it immediately with a fork to fluff it and break up any lumps. Every 5 to 10 minutes, fluff it again. After 30 minutes, the couscous will have swollen and appear almost "cooked." To fluff it even more effectively, do so using your hands. Rub the grains between the hands to remove any lumps. Taste and add salt, if needed.

Fill the bottom of a couscoussier (couscous pot) one-third full of hot water and bring it to a boil. Pour the couscous into the top of the couscoussier, cover, and let the couscous steam for 20 minutes. Transfer the cooked couscous to a large shallow dish, add the butter in small pieces, and mix with a fork. Taste and adjust the salt seasoning, as needed. Serve the meat in a shallow dish surrounded by vegetables. Serve the couscous and broth (obtained from the meat-vegetable mixture) separately.

Andrée Zana-Murat, an unparalleled cook, was consulted not only for her tips on making couscous but also for her mastery and generosity, as part of her Mediterranean heritage.

The roots of cooking . . .

leek

Leek root tempura: choose leeks with beautiful "beards" (roots). Cut off the root end to ⅛ inch (3 mm), quarter it, then wash and dry it well. Dredge it in batter (made from 1 egg yolk and ¾ cup plus 1 tablespoon/200 mL of ice water with 1 cup plus 3 tablespoons/120 g of flour, stirred just a little). Deep-fry it in oil, then drain it on paper towels and season with salt. Use the fried roots to garnish a dish or serve them as an appetizer.

Endive root with duck skin cracklins (recipe simplified by Laurent Petit*): cook 3 endive roots in chicken broth for 1 hour (reserve the broth). Halve them lengthwise, then halve 3 raw endives lengthwise. Brown all of them in butter. Arrange the endives on a serving platter and add lemon zest, then place duck skin cracklins (fried pieces of duck skin), 1 sliced shallot browned in olive oil, and some crushed walnuts on the platter. Drizzle with the reduced chicken broth, and garnish with 1 sliced raw endive.

Chef of Clos des Sens, Annecy-le-Vieux (Haute-Savoie)

endive

For the love of greens . . .

radish

Radish-leaf pesto: in a food processor, blend together radish greens, pumpkin seeds, garlic, Parmesan, and salt, then drizzle in olive oil while blending (as when making mayonnaise). This pesto offers a slightly spicy option when dolloped on pasta or spread on toast.

Carrot-greens salad: remove the stems from carrot greens and add the chopped leaves to a mâche lettuce salad with cherry tomatoes and sliced mushrooms.

carrot

Beet greens stew: cook 12 chopped beet stems, 2 peeled and chopped shallots, and some pine nuts in a little olive oil until tender. Add 7 oz/200 g ground beef, 3 tomatoes, strips of beet leaves, black pepper, and ground cumin. Let cook, partially covered, until the vegetables are softened and the beef is cooked through. Add a scant ½ cup/100 mL of water and scant ½ cup/100 g of rice, cover, and cook, until the rice is cooked through. Crush 2 garlic cloves and juice half a lemon and add them off the heat. Beet greens are high in sodium, so taste the dish before adding salt!

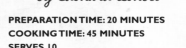

beet

School of Greens

For healthy and vitamin-rich cooking, cooks in France use all parts of fruits and vegetables: the greens (both leaves and stems), whether soft or leathery, and the roots. The country's ancestors did this for the sake of economy, but cooks today do so out of both interest and eco-consciousness.

Marie-Amal Bizalion

— ASPARAGUS PEEL —
CRÈME BRÛLÉE
by Édouard Loubet*

PREPARATION TIME: 20 MINUTES
COOKING TIME: 45 MINUTES
SERVES 10

10 asparagus stalks
2⅛ cups (½ L) whole milk
2⅛ cups (½ L) heavy cream
Salt
1 pinch agave syrup
1 pinch nutmeg
10 egg yolks
Parmesan cheese shavings
10 sliced almonds, skins on

Peel the asparagus stalks and set aside the peels. Heat the milk and cream together, season with salt, then add the agave syrup and nutmeg. When the mixture reaches a boil, turn off the heat, add the peels, then let cool off the heat. Strain and reserve the liquid. Whisk the egg yolks into the liquid, then pour the mixture into ten individual ramekins. Preheat the oven to 200°F/100°C, and bake just until set. Before serving, sprinkle with the Parmesan shavings and sliced almonds.

Two-star chef at La Bastide de Capelongue, Bonnieux (Vaucluse)

Like peas in a pod . . .

Pea pod gazpacho: take about one hundred pea pods and remove the stem end and string, then boil the pods in salted water for 45 minutes, strain.
Blend the peas to a smooth mixture with a little of the cooking water. Add 3 small containers of sheep's-milk yogurt, ½ baguette soaked and squeezed of excess water, and olive oil, and blend again until smooth. Serve chilled with chopped mint, cilantro, and a few raw peas on top.

Puréed bean pods: start with 9 oz/250 g bean pods. Clip off the ends and pull off the strings. Chop the pods, then cook them in butter, covered, for 10 minutes, or until softened. Add 2 diced potatoes and some curry, then add water to cover the contents. Cover and cook for 30 minutes. Mash the pods with a fork, season with salt and pepper, then stir in some butter and/or cream.

beans

peas

Just for the peel of it . . .

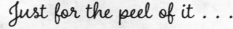

pineapple

Pineapple-peel broth: Marie Cochard* boils the peel of 1 pineapple with ¼ cup/50 g demerara sugar, 3 cups/750 mL water, ground cinnamon, cardamom, and 1 clove for 20 minutes, then lets it cool, strains the juice through a thin cloth, and drizzles it over slices of pineapple that have been browned in a skillet.

Author of Les épluchures, tout ce que vous pouvez en faire, Eyrolles, 2016

Eggplant garnish: Sonia Ezgulian* takes thin strips of eggplant peel and sautés them over high heat in a drizzle of olive oil. As soon as they are crisp, she transfers them to a paper towel to drain, then seasons them with salt and pepper. She also fries julienned strips of eggplant peel in olive oil and sprinkles them on a compote of eggplants in vinegar.

Author of Anti-gaspi, Flammarion, 2017

Carrot-peel chutney: purée 3 handfuls of carrot peels with 3 sliced shallots that have been browned in oil with some diced dried fruits (fig, apricot, dates, etc.) and lots of chile pepper, ginger, and coriander. Add a dash of vinegar and a can of beer. Simmer, stirring, until the liquid evaporates. Store in a jar.

eggplant

cucumber

carrot (peels)

Tarte au Citron (Citrus Tart)

A tangy and creamy filling, a crunchy shortbread crust, and, on top, either meringue or nothing at all, each to his own taste. Citrus tart is an absolute classic in French pastry.

Delphine Le Feuvre

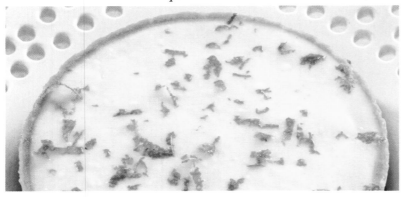

TARTE AU CITRON
by Jacques Genin

PREPARATION TIME: I HOUR
COOKING TIME: 20 MINUTES
REFRIGERATION TIME: 3 HOURS (FOR THE FILLING) + I HOUR (FOR THE CRUST)
SERVES 6

For the citrus cream filling
Zest of 3 lemons
3 large eggs
¾ cup plus I tablespoon plus I¾ teaspoons (170 g) superfine sugar
6⅓ ounces (180 g) lime juice (from 6 to 10 limes)
14 tablespoons (200 g) unsalted butter

For the dough (enough for two tarts)
I vanilla bean
13 tablespoons (175 g) unsalted butter, room temperature
I¼ cups (125 g) confectioners' sugar
2⅛ ounces (60 g) almond flour
2 large eggs plus I large egg yolk, room temperature
I pinch salt
3 cups plus 2 tablespoons (310 g) all-purpose flour

Make the citrus cream filling
In a heavy-bottom saucepan, whisk the lemon zest with the eggs and superfine sugar. Whisk in the lime juice. Heat the pan over very low heat, stirring continuously with a silicone spatula until the cream is very thick. At the first sign of bubbles, remove the cream from the heat, then immediately strain it through a fine-mesh sieve into a cold bowl. Let stand for 5 minutes, then stir in all the butter. Blend using an immersion blender. Refrigerate for at least 3 hours.

Make the dough
Split the vanilla bean lengthwise in half and scrape out the seeds with a knife; set the seeds aside. Cut the butter into small pieces. Place the confectioners' sugar and almond flour in a bowl. Work the butter into the sugar-flour mixture by crumbling it with your fingertips until you have a sandy texture. Add the eggs and vanilla bean seeds and combine using your hands. Add the salt to the flour, then incorporate the flour into the mixture to form a dough. Fold the edges of the dough in toward the center, then fold it over to form a ball. Lightly dust a work surface with flour. Place the dough on the work surface and cut it in half. Place one half on a sheet of parchment, wrap the other half in plastic wrap and refrigerate or freeze for another use. Flatten it with a rolling pin, then roll it out into a circle about 10 inches (25 cm) in diameter. Cover it with plastic wrap and refrigerate for 1½ hours. When the dough is chilled, lightly flour a work surface and roll the dough out to a thickness of about ⅛ inch (3 mm) and a diameter of 10 inches (25 cm). Place a flan ring in the center of the dough and cut out a circle, leaving a margin of ¾ inch (2 cm) beyond the edge of the ring. Place the dough circle in the freezer for 2 to 3 minutes, then remove it, and place it in the flan ring on a sheet pan, ensuring that the dough runs all the way up the sides of the ring. Fold any excess dough down and onto the sides using your fingers; run a rolling pin over the top of the flan ring to remove any excess dough. Preheat the oven to 350°F (170°C) and bake for about 20 minutes, or until golden. Once cooled, fill the crust with the citrus cream filling. Serve well chilled.

skip to
A *Tour de France* of Citrus, p. 292

Stanislas Leszczynski, King of the Baba au Rhum

His name first brings to mind the splendid square in Nancy, but "Stanislas the Benefactor" was above all a great gourmet.

Elvira Masson

Descended from great nobility, **Stanislas I ruled Poland from 1704 to 1709**. After certain political setbacks, he went into **exile at the Château de Lunéville**. In that small Versailles of the Lorraine region, he delved into philosophy alongside Montesquieu and Voltaire, and also indulged in, how shall we say, much more earthly pleasures, with good food in mind. We can thank him and his **brilliant pâtissier, Nicolas Stohrer**, for the *baba au rhum*. When his daughter Marie Leszczyńska married Louis XV, the King of the Baba became a royal father-in-law and the **history of sweets would be revolutionized**. Stohrer accompanied the royal couple to Paris, where he founded, on **rue Montorgueil, the first pâtisserie**, which still bears his name. Indirectly, we can thank Stanislas Leszczynski for countless other sweet delights, and also for a few savory ones. The accuracy of the attribution, however, is subject to debate.

True or False?

Stanislas is the inventor of:

Kugelhopf: False
The first kugelhopf molds found in Alsace date from the eighteenth century. Although King Stanislas didn't invent it, he was nevertheless a big fan.

The Baba au Rhum: True
Or supposedly true! It was the pâtissier Nicolas Stohrer who sprinkled dessert wine on a kugelhopf that his employer Stanislas deemed too dry and developed the recipe for the Baba. It was only later that the wine was replaced with rum.

Nancy Macarons: To be determined!
We know that these almond cookies were accepted currency at King Stanislas' table. Gilliers, his private chef, recounted episodes in his 1751 book, *Le Cannaméliste français*. As did Buc'hoz, his doctor, in *L'Art de preparer les aliments*, in 1787.

The Commercy Madeleine: Perhaps
During a banquet organized by the Duke of Lorraine, a servant named Madeleine Paulmier, a native of Commercy, who had come to help in the kitchen, was pleased to present him with small moist cakes, which he then named for her. According to other sources, the Madeleine originally dates back to the pilgrimage of Saint James, when a young woman named Madeleine is said to have given the pilgrims an egg cake shaped like a scallop.

The *Bergamote*: False
These little hard candy squares flavored with bergamot were invented in Nancy in the mid-nineteenth century.

skip to
The Road to Rum, p. 302;
A Sweet Tour of the Candies of France, p. 164

Strange Game

In times of scarcity, all game, both furry and feathered, provided a vital source of protein.
With game hunting now heavily regulated, some animals named below have gone out of style;
others take some getting used to.

Marie-Amal Bizalion

PROHIBITED

Hedgehog: a Gypsy treat

The food-loving Gypsy culture pays no heed to the 2007 European ban on hunting this insectivore. A favorite recipe? *Niglo ap i bus* (hedgehog kebab): stretch it out or fill with air using a tube to shave off its spines and hairs with a sharp knife. Finish the job using a flame or boiling water, then gut. Split in two, flatten, skewer, and grill over coals. Use the fat, which tastes a bit like olive oil, to brown potatoes.

Eurasian beaver: meat for Lent

Considering the semiaquatic mammal to be a fish, the Church said it could be consumed during Lent. What's more, the monks of Villeneuve-lès-Avignon made "pure beaver" sausages until the eighteenth century. Sought out for its fur and for its castor anal sac secretion, used for perfumes, only a few could still be found in Camargue in 1909. Since then the largest of European rodents has enjoyed complete legal protection.

Today there are fifteen thousand. To appreciate its liverlike taste and the sweetbread texture of its tail, head to Tierra del Fuego, where the North American beaver, introduced in 1946, proliferates. So long as the CONICET—The National Scientific and Technical Research Council in Argentina—allows it to be consumed.

The ortolan under cover

Related to the sparrow, this bird was cherished by the Romans and made Alexandre Dumas* swoon. It also drove François Mitterrand mad; he ate one eight days before he died. A law from 1999 prohibits its hunting and so it has escaped its previous cruel fate: three weeks in the dark, stuffed twelve times a day, and ultimately doused in Armagnac, in which it drowned. To savor its every bit, from brain to tripe, remember one golden rule: cover your head with a napkin. Then you'll be able to enjoy the aromas of the meat while hiding the somewhat unpalatable sight from others.

He offered several recipes in his Grand Dictionnaire de cuisine, *1873*

OUT OF STYLE

In our society that likes its food big and plentiful, there are only a few old-timers who still seek out the little bird.

Edible dormouse: smoked in the Corsican style

The *Glis glis*, a rodent in the Gliridae family, weighs no more then 9 ounces (250 g). With round ringed eyes, a long bushy tail, and soft fur, the cuddly animal isn't an endangered species but it's no longer used in recipes. And yet, from antiquity to the Renaissance, throughout the Mediterranean Basin, it was fattened with grains in earthenware jars. Corsicans continue to hunt the animal in the fall when it is most fluffy. Nests are fumigated and the dormouse is clobbered when it comes out of its hole. Then? Just like in Calabria, it's gutted and grilled with its skin. The fat is soaked up with slices of bread.

EXTREMELY RARE

French regulations now prohibit the sale of snipes, thrushes, and sarcelles. Let's turn now to the woodcock, the hunting of which requires endurance and a skillfully trained dog.

The unattainable "queen of the woods"

Grimod de La Reynière, a pioneering food critic, wrote, "This precious bird is so revered that it's paid the same homage as the Grand Lama: one need not say more than that its excrement is not only preciously collected for roasts moistened with lemon juice, but also eaten with respect by the most fervent enthusiasts."* In 2014, four chefs, including Alain Ducasse, asked permission to serve the migrating wading bird at their restaurants one day a year. Request denied. If you want to try it, you'll have to tag along with snipe hunters. The elitist caste has upheld the law enough that the bird hasn't been decimated. Yves Camdeborde** puts it in the oven without gutting it, soaks it in Armagnac, and serves it with fried porcinis. *Basta!*

* Almanach des gourmands par un vieil amateur, *1804, Éditions Maradan, pp. 37–38*
**Chef at the Comptoir du Relais, Paris 7th*

RECOMMENDED

Certain exotic species, for example the Canada goose, have become persona non grata in France. These two worrisome castrates are examples.

About the coypu

This large herbivorous rodent with orange incisors and a rat tail was imported from South America in the nineteenth century for its fur and was quickly released in nature. It immediately reproduced, destroyed riverbanks and bird nests, and transmitted leptospirosis; in short, everything to qualify it as a pest.* As a result, killing the animal by gun, trap, and burrowing is permitted year-round. So what can you do with the *Myocastor coypu*, which can grow to 22 pounds (10 kg)? Cook up its delicate, gamey meat in a terrine—with pork, eggs, spices and eau-de-vie—or in a stew marinated in Calvados.

Article R. 427-6 in the French environmental code, order of June 28, 2016

Squirrel: be aware of color

Cherished in rural areas until the middle of the twentieth century, the Eurasian red squirrel has been strictly protected since 1976. However, the related eastern gray squirrel, imported in the nineteenth century, hoards food and carries fatal viruses. The Yankee is one of the species the European Union would like to eradicate.* But you won't find them yet at the market, like in the United Kingdom . . . So you'll have to delve into the magic books of our ancestors to learn how to eat their meat, "which tastes like hare, but fattier," according to Fergus Henderson, the chef at St. John in London. Or carefully follow his recipe for watercress stew.** Allow for one animal per person, at least

Implementing regulation 2016/1141 of the EU dated 07/14/2016
**In Courier International, 01/10/2003*

skip to ....
Wild Boar, a
Bristly Beast, p. 57

Homemade mayo!
It's so much better than the commercially produced stuff.
Here the most famous sauce in French cuisine is examined.

FRANÇOIS-RÉGIS GAUDRY

mayonnaise

The classic recipe using a hand whisk

This is the recipe of our grandmothers. Some even set aside the whisk and are satisfied using a fork. This approach works very well, but it takes a little more time.

Preparation Time: 4 to 5 minutes
Makes 1 bowl

1 egg yolk
2 teaspoons (10 mL) strong mustard
3 large pinches salt
Freshly ground black pepper (about 6 turns of a pepper mill)
¾ cup plus 1 tablespoon (200 mL) sunflower oil
1 tablespoon (15 mL) wine vinegar

Place the egg yolk in a large bowl and set the bowl on a dish towel to prevent slipping. Add the mustard, salt, and pepper. Whisk thoroughly to combine, then let sit for 1 minute. Add the oil in a thin stream, very gradually and without stopping, while whisking continuously until you have a very thick mixture. Whisk in the vinegar. Store at room temperature if eaten the same day; it can rest refrigerated for up to 3 hours, if necessary, before losing its quality.

The express recipe using an immersion blender

Makes 1 bowl

Place all of the same ingredients as per the whisked mayonnaise (left) in a high-sided container, except use a whole egg (both the yellow and the white). Using an immersion blender in an up and down motion, blend until the mixture forms a thick, smooth mayonnaise. The mayonnaise should be very light in color (because of the egg white). The look of the mayonnaise will be deceiving: it will be light in color but superbly dense.

With or without mustard?

Purists are unequivocal:
Originally, mayonnaise was made with oil, egg yolk, vinegar, and salt. If you added mustard, it became what was called a rémoulade sauce.

In his *Le Guide culinaire* (1902), Auguste Escoffier includes a recipe for a mayonnaise without mustard.

Le Répertoire de la cuisine (1914) by Gringoire and Saulnier provides a recipe that uses mustard.

Sauces, réflexions d'un cuisinier (2014) by Yannick Alleno defines contemporary mayonnaise as containing mustard, and rémoulade as a mayonnaise to which "capers, cornichons, parsley, chervil, tarragon, and anchovy paste" are added.

The 5 rules of mayo

1
All the ingredients must be at room temperature. The lower the temperature of the ingredients, the lower the capacity of the oil and water to mix because the oil tends to solidify.

2
There is no need to let the egg yolk rest in the mustard. Contrary to popular belief, this does not facilitate the emulsion.

3
You can rectify a broken mayonnaise with a few grains of salt and a few drops of lemon juice. These ingredients increase the emulsive capacity of mayonnaise.

4
Do not add the oil too quickly. This risks halting the emulsion in its tracks!

5
Mayonnaise does not like the refrigerator. The oil solidifies and the mayonnaise "separates."

skip to ....
Light Mayonnaise, p. 108

Where Does Mayonnaise Come From?

A collection of popular theories.

From Mahón, the capital of Menorca in the Balearic Islands, conquered by Marshal Richelieu in 1756. He would have tasted a "mahonnaise" made with the only two ingredients available: egg and oil.
From magnonaise, from the verbs *magner* ("hurry") or *manier* ("combine"), according to Antonin Carême.
From moyeunaise or **moyennaise**, based on *moyeu* or *moyen*, referring to an egg yolk in old French, according to Prosper Montagné.
From magnonnaise, a derivative of *magnon* (Lot-et-Garonne), and from a Magnon (now the village of Fauillet) cook who popularized it first in the south of France.
From the region of Mayenne. The duke of Mayenne overindulged on a delicious sauce on the eve of the battle of Arques. The next day he fell off the bridge and lost the battle.
From the city of Bayonne, which had an emulsified sauce called *bayonnaise*.

Sauces derived from mayonnaise

Mayonnaise + Addition	= Derivative Sauce
Cooked tomatoes, brunoise of red peppers	Andalouse
Ketchup, cognac, Tabasco	Cocktail
Chopped shallots cooked in white wine, chopped scallions	Musketeer
Chopped capers, cornichons, onions, parsley, chervil, tarragon	Tartar
Baked potato, peeled, crushed in a mortar with garlic, egg yolk, lemon juice, olive oil	Aïoli
+ 1 minced garlic clove, olive oil (replacing sunflower oil)	Mayoli
+ 1 pinch curry	Mayo curry
Lemon juice, cream (whipped before serving)	Vierge or Mousseline
Chlorophyll extract (obtained by gently heating the juice from chopped and pressed chervil, parsley, watercress, spinach, and tarragon to about 158°F/70°C) and finely chopped green herbs	Green
Lemon juice instead of vinegar, very stiffly whipped cream added just before use	Chantilly
Hard-boiled egg yolks, mustard, vinegar, chopped cornichons and capers, parsley, chervil, chopped tarragon, and a short julienne of hard-boiled egg whites	Gribiche
Hard-boiled egg yolk, 1 pinch chile powder, blend of chopped scallions, parsley, tarragon, chervil, capers, and cornichons, white vinegar	Ravigote
Mustard and chopped capers, cornichons, onions, parsley, chervil, and tarragon, with a little anchovy paste	Rémoulade
½ tartar sauce + ½ green sauce, combined	Vincent
Purée of caviar and lobster seasoned with mustard and a few drops of Escoffier sauce (mayonnaise with horseradish, parsley, and chervil)	Russe
Purée made in a mortar of hard-boiled egg yolk, mustard, chopped capers, cornichons, onions, parsley, chervil, and tarragon plus anchovies	Cambridge

Balzac, the Intermittent Gourmand

Named after the patron saint of bakers (Saint-Honoré), he was born in the land of Rabelais: a gourmand by nature! Portrait of a bulimic ascetic armed with a full-flavored pen.

Stéphane Solier

PORTRAIT OF A GOURMAND

His childhood memories?
Not very happy: a strict father who ate a piece of fruit for dinner, boarding school with bland meals, and the bitter discovery of Touraine delights in his classmates' care packages!

His favorite snack?
Smoked beef tongue sneaked into his schoolbag.

His diet during creative firestorms?
Fruit and a soft-boiled egg in the morning; sardines with butter, a wing of a bird or a slice of leg of lamb at night; and of course coffee!

His celebration menu after turning in his writing?
Some hundred oysters, four bottles of white wine, twelve *pré-salé* (salt-marsh) lamb chops, a duckling with turnips, a pair of roasted partridges, Normandy sole, desserts, fruit . . . all paid for by the publishing house!

His soft spot?
Macaroni pâté: he swallowed four "in three or four gargantuan bites"!

His most extravagant meal?
In 1836, delivered by Le Grande Véfour to his cell at the Hôtel des Haricots (sic): pâtés, truffled fowl, glazed game, jellies, wines, and liqueurs!

His favorite wines?
Because Balzac didn't only love coffee: "Wine nourished my body whereas coffee maintained my mind!" White wine from Vouvray, Montlouis, Saumur, Champagne (mentioned sixty-eight times in *La Comédie Humaine (The Human Comedy)*, and mulled wine from Spain and Portugal.

His idea of happiness?
"For me, La Touraine is like pâté of foie gras up to my ears, and its delicious wine, instead of intoxicating, stupefies you and makes you happy."

His small (?!) and sweet soft spot?
"His lips quivered, his eyes lit up with happiness, his hands shook with joy upon seeing a pyramid of pears or pretty peaches . . . He was superb in vegetable pantagruelism . . ."

skip to ....
The Omelet, p. 90; Coffee: A French Obsession, p. 300

A BALZACIAN GUIDE TO GOURMAND PARIS

Boho, chic, and working-class neighborhoods: Balzac's gourmand Paris—then, as now—evolves with trends and sociology. La Comédie humaine (The Human Comedy) presents a map of gastronomical customs in the capital between 1800 and 1850.

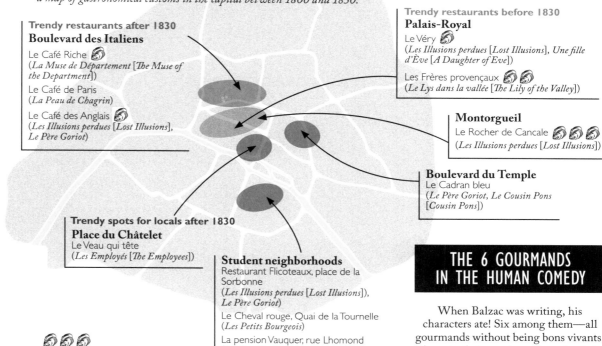

Trendy restaurants after 1830
Boulevard des Italiens
Le Café Riche
(*La Muse de Département* [*The Muse of the Department*])
Le Café de Paris
(*La Peau de Chagrin*)
Le Café des Anglais
(*Les Illusions perdues* [*Lost Illusions*], *Le Père Goriot*)

Trendy restaurants before 1830
Palais-Royal
Le Véry
(*Les Illusions perdues* [*Lost Illusions*], *Une fille d'Ève* [*A Daughter of Eve*])
Les Frères provençaux
(*Le Lys dans la vallée* [*The Lily of the Valley*])

Montorgueil
Le Rocher de Cancale
(*Les Illusions perdues* [*Lost Illusions*])

Boulevard du Temple
Le Cadran bleu
(*Le Père Goriot, Le Cousin Pons* [*Cousin Pons*])

Trendy spots for locals after 1830
Place du Châtelet
Le Veau qui tête
(*Les Employés* [*The Employees*])

Student neighborhoods
Restaurant Flicoteaux, place de la Sorbonne
(*Les Illusions perdues* [*Lost Illusions*]), *Le Père Goriot*)
Le Cheval rouge, Quai de la Tournelle
(*Les Petits Bourgeois*)
La pension Vauquer, rue Lhomond
(*Le Père Goriot*)

Balzacian Distinctions

— Balzac the gourmand in words —

"Pons missed certain creams, true poems! Certain white sauces, masterpieces! Certain truffled fowl, darlings! And, above all, the famous Rhine carps . . . that came with a sauce that was clear in the gravy boat but thick on the tongue, a sauce that deserved to win the Montyon Prize!"
Le Cousin Pons (Cousin Pons), 1847

"He walked into the Véry and, to become acquainted with the pleasures of Paris, ordered a dinner that consoled his despair. A bottle of wine from Bordeaux, oysters from Ostend, fish, a partridge, a macaroni dish and fruit were the ne plus ultra of his desires. He savored this small debauchery and thought about how he might reveal his wit tonight to the Marquise d'Espard . . . He was drawn out of his reverie by the total of the bill . . ."
Les Illusions perdues (Lost Illusions), 1843

"In the provinces, the lack of occupation and the monotony of life draw the mind to the activity of cooking. One does not dine as luxuriously in the provinces as one does in Paris, but one dines better: dishes are considered, studied there. In the depths of the countryside, there are Carêmes in petticoats, unknown geniuses, who can turn a simple dish of haricots verts into something worthy of a nod from Rossini, his way of acknowledging a perfect success."
La Rabouilleuse (The Black Sheep), 1842

THE 6 GOURMANDS IN THE HUMAN COMEDY

When Balzac was writing, his characters ate! Six among them—all gourmands without being bons vivants, slaves to their mania—all soothe their misfortunes with edible delights.

DULL HUSBANDS
The **Count de Montperson** (*Le Message*), **Monsieur de Watteville** (*Albert Savarus*), and the **Vicomte de Beauséant** (*Le Père Goriot*) compensate for the disillusions of their marriages with refined meals.

THE IMPOTENT
Doctor Rouget, who is sexually impotent (*The Black Sheep*), and **Sylvain Pons**, who is monstrously ugly (*Cousin Pons*), console themselves about their physical deficiencies with the pleasure of food. And we can thank the latter's servant from Berry for the unique recipe in *The Human Comedy* for the frothy omelet.

THE HAPPY GOURMAND
The only happy gourmet in *The Human Comedy* is the young **Oscar Husson** (*Un début dans la vie* [*A Start in Life*]). But his feasts are only imaginary; a gastronomic paradise that in every way matches the Balzacian ideal: hors d'oeuvre, soup, daube, beef tongue, stewed pigeon, *timbale de macaroni*, eleven fruit desserts, and wines!

Cakes to Carry

Created as a result of the rise in tourism and paid holidays, these *gâteaux voyages* ("traveling cakes")
befit their name: cakes that can travel easily and keep well because they have no fillings.
Their scent evokes memories of picnics in the grass or afternoon snack time.

Marie-Laure Fréchet

THE HISTORY

The concept has existed since Roman times, when legionnaires would pack and carry food with them for snacking. This sort of snack was known as the *panis militaris*, a kind of very hard cookie. The warriors of Genghis Khan carried a cake of honey and spices in their satchels. This cake was brought to Europe by the Crusaders, before the so-called *pain d'épices* (similar to gingerbread) found its fame in Dijon and Alsace. The development of tourism, thanks to railways, paid holidays, and the popularity of picnics, encouraged the development of cakes without fragile cream fillings, making them more practical to transport and to store. Cookbooks for home cooks published during the 1950s taught young French women easy recipes to share with family.

The First Ones

Beauvilliers bear the name of one of the first great restaurant owners of Paris in the middle of the nineteenth century, whose pastry chef created a cake made from crushed almonds that was carried wrapped in a thin sheet of tin. This cake has fallen into culinary oblivion.

Financiers were inspired by the oval almond cakes made in the Middle Ages by the Vistandine nuns. Around 1890, a pastry cook settled in Paris near the stock exchange and had the idea of baking them in the shape of gold ingots and selling them to stockbrokers, who were delighted to be able to enjoy them on the go between transactions.

The Cakes

Whereas for English speakers the word *cake* designates all kinds of cakes, in France it refers only to rectangular loaf cakes, baked in a loaf pan.

The fruit cake was inspired by the English plum cake. It is filled with raisins and a mixture of rum-soaked candied fruits.

The lemon or "weekend" cake, created in 1955 by Dalloyau, is a cake made with lemon zest and coated in a thin white icing and one that the Parisians took away with them on weekends.

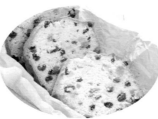

The marbled cake appeared in the 1950s, possibly inspired by the *babovka*, a sort of traditional marbled Czech cake. It was popularized in supermarkets in France under the brand Savane. *To make, beat 4 large eggs with 1½ cups (250 g) of sugar, then incorporate 14 tablespoons (200 g) of melted butter. Add 2½ cups (250 g) all-purpose flour and 1 teaspoon (4 g) baking powder. Melt 7 ounces (200 g) dark chocolate and fold it into half the batter. Scrape the two batters into a greased loaf pan, alternating them in equal portions. Bake for 35 minutes at 350°F (180°C), or until golden on top.*

Quatre-quart, known since the late nineteenth century, consists of four ingredients in four equal parts (similar to pound cake): *9 ounces (250 g) each of eggs (4 to 5), sugar, flour, and butter (melted). Whisk the eggs and sugar together, then stir in the flour, then the melted butter. Scrape the batter into a greased loaf pan and bake for 45 minutes at 350°F (180°C), or until golden on top.*

——— FINANCIERS ———

PREPARATION TIME: 20 MINUTES
COOKING TIME: 15 MINUTES
MAKES ABOUT 12 FINANCIERS

4 tablespoons plus ¾ teaspoon (60 g) + 1 tablespoon plus
1 teaspoon (20 g) demi-sel butter
¼ cup plus 1 tablespoon (30 g) all-purpose flour
2⅛ ounces (60 g) almond flour
3 large (90 g) egg whites
¾ cup plus 2 tablespoons plus 1½ teaspoons (90 g)
confectioners' sugar
½ teaspoon (2 g) vanilla extract

Preheat the oven to 350°F (180°C). Melt the 4 tablespoons plus ¾ teaspoons (60 g) of butter in a saucepan over medium heat until the solids have fallen to the bottom of the pan and browned; set aside to cool slightly. Meanwhile, sift together the all-purpose and almond flours, then gradually stir in the egg whites, then the melted butter, sugar, and vanilla extract. Stir gently just until combined. Pipe the batter into financier molds greased with the remaining butter. Bake for 12 to 15 minutes, or until golden. Once cooled, sprinkle with the remaining sugar.

Today's Gâteaux Voyages

The yogurt cake is known as the perfect cake for making with kids. It became very popular during the 1970s with the development of commercially produced dairy products. *The basic recipe: Stir together 1 container of yogurt, ½ yogurt container of flavorless oil, 2 yogurt containers of granulated sugar, 3 yogurt containers of all-purpose flour, 3 eggs, and 1 teaspoon (4 g) baking powder. Bake in a greased cake pan for 30 minutes at 350°F (180°C).*

Fondant au chocolat is a cake with a dense and melting texture, one that is intentionally underbaked. This cake is not to be confused with the chocolate *mi-cuit* ("molten chocolate cake") created in 1981 by Michel Bras.

Moelleux au chocolat has an airy texture thanks to the addition of beaten egg whites.

The BN: From WWI Soldiers to Schoolchildren

Created in 1896 in Nantes, Biscuiterie Nantaise (BN) is a family business that produced the "Petit Breton," madeleines, and macarons until World War I, when it was requisitioned to make breads for soldiers at the front. In the aftermath of the war, the cookie factory launched its "Snack BN," a simple and economic cookie that became the standard cookie of the working class and for schoolchildren. It was improved in 1933 with the addition of a chocolate filling. But it wasn't until the end of World War II that the chocolate version, the "Choco BN," became popular.

It Smells like Sulfur!

In the world of wine, sulfur is used to combat the effects of oxygen on wine. A source of many debates, its use is challenged by some winemakers who consider it harmful.
Jérôme Gagnez

SULFUR—THE VIRTUES
Sulfur dioxide (SO_2) is a food additive with antioxidant and antiseptic properties. It protects wine from oxidation and prevents deviations due to the activity of bacteria and yeasts. The absence of sulfur can also lead to the transformation of wine into vinegar.

SULFUR—THE CHALLENGES
An aggressive use of SO_2 blocks the aromatic expression of wine. Even worse, it causes headaches, which can sometimes be quite acute.

THE ORIGINS
By adding sulfur to wine barrels in the seventeenth century (they burned a wick of sulfur in the barrel), Dutch merchants who crossed Europe discovered the protective virtues of sulfur on wine.

WHAT TYPE OF SULFUR IS USED?
There are two types of sulfur: **volcanic sulfur**, which is a natural product, and **chemical sulfur,** which is, as its name suggests, much less natural.

Volcanic sulfur is much less likely to cause a pounding headache after waking up the next day from an evening of celebration. But with common sense not always reigning supreme over the legislation of French wines, volcanic sulfur is banned, while chemical sulfur is allowed.

skip to
Natural Wine, p. 86

DOSES
French legislation regulates the use of sulfur dioxide. The maximum concentration is:
0.005 ounce per 34 fl ounces (150 mg per liter) for red wines.
0.006 ounce per 34 fl ounces (185 mg per liter) for sparkling wines.
0.007 ounce per 34 fl ounces (200 mg per liter) for white and rosé wines.

0 SULFUR?
To assume wines have no sulfur is a mistake. During fermentation, yeasts naturally produce from 0.0001 to 0.001 ounce (5 to 30 milligrams) per 34 fl ounces (1 liter) of sulfur dioxide.

Are French wines treated with sulfites today?

The overwhelming majority of wines marketed today are treated with sulfites. The challenge is knowing in what proportion. It's important therefore to **favor winemakers who use sulfur moderately**. Their wines are better, not only in terms of their aromatic expression but also in terms of their digestibility. Some winemakers experiment with the total absence of sulfur. Unfortunately, very few are able to produce good, quality wines.

The Hams of France

Ham (*jambon*) is the part of the pig that makes up most of the thigh. When cooked, it is typically enjoyed on a sandwich. When raw, it is enjoyed salted, dried, and sometimes smoked—and just about everywhere in France.
Charles Patin O'Coohoon

Classification of ham according to the Code of Use for cured meats

"Superior": contains no polyphosphates or gelling agent, and no more than 1 percent sugar. It represents more than 80 percent of French production.
"Choice": contains no gelling agent and represents 15 percent of French production.
"Standard": allows the use of additives. It represents only 5 percent of French production.

Let it be known, jambon de Paris ("ham from Paris") does not come from Paris!
This ham is ordinary ham that has been salted, cooked in water, boned, placed in a terrine with the rind underneath, and pressed while chilled, a process standardized by chef Jules Gouffé in 1869. Today, *jambon de Paris* refers to a boneless, salted pork thigh placed in a rectangular dish and cooked in an aromatic broth.

Ham	Origin	Label	Pig Breed	Salting	Smoking	Drying	Aging	Color
Jambon sec des Ardennes	Ardennes	PGI 2015					9 months minimum	red
Jambon de l'Ardèche	Ardèche	PGI 2010		rubbed with pepper	sometimes, with chestnut wood		7 months minimum	dark red
Jambon d'Auvergne	Auvergne	PGI 2016		dry salted			9 months	dark brown
Jambon de Bayonne	Béarn	PGI 1998		with salt from Adour			7 months minimum	dark brown
Jambon de Lacaune	Languedoc	PGI 2015					9–12 months	dark brown
Jambon de Luxeuil	Haute-Saône	not labeled		macerated in Arbois wine	over pine wood shavings		8 months	light brown
Jambon de Savoie	Savoie, Haute-Savoie	not labeled			over beech wood		6 months	light brown
Jambon de Vendée	Vendée and neighboring cantons	PGI 2014		rubbed with herbs and eau-de-vie				reddish brown
Jambon Noir de Bigorre	Hautes-Pyrénées, Gers, Haute-Garonne	AOP 2015	Gascon pig	with salt from Adour		10 months	10 months	dark red
Prisuttu	Corse	AOP 2011	Nustrale pig		sometimes, over chestnut wood		12–18 months	red

Discovering the Madeleine

The most celebrated little cake in literature is also a pinnacle of gourmandise when it is made well—and doing so is not that easy!
François-Régis Gaudry

The Madeleine of Proust

This is the day when little Marcel made his childhood memories in Combray return by eating just a few crumbs of madeleine . . .

She sent for one of those squat, plump little cakes called "petites madeleines," which look as though they had been moulded in the fluted valve of a scallop shell. And soon, mechanically, dispirited after a dreary day with the prospect of a depressing morrow, I raised to my lips a spoonful of the tea in which I had soaked a morsel of the cake. No sooner had the warm liquid mixed with the crumbs touched my palate than a shudder ran through me and I stopped, intent upon the extraordinary thing that was happening to me. An exquisite pleasure had invaded my senses, something isolated, detached, with no suggestion of its origin. And at once the vicissitudes of life had become indifferent to me, its disasters innocuous, its brevity illusory—this new sensation having had on me the effect which love has of filling me with a precious essence; or rather this essence was not in me it was me.

À la recherche du temps perdu, Du côté de chez Swann (*In Search of Lost Time, Swann's Way*), 1913, by **Marcel Proust**

ITS ORIGINS

The one fact that is nearly certain: the madeleine was born in Commercy, in Lorraine. The only problem is identifying its inventor, and it's here where the details get mixed up . . .

In the Middle Ages, a cook called Madeleine prepared small brioche shaped like scallop shells to feed the pilgrims along the Way of St. James.

In the seventeenth century, Paul de Gondi, cardinal of Retz, uncle of Madame de Sévigné, and a complete rebel, had been exiled to his lands at Commercy. In 1661, his cook, Madeleine Simonin, had the idea of modifying a beignet batter to make a new treat, one which he thought the Duchess of Longueville would love. The cake was completed, and madeleines were associated with Commercy forever.

A century later, another famous exile, Stanislas Leszczynski (former king of Poland, father of Queen Mary, and father-in-law of Louis XV, who offered him the duchy of Lorraine), had a cook (one named Madeleine of course) who had the idea of serving him this forgotten pastry. He revived, therefore, this famous cake.

Why Does It Have a Bump?

Even chemists struggle to explain why this happens, but there are several hypotheses:

🐝 The madeleine's famous bump results from the **heat shock** between the cold batter and the hot oven. This can be refuted because even when the batter is not refrigerated, the bump still forms.

🐝 The bump forms **over the deepest point in the mold**, where the baking powder content is the most concentrated.

🐝 For the famous pastry chef Antonin Carême, this swelling was a defect linked to having **worked the dough too much**, which made the madeleine puff.

THE RECIPE
*by Fabrice le Bourdat**

This is the sweet madeleine of the chef of the bakery Blé sucré and was at the top of the list of the fifteen best Parisian madeleines in *Figaroscope* in 2014. It is perfection. And a little crackly icing makes it even more indulgent.

RESTING TIME: 2 TO 3 HOURS
BAKING TIME: 9 TO 10 MINUTES
MAKES 12 MADELEINES

Equipment
1 metal twelve-cavity madeleine mold

Ingredients
2 eggs
½ cup (100 g) granulated sugar
2 tablespoons plus 2 teaspoons (40 g) milk
1¼ cups (125 g) all-purpose flour, sifted, plus more for dusting
⅛ ounce (5 g) baking powder
9 tablespoons plus 2 teaspoons (140 g) unsalted butter, melted and kept warm, plus more at room temperature for greasing the mold

The icing
1 cup plus 3 tablespoons plus 1 teaspoon (120 g) confectioners' sugar
2 tablespoons (30 g) orange juice

Whisk together the eggs and granulated sugar. Whisk in the milk. Sift the flour with the baking powder. Using the whisk, stir in the flour, then stir in the warm melted butter until thoroughly combined. Let the batter rest in the refrigerator for 2 to 3 hours. Grease the mold with butter, then dust with flour, tapping out any excess. Fill each cavity with the batter and bake for 9 to 10 minutes at 400°F (210°C).

For the icing, stir together the confectioners' sugar and orange juice. Using a pastry brush, coat the madeleines with the icing.

**Baker-pastry chef of Blé sucré, 7, rue Antoine-Vollon, Paris 7th*

FAUX PAS

Adding honey
Adding vanilla
Adding lemon: zest or juice

The Grand Aïoli

This is a dish for sharing which, according to Frédéric Mistral, "epitomizes the heat, the power, and the joy of the Provençal sun." Here is all you need to succeed in creating your own.

François-Régis Gaudry

TO SIMPLIFY IT

Aïoli

Aïoli was originally made with just garlic and olive oil. But it is permissible to do as chef Édouard Loubet does and add an egg yolk, water, and lemon juice to help the emulsion.

If you are reluctant to use a mortar and pestle, you can make a "mayoli": just make a mayonnaise with olive oil using a whisk or blender and season it at the end with a garlic purée.

Cod

If you do not have time to desalt cod, choose fresh cod and dip it in cold, salted water (½ oz/15 g of salt per 4¼ cups/1 liter of water) for 1½ hours. The flesh will firm up. Just steam it for 10 to 15 minutes.

THE RECIPE
by Édouard Loubet

Here master chef Édouard Loubet* offers a sublime version of this specialty. Purists may choose to remove the zucchini and cuttlefish, which are not part of the traditional recipe.

DESALTING THE COD: 24 HOURS
DISGORGING THE WHELK: 1 HOUR
PREPARATION & COOKING TIME:
2 HOURS 30 MINUTES
SERVES 6

3⅓ pounds (1.5 kg) salt cod
1⅔ pounds (750 g) whelks
1 handful coarse salt
6 peppercorns
1 bouquet garni
1 onion
2 cloves, for piercing the onion
2 tablespoons plus 2 teaspoons (40 mL) pastis
6 eggs
6 potatoes
6 baby carrots
1⅛ pounds (500 g) string beans
3 small zucchini
3 small bulbs fennel
1 small cauliflower
1¾ pounds (800 g) small cuttlefish
2 tablespoons (30 mL) olive oil
Salt and freshly ground black pepper

The aïoli
6 cloves garlic
1 egg yolk
1 pinch salt
1½ cups (350 mL) olive oil
Juice of ½ lemon

The cod

Cut the cod into pieces. Place the pieces in a strainer and immerse them in cold water. Let the cod soak for 24 hours to remove excess salt, changing the water three times during this period. Two hours before preparing the aïoli, disgorge the whelks by covering them for 1 hour in the coarse salt; rinse them well. Cook the whelks for 25 minutes in 3 quarts (3 L) of water with the peppercorns, bouquet garni, onion (studded with the cloves), and pastis; drain and set the whelks aside. Boil the eggs for 10 minutes, or until hard boiled. Using some of the soaking water from the cod, cook the potatoes and carrots for 15 minutes. Snap off the stems and remove the strings from the string beans. Peel the zucchini, then slice into long sticks. Separate the fennel layers. Cook the string beans, zucchini, and fennel together in a pan of boiling water for 10 minutes; drain. Cut the cauliflower into florets and cook them, separately, for 15 minutes in salted boiling water.

The aïoli

Peel and crush the garlic. Add the egg yolk and salt. Add the oil in a thin stream while whisking continuously in the same direction. After adding about ¼ cup (50 mL) of oil, add 1 teaspoon (5 mL) of water and the lemon juice. Continue to whisk until the aïoli thickens.

Finishing and presentation

Drain the cod. In a saucepan, cover it with cold water and bring it almost to a boil. Remove the pan from the heat and let the cod poach for 5 to 8 minutes, covered. Slice open the cuttlefish bodies, then rinse them. Cook for 5 minutes over high heat in the oil (starting in cold oil to prevent them from firming up). Remove the skin and any bones from the cod, then place it on a very large serving platter. Peel and halve the boiled eggs. Arrange them and the cooked vegetables around the cod, cuttlefish, and whelks.

Domaine de Capelongue in Bonnieux (Vaucluse). Recipe taken from Cuisinier provençal, Les 100 recettes incontournables, *Éditions Skira.*

skip to
Mayonnaise, p. 100

Let's Talk Salad!

Originating in rural areas and increasing in popularity due to the increase in tourism, composed salads throughout France are plentiful. And each region has developed its own signature one. Here are eleven of them to try!

François-Régis Gaudry

1 La Lyonnaise (Lyon)

This is one of the specialties in restaurants in Lyon. It's an urban variation of a dandelion salad that has bacon from the mountains of Lyon.

Lettuces used: curly endive or lion's tooth (dandelion).

Suggested additions: soft-boiled eggs, smoked bacon, parsley, croutons (maybe rubbed with garlic).

Suggested dressing and seasoning: sunflower or walnut oil, aged wine vinegar, salt and pepper.

A faux pas: replacing the curly endive with lettuce, as often happens in Lyon.

2 La Vigneronne

This rustic salad was traditionally prepared by families in Burgundy using wild greens growing in the vineyards.

Lettuces used: dandelions, sometimes Capuchin's beard or mâche lettuce.

Suggested additions: bacon fried in lard, in which the dandelions are briefly "dropped."

Suggested dressing and seasoning: melted lard for fat, wine vinegar, salt and pepper.

A faux pas: eating it in Bordeaux!

3 La Niçoise

Salada nissarda was served elaborately by Auguste Escoffier, before being updated by the former mayor of Nice, Jacques Médecin.

Lettuces used: wild lettuces (arugula, purslane, etc.), sometimes mesclun.

Suggested additions: tomato, cucumber, small beans, small trimmed artichokes, bell peppers, scallions (or young onions), basil, garlic, hard-boiled eggs, tuna in oil and/or anchovies, niçoise olives.

Suggested dressing and seasoning: olive oil, salt and pepper. Never vinegar.

A faux pas: adding cooked ingredients other than a hard-boiled egg, such as string beans, potatoes, or rice.

4 La Parisienne

A classic in local brasseries—neon and Formica included.

Lettuces used: batavia lettuce.

Suggested additions: diced pressed ham, diced Emmental cheese, hard-boiled eggs, sometimes white button mushrooms.

Suggested dressing and seasoning: sunflower oil, mustard, vinegar, salt and pepper.

A faux pas: adding black olives, corn, or hearts of palm.

5 La Landaise

Since the 1950s, this salad has been served with conviction in restaurants throughout France.

Lettuces used: lettuce, mesclun, mâche.

Suggested additions: duck in all its forms (gizzards, strips of meat, duck breast, foie gras, etc.), pine nuts or walnuts, garlic croutons, tomato or apple (depending on the season).

Suggested dressing and seasoning: olive or walnut oil, vinegar, salt and pepper.

A faux pas: serving it to a vegan!

6 La Vosgienne

Also called "warm *meurotte* salad," traditionally prepared in the countryside during Lent.

Lettuces used: dandelions.

Suggested additions: potatoes boiled in water, bacon.

Suggested dressing and seasoning: the "meurotte" is a warm vinaigrette prepared with the fat from cooked bacon, chopped shallot, wine vinegar, salt and pepper. The warm dressing helps tenderize the dandelions.

A faux pas: using commercially processed bacon that produces more water than fat.

7 La Savoyarde

This salad made its appearance in the 1960s as part of the winter sports season, but it may have origins in alpine chalets.

Lettuces used: dandelions, iceberg lettuce, or sugarloaf chicory.

Suggested additions: slices of Savoy ham or grilled bacon, walnuts, diced Beaufort cheese.

Suggested dressing and seasoning: sunflower oil, mustard, vinegar, salt and pepper.

A faux pas: adding tomatoes in winter!

8 La Chèvre Chaud

This warm goat-cheese salad, whose origins can be traced to the Berry and Minervois regions, was the star in French bistros in the 1980s.

Lettuces used: oak leaves, mâche, batavia lettuce.

Suggested additions: fresh goat cheese, such as crottin de Chavignol, placed on a puff pastry crust or a slice of country bread and briefly broiled, sometimes with cumin or caraway.

Suggested dressing and seasoning: rapeseed, peanut, or walnut oil, onions, wine vinegar, salt and pepper.

A faux pas: a commercial log of goat cheese placed on toasted sandwich bread.

SALADS WITHOUT LETTUCES

Lentil salad: cook Puy AOP lentils (boiled in three times their volume of cold, unsalted water, 20 to 25 minutes once the water reaches a boil), drain, and mix with lardons, chopped shallot, chopped parsley, and a good mustard vinaigrette.

Chickpea salad: combine cooked chickpeas (see page 56) with canned sardine fillets, garlic, and minced onion. Season with lemon and olive oil.

Beet salad: dice cooked beets and combine them with pieces of Comté cheese, hard-boiled eggs, optional sunflower seeds, and a mustard vinaigrette.

skip to
Vinegar, p. 226; Lettuces and Chicories, p. 337

Michel Guérard

Heavyweight of cuisine minceur
(born in 1933)

A pioneer of Nouvelle Cuisine, Michel Guérard is the iconic chef from Eugénie-les-Bains.

A little cleanse in his world.

Charles Patin O'Coohoon

A STROKE OF GENIUS IN EUGÉNIE!

In the mid-1970s, he moved to the Eugénie-les-Bains spa with his wife, Christine Barthélémy, heir to the company Chaîne Thermale du Soleil. Very quickly, he gave shape to *cuisine minceur* (healthy cooking). The idea was to offer light, gourmet cuisine to guests at the spa. Within three years, he was awarded three stars and his stoves became a genuine laboratory. He partnered with frozen food brands and continues to develop his own research on diet.

HIS BIOGRAPHY IN 10 DATES

1933
Born in Vétheuil
(Val-d'Oise department)

1956
Becomes head pastry chef
at the Hôtel Crillon

1958
Wins Best Craftsman of France
(MOF) for pastry

1965
Purchases Le Pot-au-Feu
at auction in Asnières

1971
Le Pot-au-Feu earns its
second Michelin star

1974
Moves with his wife to
Eugénie-les-Bains, a spa
in the Landes department

1976
Publication of
La grande cuisine minceur
by Éditions Robert Laffont

1976
Appears on the cover of *Time*

1977
Les Prés d'Eugénie earns
a third Michelin star

2013
Founds a school for healthy
cooking

His 3 signature dishes

THE SALADE GOURMANDE (1968)
Scandalous at the time. He combined asparagus, string beans, and foie gras in a single salad with vinegar dressing. Vinaigrette with foie gras! Once unthinkable, it is now listed in brasseries under the name *salade folle* (crazy salad).

L'OREILLER MOELLEUX DE MOUSSERONS ET DE MORILLES AUX ASPERGES DU PAYS (1979) (SOFT PILLOW OF WILD MUSHROOMS AND MORELS WITH ASPARAGUS)
The chef offers this description on his menu: "A silky symphony of vegetables, invented in 1978 upon return from a trip." This ravioli dish was inspired by time spent in China.

LE HOMARD IVRE DES PÊCHEURS DE LUNE (2007) (MOON FISHERMAN'S DRUNKEN LOBSTER)
The lobster is killed by being plunged in Armagnac (eau-de-vie), which soaks its flesh. It is served as an iridescent carpaccio.

WARM STRAWBERRY TARTS

SERVES 8
4½ pounds (2 kg) strawberries (preferably wild Mara strawberries)
1 cup (200 g) + ¼ cup plus 2 tablespoons (85 g) sugar, plus more for sprinkling
3 egg yolks
½ cup (120 g) lemon juice, divided (about 4 lemons)
1 sheet gelatin (0.08 oz/2.5 g), softened in cold water
7 tablespoons (100 g) unsalted butter, room temperature
Zest of 1 lemon
¾ cup plus 1 tablespoon (200 g) heavy cream, whipped
8 rounds of puff pastry (5½ inches/14 cm in diameter and ¹⁄₁₀ inch/2 mm thick)

Several hours before serving, halve the strawberries and arrange them on an ovenproof baking pan with holes (such as a perforated pizza pan) so that the juice drains (reserve the juices by placing a sheet pan under it to catch them). Sprinkle the strawberries with the 1 cup (200 g) of sugar and bake them in the oven at 350°F (180°C) for 20 minutes. Remove from the oven and place them on paper towels for several hours so that their water releases. In a saucepan, reduce the reserved juice until thickened.

• Make the lemon cream. Whisk the egg yolks with the ¼ cup plus 2 tablespoons (85 g) of sugar and ¼ cup (60 g) of the lemon juice. Bring this mixture to a boil for 2 minutes. Add the softened gelatin off the heat. Let the mixture cool to 131°F (55°C) and whisk in the butter. Once the mixture has completely cooled, stir in the zest and remaining lemon juice, and fold in the whipped cream. Arrange the strawberries on the puff pastry circles, leaving a ½-inch (1.5 cm) border. Bake them on a sheet pan for 20 minutes at 400°F (200°C). Before serving, brush the tarts with the reduced juice, then sprinkle with sugar. Serve them with the lemon cream.

Knives 101

From an apprentice cook to a chef, every cook's essential tool is the knife.
The shapes of their blades are as diverse as their uses.
Marielle Gaudry

1

Butter knife
Blade: 1½ to 2¾ inches (4 to 7 cm), slightly sharp.
Function: Spread butter.

2

Oyster knife
Blade: 1½ to 2¾ inches (4 to 7 cm), thick.
Function: open oysters.

3

Bird's beak
Blade: 2 to 2¾ inches (5 to 7 cm), curved tip.
Function: peel fruits and vegetables.

4

Paring knife
Blade: 2¾ to 4 inches (7 to 10 cm), pointed.
Function: peel, trim, and slice fruits and vegetables.

5

Tomato knife
Blade: 4 to 5½ inches (10 to 14 cm), pointed and microserrated.
Function: slice tomatoes.

6

Boning knife
Blade: 4¾ to 6 inches (12 to 16 cm), thin and curved.
Function: bone poultry and fish.

7

Slicing knife
Blade: 6 to 9¾ inches (15 to 25 cm).
Function: cut up and carve meat and shellfish carcasses.

8

Bread knife
Blade: 7 to 12 inches (18 to 30 cm), rigid and serrated.
Function: slice bread.

9

Utility knife
Blade: 6 to 12 inches (15 to 30 cm), thick.
Function: chop, mince; slice hard foods.

10

Chef's knife
Blade: 9¾ to 12 inches (25 to 30 cm), beveled.
Function: split and crush meat bones.

11

Cleaver
Blade: 8½ to 12 inches (22 to 30 cm), thick and curved.
Function: chop meat carcasses.

12

Honing steel
Blade: 8 to 12 inches (20 to 30 cm), cylindrical, sometimes diamond-coated.
Function: sharpen knives.

Thanks to cutler Sabatier (Thiers).

CUTS OF VEGETABLES
• Brunoise
Cut into ¹⁄₁₀-inch (2 mm) dice; for sauces, garnishes, or fillings.
• Macédoine
Cut into ⅛-inch (3 mm) dice; for a side dish or making a vegetable mixture.

• Mirepoix
Cut into ⅓-inch (1 cm) dice; for accompaniments for meat and fish.
• Julienne
Cut into sticks 2 inches (5 cm) long and ¹⁄₁₀ inch (2 mm) thick; for decorative garnishes or for salads.

skip to ....
The Knives of France's Provinces, p. 196

Sausage Rougail

If there was only one dish to choose to taste while in Réunion, it would be this spicy pork dish.
Thierry Kasprowicz*

3 Things to Know

Rougail is a word originating in India—from *ouroukaille*, which in Tamil means candied green fruit or chile pepper—designating a paste or sauce made from tomatoes, onions, and chile, enriched with various ingredients according to the recipe. Sausage rougail (*rougail saucisse*) is the most popular dish.

Sausage rougail prepared over a wood fire wins hands down: it has an unmatched smoky quality.

Its recipe varies according to the areas of the island, and to each family. Some add garlic, ginger, thyme, and turmeric.

SAUSAGE ROUGAIL
by Christian Antou**

SERVES 6

12 fresh or smoked sausages (preferably Toulouse)
2 tablespoons (30 mL) vegetable oil
5 red onions
1 or 2 green chile peppers (depending on your tolerance for heat), crushed
5 very ripe tomatoes

Submerse the sausages in a large volume of cold water in a large pot. Simmer over medium heat for about 25 minutes to desalt them. Discard the water in the pot and set the sausages aside to drain. In the same pot, lightly brown the sausages in the vegetable oil, piercing them and skimming off some of their fat, if necessary. Remove the sausages and cut them into ⅓-inch- (1 cm) thick pieces. Peel and mince the onions, then fry them without letting them brown, and place the pieces of sausage back in the pot. Add the chile and cook until softened. Finely chop the tomatoes and add them to the pot. Let simmer, covered, over low heat for 25 minutes. The sauce should be reduced and thickened and not greasy. Serve with white rice and some lentils from Cilaos, another local specialty!

**An ardent defender of traditional Réunion cuisine (goutanou.re), now deceased

5 ADDRESSES FOR TRADITIONAL RÉUNION CUISINE

Chez Ti Fred à Petite Île: cooking done over a wood fire in a friendly setting.
Le Reflet des Îles à Saint-Denis: a renowned location for traditional cuisine from the capital.
Le Tamaréo à La Nouvelle, Cirque de Mafate: inn accessible only by foot. Local chicken curry, pistachio rougail . . . all a good reason for a hike!
Le Gîte de l'Îlet à l'Îlet à Cordes, Cirque de Cilaos: a family-style ambience in this magical and elaborate space.
Ferme-Auberge Annibal à Bras-Panon: Vanilla Duck by Madame Eva Annibal, still the keeper of the recipe.

*Creator of Guide Kaspro, *premier food guide of Réunion*

skip to
Sausages, p. 385; The Best of the French West Indies, p. 350

Gone Too Soon

Suicides, heart attacks . . . these twelve symbols of French haute cuisine were lost before the age of sixty.
François-Régis Gaudry

**FRANÇOIS VATEL
(1631–1671)**
Supervisor of the kitchens at Château de Chantilly (Oise)
† Died in Chantilly at the age of 40
Cause of death: suicide

**ANTONIN CARÊME
(1784–1833)**
Chef and pastry chef, author of the encyclopedia *L'Art de la cuisine française*
† Died in Paris at the age of 49
Cause of death: lung disease (toxic fumes from his charcoal oven)

**FERNAND POINT
(1897–1955)**
Chef of La Pyramid in Vienna (Isère)
† Died in Vienna at the age of 58
Cause of death: long illness

**PAUL LACOMBE
(1913–1972)**
Chef of Léon de Lyon (Lyon)
† Died in Lyon at the age of 58
Cause of death: exhaustion (was diabetic with heart problems)

**JACQUES LACOMBE
(1923–1974)**
Chef (native of Annecy) of Lion d'Or in Cologny (Switzerland)
† Died in Martigny (Switzerland) at the age of 51
Cause of death: car accident

**JEAN TROISGROS
(1926–1983)**
One of the Troisgros brothers (Loire)
† Died in Vittel (Vosges) at the age of 57
Cause of death: heart attack during a tennis game

**ALAIN CHAPEL
(1937–1990)**
Three-star chef from Mionnay (Ain)
† Died in Saint-Rémy-de-Provence at the age of 53
Cause of death: infarction

**JACQUES PIC
(1932–1992)**
Three-star chef of La Maison Pic in Valence (Drôme)
† Died in Valence (Drôme) at the age of 60
Cause of death: heart attack

**BERNARD LOISEAU
(1951–2003)**
Three-star chef of La Côte d'Or in Saulieu (Côte-d'Or)
† Died in Saulieu at the age of 52
Cause of death: suicide

**BENOÎT VIOLIER
(1971–2016)**
Three-star chef of Restaurant L'Hôtel de Ville in Crissier (Switzerland)
† Died in Crissier at the age of 45
Cause of death: suicide

**MICHEL DEL BURGO
(1962–2017)**
Former three-star chef of L'Atelier Robuchon Hong Kong
† Died in Paris at the age of 54
Cause of death: long illness

**LAURENT JEANNIN
(1968–2017)**
Pastry chef at the Bristol Hotel in Paris
† Died in Paris at the age of 49
Cause of death: heart attack

The Oldest of the New World Wines

The wine-producing industry of Corsica (France's Île de Beauté) combines two qualities: exoticism and namesake. Its vineyards offer wines, both unique and seductive, for export that maintain their connection to their *terroir*. Here is the proof in twelve exceptional cuvées.

Nicolas Stromboni

Domaine d'Alzipratu
Lume
White
A very Mediterranean approach for this wine of Vermentino. Luscious and sexy, but without being teasing. It has an immediate seduction, yet exhibits restraint.
To drink with: a creamy and aged cheese

Domain Gentille
Muscat Authentica
White
The essence of Corsican citrus fruits—both fresh and candied—with rose and lychee precisely captured. A Muscat that suggests a composer could write an opera after a mere sip.
To drink with: Ispahan tart

Domaine Giudicelli
Foudre
Red
A gentleman farmer, a very civilized bottle but without pretension; the juice and strength of Nielluccio without a single constraint; a very Piedmontese bottle.
To drink with: a red wine risotto with chanterelles

Domaine Pieretti
Marine
White
When the salt of the earth meets the salt of the sea. A Vermentino that gives meaning to the word *minerality*. A kind of fresh and pure taste of water from rock, dense and crystalline.
To drink with: a lightly poached spider crab

Domaine Antoine Arena
Carco
White
From the pope of Corsican wines. A tale that tells a singular way of isolating, in a Vermentino, the sun, the earth, the wind, and the elements. To experience without moderation.
To drink with: a Mediterranean fish

Clos Venturi
Chiesa Nera
White
When geometry is made into wine. A grand righteousness, almost a cathedral wine, but a baroque cathedral for this trio of Vermentino, Biancu Gentile, and Genovese. This wine brings people together in communion.
To drink with: wild oysters

Abbatucci Estate
Diplomate
White
A wine made like those of yesteryear. This is an expert blend of Vermentino and old endemic varietals; liquid aristocracy.
To drink with: a nice lobster delicately roasted in olive oil

Enclos des Anges
Domaine
Red
A tribute to the Mediterranean Burgundy, by its English winemaker, from whole cluster Grenache. A multicultural and delicious bottle.
To drink with: a confit of lamb

Clos Canereccia
Amphore de Carcaghjolu
Neru
Red
When a civilization comes to the rescue of another civilization; the domestication, in the Greek sense, of this old fleshy varietal Carcaghjolu, fiery, muscular, and wild but so familiar; a wine you will immediately appreciate.
To drink with: osso bucco

Domaine Zuria
Domaine
Rosé
When a terroir is large, whether its wine is dark or light pink, pleasure is not without expression. One of the first bottles of Sciacarellu that marks the renaissance of the great terroir of Bonifacio. Do not hesitate, as the whole world will want to taste it.
To drink with: carpaccio of langoustine

Clos Canarelli
Biancu Ghjentile
White
An accent of Condrieu; a very local expression of the old varietal Biancu Gentile, a very sweet but energetic juice. A beautiful compromise between vitality and charm.
To drink with: a seviche of white fish and mango

Domaine Sant'Armettu
Minustellu
Red
Strength and delicacy for this bottle from a wonderful old varietal, Minustellu. An athletic body in a ballerina's dress.
To drink with: a barely cooked *picania* of beef

skip to
The Island of Cheeses, p. 135

BUTTERED UP

In France, fat gets good press; English-speaking world, not so much. Cooking with butter and cream doesn't mean the French aren't healthy. You can have a slim waist and eat Tarte Tatin: yes, it's a paradox, but not a contradiction!

Aurore Vincenti

Kitchen Latin

The word *butter* comes from the Latin **butryum**, which comes from the Greek **bouturon**. It was primarily used by the Greeks and Romans as an ointment. The word is formed by the combination of two terms: the Greek **bous** and the Indo-European word **turos**. The former means beef or cow, and the latter, cheese. Butter was therefore originally considered to be **cow cheese**!

No teeth

Both in Latin and Greek, the word used to designate butter includes the **[t]** sound. In English and German, you find the letter in the word: **butter**. You also find it in Dutch: **boter**. But in French, the consonant, which is considered "dental," disappeared. Probably **because you don't bite into butter**. That's moreover the first quality that universal wisdom imparts about this foodstuff: **it melts!** One says "melts like butter" and also "smooth as butter." The hard "t" had to go in French so that the word could melt over your tongue.

The price of butter

Butter is valued both in the French language and in French society! It's often the **sign of a certain level of wealth**. Hence the value-ridden French expression to **"butter your spinach"** (earn a bit extra).

Cooking with butter

❧ **"Making your butter"** in French means making a living. In Wallonia, however, when someone says that you have your **butt in butter**, you can **bet that things will be easy** because you were born rich.

❧ In Émile Zola's *L'Assommoir*, Coupeau sarcastically suggests to his wife who has been complaining about walking the streets: **"Woman! If it means butter for the spinach!"** *"Mettre du beurre dans les épinards"* means making everyday life easier with additional income. That's **a dab of pleasure on top of the ordinary**.

❧ Nevertheless, don't push it, you can't **"push grandma into the nettles" once you have butter for the spinach or bread** (not to mention the "dairywoman's ass"—you can't have your cake and eat it, too) . . . **You have to learn to appreciate simple pleasures**.

❧ "He left the room, went back into the kitchen, **opened the cupboard**, took out a six-pound loaf of bread, **cut off a slice**, and carefully gathered the crumbs in the palm of his hand and threw them into his mouth, so as not to lose anything. Then, with the end of his knife, he scraped out **a little salt butter** from the bottom of an earthen jar, spread it on his bread and **began to eat slowly**, as he did everything."

Le Vieux (*The Old Man*), Guy de Maupassant

A kitchen without butter

❧ But butter hasn't only been a sign of wealth. You'll have nothing more than . . . **butter on a skewer, on a stick, on your hand, on your ass**. So many ways to say it: no, you'll get **nothing, nothing at all**. The idea is negative in this case, and yet butter is still value-laden because **its absence is noteworthy**.

❧ In our times, butter has an inferior value in the French expression **"counted as butter."** If you play cards for butter, for example, no price will be assigned to the round. **No bets are made and no points counted.**

❧ Totally buttered or bombed? Buttered bread **always falls down on the wrong side**. In French, if you're buttered, you, too, run the risk of falling on the wrong side of language. Your **words will be crude (and greasy)**. The French have used the word "buttered" since the beginning of the twentieth century because, in drunken stupor, the word for **bombed** (*bourré*) sounds like the word for **buttered** (*beurré*). **Dizzy paronymy for someone seeing blurry . . .**

❧ **Little butter pot, when *dépetitpotdebeurreriseras-tu?*** In Charles Perrault's tale, Little Red Riding Hood brings her grandmother a **"a biscuit and a little butter pot."** It was the wolf's **palm she should have greased,** though. Maybe if she had come with a butter dish, and not a little butter pot, the wolf would have been frightened off; because a "beurrier" in French (**butter dish**), before designating a container, **meant someone who made or sold butter**. That sense has been lost.

Skip to: At the Dairy, p. 316

LA BOUILLABAISSE
DE MARSEILLE

Bouillabaisse from Marseille is as well known as the Marseillaise! What started as a poor fishermen's soup has become a star in the French repertoire. And you can even make it at home . . .

Marie-Amal Bizalion

A PROTECTED SOUP

To protect its standards, the methods for making this fish soup were outlined in a charter in 1980 by a group of local restaurateurs. Starting from what was nothing more than a simple soup made from unsold fish and brought by Greek settlers to the shores of Lacydon, bouillabaisse has now become a complex and expensive dish. However . . .

APPROACH IT INSTINCTIVELY

If after an unsuccessful fishing trip, or a disappointing trip to the fish market, you have no desire to check the "real" recipe, **instead of becoming tied down by what the purists insist upon, just follow these three basic rules when making bouillabaisse:**
- Use only Mediterranean fish.
- Include a good variety of types of fish (from finer to more common).
- Pay close attention to the best cooking times for each type of seafood used.

La Recette

Skin all the fish, cut off the heads, then remove the entrails and clean the bodies. Cut the large fish into smaller pieces; set aside. In a large pan, heat olive oil and cook some onions, freshly chopped tomatoes, and peeled and crushed garlic cloves. Add the various Mediterranean fish (such as those from the rockfish group), the heads of any other fish, and, if desired, 1 or 2 crabs. Stir until everything is well combined, then add 2⅛ to 3⅛ quarts (2 to 3 L) of water, salt and pepper, 2 pinches of ground saffron, parsley, and half a fennel bulb with the stalks (or add a splash of pastis), and let simmer for 1 hour. Using an immersion blender, blend the mixture until smooth, then strain the contents through a fine-mesh sieve. Return the soup to the heat, then add quartered potatoes. Halfway through the cooking time, add any firm-fleshed fish—such as John Dory or Conger. Add the most delicate seafood (such as weever or tub gurnard) a few minutes before the end of the cooking time. The bouillabaise is now ready, yet it must be served with a *rouille* sauce, without which the dish is not up to its best: take 2 or 3 cooked potatoes and mash them with several cloves of garlic, egg yolks, saffron, black pepper, salt, and chile pepper, all whisked with olive oil until smooth. Serve the sauce with a crusty bread (that can also be used to soak up the soup broth).

WITHOUT FISH IS POSSIBLE, TOO!

The recipe that Reboul* called a "one-eyed bouillabaisse," but which pleased chef Marcel Pagnol when he could not buy fish, starts in the same way as the traditional one, but instead of adding fish and fennel, add to the broth (without blending): orange peel, bay leaf, saffron, and sliced potatoes. Once cooked, poach eggs in the broth for 3 minutes. Place a slice of bread on the bottom of each serving dish, gently place a poached egg on top, then surround it with potatoes and drizzle it with the broth.

*Author of La cuisinière provençale, *1897*

skip to . . . .
The Art of Drowning Fish, p. 334

Cheeses for Melting

It's difficult not to melt with pleasure over these melty cheeses, which have become a must-have indulgence for cold winter evenings.
Marielle Gaudry

	Tartiflette	Raclette	Fondue Savoyard	Aligot	Cancoillotte
A LITTLE HISTORY	Not exactly an old dish, *tartiflette* takes its name from *tartiflâ*, a Savoyard potato, and was invented in the 1980s by the Interprofessional Reblochon Syndicat to boost the sales of cheese. The dish was inspired by another famous dish: *la pela*, a rustic recipe from the Aravis (Haute-Savoie) made with potatoes, onions, and reblochon cheese melted in a long-handled pan (called a *péla* in local dialect).	Its origins are Swiss (from the canton of Valais). Before the "raclette" of the twentieth century, there was the "roasted cheese" consumed by shepherds in the Middle Ages, which was a half round of cheese set by the fire and its melting interior scooped up for eating. The rise in popularity of winter sports in the 1960s and the launch of cookware manufacturer Tefal's first raclette machine in 1978 gave rise to its popularity.	Fondue did not become part of traditional Savoyard culture until after World War II. The concept is to dip small pieces of bread into cheese melted in a fondue pot. This dish has relatives: the fondue of Mont-Doré (Cantal and Saint-Nectaire cheeses) in Auvergne; and fondue Camembert-Pont l'Évêque-Livarot with Calvados in Normandy.	This dish from Auvergne was originally a mixture of bread and fresh tomme cheese that the monks of Aubrac in the twelfth century served for pilgrims en route to Santiago de Compostela (the Way of Saint James). In the seventeenth century, following disastrous wheat harvests, bread was replaced by potatoes.	This Franconian specialty of a jarred, runny cheese has uncertain origins, but its name is sometimes attributed to the Latin *concoctum lactem* found in writings from the Gallo-Roman period, or sometimes attributed to a mistake made on a sixteenth-century farm while preparing another dish. We owe its notoriety to Laurent Raguin who, during World War I, had the idea to sterilize and package it in cans to supply soldiers from the Franche-Comté located at the front.
CHEESES USED	Reblochon, but unlike in *la pela*, bacon and a little white wine are added. The recipe from commercial manufacturers was certified as a Label Rouge ("Red Label") in 2014, which requires that the reblochon be Savoie AOP, and that the entire dish be baked in a traditional oven. **1 whole wheel of reblochon for 4 people.**	Raclette cheese! Or Swiss cheese of Valais (with an AOP), or the raclette of Savoie (with a PGI since 2017). Other delicious additions are allowed, too: Morbier, fourme d'Ambert, or a sheep's-milk tomme. **2¼ pounds (1 kg) of raclette cheese for 4 people.**	There are different schools of thought when it comes to fondue. Most lean toward Switzerland's famous half Vacherin and half Swiss Gruyère, but the Savoyard version is traditionally prepared with Beaufort, Comté, and Gruyère de Savoie. **12 ounces (350 g) of Beaufort, 12 ounces (350 g) of Comté, and 12 ounces (350 g) of Savoyard Gruyère for 4 people.**	A fresh tomme de l'Aubrac cheese, which is also referred to as *tome d'aligot*, is a by-product from the production of Laguiole, Salers, and Cantal cheeses. More of a curd than a cheese, it's firmly pressed, then slightly fermented. It has the ideal texture for creating aligot's signature runny and ropelike consistency. **1⅛ pounds (500 g) of fresh tomme de l'Aubrac for 4 people.**	Warning: strong cheese! *Cancoillotte* is made with a mixture of metton cheese, a curdled and aged skimmed milk (referred to as "spoiled"), with water and butter added at the end of preparation. **One 9-ounce (250 g) jar for 4 people**
FAUX PAS	Using crème fraîche in a *tartiflette*, which purists frown upon.	Stealing the contents of your neighbor's pan. Remember, raclette is synonymous with sharing and conviviality!	Losing a piece of bread in the fondue pot. The guilty party must accept a dare if this happens—it's a well-known tradition! Sending them to roll naked in the snow is always an effective deterrent.	Breaking the string. It's not so easy to master stirring the mixture to the right stringiness to lift it with a spoon up to more than 3 feet (1 m) without breaking it!	You should avoid the pronunciation *co-coillotte*, but instead say *kan-koi-yotte*, as it is pronounced in northern Franche-Comté, or *kan-ko-yotte*, as in southern Jura. If you want to practice pronouncing it, follow the singing advice of Hubert-Félix Thiéfaine (*La Cancoillotte*, 1978).
HOW TO TASTE IT	Serve it hot directly from the cast-iron pan, with a green salad.	Since a raclette machine has individual pans, it can be adapted to the number of guests and arranged in the center of the table. As a half round placed under a heat source. With a baked potato, a platter of cured meats, including *tavaillon* (slices of cured beef), cornichons, and a salad.	The fondue pot is placed in the center of the table next to cubes of stale, rustic bread, accompanied by cooked or raw pieces of ham, local dried sausages, and a green salad.	An obvious accompaniment: a good local country sausage, oozing with fat!	Plain or with garlic, walnuts, or vin jaune in which to dip crudités. Enjoyed cold, with just a spoon; or spread on a slice of toasted bread. Enjoyed hot, on potatoes, accompanied by a Morteau sausage and a green salad.
	Wine: a white from Savoie (Chignin-Bergeron)	**Wine: a white from Savoie (Apremont)**	**Wine: a white from Savoie (Roussette)**	**Wine: an Aveyron red (Marcillac)**	**Wine: a white wine from Jura (Arbois)**

FONDUE SAVOYARD

SERVES 4
1 large crusty loaf of bread, a little stale
12 ounces (350 g) Beaufort cheese
12 ounces (350 g) Comté cheese
12 ounces (350 g) Savoyard Gruyère
1 clove garlic, peeled
½ bottle (375 mL) white wine (preferably Apremont)
Freshly ground black pepper

Cut the bread into cubes and set it aside to dry out. Small dice all the cheeses. Rub the inside of a fondue pot with the garlic clove and place the pot over medium heat. Pour the wine into the pot. As soon as it begins to simmer, add the cheeses. Stir with a wooden spoon until the cheeses are melted. Season with pepper and continue to stir. Place the fondue pot over a heat source (such as on a trivet set over a burner) in the center of the table and enjoy.

2 tips
→ If the fondue mixture becomes too liquid, add a teaspoon of potato starch.

→ Crack an egg into the fondue pot after all the fondue has been eaten, for a more complete finish to the meal!

TARTIFLETTE

SERVES 4
2¼ pounds (1 kg) potatoes
2 onions
2 tablespoons (30 g) unsalted butter, plus more for greasing
7 ounces (200 g) lardons of bacon
1 pound (450 g) good-quality reblochon cheese
Salt and freshly ground black pepper

Peel and wash the potatoes. Submerge the potatoes in a saucepan of cold salted water, bring to a boil, and let cook for 20 minutes; drain. Peel and chop the onions. In a flameproof casserole dish, heat the butter and cook the onions for 5 minutes, or just until translucent. Add the lardons and cook for a few more minutes, until the lardons are lightly browned. Preheat the oven to 350°F (180°C). Grease a baking dish with butter, then slice the potatoes into rounds, and slice the reblochon. Start by arranging half the potato slices in the baking dish, then half the onions and bacon, and finally a layer of cheese. Repeat this step until all the ingredients are used. Season with salt and pepper. Bake for 20 minutes, or until the cheese is completely melted.

Regional variations
Very similar to *tartiflette*, *reblochonnade* uses crème fraîche rather than lardons. In Franche-Comté, the local *tartiflette* is *morbiflette*, made with Morbier cheese. In Cantal, it is called *truffade*, made with Salers or Cantal cheeses.

ALIGOT

SERVES 4
2¼ pounds (1 kg) potatoes (preferably Bintje)
1⅛ pounds (500 g) fresh tomme de l'Aubrac cheese
9 ounces (250 g) crème fraîche (preferably from Aubrac)

Peel and wash the potatoes. Place them in a saucepan of cold salted water and cook them for 20 minutes starting from the boiling point. Cut the tomme into strips and set them aside. When the potatoes are cooked, drain them, then process them through a potato masher to obtain a thin paste. Place the mashed potatoes back in the saucepan, which has been drained of any excess water, and add the crème fraîche. Stir with a wooden spoon to combine. Over very low heat, add the cheese and stir vigorously, in a figure eight, to melt the cheese. By stirring vigorously, the mixture should become stringy and stretch. When this happens, the *aligot* is ready.

Bake It!
Mont d'Or cheese is baked in its box in Franche-Comté.

With the lid placed under the box, scoop out a hole in the center of the cheese, then pour in a scant ¼ cup (50 mL) of dry white wine from Jura, then add a minced garlic clove. Bake at 425°F (220°C) for 30 minutes. Enjoy with warm skin-on potatoes and Morteau sausage.
**Quantity: 1 Mont d'Or for 4 people.
Wine: a white from Jura
(Côtes-du-Jura)**

skip to
Tarte au Maroilles, p. 245

Roger Vergé

Behind an iconic mustache hides one of the major chefs of Nouvelle Cuisine. He authored several influential books filled with his Mediterranean recipes and hoisted Mougins to the peak of fine food.
Charles Patin O'Coohoon

1930: born in Commentry (Allier)

1961: chef and manager of Club de Cavalière, the two-star restaurant in Le Lavandou (Var)

1969: opens the Moulin de Mougins (Alpes-Maritimes)

1972: receives the Meilleur Ouvrier de France (MOF)

1974

Receives three Michelin stars for Moulin de Mougins

★ ★ ★

1978: publishes *Ma Cuisine du Soleil*

1982: together with Gaston Lenôtre and Paul Bocuse, opens the restaurant Les Chefs de France in the France Pavilion at Walt Disney World in Florida

1992: publishes *Les Légumes de mon moulin*

2006: the Festival International de la Gastronomie in Mougins is founded in his honor

2015: dies in Mougins. The *New York Times* publishes a full-page obituary: "Audacity was part of his repertoire. Without hesitation, he offered diners humble ingredients previously unthinkable in a three-star restaurant."

The Riviera Genius
(1930–2015)

"In short, indulge. And you'll know how to cook."

Signature Dishes

Artichokes à la *barigoule* (stuffed with chopped mushrooms and ham, then braised)
 Squash blossom *pupton* with Vaucluse black truffles and mushroom butter
 Lobster fricassee with pink peppercorns
 Fillet of line-caught turbot with a vegetable matignon, *vin de palette* wine sauce

MOUGINS
The red carpet
Being so close to Cannes, his restaurant drew celebrities from the film festival, including Richard Burton, Elizabeth Taylor, James Coburn, Danny Kaye, Fred Astaire, Gérard Depardieu, Gunter Sachs, and John Travolta. In 1993, the Moulin hosted the first amfAR gala (The Foundation for AIDS Research), a prestigious fund-raiser.
The museum
The former mill was turned into a small museum of contemporary art. Being a friend to many artists and with the École de Nice nearby, Roger Vergé quickly opened the Moulin's doors to creative visions. An experimental laboratory exhibited works by César, Jean-Michel Folon, Arman, Jean-Claude Farhi, Theo Tobiasse, and Niki de Saint Phalle.

HIS SOUP AU PISTOU

SOAKING TIME: 12 HOURS
PREPARATION TIME: 40 MINUTES
COOKING AND FINISHING TIME: 1 HOUR
SERVES 6

7 ounces (200 g) dry white beans (such as large white kidney beans)
1 bouquet garni
Salt
2 carrots
2 turnips
2 long zucchini
1 white onion
1 large handful string beans, preferably long and flat
1 leek (white portion only)
2 tender stalks celery
⅓ cup plus 1 tablespoon (100 mL) olive oil
2 bouillon cubes (beef or chicken)
1 potato (3½ oz/100 g)
4 large ripe tomatoes (3 oz/80 g each)
6 cloves garlic
30 basil leaves
Freshly ground black pepper

Soak the beans for 12 hours in 3⅛ quarts (3 L) of cold water; drain, then cook in 2⅛ quarts (2 L) of water with the bouquet garni. Salt the water after 5 minutes of boiling, and simmer for 1 hour, or until tender.

Cut the carrots, turnips, zucchini, onion, and string beans into ⅓-inch (1 cm) cubes. Finely chop the leek and celery stalks. Place the vegetables in a pot with ¼ cup (60 mL) of the oil and ¼ cup (60 mL) of cold water.

Cook over medium heat for 10 minutes, stirring with a wooden spoon until there isn't any more water, but the vegetables have not browned. Cover with 4¼ quarts (4 L) of cold water and add the bouillon cubes. Cook over high heat. Salt the water after 5 minutes of boiling. Dice the potato the same size as the other vegetables and add it to the pot after 20 minutes.

Meanwhile, cut off any stems from the tomatoes and halve the tomatoes horizontally. Squeeze to remove their seeds and juice, then dice them. Peel the garlic cloves and pick the basil leaves from their stems, crush them with a mortar and pestle. Add the diced tomatoes. Crush the mixture to obtain a smooth texture (absent of any seeds).

Drizzle in the remaining oil and mash thoroughly.

Remove the bouquet garni from the beans. Add the beans and their broth to the pot with the cooked vegetables. Bring to a boil. Move the pot off the heat and add the garlic-tomato mixture. Mix well with a wooden spoon. Season with salt and pepper to taste. Be careful not to let the soup come back to a boil if reheated. Serve the soup in a soup terrine brought to the table; the enticing aroma will follow you and all your guests will recognize the delicious soup you're about to serve.

Excerpt from Ma Cuisine du Soleil, *Robert Laffont*

Land and Sea Pairings

The flavors of land and sea collide in both French culinary traditions and chef-created dishes. Here is a list of some of the most delicious combinations of "surf and turf."

François-Régis Gaudry

VEAL ✚ OYSTER

Veal tartare with oysters

One of the most controversial combinations of Parisian gastronomy since 2010. Many of these creations are the crowning achievements of the new generation of chefs, from Shinichi Sato (Passage 53, Paris) to Bertrand Grébaut (Septime, Paris), who have executed them so perfectly as tartares.

SERVES 4

Cut up 9 ounces (250 g) of veal to make a tartare: first thinly slice the meat, then cut it into strips, and finally cut it into small dice. Open 8 oysters and remove them from their shells. Dice them. Peel and finely chop 1 shallot. In a bowl, gently combine the veal, oysters, shallot, a dash of lemon juice, a pinch of fleur de sel sea salt, and a drizzle of olive oil. Serve.

⟶ skip to
Whelk Stands Out!, p. 373

Beef ✚ Anchovies

L'agriade of Saint-Gilloise

Also called *broufade*, *broufado*, or *fricot des barques*, this simmering ancestral specialty from Camargue was a common dish made by boatmen on the Rhône.

SERVES 6

Place 3⅓ pounds (1.5 kg) of beef cheeks or chuck (ideally Camargue bull) cut into ¾-inch (2 cm) slices in a bowl with 6 cloves of peeled and chopped garlic, 2 bay leaves, 2 cloves, 1 pinch of freshly grated nutmeg, and ¼ cup (60 mL) of olive oil. Mix well, then refrigerate to marinate overnight. The next day, preheat the oven to 300°F (150°C). Peel and slice 6 onions. Roughly chop together 20 cornichons, 5¼ ounces (150 g) of capers, and 5¼ ounces (150 g) of anchovies. Combine this mixture with the onions. Add the marinade and ¼ cup (60 mL) of aged wine vinegar, and stir to combine. In a flameproof casserole dish, arrange a layer of the meat, then a layer of the onion mixture with a pinch of black pepper. Repeat these layers until all the ingredients are gone, finishing with a layer of the meat. Do not add salt (the anchovies will take care of that!). Pour in about 1 cup (250 mL) of water. Cover and bake for 4 hours. Serve this delicious stew with Camargue rice. Reheated the next day, this dish will be even better.

Thanks to Marie-Geneviève "Miquette" Delmas, the mother of Laurent Delmas (the movie animator of France Inter), for this delicious recipe.

Oyster ✚ Crépinette

This is a marriage of love, traditionally served around the Arcachon basin and in the Gironde region, especially during year-end holiday celebrations. All it requires is arranging opened oysters and grilled *crépinette* sausages on a tray (*crépinettes* are sausages made of minced meat, such as pork or sometimes poultry or wild game, encased in a membrane, then flattened). In Bordeaux, a gourmet alternates eating a fresh oyster then a hot *crépinette*.

SQUID ✚ BOUDIN

Squid with pig's blood

In the 2010s, Alexandre Gauthier, the brilliant cook at Grenouillère (La Madeleine-sous-Montreuil, Pas-de-Calais), stood out when he created this remarkable combination!

SERVES 4

Slice open the casing of 2 boudins noir (black blood sausages) and press the meat through a strainer to create a pastelike texture. Taste and adjust the seasoning, as needed, and set the meat aside at room temperature. Sort and wash 2 handfuls of lettuce sprouts (arugula, watercress, dandelion, etc.). Make a dressing with olive oil, mustard, and minced shallot, and set this aside. Sauté 4 squid, each weighing between 3 to 4¼ ounces (80 to 120 g), in very hot olive oil until lightly browned on all sides; remove the squid from the heat and cut them into large pieces. Using a spatula, spread the raw boudin paste on a serving platter in a large flat diagonal, about ⅛ inch (3 mm) thick, then arrange the squid on top in sections. Briefly toss the sprouts in the dressing, then pile them loosely on top of the squid. Finish with a few turns of a pepper mill and a drizzle of olive oil. Serve.

The Imaginary Museum of the French Table

The table has been abundantly represented in French art. Our historian, the author of a tome on the subject,* has selected and presented five pieces from different periods.

Patrick Rambourg

Très riches Heures du duc de Berry
(*The Very Rich Hours of Duke de Berry*)
(between 1410 and 1416)
The Limbourg Brothers

This illuminated manuscript depicts the ducal table on the day of wishes and gifts. The nave to the right and the gold china cabinet to the left point to the figure's importance. Before him is the steward in charge of cutting the roasted meat. The servant in blue, not far from the cabinet, is the wine steward, charged with serving the prince. This image shows the sophistication of the medieval table.

Le Déjeuner (*The Luncheon*, 1868)
Claude Monet

The artists of the nineteenth century often depicted well-off families in dining rooms as a way to present the joy of family. In this painting, the mother and child await the arrival of the father. His seat is indicated by the newspaper at the table and by the eggs ready to be eaten. The meal has already been served, which was customary during that time.

La scène des Femmes à table en l'absence de leurs maris (*The Scene of Women at the Table without Their Husbands*, 1636)
Abraham Bosse

This scene, based on an engraving by Abraham Bosse, takes place in a room with a prominent bed. The women converse while eating around a filled table covered with a white cloth. The dining room did not really exist at this time; it emerged gradually only during the seventeenth century and became established during the Enlightenment.

L'Art et la table, Paris, Citadelles & Mazenod, 2016

Armenonville, le soir du Grand Prix de Longchamp (1905)
Henri Gervex

This piece presents a luxurious restaurant in the Bois de Boulogne during a time when Paris was the capital of the arts, fashion, and gastronomy. Renowned since the mid-nineteenth century, it was a gathering place for high society and elegant ladies. Guests came to appreciate food in an antique setting with large windows looking outside.

Table bleue (*Blue Table,* 1963)
Daniel Spoerri

In 1960, Daniel Spoerri turned food and eating habits into the source of performance. The remains of food became works of art. The *Table Bleue* from the Galerie J illustrates the end of a meal with dirty plates, empty bottles, and used cutlery. The objects are glued to a wood panel or onto a table top, then exhibited as a "tableau piège" ("snare picture").

La Famille Pâte à Choux

From the time it was called *pâte à Poplin* under Catherine de Médicis to today's well-known croquembouche made of colored and stacked cream puffs, pâte à choux (cream puff dough) has left its mark throughout the centuries in French pastry.

Elvira Masson

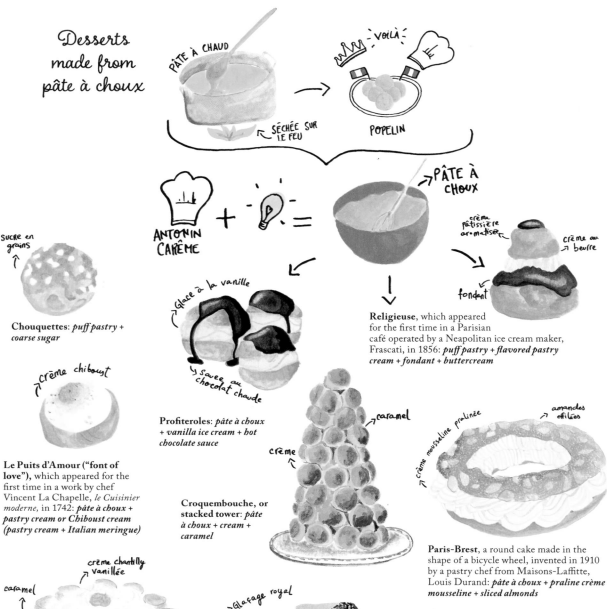

Desserts made from pâte à choux

PÂTE À CHAUD — SÉCHÉE SUR LE FEU — POPELIN — VOILÀ

ANTONIN CARÊME + 💡 = PÂTE À CHOUX

Chouquettes: *puff pastry + coarse sugar* — sucre en grains

Le Puits d'Amour ("font of love"), which appeared for the first time in a work by chef Vincent La Chapelle, *le Cuisinier moderne,* in 1742: *pâte à choux + pastry cream or Chiboust cream (pastry cream + Italian meringue)* — crème chiboust

Profiteroles: *pâte à choux + vanilla ice cream + hot chocolate sauce* — Glace à la vanille — Sauce au chocolat chaude

Croquembouche, or stacked tower: *pâte à choux + cream + caramel* — caramel — crème

Religieuse, which appeared for the first time in a Parisian café operated by a Neapolitan ice cream maker, Frascati, in 1856: *puff pastry + flavored pastry cream + fondant + buttercream* — crème pâtissière aromatisée — crème au beurre — fondant

Paris-Brest, a round cake made in the shape of a bicycle wheel, invented in 1910 by a pastry chef from Maisons-Laffitte, Louis Durand: *pâte à choux + praline crème mousseline + sliced almonds* — crème mousseline pralinée — amandes effilées

The Saint-Honoré, created around 1850 by the Chiboust pastry chop at the Palais-Royal in Paris: *pâte à choux + puff pastry (brisée or sablé) + vanilla pastry cream + caramel + vanilla whipped cream or Chiboust cream* — crème chantilly vanillée — caramel — pâte feuilletée — crème pâtissière à la vanille

Salambo, or "acorn" pastry, invented in 1890 after an opera by Reyer, adapted from Flaubert's novel, *Salammbô*: *pâte à choux + pastry cream + royal icing* — Glaçage royal — crème pâtissière

Polka: *pâte brisée (flaky pastry) + pâte à choux + pastry cream* — crème pâtissière — pâte brisée

Pont-neuf: *pâte brisée (flaky pastry) + pâte à choux + pastry cream* — pâte brisée — crème pâtissière

The éclair: *a long piped shell of pâte à choux + flavored pastry cream + fondant icing* — Fondant — crème pâtissière aromatisée

Noix Charentaise: *pâte à choux + buttercream + walnut praline + dark chocolate icing + a piece of walnut* — cerneau de noix — crème au beurre — glaçage au chocolat noir — praliné aux noix

Le Divorcé: *pâte à choux + chocolate pastry cream and coffee pastry cream* — crème pâtissière au chocolat — crème pâtissière au café

Pets de nonne, created during the fifteenth and sixteenth centuries: *fried pâte à choux* — pâte à choux frite

---

PÂTE À CHOUX
by Christophe Michalak

PREPARATION TIME: 20 MINUTES
COOKING TIME: 25 MINUTES
MAKES ABOUT 12 CREAM PUFFS

¼ cup plus 1 tablespoon plus ½ teaspoon (75 g) water
¼ cup plus 1 tablespoon (75 g) whole milk
¾ teaspoon (3 g) superfine sugar
½ teaspoon (3 g) salt
4 tablespoons plus 1¾ teaspoons (65 g) unsalted butter
¾ cup plus 1 tablespoon (80 g) all-purpose flour
5⅛ ounces (145 g) whole egg (about 3 large eggs)

Preheat the oven to 400°F (210°C). Combine the water, milk, sugar, salt, and butter in a saucepan and bring to a boil. Add the flour all at once and stir until a smooth paste is achieved. The dough will detach from the sides of the pan when it is stirred. Transfer the dough to a bowl and stir in the eggs one at a time with a wooden spoon until the dough forms a fairly firm point, similar to a bird's beak, when lifted with the spoon. Fit a pastry bag with a plain piping tube of the desired width and pipe the dough onto a lined baking sheet in the shape and size of your choice. Place in the oven, then immediately turn off the oven and bake for 10 minutes. Set the oven temperature to 300°F (150°C) and continue baking for another 25 minutes.

Key Dates

Late eighteenth to early nineteenth centuries, chef Antonin Carême modernizes pâte à choux and invents the croquembouche; profiteroles are created as cream puffs filled with pastry cream and topped with chocolate sauce; future croquembouches (1860) are cream puffs filled with pastry cream or whipped cream. Duchesses (elongated pâte à choux shells rolled in almonds) evolve into the éclairs we know today.

skip to
Cakes of Yesteryear Rise Once Again, p. 52

KIDNEYS VS SWEETBREADS

Each of these two types of organ meats taken from veal has its fans. Let's match them up to compare them.
Charles Patin O'Coohoon

● KIDNEYS

What: calf's kidney
From where: from the back of the abdomen in the lower-back area
In literature: "She ate yesterday, alone, half the meal, I saw it—the piece of kidney, so fat, so shiny, for her only—a sin, a real sin." *Joie* by George Bernanos, 1929
Average weight: 1⅛ pounds (500 g)
Preparation: remove the surrounding clear membrane, the nerves, and the fat
Cooking: cut up and grilled on skewers or panfried in browned butter
Pairing: a mustard sauce, or a Madeira sauce
Texture: plump with a slight resistance. Delicious paired with rosé
Flavor: once devoid of its urine smell (after scalding them), kidneys have a delicate flavor
Recycling: the fat from the cooked kidneys is collected. Since the eighth century, soup has been made using fat from the kidneys of Normande calves
Virtues: rich in iron
Per 3½ ounces (100 g), 163 cal, 1 ounce (26 g) of protein

● SWEETBREADS

What: the thymus glands
From where: a gland found at the front of the chest in front of the trachea, and which disappears in the adult animal
In literature: "Finely slice 4 veal sweetbreads previously sautéed in water in which a little lemon is added. Place them in a medium hot oven for 40 minutes, basting them frequently. Add 1 dl [⅓ cup plus 1 tablespoon/100 mL] heavy cream off the heat. Serve with egg whites beaten to very stiff peaks." Veal sweetbreads "my way," extract from George Perec's *Penser Classer*
Average weight: 10½ ounces (300 g)
Preparation: soak for 5 hours in cold water, then boil, drain, and pat dry before removing the filaments
Cooking: braised in a stir-fry pan or fried in slices
Pairing: in a *vol-au-vent*, with morel mushrooms
Texture: ultrasoft, supple, and melting
Flavor: delicate and very refined
Recycling: fry the sweetbreads in butter, onions, and 2 tablespoons (30 mL) of wine; strain to obtain a delicious sauce
Virtues: they contain few saturated fats. It is the least fatty organ, second only to tripe. It is rich in vitamins and minerals
Per 3½ ounces (100 g), 125 cal, ¾ ounce (22 g) of protein

The middle ground
— LA BEUCHELLE TOURANGELLE —

The recipe for this stew of blanched kidneys and sweetbreads, simmered with herbs and spices, mushrooms, and cream, was standardized by chef Édouard Nignon.

Once the sweetbreads are prepped, dice 2 kidneys, sauté them, then flambé them in cognac. Thinly slice the sweetbreads and sauté them in butter. Add some cognac, flambé, then add ⅔ cup (150 mL) of cream, and season with salt and pepper. In a separate pan, sauté 1¾ ounces (50 g) morel mushrooms. Combine the three preparations, and serve immediately.

skip to
Édouard Nignon, p. 344

The Kings of Pain d'Épices

Flour, honey, spices—it is this trio of ingredients that makes the texture and flavor of *pain d'épices* so unique and special.
Marielle Gaudry

A PROSPEROUS TEDDY BEAR?

The mere mention of a "Youpla Boum," or of the name *Prosper*, evokes the image of the brand Vandamme, whose teddy bear mascot named Prosper was launched in 1980 as part of the "king of pain d'épices" campaign to reinvigorate sales of the commercially produced version of pain d'épices, which was based on rye flour and produced in the Unimel factory in Besançon. This version was a precut rectangular loaf with a sticky and compact crust, and one that children loved . . .

ITS SECRETS

Should it be spelled *pain d'*épices or *pain d'*épice? Both spellings are allowed. The different spellings indicate if the recipe contains one or more spices (cinnamon, anise, nutmeg, ginger, clove, etc.). The basic batter is a mixture of flour, water, and honey, which rests from 3 weeks to 6 months before it's completed by adding the spices—a traditional artisanal manufacturing process that is difficult to reproduce at home. The name "pure honey" (*pur miel*) indicates that the recipe uses only honey as a sweetener, as opposed to "with honey" (*au miel*), which means it contains honey and other sugars. To have the right to use the name "pain d'épices," the recipe must contain at least 50 percent honey.

Pain d'épices is sold throughout Dijon under the name *nonnette*, and also found in the Reims and Lyon regions as well as Lorraine. This particular cake was originally made in convents by nuns, hence its name, and is a round cake topped with a glaze and traditionally filled with orange jam.

In Alsace, pain d'épices takes the form of little characters decorated with a colored glaze, called *Mannele*. They are traditionally an offering for Saint Nicholas Day.

— THE RÉMOISE — RECIPE
by Éric Sontag*

PREPARATION TIME: 10 MINUTES
RESTING TIME: 24 HOURS
COOKING TIME: 30 TO 45 MINUTES
MAKES 1 RECTANGULAR LOAF

2⅛ ounces (60 g) chestnut honey
2 tablespoons plus 1¼ teaspoons (30 g) sugar
2 tablespoons (30 g) butter
⅛ ounce (2.5 g) spice mix (cinnamon, anise, nutmeg)
⅓ cup (80 mL) water
1 tablespoon plus
1 teaspoon (20 mL) pastis
1 ounce (30 g) candied oranges, finely chopped
1 ounce (30 g) candied lemons, finely chopped
1 cup plus 1 tablespoon plus 1 teaspoon (108 g) all-purpose flour
2¼ teaspoons (9 g) baking powder

Preheat the oven to 350°F (180°C). In a saucepan, melt the honey, sugar, and butter. Stir in the spices. Let cool. Add the water, pastis, and candied fruits to the cooled mixture. Using a whisk, mix the flour and baking powder, then add to the cooled mixture. Fill a greased loaf pan three-quarters full with the batter. Bake for 30 to 45 minutes, or until the top is darkened.

*Baker-pastry chef at L'Atelier d'Eric, 32, rue de Mars, 51100 Reims

skip to
French Honey, p. 378

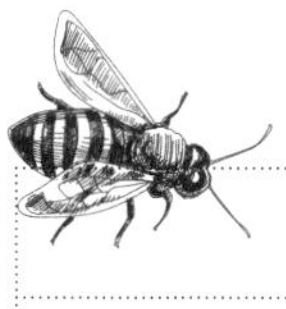

The Pain d'Épices Capitals

	REIMS	DIJON	GERTWILLER
Flour	rye	wheat	wheat
Honey	acacia	acacia	chestnut
Top Stores	Fossier (1756)	Mulot & Petitjean (1796)	Fortwenger (1768) Lips (1806)

Although it no longer has a factory today, **Vercel-Villedieule-Camp** (Doubs) also produces its own traditional pain d'épices made from mountain or fir-tree honey, with anise for its only spice, in its version dating back to the thirteenth century.

Alain Senderens

This hero of Nouvelle Cuisine passed away in 2017. This is a portrait of a visionary and iconoclastic three-star chef.
François-Régis Gaudry

AN EXPERT ON PAIRING FOOD AND WINE

The chef Michel Guérard sat down at Alain Senderens's restaurant in the late 1960s. He was disappointed with the wines. Vexed, Senderens considered the matter until a meeting in the 1980s with Jacques Puisais, an influential oenologist, changed everything. Starting in 1987, the Lucas Carton chef became the first to propose a menu along with suggestions for wine by the glass for each dish. His audacious coupling of Touraine goat cheese and Vouvray Sec—in other words, the first time a white wine was introduced with cheese—was deemed scandalous at the time. Today, it's a classic.

DUCK APICIUS

In 1985, Jean-François Revel (former editor-in-chief at *L'Express*) and Claude Imbert (founder of *Le Point*), both members of the Club des Cent, asked Senderens to prepare a Roman menu of influence. The chef dove into ancient archives and created this reinterpretation of a recipe invented by Apicius, Emperor Tiberius's official cook. A whole duck is poached in a vegetable bouillon with caraway, browned over high heat, then coated with honey and spices and served with an apple-quince compote with saffron and a mint-date purée. The dish established a worldwide reputation in just a few months . . .

HIS FAMOUS STUDENTS

Alain Passard: the three-star chef on Rue de Varenne (Paris 7th) is closely tied to his mentor, whom he still called "chef" more than twenty years after buying L'Archestrate from him, which he renamed L'Arpège.
Jérôme Banctel: he was Senderens's executive chef from 2006 to 2013. Alain Senderens considered him a son. But also: **Dominique le Stanc** (La Merenda in Nice), **Christian le Squer** (George V in Paris), **Frédéric Robert** (La Grande Cascade in Paris), **Patrick Jeffroy** (Hôtel de Carantec in the Finistère), **Bertrand Guéneron** (Au Bascou in Paris), **Jérôme Banctel** (La Réserve in Paris), **Dimitri Droisneau** (La Villa Madie in Cassis), **Alain Solivérès** (Taillevent in Paris).

skip to
The Club des Cent, p. 240; Gault & Millau guide, nouvelle cuisine, p. 206

Respected authority of Nouvelle Cuisine
1939–2017

HIS KEY DATES

December 2, 1939
born in Hyères (Var)

1962: joins La Tour d'Argent (Paris 5th)

1978: third star for L'Archestrate (Paris 7th)

1985: purchases Le Lucas Carton (Paris 8th)

2005: surrenders the three Michelin stars. The Lucas Carton is renamed the Senderens.

June 25, 2017
dies in Saint-Setiers (Corrèze)

★

TRAVELS TO CHINA

Upon his return from a trip to China in the late 1970s, Senderens was the first to introduce soy sauce into French cuisine. He invented Salmon Shizuo, a revolutionary dish with beurre blanc flavored with soy sauce.

★

DUCK APICIUS 2010 VERSION

COOKING TIME: 20 MINUTES
RESTING TIME: 18 HOURS
SERVES 4

For the Apicius spice blend
2 tablespoons (10 g) coriander seeds
2 tablespoons (20 g) coarse-ground peppercorns
3 tablespoons (7 g) dried oregano
1½ teaspoons (4 g) caraway seeds

1 duckling (4¾ lb/2.2 kg)

4¼ cups (1 L) clarified chicken stock
¼ cup (80 g) mountain or *toutes fleurs* ("all-flower") honey
¾ cup plus 1 tablespoon (200 mL) dry white wine
3 Granny Smith apples
¼ cup (50 g) sugar
1 pinch (2 g) saffron, plus a few threads for garnish
12 fresh Tunisian dates
1 small bunch fresh mint

CREATED IN **1981**

Combine all the spices for the Apicius spice blend. Cut up the duck and keep only the carcass with the two breast fillets attached. Make a broth using the clarified chicken broth and a few pinches of the spice blend. Bring to a boil in a saucepan. Immerse the duckling carcass into the broth, turn off the heat, then let the duck poach for 15 minutes. Combine the honey, wine, and the remaining spice blend. Coat and marinate the duck for 12 to 18 hours in this mixture. After this time, pat the duck to remove any excess marinade; reserve the marinade. Cook the duck in a very hot skillet until browned on all sides. Preheat the oven to 350°F (180°C) and roast the duck in the oven for 8 minutes. Meanwhile, peel and quarter the apples, and cook them in a syrup made of 4 cups (1 L) of water, the sugar, and the saffron. Remove the skin from the dates (immerse them in boiling water for 1 minute, then peel them), then remove the pits. Fill the dates with fresh mint leaves. Remove the duck from the oven. Brush it with the reserved marinade. Slice the duck breasts and serve them with the dates decorated with a mint leaf and the apple quarters garnished with a thread of saffron.
Suggested wine: a sweet white wine

FOIE GRAS OF LANDES DUCK WITH STEAMED CABBAGE

8¾ ounces (4 kg) green cabbage
1⅓ pounds (600 g) duck foie gras (preferably from Landes)
⅛ ounce (4 g) sel de Guérande sea salt
⅛ ounce (4 g) coarsely ground white peppercorns

Separate all the cabbage leaves and immerse them in boiling water for 2 minutes. Drain on a dry cloth.

Thinly slice the foie gras into 2½-ounce (70 g) slices. Season with the salt and pepper, then wrap each slice in a cabbage leaf. Steam for 4 minutes.

Arrange on very hot plates (2 pieces per person).

BRITTANY LOBSTER WITH VANILLA

4 female lobsters (each weighing 1¼ lb/550 g)
2 Madagascar vanilla beans
3 ounces (80 g) shallots, peeled and chopped
⅓ cup plus 1 tablespoon (100 mL) Champagne
1¼ cups (300 mL) heavy cream
2½ ounces (70 g) spinach sprouts
1¾ ounces (50 g) sorrel
1¾ ounces (50 g) rice vermicelli
½ lemon
7 tablespoons (100 g) unsalted butter
¼ ounce (6 g) pickled ginger
3 tablespoons plus 1 teaspoon (50 mL) olive oil

Cook the lobsters
Steam the lobsters for 5 minutes, then let them cool. Slice the tails lengthwise in half and keep the bodies. Empty the body cavities, then cut off and reserve the heads.

Prepare the sauce
Split the vanilla beans and scrape out the seeds (keep the empty pods). Cook the shallots and vanilla seeds together until the shallot is softened. Deglaze with the Champagne, then cook until the liquid is slightly reduced. Add the cream and cook for 15 minutes, or until thickened; strain. Remove the spinach and sorrel leaves from the stems and wash the leaves. Cook the vermicelli in boiling water, then let cool. Remove the rind from the lemon, then blanch the rinds twice in boiling water, starting with cold water.

Assemble and finish
Reheat the lobster pieces. Reheat the vermicelli in one-fourth of the sauce with a little lemon juice and pickled ginger. Reheat the remaining sauce, whisk in the butter, and add the remaining juice from the lemon. Heat the oil in a skillet and very lightly sauté the spinach and sorrel. Drain on paper towels.

Spoon the sauce onto serving plates into a 4-inch (10 cm) circle. Place the vermicelli and lobster tails on top, the claws in the middle, then the spinach and sorrel around the edge. Using the remainder of the sauce, create a foam (using an immersion blender or nitrous oxide canister). Use the lobster heads and empty vanilla bean pods as additional decoration, if desired.

These recipes have been rewritten by Jérôme Banctel, former executive chef of Alain Senderens, and photographed by Julie Limont.

Endangered Hors d'Oeuvre

Deposed by the French "apéro" and "entrée" (appetizer), the hors d'oeuvre has been somewhat forgotten.
What if we were to revive the great classics of Sunday lunch? Back to the future . . .

Marie-Laure Fréchet

A SHORT HISTORY

In architecture, it's an outbuilding. In cooking, starting in the seventeenth century, the word *hors d'oeuvre* described dishes served especially to relieve the hunger of guests as they waited for dishes worthy of appearing on the menu. There were also "assiettes volantes" (flying saucers), which designated what came before the soup and fish. Until the beginning of the twentieth century, food critics, with Ali Bab at the fore, agreed that "hors d'oeuvre are insignificant dishes," and that one "could easily eliminate them without in any manner disturbing the order of menus." Auguste Escoffier was offended by their existence, which he called "nonsense" and derided for introducing an excess of flavor to the palate. In *Livre de la ménagère*, Urbain Dubois is more concerned about the "stomach's hygiene" and recommends "dishes that are light and subtle in taste instead because the mouth is still fresh."

1950: THE GOLDEN AGE

On the flip side of culinary history, during the 1950s, hors d'oeuvres were at their peak. They were exclusively served at lunch, as was recommended by *L'Art culinaire moderne*, or at dinners that did not include a soup course. The book offers more than one hundred fifty extremely codified recipes and distinguishes between hot hors d'oeuvres and cold, salads and pickled fish, croustades and cassolettes, timbales and croquettes: "Hors d'oeuvre must be handsome and tasty, with few ingredients. They must be freshly prepared, artistically presented and stylishly served."

skip to

Oeuf Mayonnaise, p. 75;
Restaurants Routiers, p. 44;
Raymond Oliver, p. 359

Cooking at Home

In the 1960s, housewives took off their aprons. They would no longer be breading croquettes after work. Hors d'oeuvres became simpler. Three cheers for deviled eggs, celery rémoulade, and grated carrots. For the French, that might bring up bad memories of school lunches with beet salads and a half a grapefruit . . . At grand Sunday tables, hors d'oeuvres held down the fort in France until the 1980s, when, under the influence of recipe cards and the democratization of restaurants, the dishes, a symbol of homemade cooking, were relegated instead to bistros, roadside restaurants, and delicatessens, ousted by more creative appetizers.

RAVIER REVIVAL

The *ravier* is specially dedicated to the hors d'oeuvre, and more specifically to the radish. Etymologically, it is related to *raves*, a type of radish in French. It was once a staple in French homes and on wedding registries. This small, oblong, porcelain dish has now been relegated to a box in the attic. You can hunt for them in secondhand stores.

THE CANAPÉ

The canapé gets its name from its cushionlike shape (in French, "canapé" means sofa). It once was considered an hors d'oeuvre but then was relegated to being served with the aperitif in the 1970s, and was later replaced by mass-market crackers and verrines. It is still a staple at cocktail parties. The great classics: smoked salmon, lumpfish roe, and asparagus spears on white bread cut into squares or triangles.

GREEK MUSHROOMS
Recipe by Raymond Oliver

COOKING TIME: 30 MINUTES
SERVES 4

1⅛ pounds (500 g) white button mushrooms (choose very small ones)
¼ cup (60 mL) flavorless cooking oil
Zest of 1 lemon
1 sprig thyme
2 bay leaves

A few coriander seeds
3⅛ cups (¾ L) white wine
¼ cup (60 mL) tomato paste
Salt and freshly ground black pepper

Clean the mushrooms and keep them whole, with their stems. In a flameproof casserole dish, heat the

oil. Add the mushrooms, lemon zest, herbs, coriander seeds, wine, and tomato paste. Season with salt and pepper. Cook for about 30 minutes over medium heat, uncovered. The sauce should coat the mushrooms. Remove from the heat and let cool. Enjoy!

Crab or Shrimp Avocado Cocktail

The idea: half an avocado, with crumbled crab or whole shrimp arranged in the center, and a cocktail sauce (mayonnaise, tomato sauce, cognac or whiskey, Tabasco). This dish provided a hint of exoticism in the mid-seventies. The empty avocado hulls were even used for serving.

Serve it again? yes, if served for dinner to a relative coming from the countryside, before an evening at home watching old family slides.

Celery Rémoulade

The idea: this julienne of raw celery root gets its name from its rémoulade sauce dressing, which is a mustard-mayonnaise.

Serve it again? yes, with a perfectly executed homemade mayonnaise. And without necessarily adding grated carrots, like grandma used to do.

Mushrooms à la Grecque (Greek Mushrooms)

The idea: the term *à la grecque* refers to a technique for preparing vegetables in which they are cooked in aromatics and served cold. A must for all salad bars.

Serve it again? perhaps, if making this bygone dish using the recipe by Raymond Oliver (shown opposite), or purchasing it premade from a fine food store.

Macedonian Ham

The idea: a slice of pressed white ham wrapped around a vegetable Macedonia (a mixture of diced vegetables) with mayonnaise. It's also called a *cornet de jambon à la russe* (Russian-style ham wrap), as is the salad of the same name (invented by Belgian chef Lucien Olivier in the 1860s for a Moscow restaurant).

Serve it again? yes, and you can make a homemade Macedonia (and a homemade mayonnaise, obviously), even if it takes a little time. Be sure to find a good cooked ham, however.

Cantaloupe and Port

The idea: since ancient times, people have suggested drinking a sweet wine with cantaloupe to help digest the cantaloupe better. Now you know how these two ingredients came together.

Serve it again? yes, as recommended by Alexandre Dumas, who was fond of cantaloupe: this course is to be enjoyed between cheese and dessert, seasoned with salt and pepper. Be sure to drink the port.

Oeuf Mimosa (Deviled Egg)

The idea: not to be confused with the *oeuf mayonnaise*, which the oeuf mimosa has dethroned. The hard-boiled egg is cut in half and its yolk is scooped out and mixed with mayonnaise, then spooned back into the empty egg white. It is then sprinkled with another egg yolk that has been finely crumbled, making it resemble the mimosa flower.

Serve it again? yes, because it's a little less filling than the *oeuf mayonnaise*, though less iconic.

Leeks in Vinaigrette

The idea: young leeks, trimmed of their rough green leaves, tied together and slightly cooked in simmering salted water, between 8 and 15 minutes depending on their size, then seasoned with an herb vinaigrette.

Serve it again? it's best not to change this classic bistro dish.

Radishes with Butter

The idea: it would be difficult to find a dish that is any simpler: radishes eaten with flaky salt and a good-quality butter, which tempers their heat.

Serve it again? definitely! With some slices of *sauciflard* sausages as a bonus.

Tomato Salad

The idea: tomatoes are peeled and thinly sliced, then seasoned with vinaigrette, garlic, and parsley. Dethroned in the 1990s by the caprese salad (thin slices of mozzarella and tomato).

Serve it again? yes, if using perfectly ripened heirloom tomatoes, enhanced with a drizzle of good olive oil.

Sardines in Oil

The idea: sardines are arranged in a round shallow dish, accompanied by slices of fluted lemons. The hors d'oeuvre of the pressed-for-time housewife.

Serve it again? yes, in their vintage tins.

The Brotherhoods of French Gastronomy

With long dresses, proud banners, and absolute devotion, these brotherhoods wear their monomaniac gourmandise loud and clear. From *chouquettes* to *tête de veau*, here is a *tour de France* of these gastronomic groups.

Charles Patin O'Coohoon

UNIVERSAL ACADEMY OF TÊTE DE VEAU
The item: calf's head
Headquarters: Pessac (Gironde)
Founded: 1992

BROTHERHOOD OF THE KNIGHTS OF CAMEMBERT
The item: cow's-milk cheese with raw milk and flowery crust
Headquarters: Vimotiers (Orne)
Founded: 1985

BROTHERHOOD OF THE CÈPE MUSHROOM
The item: the famous cèpe (porcini) mushrooms
Headquarters: Saint-Saud-Lacoussière (Dordogne)
Founded: 1996

BROTHERHOOD OF THE BLUE SOLAIZE LEEK
The item: the blue leek
Headquarters: Solaize (Rhône)
Founded: 1995

BROTHERHOOD OF PINK GARLIC FROM LAUTREC
The item: slightly pink garlic (cluster)
Headquarters: Lautrec (Tarn)
Founded: 2000

BROTHERHOOD OF THE CACASSE À CUL NU
The item: an iconic dish of potatoes and onions
Headquarters: Aiglemont (Ardennes)
Founded: 2001

BROTHERHOOD OF THE TRICANDILLE
The item: the dish *tricandille* (a Bordelaise specialty with pork intestines)
Headquarters: Blanquefort (Gironde)
Founded: 2004

BROTHERHOOD OF THE ROSCOFF ONION
The item: the pink onion
Headquarters: Roscoff (Finistère)
Founded: 2010

BROTHERHOOD OF THE BLACK DIAMOND
The item: the *Tuber melanosporum* (black truffle)
Headquarters: Richerenches (Vaucluse)
Founded: 1982

BROTHERHOOD OF THE TEURGOULE
The item: a rice pudding flavored with cinnamon and cooked for about 5 hours
Headquarters: Dozulé (Calvados)
Founded: 1978

BROTHERHOOD OF THE KNIGHTS OF SARTHOISES RILLETTES
The item: a preparation of pork cooked in fat
Headquarters: Mamers (Sarthe)
Founded: 1968

BROTHERHOOD OF THE KNIGHTS OF THE ORDER OF THE CAVAILLON MELON
The item: the melon (southern France)
Headquarters: Cavaillon (Vaucluse)
Founded: 1988

BROTHERHOOD OF FROG-THIGH EATERS
The item: the frog
Headquarters: Vittel (Vosges)
Founded: 1972

BROTHERHOOD OF THE SAINT-NICOLAS-DE-PORT POTÉE PORTOISE
The item: *potée portoise* (a local port stew)
Headquarters: Saint-Nicolas-de-Port (Meurthe-et-Moselle)
Founded: 1975

BROTHERHOOD OF THE COASTAL HERRING
The item: herring
Headquarters: Berck-sur-Mer (Pas-de-Calais)
Founded: 1991

THE LODGE DU CLOS MONTMARTRE
The item: wine made on Montmartre
Headquarters: Paris
Founded: 1983

BROTHERHOOD OF THE TRUE FLAMEKUECHE
The item: an Alsatian tart cooked over a fire
Headquarters: Saessolsheim (Bas-Rhin)
Founded: 1979

THE LODGE OF SAINTEMAURE-DE-TOURAINE CHEESE
The item: raw goat's-milk cheese from Sainte-Maure-de-Touraine
Headquarters: Sainte-Maure-de-Touraine (Indre-et-Loire)
Founded: 1972

BROTHERHOOD OF PORK LIVER TERRINE
The item: pork liver terrine
Headquarters: Cousolre (North)
Founded: 1986

BROTHERHOOD OF THE ARIÈGE SNAIL
The item: a little gray snail
Headquarters: La Tour du Crieu (Ariège)
Founded: 2001

THE MERRYMAKING BROTHERHOOD OF THE BOUTIFARRE DU CONFLENT EATERS
The item: Catalan boudin (blood sausage)
Headquarters: Prades (Pyrénées-Orientales)
Founded: 2009

BROTHERHOOD OF THE AMIÉNOISE PICARDE FICELLE
The item: a baked crêpe filled with ham and mushrooms
Headquarters: Amiens (Somme)
Founded: 2013

BROTHERHOOD OF THE KNIGHTS OF THE ANDOUILLE EATERS
The item: andouillette from Jargeau
Headquarters: Jargeau (Loiret)
Founded: 1971

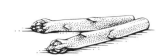

BROTHERHOOD OF ASPARAGUS FROM BLAYE
The item: white asparagus
Headquarters: Reignac (Gironde)
Founded: 1973

BROTHERHOOD OF THE GARBURE BIGOURDANE
The item: a soup of cabbage, cassoulet (tarbais) beans, and cured ham
Headquarters: Argelès-Gazost (Pyrénées-Orientales)
Founded: 1997

BROTHERHOOD OF PÂTÉ LORRAIN
The item: pâté in a flaky crust
Headquarters: Chatenois (Bas-Rhin)
Founded: 1990

BROTHERHOOD OF THE KNIGHTS OF THE WINE TASTERS
The item: Burgundy wines
Headquarters: Vougeot (Côte-d'Or)
Founded: 1934

BROTHERHOOD OF THE ITXASSOU CHERRY
The item: the black cherry of Pays Basque
Headquarters: Itxassou (Pyrénées-Atlantiques)
Founded: 2007

BROTHERHOOD OF POTATO PÂTÉ
The item: a pastry pie with potatoes and crème fraîche
Headquarters: Montmarault (Allier)
Founded: 2004

BROTHERHOOD OF FIADONE
The item: a Corsican cake made with brocciu cheese
Headquarters: Ajaccio (Corse-du-Sud)
Founded: 2013

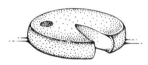

BROTHERHOOD OF REBLOCHON
The item: a soft, raw cow's-milk cheese
Headquarters: Thônes (Haute-Savoie)
Founded: 1994

BROTHERHOOD OF THE MANGE-TRIPES
The item: tripe, made in the Alésian style
Headquarters: Alès (Gard)
Founded: 1999

BROTHERHOOD OF THE COMPAGNONS DE LA BRÉJAUDE
The item: a soup from Limousin with potatoes and bacon
Headquarters: Saint-Junien (Haute-Vienne)
Founded: 1989

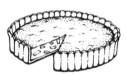

BROTHERHOOD OF THE QUICHE LORRAINE
The item: quiche lorraine
Headquarters: Dombasle (Meurthe-et-Moselle)
Founded: 2015

BROTHERHOOD OF THE ADMIRERS OF THE MARENNES-OLÉRON OYSTERS
The item: oysters from the world-famous oyster bed of Marennes-Oléron
Headquarters: Marennes (Charente-Maritime)
Founded: 1954

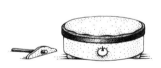

THE BROTHERHOOD OF THE PIPERIA GALETTE
The item: the buckwheat galette
Headquarters: Pipriac (Ille-et-Vilaine)
Founded: 1998

BROTHERHOOD OF THE SAULXURONNE-SUR-MOSELOTTE RASPBERRY
The item: the raspberry
Headquarters: Saulxures-sur-Moselotte (Vosges)
Founded: 1975

BROTHERHOOD OF THE VOUTEZAC PEACH TASTERS
The item: the peach
Headquarters: Voutezac (Corrèze)
Founded: 2008

BROTHERHOOD OF THE ROYAL VIN JAUNE
The item: the white wine of Jura
Headquarters: Arbois (Jura)
Founded: 1989

BROTHERHOOD OF PHEASANT FARMING
The item: pheasant terrine
Headquarters: Sully-sur-Loire (Loiret)
Founded: 1987

BROTHERHOOD OF THE BAZONCOURT HAM
The item: grilled pig shank
Headquarters: Bazoncourt (Moselle)
Founded: 1985

BROTHERHOOD OF THE MASTER CHOUQUETTE MAKERS OF GÂTINAIS
The item: the *chouquette* (cream puffs studded with sugar)
Headquarters: Ouzouer-des-Champs (Loiret)
Founded: 1999

BROTHERHOOD OF THE HOUDAN HEN AND HOUDAN PÂTÉ
The item: a breed of chicken from Houdan
Headquarters: Havelu (Eure-et-Loir)
Founded: 2016

BROTHERHOOD OF THE ARCONSAT CABBAGE SAUSAGE
The item: cabbage sausage
Headquarters: Arconsat (Puy-de-Dôme)
Founded: 2000

Insects in French Food

Common during ancient times, eating insects is no longer France's custom. The main reason? During the fourth century, Jerome, the father of the Catholic Church and the official translator of the Bible, notably attributed the decline of Rome to the appetite for larvae and wood-eating insects among its prominent citizens. Such food then became the symbol of rot. Nevertheless, the French remained entomophagous for a long time.

Marie-Amal Bizalion

WHICH INSECTS ARE ON THE MENU?

Some French people still delighted in them until the beginning of the twentieth century. Here's a short inventory of flying, climbing, furry, and sticky delicacies, based on reliable sources.

Bumblebees: in the first part of the nineteenth century, the anatomist Pierre-André Latreille described the consumption of these members of the Apidae family. According to him, they were "much loved by children who took their lives in order to suck on the honey inside their bodies." In Georges Cuvier, *Le règne animal distribué d'après son organisation,* volume III, p. 525 (1817).

Spiders: they were the guilty pleasure of Lalande, the astronomer (1732–1807), as the French writer Étienne-Léon de Lamothe-Langon recounts.

"I saw him place his hand into his snuffbox or candy box: he took out something that I could not make out. He raised it to his mouth, placed it on his lip and began to suck on it with such sensual delight that it seemed performed. Monsieur de Courchamps, my neighbor, noticing my curiosity, leaned toward my ear: 'They're spiders,' he said. 'Spiders!'

I cried rather loudly, and in a manner so as to be heard. 'Listen! Why not, sir,' the astronomer replied, 'they have a delicate taste that resembles strawberry and artichoke; I like them very much and invite you to share in my feast, if your heart so desires.'" *Mémoires et souvenirs d'un pair de France*, volume III, p. 120 (1840).

Grasshoppers: during the American Revolutionary War, Colonel Nathaniel Freeman—the author's father—was concerned about the odd behavior of French troops who were encamped separately from Americans.

"Perceiving that they had kindled numerous fires in the adjoining fields, and were running about in strange disorder, Maj. Osgood and himself [Nathaniel Freeman], accompanied by Gen. Washington and other officers, mounted horses and rode to the encampment. It was found that the Frenchmen were enjoying rare sport in a campaign against the grasshoppers, which were unusually numerous at that time. These insects, as soon as captured, were impaled upon a sharpened stick or fork and held for a moment over the fire and then eaten with great gusto. The fires were furnished with fuel of deposits from cattle in the fields, made by the excessive heat and drought of the autumn sufficiently dry and combustible." Frederick Freeman, *The History of Cape Cod*, volume I, p. 524 (1858).

Beetle larvae: they were nicknamed "white worms" in *La Gazette des campagnes* (1870). The lawyer Henry Miot even offered a high-protein recipe.

"Roll the white worms, which are oily and short, in flour mixed with bread crumbs, salt and pepper, then wrap them in parchment with liberal amounts of butter; place within hot coals; cook for twenty minutes."

Beetles: on February 12, 1878, Achille Testelin, a Nord senator in France, described an original specialty before the Senate. What's more, it's the only recipe published to this day in the *Journal officiel de la République française.*

"Take beetles, grind them, and toss them in a sieve. If you'd like to make a light soup, pour water on top. If possible and if you would like to make a fatty soup, add bouillon. It has a delicious taste, appreciated by gourmets." In Bruno Fuligni's *Les gastronomes de l'extrême*, Éditions du Trésor (2015), the author specifies: "The writer Catulle Mendès, during that same period, preferred sucking them up raw once the anterior wings and legs had been removed. He found that they had the slight taste of unsalted chicken."

Today in France . . .

In Réunion, mason wasp larvae (*Polistes hebraeus*) are cherished. They are eaten fried or stewed in a ragout of spicy tomato and ginger.

---

skip to
Strange Game, p. 99

Who's Eating Whom?

Humans fond of insects are entomophagous. Whereas animals are insectivores.

Everyone's entomophagous!

Did you think the custom only dated back to tribes long ago? Everyone in France eats insects, most often without knowing it. Overall, 1⅛ pounds (500 g) per year and per capita. Which ones?

Mealworms, who love cereal.
Carminic acid produced by the scale insect, called E120, which is the dye used for merguez sausages, sodas, and more.
Maggots, which produce the Corsican sheep's-milk cheese "casgiu merzu."
Flour mites, the acari that sculpt and add flavor to the rinds of tomme cheese from Savoie to the Pyrénées.
Aphid "juice": fir or scrub honey is packed with this juice, discreetly called honeydew, which bees adore.
Gnats and spiders swallowed while sleeping, yawning, etc.

BETWEEN LOCAL CUSTOM AND SNOBBERY

→ In Saint-Jean-le-Centenier (Ardèche), silkworm omelets were still being served at the beginning of the twentieth century. *Source* INRA, Alain Fraval, 2009.
→ In the Jura, panfried bee larvae were enjoyed.
→ Along the marshes in the Massif Central, children would suck on firefly bellies, which are very sweet.
→ In Paris, Paul Corcellet, a purveyor of fine foods on Avenue de l'Opéra, offered chocolate-dipped termites until 1989.

Pâté en Croûte

A special brotherhood honors it, a world championship has crowned it, and each year the French consume 6½ metric tons of it . . . Let's examine this little slice of heaven containing pâté in a pastry crust—*le pâté en croûte.*

Charles Patin O'Coohoon

6
CITIES FOR ENJOYING A SLICE

Le pâté Pantin
(Seine-Saint-Denis)
Pork and veal. Oblong; made by hand and baked without a mold.

Le pâté de Houdan (Yvelines)
Hen from Houdan and pistachios. Rectangular.

Le pâté de Chartres
(Eure-et-Loir)
Game birds (partridge and pheasant). With or without foie gras. Rectangular.

Le pâté de Périgueux
(Dordogne)
A classic base with a whole duck foie gras. Rectangular.

Le pâté d'Amiens (Somme)
Duck base with Reinette apples. Rectangular.

Le pâté de Brantôme
(Dordogne)
Pork, veal, woodcock. Rectangular.

skip to .....
Chicken liver terrine, p. 206

"Shame to anyone who serves faithful guests without pâté-croûte."

This is the motto of the World Pâté en Croûte Championship, organized each year since 2009 in Tain-l'Hermitage (Drôme). Its prestigious panel of judges is composed of Best Craftsmen of France (MOFs) and other renowned chefs.

THE SUPERB AND RUSTIC PÂTÉ EN CROÛTE
by *Yohan Lastre**

Equipment
1 rectangular metal pâté en croûte mold measuring 12¼ by 3 inches (31 by 8 cm) or 1 oval metal pâté en croûte mold measuring 8¼ by 5 inches (21 by 13 cm)
1 instant-read thermometer

For the flaky pastry dough
11 tablespoons plus 1 teaspoon (160 g) unsalted butter
1 egg
1 pinch sugar
1 teaspoon salt
3 tablespoons plus 1 teaspoon (50 g) water
2½ cups (250 g) all-purpose flour

For the filling
12 ounces (350 g) boneless and skinless chicken breasts
10½ ounces (300 g) boneless chicken thighs
12 ounces (350 g) pork belly, trimmed of fat
12 ounces (350 g) pork tenderloin
1 ounce (28 g) fleur de sel sea salt
Freshly ground black pepper (about 15 turns of the pepper mill)
1 pinch quatre épices spice blend
⅓ cup (80 mL) white wine
4¼ ounces (120 g) pistachios
1 tablespoon (14 g) butter, softened, for greasing the mold

For the gelée
1⅛ ounces (32 g) gelatin sheets
4¼ cups (1 L) chicken or vegetable broth
¼ cup (60 mL) ruby port

Two days before
Make the flaky pastry dough. Melt the butter, let it cool, then pour it into a mixing bowl. Add the remaining ingredients. Beat for 20 seconds, pour it out onto a work surface, and knead it with your hands just until a dough forms. Wrap the dough in plastic

.....

THE CRUST
The pâté is made with a base of veal and pork enriched with poultry or wild game and wrapped in a *pâte brisée* (flaky pastry) or a *pâte feuilletée* (puff pastry). The dough was first used only for cooking and preserving the meat it encased. It was not until the Middle Ages that the crust was made for eating. In the *Viandier*, the bible of Medieval cuisine, the cook for Charles V, Guillaume Tirel, also known as Taillevent, developed no less than 25 recipes for meat pâtés.

wrap and place it in the refrigerator. Make the filling. Cut all the meat into 1-inch (3 cm) pieces. Process the pork belly and chicken thighs through a meat grinder fitted with a grinding plate with large holes. Combine the meat with the remaining filling ingredients, wrap the mixture in plastic wrap, and place it in the refrigerator.

The day before
Grease the mold with the butter. Roll out the dough to a thickness of about ⅛ to ¼ in (4 to 5 mm), then line the mold with the dough, going all the way up the sides. Scrape the filling into the mold (do not fold the dough over the top). Preheat the oven to 400°F (200°C). Bake the pâté for about 25 minutes, or until beautifully golden brown, then lower the oven temperature to 275°F (140°C) and bake until the center reaches 149°F (65°C) on the instant-read thermometer. Meanwhile, make the gelée. Melt the gelatin in the warm broth, then stir in the port. Remove the pâté from the oven and fill it with the warm gélee. Repeat this step four or five times in about 30-minute intervals. Refrigerate the pâté and any remaining gelée overnight.

The next day
Heat the remaining gelée and pour it over the top of the pâté. Place the pâté back in the refrigerator until the gelée has set. To unmold the pâté en croûte, gently warm the mold in the oven to loosen the pâté crust from the pan. Slice and serve.

Chef's tip: for a pâté that is stronger in flavor, add 2 tablespoons (30 mL) of brandy.

*Pâté en croûte World Champion and founder of Lastre sans apastrophe (Paris 7th).

Pâté croûte or pâté en croûte?
Throughout much of France, the French say "pâté *en* croûte," but in Lyon, they say simply "Pâté *croûte*." This is merely their way of swallowing words as much as the famous pâté itself . . .

Julia Child, the French Chef

She is the most French of all American chefs. A star of the small screen on her television show *The French Chef*, a bestselling author, and an uninhibited cook, Julia Child was a passionate ambassador of French gastronomy, introducing coq au vin, ratatouille, and beef bourguignon to the United States.

Camille Pierrard

The birth of a chef
1912: born Julia Carolyn McWilliams in Pasadena, California.

An American in Paris
Julia Child followed her diplomat husband, Paul Child, to Paris where she started chef training at Le Cordon Bleu. She graduated in **1951**. She met French natives Simone Beck and Louisette Bertholle, with whom she started a cooking school called L'École des Trois Gourmands (the School of the Three Gourmands). Together they wrote a cookbook for American housewives.

The publication of cult cookbooks
Their cookbook was written in English, with the addition of detailed instructions to allow readers to easily reproduce traditional French techniques and recipes at home. There was enormous enthusiasm for their book, *Mastering the Art of French Cooking*, published in **1961**, with more than 1.6 million copies sold to date. Other volumes followed.

A true television success
1963: the launch of her own television show, *The French Chef*. In each episode, she would make a recipe and any blunders or mishaps would not be removed, a style that viewers found relatable. The show was broadcast for ten years, winning an Emmy in **1966**.

A legacy of pleasure
Julia passed away in **2004**, but left a lasting imprint on the culinary culture of the United States thanks to her philosophy on eating well and cooking at home from scratch.

★ ★ ★

FROM SMALL TO BIG SCREEN
Meryl Streep played Julia Child in Nora Ephron's film *Julie and Julia* (2009), a cross-adaptation of two books: Julia Child's autobiography, *My Life in France*, and the story of Julie Powell (played by Amy Adams), a blogger and writer who attempted to make each recipe from the book *Mastering the Art of French Cooking* in only one year.

3 Dishes Julia's Way

Unmolded soufflé
A never-fail cheese and tomato soufflé, which, even if it does not rise as much as a traditional soufflé, will almost never fall. It is cooked slowly in a bain-marie set in the oven, then unmolded.

Gratin dauphinois
A gratin made with potatoes precooked in milk and Provençal cream, to which grated cheese is added.

Coulis de tomates à la Provençal
In this recipe for fresh tomato purée, Child does not limit its ingredients to just those traditionally considered Provençal—such as thyme, basil, and bay leaf—but enhances it with a little dried orange peel.

LA REINE DE SABA

This classic French pastry is one of the iconic recipes in *Mastering the Art of French Cooking*. This is an abridged version.

PREPARATION TIME: 30 MINUTES
COOKING TIME: 25 MINUTES
SERVES 6 TO 8

4 ounces (113 g), or 4 squares semisweet chocolate
2 tablespoons (30 mL) rum or coffee
8 tablespoons (113 g) unsalted butter, softened
⅔ cup (133 g) + 1 tablespoon (13 g) sugar
3 large eggs, separated
1 pinch salt
⅓ cup (40 g) pulverized almonds
¼ teaspoon (4 mL) almond extract
½ cup (50 g) cake flour
For the chocolate-butter icing
2 ounces (57 g), or 2 squares semisweet baking chocolate
2 tablespoons (30 mL) rum or coffee
5 to 6 tablespoons (65 to 78 g) unsalted butter
A few almonds

Preheat the oven to 350°F (180°C). Grease and flour an 8-inch (20 cm) round cake pan. Place the 4 ounces (113 g) of chocolate and the rum in a bowl, cover, and place the bowl in a bain-marie to melt the chocolate. Using an electric mixer, cream the butter and ⅔ cup (133 g) sugar together until they form a pale yellow, fluffy mixture. Beat in the egg yolks until well blended. Beat the egg whites and salt in a separate bowl until soft peaks form; sprinkle in the 1 tablespoon (13 g) of sugar, and beat until stiff peaks form. Blend the melted chocolate into the butter and sugar mixture, then stir in the almonds and almond extract. Immediately stir in one-fourth of the beaten egg whites to lighten the batter. Delicately fold in one-third of the remaining egg whites and when partially blended, sift in one-third of the flour and continue folding. Alternate rapidly with more egg whites and more flour until all the egg whites and flour are incorporated. Scrape the batter into the cake pan and bake for about 25 minutes. The cake is done when it has puffed, and 2½ to 3 inches (6 to 7½ cm) around the circumference are set so that a needle inserted into that area comes out clean; the center should move slightly if the pan is shaken, and a needle comes out oily. Let the cake cool in the pan for 10 minutes. Unmold, and allow it to cool for 1 to 2 hours.
Make the chocolate-butter icing
Place the chocolate and rum in a bowl, cover, and place the bowl in a bain-marie for about 5 minutes to melt the chocolate until perfectly smooth. Lift the bowl out of the bain-marie, and beat in the butter 1 tablespoon (14 g) at a time. Place the bowl over a bowl of ice cubes and water and beat until the chocolate mixture has cooled to spreading consistency. At once, spread it over the cake. Decorate it with a few almonds.

skip to
Soufflés Are Full of Air!, p. 374;
Gratin Dauphinois (Scalloped Potatoes), p. 197

Ernest Hemingway's Paris

He's the most Parisian of all American writers. Immigrating to France in 1921, young Hemingway quickly became an artistic and bohemian figure of Paris. Here is a compilation of some of his most famous—and fascinating—gastronomic haunts.

Estelle Lenartowicz

Brasserie Lipp and Le Pré-aux-Clercs

Hemingway often whiled away his lunches at these two temples of Parisian gastronomy. At Brasserie Lipp, he would order a humble salad of *pommes à l'huile* (potatoes in olive oil) with a draft beer. At Le Pré-aux-Clercs, he would opt for the menu of the day for twelve francs and a bottle of wine for sixty centimes. These bistros are located close to the bookstore Shakespeare and Company, founded in 1919 by Sylvia Beach, where Hemingway would visit regularly to replenish his supply of books and to retrieve his mail, like many expatriates at that time.

→ *51, bd Saint-Germain and 30, rue Bonaparte, Paris 6th*

Les Blés d'Ange

A modest bakery, now gone, where the future Nobel Prize winner, who lived just in front, would regularly come to buy pastries. He would enjoy them during his daily walks in the Luxembourg Gardens, where he would sometimes hunt pigeons!

→ *151, bd du Montparnasse, Paris 6th*

La Rotonde

Along with restaurant-cafés Le Dôme and Le Select, this is one of the must-see establishments in the Montparnasse neighborhood. "No matter what café in Montparnasse you ask a taxi-driver to bring you to from the right bank of the river, they always take you to the Rotonde."

(*The Sun Also Rises*)

→ *105, bd du Montparnasse, Paris 6th*

La Closerie des Lilas

A landmark of literary Paris where John Dos Passos, Ezra Pound, and Henri Miller also dined. After long sessions of writing here, punctuated with cafés crème (this is where Hemingway wrote *The Sun Also Rises*), Hemingway would often stay for dinner. On the menu at the time: oyster tower and plates of Pont-

> "If you are lucky enough to have lived in Paris as a young man, then wherever you go for the rest of your life, it stays with you, for Paris is a moveable feast."

l'Évêque (one of his favorite cheeses), washed down with a very chilled Sancerre. "*It was one of the best cafés in Paris. It was warm inside in the winter and in the spring and fall it was fine outside with the table under the shade of the trees on the side where the statue of the Marshall Ney was, and the square, regular tables under the big awnings along the boulevard.*"

(*A Moveable Feast*)

→ *171, bd du Montparnasse, Paris 6th*

Le Dingo ("whacko" in English).

As attested in *A Moveable Feast*, it is in this famous watering hole that Hemingway met F. Scott Fitzgerald. Their drinking festivities took place under the ownership of Jimmy Charters, a former boxer turned "father confessor of Montparnasse." Here Hemingway invented some of the cocktails depicted in his novels, including Long Island Iced Tea. The bar has since been replaced by an Italian restaurant, but the old wooden counter is still there!

→ *10, rue Delambre, Paris 14th*

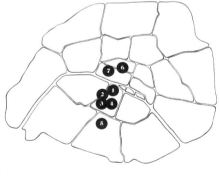

Stroll through Hemingway's Paris in the Two Books He Dedicated to the City of Light

★ *The Sun Also Rises* (1926), his first novel, inspired by his life as a penniless writer in Europe between the First and Second World Wars.

★ *A Moveable Feast* (1964), his ultimate posthumously published text, which traces his life on the Left Bank during the Roaring Twenties.

Harry's Bar

Centered on the small rue Daunou near the Opera Garnier, this New York City–style bar opened its doors in 1911 on Thanksgiving Day. A friend of the owners, Hemingway made it one of his headquarters . . . it was within its wood-paneled walls that the Bloody Mary and the Side Car cocktails were born.

→ *5, rue Daunou, Paris 2nd*

And also . . . the liberated Ritz

"*When I dream of afterlife in heaven, the action always takes place in the Paris Ritz,*" he liked to say about his favorite palace. At the end of the Second World War, Hemingway was embedded in the 4th Infantry Division of the United States, and he was determined to be "the first American to personally liberate Paris" and its famous five-star hotel. So there he was, in the middle of the summer of 1944, staging this "liberation": dressed in the uniform of a war correspondent, machine gun in hand, he crossed Place Vendôme in a jeep and, accompanied by a group of Resistance fighters, burst into the lobby of the Ritz. "Where are the Germans? I'm coming to liberate the Ritz!" he demanded of the hotel manager Claude Auzello. "Of course, Mr. Hemingway, but please leave your gun at the door," the manager stated. The novelist obeyed, then returned to make a trip down to the cellars of the hotel where he found a stock of excellent brandy. The evening continued in the bar, where, according to legend, it ended with Hemingway ordering a record fifty-one Martinis. . . . Who can top that?

→ *15, place Vendôme, Paris 1st*

skip to

The Cocktail Savants of Harry's Bar, p. 268

The Brits Have It!

Several recipes from France's culinary repertoire boast of having origins in England.
What did the French really borrow from their neighbors across the Channel?

Loïc Bienassis

Crème anglaise?

Was it the importance of vanilla custards from across the Channel that led the French to christen their own vanilla custard (which has a more liquid consistency than the English variety) as "*crème anglaise*"? It's a mystery. Grimod de La Reynière mentions a "*crème à l'anglaise*" (English cream) in 1806 but a bit of gray area endured for a long time: "vanilla creams," so named but containing gelatin, as well as "crème anglaise sauces" . . . The version without gelatin became the standard recipe during the first half of the twentieth century. The most recent edition of *Larousse gastronomique* mentions "*crème anglaise collée*" ("jellied crème anglaise") for the version made with gelatin.

Cooking à l'anglaise?

For a Frenchman in 1810, a meat cooked *à l'anglaise* ("in the English style") was one cooked very little, or with blood still present—and not much to the Frenchman's liking. "The English love meat cooked only to medium rare, whereas Italians and Spaniards eat meat well done, and even burnt" (A. Viard, *Le cuisinier royal*, 1820). It's not too far from the truth!

Over the decades, the term *à l'anglaise* began to be used more and more to refer to boiling vegetables in salted water—again a common practice on the other side of the Channel. This style of cooking would eventually be applied to meats. The *Larousse gastronomique* of 1938 attests to this; it defines the method *à l'anglaise* as one that applies "to various preparations cooked most often in water (*gigot de mouton*) or in a white stock (*poularde à l'anglaise*)."

The "assiette anglaise" (the English plate)?

There is direct evidence that this preparation appeared in the 1890s. The Anglomania occurring during this time may have contributed to its moniker. This dish is defined mainly by the predictable presence of roast beef, and it very quickly became a classic dish for lunch in cafés and bistros in France. This hors d'oeuvre, which is an assortment of cold meats arranged on a plate or platter, has a clear definition: it includes cooked ham, pickled beef tongue, beef rib, tenderloin, or roast beef (*Larousse gastronomique*, 1938), garnished with diced gelée, watercress, and cornichons.

skip to
The Classic Crème Anglaise, p. 29

13 Desserts for a Provençal Christmas

The tradition of serving thirteen desserts for Christmas was established in the 1930s. The custom of thirteen *pachichoio* was decided upon by the Félibriges, an association founded by Provençal writers to promote the Provençal language and literature. The number represents Christ and his apostles, and the desserts replaced the thirteen loaves of bread that had been served during Christmas for four centuries. *Marie-Amal Bizalion*

A UNIQUE TRADITION

With living nativity scenes, figurines of the baby Jesus, and pastoral settings, no region in France (apart from Alsace) celebrates the Nativity with more zeal than Provence. Beginning as early as December 4, on the day of Saint Barbara, locals sow wheat in three shallow bowls and place the tall sprouted wheat on the table along with three tablecloths on Christmas Day. Before the meal, the eldest and the youngest perform a ritual called *cacho-fio*, just as it was performed in the sixteenth century: they place a log on the hearth, sprinkle it with wine, and say a prayer ending with: *Se noun sian pas mai, que noun fuguen not mens* (If next year we have not more, then we ask to have no less).

THE 9 ESSENTIAL DESSERTS

Nougat noir (dark nougat), nougat blanc (white nougat), candied fruits, dates, oranges, and four *mendiants* (beggars): fig, raisin, walnut, and almond.

THE 4 RECOMMENDED DESSERTS

The four remaining desserts can be chosen from among many options, including apples, fresh grapes, tangerines, and any local specialty such as *calisson d'Aix* (candied fruit paste with royal icing), *ganse du Var* (a braided pastry), *pompe à l'huile de Marseille* (made from flour, olive oil, sugar, and orange blossom), *tourte de blettes niçoise* (Nicoise Swiss chard pie), or *fougasse* with pork cracklins from Arles. These desserts should be broken or torn with the hands; using a knife is considered bad luck.

SWISS CHARD PIE
by Camille Oger*

PREPARATION TIME: 1 HOUR 30 MINUTES
RESTING TIME: 2 HOURS
COOKING TIME: 40 MINUTES
SERVES 10

For the pastry
5 cups (500 g) all-purpose flour
2 large eggs
⅛ ounce (5 g) active dry yeast
½ cup (100 g) granulated sugar
⅓ cup plus 1 tablespoon (100 mL) water
8 tablespoons (100 g) olive oil
Zest of 1 lemon
1 pinch salt

For the filling
20 Swiss chard leaves, stems removed and discarded
Salt
3 pears, cored and diced
⅓ cup plus 1 tablespoon (100 mL) pastis
1¾ ounces (50 g) raisins
5¼ ounces (150 g) turbinado sugar
2⅛ ounces (60 g) grated Parmesan cheese
1 tablespoon (15 mL) olive oil
2 eggs
1¾ ounces (50 g) pine nuts
Confectioners' sugar, for dusting

Make the pastry. In a large bowl, make a well in the center of the flour. Lightly beat the eggs, then add them to the well with the remaining ingredients. Knead the mixture by hand until a smooth dough is formed. Set the dough aside at room temperature for 2 hours to rise, covered with a cloth.

Make the filling. Cut the chard leaves into strips, sprinkle with salt, then toss to coat. Set aside for 2 hours, tossing them two or three times again. Cook the diced pears with a little water for 45 minutes over low heat in a heavy-bottom saucepan, covered, until softened; drain. Pour the pastis over the raisins to macerate them. Place the chard leaves in a salad spinner to dry them completely. Combine all the filling ingredients (except the confectioners' sugar) to make the filling.

Preheat the oven to 350°F (180°C). Grease a cake pan, then roll out half the dough and line the pan. Scrape the filling into the pan. Roll out the remaining dough on a floured work surface, fold the dough over two or three times, and roll it out again. Place the dough on top, and then tuck the excess dough into the edges of the pan to create a border. Score the dough, and bake for 40 minutes, or until golden. Let cool, dust with the confectioners' sugar, and serve.

*Journalist and author of the blog lemanger.fr

skip to
Nuts for Nougat!, p. 270

🐴 A Horse in the Vineyard?

Draft horses have been put back to work in vineyards for some twenty years. While some chateaux treat themselves to the latest tractors, winemakers prefer using animals (once again). It's not backward-looking nostalgia; it's a true "solution" for the future.

Pierrick Jégu

FOUR WINEMAKERS ON HORSEBACK

8 reasons to use a horse in your vineyard

1 Horses are clearly less **polluting** than a tractor, which guzzles a lot of fuel and harms air quality!

2 Horses never step twice in the same spot . . . **So they don't pack down the ground**, unlike tractors. A compacted soil is less aerated and therefore less alive.

3 When winemakers plow from behind a horse, they are in direct contact with the ground and get to know it in a very precise way: its **textures, colors, and smells**.

4 Horses allow for **a more delicate** and less systematic approach to winemaking. Certain tasks, like loosening up the soil between vines, can damage the vine stocks. A well-controlled horse can allow for more precise maneuvering.

5 By using draft horses, winemakers aren't looking to go back in time and draw on past processes: **animal traction has evolved,** especially with more effective equipment.

6 Bringing horses back into vineyards helps save certain races (Comtois, Percheron, Breton, and the Auxois, for example), but also spurs **economic development** and therefore enriches the social fabric by supporting different professionals in the equestrian world: breeders, service providers who go to domaines with their own animals, makers of plows and horse-pulled pulverizers, etc.

7 A winemaker can develop **trust** and even a bond with horses.

8 A tractor costs about 140,000 euros ($165,000) . . . Figure on about **5,000 euros ($6,000)** for a horse and its harness.

"We never had tractors, just a small motorized tiller for a while. We've almost always used horses, first through a service provider, then Skippy."

DOMAINE HAUSHERR, in Eguisheim, in Alsace
The winemakers: Hubert and Heidi Hausherr
The horse: Skippy, an eleven-year-old Auxois with a blond mane, arrived at the domaine in 2009. The winemakers are looking for a second horse to relieve him some.
Its tasks: tillage, biodynamic processes, harvesting. Skippy is very talented.

CHRISTIAN DUCROUX, in Lantignié, in Beaujolais
The winemaker: Christian Ducroux
The horses: without shoes or bits. Hevan, a twenty-year-old Comtois-Breton crossbred mare, "small and very self-willed," has been at the domaine for eighteen years. She lives with two other horses: Kaïna, an eighteen-year-old large Comtois weighing 1,653 pounds (750 kg), and Écho, a three-year-old gelded Comtois, still "in training."
Their tasks: plowing, tilling, spraying of biodynamic preparations, protective spraying (partial), harvesting.

"At first, we got a horse so that our fragile soil would be less compacted. Then, when I started harvesting with a horse, I got another one so that I wouldn't need a tractor anymore."

ALEXANDRE BAIN, in Tracy-sur-Loire, in the Pouilly-Fumé vineyard
The winemaker: Alexandre Bain
The horses: two gelded Percherons. Phénomène, age fourteen, has been at the domaine for eleven years and is "very professional." Viaduc, age eight, has been at his side for three years. He's "very powerful and intelligent."
Their tasks: mounding, aeration, loosening and plowing soil around and between stocks, spraying of biodynamic fertilizers . . . everything but harvesting!

"We're able to do everything using animal traction on the 27 acres (11 hectares), which is not a small plot of land."

LES CLOSERIES DES MOUSSIS, in Arsac, in Médoc
The winemakers: Laurence Alias and Pascale Choime
The horse: Jumpa, Breton draft, age nineteen, has been at the domaine since 2013. It's Laurence Alias who leads this Alazan that's 5 feet 2 inches (1.60 m) to the withers—so not very tall, but stocky and strong.
Its tasks: all plowing and tilling, mounding, loosening soil and plowing around vine stocks, etc., but no spraying.

"Little in size and very compact . . . we needed either a horse, or a high-clearance tractor that's heavy and compacts the ground . . . We made our choice!"

skip to
Natural Wine, p. 86

Cherry Season

Whether enjoyed straight off the stem or used to adorn plates or desserts, cherries are a gift from nature.
Here are several varieties along with a few recipes.

Alvina Ledru-Johansson

Folfer
Harvest mid-May to June.
Dark red skin with red flesh.
Crisp, juicy, sweet, and mild.

Giant Red
Harvest mid-May to June.
Dark red skin with burgundy flesh.
Firm and balanced.

Ferdouce
Harvest mid-May to June.
Dark red skin with dark red and white flesh.
Firm, sweet, and very mild.

Celeste
Harvest mid-May to June.
Red skin with red flesh.
Juicy, sweet, and tart.

La bellise
Harvest June.
Dark red skin with dark flesh.
Crisp, juicy, sweet, and mild.

Sweetheart
Harvest June and July.
Red with white flesh.
Crisp, juicy, sweet, and tart.

Florie
Harvest mid-May to June.
Dark red skin with two-tone flesh.

Bigalise
Harvest in June.
Dark red skin with two-tone flesh.
Very firm, juicy, sweet, and slightly acidic.

Napoléon
Harvest mid-June.
White to pink skin with red flesh.
Firm, juicy, sweet, and mild.

Earlise
Harvest May to early June.
Black skin with black flesh.
Tender, juicy, and balanced.

Canada Giant
Harvest June and July.
Red skin with white flesh.
Juicy, sweet, and flavorful.

Early Red
Harvest mid-May to early June.
Black skin with black flesh.
Firm and sweet.

● THE CLASSIC

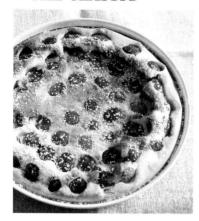

SERVES 8
½ vanilla bean
2½ cups (250 g) all-purpose flour
5 eggs
4 tablespoons (50 g) granulated sugar
1 pinch salt
2⅛ cups (½ L) milk
Butter, for greasing the baking dish
1⅛ pounds (500 g) ripe cherries, with pits
Confectioners' sugar (optional)

Split the vanilla bean lengthwise in half and scrape out and reserve the seeds. Whisk together the flour, eggs, granulated sugar, salt, and vanilla bean seeds. Gradually whisk in the milk, until the mixture forms a smooth batter. Grease a baking dish with butter. Arrange the cherries (do not pit them) in the bottom of the dish. Pour the batter over the cherries. Bake at 400°F (200°C) for about 30 minutes, or until golden. Carefully lift the clafoutis out of the baking dish and onto a serving platter. Dust with confectioners' sugar, if desired.

● THE CRUMBLE
by Philippe Conticini

SERVES 8
For the crumble topping
5 tablespoons (70 g) unsalted butter, softened
2¼ tablespoons (30 g) brown sugar
3½ ounces (100 g) speculaas cookies, crushed

For the batter
3 vanilla beans
3 eggs
½ cup (70 g) hazelnut flour
⅔ cup plus ½ teaspoon (135 g) demerara sugar, plus more for sprinkling
½ cup plus 2½ teaspoons (55 g) all-purpose flour
½ teaspoon (3 g) fleur de sel sea salt
1 teaspoon (2 g) ground cinnamon
1 ounce (25 g) crème fraîche
½ cup plus 1 tablespoon plus 1½ teaspoons (140 mL) low-fat milk
Zest of 1 organic orange
2 tablespoons (30 mL) crème de cerises cherry liqueur (optional)
1 tablespoon (15 g) butter, for greasing the dish
1⅛ pounds (500 g) cherries

Preheat the oven to 325°F (160°C). Make the crumble topping. Combine the butter, brown sugar, and cookies in a bowl. Spread the topping onto a baking sheet and bake for 15 to 20 minutes, or until golden. Increase the oven temperature to 350°F (180°C). Make the batter. Split the vanilla beans lengthwise and scrape out and reserve the seeds. Using an electric mixer, beat the eggs until foamy. Add all the dry ingredients, and beat until combined. Add the crème fraîche, milk, zest, and crème de cerises, if using. Beat for about 30 seconds until smooth. Let stand for 15 minutes. Grease a cake pan with the butter and arrange the cherries in the bottom of the pan, then scrape the batter into the pan. Cover the top with the crumble, then sprinkle with demerara sugar. Bake for 30 to 40 minutes, or until golden.

Pits or No Pits

Some claim the pits in the cherries should be retained so that the cherries do not seep their juices into the cake, plus the pits impart an incomparable, slightly bitter taste. Others say it's easier to enjoy the cake without having to spit out the pits, making the cakes more pleasant for children, and perhaps grandma, to eat!

The orchard of Christian Jean-Pierre

This son of farmers grew up in Céret, in the Pyrénées-Orientales. After a career working in customs, he returned to his first love: growing fruit. Today, he and his wife devote 9.8 acres (4 hectares) to growing red stone fruits on their family farm. There, the main varieties of cherries (shown opposite) can be found.

The Céret basin: the basin of cherries

It is in the Céret commune of France that the first cherries of the year appear, starting in mid-April. For over a century, this region has provided France with its bounty of plump and fleshy fruits. Since 1932, the tradition has been to send a crate of the season's first fruits each year to the President of the Republic.

skip to
France's Wild Berries, p. 382

The Island of Cheeses

The reputation of Corsica's cheeses is well known. But did you know that there are five different types of cheese that come from the island?
Frédéric Laly-Baraglioli

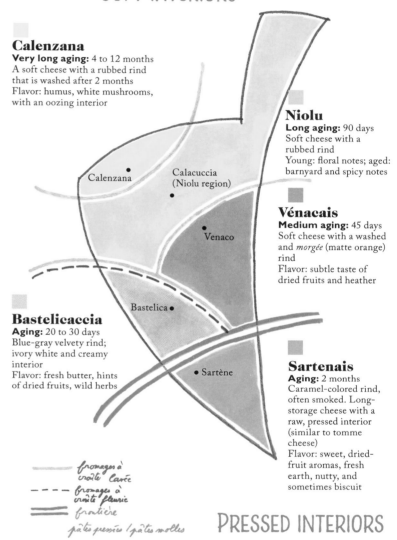

SOFT INTERIORS

Calenzana
Very long aging: 4 to 12 months
A soft cheese with a rubbed rind that is washed after 2 months
Flavor: humus, white mushrooms, with an oozing interior

Niolu
Long aging: 90 days
Soft cheese with a rubbed rind
Young: floral notes; aged: barnyard and spicy notes

Vénacais
Medium aging: 45 days
Soft cheese with a washed and *morgée* (matte orange) rind
Flavor: subtle taste of dried fruits and heather

Bastelicaccia
Aging: 20 to 30 days
Blue-gray velvety rind; ivory white and creamy interior
Flavor: fresh butter, hints of dried fruits, wild herbs

Sartenais
Aging: 2 months
Caramel-colored rind, often smoked. Long-storage cheese with a raw, pressed interior (similar to tomme cheese)
Flavor: sweet, dried-fruit aromas, fresh earth, nutty, and sometimes biscuit

fromages à croûte lavée
fromages à croûte fleurie
frontière
pâtes pressées / pâtes molles

PRESSED INTERIORS

WHICH MILK?
Pastoral traditions allow Corsican cheeses to be made from sheep's or goat's milk. The differences in the cheeses lie in how they are prepared and aged.

WHAT IS THE VOLATILE CORSICAN CHEESE FROM *ASTÉRIX EN CORSE*? (*ASTERIX IN CORSICA*)
Here are some potential and plausible causes for the myth of the stinky Corsican cheese **casgiu merzu,** a specialty of southern Corsica, which is made by letting the cheese ripen long enough for it to obtain extra flavor thanks to the introduction of . . . live *Piophila* fly larvae! This "inhabited cheese," which is not produced commercially, offers a very strong cheese-tasting experience.
Pignata or **casgiu minatu:** the preparation of this cheese is confidential and almost endangered. A mixture is prepared with remnants of old cheeses, with oil, garlic, and brandy added to create a spreadable and unique tasting experience!

skip to
Brocciu, and the Art of Whey, p. 260

Blanquette de Veau

This flagship of bourgeois cuisine is one of France's favorite dishes. Let's explore this classic dish of veal in white sauce!

Charles Patin O'Coohoon

IT'S WHITE!

The recipe's origins are uncertain, but it is of aristocratic lineage.
→ **Vincent La Chapelle** is the first to have documented its preparation in his book *Le Cuisinier moderne*, published in 1735. It was composed of the leftovers of roasted white meats, served as a starter with white button mushrooms and onions.
→ In 1752, the dictionary of **Trevoux** says that a *blanquette* is a dish very common among the bourgeois when they are dining at home.
→ Starting in 1867, chef **Jules Gouffé** creates a recipe by replacing roasted meats with raw meats, boiled in a flavored broth and thickened with a roux.

WHAT CUTS OF MEAT?

The foreribs: the abdominal wall of the calf with fat and cartilage; a lean portion.
The flank: the lower part of the abdominal wall. A soft and gelatinous piece. This is one of the best cuts for blanquette.
The neck: the neck muscle, perfect for simmering.
The shoulder: the anterior muscle prepared in many ways: roasted, braised, or sautéed.

The 5 golden rules

Prepare a blanquette in an enameled pot, to ensure it maintains its white color.

Never brown the food before adding it to the pot.

Never bring the contents to a boil, as the sauce may clump.

Bind (thicken) the blanquette with egg yolks or with a roux.

Serve with Creole white rice.

4 BLANQUETTES OF MASTER CHEFS

MÈRE BRAZIER
Unique additions: cornichons
The method: this famous Lyonnaise mother of modern French cooking from rue Royale used to add in minced cornichons to liven up her traditional blanquette.

ROGER VERGÉ
Unique additions: lamb
The method: following the classic recipe, this top chef replaced veal with simmered lamb's shoulder and diced lamb's feet.

ALAIN DUCASSE
Unique additions: vegetables
The method: at Allard, his Parisian bistro, the chef adorns his stew with baby (pencil) leeks and asparagus tips.

GUY MARTIN
Unique additions: morels
The method: the chef of Le Grand Véfour in Paris replaced white button mushrooms with morel mushrooms in a traditional base.

BLANQUETTE DE VEAU (Veal in White Sauce)
by Christian Constant*

SERVES 4
2¼ pounds (1 kg) assorted veal meats (neck, shoulder, etc.)
1 yellow onion
3 cloves garlic
2 carrots
4 cloves, for piercing the onion
1 bouquet garni (leek green, parsley, and thyme sprigs)
1 bay leaf
Salt
5¼ ounces (150 g) white button mushrooms
1 lemon, halved
3 tablespoons (50 g) unsalted butter
¾ cup plus 1 tablespoon (200 mL) heavy cream

For the white roux
2 tablespoons plus 1 teaspoon (35 g) unsalted butter
⅓ cup plus 1 teaspoon (35 g) flour

Cut the pieces of veal into large cubes. Peel the onion and garlic cloves. Peel and cut the carrots into thick rounds. Pierce the onion with the cloves. In a deep pot, combine the onion, carrots, garlic, bouquet garni, bay leaf, and veal meats. Cover the contents with cold water and add a pinch of salt. Cook, covered, over low heat for 3 hours. From time to time, skim any impurities off the surface using a skimmer or slotted spoon. Meanwhile, make the white roux. In a small saucepan, melt the butter, then stir in the flour. Stir well to combine and cook for 2 minutes. Remove the roux from the heat and set it aside in the refrigerator. Cut the stems off the mushrooms. Cut the mushrooms into 6 or 8 pieces, depending on their size. In a saucepan, add a scant ½ cup (100 mL) of cold water, the 3 tablespoons (50 g) of butter, and the juice from one half of the lemon. Bring to a boil. Add the chopped mushrooms and boil for 3 to 4 minutes; drain, reserving the cooking liquid to add to the veal broth. Check that the meat is cooked by taking a piece between your fingers and squeezing it; it should feel tender. Drain the meat, reserving the cooking liquid, and set the meat aside. Finish the sauce by reducing the reserved cooking liquids (from the veal and mushrooms) to about 5¼ cups (1¼ L), then strain it through a fine-mesh sieve to remove any impurities. Add the cream. Whisk the cold roux into the liquid to thicken it; it should have a velvety consistency. If necessary, you can add a little water if it is too thick or reduce it if it is too liquid. Finish by seasoning with salt, a few turns of the pepper mill, and the juice from the remaining lemon half. Add the meat and the mushrooms to the sauce and serve.

Chef of Violon d'Ingres, Paris 7th

skip to
Curnonsky, p. 328

Light Up the Mussels!

Healthy, inexpensive, and light, these bivalve mollusks are ready for your stovetop, or for a cookout.

François-Régis Gaudry

LEXICON

Mussel farming: raising mussels is called *mytiliculture* in French, from the Latin *mytilus* ("mussel").

Mussel bed: made of wood, used to support mussels. This kind of mussel breeding has existed in France since 1235.

Mont-Saint-Michel: bouchot mussels from this bay have been protected by the AOP (*appellation d'origine protégée*) since 2011.

★ ★ ★

2 rules

Mussels have to be cleaned (scrubbed, washed, and debearded).

For a meal, you'll need about 4 cups (1 L) of mussels per person; that's about 1½ to 1¾ pounds (700 to 800 g). As an appetizer, figure on about 2 cups (0.5 L) per person.

ECLADE DE MOULES: LIGHT IT UP!

Called *terrée* (earth) when made on the dried mud of a shore, mussels cooked by fire might have been invented by the Cro-Magnons; or maybe it was the French Boy Scouts. From time immemorial, fishermen from Charente have cooked mussels right on top of a natural fire on-site. Here's an outdoor demo (don't forget to use caution when cooking with an open flame).

1 Choose a big piece of untreated wood, preferably pine, 3 by 3 feet (1 by 1 m). Drive four nails through the middle of the board. Generously rinse the board with water (so it won't burn while cooking). Place it on the ground in an uncluttered area.

2 Wedge the first four mussels in a cross on the nails, hinges facing up. The mussels can't be too upright because they'll open somewhat with the heat and shouldn't flip over (ashes in mussels don't taste so good).

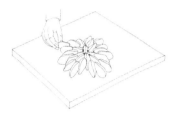

3 Arrange the other mussels, forming concentric circles and packing them as tightly together as possible. Figure on a ½ pound/0.5 liter of mussels for a hearty appetizer.

4 Cover the mussels with a thick layer of very dry pine needles. Light the fire.

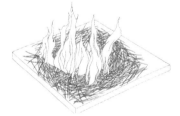

5 As soon as the flames go out (about 5 minutes), it's ready. Ventilate with cardboard to scatter the ashes.

Eat with your fingers, buttered bread, and a good glass of dry white wine (a muscadet!). The mussels will have a delicious forest taste.

4 recipes for mussels

MUSSELS AU NATUREL

Plain mussels at their simplest.

Cooking mussels in a covered pot over low heat while stirring them carefully with a wooden spoon allows the mussels to open. After a few minutes (time will vary depending on the quantity), when all the mussels are open, just enjoy.

 shallots, butter, flat-leaf parsley, thyme, bay leaf, and white wine

 crème fraîche

  egg yolk, crème fraîche, curry

 MUSSELS MARINIÈRE

Peel and finely mince 2 shallots, then brown them with a large dollop of butter in a pot with some chopped parsley. Add a sprig of thyme, 1 bay leaf, and about ¾ cup (200 mL) of white wine. When the shallots are softened, add the mussels, cover the pot and place it over high heat, and shake it regularly so that the mussels cook evenly. Add more chopped parsley leaves at the end of the cooking time and enjoy.

 MUSSELS IN CREAM

Cook the mussels in the *marinière* style and, at the end of the cooking time, add 4 rounded spoonfuls of crème fraîche. If there's too much liquid, strain it after removing the mussels and reduce it by one-third over low heat, then add cream.

 MUSSELS MOUCLADE

Cook the mussels in the *marinière* style. Strain the liquid and reduce it by one-third over low heat. In a separate bowl, mix 2 egg yolks with ¼ cup (60 mL) of crème fraîche and a pinch of curry.

Add the mixture to the liquid, whisking for a velvety texture. Note: In the city of Fouras, Mussels Mouclade are made with curry, but in Saintonge, saffron is added.

The Victuals of NOAILLES

Noailles is the belly of Marseilles, the liveliest neighborhood in the city,
the most authentic, and the most sincere. Let's go food shopping at our favorite spots!

*Julia Sammut**

In **Noailles**, they'll look you right in the eye and hand you a **brioche with cardamom**
that you'll never forget, **fresh mint** and **lemons**, **chickpeas** already soaked, homemade
feuilles de brick, **harissa**, warm **pita bread**, **halloumi** for grilling, **curdled milk**.

Unending inspiration . . .

JOURNO

Maison Journo, which has been located on rue Pavillon for ages, is the king of fricassees: little fried Tunisian sandwiches stuffed with tuna, harissa, and vegetables with vinegar. They also make a lemonade to die for, cakes, of course, and individual loukoum that even my Tunisian friends crave!
28, rue Pavillon

LE PÈRE BLAIZE

The city's legendary herbal shop that recently celebrated its bicentennial, no less. Unrivaled teas. The Tisane Dynamisante will wake you up better than coffee!
4/6, rue Meolan

LE CARTHAGE

Go next door for your morning honey or sugar beignet. Tunisian atmosphere a given. You can have the fritter if it's before ten o'clock in the morning, and if not, connoisseurs know they've got a handle on Tunisian snacks and fresh feuilles de brick.
8, rue d'Aubagne

CHEZ YASSINE

An authentic Tunisian market eatery with *keftaji* (grilled peppers, fries, and eggs cut with two knives at the speed of light), *leblebi* (chickpea soup), feuilles de brick with egg and tuna, and other little delights from everyday Tunisian cuisine. Soak it all up with the restaurant's bread.
8, rue d'Aubagne

EMPEREUR

There's nothing like it! A huge hardware store with everything from electrical supplies to kitchen utensils. No one else has what they have.
4, rue des Récolettes

SAUVEUR

Fabrice Giacalone took over the premier pizzeria in Marseille and met the legendary Sauveur di Paola who shared his secrets. Half tomato and Emmental cheese, half tomato and anchovies: an unbeatable pizza. Adding garlic oil gives it a flavor that is so reminiscent of Sauveur!
10, rue d'Aubagne

MURAT

Madame and Monsieur Murat have filled their stalls with Eastern delights: tahini, dried fruit, Greek yogurt, fresh phyllo dough, pastirma . . . They'll make you an Armenian brioche with cardamom that's out of this world.
13, rue d'Aubagne

CHEZ JACQUES

Curdled milk, raw milk, fermented milk—you'll find it at Chez Jacques, owned by a family of Italians in the Saint-Antoine neighborhood who have been in the game for fifty years. They sell their products in an *estanco* shop on the corner of rue d'Aubagne
14, rue d'Aubagne

AU GRAND SAINT-ANTOINE

People from all over the city come here for the Bossens family's smoked *magret de canard* and *caillette* meatballs. A neighborhood must.
11, rue du Marché-des-Capucins

SALADIN

The king of spices. Thousands of kinds sold in bulk. Also the king of dried fruit and olives dished out with ladles. This shop on rue Longue des Capucins is sure to put a spell on you.
10, rue Longue des Capucins

LE CÈDRE DU LIBAN

Every day around eleven o'clock in the morning, the hot pitas come tumbling down a stainless steel chute before being packed up. And the two brothers talk about their Lebanon, their dishes, and their pita bread with love . . .
39, rue d'Aubagne

TAMKY

You first have to meet the Tamky brothers and sisters to understand. There are thirteen of them. Originally from Vietnam, they speak with a Marseille accent that cuts like a knife. The enormous store focuses on Asia, of course, and on a range of things exotic. Fresh ingredients for Asian broths are in the front, like galanga and scallions. Prepared foods can be found upstairs, like Vietnamese sausages, spring rolls, and more.
5, rue des Halles-Delacroix

*Owner of the L'Idéale, 11, rue d'Aubagne, Marseille (Bouche-du-Rhône). In the heart of the Noailles neighborhood, which goes without saying . . .

138

Intensely Chocolate

Whether you prefer a *moelleux* (molten chocolate cake) or a *mi-cuit* (soft chocolate cake) for a birthday dessert or for a romantic dinner, either recipe will provide a pure chocolate experience.
Marielle Gaudry

Before chocolate cake there was the chocolate drink

1528: Hernan Cortès brings a cocoa-based drink from Mexico to the Spanish court.
1609: Jewish chocolatiers from Spain flee the Inquisition and settle in Bayonne.
1615: chocolate is introduced to the French court by Anne of Austria, who marries Louis XIII.
1659: David Chaillou, the first known chocolatier in history, was granted by Louis XIV the right to make and sell chocolate for drinking.
1780: the first chocolate factory opens in Bayonne.
1836: the first French wrapped tablet of chocolate is created by Antoine Menier.

— CHOCOLATE MOUSSE —

Here is a delightful chocolate mousse recipe for making at home that has many virtues: zero added sugar, zero cream, and zero butter—but generous in chocolate. A mousse in its simplest form!

SERVES 6
9 ounces (250 g) dark chocolate (such as Nestlé dessert Noir 52% cacao, or better yet Nestlé dessert Corsé 65% cacao)
4 eggs, separated
1 pinch salt
1 teaspoon (5 mL) brewed espresso

Chop the chocolate and melt it in a bain-marie or over a double boiler, then pour the chocolate into a large mixing bowl to cool slightly. Stir the egg yolks into the chocolate until thoroughly combined. Beat the egg whites with the pinch of salt, starting on medium speed, then increasing to medium-high once the whites start to foam. Add the espresso to the chocolate and stir to combine. Using a spatula, gently stir one-fourth of the beaten egg whites into the chocolate mixture, then gently stir in the remaining egg whites. Spoon the mousse into serving dishes and refrigerate for at least 3 hours.

THE MOELLEUX
by Michel Bras

The cake with the runny chocolate center was created in 1981 and has spread around the world.

SERVES 6
For the chocolate centers
4¼ ounces (120 g) dark chocolate couverture
¾ cup plus 1 tablespoon plus 1¾ teaspoons (200 mL) heavy cream
3 tablespoons plus 1¾ teaspoons (50 g) butter

For the batter
6 pastry rings measuring 2¼ inches (55 mm) in diameter and 1½ inches (40 mm) in height
3 tablespoons plus 1¾ teaspoons (50 g) unsalted butter, room temperature, plus more for greasing the parchment
Cocoa powder
3¾ ounces (110 g) dark chocolate couverture
1½ ounces (40 g) almond flour
1½ ounces (40 g) rice flour
2 eggs, separated
¼ cup plus 3 tablespoons plus ½ teaspoon (90 g) sugar
Parchment paper (measuring 2¾ by 10 in/70 by 250 mm)

The night before, make the chocolate centers. In a bain-marie or over a double boiler, melt the chocolate with the cream, butter, and ¼ cup (60 mL) of water. Pour the chocolate mixture into 6 round molds measuring 1⅓ inches (45 mm) in diameter and place in the freezer. Cut out six strips from the parchment paper, grease them with butter, then line the pastry rings with the strips. Dust the insides of the molds with cocoa powder. A few hours before serving, unmold the chocolate centers, then place them back in the freezer. Chop the chocolate and melt it in a bain-marie or over a double boiler. Off the heat, add the butter, almond flour, rice flour, and egg yolks and stir to combine. Beat the egg whites to stiff peaks, adding the sugar to the whites while they are beating. Fold the meringue into the chocolate mixture. Using a piping bag, pipe some batter into the bottom of each pastry ring, then place a frozen chocolate center in the batter. Finish filling the rings with the remaining batter, lightly tapping the side of each ring to level out the batter, then place the rings in the freezer for 6 hours. Preheat the oven to 350°F (180°C). Place the frozen cakes on a baking sheet and bake for 20 minutes. Unmold the cakes and serve.

THE MI-CUIT
by Suzy Palatin

This is a cake to die for, the "best in the world" according to legendary French pastry chef Pierre Hermé.

In this recipe from Suzy Palatin, the order in which the ingredients are incorporated makes a big difference, as does the baking time, which gives this cake a melting texture.

SERVES 6
9 ounces (250 g) dark chocolate (preferably a Valrhona Guanaja)
18 tablespoons (250 g) unsalted butter
1¼ cups (250 g) sugar
¾ cup minus 2 teaspoons (70 g) all-purpose flour, sifted
4 eggs

Preheat the oven to 400°F (200°C). Melt the chocolate in the microwave for 3 minutes, then add the butter and melt again for 1 minute; stir to combine. Add the sugar, then the flour, mixing well between each addition. Lightly beat the eggs with a fork until blended, then stir them into the chocolate mixture. Pour the batter into a 9½-inch (24 cm) round greased and floured cake pan. Lower the oven temperature to 350°F (180°C), place the pan in the oven, and bake for 25 minutes. Let the cake cool to room temperature before unmolding.

Which Chocolate Should You Choose?
A high-quality couverture chocolate or one used for pastry making (a plain dark chocolate) and without lecithin or fats other than cocoa butter:
• **Dark chocolate, 70% cacao** for cakes
• **Dark chocolate, 50% to 65% cacao** for mousses
• **Couverture chocolate** for ganaches

skip to ....
Grand Cru Chocolate Bars, p. 204

Alain Passard

A roaster, vegetable genius, and visual artist, Alain Passard is one of the most admired chefs in the world.

François-Régis Gaudry

ABSOLUTE CHEF

1956: born in La Guerche-de-Bretagne (Ille-et-Vilaine)

1970: begins apprenticeship with Michel Kerever, at Le Lion d'Or in Liffré (Ille-et-Vilaine department)

1976–1977: serves as chef at Gérard Boyer's La Chaumière in Reims

1980–1984: serves as chef at Le Duc d'Enghien, at the Casino d'Enghien. At age twenty-six, he becomes the youngest chef to be awarded two stars

1978–1980: serves as chef at Alain Senderens's L'Archestrate, 84, rue de Varenne in Paris

1985: receives two Michelin stars at the Brussels Carlton

1986: purchases L'Archestrate from his mentor Alain Senderens, which becomes L'Arpège

1996

Receives three Michelin stars ten years after opening L'Arpège

❀❀❀

2001

"The rupture with animal tissue." Passard stops cooking red meat and turns to vegetables. Purchases his first garden in Fillé-sur-Sarthe; two others would follow in the Eure and Manche departments

2011: work is featured in the book *En Cuisine avec Alain Passard* by Christophe Blain (Gallimard)

2016: appears in the documentary *Chef's Table* (season 5), directed by David Gelb for Netflix

2017: participates in "Open Museum" at the Palais de Beaux-Arts in Lille

Chef, gardener, artisan, artist
(born in 1956)

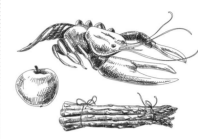

His Strokes of Genius

→ He cuts **lobster** vertically into fillets and cooks it with a yellow wine sauce
→ He roasts **asparagus** vertically with unsalted butter for three hours
→ He cooks vegetables in a salt crust
→ He combines a **half chicken** and a **half duck** together to create the most haute couture union in gastronomy!
→ He cuts **apples** in spirals to transform an apple tart into a bouquet of roses

STRING BEANS, WHITE PEACH, FRESH ALMONDS

The peach makes the perfect refreshment when in season, with its gentle sweetness and delicate flavor of white flower. Pairing it with string beans provides a nice duo of textures, and an especially harmonious marriage of flavors. Almonds, meanwhile, bring a fabulously fresh crunch.

1⅓ pounds (600 g) string beans
Salted butter
Olive oil
12 unshelled raw almonds
1 plump white peach
A few sprigs purple basil
Fleur de sel sea salt

Immerse the string beans in simmering water and blanch until they are just al dente. Remove them with a slotted spoon and immediately immerse them in a cold-water bath to stop the cooking and preserve their color. Set them aside to drain, then sauté them in a large pan over low heat with a little salted butter and a good drizzle of olive oil. Shell the almonds, then add them to the pan. Pit the peach and cut it into 12 wedges, then add the wedges to the pan with a few of the best basil leaves. Sprinkle everything with sea salt and add a few turns of the pepper mill. Do not stir the contents in order to maintain the beautiful appearance of the peaches!

Arrange on four warmed plates and serve immediately.

A MAN OF ART

We all know Alain Passard the chef, but there is also Alain Passard the sculptor, who creates bronze lobsters more than 6½ feet (2 m) high, as well as the artist, who arranges newspaper clippings to carefully construct collages of plated dishes.

---◇---

Here is what he says about how his art began:

"**It was** 2004 or 2005. **I was traveling to Japan.** One night **I had insomnia** because of jet lag. I called the reception desk to **ask for some glue and scissors**, and I started cutting up **newspapers in my room** and creating collages. . . . I constructed **a mozzarella tomato salad, a cantaloupe with fourme d'Ambert**, etc. When I returned to Paris, I continued to make collages in this way. The publisher Gallimard ordered **a book with 50 recipes illustrated** with my creations. Today, my art has become my **private sanctum**. I do it in Paris or during the weekend in my vegetable garden near Evreux or the one in Sarthe. **I have developed a rapport with this medium**, seeing it now as an extension of **what I do in the kitchen**."

---◇---

PURPLE TURNIP AND NEW POTATOES WITH RED TOMATO

Alain Passard says, "I combined these ingredients just out of curiosity. This is an unusual but succulent trilogy, a nice balance between the graceful bitterness of the turnip, the juiciness of the tomato, and the tender texture of the potato. The aniseed-like flavor of the tarragon contributes a contemporary and lively flavor!"

SERVES 4

4 large turnips
1 tablespoon (14 g) salted butter
¼ cup (60 mL) olive oil
12 new potatoes, skin on
4 medium red tomatoes
Fleur de sel sea salt and freshly ground black pepper
2 sprigs tarragon, leaves only

Quarter the turnips. Heat the butter and oil in a large skillet over low heat and add the turnips and potatoes. Add just enough water to cover the vegetables, and cook until the vegetables are very tender and the liquid has evaporated. When all the liquid has evaporated, quarter the tomatoes and add them to the pan; season with sea salt and pepper. When the tomatoes are just warmed through, serve immediately (you want to enjoy the tomatoes hot but not cooked!). You can enhance this dish with various fresh herbs, including fresh tarragon leaves sprinkled on the potatoes and tomatoes.

JULY'S GARDEN WITH TURNIP PETALS, FLAVORS OF OLIVE, LEMON, HONEY

A beautiful classic from the cuisine of L'Arpège . . . Surprising, and particularly refreshing in the summer! The tangy flavors of lemon and honey amplify the taste of this collage of garden vegetables. The turnip petals serve as a wrap, similar to a ravioli, for each composed bite . . . The dish offers a wonderful sweet and sour contrast and a clever play between raw and cooked ingredients!

SERVES 4

2 beets (red, yellow, or white)
4 yellow carrots
4 orange carrots
4 black radishes
4 purple turnips (for making turnip "petals")
2 Black Crimea tomatoes
4 red radishes
½ cucumber
1 zucchini
1 bunch mesclun

For the "olive-lemon-honey" essence
2 lemons
2½ ounces (70 g) acacia honey
¾ cup minus 1 tablespoon (150 g) olive oil

Select medium-size fresh vegetables from the market. In simmering water, cook the beets, carrots, and black radishes separately, with peels on to preserve their colors, until just al dente. Let cool while in their cooking water, then peel them, except for the radishes to keep their beautiful color.

Set the cooked vegetables aside on a plate. Using a mandoline, very thinly slice the turnips to make the turnip "petals." They must be very thin and translucent. Immerse the turnip slices for 3 to 4 seconds in boiling water, then immediately transfer them to a bowl of cold water with a few ice cubes, to stop the cooking. Set them on a flattened kitchen towel to drain. Make the "olive-honey-lemon" essence. Juice the lemons, then stir together the lemon juice, honey, and oil by gradually adding the juice while stirring; the mixture must be beautifully smooth, homogeneous, and slightly thick. Transfer the mixture to a sauce dish. On a plate or serving platter, arrange the raw vegetables (tomatoes, red radishes, cucumber, and zucchini, also sliced thin with a mandoline) together with the cooked vegetables (beets, carrots, and black radishes). Arrange the turnip petals in a decorative pattern on top of the vegetables to cover them, then surround the vegetables with the mesclun leaves. Serve with the olive-lemon-honey essence for drizzling, and enjoy the deliciousness!

Foie Gras: The Art of the Terrine

How do you like your foie gras prepared? In a terrine, microwaved, or poached in sangria? Here are three recipes to satisfy any preference.

Marielle Gaudry

A BEAUTIFUL ETYMOLOGY

The Latin origin of the French word for liver ("*foie*") tells us a lot about the tradition of foie gras under the Roman Empire: *jecur ficatum* (or simply *ficatum* in the elliptical form that followed) referred to fig-stuffed liver fattened from feeding figs to geese in the form of dried dumplings, as described by Pliny the Elder.

AN ALSATIAN CRADLE

Before the southwest of France was proclaimed as the home for foie gras production (the regions of Aquitaine and Midi-Pyrénées now account for two-thirds of the breeders), foie gras as a food originated in Strasbourg. Appearing around 1780, foie gras as a dish was created by Jean-Paul Clause, cook for the governor of Alsace, who was asked to create an exceptional recipe. He created what Brillat-Savarin later described in his writings as the "Gibraltar of Strasbourg Foie Gras," a kind of pâté en croûte with whole foie gras stuffed with bacon and finely chopped veal meat.

A PGI

Thanks to the efforts of a handful of producers from southwest France, under the Renaissance Committee, the PGI (Protected Geographical Indication) label was requested in 1992 and granted in 1999. The PGI for duck foie gras from the southwest guarantees that duck products are processed in the region, and that they respect traditional methods of production.

MICROWAVE FOIE GRAS TERRINE

This is an ultrasimple and fast cooking method for terrine of foie gras. Devein a duck foie gras, then cut it into pieces, and season it with salt and pepper. Place the liver pieces on a microwavable plate, cover them in plastic wrap, and microwave for 1 minute 30 seconds (at 700 watts). Place the liver pieces in a terrine, pressing them down firmly, then place a weighted board or plate on top to keep the liver pressed. Refrigerate for 24 to 48 hours, then serve.

SANGRIA-POACHED FOIE GRAS TERRINE
by Hélène Darroze

A sophisticated dish representing this chef from Landes.

SERVES 12

For the sangria
8½ cups (2 L) Spanish red wine
2¼ cups (¼ L) peach liqueur
⅓ cup plus 1 tablespoon (100 mL) Armagnac
½ cup (100 g) superfine sugar
2¼ pounds (1 kg) unwaxed oranges
1⅛ pounds (500 g) unwaxed lemons
1⅛ pounds (500 g) peaches (if in season; if not, use mangoes)
1⅛ pounds (500 g) Golden apples
1⅛ pounds (500 g) strawberries
2 cinnamon sticks
1 vanilla bean

For the terrine
2 lobes of premium duck foie gras (1⅓ pounds/600 g each)
Fine salt and freshly ground black pepper

The sangria
Prepare the sangria 48 hours before preparing the foie gras terrine by combining all the ingredients and placing them in the refrigerator.

The terrine
Prepare the terrine at least 48 hours before serving it. Season the foie gras lobes with 2 teaspoons (12 g) of salt and 2½ teaspoons (6 g) of black pepper for each 2¼ pounds (1 kg) of foie gras. Refrigerate the foie gras to marinate overnight. The next day, heat the sangria to 176°F (80°C), then poach the lobes in the sangria for 25 to 30 minutes, depending on their size; the center of the foie gras should be tender. Drain the lobes, then cut them in half lengthwise. Place them in a terrine, place a piece of parchment paper on top, and place a weighted container on top of the parchment. Choose a container that will fit inside the terrine to keep the lobes pressed down. Place the terrine in the refrigerator for several hours. Enjoy sliced, on top of slices of rustic bread.

Recipe from Mes recettes en fête, *photographs by Pierre-Louis Viel, Éditions Cherche Midi*

WHAT IS *MI-CUIT* FOIE GRAS?

Foie gras prepared in this way is partially preserved, cooked at a temperature of between 158°F to 185°F (70°C to 85°C). A "cooked" foie gras has been heated to a temperature of between 200°F to 230°F (90°C to 110°C). Low-temperature cooking ensures the foie gras retains its freshness and aroma, but it needs to be served soon cooking since it spoils quickly.

TERRINE OF FOIE GRAS IN A BAIN-MARIE

The traditional approach to a terrine using the oven.

At room temperature, separate the two lobes of a raw foie gras and devein them. Season with salt and pepper and ½ teaspoon (2 g) of sugar. Sprinkle the lobes with port or Sauternes, according to your taste, and cover them with plastic wrap. Preheat the oven to 300°F (150°C). Place the foie gras in a terrine, place the terrine down into in a larger pan filled with water, then place the pan in the oven. Immediately lower the oven temperature to 225°F (110°C) for 15 minutes, then to 200°F (90°C) for 35 minutes. Lift the plastic wrap to check the core temperature of the foie gras. It should register between 113°F and 131°F (45°C and 55°C) on an instant-read thermometer. Refrigerate the terrine for 3 days before serving.

skip to
Pâté en Croûte, p. 129

French Infusions

And to think they're sometimes called *pisse-mémé* ("grandma pisser") in French!
But these herbal hot beverages are an art, bringing together medicinal benefits with enjoyable taste.
Angèle Ferreux-Maeght

DEFINITION

Infusion is a process that consists of extracting the active properties and aromas from a plant using hot water. It's one of the methods of phytotherapy.

It's particularly suitable for flowers, soft leaves, and aromatic plants, whereas decoction, which is prolonged boiling of leaves, is better for thicker and tougher leaves, roots, and peels.

Directions for Use

Store dried plants in hermetically sealed jars or paper sachets away from light.

Heat water, preferably filtered and low in minerals. Remove from the heat as soon as it reaches 185°F to 200°F (85°C to 90°C), or when large bubbles form, so that the plant's active properties aren't lost.

Once the water is removed from the heat, add selected plants (⅓ to 1 oz/10 to 30 g of dried plants per 4¼ cups/1 L of water), or pour the hot water over the plants in a pot. Cover the infusion so that the aromatic components don't evaporate. Steep for 2 to 5 minutes to fully reap the benefits of the plant's aromatic components, and for 10 minutes for the non-aromatic components (bitters, tannins, etc.).

Store the infusion with the plants removed for no longer than a day at room temperature, for 48 hours maximum in the refrigerator, and for several weeks in ice in the freezer.

skip to ....
Aromatic Plants, p. 295

Thyme
(Grasse region, Maine-et-Loire)
Latin name: *Thymus vulgaris*
Family: Lamiaceae
Taste: strong, slightly bitter, with menthol and lemon
Properties: stimulant, expectorant, antispasmodic, and antiseptic. Consume several times per day.

Rosemary
(Mediterranean region)
Latin name: *Rosmarinus officinalis*
Family: Lamiaceae
Taste: deep and strong, resinous
Properties: stimulant, digestive, carminative (helps evacuate intestinal gas), and cholagogue (facilitates the evacuation of bile). Recommended for digestive and liver problems. Consume after meals.

Linden
(Carpentras, Vaucluse)
Latin name: *Tilia vulgaris*
Family: Malvaceae
Taste: gentle, honey, some menthol
Properties: sedative and soothing, recommended for sleep problems. Consume at night at bedtime.

Mint
(Milly-la-Forêt, Essonne)
Latin name: *Mentha piperita* or *Mitcham milly*
Family: Lamiaceae
Taste: very mentholated, strong and lingering
Properties: stimulant, digestive, and carminative (helps evacuate intestinal gas). An infusion (five or six leaves) is therefore recommended for digestive problems, bloating, nausea, and spasms. Consume after every meal.

Chamomile
(Chemillé, Maine-et-Loire)
Latin name: *Anthemis nobilis* or *Chamaemelum nobile*
Family: Asteraceae
Taste: floral, gently bitter
Properties: soothing, recommended for sleep problems. To be consumed at night before bedtime. Also effective with stomachaches and digestive problems thanks to its effects as a tonic, digestive, antispasmodic, and analgesic. Consume after every meal.

Au pied de cochon
Restaurant
6. rue Coquillière.

Téléphone:
CENTRAL 11-75
„ 11-76

Halles centrales de Paris, entre la Bourse de Commerce et Saint Eustache...

OUVERT JOUR ET NUIT

NOS HORS-D'ŒUVRE
Melon glacé de Cavaillon	4.—
Pamplemousse frappé	2.50
Salade de Tomates	2.50
Salade de Concombre	2.50
Salade Niçoise	4.50
Assiette de Crudités	4.50
Œuf en gelée ou mayonnaise	2.50
Langoustines mayonnaise	7.—
Sardine à l'huile	2.50
Thon à l'huile	3.—
Maquereau au vin blanc	3.—
Assiette de Cochonaille	4.50
Médaillon foie gras truffé	12.—
Jambon de Paris	4.—
Jambon de Bayonne	5.—
Saucisson sec par Porc	3.—
Terrine du Chef	4.50
Pâté de Campagne	2.50
Rillettes	2.50
Andouille de Vire	3.—
Saumon fumé	9.50
Caviar avec Toast et Citron	13.—

NOS PLATS D'ŒUFS
Omelette aux Fines Herbes	2.50
Omelette au Fromage	3.—
Omelette au Jambon	3.—
Œufs plat au Bacon	3.—

NOS POISSONS
Truite aux Amandes	6.50
Truite du Vivier au Bleu	6.50
Sole Belle Meunière	7.—
Langouste Mayonnaise	S.G.
Coquilles Saint-Jacques	7.—
Turbot grillé sauce Béarnaise	8.50

Le Pied de Cochon
vous recommande

Soupe à l'Oignon gratinée	2.50
Grenouilles Provençale	8.50
Escargots de Bourgogne, la dz.	5.—
Coquilles St-Jacques provençale	7.—
Terrine du Chef	4.50
Pied de Cochon grillé	5.50
Pied de Cochon farci Truffé	5.50
Plateau grillé Saint-Antoine	5.50
Andouillette grillée	5.50
Saucisson chaud par Porc	5.50
Tête de Veau ravigote	5.50
Choucroute au Riesling	6.—
Brochette de Rognons	6.50
Rognon de Veau flambé Armagnac	9.50
Tournedos Béarnaise	8.50
Tournedos Rossini	9.—
Steak au poivre	8.50
Entrecôte Bercy	8.—
Entrecôte à la Moelle	
"Fût des Halles" (2 p.)	18.—

et

Sa Spécialité

NOS VIANDES
Entrecôte à la Moelle (2 p.)	18.—
Entrecôte Minute	7.50
Entrecôte Bercy	8.—
Tournedos Béarnaise	8.50
Tournedos Rossini	9.—
Steak au poivre	8.50
Steak Tartare	8.—
Côte de Bœuf (2 pers.)	19.—
Côtes d'Agneau Vert-Pré	8.—
Côte de Porc Milanaise	6.50
Côte de Veau Mandataire	7.—
Cervelle de Veau	7.50
Tripes à la Mode de Caen	5.—
Boudin de Campagne	3.—
Saucisses de Francfort Garnies	3.—

NOS FROMAGES
Fromages	
Yoghourt	
Crème fraîche	

GARE St LAZARE
15, PLACE DU HAVRE

Poutéla
TRAITEUR

PETITS DÉJEUNERS · PATISSERIES FINES · SALON DE THÉ

EUROPE 35-14 et 15   R.C. 866-806

Au vrai
Saumur
F. LAUR, Pre

GRAND COMPTOI
BRASSERIE - BUFFET-FRO

1, CHAUSSÉE DE LA MUET
PARIS-16e ◆ AGENCE HAV
TÉL. : JASMIN 47-84 - 47-85 - 47-

Brioche ....   Cake 40
SUPPLÉMENT PAR PERSONNE

ARRIVAGE DIRECT D'HUITRES
toute l'année.
ooo
BELONS N°1 .... la dz
(avec pain - beurre - citr

Tarte aux Poireaux	
Jambon Persillé Spécialité	
Hareng Baltique	
Crème Fraîche Oignons Pommes à l'Air	

ENTRÉES
Potage aux Légumes	
Œufs Mayonnaise	
Assiette de Crudités	
Fromage de Tête	
Cervelas Rémoulade	
Salade Niçoise	
Pâté en croûte	
Jambon de Parme	
Jambon Fumé de Forêt Noire	
Hure pistachée	
Foie Gras Frais de Canard des Landes préparé par la Maison	
Pâté de Grives de l'Aveyron au Foie Gras	
Soupe à l'Oignon Gratinée	

FROID
Quart Poulet Mayonnaise	
Steack Tartare	

SPÉCIALITÉS
SORTIE DE THÉATRE
X Sortie de Théâtre Queues Oreilles de Cochon Grillées	
Poule au Pot	
Goulach à la Hongroise	
Jarret de Porc à la Choucroute	
Choucroute Garnie	
Tripoux de l'Aveyron	
X Pied Jamet (Désossé, Farci, Truffé)	
Andouillette de Troyes Pommes Mousseline	
Foie de Veau Meunière garni Gratin Dauphinois	

GRILLADES (15 minutes)
Hamburger Pommes	
Rognons d'Agneau Grillés	

LE MUNICHE
25-27 rue de Buci Paris 6
MÉDicis : 62-09

*tous les jours
service sans interruption
de midi à 3 heures du matin*

GARNIER

111, RUE SAINT-LAZARE - PARIS 8e ARR'
TÉL. : EUROPE 50-40 (4 lignes groupées) - PARIS-INTER

CONSIGNE

Aujourd'hui

Filets de Lotte Normande	250.
Sole Frite au Citron	300.

- Plats du Jour -
Le Vol au Vent Financière	250.
Andouillette de Troyes Grillée sur Pré	175.
Filet de Porc rôti Pom. Mousseline	225.
Poulet Sauté à l'Armagnac	375.
Asperges à l'huile	120.
Desserts (Fraises des Bois au sucre	150.
Poire Tasse Crataux 150. Mystère 125.	
Pâtisseries 125.	

FURSTEMBERG
BAR CLIMATISÉ
au sous-sol
ODÉon : 79-51

US LES SOIRS À 21 H
Piano : ANDRÉ PERSIANY
la Batterie : PARA-BOSCHI

Catégorie
R. C. Seine : 53.080

Bière de Ch

Vins.	la blle	la 1/2	le 1/4	
Rouge	110	70	35	
Blanc	160	80	40	

Chez Honori

Couvent .15

Pain toop a la comm
MAISON CAVE

Mercredi 1er Septem

8. BOULEVARD DELESSERT. — PARIS (16e)
Téléphone : TROCADÉRO 55-12

Hors d'Œuvres —
La salade de tomates	50	Le Bœuf marmi
Les soissons nouveaux en salade	60	Le Sauté de 8
La salade de Concombre	80	La Côte de Ve
La salade de pommes	60	Le Carré de mou
Les radis roses	60	Le rôti de Veau
Le Melon glacé	100	Le Poulet sauté
L'Œuf dur mayonnaise	75	Le Poulet froid
Le Saucisson	70	Le Poulet rôti
Les Filets de Harengs marinés	80	Le Pigeon sur
Les anchois marinés	80	

Entrées —
Les œufs au plat les 2.	80	La Pomme
Le Jambon de Paris	100	Les Haricots nou
Le Colin froid mayonnaise	170	L'Artichaut
Le Filet de sole à la Russe	190	La Salade de
La Sole meunière	250	

Desserts —
La Pêche Abricot 70 . La Pêche 70 . Les
Les Figues fraîches 75 . Les Fraises des Bois . 100
Le Melon glacé 100

L'Oiseau Bleu

Pâtisserie ___ Confiserie

Salon de thé ___ Restaurant

47, Boulevard Haussmann, PARIS-9e
OPÉra 36-76   (face au Printemps)

AUBERGE
SAINT-JEAN-DE-LUZ
25, RUE LESUEUR   TÉLÉPHONE
PARIS-16e   PASSY 65-15

MENU

Couvert 41

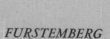

By the Menu

A veteran restaurateur, Jérôme Dumant is one of the greatest French *missuphilists* (collector of menus). For more than thirty years, the owner of the Relais Routier Les Marches in Paris has collected old restaurant menus found at flea markets and auctions. He has more than a thousand, with a predilection for those from bistros from the 1930s to 1960s. Displayed here are some of those from his collection.

Jordan Moilim

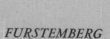

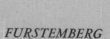

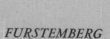

LA ROMANÉE 1942 .. 700. »
CHAMBERTIN 1942.. 700. »
USULES 1947 .. 700. »

Sauté d'Agneau en Cassoulet
JEUDI
La Petite Marmite
VENDREDI

Cervelas mayonnaise 90. »   Andouille de Vire 90. »

VIANDES FROIDES
Poulet froid mayonnaise, le 1/4 375. »   Jambon des Gourmets
Jambon de campagne fumé 250. »   Foie gras truffé à la gelée charentais

---

CIDRE
Bouto

BORDEAUX
CHATEAU
1er CRU
CHAT. 1er CRU
CHAT. 5e
HAUT SA

CHABLIS
MEURSAU
CORTON

VINS

144

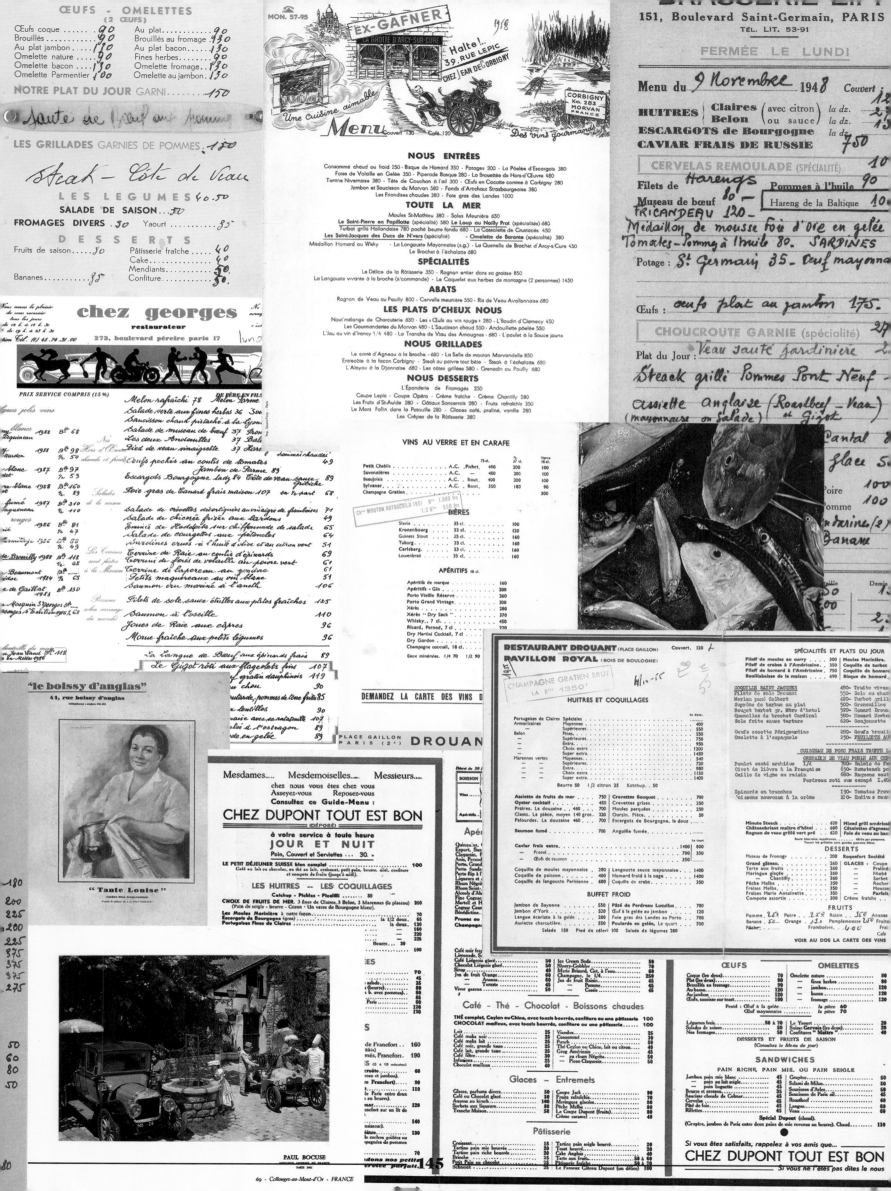

ŒUFS - OMELETTES
(2 ŒUFS)

Œufs coque	90	Au plat	90
Brouillés	90	Brouillés au fromage	130
Au plat jambon	130	Au plat bacon	130
Omelette nature	90	Fines herbes	90
Omelette bacon	130	Omelette fromage	130
Omelette Parmentier	100	Omelette au jambon	130

NOTRE PLAT DU JOUR GARNI 150

Sauté de Bœuf aux pommes

LES GRILLADES GARNIES DE POMMES . 150

Steak - Côte de Veau

LES LEGUMES 40.50

SALADE DE SAISON ... 50

FROMAGES DIVERS . 50   Yaourt 35

DESSERTS

Fruits de saison	50	Pâtisserie fraîche	40
Cake	40		
		Mendiants	50
Bananes	35	Confiture	50

---

chez georges
restaurateur
273, boulevard péreire paris 17

PRIX SERVICE COMPRIS (15 %)   DE PÈRE EN FILS

Melon rafraîchi 78   Melon Pomme

Salade verte aux fines herbes 36
Saucisson chaud pistaché à la lyonnaise
Les deux Andouilles 37
Salade de museau de bœuf 37
Hors d'Œuvre   Pied de veau vinaigrette 37
Œufs pochés au coulis de tomates 49
Jambon de Parme 89
Escargots Bourgogne 84   Côte de veau sauce Grébiche 89
Foie gras de Canard frais maison 107   en 1/2 part 68

Salade de crevettes décortiquées au vinaigre de framboises 71
Salade de chicorée frisée aux lardons 49
Emincé de Haddock sur chiffonnade de salade 65
Salade de courgettes aux pétoncles 64
Sardines crues à l'huile d'olive et au citron vert 51
Terrine de Raie au coulis d'épinards 69
Terrine de foies de volaille au poivre vert 61
Terrine de lapereau au genièvre 61
Petits maquereaux au vin blanc 51
Saumon cru mariné à l'aneth 106

Filets de sole sauce étrilles aux pâtes fraîches 135
Saumon à l'oseille 110
Joues de Raie aux câpres 96
Morue fraîche aux petits légumes 96

La Langue de Bœuf aux épinards frais 89
Le Gigot rôti aux flageolets fins 107
gratin dauphinois 119
chou 90
lentilles 90
raie avec sa ratatouille 107
à l'estragon 89
en gelée 89

"le boissy d'anglas"
41, rue boissy d'anglas

"Tante Louise"

180
200
225
200
225
375
375
275

50
60
80
50

EX-GAFNER
LA GROTTE D'ARCY-SUR-CURE
Halte !..
39, RUE LEPIC
CHEZ JEAN D'ORBIGNY
CORBIGNY Km. 283 MORVAN FRANCE
Une cuisine aimable
Menu Couvert 130   Café 120
Des vins gourmands

NOUS ENTRÉES
Consommé chaud ou froid 250 - Bisque de Homard 350 - Potages 200 - La Poêlée d'Escargots 380
Foies de Volaille en Gelée 350 - Piperade Basque 280 - La Brouettade de Hors-d'Œuvre 480
Terrine Nivernaise 380 - Tête de Couchon à l'ail 300 - Œufs en Cocotte comme à Corbigny 280
Jambon et Saucisson du Morvan 580 - Fonds d'Artichaut Strasbourgeoise 380
Les Friandises chaudes 380 - Foie gras des Landes 1000

TOUTE LA MER
Moules St-Mathieu 380 - Soles Meunière 650
Le Saint-Pierre en Papillotte (spécialité) 580 Le Loup au Noilly Prat (spécialité) 680
Turbot grillé Hollandaise 780 poché beurre fondu 680 - La Cassolette de Crustacés 680
Les Saint-Jacques des Ducs de N'vers (spécialité) - Omelette de Barante (spécialité) 380
Médaillon Homard au Wisky - La Langouste Mayonnaise (s.g.) - La Quenelle de Brochet d'Arcy-s/Cure 450
Le Brochet à l'échalotte 680

SPÉCIALITÉS
Le Délice de la Rôtisserie 350 - Rognon entier dans sa graisse 850
La Langouste vivante à la broche (s'commande) - Le Coquelet aux herbes de montagne (2 personnes) 1450

ABATS
Rognon de Veau au Pouilly 800 - Cervelle meunière 550 - Ris de Veau Avallonnaise 680

LES PLATS D'CHEUX NOUS
Nout'mélange de Charcuterie 650 - Les « Œufs au vin rouge » 480 - L'Boudin d'Clamecy 450
Les Gourmanderies du Morvan 480 - L'Saucisson chaud 550 - Andouillette poêlée 550
L'Jau au vin d'Irancy 1/4 480 - La Tranche de Viau des Amougnes - 680 - L'poulet à la Sauce jaune

NOUS GRILLADES
Le carré d'Agneau à la broche - 680 - La Selle de mouton Marvandelle 850
Entrecôte à la façon Corbigny - Steak au poivre tout bête - Steak à l'échalotte 680
L'Alayou à la Dijonnaise 680 - Les côtes grillées 580 - Grenadin au Pouilly 680

NOUS DESSERTS
L'Epanderie de Fromages 250
Coupe Lepic - Coupe Opéra - Crème fraîche - Crème Chantilly 280
Les Fruits de St-Aulde 280 - Gâteaux Sancerrois 280 - Fruits rafraîchis 350
Le Mont Follin dans la Patouille 280 - Glaces café, praliné, vanille 280
Les Crêpes de la Rôtisserie 350

VINS AU VERRE ET EN CARAFE

			75 cl.		Verre 10 cl.
Petit Chablis	A.C.	Pichet.	400	200	100
Savennières	A.C.		400	200	100
Beaujolais	A.C.	Bout.	400	200	100
Sylvaner	A.C.	Bout.	350	180	90
Champagne Gratien					

Ch. MOUTON ROTHSCHILD 1951 Bttle 1.000 frs
1/2 Bttle 550 frs

BIÈRES
Slavia	33 cl.	100
Kronenbourg	33 cl.	120
Guiness Stout	25 cl.	160
Tuborg	33 cl.	160
Carlsberg	33 cl.	160
Lowenbräu	33 cl.	160

APÉRITIFS 10 cl.
Apéritifs de marque		160
Apéritifs - Gin		200
Porto Vieille Réserve		260
Porto Grand Vintage		300
Xérès		280
Xérès " Dry Sack "		370
Whisky, 3 cl.		270
Ricard, Pernod, 7 cl.		220
Dry Martini Cocktail, 7 cl.		
Dry Gordon		
Champagne cocktail, 18 cl.		

Eaux minérales. 1/4 70 1/2 90

DEMANDEZ LA CARTE DES VINS
PLACE GAILLON PARIS (2e)   DROUANT

Mesdames... Mesdemoiselles... Messieurs...
chez nous vous êtes chez vous
Asseyez-vous   Reposez-vous
Consultez ce Guide-Menu
CHEZ DUPONT TOUT EST BON
(DÉPOSÉ)
à votre service à toute heure
JOUR ET NUIT
Pain, Couvert et Serviettes ... 30.

LE PETIT DÉJEUNER SUISSE bien complet
Café au lait ou chocolat, ou thé au lait, croissant, petit pain, beurre, miel, confiture
et compote de fruits (jusqu'à midi).   100

LES HUITRES — LES COQUILLAGES
Catchup - Pickles - Piccalilli ...
CHOIX DE FRUITS DE MER : 3 fines de Claires, 3 Belon, 3 Marennes (le plateau) 210
(Pain de seigle - beurre - Citron - Un verre de Bourgogne blanc).
Les Moules Marinière à notre façon.
Escargots de Bourgogne (la douz.)
Portugaises Fines de Claires

Café - Thé - Chocolat - Boissons chaudes
THÉ complet, Ceylan ou Chine, avec toasts beurrés, confiture ou une pâtisserie 100
CHOCOLAT meilleux, avec toasts beurrés, confiture ou une pâtisserie 100

Glaces - Entremets

Pâtisserie

Si vous êtes satisfaits, rappelez à vos amis que...
CHEZ DUPONT TOUT EST BON

BRASSERIE LIPP
151, Boulevard Saint-Germain, PARIS
TÉL. LIT. 53-91

FERMÉE LE LUNDI

Menu du 9 Novembre 1948   Couvert

HUITRES	Claires (avec citron)	la dz.	12
	Belon (ou sauce)	la dz.	27
ESCARGOTS de Bourgogne		la dz	
CAVIAR FRAIS DE RUSSIE			750

CERVELAS REMOULADE (SPÉCIALITÉ) 10

Filets de Harengs   Pommes à l'huile 90
Museau de bœuf 80 —   Hareng de la Baltique 100
TRICANDEAU 120 —
Médaillon de mousse foie d'oie en gelée
Tomates - Pommes à l'huile 80. SARDINES
Potage : St Germain 35 - Œuf mayonnaise

Œufs : œufs plat au jambon 175.

CHOUCROUTE GARNIE (spécialité) 27

Plat du Jour : Veau sauté jardinière 2.
Steack grillé Pommes Pont Neuf
Assiette anglaise (Roastbeef - Veau)
(mayonnaise ou salade) et Gigot

Cantal
Glace 5
Poire 100
Pomme 100
Mandarine (2)
Banane

RESTAURANT DROUANT (PLACE GAILLON)   Couvert 120
PAVILLON ROYAL (Bois de Boulogne)

CHAMPAGNE GRATIEN BRUT
LA Bttle 1350

HUITRES ET COQUILLAGES

	Le doz.
Portugaises de Claires Spéciales	400
Armoricaines Moyennes	450
Supérieures	550
Belon — Fines	550
Supérieures	750
Extra	950
Choix extra	1200
Super extra	1400
Marennes vertes Moyennes	550
Supérieures	720
Extra	880
Choix extra	1150
Super extra	1400

Beurre 50   1/2 citron 25   Ketchup, 50

Assiette de fruits de mer	750	Crevettes Bouquet	700
Oyster cocktail	450	Crevettes grises	250
Prâtres. La douzaine	460	Moules parquées	250
Clams. La pièce, moyen 140 gros.	220	Oursin. Pièce.	50
Palourdes. La douzaine 460		Escargots de Bourgogne, la douz	700

Saumon fumé 700   Anguille fumée.

Caviar frais extra		Le lourd
Pressé		1400 800
Œufs de saumon		700 300
		350
Coquille de moules mayonnaise	280	Langouste sauce mayonnaise 1400
Coquille de poisson	400	Homard froid à la nage 1400
Coquille de langouste Parisienne	350	Coquille de crabe. 350

BUFFET FROID
Jambon de Bayonne	450	Pâté de Pordreau Lucullus	780
Jambon d'York	420	Œuf à la gelée au jambon	120
Langue écarlate à la gelée	420	Foie gras des Landes au Porto	780
Assiette charcutière	550	Poularde en gelée, le quart	700

Salade 150 Pied de céleri 100 Salade de légumes 280

SPÉCIALITÉS ET PLATS DU JOUR
Pilaff de moules au curry	300	Moules Marinière.	
Pilaff de crabes à l'Américaine	350	Coquille de turbot	
Pilaff de homard à l'Américaine	750	Coquille de homard	
Bouillabaisse de la maison	750	Bisque de homard	

COQUILLE SAINT JACQUES   450
Filets de sole Drouant	550
Merlan pané Colbert	420
Suprême de barbue au plat	500
Rouget barbet gr. Mtre d'hotel	520
Quenelles de brochet Cardinal	580
Sole frite sauce tartare	620

Œufs cocotte Périgourdine 280
Omelette à l'espagnole 250

CUISSEAU DE PORC FRAIS TRUFFÉ
Poulet sauté archiduc 1/4	760	Salmis de faisan
Civet de lièvre à la Française	650	Rumsteck poêlé
Caille de vigne au raisin	420	Rognons sauté
		Perdreau rôti sur canapé 1.40

Epinards en branches 190
Petits pois nouveaux à la crème 200

DESSERTS
Plateau de Fromage 200   Roquefort Société
Grand gâteau. 260   GLACES : Coupe
Tarte aux fruits 260   Praliné
Meringue glacée 260   Moka
Chantilly 260   Sorbet
Pêche Melba 350   Nesrou
Fraises Melba 350   Mousse
Fraises Marie Antoinette 350   Parfait
Compote assortie 300   Crème fraîche

FRUITS
Pomme 250 Poire 250 Raisin 350 Ananas
Banane 50 Orange 120 Pamplemousse 400 Fruits
Pêcher 350 Framboises 400

VOIR AU DOS LA CARTE DES VINS

ŒUFS		OMELETTES	
Coque (les deux)	70	Omelette nature	90
Plat (les deux)	70	fines herbes	90
Brouillés au fromage	120	bacon	120
au bacon	120	jambon	120
au jambon	120	fromage	120
Œufs, saucisse sur toast	120		

Froid : Œuf à la gelée la pièce 80
Œuf Mimosa pétronille la pièce 70

Légumes frais 50 à 70 Le Yaourt 50
Salades de saison Crème Gervais (les deux)
Nos fromages Fromages " Médaine "

DESSERTS ET FRUITS DE SAISON
(Consultez le Menu du Jour)

SANDWICHES
PAIN RICHE, PAIN MIE, OU PAIN SEIGLE
Jambon pain mie blanc	45	Truite
pain au mie seigle	45	Salami de Milan
pain baguette	45	Saucisson d'Arles
Beurre et cornichons	45	Saucisson de Paris ail
Saucisse chaude de Colmar	45	Roastbeef
Foie de bœuf	45	Langue
Rillettes	45	Veau

Spécial Dupont (chaud)
(Gruyère, jambon de Paris entre deux pains de mie revenus au beurre). Chaud ... 110

CHEZ DUPONT TOUT EST BON
Si vous n'êtes pas dites le nous

145

✳ Miss K ✳

Here is the famous salted butter caramel *religieuse* recipe of Christophe Michalak,
referred to in his shops as "Miss K." Finally, the veil is lifted on how it's made.

Émilie Franzo

A MYTHICAL CAKE

It was in 2002, when he was pastry chef at the Plaza Athénée, that Christophe Michalak invented the dessert that became his signature and one of the great symbols of his career: the salted butter caramel religieuse. Composed of two cream puffs crowned with a delicate crackly topping and filled with a caramel *crémeux* filling, this is now the most requested pastry in his shops.

MICHALAK IN 3 DATES

1973: born in Senlis (Oise)
2000: becomes pastry chef at the Hotel Plaza-Athénée in Paris
2005: becomes World Pastry Champion

A SHORT HISTORY OF THE CRACKLY TOPPING

Thanks to the crunch and to the aesthetic quality that it brings to the pastry, this mixture of butter, flour, and brown sugar is, according to Michalak, a must-have for every self-respecting cream puff. However, this simple pâte sablée dough was not always popular among other pastry chefs. Michalak learned the technique during his apprenticeship in Belgium, but did not apply it until the 2000s after seeing Best Craftsman of France (MOF) chef Stéphane Leroux modernize the recipe. The idea clicked and now many pastry shops prepare their religieuse pastries in this way.

——— THE RECIPE ———

MAKES 10 RELIGIEUSE PASTRIES

For the caramel crémeux filling
2¼ cups (550 g) whole milk
1 vanilla bean
1 cup minus 2½ teaspoons (190 g) +
2 tablespoons plus 1¼ teaspoons (30 g)
superfine sugar
4 large (90 g) egg yolks
1½ ounces (40 g) pastry cream powder
⅓ teaspoon (2 g) fleur de sel sea salt
21½ tablespoons (305 g) unsalted butter, room temperature
For the caramel whipped cream
½ cup plus 2 tablespoons plus 1 teaspoon (150 g) ultra-pasteurized light cream (35% fat)
⅓ ounce (10 g) gelatin
¼ cup (50 g) superfine sugar
For the pâte à choux (cream puff dough)
¼ cup plus 1 tablespoon plus ½ teaspoon (75 g) water
¼ cup plus 1 tablespoon (75 g) whole milk
¾ teaspoon (3 g) superfine sugar
½ teaspoon (3 g) salt
4 tablespoons plus 1¾ teaspoons (65 g) unsalted butter
¾ cup plus 1 tablespoon (80 g) all-purpose flour
3 large (145 g) eggs
For the crackly choux topping
3 tablespoons plus 1¾ teaspoons (50 g) butter
2⅛ ounces (60 g) turbinado sugar
½ cup plus 1 tablespoon plus 2 teaspoons (60 g) all-purpose flour

Small fudge cubes, for decoration
Almond paste, for finishing

Make the caramel crémeux filling.
Warm the milk with the vanilla bean. In a heavy-bottom saucepan, heat the 1 cup minus 2½ teaspoons (190 g) of superfine sugar, adding it slowly in three batches, until it turns a smooth dark brown caramel. Add the warm milk to the caramel in three batches, while stirring, then remove the caramel from the heat. In a saucepan, whisk together the egg yolks, the 2 tablespoons plus 1¼ teaspoons (30 g) of superfine sugar, the pastry cream powder, and the sea salt. Add the caramel to the

yolk mixture, and bring the mixture to a boil for 30 seconds, while stirring continuously. Add the butter in pieces and emulsify the cream using an immersion blender. Transfer the cream to a bowl and cover the surface with plastic wrap. Refrigerate for at least 2 hours.

Make the caramel whipped cream. Warm the cream and incorporate the gelatin until the gelatin is melted. In a heavy-bottom saucepan, heat the sugar, adding it slowly in three batches, until it turns to a smooth dark brown caramel. Off the heat, carefully pour the warm cream into the caramel while stirring. Let the caramel cool, then refrigerate it until it's completely chilled. Whip the caramel cream to soft peaks, then keep it refrigerated.

Make the cream puff dough. See the recipe for pâte à choux on page 120 (piping two different sizes: small and large).

Make the crackly choux topping. Stir together the butter, turbinado sugar, and flour until you have a smooth paste. Thinly spread the mixture between two sheets of parchment paper and let it cool for 20 minutes, or until set. Cut out two sizes of rounds, one size measuring 2 inches (5 cm) and the other size measuring 1⅛ inches (3 cm) in diameter. Place the rounds on top of the baked cream puffs according to their size. Preheat the oven to 400°F (210°C). Place the cream puffs in the oven, turn off the oven, and bake them for 10 minutes. With the puffs still in the oven, turn the oven back on to 300°F (150°C) and continue baking the puffs for 25 minutes.

Assembly: Fill the cream puffs with the caramel crémeux. Roll out the almond paste and cut out ten disks measuring 2¼ inches (6 cm) in diameter. Place an almond paste disk on top of each of the larger cream puffs, then place the smaller cream puffs on top, bottom side down. Finish with a rosette of caramel whipped cream and top with a cube of fudge.

> **HOW DO YOU RECOGNIZE A BAD RELIGIEUSE?**
> ☞ *a grainy cream filling*
> ☞ *a soggy cream puff*

skip to ......
The Paris-Brest, p. 319

The Forgotten Cabbage

It is said to be "forgotten," but it persists despite its reputation as a rustic and smelly vegetable. However, when prepared stuffed, it is a monument to French gastronomy!

Xavier Mathias

STUFFED CABBAGE
by Denise Solier-Gaudry

PREPARATION TIME: 30 MINUTES
COOKING TIME: 1 HOUR 45 MINUTES
SERVES 6

1 large head cabbage
4 slices bread
⅔ cup (150 mL) milk
4 sprigs parsley
1 clove garlic
7 ounces (200 g) raw foie gras
9 ounces (250 g) ground sausage
7 ounces (200 g) ground veal
7 ounces (200 g) ground beef
2 eggs
Salt and freshly ground black pepper
4¼ cups (1 L) chicken broth
2 sprigs thyme
Kitchen twine

Remove and discard the outer leaves of the cabbage. In a pot of boiling salted water, blanch the cabbage, whole, for 15 minutes. Drain it in a colander, then let it cool. Dip the bread slices in the milk, then squeeze out the excess milk. Wash the parsley and remove the leaves. Peel the garlic clove, then chop it together with the parsley leaves. Cut the foie gras into large cubes.

In a large bowl, thoroughly combine the ground meats, bread, garlic, parsley, and eggs; season with salt and pepper. Place the cabbage down on a towel and gently spread the leaves open, all the way to the core. If there is still too much water in the cabbage, blot it with paper towels. Remove the cabbage heart with a knife, finely chop it, and add it to the meat mixture. Incorporate the foie gras, then fill the center of the cabbage with the stuffing. Close the leaves up to encase the stuffing. Tie the cabbage closed with kitchen twine, as if tying a package, and place the cabbage in a flameproof casserole dish. Pour the broth all around it, add the thyme sprigs, and cook over low heat for 1 hour 30 minutes (although a longer cooking time will not hurt it).

To serve, place the cabbage in a shallow serving dish and carefully remove the twine. Pour the cooking liquid all around it. Slice it into thick wedges, and serve.

Cabbage—a large family!
GENUS *BRASSICA*

SPECIES *OLEACERA*

Botrytis
Type: cauliflower
Varieties: Boule de Neige, d'Angers

Capitata
Type: cabbage (smooth leaves)
Varieties: Coeur de boeuf, de Châteaurenard, Filderkraut, Quintal d'Alsace, Rodynda (red)

Sabellica
Type: curly, green (kale)
Varieties: Westlandse Winter, Beurré de Jalhay

Cymosa
Type: broccoli
Varieties: Noir de Toscane

Gemmifera
Type: Brussels sprouts
Varieties: De Rosny

Gongylodes
Type: kohlrabi
Varieties: Blanc Hâtif, de Vienne

Ramosa
Type: perennial kale
Varieties: De Daubenton

Sabauda
Type: savoy cabbage (crinkled leaves)
Varieties: De Pontoise, Plainpalais

Costata
Type: Tronchuda kale
Varieties: Tronchuda

SPECIES *RAPA*

Chinensis
Type: Chinese cabbage
Varieties: bok choy

Pekinensis
Type: Chinese cabbage
Varieties: pe-tsai

skip to
Good Soups All Around!, p. 170

Grimod de la Reynière

A literature and theater critic, he also invented gastronomic writing. His famous supper was an event ahead of its time.
Laurent Séminel

The strange Monsieur Grimod de La Reynière
(1758–1837)

A rich family
Alexandre's father, Laurent Grimod de La Reynière, was a *fermier general* tax collector and post office administrator. As such, he amassed a fortune.

His grandfather, who "suffocated on piece of pâté de foie gras" and died on February 10, 1754, owned the best restaurant in Paris.

An illness
Alexandre was born with deformed hands. His father had artificial hands made for him in Switzerland. Always gloved, his prostheses enabled him to write.

Famous friends
His grandfather was associated with Voltaire and his daughter Maria in the commune of Malesherbes.

Grimod's friends included Beaumarchais.

Bibliothèque d'un Gourmand

A Grimod chronology

November 20, 1758: birth of Alexandre Balthasar Laurent Grimod de La Reynière. He is the son of Laurent Grimod de La Reynière and Suzanne Françoise Élisabeth Jarente de Sénar d'Orgeval.

1774–1775: studies at Louis-le-Grand

1775–1776: travels through family territory in the provinces of Bourbonnais and Lyonnais, then through Dauphiné, Geneva, and Lausanne, where he stayed for ten months.

1777: after earning a degree in law, Grimod becomes a lawyer. He also contributes to the *Journal de Théâtres*.

1780: serves as a lawyer in the Paris Parliament and moves to the Château des Tuileries.

1782: moves to his parents' estate at 1, rue des Champs-Élysées. He founds the Société des Mercredis. Dinners are served at the Hôtel des Champs-Élysées until 1796, and then at the Rocher de Cancale until 1810.

1783: publication of *Réflexions philosophiques sur le plaisir*. On February 1, Grimod de la Reynière hosts his famous supper.

September 28, 1784: launch of his *Déjeuners philosophiques* (philosophical dinners).

1786: grimod is forced into exile at the abbey in Domèvre-sur-Verouze, following a royal letter condemning him for a scathing pamphlet. He stays at the abbey until 1788 before traveling to Zurich, Lausanne, Geneva, and Lyon.

1789: travels through Provence, Switzerland, and Germany. Moves to Lyon, where he opens a shop selling groceries. It goes bankrupt in 1792.

1797–1798: publication of *Le Censeur dramatique*.

1803: publication of the first volume of *L'Almanach des gourmands* and establishment of the tasting jury.

1808: publication of *Manuel des amphitryons*.

December 25, 1837: dies in Villiers-sur-Orge.

skip to
The Gastrocrats, p. 354

Bottarga: Mediterranean Caviar

The Greeks say they invented it; Tunisian Jews claim it as their own; Sardinians and Sicilians delight in it; but bottarga has also found a home in the south of France.
Frédéric Laly-Baraglioli

WHAT IS IT?
→ The roe pouch of gray mullets, which spawn in ponds. It's covered in salt, pressed between two boards, and exposed to wind. Presented as two orange lobes.

→ Primarily produced in Martigues (Étang de Berre) or on the eastern coast of Corsica (ponds of Palau, Urbino, Diana and Biguglia).

→ Its taste is iodized and addictive, and so is its cost (about 180 euros—$212—per 2 pounds/1 kg), which makes this the poor man's caviar.

A DISH WITH PRESTIGE
Rabelais may have discovered it along the ponds of Languedoc when he was studying medicine in Montpellier and turned it into one of Grandgousier's beloved dishes in *Gargantua*. It's also one of Casanova's cherished foods, which confirms Curnonsky's hypothesis, who touted it as an aphrodisiac. More recently, Albert Cohen named it as the connection between the Provence of his childhood and the Corfu of his ancestors.

HOW TO ENJOY IT
→ **Plain,** in thin slices, with bread, olive oil, or butter and perhaps a bit of lemon.

→ **With scrambled eggs,** a chickpea or white bean salad, or even a risotto.

→ **With pasta:** for two people and 10½ ounces (300 g) of spaghetti or linguini, grate 1 ounce (30 g) of bottarga, and 1 ounce (30 g) of Parmesan. Make a sauce by combining 5 tablespoons (75 mL) of olive oil, pepper, a third of the bottarga and cheese, and 3 to 4 tablespoons (45 to 60 mL) of cooking water from the spaghetti. Add the pasta gradually, then add the rest of the bottarga and cheese little by little. Serve with a few slices of bottarga on each plate and a drizzle of olive oil. Finely grated orange zest will enhance the dish.

B OR P?

The pronunciation "poutargue," indigenous to Martigues, seems to have established itself without due cause, but the word emerged in the French language initially with the *b*, just as one will find in the Corsican *butaraga*, the Provençal *butargo*, the Italian *bottarga*, the Portuguese *butarga* and also the Arabic *bittarikha* and *butarik*. The root of each is the Coptic *outarakhon* and the Green *oion tarichon*, meaning "egg prepared by salting."

skip to
Caviar and France, p. 254

The Other Whiskey Country

For France, whiskey used to be mostly a matter of consumption: the French were among the very first to drink it! Wake-up call: today, the French have begun making it. And amazing eaux-de-vie malts are coming out of French microdistilleries . . .

Jérôme Lefort

WHAT'S WHISKEY?

It's the generic name for various eaux-de-vie, made by distilling malted and nonmalted grains. Scotland and Ireland both claim to have invented it, the New World (the United States and Canada) adopted it, as did Japan as early as the twentieth century . . . and France is joining the party.

PREMISES AND GRIMACES

For a long time, French distillers were chasing after something outside their reach: Scotch whiskey. It was invented centuries earlier and based on an industrial model, and the French, with their small facilities, couldn't imitate it properly. The result? A French production without a French soul.

ARTISANS AND PARTISANS

This time the French didn't count on the indomitable Gauls. Instead, a new quest, one for a French whiskey: an artisanal approach, both uninhibited and experimental. Everywhere in France brewers use buckwheat, make peat from barley grains after germination and drying, draw on strains of homemade yeast, and distill through pressure to obtain sweeter extracts . . .

THE FRENCH ADVANTAGE

Top-quality grain production

•

The art of malting as reinvented by Frenchmen Nicolas Galland and Jules Saladin at the end of the nineteenth century

•

The science of fermentation as developed by Louis Pasteur

•

Mastery of small alembics, viable barrels, and farming know-how that's respected worldwide

★ PROMISING NUMBERS

In 2017, some **fifty** French distilleries produced close to **800,000** bottles of whiskey. **More than three million** are forecasted by 2020!

★

French expert picks

Nicholas Julhès, founder of the Distillerie de Paris
Philippe Jugé, director of the Fédération du Whiskey de France

Warenghem (Brittany)

Whiskey distiller since 1987: the first French whiskey is from Brittany. In Lannion, extralarge alembics inspired by the Scottish kind; double distillation and aging, for certain eaux-de-vie, in barrels made from oak from the forests of Brittany.
Armorik Single Malt Double Maturation: woody, full-flavored, caramelized.

Distillerie des Menhirs (Brittany)

Buckwheat whiskey distiller since 2002: legendary producer of Pommeau de Bretagne with AOC designation at the family distillery in Plomelin. Guy Le Lay heads the distilling of, yes, buckwheat!
Eddu Silver Brocéliande: strong, roasted, buckwheat, spicy.

P&M (Corsica)

Whiskey distiller since 1999: distilled beer aged in barrels? Whiskey! Hence the partnership between the Pietra brewery and the Mavela distillery, with help from the water from the Col Saint-Georges mountain pass and the white wine and Muscatel barrels from the Domaine Gentile.
P&M Single Malt, 7 years: original, pine sap, sunny, masculine.

G. Rozelieures (Lorraine)

Whiskey distiller since 2000: a grain grower and distiller eager to create a whiskey in a region that produces a large amount of brewing barley. The oak forests are used for the best barrels and the springs are pure.
Single Malt Fumé Collection: woody, delicate, caramel, fluid, long.

Domaine des Hautes Glaces (Rhône-Alpes)

Whiskey distillers since 2014: at 2,952 feet (900 m) in altitude, between Écrins and Vercors, a unique farm and distillery. Homegrown organic barley; naturally low air pressure; wood-burning heat. It was purchased in 2017 by Rémy Cointreau.
Single Malt Moissons: herbal, grainy, very easy, balanced, long.

Les Bienheureux (Aquitaine)

Whiskey blenders since 2015: not distillers, no, but blenders and agers. The fruit of a partnership between Jean Moueix, CEO of the holding company Videlot, notably the owner of Petrus, and Alexandre Sirech, trader. Each time, they blend three French single malts, before final aging in Charente.
Blue Label, Triple Malt: silky, sophisticated, delicate, fruity, accessible.

skip to . . . .
The Good Tubes of the Alembic Still, p. 70

The Tarte au Sucre (Sugar Tart)

Alex Croquet, a baking genius from Lille, is a pro when it comes to making this brioche, which is common in the north of France, but can also be found in Belgium.

Marie-Laure Fréchet and Loïc Bienassis

TARTE AU SUCRE
by Alex Croquet (Lille)

MAKES ABOUT 10 INDIVIDUAL TARTS

For the brioche
2¼ pounds (1 kg) pastry flour (Type 45 or 55)
1¼ pounds (550 g) whole eggs
3 tablespoons plus 1 teaspoon (50 g) water
1½ ounces (40 g) fresh compressed yeast
1 tablespoon plus 1 teaspoon (25 g) salt
½ cup plus 1 tablespoon plus 1¾ teaspoons (120 g) coarse sugar
⅓ cup plus 1 tablespoon plus 1¾ teaspoons (100 g) heavy cream
1⅛ pounds (500 g) unsalted butter, cubed and chilled

For the filling
7 tablespoons (100 g) unsalted butter
3 tablespoons plus 1 teaspoon (50 g) heavy cream
1½ ounces (40 g) egg yolk (about 2 yolks)

For finishing
½ cup minus 2 teaspoons (100 g) light brown sugar

The brioche
Knead together the flour, eggs, water, and yeast for 10 minutes. The dough should be smooth. Add the salt, coarse sugar, and cream. Knead for another 10 minutes. Finally, add the cold butter. Knead the dough for another 10 minutes. Shape the dough into a ball. Let the dough stand for 30 minutes at room temperature. Punch down the dough, then knead it briefly again by folding it over, and let it rest another 30 minutes at room temperature. Repeat this step twice more. After 1½ hours, divide the dough into 9-ounce (250 g) pieces. Shape each piece into a ball and let them rest for another 30 minutes at room temperature. Roll out each piece of dough to form circles 6 to 7 inches (16 to 18 cm) in diameter. Set them aside for 1 hour to rise.

The filling
Melt the butter, then add the remaining ingredients and whisk to thoroughly combine.

Assembly
Using your fingers, create indentions in each of the dough circles. Pour the filling into the indentions, then sprinkle each tart liberally with the brown sugar. Bake for 10 to 12 minutes at 375°F (190°C). Enjoy warm.

A Sweet Lexicon

 Sucre en poudre: also called *sucre semoule.* Superfine sugar made by sifting granulated sugar. It is the primary sugar used in most dessert recipes.

 Cassonade: coarse brown sugar (similar to turbinado) made from sugarcane, with an amber color and a fragrance of rum. From the word *casson,* a term used to describe raw sugar in the sixteenth century.

 Vergeoise: light or dark brown sugar, moist, made from the cooking of syrup from sugar beets. Used in making speculaas or *tarte au sucre.* Beware of confusion: Belgians refer to it as *cassonade.*

 Sucre candi roux: brown rock sugar. Large sugar crystals obtained by slow crystallization for several days of a concentrated sugar syrup.

 Sucre glace: confectioners' sugar, made by very finely grinding white granulated sugar. It is often used in icing glazes, for decorating desserts, or dusted on waffles.

 Sucre pour confitures: jam sugar. A sugar to which pectin from natural fruits has been added (0.4 to 1 percent), along with citric acid. Used to facilitate setting jams and *gelées* (gelled liquids).

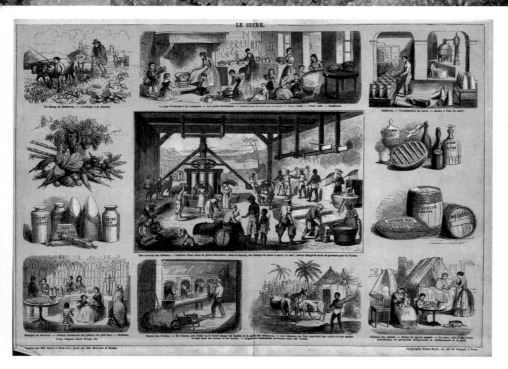

FROM CANE TO BEET
On the eve of the French Revolution, through its West Indian territories, France provided one-third of world's production of sugarcane; in other words, 100,000 metric tons per year.
Starting in 1806, with Napoléon's Continental Blockade and English retaliation, Europe was deprived of American sugar. Napoléon sought to encourage the development of a substitute industry.
In 1812, the emperor visited Benjamin Delessert's factory in Passy. Excited about the beet-sugar bread he was presented, he took off his own Légion d'Honneur to honor the entrepreneur.
Starting in the 1830s, the beet-sugar industry took off. Beet sugar was set to rival sugarcane both in terms of quantity and quality thanks to great technical advances.
Starting in the 1870s, osmosis as a system took root in France. Beets were cut into slices called "cossettes," which were then plunged in a stream of water loaded with sucrose before being filtered and undergoing evaporation. The method is still used today.

skip to
Caramel: The Alchemy of Sugar, p. 392

Chabrolienne Stew

Filmmaker Claude Chabrol was a big fan of dishes served in a sauce, even using them often in his movies. His beef stew recipe is a hearty rendition . . .

Laurent Delmas

The film: *Que la bête meure* (*This Man Must Die*), 1969

The hero (detestable): Paul Decourt, aka Jean Yanne

The scene: at a family luncheon, Paul Decourt humiliates his wife, played by Anouk Ferjac, over her beef stew.

The reply: "Well, this stew is just disgusting! The sauce is watery! Why didn't you reduce it?"

The recipe: beef stew

Cooking advice: Paul Decourt to his wife: "I told you twenty times, when the meat is cooked, you keep it warm, and the sauce, you reduce it separately in a saucepan. Separately!"

The peremptory conclusion: Paul Decourt, always to his wife: "Cooking is the only art that does not lie. A person can mess up when painting or creating music, but with food, no, it's either good or it's bad."

BEEF STEW

5½ tablespoons (80 g) unsalted butter
2¼ pounds (1 kg) beef coulette (top sirloin cuts), cubed
3 onions, peeled and chopped
½ cup plus 1 tablespoon (60 g) all-purpose flour
1 clove garlic, peeled and chopped
1 bouquet garni (rosemary, thyme, bay leaf, or other herbs of your choice)
Salt and freshly ground black pepper
1⅔ cups (400 mL) white wine
1⅛ pounds (500 g) turnips, peeled and chopped
1⅛ pounds (500 g) carrots, peeled and sliced into rounds
1⅛ pounds (500 g) potatoes
1⅛ pounds (500 g) fresh peas, shelled

Melt the butter in a flameproof casserole dish and brown the beef cubes. Add the onions and brown them. Sprinkle in the flour and let it cook until browned. Add the chopped garlic and the bouquet garni, then season with salt and pepper. Add the wine and ½ cup (125 mL) of water. When the liquid starts to simmer, lower the heat, cover, and cook over low heat for 1 hour 30 minutes.

Add the turnips and carrots. Cook over low heat for 50 minutes. Peel and quarter the potatoes, then add them to the pot. Add the peas, then cook for another 40 minutes, or until the vegetables are tender.

Terroir, a Very French Word

The French like to remind the world that the word cannot not be translated, as if it did not exist elsewhere . . . Really?

Loïc Bienassis

AN OFFICIAL DEFINITION

There is an official definition, concocted by the INRA (French National Institute of Agricultural Research), the INAO (The French National Institute for Origin and Quality), and UNESCO:

"A Terroir is a geographical limited area where a human community generates and accumulates along its history a set of cultural distinctive features, knowledges, and practices based on a system of interactions between biophysical and human factors. The combination of techniques involved in production reveals originality, confers typicity, and leads to a reputation for good originating from this geographical area, and therefore for its inhabitants. The terroirs are living and innovating spaces that cannot be reduced only to tradition."

HOW DO YOU SAY IT IN OTHER
LANGUAGES?

German, English, Italian, Japanese, Portuguese, Russian, and other languages adopt the French word. The Spanish *terruño* is sometimes given as a synonym, but it continues to primarily mean "little homeland."

History of the Word

→ The term appeared in the French language as early as the thirteenth century to designate the territory of a village—"the *manans* [peasants] and *habitans* [inhabitants] of said place and terroir," reads one eighteenth-century land register. In the seventeenth and eighteenth centuries, it also became synonymous with "soil." A good terroir is a land where wheat grows well—"the foundation of agriculture is the knowledge of the nature of terroirs," Olivier de Serres tells us (1600).

→ On the other hand, a wine that "smells like terroir" was thought to be coarse. The vague idea wherein a land and climate conferred specific properties to the food it yielded was certainly accepted, but the notion was not associated with "terroir."

→ And during the nineteenth century, when "terroir" came to designate a space united by a common history and culture—the Norman, Provençal, even French terroir—the "product of a terroir" also referred to its connection to a place, but in the simple sense of it being "local," without any particular emotional value.

→ It was later, notably in the 1970s, that it acquired its current sense and became eminently positive.

Anne-Sophie Pic

The only woman to earn three stars in the Michelin Guide, the heir to an amazing culinary venture in Valence is at the peak of her art. The proof is in the recipes!
François-Régis Gaudry

➡ FOUR GENERATIONS OF PICS

Sophie Pic (1870–1952)
Establishes L'Auberge du Pin in Saint-Péray in 1889. The restaurant moves to Valence and becomes the Maison Pic in 1936.

André Pic (1893–1984)
Receives three stars in 1934 and in 1939.

✿✿✿

Jacques Pic (1932–1992)
Becomes chef in 1950.
Two stars in 1956 and three stars in 1976.

✿✿✿

Anne-Sophie Pic (born in 1969)
Becomes chef in 1997.
Three stars in 2007.

✿✿✿

Bistro 7 opens in Valence in 2006.
Opens the Beau-Rivage Palace restaurant in Lausanne in 2009.
La Dame de Pic opens in Paris in 2012.
La Dame de Pic opens in London in 2017.

The only woman to earn three stars as a chef in France
(Born in 1969)

➡ PIC AT THE RESTAURANT

BLUE LOBSTER WITH RED FRUITS (2008)
The king of crustaceans wades in a delicate dashi bouillon made with raspberries, strawberries, and cherries . . . Elegant in color, subtly sharp, intensely aromatic.

OYSTER WITH COFFEE (2014)
A Tarbouriech oyster from the Etang de Thau pond, titillated by sharp rhubarb notes and by an extract of spiced coffee and whiskey.

➡ PIC AT HOME

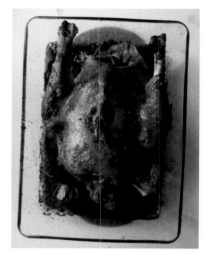

MY MOTHER'S TARRAGON CHICKEN
A recipe for Sundays with the family. You'll need a big bouquet of tarragon. Line the bottom of a baking dish with the tarragon and drizzle it with olive oil. Stuff the chicken with it and coat the chicken with olive oil. Bake for 1 hour 30 minutes to 2 hours at 350°F (170°C). Turn the chicken over every 15 minutes so that each part (thigh, breast, etc.) is well cooked. By the end, it'll practically be chicken confit! I deglaze the pan quickly with water to make the typical and delicious sauce!

BEATEN EGG WHITES WITH BEER
Choose a sweet, white beer. Gently beat egg whites and very carefully add a few tablespoons of beer. The beer will lend fermented notes and give the egg whites a rather firm texture.

JUNIPER-LEMON BUTTER
Knead the butter until it becomes creamy, then add finely crushed juniper berries. Add lemon zest. Refrigerate for 2 hours. This butter is perfect with cabbage or leeks. Add the butter to cooked vegetables. The aroma is extraordinary!

A SURPRISE IN THE PEPPER MILL
Fill your pepper mill with different varieties of peppercorns (voatsiperifery, selim, etc.) and add a bit of licorice root and good ground coffee. This very aromatic blend is perfect on roasted beef.

Freshwater Fish

Thirty edible species of fish inhabit the rivers of France. Before the era of refrigerated transport, local freshwater fish from France's rivers were more popular for eating than fish from the sea, due to availability. Today, French chefs do include fish from the sea on their menus, but the fish is still much less available than freshwater fish at the markets.

Marie-Amal Bizalion

A LITTLE BACK AND FORTH

Freshwater fish that breed in ocean saltwater are called *catadromous*. These include eel, mullet, and flounder, which are all edible. Other species do exactly the opposite, swimming from the ocean to freshwater to breed. These fish, such as Atlantic salmon, shad fish, and lamprey, are called *anadromous*.

FARMED OR WILD?

Minimum sizes, fishing blackout periods . . . The regulations governing the fishing of each fish species in France are so complex that anyone wishing to fish France's waters should consult each department's rules before baiting their hooks. Anyone hoping to return home with a basket of fresh trout caught in mountain streams, for example, should dare not dream—its fishing and sale are strictly forbidden. Otherwise, the river (brown) trout or brook trout, organically farmed, will work perfectly in the mythical and now mostly abandoned recipe for trout amandine from the 1970s.

WHICH FISH LIVE WHERE?

Fast-flowing rivers	Still waters (ponds, lakes, canals)	High-altitude lakes	At home in all waters
Chub	Carp	Broad whitefish	Eel
Gudgeon	Bream	Freshwater burbot	Lamprey
Atlantic salmon	Roach fish	Arctic char	Freshwater pike perch
	Tench		Brook trout
	Perch		Trout (rainbow, river [brown], lake)
	Pike		
	Silurid		
	Catfish		

SILURID AND CATFISH, SAME FIGHT

These two related fish share a frightening trait and a bad reputation. Silurid settle in France's rivers, decimating crayfish, pike, marsh birds (gallinules), and ducks. The record for the largest one caught was from the Rhône in 2015, measuring 8 feet 11 inches (2.73 m) and weighing 287 pounds (130 kg). Such a fish provides flesh that is good for eating, indeed, but for health concerns, make sure the fish does not exceed 3 feet (1 m). Although typically much smaller than this, catfish are the scourge of ponds, impossible to eradicate. Their taste and texture are similar to eel, but cleaning them is daunting and the skin is leathery. Cooked boneless on a barbecue, however, they can be excellent.

INSIDER'S TIP

Freshwater burbot? Who knew? There are plenty in the bottom of France's alpine lakes, and fishermen, hoping to catch arctic char in their nets, pull out 4 to 6 metric tons of them per year. It should be known that burbot, the cousin of hake (but not monkfish), has few bones and a fine, tasty flesh. Its liver, lightly sautéed in butter and seasoned with salt and pepper, has no equal when served on toasted bread.

BROAD WHITEFISH IS ENJOYING ITS HEYDAY

Endemic to alpine lakes, broad whitefish declined in the 1920s, but owes its prolific return to the intentional injection of fish larvae in Lake Neuchâtel in Switzerland. Smoked, raw, grilled, poached, panfried—every cooking method benefits its firm and delicately flavored flesh. Its smoked roe is the bestseller of Laurent Petit, chef of Clos des Sens (Annecy-le-Vieux). And its liver, when sautéed in oil, accompanied by chopped shallots flambéed with rum, and served with a sauce with herbs,* is a real treat.

A suggestion from Éric Jacquier, fisherman on Lake Geneva, who supplies the greatest chefs, from Emmanuel Renaut to Pierre Gagnaire. In his fishery, he offers it fresh, smoked, or prepared in a terrine. 65, Route Nationale, 74500 Lugrin, 09 77 79 00 87

skip to
The Fishmonger's Stall, p. 218

SMOKED AND GRILLED EEL IN PEAR CIDER

Recipe from the book Banquet gaulois: 70 recettes venues directement de nos ancêtres . . . ou presque! (Larousse)

PREPARATION TIME: 20 MINUTES
SOAKING TIME: 1 HOUR
COOKING + SMOKING TIME: 20 MINUTES
SERVES 6

2 cups (500 mL) pear cider
2½ pounds (1.2 kg) eels, cleaned, spinal column removed, skin on
Salt and freshly ground black pepper
Cooking oil, for the grill

For the smoking (which is only possible over a wood-burning grill), use 1 handful of wood chips or shavings from the wood of a fruit tree (such as apple or cherry). Soak the chips for 1 hour in a bowl of water.

In a small saucepan, boil the cider over medium heat for about 10 minutes, or until it has reduced by four-fifths its volume. Chop the eels into two or three pieces, depending on their size. Season with salt and pepper. Lightly oil the grill using a brush. Grill the eels on both sides over medium heat for up to 10 minutes total, but no longer, while basting several times with the reduced cider. At the end of the cooking time, squeeze the wood chips with your hands to wring them of excess water and distribute them over the hot embers. Place a lid over the eels and let them smoke for 5 minutes.

TROUT AMANDINE

PREPARATION TIME: 10 MINUTES
COOKING TIME: 15 MINUTES
SERVES 4

4 whole trout, or 8 trout fillets
Salt and freshly ground black pepper
4 tablespoons (57 g) unsalted butter
2 tablespoons sliced almonds
1 lemon, sliced

Season the inside and outside of each trout with pepper. In a skillet, heat half the butter until warm, then fry the trout for 8 minutes on each side (4 minutes if using fillets). Season with salt and pepper. Meanwhile, melt the remaining butter in a separate skillet, add the almonds, and lightly brown them; remove them from the heat to stop the cooking. Place the trout on a dish, top with the almonds, and drizzle with the melted butter from the pan. Decorate with lemon slices.

The Influence of French Cuisine on the United States

Either born or trained in France, these chefs have helped change the tastes of the United States, a country now abundant with excellent French products and chefs.

Estelle Lenartowicz

skip to ....
Daniel Boulud, p. 155

Frenchies who realized their American dreams

1 Jean-Baptiste Pasyplat (1753–1805): former cook for the Archbishop of Bordeaux. He opened Julien's Restorator in 1793, one of the first restaurants in Boston. **Most popular dish:** sea turtle soup.

2 Charles Ranhofer (1836–1899): chef of Delmonico's (New York City) from 1862 to 1898, a French restaurant declared the best in the country at the time. Author of *The Epicurean* (1893), containing over 3,500 recipes. **Most popular dish:** lobster Newberg (made with butter, cream, and Madeira).

3 Henri Soulé (1903–1966): native of Bayonne. In 1942, he opened Le Pavilion in New York City, then La Côte Basque, offering French dishes popular with Jackie Kennedy-Onassis and Frank Sinatra, among others (despite his reputation of having an unpleasant personality). **Most popular dish:** pike dumplings with Nantua sauce.

4 René Verdon (1924–2011): hired into the White House by the Kennedys in 1961. Departed under the presidency of Lyndon B. Johnson, who was not very fond of his talent. In 1972, his restaurant Trianon (San Francisco) became a hit. **Most popular dish:** scallop mousseline.

5 Daniel Boulud (born 1955): famous chef of restaurant Daniel, three Michelin stars, in New York City, which he opened in 1993. He has thirteen restaurants and three fine food stores spread over three continents. **Most popular dish:** foie gras and truffle burger.

6 Jean-Georges Vongerichten (born 1957): born in Alsace. Opened his first bistro in New York City in 1991, which was a pioneer of Asian-French fusion. He currently heads a world empire, including the Michelin-starred Jean-Georges (New York City). **Most popular dish:** crab toast with sriracha mayonnaise.

7 Ariane Daguin (born 1958): born in France. Created the food company D'Artagnan in 1985, then the sole supplier of foie gras to the United States. Products from her well-bred feathered and furry animals entice all chefs. **Most popular product:** Green Circle Chicken, an old breed raised on the grains and vegetables from the Amish in Lancaster, Pennsylvania.

8 Dominique Crenn (born 1965): in 1988, she left France with great courage to work under the direction of Californian chef Jeremiah Tower. In 2011, she opened Atelier Crenn (San Francisco). She was the first woman in the United States to be awarded 2 Michelin stars. Named Best Female Chef in 2016 by the World's 50 Best list. **Most popular dish:** Kir Breton— a cocoa butter shell filled with apple cider, with crème de cassis.

9 Éric Ripert (born 1965): born in Antibes, trained at La Tour d'Argent and under Joël Robuchon (Paris). Chef of Le Bernardin (New York City) since 1991. **Most popular dish:** thin slices of raw tuna on toasted baguette with foie gras, olive oil, shallots, and lemon juice.

10 Dominique Ansel (born 1978): sharpened his skills at Fauchon, then became pastry chef of Daniel (by Daniel Boulud). Opened his own pastry shop in New York in 2011. **Most popular item:** the Cronut, a croissant-donut hybrid created in 2013, for which people line up every morning to purchase.

American chefs who became part of the French melting pot

11 Julia Child (1912–2004): learned cooking in Paris from top chefs. Her show *The French Chef* (1963–1973) demystified French cooking for millions of Americans. **Most popular dish:** boeuf bourguignon.

12 Alice Waters (born 1944): one year in Paris changed her perspective on food. In 1971, she created the concept of farm-to-table in her bistro Chez Panisse (Berkeley, California), which became a world symbol of cooking dedicated to involvement with local and organically grown products. **Most popular dish:** blackberry ice cream.

13 Thomas Keller (born 1955): trained under Roland Henin in Rhode Island, then at Guy Savoy and Taillevent in Paris. His restaurants the French Laundry (Napa Valley) and Per Se (New York City), each have three Michelin stars. **Most popular dish:** pearl tapioca with oysters with caviar.

14 Anthony Bourdain (1956–2018): stirred with emotion as a child after eating an oyster in France, he served classic French dishes at Brasserie Les Halles (New York City; closed in 2017). Became a frank-speaking popular TV host; tragically died in 2018. **Most popular dish:** snails in garlic butter.

Daniel Boulud

This Michelin-starred chef, based in New York City, was raised the son of French farmers and now runs a culinary empire spread over three continents.
Marie-Amal Bizalion

As a result of time spent on the family farm as a child, Daniel Boulud's approach to cooking is to maintain the flavor of fresh, simple products, which he loved cooking with his grandmother. He began his apprenticeship with a Lyon chef at age fourteen, eventually refining his approach to French cuisine before landing in New York, where he has remained.

An alliance of French techniques and local flavors

Boulud opened his own fine-dining restaurant, Daniel, in New York. In 2001, on the menu of DB Bistro Moderne (his contemporary casual restaurant), he introduced a burger with foie gras and truffle, ingredients that were not found on burgers in the United States. Sinfully moist with an elaborate presentation, the dish embodies the fusion of French and American cultures. Today it remains a bestseller, along with other dishes emblematic of the two cultures, such as Boulud's crisp potato paupiette of sea bass.

KEY DATES

March 25, 1955
Born in Saint-Pierre-de-Chandieu, near Lyon (France).

1969: begins an apprenticeship at Nandron, a Michelin-starred restaurant in Lyon. Experiences a culinary epiphany after tasting caviar.

1972–1980: sharpens his skills working at restaurants under famous French and Danish chefs.

1982: arrives in New York City.

1986: serves as executive chef of Le Cirque until 1992; it's a restaurant with one of the most sought-after tables in New York.

May 1993: opens his restaurant Daniel.

2006: launch of the 1st edition of the New York Michelin Guide. Earns two stars for Daniel and one star for Café Boulud.

2010: Restaurant Daniel earns three Michelin stars

2018: owns thirteen restaurants and three fine food stores spread over three continents.

> *"Meeting Daniel's dad, one begins to understand the roots of his perfectionism."*
> Anthony Bourdain, on CNN's *Parts Unknown*

THE DB BURGER

Once this burger is completed, serve it right away. The first step is to prepare beef rib eye by flouring and browning it. In the same pot, cook a mirepoix of carrots, celery, onion, garlic, thyme, and a little tomato paste. Deglaze the pot with red wine, and braise the meat in the wine for 4 hours over low heat. Remove the meat, let it cool, then shred it. Thoroughly combine the meat with the cooked vegetables. Shape the mixture into large patties with a cube of foie gras and shavings of black truffle enclosed in the center of each. Halve Parmesan and poppy seed brioche buns (homemade buns are best), and in a skillet brown the undersides of the buns in butter. Spread a French mustard on top of the bottom bun, then spread on some tomato compote. Add a layer of freshly grated horseradish, rings of raw red onion, thin slices of *fresh* tomato, and some leaves of frisée. Just before serving, gently grill the meat patties on all sides and let them rest for several minutes in a warm oven before placing them on the buns, with or without additional shaved truffle, as desired. Serve with homemade fries!

HIS FRENCH MENTORS
→ **Georges Blanc** (Mère Blanc), "A young entrepreneur passionate about his region"
→ **Roger Vergé** (Moulin de Mougins), "a cosmopolitan, in love with Provence"
→ **Michel Guérard** (Les Prés d'Eugénie), "a culinary poet, one with delicacy and finesse"

HIS SUCCESSFUL STUDENTS
→ **Gavin Kaysen,** Spoon & Stable, Minneapolis, Minnesota
→ **Andrew Carmellini,** operates a dozen restaurants and bars in New York and Miami, such as Locanda Verde and the Dutch.
→ **Dominique Ansel,** pastry chef with shops in New York, Los Angeles, Tokyo, and London
→ **Melissa Rodriguez,** chef of Del Posto, New York
→ **Hooni Kim,** chef of Danji and Hanjan restaurants, New York
→ **Gregory Stawowy,** chef of Le Suprême, Lyon (France)

★ ★ ★

What evokes nostalgia . . .
The taste of strawberries from the woods of Provence and the truffle of Périgord.

Giving back
For twenty years, he has served as president of Citymeals on Wheels, a charitable organization that serves 18,000 meals per week to the poor.

Proud moments
His French Legion of Honor award. His mosaic portrait by Vik Muniz in the 2nd Avenue subway station in Manhattan.

Upcoming new location?
Mexico City, employing the best ingredients and chefs.

★ ★ ★

This Is Boudin!

Here is a *tour de France* of this famous recipe that uses warm blood!

Blandine Boyer

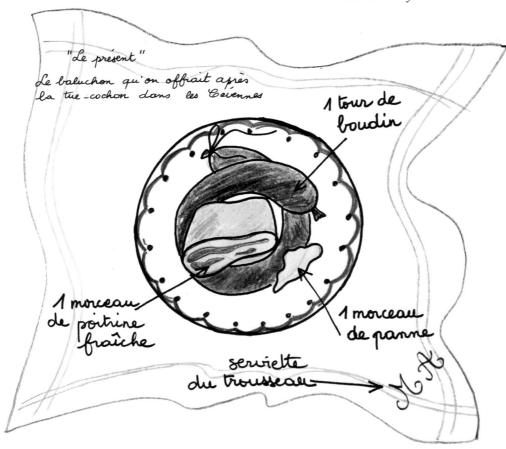

"Le présent"
Le baluchon qu'on offrait après
la tue-cochon dans les Cévennes

1 tour de boudin

1 morceau de poitrine fraîche

1 morceau de panne

serviette du trousseau

Here are the boudins!

Thanks to the trend in bistro dining, artisanal boudin has surged in popularity. Throughout France, pork butchers continue to defend their boudins and offer them in numerous regional, and even local, variations.

"Tomatoes in summer, boudin in winter . . ."

In the past, just after the blood had been collected from a newly slaughtered pig, boudin was made immediately and **eaten the same day**. Blood is very sensitive to heat, and even today in the south of France, serious pork butchers are reluctant to make boudin in the summer. A boudin without preservatives should be **eaten within 3 days** of being made, and it must not be frozen or else it becomes grainy and inedible.

IN PIÉMONT CÉVENOL, A VEGETABLE-BASED BOUDIN

Until the 1950s, boudin was still locally made from wild lettuces, usually bitter lettuces, such as sow thistle, poppy, arugula, salsify, fennel, mallow, or chicory . . . but also made with spinach and lettuces from the garden (except not chard or cabbage). Picking, sorting, washing, cooking, and chopping lettuces to prepare boudin was long and difficult work for the women who were tasked with the job.

To prepare a vegetable boudin, a large amount of herbs, spinach, and sweet onions of Cévennes are slow cooked in lard without browning them. Warm blood is then added, and the mixture is seasoned with salt and pepper. Lots of thyme and quatre épices spice blend (preferably blended and ground at home; the difference in flavor is incomparable) are added with, as an added bonus, perhaps star anise or a good dousing of pastis!

Another unusual ingredient is orange blossom, which should be added in very meticulously measured quantities. If you notice it when tasting the boudin, it means there is too much! All the ingredients are thoroughly combined before encasing the sausages, which should be tied together in 24-inch (60 cm) sections (with 1 twist), then poached in water at 176°F (80°C) before hanging them for several hours to dry and cool.

THE CUSTOM OF THE GIFT

Before the existence of refrigerators and freezers, pigs were killed during the coldest part of the winter, and the meat salted and stored in jars the same day. Each time a pig was killed, its owners would present to their neighbors and friends *le présent* ("the gift") of a bundle containing a plate of boudin, lard, and pork belly (or a tenderloin when feeling most generous), which allowed the recipient to eat a little fresh pork all winter long.

A FEW RECIPES

With quince

Slow cook some quince in demi-sel butter, a little brown sugar, and quatre épices spice blend. Spread the mixture out onto sheets of *feuille de brick* (or phyllo dough), top it with slices of boudin (casing removed), then fold the dough over into a pocket and panfry it very gently in a little lard. Drain on paper towels and serve immediately.

As in Cévennes

Cook pork belly cut into large dice over low heat until browned. Slice some herbed boudin into rounds and gently peel away the casing. Cook the meat over low heat in a little lard until the surface has crisped. Serve the boudin and pork belly with mashed potatoes drizzled with the cooking juices of the meat deglazed with a little water.

As a Parmentier

Make a potato–Jerusalem artichoke purée with cream, a pinch of nutmeg, and 1 whole egg. Cook some onions in a little butter. Combine the flesh from boudin (casing removed) with the onions in a gratin dish. Cover with the purée, then distribute small pats of butter on top, and bake in the oven for 20 minutes, or just until browned on top.

Land and sea

Clean some small cuttlefish. Coarsely chop the heads and tentacles and brown them in a little olive oil. Combine them with coarsely chopped Catalan boudin and stuff the body of the cuttlefish with the mixture. Close the cuttlefish using toothpicks and brown them in olive oil. Simmer them in a little tomato sauce generously seasoned with garlic, thyme, and Espelette pepper.

A multitude of recipes

Boudin is first and foremost made with fresh pork blood, even though dehydrated blood is common! Raw onions, or onions gently cooked in lard, are the most typical additions, along with quatre épices spice blend and cream.

Other ingredients can then be added for either a more refined or coarser texture, such as pork rind, bacon, offal, vegetables, fruits, bread, eggs, herbs and spices, alcohol, or milk . . . basically any additions can be attempted.

All the ingredients are then combined and encased in pork (or sometimes beef)

casings, then poached or steamed before being cooked. Large boudins containing large pieces of other ingredients, which are a sort of hybrid of boudin and headcheese, are eaten cold, or sliced and panfried.

There are also quick versions of boudin that are prepared with the blood and other ingredients cooked directly in the pan.

Small subjective inventory of current or forgotten recipes

Region	Alias	Typical Ingredients in Addition to Blood (not exhaustive)
Alsace		Onions, chopped Reinette apples, cream
Brittany		Apples, onions, chervil
Cévennes		Spinach and bitter lettuces, anise, orange blossom
Anjou	*Gogue*	Cream, milk, chard, eggs, encased in the large intestine
Catalonia	*Boutiffara (boutifar, botiffara)*	Pork, lardons, chile
Lyon		Onions, cognac, herbs, shallots / Cream, onions, chard
Nancy		Onions, cream, apple compote
Quercy		Cheek and jowl, citrus zest, orange blossom, cognac
Poitou		No pork fat but includes milk, eggs, spinach, couscous, or ladyfingers
Saint-Quentin		Onions, eggs
Paris	*Boudin de Paris*	Blood, pork fat, and onions, in equal parts
Maine	*Boudin de Maine PGI*	Blood, fat and throat, and onions, in equal parts
Occitanie	*Galabar*	Head, pork rind, offal, bread, and large intestine, cold or fried and sliced
Limousin		Brined pork, chestnuts
Béarn		Beef head, throat, lung, vegetable stock
Nice	*Trulle*	Chard, rice
Corsica	*Sangui and ventru*	Chard, herbs of the maquis (mint, calament de Corse, chestnuts, or walnuts)
Réunion		Lard, scallions, parsley, sweet potato brèdes (edible leaves), chile
West Indies	*Boudin créole*	Scallions, spices, thyme, bois d'Inde spice, chile, cooked in banana leaves
Burgundy		Milk, rice
Strasbourg		Tongue, diced bacon, beef casing
Audes		Head, throat, pork rind, feet
Coutances		Raw onion, pork intestine
Auvergne		Head, milk

When the pig is killed . . .

In winter, many villages still perpetuate Saint Cochon (*Pig*) Day, a festival or day for enjoying pork. Parishioners and elected officials from both sides forget their differences for a moment to commune elbow to elbow around the divine boudin.

In former times, France revered the pig: it fed the country during the winter. Some referred to it as "Moussu" ("monsieur") or even "minister" to avoid calling it by name. The tradition of butchering or processing a pig on the farm among family or friends who share the passion for it (with ideally a *monsieur* weighing at least 330 lb/150 kg, and fed on acorns or chestnuts), is experiencing a resurgence everywhere in France.

From one region to another, France mainly talks about *tue-cochon* (pig butchering) or other grammatical inventions: *tuaille, tuade, tuaison,* or even *tuerie* . . . In Occitanie, the expression is to "break up" the pig: *pele-porc, pélaporc, péléra,* while in Corsica it is "cut down": *a tumbera.*

Today, the slaughterhouse has taken over the processes of the butchers (called *mataporc* in the Pyrénées or *sagnaïre* in Languedoc), making slaughtering them at home illegal.

skip to ....
Tripe on the Table, p. 338

A *Tour de France* of Breads

Each region of France is known for its own style of bread. Like cheeses, breads are part of French culinary heritage. Here is a tour of many of France's varieties.

Marie-Laure Fréchet

Some favorite breads, from north to south

FALUCHE (Hauts-de-France)
A small crustless sourdough with a tender crumb and a short rising and baking time. It is wrapped in a cloth at the end of the baking time so that the steam can soften it. It gets its name from the black velvet beret worn by students in Lille. ㉑

PAIN TABATIÈRE (Picardy)
A boule in which one-fourth of the dough is rolled out and folded over the top. This bread can also be found in the Jura. ㉔

PAIN BRIÉ (Normandy)
A bread with a compact crumb, obtained by beating the dough (the dough used to include Brie cheese, hence its name). The dough is made with butter and scored with shapes of leaves or ears of wheat. ⑯

PAIN PLIÉ OF MORLAIX (Brittany)
A boule of white bread, folded, then shaped in such a way that the "head" folds down onto its "belly." ③

PAIN CHAPEAU (Finistère, Brittany)
A large boule of bread topped by a smaller one, and pierced with a hole in the center using the finger. ④

PAIN RÉGENCE (Oise)
A bread consisting of five balls of dough. It was one of the first breads to use yeast, which appeared as early as the seventeenth century. It was considered a premium bread. ⑳

BAGUETTE PARISIENNE
A loaf weighing 9 to 10½ ounces (250 to 300 g), shaped to 24 by 25½ inches (60 by 65 cm) and slashed five times. ㉚

FOUÉE DE TOURAINE
A flattened dough baked in a very hot oven so that it "inflates." It owes its name to the wood oven in which it is cooked, the *fou* (or "fire") in Old French. ㊺

PAIN CORDON DE BOURGOGNE
An oblong-shaped bread topped with a cord of dough, which causes the bread to split when baked. ㊲

COURONNE BORDELAISE
This bread consists of seven 3-ounce (80 g) balls of dough stuck together by a disk folded in the center. (52)

COURONNE LYONNAISE
A boule indented in the center using the elbow or the palm of the hand, then stretched into a large hole using the thumbs and hands. ㊾

PORTEMANTEAU DE TOULOUSE (Haute-Garonne)
A 1⅛-pound (500 g) butter-dough package elongated and rolled up to one-third its length. (66)

FOUGASSE (Midi-Mediterranean)
A boule spread out to form an oval, made from a dough using olive oil, scored on each side to resemble a palm leaf. It was originally designed to allow the bread baker to make sure the oven was at the proper temperature before baking other breads. (57)

PAIN DE BAUCAIRE (Languedoc)
A *pain de mie* (white bread loaf) with a very honeycombed crumb achieved from a lengthy kneading time and shaped so that a crack appears during baking. (73)

PAIN VAUDOIS DE SAVOIE
A bread of Swiss origin, round with a crisscross scored in the top. (51)

MICHETTE DE PROVENCE
A small elongated 9-ounce (250 g) bread split in the middle. (78)

MAIN DE NICE
A bread of Italian origin in the form of a four-fingered croissant. (79)

AUVERGNAT
A 1⅛-pound (500 g) boule with a 1¾-ounce (50 g) elongated strip of dough baked on the top.

TORDU (Southwest)
A long, twisted bread. (64)

SÜBROT D'ALSACE
A 1¼-pound (550 g) elongated bread divided into two rectangles and rolled out, attached, and cut into the shape of a diamond. Its name means "penny bread." ㊴

COUPIETTE DE CORSE
A bread shaped into two detachable lobes. (80)

Also in the bread family

ARTICHAUT Bread shaped using a crenellated stick and folded over onto itself. ㉓

BENOÎTON Dark rye bread with dried currants. It owes its name to Saint Benedict, who nearly died because of a small poisoned loaf. ㉜

BOULOT A 1⅛-pound (500 g) white bread, most often sold sliced for toasting and spreads. ㉟

POLKA A round bread scored with a square or diamond pattern. ㉒

TOURTE Bread made from briefly sifted flour.

KOUIGN-AMANN, IS IT A BREAD?

Kouign-amann is made from a bread dough containing butter that is sprinkled with sugar, then rolled and folded in layers as is done with puff pastry.

During baking, the sugar caramelizes, giving the kouign-amann a tender and flaky interior and a crisp exterior. The name of this Breton specialty, which originates from Cornouaille in Brittany, comes from *kouign*, which means cake in Breton, and *amann*, which means butter.

The kouign-amann claims several origins. It was invented at a time when flour was lacking but butter was plentiful, and therefore contains an uncommon proportion of ingredients: 4 cups (400 g) of flour, 12 tablespoons (300 g) of butter, and 1½ cups (300 g) of sugar.

In the bread dough family

the pretzel

This little bread, a symbol of Alsatian and German gastronomy, has been around for at least 1,000 years, with evidence found among the Carolingians. The pretzel is also mentioned in the illuminations of the *Hortus Deliciarum*, a manuscript from the twelfth century, written at the Abbey of Hohenbourg Mont-Saint-Odile in Alsace. Its name comes from the Latin *bracellus*, or "bracelet." Its shape is reminiscent of a heart or two crossed arms. There are many legends to explain its origin.

In French, is it written as the masculine form *le bretzel* or the feminine form *la breztel*? Both spellings are acceptable.

Pretzels are made from a bread dough containing butter, then scalded (poached) in water that contains baking soda before being baked. The poaching gives them their characteristic shiny crust.

SOFT PRETZELS

by Denise Solier-Gaudry

PREPARATION TIME: 30 MINUTES
RESTING TIME: 2 HOURS 20 MINUTES
COOKING TIME: 15 MINUTES
MAKES 15 PRETZELS

5 cups (500 g) all-purpose flour + ¼ cup (30 g) for the work surface
¼ ounce (10 g) active dry yeast
1 teaspoon (6 g) salt
1 teaspoon (4 g) sugar
1 cup (250 mL) lukewarm water
5 teaspoons (30 g) baking soda
1 egg yolk
1 handful coarse salt and/or 1¾ ounces (50 g) cumin seeds

Place the 5 cups (500 g) of flour in a large bowl and make a well in the center. Add half the yeast, then add the salt and sugar to the well. Gradually add the warm water while mixing thoroughly with your hands to make a dough; the dough must be quite firm and homogeneous. Cover the bowl with a clean cloth, and let the dough rise in a warm place for 2 hours. Lightly flour a work surface. Form separate log-shaped pieces with the dough, each measuring 2¾ inches (2 cm) in diameter and 15¾ by 19½ inches (40 by 50 cm) long. Using your hands, thinly roll out both ends, then twist the strip of dough into a figure eight. Set the pretzels aside to rise for 20 minutes. Preheat the oven to 400°F (200°C). Line two baking sheets with parchment paper.

Boil a pot of water with the baking soda and the remaining yeast. Immerse the pretzels in the boiling water. As soon as they float to the surface, take them out using a slotted skimmer and set them aside to drain.

Place the pretzels on the parchment-lined baking sheets. Using a brush, brush them with egg yolk. Sprinkle them with the coarse salt and/or cumin seeds.

Bake for 15 minutes, or until golden brown. Serve hot!

skip to
Traditional French Bread: The Art and the Method, p. 356

Breads by Region

1 Pain plié
2 Bara Michen
3 Pain de Morlaix
4 Pain chapeau
5 Bonimate
6 Miraud
7 Pain saumon
8 Monsic
9 Garrot
10 Pain de Cherbourg
11 Pain bateau
12 La couronne moulée
13 Le tourton
14 La gâche
15 Pain rennais
16 Pain brié
17 Pain à soupe
18 Pain de mie
19 Le maigret
20 Pain régence
21 La faluche

22 Pain polka
23 Pain artichaut
24 Petit pain tabatière
25 Petit pain choine
26 Petit pain pistolet
27 Petit pain auvergnat
28 Petit pain empereur
29 Petit pain miraud
30 Pain de fantaisie
31 Pain marchand de vin
32 Le benoiton
33 Pain saucisson
34 Pain fendu
35 Pain boulot
36 Pain aux noix
37 Pain cordon
38 Pain tabatière
39 Sübrot
40 Pain Graham
41 Pumpernickel
42 Pain tressé et pain natté

43 Le fer à cheval
44 Pain collier
45 La fouée
46 Le pain cordé
47 Le pain de seigle
48 Pain chemin de fer
49 La couronne
50 La couronne de Bugey
51 Le pain vaudois
52 La couronne bordelaise
53 La souflâme
54 Le méteil
55 Le seda
56 La maniode
57 La fougasse
58 Le pain bouilli
59 La rioute
60 Le gascon ou l'agenais
61 La méture
62 Le tignolet
63 La flambade, flambadelle, flambêche

64 Le tordu
65 Le quatre-banes
66 Le porte manteau
67 L'échaudé
68 Le pain de Lodève
69 Le phoenix, le pain viennois
70 Le charleston
71 Le ravaille
72 Le pain coiffé
73 Le beaucaire
74 Le pain scie
75 Le pain d'Aix
76 La tête d'Aix
77 Le charleston niçois
78 La michette
79 La main de Nice et le monte-dessus
80 La coupiette
81 Bretzel

Map of French regional breads, compiled by Lionel Poilâne in 1981 after a long survey conducted throughout France.

CHICKEN AND MORELS IN VIN JAUNE

Passionate about wine, chef François Duthey spent twenty-five years with his wife, Sylvette, at the Auberge de la Tour Penchée in Sévenans, between Belfort and Montbéliard.

VIN JAUNE: THE GOLD OF JURA

Vin jaune is a dry white wine made only in the Jura and from the Savagnin, a local white grape variety.

Production: only four AOCs (*appellations d'origine contrôlée*) are authorized for vin jaune: Château-Chalon, Arbois vin jaune, Vin jaune de l'Étoile, and Côtes-du-Jura vin jaune. The start of its production resembles that of white wine: harvesting and crushing the grapes, then placing them in tanks to ferment. After fermentation, the juice is placed in oak barrels for 6 years and 3 months. During this time, the wine is neither transferred to other barrels nor topped off in the barrel: a veil of yeast forms on the surface and naturally protects the wine from oxidation.

The bottle: the bottle is called a *clavelin* and contains only 21 fluid ounces (620 mL) of wine. This volume corresponds to the proportion of liquid that remains per each 33 fluid ounces (1 L) of wine from the barrel. The other 12 fluid ounces (380 mL) that evaporated are referred to as the "angels' share."

Flavors: vin jaune has aromas of green apple, dried fruits (including nuts), spices (such as curry and saffron), and subtle floral notes. In addition to the chicken with vin jaune recipe (below), it usually pairs well with poultry in general, but also with an aged Comté.

THE RECIPE
by François Duthey

1 handful dehydrated morels
Demi-sel butter
1 shallot, peeled and finely chopped
1 roasting chicken, cut into 6 or 8 pieces
Flour
Salt and freshly ground black pepper
Scant ½ cup (100 mL) chicken broth
½ bottle (375 mL) Savagnin wine
1 tablespoon (15 mL) heavy cream
Scant ½ cup (100 mL) vin jaune

Soak the morels for several hours in a little water to rehydrate them, then reserve the soaking liquid. Wash the morels 6 to 10 times in a large quantity of water, then set the morels aside. In a cast-iron casserole dish, melt a large pat of the butter and add the shallot, then add the chicken pieces. Sprinkle the chicken with a little flour. Season the chicken with salt and pepper, then add the broth, the Savagnin wine, and a scant ½ cup (100 mL) of the morel soaking liquid. Cook, covered, for 40 minutes, or until the chicken is cooked through. Just before serving, add the cream, morels, and the vin jaune off the heat.

2 TIPS!
❶ As in the recipe above, rather than using an expensive bottle of vin jaune, you can add about ½ cup (100 mL) only of vin jaune at the end of the cooking time for the taste, and opt instead for a Savagnin wine for the remainder.
❷ For more flavor, add chopped leek.

skip to
Wild Mushrooms, p. 68

The Wine of the Hanged

When human corpses nourished the vines . . .
*Robert Baud**

THE MYTH . . .

The *Bois des Pendus* ("Woods of the Hanged") or the *Bois de Justice* ("Woods of Justice")[1] in the Franche-Comté is where capital punishment was carried out before the French Revolution. The woods were located on high grounds near towns and villages to ensure the torture was visible and therefore would act as a deterrent. Over time, hanging bodies decomposed as they were exposed to the elements, and with the help of vultures and vermin. The resulting fluids and waste from the bodies contributed nutrients to the soil. Now, among the spontaneous vegetation growing on these lands, one can find mandrake, a plant whose root mimics the form of a human silhouette and which, as a result of this morbid past, contains elements from these wicked deeds, which contribute to the plant's supposed magical properties. Enrichment of the soil has also benefited surrounding plots of land, which were often planted with grapevines once conditions permitted.

. . . THE PRICKLY REALITY IN MONTBÉLIARD

The Principality of Montbéliard belonged, until its annexation to France in 1793, to the princes of Wurtemberg. A watercolor depicting the perspective from the city and the fortress of Montbéliard (see photo), dated June 15, 1589, represents at the top left the site of the "Woods of Justice," which includes several instruments (gallows, racks, etc.) on which corpses and human remains can be seen. The site appears closely surrounded by vineyards that belonged to the city's hospital. History suggests that the vineyard produced quality wines; Ploussard and Savagnin were part of the grape varietals, which were freed from taxes in 1654. It is not known if the flavor of these wines was influenced by the mandrake.

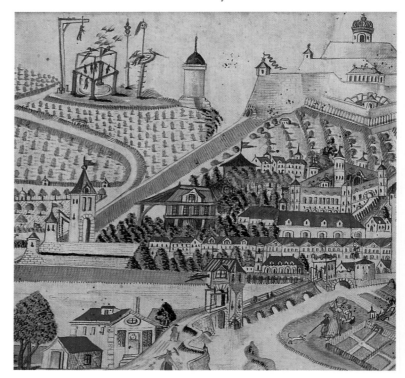

Perspective of the city and fortress of Montbéliard, kindly contributed by the Montbéliard museums. Photo by Claude-Henri Bernardot.

1. *Regarding the names "les Justice," "Bois de Justice," and "Bois des Pendus," the nomenclature used in the land registry of France (nineteenth century) attests the use of these names as granted by feudal law to Lords of "high justice" when handing down capital punishment, which occurred in the seat of each lordship. Consequently, these names were consecrated at a later time by the land registry of France and are frequently seen in reference to France's territories.*

*Passionate winemaker in Moutherot (Doubs)

skip to
Natural Wine, p. 86

Crème Chantilly: Noblesse Oblige

The quintessence of eighteenth-century French sophistication with gallant tea parties in the shade of great trees and taffeta dresses whirling to the rhythm of chatter . . . This is a spotlight (and whisk) on the best-known sweetened cream in the world!

Véronique Richez-Lerouge

Who invented crème Chantilly (sweetened whipped cream)?

4 hypotheses

François Vatel, the legendary maître d'hôtel, is said to have presented a new kind of whipped cream to Louis XIV and the court on the occasion of the famous banquet at Vaux-le-Vicomte in 1671. It was airy and sweetened. Years later, officiating at the Château de Chantilly, he mixed the cream using a branch of boxwood.

Catherine de Médicis, queen of France, is said to have brought the cream whipping technique with her from Italy, where cream was said to have been whisked using broom tree branches.

The Prince of Condé is said to have launched cream "à la Chantilly" in the hamlet he had built in 1775 near the chateau. This genuine little village, with its farm, dairy, prairie of cows, and two cottages, provided a kind of rustic banquet hall for high society.

Brice Connesson's hypothesis: "The first text attesting to the existence of this famous and very particular cream dates back to 1784. That year, **the Baronne Marie Féodorovna** was the first to mention the cream by the name Chantilly in her recounting of a banquet held in the hamlet of the same name."

Crème Chantilly: a success story

The cream began appearing in cookbooks in the nineteenth century. It is described as a "cream beaten into peaks using a whisk," sweetened in the Chantilly manner. At the start of the twentieth century, crème Chantilly became very fashionable and was consumed alone or with fruit and desserts. In the 1970s, it became widespread with the invention of the electric whisks that served as air-blowing beaters. The cream contributed to contemporary French pastries by replacing heavy butter-based creams in cakes. With the advent of electric beaters, crème Chantilly became a staple in every middle-class home.

Chantilly with Mascarpone
by Brice Connesson*

The brilliant French invention is combined with the creamiest of Italian ingredients to create the ultimate temptation!

5¼ ounces (150 g) mascarpone cheese
3⅔ cups (850 g) whipping cream (35% fat), chilled
½ vanilla bean
½ cup (50 g) confectioners' sugar

The day before, combine the mascarpone with the cream. Split the vanilla bean lengthwise in half, scrape out the seeds with a knife, and reserve the seeds and pod. Place the empty vanilla bean pod in the mascarpone-cream mixture and stir in the reserved seeds. Refrigerate overnight to infuse. The next day, remove the vanilla bean pod. Begin by gently beating the cream mixture until small bubbles form on the surface. Add half the confectioners' sugar and begin beating more vigorously. When the cream thickens, add the rest of the confectioners' sugar and continue to beat until the desired texture is obtained. This cream is ideal for filling puff pastry.

*Pastry chef and chocolatier in Chantilly (Oise), La Passion du Chocolat, 45, rue Connétable.

How to make a successful crème Chantilly?

Proportions: 4 cups (1 L) whipping cream, ¼ cup (50 g) confectioners' sugar, ½ vanilla bean.

Cream: choose a quality brand, raw or pasteurized, 35 percent fat minimum. Avoid ultra-pasteurized cream (too many additives). Reduced-fat creams should be banned. You can make crème Chantilly using heavy cream, but the texture will be thicker and more fatty.

Vanilla: infuse the half bean in the whipping cream beforehand for 12 hours in the refrigerator to best steep the aromas into the cream. But you can get away with grating the pod just before whipping.

Sugar: confectioners' sugar is lighter and blends better during whipping. Granulated sugar makes the crème Chantilly heavy.

Temperature: make your crème Chantilly in a round bowl placed in ice. Use cream that has been refrigerated at 39°F (4°C).

Whipping: using a large whisk with fine wires, beat gently while adding the sugar gradually. Maintain an even rhythm. Time: 15 minutes.

With an electric beater: efficient but there are some pitfalls. Begin at low speed, then increase the speed as the cream begins to thicken. Be sure to control the time and speed: if you beat too quickly and for too long, you'll make butter. Time: 5 to 7 minutes.

Tip: add 1 or 2 tablespoons (15 to 30 mL) of crème fraîche to introduce a slightly sour taste.

The rule: you can only lay claim to the name "crème Chantilly" if the cream is whipped using a cream with at least 35 percent fat, a vanilla bean, and confectioners' sugar.

skip to
La Famille Pâte à Choux, p. 120

Magret de Canard

How did *magret de canard* (duck breast) become a centerpiece at every gourmet restaurant in the 1960s? Here are the answers and a recipe.
Arnaud Daguin & Agnès Deville

How my father André Daguin dared to roast a magret de canard rare . . .
"What? Grilling duck breast and serving it rare? But that'll send our guests either to the toilet or hospital!" my grandfather would say to me in 1955, his brow furrowed beneath his beret. "You know duck is dirty and that only cooking it confit for a long time will make it safe." Safe for sure, but also tasteless and dry. This fine cut of red meat deserves a solo, not a supporting role in a pot. We've seen and tasted everything, and rare duck, a French favorite, is conquering the world.
Signed: inspector Magret (André Daguin)

THE "CHOUNES" RECIPE

This is how my friend Agnès Deville cooks duck breast for thirty people.

This cutting-edge method will make you popular in the most exclusive barbecues of Cap d'Agde.

This method for cooking duck breast guarantees precise portions, perfect cooking, and admiration from all your friends. Plan for 1 duck breast per 2 people. Slice each breast lengthwise in half. Using the point of the knife, score the skin in a square pattern, cutting only halfway through the fat of the skin (and not into the meat). Place the breast halves skin side down in a warm pan and heat them gradually; the fat should melt before the skin begins to brown.

Remove the breast halves and empty the fat from the pan. Make a long incision lengthwise down each breast half, stopping just an inch (3 cm) or less from the ends: the choune should open up into a rounded shape. Let them rest (go enjoy a drink with friends). Just before serving, sear the chounes on the flesh side, then turn them over for a few seconds on the skin side to finish them under the broiler. Your chounes are now ready to go.

Is it magret or maigret?

In the Gascon tradition, duck was prepared **confit** and less often **roasted whole.** It was only recently that the idea emerged to remove its *magrets* (breasts). An Occitan word, short for **magre** (thin), the *magret* is the **fillet cut from the breast** of a goose or fattened duck. We can thank my father, **André Daguin**, chef at the Hôtel de France in Auch (Gers) the year I was born (1959), for this method of preparing duck fillets. His recipe for **magret with green peppercorns** (1965) has become a classic of French gastronomy. He recommended using the French term "maigret." But nope! **It was ultimately the Gascon word that took root.**

The Day Vatel Took His Life

Born in Allaines, in the region of Picardy, in the mid-1620s, the Controller-General to the Prince of Condé supervised the festivities planned for Louis XIV's visit to the Château de Chantilly in April 1671. When suddenly . . .
Loïc Bienassis

The King arrived on a Thursday night. There was hunting, lanterns and moonlight, a leisurely walk and a light meal surrounded by daffodils: so far, all went as planned. Supper was served. A few tables did not have roasted meats on account of several unexpected guests. That overwhelmed Vatel. Several times, he said: "I am disgraced; I will not survive such an affront." He said to Gourville [House of Condé steward]: "My head is spinning, I have not slept for twelve nights. Help me give orders." Gourville consoled him as best he could. The missing roast (not at the King's table, but at some of the other twenty-five) was at the forefront of his mind . . . Night fell. The fireworks were unsuccessful; clouds obscured them. It cost six thousand francs. At four o'clock in the morning, Vatel went round and found everyone asleep. He met with a small purveyor who arrived only with two loads of fish; he asked him: "Is that all?" He answered: "Yes, sir." He did not know that Vatel had sent orders to every seaport. He waited for some time; the other purveyors did not arrive. He became excited; he believed he would not receive other fish. He found Gourville and said to him: "Monsieur, I will not survive such an affront; my honor and reputation are on the line." Gourville laughed at him. Vatel went up to his room, set his sword against the door, and thrust it through his heart, but only after the third attempt, for two others were not fatal; he fell to his death.

Nevertheless, fish arrived from north and south. Vatel was sought for its distribution. They went to his room. They knocked at the door, forced it open, and found him drowning in his blood.

Letter from Madame Sévigné
to Madame de Grignan, Paris, April 26, 1671

What is a recipe "à la Vatel?"

Antoine Carême named three of his recipes after the Condé servant (*L'Art de la cuisine fraçaise au xixe siècle: 1833–1843*): turbot fillet à la Vatel, cod fillet à la Vatel, and beef terrine à la Vatel. *Le Grand Larousse gastronomique* from 2007 states that a "Vatel soup is a consommé of sole fumet with a crayfish coulis royale garnish and diamond fillets of sole."

Vatel's suicide **had little impact** on his peers. Vatel was not a chef but rather the **maître d'hôtel**. Vatel left behind **not one** recipe, he **did not write any books**. In short: **only his death made him famous.**

3 Ways to Make an Apple Tart

Some people like apple tart hot right out of the oven, others when it's barely warm and accompanied by a scoop of ice cream . . .

Elvira Masson

— CARAMELIZED APPLE TART —
by Sébastien Dumotier

🍎 **APPLE VARIETY: CANADA GRAY**
PREPARATION TIME: 25 MINUTES
COOKING TIME: 35 MINUTES
SERVES 6

1 (8 oz/227 g) sheet all-butter puff pastry,
homemade or store-bought
3 pounds (1.3 kg) apples
1 cup (200 g) sugar
1 tablespoon plus 1 teaspoon (20 mL) rum
1 tablespoon (15 mL) vanilla extract
1 teaspoon (2 g) ground cinnamon

Line a tart pan with the puff pastry sheet; do not grease the pan. Peel and core the apples. Cut the apples in half and set them aside. Pour the sugar into a heavy-bottom pan and melt it over low heat without stirring it. When the sugar starts to caramelize, add the apples and let them cook for about 10 minutes. Pour the rum and vanilla extract over the apples and sprinkle on the cinnamon; stir gently. Preheat the oven to 350°F (180°C). Arrange the apples on the bottom of the tart pan. Use the caramel in the skillet to brush on top of the apples. Bake for 35 minutes, or until the edges of the crust are golden. Unmold the tart from the pan immediately out of the oven so that the caramel does not stick to the pan while it's cooling. Serve warm, with a scoop of crème fraîche or ice cream.

— NORMANDE TART —

🍎 **APPLE VARIETY: FUJI OR GALA**
PREPARATION TIME: 25 MINUTES
COOKING TIME: 40 MINUTES
SERVES 6

1 (8 oz/227 g) sheet all-butter puff pastry,
homemade or store-bought
2¼ pounds (1 kg) apples
Juice of ½ lemon
3 eggs
½ cup (100 g) sugar
1¼ cups (300 mL) crème fraîche
3 tablespoons plus 1 teaspoon (50 mL) Calvados
(apple eau-de-vie)

Preheat the oven to 350°F (180°C). Line a tart pan with the puff pastry sheet; do not grease the pan. Peel and core the apples. Slice the apples into medium-thick wedges, then sprinkle them with the lemon juice to prevent them from oxidizing. Arrange the apple slices on top of the dough, placing them snuggly against each other so that they almost overlap. In a bowl, whisk together the eggs and sugar until lightened. Whisk in the crème fraiche, then stir in the Calvados. Pour this mixture over the apples. Bake for about 40 minutes, or until the top is golden.

— THIN APPLE TART —
by Denise Solier-Gaudry

🍎 **APPLE VARIETY: GOLDEN**
PREPARATION TIME: 15 MINUTES
COOKING TIME: 35 MINUTES
SERVES 6

1 (8 oz/227 g) sheet all-butter puff pastry,
homemade or store-bought
3 apples
2 tablespoons (26 g) demerara sugar
1 tablespoon (15 g) unsalted butter

Preheat the oven to 400°F (200°C). Roll out the dough onto a parchment-lined baking sheet. Prick the dough with a fork. Peel and core the apples, quarter them, then thinly slice each quarter about ⅛ inch/3 mm thick. Arrange the slices in a rosette pattern on top of the dough, overlapping them slightly. Sprinkle them with the sugar and distribute the butter in small pieces on top. Bake for about 35 minutes, or until golden. Let cool slightly. Ideally the tart should be served while still a little warm.

skip to ....
Tarte Tatin, p. 67

THE APPLE TARTS OF MASTER CHEFS

Alain Passard
Shaped liked a bouquet of roses, with Pink Lady apples thinly sliced and rolled to resemble flowers.

Philippe Conticini
The dough is covered in a thin layer of apple compote, lined with Pink Lady apples, then topped by rosettes of Golden apples in the form of a pyramid.

Cyril Lignac
This apple-cinnamon amandine tart is enhanced by a touch of rum . . . consume it in moderation!

A Sweet Tour of the Candies of France

Jacques Brel preferred candy to flowers and sang the merits of candy shops in one of his best-known songs. Each French region has its own specialty. Here is a collection.

Elvira Masson & Delphine Le Feuvre

1 Angélique confite de Niort: a stick of candy dipped seven times in sugar. Used as a traditional garnish for galettes in Charente.

2 Anis de Flavigny: green aniseed coated with a flavored sugar syrup—violet, licorice, orange, etc. Made in Flavigny-sur-Ozerain, in Burgundy.

3 Bergamot de Nancy: a flat, golden square flavored with essential oil of bergamot.

4 Berlingot de Pézenas: round in shape, unlike its cousin Berlingot nantais.

5 Berlingot nantais: colorful and slightly tart.

6 Bêtise de Cambrai: a small pillow-shaped candy traditionally flavored with mint, striped with caramelized sugar.

7 Bois cassé ("broken wood"): a hard candy. A specialty in Charente.

8 Boule Boissier de Paris: a colored ball flavored with white peach, rose, mandarin, or violet.

9 Cachou Lajaunie: more than ten million yellow, round boxes of these are sold each year! This highly successful black candy has a flavor of licorice.

10 Cafétis: coffee beans coated with dark chocolate, made in the Rhône-Alpes region.

11 Calisson d'Aix: its almond shape hides a smooth paste made of candied fruits and almonds on a thin cookie, covered with a royal icing that is either white or another color.

12 Caramel au beurre salé ("salted butter caramel"): this candy has a great flavor of butter and sel de Guérande sea salt!

13 Caramel tendre d'Isigny ("sweet caramel from Isigny"): made with either crème fraîche or milk from Normandy.

14 Cassissine de Dijon: a fruit paste with black currant that reveals a center of black currant liqueur.

15 Chardon de Metz: each shell of tinted white chocolate contains an eau-de-vie. Be careful not to consume too many at once!

16 Chuque du Nord: a coffee-flavored candy filled with soft caramel, wrapped in a red-and-white striped wrapper.

17 Coque aux fruits de Morangis: multicolored with a jam center.

18 Coquelicot de Nemours ("Poppy of Nemours"): it has the color of a poppy but not its shape! A tangy taste of red berries.

19 Cotignac d'Orléans: a thick quince jelly, soft and melting. Its box is a tribute to Joan of Arc.

20 Coucougnette du Vert Galant: a toasted almond coated with dark chocolate and rolled in a raspberry, ginger, or Armagnac almond paste.

21 Coussin de Lyon ("Lyon cushion"): a chocolate ganache enrobed with almond paste flavored with curaçao.

22 Crotte d'Isard: an almond or hazelnut coated with chocolate and dusted with cocoa powder.

23 Dent de l'ours ("bear's tooth"): a cube of candied pistachio-melon almond paste, coated with white chocolate and topped with a chocolate-coated almond that resembles a bear's tooth.

24 Dragée: a traditional gift for baptisms, communions, and weddings. An almond or chocolate with a sugar coating in various colors.

25 Flocon d'Ariège: a beautiful round and white meringue with a creamy hazelnut praline filling.

26 Forestine de Bourges: almond, hazelnut, and chocolate praline in a satiny sugar shell.

27 Froufrou de Rouen: a small pillow-shaped sugar candy of various colors, filled with jam.

28 Fructicanne du Loiret: cane sugar flavored with orange or lemon in the shape of a wedge of citrus fruit.

29 Fruits confits ("candied fruits"): fruits, first candied in honey during the Middle Ages but now candied in sugar. Specialty of the Apt region in the Luberon.

30 Gallien de Bordeaux: a shell of nougatine with an almond praline center.

31 Gravillon de Gave ("gravel of Gave"): a nougatine paste, with a gray, gravel-like color.

32 Grisette de Montpellier: a small black marble of candy, flavored with honey and licorice.

33 Guimauve de Toulouse ("Toulouse marshmallow"): its unique characteristic is that it contains no egg white.

34 Le Richelieu: a square nougat filled with almond cream and pistachios.

35 Madeleine de Commercy: candies filled with crème de madeleine.

36 Masque noir ("black mask"): licorice candies in the shape of faces, lightly flavored with violet.

37 Menhir de Bretagne: a hazelnut or an almond coated with a milk chocolate ganache, dusted with cocoa. Its shape is reminiscent of megalithic stones.

38 Mini-chique de Pézenas: the lollipop version of the Berlingot de Pézenas!

39 Mousse de Lichen: Arabic gum, known for its digestive benefits.

40 Négus de Nevers: soft chocolate caramel coated with a boiled sugar syrup. Negus was the nickname of the emperor of Abyssinia (the Ethiopian Empire), who visited France at the beginning of the twentieth century.

41 Niniche: a Quiberon specialty. A flavored cylindrical lollipop. It was selected as the "best candy in France" in 1946.

42 Noix du Quercy ("Quercy walnuts"): toasted walnuts caramelized in honey, dipped in white chocolate.

43 Nougat de Sault: white or black, made from lavender honey and almonds harvested in Provence.

44 Nougatine de Nevers: a hard, brown nougat of crushed almonds and caramel, coated in royal icing. Flat and round disks.

45 Orangettes lyonnaises: candied orange peels lightly coated with dark chocolate.

46 Papaline d'Avignon: a small, colorful candy containing a center of oregano liquor from Comtat.

47 Pastille de Vichy: well known for its digestive benefits due to the mineral salts from the waters of Vichy.

48 Pâte de fruits: originally from Auvergne, the first ones were made near Clermont-Ferrand in the middle of the fifteenth century.

49 Pavé de Pouilly: a tender praline coated with nougatine, then coated entirely with ground almonds.

50 Petit poucet de Vichy: a mini candy cane with fruit, slightly tangy, wrapped in glossy paper.

51 Praline: toasted and caramelized almond, originating in Montargis, in the Loiret.

52 Praline rose: a pink sugar praline that is used to make praline tarts, a Lyonnaise specialty.

53 Quenelle de Lyon: a praline topped with white chocolate, whose name is reminiscent of the specialty of *bouchons* (restaurants) in Lyon.

54 Quernon d'Ardoise: Anjou specialty, a fine nougatine coated with white chocolate and tinted blue. The "quernon" refers to a block of shale from which slate is extracted.

55 Rigolette de Nantes: a thin shell of sugar cooked by steam, filled with a soft center flavored with fruit pulp.

56 57 Roudoudou: a colorful shell that children lick, and which supposedly cuts their lips according to Renaud in his song "Mistral Gagnant." The traditional roudoudou is made in Lalouvesc. A Belgian version exists, also.

58 Sottise de Valenciennes: the alternative to the Bêtise de Cambrai. Originally flavored with mint and decorated with a drizzle of red sugar.

59 Sucette de Pézenas: a slimmer Berlingot de Pézenas, but just as colorful.

60 Sucette du Val André: cooked in a copper kettle and shaped by hand.

61 Sucre d'orge de Moret-sur-Loing: produced since 1638, in the form of a hard candy (*berlingot*) or stick, known for helping to cure colds.

62 Sucre de pomme de Rouen: a candy stick made from apple juice, representing the Gros-Horloge de Rouen (the fourteenth-century astronomical clock in Rouen).

63 Téton de la reine Margot ("Queen Margot's teat"): praline flavored with Grand Marnier and coated with white chocolate; an homage to Queen Margot, known for her provocative necklines.

64 Violette de Toulouse: a violet flower, the symbol of the city of Toulouse, crystallized in sugar.

65 Guimauve de Bayonne ("Bayonne marshmallow"): made in the Pays Basque for the Bonbon du Palais, this is a colorful and fragrant candy made from sugar and egg whites.

66 Croibleu: little candies reputed to help cure intoxication thanks to their fresh flavors: mint, pine sap, eucalyptus, and licorice.

67 Chabernac au miel: licorice candies made from gum arabic and honey.

68 Fondant: flavored sugar paste, enjoyed at Christmastime.

69 Berlingot de Cauterets: a hard candy with a very pronounced flavor, originally used by doctors for their patients at thermal baths of Cauteret.

70 Caramel de Pézenas: a soft caramel with flavors representative of the south of France.

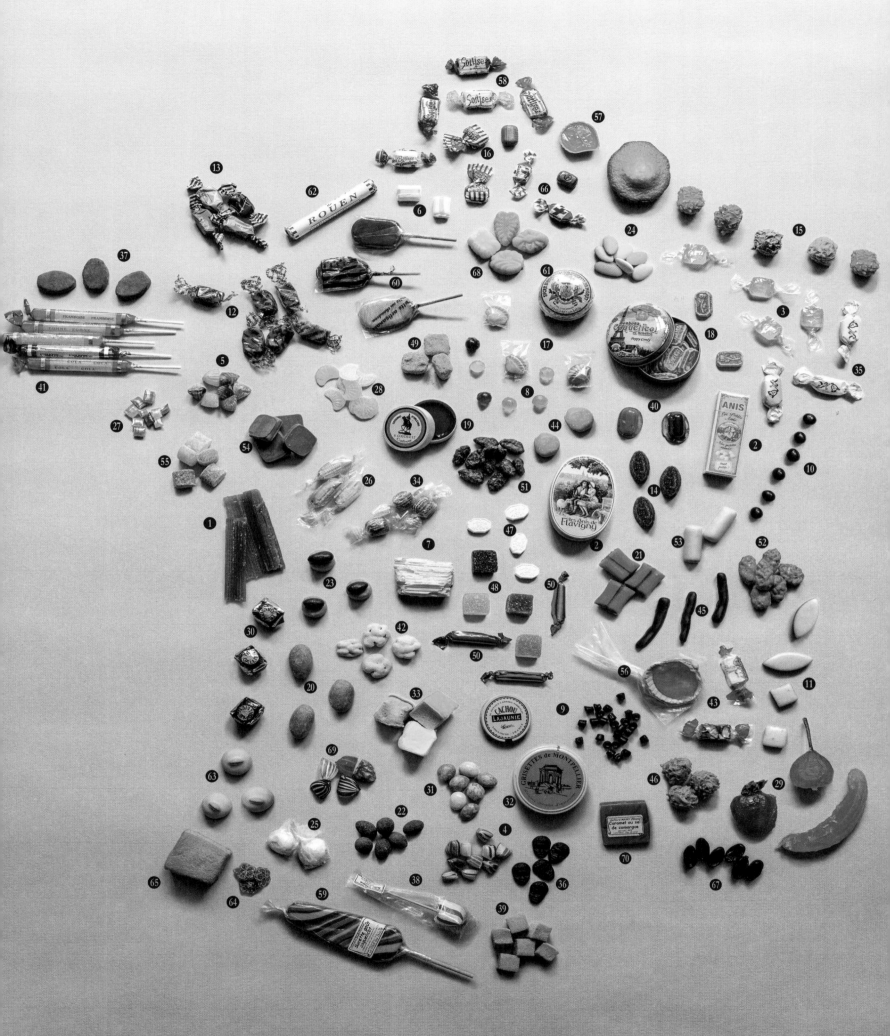

Thanks to Georges Marques who owns the most beautiful collection of the candies of France at the Bonbon du Palais, 19, rue Monge, Paris 5th

· AN INVENTORY OF THE COWS OF FRANCE ·

Each breed of cow has its own area of origin and specific quality of meat.
Here is an overview.

AUBRAC
Mixed (raised for its meat and milk)
Origin: Aubrac plateau (Massif Central)
Label: Label Rouge ("Red Label") since 1999
Physical appearance: tawny coat, ears with a black outline and lyre-shaped horns
Meat: ruby red, fine grain, rustic flavors

BAZADAISE
Origin: Bazas (Gironde)
Label: PGI (Protected Geographical Indication) since 1997
Physical appearance: slate gray coat, curved horns
Meat: marbled, with a beautiful grain, very tender

BÉARNAISE
Mixed
Origin: Béarn (Pyrénées)
Label: protected under the "Sentinelle" Slow Food project
Physical appearance: blond coat, red withers, turned horns
Meat: rustic, with great flavor and nice chewiness

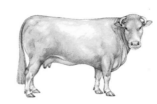

BLONDE D'AQUITAINE
Origin: Aquitaine Basin
Label: not labeled
Physical appearance: wheat-colored coat, white horns with a black tip
Meat: little marbling, very tender

BRETONNE PIE NOIR
Mixed
Origin: Brittany
Label: protected under the "Sentinelle" Slow Food project
Physical appearance: black coat mottled with white; one of the smallest French breeds
Meat: fairly marbled and strong in flavor

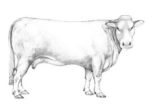

CHAROLAISE (CHAROLAIS)
Origin: Charolles (Burgundy)
Label: Label Rouge ("Red Label") since 1989
Physical appearance: white coat with cream highlights, round and white horns
Meat: deep red and marbled, very tender

CRÉOLE
Origin: Guadeloupe; the only rustic breed in a tropical environment
Label: not labeled
Physical appearance: small size, tawny coat, with a hump on the withers
Meat: rustic flavor

FERRANDAISE
Mixed
Origin: Montferrand (Puy-de-Dôme)
Label: not labeled
Physical appearance: speckled red and white coat, low lyre-shaped horns
Meat: tender, slightly rustic flavor

GASCONNE
Origin: Gascony
Label: Label Rouge ("Red Label") since 1997
Physical appearance: silver-gray coat with black tips
Meat: firm with tight fibers

LIMOUSINE (LIMOUSIN)
Origin: Limousin
Label: first breed to receive the Label Rouge ("Red Label"), granted in 1988
Physical appearance: bright wheat-colored coat, narrow horns that curve forward
Meat: bright red, not very fatty, with a fine grain

LOURDAISE
Mixed
Origin: Hautes-Pyrénées
Label: not labeled
Physical appearance: wheat-colored coat with long straight horns
Meat: very fine, also produces a rich milk

MIRANDAISE
Origin: Gers
Label: not labeled
Physical appearance: large with a light gray coat
Meat: not very fatty

NANTAISE
Mixed
Origin: southern Brittany
Label: not labeled
Physical appearance: wheat to light gray
Meat: marbled, perfect for aging

NORMANDE
Mixed
Origin: Normandy
Label: not labeled
Physical appearance: large size with speckled chestnut brown patches, or black
Meat: marbled and strong in flavor

PARTHENAISE
Origin: the region of Parthenay in Deux-Sèvres
Label: Label Rouge ("Red Label") since 2006
Physical appearance: tawny, plain coat; contoured black eyes; short horns
Meat: bright red, beautifully tender

RAÇO DI BIOU (CAMARGUE)
Origin: Camargue
Label: AOC (*appellation d'origine contrôlée*) since 2003
Physical appearance: deep black coat
Meat: red and slightly fatty with a strong flavor

ROUGE DES PRÉS
Origin: Maine-Anjou
Label: AOC (*appellation d'origine contrôlée*) since 2004
Physical appearance: red and white spotted coat
Meat: intense red with nice juiciness and a very persistent flavor

SALERS
Origin: near Salers in the Cantal
Label: Label Rouge ("Red Label") since 2004
Physical appearance: dark mahogany coat, long-haired and curly with narrow lyre-shaped horns
Meat: bright red, rustic, and finely marbled

DIAGRAM OF BEEF CUTS
1. Chuck
2. Rib, rib eye steak
3. Sirloin
4. Filet (tenderloin)
5. Round
6. Eye of round
7. Pear & whiting cut
8. Knuckle
9. Spider
10. Bottom sirloin cuts
11. Bavette (skirt)
12. Skirt
13. Prime cut
14. Sliced filet
15. Bavette (flank)
16. Top rib
17. Flat iron
18. Upper chuck
19. Chuck tender, for steaks
20. Chuck tender, for stewing
21. Blade, for stewing
22. Tail
23. Shank
24. Flank
25. Short ribs
26. Chest
27. Neck
28. Cheek
29. Tongue

· AN INVENTORY OF THE CHICKENS OF FRANCE ·

These are beautiful and ancient breeds!
From Mans to Bresse, here is the cream of the crop in the barnyard.

BARBEZIEUX
Origin: Barbezieux (Charente)
Physical appearance: large size with black plumage and simple red comb
Meat: tender

BRESSE GAULOISE
Origin: Bény (Ain). The only AOC (*appellation d'origine contrôlée*), since 1957
Physical appearance: white plumage with simple red comb
Meat: firm, fat fillets

BOURBONNAISE
Origin: the Bourbonnais (Allier)
Physical appearance: white plumage with black flecks, with a simple red comb
Meat: firm

BOURBOURG
Origin: Bourbourg (North)
Physical appearance: white plumage, simple red comb
Meat: tender

CAUMONT
Origin: Caumont (Calvados)
Physical appearance: slender with black to blue plumage, comb in the shape of a crown or cup
Meat: firm and flavorful

CHAROLLAISE
Origin: Charolles (Saône-et-Loire)
Physical appearance: white plumage with a curly red comb
Meat: plump and firm

COTENTINE
Origin: Cotentin peninsula (Manche)
Physical appearance: black plumage and simple red comb
Meat: rather rustic but very tender

COU NU DU FOREZ
Origin: Forez (Loire)
Physical appearance: bare neck, white plumage, and simple red comb
Meat: delicate and firm

COUCOU DE RENNES
Origin: Rennes (Ille-et-Vilaine)
Physical appearance: gray speckled plumage with a straight comb
Meat: delicate taste of hazelnut

FAVEROLLES
Origin: Faverolles (Eure-et-Loir)
Physical appearance: rather imposing; five toes on the claw and a bright salmon-colored plumage; simple red comb
Meat: delicate

GÂTINAISE
Origin: the Gâtinais (south of Île-de-France)
Physical appearance: rustic breed with white plumage and simple red comb
Meat: nice firmness

GAULOISE DORÉE
Origin: the symbol of France; oldest European race
Physical appearance: colorful plumage
Meat: brown and dense

GÉLINE DE TOURAINE
Origin: Touraine
Physical appearance: farm poultry with black plumage and a red comb
Meat: dense, white, and delicate

GOURNAY
Origin: Gournay-en-Bray (Seine-Maritime)
Physical appearance: small, rustic breed with tight black plumage speckled with white
Meat: delicate, called Bresse Normande

HOUDAN
Origin: Houdan (Yvelines), dates back to the fourteenth century
Physical appearance: crest of feathers and comb that resemble the shape of oak leaves. The only breed, along with the Faverolles, to have five toes on the claw
Meat: firm and flavorful

LA FLÈCHE
Origin: La Flèche (Sarthe). It was used to make the famous chicken stew for Henri IV
Physical appearance: black plumage and double horn-shape comb
Meat: brown, delicate, and firm

LE MANS
Origin: Le Mans (Sarthe)
Physical appearance: black coat with green hues, red comb
Meat: very delicate

DIAGRAM OF CHICKEN CUTS

1. Breast
2. Drumstick
3. Thigh
4. Wing
5. Back
6. Neck

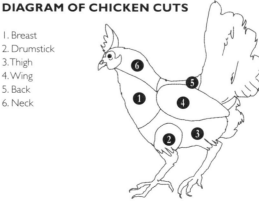

· AN INVENTORY OF THE PIGS OF FRANCE ·

In France, there are six rustic breeds of pigs raised in the open. And everything on them is delicious.

CUL NOIR DU LIMOUSIN
Origin: Limousin
Physical appearance: white coat with black staining, very silky; drooping ears
Meat: red with a nice tenderness

GRAND BLANC DE L'OUEST
Origin: Normandy
Physical appearance: uniformly white, slightly pinkish, with white bristles forming near the kidneys; drooping ears
Meat: excellent meat. Used historically to make *jambon de Paris*

PIE NOIR
Origin: Pays Basque
Physical appearance: distinctive black and white coat: black head and black butt; drooping ears
Meat: feeds on acorns, herbs, and chestnuts. The symbol for cured meats from the southwest

PORC DE BAYEUX
Origin: Normandy
Physical appearance: pink coat, with rounded black spots; dangling ears
Meat: provides many dairy products, its meat is soft and tender

PORC GASCON
Origin: Hautes-Pyrénées
Physical appearance: black coat with long, stiff bristles, thicker and tighter toward the back; dangling ears
Meat: fine and marbled, produces high-quality deli meats

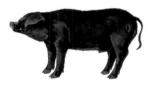

PORC NUSTRALE
Origin: Corsica
Physical appearance: dark coat that changes between brown and black; drooping ears
Meat: feeds on mountain pastures during the summer, acorns and chestnuts during the winter. Because of its diet, this Corsican pig produces one of the best cured meats from the island

DIAGRAM OF PORK CUTS

1. Head	6. Loin	11. Shoulder
2. Ear	7. Rump	12. Hock
3. Jowl	8. Ham	13. Feet
4. Butt	9. Belly	14. Tail
5. Rib rack	10. Chop	

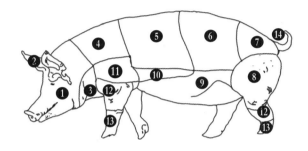

· AN INVENTORY OF THE SHEEP OF FRANCE ·

These are some of the finest sheep breeds of France.

BARÉGEOISE
Origin: Hautes-Pyrénées
Label: Barèges-Gavarnie mutton AOC (*appellation d'origine contrôlée*) since 2003
Physical appearance: white head with short spiral horns; white, black, or brown fleece
Meat: red, with a flavor of mountain herbs and a slight licorice taste

BLANCHE DU MASSIF CENTRAL
Origin: mountainous region of Margeride
Label: Lozère sheep PGI (Protected Geographical Indication) since 2008
Physical appearance: small white head; long, drooping ears; white fleece
Meat: pink and tender, a scent of meadow grasses

CORSE
Mixed
Origin: Corsica
Label: Nustrale young mutton PGI (Protected Geographical Indication) in process
Physical appearance: small head; long fleece with black streaks, russet and white, or gray
Meat: light pink, with aromas of the Mediterranean maquis (coastal shrubland)

LACAUNE
Mixed
Origin: Aveyron
Label: free-range lamb of Pays d'Oc since 1992
Physical appearance: white and small head; white fleece with silver tones
Meat: light pink, sweet and delicate flavor

LIMOUSINE
Origin: Limousin
Label: Limousin lamb PGI (Protected Geographical Indication) since 2000
Physical appearance: white head with short neck; white fleece with long locks
Meat: pink, tender, scent of meadow grasses

PRÉALPES DU SUD
Origin: Alpes-de-Haute-Provence and Hautes-Alpes
Label: Sisteron lamb Label Rouge ("Red Label") since 1995
Physical appearance: fine, elongated white head; white fleece with short locks
Meat: light pink, sweet flavor and very tender

SOLOGNOTE
Origin: Sologne
Label: protected under the *Arche du goût* Slow Food project
Physical appearance: brown head and legs; medium-length white fleece
Meat: delicate pink, similar to duck

TARASCONNAISE
Origin: Central Pyrénées
Label: Pyrénées lamb PGI (Protected Geographical Indication)
Physical appearance: white head with spiral horns; white fleece of soft, tight wool
Meat: light pink, with aromas of hazelnut

DIAGRAM OF LAMB CUTS

1. Neck
2. Cross rib
3. Rib chop and front rib
4. Filet mignon and loin chop
5. Saddle
6. Trimmed leg
7. Whole leg
8. Breast
9. Rib cutlets
10. Shoulder

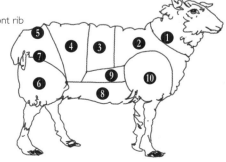

CARNIVORE DETOUR

Aurore Vincenti

The word *viande* (meat)

Comes from the Latin **vivanda**, literally **"necessary for living."** From the ninth to the fourteenth century, the use of the word referred to **all food,** and it was not before the end of the fourteenth century that the word designated flesh of mammals and birds. Nevertheless, its general meaning is still common in French expressions like "it's not meat for him" (it's something above his means). The French word **viandard**—which once meant a fat horse, a hunter thirsting for blood, an unscrupulous profiteer, and a lecherous man—now means a big red-meat eater.

A first hypothesis connects the French **barbaque** (roasted meat) to the Mexican (1518) **barbacoa** (a grill used to smoke meat). In that case, barbaque and **barbecue** would belong to the same family. A second hypothesis, this time Romanian, connects it to **berbec,** meaning "mutton." Otherwise, one could decide to rely on its first French use dating from 1813, which has the word coming from the **nickname** given to a butcher from La Chapelle. Barbaque and **bidoche (meat),** the exact origins of which are unknown, at first designated poor-quality meats. Today, the French use those terms as slang, whether the meat is good or bad . . .

The word *billot* (butcher's block)

Comes from the Gallic **bilia**, which means "tree trunk" and, more specifically, **a section of wood** on which things can be placed, cut, and crushed. In butcher jargon, it's a piece of furniture **used to cut meat**. One can't help but associate the French word *billot* with its other meaning, a headrest for someone who had received the **death sentence**. That's enough to make you vegetarian.

★

LOUCHÉBEM OR LOUCHERBEM (BUTCHER PIG LATIN)

is slang that was used by butchers in Lyon and Paris in the first half of the nineteenth century. It involves taking the first consonant of a word and moving it to the end of the word, then replacing it with an "l" and, at the end of the word, a slang suffix.

Boucher (butcher)
=> oucherb
=> loucherb
=> loucherbem

★

The Bäckeoffe

This Alsatian term means "baker's pot." In the past, townspeople provided their stews in terrines early in the morning to the town baker, who would place them in the bread ovens to be ready by lunchtime. Today, this full-meal dish is one of the pillars of Alsatian cuisine.

Delphine Le Feuvre

1 bay leaf
1 sprig thyme
10 peppercorns
5 cloves
1 bottle (750 mL) dry white wine (Sylvaner)

3⅓ pounds (1.5 kg) potatoes
2 carrots
1 large leek
1 large onion
1 raw pig's foot
Salt and freshly ground black pepper
1 cup (100 g) all-purpose flour

PREPARATION TIME: 30 MINUTES
RESTING TIME: 12 HOURS
COOKING TIME: 2 HOURS 30 MINUTES
SERVES 4

For the marinade
2 onions
3 sprigs parsley
14 ounces (400 g) pork tenderloin
14 ounces (400 g) beef chuck
14 ounces (400 g) boneless lamb shoulder

Make the marinade. Peel the 2 onions and thinly slice them. Wash the parsley and pick the leaves off the stems. Cut all the meats (except the pig's foot) into large cubes, then place them in a bowl with the onions, parsley, bay leaf, thyme, peppercorns, and cloves. Add the wine and refrigerate for 12 hours to marinate.

Preheat the oven to 350°F (180°C). Wash, peel, and thinly slice the potatoes, carrots, and leek. Peel and slice the large onion. Remove the meat from the marinade (reserve the liquid). In a lidded terra-cotta terrine, or in a *bäckeoffe* dish (or a regular lidded flameproof casserole dish), place the pig's foot, then alternate a layer of cubed meat, a layer of vegetables, and a layer of sliced onion. Repeat the layering twice more. Season with salt and pepper, and add the marinade liquid. Place the lid on the pot. Combine the flour with a little water to make a fairly soft and pliable dough, then roll the dough into a long narrow log. Seal the lid to the pot all the way around using the dough. Bake for 2 hours 30 minutes. Bring the dish to the table, and remove the lid in front of the guests.

Meats Rub Shoulders in These Dishes!

Cassoulet: pork and duck mingle happily together in all their forms (fat, sausage, confit, rind, etc.) in this specialty from the southwest (see page 209).
Bouchées à la reine ("the queen's bites"): veal dumplings and chicken cutlets, along with mushrooms, all cooked in a cream sauce, in rounds of puff pastry.
Kig ha farz: pork shank and beef ribs are cooked together in this Breton stew (see page 308).
Potjevleesch: meaning "little pot of meat" in Flemish, this is a mixture of hen, rabbit, pork, and veal meats, cold, set in a lightly vinegary gelée.

Good Soups All Around!

After learning to master fire about 15,000 years ago, man added roots, bones, herbs, and grains to pots to create thickened broths. In the thirteenth century, the word *soup* was born. Here is a *tour de France* by spoon.

Marie-Amal Bizalion

Throughout France's regions . . .

It's difficult to date the origin of these recipes: some seem unchanged since their beginnings, others have been enhanced and changed over time—but all have an invigorating rustic quality.

❶ *Cévennes*
Bajana: a winter soup, served to sheepherders after a long stay in the mountains.
Ingredients: contains chestnuts dried over a wood fire, boiled in water until crumbling, then drizzled with a little milk or wine.

❷ *Provence*
Soupe au pistou: a Genoese recipe enjoyed from Nice to Marseille.
Ingredients: includes beans (including string, flat, and white beans), zucchini, tomatoes, potatoes, pasta, and Parmesan rind or Italian sausage, served with a basil-garlic olive oil.

❸ *Haute-Savoie*
Soupe châtrée: a peasant dish created for using leftovers, common in Samoëns.
Ingredients: onions browned in butter then cooked in white wine and water. The broth is placed in a soup tureen that is then filled with crusty breads and slices of tomme cheese and baked in the oven.

❹ *Alsace*
Biersupp ("beer soup"): a soup with "medicinal" benefits, originating in the thirteenth century.
Ingredients: onions, chicken broth, beer, and bread crumbs, served with crème fraiche and croutons fried in butter.

❺ *Limousin*
Fricassee au tourain: a broth-based peasant soup containing rare winter vegetables.
Ingredients: includes salt pork; onions browned in lard, sprinkled with flour, then moistened with water; and chopped sorrel.

Dordogne
Jemboura: a fatty broth made by families after butchering a pig at the end of Lent.
Ingredients: onions, leeks, carrots, kohlrabi, turnips, and herbs. Cooked with boudin, which swells in the cooking liquid.

❻ *Normandy*
Soupe à la graisse Norman: in the Middle Ages, during a time of scarcity, a priest invented this recipe using tallow cooked with vegetables to give the broth a taste of meat.
Ingredients: includes pork fat and fat from beef kidney stewed with vegetables and herbs, strained, and allowed to solidify, then added to a soup of potatoes, beans, string beans, and garlic.

❼ *Poitou-Charentes*
Soupe au giraume: *giraume* is the name of a cucurbit (turban squash) brought back from Tahiti by Louis Antoine de Bougainville in the eighteenth century.
Ingredients: turban squash cooked in water, then boiled in milk with sugar, salt, and pepper.

❽ *Pays basque*
Elzekaria: local variant of a *garbure* (ham and cabbage stew).
Ingredients: includes white cabbage, onions, beans, bacon, garlic, Espelette pepper, and vinegar.

❾ *Corse*
Corsican soup: see page 95.

❿ *Paris*
Gratinée à l'oignon (onion soup): see page 22.

DIFFERENT WORDS FOR DIFFERENT SOUPS

SOUPE (from the lower Latin *suppa*, from the Germanic *suppa*): a potage or broth served on slices of bread.

★

POTAGE (from the word *pot*): a liquid preparation, thin or thickened, served hot or cold, at the beginning of the meal.

★

VELOUTÉ ("velvet"): a potage with a white stock base, enriched with egg.

★

CONSOMMÉ ("to consume"): a clarified beef or poultry broth.

GARBURE À LA BÉARNAISE

SOAKING TIME: 12 HOURS
PREPARATION TIME: 1 HOUR
COOKING TIME: 3 HOURS
SERVES 6

9 ounces (250 g) dried white beans
10½ ounces (300 g) plain thick bacon, large dice
6 small turnips
2 onions
3 cloves garlic
1 bouquet garni (rosemary, thyme, bay leaf, or any herbs you prefer)
Salt and freshly ground black pepper
1 green cabbage
6 potatoes
4 duck legs confit
6 slices toasted rustic bread

The day before, soak the beans for several hours in water; drain. The next day, in a large pot, brown the bacon, then add the beans. Quarter the turnips, peel and chop the onions, and peel the garlic. Add the turnips, onions, garlic, and bouquet garni to the pot. Add 5¼ quarts (5 L) of water, and season with salt and pepper. Bring to a boil, and let simmer for 1 hour and 30 minutes. Meanwhile, slice the cabbage and blanch it for 5 minutes in boiling water, then rinse it in cold water, and add it to the pot. After 1 hour of cooking time, quarter the potatoes and add them to the pot, then add the duck legs. Let simmer for 30 more minutes. Place each bread slice in the bottom of a soup plate, ladle in the broth, then add the meats and vegetables.

skip to

All in the Soup Family!, p. 246

Where Are They Now?

They were less than thirty years old in the 1980s. Most of them today have become stove stars.
Can you recognize Alain Ducasse, Michel Troisgros, and Alain Passard?

François-Régis Gaudry

FOR THE RECORD

Browsing through an old issue of *Cuisine & Vins de France* dated September 1984, I came across a double-page spread, by Maurice Rougemont, with the enticing headline "Who'll be the chefs in the year 2000?" Gilles Pudlowski had selected nineteen chefs, age twenty-six on average. It goes without saying that the food critic had flair. Save for a few who fell into oblivion, many of these young go-getters did indeed become great, famous, and respected chefs thirty years later. One among them even became part of the team of commentators on *Let's Eat France* on public radio channel France Inter. Figure out who.

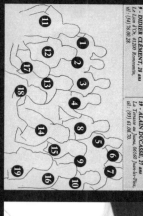

★
1 - PATRICK CIROTTE, 26 ans
La Coupole, 46, rue de Naples, Paris 8e.
tél.: 565.28.92.

★
2 - PHILIPPE ROSTANG, 24 ans
La Bonne Auberge, 06600 Antibes.
tél.: (93) 33.36.65.

★
3 - MICHEL HUSSER, 25 ans
Le Cerf, 67520 Marlenheim,
tél.: (88) 87.73.73.

★
4 - JEAN-MICHEL LORAIN, 25 ans
La Côte Saint-Jacques, 14, Fb Paris,
89300 Joigny. tél.: (86) 62.09.70.

★
5 - XAVIER AUBRUN, 25 ans
La Barrière à Clichy, 1 rue de Paris,
92110 Clichy. tél.: 739.05.18.

★
6 - JEAN-PIERRE JACOB, 29 ans
Le Bateau Ivre, 73370 Le Bourget-du-Lac.
tél.: (79) 25.02.66.

★
7 - MICHEL TROISGROS, 24 ans
Troisgros, place de la Gare, 42300 Roanne.
tél.: (77) 71.66.97.

★
8 - GILLES CLÉMENT, 28 ans
Gill, 60 rue Saint-Nicolas, 76000 Rouen.
tél.: (35) 71.16.14.

★
9 - DIDIER CLÉMENT, 26 ans
Le Lion d'Or, 41200 Romorantin.
tél.: (54) 76.00.28.

★
10 - DOMINIQUE LE STANC, 25 ans
Le Sanc, 18 bd des Moulins, Monte-Carlo.
tél.: (93) 50.63.37.

★
11 - ALAIN PASSARD, 28 ans
Le Duc d'Enghien, 95880 Enghien-les-Bains, tél.: 412.90.00.

★
12 - PHILIPPE GAERTNER, 28 ans
La Fleur de Lys,
68770 Ammerschwihr.
tél.: (89) 47.10.12.

★
13 - MARC HAEBERLIN, 29 ans
Auberge de l'Ill, 68150 Illhaeusern,
tél.: (89) 71.83.23.

★
14 - ARNAUD DAGUIN, 25 ans
Hôtel de France, 32000 Auch,
tél.: (62) 05.00.04.

★
15 - PATRICK FULGRAFF, 29 ans
Le Fer Rouge, 52, Grand-Rue,
68000 Colmar. tél.: (89) 41.37.24.

★
16 - PATRICK MICHELON, 29 ans
L'Hostellerie de la Poste,
Taillades, tél.: (25) 82.31.13.

★
17 - GÉRARD PASSÉDAT, 24 ans
Le Petit Nice, 13007 Marseille.
tél.: (91) 52.14.39.

★
18 - GILLES ÉPIÉ, 23 ans
La Papillote des Princes, 69 av. de la Porte
d'Auteuil, Paris 16e. tél.: 605.65.50.

★
19 - ALAIN DUCASSE, 27 ans
La Terrasse au Juana, 06160 Juan-les-Pins,
tél.: (93) 61.08.70.

The Tarte Bourdaloue

This pear tart, served warm, was invented in Paris in the 1850s, and is a staple of French pastry.
It's time to reveal the mystery of this French pear tart!

Delphine Le Feuvre

THE ORIGINS OF THE TART

The first known person to carry the name of *Bourdaloue* was the Jesuit Louis Bourdaloue, who was preaching in the seventeenth century in Paris. His name was given to a small street in Paris, but it is not to him that we can attribute the invention of the tarte Bourdaloue, whose recipe has gone unchanged, or perhaps only slightly changed, since its creation. It was the pastry chef Fasquelle who invented it in the middle of the nineteenth century, and he named the tart for the small street on which he worked, in the 9th arrondissement of Paris. Thus, the tarte Bourdaloue was born.

THE TRADITIONAL INGREDIENTS OF THE TARTE BOURDALOUE

→ A sweet crust
→ Almond cream
→ Williams pear halves, poached in syrup
→ Pieces of macaron shells

Spotlight on Sébastien Gaudard
The son of a pastry chef, Sébastien Gaudard nostalgically takes the recipes of yesteryear from old books to update them into true delicacies for today's gourmands.

Where do you find Sébastien Gaudard's tarte Bourdaloue?
Pâtisserie des Martyrs,
22, rue des Martyrs, Paris 9th
Pâtisserie–salon de thé des Tuileries, 1, rue des Pyramides,
Paris 1st

THE TARTE BOURDALOUE (FRENCH PEAR TART)

by Sébastien Gaudard

PREPARATION TIME: 45 MINUTES
COOKING TIME: 1 HOUR
SERVES 6

Pears poached with vanilla
See the recipe for the yule log, page 79

For the tart dough (enough for two tarts)
1½ cups plus 1 tablespoon plus 2 teaspoons (160 g) all-purpose flour
½ cup plus 2 tablespoons (90 g) potato starch
12 tablespoons plus 2 teaspoons (180 g) unsalted butter, slightly softened
1 teaspoon (6 g) fine salt
1 level teaspoon (5 mL) honey
1 egg yolk
3 tablespoons plus 1 teaspoon (50 mL) water

For the almond cream
⅓ cup (80 g) whipping cream
7 tablespoons (100 g) unsalted butter, slightly softened, plus more for brushing the pears
1 cup (100 g) confectioners' sugar, plus more for dusting
1 cup minus 2 tablespoons (125 g) almond flour
1 tablespoon (8 g) cornstarch
2 tablespoons (30 mL) dark rum
2 or 3 eggs (125 g)

Crushed pieces of macaron shells or cookies

Poach the pears in the syrup according to the recipe on page 79.

Make the tart dough. Sift together the flour and the potato starch. In a bowl, cream the butter with a spatula until it's smooth. Add the salt, honey, egg yolk, and water to the bowl while stirring to combine. When the mixture is smooth, gradually incorporate the flour mixture. Once a smooth dough is obtained, flatten the dough, wrap it in plastic wrap, and refrigerate it for at least 2 hours. Roll out the chilled dough to ⅒ inch (2.5 mm) thick. Grease a flan ring (or a tart pan) measuring 7 inches (18 cm) in diameter and place on a sheet pan. Line the ring with the dough, prick it all over with a fork, and place a round of parchment paper on top. Pour dried beans or pie weights onto the parchment paper. Place the ring in the refrigerator for 30 minutes. Preheat the oven to 325°F (160°C). Bake the tart crust for 25 minutes, or until golden. If making only one tart, wrap the other half of the dough in plastic wrap and freeze it for long-term storage.

Make the almond cream. Whip the cream. Briefly beat the butter until creamy, then add all the remaining ingredients to the butter, one by one, while continuing to beat on slow speed. Finally, gently beat in the whipped cream.

Compose the tart. Preheat the oven to 350°F (180°C). Drain the pears, and cut them into 16 slices starting from the top of the pear down, keeping the slices together. Spread a ½-inch- (1.5 cm) thick layer of the almond cream in the cooled tart shell, spread the sliced pears on top (keeping the slices of each pear together by gently pressing them down to fan them out), then brush the pears with a little melted butter. Bake for 35 to 45 minutes, or until golden.

Once the tart has cooled, dust it with confectioners' sugar and, between the pears and in the center, sprinkle broken pieces of macaron shells or cookie crumbs.

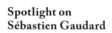
skip to
Cakes of Yesteryear Rise Once Again, p. 52

The Art of Roast Chicken

The chicken is the shining star of every barnyard. When roasted, it becomes a monumental family meal.
Here are some rules to ensure your roast chicken is the star of your Sunday meals at home.
Charles Patin O'Coohoon

"It does not take a lot of thinking to cook a chicken; and yet we see men who, all their lives, are bad at roasting them."

LUC DE CLAPIERS, MARQUIS DE VAUVENARGUES, 1746

♥ What to do . . .

Select a well-bred chicken (farm or organically raised).

Leave it at room temperature before roasting it.

Choose a pan large enough for the chicken to have room.

Salt the outside of the chicken before cooking it to absorb moisture from the skin and make it crisp when baked.

Turn the chicken frequently while roasting it.

🚫 What not to do . . .

Never put water in the bottom of the roasting pan.

Do not pepper the chicken before or during cooking. Cooked pepper is very bitter.

---

3 WAYS TO PREPARE YOUR CHICKEN

OVER HIGH HEAT
by Frédéric Ménager
Chicken breeder and cook at Ferme de la Ruchotte, Bligny-sur-Ouche (Côte-d'Or)

🍗 **CHICKEN: ABOUT 4½ POUNDS (2 KG)**
⏱ **COOKING TIME: 1 HOUR 10 MINUTES (REST: 30 MINUTES)**
🌡 **OVEN TEMPERATURE: PREHEAT TO 475°F (250°C)**
COOKING FAT: 10 TBSP (150 G) SOFTENED BUTTER

Place a lemon, some thyme, some garlic cloves, and a teaspoon of coarse salt in the cavity of the chicken. Season the chicken all over with salt and coat it with the softened butter. Sear the chicken on the stovetop on its back in a cast-iron casserole dish for 10 minutes. Turn it over on its left thigh and let it cook for another 10 minutes, then turn it over on its right thigh and let it cook for another 10 minutes. Lower the oven temperature to 300°F (150°C). Turn the chicken over again onto its back in the casserole dish and place it in the oven. Baste it every 5 minutes for 30 minutes. Remove it from the oven and let stand for 30 minutes, then lower the oven temperature to 200°F (100°C) and roast the chicken for another 10 minutes; serve.

Result: after 1 hour of cooking, the skin is crunchy; the chicken is slightly less juicy than when cooked using other methods but its flesh is incredibly tender.

OVER GENTLE HEAT
by Arthur Le Caisne
Author of La Cuisine c'est aussi de la chimie, Éditions Hachette Cuisine

🍗 **CHICKEN: ABOUT 4½ POUNDS (2 KG)**
⏱ **COOKING TIME: 3 HOURS**
🌡 **OVEN TEMPERATURE: PREHEAT TO 275°F (140°C)**
COOKING FAT: BUTTER AND OLIVE OIL

Place 2 tablespoons (28 g) of butter and some garlic cloves and herbs in the cavity of the chicken. Spread 2 tablespoons (28 g) of softened butter all under the skin of the chicken and coat the outside of the chicken with olive oil. Season the chicken all over with salt. In a baking dish just slightly larger than the chicken, place the chicken on its side. Roast it for 15 minutes, then turn it over on its other side. Let roast for another 15 minutes, then turn the chicken breast side down. Roast for another 2 hours and 30 minutes. Remove it from the oven, season with salt and pepper, then carve it and serve. After 3 hours of cooking, the skin isn't too crispy, but the chicken keeps all its juiciness.

IN A BRINE
by Fabien Beaufour
Chef at Dyades, in Massignac (Charente)

🍗 **CHICKEN: 3½ POUNDS (1.6 KG)**
⏱ **COOKING TIME: 50 MINUTES (REST: 10 HOURS)**
🌡 **OVEN TEMPERATURE: PREHEAT TO 350°F (180°C)**
COOKING FAT: ¼ CUP (60 ML) OLIVE OIL

Make a brine. Boil 4 cups (1 L) of water with 2 tablespoons (19 g) of salt, 1 cup (200 g) of sugar, and ¾ cup (200 g) of soy sauce. Add 12 cups (3 L) of water, 1 teaspoon (3 g) of ground black pepper, 1 lemon slice, and 3½ ounces (100 g) of chopped onion. Submerge a Barbezieux chicken (see page 167) in the brine for 6 hours. Drain and let dry for 3 hours. Place 1 tablespoon (3 g) of rosemary, 3 bay leaves, and 1 crushed garlic clove in the cavity of the chicken. Rub the chicken all over with the olive oil mixed with ¾ teaspoon (5 g) of paprika and ¾ teaspoon (5 g) of cayenne pepper. Let dry for 1 hour. Roast the chicken on its back for 20 minutes at 350°F (180°C), then turn it over to roast for 15 minutes on each side. Remove from the oven and let it rest for 20 minutes before serving.

DO NOT CONFUSE THE OYSTER MEAT WITH THE WISHBONE

What the less-experienced cook often forgets about when roasting chicken are the two delectable pieces of meat called the oysters, lodged inside the body of the chicken along the backbone. The other often-forgotten piece of the chicken is the furcula (the wishbone), which provides a lot of joy. Each person grabs hold of one side of the wishbone and pulls it toward himself. The bone will break, and the person left with the largest piece will have his wish fulfilled.

skip to An Inventory of the Chickens of France, p. 167

A Paris Restaurant during the Occupation

Menus are evidence of French culinary passions and also of French history.
Here's the story of the Paris restaurant Leprince* during the German Occupation.

Patrick Rambourg

THE CONTEXT

The German Occupation during the Second World War deeply marked the French and their relationship to food: for example, **rutabaga** and **topinambour (Jerusalem artichoke)** were unwanted for a long time because they brought back bad memories. As early as September 1940, with the **first ration cards**, the French entered a long period of limited foodstuffs. In the capital, restaurants needed to adapt to the situation and find solutions in the face of an increasing shortage of foods.

MENU FOR AUGUST 30, 1939

A few days before the war erupted, Leprince smelled sweetly of cooking from the French provinces: lobster *à l'américaine* with wine and herbs, Roscoff crayfish with mayonnaise, Volga fresh caviar, celery rémoulade, simple foie gras, cold turbot with green sauce, roasted duckling with green peas, Normandy fattened chicken, etc. And then there were vegetables, cheeses, fruit, and desserts. The situation quickly worsened and laws became strict. As early as November, Mondays became days without butcher meat and Tuesdays, days without beef. Starting on December 15, Fridays became days "without meat of any kind." In October 1940, ration cards were required in restaurants. More and more was missing from the establishment's menus: on the evening of October 15, there was no butter with the hors d'oeuvres and there was no coffee.

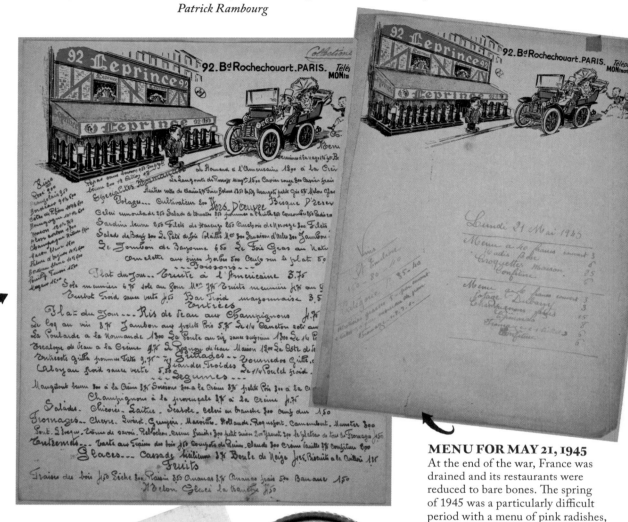

MENU FOR MAY 21, 1945

At the end of the war, France was drained and its restaurants were reduced to bare bones. The spring of 1945 was a particularly difficult period with a menu of pink radishes, homemade croquettes, and jam for forty francs. When the war ended, it would still take several months before guests would have access to the mouthwatering dishes from 1939 and the à la carte system.

*92, boulevard Rochechouart, Paris 18th

THE CAKE DE GUERRE (Wartime Cake)

1¾ cups minus 1 tablespoon (170 g) all-purpose flour
¼ cup plus 3 tablespoons plus ½ teaspoon (90 g) sugar
½ teaspoon (3.5 g) baking soda
1 egg
½ cup plus 1 tablespoon plus ¾ teaspoon (140 g) whole milk

Whisk together the flour, sugar, and baking soda. Make a well using your fingers, then add the egg and milk to the well. Mix quickly to combine. Preheat the oven for 5 minutes to 350°F/180°C (no longer, as the cake dries out easily). Scrape the batter into an 8-inch (20 cm) round cake pan. Bake for 20 minutes.

Thoughts from Estérelle Payany

This cake tends to dry out quickly and is relatively sweet, so it's imperative to eat it the same day it is made. Eating it causes you to reflect on life and to think about the preciousness of those things in life we take for granted. This must have been especially true when, during times of war, chicory was the only beverage available to moisten this cake!

Her tips

To make it more up to date without adulterating it, there are several approaches to take:
- replace the milk with pure buttermilk for more moisture
- add lemon zest or a few drops of pure vanilla extract for more flavor
- use it as a base for a dessert and cover it with fruit: raspberries, cherries, slices of apple, etc.

Nadia Chougui, the production manager of *Let's Eat France* on France Inter, inherited from her aunt Simone Blézot a moving notebook of recipes dating from the Second World War. Our commentator Estérelle Payany tried the wartime cake recipe and improved on it.

Michel Bras

To pronounce the final "s" in Bras is already to pay homage to one of the most celebrated names in contemporary gastronomy.
François-Régis Gaudry

Key dates

November 4, 1946
Born in Gabriac in the Aveyron department, into a family of restaurant owners. "Mémé Bras," his mother, whipped up tasty home cooking at the Lou Mazuc in the commune of Laguiole. Her *aligot* was famous.

1978: takes the reins of his mother's restaurant with his wife, Ginette

1992: Le Suquet is established atop a prominent hill in Laguiole

❀❀❀

1999

Third star in the Michelin guide

2002: the restaurant Toya opens on the island of Hokkaido in Japan

2009: the business passes down to his son Sébastien

The genius from the village of Aubrac
(born in 1946)

Le Gargouillou, a legendary dish

This invention, at once rural and radical, rustic and modern, was developed in 1980 and then earned worldwide recognition.

WHERE DOES IT GET ITS NAME?
Traditionally, in Auvergne, *gargouillou* designated a potato dish, moistened with water and paired with a slice of cured ham.

WHAT'S IT LIKE?
It's a mix of wild plants, herbs and young vegetables that vary with the seasons. Ferns, amaranth, white borage, Rocambole garlic, clover, cauliflower stalk, peas, tuberous chervil, nasturtium, rampion, pattypan squash, scallion, chicory, chickweed, pink radish, salsify, tomato, spring onion, alpine fennel . . . and other vegetables, young shoots, leaves, flowers, stalks, grains, and roots, are combined into a plant-based dish bursting with flavor and color, thickened only with eggnog and juices from a cured ham cooked in a bouillon.

HOW DID MICHEL BRAS INVENT IT?
The chef explains how it came into being: "Jogging regularly gives me a feeling of

well-being where everything is fluid. A kind of trance takes me to another level of unsuspected sensations. Le Gargouillou appeared during one of those 'voyages inward' in the month of June, when the pastures of Aubrac are flooded with myriad flowers, with scents and light. It's truly like fireworks, a hymn to the season."

CAN YOU TRY IT AT HOME?
Le Gargouillou is inextricably linked to Aubrac, so trying to reproduce it elsewhere would be in vain. Your best option is still to savor it at the Laguiole restaurant now run by Sébastien, Michel's son, or to adapt it to your own biotope. To do so, gather young vegetables in season and a selection of herbs and edible plants, all local. Here's Bras's secret for adding flavor: "In a pan, brown a few slices of *jambon de pays* (a cured country ham). Deglaze with a vegetable stock. Add a dollop of butter to emulsify the ham broth. Toss and heat the vegetables in it. Plate with care. Garnish with sprigs of springtime herbs from the field and sprouts, and play with dabs and touches of flavor."

THE WINES OF FRANCE

Locating the AOC

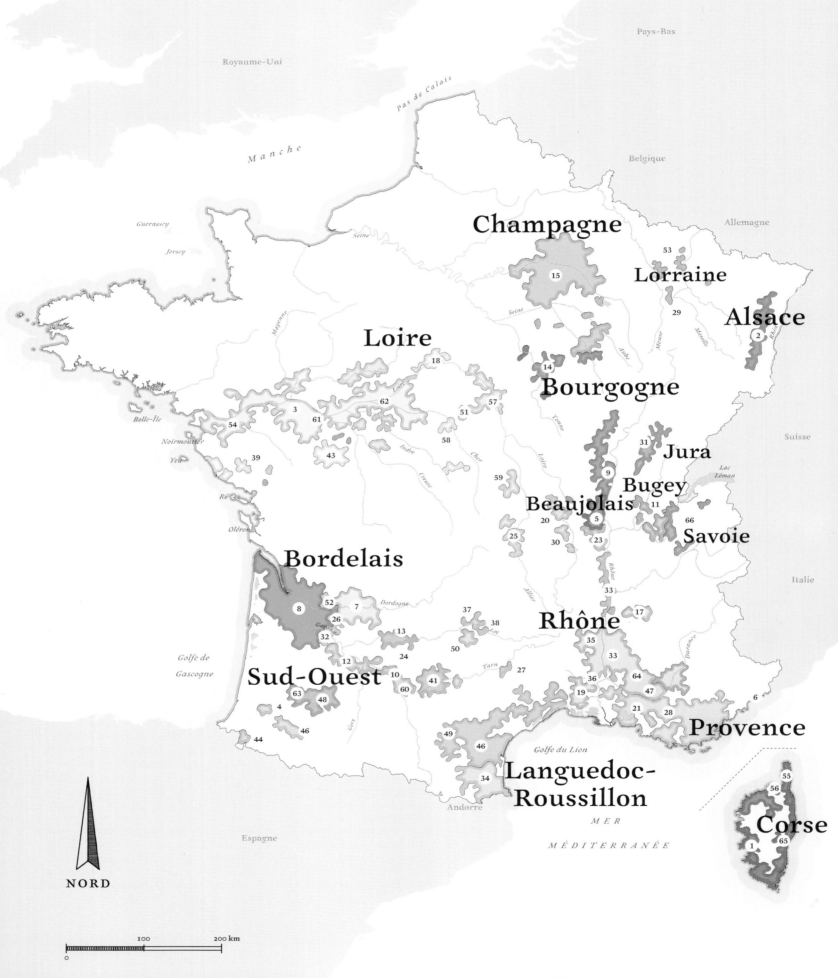

NORD

100   200 km

0

1   Ajaccio

2   Alsace or Vin d'Alsace / Alsace Grand Cru / Crémant d'Alsace / Marc d'Alsace

3   Anjou / Anjou Villages / Anjou Villages Brissac / Anjou-Coteaux de la Loire / Bonnezeaux / Cabernet d'Anjou / Coteaux de l'Aubance / Quarts de Chaume / Rosé d'Anjou / Savennières / Savennières Coulée de Serrant / Savennières Roche aux Moines

4   Béarn / Pacherenc du Vic-Bilh

5   Beaujolais / Brouilly / Chénas / Chiroubles / Côte de Brouilly / Fleurie / Juliénas / Morgon / Moulin-à-Vent / Régnié / Saint-Amour

6   Bellet or Vin de Bellet

7   Bergerac / Côtes de Bergerac / Monbazillac / Pécharmant / Rosette / Saussignac

8   Bordeaux / Barsac / Blaye / Bordeaux supérieur / Bourg or Côtes de Bourg or Bourgeais / Cadillac / Canon Fronsac Cérons / Côtes de Blaye / Côtes de Bordeaux / Côtes de Bordeaux-Saint-Macaire / Crémant de Bordeaux / Entre-deux-Mers / Fronsac Graves / Graves de Vayres / Graves supérieures / Haut-Médoc / Lalande-de-Pomerol / Listrac-Médoc / Loupiac / Lussac-Saint-Émilion / Margaux / Médoc / Montagne-Saint-Émilion / Moulis or Moulis-en-Médoc / Pauillac / Pessac-Léognan / Pomerol / Premières Côtes de Bordeaux / Puisseguin Saint-Émilion / Saint-Émilion Grand Cru / Saint-Estèphe / Saint-Georges-Saint-Émilion / Saint-Émilion / Saint-Julien / Sainte-Croix-du- Mont / Sainte-Foy-Bordeaux / Sauternes

9   Bourgogne / Aloxe-Corton / Auxey-Duresses / Bâtard-Montrachet / Beaune / Bienvenues-Bâtard-Montrachet / Blagny / Bonnes-Mares / Bourgogne Aligoté / Bourgogne Mous Seux / Bourgogne Passe-tout-grains / Bouzeron / Chambertin / Chambertin-Clos de Bèze / Chambolle-Musigny / Chapelle-Chambertin Charlemagne / Charmes-Chambertin / Chasagne-Montrachet / Chevalier-Montrachet / Chorey-lès-Beaune / Clos de la Roche / Clos de Tart / Clos de Vougeot or Clos Vougeot / Clos des Lambrays / Clos Saint-Denis / Corton / Corton-Charlemagne / Côte de Beaune / Côte de Beaune-Villages / Côte de Nuits-Villages Coteaux Bourguignons or Bourgogne Grand Ordinaire or Bourgogne Ordinaire / Crémant de Bourgogne / Criots-Bâtard-Montrachet / Echezeaux / Fixin / Gevrey-Chambertin / Givry / Grands-Echezeaux / Griotte-Chambertin / Irancy / La Grande Rue / La Romanée / La Tâche / Ladoix / Latricières-Chambertin / Mâcon / Maranges / Marsannay / Mazis-Chambertin / Mazoyères-Chambertin / Mercurey / Meursault / Montagny / Monthélie / Montrachet / Morey-Saint-Denis / Musigny / Nuits-Saint-Georges / Pernand-Vergelesses / Pommard / Pouilly-Fuissé / Pouilly-Loché / Pouilly-Vinzelles / Puligny-Montrachet / Richebourg / Romanée-Conti / Romanée-Saint-Vivant / Ruchottes-Chambertin / Rully / Saint-Aubin / Saint-Bris / Saint-Romain / Saint-Véran / Santenay / Savigny-lès-Beaune / Viré-Clessé / Volnay / Vosne-Romanée / Vougeot / Fine de Bourgogne / Marc de Bourgogne

10 Brulhois

11 Bugey / Roussette du Bugey

12 Buzet

13 Cahors

14 Chablis / Chablis Grand Cru / Petit Chablis

15 Champagne / Coteaux Champenois / Rosé des Riceys

16 Châteaumeillant

17 Châtillon-en-Diois / Clairette de Die / Crémant de Die

18 Cheverny / Cour-Cheverny

19 Costières de Nîmes

20 Côte Roannaise

21 Coteaux d'Aix-en-Provence

22 Coteaux du Giennois

23 Coteaux du Lyonnais

24 Coteaux du Quercy

25 Côtes d'Auvergne

26 Côtes de Duras

27 Côtes de Millau

28 Côtes de Provence / Bandol / Cassis / Coteaux Varois en Provence / Les Baux de Provence / Palette / Pierrevert

29 Côtes de Toul

30 Côtes du Forez

31 Côtes du Jura / Arbois / Château-Chalon / Crémant du Jura / L'Etoile / Macvin du Jura

32 Côtes du Marmandais

33 Côtes du Rhône / Beaumes de Venise / Château-Grillet Châteauneuf-du-Pape / Condrieu / Cornas / Côte Rôtie / Côtes du Rhône Villages / Crozes-Hermitage or Crozes-Ermitage / Gigondas / Hermitage or Ermitage or l'Hermitage or l'Ermitage / Lirac / Muscat de Beaumes-de-Venise / Rasteau / Saint-Joseph / Saint-Péray / Tavel / Vacqueyras / Vinsobres

34 Côtes du Roussillon / Banyuls / Banyuls Grand Cru / Cabardès / Collioure / Côtes du Roussillon Villages / Crémant de Limoux / Fitou / Grand Roussillon / Limoux / Maury

35 Côtes du Vivarais

36 Duché d'Uzès

37 Entraygues–Le Fel

38 Estaing

39 Fiefs Vendéens

40 Fronton

41 Gaillac / Gaillac Premières Côtes

42 Grignan-les-Adhémar

43 Haut-Poitou

44 Irouléguy

45 Jurançon

46 Languedoc / Clairette de Bellegarde / Clairette du Languedoc / Corbières / Corbières-Boutenac / Faugères / Minervois / Minervois-La Livinière / Muscat de Frontignan or Frontignan or vin de Frontignan / Muscat de Lunel / Muscat de Mireval / Muscat de Rivesaltes / Muscat de Saint-Jean-de-Minervois / Picpoul de Pinet / Rivesaltes / Saint-Chinian

47 Luberon

48 Madiran

49 Malepère

50 Marcillac

51 Menetou-Salon

52 Montravel / Côtes de Montravel / Haut-Montravel

53 Moselle

54 Muscadet / Coteaux d'Ancenis / Gros Plant du Pays Nantais / Muscadet Coteaux de la Loire / Muscadet Côtes de Grandlieu / Muscadet Sèvre et Maine

55 Muscat du Cap Corse

56 Patrimonio

57 Pouilly-sur-Loire / Pouilly-Fumé or Blanc Fumé de Pouilly / Sancerre

58 Quincy

59 Saint-Pourçain /

60 Saint-Sardos

61 Saumur / Saumur-Champigny / Cabernet de Saumur / Chinon / Coteaux de Saumur / Coteaux du Layon

62 Touraine / Touraine Noble Joué / Bourgueil / Coteaux du Loir / Coteaux du Vendômois / Crémant de Loire / Jasnières / Montlouis-sur-Loire / Orléans / Orléans-Cléry / Reuilly / Rosé de Loire / Saint-Nicolas-de-Bourgueil / Valençay / Vouvray

63 Tursan

64 Ventoux

65 Vin de Corse or Corse

66 Vin de Savoie or Savoie / Roussette de Savoie / Seyssel

Philosophers around the Table

What if feeding the soul wasn't enough for fine French minds? Sometimes philosophers might want to chew on very worldly things. Or reflect on the contents of their plates, on food phobias, on table manners, and the like. Here are select bits and pieces from Montaigne to Gilles Deleuze.

Thibaut de Saint-Maurice

Je ne suis excessivement desireux ny de salades, ny de fruits, sauf les melons. Mon pere haïssoit toute sorte de sauces; je les aime toutes. Le trop manger m'empeche; mais, par sa qualité, je n'ay encore cognoissance bien certaine qu'aucune viande me nuise; comme aussi je ne remarque ny lune plaine, ny basse, ny l'automne du printemps. Il y a des mouvemens en nous, inconstans et incogneus; car des refors, pour exemple, je les ay trouvez premierement commodes, depuis facheux, present de rechef commodes. En plusieurs choses je sens mon estomac et mon appetit aller ainsi diversifiant :

> Montaigne, *Essais (Essays)*, III, 9, 1580
> *(modernized text)*

Melon according to Montaigne

Montaigne deeply believed that the soul is affected by what the body absorbs. It's an idea that stems from reading the philosophers of ancient times. What matters is eating well, in other words, extracting measured and balanced pleasure from what one eats. And yet Montaigne had a soft spot: melon. For example, in the notes he took on his travels to Italy, he delighted in eating the first melon of the season and even preciously wrote down the name of the village.

But why did Montaigne so love melons? Undoubtedly because the fruit perfectly embodies that ideal of balance and moderation he so often sought. Melon is earthy and yet it's sweet and musky. It can be eaten both as an appetizer and as a dessert; its natural sugar pairs well with salt; it comes from the East and nevertheless became popular in the West; in other words, it's the most balanced natural fruit there is.

Milk according to Jean-Jacques Rousseau

On craint le lait trié ou caillé : c'est une folie, puisqu'on sait que le lait se caille toujours dans l'estomac. C'est ainsi qu'il devient un aliment assez solide pour nourrir les enfants et les petits des animaux : Notre premier aliment est le lait; nous ne nous accoutumons que par degrés aux saveurs fortes; d'abord elles nous répugnent. Des fruits, des légumes, des herbes, et enfin quelques viandes grillées, sans assaisonnement et sans sel, firent les festins des premiers hommes★.

> Rousseau, *Émile*,
> 1762

For Rousseau, eating was nothing more than the occasion to satisfy a vital need. Although he was an architect of the French Revolution, notably through his political writings, in all other concerns, he tended to side more with critics of progress. For example, on culinary matters, he challenged all excessive preparation of food and promoted the merits of a diet made from provisions left as is: fruits, vegetables, grains, and eggs. But for Rousseau, milk was above all the perfect food. Prescribed by nature to man, it is the first food, the one with which we all begin and that makes us grow. It is gentleness and innocence, its taste simple and pure. Another property of milk: it ferments without the artificial intervention of man. In short, milk does not lie. It is the original food that must not be surpassed; one must always return to it so as not to run the risk of losing one's way in corrupted tastes and tampered flavors.

Forbidden foods according to Voltaire

Despite the problems he had digesting what he ate, Voltaire was one of the biggest dinner hosts of the entire late Enlightenment. Voltaire didn't really have preferences, except for "pâtés stuffed with truffles," which became the symbol of that philosophical conviviality: they were exchanged and shared as much as arguments. Voltaire was the apostle of tolerance against religious fanaticism. He even took that fight into kitchens and strongly opposed food being forbidden by religions. In the eighteenth century, fish was on average two to four times as expensive as meat. To forbid meat and prescribe fish was therefore a way of punishing the poor by starving them and of saving the rich by making the obligation of asceticism easier. The only original recipe of a Voltairian dinner is the following: free the table of prescriptions and fanaticism so as to taste together the pleasure of being guests at the same dinner, despite all our differences.

Pourquoi Jésus jeûna-t-il quarante jours dans le désert où il fut emporté par le diable, par le *Knathbull*? Saint Matthieu remarque qu'après ce carême il eut faim; il n'avait donc pas faim pendant ce carême?

Prêtres idiots et cruels! à qui ordonnez-vous le carême? Est-ce aux riches? ils se gardent bien de l'observer. Est-ce aux pauvres? ils font carême toute l'année.

> Voltaire, *Dictionnaire philosophique*,
> "Carême," 1764

Steak with fries according to Roland Barthes

Roland Barthes saw cooking, meals, and food as books, sentences, and words. Cooking has meaning because it is a language. Recipes and technique are like grammar and cooking like a narrative that can tell stories, which Barthes called "Mythologies." Steak and fries (aka *steak frites*) are two characters in the great national culinary novel. Present at every table, they are foods that are at once simple and fortifying and so reflect France itself.

Steak represents blood. The way it's cooked, for example, is not expressed in terms of heat but "in images of blood": the French use the terms *cru* (raw), *saignant* (bloody), and *bleu* (blue). Eating a steak is therefore a kind of transfusion through which the body and character are rejuvenated. That image makes it similar to wine and therefore a "basic element, nationalized even more than socialized." When one explains how he wants his steak cooked, a euphemism is used to describe how: it is *à point* (just right).

Frites represent the land. To eat them is to participate in the "ritual of approbation reclaiming French ethnicity." Besides, outside of France, they're known as French fries.

The art of the regimen according to Michel Foucault

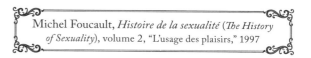

En somme, la pratique du régime comme art de vivre est bien autre chose qu'un ensemble de précautions destinées à éviter les maladies ou à achever de les guérir. C'est toute une manière de se constituer comme un sujet qui a, de son corps, le souci juste, nécessaire et suffisant. Souci qui traverse la vie quotidienne; qui fait des activités majeures ou courantes de l'existence un enjeu à la fois de santé et de morale; qui définit entre le corps et les éléments qui l'entourent une stratégie circonstancielle; et qui vise enfin à armer l'individu lui-même d'une conduite rationnelle.

> Michel Foucault, *Histoire de la sexualité* (*The History of Sexuality*), volume 2, "L'usage des plaisirs," 1997

Le bifteck et les frites

Manger le bifteck saignant représente donc à la fois une nature et une morale. Tous les tempéraments sont censés y trouver leur compte, les sanguins par identité, les nerveux et les lymphatiques par complément. Et de même que le vin devient pour bon nombre d'intellectuels une substance médiumnique qui les conduit vers la force originelle de la nature, de même le bifteck est pour eux un aliment de rachat, grâce auquel ils prosaïsent leur cérébralité et conjurent par le sang et la pulpe molle, la sécheresse stérile dont sans cesse on les accuse.

> Barthes, *Mythologies*, "Le bifteck et les frites," 1957

Springing off of conceptions of diet and regimen from antiquity, Foucault shows that a dietary regimen is a "strategic art" that begins when man's nourishment tears away from simple natural prescriptions. Regimen becomes an "art of living" because instead of forbidding all pleasures, it simply invites one to better know and question them. The practice of following a regimen is therefore not a negation of the pleasure of eating, but a "stylization" of that pleasure based on the reflections of each person. The art of the regimen according to Foucault therefore implies knowledge of the self. The practice of a regimen is a particular way to "stylize our freedom," exactly like the master chef who incorporates each ingredient in accordance with the rules of his taste and reveals individual style and subjectivity.

FOR FURTHER READING: MICHEL FOUCAULT, *HISTOIRE DE LA SEXUALITÉ (THE HISTORY OF SEXUALITY)*, VOLUME 2, "L'USAGE DES PLAISIRS," GALLIMARD, COLL. TEL. 1997.

Alcohol according to Gilles Deleuze

Deleuze admitted it right away: he drank a lot. For most people, an alcoholic is someone who has lost all sense of limits. Deleuze, however, explains that alcohol leads to a better understanding of one's own limit because the alcoholic "evaluates what he can hold . . . without collapsing." If he really drank without limits, he wouldn't get up again and wouldn't be able to start over the next day.

So "to drink is a matter of quantity." The paradoxical wisdom of alcohol is that it reveals our limit. But why give in to alcohol? Deleuze's explanation is directly philosophical. Drinking allows one to bear that which is too heavy in life. Feeling challenged and overwhelmed by the power of life, the alcoholic gives in to drinking by precisely seeking to "hold alcohol," to limit it by not going all the way so as to re-create a limit that does not exist in life.

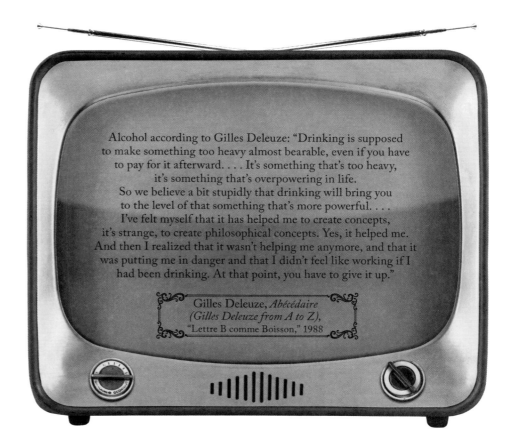

Alcohol according to Gilles Deleuze: "Drinking is supposed to make something too heavy almost bearable, even if you have to pay for it afterward. . . . It's something that's too heavy, it's something that's overpowering in life. So we believe a bit stupidly that drinking will bring you to the level of that something that's more powerful. . . . I've felt myself that it has helped me to create concepts, it's strange, to create philosophical concepts. Yes, it helped me. And then I realized that it wasn't helping me anymore, and that it was putting me in danger and that I didn't feel like working if I had been drinking. At that point, you have to give it up."

> Gilles Deleuze, *Abécédaire*
> (*Gilles Deleuze from A to Z*),
> "Lettre B comme Boisson," 1988

Olivier Roellinger

From his hometown of Cancale, Olivier Roellinger has wedded his fish-based cuisine with exotic flavors.
On deck with one of the greatest adventurers of the kitchen!

Charles Patin O'Coohoon

Olivier Roellinger

HIS KEY DATES

1955: born in Cancale
1976: studies chemistry
1982: establishes a restaurant in his family home, Les Maisons de Bricourt
1984: Les Maisons de Bricourt obtains its first star
2004: Roellinger opens his spice store
2006: obtains the third star
2008: surrenders his stars
2016: his son, Hugo, takes over Les Maisons de Bricourt and develops his brand

Cancale: Port of Registry

Born at his home in Bricourt, a 1760 estate in the *Malouinière* style, the *corsaire* chef (a chef who cooks with the flavors and the products of the sea) has never left Cancale, filling the Breton town with life. Olivier Roellinger has built an entire gourmet ecosystem at the heart of the seaside city.

One can learn signature dishes at his school called **La Cuisine Corsaire**, from Saint Peter Returns from India to **Vanilla Bean**, a teatime pastry.

At **La Maison du Voyageur**, the chef becomes an alchemist who stews, roasts, grinds, crushes, weighs, measures, and combines raw spices that are then sold in his épicierie (spice store). In the hills, facing the Mont-Saint-Michel Bay, there reigns the **Château Richeux**, an estate from the 1920s that became the venture's headquarters. Inside are eleven rooms and the Michelin-starred restaurant **Le Coquillage**.

The most recent initiative, **La Ferme du Vent**, is a compound of *kleds* ("wind cottages" in Breton).

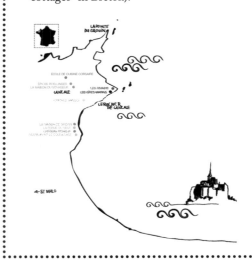

Olivier Roellinger
(born in 1955)

EPIPHANY

When he was a student, he was brutally attacked along the Saint-Malo ramparts by a gang that left him for dead on the beach. The outcome: a few weeks in a coma and two years in a wheelchair. After that trial, he abandoned science and turned to cooking. Devouring books by Antonin Carême and Édouard Nignon, he learned to make beurre blanc sauce and ultimately earned his CAP cuisine diploma.

THE REALM OF SPICE

His whole childhood was immersed in the scent of spice. His maternal grandfather, Eugène Chouan, sold spices wholesale in Rennes. When he launched into his cooking ventures in Cancale, he met a college student who had written a thesis on the French East India Company. That's when he invented his first mixture: Return from India, a blend of turmeric, coriander, star anise, mace, Szechuan pepper, and cumin, all spices found in eighteenth-century Saint Malo.

MY FRIEND GILDAS'S TOMATOES, CLAMS, SEAWEED, AND CURRY CORSAIRE
by Hugo Roellinger

Olivier's son, Hugo, was on his way to a career as an officer in the French Navy when he moored instead to cooking. Like his father, he connects land to sea by using local products like the tomatoes grown by Gildas Macon, an organic farmer in Sains in the Ille-et-Vilaine department.

SERVES 4

¼ cup plus 2 tablespoons (40 g) Corsaire curry powder (or a mixture of ground coriander, ginger, turmeric, and cardamom)
1 cup (200 g) organic grapeseed oil
3 black tomatoes, preferably Black from Tula
2 red tomatoes, preferably Paola
3 teaspoons seaweed mixture, preferably Jardin Marin by Roellinger
1 pinch ground guajillo pepper
1 tablespoon (15 mL) sherry vinegar
3 tablespoons (45 mL) olive oil
1 pinch salt
1 handful string beans
24 palourde clams
Fleur de sel sea salt
Cilantro flowers

To make the Corsaire curry powder–infused oil, toast the curry in the oven at 350°F (180°C) until fragrant. Infuse the curry with the grapeseed oil for 7 minutes heated to 158°F (70°C), then strain it through a coffee filter. Make a vinaigrette by blending together 2 of the black tomatoes and the 2 red tomatoes in a blender for 5 seconds. Add the seaweed mixture, guajillo, vinegar, oil, and salt.

Cook the string beans. Gently pry open the clams, warm the vinaigrette, and slice the remaining black tomato into four slices. Arrange the clams and string beans in the center of each of four serving plates, cover each with a slice of tomato, then season with the sea salt. Add a drizzle of the curry oil, and garnish each plate with a cilantro flower. Pour a little of the warm vinaigrette on top and serve.

MY LITTLE LAMBS

It's difficult to think of an Easter meal in France without lamb! There are essential things to know
when it comes to preparing this meat suitably for any occasion.
Marielle Gaudry & Michel Rubin

LEG OF LAMB 5 WAYS

Far from being a dish for just special
occasions, leg of lamb, considered
the most desirable part of the lamb,
fits any occasion. Michel Rubin*
demonstrates this in these five
gourmet variations.

*Author of *Le goût de l'agneau: traité de
recettes monothéistes, méditerranéennes &
moyenorientales* (Encre d'Orient, 2011)

Classic roast leg of lamb

Recipe: make small incisions in a leg
of lamb weighing 5½ pounds (2.5 kg),
then place the lamb in a roasting
pan. Season with salt and pepper and
drizzle it with 2 tablespoons (30 mL)
of olive oil. Add 4 cloves of garlic
and some bay leaves and sprigs of
thyme to the pan, or, instead of the
garlic and herbs, sprinkle the lamb
with ½ teaspoon of paprika. Roast for
50 minutes to 1 hour at 350°F (180°C).
Meat: tender and pink
Sides: baked apples and ratatouille

"Crying" leg of lamb

Recipe: peel and halve 2 onions,
then slice them crosswise (you might
shed a tear!). Peel and thinly slice
3 cloves of garlic. Wash, peel, and
slice 2¼ pounds (1 kg) of potatoes.
Make 6 incisions in the leg of lamb
and slip some of the garlic slices into
the incisions. Rub the leg with salt,
pepper, and 1 tablespoon (15 mL) of
olive oil. In a baking dish, arrange the
onions and the remaining garlic slices
and cover them with the potato slices.
Distribute 3 tablespoons (50 g) butter
on top, broken into pieces. Roast
the potatoes in the oven at 300°F
(150°C) for 15 minutes, then add the
leg of lamb to the dish. Immediately
raise the oven temperature to 350°F
(180°C) and roast for another
40 minutes.
Meat: tender and medium rare
Sides: potatoes gratin

7-hour "spoon" leg of lamb

Recipe: place the leg of lamb in a
flameproof casserole dish and brown
it in olive oil on all sides; set the lamb
aside. In the same casserole dish, fry
4 or 5 cloves of peeled garlic, a carrot
cut in mirepoix (small dice), a bouquet
garni (thyme, bay leaf), and a peeled
and minced onion. Season with salt
and pepper. Return the leg to the
casserole dish and roast it in the oven
for 7 hours at 250°F (120°C).
Meat: so melting it can be eaten
with a spoon
Sides: sautéed potatoes

40-garlic leg of lamb

Recipe: place a 5½-pound (2.5 kg)
leg of lamb in a roasting pan, and
pour in a little olive oil. Season
the leg with salt and pepper. Add
unpeeled garlic cloves from 4 to
5 heads of garlic, then sprinkle
the lamb with thyme. Bake for
50 minutes at 350°F (180°C).
Meat: tender and pink
Sides: white beans

Lacquered leg of lamb

Recipe: rub a leg of lamb with honey
(it will caramelize in the oven),
then add pinches of various spices
(cinnamon, ground clove, grated
nutmeg) over the lamb. Bake at 350°F
(180°C) for 1 hour. Deglaze the pan
with a little vinegar for a hint of
acidity.
Meat: caramelized
Sides: sweet potatoes and beans

DISHES FROM TIMES PAST

Pascaline d'agneau à la royale: a boneless lamb, stuffed with lamb meat,
hard-boiled egg yolks, stale bread crumbs, herbs, and spices, then roasted.
Issue d'agneau: a stew consisting of the head, heart, lungs, sweetbreads,
liver, and lamb's feet steamed and served as a soup, thickened with raw
egg yolks and lemon juice.
Épigramme d'agneau aux pointes d'asperges: breaded breast of lamb and
sautéed lamb chops, served with asparagus tips and a béchamel sauce.

LE NAVARIN
Why the name?
The name *navarin* is a play on
words from 1847 that uses the
French word for "turnip" (*navet*)
as a derivative of the Greek city
Navarino, the scene of a famous
naval battle in 1827. The turnip is
the featured vegetable in the dish.
What part of the lamb?
Lamb shoulder
Best time to prepare it?
In the spring

NAVARIN
by Denise Solier-Gaudry

SERVES 6
3 onions
4 sprigs parsley
1 clove garlic
3 tablespoons (45 mL) sunflower oil
1⅓ pounds (600 g) lamb neck
1⅓ pounds (600 g) boneless lamb shoulder,
cut into pieces
3 sprigs thyme
1 bay leaf
Salt and freshly ground black pepper
14 ounces (400 g) peas
14 ounces (400 g) carrots
14 ounces (400 g) turnips
14 ounces (400 g) firm-flesh potatoes

❶ Peel the onions and slice them.

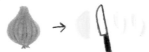

❷ Wash and remove the parsley
leaves. Peel the
garlic clove and
chop it with the
parsley leaves; set
aside.

❸ Pour the oil into a skillet, brown
the pieces of meat, then transfer the
meat to a cast-iron pot.

❹ In the same skillet, cook the
onions over low heat for 5 minutes,
then transfer them to the pot.

❺ Add the chopped garlic and
parsley, the thyme, and the bay leaf.

❻ Season with salt and pepper, and
cover with water.

❼ Simmer for 1 hour over low heat.

❽ Meanwhile, prepare the
vegetables: shell the peas. Peel the
carrots and turnips, then wash
and chop them. Peel and wash the
potatoes and halve them.

❾ After 1 hour of cooking the meat,
add the peas, carrots, and turnips and
cook for 45 minutes. Twenty minutes
before the end of the cooking time,
add the potatoes.

OYSTERS: SPECIAL FRENCH PEARLS

French oyster farming has its *terroirs*, its signatures, its techniques, and its *grands crus*!
From Normandy to the Mediterranean, here's a look at the oysters
you have to try at least once in your life.

Garry Dorr*

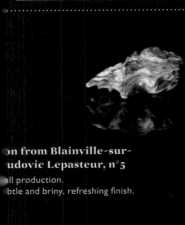
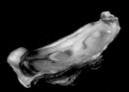

**…on from Blainville-sur-
…udovic Lepasteur, n°5**
…ll production.
…btle and briny, refreshing finish.

**Spéciale Saint-Vaast, Jean-
François Mauger, n°4**
Known and recognized appellation, linked
to the name of an oyster farmer with
rigorous farming methods.
Taste: very briny, an oyster with character!

**Spéciale Isigny-sur-Mer, Sylvain
Perron, n°3**
Medium size and meaty without being excessive.
Taste: more delicate than strong, subtle salinity.

**Spéciale Utah Beach,
Jean-Paul Guernier, n°2**
An influential terroir that's rich in…
Taste: meaty and subtle, sweet w…

ÎLE DE RÉ

**Belon Cadoret, Jean-Jacques
Cadoret, n°00000**
The name Cadoret designates its own
brand of flat oysters from Belon.
Taste: unique woody and grainy
aromas, crisp and meaty texture.

**Fine from l'île de Ré,
Réglin, n°3**
Raised in lanterns (tubular
with stiff trays).
Taste: ocean, seaweed not…
meat, perfect as an appetiz…

**…rom Prat-Ar-Coum,
…Madec, n°3**
… from the coasts of Brittany,
…ed for two years.
… very balanced oyster,
…bly consistent.

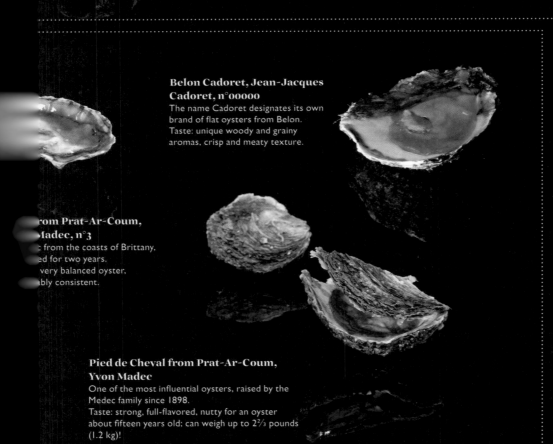

**Pied de Cheval from Prat-Ar-Coum,
Yvon Madec**
One of the most influential oysters, raised by the
Medec family since 1898.
Taste: strong, full-flavored, nutty for an oyster
about fifteen years old; can weigh up to 2⅔ pounds
(1.2 kg)!

**Owner of Le Bar à Huit
restaurants in Paris.*

NOIRMOUTIER

Fine from l'île de Noirmoutier, Alain Gendron, n°2
Produced as part of the island's cooperative oyster-farming tradition.
Taste: very salty notes, delicate meat and a touch bitter.

POITOU-CHARENTES

Spéciale Gillardeau, n°3
An emblematic brand since the 1980s. The oysters are born and raised in Normandy before being matured in Marennes.
Taste: balanced, subtly briny, refreshing, supple texture.

Fine de Claire, David Hervé, n°2
David Hervé's oysters are simply inimitable, the Rolls Royce of oysters!
Taste: possibly the best oyster in the world; plump, smooth, long finish.

AQUITAINE

Wild oyster from Île aux Oiseaux, Olivier Laban
Unique oyster with no human intervention, hence its irregular shape and its method of hand "harvesting."
Taste: natural, no maturation, strong taste of seaweed and salt. Uncompromising!

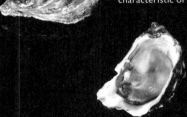

Papillon from the Dune du Pilat, Olivier Laban , n°5
The smallest in size, produced in very small quantities . . . Love from the Dune du Pilat!
Taste: briny, with the almost metallic finish that's characteristic of oysters from Arachon Bay.

MEDITERRANEAN

Bonbon Rose, n°5
A tiny oyster, sometimes even available as n°6! A true plump candy drop, nicely meaty.
Taste: subtly briny, almost sweet, both smooth and crisp.

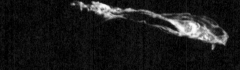

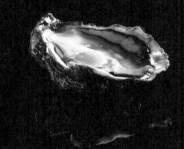

Rose Spéciale, Florent Tarbouriech, n°00
Exceptional oyster directly from the Étang de Thau lagoon, raised using the "collage" technique. Removed from water daily via a mechanical system involving solar panels. Its shell turns pink and iridescent.
Taste: subtly briny, almost sweet, between smooth and crisp. Impressive size.

CORSICA

Plate de Diana Nustrale, Alain Sanci
From Étang de Diana, a lagoon situated on the eastern plain of the Île de Beauté (Corsica). The Romans had already discovered these.
Taste: meaty, extreme sea taste and nutty, very long finish.

Huître Creuse from the Étang d'Urbino, Bronzini di Caraffa family
Very small production of huîtres creuses (*Crassostrea*) along the eastern coast of Corsica, mostly for local consumption.
Taste: salty, complex, not numbered because Corsican oysters are not ranked, but fabulous!

The Art of the Potée

◆

This stew takes its name (*potée*) from the pot in which it is cooked. A unique pork stew prepared in the countryside during holidays, the potée is a mixture of meats (typically pork) and vegetables cooked in broth.

Valentine Oudard

THE AUVERGNE POTÉE

Recipe from the CNAC, Inventory of French Culinary Heritage in Auvergne

COOKING TIME: 3 HOURS
SERVES 6

1⅛ pounds (500 g) salt pork (lightly salted)
2¼ pounds (1 kg) pork shoulder (lightly salted)
1 head cabbage
6 carrots
2 turnips
2 onions
2 cloves
2 cloves garlic
2 tablespoons (29 g) lard or butter
6 leeks (white portion only)
2 stalks celery
1 bouquet garni (thyme, parsley, bay leaf, leek green)
6 potatoes
1 *saucisson à cuire* (a specialty pork shoulder sausage from Lyon)
Salt and freshly ground black pepper

Submerge the meats in cold water and let them desalt for 1 hour. Dab the meats dry with a cloth. Remove and discard the outer leaves of the cabbage, quarter the cabbage, and cut out the core. Blanch the cabbage quarters for 5 minutes in boiling salted water; drain. Peel the carrots and turnips, and cut them into large pieces. Peel the onions. Pierce one of the onions with the cloves, and quarter the other onion. Peel and halve the garlic cloves. Heat the lard in a large flameproof casserole dish. Add the meat and brown it on all sides. Add the carrots, leeks, celery, bouquet garni, and garlic. Cover the contents with water, bring to a boil, then add the cabbage quarters. Cover and simmer over low heat for 2 hours and 30 minutes. Peel the potatoes and add them to the casserole with the sausage. Season with salt and pepper. Continue cooking for 30 minutes. Ladle the meat and vegetables into a soup dish. Just before serving, pour the broth over the top.

"These stews are where all the meats from the farm and all the vegetables from the gardens mingle, and are those that all the farming communities enjoy during their hours of serenity."

Biographie de mes fantômes (1901–1906), Georges Duhamel

"The evolution of girls from Craon, which the potée and cold bacon make fat too soon."

Vipère au poing (1948) by Hervé Bazin

The champenoise "of the grape harvesters": *pork shoulder, shank, spare ribs, bacon, smoked sausage, carrots, leeks, turnips, potatoes, cabbage heart, bouquet garni.*

The lorraine: *also called "potaye" or "retirage." Smoked pork shoulder, smoked lean bacon, pig's tail, pork, smoked Lorraine sausages, green cabbage, turnips, carrots, leeks, onions, celery stalk, potatoes, white beans, string beans, fresh beans, peas, bouquet garni.*

The bourguignonne: *bacon, pork shank and shoulder, sausage, cabbage, carrots, turnips, leeks, potatoes, onion, bouquet garni.*

The alsacienne: *locally called "bäckeoffe," or "potée boulangère" (baker's pot) in reference to the Alsatians who entrusted their preparations to the local bakers in the mornings to cook in the bread ovens and to be ready to enjoy by lunchtime. Spare rib, pork leg and tail, beef chuck, boneless mutton shoulder, Riesling, potatoes, onions, garlic, bouquet garni.*

The bretonne: *salt pork (lightly salted or smoked), rib, pork knuckle, fresh or smoked sausages, carrots, cabbage, leeks, onions, potatoes, turnips.*

The berrichonne: *red beans, sausages (cured or raw), onions, thyme, bay leaves, cooked in red wine.*

The franc-comtoise: *bacon, pork belly and shoulder, Morteau sausage, cabbage, kohlrabi, carrots, turnips, leeks, potatoes, bouquet garni.*

The limousine: *salt pork, smoked bacon, green cabbage, carrots, turnips, leeks, onions, potatoes, garlic, bouquet garni. Optional: pork knuckle, sausage, mique (a dumpling), or andouille sausage.*

The savoyarde: *diots (sausages), garlic sausage, pork shank and belly, smoked bacon, cabbage, potatoes, carrots, onions, white wine, bouquet garni.*

The albigeoise: *smoked raw ham, raw sausage, beef shank, veal shank, goose confit, white cabbage, carrots, turnips, celery stalk, leek whites, white beans.*

The dauphinoise: *cervelat sausages, tongue, beef rib, bacon, pork rind, ham hock, pork shoulder, split pig's feet, veal feet, onions, potatoes, cabbage, carrots, turnips, celery stalk, bouquet garni, herbs.*

The antillaise: *pork shoulder and spare ribs (lightly salted), pork knuckle, smoked bacon, flowering kale (cabbage), carrots, turnips, sweet potatoes, yams, green bananas, plantains, peppers, scallions, lime, herbs and spices.*

Pierrot: "It's not bad, this little potée."
Jean-Claude: "Yes. Not enough to write a thesis."

Les Valseuses (1974) by Bertrand Blier & Philippe Dumarçay

skip to ....
The Bäckeoffe, p. 169

They collect restaurants and stars. They strengthen French gastronomy abroad . . .

. . . a duel between the two "frenemies" of French gastronomy.
Emmanuel Rubin

Battle of the Toques

		ALAIN DUCASSE	JOËL ROBUCHON
	AGE	62 years old (born on September 13, 1956 in Castel-Sarrazin).	73 years old (born on April 7, 1945 in Poitiers).
	NATIONALITY	Naturalized Monégasque in 2008.	French.
	TRAINING	Left Talence hotel school.	Petit Séminaire in Mauléon, then Compagnons du Devoir (cooking) after his "tour de France."
	NICKNAMES	Dudu, Ducasse-couilles, Ducash.	JR.
	GUIDING CHEFS	Michel Guérard, Roger Vergé, and Alain Chapel.	Jean Delaveyne.
	RESTAURANTS	25 restaurants in 7 countries (France, Monaco, England, USA, Doha, Japan, China-Hong Kong).	25 restaurants in 9 countries (France, Monaco, England, USA, Japan, China, Canada, Singapore, Thailand).
	SIGNATURE DISHES	Vegetable cookpot, vegetable salad with truffles.	Mashed fingerling potatoes, gelée of caviar with cauliflower cream.
	STARS	18, including three stars 3 times.	31, including three stars 5 times.
	HONORS	Chevalier de la Légion d'Honneur.	Officier de la Légion d'Honneur, Best Craftsman of France (MOF).
	BUSINESS	Aside from restaurants, the Groupe Alain Ducasse includes a cooking school, a chocolaterie, a training and consulting program, a publishing house, and the chain Châteaux & Hôtels Collection.	Aside from restaurants, cellars, and shops, JR also acts as a consultant in gastronomy and food processing. From 1999 to 2012, he directed several cooking shows on television (TF1, France 3) and presided over the channel Gourmet TV (2002–2004).
	SALARY	12 million euros ($14 million) per year (source: Forbes 2016).	7 million euros ($8 million) per year (source: Capital-Infogreffe 2016).
	CONSULTING	Since 2006, he has developed recipes for space in partnership with the CNES, the French space agency.	A specialist in the matter (he was advisor for Reflets de France and created recipes for Fleury-Michon).
	THAT DAY WHEN . . .	On August 9, 1984, he was the sole survivor of a plane crash—a miracle that deeply changed his approach to life.	In 1995, he retired at age 50 only to come back 6 years later with a new vision for his career.
	INFLUENCE	Cofounder of the Collège Culinaire de France. The Plaza Athenée (Paris) is ranked 13th in the World 50 Best Restaurants 2017.	Cofounder of the Collège Culinaire de France.
	BOOKS	Some 50 books, and a publishing house, Alain Ducasse Éditions, which publishes one on Robuchon, among others.	Some 30 books translated throughout the world, and editor, in 1996, of the famous *Larousse Gastronomique*.
	DISCIPLES	Franck Cerutti (Le Louis XV, Monaco), Bruno Cirino (Hostellerie Jérôme, La Turbie), Jean-François Piège (Le Grand Restaurant, Paris), Hélène Darroze (Paris, London), Jean-Louis Nomicos (Les Tablettes, Paris), Christophe Saintagne (Papillon, Paris) . . .	Frédéric Anton (Pré Catelan, Paris), Olivier Belin (Auberge des Glazicks, Plomodiern), Éric Ripert (Le Bernardin, New York) . . .
	FLOPS	BE, a boulangerie and épicerie in Paris; the restaurant Marcel in the Drugstore Publicis.	Le Grand Restaurant in Bordeaux, open for just about a year and then gone!
	QUOTATION	"Leadership is a leader's capacity to move forward while ensuring the full support of the people he works with."	"Great French cuisine bores the hell out of me . . ."

Bring On the Sauce!

"England has two sauces and three hundred religions. France, on the other hand, has two religions but more than three hundred sauces," wrote Talleyrand. Here is an in-depth exploration of this fabulous heritage through the families of sauces.

François-Régis Gaudry & Éric Trochon

Stocks, roux, and jus are "the keystones of cooking" according to Auguste Escoffier, who largely contributed to the standardization of France's repertoire of sauces. Coauthor of the *Repertoire des sauces* (Éditions Flammarion) with Brian Lemercier, chef Éric Trochon, Best Craftsman of France (MOF), explores French heritage through four major families of sauces: those made with a white stock, those made with a brown stock, those derived from béchamel, and those derived from a béarnaise sauce. His goal is also to help prevent béchamel, Mornay, and choron sauces from disappearing into culinary oblivion . . .

STOCKS

These form the base of numerous French sauces. These are broths or juices, fat or lean, made from meat, vegetables, and herbs cooked for several hours in water, then strained. They are used to make a sauce or to add to dishes while braising.

A differentiation:
- **"White" stock:** made from white meats (veal or poultry) and aromatics placed in a cooking liquid (water).
- **"Brown" stock:** made from beef, veal, or poultry, which are first browned before adding them to the cooking liquid, and accompanied by aromatics.
- **Fish stock**, also called *fumet*.

ROUX

A mixture of flour and butter (half each), cooked and browned over medium heat.
A differentiation:
- **White roux or velouté:** a base for béchamel and other white sauces.
- **Blond roux:** has a hazelnut flavor; serves as a thickener for dishes with white meat or fish, and as a base for béchamel sauce.
- **Brown roux:** a base for brown sauces that accompany red meats.

BEURRE BLANC

Makes about 1 cup (250 g) of sauce
⅓ cup plus 1 tablespoon (100 mL) dry white wine (from Pays Nantais)
3 tablespoons plus 1 teaspoon (50 mL) vinegar
2 shallots, peeled and chopped
28 tablespoons (400 g) unsalted butter, cubed and chilled
Salt and freshly ground black pepper

Combine the wine and vinegar with the shallots and reduce the mixture by three-fourths its volume. Whisk in the cold butter. Season with salt and pepper.
Accompaniment: fish poached in a court-bouillon or grilled.

White stock and its derivative sauces

A white stock is achieved simply by simmering crushed bones with herbs and vegetables.

THE BUILDING BLOCKS

WHITE STOCK
→ + cream + butter + lemon **SUPREME SAUCE**
  → + tomato + butter **AURORE**
  → + Glace de Viande + red pepper butter **ALBUFERA**
→ + egg yolks + cream **PARISIENNE (OR ALLEMANDE)**
  → + mushroom + parsley + lemon **POULETTE**

THE RECIPES

White stock
Cooking time: 5 hours for veal stock / 1 hour for chicken stock
Makes 8 cups (2 L)
2¼ pounds (1 kg) veal bones and trimmings or chicken bones and carcasses
5¼ ounces (150 g) carrots
5¼ ounces (150 g) onions
1 clove
5¼ ounces (150 g) leeks
1¾ ounces (50 g) stalks celery
½ clove garlic
1 bouquet garni

Place the bones and trimmings or carcasses in a cast-iron pot and cover them with room-temperature water. Bring to a simmer. Add all the vegetables (whole) and the bouquet garni. Let simmer, frequently skimming the surface of any fat or foam. Strain through a fine-mesh strainer, and store the stock.

Supreme Sauce
Thicken 2 cups (500 mL) of white chicken stock with 1 ounce (30 g) of white roux (made from 2 tablespoons/15 g of flour + 1 tablespoon/15 g of butter). Bring the mixture to a boil. Add ⅓ cup plus 1 tablespoon (100 mL) of cream and reduce the mixture until slightly thickened (it should coat a spoon). Add 2 tablespoons (30 mL) of lemon juice and 1 tablespoon plus 2 teaspoons (25 g) of butter. Season with salt and pepper, then add a pinch each of cayenne pepper and nutmeg.
Accompaniment: poultry.

Parisienne (or Allemande)
Thicken 3¾ cups (900 mL) of white veal stock with a white roux (made from ½ cup plus 1 tablespoon/60 g of flour + 4 tablespoons/60 g of butter). Incorporate 3 large (60 g) egg yolks with 1 teaspoon (5 mL) of lemon juice, ¾ cup plus 1 tablespoon (200 mL) cream, and a portion of the veal stock–roux mixture. Once incorporated, add the remaining veal stock–roux mixture and stir to combine. Bring to a simmer and let cook until the desired consistency is achieved. Adjust the seasoning as needed.
Accompaniment: vol-au-vent.

Albuféra
2 cups (500 mL) Supreme Sauce + ⅓ cup plus 1 tablespoon (100 mL) Glace de Viande (see page 187) + 3 tablespoons (50 g) red pepper butter.
Accompaniment: poached or braised poultry.

Aurore
1⅔ cups (400 mL) Supreme Sauce + ⅓ cup plus 1 tablespoon (100 mL) tomato sauce + 5 tablespoons (75 g) butter.
Accompaniment: eggs, pork, veal, rabbit, or poultry.

Poulette
Slightly reduce 3 tablespoons plus 1 teaspoon (50 mL) liquid obtained from cooking mushrooms, then add 2 cups (500 mL) Parisienne (or Allemande) sauce. Boil for 5 minutes. Off the heat, whisk in 5 tablespoons (75 g) of butter. Add 2½ tablespoons (10 g) chopped parsley, and a drizzle of lemon juice.
Accompaniment: hedgehog mushrooms, eggs, legumes.

Brown stock and its derivative sauces

Brown stocks are made simply from bones browned in the oven (hence the dark color), then added to simmering water with herbs and vegetables.

THE BUILDING BLOCKS

BROWN STOCK

→ + brown roux + mirepoix + tomato **ESPAGNOLE**

→ + red wine + anchovy + onion + carrot + Demi-Glace de Viande **GENEVOISE**

→ Reduced **DEMI-GLACE DE VIANDE**

→ Reduced **GLACE DE VIANDE**

→ + fish court-bouillon + mushroom **MATELOTE**

→ + onion + tomato **BRETONNE**

→ + white wine + shallot + cayenne **DIABLE**

→ + 2⅛ ounces (60 g) chopped cornichons **COLBERT SAUCE**

→ + white wine + shallot + parsley **BERCY**

→ + red wine + shallot **BORDELAISE**

→ + white wine + onion + mustard **ROBERT**

→ + white wine + mushroom **CHASSEUR**

→ + Madeira **MADÈRE**

THE RECIPES

Brown stock
Cooking time: 5 hours with bones / 2 hours with pieces only (tail, tendons)
Makes 8½ cups (2 L)
2¼ pounds (1 kg) veal bone, tendon, shank, foot, and trimmings
5¼ ounces (150 g) carrots
5¼ ounces (150 g) onions
2½ ounces (75 g) celery
1 bouquet garni (rosemary, thyme, bay leaf, or any herbs you prefer)
1 tablespoon plus 1 teaspoon (20 g) tomato paste
7 ounces (200 g) fresh tomatoes (optional)
½ head garlic
1 pinch coarse salt

In a roasting pan, heat the bones and trimmings in the oven just until browned. Skim the fat from the pan, and add the vegetables, bouquet garni, and tomato paste; let simmer to reduce. Deglaze the roasting pan with a little water. Place all the ingredients in a large pot and add 4 quarts (4 L) of water. Simmer, then strain through a fine-mesh sieve and store the stock.

Espagnole
Boil 4 quarts (4 L) of brown stock, and thicken it with 10½ ounces (300 g) brown roux. Let cook slowly, and skim the fat off regularly. Cut thick bacon into small cubes and fry it in a skillet, then add a *brunoise* (small dice) made with 4½ ounces (125 g) carrots, 2½ ounces (75 g) onions, thyme, and bay leaves. Cook until the bacon and onions are browned and fragrant, then add this mixture to the sauce. Deglaze the skillet with white wine, reduce the liquid by half, and add this reduction to the sauce. Cook 1 hour and strain through a fine-mesh sieve, pressing down on the contents to release all the liquid. Add 4 cups (1 L) of the stock, and cook for another hour. The next day, add 4 cups (1 L) of the remaining stock to 1⅛ pounds (500 g) of tomato sauce. Bring to a boil, then let reduce over low heat for 1 hour, regularly skimming off any fat. Strain through a cheesecloth.
Accompaniment: pork, veal, poultry, game, or fish.

Genevoise
Espagnole sauce + 4 cups (1 L) red wine + 1 ounce (25 g) anchovies + 3½ ounces (100 g) onions + 3½ ounces (100 g) carrots + Demi-Glace
Accompaniment: salmon or trout.

Demi-Glace de Viande
A brown stock reduction, with a concentrated texture. 8½ cups (2 L) brown stock + ⅓ cup plus 1 tablespoon (100 mL) port or Madeira + 5¼ ounces (150 g) white button mushrooms + 1 tablespoon (15 g) butter + 1 hour to 1 hour 30 minutes of cooking = 2 cups (500 mL) Demi-Glace de Viande.

Glace de Viande
A brown stock reduction, with a syrupy texture. 8½ cups (2 L) brown stock + 1 hour 30 minutes of cooking = ¾ cup plus 1 tablespoon (200 mL) Glace de Viande.

Matelote
Reduce 1¼ cups (300 mL) of fish stock with red wine and 1 ounce (30 g) of chopped mushrooms. Add ¾ cup plus 1 tablespoon (200 mL) of Demi-Glace de Veau (veal). Strain. Whisk in 2 tablespoons (30 g) of butter. Season with salt and pepper.
Accompaniment: eel, fish.

Bretonne
Brown 3½ ounces (100 g) chopped onions in butter. Add 3 tablespoons plus 1 teaspoon (50 mL) of white wine. Reduce. Add 1¼ cups (300 mL) of Demi-Glace de Veau (veal). Add ¾ cup plus 1 tablespoon (200 mL) of tomato sauce, 7 ounces (200 g) diced fresh tomatoes, and ⅓ ounce (10 g) crushed garlic. Cook 7 to 8 minutes, then strain through a fine-mesh sieve. Whisk in 1 tablespoon plus 1 teaspoon (20 g) of butter and stir in 5 tablespoons (20 g) chopped parsley.
Accompaniment: a base for beans and dried legumes.

Diable
Reduce 3 tablespoons plus 1 teaspoon (50 mL) of white wine with 1 tablespoon plus 1 teaspoon of vinegar (20 mL), 1½ ounces (40 g) of finely chopped shallot, ⅛ ounce (3 g) of pepper, and ⅓ ounce (10 g) of tarragon. Add 1⅔ cups (400 mL) of Demi-Glace de Veau (veal) and bring to a boil for 2 minutes. Let infuse for 15 minutes off the heat. Strain through a fine-mesh sieve and whisk in 2 tablespoons plus 2 teaspoons (40 g) of butter. Add a pinch of cayenne pepper.
Accompaniment: poultry or grilled fish.

Bercy
Gently cook 1 ounce (30 g) of shallots. Add 3 tablespoons plus 1 teaspoon (50 mL) of white wine, and reduce to one-tenth its volume. Add 2 cups (500 mL) of Demi-Glace de Veau (veal), and reduce to two-thirds its volume. Whisk in 7 tablespoons (100 g) of butter. Add 2½ tablespoons (10 g) of chopped parsley and 3 tablespoons plus 1 teaspoon (50 mL) of white wine. Season with salt and pepper.
Accompaniment: steak, tournedos.

Bordelaise
Sauté 1 ounce (30 g) of shallots with black pepper, thyme, and bay leaf. Add 2 cups (500 mL) Bordeaux red wine and reduce it to one-fourth its volume. Add 1⅔ cups (400 mL) of Demi-Glace de Veau (veal). Strain through a fine-mesh sieve, and add diced poached beef bone marrow.
Accompaniment: small servings of meat.

Robert
Gently cook 3½ ounces (100 g) of onions with 2 tablespoons (30 g) of butter. Add ⅔ cup (150 mL) of white wine and 3 tablespoons plus 1 teaspoon (50 mL) of vinegar, then reduce by two-thirds its volume. Add 1⅔ cups (400 mL) of Demi-Glace de Veau (veal). Reduce again, and add 3 teaspoons (20 g) of Dijon mustard and 1¼ teaspoons (5 g) of sugar. Strain through a fine-mesh sieve. Season with salt and pepper; do not boil.
Accompaniment: tongue, small game, poached eggs.

Colbert
Add 2⅛ ounces (60 g) chopped cornichons to a Robert sauce.
Accompaniment: vegetables, fish, grilled meats.

Chasseur
Sauté 9 ounces (250 g) of white button mushrooms with 1 tablespoon plus 2 teaspoons (25 g) of butter. Add 1 ounce (30 g) of chopped shallots and 3 tablespoons plus 1 teaspoon (50 mL) of cognac. Reduce, and add 2 cups (500 mL) of white wine. Reduce again. Add 1⅔ cups (400 mL) Demi-Glace de Veau (veal), then whisk in 2 teaspoons (10 g) of butter. Stir in ⅓ ounce (10 g) chopped chervil and tarragon. Season with salt and pepper.
Accompaniment: poultry, rabbit, veal, sweetbreads.

Madère
Heat ¾ cup plus 1 tablespoon (200 mL) of Demi-Glace de Veau (veal) and add 3 tablespoons (45 mL) of Madeira; do not let it boil.
Accompaniment: small servings of meat, such as tournedos.

continued

Béarnaise sauce and its derivatives

Béarnaise is part of the family of so-called "warm semicoagulated emulsified sauces."

THE BUILDING BLOCKS

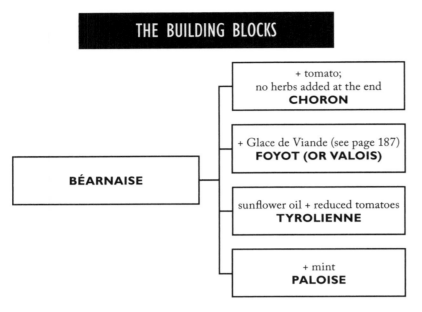

BÉARNAISE	+ tomato; no herbs added at the end **CHORON**
	+ Glace de Viande (see page 187) **FOYOT (OR VALOIS)**
	sunflower oil + reduced tomatoes **TYROLIENNE**
	+ mint **PALOISE**

THIS SAUCE IS REALLY A *BÉARNAISE*?

Nothing could be less certain! The béarnaise sauce was prepared for the first time at Pavillon Henri IV in Saint-Germain-en-Laye. It was perhaps so named in memory of King Henry IV, the Grand Béarnais. The chef was none other than Monsieur Collinet, to whom we also owe the invention of *pommes soufflées* (souffléed potatoes).

THE RECIPES

Béarnaise

Makes 1⅔ cups (400 mL); enough for 8 people

⅓ cup plus 1 tablespoon (100 mL) white vinegar
1¾ ounces (50 g) finely chopped shallot
Freshly ground black pepper
¾ ounce (20 g) chopped tarragon
5 egg yolks
10½ ounces (300 g) clarified butter
⅓ ounce (10 g) chopped chervil

Reduce the vinegar with the shallots, some pepper, and half the tarragon. Once the mixture is well reduced by half, stir in the yolks. Using a balloon whisk, whisk the mixture vigorously to create a sabayon (thick and billowy), gradually adding the clarified butter while continuing to whisk. Strain through a fine-mesh sieve. Whisk in the remaining tarragon and the chervil.
Accompaniment: grilled meats or fish.

Choron

Add 3½ ounces (100 g) of crushed tomatoes to 10½ ounces (300 g) of béarnaise.
Accompaniment: beef ribs, steaks, grilled red meats.

Foyot (or Valois)

Add 1⅔ cups (400 mL) of béarnaise to 3 tablespoons plus 1 teaspoon (50 mL) of Glace de Viande.
Accompaniment: grilled red meats.

Tyrolienne

Substitute the butter in a béarnaise with sunflower oil, and add 10½ ounces (300 g) of the béarnaise to 3½ ounces (100 g) of reduced tomatoes.
Accompaniment: steaks, tournedos, grilled red meats.

Paloise

In a béarnaise, replace the tarragon with fresh mint (when reducing and finishing).
Accompaniment: lamb, red meats.

Hollandaise and its derivatives

Hollandaise and its derivatives, like béarnaise, are so-called "warm semicoagulated emulsified" sauces.

THE BUILDING BLOCKS

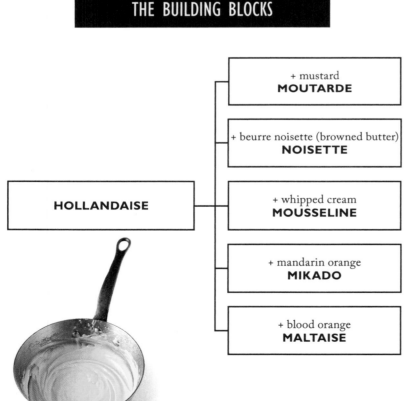

HOLLANDAISE	+ mustard **MOUTARDE**
	+ beurre noisette (browned butter) **NOISETTE**
	+ whipped cream **MOUSSELINE**
	+ mandarin orange **MIKADO**
	+ blood orange **MALTAISE**

THE RECIPES

Hollandaise

Makes 1⅔ cups (400 mL); enough for 8 people

¼ cup (60 mL) water
5 egg yolks
35 tablespoons (500 g) butter
Juice of 1 lemon
Salt and freshly ground black pepper

Vigorously whisk together the water and the egg yolks over low heat to make a sabayon (thick and billowy). While continuing to whisk vigorously, gradually add the butter. Whisk in the lemon juice and a pinch of salt and pepper.
Accompaniment: fish, asparagus.

Moutarde

Add 1⅔ cups (400 mL) of Hollandaise to 3 tablespoons (45 mL) of strong mustard, a pinch of salt and pepper, and the juice of half a lemon. Stir in ¾ cup plus 1 tablespoon (200 mL) of crème fraîche.
Accompaniment: fish.

Noisette

Add 2½ ounces (75 g) of *beurre noisette* (browned butter) to 1⅔ cups (400 mL) of Hollandaise at the end.

Accompaniment: white asparagus, vegetables, salmon, poached trout.

Mousseline

Add ⅓ cup plus 1 tablespoon (100 mL) of cream whipped to stiff peaks to 1¼ cups (300 mL) of Hollandaise. Stir in the whipped cream off the heat. Keep warm and serve.
Accompaniment: grilled fish, asparagus.

Mikado

Julienne the zest of 2 mandarin oranges and blanch them for several minutes. Juice the mandarins. Add the juice and zests to 1⅔ cups (400 mL) of Hollandaise. Add a small pinch of cayenne pepper.
Accompaniment: white asparagus, vegetables.

Maltaise

Add the zest and juice of a blood orange to 2 cups (500 mL) of Hollandaise. Strain through a fine-mesh sieve.
Accompaniment: white asparagus.

Béchamel sauce and its derivatives

Béchamel is a white sauce made from roux (a mixture of flour and butter).

1 Béchamel, 2 Schools

Here is a match-up of recipes between two great French chefs: Antonin Carême (1784–1833) and Auguste Escoffier (1846–1935).

Laurent Séminel

Ingredients

Auguste Escoffier: butter, flour, and milk, to which onion, thyme, pepper, nutmeg, salt, and veal can be added.

Antonin Carême: a few strips of lean ham cushion (from the shoulder), 1 veal cushion (from the shoulder), 1 bottom round of veal, 1 veal rump, 2 large chickens, and enough chicken broth to cover the meat, plus heavy cream, white button mushrooms, butter, and flour.

The details

Auguste Escoffier: "Combine the roux [the butter and flour] with boiling milk; bring back to a boil, stirring, and add the seasoning and herbs, and the veal, which has been parboiled. Cook gently for 1 hour; strain through cheesecloth, and mop the surface of the sauce with a piece of butter. When the béchamel sauce is intended for serving with lean dishes, the veal is removed from the recipe, but the indicated spices must be maintained."

Antonin Carême: "After you have lightly buttered the bottom of a large saucepan . . . add a few slices of lean ham cushion, the veal cushion, bottom round, veal rump, two large chickens, and the quantity of broth necessary to just cover them all. Then, place the covered pan on a hot stove. After a few hours you will have a velouté, which should not be browned. It is then mixed into a roux composed of butter and flour, to which is then added mushrooms and a bouquet garni. Then, an hour and a half later, you pour in 3 pints of good heavy cream, which should quickly give you a silky, white, and perfect béchamel."

The result

These two versions of béchamel are very different.

The version by Antonin Carême is extremely delicate. The broth is made with lean, high-quality morsels of meat. The result is amazing and is closer to a Japanese dashi than to a classic veal broth made with bones and trimmings. Auguste Escoffier has, in fact, completely revolutionized the béchamel by simplifying it and making it accessible to as many people as possible.

THE BUILDING BLOCKS

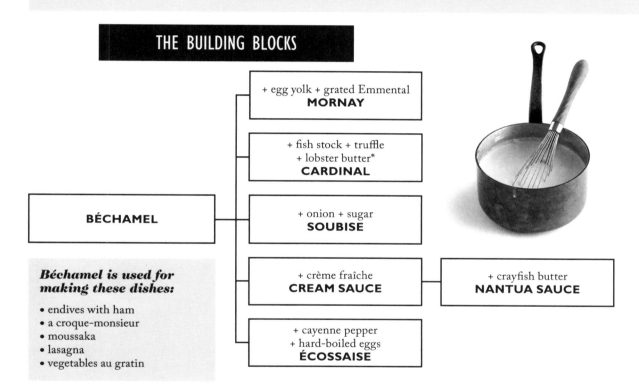

BÉCHAMEL

+ egg yolk + grated Emmental
MORNAY

+ fish stock + truffle
+ lobster butter*
CARDINAL

+ onion + sugar
SOUBISE

+ crème fraîche
CREAM SAUCE

+ crayfish butter
NANTUA SAUCE

+ cayenne pepper
+ hard-boiled eggs
ÉCOSSAISE

Béchamel is used for making these dishes:

- endives with ham
- a croque-monsieur
- moussaka
- lasagna
- vegetables au gratin

DID YOU KNOW?

Béchamel is attributed to Louis de Béchameil, maître d'hôtel of Louis XIV. Béchameil lost its "i" over the course of time, and it must not be spelled with two "l's" and an "e" at the end.

Béchamel

Makes about 4 cups (1 L); enough for 10 people
5 tablespoons (70 g) unsalted butter
¾ cup minus 2 teaspoons (70 g) flour
4 cups (1 L) milk
Nutmeg
Fine salt and ground white pepper

In a saucepan, melt the butter, add the flour, and whisk until thoroughly combined. Pour in the cold milk, little by little, while whisking. Whisk quickly to dissolve the roux. Bring to a boil and cook for 4 to 5 minutes, stirring continuously. Season with nutmeg, salt, and pepper. Strain through a fine-mesh sieve and let cool.

Mornay

Add 3 egg yolks and 3½ ounces (100 g) of grated Emmental cheese to 4 cups (1 L) of béchamel.

Accompaniment: eggs and vegetables, such as in Swiss Chard au Gratin.

Cardinal

Add ⅓ cup plus 1 tablespoon (100 mL) of fish stock and 3 tablespoons plus 1 teaspoon (50 mL) of truffle oil to ¾ cup plus 1 tablespoon (200 mL) of béchamel. Bring to a boil. Add ⅓ cup plus 1 tablespoon (100 mL) of cream and 1¾ ounces (50 g) of lobster butter* and whisk to combine. Season with salt and pepper, and add 1 small pinch of cayenne pepper.

Accompaniment: a high-quality fish.

Soubise

Gently cook 4½ ounces (125 g) of sliced onions in butter. Add 1 tablespoon plus 1¾ teaspoons (20 g) of sugar and 3 tablespoons plus 1 teaspoon (50 mL) of béchamel and stir to combine. Bring to a boil, and

strain through a fine-mesh sieve. Add ½ cup (120 mL) of crème fraîche and reduce to a thick consistency. Season with salt and pepper.

Accompaniment: roast veal, boiled eggs, vegetables.

Cream Sauce

Reduce 1⅔ cups (400 mL) of béchamel with ¾ cup plus 1 tablespoon (200 mL) of cream to obtain a thickened sauce. Season with salt and pepper.

Accompaniment: vegetables, poultry, eggs.

Nantua

Reduce ¾ cup plus 1 tablespoon (200 mL) of Cream Sauce with ⅓ cup plus 1 tablespoon (100 mL) of crayfish stock (or reduced fish stock). Whisk in crayfish butter.* Add ½ cup (120 mL) of cognac and a pinch of cayenne pepper. Strain through a fine-mesh sieve.

Accompaniment: Lyonnaise dumplings.

Écossaise

Whisk together 1 small pinch each of cayenne pepper and nutmeg, and the finely chopped whites and yolks of 4 hard-boiled eggs, with 2 cups (500 mL) of béchamel.

Accompaniment: cod.

*Lobster butter or crayfish butter (makes 9 oz/250 g): melt 14 tablespoons (200 g) of butter in a bain-marie and add 9 ounces (250 g) lobster (or crayfish) shells and claws, stirring regularly. Strain through a fine-mesh sieve when the butter is browned and fragrant. Cool, and use within 2 to 3 days.

skip to
Mayonnaise, p. 100

Slices of Sausage

A good-quality sausage makes for a delicious appetizer. Even if years of commercially produced sausages have tainted the image of this symbol of French gastronomy, there are still artisan sausage makers who continue to produce perfect examples. Here are some of the best ones for serving up.

Jordan Moilim

❶ PORC DE BAYEUX SAUSAGE
Producer: Ferme de l'Hôtel Fauvel in Saint-Maurice-en-Contentin (Manche)
Composition: 80 percent lean, 20 percent fat
Aging: 3 weeks
Taste: refined, grassy

❷ PORC NUSTRALE SAUSAGE
Producer: Félix Torre in Cuttoli (Corse-du-Sud)
Composition: 80 percent lean, 20 percent fat
Aging: 4 months
Taste: rustic, slightly nutty, notes of fresh butter, long finish

❸ PORC GASCON SAUSAGE
Producer: Thierry Pardon in Coarraze (Pyrénées-Atlantiques)
Composition: 90 percent lean, 10 percent fat
Aging: 9 weeks
Taste: smoky notes, chestnut

❹ PORC CUL NOIR SAUSAGE
Producer: Pierre Giraud in Vigeois (Corrèze)
Composition: 65 percent lean, 35 percent fat
Aging: 1 month
Taste: peppery and lightly smoky notes

❺ PIE NOIR DU PAYS BASQUE SAUSAGE
Producer: Pierre Oteiza at Aldudes (Pyrénées-Atlantiques)
Composition: 90 percent lean, 10 percent fat
Aging: 6 to 8 weeks
Taste: notes of acorn and chestnut

❻ TAUREAU (BEEF) SAUSAGE
Producer: Maison Bignalet in Habas (Landes)
Composition: 60 percent lean beef, 40 percent lean pork meat and pork fat
Aging: 4 weeks
Taste: peppery, slightly garlicy, "animal-like" finish

❼ DUCK SAUSAGE
Producer: Patrick Duler in Lascabannes (Lot)
Composition: 10 percent duck fat, 80 percent duck breast, 10 percent wine lees
Aging: 3 weeks
Taste: very fragrant, flavors of coq-au-vin

❽ PIE NOIRE BEEF SAUSAGE
Producer: Agnès Bernard in Courgenard (Sarthe)
Composition: 70 percent lean, 30 percent fat
Aging: 3 months
Taste: leather, animal

Should You Eat the Skin?

When eating commercially produced sausages made using plastic casings and covered with rice flour or talc, it is best to avoid eating the skins. For "real" sausages (those made by artisan producers), you can obviously eat the skin. These sausages and cured meats are all made with natural casings, and their whitish appearance on the outside is due to a natural fungus: the penicillium. This fungus is also good for intestinal flora. Everything is good in a well-made sausage!

Benoît Violier

The shooting star
(1971–2016)

In December 2015, his restaurant, the Hôtel de Ville, was distinguished as the "best in the world." His suicide a month and a half later sent shock waves through the food world. A look at the life of a shooting star.

Hadrien Gonzales

A MYSTERIOUS SUICIDE

Benoît Violier laughed with joy when he was told during an interview* that his establishment had just been distinguished as the best in the world. He had already received three Michelin stars and a grade of 19/20 in Gault & Millau. His eyes then filled with tears when he spoke of the deaths of his mentor, Philippe Rochat, and his father in the same year. Later there was a moment of hesitation in the restaurant smokehouse . . . On January 30, 2016, he was found dead in his room above the restaurant. He had taken his own life with a hunting rifle. The reasons remain unknown. Since February 2016, the establishment has been managed by his wife, Brigitte Violier.

Le Figaro, December 2015

EXPRESS BIO

1971: born in Saintes
1990: enters the Compagnons du Tour de France des Devoirs Unis
1996: qrrives at the Hôtel de Ville in Crissier
1999: serves as chef at the Hôtel de Ville
2000: achieves Best Craftsman of France (MOF)
2003: Compagnon du Tour de France
2012: with his wife, Brigitte, he takes the helm of the Hôtel de Ville
2015: receives recognition as meilleur restaurant du monde (best restaurant in the world) according to La Liste

HIS SIGNATURE DISHES

Fillettes *and* bourgeoises Pertuis asparagus served with a mimosa sauce and Imperial Ossetra caviar

Blue lobster blanched with salted butter, spiced melba toast

Panfried chamois chops with green peppercorn

HE EVOKED HIS MENTORS

Alain Chapel (1937–1990)
"Madame Chapel often tells me that I know her husband better than some chefs who worked for him. My greatest regret is to never have worked with him."

Benoît Guichard (born in 1961)
The executive chef of Jamin, in Paris, was Benoît Violier's first maitre d'hôtel when Violier joined Joël Robuchon's staff in Paris in 1994. "He was a stupendous professional, a model."

Frédy Girardet (born in 1936)
Benoît Violier joined the Hôtel de Ville's kitchen staff in 1996 under his orders: "When I was fifteen or sixteen years old, I clipped out articles about Girardet and his recipes and kept them in a file."

Philippe Rochat (1953–2015)
Philippe Rochat succeeded Girardet at the helm of the Hôtel de Ville in December 1996. "I have never seen anyone with such a developed sense of taste."

———— PANFRIED CHAMOIS CHOPS WITH GREEN PEPPERCORN ————

SERVES 4
For the Green Peppercorn Sauce
1 tablespoon (10 g) green peppercorns, crushed
1¾ ounces (50 g) shallots, peeled and finely chopped
2½ tablespoons (37 g) unsalted butter
Salt
1 tablespoon plus 1 teaspoon (20 mL) cognac, plus more for drizzling
¾ cup plus 1 tablespoon (200 mL) white wine
1¼ cups (300 mL) game or veal brown stock (previously made)
3 tablespoons plus 1 teaspoon (50 mL) cream
1 bunch thyme

4 (6⅓ oz/180 g) racks of chamois or deer, perfectly trimmed
Salt
A mixture of game meat spices
3 tablespoons plus 1 teaspoon (50 mL) peanut oil
3 ounces (80 g), about 16 cloves, garlic, unpeeled
¾ ounce (20 g), about ½ bunch, sprigs thyme
¾ ounce (20 g), about ½ bunch, sprigs savory
3½ ounces (100 g) shallots, split in two
10 juniper berries, crushed
5½ tablespoons (80 g) unsalted butter, small dice

Green peppercorn sauce
Sauté the peppercorns and chopped shallots in 2 tablespoons (30 g) of

the butter. Season with salt. Add the cognac and ignite it using a long match. Add the white wine to deglaze the pan and reduce the liquid in the pan by one-third. Add the stock and let it simmer for 5 minutes. Add the cream, whisk in the remaining butter, and add a drizzle of cognac. Adjust the seasoning as needed and add the thyme.

Chamois ribs
Preheat the oven to 350°F (180°C). Season the rib racks with the salt and game meat spices. Heat the oil in a large skillet, and brown the rib racks on all sides. Add the racks,

vegetables, herbs, juniper berries, and butter to a large roasting pan and roast for about 5 minutes, basting regularly and watching the butter carefully so that it does not burn. The center of the meat should register 95°F (35°C) for a pink center. Remove the racks from the oven, then place them on cooling racks and let them rest for 15 minutes, covered with foil.

Before serving, heat the ribs in the oven at 350°F (180°C) for 3 minutes, then trim off the ends. Warm the green peppercorn sauce and stir it briefly, then serve separately alongside the ribs. Accompany with seasonal vegetables.

Pissaladière and Company

Pissaladière is the pizza of Nice, but all the local Provençaux will cheerfully share it! But first, they have to agree on what ingredients should be on it . . . Here are our recipes *aux petits oignons* ("with love and care").

François-Régis Gaudry

THE PISSALADIÈRE IN 4 INGREDIENTS

The dough
Originally, the crust was made using a bread dough with olive oil, a sort of cousin of focaccia from neighboring Liguria. But the use of a *pâte brisée* flaky dough began to appear in modern recipes. This wasn't a scandalous change, although not a great one either . . .

The onions
The onion lies at the heart of the pissaladière. A white and sweet onion is preferable, and it must first be cooked and browned, almost caramelized, before it is added to the pizza—and in sufficient quantity. Tradition states that the layer of onions should be as thick as the dough.

The olives
Olives are a must, and they should be Niçoise olives. Look for the AOC olive "Appellation Olive de Nice Protégée." This is the authentic Niçoise olive, nicknamed the *caillette*, whose color varies from green-yellow to slate to near brown. If you use the *taggiasche* olive, its Italian cousin, you'll be forgiven . . .

The anchovies
The name *pissaladière* comes from *pissalat* (or *peis salat*, "salt fish," in Nissart, a regional variety of the Occitan language), which describes a salty cream made from fermented anchovy larvae, proof that the *pissaladière* has anchovies! However, anchovy fillets have replaced this ingredient in today's versions.

ITS COUSINS
The tarte de Menton: a pissaladière without anchovies.
The pichade de Menton: a kind of pizza, topped with anchovies, tomato sauce, onions, black olives, and garlic.

Thanks to Dominique Le Stanc for his recipe for the tarte de Menton, which you can enjoy at La Merenda, 4, rue Raoul Bosio, Nice (Alpes-Maritimes)

skip to
A *Tour de France*—Onions, p. 20

1 Dough, 3 Possibilities

MAKES I DOUGH SERVING 6
I TART (OR PIZZA) PAN MEASURING 12 INCHES (30 CM) IN DIAMETER

⅔ cup (150 mL) whole milk
1 ounce (30 g) fresh compressed yeast, preferably organic
3 cups (300 g) all-purpose flour
Salt
⅔ cup (150 mL) olive oil

Heat the milk in a saucepan, but do not boil it; it should be warm, but cool enough to touch without burning. Add the yeast and stir it thoroughly into the milk. In a large bowl, combine the flour and a pinch of salt and form a well in the center of the flour. Pour the milk-yeast mixture into the well, add the oil, then knead the mixture with your fingers just until you have a smooth ball of dough, but without overworking it. Place the dough in the center of a lightly oiled pan and spread the dough out with your fingers. Cover the dough with a cloth and place the pan in a warm place away from the sun. Allow it to rise for at least half an hour; it should be doubled in volume.

TARTE DE MENTON

3⅓ pounds (1.5 kg) onions (preferably sweet, such as Cévennes)
2 tablespoons (30 mL) olive oil, plus more for drizzling
1 bay leaf
1 sprig thyme
2 cloves garlic, peeled
3½ ounces (100 g) Niçoise olives, pitted
Salt

Peel the onions and thinly slice them. Heat the oil in a flameproof casserole dish over medium heat. Add the onions, bay leaf, thyme, and whole garlic cloves, and cook until the onions are very soft but are not too browned. If the onions seem dry, add 1 or 2 tablespoons (15 or 30 mL) of water. If they do not taste sweet enough, add a spoonful of superfine sugar. Season with salt. After the onions are cooked, remove the garlic cloves. Cover the dough with the onions and bake the pizza for about 30 minutes at 400°F (200°C), or until golden. Remove the pizza from the oven, add the olives on top, and add a drizzle of good olive oil. Serve warm (not hot!).

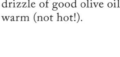

+ 20 anchovy fillets in olive oil

= A PISSALADIÈRE

When cooking the onions, add half the anchovy fillets, chopped. These will soften and cook with the onions. Distribute the onion-anchovy mixture on top of the dough, and bake until golden. Remove the pizza and let it cool slightly. Add the remaining anchovy fillets and the olives on top.

+ 4 ripe tomatoes, peeled and crushed, or 1 (14 ounce/400 g) can of crushed tomatoes

= PICHADE DE MENTON

When cooking the onions with the anchovies, add the tomatoes, and let reduce until the water from the tomatoes has evaporated. Distribute the onion-anchovy-tomato mixture on top of the dough, and bake until golden.

Lights, Camera, Action: Eat!

Cozy little bistros, luxurious restaurants, crowded brasseries, or open-air cafés . . . You can always revisit your favorite spots by watching the movies that were filmed there.
Laurent Delmas

LE GARET

The Clockmaker (1974), the first film by Lyonnais director Bernard Tavernier, is an ode to the "capital of Gauls and gullets." Philippe Noiret plays Paul Descombes, a quiet watchmaker initially living a conventional existence in the city's historic center. This setting is a picture-perfect evocation of a traditional restaurant in the heart of Vieux-Lyon.

On the menu
Calf's brains meunière, tête de veau, breaded beef tripe, and other such delicacies, all washed down with wine from the nearby vineyards of Beaujolais.

7, rue du Garet, Lyon (Rhône)

BRASSERIE LIPP

A famous scene in Étienne Chatiliez's *Tanguy* (2001) takes place within the mirrored walls of this Parisian brasserie. Sabine Azéma, Hélène Duc, and André Dussollier are dining here when Tanguy announces he's finally found an apartment . . .

On the menu
Pickled herring, sauerkraut with pork knuckle, baba au rhum . . .

151, boulevard Saint-Germain, Paris 6th

CABARET NORMAND

Henri Verneuil's *A Monkey in Winter* (1962) takes place in the imaginary town of Tigreville (actually Villerville), a village on Normandy's Côte Fleurie. Belmondo and Gabon raise drunken binging to the level of a fine art in the restaurant Cabaret Normand.

On the menu
Traditional Norman dishes.

2, rue Daubigny, Villerville (Calvados)

Lapérouse

In Henri-Georges Clouzot's *Quai des Orfèvres* (1947), Brignon (Charles Dullin) invites Jenny (Suzy Delair) to one of the notorious private dining rooms in Lapérouse, provoking the wrath of her husband Maurice (Bernard Blier). This *hôtel particulier* on the bank of the Seine dates from 1766 and is an integral part of the capital's culinary and cultural heritage.

On the menu
Cuisine that varies with changing seasons and shifting ownerships . . .
51, quai des Grands-Augustins, Paris 6th

AU PUITS DE JACOB

This kosher restaurant is featured in *Would I Lie to You?* (1997). José Garcia, Richard Anconina, and Antony Delon are dining here together when they meet the owner's daughter played by Amira Casar.

On the menu
A 100 percent kosher couscous. Let's go!

54, rue de Godefroy-de-Cavaignac, Paris 11th

AUBERGE PYRÉNÉES CÉVENNES

The idiot secret agent of *OSS 117 – Cairo, Nest of Spies* (2006), directed by Michel Hazanavicius, dines with his boss in this cozy restaurant with exposed beams and checkered tablecloths and napkins.

On the menu
Herring with potato salad, warm sausages, gratin dauphinois . . . Hubert Bonisseur de la Bath, alias OSS 117, decides on the blanquette (because "the blanquette's good here," he explains) washed down with a nice glass of Brouilly. Just this once, he's got the right idea.

106, rue de la Folie-Méricourt, Paris 11th

Chartier

It's an institution! In *A Very Long Engagement* (2004) directed by Jean-Pierre Jeunet, Jodie Foster dines here with her newfound love.

On the menu
Soup du jour, avocado with cocktail sauce, chicken with frites, and crème caramel are the modestly priced, speedily served standards here.

7, rue du Faubourg-Montmartre, Paris 9th

skip to ....
French Movie Chefs, p. 387

193

Champagne

It's served at glamorous Parisian fashion shows, makes a special appearance at family celebrations, and elicits oohs and ahhs with its recognizable "pop" during gourmet dinners. Let's unveil some of Champagne's fascinating details.

Antoine Gerbelle

Key Numbers

4,700,000,000

in sales for Champagne, including €2.6 billion ($3 billion) in exports

1,045,014 bubbles in a bottle of Champagne

268,000,000 bottles average yearly production

15,800 wine growers

of whom 4,720 sell their own Champagne

83,522

acres (33,800 hectares) of vineyard area in France

115,000 *grape pickers* because manual harvesting is required

300 Champagne houses

136 *cooperatives*

of whom 43 sell Champagne

---

*"I drink **Champagne** only twice, when I'm **in love** and **when I'm not**."*
Coco Chanel

---

*"**Snobbery** is a Champagne bubble that hesitates between **burping** and **farting**."*
Serge Gainsbourg

OPEN A BOTTLE OF CHAMPAGNE IN 3 MOVES

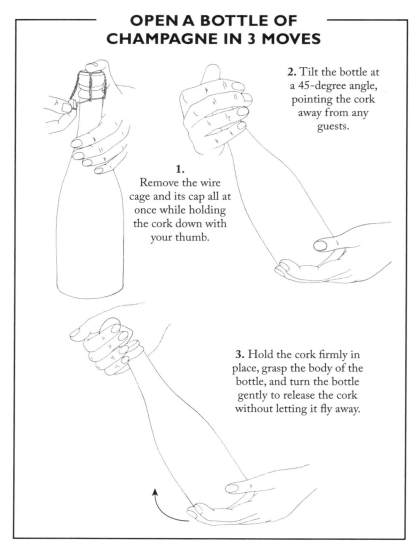

2. Tilt the bottle at a 45-degree angle, pointing the cork away from any guests.

1. Remove the wire cage and its cap all at once while holding the cork down with your thumb.

3. Hold the cork firmly in place, grasp the body of the bottle, and turn the bottle gently to release the cork without letting it fly away.

A LITTLE BIO

La Champagne — DOM PÉRIGNON découvrant la mousse
(D'après le fragment d'un tableau d'Armand Gabry)

Dom Pérignon (1638–1715)

It was not with Dom Pérignon where the effervescent effects of Champagne began, as the legend portrays. On the contrary, this Benedictine monk sought to reduce the consequences of effervescence in wine, which was considered a defect, therefore bestowing the nickname "wine of the devil" on the wines of the region with this characteristic. The process of making sparkling Champagne was a collective and long-term endeavor—in which Dom Pérignon played a major role—but more important, he contributed to the development of the art of blending the vintages of "the mountains" (in Reims) and "the river" (of the Marne Valley).

The 10 Major Markets

France: 157.9 million bottles

England: 31.1 million bottles
United States: 21.8 million bottles
Germany: 12.4 million bottles
Japan: 10.9 million bottles
Belgium: 8.3 million bottles
Australia: 7.8 million bottles
Italy: 6.6 million bottles
Switzerland: 5.7 million bottles
Spain: 3.9 million bottles

Surprisingly, China still does not make the top ten Champagne markets. The trend of sparkling wines is gaining traction there slowly.

CHAMPAGNE AND THE 7 GRAPES

Just as important as remembering the names of the seven dwarfs in *Snow White*, how well do you remember the names of the seven grape varieties authorized in Champagne? Here is a hint to help you. The three dominant varieties of the appellation? **Pinot Noir** (38 percent of the total area of grape production), which dominates the Montagne de Reims and the Côte des Bars (Aube) regions, and which grows in cool limestone soils. **Meunier** (32 percent of the total area of grape production), sometimes called Pinot Meunier, which is also a black grape with white juice, and is the king of the Marne Valley. And, of course, **Chardonnay** (30 percent of the total area of grape production), which flourishes on the white chalk of the Côte des Blancs. There is a group of four marginal varietals, which are talked about more and more. These are four white-grape varieties: Arbane, Petit Meslier, Pinot Blanc, and Pinot Gris. They are considered "marginal" because today they represent less than 0.5 percent of the wine-growing regions. The Comité interprofessional des vins de Champagne (Interprofessional Committee for Champagne), which is the governmental authority regulating the region of Champagne, only allows their planting in very small quantities. Why? Champagne's image is one that was founded on the reputation of the three dominant grape varieties, and it should therefore not be clouded with more obscure varietals. Does this provide clarity for the market, or is it perhaps just a matter of overmarketing?

THE CREATION OF CHAMPAGNE (IN 6 STEPS)

1. Pressing
Pressing the grapes and fermenting the still wine in vats.

2. Bottling
Bottling the still wine with the addition of sugar and yeast to induce a second alcoholic fermentation.

3. Prise de mousse
Mounting pressure within the bottle (between 87 and 101 psi/6 and 7 bars) creates Champagne's bubbles. This process, known as *prise de mousse*, takes one to three months.

4. Aging and prise de mousse in cellars
Referred to as *sur lattes* (on slats) because the shelves of bottles are separated by wooden racks. This process of aging on the lees takes at least fifteen months for nonvintage Champagnes, three years for vintages, and much longer for the finest wines.

5. Disgorgement and capping
Using internal pressure, this step forces the expulsion of the plug of yeast in the neck of the bottle—which has first been frozen to facilitate the process.

6. Dosage and corking
Disgorgement leaves space in the bottle that is refilled with Champagne and a sweetened liquid. Then the bottle is corked and receives the decorative little cap (*plaque*) beneath the wire cage (*musulet*) that brings delight to those collectors of Champagne esoterica known as placomusophiles.

2012, the Last Great Vintage

In the past, Champagne producers named only the most exceptional harvests as vintages. Identified as prodigies at the outset, the wines were jealously guarded. They were rare indeed, and wine specialists took infinite care of them. But these days, global marketing campaigns have taken over. Growers and houses designate a portion of each year's production as vintage, one after another, just as in other wine-producing regions. **But is Champagne just another wine?** Global warming makes for warmer winters around Reims, but truly great years remain the exception. Over the last twenty years, only 2002, 2008, and, most important, 2012 are contenders for the pantheon of legendary vintages. **The first 2012 bottlings began to emerge from the cellars in 2017. They'll start to become more widely available in the early 2020s and over the next thirty years.**

*"**France** is a magical country where in the **most unassuming little bar** you'll be served a great **Champagne** at the perfect temperature no matter what time of day."*
Amélie Nothomb

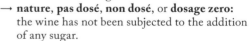

*"Champagne is the **only wine** that leaves a woman beautiful **after she drinks it**."*
Marquise de Pompadour

DECODING NOTATIONS ON CHAMPAGNE LABELS

Every Champagne label bears two letters that indicate who produced the bottle. A registration number is issued by the trade association known as Comité Champagne.

RM for a *récoltant manipulant*, a grower who processes his own grapes.

NM for a *négociant manipulant*, a producer who purchases the grapes or wines.

CM for a *coopérative de manipulation*, a co-op that makes wine from its members' grapes.

RC for a *récoltant coopérateur*, a member who sells the same wine as the co-op's, but under his name.

SR for a *société de récoltants*, an association of wine growers (often family members)

who share production and marketing activities, often affiliated with a cooperative that provides services.

ND for a *négociant distributeur*, a merchant who purchases bottles for resale under his own name.

MA for a *marque d'acheteur*, a producer who makes the wine on behalf of another entity (e.g., restaurateur, merchant, supermarket chain).

Blanc de Blanc simply indicates that only white grapes were used in the bottle.

Blanc de Noir indicates a red wine grape that was pressed rapidly to produce a white juice referred to as Blanc de Noir. QED.

Brut, Extra-brut, Nature . . .
A sweetened liquid is often added after the Champagne is disgorged. Champagne producers refer to it as the "dosage."
→ **nature, pas dosé, non dosé,** or **dosage zero:** the wine has not been subjected to the addition of any sugar.
→ **extra-brut:** between 0 and 0.211 ounce/quart (0 and 6 g/L) of sugar
→ **brut nature:** less than 0.105 ounce/quart (3 g/L)
→ **brut:** less than 0.423 ounce/quart (12 g/L)
→ **extra-dry:** between 0.423 and 0.599 ounce/quart (12 and 17 g/L)
→ **sec (or dry):** between 0.599 and 1.129 ounces/quart (17 and 32 g/L)
→ **demi-sec:** between 1.129 and 1.764 ounces/quart (32 and 50 g/L)
→ **doux:** more than 1.764 ounces/quart (50 g/L)

skip to

A "Fantasy" in the Glass, p. 60

What passerby on the streets of Paris has never stopped to gaze at the magnificent display
of artisanal blades adorning the window of the famous cutler Courty*?

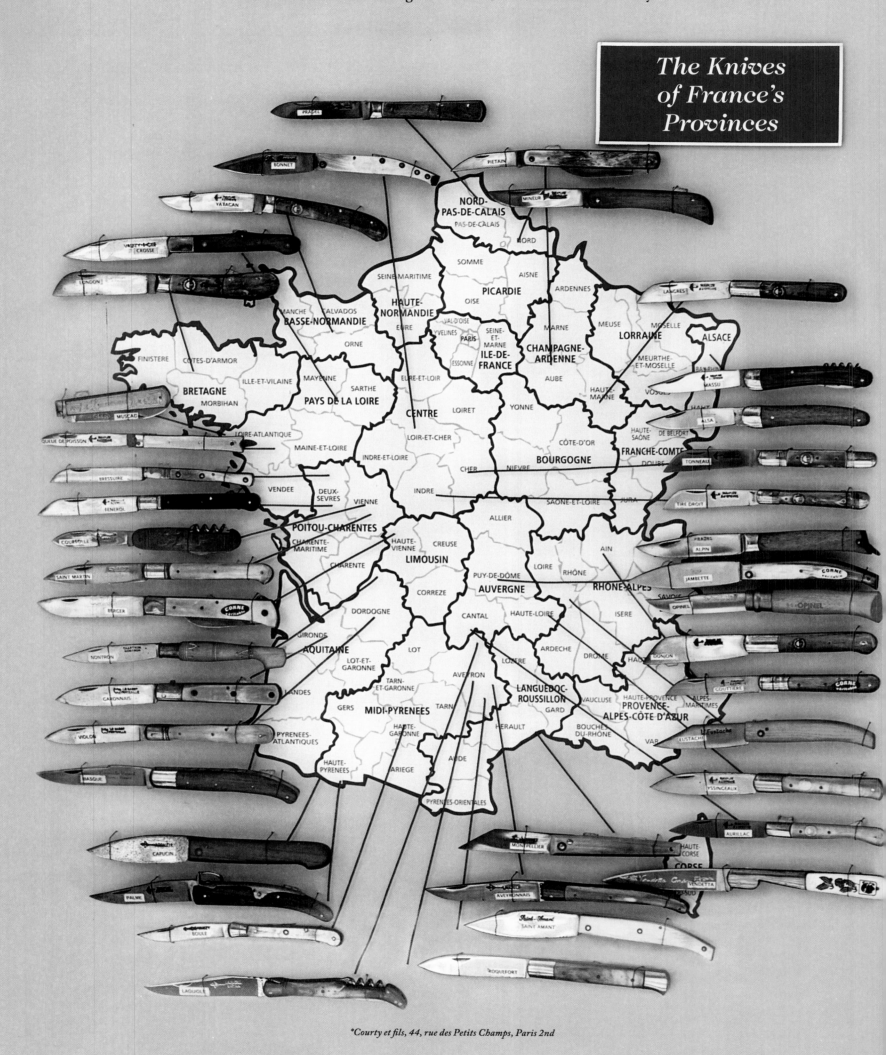

The Knives of France's Provinces

Courty et fils, 44, rue des Petits Champs, Paris 2nd

Hats Off to Marc Veyrat!

Some jeer at his megalomania, his cult of personality, and his bad temper. But the wizard of the Alps has forever left his mark on French gastronomy.

François-Régis Gaudry

**The mountain druid
(born in 1950)**

Here are 5 important facts that will assure his legacy

★ He's the only chef in history to have obtained three stars twice in the Michelin Guide and 20/20 twice in Gault & Millau for his two establishments, L'Auberge de l'Eridan in Veyrier-du-Lac and La Ferme de mon père in Megève, in Haute-Savoie.

★ As early as the 1990s, he was the ingenious pioneer of an ecological, utopian, and experimental cuisine based on foraging wild plants and the use of molecular techniques. Along with the ethnobotanist François Couplan, he has introduced wood sorrels, burnet, fonio, and more into cooking.

★ He traded in his white chef's toque for a black hat, an homage to his grandfather who presented him with his felt hat after school with blueberries, raspberries, and strawberries on top.

★ He has nurtured an exceptional generation of chefs. Emmanuel Renaut, Jean Suplice, and David Toutain, among others, have named him as an influence.

★ Following several dramatic events—several fires in his restaurants and a ski accident in 2006 that almost took his life—Marc Veyrat has found the strength to get back up on his feet. He founded the Maison des Bois in Manig.

EGG IN SHELL, WOOD SORREL, NUTMEG FOAM

A signature dish where wood sorrel imparts its sour and lemon notes.

SERVES 4

The eggs
Using small scissors, cut off the tops of the shells off of 4 raw eggs, empty and reserve their contents, and rinse the shells with cold water. Separate the egg whites from the egg yolks, and put the yolks back in the shells. In a baking dish, cook the yolks in their shells for 2 hours at 149°F (65°C), with the shells sitting upright on coarse salt.

The wood sorrel sauce
Warm ¾ cup plus 1 tablespoon (200 mL) of light cream with ⅓ ounce (10 g) of wood sorrel; let infuse for 10 minutes. Add 1 tablespoon plus 2 teaspoons (25 mL) of white vinegar. Stir to combine, strain, then let cool. Fill four syringes halfway with the sauce, then refrigerate them.

Nutmeg mousse
Soak 1 sheet of gelatin in cold water for 5 minutes. Heat together ¾ cup plus 1 tablespoon (200 mL) of cream, 3 tablespoons plus 1 teaspoon (50 mL) of vegetable broth, and ⅛ ounce (5 g) of lightly crushed nutmeg seed. Let infuse for 10 minutes. Add 1/16 ounce (2 g) of chicken stock and ¼ teaspoon (1 g) of sugar. Stir to combine. Strain, then stir in the gelatin until melted. Pour the mixture into a whipped cream dispenser fitted with one gas canister. Shake the canister, and set it aside in the refrigerator.

Assembly
Shake the whipped cream dispenser well and hold it upside down to dispense the nutmeg foam onto to the surface of the egg yolks. Inject the wood sorrel sauce into the bottom of the egg shells using one syringe for each shell.

skip to
France's Wild Berries, p. 382

Gratin Dauphinois (Scalloped Potatoes)

A grand family classic, this potato dish has gone well beyond the borders of its native Dauphiné. It's always worth revisiting a classic . . .

François-Régis Gaudry

4 RULES

❶ The potato
The Gratin Dauphinois at Guy Savoy uses the (new) Charlotte potato variety, while chef Jean-Pierre Vigato campaigns for using the (old) Bintje variety. Firm-fleshed potato varieties are excellent choices, including Charlotte, Roseval, or Amandine.

❷ The slicing
One-tenth inch (2 mm) is the recommended thickness for the potato slices. It is important not to rinse the slices because their starch is vital in developing the texture of the dish.

❸ The garlic
This is an essential ingredient! Take a peeled garlic clove and rub the inside of the baking dish with it so that its flavor infuses into the butter-cream mixture.

❹ The texture
Properly cooked scalloped potatoes must be well browned. At the end of the cooking time, the potatoes should not be floating in the cream, but they should not be too dry either.

THE RECIPE
by Denise Solier-Gaudry

PREPARATION TIME: 30 MINUTES
COOKING TIME: 1 HOUR
SERVES 6

1 clove garlic
1⅔ cups (400 mL) whole milk
1⅔ cups (400 mL) cream
Fresh nutmeg
2½ pounds (1.2 kg) firm-fleshed potatoes
1 tablespoon plus 1 teaspoon (20 g) unsalted butter
Salt and freshly ground black pepper

Preheat the oven to 400°F (200°C). Peel the garlic clove, remove the germ from the center, and cut the clove in half. Rub the gratin dish with the garlic, then finely chop the garlic, and place it in a saucepan with the milk and cream. Add a pinch of salt, grate in some nutmeg, and stir to combine. Heat the mixture until boiling. Peel, wash, and wipe the potatoes dry. Slice the potatoes into 1/10-inch (2 mm) rounds. Arrange the rounds in the dish, in layers, slightly overlapping each other. Season each layer with salt and pepper. Pour the milk-cream mixture onto the potatoes, pressing any down that peek out of the liquid. Distribute the butter in pieces over the top, and bake for about 1 hour, or until the top is nicely golden.

2 Regional Variations

Gratin Dauphinois ➕ grated cheese ➖ Gratin Savoyard
Use 5¼ ounces (150 g) of cheese distributed between the layers of potatoes and 1¾ ounces (50 g) of cheese for the top.

Gratin Dauphinois ➕ porcini mushrooms ➖ Gratin Bordeaux
Use 14 ounces (400 g) of porcini mushrooms. Clean the porcinis and peel the stems. Thinly slice the porcini, but not too thin. Wash some parsley sprigs and remove the leaves. Chop the parsley leaves with a peeled garlic clove. Sauté the porcini and garlic-parsley mixture together. Spread the mushroom mixture between the potato layers.

Squash: Is It a Fruit?

━━━ ❖ ❖ ━━━

And to think that once upon a time, French squash was used only to feed cows in winter.
Originally from South America, the large *Cucurbita* genus has finally revealed all its charms!
Xavier Mathias

IT'S A FRUIT!

While *legume* is a word borrowed from cooking and means the part of a plant served as garnish (fruit, flower, leaf, root, tuber, etc.), *fruit* is a botanical word signifying, simply put, an organ resulting from the fertilization of a flower and containing seeds. Squash, like eggplant, peppers, cucumbers, and tomatoes, are therefore indeed fruit but are generally prepared like vegetables.

A KIND OF WHAT EXACTLY?

Squash, pumpkins, gourds, etc.—it can be tricky figuring out what's what in the whole maelstrom of names used to designate the species in the vast Cucurbitaceae family:

GOURDS (*CUCURBITA*)

Let's try to find out what's hidden behind all those very common names, the origins of which are somewhat nebulous.

Squash: Squash is the name for all the different consumed species as presented in the family tree. It's the generic word.

Pumpkin: Even if the word is now used improperly, pumpkins are, according to Charles Victor Naudin, *Cucurbita pepo,* the shape of which is more oblong than round. What you use to make a **jack-o'-lantern** is therefore a pumpkin, as is **spaghetti squash**.

Winter squash: Again according to Naudin's standard reference, *Cucurbita maxima* include, for example, the famous **Rouge vif d'Etampes** and the **Blanc de Paris.** Sorry Disney, Cinderella's carriage isn't a pumpkin.

Zucchini: These are small squash, as the "ini" suggests. They belong to the *pepo* species, which the name *zucchini* does not suggest, however.

Gourds: Here's a good example of a mistake that could have troublesome consequences. What is called the gourd, which belongs to the *pepo* species, is in fact called *coloquinelle* or *fausse coloquinte* in French, and false colocynth in English. True colocynths are *Citrullus colocynthis,* which are toxic, unlike small ornamental gourds, which can prove to be bitter and sometimes inedible, but aren't really dangerous.

Potimarron: For this word, we can thank Philippe Desbrosses who, upon bringing them back from Japan, coined the brilliant name. Potimarrons are not a variety, strictly speaking. The term designates a group of varieties of *Cucurbita maxima,* generally orange (there are also green and blue ones), shaped like a top, with a chestnut flavor that's more or less defined: **Red Kuri, Uchiki Kuri,** and **Green Hokkaido** are potimarrons.

SPECIES	VARIETIES	TRAITS
argyrosperma	Coïchiti pueblo	Angular stalk, flared where enters fruit. No tendrils.
ficifolia	Figleaf gourd	Black seeds. Perennial, not hardy. Leaves resemble fig leaves.
maxima	Winter squash, potimarrons, Rouge vif d'Etampes, Galeux d'Eysines, Giraumons, etc.	Thick cylindrical stalk that becomes corklike with age. Soft hairs on leaves and stems.
moschata	Butternut, Longue de Nice, Musquée de Provence, Pleine de Naples, Sucrine du Berry	Hard, angular stalk, splayed where enters fruit. Dark green leaves with white markings.
pepo	Squash in general. Pommes d'or, spaghetti squash, false colocynth, pâtissons, etc.	Very hard and short stalk. Very angular leaves, sometimes with white markings.

━━━ **3 RECIPES** ━━━

by Jean-Christophe Rizet*

A potimarron? Make a velouté

Wash the potimarron. Cut in in half and scrape out the seeds and fibers; do not peel it. Cut it into large cubes. Peel then chop 1 onion. Crush 2 cloves of garlic and remove their germs. In a casserole dish, gently cook the onion and garlic in 5½ tablespoons (80 g) of butter over low heat, then add the cubed potimarron. Add several peeled slices of ginger. Sauté for a few minutes, and add 2 tablespoons (30 mL) Noilly Prat vermouth, then cover halfway with water and cook for about 20 minutes. Add ⅔ cup (150 mL) of cream at the end of the cooking time, then transfer to a blender and blend, or use an immersion blender. Blend until the mixture is very smooth. Season with salt and pepper, and stir in some water if the texture is too thick. Serve the velouté with roasted squash seeds.

A butternut squash?
Roast, and serve with brousse cheese

Wash the squash. Cut it in half and scrape and scoop out the fibers and seeds. Cut the squash into 1½-inch (4 cm) cubes. Arrange the pieces of squash in a gratin dish with 4 cloves of whole garlic, a drizzle of olive oil, a spoonful of honey, and a sprig of rosemary and thyme. Season with salt, and stir. Preheat the oven to 400°F (200°C). Roast the squash for 25 to 30 minutes, being careful to stir regularly during cooking so that the squash browns on all sides. When done cooking, the flesh must be very soft and slightly caramelized. Let cool, and toss in a salad with a dash of sherry vinegar and olive oil. Divide among plates, spoon some brousse cheese on onto the cubes of squash, and sprinkle squash seeds (previously roasted for several minutes in a dry hot pan) on top, and serve.

An acorn squash? Make a *millas*

"A milla *was originally a cake made from grains (corn, millet, wheat, rice). My grandmother adapted it to use squash from the garden."*

Peel, and scrape and scoop out the fibers and seeds of 2 pounds (1 kg) of acorn squash. Cut the squash into large dice, then steam it. When the flesh is very tender, blend it in a blender or using an immersion blender. Combine 1¼ cups (250 g) of sugar with 3 whole eggs plus 1 egg yolk.

Stir the puréed squash to this mixture, then incorporate 1½ cups (150 g) of sifted flour and ⅓ cup (80 mL) of cream. Set aside. Cook 1½ cups (300 g) of rice in 2 cups (500 mL) of milk with 3 tablespoons (40 g) of sugar and the seeds and empty pod of 1 vanilla bean. Let cool to room temperature. Preheat the oven to 350°F (180°C). Remove the pits from 9 ounces (250 g) of prunes, and sprinkle the prunes with a few tablespoons of cognac. Combine the rice with the pumpkin mixture. Grease and flour a cake pan. Place the prunes in the bottom of the pan, then scrape the batter into the pan. Bake for 35 minutes.

1. Longue de Nice
2. Potimarron Red Kuri
3. Melonette Jaspée de Vendée
4. Sucrine du Berry
5. Butternut
6. Sweet Dumpling or Patidou
7. Violine (Violin)
8. Chayote (Chouchou or Christophine)
9. Tonda Padana
10. Spaghetti
11. Delicata
12. Futsu Black
13. Pomme d'or (Golden Apple)
14. Kiwano or Concombre Cornu d'Afrique
15. Pleine de Naples

A Tour de France—Cheese

There are more than 1,200 varieties of cheeses in France. To date, only forty-five of these cheeses—whether soft or hard, bloomed or blue-veined, and each well established in their respective regions—have obtained an AOP (*appellation d'origine protégée*) certification, while only nine have obtained a PGI (Protected Geographical Indication) certification.

By Marielle Gaudry

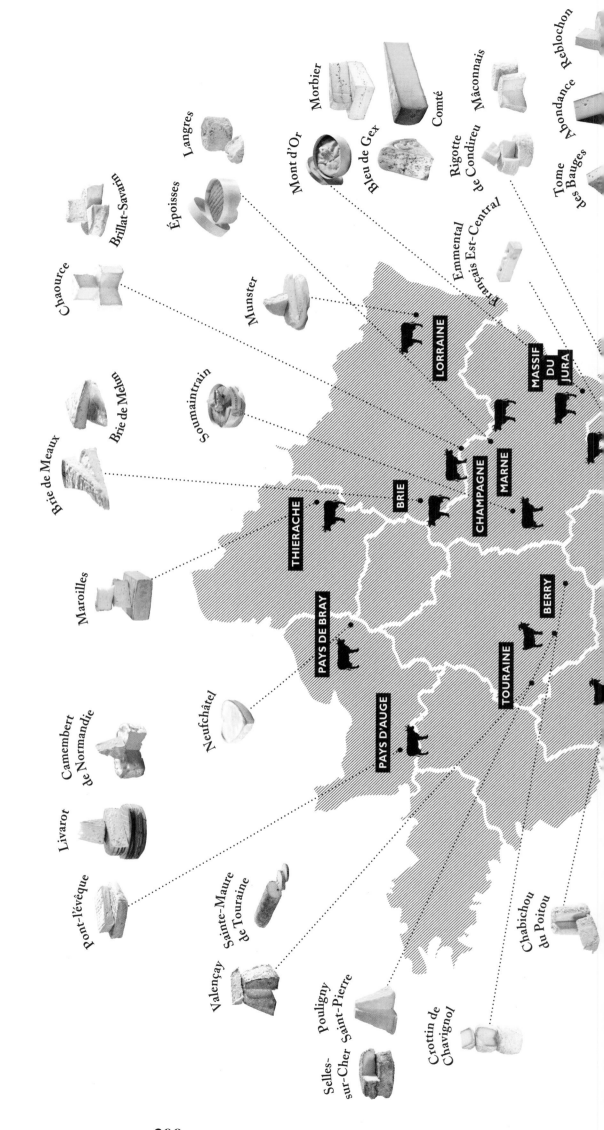

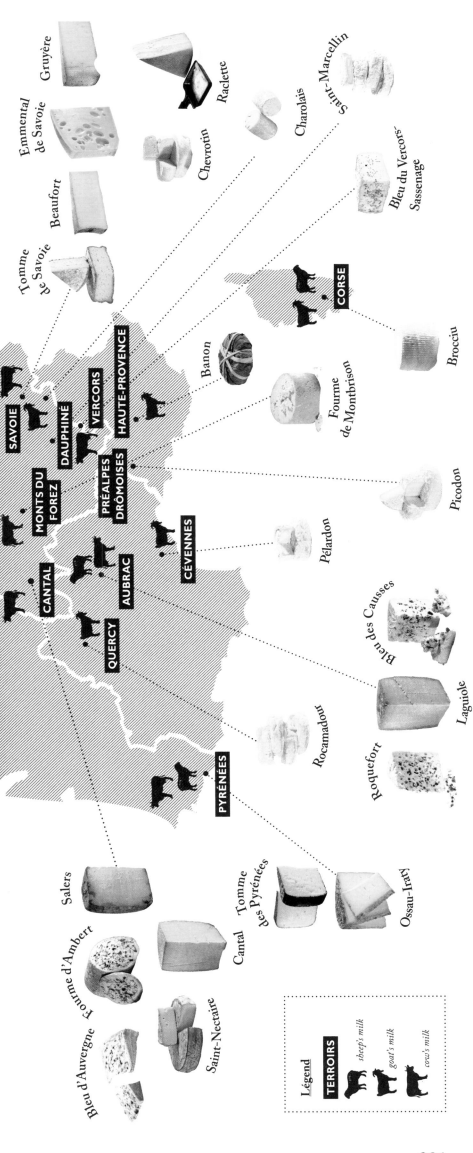

Gruyère

Raclette

Saint-Marcellin

Charolais

Emmental de Savoie

Chevrotin

Beaufort

Bleu du Vercors-Sassenage

Tomme de Savoie

CORSE

Banon

Brocciu

SAVOIE

VERCORS

HAUTE-PROVENCE

DAUPHINÉ

Fourme de Montbrison

MONTS DU FOREZ

PRÉALPES DRÔMOISES

Picodon

CANTAL

CÉVENNES

Pélardon

AUBRAC

QUERCY

Bleu des Causses

Laguiole

Rocamadour

Roquefort

PYRÉNÉES

Salers

Tomme des Pyrénées

Ossau-Iraty

Fourme d'Ambert

Cantal

Bleu d'Auvergne

Saint-Nectaire

Légende

TERROIRS

sheep's milk

goat's milk

cow's milk

THE AOPs

Abondance
(AOP since 1996)
Production area: Haute-Savoie
Interior (pâte) type: pressed half-cooked
Aging: 3 months
Appearance: orange-brown crust, ivory-yellow interior
Flavor: fruity and nutty, slightly funky taste with a hint of bitterness

Banon
(AOP since 2007)
Production area: Alpes-de-Haute-Provence
Interior (pâte) type: soft with a natural rind
Aging: 2 weeks to 2 months
Appearance: small disk packed in chestnut leaves; creamy interior
Flavor: intensely rustic (goatlike) and nutty

Beaufort
(AOP since 1996)
Production area: Savoie
Interior (pâte) type: cooked
Aging: 5 months minimum
Appearance: round, smooth brown crust spotted with white; more or less yellow interior, depending on the season
Flavor: aromas of butter, dried fruits, and sometimes pineapple

Bleu d'Auvergne
(AOP since 1996)
Production area: Puy-de-Dôme/Cantal
Interior (pâte) type: blue veining
Aging: 3 months
Appearance: white to ivory flat cylinder with blue-green mold veining
Flavor: blue-cheese, undergrowth, and mushroom aromas

Bleu de Gex
(AOP since 1996)
Production area: Jura/Ain
Interior (pâte) type: blue veining
Aging: 2 months
Appearance: round, yellowish rind engraved with the word *Gex*; ivory interior with blue-green veining
Flavor: aromas of hazelnut and mushroom

Bleu des Causses
(AOP since 2009)
Production area: Aveyron/Lot/Lozère
Interior (pâte) type: blue veining
Aging: 3 months
Appearance: white to ivory flat cylinder with blue-green mold veining
Flavor: intense flavor of blue cheese

Bleu de Vercors-Sassenage
(AOP since 2001)
Production area: Drôme/Isère
Interior (pâte) type: blue veining
Aging: 2 months minimum
Appearance: cylinder with a fuzzy gray rind, ivory interior, and thin blue-gray veining
Flavor: aroma of hazelnut

Brie de Meaux
(AOP since 1996)
Production area: Seine-et-Marne/Loiret/Meuse/Aube/Haute-Marne/Marne/Yonne
Interior (pâte) type: soft with a bloomy rind
Aging: 8 weeks minimum
Appearance: flat disk with fuzzy white rind, ivory interior pocked with small holes
Flavor: undergrowth and barnyard aromas

THE PGIs

Brillat-Savarin
(PGI since 2017)
Production area: Aube/Côte-d'Or/Seine-et-Marne/Saône-et-Loire/Yonne
Interior (pâte) type: soft (fresh) or bloomy rind (aged)
Aging: 2 weeks
Appearance: rindless cylinder (fresh) or fuzzy smooth white and white (aged)
Flavor: aromas of butter and mushroom

Emmental de Savoie
(PGI since 1996)
Production area: Savoie
Interior (pâte) type: cooked interior
Aging: 75 days minimum
Appearance: yellow to brown rind; yellow interior with holes
Flavor: fresh and fruity, without being spicy

Emmental Français Est-Central
(PGI since 1996)
Production area: Haute-Saône/Territoire de Belfort/Haute-Marne/Vosges/Côte-d'Or/Doubs/Jura/Saone-et-Loire/Ain/Haute-Savoie/Rhône/Savoie/Isère
Interior (pâte) type: cooked interior
Aging: 12 weeks
Appearance: wheel with a yellow rind; bright yellow interior pocked with "eyes"
Flavor: fresh taste, sweet fruity notes

Gruyère
(PGI since 2013)
Production area: Savoie/Franche-Comté
Interior (pâte) type: cooked interior
Aging: 120 days
Appearance: round, brown rind; pale yellow (winter) to golden yellow (summer) interior pocked with holes
Flavor: sweet, fruity, and flowery

THE AOPs (continued)

Brie de Melun
(AOP since 1996)
Production area: Seine-et-Marne/Yonne/Aube
Interior (pâte) type: soft with a bloomy rind
Aging: 10 weeks minimum
Appearance: flat disk with a white rind mottled with brown spots; yellow interior
Flavor: nutty aromas and notes of mushroom

Brocciu
(AOP since 2003)
Production area: Haute-Corse/Corse-du-Sud
Interior (pâte) type: fresh
Aging: 21 days minimum (brocciu passu)
Appearance: white cylinder presented in a basket; white interior
Flavor: aromas of fresh sheep's milk or goat's milk

Camembert de Normandie
(AOP since 1996)
Production area: Orne/Calvados/Eure/Manche
Interior (pâte) type: soft with a bloomy rind
Aging: 1 month
Appearance: white cylinder with a fuzzy rind; ivory to light yellow interior
Flavor: dairy aromas, undergrowth notes

Cantal
(AOP since 1996)
Production area: Cantal
Interior (pâte) type: uncooked pressed
Aging: 1 month minimum (young) to more than 8 months (aged)
Appearance: cylinder with a light gray to golden brown rind; ivory to dark yellow interior
Flavor: hazelnut and vanilla

Comté
(AOP since 1996)
Production area: Jura/Doubs/Ain
Interior (pâte) type: cooked interior
Aging: 4 months minimum
Appearance: round, brown rind; creamy yellow to yellow interior
Flavor: buttery, roasted, and woody

Époisses
(AOP since 1996)
Production area: Côte-d'Or/Yonne/Haute-Marne
Interior (pâte) type: soft washed rind
Aging: 4 weeks minimum
Appearance: cylinder, enclosed in a box; ivory-orange to brick red rind; light beige interior
Flavor: slightly spicy cream

Fourme d'Ambert
(AOP since 1996)
Production area: Puy-de-Dôme
Interior (pâte) type: blue veining
Aging: 28 days minimum
Appearance: tall cylinder with fuzzy gray rind; creamy interior with blue-gray spots
Flavor: rustic aromas of blue cheese

Fourme de Montbrison
(AOP since 2010)
Production area: Loire/Puy-de-Dôme
Interior (pâte) type: blue veining
Aging: 3 weeks minimum
Appearance: tall cylinder with orange rind; cream interior with blue veining
Flavor: fruity sweetness and a light taste of blue cheese

Laguiole
(AOP since 2008)
Production area: Aveyron
Interior (pâte) type: uncooked pressed
Aging: 3 months minimum
Appearance: cylinder with pale gray rind; yellow marbled interior
Flavor: acidic with aromas of butter

Morbier
(AOP since 2002)
Production area: Doubs/Ain/Jura
Interior (pâte) type: uncooked pressed
Aging: 45 days minimum
Appearance: flat cylinder with pink to orange-beige rind; ivory to pale yellow interior with a thin layer of ash through the center
Flavor: taste of cream, slightly vanilla and lemony aromas

Munster
(AOP since 1996)
Production area: Bas-Rhin/Haut-Rhin/Meurthe-et-Moselle/Vosges/Moselle/Territoire de Belfort/Haute-Saône
Interior (pâte) type: soft washed rind
Aging: 21 days minimum
Appearance: flat cylinder with orange-pink rind; cream-colored interior
Flavor: lactic, woody aromas, hints of dry seeds

Neufchâtel
(AOP since 1996)
Production area: Seine-Maritime/Oise
Interior (pâte) type: soft with a bloomy rind
Aging: 10 days minimum
Appearance: heart-shaped, fuzzy white rind; creamy yellow interior
Flavor: salty aromas of cream and fresh milk

Ossau-Iraty
(AOP since 2003)
Production area: Pyrénées-Atlantiques/Hautes-Pyrénées
Interior (pâte) type: uncooked pressed
Aging: 2½ to 12 months
Appearance: cylinder with a yellow to gray crust; white interior
Flavor: notes of hazelnut and intensely rustic

Pélardon
(AOP since 2001)
Production area: Aude/Gard/Hérault/Lozère/Tarn
Interior (pâte) type: soft with a natural rind
Aging: 11 days minimum

Rigotte of Condrieu
(AOP since 2013)
Production area: Loire/Rhône
Interior (pâte) type: soft with a natural rind
Aging: 8 days minimum
Appearance: small puck shape with ivory rind spotted with blue-gray; white and dense interior
Flavor: intensely rustic (goatlike) and nutty

Rocamadour
(AOP since 1999)
Production area: Lot
Interior (pâte) type: soft with a natural rind
Aging: 6 days minimum
Appearance: small white to bluish fuzzy disk; ivory-cream interior
Flavor: cream and butter flavors

Roquefort
(AOP since 1996)
Production area: Aveyron
Interior (pâte) type: blue veining
Aging: 3 months minimum
Appearance: blue-, gray- and green-veined cylinder
Flavor: powerful aromas of humus and moist cave, salty taste, intensely rustic (sheeplike)

Saint-Nectaire
(AOP since 1996)
Production area: Cantal/Puy-de-Dôme
Interior (pâte) type: uncooked pressed
Aging: 28 days minimum
Appearance: flat cylinder with a rustic rind spotted with white, brown, or gray; cream-colored shiny interior
Flavor: nutty aromas

Sainte-Maure de Touraine
(AOP since 1996)
Production area: Indre-et-Loire/Vienne/Indre/Loir-et-Cher
Interior (pâte) type: soft with a natural rind
Aging: 10 days minimum
Appearance: log with a gray and blue wrinkled rind; dense white interior
Flavor: intensely rustic (goatlike) and hay aromas (in summer), hazelnut (in winter)

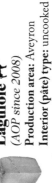

Raclette de Savoie
(PGI since 2017)
Production area: Savoie
Interior (pâte) type: uncooked pressed
Aging: 2 months minimum
Appearance: flat cylinder with yellow to brown rind; white to straw-colored interior
Flavor: floral and fruity aromas, roasted and spicy notes

Saint-Marcellin
(PGI since 2013)

Production area: Isère
Interior (pâte) type: soft with a bloomy rind
Aging: 12 to 28 days
Appearance: small puck with a fine and off-white fuzzy rind; cream-colored interior
Flavor: aromas of fresh milk and honey

Soumaintrain
(PGI since 2016)

Production area: Yonne
Interior (pâte) type: soft washed rind
Aging: 21 days minimum
Appearance: cylinder with an ivory to orangey rind; ivory to honey-colored interior
Flavor: vegetal aromas of mushroom and hay

Tomme de Savoie
(PGI since 1996)

Production area: Savoie
Interior (pâte) type: uncooked pressed
Aging: 10 weeks
Appearance: cylinder with spotted gray rind; white to yellow interior
Flavor: sweet and nutty

Tomme des Pyrénées
(PGI since 1996)

Production area: Pyrénées-Atlantiques/Hautes-Pyrénées/Ariège/Haute-Garonne/Aude
Interior (pâte) type: uncooked pressed
Aging: 21 days minimum
Appearance: cylinder with gold rind (or black wax); ivory to yellow interior
Flavor: full-bodied (gold rind), tart (black rind)

Salers
(AOP since 2003)

Production area: Cantal/Haute-Loire/Puy-de-Dôme/Aveyron/Corrèze
Interior (pâte) type: uncooked pressed
Aging: 3 months minimum
Appearance: cylinder with a golden brown rind; marbled yellow interior
Flavor: aromas of dried fruits and butter

Selles-sur-cher
(AOP since 1996)

Production area: Loir-et-Cher/Cher/Indre
Interior (pâte) type: soft with a natural rind
Aging: 10 days minimum
Appearance: puck shape with a powdery and gray rind; dense white interior
Flavor: intensely rustic (goatlike), delicate aromas of hazelnut

Tome des Bauges
(AOP since 2007)
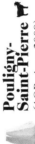
Production area: Savoie/Haute-Savoie
Interior (pâte) type: uncooked pressed
Aging: 5 weeks minimum
Appearance: cylinder with a blotched gray rind; yellow interior pocked with a few holes
Flavor: fruity and woody aromas, mushroom notes

Valençay
(AOP since 2004)
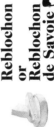
Production area: Cher/Indre/Indre-et-Loire/Loir-et-Cher
Interior (pâte) type: soft with a natural rind
Aging: 11 days minimum
Appearance: pyramid shape with a light gray to bluish rind; dense white interior
Flavor: aromas of fresh nuts, dried fruits, and hay

Chabichou du Poitou
(AOP since 1996)

Production area: Haut-Poitou
Interior (pâte) type: soft with a bloomy rind
Aging: 10 days minimum
Appearance: small cylinder with white and yellow wrinkled rind; white interior
Flavor: intensely rustic (goatlike) and light hazelnut flavor

Chaource
(AOP since 1996)

Production area: Aube/Yonne
Interior (pâte) type: soft with a bloomy rind
Aging: 15 days minimum
Appearance: small cylinder with white interior
Flavor: fruity and nutty

Charolais
(AOP since 2014)

Production area: Saône-et-Loire/Rhône/Loire/Allier
Interior (pâte) type: soft with a natural rind
Aging: 15 days minimum
Appearance: small flat cylinder with a white or blue bloomy rind; firm white interior
Flavor: salty taste with aromas of hazelnut

Crottin de Chavignol
(AOP since 1996)
Production area: Cher/Nièvre/Loiret
Interior (pâte) type: soft with a natural rind
Aging: 10 days minimum
Appearance: small flat cylinder with a white or blue bloomy rind; firm white interior
Flavor: intensely rustic (goatlike), then slightly hazelnut

Chevrotin
(AOP since 2005)

Production area: Savoie/Haute-Savoie
Interior (pâte) type: uncooked pressed
Aging: 21 days minimum
Appearance: cylinder with orange crust
Flavor: nutty and woody aromas

Langres
(AOP since 2009)

Production area: Haute-Marne
Interior (pâte) type: soft washed rind
Aging: 40 days minimum
Appearance: cylinder with pale yellow to orange rind; white interior
Flavor: fresh, acidic flavors of curd

Livarot
(AOP since 1996)

Production area: Calvados/Eure/Orne
Interior (pâte) type: soft washed rind
Aging: 3 weeks to 3 months
Appearance: cylinder wrapped in strips of reed, brown-red to brown rind; shiny ivory interior
Flavor: aromas of leather and smoked meats

Mâconnais
(AOP since 2009)

Production area: Rhône/Saône-et-Loire
Interior (pâte) type: soft with a natural rind
Aging: 10 days minimum
Appearance: small cylinder with cream to bluish rind; smooth white interior
Flavor: intensely rustic (goatlike) aromas and mineral notes

Maroilles or Marolles
(AOP since 1996)
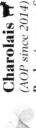
Production area: Aisne/Nord
Interior (pâte) type: soft washed rind
Aging: 2 to 4 months
Appearance: thick square, orange rind; creamy blond interior
Flavor: milky taste, slightly salty, with a hint of bitterness

Mont d'Or or Vacherin du Haut-Doubs
(AOP since 1996)

Production area: Haut-Doubs
Interior (pâte) type: soft washed rind
Aging: 21 days
Appearance: cylinder enclosed in a spruce box; beige to rosy rind; shiny white interior
Flavor: cream and woody aromas

Raclette de Savoie (continued top)

Pont-l'Évêque
(AOP since 1996)

Production area: Calvados/Manche/Eure/Orne/Seine-Maritime
Interior (pâte) type: soft washed rind
Aging: 18 days minimum
Appearance: thick square, pinkish rind; light yellow interior with occasional holes
Flavor: creamy, fruity, and nutty

Pouligny-Saint-Pierre
(AOP since 2009)

Production area: Indre
Interior (pâte) type: soft with a natural rind
Aging: 10 days
Appearance: pyramid shape with a white fuzzy rind; white and dense interior
Flavor: intensely rustic (goatlike) and dried fruit aromas

Picodon
(AOP since 1996)

Production area: Ardèche/Drôme/Gard/Vaucluse
Interior (pâte) type: soft with a natural rind
Aging: 14 days minimum
Appearance: small puck with creamy white to blue rind; dense white interior
Flavor: intensely rustic (goatlike) aromas, hazelnut notes

Reblochon or Reblochon de Savoie
(AOP since 1996)

Production area: Savoie/Haute-Savoie
Interior (pâte) type: uncooked pressed
Aging: 3 to 4 weeks
Appearance: flat cylinder with saffron yellow rind; ivory interior
Flavor: creamy velouté-like aromas and notes of hazelnut

Appearance: small puck shape with thin cream to blue rind; white interior
Flavor: intensely rustic, dried hay, honey and hazelnut aromas

Grands Cru Chocolate Bars

While most chocolate makers turn to already-processed cacao to make their chocolate, a handful of artisans are scouring the globe for the best beans, then turning them into chocolate bars. Here are some of the best.

Marielle Gaudry & Jordan Moilim

❶ Bernachon
Chuao 55%/Venezuela
Pronounced flavors of black fruits, notes of toasted almonds

❷ Chapon
Pure Origin Rio Caribe 100%/ Venezuela
Slight astringency, subtle notes of tobacco and dried fruits

❸ Bonnat
Maragnan 75%/Brazil
Floral and fruity notes, citrus nuances

❹ Ducasse
Forastero 75%/Cameroon
Lively, tangy, and vegetal

❺ Cluizel
Los Anconès Organic 67%/ Santo Domingo
Aromas of licorice root, candied fruits, and green olives

❻ Valrhona
Porcelana El Pedregal 64%/ Venezuela
Subtle notes of honey and ripe fruit

❼ Pralus
Tanzania Organic 75%/Tanzania
Raisin notes, spicy nuances, and dried wood

❽ Morin
Ekeko 48%/Bolivia
Notes of caramel, coconut, almonds, and gingerbread

skip to
Intensely Chocolate, p. 139

Never-Fail Ratatouille

Do not be fooled by the dictionary definition of this dish, which describes it as a "large mixture of summer vegetables made into a 'thickened ragout.'" Made famous in the film *Ratatouille* by Pixar Studios, this dish requires some effort to complete with finesse. The secret: cooking all the vegetables separately.

François-Régis Gaudry

The Golden Rules

1

Cook the vegetables separately: this approach is more time consuming, but it guarantees the vegetables will be perfectly tender. Always remember that ratatouille is a compote of vegetables.

2

Do not make ratatouille in the winter, unless you enjoy eating vegetables grown in greenhouses or under aggressive farming methods.

3

Ratatouille is even better when heated the next day. Do not hesitate to prepare a lot at once, especially since it is also delicious cold.

ITS ORIGINS

It is Provençal, and more specifically from Nice. But when you think about it, all the vegetables that compose the ratatouille come from South America, with the exception of onion and garlic. According to the *Lou Tresor dou Felibrige*, the Occitan dictionary of Frédéric Mistral, *ratatouio* is not a very flattering term: it translates as *salmigondis* (hodgepodge) or *galimafrées* (mishmash). Attested in French in 1778, it referred to a "thickened ragout." It was only during the twentieth century that ratatouille became a respected dish.

Official ingredients
Eggplant
Zucchini
Onion
Tomato
Bell pepper
Garlic
Thyme
Bay leaf
Basil and/or parsley
Olive oil

Forbidden ingredients
Celery
Carrot
Bacon
White wine
Olives
Pine nuts

RATATOUILLE'S 3 FIRST COUSINS

BYALDI CONFIT

A dish inspired by a Turkish specialty, updated by chef Michel Guérard in 1976, and popularized by the American chef Thomas Keller, who served as consultant on the animated film *Ratatouille*. The vegetables (onions, tomatoes, zucchini, eggplants, and garlic) are sliced into thin strips, placed on a baking sheet with a piperade (page 208) of grilled peppers, baked without fat, and served with a balsamic vinaigrette.

VEGETABLE TIAN

Tian is an Occitan name for a glazed terra-cotta dish in which vegetables, meats, fish, and eggs are coated in olive oil and baked. The recipe is very different from ratatouille, but when the tian contains only vegetables, they are the same as those used in ratatouille.

THE BOHEMIAN

This is a ratatouille without zucchini, originating from Avignon and the former Comtat Venaissin.

THE RECIPE

Makes a good family-style ratatouille, best for enjoying the next day.

4 eggplants
5 zucchini
3 bell peppers (preferably 1 red, 1 green, 1 yellow)
5 large ripe tomatoes, or 9 ounces (250 g) canned tomato sauce
2 large onions
3 cloves garlic
A few sprigs basil
1 sprig thyme
⅔ cup (150 mL) olive oil
Salt

Wash the eggplants, zucchini, and bell peppers. Remove their stems. Seed the bell peppers, then cut each of the three vegetables into ⅓-inch (1 cm) dice, keeping them separate from each other.

Score an "x" in the skin of the tomatoes, then lower them into boiling water for 1 minute. Rinse them under cold water, then peel and chop them; set them aside. Peel the onions and garlic, thinly slice them, and chop the basil leaves.

In a large flameproof casserole dish, heat a drizzle of olive oil, add ½ garlic clove, and cook the onions until lightly browned.

In separate pots, repeat these steps with the diced zucchini, eggplant, and bell peppers, adding a few tablespoons of water. The vegetables

should be allowed to soften over medium heat for at least 15 minutes, but without overbrowning them.

Transfer all the vegetables to the casserole dish and add the tomatoes, the remaining garlic, the basil, and the thyme sprigs. Season with salt, and simmer, uncovered, over low heat for at least 1 hour.

skip to ....
La Ratatouille à la Pagnol, p. 74

GAULT et MILLAU se mettent À TABLE

Henri Gault and Christian Millau: the famous duo founded Nouvelle Cuisine in the 1970s, a creative and liberating movement that changed the face of gastronomy in France and the world over.

François-Régis Gaudry

GAULT & MILLAU IN 10 DATES

1963: publication of *Guide Julliard de Paris*

1966: publication of *Guide Julliard des environs de Paris*

1969: establishment of the commercial brand Gault & Millau as well as a monthly gastronomy magazine

1972: establishment of *Guides Gault & Millau*

1973: creation of Nouvelle Cuisine and its 10 commandments

1980: Henri Gault and Christian Millau appear on the cover of *Time*

1986: Henri Gault and Christian Millau separate

1987: the duo sells their publishing house

July 9, 2000: Henri Gault dies

August 5, 2017: Christian Millau dies

Nouvelle Cuisine
In **issue 54** of the monthly *Gault & Millau*, dated **October 1973**, the food critics Henri Gault and Christian Millau first announced the arrival of "**Nouvelle Cuisine Française**." It was a way to break away from the dogmas of old-style, time-consuming cooking that had emerged from the codes Auguste Escoffier established at the beginning of the twentieth century.

THE 10 COMMANDEMENTS OF NOUVELLE CUISINE

Declared in 1973 by the partners Gault and Millau, these rules were meant to offer young chefs a new code of conduct.

I. Thou shalt not overcook.
II. Thou shalt use fresh, quality products.
III. Thou shalt lighten thy menu.
IV. Thou shalt not be systematically modernist.
V. Thou shalt nevertheless seek out what the new techniques can bring you.
VI. Thou shalt avoid pickles, cured game meats, fermented foods, etc.
VII. Thou shalt eliminate rich sauces.
VIII. Thou shalt not ignore dietetics.
IX. Thou shalt not doctor up thy presentations.
X. Thou shalt be inventive.

☞ Nouvelle Cuisine abhors
Jelled bone broth
Fish in gelée (jelled)
Roux and white sauces (béchamel)
Marinades and aged meats
Flambés
Tournedos Rossini
Coq au Chambertin
Trout Amandine
Lobster Thermidor

☞ Nouvelle Cuisine adores
Crisp vegetables
Truffles with just a sprinkling of salt
Green peppercorn
Pink fish with bones
Raw salmon
Game with a bloody flavor
Fat-free sauces
Vegetable mousses
Chilled reds served with oysters

The 13 Chefs
These are the holy fathers of the movement, a club known as the "Nouvelle Grande Cuisine Française."
Paul Bocuse (Collonges-au-Mont d'Or)
Paul Haeberlin (Illhaeusern)
Pierre and Jean Troisgros (Roanne)
Alain Chapel (Mionnay)
Roger Vergé (Mougins)
Michel Guérard (Eugénie-les-Bains)
Charles Barrier (Tours)
Raymond Oliver (Paris)
René Lasserre (Paris)
Gaston Lenôtre (Paris)
Louis Outhier (La Napoule)
Pierre Laporte (Biarritz)

5 INFLUENTIAL DISHES

La soupe VGE (soup with black truffles) by Paul Bocuse (1975)

La salade gourmande (a salad with truffles and fois gras) by Michel Guérard (1968)

La mousseline de grenouille (frog mousseline) by Paul Haeberlin (1967)

Le loup au caviar (fillet of bass with caviar) by Jacques Pic (1973)

Le saumon à l'oseille (salmon in sorrel) by the Troisgros brothers (1963)

Pâté: What Am I, Chopped Liver?

Everything on a pig is good.* These pâtés, passed down through my family of Ardèche butchers, are tasty and easy to make. Terrine stamp of approval!

Stéphane Raynaud

CHICKEN LIVER TERRINE

PREPARATION TIME: 30 MINUTES
COOKING TIME: 2 HOURS
MAKES A 2¼-POUND (1 KG) TERRINE

2 onions
1 tablespoon duck fat
10½ ounces (300 g) chicken livers
2 tablespoons plus 2 teaspoons (40 mL) cognac
3½ ounces (100 g) smoked bacon
10½ ounces (300 g) fresh pork belly
7 ounces (200 g) pork spare ribs
2 shallots
1 teaspoon quatre épices spice blend
2 eggs
¾ cup plus 1 tablespoon (200 mL) cream
2 sprigs thyme
Salt and freshly ground black pepper

Peel the onions and chop them. Heat the duck fat until melted and fry the onions until lightly browned. Add the chicken livers and cook them until browned. Add the cognac, and ignite it with a long match. Cut the smoked bacon into thick cubes. Finely chop the pork belly and spare rib meat. Peel and chop the shallots. Combine the bacon with the chopped meat, then add the chicken livers, cooked onions, shallots, quatre épices spice blend, eggs, cream, and thyme leaves. Combine everything with a spoon and season with salt and pepper. Bake in a covered terrine in a bain-marie at 400°F (200°C) for 2 hours.

EQUIPMENT
A terra-cotta or porcelain dish with a lid and a 5-cup (1.2 L) capacity; 1 meat grinder with a grinding plate with ¼-inch (7 mm) holes.

COOKING IN A BAIN-MARIE
Use any pan or dish larger than the terrine and filled with hot water to create the bain-marie. Three-fourths of the terrine must be submerged when placed down in the water.

TERRINE BEAUJOLAISE

PREPARATION TIME: 30 MINUTES
MARINATING TIME: 24 HOURS
COOKING TIME: 2 HOURS
MAKES A 2¼-POUND (1 KG) TERRINE

3 carrots
4 cloves garlic
4 onions
10½ ounces (300 g) pork neck
10½ ounces (300 g) pork spare ribs
7 ounces (200 g) pork liver
1 bay leaf
1⅔ cups (400 mL) Beaujolais wine
⅓ cup plus 1 tablespoon (100 mL) ruby port
Salt and freshly ground black pepper
1 piece caul fat (purchased at the butcher's counter)

Peel and thinly slice the carrots, garlic, and onions. Cut all the pork meat into cubes. Place the meat and all the vegetables in the Beaujolais and port to marinate for 24 hours. Process all the meat and vegetables through a meat grinder; season with salt and pepper. Combine the mixture with half the marinade liquid. Transfer the mixture to an earthenware terrine and cover the top with the piece of caul fat, taking care to completely and neatly cover the top of mixture. Preheat the oven to 350°F (180°C). Bake the terrine in the bain-marie for 2 hours, uncovered. The terrine must be browned on the top. Serve cold.

*Cochon & Fils, Marabout, 2011.
Terrines, Marabout, 2009.

skip to
Pâté en Croûte, p. 129

Olive Oil, Liquid Gold

Because they flourish in dry soil and abhor frost, France's olive trees are cultivated near the Mediterranean coastline.
They've been cultivated there for some 7,000 years.

Marie-Amal Bizalion

GEOGRAPHIC RANGE

Along the coast: from Menton to the Spanish border
Inland: Alpes-de-Haute-Provence, Drôme Provençale, Ardèche, and the environs of Carcassonne

THE 3 MAJOR TYPES

Fruity green: oil from olives harvested before ripening
Fruity ripe: oil produced from olives harvested when ripe
Fruity black: produced from olives that have undergone fermentation before pressing

Fruity green

Aromas: herbaceous, pungent, peppery, sometimes even bitter, suggesting basil, fresh almonds, and artichoke
Recommended for: crustaceans, fish, cooked vegetables, crudités
The intense, almost peppery flavor is particularly marked in the months immediately following the harvest, and lends balance to foods that may otherwise seem a bit bland. It can be added at the end of the cooking time to any salt or freshwater fish, a tuna tartare, or a beef carpaccio. It's delicious over fully ripe tomatoes with basil, and pairs beautifully with balsamic vinegar in a mâche-roquefort-pear salad. Try it in shrimp sautéed with lemongrass or an eggplant purée with a sesame cream.

Fruity ripe

Aromas: ripe fruit, dried fruit, flowers
Recommended for: fish, white meats, cooked vegetables, pastry, fruits
Use to flavor a clafoutis with olives, Parmesan, and cherry tomatoes, or endives braised in orange juice. Enlivens any white meat, whether steamed or broiled. As a cooking ingredient, it's ideal for ratatouille or fried eggs. A few drops will transform vanilla ice cream or a salad of strawberries with mint. Try a few drops in a sweet or savory cake batter, with almonds, for example.

Fruity black

Aromas: dominant woodsy notes, cocoa, mushrooms
Recommended for: lamb, game, ethnic dishes, garlicky salads
With its concentrated aroma of the olive fruit, this oil retains all its intensity in a spicy tagine or a dish of stewed boar or lamb shoulder. Uncooked, it's perfect on a frisée aux lardons, a serving of anchovies with garlic, or a raw white mushroom salad

with lemon juice, shallots, and Italian parsley. And try pouring a few drops on a very lightly sweetened dark chocolate mousse.

PRINCIPAL VARIETIES AND GROWING REGIONS

Aglandau (Vaucluse), lucques (Languedoc), négrette (Gard), petit ribier (centre Var), picholine (Gard, Bouches-du-Rhône), rougette (Hérault), salonenque (Salon-de-Provence), and cailletier (Nice).

THE 7 AOPS

Aix-en-Provence, Corsica, Haute-Provence, Nice, Nîmes, Nyons, Vallée des Baux-de-Provence.

THE ONLY AOC

Olive oil from Provence, which encompasses southeastern France.

A few recommendations

Olivier Morati's Corsican AOP.
Pressed when very ripe, his Biancaghja olives, a unique local variety, yield a very sweet oil with the flavor of fresh almonds.
→ Santu-Pietru di Tenda, 04 95 37 71 98

L'huile H, Domaine Leos.
A pungent, peppery, fruity green oil made primarily from Aglandau olives, with aromas of artichoke, banana, and apples. Organic.
→ L'Isle-sur-la-Sorgue (Vaucluse), www.huilehoriginelle.com

AOC ripened olives from Provence, Huilerie Sainte-Anne.
Traditional fabrication methods create pronounced aromas of licorice and cocoa.
→ 138, route de Draguignan, Grasse, Alpes-Maritimes 04 93 70 21 42

L'AOP Nice Cru Amandine, from Soffiotti & fils.
An organic ripe fruity oil, 100 percent Cailletier, extremely rich with aromas of hazelnuts and crème fraîche.
→ Col Saint-Jean, Sospel (Alpes-Maritimes) 04 93 04 08 81

WHAT'S TO BLAME?

There are about **49,421** acres (**20,000** hectares) of olive groves **in France**, producing an average **52 gallons (200 liters) of oil** per hectare, compared with **200 to 260 gallons (800 to 1,000 liters) in Spain and Morocco.**[*]

The culprit is the **olive fruit fly**, which has become increasingly destructive since 2010. The 2014–2015 crop was **down 60 percent**, which explains the sometimes prohibitive cost of French olive oils.

* Source: Afidol (Association Interprofessionnelle Française de l'Olive)

☞ USEFUL TIP

A **precautionary swig** of olive oil before a heavy holiday meal coats the stomach, preventing digestive problems. It also significantly slows the rise in the body's blood alcohol level. Cheers!

Chiles!

From France's cities to its overseas territories, here is an overview of the nightshades that bring a little pep to French cuisine.

Jacques Brunel

NATIVE TO AMERICA, the chile pepper is a sort of Janus with two opposite faces: one smiling, the other scary. Which side makes an appearance when you consume the chile all depends on the chile's capsaicin content. Capsaicin is a substance secreted from the plant that serves as an irritant to help ward off predators, but one that is appreciated by humans for its spiciness and its stimulation of the salivary glands, not to mention its slimming effects and anticancer benefits.

THE SCOVILLE SCALE rates chiles based on their level of spicy heat, using a scale of 0 to 2 million. Scoville units indicate the number of capsaicin molecules present in the chile. The peppers indicated here establish a relationship between bell peppers—with a neutral heat level—and their most ferocious relatives, up to just over 300,000 units.

The mild

❼ The bell pepper (le poivron)
(*Capsicum annuum*)

Larger than other types of sweet peppers, this pepper does not contain capsaicin, although its pollen can be irritating. It is grown in France under many varieties: petit vert de Marseille, carré de Nice, poivrons doux (sweet peppers) de Valencia or des Landes, etc.
Scoville scale: 0

❻ The Landes pepper (piment des Landes)
(*Capsicum annuum*)

A hundred times stronger than bell pepper, this long red pepper (which is also consumed when green) cooks down without being spicy and is used in many of the meat recipes in Landes.
Scoville scale: 0–100 (neutral)

❺ The Anglet pepper (piment d'Anglet)
(*Capsicum annuum*)

"It does not burn," say the Basques, who nevertheless use it in their *aixoas*, piperades, chile omelets, and local chicken dishes. Although accustomed to growing in gardens, this green chile is most adapted to growing in greenhouses.
Scoville scale: 0–100 (neutral)

❷ The bonnet pepper (piment végétarien)
(*Capsicum chinense*)

A false relative of the extremely spicy habanero, this small vegetable from the West Indies is as mild as a bell pepper but with a big crunch, and it is very aromatic but without an ounce of spice. Serve to children and pyrophobic tourists; it can also lend its aromas to hot dishes in which spicy chile peppers are used.
Scoville scale: 0–100 (neutral)

The spicy

❹ The Espelette pepper (piment d'Espelette)
(*Capsicum annuum*)

When grown in Pays Basque, this beautiful long pepper tends to have less heat than those originally found in the West Indies, and therefore falls to the midrange of the Scoville scale. Produced under the variety Gorria around Espelette, a beautiful village in the Labourd (where it is a popular product for tourists) and protected by an AOP (*appellation d'origine protégée*), this "purple caviar" is consumed in jelly or used ground in powder form. It is the alter ego of peppercorn, with its delicate spiciness giving pep to Basque cured meats, squid, cheese, foie gras, etc.
Scoville scale: 1500–2500 🔥

The Bresse chile (piment de Bresse)
(*Capsicum annuum*)

Less spicy than its cousin the Espelette, this pepper, adapted to the cold, serves as seasoning in Bressannes specialties. After falling into disuse after World War II, its cultivation has been revived today thanks to some enthusiastic farmers and restaurateurs.
Scoville scale: 1500–2500 🔥

The incendiary

❸ The African bird's eye pepper (piment-oiseau)
(*Capsicum frutescens*)

Rated a degree higher than the Bresse chile, this long red and green chile pepper makes traditional dishes of the West Indies and Réunion dance: *rougails, accras, gratins de christophines*, etc. Sold on the islands in sauces and freshly ground into powders, it is used sparingly, with the knowledge that only fat (not water) can tame its fire.
Scoville scale: 50,000–100,000 🔥🔥🔥

❶ The habanero (piment habanero)
(*Capsicum chinense*)

Although there are still other chiles stronger than the habanero, this small lantern-shaped pepper has a heat that, although harmless to the stomach, can attack the eyes and skin (always wear gloves when handling it). One might say those on France's islands are crazy, to the point of sometimes consuming it raw. On Réunion it goes by the name *piment cabri*; in the West Indies by the name *Bondamanjak* (translated as "the buttocks of Madame Jacques, presumed volcanic"). What doesn't kill you makes you stronger.
Scoville scale: 100,000–325,000 🔥🔥🔥🔥

Note: Cayenne pepper is not included in this list. First, because it is not very prevalent in French Guyana (although its name is derived from the capital city). Second, because its name is ambiguous: it sometimes denotes the hot pepper found in Asia and South America, and sometimes sweet pepper or paprika.

PIPERADE

There are only hot chile peppers and no bell peppers in the piperade, as the name suggests: *Biper/piper* means "hot pepper" in the language of Basque! It is almost always made with eggs.
SERVES 6 TO 8

In a skillet, sauté 5 slices of chopped Ibaïona ham and 2 peeled and chopped onions in olive oil. Cook until the onions are very soft. Add 1 or 2 cloves of garlic, minced, and 10½ ounces (300 g) of Landes (or Anglet) chile peppers, seeded and cut into strips. Cook the peppers until softened and add 5 large tomatoes, cut up and crushed. Season with salt and add a pinch of ground Espelette pepper. Cook over low heat for 45 minutes to 1 hour, or until all the vegetables are softened and the liquid has evaporated. Briefly beat together 8 eggs, pour them over the peppers, stir to combine, and remove from the heat as soon as the eggs are cooked.

Cassoulet

Originally from Castelnaudary, this flagship dish of French gastronomy also simmers in Carcassonne and Toulouse.

Charles Patin O'Coohoon

THE CASSOULET WAR

Although it originated in Castelnaudary, cassoulet developed different styles in Carcassonne and Toulouse.

	In Castelnaudary	In Carcassonne	In Toulouse
Bean	■	■	■
Pork loin	■	■	■
Ham	■	■	■
Pork shank	■	■	■
Sausage	■	■	■
Pork rind	■	■	■
Bacon			■
Partridge		■	
Lamb leg and shoulder	■	■	
Goose confit	■		
Duck confit			■
Toulouse sausage			■

CASSOULET
by Alain Dutournier*

SERVES 6 TO 8

1⅛ pounds (500 g) dried beans
1 dry-cured ham hock
1 boneless lamb shoulder
5¼ ounces (150 g) dry-cured ham
5¼ ounces (150 g) pork rind, fat trimmed and reserved
Scant ½ cup (100 mL) dry white wine
3 duck legs confit
1 duck wing confit
1⅓ pounds (600 g) pork sausage
6 goose gizzards confit

For the aromatics
1 onion, 2 carrots, 3 cloves garlic, 1 ripe tomato, 1 clove, 1 grated nutmeg, 1 bouquet garni

Soak the beans and the ham hock overnight in cold water. Blanch the ham hock in boiling water. Cut the lamb shoulder into large cubes, then blanch them and drain. Drain the beans and rinse them under cold water. Peel the onion and carrots. Chop the onion, cut the carrots into *brunoise* (small dice), and crush the garlic cloves in their skins. Blanch and seed the tomato. Cut the dry-cured ham into cubes. Cut the pork rind into strips. Brown the lamb with its fat trimmings in a cast-iron casserole dish, add the strips of rind, then add the carrots, onion, garlic, and dry-cured ham. Cook until browned and caramelized. Skim off the fat from the surface, and deglaze the pot with the wine and a scant ½ cup (100 mL) of water. Preheat the oven to 275°F (140°C). Add the rest of the aromatics (clove, nutmeg, bouquet garni) and the ham hock to the pot. Add the beans, then add just enough water to cover the ingredients. Cook on the stovetop, frequently skimming off any foam that forms on the surface. In a roasting pan, roast the duck leg and wing confit pieces for 20 minutes in the oven, frequently and thoroughly basting them. Add the sausages to the pan with the duck and roast until cooked through, then add the gizzards and roast until cooked through. After the beans have cooked for 1 hour, add the duck meats, sausages, and gizzards to the pot and cook for 30 another minutes.

And what should you drink with cassoulet? "Serving cassoulet without wine is like having a priest who can't speak Latin," says Pierre Desproges. Choose the finesse of a Fronton en Haute-Garonne wine.

Michelin two-star chef at Carré des Feuillants.

THE GOLDEN RULES OF CASSOULET

Choose a variety of white beans from southwest France.
Cook the cassoulet in its traditional cooking vessel (a *cassole*).
Add a third meat. Mandatory since the États généreux de Gastronomie française in 1966, which defined the proportions of meats to the other ingredients.
Banish any frankfurters.

Pork rind is a must, as it releases collagen to thicken the liquid.
Never stir the cassoulet.
Break the top crust at least six times during cooking.

skip to
Sausages, p. 385

Cooking with Feet

France has a sort of mania when it comes to exploiting a beast from the head to the tail, all the way down to its feet.

Marie-Amal Bizalion

In praise of slow cooking

Popular starting from the Middle Ages until the nineteenth century, the time-consuming art of cooking animal feet has now largely been lost among home cooks. However, whether it is mutton, pig, veal, or beef, this meat can treat an entire table of guests for very little cost.

What's your favorite?
Veal: a Lyon-style salad.
Simmer veal feet for 2 hours in salted water with carrots, onions, and a bouquet garni. Bone the feet, dice the meat, and serve it warm in a sauce of mustard, vinegar, chopped shallots, capers, fromage blanc, and chopped parsley.

Mutton: in a poulette sauce.
Boil sheep's feet for 5 to 6 hours with carrots, 1 onion pierced with a few cloves, a bouquet garni, and salt. Drain (reserve the broth) and remove the bone. Brown some mushrooms in a skillet, then add them to the reserved broth and simmer. Remove 1 cup (250 mL) of the broth, combine it with a flour-butter roux, and make a reduced sauce. After 10 minutes, remove the sauce from the heat, then add a small bowl of cream beaten briefly with 2 egg yolks and the juice of ½ lemon. Stir to combine.

Pig: Sainte-Menehould–style.
A specialty of the city of the same name, created in 1730 from meat left all night over hot embers. Wrap the pigs' feet in a cloth so that they stay whole, then cook them for 7 hours in water with vegetables and herbs. Split the feet lengthwise, dredge them in egg yolk and then in bread crumbs, and fry them in butter. Vincent La Chapelle* also likes them fried in a light batter. Do not forget to chew the crushed bones (when cooked) to suck out the marrow.
La Cuisine moderne, volume 3, pp. 109, 110, 1735

Beef: in a pot-au-feu. When added to the stew with other pieces of meat, feet provide a silky substance to the broth.

PIEDS PAQUETS
(STEWED LAMBS' FEET "PACKAGES")
From *Le Reboul*, the bible of Provençal cuisine

PREPARATION TIME: 1 HOUR 30 MINUTES
COOKING TIME: 8 HOURS
SERVES 8

For the stuffing
10½ ounces (300 g) salt pork, finely chopped
4 cloves garlic, peeled and finely chopped
4 sprigs parsley, finely chopped
Salt

2 lamb intestines, cleaned, cut into 3 by 3-inch (8 by 8 cm) squares
8 lamb's feet
Flour

For the sauce
3 onions
3 whole cloves (for piercing 1 onion)
7 ounces (200 g) diced bacon
2 leeks
2 carrots, peeled and sliced
4 tomatoes, chopped
2 garlic cloves, crushed
1 bouquet garni (use any preferred herbs)
4 cups (1 L) white wine
3 quarts (3 L) chicken or vegetable broth
Salt and freshly ground black pepper

Thoroughly combine all the ingredients for the stuffing. Cut a small slit in the corner of each square piece of intestine, and spoon one small mound of stuffing in the center. Slip the other corners into the slit (or you can gather up and tie the corners together). Peel and chop 2 of the onions and pierce the remaining whole onion with the cloves. In a cast-iron casserole dish, brown the bacon, gently cook the leeks and chopped onions, then add the carrots, tomatoes, whole onion, garlic, bouquet garni, wine, and broth. Season with salt and pepper. Place the feet at the bottom of the casserole dish, then add the stuffed intestine "packages." Place the lid of the casserole dish on top and seal it completely using a long dough log made from flour and water, and placed between the rim of the pot and the lid. Set the casserole dish in hot embers, or over a small fire, and let cook overnight. Serve with steamed potatoes.

In the commune of Sisteron, they add orange peels, too!

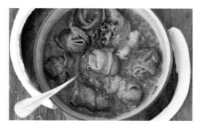

skip to
Tripe on the Table, p. 338

City Beers, Country Beers

France, the country of wine, also offers beer lovers an enormous variety across all its regions, whether in the city or the countryside. The country's regions are abuzz with new up-and-coming breweries, so no doubt you'll discover a favorite somewhere nearby.

Elisabeth Pierre

Aix-Noulette · 22
Trélou-sur-Marne · 32
Strasbourg · 4 · 9
Théméricourt · 24
7 · 27
13 · 26 · 1
21
Landévennec · 12 · 33
Tours · 19
37
31 · 30
Bletterans · 14
15
Verchaix
Chambretaud · 23
10 · 11 · 17 · 8
28
18 · 38
3
36 · 5
Montauban · 6
IRON
2
35
16
Miramas · 20
Sommières
Marseille · 25
29
Puivert · 34
39

FRANCE, A LAND OF BREWING

In 1900, France had 4,000 breweries. All the major cities at that time had their own local breweries. However, most of them disappeared in the middle of the twentieth century. In 2017, France experienced a revival, with more than 1,100 new local microbreweries. One new brewery is established every day.

OLD STYLES

→ **The Cervoise:** a Gallic recipe, distinguished by the addition of herbs, spices, and honey.

→ **The Black Porter of Lyon,** or **black beer of Lyon:** well known in the nineteenth century outside of France, it has returned with force, adorned with aromas of caramel and chocolate.

→ **Bières de table ("table beers"):** delivered by brewers to homes, these beers were found on all family tables in the nineteenth century. Today, they are known for their low alcohol content (less than 3.5 percent) and their aromatic hops.

→ **Bières de garde ("beers for keeping"):** the beers were made up until the nineteenth century and included a process for preserving beers made during the winter for drinking in the summer. This historical French style is known internationally.

skip to ....
Flemish Carbonade, p. 71

FOR THEIR LIGHT QUALITY

Beers light in alcohol, called "table beers" or "sessions." All the flavor with little alcohol!

Brasserie BapBAp, Paris (75): **1** Poids Plume, 3 percent (table beer): yellow fruit, apricot, and floral aromas, honeysuckle, vegetal and cereal notes, dry finish, fruity bitterness.

Brasserie L'Excuse, Mauvezin (32): **2** L'Exotique, 3.5 percent (session IPA): ultrahoppy, citrus aromas, exotic fruits and green herbs, aromatic and refreshing.

FOR THEIR FRESH QUALITY

Balanced and refreshing beers, fermented at low temperatures, with a long, cold storage.

Brasserie de l'Alagnon, Blesle (43): **3** La Damoiselle de Printemps, 5 percent (lager): aromas of cereals and grains, refreshing, floral, and dry.

Brasserie La Perle, Strasbourg (67): **4** Perle Lager, 4.5 percent (pils): honey and cereal aromas, floral and herbaceous bitterness.

FOR THEIR ACIDIC QUALITY

Bitter beers with controlled acidity, inspired by old Germanic styles, such as the Berliner Weisse, Gose, and Grätzer.

Brasserie Haut Buëch, Lus-La Jarjatte (26): **5** Grätzer, 6 percent (smoked wheat beer): smoked sausage on the nose, sparkling, tart and bitter, dry.

Brasserie Iron, Montauban (82): **6** Sanguine, 4.5 percent (wheat sour hibiscus): intense raspberry color, creamy, lactic, acidity balanced by the fruitiness of the infused hibiscus flowers.

FOR THEIR GREEN BITTERNESS, VEGETABLE, AND FRUITY QUALITY

Beers marked by hops, used at the end of boiling or for long storage, more or less herbaceous, resinous, or floral according to their origin.

Brasserie du Grand Paris, Saint-Denis (93): **7** IPA Citra Galactique, 6.5 percent (American IPA): an explosion of hops, citrus and tropical fruits, and flowers; resinous, sparkling, fresh, dry, and bitter.

Brasserie de la Vallée du Giffre, Verchaix (74): **8** Alt Sept 65, 8.3 percent, (Imperial IPA): resinous, mellow, with a long bitterness.

FOR THEIR BITTER COFFEE QUALITY

Beers highlighting very roasted malts or roasted malts associated with hops, evoking Italian *ristretto* or bitter chocolate with mint . . .

Brasserie Bendorf, Strasbourg (67): **9** Rêves d'Étoiles, 7.9 percent (black IPA): bitter chocolate on the nose, strong coffee flavors, then dark chocolate melted with hops.

Brasserie La Canaille, Sail-sous-Couzan (42): **10** Barricade Puebla, 7.5 percent (Cascadian dark ale): roasted aromas of coffee with resinous touches, intense coffee taste interspersed with fruity notes (red fruits, exotic fruits), bitter coffee finish.

FOR THEIR STRONG QUALITY

Triple beers are descended from old monastic beers, with three times more alcohol than normal beer—expect stoutness, roundness, spicy and fruity esters.

Brasserie Stephanoise, Saint-Étienne (42): **11** Glütte Triple, 7.5 percent, (triple): yellow fruit aromas, toast, spicy notes, peppery, well-established malt base.

Brasserie du Bout du Monde, Landévennec (29): **12** Térénez Triple, 6.7 percent (triple): spices on the nose, fruits, cereals, round, unctuous, and stout.

FOR THEIR SMOKY QUALITY

Smoked beers made with smoked malts, mostly with beech wood or peat.

Brasserie La Baleine, Paris (75): **13** Gitane, 5 percent (smoked ale): light rust, sweet, intensely peaty aromas, taste of toasted bread.

Rouget de l'Isle Brewery, Bletterans (39): **14** Vieux Tuyé, 6 percent (smoked lager): caramel nose and smoked sausage, sweet, roasted, smoked.

Brasserie La Farlodoise, Chazelles-sur-Lyon (42): **15** La Farlodoise Fumée, 5.5 percent (smoked ale): sausage, cured meats on the nose, rounded mixture of toasted and smoked flavors.

FOR THEIR SWEET QUALITY

Beers registering close to maltiness, with residual sugars and fatty and ample textures, like barley or wheat wine.

Brasserie des Garrigues, Sommières (30): **16** Sacrée Grôle, 12.6 percent (barley wine): bright orange color, candied fruit and caramel on the nose, rich, intense sensation of pear jam and smoky notes.

Brasserie Ninkasi, Lyon (69): **17** Ninkasi Grand Cru Wheat Wine, 12 percent (wheat wine): citrus and pine aromas, velvety, candied fruit, and peppery notes.

FOR THEIR CARAMEL QUALITY

Malty beers with red, mahogany, or tawny amber colors, with a wide range of gourmet sensations.

Brasserie de la Loire, Saint-Juste-Saint-Rambert (42): **18** 109, 6 percent (amber ale): fresh hazelnuts.

FOR THEIR TOASTED QUALITY

This spectrum is wide: from toasted wheat beers to dry or creamy stouts.

Brasserie La P'tite Maiz, Tours (37): **19** Goat Me a Stout, 6.6 percent (oatmeal stout): coffee, chocolate, roundness in the mouth, silky.

NEW TRENDS

WILD BEERS

These beers (wild ales) are inspired by the Belgian Lambic, traditional beers of spontaneous fermentation (caused by microorganisms present in the ambient air).

Brasserie de Sulauze, Miramas (13): **20** Ta Mère Nature, 5 percent (wild beer): blend of three wild beers made in barrels, tart and woody, vanilla and pineapple notes.

BEERS AGED IN BARRELS

The Gauls used barrels to ferment and store beer. Today, this practice uses new barrels, or barrels that previously contained wine or spirits. These are typically vintage beers, with the date of bottling and brewing ideally indicated on the label.

Brasserie de la Vallée de Chevreuse, Bonnelles (78): **21** Volecelest, 8 percent (triple raised in new French-oak barrels): fig on the nose, honey and sugar, sweet, candied orange notes, dried apricots, and woody.

Brasserie de Saint Germain, Aix-Noulette (62): **22** Belgian Dubbel, 7.9 percent (brown Belgian-style, fermented in Burgundy red-wine barrels): intense nose of roasting, soft, taste of dark chocolate, notes of black cherries.

ADDED INGREDIENTS

These beers include fresh fruits used in macerations, dried flowers, and various seasonal spices used at various stages of production.

Brasserie Mélusine, Chambretaud (85): **23** Love & Flowers, 4.2 percent (wheat beer with dried rose petals): wheat and floral aromas, violet, rose, fine bubbles, mineral, elegant.

Brasserie du Vexin, Théméricourt (95): **24** Véliocasse, 7 percent (blond beer with honey): toasted bread on the nose, caramel and honey, velvety, candied fruit, gourmand.

CITY BEERS, COUNTRY BEERS

It all began in the 1980s with the Coreff brewery in Brittany. Since then, new brewers have enjoyed growing appreciation among consumers.

IN CITIES . . .

Urban brewers play an active role in the life of neighborhoods, developing urban economic plans and sometimes acting as neighborhood bar and cellar.

Brasserie de la Plaine, Marseille (13): ㉕ HAC, Houblonnée à Cru, 5.5 percent (blond ale): Aroma of white blossoms and exotic fruit, slightly acidic, fruity bitterness.

Brasserie de l'Être, Paris (75): ㉖ Sphinx, 4.5 percent (seasonal): yeast and citrus notes, slightly acidic, dry and bitter.

La Montreuilloise, Montreuil (93): ㉗ Fleur de Montreuil, 5 percent (amber with elder tree flower): floral aroma with caramel, slightly acidic, fruity with a roasted malt base.

Brasserie Grizzly, Clermont-Ferrand (63): ㉘ Velours Noir, 4.3 percent (creamy stout): coffee aroma, creamy, gentle and chocolaty palate.

L'Antre de l'Échoppe, Narbonne (11): ㉙ Chimère de Cendre, 4.8 percent (dry stout): intense roasting aroma, feel of bitter dark chocolate, earthy and dry.

IN VILLAGES . . .

Breweries are bringing new life to French villages and have become event spaces for exhibitions and concerts.

La Rente Rouge, Chargey-lès-Gray (70): ㉚ Insomnuit, 6.5 percent (dark beer aged in Nuits-Saint-Georges barrels): notes of milky coffee, juicy, woody, dry fruit, black cherry aftertaste.

Brasserie des Trois Fontaines, Bretenière (21): ㉛ Mandubienne Brune, 7 percent (dark ale): coffee and red berry notes, full flavored and rustic, nice roasted bitterness.

Brasserie Les Trois Loups, Trélou-sur-Marne (02): ㉜ Triple, 8.5 percent (Belgian-style tripel): fruity esters, complex palate, herbal and floral, soft and resinous.

Brasserie An Alarc'h, La Feuillée (29): ㉝ Kerzu, 7 percent (creamy Imperial stout): notes of coffee, red berries and vanilla, chocolaty then intense coffee, silky, unending.

Brasserie du Quercorb, Puivert (11): ㉞ La Ninfas, 5 percent (Vienna lager): aroma of caramel and licorice, gentle, creamy, toasted bread, light, sharp at end.

IN THE FIELDS: TERROIR BEERS BREWED BY FARMERS

These farmers add value to their grain crops (barley, wheat, oats, rye, spelt) by transforming them at the farm to produce true terroir beers. The grains are sometimes malted at the farm, but generally undergo the process at a local micromalthouse. Hops farming is on the rise.

Ferme-Brasserie La Caussenarde, Saint-Beaulize (12): ㉟ L'Avoinée, 5.5 percent (dark ale with oats): roasted grain notes, almond cake, toasted bread, velvety and full flavored, dry and bitter at the end.

Brasserie des Trois Becs, Gigors-et-Lozeron (26): ㊱ Bière à l'ortie, 6.5 percent (aromatic herbal beer): herbal aroma, full palate, then mineral, fresh over roasted malt base.

Brasserie Popinh, Vaumort (89): ㊲ Icauna, 4.8 percent (pale ale): floral sensation, lemony, resinous, fresh and mellow at the same time, lemony bitterness as aftertaste.

Ferme de la Quintillière, Saint-Maurice-sur-Dargoire (69): ㊳ La Busard Seigle, 5 percent (three-grain ale): a beer you can eat, all grain, velvety and spicy.

Ribella, Pahimonio (2B): ㊴ La Ribella Mistica, 8 percent: base of Corsican organic barley, farmed hops, and Nebbio chestnuts.

Lexicon of Brewing Terms

Ale
Generic term describing yeast beers fermented at high temperature. In England, the word originally designated traditional, amber beers brewed without hops.

Barley Wine
Designates a high-fermentation beer with strong alcohol content, dense, liquorlike, and often aged in barrels, that can improve over time. Wheat wine is its counterpart made with wheat and barley.

Dunkelweizen
Literally "dark wheat." Brewed with roasted wheat malt. Wheat beers in France are generally called *bières blanches* (white beers).

Cervoise
Designates a beer from the Gallic tradition, in all likelihood originally brewed without hops.

Doppelbock
Double-Bock: *bock* is a German word meaning a low-fermentation beer with high alcohol content. The color ranges from copper blond to dark brown. The word *double* used before the style name indicates a beer that is stronger in alcohol content.

Grätzer
Originally a Polish beer made from oak-smoked wheat malt.

Dry Hopping
Dry hopping involves adding hops to the cask, cold. The technique is widely used for American-style hops beers.

IPA
Acronym signifying *India Pale Ale*, designating a hoppy beer style originally from England. The name comes from beers sent to English colonies. Additional hops were said to be added so that the beverage would survive the trip from England to India. In truth, these hoppy beers existed before this time, and were related to beers brewed in October and meant to be stored. Depending on the hops used, a distinction is made between American IPAs, English IPAs, etc.

Lager
Generic name given to yeast beers brewed at low temperatures. The beer is then stored cold (the German word *lagern* means "storeroom"). Originally a German process dating back to the mid-nineteenth century.

Pale Ale
Designates an originally English beer, brewed with pale malt.

American Pale Ale
Pale ale brewed with American hops.

Porter
High-fermentation dark beer originally from eighteenth-century London, with roasted aromas of cacao and chocolate. A Baltic porter is a strong, low-fermentation version, adapted from Baltic styles.

Session
Originally an American term used to designate beers with low alcohol content. Equivalent to *bières de table* (table beers). Today there are many styles of session beers.

Stout
High-fermentation black beer, originally called "stout porter." Today, stout can be dry and light (Irish stout), creamy (sweet stout, milky stout), strong (double stout, Imperial stout), hoppy (India stout), barrel-aged, etc.

Sour
Describes beers in which the predominant flavor is acidity . . . Different techniques create acidity in beers, notably the addition of lactic acid bacteria. A wheat sour is brewed with wheat.

Tripel
Beer with strong alcohol content, originally Belgian, that draws on beers brewed in monasteries during the Middle Ages: a single is 3 percent alcohol, a double is 6 percent alcohol, and a triple is 9 percent. These are generally blond.

Vienna Lager
Designates a low-fermentation beer brewed with Vienna malt, which lends a roasted and toasted aroma.

My Kitchen Library

What are the influential cookbook series and bestsellers that have left their mark on the history of French cookbooks? Let's browse the shelves . . .

Déborah Dupont*

Legendary Collections

ELLE Encyclopédie
In the 1950s, the women's magazine released a remarkable encyclopedia written for the most part by Mapie de Toulouse-Lautrec.

Les trois cuisines de France, Robert Laffont
A series of subject-based cookbooks from the 1990s. There were many editions with different covers. It's up to the reader to seek out recipes by Michel Guérard, Pierre Gagnaire, Marc Meneau, and others, identified by their initials.

Cuisines régionales de France, Éditions Time Life
The other series published by Time Life is more recent (1990s), and presents French regional specialties along with a few deliciously dated photographs.

Recettes et paysages, Éditions des Publications Françaises
Dive into the 1950s with these five hardcover volumes. Curnonsky and other famous writers wrote some of the prefaces, emphasizing culinary nationalism.

L'inventaire du patrimoine culinaire de la France, Albin Michel
Copublished by the Conseil National des Arts Culinaires at the end of the 1990s, this unique book of knowledge presents regional products and traditional recipes by region (except for Réunion, which has not yet been written).

Recettes originales de . . . , Robert Laffont
Inextricably linked to the Nouvelle Cuisine of the 1970s, this series edited by Claude Lebey symbolized the chefs bursting onto the kitchen scene.

Cuisiner mieux, Éditions Time Life
Written by journalists from several countries in the early 1980s, this twenty-seven-volume series presents the major themes of cooking with illustrated step-by-step recipes. An international success!

Dix façons de préparer . . . , L'Épure
Twenty-four-page booklets on colored and textured paper. Sewn by hand with linen thread to be untied with a letter opener . . . With 289 volumes published since 1989, this series is still exciting collectors.

Best of, Ed. Alain Ducasse
The newest member of the library of legendary cookbook series, launched in early 2008. It brings together present-day chefs and pâtissiers, through some dozen signature dishes explained in step-by-step photographs.

Bestsellers

By *bestseller*, we don't necessarily mean the books with the most sales, but rather the books that have found true success having been published in multiple editions, sometimes translated for other countries, and commonly found in French kitchens.

→ **Michel Oliver,** *La cuisine est un jeu d'enfants,* Plon (1963)
→ **Michel Guérard,** *La grande cuisine minceur,* Robert Laffont (1976)
→ ***Larousse de la cuisine,*** Larousse (1990)

→ **Ginette Mathiot,** *Je sais cuisiner,* Albin Michel (1932)
→ **Françoise Bernard,** *Les recettes faciles,* Hachette (1965)
→ **Gaston Lenôtre,** *Faites votre pâtisserie comme Gaston Lenôtre,* Flammarion (1980)
→ **Sophie Dudemaine,** *Les cakes de Sophie,* Minerva / La Martinière (2000)
→ **Christophe Felder,** *Pâtisserie!,* La Martinière (2011)
→ **Jean-François Mallet,** *Simplissime,* Hachette (2015)

*Owner of La Librairie gourmande, 92–96, rue Monmartre, Paris 2nd

skip to
Édouard Nignon, p. 344

The Chestnut

Hidden in its shell, the chestnut suffers from an extreme lack of recognition. Every winter, however, the story changes with the start of the holidays, as the chestnut is brought out of its shell to steal the show as part of France's holiday dishes and customs. Let's finally learn to appreciate everything good about the chestnut!

Jill Cousin

THE MATCH-UP

❀ Ardèche vs Corsica ❀
The 2 major producing regions

	ARDÈCHE	CORSICA
The varieties	Of the **65 recognized varieties**, the principal ones are: Aguyane, Précoce de Vans, Pourette, Sardonne, Bouche Rouge, Comballe, Garinche, Bouche de Clos, and Merle.	Of the **47 recognized varieties**, the main ones are: Insitina, Bastelicaccia, Tricciuta, Insetu Pinzutu, Carpinaghja.
Production area	From Saint-Victor to Les Vans via Montpezat and Aubenas.	Corsica alpine, to the northeast and around the line connecting Corte to Solenzara.
Production (metric tons in 2010)	4,200	1,000
A protected hunting ground	Obtained an AOP in 2014 that concerns the fruit in all its forms (whole, dry, flour). The geographical area of the AOP "Châtaigne d'Ardèche" covers 188 towns in Ardèche and a few neighboring towns in Gard and Drôme (9 in total).	Since 2010, the "Corsican chestnut flour" is protected by an AOP. To qualify for the name, the flour must come from chestnut groves located in mountain or mid-mountain areas, the preferred area of the tree being between 1,300 and 2,600 feet (400 and 800 m) in altitude. No chemical treatment is allowed.
It's a party!	In autumn, France celebrates the harvest around the "**castagnades**."	In December, the village of Bocognano celebrates the chestnut during the "**Fiera di a castagna**."
The recipes	**Le cousina:** a soup made of cooked chestnuts and fresh cream. **Confiture des châtaignes ("chestnut jam"):** the fruit is mashed, then cooked with sugar and vanilla bean. **L'ardéchois:** a moist cake made of chestnut cream.	**La pulenda:** a mixture of water, sifted flour, and a little salt, cooked in a kettle. It can be eaten in slices, hot, with eggs, brocciu cheese, or figatelli sausage, or savored the next day fried in a little olive oil. **Les Fritelle Castagnines:** sweet doughnuts of chestnut flour with brocciu cheese.

WHICH CHESTNUT IS EDIBLE? THAT IS THE QUESTION

Horse chestnut (*Aesculus hippocastanum*) is not edible. What is incorrectly referred to as *marron* in French **is actually a variety of chestnut** grown by *castanéiculteurs* (chestnut tree farmers). The thorny shell contains only one fruit. It is a version of the sweet chestnut (*Castanea sativa*) cultivated by humans and harvested starting in October.

THE CHESTNUT, A NOURISHING TREE

For a very long time, the chestnut has played a vital role in the diet of the populations of southern France and the Mediterranean region. Nicknamed "the bread tree," the chestnut provided flour when wheat flour was lacking.

CHESTNUT POLENTA WITH FIGATELLI AND BROCCIU

Recipe from *Du Pain, du vin et des oursins* by Nicolas Stromboni

PREPARATION TIME: 15 MINUTES
COOKING TIME: 1 HOUR
SERVES 8

2¼ pounds (1 kg) sifted chestnut flour
2 figatelli sausages (a Corsican fresh sausage)
8 eggs
1 wheel brocciu cheese (2¼ lb/1 kg)

In a pot, bring 8 cups (2 L) of salted water to a boil. Sprinkle in the chestnut flour, stirring with a *pulendaghju* (a round wooden stick measuring 19½ inches/50 cm long) or a long wooden spoon. The heat should be high. Never stop stirring, attempting as you stir to scrape the flour off the sides of the pot. Cook for 30 minutes, or until the flour forms a compact brown paste. Remove the pot from the heat and stir the polenta for about 1 minute, vigorously stirring and scraping the polenta off the sides of the pot with a spatula. Sprinkle chestnut flour onto a dry cloth, then scrape the polenta onto the towel. Let it rest for a few minutes, covering it with another towel. Cut the polenta into ¾-inch- (2 cm) wide slices with a kitchen string or a thin wire. Cook the figatelli over a wood fire, fry the eggs in a pan, and cut the cheese into 8 portions. Serve each warm slice of polenta with a slice of the cheese, a piece of sausage, and a fried egg.

Etiquette according to the Baronne Staffe

What if we dined today according to the norms established by the triumphant bourgeoisie in the nineteenth century? Are you ready for the challenge?

Loïc Bienassis

A true bestseller!

The most influential treatise on etiquette in the nineteenth century was a book by a woman, Blanche Soyer (1843–1911), who was best known by her pseudonym, the Baronne Staffe. Her book *Usages du Monde: Règles du savoir-vivre dans la société moderne* was published in 1889. There are several editions. It instructed readers in the proper conduct at life's major events (baptisms, weddings, etc.) and in all social situations (visits, conversations, etc.).

As a host in the know, how many glasses have you made available for each guest?

The plate "is preceded by five glasses (or two): a large one for mixing ordinary wine with water (or to drink pure), a second of special size for the Madeira wine, the third for the Burgundy wine, the fourth for the Bordeaux wine, the fifth, a flute or coupe, for Champagne; in many homes, the flute prevails. For wines from Greece, Sicily and Spain, which one drinks for dessert, one must have a very small glass of decorated crystal: Rhine wine requires a green glass the color of that river."

You love the soup. Might you ask for more?

The answer is no. For one very simple reason: "If too much of this practically liquid dish is absorbed, the stomach will be loaded, immediately full, which will make it impossible to receive other foods."

Some soup remains at the bottom of your plate . . . How might you finish with distinction?

You will not finish it! There must always remain a bit of soup at the bottom of the plate because it would be unthinkable to tip it to one side or other to finish it. The Baronne does not even introduce the possibility of soaking it up with bread.

USAGES du MONDE

Règles du Savoir-Vivre

dans la

Société Moderne

par

la Baronne Staffe

PARIS

VICTOR-HAVARD, ÉDITEUR

1894

Do you know how to elegantly cut the bit of bread on the side?

But bread is not to be cut! Are you aware of the danger of such an operation? The Baronne reminds you—even though she should not have to—that "It is pointless . . . to say that one breaks one's bread. Why not cut it? Because particles of the crust could, by the dint of the knife, jump before the eyes of neighbors and onto the bare shoulders of ladies."

The lady sitting next to you is thirsty. You serve her a glass of wine. Both wrong! Why?

Because it is not your role to serve her and because you did not take the time to pour water into her wine. Know that between each guest, carafes of wine and water must alternate: "The carafe of wine is within reach of the male guest, who is in charge of serving the lady he has brought to the table. He always offers her water. Except for at dessert, a woman only drinks diluted wine."

Which foods are you permitted to touch with your hands?

Bread and only bread. The golden rule, the iron law: aside from bread, you do not touch anything with your fingers. All fruits are peeled and eaten with a fork and dessert knife. Prick, peel, and pit: that is how you are to eat them.

The cherry challenge. What to do with the pits?

"When one eats cherries or other pitted fruit, which cannot be cut into pieces, one must not spit out the pits into the plate; nor gather them in one's hand so as to place them on the plate. One must instead bring the dessert spoon to the mouth and dispose of the pit in it. It is a small maneuver that can be easily accomplished with one's lips, and from there, put the pit on the plate. Practice at home with your family and you will be able to successfully perform all these movements."

The menu is pretty. You would like to bring it back home to add to your collection. How to do so?

Quite simply, take it. No, it will not be held against you. A menu is placed before each guest, either plainly written on heavyweight paper or in a "very elegant, very artistic" manner. It is therefore natural to take it with you. Remember that the back of the menu, where the name of the guest appears, is turned toward this guest.

The Baronne recommends that you turn it over as soon as you are seated.

skip to

So Long as There Is Inebriation, p. 49

Rice in Desserts

It is an inexpensive grain, and a household staple that is quickly consumed! It's also an essential ingredient in many French dishes, including on dessert menus. Here is the proof in a few recipes!

Elvira Masson

"Rice can be used in so many ways that a person could vary its preparation for three hundred and sixty-five days of the year without experiencing any fatigue," writes Auguste Escoffier in 1927 in his book *Le riz, l'aliment le meilleur, le plus nutritif, 120 recettes pour l'accommoder* (*Rice: The Best and Most Nutritious Food and 120 Recipes for Preparing It*). At the time, it was a little-known grain in France and was snubbed by chefs, a situation that Escoffier tried to overcome by emphasizing that it was much more nutritious than the potato, inexpensive, and went well with salty or sweet preparations: **"Mixed with sugar, cooked with caramel, it's a real treat,"** he stated. Among the recipes he proposed are Peaches with Couscous (a rice pudding thickened with egg yolk and prepared with peaches in syrup), Banana Soufflé with Creole Rice, and English Rice Pudding.

GÂTEAU DE RIZ (RICE CAKE)

A dish of childlike simplicity, this dessert can be enjoyed hot, warm, or cold.

PREPARATION TIME: 30 MINUTES
COOKING TIME: 30 MINUTES
SERVES 6

7 ounces (200 g) short-grain rice
I vanilla bean
4 cups (I L) milk
2 eggs
¾ cup (150 g) superfine sugar
3 tablespoons plus I teaspoon (50 mL) heavy cream

For the caramel
3 tablespoons (45 mL) water
¼ cup plus 2 tablespoons (75 g) sugar

Rinse the rice with cold water, then place the rice in a saucepan. Cover the rice with water, bring it to a boil for 3 to 4 minutes, then drain. Rinse the rice under cold water to stop the cooking. Split the vanilla bean lengthwise in half and scrape out the seeds with a knife. Boil the milk with the empty vanilla bean pod and the seeds. Add the rice and cook over low heat for 30 minutes. Remove the vanilla bean pod. Whisk the eggs with the sugar and cream, then add this mixture to the rice. Stir well to combine.

Preheat the oven to 350°F (180°C). Prepare the caramel by cooking the water and sugar together in a heavy-bottom saucepan until the syrup turns a light amber color. Pour a little of the caramel into the bottom of a heatproof glass bowl or dish (or into six individual serving dishes). Pour the rice mixture into the bowl, and cover it with a piece of parchment paper. Place the bowl into a bain-marie and bake for about 30 minutes, or just until set. Invert and unmold the cake once cooled.

RICE PUDDING
by Bruno Doucet

Bruno Doucet serves this dessert in his Paris La Régalades restaurants (1st, 9th, and 14th). Topped with caramel, it has a sweetness that never gets boring!

PREPARATION TIME: 20 MINUTES
COOKING TIME: 30 MINUTES
SERVES 4

4 cups (I L) whole milk
2 cups (500 mL) cream
I vanilla bean
7 ounces (200 g) short-grain rice
I cup (200 g) superfine sugar

For the caramel sauce (optional)
4 cups (500 g) cream
4½ cups (500 g) granulated sugar
I pinch fleur de sel sea salt

For the fresh fruits/dried fruits (optional)
Assorted fresh fruits, cubed
I handful assorted dried fruits

Prepare the rice pudding
In a heavy-bottom saucepan, combine the milk and cream. Split the vanilla bean lengthwise in half and scrape out and reserve the seeds. Add the empty pod and seeds to the saucepan. Stir in the rice and superfine sugar. Bring to a boil, lower the heat to very low, and cook for about 30 minutes, stirring frequently. When cooked, pour the rice pudding onto a plate and let it cool to room temperature, then place it in the refrigerator for 1 hour. Remove the empty vanilla pod, stir gently, then transfer the pudding to a serving bowl.

WE SERVE IT WITH . . .
- A caramel sauce: In a saucepan, heat the cream until hot; set it aside. Cook the granulated sugar in a heavy-bottom saucepan until it turns amber in color. Add the sea salt, then pour in half the hot cream, being very careful not to get burned from splattering. Bring the caramel to a boil, then add the remaining hot cream. Transfer the caramel to a large bowl, and let it cool.
- A mixture of fresh and dried fruits.

skip to ....
At the Dairy, p. 316

LA TEURGOULE NORMANDE
from the Brotherhood of the Teurgoule and Fallue of Normandy

This version of rice pudding is served hot, and it's from this fact that the recipe takes its name. It is said that *teurgoule* comes from the expression "to hurt the *ghoul* (mouth)," since it was eaten hot right out of the oven.

PREPARATION TIME: 10 MINUTES
COOKING TIME: 6 HOURS
SERVES 4

5¼ ounces (150 g) short-grain rice
¾ cup plus 2 tablespoons (180 g) superfine sugar
I pinch salt
2 level teaspoons (4 g) ground cinnamon
2⅛ quarts (2 L) whole milk

Place the rice in the bottom of an 8-cup (2 L) terra-cotta terrine. Add the sugar, salt, and cinnamon and stir with a spatula to combine. Slowly add the milk so that the rice stays in the bottom of the container. Place the terrine in a 300°F (150°C) preheated oven for 1 hour, then lower the temperature to 225°F (110°C) and bake for 5 hours. The teurgoule is cooked when the crust is golden, and when the liquid has evaporated. Serve hot or warm.

WINE WORDS

In France, wine is sacred despite its sometimes very blasphemous effect . . . Rabelais spoke of the "deific" drink, more Bacchanal than the blood of Christ, which could make one go up hill and down dale. The Way of Saint James cannot rival the wine routes one travels on pilgrimage!

Aurore Vincenti

The passion of wine

We give wine the power to fill us with joy or gloom. In that respect, the French say one can have **cheery, sad, or bad wine** (1697). There is a syntactic and organic shift between the drink and one's **mood**. You might therefore **drown your sorrows** in it, hoping to dilute some of your misfortunes, or when consumed by passion, you might be moved to add **a bit of water to your wine** to dilute conflicts.

In time

The effects of time on the body and soul are echoed by the **aging** of wine. One can hold a **wine for keeping** because it **ages well** and because its value increases with each passing year. A wine that improves in time reveals all its splendor over time. But with age, one can also become bitter. There's nothing worse than a vintage that has **turned to vinegar**. It's better, then, to know when to **pull the wine**, when to **bottle it** or put it in a carafe. There's the French expression "when the wine is pulled, you have to drink it!" for when one is **overly involved** in a matter and must back out. As a synonym for life experience, the French expression "**to have bottles**" refers to the maturity of wines that have been patiently stored. The word **vintage**, used in English and in French, also comes from winemaking culture and, in truth, from the French word **vendange** (grape harvesting). The word, very much in use today and meaning everything that bears the cachet of time, has existed since the fifteenth century when it designated the **grape harvest**. The French will instead use the word **millésime** (vintage) to date a wine.

Cheap wine

There aren't only *grands crus*. The French have a lot to say about cheap wine (*piquette*). The French verb **picoler** (to knock back) comes from the Italian **piccolo**, meaning "little." The French *petit* (little) has come to mean a **little, light wine**. The word was popular during the First World War and meant the excessive consumption of alcohol, in all likelihood because light wines go down so easily. **Picrate** (plonk), with the same "pic" (blow) that's in **picole, pinard, and piot**, comes from the Greek **pikros**, meaning "prickle, piercing," and stings as much as **piquette**. During the First World War, potassium and ammonium "picrates" were the most common explosives. Soldiers therefore quickly made the connection between an **explosive** and a wine that'll **get you bombed**. Humor was essential in the trenches. **Vinasse** (1765), meaning "cheap wine" in French, has one of the most depreciating suffixes and originally designated the cloudy liquid of a **partially sour** wine. In terms of a sour wine, in French you can also say **criquet** (cricket), which also dates from the nineteenth century, **ginguet** (sour) and **reginglard** (somewhat acidic) . . .

The Gauls: French Ancestors

And what if French cuisine were still filled with the customs and habits of the Gauls? Let's look at the legend and the reality.
Stéphane Solier

WHAT DO THE FRENCH OWE TO THE GAULS?

French cuisine today is indebted to its ancestors for the role gastronomy plays in France. "It would not be absurd to formulate the hypothesis that there is a relationship between the keen interest of the Gauls in food and French *gourmandise*," for "in Gaul, the love of food was inseparable from political and social life." (Jean-Robert Pitte, *Gastronomie française*, 1991)

→ **The French combination of leguminous plants and vegetables with a bit of fat:**
– salted pork with lentils
– cassoulet as a "févoulet" with beans, because beans only began bloating the French after Catherine de Médicis!
– sauerkraut
– peasant soup (hardy soup with beans, garbure . . .)
→ **French boiled meats:**
– The many regional varieties of pot-au-feu

– The **other meats in bouillon** in French tradition: coarse-salted beef, in a hot pot, beef miroton, blanquette de veau, tripe dishes (cow's head, tongue, cheek), pigs' knuckles and pork shoulder, whole chicken in a pot . . .
→ **French cured meats**: hams, bacon, rillettes, boudins, the art of which the Gauls had already perfectly mastered!
→ **French cooking with butter**: the use of butter was common in Gallic cuisine, much more so than olive oil, which was rare and expensive, reserved for the elite (Pliny the Elder).
→ **French symbols of gastronomy**: frog legs and escargots, which the Gauls adored.
→ **Brewing practices** in the northern parts of France, which perpetuate Gallic know-how with respect to beer.
→ **French love of wine**, introduced in Gaul by the Greeks (in 600 BC) and enthusiastically adopted by the Gallic elite (Plato, *The Laws*, Titus Livius, *The History of Rome*, V, 33).
→ **Certain French regional sweets**:
– *Cornue du Limousin*: tricornered brioche consumed on Palm Sunday.
– **Pithiviers**.
– **Quatre-quarts Breton**, a direct descendent of Carnute honey cake (the Carnutes were a Gaulish people who occupied present-day Eure-et-Loir).
– **Galette des Rois**: with its round shape and golden crust, it parallels the Gallic (and Roman) tradition of celebrating what's missing most at the time of the winter solstice: sun and sunlight.

TRUE / FALSE	TRUE	FALSE
Boar was the favorite dish of the Gauls		Remains of the famous boar have rarely been found in the waste of Gallic kitchens. It was reserved for the elite.
The Gauls were big drinkers	The writers of antiquity (Plato, Athenaeus, Appian, Diodorus Siculus, Pliny the Elder) often evoked the consumption of drinks among the Celts. They were offended by their manner of drinking wine (without mixing it with water) and the quantities in which they drank it, which they deemed excessive.	
The Gauls often organized large community banquets	Historical sources and archaeological excavations attest to the lavish festivities held in specially built structures.	
The Gauls ate lying down, like the Romans		They ate sitting on small benches or on very low mattresses.

skip to
Asterix's Gastronomic Tour of Gaul, p. 310

WITH OVER 11,000 MILES (19,000 KM) OF COASTLINE, FRANCE IS A LOVELY FISHING GROUND, FOR EVERYTHING FROM BLUE FISH TO SQUID TO OCTOPUS. HERE IS A TOUR OF THE SEAFOOD SHOP OF BEST CRAFTSMAN OF FRANCE (MOF) ARNAUD VANHAMME (PARIS 15TH).

Charles Patin O'Coohoon

Blue Fish

———◆———

These fish are referred to as fatty because of their fat content between 5 percent and 12 percent. Thanks to their blue-green back that protects them from being spotted by birds, they spawn in the pelagic zone (the area of the ocean's waters closest to the surface).

MACKEREL

Scomber scombrus

FAMILY: SCOMBRIDAE
SEASON: FROM MARCH TO MAY
FLESH: WHITE AND OILY (ADDICTIVE RAW OR COOKED)
PREPARED: BRUSHED WITH MUSTARD AND BAKED EN PAPILLOTE

ATLANTIC HORSE MACKEREL

Trachurus trachurus

FAMILY: CARANGIDAE
SEASON: FROM FEBRUARY TO JUNE
FLESH: TRANSLUCENT, DELICIOUS AND FIRM, A COUSIN OF THE MACKEREL
PREPARED: RAW, ROASTED IN THE OVEN, OR STEAMED EN PAPILLOTE

SARDINE

Sardina pilchardus

FAMILY: CLUPEIDAE
SEASON: FROM OCTOBER TO FEBRUARY
FLESH: HALF FAT, WITH THIN BONES, THE SMALLEST ARE THE BEST
PREPARED: CANNED, RAW, OR GRILLED

ANCHOVY

Engraulis encrasicolus

FAMILY: ENGRAULIDAE
SEASON: APRIL TO OCTOBER
FLESH: FINE AND FRAGILE
PREPARED: FILLETED, SALTED, AND PLACED IN STRIPS ON A PIZZA—OF COURSE!

Flatfish

These are the species that populate the bottoms of the seas. Many benthic fish are flattened, either on their bellies, such as skate and monkfish, or on their sides, such as sole. The side facing the sea bottom is always white.

TURBOT
Psetta maxima
FAMILY: SCOPHTHALMIDAE
SEASON: ALL YEAR, PEAKS FROM APRIL TO JULY
FLESH: FINE, WHITE, AND LEAN. THE FINEST OF THE FLAT FISHES
PREPARED: ROASTED WHOLE IN THE OVEN

BARBUE
Scophtalmus rhombus
FAMILY: SCOPHTHALMIDAE
SEASON: ALL YEAR
FLESH: WHITE AND FINE, LESS EXPENSIVE THAN ITS COUSIN THE TURBOT
PREPARED: POACHED WHOLE IN A COURT-BOUILLON

LEMON SOLE
Microstomus kitt
FAMILY: PLEURONECTIDAE
SEASON: MAY TO OCTOBER
FLESH: THIN AND LESS FINE, SO LESS EXPENSIVE, THAN ITS COUSIN THE SOLE
PREPARED: PANFRIED OR ROASTED

SOLE
Solea solea
FAMILY: SOLIDAE
SEASON: FROM DECEMBER TO MARCH
FLESH: FINE AND FIRM, THE FILLETS REMOVE IN ONE PIECE
PREPARED: BROILED IN BROWN BUTTER. PREPARED IN THIS WAY IT IS A SPECIALTY IN BRASSERIES

White-Fleshed Fish

These species live just above the seabed in the ocean's demersal zone.
They are very mobile but very dependent on the ocean floor from which they derive their food.
Among them are hake, whiting, and bream. Their colors vary from silver-gray to red.

WHITING
Merlangius merlangus

FAMILY: GADIDAE
SEASON: ALL YEAR
FLESH: LEAN, FINE, AND FLAKY, WITH A DELICATE TASTE
PREPARED: FRIED IN BREAD CRUMBS. THE FINEST VARIETY IS THE COLBERT WHITING

MEAGRE
Argyrosomus regius

FAMILY: SCIAENIDAE
SEASON: ALL YEAR, PEAKS BETWEEN DECEMBER AND FEBRUARY
FLESH: FINE, WHITE, WITH A "SKINNY" APPEARANCE, FROM WHICH IT GETS ITS NAME
PREPARED: COLD WITH MAYONNAISE, IT'S "OVER THE TOP"

SEA BASS
Dicentrarchus labrax

FAMILY: MORONIDAE
SEASON: FROM NOVEMBER TO MARCH
FLESH: THIN AND VERY FINE WITH FEW BONES
PREPARED: IN A SALT CRUST

EUROPEAN HAKE
Merluccius merluccius

FAMILY: MERLUCCIIDAE
SEASON: FROM MARCH TO JULY
FLESH: WHITE AND FIRM, HOLDS TOGETHER PERFECTLY WHEN COOKED
PREPARED: THIS LITTLE HAKE IS BEST WHEN SIMPLY ROASTED IN THE OVEN

RED PORGY
Pagrus pagrus

FAMILY: SPARIDS
SEASON: FROM JUNE TO OCTOBER
FLESH: LESS FINE THAN DAURADE
PREPARED: COOKED WHOLE À LA PLANCHA

GILT-HEAD SEA BREAM
Sparus aurata

FAMILY: SPARIDS
SEASON: FROM SEPTEMBER TO NOVEMBER
FLESH: DELICATE, WHITE, THIN, VERY TASTY WITH A BEAUTIFUL SOFTNESS
PREPARED: BARBECUED, ROYAL

The Crustaceans

———— ❖ ————

They derive their name from the Latin *crusta*, or "crust." Underneath their shells and behind their two pairs of antennae and their mandibles hides a species full of trace minerals.

GRAY SHRIMP

Crangon crangon

FAMILY: CRANGONIDAE
SEASON: ALL YEAR
FLESH: TENDER AND FRAGILE
PREPARED: TO EAT FROM HEAD TO TAIL, PEPPERED AND PANFRIED AS AN APPETIZER

COMMON LOBSTER

Homarus gammarus

FAMILY: NEPHROPINÉ
SEASON: PLENTIFUL FROM MAY TO AUGUST
FLESH: SWEET AND MILD
PREPARED: SIMPLY BAKED

LANGOUSTINE

Nephrops norvegicus

FAMILY: NEPHROPINES
SEASON: FROM APRIL TO AUGUST
FLESH: DELICATE AND TENDER
PREPARED: WITH MAYO, AS AN APPETIZER

Is it à l'Armoricaine or à l'Américaine ?

Pierre Fraysse is credited with the origin of this recipe in the middle of the nineteenth century. Back from the United States, this Sète-based chef cooked, in his Chez Peter's Americana restaurant, the famous lobster dish with tomatoes, onions, and white wine, called "American-style." The name "Armorican" appeared later by suggestion (pressure) from the inhabitants of Breton, whose blue crayfish remains one their symbols.

A few tricks with lobster

THERMIDOR
Cut the lobster in half lengthwise, break the claws, season the flesh with salt and pepper, and drizzle it with a few drops of oil. Turn the lobster halves over shell side down and bake them in a hot oven for 15 minutes. For the sauce, make a roux with 3 tablespoons (50 g) of butter and 2 tablespoons (12 g) of flour. In a saucepan, cook the roux for 15 minutes without letting it brown, then add 1 cup (250 mL) of milk and some salt, and let boil for 1 minute. Off the heat, add an egg yolk diluted with 2 tablespoons (30 mL) of cream, then add a dollop of strong mustard, and stir to combine. Remove the lobster meat from the shells and slice it; coat the meat with some of the sauce, and place it back in the shells. Bake just until cooked through. Serve.

IN A BISQUE
Crush 2 lobster carcasses and sauté them in oil. Add 2 peeled cloves of garlic and 3 chopped shallots. Add ⅓ cup plus 1 tablespoon (100 mL) of brandy and ignite it with a long match. Add 14 ounces (400 g) of skinned and diced tomatoes. Add 3 cups (750 mL) of fish stock. Cook over medium heat for 40 minutes. Stir to combine, strain, and serve.

AS A CARPACCIO
Cook the lobster in a court-bouillon, peel it, then wrap the tail in plastic wrap and place it in the freezer. Once frozen, thinly slice it with an electric carving knife, sprinkle the slices with a vanilla vinaigrette, and serve.

IN MAYONNAISE
In the method of Paul Bocuse, cook the lobster in a court-bouillon. Let it cool, remove the meat from the shell, and thinly slice it. Season the meat with salt and pepper, then drizzle it with a few drops of vinegar and oil. Fill a large bowl with chopped lettuce, then place the lobster slices on top. Coat with a mayonnaise sauce and garnish with anchovy fillets, wedges of hard-boiled eggs, capers, and heart of lettuce.

AMERICAN STYLE (À L'AMÉRICAINE)
Once the lobster has turned red during cooking, remove it and pull it apart. Reserve the coral (roe), cut the tail into pieces, and fry it in butter. Peel and crush 2 tomatoes. Reserve. Chop 1 carrot, 1 onion, 2 shallots, and 1 clove of garlic, and cook them in 3 tablespoons (50 g) of butter, then add the lobster and ¾ cup (200 mL) of white wine. Add a shot of cognac and ignite it with a long match. Add the tomatoes and 2 tablespoons (30 mL) of tomato paste. Remove the lobster and reduce the sauce over high heat. Whisk in 3 tablespoons (50 g) of butter and the lobster coral. Pour this mixture over the lobster.

COOKING
In a court-bouillon, 8 to 10 minutes for a lobster weighing 1⅓ pounds (600 g), 15 minutes for a lobster weighing 2¼ pounds (1 kg).

CARDINALISATION
This is the color change that a lobster undergoes when cooked. Its bright red color evokes that of a cardinal's robe.

Cephalopods

From the Greek words *kephalé*, meaning "head", and *pod*, meaning "foot," cephalopods are mollusks whose feet surround their heads. And despite their sea-monster image—with their soft skulls, hard beaks, and tentacles with suckers—they are delicious when cooked.

OCTOPUS
Octopus vulgaris

FAMILY: OCTOPODIDAE
SEASON: FROM AUGUST TO MAY
FLESH: FIRM AND VERY BRINY
PREPARED: MARINATED IN A VINAIGRETTE

Briny Ideas

SQUID

Loligo vulgaris

<u>FAMILY</u>: LOLIGINIDAE

<u>SEASON</u>: FROM AUGUST TO FEBRUARY

<u>FLESH</u>: SOFT AND SLIGHTLY ROUNDED

<u>PREPARED</u>: SEARED WITH GARLIC AND PARSLEY

Jacques Maximin*
QUATRE-QUARTS SAUCE

Roast a whole gilt-head sea bream in the oven. Create a sauce by combining equal portions (any quantity to suit the amount of sauce desired) of olive oil, water, lemon juice, and melted butter, and pour this over the roasted fish. Serve, with some nice olives on the side.

Former chef of Bistrot de la Marine, Cagnes-sur-Mer (Alpes Maritimes)

Emmanuel Renaut*
MACKEREL IN WHITE WINE

SERVES 4

4 (12 oz/350 g) whole mackerels	1 bottle (750 mL) dry white wine
2 carrots	1 cup (250 mL) white vinegar
1 stalk celery	Salt and freshly ground pepper
8 spring onions	
4 cloves garlic	1 sprig rosemary
1 organic lemon	2 sprigs lemon thyme
8 black peppercorns	2 bay leaves
2 tablespoons (30 mL) olive oil	2 cloves

Clean and gut the mackerels, carefully remove the fillets, then remove the bones. Rinse the fillets in cold water and dry them well. Peel the carrots, celery, and onions, and thinly slice them. Peel the garlic cloves. Slice the lemon. Lightly crush the peppercorns. In a casserole dish, prepare a marinade: heat the olive oil until warm, then add the carrots, celery, onions, and garlic and cook for about 5 minutes, or just until softened; do not let them brown.

Add the wine and vinegar and bring to a boil. Season the mackerel fillets with salt and pepper. In a separate casserole dish, arrange the slices of lemon, fillets, rosemary, lemon thyme, bay leaves, cloves, and peppercorns, then add the warm vegetables (the marinade). Bring to a boil, remove from the heat, and let cool in the pan. Let stand at least 12 hours in the refrigerator before serving.

Chef of Flocons de sel, Megève (Haute-Savoie)

Philippe Emanuelli*
WHITING FISH IN TABASCO

SERVES 4

4 small whiting fish, about 9 ounces (250 g) each, scaled and cleaned	1½ teaspoons (9 g) fine salt
	1½ teaspoons (4 g) ground Espelette pepper
3 tablespoons (18 g) all-purpose flour	8 cups (2 L) oil, for frying
4 eggs	Smoked Tabasco
7 ounces (200 g) white bread crumbs	

Wash the fish and dry them. Bend each one so that it bites its tail (their sharp and compact teeth will make this possible). Place the fish in a plastic bag with the flour and shake it gently. Lightly beat the eggs and pour them into a shallow plate, then combine the bread crumbs, salt, and Espelette pepper, and spread this mixture out into a second shallow plate. Heat a grill. Dredge the floured fish in the eggs, then in the bread crumbs, then place each one on the grill as you go. Heat the oil to 350°F (180°C). Submerge the fish, two at a time, in the hot oil and fry them for about 6 minutes, or until golden. Place the fish on paper towels to drain. Serve hot, with Tabasco on the side.

Author of Fish, Marabout, 2014

Jean-Pierre Montanay*
SQUID STUFFED WITH SPINACH

SERVES 4

4 squids, measuring 7 inches (18 cm) each	1⅓ pounds (600 g) fresh spinach
2 onions, finely chopped	3½ ounces (100 g) broken rice
Oil, for sautéing and for greasing the dish	⅓ cup plus 1 tablespoon (100 mL) white wine
1 teaspoon (2 g) ground cumin	Salt and freshly ground black pepper

Preheat the oven to 350°F (180°C). Thoroughly clean the squid, remove the heads, and cut the tentacles into small pieces. In a casserole dish, fry the onions in a little oil, just until softened, then add the squid tentacles. Cook for 2 minutes. Add the cumin and season with salt. Add the spinach and cook, covered, just until the spinach is wilted. Add the rice, and a little water if the pan seems too dry. Cook, covered, for 20 minutes. Stuff the squids with the rice mixture, then close the squids using toothpicks. Season with salt and pepper. Grease a baking dish with some oil, then arrange the stuffed squid in the dish, and add the wine. Bake for 25 minutes. Serve.

Author of Poulpe, Hachette Pratique, 2015

Artichokes à la Barigoule

This is a Provençal dish par excellence—from Alpilles, to be exact. It is a stew made with poivrade artichokes, and has gone from an obscure peasant dish to one included in the repertoire of great chefs.

François-Régis Gaudry

Barigoule?

→ The *barigoule* (*barigoulo* in Provençal) is a mushroom of the agaric type. Other sources claim that the recipe is derived from *berigoula* or *barigoule*, the vernacular names of the mushroom *Pleurotus eryngii*, also called King Oyster mushroom.
→ One fact is certain about this dish: the artichokes were originally simmered with mushrooms, bacon, and various herbs.
→ In 1742, in Menon, mushrooms were no longer included in the recipe, but the name remained.

ARTICHOKES À LA BARIGOULE
by Denise Solier-Gaudry

PREPARATION: 20 MINUTES
COOKING TIME: 35 MINUTES
SERVES 4

8 small purple artichokes, or 12 poivrade artichokes
1 lemon
1 tablespoon (15 mL) vinegar
1 large carrot
1 small stalk celery
2 small spring onions
1 clove garlic
4 sprigs parsley
1 tablespoon (15 mL) olive oil
3½ ounces (100 g) lardons (thick-cut cubed bacon)
3 tablespoons plus 1 teaspoon (50 mL) white wine
1 sprig thyme
Salt and freshly ground black pepper
1 tablespoon (6 g) all-purpose flour

Prepare the artichokes: cut off the stems to 1⅛ inches (3 cm) from the base, then peel the remaining stem sections. Remove the first layers of artichoke leaves and snip off the tips of the remaining leaves. Trim the artichokes with a short knife so that they are equal in size. Sprinkle them with a squeeze of lemon juice and soak them in water with the vinegar. If you are using purple artichokes, which are a little larger, cut them in half before cooking them, and remove the choke using a melon baller. Coat them well in lemon juice. Peel the carrot and cut it into small dice. Chop the celery into small pieces. Peel the onions and garlic, thinly slice the onions, and chop the garlic with the parsley. Heat the oil in a pan and sauté the carrot, onions, and celery for 5 minutes, then add the lardons and minced garlic and parsley. Add the wine and cook for 2 minutes, or until the wine has evaporated. Add the artichokes and thyme, season with salt and pepper, then sprinkle in the flour while stirring to ensure the ingredients are coated well. Add just enough water to almost cover the artichokes (the water should be just level with the artichokes). Cover the dish and cook over low heat for 30 minutes. Check the doneness by pricking the artichokes with the tip of a knife to see if they are tender. If the liquid evaporates too quickly, add a little water. If there is too much liquid at the end of the cooking time, increase the heat just until the liquid has evaporated. Transfer to a serving dish and serve. **What should you drink?** A rosé from Provence.

skip to
Brocciu, and the Art of Whey, p. 260

Georges Perec: The Little Kitchen of Writing

Cupboards are full of victuals and the names of dishes fill many pages in Georges Perec's writing: there's drink, food, and the memory of country magic cooked up by great chefs.

Estérelle Payany

Starting with his first book, *Les Choses* (*Things*, 1965), the accumulation of dishes and culinary matters was paired with a critique of consumer society. In his second one, *Quel petit vélo à guidon chromé au fond de la cour?* (*Which Moped with Chrome-plated Handlebars at the Back of the Yard?*, 1966), the back cover enticed the reader by promising "a recipe for rice with olives that should satisfy the pickiest." We sought for it in vain in its pages, but it launched a fine series of rice salads that would regularly punctuate his work. Was he a gourmand? Not particularly, even if his *Tentative d'inventaire des aliments liquides et solides que j'ai ingurgité au cours de l'année mil neuf cent soixante-quatorze* (*Attempt at an Inventory of the Liquid and Solid Foodstuffs Ingurgitated by Me in the Course of the Year Nineteen Hundred and Seventy-Four*) proved to be impressive, with lamb brain, creamed radicchio, and guava sorbet, not to mention a fine number of smoked fish and glasses of vodka, a discreet sign of his Polish origins. In the book *Penser/Classer*, eighty-one recipe cards for beginners use combinatorial mathematics to imagine recipes for sole, sweetbread, rabbit, and young rabbit . . . and in *La Vie mode d'emploi* (*Life: A User's Manual*, 1978), the action takes place on June 23, 1975, at precisely eight o'clock at night, when all the residents of the building described are supposed to be sitting down to eat. Even in *La Disparition* (*A Void*, 1969), a pangrammatic lipogram written without a single "e," lobster with cumin, Balkan sausage with paprika, and Souvaroff chaudfroid ortolans are enjoyed. But it is in no way colorful, there is no quality of taste or gastronomic pleasure: capturing meals, noting what is being eaten, means freezing time, attempting to save what's ephemeral in our lives from oblivion. And from Proust to Perec, mealtime becomes a way to travel back in time.

Strawberry Cream

Georges Perec, *La Vie Mode d'Emploi* (*Life: A User's Manual*, 1978)
"The book is placed on a music stand. It is open at an illustration of a reception given in 1890 by Lord Radnor in the drawing rooms of Longford Castle. Printed on the left-hand page in a frame of art-nouveau colophons and garland decorations is a recipe for Strawberry Cream: Take 10 ounces (300 g) wild or cultivated strawberries. Strain them through a fine-mesh sieve. Whip 2 cups (464 g) of cream until very firm, and fold the beaten cream into the mixture. Spoon the mixture from the bowl into small round paper cups, and cool for two hours in a cellar that is not too cold. To serve, place a large strawberry in each cup."

LE PARFAIT AU CASSIS

Estérelle Payany, inspired by *La Disparition*

Serves 6 gracious guests
Egg yolks – 4 large
Syrup – 4¼ ounces (120 g)
Fresh black currants – 9 ounces (250 g)
Crème de cassis (as used in a Kir) – 3 tablespoons plus 1 teaspoon (50 mL)
Milk fat – 1⅔ cups (400 mL)

Beat together the yolks + syrup until lightened. Combine the black currants + crème de cassis, ensuring they are well combined before using them. Beat the milk fat as when making a whipped cream. Thoroughly combine all the mixtures. Scrape the mixture into a long serving dish, then refrigerate it for 12 hours, or long enough to ensure it's very cold. Slice, and serve to the guests.

HAPPINESS IN BOTTLES

by Gwilherm de Cerval

Oversize wine bottles are often associated with Champagne. The custom of using oversize bottles was created mainly by Champagne traders in the nineteenth century. The largest of these bottles usually bear the names of biblical figures. Here is a short review of the principal sizes to remember.

N°1 • QUART (or piccolo)
Must contain at least 6.3 fluid ounces (187.5 mL)
Height: 8 inches (20 cm)
Capacity: 6.7 fluid ounces (200 mL)
Number of glasses: 1.5
Occasion: on the plane
Probability of uncorking it: low—only airlines offer them to their passengers

N°2 • DEMIE (or "little girl")
Corresponds to half a standard wine bottle of 25.3 fluid ounces (750 mL)
Height: 10.2 inches (26 cm)
Capacity: 12.6 fluid ounces (375 mL)
Number of glasses: 3
Occasion: when your wife is pregnant
Probability of uncorking it: weak—with the introduction of wines by the glass in the food industry, its production has dropped considerably

N°3 • BOUTEILLE (or champenoise)
Comes from the word *botele*, Old French for a type of container
Height: 12.6 inches (32 cm)
Capacity: 25.3 fluid ounces (750 mL)
Number of glasses: 6
Occasion: no need for a special occasion
Probability of uncorking it: very high—a French person consumes about 1,495 fluid ounces (44.2 L) of wine per year (the equivalent of sixty standard bottles)

N°4 • MAGNUM
Means "large" in Latin
Height: 14.9 inches (38 cm)
Capacity: 50.7 fluid ounces (1.5 L)
Equivalent: 2 bottles
Number of glasses: 12
Occasion: Valentine's Day
Probability of uncorking it: very high—it is often said that this is the most suitable format for wine

N°5 • JÉROBOAM (or double magnum)
The first biblical king of northern Israel
Height: 19.5 inches (50 cm)
Capacity: 101.4 fluid ounces (3 L)
Equivalent: 4 bottles
Number of glasses: 24
Occasion: for aging
Probability of uncorking it: high—this is a bottle that is very popular among winemakers themselves, particularly for their own consumption

N°6 • REHOBOAM
The son of King Solomon
Height: 22 inches (56 cm)
Capacity: 152.2 fluid ounces (4.5 L)
Equivalent: 6 bottles
Number of glasses: 36
Occasion: having a toast to celebrate retirement
Probability of uncorking it: very weak—this format has not found a wide audience, and only a few specialized wine merchants offer it

N°7 • MATHUSALEM (or imperial)
The son of Enoch: synonymous with longevity, he lived 969 years
Height: 24 inches (60 cm)
Capacity: 202.9 fluid ounces (6 L)
Equivalent: 8 bottles
Number of glasses: 48
Occasion: an endless meal with friends
Probability of uncorking it: weak

N°8 • SALMANAZAR
This surname was held by five Assyrian kings
Height: 26.3 inches (67 cm)
Capacity: 304.3 fluid ounces (9 L)
Equivalent: 12 bottles
Number of glasses: 72
Occasion: a Christmas party with a large family
Probability of uncorking it: very low—unless you spend all your evenings in high-end clubs

N°9 • BALTHAZAR
One of the three wise men, representing Africa
Height: 29.1 inches (74 cm)
Capacity: 405.8 fluid ounces (12 L)
Equivalent: 16 bottles
Number of glasses: 96
Occasion: a holiday celebration with your neighbors
Probability of uncorking it: very weak—mostly associated with the vineyards of Champagne

N°10 • NABUCHODONOSOR
The greatest king of Babylon between 605 and 562 BC
Height: 31.1 inches (79 cm)
Capacity: 507.2 fluid ounces (15 L)
Equivalent: 20 bottles
Number of glasses: 120
Occasion: Labor Day with friends and family
Probability of uncorking it: very low—unless you like to spend your holidays on the beach making new friends

N°11 • SALOMON (or Melchior)
One of the three wise men, representing Europe
Height: 33.8 inches (86 cm)
Capacity: 608.7 fluid ounces (18 L)
Equivalent: 24 bottles
Number of glasses: 144
Occasion: your birthday
Probability of uncorking it: very low—it is rare for Champagne houses to produce it each year

N°12 • PRIMAT
Comes from postclassical Latin, meaning "firstrate"
Height: 40.1 (102 cm)
Capacity: 913 fluid ounces (27 L)
Equivalent: 36 bottles
Number of glasses: 216
Occasion: in commemoration of May 8, 1945 (VE Day) in France (Drappier was the favorite Champagne of General de Gaulle)
Probability of uncorking it: almost zero—only Champagne Drappier produces it

N°13 • MELCHISEDECH
King of Salem, priest of the Most High God. The name means "King of Justice"
Height: 43.3 inches (110 cm)
Capacity: 1,014 fluid ounces (30 L)
Equivalent: 40 bottles
Number of glasses: 240
Occasion: your wedding
Probability of uncorking it: very weak—unless you decide to marry several times in your life

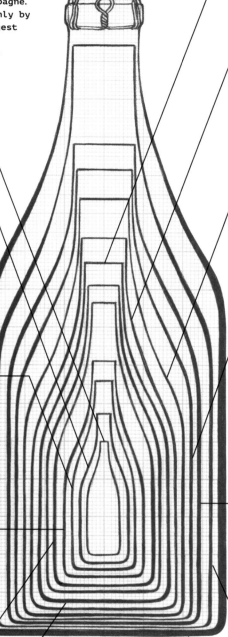

DIAGRAM
Side view of bottle sizes

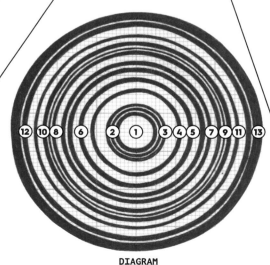

DIAGRAM
Top view of bottle sizes

Vinegar

Without vinegar, French cuisine would be bland. France is full of these nectars, which are as refined as they are varied, and which are developed by high-quality producers and craftspeople who follow ancestral traditions. From Orléans to Banyuls, here is a decryption of this addictive acid.

Marie-Amal Bizalion

A CHEMISTRY LESSON

Louis Pasteur discovered the secret of this preservative and flavor enhancer in 1865. When it comes into contact with air and heat, fermented alcohol becomes bitter. To prevent the proliferation of bad bacteria, wine that is too strong is cut with water and vinegar is added; in hot weather, a "plant," the *Mycoderma aceti*, spontaneously forms a thin membrane that quickly covers the entire surface of the liquid. By absorbing the oxygen from this liquid, a process of combustion within the alcohol begins that eventually turns the alcohol into acetic acid.

Homemade vinegar in 6 steps

Equipment: a *vinaigrier* (vinegar cask), made of wood, sandstone, or earthenware, with a tap.

Store the vinegar in a room heated to a minimum of 68°F (20°C).

Fill the cask two-thirds full with equal parts of a good, low-alcohol wine and vinegar.

Replace the cap with a piece of gauze, secured by a tie.

Watch for the appearance (it happens very soon) of a translucent veil on the surface.

After three weeks, taste the vinegar on a regular basis.

When the vinegar is ready (from three weeks to two months, depending on the room temperature), remove a little of the vinegar and replace it with the same amount of wine, without breaking the veil that has formed on the surface.

CHICKEN WITH VINEGAR
by *Marion Monnier**

The title of this recipe is the title of a famous film by extreme gastronome and director Claude Chabrol, with Jean Poiret playing the role of the "chicken." This is also an old and very common recipe that was prepared in nineteenth- and twentieth-century bourgeois family kitchens.

PREPARATION TIME: 25 MINUTES
COOKING TIME: 1 HOUR
SERVES 4

2 carrots, roughly chopped
1 onion, peeled and roughly chopped
1 clove garlic, peeled and roughly chopped
1 stalk celery, roughly chopped
A few sprigs thyme
1 bay leaf
Salt and freshly ground black pepper
2 chicken wings
1 chicken neck
Scant ½ cup (100 mL) vinegar, plus a few tablespoons for the livers
Breasts and thighs from a free-range chicken
Butter, for cooking
Beurre manié ("kneaded butter"): thoroughly combine 2 tablespoons/30 g of very soft butter with ¼ cup plus 1 tablespoon/30 g of flour
Raw chicken livers

Place all the vegetables, herbs, and chicken wings and neck in a casserole dish and cover them with water. Bring to a boil. When the liquid reduces by half, strain and reserve the liquid, and add the vinegar. In a saucepan, simmer the strained broth and reduce it again by one-third. Meanwhile, brown the chicken breasts and thighs in butter in the casserole dish, cover, and cook over low heat for 35 minutes. Bring the reduced broth to a boil, lower the heat, and stir in the *beurre manié* to thicken the broth. Off the heat, add the reduced broth and raw livers (combined with a little vinegar) to the casserole dish with the chicken breasts and thighs. Serve immediately.

*Chef of La Caillebotte bistro, Saintes (Charente-Maritime)

skip to
Lettuces and Chicories, p. 337

4 TECHNIQUES WITH VINEGAR

1

Deglazing

Brown veal liver, fish, or poultry in a pan or a casserole dish. Pour off the fat, heat the pan over very high heat, and add a splash of good vinegar. Deglaze the pan by scraping up the browned bits. Let reduce for a few minutes, then add the meat pieces back to the pan.

2

Preserving

Before the era of freezers, vinegar was used to extend the life of food. Vinegar can change the flavor of food by improving it. This is the case when cooking saffron milk cap mushrooms, whose pungency often disappears after the mushrooms are cooked until dry in a pan. To the pan with the cooked mushrooms, add olive oil, onions, crushed garlic, herbes de Provence, and a scant ½ cup (100 mL) of good red vinegar (one whose aroma is strong). Simmer for 15 minutes, then transfer the entire mixture to a jar; top it off with olive oil. When enjoyed still warm, this treasure of the woods satisfies any hunger.

3

Invigorating

To invigorate a homemade mayonnaise, add a dash of vinegar to it at the end. Strawberries, raspberries, and melons love a small amount of white Banyuls vinegar with three crushed mint or basil leaves. For those with high blood pressure (hypertension), vinegar can be a satisfying replacement for salt.

4

Marinating

An extended dip in an acidic solution will tenderize meat. Whether using red or white vinegar, the quartet of honey–olive oil–vinegar–mustard works perfectly on grilled meats. In Provence, boar or beef stews are given pep by adding a dash of vinegar to their marinade.

The Vinaigrettes of Top Chefs

COUNTRY STYLE
by Éric Frechon*

Stir together 2 tablespoons (30 mL) of sherry vinegar with 3 pinches of salt. Whisk in 1 tablespoon plus 1 teaspoon (20 mL) of hazelnut oil, ⅓ cup (80 mL) of peanut oil, and 1 pinch of black pepper. This vinaigrette is perfect with a salad of green beans, artichoke hearts, shallots, and pan-roasted and crushed hazelnuts.

*Chef of Épicure restaurant, Paris 8th.

HIGH IN VITAMINS
by Alain Ducasse*

Juice 4 skinned blood oranges. Add 1 tablespoon (15 mL) of red wine vinegar and 4 tablespoons (60 mL) of olive oil, and season with salt and freshly ground black pepper. This vinaigrette is perfect with a salad of blood oranges, celery, minced red onion, Niçoise olives, diced feta cheese, and chopped parsley.

*Chef of Le Louis XV, Monte-Carlo, and Le Plaza Athénée restaurants, Paris 8th.

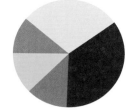

WILD
by Frédy Girardet*

Vigorously whisk together 1 teaspoon (5 mL) of red wine vinegar, 2 tablespoons (30 mL) of white wine vinegar, 1 tablespoon (15 mL) of peanut oil, 1 tablespoon (15 mL) of walnut oil, and 2 tablespoons (30 mL) of truffle juice. Season with salt and pepper. Add 1 ounce (30 g) of truffle and 1 coarsely chopped hard-boiled egg. Heat everything without boiling. This vinaigrette is perfect with warm wild asparagus tips that have been immersed for 5 minutes in salted boiling water.

*Former chef of the restaurant of the Hôtel de Ville, Crissier (Switzerland).

CREATIVE
by Reine and Nadia Sammut*

In a blender, blend 1 small peeled and cooked beet, 1 tablespoon (15 mL) of pomegranate molasses, 1 tablespoon (15 mL) of white Banyuls vinegar, 6 tablespoons (90 mL) of Cucuron olive oil, salt, and freshly ground Sarawak white pepper. This vinaigrette is perfect with a pot-au-feu enjoyed the next day, or over baby (pencil) leeks.

*Chefs of l'Auberge de La Fenière, Cadenet (Vaucluse).

A Tour de France of Vinegar Appellations

Orléans
Origin: 1394, created by the Corporation of Vinegar Makers of Orléans. There were three hundred vinegar makers in the eighteenth century, but only one remains today. **Ingredients:** French wines and a vinegar base.

Banyuls
Origin: from grapevines planted in the eighth century BC by the Greeks. A vinegar whose production is still confidential; sold since 1976. **Ingredients:** sweet wine of Banyuls and acetic bacteria.

Reims
Origin: associated since the eighteenth century with the wines of Champagne.

Ingredients: enhanced using the disgorged portion from Champagnes made from Chardonnay, Pinot Noir, and Pinot Meunier grapes. Aged in oak barrels.

Bordeaux
Origin: there were many factories in the city during the eighteenth century. Now, these are entrusted to rare vineyard domains. **Ingredient:** AOC Bordeaux, aged in oak barrels.

Lagny
Origin: around 1875, phylloxera ravaged the vineyards of the Île-de-France region. The commune of Lagny-sur-Marne turned to the production of clear alcohol. Lagny vinegar was created in 1890. **Ingredients:** sugar-beet alcohol and beech chips macerated in oak barrels; flavored with fruits.

Vin de pommes basque (Basque apple wine)
Origin: made from Sagarno (apple wine), a "near cider," without bubbles or sugar. **Ingredient:** fermented local apple pulp.

Pineau des Charentes
Origin: 1589, from the accidental creation of a divine liquid from a combination of grape must with forgotten brandy. The vinegar was created as a result. **Ingredients:** Pineau des Charentes AOC. A slow acidifying process, aged in oak.

Vin jaune du Jura
Origin: since the Crusades, exceptional wine had been deemed inappropriate for making vinegar. In 1993, success was achieved by Philippe Gonet after three years of testing. **Ingredients:** Savagnin grape wine. An acetification process adhering closely to the principles applied by Pasteur.

Limousin Cider
Origin: from the region of sweet apples, using traditional farming methods. Producers of this vinegar should be sought out in local markets. **Ingredient:** locally produced cider aged in chestnut wood, hence its unique flavor.

ALL ABOUT THE MOTHER
The belief is firmly rooted that the famous "mother" of vinegar, thick and viscous, should be used, with devotion, to begin a new vinegar. But this is only a layer of dead bacteria, which ends up sinking to the bottom of the bottle. It's fine to discard it.

THANKING THIEVES
In 1628, the plague was ravaging Toulouse. Four apparently immune bandits robbed many of the patients. These thieves were condemned to be burned alive, unless they revealed the secrets of their immunity from the disease. They admitted to being dunked in a complex mixture of plants steeped in white vinegar. As thanks, they were still hanged, but their formula for this mixture was entered into the codex of French pharmacopoeia in 1748. It consisted of a white vinegar containing, among other ingredients, absinthe, rosemary, sage, garlic, and several spices.

BEWARE OF CLAIMS
"Tradition," "réserve," "vieilli en fût de chêne" ("aged in oak barrels") . . . these words do not guarantee that the vinegar has been produced with traditional methods. Even the most organically produced vinegars cannot guarantee their traditional production unless the word *traditionnel* appears on the bottle, which must be indicated in full on the label of each container of vinegar.

THE MATCH-UP

● COMMERCIAL
98 percent of all production
Produced in large steel tanks, heated to 86°F (30°C). The alcoholic solution is injected with microbubbles loaded with acetic bacteria. Vinegar is achieved after 24 hours.

● ARTISAN
2 percent of all production
Fermented in wooden casks, aged a minimum of three weeks, then aged at least six months in cellars. Often less acidic, and always more subtle.

The address
Vinaigrerie Laurent Agnès, Saint-Jean-d'Angély (Charente-Maritime), 05 46 26 18 45. Sumptuous artisanal vinegars, carefully produced from a base of cider or wine, and either plain or flavored.

The Cake of Love

"Prepare your . . . prepare your dough. . . ." This is part of the famous recipe for the "cake d'amour," featured in a song in the film *Peau d'âne* (*Donkey Skin*), by Jacques Demy. Legendary French pastry chef Pierre Hermé offers his reinterpretation here.

Camille Pierrard

AN ICONIC SCENE

When adapting the story of Perrault in 1970, Jacques Demy decided to set to music the scene in which this cake is prepared, inspired in particular by his own mother who was skilled at making pastry and who loved to sing. He entrusted the responsibility of composing the music for the film with care to Michel Legrand—with whom he had already collaborated on *Les Demoiselles de Rochefort* (*The Young Ladies of Rochefort*), *Les Parapluies de Cherbourg* (*The Umbrellas of Cherbourg*), and *Lola*. It's a light and crazy song that made the cake d'amour the undisputed star of fictional cakes. Michel Legrand, nevertheless, seemed to have favored rhyme and rhythm at the expense of the creating a truly edible cake!

In the film's cult-classic scene, Catherine Deneuve, with her Botticellian features, flips through the pages of her cookbook in search of a perfect recipe. After skipping past several equally imaginative recipes for pastries, such as *Chenonceau au rhum* (Chenonceau with Rum) or *délice à la noix* (Walnut Delight), she finally stops on the cake d'amour. She then puts on her sun-colored dress and starts to work.

Once upon a time . . . A young princess took refuge in a cabin in the woods. A prince discovered her and was surprised. Lovesick, he wanted nothing more than a cake made from her hand. As the princess, Peau d'âne, placed the cake in the hearth, one of her gold rings fell into the batter, which would be discovered by her beloved.

According to the scene in the film, the cake recipe is very difficult to execute. Here pastry chef Pierre Hermé delivers his tasty version.

Makes 3 cakes d'amour

Two or three days before making the cake d'amour, crystallize the rose petals.

CRYSTALLIZED ROSE PETALS

Red rose petals
2 large (50 g) egg whites
½ cup (100 g) superfine sugar

Select the most beautiful petals. Using a brush, coat the petals with a thin layer of egg white, then dredge them in the sugar, and let them drain. Place them on a rack in a cool, dry place, protected from any moisture, to dry and crystallize for 2 or 3 days. Use them right away or store them in an airtight container.

ROSE-ALMOND SPONGE CAKE

2 cups (270 g) almond flour
2½ cups plus 1 tablespoon (260 g) confectioners' sugar
2 tablespoons plus 2 teaspoons (40 g) whole milk
1 teaspoon (5 g) rose extract (alcohol based)
1 drop (1 g) red liquid natural food coloring (adjusted as needed, according to the strength of the color)
18½ tablespoons (260 g) unsalted butter, softened
5 large (95 g) egg yolks
1 whole (55 g) egg
5 large (145 g) egg whites
¼ cup plus 2½ teaspoons (60 g) superfine sugar
1⅓ cups (130 g) all-purpose flour, sifted

In a large bowl or on a piece of parchment paper, sift together the almond flour and confectioners' sugar. Combine the milk, rose extract, and the food coloring. In the bowl of a stand mixer fitted with the flat beater, beat the butter with the confectioners' sugar–almond flour mixture. Attach the whisk beater. Add the egg yolks and the egg, and beat for another 2 minutes. Carefully add the milk mixture. Scrape the batter into a large bowl and set it aside. In the bowl of a stand mixer fitted with the whisk beater (thoroughly clean the bowl and beater if you have only one), beat the egg whites just until medium peaks (not too firm) form, gradually adding the superfine sugar while beating them; the whites will create a peak that will bend slightly into what is a called *bec d'oiseau* ("bird's beak") when the beater is raised. Using a spatula, fold the beaten egg whites into the first mixture, then sift the flour over the top of the batter, and carefully fold it in. Fill the pans.

FILLING THE PANS

1 tablespoon plus 2 teaspoons (25g) unsalted butter
¾ cup minus 2 teaspoons (70 g) all-purpose flour
1 recipe Rose-Almond Sponge Cake (recipe left)
9 ounces (250 g) fresh raspberries (use remaining raspberries as decoration)
3 round rosette cake pans measuring 6 inches (16 cm) in diameter and 2 inches (5 cm) in height

Preheat a convection oven to 350°F (180°C). Gently soften the butter in the microwave; then grease the entire interior of the pans with the butter using a pastry brush. Sprinkle some of the flour into each pan then turn the pans to completely coat the bottoms and sides with the flour. Turn the pans upside down to tap out any excess flour. Place the pans on a baking sheet. Using a piping bag fitted with a #12 plain piping tube, pipe 7 ounces (200 g) of the rose-almond sponge cake batter into each pan. Place 1 ounce (30 g) of fresh raspberries on top, taking care not to place them too close to the edge, then cover the raspberries with 3 ounces (80 g) of the batter, followed by another 1 ounce (30 g) of fresh raspberries placed in the same manner on top. Cover the raspberries with 4¼ ounces (120 g) of the rose-almond sponge cake batter, smooth the top, and place them immediately in the oven.

BAKING

As soon as the cakes are placed in the oven, reduce the temperature of the oven to 300°F (150°C), and bake for about 1 hour and 30 minutes to 1 hour and 40 minutes. Check the doneness of the cake using the point of a knife; the point should come out clean when inserted into the center of a cake. Remove the cakes from the oven, immediately unmold them onto a rack, and let them cool to room temperature. Refrigerate the cooled cakes, wrapped in plastic wrap, or decorate them right away with the pink fondant.

PINK FONDANT

1⅛ pounds (500 g) premade fondant
3 tablespoons plus 1 teaspoon (50 g) water
A few drops of red liquid natural food coloring
Knead the fondant by hand to make it more supple and smooth, then transfer it to a saucepan with the water and the food coloring. Gently warm it to 99°F (37°C). Use immediately.
Note: The temperature of the fondant should not exceed 99°F (37°C).

PINK PRALINES

Several pink pralines
Using a rolling pin, coarsely crush the pink pralines. Use them immediately, or store them in an airtight container.

ASSEMBLY

5 tablespoons (100 g) apricot preserves
Heat the apricot preserves to about 113°F (45°C). Brush the cakes all over with the heated preserves. Then, using a ladle, glaze the cakes with the softened fondant. Sprinkle the top of each cake with pink praline pieces, and decorate each with a crystallized rose petal and raspberries. Store refrigerated.

TIPS FOR SERVING

Take the cake out of the refrigerator 2 hours before serving it. The cake should be enjoyed at room temperature.

SUGGESTED DRINKS

Water; Ispahan teas

skip to ....
Bad Taste, p. 261

Is Coca-Cola a French Invention?

Does that legendary soft drink from Atlanta boast a
Corsican lineage?

François-Régis Gaudry

A LITTLE HISTORY

In a genuinely scholarly study,* the
American author Mark Pendergrast
asserts that Coca-Cola's ancestry
can be traced to French Wine
Coca, an alcoholic beverage with
a base of coca leaves, kola nuts,
and leaves of the damiana plant (a
shrub that grows in Texas and Latin
America). When the pharmacist
John Pemberton formulated
this concoction in 1885, he was
apparently inspired by Vin Damiani,
a medicinal tonic based on Bordeaux
wine and Peruvian coca, originally
devised by the Corsican chemist
Angelo Mariani in 1863. This
elixir was renowned as a treatment
for flu, impotence, anemia, and
neurological ailments. Pope Leo
XIII was a devotee, and the potion
earned a worldwide reputation,
probably finding its way into the
glass of that American pharmacist.
With the advent of Prohibition,
John Pemberton and his colleague
Ed Holland established the Coca-
Cola trademark and invented the
carbonated nonalcoholic drink whose
formula remains a closely
held secret to this day.

*For God, Country & Coca-Cola: The
Definitive History of the Great American Soft
Drink and the Company That Makes It,* 1993

THE RECIPE FOR VIN À LA COCA

MAKES 2 CUPS (500 ML)

2⅛ ounces (60 g) coca leaves
1 cup (250 mL) Bordeaux red wine
¾ cup plus 1 tablespoon (200 mL) cognac
2 tablespoons (30 g) cane sugar

Combine all the ingredients in a tightly sealed jar. Let macerate for
3 months, swirling the jar frequently to keep the ingredients thoroughly
combined. Drain through a strainer lined with cheesecloth and transfer
to a bottle. Actually, we've omitted one minor detail: it would be a
challenge to find any coca leaves for this concoction. The substance
is illegal in France and the United States, and the United Nations
included it in their list of proscribed drugs published in 1961.
With good reason: it's the source of cocaine.

When Dining in Paris Was a Dangerous Sport

Paris, the world's gastronomic capital? That was far from being
the case in the eighteenth and nineteenth centuries. Its taverns
and tables were widely regarded as hellholes. A brief compilation
of the most devastating reviews.

François-Régis Gaudry

TOBIAS SMOLLETT
English writer
"The bedrooms [of French inns] are
generally cold and comfortless, the
beds narrow, the cuisine execrable,
the wine poisonous, the service bad,
the patrons insolent. And the bill is
highway robbery."
Voyages à travers la France et l'Italie
(*Travels through France and Italy,*
1763)

TAXILE DELORD
**Author of a popular little guide,
warning foreign visitors of the
perils of international travel**
"Poor foreign visitors, how
monstrously [they] are exploited!
And then they return to their homes
in England, Prussia, Switzerland,
and Asia Minor. They claim that
French cuisine is nothing but a
myth, that there's no such thing,
that it's one plate of stew after
another, a perpetual mishmash,
that our vaunted French wines
are an atrocious scam, composed
of logwood juice and bleach. It is
not the fault of France—it's the
misguided path that they've followed.
Why have they wandered blindly
into their hotel's dining room?"
Paris-Étranger, coll. "Petits-Paris"
(1855)

JOACHIM-CHRISTOPH NEMEITZ
German Privy councilor to the Prince of Waldeck
"Almost everyone is under the impression that you'll eat well in France,
especially in Paris: that's not true . . . You'll eat pretty poorly in inns where the
food isn't well prepared and the menu offers little variety. You'll be served a
soup, a piece of broiled or boiled meat, a fricassee of veal or some chops, a few
vegetables, a roast, and for dessert milk, cheese, small cakes, seasonal fruits,
the same thing all year long."
Séjour de Paris pour les voyageurs de condition (1718)

LOUIS-SEBASTIEN MERCIER
French writer
"Foreigners find the dining
rooms intolerable, but there is no
alternative. You are forced to eat
surrounded by a dozen strangers
after taking your place. Anyone
endowed with a modicum of good
manners won't get the dinner he's
paid for. The center of the table, near
what is referred to as the pièces de
résistance, or the meal's main dishes,
is occupied by habitués who seize
the available spaces and unleash a
stream of the day's gossip. Armed
with tireless jaws, they set to work
devouring at the first signal. Woe to
anyone who is slow to eat his meager
portion. In the midst of these
greedy, agile birds of prey, he'll fast
rather than feast."
Tableau de Paris (1781–1788)

JEAN ANTHELME BRILLAT-SAVARIN
Essayist on gastronomy
"By 1770, after the glorious reign
of Louis XIV, the debaucheries of
the Regency, and the long peaceful
ministry of Cardinal de Fleury [under
Louis XV], foreign visitors to Paris
had very little in the way of resources
available at a reasonable cost."
Physiologie du goût (*The Physiology
of Taste,* 1825)

skip to ....
Gastronomy or French
Decadence?, p. 16

Dumas's Dictionary

The best way to cook a piece of beef? Season a frog's-leg potage? Serve bear, shark, or elephant? The answers to all these questions, ranging from whimsical to earnest, can be found in *Le Grand Dictionnaire de Cuisine* by Alexandre Dumas. Let's explore this monument of gastronomic literature.

Estelle Lenartowicz

A selection (obviously subjective) of the 15 best definitions

Convinced that his culinary reputation would ultimately outstrip his literary renown, Alexandre Dumas (1802–1870) dedicated the last years of his life to the compilation of his delightful gastronomic treatise, the vast *Grand Dictionnaire de Cuisine* (1872). Comparable to the imposing scope of his oeuvre *The Three Musketeers* (1844), the work encompasses more than three thousand foods, spices, drinks, and recipes—everything that can, might, or conceivably could be eaten. Crammed with technical descriptions and personal anecdotes, and garnished with historical digressions of every kind, it is the most novelistic manual of cuisine ever written.

Bread
The most proverbial
"It's commonly said that bread must be a day old to be good to eat; that flour must be a month old to make dough; that grain must be a year old before being milled."

Cake
The most debatable
"The word for cake (*gâteau*) no doubt derives from the prodigality with which children are spoiled (*gâtés*) by adults handing out cakes as a gastronomic reward or inducement."

Turtle
The most heartless
"Tie the turtle to a ladder, and attach a 55-pound (25 kg) weight to the neck; using a heavy knife, cut off its head and allow it to bleed for five to six hours. Lay it down on its back on a table, detach the plastron from the shell, remove all the intestines, cut off the fins with their skin by pushing down your knife on the shell."

Truffle
The most reverent
"Herewith we arrive in the sanctum sanctorum of gastronomes, at that name that gourmands of every era have never uttered without a tip of the hat, to the *Tuber cibarium*, to the *Lycoperdon gulosorum*, to the truffle. . . . You have interrogated the truffle itself, and the truffle has answered: 'Eat me and praise the Lord.'"

Figs
The most anecdotal
"The nursery keeper of the Jardin des Plantes had ordered a simpleminded servant to take two beautiful fresh figs to the famed naturalist Buffon. En route, the servant succumbed to temptation and ate one of them. Buffon, aware that he should have received two figs, demanded the other one from the servant, who admitted his guilt. 'How could you have done this?' cried Buffon. Placing the remaining fig in his mouth, the servant swallowed and explained 'Like this!'"

Salmon
The most poetic
"They leave the sea in the spring to spawn, traveling in numerous schools. These nomads maintain a remarkable order, gathered in two lines that join as they move forward in a V-shaped formation. It's the same organization observed in migratory birds flying through the air. They usually climb slowly, as if at play; this raises a loud noise, but if they sense a threat, the eye cannot follow the speed with which they react. It is surpassed only by that of light. Neither seawalls, nor waterfalls can stop them. They fling their flanks on stones, arch their bodies powerfully, and violently struggling, project themselves into the air and hurl themselves over the obstacle. Thus they pass through the rivers, sometimes more than eight hundred leagues from the seacoast."

Baker, bakery
The most fortunate
"Saint Louis did yet more: he exempted bakers from military service, and this favor was all the more important in that, during wartime, all his subjects, unless beneficiaries of special privileges, were obliged to report to the army when so commanded by their lords."

Shark
The most honest
"For those who enjoy shark or who have contemplated sampling it, we recommend this recipe: [a shark croustade with the stomachs of young sharks] but admit in advance that we can express no opinion on these foods, never having sampled them and having no desire to do so."

Eagle
The most merciful
"The grandeur, nobility, and pride of this king of birds do not make for tender, delicately flavored flesh. Everyone knows that it is tough, stringy, and evil-tasting and was forbidden by Jewish law. Let us therefore allow him to soar and rival the sun, and avoid eating him."

Water
The most sober
"For the last fifty or sixty years of my life I have drunk nothing but water—never Grand-Laffite or Chambertin. Never have they offered the wine connoisseur the same delights as I have experienced drinking water from a cool spring whose purity is unmarred by any taint of earthy minerals."

Dinner
The most demanding
"A daily and vitally important activity that cannot be worthily accomplished except by men of intelligence: it does not suffice merely to eat at dinnertime; one must speak with a note of cheerfulness that is both subtle and serene. The conversation must sparkle as brightly as the ruby gleam of wines and ices; it must assume a delectable smoothness with dessert sweets and take on true depth with the coffee."

Swan
The most disagreeable
"The swan is a true anomaly in the eyes—or rather the ears—of ornithologists: naturalists have applied the name of *Cygnus musicus* to this creature. But anyone who has heard the famous swan's song will agree that it is the most disagreeable they've ever heard."

Burning
The most understanding
"Burning food is among the most frequent mishaps that can afflict a conscientious and practiced cook. We extract from Monsieur Lorrain's *Traité des préparations* instructions on recognized remedies as well as those likely to prevent future mishaps."

Salad
The most scientific
"The technique consists of saturating the salad with oil seasoned with salt and pepper before adding vinegar; these measures will produce a salad that is never too vinegary because the vinegar slips over each oil-coated leaf. Thus, even if too much vinegar has been added, as we all agree happens far too often, one will never have to repent because the vinegar will always collect at the bottom of the salad bowl where, as Monsieur Chaptal has so carefully demonstrated, it must end up by virtue of the laws of specific gravity pertaining to oil."

Bouillon
The most patriotic
"There is no good cooking without good bouillon; French gastronomy, the foremost of all cuisines, owes its superiority to the excellence of French bouillon."

GREEN PEAS À LA FRANÇAISE

Place 8 cups (2 L) of very small green peas in a pot with a bit of butter and water. Mix with the hands, empty out the water, and add a bouquet of parsley, a small onion, a lettuce heart, a pinch of salt, and a small spoonful of sugar. Cover the pot and cook for 30 minutes over low heat. Remove the parsley and the onion, arrange the lettuce on a plate, and thicken the peas with a generous pat of butter kneaded with a little flour. Sauté them on the stove until they are well mixed and turn them out on top of the lettuce. Or skip this step: fresh peas will thicken on their own.

Be careful: to prevent the peas from drying out during the cooking process, replace the pot lid with a plate heated with water. You can also make a similar preparation, but without the lettuce, and enrich the peas with egg yolks and a piece of fresh butter instead of the butter-flour mixture.

Arnaud Lallement* reveals the code
"I love green peas and their faintly acidic edge; this vegetable has everything, with a crunchy exterior and creamy center. Peas are versatile, and you can enjoy experimenting with them in innumerable recipes: whole, puréed, in a mousse, or a sauce. The color reminds me of summer and fresh vegetation.

"The modern cook's goal is to make dishes as light as possible while eliminating the superfluous. I'd prefer a reduction of baby peas to peas prepared with a roux. That gives the maximum concentration of flavors.

"For even more richness and body, you can cook the peas with some bacon or even carrots. The lettuce lends freshness to the peas. It's a trio that's always worked well together. You'll still find traditional peas à la française served today, because it's a dish that's never out of style. To my mind, there's no boundary between classic and contemporary cuisine.

"It's misguided to try to categorize cuisines this way. The essence of cooking is taste and pleasure, not passing fads."

Chef of l'Assiette Champenoise, Tinqueux (Marne)

OMELET WITH SHRIMP

Boil the shrimp until just cooked through, then clean and peel them. Take beaten eggs, season with salt and pepper, stir in your shrimp bisque, and cook the omelet as usual. Follow the same procedure for scrambled eggs with shrimp. If you happen to have some chicken bouillon, go ahead and combine it with the bisque. Then toss the bisque and shrimp all together with the beaten eggs (reserve 1 egg white for every 3 eggs) and stir and scramble your eggs as you would asparagus tips. You can also peel the cooked shrimp, crush and marinate them in oil and vinegar, and press them through a sieve. Take this cold preparation and pour it over salad leaves seasoned with salt and pepper.

Arnaud Lallement* reveals the code
"It's an appealing dish because Alexandre Dumas's omelet recipe is very ambitious. He could have just combined the eggs with the shrimp. Dumas clearly respected the flavor of the shrimp: you can really imagine the taste of them in your mouth. The unfortunate thing is that you lose the texture of the shrimp. There's just the taste. I wouldn't cook shrimp in salted white wine because I find it gives the shrimp that 'canned fish' taste. The secret of the omelet is controlling the cooking temperature, which has to be high enough for the eggs to coagulate slowly, without taking on color and overwhelming the flavor. The temperature has to be consistent throughout the omelet. This dish is often taken for granted, and that's regrettable. It can really be extremely good, but ultimately it's not easy to do right—it demands a certain savoir-faire."

Chef of l'Amphitryon, Lorient (Morbihan)

skip to
The Omelet, p. 90

Recipes from *Dico Dumas: le grand dictionnaire de cuisine*, Alexandre Dumas, preface by Pascal Ory, Menu Fretin (2008)

Phylloxera: Wine Enemy No. 1

In 1864, a devastating crisis struck French vineyards. Emanating from the United States, the insect known as phylloxera first attacked the Lirac region in Gard. Over the next 30 years, the ravages of this pest destroyed 6.1 million acres (2.5 million hectares) of vines.

Gwilherm de Cerval

DESTRUCTION DU PHYLLOXERA EN BOURGOGNE

Devant les autorités départementales et locales. — Dessin de P. Kauffmann.

WANTED

Name: Phylloxera
Family: Phylloxeridae
Genus: *Daktulosphaira vitifoliae*
Size: from 0.01 to 0.05 inch (0.3 to 1.4 mm)
Target of attacks: leaves and roots

THE TWO TYPES OF PHYLLOXERA

1. **Phylloxera gallicola:** feeds on leaves and produces a type of gall. Usually not seriously harmful to the plant.
2. **Phylloxera radicicola:** feeds on the roots of the grapevine and produces nodes and swellings. The plant dies within three years.

THE SOLUTION

Having unleashed this scourge in France, it was incumbent on the United States to provide the miracle cure. The solution: grafting American rootstocks that were more resistant to the pest onto European vines. Today, virtually all French vineyards have been treated in this way.

THE SURVIVORS

Vines that successfully resisted the phylloxera attack are rare these days. A few survivors are found from time to time scattered in parcels of various vineyards. These are vines so old that they have weathered at least 150 harvests. Here are two wines that Émile Zola might have sampled:
- Champagne Bollinger Grand Cru Cuvée "Vieilles Vignes Françaises"
- AOC Saint-Mont Cuvée "Vigne de la Ferme Pédebernade"

UNGRAFTED VINES

Although phylloxera still exist in wine-growing regions, these destructive pests cannot readily attack roots planted in sandy soils because the sand prevents the insects from digging their underground tunnels. In recent years, a few dedicated wine growers have experimented with replanting ungrafted vine stocks that are known as *francs de pied*. Here are our favorites:
- AOC Chinon red cuvée "Franc de pied" Domaine Bernard Baudry
- AOC Touraine red cuvée "Renaissance" Domaine Henry Marionnet
- AOC Bourgueil red cuvée "Franc de pied" Domaine Catherine et Pierre Breton
- AOC Pouilly Fumé white cuvée "Astéroïde" Domaine Didier Dagueneau
- AOC Montlouis-sur-Loire white cuvée "Les Bournais Francs de pied" Domaine François Chidaine

skip to
Natural Wine, p. 86;
The Wine of the Hanged, p. 160

Anchoiade

Whether spread on grilled bread or used to dip seasonal raw vegetables, this anchovy paste is *the* Provençal spread!

François-Régis Gaudry

ANCHOIADE OR QUICHÉ?

Originally, anchovies were pounded in a mortar with garlic, and the mixture was then blended with olive oil to make an **anchoiade**, which is an emulsion that one spreads on slices of bread toasted over a fire.

The *quiché* was its equivalent, yet not in a spread: whole anchovies were placed in a deep dish, garnished with garlic and olive oil, then placed on the bread and crushed with a fork.

THE RECIPE
*by Edouard Loubet**

To taste it is to yield to its addiction. Chef Loubet's secret: a touch of sugar, which changes everything!

PREPARATION TIME: 15 MINUTES
SERVES 4

½ onion
1 clove garlic
2 sprigs flat-leaf parsley
5 celery stalk leaves
½ teaspoon (2 g) sugar
9 ounces (250 g) anchovies in oil and salt
1⅓ cups (330 mL) olive oil

Peel the onion and garlic. Remove the germ from the center of the garlic clove. In a blender, blend the onion and garlic with the parsley, celery leaves, and sugar until smooth. Add the anchovies. Pour in the olive oil and blend to a creamy consistency. Add an ice cube to the blender, and blend again until smooth (this will help firm up the mixture). Transfer the mixture to a serving dish. An extra tip: drop a spoonful of anchoiade into a pan to deglaze it after cooking a steak.

Chef of Domaine de Capelongue in Bonnieux (Vaucluse)

ANCHOVY IN ALL ITS FORMS!

Engraulis encrasicolus is a fish of 2¾ to 8 inches (7 to 20 cm) in length, with a slender, silver-colored body with blue-green hues. When salted, it represents a source of important proteins for every age. Here are some of its variations.

The sausson: a sauce from Var made with anchovies, almonds, fresh fennel, mint, and olive oil.

Provençal mustard: crushed, cooked garlic with anchovies, to accompany leg of lamb.

The pissalat: from Niçois meaning *peis salat* ("salted fish"), this Niçoise sauce is prepared with fermented anchovy larvae (see Pissaladière and Company, page 192). The *melet* is its equivalent in Martigues and the west side of the Mediterranean.

La bagna cauda: a fondue enjoyed by the Niçois, borrowed from the Piedmontese. It consists of a hot sauce with anchovies, garlic, and olive oil, in which raw vegetables are dipped.

Anchovies à la bastiaise: anchovies in olive oil, garnished with garlic and parsley.

THE ANCHOVIES OF COLLIOURE

This small Mediterranean fishing port of the Côte Vermeille (Pyrénées-Orientales) has made this silver fish its specialty. Whether in a brine, oil, or salt, it is protected by a PGI (Protected Geographical Indication).

skip to
Olive Oil, Liquid Gold, p. 207

Cheeses and Wines, Our Aged Friends

Let's end that common pairing of Bordeaux red wine and Camembert. With a few exceptions, it is more accepted to pair a white wine with cheese, and AOP cheeses are often produced in wine-growing regions. Enjoy!

Gwilherm de Cerval

Crottin de Chavignol
Type: soft-ripened, crumbly
Milk: goat
Flavors: floral
Aging: from 10 days to 2½ months

White Sancerre
Region: Loire Valley
Grape: Sauvignon
Flavors: floral
Serving temperature: 50°F to 54°F (10°C to 12°C)
A producer: Romain Dubois
A vintage: White Sancerre "Harmony," Domaine Vincent Pinard

➡ **The pairing:** the floury texture of a young Crottin de Chavignol has a tendency to coat your gums. When it is paired with a recent vintage of this wine, the wine rinses your palate thanks to its liveliness.

Camembert de Normandie
Type: soft cheese with a floral rind
Milk: cow
Flavors: fruity
Aging: minimum 21 days

Dry (Brut) Cider
Region: Normandy
Fruit: apple
Flavors: fruity
Serving temperature: 50°F to 54°F (10°C to 12°C)
A producer: Patrick Mercier Domaine Éric Bordelet
A vintage: Sydre brut "Argelette"

➡ **The pairing:** the longer Camembert is aged, the more fluid its interior becomes. The light bubbles of this winelike cider wash your mouth, leaving you with beautiful fruity aromas.

Munster
Type: soft cheese with a washed rind
Milk: cow
Flavors: spicy
Aging: minimum 21 days

Gewürztraminer
Region: Alsace
Grape: Gewürztraminer
Flavors: exotic fruits
Serving temperature: 50°F to 54°F (10°C to 12°C)
A producer: Hubert Pierrevelcin
A vintage: Gewurztraminer "Tradition," Domaine Albert Mann

➡ **The pairing:** with a soft interior and a salty and oozing rind, this cheese displays character and length in the mouth. The slight residual sugar of this wine tempers the power of the cheese and cleanses your mouth with the freshness of its exotic notes.

Brocciu
Type: fresh
Milk: sheep and/or goat
Flavors: floral
Aging: from 2 days to more than 21 days

Ajaccio white
Region: Corsica
Grape: Vermentinu
Flavors: floral
Serving temperature: 50°F to 54°F (10°C to 12°C)
A producer: Mireille and Jean-André Mameli
A vintage: Ajaccio white "Granite," Domaine de Vaccelli

➡ **The pairing:** when fresh, brocciu has a supple and creamy texture with a sweet and milky scent. This Corsican wine, with its aromas of hawthorn and delicate spices, does not overwhelm the palate, and accompanies the cheese perfectly thanks to its fresh and salivating finish.

Ossau-Iraty
Type: uncooked pressed interior
Milk: sheep
Flavors: dried fruits
Aging: from 80 days to 12 months

Irouléguy
Region: southwest France
Grapes: Gros Manseng, Petit Manseng, and Petit Courbu
Flavors: exotic fruits
Serving temperature: 50°F to 54°F (10°C to 12°C)
A producer: Manu and Marion Ossiniri
A vintage: Irouléguy white "Hegoxuri," Domaine Arretxea

➡ **The pairing:** aged for several months, Ossau-Iraty adopts a fairly brittle texture with flavors of hazelnut. The rich and plump wine complements the creaminess of the cheese with its sweet scent of exotic fruits.

Abondance
Type: cooked pressed interior
Milk: cow
Flavors: herbaceous
Aging: more than 100 days

Roussette de Savoie
Region: Savoie
Grape: Roussette
Flavors: citrus
Serving temperature: 50°F to 54°F (10°C to 12°C)
A producer: Patrick Charvet
A vintage: Roussette de Savoie blanc "El Hem," Domaine Gilles Berlioz

➡ **The pairing:** when young, Abondance reveals aromas of grass and barnyard. Its texture, both firm and melting on the palate, blends perfectly with the roundness and vivacity of this wine.

Roquefort
Type: blue-veined interior
Milk: sheep
Flavors: humus
Aging: minimum 3 months

Maury red
Region: Languedoc-Roussillon
Grapes: Black Grenache and Carignan
Flavors: cocoa
Serving temperature: 61°F to 64°F (16°C to 18°C)
A producer: Yves Combes
A vintage: A red Maury "Op. Nord," Domaine les Terres de Fagayra

➡ **The pairing:** with a crumbly and creamy texture, Roquefort is a powerful cheese. The tannins and sugars brought by this wine soften the cheese's strong character.

Saint-Nectaire
Type: uncooked pressed interior
Milk: cow
Flavors: earthy
Aging: minimum 28 days

Côte Roannaise red
Region: Auvergne
Grape: Gamay Saint-Romain
Flavors: spicy
Serving temperature: 61°F to 64°F (16°C to 18°C)
A producer: Chassard family
A vintage: Red Côte Roanne "Clos du Puy," Domaine des Pothiers

➡ **The pairing:** Saint-Nectaire is rather soft and mellow in the mouth. The structure of the rind, with its earthy texture and aromas, is very supportive of the Gamay's delicate tannins, which are slightly refined by oak.

Comté
Type: cooked pressed interior
Milk: cow
Flavors: hazelnut
Aging: from 4 to 41 months
An Affineur: Marcel Petite

Arbois
Region: Jura
Grape: Chardonnay
Flavors: walnuts
Serving temperature: 50°F to 54°F (10°C to 12°C)
A vintage: White Arbois "Les Bruyères," Domaine Stéphane Tissot

➡ **The pairing:** when young, Comté reveals floral and fruity aromas. When aged for several months, the texture becomes granular and takes on roasted and hazelnut flavors. The mild oxidation of this wine will perfectly accompany the aromas of the cheese.

Époisses
Type: soft cheese with a washed rind
Milk: cow
Flavors: undergrowth
Aging: 6 to 8 weeks

Burgundy Côtes d'Auxerre white
Region: Burgundy
Grape: Chardonnay
Flavors: florals
Serving temperature: 50°F to 54°F (10°C to 12°C)
A producer: Alain and Caroline Bartkowiez
A vintage: Burgundy Côtes d'Auxerre white, Domaine Goisot

➡ **The pairing:** with a creamy and smooth texture, Époisses is less strong than its smell might suggest. This lively and salivating wine, with aromas of undergrowth, will comfortably rinse your palate.

skip to .... A *Tour de France*—Cheese, p. 200

Mad for Meringues

Its silky and billowy texture calls out to the palates of all gourmands. And there are three types to enjoy: French, Italian, or Swiss.

Marie-Laure Fréchet

French Meringue

CRUNCHY AND TENDER

This is the simplest of the meringues. Sugar is beaten into the egg whites at double the weight of the egg whites. Superfine sugar is used, or a mixture of an equal quantity of superfine sugar and confectioners' sugar. Start by beating the whites on low speed, and when they become foamy, gradually start adding the sugar while beating them at the highest speed. The meringues are then piped or spooned out and baked at between 212°F and 250°F (100°C to 120°C) for 1 hour and 15 minutes to 2 hours, depending on their size; this is a drying process, not a cooking process. They can also be baked for 20 minutes at 325°F (170°C), then for 2 hours at 275°F (140°C). Baked in this way, the sugar in the meringue caramelizes slightly. The meringues develop some color and become richer in flavor. This is the Botterens method of making meringues, from the Botterens bakery in Switzerland.

> *"There is not a single reunion where each guest can resist biting into several, as these kinds of cakes are the jewels of ladies, and gourmands make a pleasing homage to them."*
>
> **Antonin Carême**

THE ETYMOLOGY

The term is one of the known culinary enigmas. Neither the Swiss theory (from Meiringen, the city of pastry chef Gasparini, who served this dessert in 1720 to Marie Leszczyńska, future wife of Louis XV) nor the Polish theory (from *murzynka*, "negress," which designates a chocolate meringue) have convinced the academicians of its origins.

THE HISTORY

The principle of the snowlike texture that is obtained by beating egg whites seems to have been discovered as early as the sixth century by the Byzantine doctor Anthime. But it was not until the Renaissance in France that it developed interest for culinary use. In 1651, in *Cuisinier François*, La Varenne gives the recipe for a meringue and "sugar cakes in snow," according to a technique close to that of Italian meringue. Queen Marie Antoinette was attempting to make a vacherin at the Petit Trianon. The meringue was simply spooned at that time, and it was Antonin Carême who had the idea to pipe it. His "Parisian meringues" were flavored with rose or Seville orange and sprinkled with pistachios.

As the egg whites foam, the albumin of the egg traps air bubbles. When cooked, these air bubbles expand under the influence of heat up to 284°F (140°C). Beyond that, they coagulate and harden, which has the effect of definitively setting the volume of the meringue.

THE TECHNIQUE

Egg whites and sugar are whipped cold or warm, depending on their use.

In the French meringue family

Pavlova: a crown of meringue adorned with whipped cream and fresh fruit. It was created during Russian ballerina Anna Matveïevna Pavlova's tour of Australia and New Zealand in the 1920s. Both countries claim its origination, but evidence seems to point to New Zealand ancestry.

Vacherin: a cold dessert consisting of stacks of meringue filled with ice cream or sorbet and decorated with whipped cream. Its name comes from its resemblance to the cheese of the same name.

Tête-de-nègre: a meringue ball topped with chocolate buttercream and covered with chocolate vermicelli. It is also seen under the more politically correct name Othello.

Île flottante: meringues cooked in a bain-marie in a mold, then dusted with sugar and surrounded with crème anglaise.

Merveilleux: two meringue disks separated by a layer of whipped cream, topped with more whipped cream, and covered with chocolate shavings. A traditional pastry from Belgium and northern France.

Oeufs à la neige: egg whites are beaten with sugar (equal parts superfine and confectioners' sugar), then poached in simmering water or in milk (it also works very well in the microwave). They are served with a crème anglaise made with egg yolks.

Dacquoise: a French meringue to which hazelnut or almond flour is added. Its batter is very similar to that of macarons, and is used to make a Progrès, a cake topped with buttercream flavored with coffee, praline, or chocolate, or a Succès, a similar cake created by Lenôtre, topped with a crunchy nougatine cream.

Italian Meringue

SILKY

Made with a sugar syrup. Between 1 ounce (30 g) and 1¾ ounces (50 g) of sugar per egg white. The sugar is boiled to between 244°F and 248°F (118°C and 120°C), then gradually poured into the egg whites while beating them, and continuing to beat them until the meringue has cooled. This meringue does not need to be baked. It can be browned under the oven broiler or using a blowtorch.

The Italian meringue family

Tarte au citron meringuée (Lemon meringue tart): the gourmet version of a pastry classic.

Polonaise: a Parisian brioche soaked in a rum or kirsch syrup, filled in the center with a pastry cream and covered with Italian meringue, then sprinkled with sliced almonds.

Chiboust cream: a mixture of pastry cream and Italian meringue. This is the cream used to fill the Saint-Honoré cake. It was invented by the pastry chef of Maison Chiboust, in Paris, around 1850.

Omelette norvégienne (Norwegian omelet): a dessert consisting of a génoise sponge cake and vanilla ice cream, covered completely in Italian meringue, browned in the oven, then finally flambéed at the table. It was created thanks to physicist Benjamin Thompson, Earl of Rumford, who demonstrated that egg whites do not conduct heat. His work inspired the chef of the Grand Hôtel de Paris during the 1867 World's Fair, who created this dessert as a tribute to science.

Swiss Meringue

BRITTLE

Egg whites and confectioners' sugar are beaten in a bain-marie until thickened. When the mixture reaches 122°F (50°C), it is beaten off the heat until completely cooled. This creates a smooth and shiny appearance. It is then baked for 30 minutes to 1 hour (depending on the size of the pieces) at 212°F (100°C).

In the Swiss meringue family

Meringue de boulangerie: plain or tinted, a timeless classic found in the windows of most boulangeries.

Champignons: piped meringue mushrooms for yule logs.

A VEGAN MERINGUE?

It's possible!

This technique is revolutionary for vegans. You can make incredible meringues using the cooking liquid of chickpeas. Like egg whites, chickpea liquid contains about 10 percent protein (vegetable) and about 90 percent water. This discovery was made in 2014 by Joël Roessel, a French tenor by profession and author of the blog revolutionvegetale.com, then passed on to an American foodie, Goose Wohlt, who christened the liquid "aquafaba" (literally "bean water"). Since then, the recipe has traveled the globe.

NORWEGIAN OMELET

PREPARATION TIME: 30 MINUTES
COOKING TIME: 5 MINUTES
SERVES 6

1 génoise sponge cake, preferably homemade
1 quart (1 L) vanilla ice cream
For the syrup
⅓ cup plus 1 tablespoon (100 mL) water
¼ cup plus 3 tablespoons (90 g) superfine sugar
2 tablespoons (30 mL) Grand Marnier orange liqueur
For the Italian meringue
½ cup (120 mL) water
1½ cups (300 g) superfine sugar
6 large (180 g) egg whites

Make the syrup by boiling together the water and sugar. Off the heat, add the Grand Marnier. Trim the sponge cake into the shape of a rectangle. Brush the cake thoroughly with the syrup. Spread the ice cream over the cake so that it matches the shape of the cake. Store in the freezer.

Make the Italian meringue: Place the water and sugar in a saucepan. Bring to a boil without stirring, and cook until the syrup reaches between 212°F and 250°F/100°C to 120°C (measure the temperature using a sugar thermometer or use the ball technique). While the syrup is cooking, begin beating the egg whites. When the syrup reaches the correct temperature, pour it into the egg whites while continuing to beat them; continue beating the meringue until cooled. Take the ice cream cake out of the freezer. Preheat the oven to 475°F (240°C). Using a spatula, cover the cake completely with the Italian meringue, then use a piping bag to pipe some of the meringue into a weave design. Bake just until the meringue is lightly browned. Out of the oven, you can flambé the dessert with 1 tablespoon (20 mL) of heated Grand Marnier.

skip to
Mont Lozère with Honey and Chestnuts, p. 311

LE MERVEILLEUX

PREPARATION TIME: 1 HOUR
RESTING TIME: AT LEAST 3 HOURS
COOKING TIME: 2 HOURS
FOR A GRAND OCCASION

5 large (150 g) egg whites
¾ cup (150 g) superfine sugar
1 cup (200 g) confectioners' sugar, sifted
1 vanilla bean
2 cups (500 mL) whipping cream
1 small bar chocolate (dark or white), for grating

Beat the egg whites until foamy, then gradually add the superfine sugar until stiff peaks are formed. Using a spatula, carefully fold in ¾ cup (150 g) of the confectioners' sugar. Using a piping bag without a piping tube, pipe two disks measuring 8 to 9¾ inches (20 to 25 cm) in diameter onto two baking sheets (one on each baking sheet) lined with parchment paper, starting at the center and continuing outward in a spiral. Preheat the oven to 212°F (100°C), and bake the disks for 2 hours. Let cool completely. Split the vanilla bean lengthwise in half and scrape out the seeds. Whip the cream with the vanilla bean seeds and the remaining confectioners' sugar. Spread a layer of the whipped cream onto the first cooled meringue disk. Place the second meringue disk on top, and spread a layer of the whipped cream on top. Cover the entire cake with the remaining whipped cream. Grate the chocolate bar to create chocolate shavings or curls, and sprinkle them on top of the cake. Refrigerate the cake for at least 3 hours, or until completely chilled.

Note: this dessert can also be made into individual 3-inch (8 cm) cakes.

Singing the Praises of the Moussette

No need to open your *Petit Robert* French dictionary—the term *moussette* does not appear there. Only a small population of Norman and Breton eaters revel in this ultraconfidential pleasure: a young spider crab with an extraordinary taste. Oh my, how good it is!

François-Régis Gaudry

WHAT IS IT?

Also known as a "moss crab," this animal was long considered its own species. However, the scientific reality is quite different: the moss crab is just the juvenile form of *Maja brachydactyla*, the Atlantic spider crab. (Since 2008, it has been distinguished from its sister in the Mediterranean, *Maja squinado*.) This youngster crab is under 2 years old, while the adult spider crab can live for up to 8 years. It is referred to as the "moss crab" because it is covered in fuzz and the ends of its hind legs remain soft.

WHERE DOES IT LIVE?

Spider crabs thrive in the North Atlantic, where they live in waters up to 390 feet (120 m) deep. In the spring, babies migrate en masse to coasts, bays, or estuaries with sandy-muddy bottoms at depths of 0 to 65 feet (0 to 20 m). These nurseries are located in Manche-Ouest, in the bay of Saint-Brieuc, and on the west coast of Cotentin.

HOW DO YOU FISH THEM?

The two most commonly practiced techniques are underwater fishing and boat-trap fishing. The fishing season is very short: it varies from early April to early June and depends heavily on weather conditions.

WHERE DO YOU BUY THEM?

Out of the bottom of boats on the port of Grandville, in the markets of Cotentin, and in some fish markets in Honfleur, Deauville, and Paris. But its consumption remains seasonal and very localized. Its price is particularly cheap: between €5 and €11 ($6 and $13) per pound (½ kg), according to the quantity fished that season. Compared to the lobster, which can be priced around €30 ($35) per pound (½ kg), that's a bargain! If you are in Gouville-sur-Mer (Manche), fishmonger Laurent

Macé is recommended. He also comes to the market at Place Sainte-Catherine in Honfleur (Calvados) on Saturday mornings: 02-33-47-86-13 and 06-84-37-44-12.

WHAT FLAVOR DOES IT HAVE?

The moss crab is renowned for the delicacy and tenderness of its meat. It is slightly salty and sweeter than the meat of adult spider crabs.

HOW DO YOU PREPARE IT?

You can't go wrong if you follow the advice of Philippe Hardy, chef of Le Mascaret,* who prepares it in the simplest way: "They are immersed in a large pot of unsalted cold water, then, when the water just begins to barely simmer, they are cooked for 7 to 10 minutes. They are then cooled and are eaten at room temperature with a good homemade mayo."

Le Mascaret, 1, rue de Bas, Blainville-sur-Mer (Channel), 02 33 45 86 09

DO THEY KEEP?

Restaurant La Poissonnade* in Cherbourg offers this advice: "Once cooked, drain them. Dip a tea towel into the cooking liquid. Spread out the towel onto a work surface and place the crab on it and wrap it up. Place the entire thing into a plastic bag and tightly seal it. Let cool, then place it in the fridge as is. In this way, you can keep your moss crab fresh for 2 to 3 days!"

La Poissonnade, 10, Grande Rue, Cherbourg (Manche)

THE TASTING: A TRUE RITUAL!

1

You need one moss crab per person, at a minimum. Perhaps two or three per person if it is a main course.

2

Using a crab cracker is forbidden! The shell and cartilage are not too hard. You only need to use your hands when pulling it apart.

3

Begin with the ten legs: break them at the joints, pull and—a miracle! What is revealed is a lightly sweet whitish flesh that you then dip in mayonnaise. So easy!

4

Continue on to the body shell: the lower part of the body separates very easily from the top. Discard the brown parts of the head (although some love to eat these!), then dig into the bowels of the beast. Here you'll find some unexpected pieces of meat to enjoy.

The Cuisine of Statesmen

Important political figures very often boast refined palates. Some have actually inspired recipes, many of which have faded into oblivion. Let's return to a few of those dishes rescued from the politico-cultural archives.

Camille Pierrard

Henri IV's chicken in every pot

A little history: as related by Hardouin de Péréfixe, the private tutor of Louis XIV, in his 1661 *Histoire du roy Henry le Grand*, Henri IV once declared to the Duke de Savoie: "If God grants me life, I will see to it that there will be no laborer in all my kingdom without the means to have a chicken in his pot." Emblematic of societal well-being and integral to the legend of "Good King Henri," the chicken in every pot was promised anew by Louis XVIII during the Restoration.
Legacy: a founding myth of the French culinary and political collective imagination.

Sauce Soubise

A little history: Charles de Rohan, Prince of Soubise, maréchal and minister of Louis XV and subsequently of Louis XVI, was the inspiration for a sauce made of puréed onions, akin to a coulis. In the early twentieth century, Auguste Escoffier codified the recipe, suggesting it as a particularly happy accompaniment for poached or coddled eggs and roasts.
Legacy: continues to hold an honored place in the sometimes slightly dusty pantheon of traditional sauces.

Senator Couteaux's hare à la royale

A little history: in 1898, Senator Aristide Couteaux published his recipe for hare simmered in wine with 40 cloves of garlic and 60 shallots. The senator thus entered into a rivalry with Antonin Carême, who had published his own recipe for hare à la royale embellished with foie gras in the late eighteenth century. It was subsequently codified by Henri Babinski.
Legacy: minimal, aside from a few factional squabbles.

Le poulet Gaston Gérard

A little history: invented on the occasion of a dinner held in 1930 in honor of the famed gastronomic pundit Maurice Curnonsky, this recipe, like so many others, is the fruit of serendipity. Rose Geneviève Bourgogne, wife of Gaston Gérard, mayor of Dijon, accidentally spilled paprika in the dish of chicken in mustard sauce that she was preparing. In an effort to rectify this mistake, she added grated Comté cheese, crème fraîche, and white wine.
Legacy: unfairly enough, it's the cook's husband who's commemorated in the name of the dish.

"Soupe VGE"

A little history: this soup, concocted from black truffles and foie gras simmering beneath a thin layer of puff pastry, was created by Paul Bocuse in 1975. The occasion? A banquet organized by Valéry Giscard d'Estaing in honor of the chef's elevation to the rank of Chevalier de la Légion d'Honneur.
Legacy: a monument to the opulent cuisine of the Fifth Republic, along with the songbirds known as ortolans and tête de veau, a rich veal dish.

GASTON GÉRARD'S CHICKEN

PREPARATION TIME: 30 MINUTES
COOKING TIME: 50 MINUTES
SERVES 6
1 Bresse chicken (about 3⅓ lb/1.5 kg)
3 tablespoons (50 g) unsalted butter
Salt and freshly ground black pepper
1 tablespoon (7 g) paprika
⅓ cup plus 1 tablespoon (100 mL) very dry white wine
5¼ ounces (150 g) grated Comté cheese, plus more for sprinkling
14 ounces (400 g) crème fraîche
1 tablespoon (15 mL) Dijon mustard
3 tablespoons (21 g) bread crumbs

Cut up the chicken and remove the bones. In a casserole dish, heat the butter and brown the chicken pieces on both sides. Season with salt and pepper, and add the paprika. Cover and cook over low heat for about 30 minutes. Remove the chicken pieces from the casserole dish and place them in a baking dish. Preheat the oven to 350°F (180°C). Add the white wine to the cooking juices in the casserole dish, then the grated cheese. Stir to gently melt the cheese. Stir in the crème fraiche, then stir in the mustard. Bring to a boil and pour the sauce over the chicken. Sprinkle the top of the chicken pieces with the bread crumbs and a little Comté. Bake for several minutes, or until the chicken is cooked through.

Commemoratively named dishes by Auguste Escoffier

Peach Melba, Pommes de Terre Mireille, Mornay Sauce . . . the king of chefs paid homage to a bevy of celebrities by naming dishes in their honor. Statesmen are not without rivals in the realm of cuisine.

GARNITURE RICHELIEU
Intended to accompany roasts, it combines stuffed tomatoes, mushrooms, braised lettuce, and potatoes. In a Garniture Richelieu, "tomato is rigueur; it represents the cardinal's cap."
(*Ma Cuisine*, 1934)

CHICKEN BREAST OR TOURNEDOS HENRI IV
These dishes share a distinctive garnish of artichoke hearts and small browned potatoes served with béarnaise sauce.

BEURRE COLBERT
Bearing the name of Louis XIV's celebrated minister, the recipe calls for adding meat glaze to maître d'hôtel butter. Colbert's name is also attached to a breaded and fried fish preparation, as well as a clear chicken consommé with poached eggs and spring vegetables.

EGGS, TIMBALE DE CANETON, AND ENTRECOTE MIRABEAU
Anchovies, olives, tarragon, and/or truffles are the distinctive features of the egg, duckling, and steak dishes named after this revolutionary figure.

SADDLE OF VEAL, ROAST CHICKEN, AND FILLET OF SOLE À LA TALLEYRAND
The distinguishing feature of the many specialties named for this expert negotiator at the Congress of Vienna (1815) is a side dish of pasta, grated Parmesan, diced foie gras, and sliced or slivered truffle.

SOUP OR LAKE TROUT CAMBACÉRÈS
These shrimp dishes bear the name of the arch-chancellor of the First Empire, a gastronome acclaimed for his splendid table. Escoffier also used his name for a timbale of foie gras served with truffle purée.

Noire de Caromb
Fruit 2x/year • Taste quality: ✹✹
Uses: fresh; in jam

Negronne
Fruit 2x/year • Taste quality: ✹✹
Uses: fresh; in jam; dried

Sultane
Fruit 2x/year • Taste quality: ✹
Uses: fresh; in jam

Ronde de Bordeaux
(Round of Bordeaux) ♥
Fruit 1x/year • Taste quality: ✹✹✹
Uses: fresh; in jam; dried

Pastilière
Fruit 1x/year • Taste quality: ✹✹
Use: fresh

Col de Dame Noir ♥
Fruit 1x/year • Taste quality: ✹✹✹
Uses: fresh; in jam; dried

Doree
Fruit 2x/year • Taste quality: ✹✹
Uses: fresh; in jam

Longue d'Août
Fruit 2x/year • Taste quality: ✹
Use: fresh

Dauphine
Fruit 2x/year • Taste quality: ✹✹
Uses: fresh; in jam

Violette de Sollies
(Bourjassotte Noir)
Fruit 1x/year • Taste quality: ✹✹
Uses: fresh; in jam

Madeleine des Deux Saisons
Fruit 2x/year • Taste quality: ✹✹
Uses: fresh; in jam

Alma
Fruit 1x/year • Taste quality: ✹✹✹
Uses: fresh; in jam

> ♥ **Pierre Baud's favorites**
>
> **HARVEST**
> **Fruit 1x/year:** a harvest at the end of summer
> **Fruit 2x/year:** two harvests, one at the beginning of summer (figs-flowers), and a second at the end of summer or early autumn
>
> **TASTING QUALITY**
> Good: ✹
> Very good: ✹✹
> Excellent: ✹✹✹

Grise de Saint-Jean
Fruit 2x/year • Taste quality: ✹✹
Uses: fresh; in jam; dried

Cendrosa
Fruit 1x/year • Taste quality: ✹✹✹
Uses: fresh; in jam

Dalmatie
Fruit 2x/year • Taste quality: ✹✹
Uses: fresh; in jam

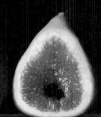

Blanche
Fruit 2x/year • Taste quality: ✹✹
Uses: fresh; in jam; dried

Col de Dame Blanc
Fruit 1x/year • Taste quality: ✹✹✹
Uses: fresh; in jam; dried

Verdal ♥
Fruit 1x/year • Taste quality: ✹✹✹
Uses: fresh; in jam; dried

Tena
Fruit 2x/year • Taste quality: ✹✹
Uses: fresh; in jam; dried

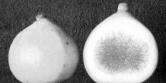

Figue de Marseille ♥
Fruit 2x/year • Taste quality: ✹✹✹
Uses: fresh; in jam; dried

Marseillaise
Fruit 1x/year • Taste quality: ✹✹
Uses: fresh; in jam; dried

Panachée ♥
Fruit 1x/year • Taste quality: ✹✹
Uses: fresh; in jam.

Figs, Little Sweet Bombs

Ah! Nothing is better than nap time in the shade provided by the broad leaves of a fig tree, with its fresh and delicate scent . . . Originally from Asia Minor, the fig tree has flourished in the Mediterranean sun since the Tertiary period. France warmly welcomed it, for both botanical and culinary reasons.

François–Régis Gaudry

A TASTING LESSON

In Provençal orchards, it is often said that "For a fig to be 'candylike,' it must have its head bowed, its 'dress' torn, and a tear in its eye!" It is said, moreover, that a fig "weeps" or "makes a pearl." These are the characteristics of an overripe fig—a real treat, but one that is too short-lived for a someone to experience who lives far from the orchards of the countryside, where fresh figs right off the trees are readily available. The skin of the fig, usually untreated with chemicals, can also be eaten! If the outer skin is too elastic, however, you can use a kitchen knife to make two cross cuts across the top to create four flaps that are gently pulled back toward the eye (the ostiole) of the fruit.

A BOTANICAL MIRACLE

The fig tree, or *Ficus carica*, belongs to the Moraceae family, like the mulberry tree. This tree lives in symbiosis with the insect that pollinates it. The flowers are male or female and are numerous and enclosed in a fleshy receptacle. André Gide explained it in *Les Nourritures terrestres*: "Its flower is folded, as if in a closed room where the wedding is celebrated." The fig is not a fruit, strictly speaking, but instead an "envelope" that contains a multitude of fruits. The achenes (seeds), which crunch when eaten, are, in a botanical sense, many fruits of the fig tree. Thus, starting out as a kind of "bouquet" of flowers, the fig eventually develops into a "basket" of fruit.

The Profession of Cultivating Figs

Arborist, nurseryman, and fig grower **Pierre Baud** cultivates, through organic farming, **more than 300 varieties of figs in his orchard** in Le Palis, near Vaison-La-Romaine (Vaucluse). The 22 varieties of figs (opposite) are from his orchard.

skip to ....
Dumas's Dictionary, p. 230

CANISTRELLI (FIG COOKIES)
by *Denise Solier-Gaudry*

MAKES ABOUT 40 COOKIES

5 cups (500 g) all-purpose flour
¾ cup plus 2 tablespoons (180 g) granulated sugar
¾ cup (180 mL) sunflower oil or a very sweet olive oil
¾ cup (180 mL) hot, but not boiling, white wine
12 dried figs, cut into cubes
1 packet (8 g) active dry yeast
Salt

Preheat the oven to 400°F (200°C). In a bowl, combine all the ingredients to form a smooth dough (do not overwork the dough; it should be soft and not stick to the fingers). Divide the dough into narrow rectangular strips, then shape them with your hands so that they are all equal in width. Using a knife or a rolling cutter, cut crosswise into rectangles measuring 1⅛ to 1½ inches (3 to 4 cm) in length. Using a spatula, transfer the rectangles to a parchment-lined baking sheet and bake for about 15 minutes, or until golden. Check the cookies while they are baking to ensure they are not overbrowning.

FIG ANCHOIADE

Incorporating sugar, the scent of fig, salt, and the slight bitterness of anchovies, this recipe offers unusual and surprising flavors!

1 large clove garlic
12 to 14 ounces (350 to 400 g) ripe figs
6 anchovies, in oil
10 capers
1 drizzle olive oil

Blanch the garlic clove for 2 minutes in its skin. Peel the figs. In a blender, blend the anchovies and capers together for a few seconds. In a mortar, mash together the fig pulp, the anchovies and capers mixture, and the blanched garlic (discard the peel). While stirring, gradually add a drizzle of olive oil until a smooth paste is achieved. Serve as a spread with toasted bread.

3 GOURMET IDEAS FROM D'ALAIN PASSARD*

Fig gratin with cinnamon
Grease a baking dish with butter, and cover the bottom with slices of peeled figs, about ½ inch (1.5 cm) thick. Place them together snugly, but without overlapping. Sprinkle them with coarse sugar, then grate some cinnamon over them. Distribute small pieces of butter on top, and place under the oven broiler for 6 to 7 minutes. Serve with a side of heavy cream for drizzling.

Fig caviar
In a skillet, heat 1 tablespoon (15 mL) of olive oil. Add 4 small sliced white onions, 3 medium tomatoes (seeded and peeled), and 8 to 10 peeled figs. Let cook gently in the pan for 25 to 30 minutes. Let cool, then blend the mixture in a blender while gradually adding ¼ cup (60 mL) of olive or peanut oil that has been briefly infused (through a cold infusion) with half a chile pepper. Season with salt and pepper, then squeeze in a little fresh lemon juice. Enjoy this caviar with hot toasted bread and a very chilled dry white wine.

Figs coated with sesame seeds
Peel a large quantity of figs, dip them in 1 lightly beaten egg, then dredge them in a plate of white sesame seeds. Over low heat, melt some salted butter until foamy, then fry the figs for 40 minutes, turning them over continuously. Roll in coarse sugar, and serve with a quenelle of vanilla ice cream.

Chef at l'Arpège, 84, rue de Varenne, Paris 7th

It's "mi-figue, mi-raisin"

This expression appeared **in 1487** among **Venetian merchants** who imported parcels of grapes from Corinth, and who uncovered the fraudulent practice of sellers **mixing grapes with dried figs** in order to make their parcels cost them less. According to *Le Petit Robert*, the French expression *mi-figue, mi-raisin* ("half fig, half grape") means **"both satisfactory and dissatisfactory at the same time."**

The Club des Cent

The Club des Cent (Club of One Hundred) is Paris' most gourmet private club. Its members, selected from the upper crust of finance, industry, and media, come together every week to honor their love of gastronomy together. What do we know about this brotherhood of dining?

Estelle Lenartowicz

THE CLUB'S BEGINNINGS

"You have to be someone who can eat on the run, but is then overtaken by an expert's enjoyment of good, fine food."

Louis Forest

Founded in January 1912 by the liberal Dreyfus supporter and journalist Louis Forest, the club brought together a handful of notables who crisscrossed the country by car to seek out quality inns and restaurants. The gastro-nomads were committed to sharing their best addresses: "We would like to compile the full list of the lone good inns, the lone and especially French establishments where very good things can be eaten on clean dishes and white tablecloths," Forest stated in a members' letter.

The club's founding was also tinted by strong nationalism on the eve of World War I: to defend French excellence was to poke at the great German rival!

THE PRINCIPLES

→ Promotion of French gastronomy via its influential members
→ Spirit of camaraderie and the art of conversation
→ Goodbye to snobbery

THE SACROSANCT THURSDAY LUNCH

The lunch takes place from 12:40 p.m. to 2:30 p.m. exactly, most often in a restaurant, almost always in Paris or its immediate outskirts. Each person pays his own bill, between 70 and 150 euros (80 and 115 dollars).

The club is never fully attended and depends on what the restaurant can accommodate.

At the helm, a member designated as brigadier is responsible for choosing the location, the menu, and the selection of wines.

Each meal is followed by a critique, "accurate and sharp," which is launched by a dinner guest selected

Curnonsky, in good company

HOW DOES ONE BECOME A MEMBER?

Submit an application form with the support of two official members. And you have to have the necessary profile requirements! The Club recruits members who vary in age, experience, and interest. For the moment, no candidates between the age of forty-five and sixty-five and no doctors.

The exam, a particularly selective step: nine out of ten candidates fail. Sample questions include: Do you prefer Bordeaux or Burgundy wines? What distinction do you make between a gourmet meal and a gourmand meal? Tell us about your last very good meal. Which bean must you chose for mutton with beans? What is *zist*? What wine should be served with asparagus? Which poet from the early twentieth century made a good *tête de veau*? What do you call the flat little fish, similar to sole, that is fished from Aquitaine waters?

A training period, which can last between a few weeks and a few years, until a full membership position becomes available.

Induction, in which each member (known as a *centiste* in French) is given a number. Except in very rare cases, one is a member for life.

in advance. Every year, a prize for criticism and presentation is awarded to the member who has proven to be the most exceptional.

AT THE TABLE OF ONE HUNDREDS

A temple of insulated peers, the club is open to the most influential and wealthy gastronomes in France.

Big bosses: Martin Bouygues, Patrick Ricard, Robert Peugeot, Éric Frachon (Évian), Claude Bébéar and Henri de Castries (Axa), Jean-René Fourtou (Vivendi), Jean-François Cirelli (GDF-Suez), Daniel Bouton (ex-CEO of Société Générale), the banker Michel David-Weill, Alain Boucheron, and also Jean Solanet, the club's president . . .

Aristocrats: Jean de Luxembourg, Éric de Rothschild, Albert II Prince of Monaco . . .

A priest! (Father Six)

Media personalities and figures from the arts: Erik Orsenna, Philippe Bouvard, Claude Imbert, Nicolas d'Estienne d'Orves, Bernard Pivot, the historian Jean Tulard, ENA alumnus and Armagnac producer Jean Castarède, and actors including Pierre Arditi, Jacques Sereys, and Guillaume Galienne.

Politicians and star barristers: Jean-Pierre Raffarin, Xavier Darcos, lawyer Paul Lombard . . .

Five-star chefs, exempt from the entrance exam: Paul Bocuse, Joël Robuchon, Alain Ducasse, Bernard Pacaud, and Jean-Pierre Vigato. Every year, members also award an honorary degree, the Diplôme du Club des Cent, a certificate of excellence that is prized by restaurant wizards.

Where are the women?

Alas, women are not admitted. Madame **Sarah Bernhardt** is said to have regretted two things in her life: not being able to have **a tiger's tail** surgically attached to her body and also, not having been able to enter the **Club des Cent!**

skip to . . . .
Duck Apicius, p. 122

Galettes

Brittany is a land divided into Upper Brittany and Lower Brittany, and where a culinary line
is also drawn: on one side a crêpe is not a galette, and a galette is far from being a crêpe.
Jill Cousin

A BORDER OF FOOD AND SEMANTICS

In Gallo country, Upper Brittany, one refers to it as a "galette," a name and dish defended and promoted by the Piperia Brotherhood of the Galette; here the galette is made entirely of buckwheat flour, with a thin and tender result. In Lower Brittany, one calls it a "buckwheat crêpe" (*crêpe de blé noir*), and it is made with a combination of buckwheat flour and wheat flour (wheat flour is never more than 30 percent of the total quantity of flour). When cooked, the crêpe is crispier than its galette cousin. Fortunately, all Bretons do agree that a crêpe made from wheat flour should be used for making sweet desserts!

GO STADE RENNAIS!

Founded more than twenty years ago by two supporters of the Stade Rennais soccer club, the Association of the Protectors of the Galette-Saucisse Bretonne promotes the "*galettes-saucisse*" specialty beyond the borders of the Pays Bigouden (southwest Brittany). This specialty is a bit like the Breton hot dog: a grilled pork sausage is rolled in a cold buckwheat galette. It can be purchased from food carts and in main markets throughout the region.

 The Crêpe beyond Brittany . . .

Bretons do not have a monopoly on the crêpe. In the ch'ti vernacular (a variant of the Picard dialect of northern France in Nord-Pas-de-Calais), the population **prepares what they call *ratons***, a crêpe leavened with yeast added to the batter. **In Nice, the French enjoy *socca*,** a galette made from chickpea flour and baked in a pizza oven. **In the Southeast, it is the *matefaim*** or *matefan* in Franco-Provençal. From a potato galette, the *matefaim* evolved into a crêpe made from flour, eggs, mashed potatoes, and cheese. So nourishing!

BUCKWHEAT GALETTE BATTER*

PREPARATION TIME: 15 MINUTES
**REFRIGERATION TIME: 3 HOURS
(MINIMUM) TO 12 HOURS**
MAKES ABOUT 24 GALETTES

2¼ pounds (1 kg) organic stone-ground buckwheat flour (if you have an electric *bilig*, replace 10 to 20 percent of the buckwheat flour with wheat flour)
6 cups (1.5 L) filtered water
1½ tablespoons (30 g) coarse salt from Guérande
Option 1: 1 egg
Option 2: a little sparkling water, beer, or cider, or any fermented beverage that helps to aerate the batter. Add a small amount in place of some of the filtered water.

Using a wooden spoon, combine the flour, 4 cups (1 L) of the water, and the salt to obtain a soft dough. Work the dough by hand to aerate it; bubbles should form on the surface. When the dough is smooth, incorporate one of the desired options (egg or sparkling water) into the dough, and let the dough rest in the refrigerator, ideally for 12 hours, but for a minimum of 3 hours. The next day, add the remaining water and stir well to combine. If possible, take the dough out of the refrigerator at least 1 hour before cooking it; it should be at room temperature.

Recipe from Breizh Café *by Bertrand Larcher, Éditions La Martinière*

THE "FULL MEAL" GALETTE: EGG, HAM, AND CHEESE*

PREPARATION TIME: 10 MINUTES
COOKING TIME: 3 MINUTES
MAKES 1 GALETTE

5¼ ounces (150 g) buckwheat crêpe batter
1 tablespoon (15 g) Bordier demi-sel butter +
1 tablespoon (15 g) for finishing
1 organic egg
1¾ ounces (50 g) Comté cheese, aged six months, grated
1¾ ounces (50 g) pressed ham slices (without preservatives or dyes)

Pour the batter out onto a heated *bilig* (or into a crêpe pan) until cooked, then spread 1 tablespoon (15 g) of the butter onto the finished galette. Break the egg in the center of the galette, and spread the egg white out a little, separating it somewhat from the yolk. Add the grated cheese and ham around the egg. Fold over each of the four sides of the galette in toward the center, and cook for an additional 3 minutes. Add the remaining butter on top, and serve.

Recipe from Breizh Café *by Bertrand Larcher, Éditions La Martinière*

skip to Crêpes, p. 88

Hungry for Haricots

Beans (*haricots* in French) are a valuable source of vegetable protein, and are used as a natural fertilizer. This large family of legumes is also a culinary bonanza.

Xavier Mathias

WHERE DOES THE WORD *HARICOT* COME FROM?

The term is probably derived from the verb *harigoter*, an ancient term meaning "cut the meat into small pieces for making a stew." The bean, which found its perfect home in stews, would eventually adopt the term itself as its name.

GREEN, BUTTER (LIMA), DRY, OR SEMIDRY BEANS?

In all cases, beans come from the same plant: the *Phaseolus vulgaris*, brought from the Andes mountains by the conquistadores. The plant quickly replaced another species of plant growing in France, the *Vigna* (to which *Phaseolus vulgaris* was closely related); its production was greater than that of the *Vigna*. This new plant was soon cultivated throughout Europe. After several centuries of selection, many varieties began to appear, each harvested at different stages of maturity.

String beans (*haricot verts*) and butter beans (*haricots beurre*): the pods are harvested when immature and the seeds contained within are invisible.

Semidry beans or fresh beans: the pod begins to bulge significantly, yet remains very soft. The seed that forms inside has reached its optimal stage of development, but has not yet begun to dry out.

Dry beans: the pod turns yellow and dries up completely. Inside, the seeds have hardened and dehydrated; these beans must be soaked for several hours before cooking.

"LA FIN DES HARICOTS" ("THE END OF BEANS")?

When sources of protein were obtained mostly from consuming vegetables, shortages of beans often occurred after the winter and before new crops could replenish them. All throughout France, the expression *la fin des haricots* ("the end of beans") began to simply mean that another harsh period of hunger was likely to follow.

CHILI CONCARNEAU
by Arnaud Daguin

PREPARATION TIME: 20 MINUTES
COOKING TIME: 1 HOUR 15 MINUTES
SERVES 4

1⅛ pounds (500 g) dried tarbais beans (cassoulet white beans)
1 large red onion
4 cloves garlic
1 bunch flat-leaf parsley
2 cups (½ L) dry white wine
2¼ pounds (1 kg) assorted clams: prairie, palourde, wedge, etc.
A few pinches ground Itxassou (Espelette) pepper

Soak the beans in twice their volume of cold water for at least 12 hours.

After this time, peel and finely chop the onion and garlic. Chop the parsley. Add the white wine to an ovenproof casserole dish, then add the onions, garlic, and parsley, and cook them until the onions have softened. Add the beans, stir to combine, and add just enough water to cover the beans. Cook over low heat for just under 1 hour. Preheat the oven to 300°F (150°C). When the beans are almost cooked, add the clams, give two stirs with a spoon, and place in the oven for 15 minutes. When serving, sprinkle with a little of the ground pepper.

MOGETTE BEAN AND LEMON FINANCIER
by Gilles Daveau*

PREPARATION TIME: 20 MINUTES
COOKING TIME: 15 TO 20 MINUTES
SERVES 4

4¼ ounces (120 g) canned white beans
¼ cup (80 g) demerara sugar
½ vanilla bean, split lengthwise and its seeds scraped out and reserved
1 tablespoon (15 mL) rum
Zest of 1 lemon
2 eggs, separated
3 tablespoons (50 g) unsalted butter, melted
2 tablespoons (20 g) cornstarch

Preheat the oven to 325°F (160°C). Drain and rinse the beans. In a large bowl, combine the beans, sugar, vanilla bean seeds, rum, and zest. Add the egg yolks, melted butter, and cornstarch, and whisk to combine. Beat the egg whites to stiff peaks, then gently fold them into the mixture.

Scrape the mixture into small individual financier molds, or into one large cake pan lined with parchment paper, filling the pans to about ¾ inch (2 cm) deep. Bake for 15 to 20 minutes. The cakes are done when the tip of a knife inserted into the center comes out clean.

You can moisten these cakes with the juice of the lemon combined with a little sugar.

Coauthor of the book Savez-vous goûter . . . les legumes secs, Éditions Les Presses de l'EHESP

DRIED-BEAN MAYONNAISE

Adapted from Gilles Daveau's *Manuel de cuisine alternative*.

PREPARATION TIME: 10 MINUTES
MAKES ENOUGH FOR 1 SMALL JAR

3½ ounces (100 g) white beans (mogettes or coco), cooked, drained, and rinsed
1¾ ounces (50 g) mixed oils (such as rapeseed and olive)
¾ ounce (20 g) sliced shallots
¾ ounce (20 g) mustard
⅓ ounce (10 g) vinegar

In a blender or using an immersion blender, blend all the ingredients together until smooth.

Use the mayonnaise to accompany a hard-boiled egg or langoustines, as a rémoulade, or as a dip for crudités.

Mogettes, Lingots, Cornilles, and Other "Fayots"

In everyday French, there are many names for the bean . . .

Fayot: slang and pejorative, this word is a negative form of the Latin *Phaseolus*. It is generally reserved—with condescension—for all forms of beans, whether in seeds, dried, or fresh.

Lingot: in the North, in Castelnaudary, or in the Pays de la Loire, the *lingot* most often refers to a white bean, dry or semidry, also called "*mogette*" in Vendée.

Mogette: the name comes from *mongette* from the south of France, formed on the Occitan *monge*, which means "monk," because the white bean was one of the staples of monastic cuisine.

Coco: in Paimpol, this name refers to a fresh white bean, shelled, which has an AOP (*appellation d'origine protégée*). Some may also be red in color.

Cornille: the black-eyed cowpea or black-eyed pea, this fabaceae (legume) of the genus *Vigna* is probably native to Africa.

Flageolet: a semidry bean variety that retains its beautiful green color. Indispensable for serving with a Sunday leg of lamb for family.

skip to
Cassoulet, p. 209

Coco Rouge de Prague

Iroquois

Nombril de Bonne Soeur

Saint Esprit à OEil Rouge

Flageolet Rouge

Merveille du Marché

Coco Jaune de Chine

Cor des Alpes

Borlotto Langue de Feu

Red Calypso

Lingot Brun Panaché

Nombril de Bonne Soeur

Pont l'Abbé

Velour

Soja Noir

PeaBean

Pont l'Abbé

Soja Noir

Coco Brun Panaché

Coco Jaune Jaune à Oeil Noir

Borlotto

Flageolet Rouge

Oeil-de-perdrix

Dolique Lab lab

Coco Nain Blanc Précoce

Coco Bicolore Prolifique

YinYang

Orteil du Pêcheur

Espagne

Petit Riz

Montbarry

Borlotto

Lima

Plein le Panier

Couvent Vogel

Mungo

Scarlet Emperor

Lima dit de Chabannais

AAAAArgh, Andouillette!

This tripe specialty divides France into three groups: those who pinch their noses at the mere thought of this sausage, those who buy it only in supermarkets, and those devotees who would crawl on their knees to Troyes for the artisanal version.

Marie–Amal Bizalion

ITS ORIGINS

It was probably created in Troyes, yet its origin remains a mystery. Until the middle of the nineteenth century, the word *andouillette* meant nothing but a small andouille sausage. Troyes excels in the current pure pork version, but in former times used sections of veal, all the way from the teat to the small and large intestines—a recipe transcribed in the *grimoire* (spell books) until the beginning of the last century. In 1885, a serious review cited a race of Franco-British pig "with fat of an exquisite taste, and sufficiently attested by the pigs' feet from Saint-Menehould, and andouillettes of Troyes. . . ." Before 1960, however, and the emergence of aggressive breeding practices, pork was not common.

THE FRENCH EXCEPTION

Andouillette is typically considered a specialty of bistros in mainland France. Throughout the regions, you can find andouillette originating from Chablis, Jargeau, Rouillac, Périgord, Troyes, Clamecy, Beaujolais, Burgundy, Lorraine, Provence, and Rouen. The Lyonnaise variety, from Cambrai and Alençon, suffered from the ban that occurred in the 1990s on using veal chitterlings (small intestines and large intestines), which was linked to mad cow disease, until the lifting of the ban at the end of 2015.

skip to

A Parade of Labels, p. 275;
The Degree of Stench!, p. 372

Once You Purchase It, Then What?

COOKING METHODS

Enjoyed plain as a cold sausage, served with an aperitif.
The pairing: chilled Champagne. A treat for Champagne producers.

Baked for 15 minutes at 400°F (200°C),
then placed on a grill to brown all sides.
The pairing: Chaource cheese. To coat in a sauce: remove the rind of the cheese, dice it, then cook it in cream and whole-grain mustard. As a gratin: alternate slices of cooked potatoes, andouillette, and cheese in two layers, then bake for 20 minutes.

Steamed for 15 minutes, to create a unique softness.
The pairing: watercress. Blanched, rinsed in cold water, puréed in a blender, and added to a homemade butter-cream purée.

Poached for 20 minutes over very low heat in a seasoned broth.
The pairing: porcini mushrooms. In large slices, and browned in butter.

Sautéed for 10 minutes in butter, until browned on all sides,
over low heat.
The pairing: a creamy mustard. In the cooking juices of the sausage, cook chopped shallots, then add white wine and mustard, thicken with some cream, and reduce by half.

Wood fired Cooked for 5 minutes in hot embers,
then 10 minutes over low heat.
The pairing: homemade fries and a strong mustard.

THE ARTISAN APPROACH, MADE BY "PULLING THE STRING," IS . . .

. . . **difficult work:** in this method, pieces of tripe (pork intestines and pork stomach in most cases) are washed, washed again, degreased, blanched, cut into long strips, seasoned (with herbs, spices, local wine, mustard, etc.), then coiled up with a string threaded through the center. An intestine casing attached to the string is placed over two fingers, the string pulled, and voilà, the contents are pulled into the casing. The andouillette is then cooked at 200°F (90°C) maximum for at least 5 hours, in a seasoned broth.

AAAAA AMUSES THE TRIPE MERCHANTS

Since 1960, the Association Amicale des Amateurs d'Andouillette Authentique (whose acronym AAAAA was created to the amusement of one of its founders Henri Clos-Jouve) wanted to be informal, but desired to set regulations for the sausage in the charcutier world. Chaired by author Jacques-Louis Delpal, the association's members—made up of mostly food critics—award the "AAAAA" label to any producer whose andouillette is considered exceptional. Those made using a string are preferred since they are made with great care, but this is not always a consistent requirement.

NOW AWARDED A RED LABEL. BUT IS IT STILL GOOD?

The Label Rouge ("Red Label") indicating *andouillette supérieure pur porc** places strict requirements for andouillette: Red Label pork must total 95 percent of the sausage's ingredients, it must be made of strips at least 4 inches (10 cm) long, baked for at least 7 hours, and cannot exceed more than 18 percent fat content. These standards do not mean it is artisanal, or even tasty; however, the long cooking time requirement at least gives assurances that it will be a soft product.

**The Label Rouge was submitted and obtained by the manufacturer Gilles Amand, after a decree of the Official Journal of November 19, 2016*

IF IT SMELLS LIKE S*** . . .

. . . run away. The intestinal sections adjoining the anus must undergo a very strict cleaning. On the other hand, if the sausage smells like pig, it's a very good sign.

A must-know address for andouillette

→ Maison Thierry, 73, avenue Gallieni, Sainte-Savine, 03 25 79 08 74

Tarte au Maroilles

There are two recipes that use the only AOC cheese from the Hauts-de-France region: the *Flamiche au Morailles*, a traditional Flemish leek tart with Maroilles cheese from the Avesnois, and the *Goyère*, a specialty of Valenciennes.
Marie-Laure Fréchet

THE FLAMICHE AU MAROILLES

PREPARATION TIME: 20 MINUTES
RESTING TIME: 1 HOUR 30 MINUTES
COOKING TIME: 30 MINUTES
MAKES 1 LARGE PIE

⅓ ounce (10 g) baker's yeast
1 teaspoon (4 g) sugar
3 tablespoons (45 mL) warm milk
2½ cups (250 g) all-purpose flour or T55 flour
½ teaspoon (3 g) salt
2 tablespoons (30 mL) oil
2 eggs
3½ ounces (100 g) crème fraîche
6 ounces (180 g) Maroilles cheese (about ¼ of the square)
Freshly ground black pepper

Stir the yeast and sugar into the warm milk. Place the flour in a bowl. Make a well in the center of the flour, and add the salt, oil, and eggs to the well. Stir to thoroughly combine, then add the dissolved yeast mixture. Knead the dough until it becomes soft and is no longer sticky. Place the dough back in the bowl, cover the bowl with a towel, and set it in a warm place to allow the dough to rise to about double its volume, about 1 hour and 30 minutes. Pour the dough out onto a floured work surface, and roll it out to a thickness of ¹⁄₁₀ inch (0.5 mm). Line a butter-greased pie dish with the dough. Prick the dough with a fork. Preheat the oven to 350°F (180°C). Scrape the crème fraîche into the pie dish and spread it out over the bottom. Cut the Maroilles into thin slices, and arrange the slices on top of the crème fraîche. Season with pepper. Do not add salt. Bake for 20 to 30 minutes, or until golden.

> "**Passionately** Maroilles, the **king** of cheeses, whose **thunderous** flavor **resonates** like the sound of the saxophone in a **symphony** of cheeses . . ." **Curnonsky**

LA GOYÈRE* AU MAROILLES

PREPARATION TIME: 20 MINUTES
RESTING TIME: 1 HOUR 30 MINUTES
COOKING TIME: 25 MINUTES
MAKES 1 LARGE PIE

6 ounces (180 g) Maroilles cheese (about ¼ of the square)
3½ ounces (100 g) fromage blanc or crème fraîche
3 eggs, separated
Salt and freshly ground black pepper
1 (8-oz/113 g) pie dough or puff pastry sheet

Remove the rind from the cheese. Using a fork, mash the cheese with the fromage blanc. Incorporate the egg yolks. Beat the egg whites to stiff peaks. Carefully fold the egg whites into the cheese mixture. Season with salt and pepper, as needed. Roll out the dough to a thickness of ¼ inch (5 mm). Preheat the oven to 400°F (200°C). Grease a pie dish with butter. Line the dish with the dough, and prick the dough all over with a fork. Scrape the cheese mixture into the pan, and bake for 25 minutes, or until puffed and golden.

A puffed brioche pie, common in the North.

skip to
The Gougère, p. 288

B Is for Bernard Pivot

It's all about culture. Even his taste in wine! Born near vineyards, the renowned talk show host has been in the wine world for ages. Here's proof with three key words that start with the letter B.
Estelle Lenartowicz

Journalist in love with wine
(born in 1935)

B IS FOR BEAUJOLAIS

In bourgeois circles, he's criticized for liking such a riffraff wine, a wine for commoners, a wine for when you're thirsty, bar wine, festival wine, a wine for between meals. Whatever! Loyal to his first loves, this grocer's son who became a critic has never turned his back on his beloved Beaujolais, to which he owes his "initiation to pleasure." From age six to ten, the young Bernard played in the vineyards and went to school in Quincié-en-Beaujolais, at the foot of Mont Brouilly. As a teenager, his first pay came from wine harvesting. He says that wine taught him about freedom, sensuality, and patience. And the art of the gab!

B IS FOR BUKOWSKI

It was on Pivot's show that the now-legendary booziest episode on French TV occured. On September 22, 1978, the writer Charles Bukowski, already inebriated, walked onto the set of the prestigious show *Apostrophes*. After the usual series of questions and answers, the drunkard, reduced to silence, began knocking back bottles of Sancerre, of course. With all his grumbling and groans, the provocateur made it so that others couldn't speak. "Shut up, Bukowski!" shouted Cavanna. Bukowski shamelessly responded by groping the knees of Catherine Paysan, sitting next to him. "Oh! Well, that takes the cake!" she exclaimed. Watched by thousands of bewildered viewers, the former bum walked off the show wobbling, drunk as a skunk. As he left, he threatened a security guard with a knife. American class . . .

B IS FOR BINGE DRINKING

In his *Dictionnaire Amoureux du Vin* (Plon), Pivot pays homage to the incredible quantity of French words used to designate the drunkard. Here's an excerpt: "The *soûlographe*, the *soûlard*, the *soûlot*, the *alcoolique*, the *poivrot*, the *picoleur*, the *bituré*, the *biturin*, the *pionard*, the *pochard*, the *pochetron*, the *sac à vin*, the *éponge à vin*, the *ouvre à vin*, the *boit-sans-soif*, the *arsouille*, the *biberonneur*, the *cuitard*, the *vide-bouteilles*, the *meurt-de-soif*, the *soiffard*, the *galope-chopine*, the *siroteur*, the *relicheur*, the *vinassier*, the *alambic* . . ." Who can top that?

skip to
So Long as There Is Inebriation, p. 49

All in the Soup Family

Soups comprise a great segment of classic French cuisine. From the treatises of Auguste Escoffier to the manual of bourgeois cooking, there are dozens of different recipes to accommodate the crops from the garden. The problem: unless you are a Best Craftsman of France (MOF), there is every chance of drowning in all the terminology. This is a small survival guide to help you navigate through the soup.

François-Régis Gaudry

In the seventeenth century *the word* soup *did not have the same meaning. It was used to refer to* ***large meat or fish dishes boiled*** *with vegetables.*

"Nevertheless, a soup is brought: ***A rooster*** *appeared in its pompous garb."*
(Boileau, Third Satire, 1666)

SOUP METHODS
→ All the recipes serve 6.
→ For a vegetarian version of these soups, replace the chicken broth with water.
→ Rice, the preferred binding agent in the conventional kitchen, can be replaced by the same weight in bulgur, quinoa, barley flakes, or peeled and cubed potatoes.
→ Just before serving, do not forget to incorporate a pat of fresh butter, a few cubes of bread fried in butter, and some sprigs of chervil.

THE GREAT FAMILY OF SOUPS
According to *Larousse gastronomique*, soup is a "liquid dish served most often hot in soup plates, at the beginning of meals, and especially essential in the evening."

Among the various types of soups are:
Clear soups: broths and consommés made from meat, poultry, fish, or shellfish.
Enriched soups: liquid dishes enriched with butter, cream, béchamel, tapioca, rice, arrowroot, egg yolk, etc.

Among the enriched soups, we find:
Cream-based soups: preparations of fish, shellfish, meat, and vegetables, enriched with cream and/or béchamel.
Veloutés: soups whose basic element (vegetable, meat, fish, shellfish) is cooked in white stock, then enriched with egg yolk and cream.
Purées: liquid purées, purées of starchy vegetables or legumes, shellfish purées (bisques), or purées of fish, meat, or vegetables enriched by adding rice, potatoes, or bread—it is this category that is explored here in more detail.

Legume-based soups

Condé
Legume: the red bean
Origin: a soup dedicated to the Grand Conde, a French prince in the seventeenth century, and his descendants, by their cooks.
Recipe: place 12 ounces (350 g) of washed red beans in 6 cups (1.5 L) of cold water. Boil, skim off the foam, season with salt, then add an onion pierced with a clove, a bouquet garni, a peeled and sliced carrot, and a fresh pork heel, if desired. Add a scant ½ cup (100 mL) of red wine. Let simmer gently, then blend using an immersion blender.

Esau (or Conti)
Legume: the lentil
Origin: Esau is a character in the Bible who gives his birthright to his brother Jacob for a dish of lentils.
Recipe: place 12 ounces (350 g) of washed Puy lentils in 6 cups (1.5 L) of cold water. Boil, skim off the foam, season with salt, then add an onion pierced with a clove, a bouquet garni, a peeled and sliced carrot, and a fresh pork heel, if desired. Add a scant ½ cup (100 mL) of red wine. Let simmer gently, then blend using an immersion blender.

Saint-Germain
Legume: split peas (previously fresh peas)
Origin: even though Saint-Germain-en-Laye specialized in the cultivation of peas during its beginnings, we owe this name to the Count of Saint-Germain, minister of war for Louis XVI.
Recipe: soak 12 ounces (350 g) of split peas in cold water for 2 hours. Drain, and add 6 cups (1.5 L) of cold water. Boil, skim off the foam, and season with salt. Let simmer. In another saucepan, cook a peeled and sliced leek green and half a peeled and chopped onion in 1 tablespoon (20 g) of butter. Add the split peas, then blend using an immersion blender. Serve topped with fried lardons and a dollop of crème fraiche.

Soisonnais
Legume: the white bean
Origin: Soissons, the historical land of bean cultivation in France.
Recipe: place 12 ounces (350 g) of washed white beans in 6 cups (1.5 L) of cold water. Boil, skim off the foam, season with salt, then add an onion pierced with a clove, a bouquet garni, a peeled and sliced carrot, and a fresh pork heel, if desired. Add a scant ½ cup (100 mL) of red wine. Let simmer gently, then blend using an immersion blender.

One-vegetable soups

Argenteuil
Vegetable: white asparagus
Origin: Argenteuil (Val-d'Oise) has been famous for the cultivation of white asparagus since the seventeenth century.
Recipe: brown 14 ounces (400 g) of white asparagus tips in 3 tablespoons (50 g) of butter. Add half an onion and a pinch of salt. Add 4 cups (1 L) of chicken broth, and ½ cup (100 g) of rice. Let simmer, covered. Blend using an immersion blender, then add ¾ cup (200 mL) of crème fraîche.

Choisy
Vegetable: lettuce
Origin: Choisy was known in the eighteenth century for its lettuce. King Louis XV, whose favorite residence was the château of Choisy-le-Roi, encouraged its cultivation.
Recipe: fry 1 minced onion in 2 tablespoons (30 g) of butter. Add 3 cups (750 mL) of broth, 9 ounces (250 g) of potatoes, and 2 cups (250 mL) of milk. Season with salt. Let boil just until the potatoes are tender. Add 9½ ounces (270 g) of chopped lettuce, bring to a boil, and cook for 5 minutes. Blend using an immersion blender.

Crécy
Vegetable: carrot
Origin: Crécy-la-Chapelle (Seine-Marne) was once known for its production of carrots called "de Meaux" (a long-rooted variety, orange in color, nearing red).
Recipe: brown 1⅛ pounds (500 g) of sliced carrots in 3 tablespoons (50 g) of butter; add half an onion and a pinch of salt. Add 4 cups (1 L) of chicken broth and ½ cup (100 g) of rice and simmer, covered. Blend using an immersion blender.

Du Barry
Vegetable: cauliflower
Origin: a tribute to the white and voluptuous skin of the Comtesse du Barry, the last lover of King Louis XV.
Recipe: blanch 14 ounces (400 g) of cauliflower cut into pieces in salted boiling water; drain. Cook the cauliflower together with 9 ounces (250 g) of potatoes in 2⅔ cups (600 mL) of milk with a pinch of salt. Add just over ⅓ cup (100 mL) of milk or chicken broth. Blend using an immersion blender.

Freneuse
Vegetable: turnip
Origin: Freneuse is a town of Yvelines, formerly specializing in the cultivation of turnips.
Recipe: brown 1⅛ pounds (500 g) of sliced turnips in 3 tablespoons (50 g) of butter with a pinch of salt. Add 3 cups (700 mL) of chicken broth and 9 ounces (250 g) of potatoes. Simmer, covered. Blend using an immersion blender.

Germiny
Vegetable: sorrel
Origin: the chef of Café Anglais invented this soup as a tribute to one of his clients, Count de Germiny, governor of the Banque de France.
Recipe: wash and chop 14 ounces (400 g) of sorrel in 3 tablespoons (50 g) of butter. Add 5 cups (1.2 L) of chicken broth. Blend using an immersion blender, then blend 4 egg yolks with 1¼ cups (300 mL) of crème fraîche in another saucepan. Carefully incorporate this mixture into the sorrel soup, stirring constantly with a whisk, until the soup thickens and traces of the whisk appear. Warm slightly, but without boiling.

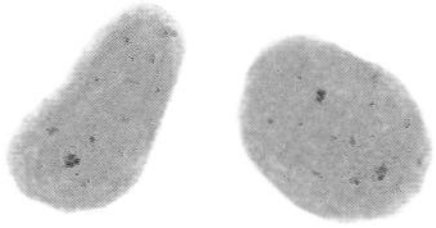

Parmentier
Vegetable: potato
Origin: a tribute to the pharmacist Antoine Parmentier (1737–1813), a great promoter of the potato in France.
Recipe: brown two sliced leeks in 1½ tablespoons (25 g) of butter. Add 1⅛ pounds (500 g) of quartered potatoes. Add 4 cups (1 L) of chicken broth, season with salt, and boil until the potatoes are tender. Blend using an immersion blender. Thin the soup out, if necessary, by adding a few spoonfuls of broth.

Solferino
Vegetable: tomato
Origin: a definite relation to the battle that took place in 1853 in the famous Lombardy commune. At the time, the tomato was associated with Italy.
Recipe: brown 3 sliced leeks in 2 tablespoons (30 g) of butter. Add 1½ pounds (700 g) of seeded and quartered tomatoes, a bouquet garni, and a crushed garlic clove. Add 6 cups (1.5 L) of chicken broth and 4 potatoes. Boil until tender. Remove the bouquet garni, blend using an immersion blender, and thin the soup out, if necessary, with a little extra broth.

Multivegetable soups

Le cultivateur ("The Farmer")
This is the "grand chef" version of the good old vegetable soup with bacon.
Recipe: cut up 3 ounces (80 g) of pork belly and brown it in 2 tablespoons (30 g) of butter. Add assorted chopped vegetables (except potato), and cook just until the vegetables are tender. Add 4 cups (1 L) of chicken broth, season with salt, and bring to a boil. Add cabbage and potatoes and boil until the potatoes are tender. Do not blend. When in season, add fresh peas and sliced green beans. Serve.

Le Bonne Femme ("The Good Wife")
This recipe was found in all bourgeois cookbooks of the nineteenth century and the first half of the twentieth century. It is the household version of the rustic peasant leek and potato soup.
Recipe: gently cook 3 sliced leek whites in 1 tablespoon (20 g) of butter. Add 6 cups (1.5 L) of chicken broth. Peel potatoes and slice them. Season with salt. Bring to a boil and cook just until the potatoes are tender. Do not blend. Incorporate a few pats of butter and top with croutons.

skip to
Good Soup All Around!, p. 170

Les Halles, the Belly of Paris

An architectural masterpiece and a shrine of Parisian popular culture, Les Halles remained the capital's principal source of food supply for well over a century. Immortalized by Zola, Huysmans, and many artists, Les Halles left an indelible mark on the French imagination.

Estelle Lenartowicz

LES HALLES WAS:

A food market covering 81 acres (33 hectares), built between 1854 and 1874 by Victor Baltard, at the initiative of Napoléon III and Baron Haussmann.
Twelve pavilions in an exuberantly modern architectural style, featuring vast canopies of glass and steel, connected by covered streets teeming with bustling throngs.
A group of pavilions each dedicated to a food category: fish (*Pavillon de la Marée*), poultry and game (*Pavillon de la Vallée*), as well as charcuterie and offal, fruits and vegetables, cut flowers, bread, butter, eggs, and cheese . . .
The source of employment for more than 5,000 people: producers, middlemen, carters, and vendors of all descriptions. Many of them were transplants from the provinces trying their luck in the French capital.
Bustling night and day with tons of agricultural commodities flooding in from every region of France. Selling began at the stroke of one o'clock each morning and continued all day, but never later than eight o'clock in the evening.
The capital's source of nourishment: in the early twentieth century, more than 1,000 tons of Gruyère cheese, 26,000 tons of fish, 10,000 tons of mussels and shellfish, 19,000 tons of fruits and vegetables, and 23,000 tons of meat passed through the market annually.
The most lively, festive neighborhood in Paris, surrounded by dozens of restaurants and cafés open 24 hours a day. Beloved haunts included La Poule au Pot, Le Café Pierre, La Cloche des Halles, Le Chien Qui Fume, and Au Chou Vert. Some of them offered camp beds and served as dormitories for weary carters.
Finally demolished in the 1970s. Ever more congested, increasingly insalubrious, and inadequate for the demands of the modern city, Les Halles' closing knell came in the early 1970s, shortly after General de Gaulle inaugurated the new market in Rungis.

The fishmonger's stall by Émile Zola

"There on the marble slab lay a **magnificent salmon**, exhibiting the pearlescent pinkness of its flesh; **turbot** white as cream; **eels,** stuck with black pegs to mark where they should be sliced; pairs of soles, **mullet**, sea bass, all arranged in an extravagant display. And in the midst of these fish with their **living eyes**, their gills still bleeding, stretched an **immense skate**, reddish in color, mottled with dark patches, splendid in its strange tonalities; but the enormous skate was **putrefying, its tail sagging**, the cartilage of its wings breaking through the rough skin."

Le Ventre de Paris (*The Belly of Paris,* 1873)

ARTISANAL TRADES OF YESTERYEAR'S MARKET

The strong men of Les Halles: easily identifiable by their enormous hats, these strapping merchandise handlers were the aristocrats of the market. The strongest could carry up to 551 pounds (250 kg) on their backs.
The pilot fish: they'd earn a few pennies for guiding carts through the market's labyrinth.
The loaders: they earned their bread by assembling imposing pyramids of fruits and vegetables in the stalls.
The egg inspectors: sworn into office by the prefecture of police, they spent their days in subterranean chambers counting, measuring, and inspecting the quality of eggs brought to the market.
The guards: in exchange for a few coins, these women would watch over merchandise that was already sold and temporarily stored in the square known as Le Carreau in the center of the market.
The "Harlequin Merchants": they made the rounds of local restaurants, collecting leftover scraps (with the assistance of dumpster divers), boiling them up, and selling these dregs to the indigent masses.

THE BELLY OF PARIS, THE LOUVRE OF THE PEOPLE

Émile Zola was absolutely fascinated by "the Louvre of the people." He described Les Halles, scribbling notes like an impassioned naturalist, cramming his accounts with delirious descriptions of stalls overflowing with merchandise. His work is a vast still life set in motion, a captivating documentary survey of Les Halles and its surrounding neighborhood.
The young revolutionary Florent, the protagonist of Zola's novel *Le Ventre de Paris* (*The Belly of Paris*), is an escaped convict who arrives in Paris hidden in a shipment of vegetables. Gaining employment as an inspector within Les Halles, he soon becomes the plaything of merciless love and power struggles occurring against the backdrop of a social revolution that pitted the wealthy fat on one side against the impoverished thin on the other.
A metaphor for the crude greed of the Second Empire, Les Halles was a vast "metal belly." It was a monstrous intestine, a labyrinth of cellars, pavilions, and alleyways where anything that could not be digested would turn on itself, be ground into remnants, and be vomited forth, whatever the cost.

skip to
The Fishmonger's Stall, p. 218

Parmentier

With potatoes boiled in water and the leftovers from a pot-au-feu or just using steak,
you quickly have a casserole that can feed a large family with little effort.
This unique dish is also suitable for all kinds of vegetable and meaty variations.

Jill Cousin

This unique dish owes its name to **Antoine Augustin Parmentier,** an **apothecary, nutritionist, and hygienist—not a potato seller—** of the eighteenth century, who **promoted the benefits of the potato.** The potato was previously used only as animal fodder and was thought to lead to the development of diseases such as leprosy.

GOLDEN RULES

Use starchy potatoes (such as Bintje) or tender-fleshed potatoes (such as Banba or Agata).

Do not use ground beef from the supermarket. Instead, choose freshly ground beef from your local butcher for a better result.

This rule you will keep to yourself as your little secret: add a pinch of nutmeg to the mashed potatoes.

BEEF PARMENTIER

PREPARATION TIME: 40 MINUTES
COOKING TIME: 50 MINUTES
SERVES 6

For the mashed potatoes
2¼ pounds (1 kg) potatoes (Bintje)
⅔ cup (150 mL) whole milk
⅓ cup plus 1 tablespoon (100 g) cream
3 tablespoons (50 g) salted butter, cut into pieces

For the filling
1 carrot
1½ tablespoons (20 g) olive oil
1½ tablespoons (25 g) unsalted butter, divided
2 onions
1⅛ pounds (500 g) freshly ground beef
Salt and freshly ground pepper
7 tablespoons (20 g) bread crumbs

Peel the potatoes and quarter them. Cook them in a large volume of water for about 30 minutes, or until tender when pierced with a knife. Drain, and mash the potatoes with a potato masher. In a saucepan, warm the milk and cream. Add this mixture to the potatoes, then add the butter. Stir well to obtain a smooth texture.

While the potatoes are cooking, make the filling. Peel and chop the carrot into a fine *brunoise* (small dice). In a skillet, heat the oil and 1 tablespoon (15 g) of the butter. Cook the carrot over medium heat for 2 minutes. Peel and thinly slice the onions. Add them to the skillet. Continue cooking for 2 minutes. Add the ground beef. Season with salt and pepper. Cook for 5 minutes, stirring; skim off any fat from the surface. Preheat the oven to 400°F (200°C). Grease a baking dish with 2 teaspoons (10 g) of the butter. Place the cooked ground beef mixture in the baking dish and spread it out evenly. Cover this mixture evenly with mashed potatoes. Sprinkle the bread crumbs over the top. Bake for about 15 minutes, or until nicely golden on top.

3 VARIATIONS

DUCK AND SWEET POTATO PARMENTIER
Follow the Beef Parmentier recipe above but replace the potatoes with **2¼ pounds (1 kg) of sweet potatoes.** Shred the flesh of **4 duck legs confit.** In a frying pan, melt **1 tablespoon (15 g) of duck fat.** Peel and chop **1 shallot.** Cook the shallot for 2 minutes. Add the duck meat. Fry over high heat for 5 minutes, stirring regularly. Place the duck meat in a baking dish. Cover it with the mashed sweet potatoes and bake.

TRICOLOR PARMENTIER
Peel and cube 14 ounces (400 g) of celery root. Cook the celery root in a large volume of water for 15 minutes, or until tender. Drain and purée the celery root with 1 tablespoon (15 g) of salted butter. Season with pepper, and set aside. Peel 10½ ounces (300 g) of carrots. Cut them in half, and cook them in a large volume of water for 15 minutes, or until tender. Drain, mash them with 1 tablespoon (15 g) of salted butter, and set aside. Peel 10½ ounces (300 g) of turnips. Cut them in half. Cook them in a large volume of water for 15 minutes, or until tender. Drain, mash them with 1 tablespoon (15 g) of salted butter, and set aside. Prepare the ground beef filling according to the Beef Parmentier recipe above. Place the meat in a baking dish. Spread the three mashed mixtures over the top, and bake.

HADDOCK AND GREEN CABBAGE PARMENTIER
Pour 4 cups (1 L) of milk and 4 cups (1 L) of water into a saucepan. Place 1¾ pounds (800 g) of haddock in the saucepan, and bring to a boil. Turn off the heat, and let the fish poach for 15 minutes. Drain the haddock and crumble the flesh. In a small saucepan, boil ¾ cup plus 1 tablespoon (200 mL) of cream. Add 1 bunch of scallions. Add the haddock to the saucepan and stir to combine; set aside. Wash 14 ounces (400 g) of green cabbage. Thinly slice it. Cook the cabbage in a skillet with 1 tablespoon (15 g) of unsalted butter. Cook over low heat, covered, for 10 minutes. Transfer the haddock mixture to a baking dish. Add the cooked cabbage. Cover with mashed potatoes (see Beef Parmentier above) and bake.

The Little Seed That Clears Your Nose

It's often associated with Dijon, but it's made throughout France. Fine, strong, country-style or flavored, mustard is a staple in our cupboards, an old companion that has a lot to offer.
Marielle Gaudry

THE PLANT
An herbaceous plant belonging to the Brassicaceae family, originally from the Mediterranean region, mustard produces dried fruit called "silique," which are capsules of small yellow or black seeds. Three kinds are grown to produce the condiment:
- **white mustard,** a plant with large flowers and pale yellow seeds, mildly spicy in taste.
- **black mustard,** a plant with fuzzy leaves and red seeds that turn black with age, very spicy in taste.
- **brown mustard,** a robust plant with serrated leaves and large spicy seeds. In Burgundy, this is the species that is grown to produce Dijon mustard.

A fourth, very hardy species is **wild mustard or field mustard** (*Sinapis arvensis*). It is the most common but is considered to be a weed.

PRODUCTION
More than five hundred thousand mustard seeds are needed to produce 2¼ pounds (1 kg) of mustard paste.
Clean: to rid the seeds of grass and parasites
Soak: for a few hours, after adding the other ingredients (vinegar, white wine, brine, and a few spices)
Grind: using millstones, delicately, without heat, so as to retain all the qualities of taste
Sift: to separate the protective seed capsule ("integument" or "bran") from the mustard paste. For coarse-grain mustard, eliminate this step.

STORAGE
Unopened, in the cupboard, away from light and humidity. Once the jar is opened, keep in the refrigerator with the cover tightly shut. Because it contains vinegar, which creates its acidity, it can be stored for up to eighteen months.

THERE'S ONLY MUSTARD IN BURGUNDY, RIGHT?
Although Dijon never was the exclusive producer of mustard—it was also made in Paris, Bordeaux, Orléans, and Reims—it did make it its specialty. "*Moult me tarde,*" Old French for "Much awaits me," is attributed to Philip the Bold in 1382 when he was Duke of Burgundy and claimed his victory over the Flemish. It has become the city of Dijon's motto.

Terroir
The region has a heavy presence of vines, from which vinegar is extracted to make the yellow paste, and the land, formerly used by coal workers to carbonize their wood, is very favorable for growing mustard seed.

Ingenuity
Around 1752, Jean Naigeon, a Dijon resident, replaced the vinegar with verjus, which considerably improved the taste of mustard. The new recipe quickly grew famous and became widespread. In 1853, Maurice Grey invented a machine to make mustard and productivity increased.

In 1931, Raymond Sachot took the reins of the company Moutarde A. Bizouard and its brand Amora. He produced the first decorated mustard jars.

Designation
A decree from September 1937, followed by another one in July 2000, defined the production process. And so there is *moutarde de Dijon* (Dijon mustard) throughout the world!

Initiative
Although mustard production has been undermined since the end of World War II by the industrial drive for profit and by competition with Canada (which provides about 80 percent of seeds), producers in Burgundy began producing seeds locally again in the mid-1990s.

DON'T TOUCH MY MUSTARD!
Whereas the designation "Moutarde de Dijon" defines a production process that can be adopted throughout the world, since November 2009, the French PGI (Protected Geographical Indication) "Moutarde de Bourgogne" (Mustard from Burgundy) has certified that the production of seeds and AOC white wine, and their transformation into a condiment, has taken place entirely in Burgundy.

Paris vs Dijon
In 1351, Paris was the first city to obtain an order regulating the production of mustard. Dijon followed in 1390. Whoever violated the rules regarding the production of mustard was subject to heavy fines. Competition between the two cities became more acute in the eighteenth century when the Paris companies Bordin and Maille rivaled against the ingenuity of the Naigeon family from Dijon. Then came the industrialization of the condiment's production in the nineteenth century, which was bolstered by the innovations of Maurice Grey in Dijon and by the Bornibus company in Paris. Maille, anxious to be associated with mustard's Burgundy origins, opened a shop in Dijon in 1845. With the company changing hands several times since 1923, Maille and Amora are now both under the auspices of the Dutch-British transnational Unilever.

MUSTARD IN VEXIN
Not one mustard seed was growing in this French region until 2009, when Emmanuel Delacour began producing his own yellow paste at home in Vexin. Heading the family farm that goes back to the nineteenth century, he chose a rustic variety. Although not very productive, it has a lot of taste, and he has developed it in accordance with a whole organic farm management system. Once his mustard is harvested, he has it made by an Oise artisan who uses millstones. It is then aged for four to six months in a cellar. He offers traditional mustards made with white wine and also flavored options (absinthe, walnut, Williams pear and cider).
→ Les Moutardes du Vexin, 1, Grande Rue, Gouzangrez (Val-d'Oise)

Why does it clear your nose?
It's a chemical reaction! As the mustard seeds soak, the fermentation process brings about an oil, allyl isothiocyanate, which is the source of the spiciness. That same substance was used in mustard gas, a chemical weapon used during World War I.

The mustards of France

Mustard of Alsace
Seeds: white
Texture/appearance: smooth and pale yellow
Ingredients: vinegar, salt, spices
Flavor: quite sweet
Historic producer/shop: Alélor (founded 1873)

Mustard of Bordeaux
Seeds: black and white
Texture/appearance: dark brown
Ingredients: vinegar, sugar, and tarragon
Flavor: sweet
Historic producer/shop: Louit (founded 1825)

Mustard of Burgundy (PGI)
Seeds: black or brown
Texture/appearance: smooth and light yellow
Ingredients: verjus
Flavor: strong
Historic producer/shop: Fallot (founded 1840)

Violet Mustard of Brive
Seeds: black
Texture/appearance: smooth and violet
Ingredients: black grape must, vinegar, spices
Flavor: sweet
Historic producer/shop: Denoix (founded 1839)

Mustard of Charroux
Seeds: brown
Texture/appearance: yellow with visible seeds
Ingredients: verjus, wine of Saint-Pourçain
Flavor: spicy
Historic producer/shop: Huiles et Moutardes de Charroux (Maenner family, founded 1989)

Mustard of Dijon
Seeds: brown
Texture/appearance: smooth and pale yellow
Ingredients: verjus
Flavor: strong to very strong
Historic producers/shops: Reine de Dijon (1840), Amora-Maille (Maille founded 1747, Amora founded 1919)

Mustard of Meaux
Seeds: brown
Texture/appearance: gray with visible seeds
Ingredients: vinegar, spices
Flavor: vinegary and spicy
Historic producer/shop: Moutarde de Meaux Pommery (founded 1949)

Mustard of Normandy
Seeds: brown and white
Texture/appearance: smooth and honey yellow
Ingredients: Normandy cider vinegar, salt
Flavor: strong and aromatic
Historic producers/shops: Rondel (founded 1735), Bocquet (founded 1855)

Mustard of Orléans
Seeds: brown
Texture/appearance: smooth and bright yellow
Ingredients: Orléans vinegar, salt, spices
Flavor: strong
Historic producer/shop: Pouret (founded 1797)

Mustard of Picardy
Seeds: brown
Texture/appearance: smooth and yellow
Ingredients: cider vinegar, spices
Flavor: sweet
Historic producer/shop: Champ's (founded 1952)

The evolution of mustard crocks

They come in various shapes and are made from either earthenware, porcelain, or sandstone. Mustard crocks were originally closed by a cork, covered with a tin cap, and sealed with wax; they were as much intended to preserve the mustard they contained as they were to identify the brand. Over the years, these crocks have become much-coveted collectors' items.

UNTIL 1820
A triangular pot with a broad base or with a bulbous torso. Narrow neck. Handwritten inscriptions.
BETWEEN 1820 AND 1830
Straight cylindrical pot with a convex torso. Drooping or rounded neck. Handwritten inscriptions.

UNTIL 1850
Straight pot with a slight shoulder. Thick neck. Inscription stenciled in manganese.
UNTIL 1885
More distinct, straight. Less thick neck. Inscription stenciled in manganese.

UNTIL 1920
Straight cylindrical crock with a shoulder. Bulging neck. Printed inscriptions.
AFTER 1900
Evolution to fancy packaging such as buckets and jugs, then in the form of drinking glasses.

skip to ....
The Cornichon (or Gherkin), p. 12

RABBIT IN MUSTARD

PREPARATION TIME: 15 MINUTES
COOKING TIME: 1 HOUR
SERVES 4
4 shallots
2 tablespoons (30 g) unsalted butter
2 tablespoons (30 mL) sunflower oil
2¼ pounds (1 kg) rabbit, cut into pieces
⅔ cup (150 mL) Burgundy white wine
⅔ cup (150 mL) chicken broth
2 tablespoons (30 mL) old-fashioned Dijon mustard
2 sprigs thyme, or 1 bunch tarragon
¾ cup plus 1 tablespoon (200 mL) cream
Salt and freshly ground pepper

Peel the shallots and slice them. Heat the butter and oil in a skillet and brown the rabbit pieces over medium heat for 5 minutes. Remove the rabbit pieces and set them aside to drain. Place the shallots in the skillet and brown them for 2 minutes. Add the rabbit pieces, then add the wine, broth, mustard, and thyme. Stir to combine and let simmer for 40 minutes over low heat. Add the cream, stir to combine, and continue cooking for another 20 minutes. Season with pepper, taste, and season with salt. If the sauce has reduced too much, add a little broth.

Eureka! in the Kitchen

Inventions relating to food sometimes result from research conducted by scientists with remarkable faculties of observation and deduction. And sometimes they result from happy accidents, from unexpected circumstances and cooks abounding with ingenuity and intuition.

Jean-Paul Branlard

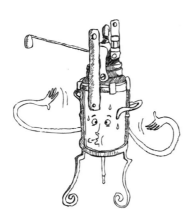

1679
Steam digester

Denis Papin (1647–1712) invented, among other things, the "digester": a thick iron cooking pot, with a safety valve. Pressure created inside was blocked by a lid and crossbar. It was a forerunner to the Cocotte-Minute pressure cooker.

1795
Appertization

Nicolas Appert (1749–1841), a confectioner in Paris, participated in a contest launched by Napoléon Bonaparte that aimed to appropriately, and quickly, resupply the armed forces. Appert began his research by placing vegetables in sealed bottles that he plunged for a period into boiling water. He thus invented the process of preserving food through the use of heat in a vacuum. Having rejected any kind of patent, he died a poor man. Society would pay homage to him by granting the name "appertization" to this kind of food preservation, which is a form of canning.

Circa 1800
Coffee percolator

Jean-Baptiste de Bellow developed the percolation system and, subsequently, invented the first coffee percolator (*percolare*, to filter, to pass through). It involves two stacked receptacles that are separated in the middle by a compartment in which ground coffee is placed. Simmering water is poured into the upper part; the grounds slowly become moist and the juice passes into the bottom receptacle. The process is not infusion but rather lixiviation, a technique that slowly sifts water through a powdered solid. "As a result, coffee has more qualities . . ." (Honoré de Balzac, *Traité des excitants modernes* [*The Pleasures and Pains of Coffee*], 1838).

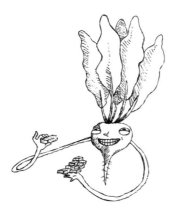

1812
Beet sugarloaf

In 1801, **Benjamin Delessert** (1773–1847), a botanist, politician, and entrepreneur, transformed an old mill into a sugar refinery. The Continental Blockade was in effect between 1806 and 1807. The ports of Europe were closed. In France, foodstuffs like cane sugar were in short supply, which incited Napoléon to support research on beet sugar. After several years of study, the first crystal loaves were produced industrially as a dry substance that could be easily broken into pieces. The emperor visited the factory in Passy on December 2, 1812. He was so enthusiastic that he took off his own cross of the Légion d'Honneur and pinned it to the breast of the entrepreneur, and then named him a baron.

1819
Chaptalization

Jean-Antoine Chaptal (1756–1832), a chemist by profession, was a student of Antoine Lavoisier. In cases when overly acidic must yields an unpleasant wine that cannot be well preserved, he suggested increasing the alcohol content. Simply adding sugar was most recommended. And that was chaptalization, which Chaptal outlined, thereby revolutionizing the art of winemaking.

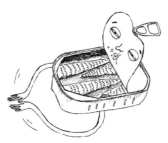

1823
Industrial canning of sardines

Joseph Colin brought sardine canning from the small-scale level to industrial production: he replaced butter with oil, and in 1824, built the first cannery in Brittany, in the industrial district around the Port de Nantes. Then he opened several French fry shops along the coast of the region. His father, Joseph, had already been keenly interested in Appert's invention: canning.

1846

Cast-iron stove

Jean-Baptiste Godin (1817–1888), the son of a locksmith, envisioned the cast-iron stove based on a workshop stove. The success of the invention was tied to the material used to make it, cast iron, which was much more effective in diffusing heat than former models made with metal. Starting in 1849, the "Godin-France" was mass-produced in Guise (Aisne). That allowed generations of chefs, both professional and amateur, to develop and enhance their cooking.

1863

Pasteurization

Louis Pasteur (1822–1895), upon the request of Napoléon III, began studying wine "diseases." He proved that variations observed in wine quality could be attributed to the presence of fungus, which changed the wine as it grew in it. To justify his opinion, he certified that in destroying the germs of such growth with heat, the development of wine diseases could be halted. That became pasteurization.

Circa 1890

Box for Camembert

Eugène Ridel, an engineer (his father was a cabinetmaker), who used a sawmill in Livarot, is said to be the inventor of the Camembert cheese box. He developed a poplar scroll, which he then stapled. Gluing the wood had proven to be unsuccessful. The box revolutionized the marketing of Camembert because it became easier to transport, especially by train.

1907

Sparkling wine in sealed tanks

Jean-Eugène Charmat, an engineer and professor at the Université de Montpellier, developed the technique for making sparkling wines in sealed vats. The process was given his name. According to this winemaking method, the second fermentation, using a still wine that has gone through a first alcoholic fermentation, occurs over ten to fifteen days in a sealed tank and not in individual bottles, the method traditionally used for Champagne. Charmat therefore paved the way for the industrial production of sparkling wines and ciders . . . and at low cost.

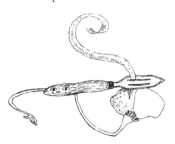

1929

Économe (vegetable peeler)

Victor Pouzet, a cutler in Thiers (Puy-de-Dôme), the birthplace of French cutlery, invented the *économe*, the affordable kitchen utensil. It was revolutionary for not cutting but economically peeling: hence its name. Its advertising slogan: "30 percent of your time and potatoes saved!" It has a stainless steel blade (inserted into a handle) at an obtuse angle and two sharp grooves. The pointed tip furthermore allows blemishes on fruit and vegetables to be removed.

1953

Cocotte-Minute (pressure cooker)

Frédéric and Henri Lescure, the great-grandsons of a traveling tinsmith, kept the family name alive through innovation, and especially through industrial technology that involved shaping a piece of metal through compression: that became stamping. Frédéric and Henri, inspired by Denis Papin's steam digester, launched into a project that led to the stamped aluminum product that has become so emblematic: the Cocotte-Minute. It was not accepted into the Household Arts Salon in Paris in 1954 (too modern!).

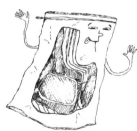

1970s

Sous-vide cooking

In the 1970s, **George Pralus** (1940–2014), a chef, developed a technique of low-temperature cooking that allowed food to be preserved. First used to cook foie gras, it was later applied to vegetables, meats, and fish. Sous-vide cooking is a temperature-controlled poaching process in a bain-marie (water bath). The food is wrapped in hermetically sealed plastic bags that are heat resistant. The food is then cooked at a lower temperature for several hours. Because sous-vide meets the demands of standardization, the food processing industry uses it to produce prepared dishes.

1990s

Oyster thread

Yves Renaut, an electrician by profession, developed a process to facilitate opening oysters. When a stainless steel thread is inserted into the shell, with part remaining outside the shell, the consumer need only pull to open. The muscle is severed and the oyster opens. A judgment made by the highest French court of appeal on October 22, 2002, recounts one of the epic trajectories of this rarely used invention.

2010

Bagues d'effervescence (sparkling wine openers)

Aldo Maffeo, a designer by profession, invented a tool that facilitates the removal of the cork from a bottle of sparkling wine (Champagne, etc.), all while reducing the muscle needed and shaking the bottle as little as possible. Once the "ring" is inserted into the notches of the cork, gently twist to easily uncork. The pressure independently ejects the cork from the bottle.

skip to
Sardines: The Little Delicacy in a Tin, p. 39

Caviar and France

Originally from the Caspian Sea and the banks of the Volga River, sturgeon spawned its way to the coasts of France. Ever since, its eggs have been harvested in the Aquitaine and Sologne regions, among others. Let's take a tour through the black gold's new world.

Charles Patin O'Coohoon

"The taste can be considered as the most **distinguished of the five senses**. Moreover, it generally **fails** to appear among the popular masses, where one does not hesitate to **deprive** oneself of **caviar** in favor of piles of **root vegetables**!"

Pierre Desproges

LES MAISONS FRANÇAISES

Caviar de Neuvic
Neuvic, Lot

La Maison Nordique
Saint Viatre, Loir-et-Cher

Le caviar Perle noire
Les Eyzies, Gironde

Sturia Saint
Genis-de-Saintonge,
Charente-Maritime

L'Esturgonnière
Le Teich, Gironde

Prunier
Montpon-Ménestérol, Dordogne

Caviar de France
Biganos, le Moulin de la Cassadotte

RAISING THE RARE PEARL

For a long time, Beluga, Osetra, and Sevruga roe were rare pearls. These three sturgeon species could be found from the rivers of the Ural Mountains to the Caspian Sea. Fishing sturgeon was banned in 2008 when it became endangered. Very quickly, farming the black gold turned into a godsend: between 2000 and 2013, the annual production of caviar went from 1,100 pounds (500 kg) to 160 metric tons. Since then, farms have cropped up across the globe. Today France is the second largest producer of caviar.

FRANCE, THE OTHER COUNTRY

The Gironde Estuary was one of the last places in Western Europe where sturgeon spawned. Caviar was produced there until the 1950s. Very quickly, France invested in farming and in 1993 the country became the first to produce caviar from aquaculture.

The Sturgeon Varieties Raised in France

BELUGA

Originally from the Danube, this fish is the largest kind of sturgeon. It can grow to close to 16 feet (5 m). The first eggs come after fifteen years and are large in size but very delicate. The caviar is light or dark gray on the outside, its membrane thin, and reveals delicate buttery notes. This is the most prestigious kind.

OSETRA

A medium-size fish, originally from the Caspian and Black Seas. It is the second most raised species in France. The first eggs appear at eight years. The caviar ranges from dark grayish brown to golden, its texture is firm, and its aroma is reminiscent of fresh walnuts.

BAERI

This fish, originally from Siberia, is a variety one finds for the most part in France. Well suited to farming, the species yields eggs as of age seven. The caviar is brown in color and has a tender texture. The eggs are average in size and have a lighter taste with subtle woody notes.

CAVIAR TALK

Among journalists: in French, *caviarder* (to caviar) means to pull a passage from a text, and by extension, the word implies censorship.

Among soccer players: a *caviar* in French is a very precise pass, perfect to within an inch. For example, when Emmanuel Petit's corner set up Zinédine Zidane's header in the final of the World Cup.

Among politicians: the term *gauche caviar* ("limousine liberal") designates an elected official who claims to be with the people but tends to keep apart.

THE STAGES OF CAVIAR PRODUCTION

1

Slaughter
The female sturgeon's belly is opened by hand. The skein, the sack containing eggs (between 10 and 15 percent of the fish's mass), is weighed.

2

Sifting
The sack containing the eggs is sifted through metal grating to rid the eggs of impurities.

3

Salting
One of the most delicate operations. It is at this stage that the eggs become caviar.

4

Drying
This step involves drying the excess water in the grains. It makes the caviar neither too dry nor too oily.

5

Packing
The caviar is placed in the traditional blue tin box, which holds 4 pounds (1.8 kg), then undergoes vacuum sealing to remove air.

6

Aging
It is at this stage that taste develops. A minimum of three months is required from the time of production for caviar to reveal its aromas. It will then be repackaged.

The Pioneer
Fernand de Robert de Lalagade

After the armistice of 1918, **Fernand de Robert Lalagade** met Soviet dignitaries eager to market caviar in Europe. In 1923, he founded the company Caviar Volga, and the same year the Maison du Caviar.
A feat of arms: he associated caviar with the jet-set and luxury lifestyle of Paris.

The Grande Maison
The Petrossian Dynasty

In the 1920s, two Armenian brothers, **Melkoum and Mouchegh Petrossian**, settled in France. They founded a fine foods store and a few years later, Petrossian caviar became the premier brand of this sought-after product. Mouchegh had four children, including Armen Petrossian, the current president of the purveyor.
A feat of arms: the purveyor was the first to commercialize and market caviar, with their famous box and brand name indicated.

The Sturgeon Fisher
Jacques Nebot

In the 1970s, **Jacques Nebot** tracked this "black gold" in the Caspian Sea. In 1981, he founded Astara, an import, processing, and distribution company. In 1985, he launched his restaurant, Le Coin du caviar, in Paris, then in 2001, the Maison Kaviari.
A feat of arms: he was one of the first to encourage the great chefs to put caviar on their menus.

MY FATHER'S FAVORITE LINE-CAUGHT AQUITAINE SEA BASS, 1971
by Anne-Sophie Pic*

SERVES 4
4 pieces of sea bass, about 3½ ounces (100 g) each
Fine salt
¼ fennel bulb, stalks removed, finely chopped
½ shallot, peeled and chopped
1 white button mushroom, stalk removed, cap cleaned and chopped
1 tablespoon (15 g) unsalted butter
1 cup (250 mL) Champagne
⅔ cup (150 mL) fish stock
2 cups (250 mL) heavy cream
⅓ cup plus 1 tablespoon (100 mL) whole milk
3 ounces (80 g) caviar, from Aquitaine
1 sheet parchment paper

The sea bass
Season the sea bass pieces with salt and steam them for 3 minutes at 212°F (100°C). Remove them from the steamer, and let them stand for 2 minutes at room temperature to finish cooking. Make the Champagne sauce. Cook the fennel, shallot, and mushroom in the butter. Add the Champagne and reduce it by half. Add the fish stock and bring it to a boil. Let the mixture reduce again by half. Add the cream and milk. Heat without reducing, and let infuse for about 15 minutes. Strain through a fine-mesh sieve. Season with salt, then adjust the flavor of the sauce with a little more Champagne, if needed.

Finishing and presentation
Spread the caviar on the sheet of parchment paper. Ensure that the Champagne sauce is well emulsified. Place the sea bass in a shallow bowl and cover it with some of the Champagne sauce. Place the caviar on the sea bass by turning the paper upside down on the sea bass, then carefully peeling it off. Finish by adding the Champagne sauce.

Daughter of Jacques Pic, Anne-Sophie Pic is the three-star chef of Maison Pic in Valencia. Recipe from Livre Blanc d'Anne-Sophie Pic, Éditions Hachette cuisine

---

THE 3 GREAT CAVIAR CREATIONS IN HISTORY

Caviar gelée with cauliflower cream by Joël Robuchon (1982): an Osetra caviar placed in a delicate jelly covered with a silk cream of cauliflower. This is one of the dishes that made the reputation of the Poitevin chef. Since then, Joël Robuchon's recipe has followed him to all his restaurants.

European sea bass with caviar by Jacques Pic (1971): a thick fillet of Mediterranean sea bass paired with a caviar from Iran. A perfect balance between the saltiness of the caviar and the fish's sweet flavor of the sea. To play with the contrast between the black caviar and the pearly sheen of the fish's flesh, the chef of Valence (Drôme) envisioned using a creamy Champagne sauce.

Puy green lentils and smoked eel caviar gelée by Alain Ducasse (2014): a magnificent timbale with coppery highlights served at the Plaza Athénée (Paris). The dish is accompanied by buckwheat blinis with raw cream—a delicious marriage between chic and rustic.

And the flesh of the fish in all this?

The sturgeon has a firm white flesh, which has long been prized. But today, it is somewhat neglected. Here are two ideas for using the sturgeon's meat.

In rillettes: chop the flesh of the steamed fillets. Season with fresh herbs and shallots.

Smoked and marinated: smoke the fish fillets in a smoker. Cube the flesh and marinate it in olive oil and fresh herbs.

BEST PAIRINGS
Potatoes
Bread and butter
Blinis
Eggs

WHAT TO DRINK WITH CAVIAR?
Although the most natural pairing is assumed to be vodka, wine also suits it very well. Champagnes with fine bubbles are excellent accompaniments, as are Burgundy Chardonnays or Muscadets.

WHY USE MOTHER-OF-PEARL?
Some metals, such as silver, oxidize on contact with caviar. It is a reaction related to the methionine and the cystine present in the metal, which form the silver sulfide. You should therefore select an inert material, such as mother-of-pearl, for spoons and dishes for serving caviar.

skip to
Bottarga: Mediterranean Caviar, p. 148

Carnivores during the Siege of Paris

September 19, 1870: Prussian soldiers besiege Paris. By October, food is in short supply; the city is shivering and dying of hunger. After devouring thousands of cats, rats, and, although taboo, sixty thousand horses and countless puppies, the City of Light went even further . . .

Marie-Amal Bizalion

THE DEVIL'S BUTCHER SHOP

During the Siege of Paris, Deboos, the owner of the English butcher shop at 173, boulevard Haussmann, launched into sordid dealings with Albert Geoffroy Saint-Hilaire, the director of the zoological garden. Zebras and buffalos, which had been given refuge at the Jardin des Plantes, bore the brunt of an initial sale. A few antelopes and kangaroos later, Saint-Hilaire surrendered his last elephants: "Please be so kind, if you accept the delivery of my animals tomorrow or before I am off duty, to give Blondel, the keeper, a letter addressed to me in which it is stated that you will pay me the price for two elephants—twenty-seven thousand francs—on Thursday morning, December 20."* On December 29, Castor was slaughtered in front of Saint-Hilaire. The agony was atrocious. Then it was Pollux's turn on December 30. Resold at a high price, they would both celebrate the New Year on the plates of the well off.

Excerpt from the collection of letters published in the weekly newspaper La joie de la maison, *p. 205, April 5, 1994.*

Exotic Christmas celebration

**Chef Choron's menu
at the Café Voisin,**
261, rue Saint-Honoré,
December 25, 1870

HORS D'OEUVRE
Butter, radishes
Stuffed donkey head
Sardines
SOUPS
Purée of red beans with croutons
Elephant consommé
ENTRÉES
Fried gudgeon
Roasted camel à l'anglaise
Kangaroo stew
Roasted bear chops with
sauce au poivre
ROASTS
Haunch of wolf in venison sauce
Cat accompanied by rats
Watercress salad
Terrine of antelope with truffles
Porcini à la bordelaise
Peas with butter
ENTREMETS
Rice pudding with jam
DESSERT
Gruyère cheese

Gourmet opinion

"Yesterday, I ordered a slice of Pollux for dinner. Pollux and his brother Castor are two elephants who were slaughtered. It was hard, coarse and fatty, and I recommend that English families, who are able to procure beef or mutton, not eat elephant." Henry Du Pré Labouchère, British correspondent for the *Daily News,* January 6, 1871

"It is not even horse that we are eating anymore. Is it perhaps dog? Is it perhaps rat? My stomach has started to hurt. We are eating the unknown." Victor Hugo, *Choses vues,* December 30, 1870

"The cat stew was in every way excellent, although somewhat hard. The dog chops were overly marinated somewhat. The plum pudding with horse marrow was delicious." Adolphe Michel, *Le siège de Paris: 1870-1871* (pp. 264–265)

January 1, 1871, Pierre Fraisse, owner of the famous restaurant Peter's, on the Passage des Princes, served the following feast:
Hors d'oeuvre: fresh butter, olives, sardines, Lyon and Boulogne sausages, marinated tuna.
Soup: *sajou* (monkey) with Bordeaux wine; blue ling with rice; *croûte-au-pot.*
Entrées: roasted mule with mashed potatoes; haunch of venison in Joussenel sauce; fillet of elephant in Madeira sauce; rack of donkey with turnips; haunch of bear bourgeois.
Roasts: chicken; duckling; leg of lamb; galantine of peacock, seasonal salad . . .

The War of the Corks

The continuing debate: should wine stoppers be made of cork or synthetic materials, or be screw caps?

Gwilherm de Cerval

WHAT IS THE "TASTE OF CAP"?
It comes from a molecule called TCA (2,4,6-trichloroanisole). It produces molds that nestle in cork and gives the wine an unpleasant smell and aroma of cork. The cork is responsible for this off flavor in 95 percent of cases. It can also come from the bark of trees polluted by insecticides, wood used in the wine cellars, or even the air.

Corks under the Magnifying Glass

To cope with the evaporation that occurs with corked bottles, or for reasons of economics (the cost of raw materials), some winemakers and industrialists choose to use other types of stoppers in their bottles:

NDtech stoppers
100 percent natural cork, individually sifted and discarded if a trace of TCA is detected
advantage: looks like a traditional cork
disadvantage: expensive

Diam stoppers
The cork's volatile compounds are extracted, thus eliminating the taste of cork
advantage: preserves the purity of the aromas
disadvantage: unattractive, and not enough information on its aging ability

Synthetic stoppers
These can have a cellular structure close to that of real cork, and can also be injected with foam or even molded
advantage: unbeatable price
disadvantage: made from petroleum, and unattractive

Screw caps
An aluminum alloy, and an airtight seal called "Saran Tin Liner" or "Saranex"
advantage: preserves the purity of the aromas
disadvantage: can reduce the perception of the wine's quality and does not have the charm of a stopper that pops!

Glass stoppers
These have a glass cylinder equipped with a waterproof plastic ring that secures the stopper
advantage: preserves the purity of the aromas and is recyclable
disadvantage: does not allow optimal aging of the wine (3 to 4 years max)

skip to
Champagne, p. 194

Let's Take a Look at Lentils

Esau was right to exchange his birthright for a bowl of lentils: they are so good!
The Bible does not say which type of lentil Esau consumed, so perhaps
it was one of the many varieties cultivated in France.

Estérelle Payany

LE PUY GREEN LENTIL
The favorite among chefs. Cultivated since the Gallo-Roman era in the region of Puy-en-Velay, and the first plant protected by an AOC in 1996 (AOP since 2008).
Appearance: thin skin, bronze color
Distinctive quality: does not burst during cooking
Popular recipe: salt pork with lentils

CHAMPAGNE LENTIL
The most "girly" of the lentils. It earned its reputation from Marie Leszczyńska, hence its nickname "Queen's lentil." It flourishes between Rethel and Troyes.
Appearance: small in size and beautiful powder pink color
Distinctive quality: particularly sweet
Popular recipe: in a warm salad

BLOND LENTIL OF SAINT-FLOUR
The least known lentil in France. Also called "Planèze lentil."
Appearance: generous in size
Distinctive quality: part of the Sentinel Slow Food project, its cultivation was saved by a narrow margin when its imminent disappearance was announced
Popular recipe: boiled with sugar, as in a jam

LENTIL DU BERRY
The same variety as that of the Puy, but grown elsewhere.
Appearance: thin skin, bronze color
Distinctive quality: protected by a Label Rouge (Red Label)
Popular recipe: in a velouté

BELUGA BLACK LENTIL
The most spectacular.
Appearance: black, turning gray when cooked
Distinctive quality: its color is distinctive enough!
Popular recipe: in risotto

RED LENTIL
The fastest to cook (15 minutes), grown mainly in southwest France.
Appearance: skinless and orange
Distinctive quality: doesn't hold up well when cooked; tends to disintegrate
Popular recipe: puréed, or in a soup

LENTIL OF CILAOS
Cultivated since the eighteenth century on the volcanic land of the island of Réunion, it comprises at least six different varieties.
Appearance: small, light brown
Distinctive quality: nicknamed "the gold of Cilaos" as much for its high price (approximately €15[$18] per 2 pounds/1 kilo) as for its delicate flavor
Popular recipe: with sausage rougail

SALT PORK IN LENTILS

PREPARATION TIME: 15 MINUTES
COOKING TIME: 2 HOURS 25 MINUTES
RESTING TIME: 12 HOURS, IF THE MEATS ARE NOT DESALTED
SERVES 6

3⅓ pounds (1.5 kg) lightly salted salt pork: backbone, hock, or knuckle
7 ounces (200 g) pork belly fat (preferably lightly salted)
1 onion
2 cloves
2 carrots
1 clove garlic
10½ ounces (300 g) Puy green lentils
1 bouquet garni (thyme, bay leaf, or other herbs of your choice)
Fine salt and freshly ground black pepper
2 tablespoons (30 mL) cream (optional)

Ask the butcher if the meat needs to be desalted or not. If you need to desalt it: soak the meat for 12 hours, changing the water twice. Peel the onion and cut it in half. Pierce each half with a clove. Peel and cut the carrots into four sections. Place the meat in a large pan. Cover the meat in cold water, add half the carrots, a half onion, and the garlic clove (unpeeled). Bring to a boil, then simmer for 1 hour and 30 minutes. Rinse the lentils and add them to a separate pan. Cover them with cold water, add the bouquet garni, the carrots, and the remaining onion. Bring to a boil, then simmer for 20 minutes; drain. Remove the meat from the first pan using a slotted spoon; reserve the broth. Cut up the meat. Place the lentils and the meats in the pan and add just enough of the broth to cover them. Bring to a boil, then simmer for 20 to 25 minutes, or until the lentils are tender but still whole. Taste and season with pepper (salt will probably not be necessary). Add the cream, if using, just before serving. The cream adds a touch of richness that some love.

skip to
Newfound Love for the Chickpea, p. 56

The Famous Pressed Duck

Pressed duck, duck à la *rouennaise*, or duck *au sang* has benefited, since its creation, from a craze that elevated the dish abroad to be one of the gastronomic symbols of France. Created in Rouen, and adapted at the grand restaurant La Tour d'Argent in Paris, the recipe has been largely copied, reworked, and reinterpreted.

Valentine Oudard

A LITTLE HISTORY

It all starts with the Duclair duck, a local breed originating from Duclair near Rouen. At the beginning of the twentieth century, farmers crossed the Seine to sell their poultry at market. They sometimes overloaded the ferry so much that some of the birds died by suffocation. Determined to sell them, the duck breeders decided to deliver the animals, still retaining their blood, to the village restaurants despite the debacle. Father Denise, innkeeper of La Poste hotel, bought these ducks (they were cheaper than the others), and consequently created a recipe using the blood of the animal to thicken the sauce. This became known as the "duckling à la Duclair."

THE FATHERS OF PRESSED DUCK

The chef of His Majesty Edward VII, **Louis Convert**, adapted Father Denise's recipe, which the chef served in his restaurant at the Cathedral in Rouen in 1900.

Michel Guéret was inspired by Louis Convert's recipe to serve the Rouennaise duck dish to members of the Rotary Club. He called it "Félix Faure," named after the ship on which he served it. In 1986, he created the Order of the Canardiers to guarantee local production and to safeguard the original recipe.

Frédéric Delair introduced the recipe to Parisians in 1890 by serving it at the restaurant La Tour d'Argent, where he worked as a chef. He created a special sauce, based on poultry consommé, Madeira, cognac, and the juices from the pressed duck. Unlike the Rouennaise duck, pressed duck at La Tour d'Argent is prepared using duck from Challans.

DUCK À LA ROUENNAISE FROM THE DIEPPE HOTEL IN ROUEN
*by Michel Guéret**

PREPARATION TIME: A LITTLE TIME AND PATIENCE
COOKING TIME: 17 TO 20 MINUTES
SERVES 2

1 bottle (750 mL) Beaune red wine
2 tablespoons (20 g) chopped shallots
A few sprigs thyme
1 bay leaf
2 cups (250 mL) veal stock
Quatre épices spice blend
1 Rouen duckling, weighing 4½ pounds (2 kg), killed but not bled
Scant ½ cup (100 mL) cognac
½ lemon
Scant ½ cup (100 mL) port
1 tablespoon (20 g) unsalted butter

In the kitchen

Prepare the Bordelaise stock. Combine the wine, shallots, thyme, and bay leaf in a saucepan and reduce the wine to two-thirds its original volume. Add the veal stock. Add the quatre épices spice blend to taste. Let stand for 1 hour; the sauce will thicken naturally. Chop up the liver and heart from the duck carcass, and press them through a fine-mesh sieve, then pour the Bordelaise sauce through the same sieve, reserving all the liquids; this creates the Rouennais stock. Place the duckling on a roasting spit and roast it for 17 to 20 minutes. Grill the duckling giblets over high heat (coat them in mustard, bread them, then grill them) and serve them on a plate with butter.

At the serving table

On a portable stove, flambé the cognac in a saucepan. Add the Rouennais stock, and warm it to almost boiling (200°F/90°C). Add the juice of the lemon half and the port, then thoroughly whisk in the butter until the mixture is creamy. In the meantime, remove the duckling breast fillets and place them on a serving dish with the giblets. Press the duck carcass to extract the blood, and add the blood to the saucepan. Heat the sauce without boiling it. Coat the fillets with the sauce. Serve on very hot plates with a side (such as a small flan of celery).

*Chef of l'Hôtel Dieppe in Rouen and founder of the Order of the Canardiers in 1986.

THE NUMBERED DUCK

When Frédéric Delair took control of La Tour d'Argent in 1890, he decided to serve pressed duck in front of the customer according to a particular ritual, and to carve it with a fork without ever touching the plate! Just as Father Denise did, he numbered each duck.

As of this writing, La Tour d'Argent has served its

1,148,787th

pressed duck

No. 328 Edward VII (1890)
No. 112,125 President Franklin D. Roosevelt (1930)
No. 236,970 Fernandel (1953)
No. 531,147 Mick Jagger (1978)
No. 536,814 Serge Gainsbourg (1978)
No. 604,200 Jean-Paul Belmondo (1983)
No. 724,025 Jacques Cousteau (1989)
No. 738,100 Charles Trenet (1990)
No. 759,216 Tom Cruise and Nicole Kidman (1991)
No. 821,208 Catherine Deneuve (1994)
No. 843,769 Jean-Pierre Marielle and Jean-Paul Belmondo (1996)
No. 1,079,006 Bill Gates (2009)

THE DUCK PRESS

This true piece of craftsmanship has been custom-made by Parisian jewelers specifically for the pressed duck recipe. Made of silver metal, it is often decorative and stylized. Each prestigious establishment, chateau, and grand restaurant has had its own duck press fabricated for its use. Those of La Tour d'Argent date to 1890 and 1911 and were created by the jeweler Christofle.

The 5 Principles of the Rouennaise Duckling Recipe

❶ The duckling must be asphyxiated. ❷ It must be cooked rare (17 to 20 minutes). ❸ The breast fillets must be removed. ❹ The carcass must be pressed to extract the blood. ❺ The sauce (Rouennais stock) must be thickened with the extracted blood.

skip to

A Taste for Blood, p. 274

Words & Foods

TYPOLOGY OF FRENCH RESTAURANTS

In France, the places where people go to be restored are not just simple establishments but veritable institutions. One does not go only for what happens on the plate and in the glass or cup, but for the atmosphere, for the sweetness of life.

Aurore Vincenti

The restaurant

When you take the time to have a bite or a drink, you are restored. To be restored, *se restaurer* in French, means **"to remake, to repair oneself."** There is nothing to do, nothing to produce. There is simply waiting, contemplation, conversation, and digestion on the program for this vacation at the heart of your day. The restaurant, which in French colloquial speech is shortened to **restau** or **resto**, bears the name of this practice, which helps us **get back on our feet.**

The café

The term *café* (coffee) emerged around 1600; it comes from the Arabic word *qâhwâ*, introduced to **the court of Louis XIV** by **Turkish** ambassadors of the Ottoman Empire. The term quickly became fashionable. It spread across the land until it lent its name to the establishments in which it is consumed. A **place for meeting**, literature, concerts, and passionate debate, cafés are famous in France and are an integral part of a certain kind of good **French living**.

The bistrot

There are extraordinary hypotheses concerning the etymology of this word: a Cossack enters a Paris cabaret in 1814 crying "**bystro**!" (quick!) so as to be served quickly; the Poitevin word **bistraud** designating the wine merchant's servant; **bistouilles** and **bistingos**, referring to obscure cabarets and questionable cocktails . . . Originally a *bistrot* was a man who owned a cabaret. Today, it is a **typically French, small café**. In the 2000s, bistros and gastronomy joined forces: the famous term **bistronomie** (bistro-style gastronomy), a beloved portmanteau of food critics, brings together quality and simplicity.

The bar

The bar is a figure of speech: a metonymy, a synecdoche! It's the wood or metal bar or counter that lends its name to a drinking establishment. The bar for the bar, **the part for the whole.**

The brasserie

The brasserie (French for "brewery") is above all where beer is made. Its **Gallic origins** are connected to the word **braces**, which designates a grain. Beer has been consumed in brasseries since the nineteenth century, but in time, the brasserie acquired a certain cachet. It is often spacious and elegant, with a very French menu that doesn't skimp on meat, and **café waiters** dressed just so and attentive to their task . . .

The estaminet

In the Walloon language, the word **stamon**, which is the origin of the word *estaminet*, designates a **post** to which a **cow is attached** near its trough. In fact, originally, an estaminet was a room with several posts. Apart from these architectural considerations, it is above all an event space, like a **cabaret**. Drinking, eating, and smoking are customary. In the early nineteenth century, it corresponded to **cafés** where pipes were smoked, as opposed to the **divan**, which was more bourgeois and where cigars and cigarettes were preferred.

The French cambuse (caboose)

In Dutch, **kambuis** designates the **kitchen on a ship**, which itself is taken from the late medieval German *kambuse*. In both languages, it is a room for storage, concoctions, and snoozing. In French, *cambuse* can be found in eighteenth-century slang to describe a place that **doesn't look so good**: a construction-site canteen, an inexpensive restaurant. Today, it's a small, unpretentious restaurant that serves as a **neighborhood eatery**. So don't be offended if "even the fries smell like fish" . . .

The winstub

Feel like a woodsy ambience, red-and-white checkered tablecloths, and a good **grumbeerekiechle** (potato pancake)? The **winstub**, literally **lounge (stub) where one drinks wine (wein)** in German, is an Alsatian or Moselle-region cabaret dating from the mid-seventeenth century. You can still go to one today to try local dishes and warm up with swigs of Gewürztraminer.

The French gargote (greasy spoon)

Everything's **mediocre** here: the food leaves something to be desired and the service is practically nonexistent. In short, it's not a very recommended place. The word originally stemmed from the French verb **gargoter** (to bubble, to have dirty food and drink), and derives from the medieval French **gorge** and **gosier** (gullet). The **lapse** therefore comes both from the customer and the service. Courtesy is left at the door. And yet, the *gargote* has a name that inspires a **certain kind of tenderness**: probably because of its ending, which sounds affectionate.

Skip to: Dining in Wine Cellars, p. 330

Brocciu, and the Art of Whey

If you have not had the opportunity to savor the sweetness, smoothness, and aroma of this AOP Corsican cheese, then you have not yet experienced the subtlety of Corsican gastronomy.

Frédéric Laly-Baraglioli

HOW DO YOU TASTE IT?

WHAT IS IT?

→ A cheese created from the by-product, or whey, that remains after the curdling of milk and the production of other cheeses.

→ Although it's a whey-based cheese, it's enriched with whole milk from Corsican sheep and/or goats, lending it a richer and fattier texture.

→ A seasonal product, molded in antique *faisselles* (molds for draining cheese) and formerly in reed baskets, which, from November to June, is ideally eaten fresh, but can also be enjoyed aged (described as *salitu*, *passu*, or *seccu*).

WHAT IT'S NOT . . .

→ The *recuech* of Auvergne, ricotta, *brousse*, *grueil* béarnais, or Basque *zemerona*—all specialty cheeses of the region. It's made only with the whey!

→ The *sérac* of Jura and the Alps, which is a mixture of whey, milk, and vinegar, smoked or aged in white wine!

IT'S CLOSE TO . . .

The Greek *mizithra* and *manouri*, Maltese *rigouta*, the Walloon *maquée*, and Romanian *urda*.

Prepared simply

Plain or sweetened: as is with a chestnut-flour galette, flattened (with sugar, brandy, coffee, or jam)

Salted: with pepper and olive oil; as a sweet component of the iconic winter dish *a pulenda* (a chestnut-flour polenta served with fried eggs, Corsican *figatellu* [a sausage], and sometimes lamb with sauce)

Cooked

Known as beignets (*fritelli*), which are served during elections, baptisms, weddings, etc., and also as part of many preparations:

Soups

Stuffed vegetables: zucchini, artichokes, onions, romaine leaves, etc.

Pasta with a stuffing made of brocciu, Swiss chard, and mint/marjoram for cannelloni, ravioli, lasagna, and *strozzapreti* (Bastiaise dumplings)

Omelets and soufflés

Fish: sardines; trout; capons stuffed with garlic, parsley, and mint; in a brandade of salt cod

Tart/pie filling: in savory pies, tarts, or popovers (with pepper, squash, Swiss chard, or onions)

Desserts: in beignets, brioche (*panetta*), turnovers, pies, tartlets, *fiadone* (Corsican cheesecake), flan, and most recently, ice cream!

— FIADONE (CORSICAN CHEESECAKE) —
by "Mamyta," Josette Solier*

This is an unorthodox recipe because it uses a food processor, but this approach has proven itself very effective!

PREPARATION TIME: 15 MINUTES
COOKING TIME: 30 MINUTES
SERVES 8

1 cup plus 2 tablespoons (226 g) sugar, divided
1 piece brocciu cheese, weighing 1⅛ pounds (500 g)
5 whole eggs
Zest of 1 unwaxed lemon
1 tablespoon (15 mL) eau-de-vie

Preheat the oven to its maximum temperature, grease a cake pan measuring 8 to 9¾ inches (20 to 25 cm) in diameter, and lightly coat the inside with 1 tablespoon (13 g) of the sugar, ensuring that the sides and the bottom are covered. In a food processor fitted with the knife blade, process together the brocciu, eggs, 1 cup (200 g) of the sugar, the lemon zest, and eau-de-vie until perfectly smooth and creamy. Scrape the mixture into the pan, place the pan in the oven, and immediately lower the temperature to 350°F (180°C). Bake for at least 30 minutes: the *fiadone* must be dark brown on the entire surface and the center must be cooked (the blade of a knife inserted in the center will come out clean). If necessary, place a piece of foil over the top if the top has browned but the center is not yet done. Remove from the oven and let cool. Once completely cooled, sprinkle the top with the remaining 1 tablespoon (13 g) of sugar, and place it in the refrigerator: this is the secret of its moisture, and its flavor!

The grandmother of François-Régis Gaudry

—ARTICHOKES STUFFED WITH BROCCIU —
by "Mamyta," Josette Solier

PREPARATION TIME: 50 TO 60 MINUTES
COOKING TIME: 45 MINUTES
SERVES 3

1 clove garlic
1 small bunch parsley
¾ of a round of brocciu, about 1⅛ ounces (500 g)
1 pinch dried marjoram, or some fresh mint leaves
Salt and freshly ground black pepper
1 egg
6 medium artichokes
½ lemon
Flour, for dredging
Sunflower or olive oil, for frying

For the sauce
1 clove garlic, peeled
1 small bunch parsley
Sunflower or olive oil, for sautéing
2 onions, peeled and chopped
2 heaping tablespoons (about 45 mL) tomato paste
Scant ½ cup to 1 cup (100 to 250 mL) white or red wine
Salt and freshly ground black pepper

❶ Make the stuffing. Finely chop together the garlic and parsley. Combine this mixture with the brocciu and a good pinch of dried marjoram. Season with salt and pepper. Add the egg and stir to combine.

Prepare the artichokes: Cut off each artichoke stem to 1½ to 2 inches (4 to 5 cm), and peel the stem section that remains. Remove the outer leaves, leaving only the most tender interior leaves. Cut the artichokes in half crosswise. Moisten them with lemon juice to prevent them from browning.

Take each artichoke between the palms of your hands and press them in the center while carefully spreading the leaves outward, to form a kind of opened-flower appearance. Remove the choke, if there is any.

❷ Fill the artichokes with plenty of the stuffing, using a fork to pack it firmly into the artichoke so that it remains in place during the double cooking process. Flour the artichokes by rolling them on their sides in flour, ensuring the stuffing is also well coated.

❸ Heat the oil in a skillet, then reduce the heat, and place the artichokes one by one upside down into the oil (the stem should be pointing up). Once the stuffing is golden brown, brown the artichokes on all sides by resting them on their sides in the oil, turning them as necessary.

Make the sauce. Finely chop together the garlic and parsley. In a pressure cooker or in a saucepan, heat a few tablespoons of the oil, sauté the onions, then add the minced garlic and parsley and sauté until the onions are softened. Add the tomato paste and wine. Stir to combine. Season with salt and pepper, and simmer over low heat. Add ½ cup (about 100 mL) of water, if necessary.

❹ In a pressure cooker, carefully arrange the artichokes in the tomato sauce, ensuring the stuffing does not come out. Close and seal the lid and cook over low heat for 20 minutes (or until the valve begins to whistle). If the tip of a knife pierces an artichoke easily, the artichokes are done. If you do not have a pressure cooker, you can cook the artichokes in a large, covered pot over low heat for a longer period of time (you may have to add a little water if cooked in this way).

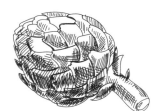

skip to
The Island of Cheeses, p. 135

BAD TASTE

Bawdy artisanal jokes or historic inventions, the names of these five specialties aim below the belt.
Sébastien Piève

LE TROU DU CRU
This cheese from Burgundy's Côte d'Or region was created in the early 1980s by the cheese maker Robert Berthaut. Its name ("asshole") is an impudent play on a common French insult and obscenity. It has a soft paste and an orange-colored rind washed with marc de Bourgogne. Reminiscent of a pungent Epoisses, it is molded into a small cylinder.

Recommendation?
It's neither made on the farm nor from raw milk (as "cru" might imply!) But try it for yourself.

LA PINE
Originating in the commune of Barbézieux-Saint-Hilaire (Charente) as a time-honored tradition, *la pine* is a pastry whose name and form cleverly allude to the male sex organ. Formerly made with puff pastry, it is offered plain or filled with custard or whipped cream. Originally served hot, and therefore hard, the delicacy is more tender with its filling . . . This local specialty is traditional in springtime, the season of new life, fertility, and Easter celebrations.

Recommendation?
Yes, but preferably along with its feminine counterpart, the *cornuelle*, a shortbread pastry in a triangular form with a hole in the center. Tasty and tasteful!

COUCOUGNETTES
These suggestively shaped oval confections were created in Pau (Pyrénées-Atlantiques) by the artisan Francis Miot (1948–2015). They are an homage to the beloved *"vert gallant"* King Henri IV, a famed seducer and the city's native son. The ingredients include almonds, chocolate, marzipan, and a hint of ginger. They are soaked in raspberry juice to give them a very distinctive pink hue.

Recommendation?
Yes, but only when accompanied by *Tétons de la Reine Margot*, another erotically named confection produced by the same boutique.

ZEZETTES
These vanilla-flavored shortbread cookies, based on a dough made from flour and white wine, feature a suggestive elongated form. They were first introduced in Sète, in Languedoc-Roussillon, by Gaston Bentata, based on family recipes from his native Algeria.

Recommendation?
Yes, dunked in coffee.

LE TOURMENT D'AMOUR
These soft, round little cakes are stuffed with coconut. They originated in the Îles des Saintes (French Antilles). The wives of sailors concocted these treats to welcome their husbands back from sea.

Recommendation?
Yes, while listening to the lyrics of Guadeloupian singer Francky Vincent: "Love's torment is like a little cake / You could find in the Saintes / And with that 'love's torment' of mine, my dear / You may find yourself pregnant." Romantic . . .

skip to
Échaudés, p. 301

Welcome Aboard

Soggy sandwiches, dishwater coffee, canned fish—cuisine aboard boats, planes, and trains generally leaves a disagreeable impression. Of course it's no simple matter to overcome the technical constraints inherent in producing the pleasures of the table while on board. Here's an overview and history of these traveling restaurants and the specialties of their chefs.

Jill Cousin

At sea . . .

Pack boats (*paquebots* in French) originally served to transport mail across the ocean, hence their name. In the early nineteenth century, the era of luxury liners opened up a new world of seaborne gastronomy under the eagle-eyed supervision of distinguished chefs.

Intérieur de l'Ile-de-France. Les Cuisines

The 1,000 members of the **kitchen** staff had to feed almost 3,000 mouths daily.

CUNARD WHITE STAR LINER "QUEEN MARY." The World's Largest and Fastest Liner.

The ship's hold was packed with staggering quantities of provisions for the voyage. The order book for a crossing from France in 1972 lists 44 tons of flour, 150 tons of fresh and frozen meat, 12,000 bottles of Champagne, 8,000 bottles of fine wines, 1,600 bottles of cognac, etc.

Every evening, the sophisticated **dining room of the *Queen Mary*** (maiden voyage in 1936) offered passengers dishes that were the last word in elegance and refined taste. The menu featured Waldorf salad and turtle soup, one of the great classics of luxury liner cuisine.

In the air . . .

Early long-haul flights required several stops for refueling. Passengers preferred to dine on terra firma when they had the option. The tray refreshments served on board consisted of simple sandwiches that were prepared and sold by the stewards. As flight conditions began to improve, more ambitious custom gastronomy appeared on board.

Business class menus.
The major airlines called upon star chefs who were media darlings to compete to develop prestigious menus adapted to the constraints imposed on airplane cuisine. The final meals on the Concorde were concocted by

Alain Ducasse, and offered a broad array of starters (Médaillons of Breton Lobster or Confit de Canard des Landes) and hot main courses (Mignons of Milk-fed Veal or Sea Bass Fillet à la Plancha), as well as two desserts. The food was prepared

several hours before the departure for New York by a team of nineteen chefs and pastry cooks from Servair and forty chefs of the distinguished professional association Les Toques du Ciel.

. . . and on land . . .

Picnics
Simple picnics were considered appropriate provender on the first long-distance luxury trains. The main line between Strasbourg and Basel was inaugurated in 1841. Neither smelly nor messy, these snacks were intended to satisfy modest appetites without inconveniencing passengers seated nearby. "Sunrises are a splendid accompaniment for railroad journeys, as are hard-boiled eggs." *Within a Budding Grove*, Marcel Proust, 1919.

Food on the move
Aware that a well-fed client is a contented client, the railway companies began to sell their own drinks and snacks from rolling carts in the late nineteenth century. They were to become ever more prevalent with the passage of time.

The dining car
Intended to shorten travel time by eliminating stops, the dining car offered meals that were loaded onto the train ready to cook or sometimes prepared on the spot. A first class offering might include the likes of Poulet Archiduc on the Train Bleu, which was inaugurated by the Compagnie des Wagons-Lits in 1866. The train originated in Calais, made a stopover in Paris, and then sped on to the sun-drenched Côte d'Azur.

WALDORF SALAD

Invented by Oscar Tschirky, the original maître d' at the Waldorf Astoria in New York, this salad, which was originally walnut-free, was destined for worldwide fame. It even appeared in Auguste Escoffier's works, as well as on the tables of some of the world's greatest palaces and steamer ships.

PREPARATION TIME: 25 MINUTES
SERVES 4

½ small celery root
2 Reinette apples
½ lemon
12 freshly shelled walnuts, chopped
3 tablespoons (45 mL) light mayonnaise

Peel the celery root and the apples, and cut them into very small dice. Immediately squeeze the lemon juice over them to prevent them from browning. Add them to a large bowl, and stir to combine, then stir in the crushed walnuts. Add the mayonnaise and stir to combine.

The Irresistible Walnut Cake

This is the recipe of Christiane Martorell. It has an incomparable moistness and a wonderful taste of walnuts. It will quickly become one of your favorites!

Delphine Le Feuvre

PREPARATION TIME: 20 MINUTES
COOKING TIME: 30 MINUTES
SERVES 6

5¼ ounces (150 g) walnuts, plus more for decoration
2 cups plus 3 tablespoons (220 g) confectioners' sugar
6 egg whites
¾ cup plus 1 tablespoon (80 g) all-purpose flour
2 tablespoons (30 mL) honey
11 tablespoons (160 g) lightly salted butter, melted and kept warm

Preheat the oven to 320°F (160°C). In a food processor, process the walnuts and sugar until finely ground. In a large bowl, whisk together the ground walnuts and the egg whites. Add the flour, and whisk until thoroughly combined. Add the honey and the butter. Stir well to combine. Scrape the batter into a greased and floured round cake pan measuring 9¾ inches (25 cm) in diameter. Arrange whole walnuts on top and bake for thirty minutes, or until slightly darkened on top. Let cool, and serve.

Walnuts and hazelnuts of France

Walnuts from Périgord
Description: four varieties are grouped under this name, all produced in the Périgord basin: Corne, Marbot, Grandjean, and Franquette.
Labels: AOC and AOP
Uses: fresh, dried, in halves, in wine, and in oil.

Walnuts from Grenoble
Description: this is the most famous French walnut, with its golden shell. It is one of the first fruits to have received an AOP, in 1938.
Labels: AOC and AOP
Uses: fresh, dried, in halves, in wine, in oil.

Hazelnuts from Cervione
Description: the only variety of hazelnut grown in Haute-Corse, the "Coutard's fertile strip." These have a small production compared to those of Italy and Turkey, but they enjoy a natural drying thanks to the winds that cradle the region.
Label: PGI
Uses: fresh, in oil, in spread.

skip to
The Chestnut, p. 214

Do You Know the OIV?

The International Organization of Vine and Wine (OIV) is located in the center of Paris. It is a tiny extraterritorial enclave where the world economy of the vine and wine is negotiated.

Bruno Fuligni

ITS HEADQUARTERS
18, rue d'Aguesseau, Paris 18th

ITS FLAG
A cluster of grapes, in which one of the six grapes is an image of Earth: this flag very clearly expresses the goals of the organization.

ITS POSITION
It is not an agency of the UN, but an old "intergovernmental organization" that continues the International Office of Wine, founded in 1924. It was established at the time of Aristide Briand and the SDN (Société des Nations), when "the spirit of Geneva" was stirring with the will to settle all conflicts through diplomatic organizations.

ITS MEMBER STATES
There are 46 of them: Algeria, Argentina, Armenia, Australia, Austria, Azerbaijan, Belgium, Bosnia, Brazil, Bulgaria, Chile, Croatia, Cyprus, Czech Republic, France, Georgia, Germany, Greece, Hungary, India, Israel, Italy, Lebanon, Luxembourg, Macedonia, Malta, Mexico, Moldova, Montenegro, Morocco, Netherlands, New Zealand, Norway, Peru, Portugal, Romania, Russia, Serbia, Slovakia, Slovenia, South Africa, Spain, Sweden, Switzerland, Turkey, and Uruguay.

China is not a member of the OIV, but Yantai City-prefecture and Ningxia Hui Autonomous Region have an **observer status**.

ITS MISSIONS

☞ In the 1920s, while Prohibition was rampant in the United States, the goal of the OIV was to promote the moderate consumption of wine.

☞ Each year, the OIV awards a **literary prize** and participates in many events.

☞ Contrary to what OPEC does for oil, the **OIV does not set any volume of production** and is not meant to serve as a cartel: its action is qualitative since it determines the international standards for winemaking and publishes worldwide wine statistics.

☞ The OIV is not only concerned with wine, but also with **all the products of the vine**, including raisins and grape juice: this is why some countries that may lack a winemaking tradition are members. Its member states represent one-fourth of the international community, and **85 percent of world grape production**. New memberships are expected: perhaps one day that of the **Vatican**, the largest consumer of wine per capita!

skip to
The Brotherhoods of French Gastronomy, p. 126

The Strawberry

This is France's favorite fruit, as evidenced by the fact that the French consume just over 6 pounds (2.8 kg) per year per household. The juicy red fruit is available from March to November to the delight of young and old.

Alvina Ledru-Johansson

A FEW DETAILS

Name: strawberry
Genus: *Fragaria*
Family: Rosaceae
Origin: the strawberry has been in Europe since ancient times. The Romans ate it and used it in cosmetics! Since the fourteenth century, it has been part of European gardens. In the seventeenth century, French botanist and sailor Amédée-François Frézier reported plans for bringing white strawberries, a large varietal of the fruit, from Chile. The problem? Male plants produce no fruit. It would not be until the work of another botanist, Antoine Nicolas Duchesne, that the plants would finally produce fruit: he noticed that the plant would produce fruit when Virginia strawberry plants were growing nearby. This was the birth of "natural" cross-fertilization, and the appearance of the "pineapple" strawberry (or pineberry), *Fragaria × ananassa*, from which today's varieties are derived.
Today: 135 varieties are listed in France (in seed catalogs), of which about a dozen represent 90 percent of sales. There is a distinction between those that bear fruit once a year versus those that bear fruit twice a year. Hence their availability until November.

LABELS, PGI, AOC

Périgord strawberry: this was the first European strawberry to obtain a PGI (Protected Geographical Indication), granted in 2004. It covers eight varieties (Gariguette, Cirafi, Darselect, Cléry, Donna, Candiss, Mara des Bois, and Charlotte) produced in thirty-two cantons of the Dordogne and nine communes of the Lot.
Nimes strawberry: this fruit has carried the PGI label since 2013 and covers the production of twenty-eight communes of the Costière plateau. The label covers Gariguette and Ciflorette varietals.
Label Rouge (Red Label) strawberries from Lot-et-Garonne: grown near Agen, they have been labeled since 2009, covering three varietals: Gariguette, Ciflorette, and Charlotte.
Plougastel strawberry: it does not have a label nor maintain a PGI or AOC. This designation concerns several varietals of strawberries including Garrigue, Seraphin, and Surprise. The vast majority are cultivated under the Saveol label in Plougastel, in the Finistère in Brittany.

DID YOU KNOW?

The strawberry is not, strictly speaking, a fruit. What we eat, the red pulp, is the receptacle of the real fruits: the little yellow dots on the outside of its flesh, which are called "achenes."

QUICK STRAWBERRY CHARLOTTE
by Caritha Ledru-Johansson

"Tested and approved hundreds of times, this ultrasimple and so-good recipe from my mother is still one of my favorite recipes—even after twenty-seven years of making it!"

PREPARATION TIME: 15 MINUTES
REFRIGERATION TIME: 4 HOURS
SERVES 8

1⅛ pounds (500 g) strawberries (a sweet variety such as Mara des Bois or Charlotte), plus 3½ ounces (100 g) for decoration
30 ladyfingers
Strawberry Syrup (recipe above)
A few drops of rum (optional)
14 ounces (400 g) fromage blanc
1 tablespoon (15 mL) crème fraîche
1 tablespoon (13 g) vanilla sugar
Granulated sugar, as needed
Equipment: a charlotte mold or a large bowl and plate

Rinse the strawberries. Quarter 14 ounces (400 g) of them and set them aside.

Slightly dilute the strawberry syrup with water, and add a few drops of rum, if using. Dip the ladyfingers in the strawberry syrup. Line the charlotte mold with some of the ladyfingers.

In a bowl, combine the fromage blanc, crème fraiche, and vanilla sugar. Add some granulated sugar to taste, taking into account the sweetness of the strawberries and the ladyfingers. Add the strawberry quarters to the bowl and stir gently to combine. Fill the mold halfway with the strawberry mixture, then cover the mixture with a layer of ladyfingers. Scrape the remaining strawberry filling into the mold, then cover this layer with another layer of ladyfingers. Cover with plastic wrap, and refrigerate for at least 4 hours. Unmold and decorate with whole strawberries.

IN THE MARIONNET NURSERIES

Since 1891, the family business Marionnet has produced red and black fruit plants (strawberries, raspberries, black currants, and red currants) in the heart of the Sologne. They also now specialize in research and development to develop more resistant and flavorful varietals, like the very famous Mara des Bois, invented by the grandfather in 1991. Today, the father, Jacques, and the son, Pascal, run the family business, which devotes more than 30,139 square feet (2,800 sq m) of space to strawberry research.

HOMEMADE STRAWBERRY SYRUP

Preparation time: 10 minutes
1¼ cups (250 g) granulated sugar
¾ cup plus 1 tablespoon (200 mL) water
9 ounces (250 g) strawberries

Cut the strawberries in half. Place the sugar and water in a saucepan and bring to a boil. Add the strawberries and let them cook for about 10 minutes. Turn off the heat and let the syrup cool completely, then strain.

Main production locations in France

50,000
total metric tons per year throughout the country

Aquitaine: 52 percent of production, mainly in Lot-et-Garonne (22 percent of national production)
Rhône-Alpes: 18 percent
Loire Valley: 10 percent
Provence: 9 percent
Midi-Pyrénées: 8 percent
Brittany: 3 percent

CAPRON

An ancient variety cultivated from the fifteenth to the nineteenth century, especially in the gardens of the king at Versailles.
Appearance: a little bigger than a wild strawberry, more oblong, slightly orange.
Flavor: white-yellow flesh with a musky taste.
Harvest: May to June.
Uses: used raw to preserve its musky taste. Its leaves are consumed, especially as a diuretic.

CHARLOTTE

A CIREF (a French grower association) varietal created in 2004.
Appearance: heart shaped, bright red, shiny.
Flavor: tender and juicy flesh, with a sweet scent of wild strawberries.
Harvest: from April to November.
Uses: raw, in salads, in pastries.

CIFLORETTE

A CIREF (a French grower association) varietal created in 1998.
Appearance: ovoid shape, orange to dark red.
Flavor: tender and juicy flesh, very sweet.
Harvest: from March to June.
Uses: jam, compotes.

DARSELECT

Variety obtained by the Darbonne nursery in 1996.
Appearance: rounded shape, light red.
Flavor: juicy, firm, sweet flesh.
Harvest: from April to June.
Uses: raw, in salad, in pastries.

GARIGUETTE

The best-selling variety in France, it is the brainchild of a researcher from the INRA (French National Institute of Agricultural Research). Its name comes from a street in Châteauneuf-de-Gadagne, in the Vaucluse, where one of the researchers on the team lived.
Appearance: fine and elongated, elongated neck and stem, vermilion red, shiny.
Flavor: sweet and tart.
Harvest: one of the first to appear in the year, from March to mid-June.
Uses: jam, compote.

MAGNUM

Created recently by nursery Marionnet, this strawberry plant produces large fruits from ¾ to 1 ounce (20 to 25 g) each.
Appearance: rounded conical shape, red to bright red, shiny.
Flavor: rather firm flesh, very fragrant, and very sweet.
Harvest: May to July.
Uses: raw, in salad, in pastries.

MANILA

Created and placed on the market in 2005 by nursery Marionnet.
Appearance: medium size, dark red, shiny.
Flavor: firm flesh with an atypical taste, very sweet.
Harvest: May to June.
Uses: jam, compote.

MARA DES BOIS

A cross between the wild strawberry and cultivated varietals; introduced to the market in 1991. One of the most-cultivated strawberries in France. Its name was inspired by its creator's name—Marionnet—and its flavor, which is close to that of the wild strawberry.
Appearance: conical shape, bright red.
Flavor: juicy flesh, sweet to very sweet, with the scent of wild strawberry.
Harvest: from May to the first frosts.
Uses: raw, in salads, in pastries.

MARIGUETTE

A cross between the Gariguette and the Mara des Bois, created by Marionnet.
Appearance: large fruit, elongated shape, bright red-orange.
Flavor: firm and even crunchy, sweet flesh, with a subtle aroma of wild strawberry.
Harvest: from May to the first frosts.
Uses: raw, in salads, in pastries.

And also . . .

MADAME MOUTOT

An old variety of strawberry par excellence, one that would have been found growing in your grandparents' orchards. Today, this varietal has almost disappeared. It produces very large, rounded red fruits.

ALPINE BLANCHE

A wild variety native to the Alps. Elongated creamy white fruit with a musky taste.

SURPRISE DES HALLES

An old variety dating back to 1925, with rounded fruits with a pink flesh. Sweet and tangy taste.

FRAISE ABRICOT

An old variety with acidulous small fruits in the shape of small white mushrooms.

STRAWBERRIES RISE AGAIN

A strawberry is said to "go back" (*remontant*) when it produces fruit several times during the year. The plant first fruits in the spring, then several times again, until the first frost.

skip to

Syrups, p. 65

The Junk Food of Yesteryear

The term "junk food" may seem very contemporary, but the consumption of altered or adulterated foods is nothing new. The practice was so widespread in the nineteenth century that the police became involved.

Bruno Fuligni

POISONOUS MUSHROOMS

The prefecture of police undertook the regulation of the mushroom trade in 1809. Numerous poisonings had occurred due to the laxity of quality control over the mushrooms flooding into Parisian markets. With the advent of the industrial revolution, the health of the urban poor suffered grievously from foodstuffs too cheap to be safe.

DOMESTIC ANIMALS

Writing during the July Monarchy (1830–1848), the prefect of police Henri Gisquet described a sickening site in Montfaucon, a veritable open-air sewer within the capital. "There I saw a fairly spacious chamber on whose walls were suspended—carefully skinned and butchered with attention to every possible detail—dogs, cats, little foals cut from the wombs of slaughtered mares, quarters of horse carcasses with the rotten sections removed," that were to be sold as pieces of rabbit or well-hung venison.

BREAD WITH PLASTER

It wasn't until 1876 that the Municipal Laboratory was established. It became the central laboratory for the prefecture of police, where consumers could verify the contents of various food products. Nevertheless, it did not prevent a number of unscrupulous operators from prospering. Commissioner Gronfier left invaluable records on the Parisian underworld, in which he recorded incidents of bread laced with plaster or chalk, cooked over wood impregnated with lead paint.

CURRANT JELLY . . . WITHOUT THE CURRANTS

As Commissioner Gronfier wrote in the late nineteenth century: "A few years ago, Monsieur Stanislas Martin, the well-known pharmacist and chemist, found 'currant jelly' in several Parisian markets that contained no trace of this fruit." It was pectin—a vegetable-based gelling agent—colored with beet juice, flavored with raspberry syrup, and solidified with gelatin.

PETROLEUM IN CAKES

Citation from an extract of a ministerial bulletin dated July 10, 1885: "Monsieur le Préfet, my attention has been drawn to the fact that, in certain pastry shops, there has been used as a replacement for butter or shortening, a product known as Vaseline, pétroléine or neutraline, an extract of heavy petroleum oils. The Public Health Advisory Committee of France, which has been charged with the duty of studying whether Vaseline may be used in food preparation without endangering public health, has noted that this substance is not subject to rancidity. This property poses a grave risk to consumers who are not alerted by the odor of staleness in the cake; they are at risk of purchasing a pastry in which the flour and eggs have already begun to spoil, not realizing the problem until the moment when the cake comes into contact with the organs of taste."

skip to
Carnivores during the Siege of Paris, p. 256

Chips Are Chic

Enjoy these fried potato petals just at picnics? No! They also work miracles on the plates of great chefs. Here is a trio of recipes to prove it.

François-Régis Gaudry

— POTATO CHIP CRUMBLE —
by Beatriz Gonzalez*

In a large bowl, combine ½ cup (50 g) of all-purpose flour, 3 tablespoons (50 g) of softened butter, and 9 ounces (250 g) of potato chips. Using your hands, combine the mixture, finely crushing the potato chips. Spread the mixture onto a baking sheet lined with parchment paper. Bake at 350°F (180°C) for 10 minutes, or until golden and crisp. Use, cold, as a topping on baked vegetables, as a topping on a compote of tomatoes, or on top of *faisselle* cheese, etc.
Result: richness and crunch!

Neva Cuisine, Paris 8th, and Coretta, Paris 17th

skip to
Fries . . . , p. 332

— THE CHIPS OMELET —
by Jacques Thorel*

For a nice omelet (4 people), beat 6 large eggs in a bowl. Season very lightly with salt. Season with pepper. Add 2 handfuls of chips, and let stand for 10 minutes.

Heat a little oil in the bottom of a pan, pour the mixture into the pan, and sauté it. Halfway through the cooking time, slide the omelet onto a plate, then invert it back into the pan. Continue cooking until cooked through. Enjoy with a green salad.
Result: like a Spanish tortilla but without having to peel and cook all the potatoes.

The former chef of L'Auberge bretonne, La Roche-Bernard, Morbihan

— CHICKEN STRIPS BREADED WITH POTATO CHIPS —
by Tomy Gousset*

Open a family-size bag of potato chips and crush them using your hands. Evenly flour several chicken breast strips, dredge them in 3 beaten egg yolks, and dredge them one by one in the bag of chips, coating them with the broken pieces. Heat cooking oil to 350°F (180°C), and fry the chicken strips until browned on both sides. Place on paper towels to drain, and enjoy.
Result: provides more taste and crunch than bread crumbs.

Tomy & Co, Paris 7th

Cooking Schools

Does your child have a natural talent for cooking? Are you needing a life change? Here is a list of some of the most famous institutions where you can don an apron and be off on a new gastronomic career.

Alvina Ledru-Johansson

A FEW NUMBERS
More than 175,000 restaurants in France

15,000
OPEN POSITIONS EACH YEAR.

CAP graduates in 2016: 32,500

ALL PATHS LEAD TO THE KITCHEN
CAP (Professional Aptitude Certificate): 2 years, 386 institutions
Brevet professional certificate: 2 years, 114 institutions
BAC (Professional and Technological Baccalaureate): 3 years, 312 institutions
BTS (Superior Technician Brevet) (BAC + 2): 2 years, 131 institutions
Bachelor's degree (BAC + 3): 3 years, several institutions

CAP CUISINE
This is the first-level diploma necessary for working in a professional kitchen and covers basic cooking and baking recipes, standards of hygiene, food management, the history of gastronomy, etc. Includes consecutive or alternating (apprenticeship) training.

APPRENTICESHIPS?
This is a way for students who are in a hurry to gain experience to put a foot in the door of a professional environment. The student, who has signed an apprenticeship contract with an employer, alternates between classes and working on-site at a business. It may be paid (depending on the age of the apprentice and the diploma).

skip to
Paul Bocuse, p. 278

➡ *THE MOST REPUTABLE SCHOOLS*

FERRANDI
Among the best known in France and recognized internationally, with a Parisian campus of 6.1 acres (25,000 sq m)
Cities: Paris, Jouy-en-Josas, and Bordeaux
Founded: 1920
Training: CAP, BAC Pro, BTS, bachelor's
Selection criteria: student records, written tests for certain courses, and an interview
Tuition: free for the CAP Cuisine, BAC Pro Cuisine, and BTS hospitality-catering. Then between €8,200 to € 22,000 ($9,500 to $25,500)
Participating apprenticeship restaurants: Le Premier et le 28 (Paris), L'Orme rond (Jouy-en-Josas), Le Piano du Lac (Bordeaux)
Alumni: William Ledeuil, Ze Kitchen Gallery (Paris); Adeline Grattard, Yam'Tcha (Paris)
International students: an international program conducted entirely in English is offered and confers a diploma, recognized by the industry
What's more: many Best Craftsmen of France (MOF) are part of the teaching staff, and renowned chefs are associate professors
→ **ferrandi-paris.fr**

INSTITUT PAUL BOCUSE
The school of Paul Bocuse and Gérard Pélisson (cofounder of the Accor Group) in the Château du Vivier
City: Ecully, near Lyon
Founded: 1990
Training: bachelor's, master's
Selection criteria: student records, written tests, and an interview
Tuition: from €10,200 to €16,400 ($11,800 to $19,000)
Participating apprenticeship restaurants: 6 between Ecully and Lyon
Alumni: Tabata Mey, Les Apothicaires (Lyon); Sébastien Bras, Le Suquet (Laguiole)
International students: they can follow the training, but a minimal level in French is required as French is the only language used in the classes
What's more: postbaccalaureate courses are taught by Best Craftsmen of France (MOF) and renowned chefs
→ **institutpaulbocuse.com**

LE CORDON BLEU
One of the oldest French cooking schools, present in 17 countries
City: Paris
Founded: 1895
Training: the Grand Diplôme (preparation for CAP), bachelor's
Selection criteria: student records
Tuition: from €10,600 to €49,500 ($12,300 to $57,300)
Participating apprenticeship restaurants: Café Cordon Bleu
Alumni: Juan Arbealez, Plantxa, Levain (Boulogne-Billancourt)
International students: provides international training par excellence; all courses provide a live interpreter
What's more: the school has an international dimension, with a strong global network
→ **cordonbleu.edu**

➡ *PUBLIC SCHOOLS*

ÉCOLE HÔTELIÈRE INTERNATIONALE, SAVOIE-LÉMAN
The oldest public school of hotel management in France, created at the time of the development of spa treatments and the many resulting luxury hotels
City: Thonon-les-Bains
Founded: 1912
Training: BAC Pro and BTS
Selection criteria: student records
Tuition: free
Participating apprenticeship restaurants: La Brasserie Antonietti and Le Savoie Leman, haute cuisine restaurant
Alumni: Georges Blanc, Restaurant Georges Blanc (Vonnas); Jean-Christophe Ansanay-Alex, Auberge de l'Île Barbe (Lyon)
What's more: the school has an educational garden where herbs, fruits, and vegetables are grown to be used in the courses
→ **school-hoteliere-thonon.com**

ÉCOLE HÔTELIÈRE ET DE TOURISME PAUL AUGIER
Founded at the turn of the twentieth century, when the Côte d'Azur became an international vacation destination
City: Nice
Founded: 1914
Training: BAC Pro, BTS
Selection criteria: The AFFELNET assignment procedure, student records, interview
Tuition: free
Participating apprenticeship restaurants: Le Bistrot des Galets, La Brasserie Capélina, and the haute cuisine restaurant La Baie des Anges
Alumni: Gérald Passédat, Le Petit Nice (Nice); Julia Sedefdjian, Les Fables de La Fontaine (Paris)
What's more: maintains partnerships with international institutions to encourage students to change location
→ **lycee-paul-augier.com**

LYCÉE JEAN DROUANT
The premier hotel management school in Paris, known as "Médéric"
City: Paris
Founded: 1936
Training: BAC Technological and Pro, BTS
Selection criteria: The AFFELNET assignment procedure and APB; student records
Tuition: free
Participating apprenticeship restaurants: Julien François, haute cuisine restaurant; and Brasserie L'Atelier Bartholdi
Alumni: Patrick Scicard, former director general of Lenôtre; Dominique Loiseau, Relais Bernard Oiseau (Saulieu)
What's more: for the BTS, an Erasmus + program allows students to carry out their 16 weeks of training in a member country of the European Union
→ **lyceejeandrouant.fr**

The Cocktail Savants of Harry's Bar

How did a small Parisian bar, founded in 1911, give birth to some of the most mythical cocktails in the world?
Here are answers and recipes . . .

Jordan Moilim

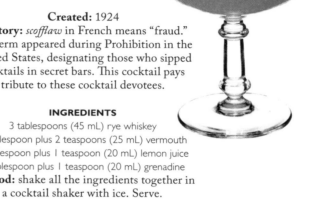

The Scofflaw

Created: 1924
History: *scofflaw* in French means "fraud." The term appeared during Prohibition in the United States, designating those who sipped cocktails in secret bars. This cocktail pays tribute to these cocktail devotees.

INGREDIENTS
3 tablespoons (45 mL) rye whiskey
1 tablespoon plus 2 teaspoons (25 mL) vermouth
1 tablespoon plus 1 teaspoon (20 mL) lemon juice
1 tablespoon plus 1 teaspoon (20 mL) grenadine
Method: shake all the ingredients together in a cocktail shaker with ice. Serve.

The Fabulous Story of HARRY'S NEW YORK BAR

Cocktails are considered an American invention, and their voyage across the Atlantic was spurred by Prohibition (1920–1933). A few expert mixologists migrated to France, including a New York bartender and his jockey friend, who dismantled their bar and moved it to Paris. The two friends created the New York Bar in 1911 in the Opéra district of the city. A decade later, Harry McElhone arrived from London to bartend in the New York Bar. Harry bought the establishment in 1923 and added his name to it. Thus, Harry's New York Bar was born and would eventually become one of the temples of the cocktail.
→ **Harry's Bar, 5, rue Daunou, Paris 2nd**

Between the Sheets

Created: 1930s
History: this cocktail, eloquently christened "Between the Sheets," recalls the debauchery of Parisian nights during the 1930s. It is said that this clever mix of spirits, with a high alcohol content, was a favorite among prostitutes, as it was a good way to prepare them for a night's work.

INGREDIENTS
2 tablespoons (30 mL) rum
2 tablespoons (30 mL) cognac
1 tablespoon plus 1 teaspoon (20 mL) lemon juice
Method: shake all the ingredients together in a cocktail shaker with ice. Serve.

The Monkey Gland

Created: 1920s
History: Harry McElhone developed this cocktail in reference to the experimentation of Dr. Voronoff, who attempted to graft monkey testicle tissue onto humans to increase longevity. Perhaps this cocktail provides the same benefits.

INGREDIENTS
3 tablespoons plus 1 teaspoon (50 mL) gin
2 tablespoons (30 mL) orange juice
2 drops grenadine
2 drops absinthe
Method: shake all the ingredients together in a cocktail shaker with ice. Serve.

skip to
Forgotten French Aperitifs, p. 348

The French 75

Created: 1915
History: this cocktail refers to the 75 mm gun used by the French and Americans during the First World War. The weapon was known for its speed as well as its ability to be deadly at first impact. This cocktail can be considered heavy artillery.

INGREDIENTS

2 tablespoons (30 mL) gin
2 dashes simple syrup
1 tablespoon (15 mL) lemon juice
2 tablespoons plus 2 teaspoons (40 mL) Champagne
Method: shake the gin, simple syrup, and lemon juice together in a cocktail shaker with ice. Strain into a cocktail glass. Top with the Champagne. Serve.

The White Lady

Created: 1923
History: the first version of this cocktail was created in London. When Harry McElhone brought the recipe to his bar, gin replaced the crème de menthe, which made the cocktail's color light and clear, and it became known for its light color— thus the name.

INGREDIENTS

2 tablespoons plus 2 teaspoons (40 mL) gin
2 tablespoons (30 mL) triple sec
1 tablespoon plus 1 teaspoon (20 mL) lemon juice
Method: shake all the ingredients together in a cocktail shaker with ice. Serve.

The Blue Lagoon

Created: 1960
History: this iconic recipe from the 1970–1980 cocktail scene was invented by Andy McElhone, Harry's son, to pay tribute to Harry. Characterized by its electric blue color, this cocktail is a variation of the famous White Lady invented by his father. Blue curaçao replaced the Cointreau, and the trend toward colorful cocktails was launched.

INGREDIENTS

2 tablespoons plus 2 teaspoons (40 mL) vodka
2 tablespoons (30 mL) curaçao
1 tablespoon plus 1 teaspoon (20 mL) lemon juice
Method: shake all the ingredients together in a cocktail shaker with ice. Serve.

The Bloody Mary

Created: 1921
History: people at the Ritz Hotel in Paris like to claim that Ernest Hemingway asked Bertin— the bartender at the hotel at the time—for a cocktail to hide the smell of alcohol to avoid being scolded by his wife, Mary. The story is a bit too good to be true, however. This cocktail seems to have been invented at Harry's Bar in Paris. The bartender, Fernand Petiot, noticed the appearance of vodka in bars at that time, which had been brought over by Russian immigrants, and which he felt was cruelly lacking in flavor. With some canned American tomato juice and a few spices added to the vodka, the Bucket of Blood cocktail was born. The name "Bloody Mary" appeared later, referencing the nickname attributed to Mary Tudor, Queen of England, for the bloody repressions she directed toward Protestants.

INGREDIENTS

2 tablespoons plus 2 teaspoons (40 mL) vodka
⅓ cup plus 2 teaspoons (90 mL) tomato juice
1 tablespoon (15 mL) lemon juice
2–3 drops Worcestershire sauce
Tabasco
Celery salt
Ground black pepper
Method: add all the ingredients to a mixing glass. Stir slowly to combine. Pour into a highball glass, and garnish with a cut celery stalk. Serve.

Mimosa

Created: 1925, Ritz Hotel Paris
History: this simple cocktail was, for a long time, a social drink that was enjoyed as an aperitif before dinner or when traveling by plane. At the time of its invention, Fran Meier, then barman of the Ritz, quickly made the connection between the cocktail and the brightest color in the garden of the hotel: the mimosa.

INGREDIENTS

5 tablespoons (75 mL) orange juice
5 tablespoons (75 mL) Champagne
Method: pour the orange juice into a flute glass. Top with the Champagne. Serve.

The Rose

Created: 1906, Chatham Hotel
History: this rather eloquent cocktail was invented by Johnny Mitta at the Chatham Hotel, a former elegant venue for Parisian parties. This relatively strong cocktail was "the" drink of the Roaring Twenties, starting the trend of delightfully kitsch cocktails.

INGREDIENTS

2 tablespoons plus 2 teaspoons (40 mL) vermouth
1 tablespoon plus 1 teaspoon (20 mL) kirsch
2 teaspoons (10 mL) liqueur de cerise
Method: shake all the ingredients together in a cocktail shaker with ice. Garnish with a maraschino cherry. Serve.

Nuts for Nougat!

Whether from Corsica or Provençe, brown or white, this sweet specialty with distant origins and nutty etymology (*nougat* comes from the word "nuts") has found its home in France! From Mesopotamia to the south of France, let's take a journey through the world of nougat.

Stéphane Solier

The different nougats

Nougat of Provence
The first mentions: fourteenth century (*pignolate*) and sixteenth century (*nogat*)
Production: Allauch and Aix-en-Provence (Bouches-du-Rhône), Sault and Signes (Vaucluse), Ollioules and Saint-Tropez (Var), Allègre-les-Fumades (Gard), Vogüé (Ardèche)

Nougat of Montélimar
The first mention: 1701
Production: Montélimar
Recipe: at least 30 percent almonds (or 28 percent almonds and 2 percent pistachios) and 25 percent honey (preferably lavender), flavored only with vanilla.

Corsican nougat
The first mention: twentieth century
Production: Bastia and Soveria (Haute-Corse), Alata and Ajaccio (Southern Corsica)
Recipes: a small cousin to the nougat of Provence, it can be brown or white, tender or hard, and made with various ingredients: between 8 and 35 percent AOC honey of Corsica, between 20 and 34 percent dried fruits and nuts (including the PGI hazelnut of Cervione), and between 5 and 10 percent candied fruits, generally Corsican (citron, clementine, fig, chestnut, myrtle berry, etc.). There is also a brown nougat that uses AOC chestnut flour.

French Catalan touron
The first mention: 1607
Production: Perpignan (Pyrénées-Orientales), Limoux (Aude), Pays Basque
Recipes: the white version is close to the *turrón* of Alicante and can be crunchy (46 percent almonds or roasted hazelnuts), tender, or even creamy (pine nuts); the brown version is almond and hazelnut, and its sugar is caramelized. There is also a praline touron, very similar to the Jijona turrón, made using a crunchy almond touron (8 percent honey and 60 percent almonds), reduced to a very fine paste and baked for a second time.

Recipes

White nougat of Provence:
30 percent honey and at least 35 percent almonds and pistachios. It is often flavored with orange blossom water.

Brown nougat of Provence
(a cooked and caramelized sweetened mixture): 25 percent honey and 15 to 50 percent toppings (almonds, pistachios, hazelnuts, walnuts, pine nuts, aniseed or coriander seeds, and candied fruits).

WHITE NOUGAT: SOFT OR HARD?
The consistency of white nougat will change according to the cooking temperature of the sugar. Soft nougat represents more than 90 percent of nougat production because of its longer shelf life (hard nougat loses its crispness faster due to humidity).

— BROWN NOUGAT —
by Denise Solier-Gaudry

PREPARATION TIME: 5 MINUTES
COOKING TIME: 20 MINUTES
SERVES 4

¾ cup (250 g) acacia or lavender honey
7 ounces (200 g) whole almonds
2 sheets crisp matzo (optional)

In a heavy-bottom saucepan, preferably with a nonstick coating, heat the honey. When the honey starts to bubble, add the almonds and cook over medium heat for 20 minutes, stirring occasionally. Line a tin mold (preferably with a lid) with pieces of matzo, pour the nougat into it, and spread it out evenly. Cover the nougat with matzo pieces and place a weight on top to press down slightly on the nougat. Slice the nougat when it's cooled to room temperature.

Cooking nougat can be monitored simply by listening: when the almonds start to crackle, the nougat is ready! The matzo can be replaced with parchment paper, but not by aluminum foil, which would be too difficult to remove.

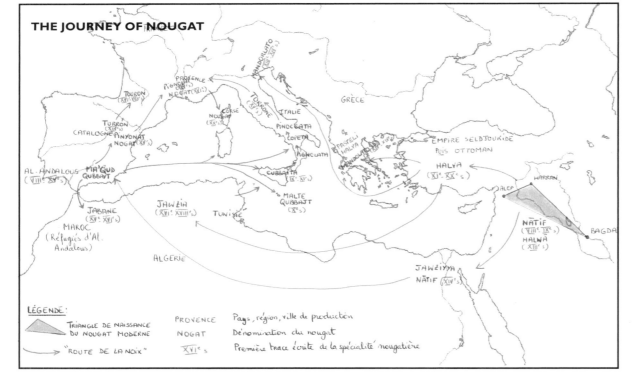

THE JOURNEY OF NOUGAT

skip to
The Irresistible Walnut Cake, p. 263

The Troisgros Dynasty

For four generations, the Troisgros family has been lighting up French cuisine and establishing themselves in Roanne, and now in Ouches—the gastronomic center of France.

Charles Patin O'Coohoon

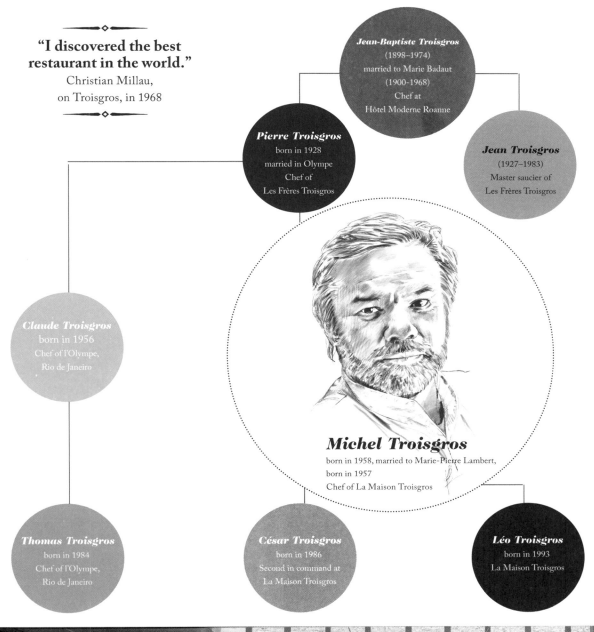

> **"I discovered the best restaurant in the world."**
> Christian Millau,
> on Troisgros, in 1968

Jean-Baptiste Troisgros
(1898–1974)
married to Marie Badaut
(1900–1968)
Chef at
Hôtel Moderne Roanne

Pierre Troisgros
born in 1928
married in Olympe
Chef of
Les Frères Troisgros

Jean Troisgros
(1927–1983)
Master saucier of
Les Frères Troisgros

Claude Troisgros
born in 1956
Chef of l'Olympe,
Rio de Janeiro

Michel Troisgros
born in 1958, married to Marie-Pierre Lambert,
born in 1957
Chef of La Maison Troisgros

Thomas Troisgros
born in 1984
Chef of l'Olympe,
Rio de Janeiro

César Troisgros
born in 1986
Second in command at
La Maison Troisgros

Léo Troisgros
born in 1993
La Maison Troisgros

– COSA CROCCANTE –
by César Troisgros

An original salad of fried carrots. The mixture is light, fresh, colorful, tangy, crisp, and vegetal.

SERVES 4

4 carrots
8 cups (2 L) sunflower oil
1 clove garlic
4 leaves green sorrel
4 leaves red sorrel
20 leaves tarragon
4 sprigs watercress
2 spring onions
A few drops of chile purée
1 lime
1 tablespoon (15 mL) hazelnut oil
20 capers

Peel the carrots. Using a vegetable peeler, make thin, long strips from all around the carrots; set the strips aside. In a large saucepan, heat the sunflower oil to 300°F (150°C). Carefully immerse the carrot strips. Cook them for 8 minutes, or until crispy. Drain, using a slotted spoon, and place them on a paper towel–lined plate. Season with salt; set aside. Peel and thinly slice the garlic. Fry the slices in the same oil used for the carrots. Set aside on paper towels to drain. Pick off the leaves from the sorrel stems and wash and dry the leaves. Slice the leaves into thin strips. Remove the leaves from the tarragon and watercress sprigs. Peel and finely chop the onions. Place all the ingredients in a large bowl. Season with the chile purée, lime juice and zest, the hazelnut oil, and the capers. Arrange the mixture in a mound in the center of four plates.

THE NEW TROISGROS LOCATION
After 87 years located in front of the Roanne train station, the Maison Troisgros moved in February 2017 to Ouches, in the heart of a 42-acre (17 hectare) country estate.

skip to
Where Are They Now?, p. 171

The Bordeaux and Burgundy Match-Up

It is often said that to know French wine, you must know the wines of Bordeaux. And that from the moment when you claim to know Bordeaux wine, you steer yourself toward the wines of Burgundy. From Bordeaux, the "terroir" produces only one to two wines. From Burgundy, each "climate" produces a specific wine. Let's review these "kings of the wine glass" for a classic match-up.

Gwilherm de Cerval

LAND AREA
(acres/hectares)

BORDEAUX
323,493 acres
(130,913 hectares)

70,015 acres
(28,334 hectares)
BURGUNDY

PERCENTAGE OF FRENCH VINEYARDS

17% BORDEAUX

3,6% BURGUNDY

POTENTIAL SELLING VOLUME
(gallons/hectoliters)

169,070,112 gallons
(6,400,000 hectoliters)

36,984,087 gallons
(1,400,000 hectoliters)

CREW MAKEUP

6,822

3,890

number of wine growers

MIDDLEMEN

33 vs. 17
co-ops

AGENTS

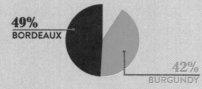

300 vs 282
trading houses

MANAGERS

Large international groups

VS

family-size groups

EXPORT MARKET
% of production

49% BORDEAUX

42% BURGUNDY

LARGEST CONSUMERS

CHINA
BORDEAUX

UNITED STATES
BURGUNDY

PACE SETTERS
% of world volume

2%   0.4%

NUMBER OF BOTTLES
185,000,000

BURGUNDY
BORDEAUX

630,000,000

BOUNTY FROM SALES
(in millions of euros)

3.6   € 1.52

the glasses

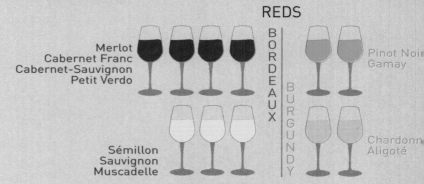

REDS

Merlot
Cabernet Franc
Cabernet-Sauvignon
Petit Verdo

BORDEAUX | BURGUNDY

Pinot Noir
Gamay

Sémillon
Sauvignon
Muscadelle

Chardonnay
Aligoté

WHITES

BARREL CAPACITY

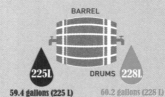

BARREL

225L DRUMS **228L**

59.4 gallons (225 L)   60.2 gallons (228 L)

APPROACH

BLENDS   SINGLE VARIETALS

OCCASIONS FOR IMBIBING

With the family for Christmas

With friends over the weekend

VOLUME OF LAND WITH ORGANIC LABELED (AB) PRODUCTION

25,795 acres
(10,439 hectares)
BORDEAUX

6,647 acres
(2,690 hectares)
BURGUNDY

HITS AND MISSES

" Lacks SIMPLICITY, a lot of SNOB APPEAL
BORDEAUX

Consistently high PRICES; few wine EVENTS organized
BURGUNDY "

GOVERNING BODIES

UNESCO World Heritage
(for the wine growing region of Saint-Émilion)

World Heritage Site of Humanity
(for the climates of Burgundy)

The Saint-Honoré

At the beginning of the twenty-first century, the *gâteau Saint-Honoré* enjoyed a resurgence of popularity, in both shops and restaurants. There have even been many fruit-based variations using seasonal fruits, and variations that highlight the imagination of pastry chefs.

Gilbert Pytel

A little history of the gâteau "Saint-Ho" in 3 dates

1846: christened with its name as a tribute to Saint Honoré, **patron saint of pastry chefs**. It was the creation of the famous pastry chef **Chiboust**, whose shop was located on rue du Faubourg-Saint-Honoré.

1863: pastry chef **Auguste Julien created the recipe** still in use today: a disk of puff pastry topped with a crown of pâte à choux (cream puff pastry) filled with whipped cream or Chiboust cream.

2009: the cake began a resurgence of popularity, in part due to pastry chef **Philippe Conticini** and his reimagined classics.

THE 5 BEST SAINT-HONORÉ IN FRANCE

→ **The salted caramel Saint-Honoré of Sébastien Bouillet (Lyon):** its creamy salted butter caramel makes it a rare variation.

→ **The vanilla Saint-Honoré of Arnaud Larher (Paris):** specially created for vanilla lovers, with a *pâte sablé* (shortcrust) base, various cream fillings, and cream puffs.

→ **The strawberry and tarragon Saint-Honoré of Hugues Pouget (Hugo et Victor, Paris):** this particular combination of flavors adds an extra freshness to the whole experience!

→ **The traditional Saint-Honoré of Frédéric Cassel (Fontainebleau):** His artistic design attracts devotees from all over the region.

→ **The Saint-Honoré of Laurent Le Daniel (Rennes):** this Best Craftsman of France (MOF) spoils us with his crispy puff pastry, little caramelized crème mousseline–filled cream puffs, and a beautiful Chantilly cream.

skip to ....
Puff Pastry, a Tour de Force, p. 342

THE SAINT-HONORÉ
by Cédric Grolet* (Hôtel Le Meurice)

PREPARATION TIME: 2 HOURS 30 MINUTES
COOKING TIME: 55 MINUTES
SERVES 10

For the laminated dough (puff pastry dough)
1¼ teaspoons (7.5 g) salt
¾ cup minus 2½ teaspoons (162 mL) water
3 cups (300 g) pastry flour or T45
1¼ cups (125 g) all-purpose flour or T55
4 tablespoons plus 1¼ teaspoons (62.5 g) melted butter, cooled
9 ounces (250 g) beurre de tourage (a cold block of roll-in butter)
Confectioners' sugar, for dusting
For the pâte à choux (cream puff pastry)
⅓ cup plus 1 tablespoon plus 1 teaspoon (100 g) milk
⅓ cup plus 1 tablespoon plus 1¾ teaspoons (100 ml) water
½ teaspoon (2 g) granulated sugar
⅔ teaspoon (4 g) salt
6 tablespoons plus 1 teaspoon (90 g) butter
1 cup plus 1 tablespoon plus 2 teaspoons (110 g) all-purpose flour
4 large (180 g) eggs
Edible gold leaf, for decoration (optional)
For the kirsch pastry cream
½ vanilla bean
¾ cup plus 1 tablespoon plus ¾ teaspoon (200 g) whole milk
1 large (18 g) egg yolk
1 tablespoon plus 1¾ teaspoons (20 g) superfine sugar
½ ounce (16 g) pastry cream powder
2 teaspoons (4 g) pastry flour (or T45), sifted
1 teaspoon (4 g) butter
1 teaspoon (5 g) kirsch cherry liqueur
For the caramel
¾ cup plus 1 tablespoon plus 1¾ teaspoons (100 mL) water
1¾ cups (300 g) superfine sugar
3 tablespoons (60 g) glucose syrup or corn syrup
For the vanilla whipped cream
2 cups plus 2 tablespoons plus 1½ teaspoons (500 g) whipping cream
1 tablespoon plus 1 teaspoon (17.5 g) sugar
2 vanilla beans

Make the laminated dough (puff pastry)

In the bowl of a stand mixer fitted with the dough hook, combine the salt and water. Add the flour and melted butter. Knead the mixture on low for 1 minute until a smooth mass forms. Scrape the dough onto a work surface, form it into a ball, then flatten it to a disk. Wrap the dough in plastic wrap and refrigerate it until chilled. Place the chilled block of butter onto a work surface and roll it into about an 8½-inch (22 cm) square. Roll out the chilled dough onto a work surface to a 10 by 20-inch (25 by 50 cm) rectangle. Place the butter square on top of the dough, flush with the top end, and fold the bottom half of the dough over it. Press the edges of the dough together to seal it. Turn the dough one quarter turn to the right and roll it out so that its length is three times its width. Fold the bottom half of the dough in toward the middle with its edge positioned at the center. Fold the top half of the dough in toward the middle with its edge against the edge of the bottom half. Fold the dough in half over onto itself (as if closing a book). Wrap the dough in plastic wrap and refrigerate for 2 hours. Repeat these steps with the chilled butter-dough package four more times, allowing a 2-hour rest in between each turn. Roll out the dough to a thickness of ¹⁄₁₀ inch (2 mm), and let it rest for several minutes. Meanwhile, preheat a convection oven to 350°F (180°C). Place the dough between two baking sheets, and bake it for 10 minutes. Cut out a 10¼-inch (26 cm) circle, then bake the circle for another 15 minutes, or until crisp and golden. Increase the oven temperature to 375°F (250°C), then sprinkle the puff pastry circle with confectioners' sugar, and place the circle back in the oven for 5 minutes to melt the sugar and glaze the circle.

Make the pâte à choux (cream puff pastry)

Preheat the oven to 350°F (180°C). In a saucepan, bring the milk, water, sugar, salt, and butter to a boil. Off the heat, add the flour all at once, place the pan back over the heat, and, using a wooden spoon or a spatula, vigorously stir the mixture until it forms a smooth mass and pulls completely away from the sides of the pan. Immediately scrape the dough into the bowl of a stand mixer fitted with the flat beater, and beat in the eggs, one at a time, to form a smooth dough. Transfer the dough to a pastry bag fitted with a plain #8 piping tube. Pipe small mounds (about 2¼ in/6 cm in diameter) onto a parchment-lined baking sheet. Bake the puffs for 10 minutes, then reduce the temperature of the oven to 325°F (160°C) and bake another 5 minutes, or until the puffs are puffed and golden.

Make the kirsch pastry cream

In a saucepan, combine the half vanilla bean and the milk and bring to a boil. In a bowl, whisk together the yolk, sugar, pastry cream powder, and flour until lightened. Strain the hot milk, then pour half of it into the yolk mixture while whisking. Pour the contents of the bowl back into the saucepan with the remaining milk and bring it to a boil for 2 minutes, while stirring. Off the heat, stir in the butter. Let cool to 39°F (4°C). Stir the pastry cream to smooth it out, then stir in the kirsch. Transfer the pastry cream to a pastry bag fitted with a plain #4 piping tube, and fill each of the cream puffs with the pastry cream by piercing the tip of the tube through the bottom of the puff.

Make the caramel

In a saucepan, boil the water with the sugar, add the glucose, and cook until the syrup caramelizes (to about a dark amber color). Immediately remove the pan from the heat, and dip the filled cream puffs into the hot caramel. Add a touch of gold leaf on top of each puff, if desired.

Make the vanilla whipped cream

Boil one-third of the cream with the sugar and the vanilla beans, split lengthwise in half. Set aside, covered, to infuse for 10 minutes, then strain the vanilla cream into the remaining cream. Refrigerate the cream until cold again. Beat the cream in a chilled bowl until soft peaks form, then transfer the cream to a piping bag fitted with a Saint-Honoré piping tube.

Assembly

Place one puff pastry circle on a work surface, pipe 7 ounces (200 g) of the kirsch pastry cream on top, and spread it out evenly. Arrange the filled cream puffs around the edge of the circle. Pipe the whipped cream on top, in short diamond-shaped strips. Top with a cream puff.

Nicknamed "the little prince of pastry," Cédric Grolet currently collects Pastry Chef of the Year titles.

A Taste for Blood

Maybe we're all vampires after all. Long regarded as abhorrent and taboo, blood is a foodstuff like no other.
French cuisine has actually elevated a number of blood-based dishes to gastronomic heights.
An autopsy and analysis of this extraordinary vital fluid.

Valentine Oudard

BLOOD IN HISTORY

Regarded as unclean and hazardous to health, the consumption of blood was long subject to religious interdiction. Étienne Boileau's *Le Livre des Métiers*, published in 1212, and *Le Mesnagier de Paris*, published in 1393, were the first works to mention blood-based dishes.

Consuming blood nevertheless remained proscribed and forbidden. It was not until the fourteenth century that a treatise on cookery alluded to a recipe that included blood. Three centuries later, it achieved the status of a recognized ingredient, but was slow to shed the notorious reputation that arose from hundreds of years of religious disapprobation. It was only in the eighteenth century that blood began to be valued as a food and its consumption became widespread.

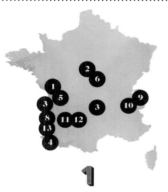

1

Fressure

Terroir: Vendée
Animal: pig
Origin of the recipe: the appearance of this blackish soup gives one pause. It is peasant fodder, combining pig's blood with offal and bacon rind, blended with stale bread, onions, and a few spices.

The word *fressure* (sounds like "frisson" or "shiver") also refers to pluck, the internal organs of a lamb. If you purchase it from a charcutier, it resembles a terrine, but when reheated, it melts and becomes a—rather frightening—soup.

Level of sangfroid required:

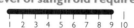

Sensitive souls had best abstain.

2

Charbonnée de porc

Terroir: Centre
Animal: pig
Origin of the recipe: this stew is prepared from the animal's offal, liver, lungs, and heart. The iridescent dark sauce, which is thickened with blood, becomes as black as coal (*charbon*), hence the name of this traditional dish.

Level of sangfroid required:

A dish that appeals to offal aficionados.

3

La sanquette or la sanguette

Terroir: Auvergne, Allier, Berry, and Bordelais
Animal: chicken, duck, or lamb
Origin of the recipe: this dish is prepared during the process of bleeding poultry. Diced bacon (or pork belly), garlic croutons, or both are placed in a shallow dish. The fowl is then bled over the dish to collect the blood, which coagulates with the other ingredients. Then everything is cooked together in a pan with goose fat and garnished with fresh parsley. This blood-based cake is said to be good for giving strength to growing children.

Level of sangfroid required:

An interesting metallic flavor note.

4

Le tripotx

Terroir: Basque country
Animal: sheep or pig
Origin of the recipe: this specialty, which originated in Sare in the Basque country, is simply a mutton-based blood sausage. Formerly made from veal, this boudin is made with the animal's tripe, stomach, lungs, and head, seasoned with Espelette pepper and thickened with blood.
Blood brother: shepherds in Saint-Étienne-de-Baïgorry waste nothing. When simmering the boudins, they consume the cooking liquid, called *tripasalda*, generally during the season of Pentecost in May.

Level of sangfroid required:

A deliciously savory sausage, dense and meltingly rich.

5

Gigourit

Terroir: Charente
Animal: pig and poultry
Origin of the recipe: during the *goraille*, the local pig butchering held during the coldest time of winter, farmers seize the opportunity to kill a few other surviving animals, including chickens that no longer lay and rabbits that no longer breed. They then prepare a pork stew that includes everything not used in the preparation of cured meats, sausages, and terrines; to this they add rabbit or chicken bones, cooking everything together for several hours. The pieces of meat are then removed from the cooking juices, stripped from the bones, and mashed with a fork. Pork blood is added at the end of the cooking time to thicken and bind the sauce.
Blood brother: *sauce de pire*, which is eaten cold as pâté, or warmed and melted to sauce a dish.

Level of sangfroid required:

Stand back—this one is a hard-core recipe.

6

Le poulet en barbouille

Terroir: Berry
Animal: rooster or chicken
Origin of the recipe: poulet en barbouille is a traditional favorite in Berry. Prepared in the kitchen of George Sand in Nohant, the dish has survived the decades and remains one of the region's iconic recipes. Mature roosters, whose meat is somewhat resistant to the cooking process, are marinated in red wine. Farmers save poultry blood to bind the sauce. It's a recipe that has been passed down from generation to generation at the Auberge de la Petite Fadette in Nohant (Indre), located just a few steps away from the home of George Sand.

Level of sangfroid required:

Blood is used only to thicken the sauce.

7

Boudin noir

Terroir: Every region has its recipe, from the environs of Paris to the overseas departments
Animal: pig
Origin of the recipe: if you follow the dictum of the Ardeche, "For it to be good, it has to be black as a crow, fat as a monk, and soft as a glove." The first recorded recipe based on blood, it's the common man's dish par excellence. Its ingredients include everything rejected by meat processors, charcuteries, and high-quality purveyors: blood, fat, head (ears and cartilage), and other remaining scraps.
Blood brother: *gimbourra*. It's based on a tradition of households in southwestern France when cooking boudins. If some of the sausages burst, the cooking liquid is kept to be mixed with blood and used as a base for vegetable soup.

Level of sangfroid required:

An absolute must among blood-based recipes.

8

Panturon de Rion-les-Landes

Terroir: Landes
Animal: lamb
Origin of the recipe: this recipe, which would otherwise have been consigned to oblivion, was resurrected by the regional association Confrérie de Rion-des-Landes. At Easter, the shepherds of the Landes highlands would kill the best of the young lambs for the master, keeping only the "innards" of the animal for their own consumption. The pluck (heart, liver, lungs), the head (which is used less and less these days), and the feet were simmered in a court-bouillon with carrots and turnips along with a nice chunk of ham. Everything was then chopped by hand and put back into the court-bouillon, and the animal's blood was added in. Lamb's blood is no longer approved for human consumption, so panturon is now prepared with veal blood.

Level of sangfroid required:

The blood creates a blackish color, but the texture is close to the Basque axoa.

9

Civet de lièvre

Terroir: Savoie
Animal: hare
Origin of the recipe: according to the old Savoyard saying, "A good hare is eaten at the end of a shotgun." Very fresh, in other words. Immediately after being killed, the hare is bled and its liver is removed; these are set aside for finishing the sauce, to which cream, a naturally occurring ingredient on Savoyard farms, is added.
Blood brothers: Flemish and Alsatian recipes for jugged hare and Poitou's hare with red sauce.
Level of sangfroid required:

1 2 3 4 5 6 7 8 9 10

Blood is used as a binding agent.

10

Fricassée de caïon

Terroir: Savoie
Animal: pig
Origin of the recipe: after a pig is killed on Savoyard farms, its blood is collected for boudin and also for preparing a fricassee of *caïon* (the local word for pig). The pieces of pork are simmered in a blend of white and red wines. At the end of the cooking time, the animal's blood is added to the dish.
Level of sangfroid required:

1 2 3 4 5 6 7 8 9 10

Only a mild taste of blood, thanks to the addition of wine.

11

La poule au pot périgourdine
or poule au pot à la farce noire et à la sauce de Sorges

Terroir: Périgord
Animal: chicken
Origin of the recipe: once gutted, the chicken is stuffed with a preparation based on offal, sausage meat, bread soaked in its blood, eggs, and seasonings. A variation features a white stuffing made with stale bread soaked in milk.
Level of sangfroid required:

1 2 3 4 5 6 7 8 9 10

A hearty, flavorful recipe.

12

Le lièvre en torchon or lièvre en cabessal

Terroir: with origins in Quercy, it came of age in the cuisines of Limousin, Rouergue, and the Périgord
Animal: hare
Origin of the recipe: in the Rouergue, *cabessal* is the local name for the twisted head cloth that women wore when carrying a bucket of water. The creator of this recipe, a native of Quercy, presented the hare in a cloth shaped like a cabessal, hence its name. A rustic version of *lièvre à la royale*, this recipe calls for marinating a whole hare overnight in a sauce based on red wine, then stuffing it with veal, fresh pork, and raw ham, and cooking it for 6 hours.
Level of sangfroid required:

1 2 3 4 5 6 7 8 9 10

A great dish!

13

Les Abignades

Terroir: Landes
Animal: goose
Origin of the recipe: once the breeders in the Landes had sold the goose confit, liver, and thighs, nothing was left but the innards—*les abignades* in the Gascon dialect. They were prepared in a stew with the heart and the giblets, cooked in a sauce thickened with blood. Éric Costedoat, chef of the Relais du Pavillon in Saint-Sever in the Landes, carries on this tradition. With a variation—since goose blood is hard to come by, he uses pork blood.
Blood brother: in Gers, there is an identical recipe based on duck, called *tripes de canard au madiran*.
Level of sangfroid required:

1 2 3 4 5 6 7 8 9 10

A dish with enduring appeal for offal fanciers.

skip to
Hare à la Royale, p. 336

A Parade of Labels

French food labels loudly proclaim the terroir, quality, and authenticity of the products within. Yet these mystifying acronyms are hard to understand—or digest. Let's take a tour of these labels and clarify their claims.

Marielle Gaudry

WHERE ARE THEY FROM?

From an ordinance dated December 2006, in application of the Agricultural Framework Law (French abbreviation "LOA") of January 6, 2006, to clarify claims of quality and promote authentic regional French products.

Who oversees this system? The Institut National de l'Origine et de la Qualité (INAO) under the supervision of the Ministry of Agriculture. According to INAO, almost 50 percent of French farmers are in the process of applying for such certifications. Inspired by the French initiative, the EU has implemented a uniform system for protecting and promoting European products with specific geographic indications. The first beneficiary of these measures was wine in 1970, followed by spirits in 1989, and then all food products in 1992.

APPELLATION D'ORIGINE CONTRÔLÉE (AOC)

Origin: the crisis in the wine industry (due to phylloxera, an aphid that ravaged French vineyards), which began in the 1860s, as well as a wide range of fraudulent practices in wine production, motivated the legislative ruling of August 1, 1905. The designation was initially reserved for wine, but was extended to cover all agricultural and food products in 1990. When a product is granted AOC status in France, it immediately enters the European process leading to an AOP designation.
Effective date: 1935, with the creation of INAO to manage its implementation.
Guarantees: origin
Certification: "Indicates a product for which all the steps of fabrication are implemented in accordance with a well-established technique within the same geographic area that gives the product its distinctive characteristics."

APPELLATION D'ORIGINE PROTÉGÉE (AOP)

Origin: the French policy of promoting agricultural products with the AOC designation inspired European regulations in 1992, which in turn gave rise to the AOP designation, the European equivalent of AOC. As of January 1, 2012, products may no longer bear anything but the European AOP label, with the exception of wines.
Effective date: 1992
Guarantees: origin
Certification: "Indicates a product whose production, processing, and preparation take place in an established geographic area with a recognized and acknowledged expertise."

LABEL ROUGE

Origin: Article 28 of the Agricultural Framework Law of August 5, 1960, stipulated the creation of this French label in response to demands by agricultural professionals, poultry farmers in particular, who were reacting to industrial-scale poultry raising. Chickens bred in the Landes region were the first product to benefit from this label.
Effective date: 1965
Guarantees: superior quality
Certification: "Attests that a product possesses an ensemble of specific characteristics establishing a level of quality that is superior to that of similar competitive products."

PROTECTED GEOGRAPHICAL INDICATION (PGI)

Origin: at least one of the steps, often the processing phase, must occur in a specific geographic area, which is more broadly defined than that imposed by an AOC designation.
Effective date: 1992
Guarantees: origin
Certification: "Designates agricultural products and food supplies whose characteristics are closely related to the geographic area where most of their production, processing, or preparation occurs."

AGRICULTURE BIOLOGIQUE (AB)

Origin: the Agricultural Framework Law of June 1980 specified the conditions for agricultural production without synthetic products.
Effective date: 1985
Guarantees: respect for the environment and animal well-being
Certification: "That the food does not include GMOs, and is at least 95 percent composed of ingredients produced in accordance with organic standards, using agricultural and breeding practices that are respectful of the balance of nature, the environment, and animal well-being."

SPÉCIALITÉ TRADITIONELLE GUARANTIE (STG)

Origin: a 1992 European regulation established this identification sign for EU agricultural products. Farmed mussels are the only French product that has received this designation.
Effective date: 2006
Guarantees: a traditional recipe
Certification: "Does not refer to product origin but is intended to designate a traditional composition or production method."

skip to
Organic Growing Boom, p. 369

The Truffle

Considered a "diamond of gastronomy" according to Brillat-Savarin, a "fairy's apple" according to George Sand, and "Sacrum sacrorum of the gastronomes" for Alexandre Dumas— the truffle is the star of all fungi. And this nugget grows everywhere in France.

Charles Patin O'Coohoon

A tour de France of truffles

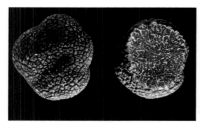

Tuber melanosporum
Nickname: Périgord black truffle
Origins: Vaucluse, Drôme, Lot, Gard, Bouches-du-Rhône, Var, Alpes-de-Haute-Provence
Appearance: black with shades ranging from purple to red
Characteristics: fragrant and subtle, the queen of truffles
Availability: mid-November to the end of March

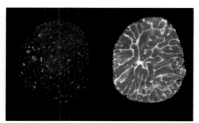

Tuber brumale
Nickname: musky truffle
Origins: Vaucluse, Drôme, Lot, Gard, Bouches-du-Rhône, Var, Alpes-de-Haute-Provence
Appearance: smaller than other truffles, with purple highlights
Characteristics: spicy fragrance with hints of musk
Availability: December to March

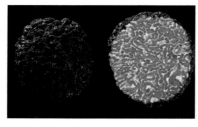

Tuber uncinatum
Nickname: Burgundy truffle
Origins: Burgundy, Champagne, Alsace
Appearance: dark chocolate color
Characteristics: undergrowth aromas
Availability: September to January

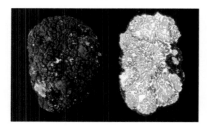

Tuber mesentericum
Nickname: truffle of Lorraine
Origins: Meuse
Appearance: black with chocolate shades
Characteristics: slightly licorice notes and almond aroma
Availability: September to December

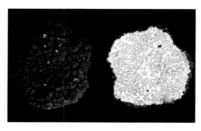

Tuber aestivum
Nickname: summer truffle
Origins: Vaucluse, Drôme, Lot, Gard, Bouches-du-Rhône, Var, Alpes-de-Haute-Provence
Appearance: brown to coffee color
Characteristics: white flesh, forest mushroom notes
Availability: May to September

IN THE SHADE OF WHICH TREES DO TRUFFLES GROW?

Young, green, and rooted oak trees and hazel trees (the only fruit-producing tree) are the trees with the most affinity for truffles. Austrian black pine, Scots pine, beech, linden, and hornbeam complete the forest family portrait of trees where you'll find truffles growing.

BIS (METHYLTHIO) METHANE?

Or 2,4-dithiapentane, an organosulfur compound. This is the famous synthetic aroma that chefs, as well as the food industry, have proliferated since the 1990s.

HOW DO YOU FIND TRUFFLES?

With a pig: the sow is particularly sensitive to a substance released by the fungus, close to the pheromones released by the animal during mating.
With a dog: dogs are more agile and have a much less greedy appetite than pigs.
With flies: flies are attracted by the smell; just follow certain species like *Suillia fuscicornis*.

3 CULT-CLASSIC TRUFFLE DISHES
The Bresse chicken *demi-deuil* ("half mourning") by Mère Brazier
Soupe VGE by Paul Bocuse
Artichoke soup with black truffle by Guy Savoy

WHOLE BLACK PÉRIGORD TRUFFLE IN COARSE SALT
by Éric Frechon*

SERVES 4

For the coarse-salt dough
1⅛ pounds (500 g) coarse salt
10 cups (1 kg) all-purpose flour
3 large (100 g) egg whites
10½ ounces (300 g) vegetale moss

For the Jerusalem artichoke mousseline
1⅛ pounds (500 g) Jerusalem artichokes
2 cups plus 2 tablespoons (500 mL) cream
Fine salt

For the "undergrowth" sponge cakes
½ cup (25 g) packed flat-leaf parsley
1 ounce (25 g) vegetale moss
½ cup (50 g) all-purpose flour
1 tablespoon plus 1 teaspoon (20 g) butter
1 pinch salt
1 pinch baking powder
¼ cup (60 mL) water, warmed
1½ large (25 g) egg yolks
1 large (40 g) egg white

4 round black truffles from Périgord, each weighing 3 ounces (80 g)

⅓ cup plus 1 tablespoon (100 mL) well-seasoned chicken stock
5½ tablespoons (80 g) butter

Make the coarse-salt dough
In the bowl of a stand mixer fitted with the flat beater, combine all the ingredients until a smooth dough is obtained. Divide the dough in half. Roll out one half of the dough to a thickness of ¾ inch (2 cm), then roll out the other half to a thickness of ⅓ inch (1 cm). Refrigerate until chilled.

Make the mousseline
Peel the Jerusalem artichokes and cut them into small pieces. Place the artichoke pieces, cream, and salt in a saucepan and cook for 20 minutes, or until the artichokes are softened. Drain, and blend the mixture into a very smooth purée. Set aside in a bain-marie to keep warm.

Make the "undergrowth" sponge cakes
In a blender, blend together the parsley, vegetale moss, flour, butter, salt, and baking powder. Add the warm water and blend. Add the yolks and egg white, blend, and strain through a fine-mesh sieve. Add the mixture to a whipped cream dispenser. Fill two paper cups three-quarters full with the mixture, and microwave them for 2 minutes. Unmold the cakes, and tear them into small pieces. Set aside.

Assembly, and cooking the truffles
Preheat the oven to 350°F (180°C). Peel the truffles, and set them aside. Chop the peels, and add them to the chicken stock. Make a small bowl-shaped well in the center of the thickest dough circle. Add the truffles, stock, and butter to the well. Cover with the second dough circle

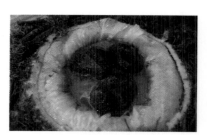

and seal tightly. Bake for 30 minutes, or until the dough has hardened.

Serving
Divide the mousseline among four serving plates, and distribute pieces of the sponge cake around it. Open the salt dough, remove the truffles, and arrange them on the plates. Spoon the cooking juices over the top.

*Excerpt from Éric Frechon, *Solar*

skip to
Salt–Crust for Crust!, p. 320

The Macaron, Squared

Its nicknames include the "Parisian" macaron, "double face," or "Gerbet." This is the sweet little burgerlike pastry that, from Paris to Tokyo and from London to New York, makes any sweet tooth swoon!
Gilbert Pytel

THE BIRTH OF AN ICONIC SWEET

The macaron, with its smooth and shiny surface, consists of two shells held together by a ganache. It is distinguished by its slightly crunchy shell and its very melting interior. The invention dates from 1862, and can be traced back to Pierre Desfontaines, grandson of the famous Parisian pastry chef Louis-Ernest Ladurée. Their design made creating them in different sizes easy: a classic individual version, and a mini-macaron called a "Gerbet," a name that serves as tribute to the pastry chef who made them his specialty. Since the last quarter of the twentieth century, the popularity of the "Parisian" macaron has grown substantially thanks to two renowned pastry chefs: Pierre Hermé and Philippe Andrieu (Ladurée).

4 IMPORTANT DATES IN THEIR SUCCESS

1997: Pierre Hermé, a consultant for Ladurée, develops the first "haute couture" Gerbet macaron recipes.
2001: Pierre Hermé opens his first Parisian pastry shop, raising the macaron to an iconic status for the twenty-first century, thanks to his many complex and subtle flavors.
2006: the international success of Sofia Coppola's film about Marie Antoinette, featuring the queen gorging herself on macarons, makes the little confection a worldwide hit.
2009: "Ça m'énerve" ("It Annoys Me"), the hit song of Helmut Fritz (which blithely mentions the creation: "It annoys me that all these people stand in line at Ladurée, all that for macarons, but hey . . . it seems that 'they are good'") greatly increases the daily sales of macarons at Ladurée.

THE FAMOUS MACARON INFINIMENT VANILLE
by Pierre Hermé

MAKES ABOUT 72 MACARONS (ABOUT 144 SHELLS)

For the vanilla ganache
2 Tahitian vanilla beans, halved lengthwise
2 Madagascar vanilla beans, halved lengthwise
2 Mexican vanilla beans, halved lengthwise
1¾ cups (400 g) light whipping cream (35% fat)
15½ ounces (440 g) Valrhona Ivoire 35% white chocolate

For the vanilla macaron shells
3 cups (300 g) confectioners' sugar
2 cups plus 2 tablespoons (300 g) ground almonds
3 vanilla beans
7 large (220 g) "liquefied" egg whites, divided*
¼ cup plus 1 tablespoon (75 mL) still mineral water
1½ cups (300 g) superfine sugar

Make the vanilla ganache

Scrape the seeds out of the vanilla beans using a knife, and stir the seeds and the empty vanilla bean pods into the cream. In a saucepan, bring the cream to a boil. Remove from the heat, then cover and let stand for 30 minutes to infuse. Chop the white chocolate, then gently melt it in a bowl set in a bain-marie. Remove the vanilla beans from the cream and wring out each one, by swiping down it with your finger, back into the cream. Pour the hot cream in thirds into the melted chocolate,

stirring to thoroughly combine after each addition. Using an immersion blender, blend the ganache until smooth, then pour the ganache into a baking dish. Cover it by gently pressing plastic wrap onto its surface. Refrigerate for at least 12 hours, or just until the ganache has developed a creamy consistency.

Make the vanilla macaron shells

Sift together the confectioners' sugar and ground almonds. Scrape the seeds out of the vanilla beans using a knife and stir the seeds into the confectioners' sugar–almond mixture. Pour half of the "liquefied" egg whites into the confectioners' sugar–almond-vanilla mixture without mixing. In a saucepan, boil the mineral water and superfine sugar to 244°F (118°C). As soon as the syrup reaches 239°F (115°C), begin beating the rest of the "liquefied" egg whites in the bowl of a stand mixer fitted with the whisk beater. When the syrup reaches 244°F (118°C), pour the syrup in a steady stream into the beaten egg whites. Beat the meringue until it cools to 122°F (50°C). Fold it with a silicone spatula into the confectioners' sugar–almond-vanilla mixture until the mixture loses volume. Transfer the batter to a pastry bag fitted with a plain #11 piping tube.

Piping and baking

Line baking sheets with parchment paper. Pipe disks about 1½ inches (3.5 cm) in diameter ¾ inch (2 cm) apart on the lined baking sheets. Rap the baking sheets on a work surface covered with a clean kitchen towel to gently smooth out the disks. Set aside for at least 30 minutes at room temperature to allow a skin to form. Preheat a convection oven to 350°F (180°C). Place the baking sheets in the oven. Bake for 12 minutes, quickly opening and closing the oven door twice during baking to release moisture. Remove the shells from the oven and slide them, still on the parchment paper, onto a work surface to cool.

Assembling the macarons

Scrape the ganache into a pastry bag fitted with a plain #11 piping tube. Turn half of the shells over with the flat sides up. Fill them with the ganache. Close them with the rest of the shells, pressing down lightly. Refrigerate the macarons for 24 hours. Remove them from the refrigerator 2 hours before eating them.

*"Liquefied" egg whites are egg whites that have been kept in a bowl set out for 2 or 3 days at room temperature.

FRANCE'S 5 BEST MACARONS

1
The Mogador macaron
(milk chocolate and passion fruit)
by Pierre Hermé
2
The coffee macaron
by Ladurée
3
The Maca'Lyon
(salted butter caramel coated with 70 percent chocolate)
by Sébastien Bouillet (Lyon)
4
The caramel/peanut macaron
by Vincent Guerlais (Nantes)
5
The Machu Picchu macaron
(Grand cru chocolate from Peru)
by Jean-Paul Hévin (Paris)

skip to
The Cake of Love, p. 228

Paul Bocuse

Monsieur Paul
(1926–2018)

The youngest Michelin-starred chef of the postwar period, Paul Bocuse, who passed away in 2018 at the age of ninety-one, was at the time of his death the oldest chef still working. He fought his entire life for the recognition of the cooking profession and established an enormous empire.

Alvina Ledru-Johansson

TRAINING
1934: begins working at eight years old in the family restaurant. "I now know what rank feels like, about the servitude that chains you to scrubbing pan bottoms, to sharpening knives, to the ovens, anyway" (*La bonne chère*, 1995).
1942: apprenticeship with Claude Maret in Lyon: "The roughest period of my life. It was the black market, we had to kill pigs and calves ourselves, cut them up before making chops in cream sauce."
1947: climbs the steep slopes of the Col de la Luère to reach La Mère Brazier and asks for a job in the kitchen. "If you've biked all the way up here, that means you've got heart. Little guy, you're hired."
1949: joins Lucas Carton (Paris) upon the recommendation of Fernand Point.
1950–1952: gets hired in Point's kitchen. He becomes his mentor. "With Fernand Point, who made me inexhaustible, I acquired simplicity."

1958

first Michelin star

❁

1960: achieves his second star.
1961: becomes Best Craftsman of France (MOF).
1965: achieves three Michelin stars.
2015: celebrates fifty years of three stars, an absolute record

❁❁❁

SOLE FERNAND POINT

PREPARATION TIME: 40 MINUTES
COOKING TIME: 25 MINUTES
SERVES 4

1 sole, weighing about 1⅓ pounds (600 g)
1 medium tomato
3 shallots
4 medium white button mushrooms
¾ cup plus 1 tablespoon (200 mL) white wine
1 large (19 g) egg yolk
7 tablespoons (100 g) clarified butter
1 tablespoon (15 mL) cream
2⅛ ounces (60 g) tagliatelle
Salt and freshly ground black pepper

Remove the fillets from the fish. Keep the head, skin, and bones to make the stock. Blanch the tomato and dice it. Peel and chop the shallots. Wash the mushrooms, cut the heads into sticks, and reserve the stems. Place the fish head, skin, and bones in a large saucepan and add just enough water to cover them. Add the wine, shallots, and mushrooms, and cook for 20 minutes. Place the egg yolk in a saucepan in a bain-marie over low heat. Add 1 spoonful (15 mL) of water, whisk, and stir in the clarified butter. Season with salt and pepper, and whisk the mixture until smooth. Strain the stock through a fine-mesh sieve. Place the fillets, mushrooms, and tomato in a saucepan and add the strained stock. Cook over low heat just until the liquid starts to boil. Remove the fillets, tomatoes, and mushrooms and reserve the stock. In a saucepan, reduce the stock. Whip the cream to soft peaks. Add the stock and whipped cream to the egg mixture in the saucepan (the sabayon). Cook the tagliatelle for 5 to 6 minutes in boiling salted water. Arrange the noodles with the tomato and mushrooms on a serving platter. Place the fillets on top. Spoon the sauce over the top. Place under the oven broiler for 2 to 3 minutes, or just until browned.

The empire

A gourmet restaurant
L'Auberge Paul Bocuse in Collonges-au-Mont-d'Or

An event space
The Abbey in Collonges-au-Mont-d'Or

Six restaurants in Lyon and Caluire

Fast-food establishments

Institut Paul Bocuse and its teaching restaurant
Seven hundred students trained every year

The Foundation d'Entreprise Paul Bocuse
For the "perpetuation of the profession's skills, knowledge and conduct."

Restaurants in the United States, Japan, and Switzerland

THE SOCIAL STATUS OF THE CHEF

Paul Bocuse fought his entire life for the proper recognition of the cooking profession.
Give the kitchen back to the cooks: a mission he learned while working with Fernand Point, who was forever repeating that phrase. At the time, only the maîtres d'hôtel enjoyed the recognition of customers and journalists. Point emphasized: "A chef has to be the owner of his business." In 1960, with a wad of bills wrapped in newspaper, Bocuse bought the Hôtel du Pont, the name of the restaurant then.
Get the cook out of his kitchen: "The dining room is a theater." Bocuse adhered to Point's precept: every night, he would go out into the dining room and shake hands, take pictures, and sign autographs.
Be proud of your profession: working with Bragard, the professional clothing specialist, he designed a new kind of jacket that was more elegant, cinched at the waist; and especially the red, white, and blue collar distinguishing the Best Craftsman of France (MOF). In 1991, he founded a contest that was given the name "Le Bocuse d'Or," which aimed to consecrate "the best chef in the world." The public went wild, there were hordes of journalists, and the chef became a star.

BRESSE CHICKEN FRICASSEE WITH MOREL MUSHROOMS

SERVES 8

1 ounce (30 g) dried morel mushrooms
⅓ cup plus 1 tablespoon (100 mL) Madeira
2½ chicken bouillon cubes
1 Bresse chicken, weighing 4 pounds (1.8 kg), cut into 8 pieces
⅓ cup plus 1 tablespoon (100 mL) Noilly-Prat vermouth
2 cups (500 mL) white wine
3 sprigs tarragon
7 ounces (100 g) white button mushrooms
6 small shallots, peeled and thinly sliced
1 tablespoon plus 1 teaspoon (20 g) butter, softened
3 tablespoons plus 1 teaspoon (20 g) flour
2 cups (500 g) crème fraîche

Place the morel mushrooms in a bowl, cover them with hot water, and let them soak for 30 minutes. Drain and slice the morel mushrooms in half. Pour the Madeira into a saucepan and reduce it until the pan is almost dry (do not let it burn). Add the morel mushrooms and a half cube of the chicken bouillon. Cover with water and cook for 40 minutes, uncovered, over medium heat.

Salt the flesh side of the chicken pieces. Pour 1 cup (250 mL) of water into a flameproof casserole dish, and add the Noilly-Prat and the wine. Rinse and dry the tarragon, then add it to the casserole dish. Cut the white button mushroom caps into sticks, then add them to the casserole dish. Add the shallots and the 2 remaining bouillon cubes. Heat over very high heat.

Place the chicken pieces in the casserole dish, and let them cook for 12 minutes, uncovered. Remove the white meat pieces. Let the brown meat pieces cook for another 13 minutes. If necessary, add a little water so that the liquid reaches the height of the chicken pieces. Meanwhile, mash the butter with a spoon until creamy. Add the flour to the butter and stir to thoroughly combine.

Remove the brown meat pieces of chicken from the casserole. Remove the tarragon. Reduce the cooking juice until it sizzles. Then add the flour-butter mixture.

Immediately add the crème fraiche and cook for 5 minutes, while stirring. Place all the chicken pieces back into the casserole dish. Turn them several times in the sauce and let them warm.

Transfer the stew to a warmed serving dish, drain the morel mushrooms and transfer them to the serving dish with the stew, and add a little chopped fresh tarragon. Serve immediately.

THE LITTLE SAYINGS OF MONSIEUR PAUL

*"I have three **stars**. I had **three bypasses**. And I still have **three women**."*

◇

*"Me, I have **my two BACs: my hot water bac (tank)**, and my **cold water bac**."*

◇

*"I encouraged **chefs** to come out of their kitchens, but sometimes they should not **forget to go back**."*

SOUPE VGE

On February 25, 1975, Bocuse was knighted by the French President Valéry Giscard d'Estaing at the Palais de l'Élysée. For this occasion, he created one of his iconic dishes.

SERVES 6

6 disks puff pastry, weighing 2⅛ ounces (60 g) each
2⅛ ounces (60 g) total of equal parts carrots, onions, celery, and mushrooms, each peeled and diced
6 tablespoons (85 g) unsalted butter
6⅓ ounces (180 g) beef upper chuck, cooked and diced
2⅛ ounces (60 g) foie gras, cut into pieces
4¼ ounces (120 g) black truffles, thinly sliced
6 tablespoons (90 mL) Noilly-Prat vermouth
6 tablespoons (90 mL) truffle juice
6 cups (1.5 L) beef consommé (or use beef broth)
3 large (57 g) egg yolks
Salt and freshly ground black pepper

Remove the puff pastry disks from the refrigerator far enough ahead so that they are supple (yet still slightly chilled) at the time of use. Preheat the oven to 425°F (220°C).

Cook the vegetables, covered, in the butter. Arrange the beef, vegetables, foie gras, and truffles in individual soup tureens. Add the Noilly Prat, the truffle juice, and the beef consommé. Trim the puff pastry disks to cover each tureen. Place a puff pastry disk over the top of each tureen, and press to tightly seal the dough all around the edges, to ensure all the flavors are concentrated inside the tureen. Brush the disks with the egg yolks, and bake for about 20 minutes. The puff pastry must have a beautiful golden color. Serve immediately. Enjoy after breaking through the pastry with a spoon. The pastry should fall in pieces into the soup.

Spring Is Rosé!

When the first rays of sun start to peek through the clouds, voilà—France pops open a rosé for an aperitif! But how do you find your way around shades of pink and red and the many labels? Simply follow the color chart.

Alexis Goujard

THE TWO MAJOR PRODUCTION METHODS

Direct press: the most popular approach to making elegant rosés. Black grapes are placed into a press; the skill of the winemaker is essential for letting the juice in the tank tint nicely, yet not too much. The juice is then left to ferment.

Maceration: this approach is used for colorful and full-bodied rosés. The grapes macerate for several hours. When the correct color and taste are reached, the must is placed in a tank to ferment. The longer the maceration, the more colorful and structured the rosé will be. This is the same procedure used for the "*saignée*" (bleeding) method, where part of the juice is used to make red wine.

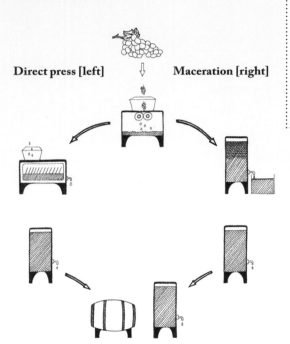

Direct press [left]   **Maceration [right]**

What does the color of a rosé tell us?

In general, the clearer the rosé, the lighter in taste it will be. The deeper the color, the more it will offer substance and structure, for serving at the table with food. Avoid any rosés whose colors are too pale or fluorescent! These wines probably will have been manipulated.

The paler a rosé is, the less alcohol it will have?

False. The very pale color suggests lightness. But pay attention: these rosés can be as strong as 12.5 to 14.5 percent in alcohol!

You should dispose of a rosé that is too pink?

False. Do you have a rosé that is too fluorescent pink in color, with flavors of a sweet tart? If so, "drown it!" Throw some ice cubes into a large glass and pour it over. They will disguise the issue.

Rosés can be stored?

True. Some rare pearls like Tavel, Palette, or Bandol are seductive after two, three, or ten years, or sometimes even longer! So, if you find an old bottle by chance in the bottom of your cellar, do not empty it into the sink, you may be surprised when you taste it.

Not a mixture of red wine and white wine! Primarily black grapes, sometimes with a small number of white grapes, are used before pressing. One exception is Champagne, where a touch of red wine can be added to white wine before it becomes sparkling.

WHAT DO YOU EAT WITH A ROSÉ?

→ With full-bodied rosés from coastal Var and Côte-de-Provence, enjoy marinated bell peppers, pizzas, pissaladières, or bouillabaisse as a few good options.

→ To pair with a Bigorre Noir or a Spanish Serrano, open a Tannat d'Irouléguy, a blend of Collioure and a Corsican Sciaccarellu.

→ Spice up Thai cuisine (beef salad, pad Thai, pet palo, etc.) with a bright and spicy Loire rosé, a Pineau d'Aunis, or a Grolleau.

→ For salted tuna cooked à la plancha, the body of a Tavel or Rosé-des-Riceys will surround the firm flesh on your palate.

Rosé Terroirs

PROVENCE
Rosés both delicate and structured.
Grape varietals: blends of Grenache, Cinsault, and Syrah in Côtes-de-Provence; Mourvèdre in Bandol; or Braquet in Bellet.

CORSICA
A strong character, firm and spicy.
Grape varietals: Sciaccarellu and Niellucciu.

RHÔNE VALLEY
Colorful and velvety alongside pale and lively options.
Grape varietals: Grenache, Syrah, Mourvèdre, and Carignan in Tavel, coastal Rhône, and Ardèche.

CHAMPAGNE
With bubbles, refined rosés; without bubbles, generous rosés.
Grape varietals: in Champagne, Pinot Noir is used alone or blended with Chardonnay and Meunier. In Rosé-des-Riceys, only Pinot Noir is used.

THE LOIRE
Tonic rosés, joyful.
Grape varietals: Gamay from Touraine, Pineau d'Aunis from the Vendômais slops, Grolleau d'Anjou, Pinot Noir of Sancerre.

BORDEAUX
It's no longer necessary to wait fifteen years before opening a Grand Cru Classé when you select a rounded and delicate rosé from the region.
Grape varietals: mainly Merlot with a little Cabernet Sauvignon.

THE SOUTHWEST
Aggressive and stimulating rosés. Lovers of sweet rosés should move on!
Grape varietals: Negrette de Fronton, Malbec de Cahors, Tannat d'Irouléguy, or Duras de Gaillac.

LANGUEDOC-ROUSSILLON
A great variety of tasty rosés with lots of fruit.
Grape varietals: Mediterranean classics such as Grenache, Syrah in Collioure and Saint-Chinian, and Cinsault in Languedoc-Cabrières.

5 GREAT ROSÉS THAT WILL MAKE YOU SING

TAVEL
Domaine de L'Anglore
Eric Pfifferling's voluptuous rosé with the generosity of southern fruit and northern freshness.
Organic.

CORSE (CORSICA)
Clos Fornelli
Raspberry and sweet spices are detected in this Sciaccarellu.
What character!

CÔTES DE PROVENCE
Roquefort Castle
Pale, modern, and slender with stony contours, this Corail sets an example.
Organic.

COTEAUX VENDÔMOIS GRIS
Patrice Colin
A pinnacle of Aunis, where the freshness of the Loire flows over the tongue.
Organic.

BANDOL
Domaine de Terrebrune
At one year old, this rosé is sanguine and floral, at ten years old, it becomes delicately spicy and flavorful. A big rosé for keeping.
Organic.

Sauerkraut

Although this is one of the favorite dishes of the French, few people dare to make it at home.
But fermented cabbage is not so complicated . . .

Frédérick e. Grasser Hermé

IN THE BEGINNING . . .

The word *sauerkraut* (*choucroute* in French) comes from the German *sauerkraut*: literally "sour cabbage," shortened eventually in French to *chou* ("cabbage") and *croute* ("crust") simply for phonetic reasons. It is indeed a dish of chopped and lacto-fermented cabbage. By extension, it refers to a dish of cabbage and its accompaniments.

OTHER SAUERKRAUTS

→ La Strasbourgeoise is cooked with goose fat or lard, accompanied by smoked pork loin, white sausages (made with veal or pork), bacon, and Strasbourg sausages
→ La Royale is sprinkled with raw Alsace Crémant (a sparkling wine)—or, even more chic, with Champagne—surrounded by smoked sausages with cumin, Frankfurt sausages, and poached pigs' knuckle
→ Ocean sauerkraut, with haddock
→ Lobster sauerkraut, flambéed with whiskey
→ Sauerkraut with roasted goose for Christmas

Lexicon
★ ★ ★

Alélor: a brand of mild and smooth Alsatian mustard, ideal for enlivening sauerkraut. A special holiday is dedicated to it every year in Reichstett. Some refer to it as "horseradish in a pot."
Kirschwasser: a colorless eau-de-vie recognizable by its very pronounced taste of cherry pit, with an alcohol content not less than 45 proof.
Torpilleur: a long earthenware dish, shaped like a ship's bow. This is the dish par excellence for serving sauerkraut, placed on a warming plate to keep the dish at the perfect temperature.

ALSATIAN SAUERKRAUT

MAKES A CROCK TO SERVE 8
3 tablespoons lard
3 ounces (80 g) finely chopped onion
4½ pounds (2 kg) raw sauerkraut
3 cloves garlic, peeled and crushed
2 bay leaves
2 sprigs thyme
1⅛ pounds (500 g) uncooked fresh pork belly
1 pork shank, desalted the day before
1⅓ pounds (600 g) smoked upper pork shoulder
1 bottle (750 mL) Sylvaner wine
Sea salt
7 juniper berries
1 teaspoon (3 g) caraway seeds
1 teaspoon (3 g) black peppercorns
2 Montbéliard sausages
8 potatoes
4 Frankfurt or Strasbourg sausages
Just over ¾ cup (200 mL) eau-de-vie, preferably Alsatian kirschwasser

In a large pot over medium heat, melt the lard. Add the onion and cook, without browning it, then add the sauerkraut, and stir well to combine with the onion. Add the garlic, bay leaves, and thyme. Push the pork belly, shank, and shoulder into the center of the sauerkraut, and cover them with the sauerkraut. Add the wine, season with salt, and add only enough water, if needed, so that the sauerkraut is submerged. Add the juniper berries, caraway seeds, and peppercorns to the pot. Bring to a simmer over medium heat. Let simmer very gently for 2 hours over low heat. The meat must be very tender. Add the Montbéliard sausages 30 minutes before the end of the cooking time. Cook the potatoes separately, either by baking or steaming. Peel the potatoes, and add them to the sauerkraut 5 minutes before the end of the cooking time. At the same time, poach the Frankfurt sausages in a pan of boiling water, cover, and allow to swell for about 5 minutes. Arrange the sauerkraut in a pile on a *torpilleur* (see left). Cut the pork belly, shank, and shoulder meat into pieces, and lay them overlapping on top of the sauerkraut. Garnish the dish with the Montbéliard sausages, sliced at an angle. Place the Frankfurt sausages, still whole, on top. Arrange the potatoes all around the edge of the dish. Serve with Alsatian mild mustard, such as Alélor, and a very chilled Riesling.

THE FORMULA FOR SAUERKRAUT

The art of fermentation is an ancient technique used for preserving vegetables and their vitamins and minerals. Choose a glazed terra-cotta crock with a gutter around the rim, filled with water, to prevent air from entering while allowing gases to release. A large glass jar is also a good option.

1 glass jar with a volume of 4 cups (1 L)
2¼ pounds (1 kg) cabbage
2½ teaspoons (15 g) salt
1 teaspoon (3 g) juniper berries
1 teaspoon (2 g) caraway seeds
½ teaspoon (1.5 g) cumin seeds

Take a large leaf of cabbage, cut out the rib, wet the leaf to soften it, and set it aside. Quarter the cabbage heads, and finely julienne the quarters into ⅒-inch- (2 mm) thick slices, preferably using a mandoline slicer. In a bowl, combine the sliced cabbage, salt, and spices. Set the bowl aside to allow the cabbage to release its liquid for about 1 hour. Transfer the mixture to the airtight jar, along with the juices. With your fist, tamp down the surface of the cabbage. Cover the cabbage with the reserved leaf, then place a weight (such as a cleaned stone) on top. Close the lid. Let the cabbage ferment for 2 days at room temperature, then 4 weeks in the refrigerator, before opening the jar. Sauerkraut can be stored for up to 1 year.

Tip: Do not rinse sauerkraut, to avoid rinsing away the probiotics, enzymes, and minerals that help with digestion.

THE OTHER SAUERKRAUT—WITH TURNIPS

Süri-rüewe is a sauerkraut prepared with fermented turnips. The cabbage is replaced by turnips peeled into long, thin, spiral strips, then prepared in the same way as the fermented cabbage sauerkraut.

Fermented Süri-Rüewe Recipe

2¼ pounds (1 kg) of large white turnips, peeled in a spiral, 2½ teaspoons (15 g) of salt, 1 tablespoon (10 g) of juniper berries, 1 large white cabbage leaf for covering, and 1 weight (such as a cleaned stone) for placing on top. Let the turnip ferment for 1 to 2 days at room temperature, then let it ferment for 3 to 4 weeks at room temperature and away from any light. For peeling the turnip, choose a vegetable lathe rather than a vegetable peeler. Use a 6-cup (1.5 L) glass jar.

An address to know

Schmid, 76, boulevard de Strasbourg, Paris 10th. An authentic Alsatian *traiteur* (prepared food market) set up opposite the Gare de l'Est since 1904. Their sauerkrauts are irreproachable.

skip to . . . .
The Quest for Fat, p. 341

Vegetable	Eggplant	Camus artichoke	Purple artichoke	Asparagus	Beet	Chard	Broccoli	Cardoon
Preparation	Thick slices	Whole	Rounded	Whole, peeled with a vegetable peeler	Whole, unpeeled	The ribs without their strings, in sections of 2¾ to 3 inches (7 to 8 cm)	Cut into small florets	Discard the large leaves, thin skin, and strings, then cut into sections of 2 to 2¾ inches (5 to 7 cm)
Boiling water		**25–40 min**	Au blanc** (see p. 285), **10 min** before braising	**8–12 min**	**60 min**	**8–10 min**	**3–7 min**	Au blanc **, **45 min** to **1 h 30 min** (must be just tender)
Steamed	Peeled, cut into cubes, disgorged **15 min** with salt, cooked **15 min**, seasoned with olive oil, garlic, scallions, and herbs	**35–50 min**		**10–15 min**		**10–15 min**	**5–8 min**	
Sweated				**15 min**			**10 min**	
Panfried, sautéed	In olive oil, with a little garlic, **15–20 min** while turning regularly		Whole or cut in half or quartered, **20 min** in olive oil with chopped garlic, adding a little water or broth			The leaves in butter, over medium heat, until their liquid has evaporated	Steamed and sautéed for a few minutes in butter until lightly browned	
Braised/glazed			Once cooked au blanc**, cut in half and braised **25 min**			Leaves and ribs in sections, **20 min**		
Fried	Deep-fried **15 min** with salt, dipped in batter*, fried **2–3 min**		Cut into 4 or 5 wedges, cooked **5 min** in boiling water, dipped in batter*, and fried **2–3 min**					Cooked in boiling water, sprinkled with parsley and lemon juice, dipped in batter*, then fried **2–3 min**
Baked	Disgorged **15 min** with salt, oiled, and grilled under the broiler **3–4 min** on each side		**8–10 min** under the broiler, brushed with olive oil, with a minced garlic clove		**1 h 30 min** at 338°F (170°C), peeled and seasoned with butter. See beetroot in salt crust, p. 320			See Cardoon Gratins, p. 26

Cooking vegetables
with Jacques Maximin

For me, the master of cooking with vegetables is Jacques Maximin. This former chef of Roger Vergé has always produced the most beautifully cooked vegetables on the Côte d'Azur. And his bible *La Cuisine des Légumes* (Albin Michel) is an absolute must-have reference. *François-Régis Gaudry*

Carrots	Celery stalk	Celery root	White button mushrooms	Green cabbage	Cauliflower	Brussels sprouts	Winter squash	Zucchini
Peeled and cut into slices, beveled sections, or sticks	Without woody stem or string, in sections of 1½ to 2 inches (4 to 5 cm)	Peeled and cut into equal pieces	Earthy stem discarded, whole	Leafless, rough leaves discarded, stem/core removed	Cut into florets	Drained, outer leaves removed	Cleaned of its strings and seeds (no need to peel the thick skin)	As "large olives" (thick rounds)
8–12 min	**10–15 min**	Au blanc**, **5–10 min**	**25 min** deep boiling water with butter, salt, and lemon juice	**15–17 min**	**8–10 min**	**8–10 min**	Quartered, **10–15 min**	**5–7 min**
10–15 min	**15–20 min**			**17–20 min**	**10–12 min**	**10–12 min**	**15–20 min**	**7–9 min**
15–20 min	**20–25 min**		**7–8 min** in butter, with crème fraiche and herbs					
In butter, over medium heat, **12–15 min**, covered, with a little water		In large slices, **15 min** in butter; in thin rounds, sautéed **5 min**	In butter, over high heat **5–10 min** then browned, seasoned with a persillade, salted. See Duxelles, p. 345	In butter: tender leaves cooked in water, drained, minced, then browned **5 min**	In butter: steamed **5–6 min** and cooked in butter until lightly browned	Cooked in boiling water and warmed in butter until soft and browned	Quartered, boiled in water, and browned in butter over medium heat	The "olives" are covered with water, butter, and sugar, cooked down until reduced, then cooked until the liquid has evaporated
In sections, with water to cover and 1 teaspoon (5 g) of sugar, 3 tablespoons (50 g) of butter, and salt, brought to a boil and then simmered until caramelized and liquid is evaporated		In chunks, **5–10 min** in boiling water, then roasted in butter with a little bit of cooking water, **10–15 min**		Cut into 4 to 6 pieces without the outer leaves, added **30 min** before the end of the cooking time in soups or pot-au-feu		Cut in 2, with water halfway up, a pat of butter, and small white onions, over low heat, until the liquid evaporates	See potimarron velouté, p. 198	In ⅓-inch (1 cm) slices, over medium-high heat, with butter and 2 tablespoons (30 mL) of water, until lightly browned
		Cut into thin slices, fried a few minutes for crispy chips			Steamed and immersed in the frying oil until hazelnut brown color			In ¼-inch (0.5 cm) slices, dipped in batter and fried in olive oil
Whole carrots, **15–20 min** at 350°F (180°C)		In large slices, brushed with olive oil, **20 min** at 350°F (180°C)		See Stuffed Cabbage, p. 147 and p. 312	Whole, roasted in oven with olive oil at 275°F (130°C) for **1 h 30 min**		Quartered, cooked in water, and placed in a gratin dish rubbed with garlic, with grated cheese and butter pieces, **15–20 min** at 350°F (180°C)	

FRENCH TECHNIQUES

Vegetables can be cooked . . .

Boiled: immersed in a large amount of boiling salted water, then drained. This approach can be used to parboil the vegetables to prepare them for frying or sautéing, or to cook them until done. This is the so-called "English" technique. The pros say "to blanch."

Steamed: placed on a steamer basket and gently steamed over boiling water. This approach does not jostle or soak the vegetables like the "English" technique (boiling), and it preserves the quality of the vegetables.

Sweated: cooked over low heat in a saucepan with a little water at the bottom, a little butter, and salt. Cooked in this way, the vegetables are said to "melt" or "sweat," then soften in their own juices.

Panfried, sautéed: this technique applies to vegetables that are raw or have already been cooked in boiling water; they are panfried in fat such as butter, olive oil, or goose fat. Vegetables can be cooked quickly over high heat.

Vegetable	Crosne (Chinese artichoke)	Endive	Spinach	Fennel	String beans	Spring turnip	Sorrel	Peas
Preparation	Ends cut off, rubbed with coarse salt in a dish towel, and washed	Core and outer damaged leaves removed	Stems removed	Stalks and outer leaves removed	Stems removed	Washed, tops removed, and peeled	Stems removed	Shelled
Boiling water	**10–11 min**	Whole, **10 min** before braising (to remove bitterness)	**3–5 min**	**15–20 min**	**3 min** (small and freshly picked)	**10–12 min**		**5–7 min**
Steamed	**12–13 min**		**5–6 min**	**20–22 min**	**12–15 min**	**12–15 min**		**7–9 min**
Sweated	Covered with water, with a little butter, and boiled until liquid is evaporated	8 endives sliced evenly, + ⅓ cup (100 mL) of water, juice of 1 lemon, 2 tablespoons (40 g) of butter, salt and a pinch of sugar; over high heat, covered, until boiling, then **30–35 min** over low heat	**3–5 min**, covered, with butter	Cut into 2, **10–15 min** in a little butter and 2 tablespoons (30 mL) of water		Cut into 2, cooked over medium heat in a little butter, with a few spoonfuls of water, until liquid is evaporated	Slow cooked, with butter, so that it loses its water; crème fraîche added at the end of cooking	With a few spoonfuls of water, in butter, covered
Panfried, sautéed	Cooked in boiling water and cooked in butter	Steamed in a pan with a little butter, **10 min** on all sides, until caramelized	Steamed and cooked over medium-high heat with a little crème fraîche		Cooked in butter, with a persillade (garlic + parsley) or in a tomato sauce	Cut in slices of ¼ inch (0.5 cm), dipped **30 seconds** in boiling water, then browned in butter **6–8 min**		à la française: 1⅛ pounds (500 g) of peas, 12 small white onions, 1 heart of lettuce, 5 tablespoons (70 g) of butter, thyme, parsley, salt, pepper, ¼ cup (60 mL) of water, covered, **20–25 min**
Braised/glazed		Cooked in boiling water and then braised with a little sugar and butter for **20 min**		Scalded **5 min**, then cooked over low heat with a little water, butter, and sugar (or the juice of an orange) until liquid is evaporated		Cut into "large olives," (thick rounds) with water to cover, butter, and a little sugar (or honey), until liquid is evaporated		
Fried								
Baked		Sweated, placed in a greased dish, covered with béchamel sauce, butter pieces, and grated Emmental cheese, **20 min** at 350°F (180°C) + **5 min** under broiler		Roasted with olive oil and some cloves of garlic, **45 min** at 350°F (180°C)				

Braised: an aromatic filling (shallots, carrot, garlic, bouquet garni) is sweated in a fat, broth is added, then the vegetables are cooked gently at a simmer, covered.
Fried: immersed in boiling oil, as with French fries. The vegetables can be raw; raw and dredged in a batter; or baked in a batter.*

Baked: whether for confit, searing, broiling, or roasting, the oven lends itself to many uses, depending on the temperature chosen. Gentle to medium: 125°F to 250°F (50°C to 125°C). Medium to hot: 250°F to 400°F (125°C to 200°C). Hot to very hot: 400°F to 475°F (200°C to 250°C).

Sugar snap peas 	Leeks 	Bell pepper 	Potato with firm flesh (Belle de Fontenay, Roseval, Charlotte, etc.)	Potato with starchy flesh (Bjinte)	New potato (Grenaille, Ratte, Noirmoutier, etc.)	Salsify 	Jerusalem artichoke (Sunchoke) 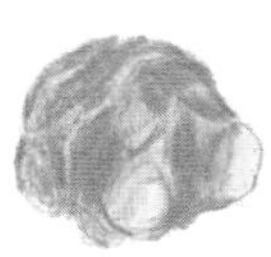
Stems removed	Roots and rough green leaves removed	Stem removed, seeded, cut into large strips	Washed	Washed	Washed, unpeeled, whole	Leaves and ends removed, peeled	Peeled (requires patience!)
4–5 min	**8–10 min**		Peeled or not, whole, in cold water, **20–25 min** from boiling	Peeled, cut into fourths, in cold water, **20 min** from boiling. See Grandma's Mashed Potatoes, p. 19	See Joel Robuchon Potato Purée, p. 19	**15 min** to au blanc**	**30 min**
5–6 min	**10–12 min**	Cooked whole with stem **8–12 min**, then peeled, and seeded	**25–30 min**	**20 min**	**10–15 min**	**20–25 min**	**30–35 min**
	Spring leeks cooked in butter with a thin layer of water, over medium heat, covered						Sliced, cooked over low heat, with butter and a thin layer of water; test with the tip of a knife
Cooked al dente in boiling water, then cooked in butter and a spoonful of water			Peeled, sliced, and cooked in a pan with butter, olive oil, or duck fat **25–30 min**		Cut into pieces and cooked with butter, olive oil, or goose fat **5 min** over high heat, then **20 min** over medium heat	Cooked in boiling water, dried, browned side by side in butter over medium heat, with or without cream	
			Chips: 2¼ pounds (1 kg) peeled, cut into strips of ⅒ inch (2 mm), washed, and dried, cooked in a single layer in a very hot frying bath **3–4 min**, stirring constantly	See World's Best Frites, p. 333		Cooked in boiling water, marinated **25–30 min** in peanut oil, lemon, and salt, then drained, immersed in batter, and fried until browned	
		Roasted whole **45 min** under the broiler to blister the peel, enclosed **5 min** in a plastic bag, then peeled, seeded, cut into strips, and covered with olive oil	Unpeeled, cut in half lengthwise, and placed on a baking sheet, flat surface up, with coarse salt, rosemary, thyme, and a drizzle of olive oil, **40–50 min** at 350°F (180°C)	Whole, unpeeled, wrapped in foil and baked **1 h 30 min** to **2 h** at 350°F (180°C), served sliced opened with crème fraîche and chopped herbs	Brushed with olive oil, cooked with coarse salt, thyme, and whole garlic cloves, **40 min** at 350°F (180°C)		

Note: Most of the time, salt and pepper are not indicated. The vegetables should be seasoned according to taste.

*BATTER

In a small bowl, dissolve 1¼ teaspoons (5 g) baking powder in 1 tablespoon (15 mL) of milk. Combine 1 cup plus 3 tablespoons (120 g) of flour, 1 egg yolk (white reserved), the baking powder mixture, and salt. Measure ½ cup (100 mL) of milk, add one-third of the milk to the flour mixture, along with 3 tablespoons (45 mL) of beer, and stir vigorously to obtain a paste without lumps. Add the remaining milk and 1 tablespoon (15 mL) of oil. Let stand for 2 hours at room temperature. Before using the batter, beat the reserved egg white to soft peaks and incorporate it thoroughly.

**COOKING "AU BLANC"

This is an English cooking method where a "white" mixture is added to boiling salted water, which prevents vegetables from browning. This method is used for cooking cardoons and celery root. Combine 2 tablespoons (12 g) of flour with 4 tablespoons (60 mL) of lemon juice, added little by little into the flour, while stirring. Heat salted water in a saucepan. Combine the lemon paste with a little hot water to obtain a clear mixture. Pour this mixture into the pan of boiling water and add in the vegetables.

To the Rescue of Pain Perdu

What an abomination to throw away stale bread! Instead, you can use it to make croutons, meatballs, stuffing, toasted bread, bread crumbs, an omelet, or a charlotte! By using its imagination, France has made its old bread the king of the table!

Frédéric Laly-Baraglioli

"Stale bread is not hard, what is hard is to live without bread."

Proverb

BREAD CRUMB TART
by Sonia Ezgulian*

PREPARATION TIME: 10 MINUTES
COOKING TIME: 30 MINUTES
SERVES 8

5¼ ounces (150 g) bread crumbs (the tart will have a very different flavor depending on the crumbs: brioche, cereal bread, rye, etc.)
1 cup (250 mL) whole milk
5½ tablespoons (70 g) sugar
5½ tablespoons (50 g) almond flour
3 eggs (3 yolks + 2 whites)
¾ cup (100 g) pine nuts, toasted
7 ounces (200 g) pâte brisée (flaky pastry dough)
2½ teaspoons (11 g) baking powder

Preheat the oven to 400°F (200°C). In a bowl, soak the bread crumbs in the milk for 15 minutes. In a separate large bowl, combine the sugar with the almond flour. Gradually stir in the egg yolks. Beat the egg whites to stiff peaks, then fold them into the almond flour mixture. Stir in the soaked bread crumbs, baking powder, and the pine nuts. Roll out the flaky pastry dough, and transfer it to a lightly greased tart pan. Scrape the filling into the pan. Bake for 25 to 30 minutes, checking from time to time to ensure it has not browned too much on top. Serve with a few strips of candied lemon slices over the top.

*Sonia Ezgulian, who specializes in cooking with leftovers, always has an idea for using stale bread. Her most daring ideas: bread French fries, and a tart crust made of bread crumbs!

	SWEET	AMOUNT OF BREAD	SALTY
		−	
SOUPS	**Milk soup,** *boued laezh* (Brittany): bread and sweet milk, reminiscent of a Colette café au lait.		**Panade:** interregional soup consisting of bread, water, and sometimes garlic or eggs. Its name, once synonymous with a terrible misery, today means a difficult situation. Dumas devoted an article to it in his *Grand Dictionnaire.*
EGGS AND BREAD	**Pastizzu** (Corsica): caramelized custard (flan) of bread (wrongly often replaced with semolina).		**Bread omelet:** made with croutons, and optional garlic and herbs.
LIGHTLY DREDGED BREAD	**Pain perdu:** indulgent slices of bread, recalling childhood, enriched with cream, calvados, pommeau, Cointreau, or rum, depending on the region.		**Brotknepfle** (Alsace): bread dumplings with shallots and nutmeg.
VARIATIONS WITH PUDDINGS	**Ch'pain d'chien** (North): a pudding (the name comes from the French *boudin*) where bread is added to milk, raisins, and, of course, turbinado or light brown sugar! **Bettelmann** (Alsace): *mendiant* or pudding with black cherries and kirsch.		**Pounti or picoussel** (Aveyron/Cantal): a pâte sucrée-savory mixture of eggs, bread, chard, sausage meat, and prunes. **Farsous (Aveyron):** small galettes of chard, bread, sausage meat, and eggs! Flour is now used instead of bread . . . **Boule auvergnate:** a salty pudding made with bacon or raw ham, eggs, parsley, garlic, and cheese.
		+	

PAIN PERDU
by Huguette Méliet*

PREPARATION TIME: 10 MINUTES
COOKING TIME: 10 MINUTES
SERVES 6

1 vanilla bean
3 eggs
3 tablespoons (50 mL) Armagnac, plus more if needed
2 cups (½ L) whole milk (raw milk, if possible)
6 thick slices of stale country bread (left out for 2 days, or for 1 day if using white sandwich bread)
10 tablespoons (150 g) butter, cut into thick slices
¾ cup (150 g) sugar

Split the vanilla lengthwise in half and scrape out the seeds using a knife. Place the empty vanilla bean pod and the seeds into a large bowl. Add the eggs and beat them lightly. Add the Armagnac and milk and stir to combine. Dip the bread slices into this mixture, turn to coat both sides, and set aside for 10 minutes. In a heavy skillet over medium heat, heat about 3 slices of the butter until melted, then add about ¼ cup (50 g) of the sugar, and 2 slices of bread. The butter will caramelize as it cooks. Stir the butter regularly. The bread will gradually brown. Sprinkle the bread slices with a little sugar before turning them over, cooking them until browned on the second side. Repeat with the remaining bread slices. When the bread and liquid have turned a caramel brown, remove the bread slices from the pan, spoon the sauce over the slices, and serve.

*Restaurateur, mother of Denis, boss of J'Go, and inspirer of the menu.

skip to
School of Greens, p. 97

Alain Chapel

He was one of the major chefs of the golden age of French gastronomy, which included Pierre Troisgros, Paul Bocuse, Alain Senderens, Michel Guérard, Jacques Pic, and Roger Vergé. Seasonal products were at the center of his plate.

Charles Patin O'Coohoon

> **"I grew up in the same *terroir* as my vegetables. For a chef, that means something."**
>
> **Alain Chapel**

A DAZZLING CHEF

1960–1967
Studies with Jean Vignard, the Lyonnais chef at Chez Juliette, and with Fernand Point. The first three-star chef at La Pyramide in Vienne.

1967
Takes over his parents' inn, La Mère Charles in Mionnay.

1969
Two stars awarded by the Michelin Guide.

1972
Best Craftsman of France (MOF).

1973
His restaurant receives a third star, making him the youngest three-star chef in France.

1983
Publishes an influential book, *La cuisine c'est beaucoup plus que des recettes*, with Robert Laffont.

1990
Dies suddenly of a heart attack.

FROM MIONNAY TO KOBE

He hoisted his town in the Dombes to the heights of French gastronomy. "No one comes to Mionnay to sunbathe, listen to Karajan, or buy the elixir from Father Souris . . . ," he wrote. He even expanded into Kobe, where he was the first French chef to open a restaurant on the archipelago.

Committed chef
(1937–1990)

ALAIN DUCASSE, THE HEIR

Joining the Mionnay kitchen at age twenty-one, Alain Ducasse was indelibly marked by his mentor. In each of the seven volumes of the culinary encyclopedia *Le Grand livre de Cuisine d'Alain Ducasse*, the dedication reads as follows: "To Alain Chapel, who taught me the pleasure of great cooking."

THE GELÉE

From red mullet on a gelée of wood pigeon, to sea urchin gelée with vieux malt, to strawberry gelée with hibiscus flower, Alain Chapel perfected this technique of extracting and capturing taste, whether savory or sweet. On his menu, Heston Blumenthal, the creative three-star chef at the Fat Duck in London, includes "Homage to Alain Chapel," quail gelée with crawfish cream.

GÂTEAU DE FOIES BLONDS

In his *Dictionnaire amoureux de la gastronomie* (Plon), Christian Millau recounts how moved his partner Henri Gault was when he tasted this liver mousse made from Bresse chickens and immersed in a sauce made from crayfish: "my eyes welled up with tears." The food critic for the *New York Times*, Craig Claiborne, wrote that this mousse "all but defied the laws of gravity, the ultimate triumph for one of the absolute cooking glories of this generation."

BRESSE CHICKEN GÂTEAU DE FOIES BLONDS*

4 very blond livers from Bresse chickens
Beef marrow bones (half the weight of the livers)
3 whole eggs
3 egg yolks
2¾ cups (650 mL) milk
Salt and freshly ground black pepper
1 tablespoon plus 1 teaspoon (20 g) butter
For the sauce
24 very fresh crayfish
4 cups (1 L) court-bouillon
1 truffle
3 tablespoons (50 g) crayfish butter (see page 189)
1 splash of brandy
⅔ cup (150 mL) crème fraîche
¾ cup plus 1 tablespoon (200 mL) hollandaise sauce

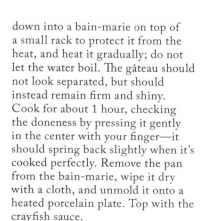

In a large bowl, combine the livers and the beef marrow. Strain the mixture through a fine-mesh sieve. Lightly beat the eggs and egg yolks together, then add them to the bowl. Stir to combine. Stir in the milk. Season with salt and pepper. Coat a 6-inch (15 cm) round mold with the butter, and pour in the liver-marrow mixture to a depth of ⅓ inch (1 cm) from the rim. Place the baking dish down into a bain-marie on top of a small rack to protect it from the heat, and heat it gradually; do not let the water boil. The gâteau should not look separated, but should instead remain firm and shiny. Cook for about 1 hour, checking the doneness by pressing it gently in the center with your finger—it should spring back slightly when it's cooked perfectly. Remove the pan from the bain-marie, wipe it dry with a cloth, and unmold it onto a heated porcelain plate. Top with the crayfish sauce.

The sauce

Cook the crayfish in the court-bouillon. Remove the claws and tails and season them with salt and pepper, then shave truffle over the top. Toss the claws and tails in the warm crayfish butter, then place them in a sauté pan. Sauté them briefly over very high heat, then add the brandy to deglaze the pan. Add the crème fraîche, cook for 1 to 2 minutes, and add the hollandaise sauce off the heat to thicken the sauce.

*Recipe from *La Cuisine c'est beaucoup plus que des recettes*, Robert Laffont

The Gougère

A golden, crisp cloud of pâte à choux with the savory saltiness of a good cheese—there is no better appetizer for your aperitif!

François-Régis Gaudry

IS THE GOUGÈRE...

Flemish? One might easily make a comparison to the *goyère*, a kind of puff pastry covered with cheese (preferably Maroilles cheese), which is a popular specialty in Flanders. But as early as the thirteenth century, "goières" were mentioned in many parts of France.

Franc-Comtoise? The almost exclusive use of Comté cheese in the recipe provides a good argument for its origins to be the Franche-Comté, but this argument does not take into account that the Counts Palatines of Burgundy ruled this region from the tenth to the seventeenth centuries.

Bourguignonne? This is the most likely possibility. The gougère has a strong resemblance to an old specialty called *ramequin*, the name of a mold in which a pâte à choux batter was baked with cheese. Grimod de la Reynière attests its Burgundian origins in his *Almanac des gourmands* in 1804.

Did you know?

In the 1920s, Prosper Montagné described the gougère as a "crown specked with cubes of Gruyère." Even if today's version has taken on the shape of a "little cabbage" (hence the name in French for the dough, *pâte à choux*, "choux" meaning "cabbages"), it is still baked in the shape of a crown in some families. The gougère is the traditional accompaniment for wine tastings, served warm or cooled.

—— BURGUNDY GOUGÈRES

MAKES ABOUT 20 SMALL GOUGÈRES OR 1 LARGE CROWN

¾ cup (175 mL) water
6 tablespoons (90 g) butter, cut into pieces
⅓ teaspoon (2 g) fine salt
1¼ cups (125 g) all-purpose flour
3 medium eggs
4½ ounces (125 g) Comté cheese
Freshly ground pepper
Nutmeg

Preheat the oven to 325°F (160°C). Bring the water, butter, and salt to a boil in a saucepan. Off the heat, add the flour all at once and stir well to combine. Lower the heat, then continue to stir the dough over low heat for several minutes to dry the dough; it should detach from the bottom and sides of the pan. Set aside to cool slightly. Off the heat, add the eggs one by one, vigorously stirring the dough between each addition (for this step, a strong arm is necessary, otherwise use a food processor). Grate half the Comté, and cut the remaining half into small cubes. Add all the cheese to the dough, and season the dough with pepper and nutmeg. Form small mounds using a spoon (or a piping bag) onto a baking sheet lined with parchment paper or onto a nonstick baking mat, and bake for 25 minutes. Do not open the oven door during the baking time! Serve warm with a white Burgundy wine.

BABETTE'S FEAST

Inspired by a short story by Karen Blixen, and an Oscar winner for best foreign film in 1988, this film by director Gabriel Axel is an ode to the exaltation of the senses.

Estelle Lenartowicz

On the stovetop

Babette (played by Stéphane Audran), a former chef in a grand Parisian restaurant, takes refuge on the wild coast of Jutland in Denmark to flee the repression of the Commune de Paris. Humbly integrated into the life of the small community, and employed as a servant in the service of two bigoted sisters, Babette wins the lottery. Rather than return to France, she has the idea of spending her fortune by creating a sumptuous meal for the inhabitants of the village.

Twelve guests

—like the twelve apostles—who, dumbfounded, attend the evening's spectacle offering the finest in French gastronomy. Each plate of food provides the taste of temptation for the austere and devout Lutherans who attend, and who are more accustomed to soups, potatoes, and rustic breads for their meals. Filmed as a mystical experience where food miraculously transfigures the guests' relationships with God, the feast allows communion, self-giving, and thanksgiving through the pleasures of the table.

The menu
On the plate

Giant turtle soup—the turtle is seen being delivered alive on a boat
Blinis Demidoff, with cream and caviar
Stuffed quails in a pastry nest, with foie gras and truffle sauce
Endive salad with walnuts
Cheeses
Baba au rhum and candied fruits
Fresh fruits (grapes, figs, pineapple)

In the glass

Sherry Amontillado—with the soup
Veuve Clicquot 1860—with the blinis
Clos de Vougeot 1845—with the quail and cheeses
Fine Champagne
Water—with the fruits
Coffee—with the baba au rhum

"This woman is capable of transforming any meal served at the Café Anglais into a sort of love affair, an ethereal and romantic love relationship where one can no longer distinguish between physical or spiritual appetites."

"Babette's Feast,"
Karen Blixen (1958)

skip to ....
French Movie Chefs, p. 387

PIONEERS IN WINEMAKING

Read on to learn about 5 domaines where wine growers have forged a path to the future of French wine.

Sylvie Augereau*

DOMAINE MARCEL LAPIERRE
Beaujolais

Marcel Lapierre was among the first to embrace natural winemaking and reckon with the consequences. He acknowledged that poorly made "natural" wines had earned shaky reputations. The use of sulfites has long been recognized in winemaking, and corrective oenology came galloping to the rescue. "It was successful, or if not, you tossed it out. Peasants didn't just put their lives on hold for wine." So he experimented, dissected, and digested everything. Then he passed on this accumulated wisdom to anyone who came to hear it, including his children. Camille and Mathieu already had the keys to the kingdom before Marcel's death in 2010, and the strong arm of Marie (their energetic mother, who also manages Château Cambon) is there to provide reassurance. We've been enjoying their Beaujolais for quite some time.

The wine: Raisin Gaulois is a magic potion imbibed by the locals as a remedy against all ills. This is a wine that really hits the spot! "Beaujolais should go straight into your system, but never stay there," proclaims the Lapierre motto.
→ Camille and Mathieu Lapierre Domaine Marcel Lapierre, rue du Pré Jourdan, Villié-Morgon (Rhône)

DOMAINE PLAGEOLES
Southwest

Plageoles is a name that's synonymous with the wine reawakening in southwestern France. Grandfather Marcel was the first member of the family to bottle the unassuming wine of Gaillac, which actually boasts a proud 2,000-year history. Then his son Robert revived neglected vines that now make the appellation a living museum with a compelling story. Myriam and Bernard are local advocates, often raising their voices when confronting regulatory authorities that have sometimes refused to allow the mention of Gaillac on their labels. Their sons, Romain and Florent, have a tendency to raise their voices even louder. The reach of the Plageole household encompasses far more than simple blood ties. The extended family embraces their employee Jérôme Galaup, their neighbor Marine Leys, and more distant relations everywhere throughout this rugby-obsessed region of France.

The wine: naturally sparkling wines are not a passing fad for the Plageoles. Their "Mauzac Nature" is an institution. The Mauzac grape, with notes of green apple, is ideally suited for this wine that stimulates appetite and satisfies thirst.
→ Myriam and Bernard Plageoles Les Très Cantous, Cahuzac-sur-Verre (Tarn), vins-plageoles.com

DOMAINE GRAMENON
Rhône

Gramenon family wines have many missions in life. Michèle Aubéry and her late husband were pioneers in natural wines, but they did not absolutely exclude the use of sulfites. "It's a luxury to do without. And it's a pleasure for the winemaker. You know that you're cutting out a dimension of the wine, that you're subtracting from its depth with additives." She doesn't shrink from complicated vintages, and she has serene confidence in herself and in her wine. Michèle loses herself in the details of biodynamic viticulture, as well as poetry.

"Wine embraces all the elements, earth and sky. We capture the sun's energy in the barrel. When you uncork a bottle, you open a window onto the year just past."
Wine has the power to convey memory, and Gramenon wines are unforgettable.

The wine: Poignée de raisin ("Handful of Grapes"). Made from young Grenache and Cinsault grapes, this wine expresses the essence of the Gramenon style, redolent of pure fruit and freshly blooming flowers.
→ Michèle Aubéry-Laurent and Maxime Gramenon Montbrizon-sur-Lez (Drôme), domaine.gramenon@club-internet.fr

CLOS DE TUE-BOEUF
Loire

Thierry and Jean-Marie Puzelat established a large family (naturally) in the department of Loir-et-Cher. They've always said that nobody's the worse for getting a little mud on their boots. They spend autumn digging the vineyard's furrows, turning over 39.5 acres (16 hectares) of soil. People from the neighborhood (and elsewhere) dined with the Puzelats and started singing their praises. They now boast a fan club that occasionally tosses them into the Indre, and they've embarked on an insanely busy life as singers. Even the famous performer Alain Souchon has come to check in on them and make sure they're still looking after their vines.

The wine: La Caillère 2015. Yes indeed! Pinot Noir grapes have been growing in Touraine since time immemorial. And when the wine is pampered like this, it rivals some very grand Burgundian labels. It's also a lot less expensive.
→ Thierry and Jean-Marie Puzelat Clos du Tue-Boeuf, 6, route de Seur, Les Montils (Loir-et-Cher), puzelat.com

CHAMPAGNE JACQUES SELOSSE
Champagne

Unlike some Champagnes that indulge simple consumer tastes, Anselme Selosse's Champagne challenges them aggressively. He raises issues even for those sampling his wine for the first time. He's a pioneer, growing vines in wooded areas, who is committed to biodynamic viticulture. Every path of inquiry leads to another, from analyzing indigenous yeasts to studying wine residues.

The wine: Substance is a wine that takes its time. Jacques adds a very old wine to a recent year's vintage to "civilize" it. And it teaches us a lesson, too, with distinctive notes of salinity and fresh sap that make us sit up and take notice.
→ Champagne Jacques Selosse 5, rue de Cramant, Avize (Marne), selosse-lesavises.com

*Journalist, taster, and grand priestess of the Dive Bouteille (the largest gathering of natural wines aficionados, held every February in Saumur), she also has vineyards located between Saumur and Angers. In collaboration with Antoine Gerbelle, she is the author of Soif d'aujourd'hui, la compil des vins au naturel, *Tana éditions, 2016.*

skip to ....
Natural Wine, p. 86

Give Me a Quiche!

No other savory dish composed of everyday ingredients has won over the hearts of so many as the quiche, a flaky crust with a simple egg-and-cream filling. It's always good to be familiar with all its variations, from the straightforward authentic Lorraine to the most whimsical.

Marie-Amal Bizalion

ONCE UPON A TIME . . .

. . . prior to the eighteenth century, a simple *migaine* (batter) made of eggs, cream, and butter would be laid upon a thin layer of bread dough left over from a week's bread baking and slid into the oven, with the goal of taking ordinary ingredients and attempting to make them, well, better. During the eighteenth century, this migaine was made into thicker fillings, and it found its refuge atop a flaky butter crust rather than leftover bread. Bacon was invited into the dish in the nineteenth century.

The quiche is, indeed, from Lorraine. If there is any doubt, just examine the words *kéich* ("cakes") and *kich* ("cuisine") from the Lorraine Franconian dialect to see that the term *quiche* undoubtedly comes from the region of Lorraine.

AND THANKS TO THE PRUSSIANS!

Without them, the quiche might have remained in the deep recesses of the region. In 1870, war broke out between France and Prussia. The French were defeated in Sedan, and consequently Alsace and Moselle were annexed. Many inhabitants from Lorraine fled the occupation and landed in Lyon, Paris, and other regions, bringing with them, as part of their belongings, this modest dish and its traditions, which have now spread across the globe and made quiche a much-beloved dish.

— THE "AUTHENTIC" QUICHE LORRAINE! —

A tested and retested recipe!
This recipe is the right compromise for a quiche, as it borrows the approaches of two great chefs from Lorraine: Cyril Leclerc and Frédéric Anton. Chef Cyril uses 8 eggs, and chef Frédéric uses 4 eggs and half the amount of cream, but with a hint of nutmeg.

The flaky pastry dough

In a bowl, combine 2½ cups (250 g) of all-purpose flour, 2 pinches of salt, and 10½ tablespoons (125 g) of diced softened butter. Mash the ingredients together using your fingers to obtain a cornmeal-like texture, then add 2 to 3 tablespoons (15 to 30 mL) of water to bring the ingredients together to form a dough. Quickly form the dough into a ball. Butter a tart or pie pan with sides high enough to accommodate all the dough, then press the dough by hand into the pan. Using the palm of your hand, press the dough along the bottom and up the edges of the pan, ensuring equal thickness all around.

The bacon

Dice 9 ounces (250 g) of bacon. Blanch it for a few minutes, drain it, and brown it in a skillet. Distribute the bacon bits over the bottom of the pan on top of the dough.

The egg mixture

Beat 3 whole (150 g) eggs with 3 large (54 g) yolks, 1⅔ cups (400 mL) cream, just over ¾ cup (200 mL) thickened, raw cream (or use crème fraiche), some pepper, and a little bit of salt, and pour this mixture into the pan. Bake at 350°F (180°C) for at least 30 minutes, or until the quiche turns a nice golden brown on top. Place it on a cooling rack to cool for at least 30 minutes. This will allow it to slightly firm up, ensuring that the slices will hold together better and be more presentable when placed on the plate. A green salad is the essential accompaniment with the quiche.

★

ITS NEIGHBORING VARIATIONS

The Vosgienne (from Vosges) quiche is made with cheese, preferably an Emmental grand cru from the Vosges. The Alsatian quiche is made with or without bacon, but always with onions cooked in butter.

★

AND IF YOU DARE . . .

With tuna
Super quick: a good can of tuna, well drained, with a little curry and parsley.

With red bell peppers
Bell peppers baked and cooled in their skins, peeled (the peel will come off easily after the pepper has been baked), and combined with eggs, cream, and cumin for a beautiful bright orange color.

With smoked salmon
Coarsely chopped, with fresh dill.

With zucchini
This version takes a little longer because you have to allow the sliced zucchini rounds to drain first, then sauté them in olive oil. Also add just a touch of garlic, a few crushed dried mint leaves, and a little brocciu cheese in small pieces. This one is even better served cold.

With green asparagus
The stalks of the asparagus are cooked al dente, drained, then distributed over the bottom of the pan on top of the dough before adding the filling; the asparagus tips are sautéed in butter, and generously coated with freshly grated Parmesan before being added to the filling.

With Maroilles cheese and leeks
Leeks diced, then browned in the fat used to fry the bacon . . . this is a very flavorful combination of quiche and *flamiche*, a tart common in the north of France.

With coconut cream (that's still cream, right?)
This version uses fewer eggs, some medium shrimp (tails removed), fresh cilantro, 1 kaffir lime leaf for a citrusy touch, grated fresh ginger, and a little hot pepper.

skip to
Pissaladière and Company, p. 192

Does the quiche lorraine contain . . .

Cheese? No, that would be a crime. **Nutmeg?** Not really, but a pinch won't hurt. **Store-bought bacon bits?** Never. Use the best fresh plain or smoked bacon, preferably fresh country bacon—and from Lorraine only, if you want to be truly authentic. **Milk?** It causes lumps. In a pinch, use a little whole milk, but using all cream is much better. **Any type of cream?** No, preferably raw and without lactic bacteria. **Puff pastry for the crust?** What a mistake, the puff pastry gets soggy. Only use a pâte brisée (a flaky tart dough). **Store-bought dough?** That would be sacrilege! A from-scratch dough can be made in 5 minutes, and it's so much better. And the crust is never prebaked. Instead, bake the entire quiche all at once.

THE LANGUAGE OF MEALTIME

We relish our meals—in French, *se repaître* (to delight in) and *repas* (meal) share the same root. It wouldn't be until the sixteenth century and its Rabelaisian orgies that *repas* took on the meaning of "a succession of dishes and drink that one has at certain times." In other words, first course, second course, and dessert . . .

Aurore Vincenti

Déjeuner

Déjeuner, like **breakfast** in English, literally means **"break the fast."** Originally, it was the **first meal of the morning.** Today, the French call breakfast *petit-déjeuner*, but in the nineteenth century, they called it **déjeuner à la tasse** (with a cup) since it consisted of a cup of milk, tea, coffee, or hot chocolate with a slice of toasted bread known as **rôtie** (roasted). In the sixteenth century, the French broke fast around 10 a.m.; in the seventeenth century, between 11 a.m. and noon; then, in the nineteenth century, the word came to designate the **midday** meal. Until then, that meal had been called *diner* (dinner) but, starting in about 1850, people spoke of a *second déjeuner* or a **déjeuner à la fourchette** (with a fork). After 1950, it was pushed back to 1 p.m. in cities.

Dîner

Dîner (dinner) is the meal whose **hour has most changed**: it went from **"repas de midi"** (noontime meal, 1532) to the nighttime one! At the end of the eighteenth century, dinner was at 4 p.m. at the latest, then it was around 5 or 6 p.m. in the nineteenth century. Nevertheless, in Belgium, Quebec, and French-speaking Switzerland, people have dinner **in the middle of the day**, and this term is still used in certain French regions.

Souper

The French *souper* (supper), which originally was the **evening meal** of soup, has almost disappeared in cities where it is, at best, a **light meal** eaten late at night—after the theater in wealthy circles. In certain regions, this use of the word persists.

Eating between meals

In wealthy circles, because meals last for hours, intentionally **hybrid** collations have emerged.

For example, **brunch**, a term the French have borrowed from English since the 1970s, has historically been a **late-morning meal**. It's a portmanteau combining **breakfast** and **lunch**. It's too late for breakfast, so let's start with lunch but still enjoy coffee and croissants. Anything is game: savory and sweet together; and coffee competes with wine or Champagne!

The French term **goûter soupatoire** (literally "supper snack," meaning high tea) emerged in the nineteenth century. The word was quickly replaced by **goûter dînatoire** (dinner snack) and *déjeuner dînatoire* (dinner lunch). Today, in France, one might also organize an **apéritif dînatoire** (cocktail dinner). The aperitif (cocktail and appetizer) is meant to **"open"** the appetite, from the Latin **aperire**. Rarely is it a true, seated meal; it's more of a **gathering** around a coffee table loaded with liquor, charcuterie, savory loaves, and carrots for various dips. When the French use the term **thé dînatoire** (dinner tea), they start with a hot beverage. But that won't stop anyone from segueing into a little kir . . .

Note: the **slunch (supper-lunch)** and the **dunch (dinner-lunch)** have tried to take root, but the French seem to prefer their *apérodinatoire* (dinner cocktail) à la française.

Skip to: B Is for Bernard Pivot, p. 245

Feel like a snack

As the name indicates, the French *en-cas* (in case) is a **snack** that helps us get back up on our feet, in case we need it, in case anything unexpected happens, in case we've got the munchies . . . A *collation* is a light meal, but originally it wasn't a matter of eating. From the Latin **collatum**, "to exchange words, to have a conversation with," the word referred to a **moment of exchange** and reading between monks. In the thirteenth century, such exchanges took place during the **evening mealtime** and so the word *collation* came to mean a light meal at night. During the Classic period, the court preferred *collation*, as the French word **goûter** (literally, "tasting," meaning afternoon snack) was considered too **common and bourgeois**. After 1789, *goûter* ultimately replaced it. As early as the eighteenth century, it mostly was something for children . . . Sometimes the French say **"le quatre-heures"** (the four o'clock). Based on the English model of five o'clock tea, some gather at teatime to munch on a few small cookies.

★

COOK UP A LITTLE SOMETHING

The French word *frichti* is said to have been introduced in **Alsace** in the nineteenth century and to have come from the German **frühstück**, "breakfast." Some linguists argue, however, that the word stems instead from the Gallo-Roman **frixicare** (to prepare fricassee). The *frichti* was initially a feast, but today the word is used more to designate **a little meal made at home**, with love.

★

A Tour de France of Citrus

They flavor, they enhance, and they season any recipe. They can be found growing in
sun in the south of France, in the heat of the West Indies, and on France's islands.
Here is a short tour of the citrus fruits cultivated throughout France and its lands.

Valentine Oudard

Michel and Bénédicte Bachès: citrus growers, orchard owners, researchers, and adventurers. Michel and Bénédicte
Bachès have become passionate about citrus and are now traveling the world looking for extraordinary varieties.
Their greenhouses are home to over eight hundred species, some originating in France!

1 Bigarade of Nice
Tree: *Citrus aurantium*
Origin: also called bitter orange, originating in China, introduced in the ninth century in North Africa and then in Italy.
Description: orange color, rough rind like that of an orange. Acidic and bitter flesh.
Season: December to January
Aromatic profile: used for essential oils, and its flower as flavoring.
Use: the flesh, which is bitter, is enjoyed cooked in jam.

2 Clementine of Corsica
Tree: *Citrus reticulata corsica*
Origin: a hybridization of a tangerine and an orange, called clementine in honor of friar Clément, who discovered the fruit near Oran.
Description: leafy, with a green bottom. Orange-red rind that is smooth and shiny. The tart flesh is seedless.
Season: November to February
Aromatic profile: tart, slightly sweet.
Use: enjoyed fresh or as a juice.

3 Mandarin of Corsica
Tree: *Citrus deliciosa*
Origin: originally from China (mandarins derive their name from the Mandarins, to whom they were offered as a gift), the mandarin tree arrived in Corsica around 1850.
Description: thin rind and an orange color, with many seeds.
Season: December to January
Aromatic profile: sweet and mild flesh, less acidic than the clementine.
Use: enjoy fresh, or in jam!

4 Tahitian lime
Tree: *Citrus latifolia*
Origin: tropical Asia.
Description: smooth and thin rind, rich in aromatic essences. When ripe, it keeps its green color but loses its shine.
Season: October to November
Aromatic profile: juice and rind are scented.
Use: the juice is used in the preparation of Tahitian-style raw fish.

5 Lemon from Menton
Tree: *Citrus limon*
Origin: located in the region since the fifteenth century.
Description: light yellow, slightly green when young, but turns a bright yellow when ripe. Very juicy, thick and rough rind.
Season: December to March
Aromatic profile: acidic and sweet. Can be eaten like an apple!
Use: the lemon tart from Menton!

6 Bergamot from Nancy
It's not the citrus fruit that is celebrated in Nancy, but the candy made with it! This is the only candy in France to have obtained a Protected Geographical Indication (PGI). The amber-colored candy is made from a sugar syrup with natural essence of bergamot, which must originate from Calabria to meet the PGI qualifications.

7 Combava (Kaffir lime)
Tree: *Citrus hystrix*, the Réunion lime or Mauritius Papeda
Origin: Southeast Asia
Description: a small lime with a lumpy and thick rind.
Season: October to February
Aromatic profile: close to lemongrass.
Use: its zest works very well with fish and shellfish. In Réunion, its leaves are used to flavor rougail.

8 Pink Pomelo
Tree: *Citrus paradisi*
Origin: West Indies
Description: smaller than a grapefruit, with a thick rind, and a smooth yellow or pinkish zest. Slightly bitter, acidic flesh.
Season: March to June
Aromatic profile: soft flesh with little bitterness.
Use: consumed plain. Excellent with avocado shrimp.

9 Tangor of Réunion
Tree: *Citrus reticulata*; 'Ortanique' tangor
Origin: discovered in Jamaica, introduced to Réunion in the 1970s.
Description: a hybrid of a tangerine and an orange. Orange-red rind, thin and rough.
Season: June to September
Aromatic profile: juicy and sweet flesh with a hint of acidity.
Use: natural or as juice.

10 Pouncem or citron (cédrat) Poncire* from Collioure
Tree: *Citrus medica*
Origin: a rare citrus fruit resulting from a hybridization between a grapefruit and a citron, present in Catalonia for three hundred years.
Description: kind of a large pomelo, an orange-yellow color when ripe. Juicy.
Season: November to January
Aromatic profile: fairly acidic juice and pulp.
Use: very present in Catalan cuisine.

*Poncire de Collioure is the name granted to the fruit by Michel and Bénédicte Bachès. It has become the common name for this citrus fruit.

11 Pomelo or shaddock or Guyanese chadek
Tree: *Citrus grandis* or *Citrus maxima*; Cayenne grapefruit
Origin: introduced to French Guyana in the seventeenth century by Captain Shaddock, from whom it gets its name.
Description: a cousin of the grapefruit, but with a thick green-yellow rind and less-juicy flesh.
Season: December to May
Aromatic profile: pungent taste and slight bitterness.
Use: consumed candied with sugar, cinnamon, and vanilla.

12 Citron (cédrat) of Corsica
Tree: *Citrus medica*
Origin: one of the first citrus to have conquered the Corsican soil.
Description: a kind of large lemon with an elongated shape and a thick, hard, and aromatic rind.
Season: November to December
Aromatic profile: the smell is reminiscent of cedar . . . hence its name in French! The juice has less flavor and acidity than lemon juice.
Use: candied, or raw cut into slices and drizzled with olive oil, or used to make cédratine, a local liqueur!

skip to
Tarte au Citron (Citrus Tart), p. 98

The Baguette, aka "La Belle Parisienne"

With a sleek silhouette, streamlined style, and becomingly tanned exterior, the baguette has plenty to boast about.
No surprise that it's a Parisian icon!

Marie-Laure Fréchet

BIRTH

→ Her age is a well-kept secret—it's impossible to determine the precise date of birth, but she's apparently a centenarian. The first mention of the word *baguette* to describe a loaf of bread was in 1920.

→ Aesthetic considerations were not a factor in her invention; there were two very pragmatic reasons for her appearance. In the late nineteenth century, ordinary loaves weighing 4½ pounds (2 kg) and measuring 27½ inches (70 cm) were taxed. By changing the size of the loaf, the tax was avoided. Also, in March 1919, a new law prohibited "the employment of workers making bread and pastries between ten o'clock at night and four o'clock in the morning." Bakers were compelled to create forms that took less time to prepare and were ready to sell to customers first thing in the morning. Birth of the baguette! Until the 1950s, the baguette was an aspirational loaf of bread—truly a luxury. But today, thirty million baguettes are sold every day in France—that's six billion a year.

MEASUREMENTS

Neither the form nor the weight of a standard baguette is regulated. The *Dictionnaire de l'Académie française* refers to a "long thin loaf weighing 9 ounces (250 g)." The number of *grignes* (the knife slashes cut into the bread to allow carbon dioxide to escape during the baking process) is traditionally set at five. Only Label Rouge (Red Label) flour is officially recognized in the ingredients specified in 2002: no. 32.89 Label Rouge flour, drinking water, salt, up to 1.5 percent yeast, five slashes, length 24 to 25½ inches (60 to 65 cm), width 2 to 2¼ inches (5 to 6 cm), and weight around 9 to 10½ ounces (250 to 300 g).

CLOSE COUSINS

The *flûte*: thicker and heavier (14 oz/400 g).
The *ficelle*: thinner and lighter (4½ oz/125 g).

skip to ....
A *Tour de France* of Breads, p. 158

The beloved jambon-beurre: 12 inches (30 cm) of bliss

The *jambon-beurre* is the most widely consumed type of sandwich in France: it represents 51 percent of total sales, or 1.2 billion units in 2016. It's also known affectionately as *le Parisien*. The recipe is no secret: a good baguette, real butter, and excellent ham. But where did it originate?

→ Louis XIV introduced what some historians consider to be the predecessor of the jambon-beurre: a little round brioche roll filled with chicken that was taken along for refreshment during strenuous hunting parties.

→ In the late nineteenth century, a *casser la croûte* ("breaking bread") referred to a meager meal based on bread that was carried by laborers and peasants working in the fields. Miners used the term *briquet* for a similar snack.

→ The jambon-beurre apparently appeared at about the same time and was popularized by the celebrated Strong Men of Les Halles, the laborers who carried the heavy loads in the wholesale market in the heart of Paris. But it wasn't until the 1950s that the baguette, neater and easier to hold, was put to use.

"BOY, BICYCLE & BAGUETTE"
Iconic French image immortalized by an American photographer, Elliott Erwitt, in 1955.

BEAUTY PAGEANTS

CONCOURS NATIONAL DE LA MEILLEUR BAGUETTE DE TRADITION FRANÇAISE

Mei Narusawa of Japan was the first woman to win this prize in the fourth annual baguette-making competition. She had trained in the Boulangerie Durrenberger in Mertzwiller (Bas-Rhin). Candidates are judged on the baguette's visual qualities, baking technique, taste, aroma, and texture of its crumb. The competition is sponsored by the Confédération Nationale de la Boulangerie et Boulangerie-pâtisserie Française.

GRAND PRIX DE LA BAGUETTE DE LA VILLE DE PARIS

This annual competition, inaugurated in 1994, honors ten winners, who are listed in order of merit and selected from the capital's best artisanal bakers. The first-prize winner receives a medal and a 4,000 euro award, and is named supplier to the Élysée Palace for a year. The 2017 winner was Sami Bouattour of the Boulangerie Brun, located in Paris 13th.

Aromatic Plants

French cuisine of the Middle Ages was smothered with spices. The food of the Grand Siècle (seventeenth century) had the taste of regional spices and fresh herbs. Here is a snapshot of just a few of those.

François-Régis Gaudry

LAMIACEAE

Common thyme (*Thymus vulgaris*)

With its cousins Corsican thyme (*Thymas herba-barona*) and lemon thyme (*T. × citriodorus*), the herb "*farigoule*" (from its Occitan name *farigola*) accompanies lamb and vegetable stews (ratatouille, artichokes with barigoule, etc.).

Wild thyme (*Thymus serpyllum*)

With a more discreet flavor than common thyme, and with slightly lemony flavors, wild thyme is used instead of common thyme in the oldest Provençal reference books.

Savory (*Satureja*, more than 150 species)

It is the herb *pebre d'ai* or *pebre d'ase* (savory) that Manon (in the film *Manon of the Spring*) picks at Pagnol. Its pungent and peppery strength goes well with rabbit and game.

Mint (*Mentha*)

Whether spearmint (*Mentha spicata*) or peppermint (*M. × piperita*), mint is typically reserved for confectionery uses, except in recipes from southern France where it can be found in Pauoise sauce, or an omelet with brocciu and mint, etc.

Sage (*Salvia*)

A family with many species whose pungent and slightly camphor taste accompanies pork throughout Provence and Languedoc.

Rosemary (*Rosmarinus*)

Its powerful resinous branches are used in stews, civets, sauces, and with grilled meats.

Oregano (*Origanum vulgare*)

Not as widely used in France as it is in Greece, Italy, or Portugal, oregano is used especially for flavoring tomato sauces.

Marjoram (*Organum majorana*)

A close cousin of oregano, but its more delicate taste is closer to thyme. It is sometimes incorrect to refer to wild marjoram as another Lamiaceae, *Calament nepeta* (lesser calament), or *a nepita* in the Corsican language.

Basil (*Ocimum basilicum*)

Its penetrating aromas of menthol and its anise accents have given birth to French pistou (a mixture of basil, garlic, and olive oil), and it accompanies many Provençal specialties.

APIACEAE

Coriander/Cilantro (*Coriandrum sativum*)

The fresh leaves have a taste of "crushed stink bug" for some, and its seeds are a classic spice.

Parsley (*Petroselinum crispum*)

The curly variety is used for garnishing dishes, such as tête de veau, and the flat-leaf variety is used for its aromatic strength. It was already being cultivated at the time of Charlemagne.

Chervil (*Anthriscus cerefolium*)

Slender leaves with a slightly aniseed taste.

ASTERACEAE

Tarragon (*Artemisia dracunculus*)

Powerful, slightly bitter, with a taste of aniseed. The taste of tarragon is very French (think béarnaise sauce). French tarragon is more aromatic than Russian tarragon.

AMARYLLIDACEAE (formerly Liliaceae or Alliaceae)

Chives (*Allium schoenoprasum*)

Long, hollow stems with a subtle taste of onion and leek. When finely chopped, it is sprinkled, raw, on top of many dishes.

LAURACEAE

Bay leaf (*Laurus nobilis*)

Originally from the Mediterranean Basin, bay leaf is used fresh or dried to flavor court-bouillons, matelots (a type of stew), ragouts, and tomato sauces.

Recipe Ideas

Rabbit with wild thyme

Place a 3⅓-pound (1.5 kg) rabbit, cut into pieces, in a casserole dish and drizzle it generously with olive oil. Add 3 cloves of crushed garlic, 4 minced onions, 1 bouquet of wild thyme, 4 carrots (sliced), and ¼ cup (60 mL) of dry white wine. Season with salt and simmer, covered, over low heat for 2 hours 30 minutes.

A sage wine

Place about 2⅛ ounces (60 g) of sage leaves in a bottle of red wine from the south of France, or from Corsica. Let macerate for 10 days, then strain. Pour into a glass, and stir in some confectioners' sugar to taste. This makes a tonic to enjoy chilled in the summer.

A persillade

Chop 3 peeled garlic cloves together with 1 bunch of parsley. Use it as a topping on string beans cooked in butter, or in butter with escargots.

A bouquet garni

A bouquet garni has been indispensable in French cuisine since the seventeenth century. This bundle of various herbs flavors many broths and sauce dishes. Tie together a small bundle of thyme, parsley sprigs, bay leaf, and leek greens. You can also add rosemary, savory, a celery stalk, tarragon, or fennel.

Home-Crafted Liqueurs

"Have some, it'll help the digestion!" "Well, just a splash, please."
It's rude to refuse. You venture a sip without knowing quite what to expect.
Blandine Boyer

WHAT ARE THEY?

They might be intensely sweet, delicately flavored, or powerfully bitter. There are countless recipes, but they're all based on the same principle: maceration in wine without fermentation, with the addition of sugar and/or alcohol, spices, and flavorings.

EXPLORING THE TOPIC

Ancestral recipes featuring vipers drowned in bottles of eau-de-vie or brownish liquid steeped in rusty nails are generally out of favor these days. We'll limit our investigations to the vegetal world, of which no corner has been left unexplored:
Leaves and flowers of trees: ash, walnut, larch cones in flower . . .
Aromatic plants: thyme, sage, rosemary . . .
The entire orchard: leaves and nuts, not to mention **red fruits**, peaches, plums, cherries, pears, blackcurrants . . .
Wild flowers: hawthorn, elderberries . . .
Things that are frankly inedible: blackthorn berries, green nuts . . .
Exotic products: citrus, spices, coffee . . .
Bitter flavors in abundance: dandelions, artichoke, wormwood, gentian . . . and even **black magic plants** (tansy), or **sulfurous** ones (absinthe) . . .

SUPERSTITION AND NOSTALGIA

These potions have had one foot in the realm of folk medicine and magic since ancient times. The process of gathering, drying, grinding, stirring, filtering, and decanting evokes the healers and witches of long ago. Plants are still harvested on Saint John's Eve. However, modern makers no longer follow the magical traditions of left hand, bare feet, and walking widdershins. (Not so long ago, these observances were practiced in a syncretic spirit that melded Christianity, animism, and superstition.)

In these more prosaic times, some makers endeavor to replicate the established favorites such as pastis, Cointreau, or Bailey's, with varying degrees of success.

Social networks are replete with shared recipes and photos of labels inscribed in cursive script: "Mom's Nut Wine," for example. There are laments that it's impossible to find an eau-de-vie worthy of the name with the current scarcity of home distilleries. In France, people embark on day trips, browsing garage sales for discarded demijohn jugs. Nostalgia exercises a powerful hold on the imagination.

THE RECIPES

In many of these recipes, the figures 1 and 4 repeat in a strangely insistent fashion. Is it just a useful mnemonic device? Who can say? That's certainly the case with these two great classics: orange wine and walnut wine.

VIN D'ORANGE
[Fortified Orange Wine]

VIN DE NOIX
[Walnut Wine]

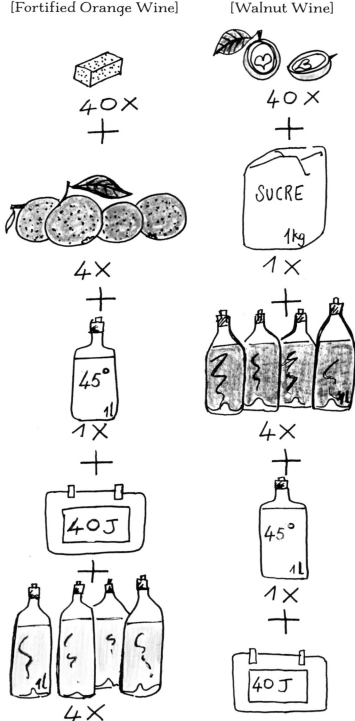

skip to ....
Forgotten French Aperitifs, p. 348

La Cartagène

Cartagène (some spell it Carthagène) of Languedoc is more precisely a *vin de liqueur* or *mistelle*, like Pineau des Charentes. You don't have to be a winemaker for this recipe—it can easily be prepared at home as long as you can get your hands on some fresh grapes.

Here's a family recipe from the area near the border between the departments of Gard and Lozère.

"You can blend various varieties, as well as mix white and red wine grapes. Pick them as ripe as possible, at the end of the harvest. Make sure to remove the seeds from the grapes by hand before pressing them to prevent bitterness. The sugar level of the must (juice) is measured with a specialized instrument known as a mustimeter; you add the amount of eau-de-vie necessary to get an alcohol level between 16 (to prevent fermentation) and 20 proof according to your taste. Just remember—never add sugar!

"Pour into demijohns and shake them daily for 20 days. Then let them rest for 2 to 5 years before straining through a paper filter and bottling."

If you drink it young, it is pinkish and the flavor of the grapes is quite pronounced. As it ages (which it can easily do for several decades), it takes on an amber hue and develops a nutty flavor. You needn't limit yourself to serving it as an aperitif; around Nîmes, it's offered with foie gras. Some people like it as a marinade for pork breast with its rind, roasted at a low temperature over coals. Barbecue sauce meets its match.

Sandwich:
The Art of Breaking Bread

Turning a piece of bread into an entire meal, that's the challenge of the sandwich.
The French love it: they eat more than two billion every year!

Marie-Laure Fréchet

THE LEGEND

The origin of the sandwich lies with from the Englishman John Montagu, Earl of Sandwich (a town in England near Dover). In the 1760s, this compulsive gambler is said to have ordered a servant to bring him bread with cold meat so that he didn't have to fold his hand.

HISTORY

→ By the Middle Ages, noblemen were using bread as a support for meat: that became the slice. Sometimes you would share it with the person sitting next to you, hence the origin of the French word *copain* (buddy, from *co-pain*, co-bread).
→ The use of the word *sandwich* in French is recent. In Balzac, they shared an *en-cas* (in case) at bourgeois tables. On the street, at the end of the nineteenth century, the word *casse-croûte* (literally "break bread") was more popular for designating a brief meal based on bread and eaten by workers and peasants. For a long time associated with the world of work, the casse-croûte has always been paid in certain French professions, as stipulated by labor laws. More recently, it has become a staple of picnics and road trips.

SANDWICH VS THE FRENCH TARTINE

The *tartine* is different from the sandwich in that only one slice of bread is garnished; in English it's called an open sandwich. In France, a sweet version is consumed at breakfast or as a snack; a savory version is common as an hors d'oeuvre (canapé). With a sandwich, the garnish is placed between two slices of bread.

JAMBON-BEURRE

The emblem of the French casse-croûte, the *jambon-beurre* (ham with butter sandwich) is said to have been made popular by the Fort des Halles haulers in Paris. Nevertheless, it wasn't until the 1950s that the baguette, which was easier to carry, was used.

THE PAN-BAGNAT: THE TASTE OF THE SOUTH OF FRANCE

Literally "bathed bread" (or wet) in Occitan, the *pan-bagnat* is a specialty of Nice. Originally it was a poor man's meal: stale bread was softened with water or with tomato juice. It's garnished with the ingredients of a *salade niçoise*, including a hard-boiled egg, the only cooked ingredient accepted by La Commune Libre du Pan-Bagnat, an association that protects the appellation.

THE PAN-BAGNAT
The official recipe of La Commune Libre du Pan-Bagnat

PREPARATION TIME: 10 MINUTES

Bread
Garlic
Olive oil
Vinegar
Salt and freshly ground black pepper
Tomatoes, quartered
Radishes and/or spring onions
Green bell pepper
String beans and/or artichoke hearts
Black olives
Tuna or anchovy
Hard-boiled egg
Basil

Slice a rounded bun in half horizontally. Scrape out some of the crumb, then rub the interior with a clove of garlic. Dab the bread generously with olive oil, then with a dash of vinegar, and season it with salt and pepper. Slice all the vegetables into rounds (except the tomatoes), then pile them on the bread with the tuna or anchovy fillets, slices of the hard-boiled egg, and some basil. Close the bread, and set it aside for at least 1 hour in the fridge before enjoying.

3
other French sandwiches

The *bokit*

This Guadeloupian sandwich is bread fried in a saucepan with oil. Also called *pain chaudière* (heater bread), it's garnished with *chiquetaille de morue* (pickled codfish), ham, cheese, crudités, tuna . . . Originally, its name came from a deformation of "johnny cake" (or journey cake), a fried Antillean specialty.

The *briquet*

In coal mines, workers had the right to take a break to have their casse-croûte, which consisted of two slices of bread with cheese or charcuterie. The name *briquet* is thought to come from its resemblance to a brick, or from the English word "break." When they came up at night, miners would give any leftovers to their children. This was known as the *pain d'alouette* (lark's bread).

The *pain surprise*

A French buffet classic, *pain surprise* (surprise bread) is an assortment of mini-sandwiches (ham, liver pâté, salmon etc.). It's probably a prepared version of a Swedish homemade specialty, the *smörgåstårta*, literally "bread cake," which consists of layers of white bread with various toppings and is traditionally served at family celebrations.

skip to ....
Let's Talk Salad!, p. 106;
The Croque-Monsieur, p. 17

Tell Me What You Eat, and I'll Tell You How You Vote

The famous food writer Curnonsky penned a column titled "The Parties and Their Gastronomy," published in September 1955 in the magazine *Cuisine et vins de France*. It's an entertaining socio-gastro-politico analysis that reveals how menu selections may indicate choices in the Freench voting booth.

 If you give the topic of gastronomy five minutes' thought, it is easy to discern that there is clearly a far right, a right, a center, a left, and an extreme left.

FAR RIGHT

True believers in "haute cuisine" that's sophisticated, rarified, and rather complicated. **It requires a great chef and top-quality ingredients—** what might be called diplomatic cuisine. You'd find it served in embassies, at formal banquets, and in palaces. The pretentious cooking of luxury hotels is often a mere parody of the real thing.

RIGHT

Supporters of "traditional cuisine" who are reluctant to accept anything but open-hearth cookery with patiently simmered dishes. They operate under the principle that **you really only eat well in your own home**, with six or eight gathered around the table. You have a cook (a faithful retainer who's served the family for thirty years), your own wine cellar . . . stocked with eaux-de-vie laid down by a great-grandfather, your own kitchen garden, orchard, henhouse, and rabbit hutch.

CENTER

Admirers of bourgeois and regional cuisine: they willingly acknowledge . . . that there are still, almost everywhere in France, good inns and excellent hotels, where they don't use prepared sauce bases and butter is butter. These centrists hold fast to and treasure **the flavors of our beloved French dishes, our specialties, and regional wines**.

They demand that foods "taste of where they're from" and are never adulterated or fussy.

LEFT

The partisans of simple cooking, without affectations or complications, sometimes eaten on the run. . . . They are perfectly happy with an omelet, a well-browned chop, an entrecôte medium rare, a fricassee of rabbit, or just a sausage or a slice of ham. They're on the lookout for little "holes in the wall" where the boss is in the kitchen. **They're delighted to discover** a modest restaurant owned by a local fellow who's proud to serve regional charcuterie. . . . You might think of them as gastronomic nomads. In fact I invented the neologism "gastronomads" expressly for them.

EXTREME LEFT

The dreamers, the restless, the innovators. . . . Always in search of new sensations and unexplored pleasures, they are insatiably curious about exotic cuisines, and every kind of recipe from the colonies or abroad. **They invent new dishes.** They like to sample the food of every time and every country. They are the most lighthearted and agile of gastronomes. **"**

Fondue Bourguignonne

This French specialty is actually a Swiss invention, based on French meat. It has nothing to do with fondue. It's a rather savory story.
Marie-Laure Fréchet

FONDUE CONFUSION

Unlike the original cheese version, there's nothing melted in this fondue. Both dishes require a heavy saucepan and long forks. The meat is cut into cubes, like the croutons of the Savoyard specialty, before being dunked in heated oil flavored with various seasonings. There are two possible explanations for the term *bourguignonne*. A high-quality beef fillet is used in this recipe, such as a cut from Charolais, a Burgundian breed. And as Georges Esenwein, the Swiss inventor of the specialty suggested, this dish goes better with a red wine rather than a white. A Burgundy, perhaps?

THE STONE AGE

During the *cuisine minceur* era in the 1980s, fondue bourguignonne was dethroned by the Pierrade. A heated stone cooking device, it was invented in 1986 by the Lyonnais restaurateur Joël Bauduret, who was inspired by the way that shepherds traditionally grilled their meat on heated flat stones. The name and device are patented.

WHAT TO BUY FROM THE BUTCHER

The French will still find cuts of beef labeled "for fondue" at the local butcher shop. It refers to a tender, lean piece of meat, generally cut from the rump. One can also use fillet or shoulder cuts.

INDISPENSIBLE SAUCES FOR FONDUE BOURGUIGNONNE

Mayonnaise
Cocktail sauce
Tartar sauce
Sauce *à l'américaine*
Béarnaise sauce
Sauce bourguignonne

Which Oil?

Choose a good vegetable oil with a high smoke point—sunflower or grapeseed oil, for example. When cooking the fondue, the oil temperature must remain stable, around 350°F (180°C). The pieces of meat must be very dry, with no trace of sauce, so that the oil won't splatter.

SAUCE BOURGUIGNONNE

PREPARATION TIME: 15 MINUTES
COOKING TIME: 15 MINUTES
SERVES 4

1 tablespoon plus 2 teaspoons (10 g) all-purpose flour
5 tablespoons (75 g) butter, softened
1 shallot
1 clove garlic
3 mushrooms
1 sprig thyme
1 cup (250 mL) red wine
Salt and freshly ground black pepper

Thoroughly combine the flour with 2 teaspoons (10 g) of the butter (this makes what is called a *beurre manié*). Peel and mince the shallot. Crush the garlic clove. Cut the mushrooms into quarters. Place the shallot, garlic, mushrooms, and thyme in a saucepan with the wine. Season with salt and pepper. Simmer over medium heat until the liquid is reduced by half. Strain this mixture through a fine-mesh sieve. Add the liquid back to the saucepan over low heat, and add the flour-butter mixture, while whisking. Add the remaining butter, and stir until the mixture is creamy.
 Serve hot or cold.

Words & Foods

THE EROTICS OF COOKING

Gastronomy meets eroticism in the mouth, with the pleasure of eating often resembling the pleasure of a kiss. And when we talk about appetite, it can be sexual or for food. Commonly, the French say that a well-rounded woman is gourmande and that she's looking for someone to chew on. And you don't have to have a twisted mind to understand that someone who's hungry or starving is craving some meat!

Aurore Vincenti

Table arts

If you had to choose the **hottest room** in the house, it'd be **the kitchen**! Its size doesn't matter; what does is what you do in there. On the counter, go for a quickie or take your time. As long as you don't get it everywhere, the kitchen opens **every appetite**.

Mise en bouche ("in mouth" appetizer), hors d'oeuvre, *plat de résistance* (main course), dessert and *mignardises* (bite-size pastries): the **foreplay** of hunger.

What inspires you on top of the table transpires **under the table**. There's a whole world above white tablecloths and social conventions. The body is **split in two**: on top, we maintain a certain amount of modesty. Below, feet seek out feet and brush against one other. One hand can gladly slip **between the thighs** of a neighbor while the other takes a piece of cake.

Forbidden fruits

Although the body is sometimes described as a landscape, one must only take a close look to find a parallel with all kinds of fruit, seafood, vegetables, and sweets. Were we to only mention one, it would the **forbidden fruit** picked by **Eve**. Some say it was an **apple**, but the biblical text is in fact rather evasive when it comes to the nature of the splendor that fell from the tree of knowledge . . .

The apple, as a motif, is like a **round breast**. Its **small stalk**, prettily planted at its center, recalls the tip of a nipple. In French, breasts are said to be **en poire** (pearlike) if the nipple, a tease, seeks to break out of the roundness, too ordinary for its taste.

Buns were being used to describe **buttocks** as early as 1875. The roundness of a behind, and its **softness**, awaken the desire to devour and knead. **All hands on the dough** (the French expression for "all hands on deck")! One caresses the rear as one might a plump loaf of bread just out of the oven, perfectly golden and dusted with flour. Talcum powder, anyone?

Open your legs and you'll find *la moule and le poireau* (mussels and leeks) . . . The metaphor is aptly spun from the analogous form and appearance. **Female genitals**, moist and viscous, recall mollusks: **mussels and oysters**. What's more, they say oysters are aphrodisiacs!

Male genitals are easy to evoke, being so shiny when turgid. Leeks are shined . . . but **cucumbers** and **bananas** are peeled. A zucchini or black radish, perhaps? On the other hand, if you **cook a carrot**, it's over, it won't get hard again. **No bones about it . . .**

Sexual practices: of food and lovers

Although there are some who do indeed like to spread food on a partner's body, there's no need to get out the little onions, as they say in French—that is, there's no need for such frills—if you want to **move on to the pan** (hop into bed). Indeed, the enterprise can seem a bit coarse—the French expression suggests there wasn't much choice in the matter or that there wasn't time to **hang around the pot** (to dillydally)—but you can always be happy you were **sautéed** (got laid), as they say in French, just like a few potatoes. Everything and anything food can be adapted to sex. First, we devour with our eyes, then we taste, lick, suck, bite, eat, and finally swallow!

The goal of the game of love is to make your lover melt. As they say in French, your have to start with liquid cream before **whipping it up**. To do so, avoid cake and opt instead for a **sweet treat**. That's probably why the French sometimes say "he's a cream dessert" (he's the cream of the crop) . . . You might also tell him to **"toss the mashed potatoes"** or **"bring in the sauce!"** And to make a splash, you'll have to at least have a **run on his bean** (be on his erection). After some petting, you just have to **dip your bread** in the soft-boiled egg. For those who prefer entering from behind, here's a French expression that turns a *cul* (ass) into a *baba au rhum*, which is moist and intoxicating: **Take it in the baba** means taking it from the rear.

Skip to: *Bad Taste,* p. 261

COFFEE—A FRENCH OBSESSION

The French love their coffee. It's the second most popular drink after water, and they consume over 11 pounds (5 kg) a year. Ninety-four percent of the population imbibes. France has left its mark on the history of coffee, just as the history of France has itself been shaped by coffee.

Hippolyte Courty

FRANCE AND ITS COFFEE TERROIRS

With its tropical departments and regions, France claims dozens of coffee-growing territories, including some of the very best for cultivating Arabicas:

→ **Le Piton des Neiges in Réunion:** it's the best known and first in historical terms. The volcanic soils and very high elevations yield one of the world's rarest and most sought-after coffees, Laurina (also known as "Bourbon pointu").

→ **Guyana** and its neighbor Surinam were among the first Latin American territories to be planted with coffee, the former by France (1719) and the latter by Holland (ca. 1720). Although these territories are at relatively low altitudes and lack volcanic soil, an embryonic coffee economy persists, particularly with plantations of Arabusta, a hybrid of Robusta and Arabica.

→ **The West Indies:** these islands have been coffee-growing territories since 1721, no doubt based on Arabica Typica plants sent from botanical gardens in Paris and Amsterdam, or perhaps from Surinam and Guyana. Later Bourbon varieties were imported from the distant island of Réunion. Coffee cultivation continues today in Guadeloupe.

→ **New Caledonia:** the Laurina variety (Bourbon pointu), brought in from Réunion, has acclimated to this Oceanic island's soil, which has a very high cobalt content. It is marketed under the name of Café Leroy (1860).

THE FRENCH LIKE IT HOT, AMERICAN STYLE . . . AND THEIR OWN WAY

The French drink coffee in all its guises (except cold).

In the north, they like strong coffee with a metallic note and a grassy, bitter chicory flavor.

In eastern France and the Alps, they like it with cream, or sometimes milk.

In the west, coffee is preferred long and mild, and often milky.

In the southeast, it's taken Italian-style, very strong, or as espresso.

In Paris, they choose the *petit–noir*, a robust espresso, sometimes tamed by a splash of milk ("noisette").

All over France, coffee is prepared using a filter (75 percent of consumption). And sometimes they add a splash of alcohol for a little lift during long evening gatherings.

Normandy: coffee + Calvados = **Café-calva**

Charentes: coffee + Cognac flambé = **Brûlot Charentais**

Lorraine: coffee + Mirabelle = **Brûlot Lorrain**

Southwest: coffee + Armagnac = **Brûlot Gascon**

Alsace: coffee + eau-de-vie (Marc de Gewurztraminer, cerise, or poire) = **Café-schnapps or Alsasische Kaffee**

Brittany: coffee + cider eau-de-vie = **Café Lambig**

North: coffee + eau-de-vie = **Café Bistouille**

Réunion: coffee + rum = **Café Rhum**

COFFEE VOCABULARY

Since coffee first entered the scene in the seventeenth century, the words used for it have proliferated in the French language: *cavé, caphé, cavhé, kaffé, canua, kawa, caoua, caowan, kahwan,* and even *chaube.* However, it's never gone by its original name—*bunn* (the word for coffee in Amharic, the language of Ethiopia).

A GRATEFUL NATION OF COFFEE ADDICTS PAYS HOMAGE TO:

Jean de La Roque: a true pioneer, the first to transport Francophone readers on a journey to the lands of coffee and coffee trees in his celebrated tome *Voyage de l'Arabie Heureuse,* 1715.

Soliman Aga Mustapha Raca: ambassador to the court of Louis XIV from the Sublime Porte, seat of the Ottoman Empire. He established a salon that attracted the entire royal entourage and inspired Molière's *Le Bourgeois gentilhomme.* He served coffee in the oriental style (heavily sweetened). Coffee won over the French court's elite.

Monsieur de La Merveille: this courageous sailor from Saint-Malo armed frigates to source directly from Aden in Arabia, which at that time was the center of the coffee trade. He hoped to establish a French agency there.

Guillaume Dufresne d'Arsel: the man who acclimated the Arabica variety exported from Yemen to the Ile de Bourbon (Réunion). He facilitated the distribution of this type of Arabica, which became known as "Bourbon" throughout the world.

Francesco Procopio dei Coltelli: known as "Procope," he founded the first elegant Left Bank café in Paris. Actors from the Comedie Français flocked there to sample coffee and sorbets. The drink became all the rage, and the venue was a mecca of sociability and sophisticated conversation.

Gabriel de Clieu: one of the founding legends of coffee and a major French contributor to the worldwide dissemination of coffee culture. He gets the credit for the arrival of the first Arabica (Typica) plants in the West Indies (Martinique), risking his life in the process.

Antoine de Jussieu: the first French botanist to describe the coffee plant.

A BIT OF COFFEE'S GEOGRAPHIC HISTORY

Marseille, often called the "Port of the Orient," was the first to experience coffee, which was introduced by visitors from the Levant, Levantines themselves, and Armenians. Most important, we remember Jean de La Roque (see right), who first served coffee around 1644.

Paris had to await the arrival of Monsieur de Thévenin in 1654, followed by his heirs—café owners and Armenian merchants—to experience this black nectar.

La Côte d'Azur boasts two jewels of the coffee industry: Malongo coffee roasters and Unic espresso machines.

Le Havre was the foremost marketplace for coffee for centuries before being eclipsed and relegated to the bottom of the list by giants of the north (Antwerp, Hamburg) and the commodity exchanges of London and New York.

THE PANTHEON OF INVENTORS

In addition to spreading coffee culture and tradition, the French invented numerous coffee-making devices.

Around 1800: the Abbot of Belloy invents the first filter coffeemaker.

1837: Jeanne Richard creates the first vacuum coffeemaker, the forerunner of Hellem and Cona devices.

Late 1910s: an unsung hero invents the so-called Neapolitan coffeemaker.

1923: Marcel-Pierre Paquet invents the modern French press coffeemaker.

1998: Jean Lenoir issues *Le Nez du Café,* which contains a selection of coffee aromas and a companion guide.

MID–LATE SEVENTEENTH CENTURY

The French discover coffee in Ethiopia and Yemen (Arabica), find it bitter, and add sugar. Europe now insists on mochas that are **aromatic, light, and heavily sweetened.**

LATE SEVENTEENTH CENTURY

Doctor Monin "invents" **sweetened café au lait,** which is warmly received. Café au lait becomes de rigueur.

EARLY EIGHTEENTH CENTURY

French and Dutch colonies become the first coffee producers. **Coffee becomes more rounded** and less aromatic than the popular mochas. Europeans discover the merits of **pure varieties.**

EIGHTEENTH CENTURY

Haiti and the West Indies become the largest coffee producers. **Blends become dominant.**

EARLY NINETEENTH CENTURY

The continental blockade imposed on France obliges the French to accustom themselves to chicory, a coffee substitute recently discovered in Germany. A bitter, **vegetal quality becomes a signature of French coffee.**

NINETEENTH CENTURY

French inventers create a multitude of gentle extraction devices (pistons, presses, etc.). Coffee is now a blend of Arabicas, **gently extracted, usually using a filtering process.**

LATE NINETEENTH AND FIRST HALF OF THE TWENTIETH CENTURY

The colonization of tropical and equatorial Africa and Asia popularizes Robusta and Liberica beans. The English promote tea drinking, while Holland endorses Arabica, and France distributes Robusta. **Powerful and bitter brews** are preferred.

TWENTIETH CENTURY

The French double down on their chicory and coffee culture, using **low-quality Robusta** in their blends. Superior beans are reserved for export.

BEGINNING IN THE 1980S

La Dolce Vita and **Italian espresso become paragons of quality for the French** market. Espresso is big, and a single brand, Carte Noire, the filter coffee par excellence, accounts for almost half the national consumption. Coffee remains a powerful presence, and filter preparation is dominant.

LATE 1990s

The French begin to eschew that coffee-ciggy habit and shift to sipping petit-noirs. Coffee pods are all the rage. Milder than the powerful brew served in local bars, they popularize **home consumption,** and coffee drinkers enjoy their high-end, colorful packaging.

2000 ON . . .

The specialty coffee revolution sweeps France, more than ten years after flooding other western countries. **Coffee is more acidic but also more complex, less bitter, and often served as a latté.**

BALZAC, A CELEBRATED COFFEE ADDICT

Honoré de Balzac wrote eighteen hours a day in his home in the Auteuil neighborhood of Paris. His secret was caffeine, in very high doses. The author of *La Comédie Humaine* drank up to fifty cups of coffee a day. Yves Gagneux, the curator of the Maison de Balzac, explains that the writer prepared a very robust brew for himself, with a blend of beans from Ile de Bourbon (Réunion), Martinique, and Yemen. Did coffee consumption hasten his death? After a grueling literary career, the writer died of systemic edema at the age of fifty-one. This is how he described his drug of choice in his *Traité des excitants modernes* (1838): "The coffee descends into your stomach . . . and immediately everything is in motion. Ideas swirl like the battalions of a vast army on the field of battle, and the battle rages. Memories charge in, banners afloat on high. The light cavalry of imagery speeds forward at a magnificent gallop; the artillery of logic races in with wagons loaded with gunpowder; inspiration arrives like advance troops; characters rouse themselves, the paper is covered with ink. Evening advances and ends in torrents of inky black water, as the battle does in black gunpowder."

*L'Arbre à Café, Paris

skip to
Vanilla—The Pleasant Pod, p. 28

Dunk Them in Water for Hot Snacks— In France, They're Called Échaudés

We're familiar with the form of Alsatian pretzels (see page 158). But not everyone is aware that every nook and cranny of France has its own little pastries, each with a distinctive form and all with a delectable crunch, known collectively as échaudés.

Frédéric Laly-Baraglioli

A TOUR DE FRANCE OF ÉCHAUDÉS

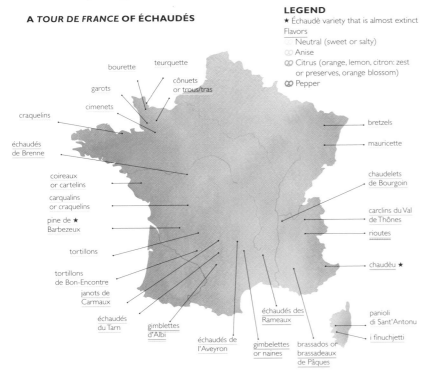

LEGEND
★ Échaudé variety that is almost extinct
Flavors
▢ Neutral (sweet or salty)
∞ Anise
∞ Citrus (orange, lemon, citron: zest or preserves, orange blossom)
∞ Pepper

bourette
teurquette
garots
cônuets or trous/tras
cimenets
craquelins
échaudés de Brenne
coireaux or cartelins
carqualins or craquelins
pine de ★ Barbezeux
tortillons
tortillons de Bon-Encontre
janots de Carmaux
échaudés du Tarn
gimblettes d'Albi
échaudés de l'Aveyron
gimbelettes or naines
échaudés des Rameaux
brassados or brassadeaux de Pâques
bretzels
mauricette
chaudelets de Bourgoin
carclins du Val de Thônes
rioutes
chaudéu ★
panioli di Sant'Antonu
i finuchjetti

WHAT MAKES AN ÉCHAUDÉ?
• A cooking technique: before being baked in the oven, the dough is first poached in boiling water. So they're *bis* (twice)-*cuits* (cooked)!
• The vestiges of a medieval technique from as early as 1260, which was practiced in Albi when Saint Louis passed through. The method is still used to make bagels and the salty nibbles called *taralli des Pouilles.*
• The same consistency— somewhere between crusty and crunchy—and the same simple ingredients: flour, water, and sometimes yeast.
• Three flavor variations: anise, citrus, or plain, salted and/or peppered.
• A variety of shapes and names: triangles, paying homage to the Trinity or conjuring demons away; circles, symbolizing the number eight or the letter omega, standing for resurrection and immortality; or cup shapes, suggesting a pilgrim's bowl. All these forms could be hung on a rope or rod for itinerant peddlers to transport for sale at pilgrimage fairs.

I FINUCHJETTI

PREPARATION TIME: 1 TO 2 HOURS
COOKING TIME: 45 MINUTES
½ ounce (12 g) baker's yeast
1 cup (250 mL) lukewarm water
5 cups (500 g) all-purpose flour
1⅔ teaspoons (10 g) salt
1 ounce (25 g) aniseed

Stir together the yeast and lukewarm water. Combine the flour, salt, and aniseed with the yeast mixture to form a dough. Knead the dough, and let it rest, covered, for 1 hour to rise. After this time, punch down the dough to release the gases, then set the dough aside for another 30 minutes to rise again. Turn the dough out, and roll it into ropes the thickness of your little finger and 9¾ inches (25 cm) in length. Shape them into figure eights, wet the ends with a little water, and press them gently to seal them. Immerse them, three at a time, in simmering water, and remove them using a slotted spoon or skimmer as soon as they float to the surface. Let them drain for a few seconds, then set them aside on a clean cloth. Repeat these steps with the remaining ones. Preheat the oven to 350°F (180°C), and bake them on a baking sheet for 10 to 15 minutes, or until dark golden.

skip to
The Gourmet Abbey, p. 77

The Road to Rum

France is one of the top nations in the production of sugarcane-derived rum, also known as *rhum agricole* (agricultural rum), which is obtained by distilling natural cane juice, as opposed to industrial rum, which is derived from molasses. From the Caribbean to the Indian Ocean, here is a spotlight on this popular eau-de-vie.

Gwilherm de Cerval

SUGARCANE

Family: grasses (genus: *Saccharum*).
Varieties: more than 4,000.
Height: up to 16 feet (5 m).
Diameter: from ¾ to 2¼ inches (2 to 6 cm).
Vegetative cycle: between 12 and 16 months.
Harvest: up to 10 times per cane before replanting.
Origins: 1,400 years before the common era, in New Guinea.
Growth: long cultivated in Persia, its distribution began in the seventh century in Europe.
Climate: needs sun and water. It is therefore cultivated in tropical or warm temperate climates.
Consumption: with more than 1.7 billion metric tons produced each year, it accounts for almost 75 percent of the world's sugar production.

THE CARIBBEAN RUM ROUTE

1493: Christopher Columbus introduced sugarcane to the Caribbean.
Sixteenth century: as users of the first alembic stills, some monks distilled rum from molasses. This was the birth of the first rums.
1654: driven from Brazil by the Portuguese, the Dutch settled in Guadeloupe and Martinique and brought a new technique for the crystallization of sugar.
1694: Father Labat perfected, in Martinique, a new alembic still that improved quality.
Early twentieth century: trade in beet sugar began to compete with that of cane sugar, thus driving down the price of sugarcane. Some producers in the West Indies, concerned about quality, proposed distilling the *vesou* (pure fresh cane juice). Thus, agricultural rum was born.

GLOSSARY

Vesou: pure juice from crushed sugarcane
Molasses: a brown and syrupy liquid made from sugar refining (noncrystallizable)
Bagasse: solid and fibrous residue resulting from the grinding of sugarcane

THE PROCESS OF MAKING AGRICULTURAL RUM

Originally, sugar was a very valuable commodity, so distilling the juice from sugarcane was unimaginable. But with the arrival of beets as a source of sugar, vesou's value decreased. Through distillation, colonial France produced the first agricultural rums, thus improving the quality of the spirit.

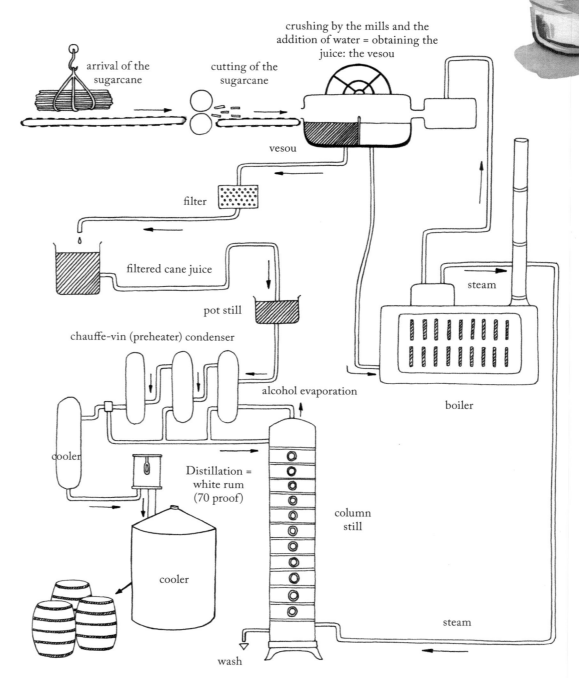

arrival of the sugarcane

cutting of the sugarcane

crushing by the mills and the addition of water = obtaining the juice: the vesou

vesou

filter

filtered cane juice

pot still

chauffe-vin (preheater) condenser

cooler

alcohol evaporation

steam

boiler

Distillation = white rum (70 proof)

column still

cooler

steam

wash

AGING

- Storage in stainless steel vats = white rum
- Storage from 1 to 1½ years in only one barrel = amber rum
- Storage for at least 3 years in one or more barrels = aged rum

MARKETING

Spring water is added to lower the alcoholic strength to between 40 and 62 proof

AN AOC
Since 1996, Martinique's agricultural rum has been the only one to hold the *appellation d'origine contrôlée* (AOC), thus preserving the process and its cultural tradition.

PGIs
(Protected Geographical Indications) It was only in 2005 that some French rums obtained the PGI. They are Rum of Guadeloupe, Rum of Réunion, Rum of Guyana, Rum of the French Overseas Departments, Rum of Baie de Galion, and Rum of the West Indies.

A RECORD
Maison Clément in Martinique and the luxury jeweler Tournaire joined forces to produce what is today the most expensive rum in the world: €100,000 ($116,000) for a bottle! Made from a vintage never sold, it is a 1966 rum that was bottled in 1991. The carafe is Baccarat crystal, and the stopper, in yellow gold and rose gold, is inlaid with four carats of diamonds. Now that's a bottle of rum!

CONSUMPTION
With 50 million bottles consumed each year, France is ranked eighth worldwide in rum consumption. White rum represents 75 percent of the market, amber rum and aged rum 25 percent.

ENVIRONMENT
Bagasse (see the Glossary opposite) is now the main source of renewable energy in France's overseas departments.

A small inventory of desserts with rum

Crêpes
Punch
Cannelé
Baba au Rhum
Caribbean Pineapple Cake
Polish Brioche
Savarin
Cake aux fruits confits
(candied fruit cake)
Oreillettes (Provence)
Merveilles (Bordeaux)
Mille-feuille
Bugnes
Croustade aux pommes
(an apple crisp)
Pithiviers
Moka, fraisier, framboisier
(cakes soaked in rum syrup)
Flambéed bananas
Stollen
Galette des rois
Birolet aux poires
(the du Berry version)
Marzipan
Diplomate
Far Breton

French Cooking Terms

Monter: to beat an ingredient or mixture to incorporate air and increase its volume.
Laisser pousser: to let [a dough] rise.

RUM RECIPE "ACCORDING TO ROGER"

For rum *arrangé*, everyone creates his or her own recipe. The idea is to macerate ingredients such as fresh fruits, spices, or even candies for several months in rum.

MAKES 1 QUART (1 L) OF RUM ARRANGÉ
1 pineapple, preferably a Victoria from Réunion
1 mango, preferably a Bassignac from Martinique
2 vanilla beans, preferably from Réunion
1 ounce (25 g) wood strips (the bark of *Richeria grandis*, an evergreen)
1½ tablespoons (20 g) turbinado sugar
3 cups (700 mL) agricultural rum

Choose a widemouthed glass container. It is important that all the ingredients fit easily into the container. Peel the fruits and keep only those parts that are edible. The riper the fruit, the more flavor it will impart. Using a thin knife, cut the fruits into equal-size pieces. Halve the vanilla beans lengthwise but do not scrape out their seeds.

Combine the fruit pieces, vanilla beans, wood strips, and turbinado sugar in the jar. Pour agricultural rum up to the level of the ingredients, ensuring all the ingredients are immersed. Taste the mixture and make any adjustments as needed, according to taste. If the flavor of alcohol is too dominant, do not hesitate to add more sugar, for example. Close the lid tightly, and invert the jar so that all the ingredients mix well.

Leave the jar at room temperature for at least 6 months. After several months, using a ladle, serve the beverage to your guests in glasses. It can be enjoyed at room temperature or over ice.

BABA AU RHUM
by Alain Ducasse

PREPARATION TIME: 35 MINUTES
COOKING TIME: 45 MINUTES
MAKES 10 BABAS

For the baba dough
¼ ounce (6 g) baker's yeast
1⅓ cups (130 g) all-purpose flour
⅛ teaspoon (1 g) salt
1 teaspoon (6 g) honey
3 tablespoons (45 g) butter
3 large (180 g) eggs
⅓ cup plus 1 tablespoon (100 mL) grapeseed oil, for greasing

For the baba syrup
4 cups (1 L) water
2¼ cups (450 g) granulated sugar
Zest of 1 lemon
Zest of 1 orange
1 vanilla bean (empty, seeds reserved for whipped cream)

For the apricot glaze
½ cup plus 1 tablespoon (125 g) strained apricot preserves
½ cup (125 g) Baba Syrup (above)
¼ cup plus 2 tablespoons (75 g) superfine sugar
1⅓ teaspoons (4 g) NH pectin*

For the soft whipped cream
1 cup plus 1 tablespoon (250 g) light whipping cream
The seeds of 1 vanilla bean (from the bean used for the syrup)
2 tablespoons (25 g) superfine sugar
Rum

NH pectin is a natural gelling agent found in the skin and seeds of fruits. It can be found in pharmacies, supermarkets, or online. In France it's sold under the brand Vitpris d'Alsa.

Prepare the baba dough
Place the yeast and flour in the bowl of a stand mixer fitted with the dough hook. Add the salt, honey, butter, and 1 egg, and knead until a dough forms that is smooth, shiny, and elastic. When the dough detaches from the sides of the bowl, add the remaining eggs, a little at a time, and knead until combined.

Place the dough on a lightly oiled baking sheet, cover it with plastic wrap, and let it rest for 20 minutes.

Prepare the baba syrup
Boil all the ingredients together in a saucepan, and let cool.

Prepare the apricot glaze
In a saucepan, combine the strained preserves and syrup and heat to 104°F (40°C), then combine the sugar and pectin, and add this mixture to the saucepan. Boil for a few minutes, and let cool.

Lightly grease ten baba au rhum molds measuring 2 inches (5 cm) in diameter.* Fill each mold with 1 ounce (30 g) of dough, and rap the pan down on the work surface to expel any air bubbles. Set the pan aside to allow the dough to rise to the top of each mold; the dough must be well risen.

Preheat the oven to 350°F (180°C), and bake the babas au rhum until golden brown.**

Dip the babas in the warm syrup. Make sure the syrup is only just warm (not hot) to avoid damaging the delicate babas, set them aside to absorb the liquid and to swell, then place them on a rack so that they drip dry.

Using a brush, cover the babas with the apricot glaze, and store them at room temperature.

Prepare the soft whipped cream
Beat all the ingredients together in a stand or handheld mixer; the cream should be light and billowy.

Place a baba in a deep dish or cup. Cut it in half, then drizzle it with rum. Serve the cream on the side.

Grapeseed oil is an odorless oil that can withstand high temperatures. It is therefore ideal for greasing your molds.

**Baking babas takes about 25 to 30 minutes. However, as these cooking times may vary from one oven to another, you must rely on the browning to know if they are done.*

skip to
The Cocktail Savants of Harry's Bar, p. 268

LE TOUR de FRANCE des biscuits

France's regions have a lot of crunch! In France, there are as many small cakes and cookies as there are regions (and sometimes even more than there are cities). From myth to reality, let's trace the most popular ones. Watch out for crumbs!

Jill Cousin

Le Macaron d'Amiens

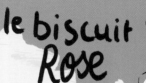

le biscuit Rose

LE PALET BRETON

le MACARON de NANCY

BEURRE demi-sel

LE BISCUIT à la CUILLÈRE

le biscuit de LU

LU PETIT-BEURRE NANTES

LE PETIT-BEURRE

MACARONS DES SOEURS

LE BOUDOIR

la Cornuelle de CHARENTE

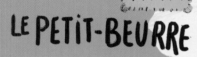

LE CROQUANT

LES Navettes des Accoules

LA NAVETTE

LE MACARON DE · St JEAN · DE · LUZ

la langue de CHAT

CALLED "BIS-CUIT"

In the Middle Ages, baking became widespread and replaced cooking over fire. The word *biscuit* (*bis* meaning "twice" and *cuit* meaning "cooked") was mentioned by John de Joinville in the fourteenth century, who talked about "those little loaves called biscuits because they are cooked two to four times."

VIN BLANC

CANISTRELLI

LE CROQUANT

Origin: Cordes-sur-Ciel during the seventeenth century. Mère Bordes, an innkeeper, created this cookie to accompany the local Gaillac wine.

Description: very light thanks to the use of egg whites. It looks like a tile, with sliced almonds.

Best bet: Biscuiterie Maison Bruyère, in Lagrave (Hautes-Alpes).

Crumbliness index: 4/5

LE PETIT-BEURRE

Origin: invented in 1886 in Nantes by Louis Lefèvre-Utile, son of Jean-Romain Lefèvre and Pauline-Isabelle Utile, founders of the company LU.

Description: Louis took inspiration from the shape of the doily used during teatime and transformed it into an allegory of time: four corner "ears," representing the four seasons, 52 "teeth" for the 52 weeks of the year, and 24 holes for 24 hours in a day. It consists mainly of butter, flour, and sugar.

Best bet: the chocolate version at pâtisserie Vincent Guerlais, Nantes (Loire-Atlantique).

Crumbliness index: 3/5

LA NAVETTE

Origin: created in 1781 by baker Aveyrous, whose bakery is located along the road near Saint-Victor abbey in Marseille.

Description: its marquis shape is like that of a boat (*navis* in Latin). Made of butter, flour, and sugar, flavored with orange blossom water.

Best bet: Biscuiterie Les Navettes des Accoules, in Marseille (Bouches-du-Rhône).

Crumbliness index: 2/5

LE CANISTRELLI

Origin: evidence indicates its origins stretch back to the short period when Genoa ruled Corsica because there are similar cookies in the Liguria region of Italy.

Description: what distinguishes it from its Italian counterpart is the presence of white wine in the dough. It is usually rolled into a log, and made with a neutral oil, not butter, then cut into a rectangle, with a very crunchy result.

Best bet: Biscuiterie Stella Inzuccarata in Cognocoli-Monticchi (southern Corsica).

Crumbliness index: 3/5

LE BISCUIT ROSE

Origin: at the end of the seventeenth century, bakers in Champagne wanted to take advantage of the heat from the ovens after the day's baking was complete. They created a dough that, after being baked, was left in the oven to dry out.

Description: a crispy rectangle made mostly of egg whites, but also with whole eggs, flour, and sugar. Carmine food coloring is added to give it a pink color. It is sprinkled with confectioners' sugar, and it can be dunked in Champagne without falling apart. So chic!

Best bet: Biscuiterie Fossier, Reims (Marne).

Crumbliness index: 5/5

LE BISCUIT À LA CUILLER

Origin: created in Paris in the sixteenth century by the cooks of Catherine de Médicis.

Description: a piped sponge cookie, soft and airy thanks to the use of egg whites beaten with sugar. It can be eaten plain or used in making charlottes or tiramisu.

Best bet: Compagnie Générale de Biscuiterie, Paris 18th.

Crumbliness index: 1/5

LE PALET BRETON

Origin: the name comes from the eponymous disk-pitching game that involves disks being thrown as close as possible to a smaller disk onto a marked playing surface or on the ground.

Description: made from a short dough, this round and sandy shortbread is usually ½ inch (1.5 cm) high. It contains on average 20 percent salted butter.

Best bet: Biscuiterie des Vénètis, Saint-Armel (Ille-et-Vilaine).

Crumbliness index: 3/5

LE BOUDOIR

Origin: it was when Prince Talleyrand dipped a cookie resting on a spoon into his glass of Madeira that Antonin Carême, the famous chef in the eighteenth century known as "the king of the chefs and the chef of kings," came up with the idea of creating a more durable cookie that would not disintegrate so quickly when dunked.

Description: elongated and crunchy, it is composed simply of sugar, flour, and eggs.

Best bet: Moulin des Moines, Krautwiller (Bas-Rhin).

Crumbliness index: 4/5

LA LANGUE-DE-CHAT

Origin: the cats have our tongues! Its origin remains a mystery. We only know that it owes its name to its resemblance to a *langue de chat* (cat's tongue).

Description: flat and oblong, 2 to 3 inches (5 to 8 cm) long. Using softened butter in the dough gives it a crisp and melting texture. Its edges are browned, and its center is pale golden.

Best bet: Ladurée (several shops in France and abroad).

Crumbliness index: 3/5

LE MACARON OF NANCY

Origin: during the decree suppressing all religious congregations (April 5, 1792), Sister Marguerite and Sister Marie-Elisabeth found refuge at the house of Doctor Gormand in Nancy. To provide for their needs, they made macarons, a recipe they had brought with them from the Monastery of the Ladies of the Blessed Sacrament.

Description: a round cake, crunchy on the outside and soft on the inside, made of a dough of crushed almonds, sugar, and egg whites.

Best bet: Maison des Soeurs Macarons, Nancy (Meurthe-et-Moselle).

Crumbliness index: 5/5

LE MACARON OF AMIENS

Origin: introduced in the sixteenth century in the medieval city by Catherine de Médicis.

Description: a Picardy specialty made from Valencia marzipan, honey, bitter almonds, and eggs. It has a grainy appearance and a soft texture.

Best bet: Jean Trogneux, Amiens (Somme).

Crumbliness index: 1/5

LE MACARON OF SAINT-JEAN-DE-LUZ

Origin: the recipe was developed by Monsieur Adam in 1660 during the marriage of Louis XIV and the Spanish Infanta Marie-Thérèse of Austria in the church in the Basque city of Saint-Jean-de-Luz.

Description: round and flattened, made with almonds, sugar, and egg whites.

Best bet: Maison Adam, Saint-Jean-de-Luz (Pyrénées-Atlantiques).

Crumbliness index: 2/5

LA CORNUELLE OF CHARENTE

Origin: its origin is uncertain. It is enjoyed during Palm Sunday. The hole in the center of the cookie allows you to insert a blessed box branch through its center.

Description: a flat sablé ("sandy") cookie in the shape of an isosceles triangle with sides measuring about 4¾ inches (10 cm), with serrated edges. The cookie is made from eggs, flour, butter, and sugar, and is brushed with egg yolk and sprinkled with aniseed before being baked.

Best bet: Boulangerie Jean Philippe, Villebois-Lavalette (Charente).

Crumbliness index: 3/5

LES CROQUANTS D'ALBI
by Mizette Momège

PREPARATION TIME: 15 MINUTES
COOKING TIME: 5 MINUTES

½ cup (75 g) hazelnuts
½ cup (75 g) almonds
1¼ cups (250 g) sugar
½ cup plus 1 tablespoon (60 g) all-purpose flour
3 large (80 g) egg whites

Preheat the oven to 400°F (200°C). Roughly chop the hazelnuts and almonds into 2 to 3 pieces each. Place them in a bowl with the sugar, flour, and egg whites, and stir well to combine.

Line two baking sheets with parchment paper. Using a small spoon, drop small mounds of the dough onto the baking sheets, spacing the mounds about 2 inches (5 cm) apart (about 12 cookies per baking sheet). Bake for 10 to 12 minutes in the oven, watching the baking time, or until they are pale golden and set. Remove them from the oven, then slide the baking paper off the baking sheets, and let the cookies cool.

Repeat these steps with any remaining dough. The cookies will keep for several days in an airtight container.

skip to
Cakes to Carry, p. 102

The Great Scallop—
The Coquille Saint-Jacques

With 5½ pounds (2.5 kg) consumed per person each year, France is the world champion in its consumption of these scallops. From Pas-de-Calais to Brittany, the country's cuisine is synonymous with coquilles Saint-Jacques.

Charles Patin O'Coohoon

THE JOURNEY OF THE GREAT SCALLOP

→ The egg laying of this hermaphroditic bivalve mollusk takes place during midsummer. The male and female gametes are expelled and the fertilization takes place in the water.

→ The larvae, measuring 0.003 to 0.009 inch (0.1 to 0.25 mm) long, develop in the water between three weeks to one month.

→ In early autumn, each larva has developed a shell, and it then settles onto the seabed.

→ The scallop then begins its silt cycle. It grows past the juvenile stage (⅓ in/1 cm at two months) to adulthood, which can take up to ten years. It can reach a size of 9 inches (23 cm) at maturity, but can be fished once it reaches 4 inches (10.2 cm) across.

→ It is fished between October 1 and May 14.

A CHRONOLOGY OF THE GREAT SCALLOP

500 million years ago: the first scallops are formed on Earth.

6 million years ago: the great scallop appears (Saint-Jacques).

Prehistoric times: the shell was used as barter.

Ancient times: in Egypt, the shell was used as a comb. It is from this use that the Latin name of the great scallop shell originates (*pecten* for *peigne* ["comb"] in French).

Eighth century BC: with the help of his mother Gaia, Cronos overthrew his father Uranus and tossed his genitals into the sea. From this, Venus was born. Riding on the sea on a scallop shell, she arrived naked on the island of Cyprus, and was admired by the gods.

830 AD: the tomb of the apostle Saint James (Saint Jacques in French), from whom the scallop got its alternative name "Saint James's shell," was discovered in Spain.

Twelfth century: in the sermon "Veneranda Dies," taken from the *Codex Calixtinus* and dedicated to Saint Jacques of Compostela, the shell was represented as the symbol of good works, representing an open hand.

1485: Botticelli painted *La Naissance de Vénus* (*The Birth of Venus*).

1758: the Swedish naturalist Carl von Linné gave the great scallop its scientific name: *Pecten maximus*.

1988: the founding of the Confrérie des Chevaliers de la Coquille Saint-Jacques (Brotherhood of the Knights of the Coquille Saint-Jacques).

2002: the great scallop from Normandy obtains a Label Rouge (Red Label).

METHODS FOR COOKING THE COQUILLE SAINT-JACQUES

Slice

Following the method of chef David Toutain (Paris 8th), cook the scallops sliced. This technique makes it possible to avoid damaging the fibers. As a result, the flesh remains soft. Cook the frilly membrane (surrounding the flesh) in water with a bouquet garni; strain, and add curry. Serve with the leaves of Brussels sprouts.

Serve as a carpaccio

According to Thierry Charrier, chef at the Quai d'Orsay kitchens: thinly slice raw scallops into 3 or 4 slices, carpaccio style, and marinate them in white wine, chopped shallots, lime juice, and olive oil. Make a vinaigrette from reduced orange juice and a vanilla bean (split, with its seeds scraped into the vinaigrette), Savora mustard (a spicy mustard), sherry, and peanut oil. Drizzle the vinaigrette on top of the scallops and serve them with cooked lentils.

Bake in the shell

Place the scallop "nut" (the white fleshy portion) inside the scallop shells with an aromatic garnish (such as minced onions, carrots, and herbs) and a dash of white wine. Make a dough (combine flour, salt, and water) and use it to seal the shells shut. Bake the shells in a hot oven for about 10 minutes. Break the dough seal, and serve immediately.

Cook the frill

Taken from *Il est frais mon passion* by Jean-Marie Baudic, La Martinière, 2012. Collect the frilly membrane that surrounds the meat. In a casserole dish, cook chopped white button mushrooms, garlic, onion, carrots, and shallots. Add the membrane, and pour in a little white wine. Let the wine reduce until evaporated, then add cider and cream. Add orange zest and a bouquet garni, and simmer over low heat for about 2 hours, covered. Serve.

Reserve the coral (roe)

Make a taramasalata with smoked codfish eggs and bread crumbs dipped in milk. Place the scallop coral in hot water for a few minutes, then let it cool. Using an immersion blender, blend, and add the roe to the taramasalata. Sprinkle with lemon juice and serve with blini.

Scallop beds of France

The scallop shell slips along the ocean floor from Picardy to Brittany. Its main sources are:

1 Dieppe and Fécamp in the Bay of Somme

2 Port-en-Bessin and Grandcamp in the Bay of Seine

3 Granville in the Bay of Mont-Saint-Michel

4 Saint-Malo in the Bay of Saint-Malo

5 Loguivy-de-la-Mer and Erquy in the Bay of Saint-Brieuc

6 Brest, Quiberon, and Oléron on the Atlantic coast

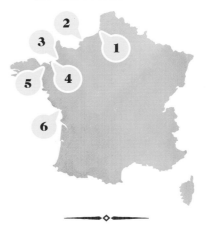

skip to
Sea Urchin—A Prickly Subject!, p. 46

François Pierre de La Varenne

He wrote the most innovative cookbook of the seventeenth century. In 1651, the book *Le Cuisinier françois (The French Cook)* established the principles of a culinary revolution: the transition from medieval cooking to great modern French cuisine.

Estelle Lenartowicz

THE FIRST GREAT CHEF OF MODERN CUISINE

Little is known about the life of François Pierre, known as La Varenne. Born in 1618 in Dijon, he is said to have learned about cooking at the court of Henri IV and Marie de Médicis. At age forty-three, he joined the kitchen of the Marquis of Uxelles. In his honor, he created the recipe that would become legendary: the "duxelles," minced mushrooms with shallots and onions sautéed in butter. The signature dish reflects a pioneering reformer with a hunger for innovation.

ESTABLISHING A MODERN CUISINE

With the motto of "health, moderation, and refinement," La Varenne proposed recipes "made from the most common and ordinary of things, the stuff of a home's pantry." In it are the first mentions of a bouquet garni, béchamel sauce, and the oldest mille-feuille puff pastry recipe. The book established cooking customs.

A role for butter: an ingredient that was until then held in contempt by the wealthy, reserved for cooking eggs and pastries. Butter was increasingly used to make all kinds of dishes.

Farewell to spices, long live herbs! appreciated for being exotic, spices (saffron, ginger, nutmeg, etc.) were replaced by aromatic garden herbs (parsley, tarragon, chervil, basil, thyme, bay leaves, chives, etc.).

New ways of cooking: shorter cooking times and less sugar were meant to preserve the tastes and textures of foods. That applied to meat—which was enjoyed once removed from the spit, in its own juices—and also to vegetables, which were eaten crisp, as they are today!

Vegetables from the garden: La Varenne was among the first to take an interest in vegetables. Cauliflowers, asparagus, artichokes, and cucumbers were used in dishes for the first time.

Le Cuisinier François (The French Cook)
(1618–1678)

LA FEUILLANTINE

Place in a bowl some pastry cream [see page 93] weighing the size of two eggs (3½ oz/ 100 g), a *quarteron* (½ cup plus 2 tablespoons/125 g) of superfine sugar, a raw egg yolk, a pinch of currants, some pine nuts, strips of lemon zest, a small amount of minced preserved lemon, 1 or 2 macarons finely crushed, a little ground cinnamon, and a good bit of rose water. You have to combine all these things together with a spatula or a silver spoon, then with a few drops of orange blossom water or lemon juice; it takes little of one, or both. Or you can make the batter using only pastry cream, white bread crumbs, or crushed cookies, a few currants, sugar, a little cinnamon, and a few drops of lemon juice. Once the dough is made, you'll roll out two portions of puff pastry the size and thickness of a small plate. Place on top of one of these portions the aforementioned mixture, which should then be spread out a little with a spatula. Then you will dab a little water all around the edge of the dough, then place the other portion of dough on top. Press the edges of the dough portions

together to seal them, in the form of a tart, and place the feuillantine in the oven to bake for 30 minutes. When the pastry is almost baked, sprinkle it with sugar and a few drops of orange blossom water, then place it back in the oven to melt the sugar. As a last step, sprinkle it with more sugar once it is removed from the oven.

Le Cuisinier françois: 400 recettes du XVIIeme siècle (The French Cook: 400 Recipes from the Seventeenth Century), François Pierre La Varenne, Éditions Vendémiaire, 2016, p. 224

A PUBLISHING PHENOMENA

Le Cuisinier françois became a resounding success as soon as it was published: a first for a cookbook! In one hundred years, there have been no less than seventy different editions. The book has been copied, imitated, plagiarized . . . As early as 1653, it was the very first French cookbook to be translated into English. Inaugurating the editorial form of the modern cookbook, this one is especially clear in its organization, with an index and numbered recipes . . . The author speaks in the first person, addressing the reader directly, which forged a new image of the modern chef. Pedagogical and didactic, its advice is abundant.

Do You Speak "French"?

The term "French" is used with many dishes, but do titles represent true French origins? What's in a name is not always what you think . . .

Baptiste Piegay

French toast

What is it?

In French it's called **pain perdu (literally "lost bread").** In the seventeenth century, this was a dish made with bread, wine, orange juice, and sugar. The use of egg became part of the equation in 1870.

Why "French" toast?

Legend has it that in 1724, an innkeeper from Albany, New York, named Joseph French, had the clever idea to use leftover bread for other purposes. Then why is it not called *French's* toast? An even more clever theory suggests that before the outbreak of the First World War, it was called *German* toast, and that its name was changed due to the conflict. But if you're ever in New Orleans, be aware that French toast is referred to exclusively as *pain perdu.*
Certificate of authenticity: None.

French press

What is it?

A coffeemaker. At the risk of offending the Italians, William Harrison Ukers in his book *All about Coffee*, published in 1922, assured us that "From the beginning, the French have given, more than any other people, continual attention to coffee." Ukers reviews a dozen coffeemaker models, but none with a press.

Why "French" press?

This coffeemaker appeared in Paris in March 1852, created by a metalworker and tradesman. It was not until the end of the 1920s that the press coffee machine gained wide popularity. In the 1980s, the term "French plunger-type" came into use in the United States. In 1993, Florence Fabricant, a food journalist for the *New York Times*, became an enthusiast of the French press method.
Certificate of authenticity: Confirmed.

French beans

What are they?

The haricot vert (string bean). This bean appeared 7,000 years ago in the Americas. Christopher Columbus reported about it during his second voyage to the Americas in 1493. But it arrived in France in 1597, much too late to justify calling it a "French" bean.

Why "French" beans?

This one seems to have no other objective other than to be a marketing tactic to make the vegetable more appealing.
Certificate of authenticity: None.

French fries

What are they?

Frites ("fried potatoes"). Are they Belgian or French? The Belgian writer Pierre-Brice Lebrun serves up the story on page 332.

Why "French" fries?

During the First World War, the allies landed in Flanders and very soon indulged in this local culinary specialty. The Belgian army was French-speaking, so the GIs are suspected of having confused the Belgians with the French.
Certificate of authenticity: Acceptable, if it pleases France's neighbors . . .

A *Tour de France:* Buckwheat

Gluten-free, rich in vitamins, proteins, and minerals—buckwheat is a very interesting substitute for wheat.
Valentine Oudard

The fabulous destiny of buckwheat

Buckwheat, native to Asia, has been grown in the western fields of France since the fifteenth century, eventually spreading to the Rhône-Alpes and Limousin. It grows in poor soils, can be harvested after three months (hence its nickname "plant of a hundred days"), resists weeds, and is not subject to diseases. But its unpredictable yield resulted in its disappearance as a crop in the 1960s to make way for a intensive agricultural practices in the cultivation of wheat and corn. Recently, however, buckwheat has gained ground thanks to the Blé Noir Tradition Bretagne Association as well as to its obtaining a Protected Geographical Indication (PGI).

A tour de France

Galettes bretonne: this was the bread of the Armoricains (in Brittany), filled with cheese, bacon, sausage or andouille, and cooked on a *bilig.*

Farz of Pays de Léon: a buckwheat porridge (*fars-gwiniz-du*), of which there is a wheat version (*farz-gwiniz*), cooked in a special bag (*farz sac'h*), then sliced or crumbled (recipe below).

Tourtous de Corrèze: made from buckwheat flour, water, and yeast. One of these thick galettes with large holes makes a complete meal.

Pous de Corrèze: it owes its name to the "pouh" sound generated when the dough releases its air when cooked. Made of buckwheat flour and milk, cooked in a cloth.

Crozets de Savoie: these pasta were originally round but in the seventeenth century became squares measuring ¼ inch (5 mm) and ¹⁄₁₀ inch (2 mm) thick. They are traditionally made from buckwheat flour and soft wheat.

Bourriols du Cantal: thick and fluffy rustic galettes made from buckwheat and wheat flours, yeast, and milk.

KIG HA FARZ

This is the Breton version of pot-au-feu.

PREPARATION TIME: 30 MINUTES
RESTING TIME: 1 NIGHT
COOKING TIME: 3 HOURS 30 MINUTES
SERVES 4

1 pork shank
1 stalk celery
1 large onion
4 leeks
6 carrots
4 turnips
1 sprig thyme
2 sprigs parsley
1 bay leaf
1⅓ pounds (600 g) upper chuck of beef
10½ ounces (300 g) pork belly
Salt and freshly ground black pepper
For the farz
4 cups (500 g) buckwheat flour
14 tablespoons (200 g) unsalted butter, softened
1 large egg
Salt
3 tablespoons (40 g) crème fraîche
Cheesecloth measuring 8 by 12 inches (20 by 30 cm)

The day before, place the pork shank in cold water, and desalt it overnight. The next day, peel all the vegetables. Chop up some of the green of the leeks and set them aside. Tie up the leeks with kitchen twine or a strip of leek green. Make a bouquet garni with the thyme, parsley, and bay leaf. Put the beef chuck and the desalted shank in a pot of water. Add the whole onion, bouquet garni, celery, and leek greens, then bring to a boil. Lower the heat and let simmer for 30 minutes. Prepare the farz. In a large bowl, combine the flour, butter, egg, a pinch of salt, and the crème fraîche. Add a little warm water to the mixture, just enough to create a smooth paste, and stir to combine. Gradually add 2 cups (500 mL) of the cooking broth to the mixture to create a liquid paste, yet one that is not too fluid. Pour the mixture onto the cheesecloth, gather the corners, and tie them together to create a sack, leaving a little space at the top as the farz swells when cooked. Immerse the bag into the pot, and cook for 1 hour 30 minutes, occasionally skimming off any foam that forms on the surface.

Add the pork belly and cook for another 30 minutes. Season with salt and pepper. Serve the meat and vegetables in the broth, along with slices of the farz.

Wine in the Pan

In the kitchens of the Hostellerie du Chapeau Rouge in Dijon, chef William Frachot pays tribute to the region of Burgundy.

Delphine Le Feuvre

EGGS EN MEURETTE

PREPARATION TIME: 1 HOUR
COOKING TIME: 50 MINUTES
SERVES 4

2⅔ cups (600 mL) chicken stock
3⅓ cups (800 mL) red wine
⅔ teaspoon (2 g) potato starch
5 tablespoons (70 g) butter, cubed
1¼ teaspoons (5 g) sugar
Salt and freshly ground black pepper
Eggs
1 cup (250 mL) red wine
Scant 3 cups (700 mL) white vinegar
8 fresh farm eggs
For the bourgugnonne garnish
3 ounces (80 g) white button mushrooms
Lemon
3 tablespoons (45 g) butter
3 ounces (80 g) lardons (thick-cut cubed bacon)
3 tablespoons (40 g) sugar
3⅛ ounces (90 g) pearl onions
Just over ¾ cup (200 mL) oil
8 slices baguette bread
1 clove garlic, peeled
A few sprigs (about ¾ oz/20 g) flat-leaf parsley, chopped

The sauce

In a saucepan, reduce the stock over low heat to just over ⅓ cup (100 mL). In a separate pan, reduce the wine over low heat to ⅓ cup (80 mL). Combine the reductions. Stir a few tablespoons of the reduction into the potato starch, then stir this mixture into the remaining reduction. Whisk gently, then whisk in the butter a few cubes at a time. Whisk in the sugar, then season with salt and pepper.

The eggs

Bring the wine to a boil in a skillet, then add 2 cups (500 mL) of the vinegar. Meanwhile, break the eggs into coffee cups (one per cup), pour a little of the remaining vinegar over each egg, and set aside for 3 minutes. The vinegar will precook the edges of the egg and make poaching easier. Poach the eggs one by one in the simmering wine and vinegar. Make a slight circular motion with a spoon in the liquid to create a swirl; this will allow the egg white to wrap around the yolk, helping to contain it. Simmer for 2 minutes, then carefully remove the egg using a slotted spoon. Dunk the poached egg into a bowl of cold water to stop the cooking.

The bourguignonne garnish

In a saucepan, cook the mushrooms in a little water with a squeeze of lemon juice, then sauté in a separate skillet in 1 tablespoon (15 g) of the butter; transfer to a plate. Sauté the bacon in the same skillet. In a separate skillet, heat the remaining butter with the sugar. Add the onions and cook until lightly browned; transfer to a plate. In the same skillet, heat the oil, then fry the slices of bread. Transfer to a plate to drain and cool, then rub with the garlic clove. Keep warm.

Serving

In a warm, shallow plate, place 2 slices of the fried bread, spoon in some of the bourguignonne garnish, then add 2 of the poached eggs, and top with the red wine sauce. Sprinkle with the chopped parsley.

William Frachot by Dates

1970
Born in Paris

1995–1996
Spends time at Bernard Loiseau, Fabrice Gillotte, and Jacques Lameloise, three chefs from Burgundy

1999
The parents of William Frachot, Dominik and Catherine, buy the restaurant Le Chapeau Rouge, a Dijon institution

2003
Receives his first Michelin star

2013
Receives his second Michelin star

COQ AU VIN

PREPARATION TIME: 45 MINUTES
MARINATING TIME: OVERNIGHT
COOKING TIME: 3 HOURS
SERVES 8

1 chicken weighing 6½ pounds (3 kg), cut up
6 cups (1.5 L) red wine
7 ounces (200 g) carrots
1 head garlic
7 ounces (200 g) white onions
1 bay leaf
1 sprig thyme
Vegetable oil, for frying
Flour
7 ounces (200 g) pearl onions
3 tablespoons (45 g) butter
1¼ teaspoons (5 g) sugar
Salt and freshly ground black pepper
7 ounces (200 g) smoked bacon
7 ounces (200 g) white button mushrooms
8 slices bread
4 tablespoons (50 g) olive oil
5¼ ounces (150 g) chicken or pork blood (ask your butcher)
A few sprigs (about ½ oz/15 g) parsley, chopped

The day before, place the chicken in the wine with half the carrots, garlic, and white onions, and the bay leaf and thyme. The next day, drain the pieces (reserving the marinade) and fry in an ovenproof casserole dish in some vegetable oil. When the chicken is browned, add the remaining carrots, garlic, and white onions, and cook until softened. Sprinkle a little flour over the chicken, and cook for 2 to 3 minutes. Preheat the oven to 350°F (180°C). Add all the reserved marinade to the casserole dish, and cook in the oven for 3 hours, covered, or cook on the stovetop over medium heat, stirring regularly.

Meanwhile, add the pearl onions to a saucepan and cover with water. Add 1 tablespoon (15 g) butter and the sugar. Season with salt and pepper. Cook until the onions are a beautiful golden color, then turn off the heat. Cut the bacon into small pieces and place in a saucepan of boiling water and cook for several minutes. Remove from the saucepan, and sauté in a skillet until lightly browned; transfer to a plate. Sauté the mushrooms in the skillet in the remaining butter. Combine the onions, mushrooms, and bacon. Cut the bread into cubes, then fry in the olive oil.

When the chicken has finished cooking, remove the pieces from the casserole dish and set aside to drain, then strain the liquid. Add the cooking liquid to a large saucepan and simmer until reduced (it should be thickened and creamy, but not too thick). Add the blood to finish the sauce, then strain again. Season to taste. Add the chicken to the saucepan, then add the cooked onions, mushrooms, and bacon. Keep the stew warm, but do not boil. Dredge the edge of the croutons in the sauce then in the parsley, then arrange the croutons, chicken, vegetables, and bacon on serving plates.

BOEUF BOURGUIGNON

PREPARATION TIME: 45 MINUTES
MARINATING TIME: 3 HOURS
COOKING TIME: 2 HOURS
SERVES 8

1 (10½-oz/300 g) onion, peeled and halved
1 clove
4½ pounds (2 kg) upper chuck of beef
10½ ounces (300 g) carrots
2 cloves garlic, crushed
1 bouquet garni (rosemary, thyme, bay leaf, or other herbs of your choice)
A few parsley sprigs
Peppercorns
Quatre épices spice blend
5 cups (1.2 L) red wine
¾ cup plus 2 tablespoons (90 g) all-purpose flour
8 cups (2 L) veal stock (unthickened, or *non lié*)
For the bourguignonne garnish
9 ounces (250 g) lardons (thick-cut cubed bacon)
9 ounces (250 g) mushrooms
1 tablespoon (20 g) sugar
4 tablespoons (60 g) butter
20 pearl onions
Several sprigs parsley, chopped

Pierce half the onion with the clove, and cut the other half into small dice. Cut the meat into 1¾-ounce (50 g) cubes. Wash and cut the carrots. Place the meat, the onion half with the clove, the diced onions, carrots, garlic, bouquet garni, parsley sprigs, peppercorns, and quatre épices spice blend in a large bowl. Pour in the wine, then set the bowl in the refrigerator, covered, to marinate for at least 3 hours. Preheat the oven to 325°F (160°C). Add a shallow pan of water to the bottom of the oven to create moisture. Remove the meat from the marinade, and reserve the marinade contents. Brown the meat in a cast-iron casserole dish. Remove the meat from the casserole dish, add the vegetables from the marinade, and cook just until warmed through. Place the meat back in the casserole dish, stir to combine, then add the flour, stirring well to coat the pieces of meat and ensure all ingredients are well combined. Add the marinade liquid, and cook until almost evaporated, then add the veal stock. Cover and place in the oven for about 2 hours.

Prepare the bourguignonne garnish. Sauté the lardons in a skillet. Mince the mushrooms, and sauté in the same skillet. In a sauté pan, heat the sugar and butter. Add the pearl onions, barely cover with water, and cook until the water has evaporated and the onions are browned. Continue cooking the sauce until it coats the back of a spoon, then strain. Place the meat, bourguignonne garnish, and the sauce back in the casserole dish, and bring to a simmer. Serve in shallow bowls, sprinkled with chopped parsley.

skip to
The Bordeaux and Burgundy Match-Up, p. 272

Asterix's Gastronomic Tour of Gaul

A quick tour of the regional and anachronistic Gallic specialties brought to us by the two Gauls in the fifth comic book of Asterix's adventures *Le Tour de Gaul d'Astérix*, published in 1965. It's definitely the most gourmand in the series.

Charles Patin O'Coohoon

THE STARTING POINT

The famous village of the indominatable Gauls is besieged by the Romans. To prove that they can travel as they please, Asterix and Obelix bet they can bring back culinary specialties from across Gaul. Their tour begins . . .

LUTÈCE (PARIS)

Specialty: ham

The recipe was mentioned for the first time in 1793. It was a pork thigh made Parisian-style: deboned, denervated, prepared, and then brined. It's cooked for hours in a bouillon. Since, it has been called *jambon de Paris*.

CAMARACUM (CAMBRAI)

Specialty: *bêtises* (stupidities or boiled sweets)

They get their name from a cooking mistake made in 1850. This caramelized sugar candy flavored with mint was listed as part of the Intangible Cultural Heritage of Humanity in 1994.

DUROCORTORUM (REIMS)

Specialty: four amphoras of Champagne: brut, dry, demi-sec, and doux

🗨 **"It's the wine of wines! It sparkles and is served on special occasions . . . For example, to inaugurate galleys . . ."**

This king of sparkling wines has been produced since the seventeenth century. Its name comes from the region where it's made.

LUGDUNUM (LYON)

Specialties: sausages and quenelles

🗨 **"Here we have sausages and quenelles"**

Lyonnais sausage is a sausage that needs to be cooked and that is generally consumed warm with potatoes. Quenelle is puff pastry mixed with pike from the ponds of the Dombes.

NICAE (NICE)

Specialty: salade niçoise brought back from the Promenade des Bretons.

🗨 **"An amphora filled with salad please . . . it's to go."**

Rule of thumb: the salad never contains cooked vegetables. It's made with tomatoes, artichokes, olives from Nice, fava beans, hard-boiled eggs, scallions, and anchovies.

MASSILIA (MARSEILLE)

Specialty: bouillabaisse

A soup made with rockfish, croutons, whole fish, and potatoes. It's the most famous Mediterranean fish ragout.

TOLOSA (TOULOUSE)
Specialty: sausage

 "It's pretty, Tolosa, and is the sausage good?" "Delicious, Obélix, delicious!"

There's lean meat and pork fat (ham, breast, shoulder), simply seasoned with salt and pepper, which is ground and stuffed into sausage casing measuring 1 to 1⅒ inches (26 to 28 mm) in diameter. You can make it as long as you'd like.

AGINUM (AGEN)
Specialty: prunes

"To start, I would like to give you this small bag of our famous Aginum prunes."

It's the dried Ente plum, grown in the Lot-et-Garonne since the fifteenth century. An antioxidant concentration of vitamins and iron, it has had a Protected Geographical Indication (PGI) since 2002.

BURDIGALA (BORDEAUX)
Specialty: amphora of white Burdigala and oysters

"Oysters are good, but you can eat boar meat even in months not containing the letter R."

Because it's so close to Arcachon Bay, the city is inundated with oysters. What does it go with? A Sémillon or a Sauvignon, the two most common grapes used to make white Bordeaux.

They're not a part of Asterix's gastronomic tour of Gaul but they're a big part of Goscinny and Uderzo's work:

CORSICA
The explosive Corsican cheese in *Astérix en Corse* (*Asterix in Corsica*).

"Smell this, my friends."

AUVERGNE
Stewed cabbage in *Le Bouclier arverne* (*The Chieftain's Shield*)

"To start, you have to have some cabbages."

NORMANDY
Fresh milk cream in *Astérix et les Normands* (*Asterix and the Normans*)

"If you don't eat your cream soup, the mean ogre will come and eat you up."

Not to forget boar, of course, which is hunted in Brittany and roasted. It's in each one of the books.

skip to
The Gauls: French Ancestors, p. 217

WILD BOAR IN A SPICE CRUST
*by Blandine Boyer**

SERVES 6 TO 8
1 piece caulfat
2 teaspoons (12 g) kosher salt
1 tablespoon (10 g) mixed peppercorns
2 tablespoons (10 g) coriander seeds
6 tablespoons (108 g) violet mustard (made from grape must) or stone-ground mustard
4 tablespoons (60 mL) olive oil
1 bunch savory or wild thyme (leaves only)
1 boar haunch (thigh and rump piece)
2 cups (500 mL) vegetable broth or water

Preheat the oven to 300°F (150°C). Rinse the caulfat under cold water, and gently unfold it onto a cloth. In a mortar, roughly crush the salt, peppercorns, and coriander seeds together. Stir in the mustard, then the oil, little by little (to make an emulsion), then the savory leaves. Coat the meat with this mixture, then wrap the meat in the caulfat. Place the meat in a large baking dish. Pour the broth into the bottom of the dish, and seal the dish tightly with foil. Roast in the oven, calculating at least 1 hour per every 2 pounds (1 kg) of meat. Every hour, add a little water to the dish, if necessary. When the meat is tender, remove it from the dish, and brown it for 15 min at 350°F (180°C) placed on a rack in the oven, with a baking sheet placed underneath it. Pour the captured juices from the baking sheet into a small saucepan and reduce them until somewhat thickened (only if they are not thick enough). Skim off any excess fat with a spoon, strain the reduced juices, then pour them over the meat, and serve.

*Excerpt from Banquet gaulois: 70 recettes venues directement de nos ancêtres . . . ou presque! *by Blandine Boyer, Larousse, 2016*

MONT LOZÈRE WITH HONEY AND CHESTNUTS
*by Blandine Boyer**

PREPARATION TIME: 30 MINUTES
COOKING TIME: APPROXIMATELY 3 HOURS
SERVES 8 TO 10
4 large (120 g) egg whites
7¾ ounces (220 g) light turbinado sugar
Scant ½ cup (50 g) chestnut flour
2 tablespoons (42 g) chestnut honey
1¼ cups (300 mL) whipping cream, chilled
Scant 1 cup (200 g) mascarpone cheese, chilled
7 ounces (200 g) chestnut jam
For the caramelized chestnuts
10½ ounces (300 g) roasted chestnuts from a jar, or roasted at home
2 tablespoons (30 mL) chestnut honey
2 tablespoons (30 g) demi-sel (lightly salted) butter

Preheat the oven to 200°F (100°C). Place the egg whites in a mixing bowl and beat them with an electric mixer. When they begin to foam, incorporate the sugar little by little, then continue beating until stiff peaks forms; the meringue should be shiny and supple. Carefully fold the chestnut flour into the egg whites using a silicone spatula. Spoon large

spoonfuls of the meringue onto a baking sheet lined with parchment paper. Drizzle the meringues with the honey, then place in the oven for at least 3 hours. During the last hour, partially open the oven door.

Prepare the caramelized chestnuts. In a nonstick skillet, sauté the chestnuts with the honey and butter over high heat until the chestnuts begin to caramelize, about 3 minutes. Spread them out onto a large piece of parchment paper and let them cool.

Before serving, whip together the cream and mascarpone until soft peaks form, then carefully fold in the chestnut jam using a silicone spatula, only partially incorporating the jam into the whipped cream to create a "marbled" effect.

On a serving platter or individual plates, arrange the meringues. Cover them with the jam cream and decorate them with the caramelized chestnuts.

In humid weather, keep the meringues in an airtight container until ready to finish and serve the dessert.

Jean Giono

His books smell like olive oil and wild herbs. With Provence in his pen and fork, Jean Giono could combine literature and *terroir* like no one else.

Estelle Lenartowicz

LE PARAÏS: A GREEN OASIS

"A palm tree, a laurel tree, an apricot tree, a kaki tree, vines, a basin as big as a hat, a fountain." That's how the writer described the small estate he bought following the success of his novel *Colline* (1929). It was there, at Lou Paraïs, near Manosque (Alpes-de-Haute-Provence), that he wrote and situated his books. An agricultural Provence, proudly rustic.

GOURMAND PROFILE OF A SON OF THE SOIL

Humble and modest tastes: instead of refined gastronomy, the author of *Le hussard sur le toit* (*The Horseman on the Roof*) preferred simple and hardy dishes, simmering for hours by the fire.

Vegetables from the garden: prepared as soups, salads, and gratins—chickpeas, white beans, lentils, cardoons but also zucchini, eggplants, and stuffed cabbage.

Olive oil: he put it on everything! He liked it fresh, mill pressed and thick, flavored and distinctly green. When he was a child, when he returned from school, his mother would give him slices of bread with olive oil and salt as a snack.

Lamb and game: he wasn't crazy about meat but admitted to having a soft spot for game birds, brochettes of small birds, and marinated quail. In exchange for this guilty pleasure: frequent attacks of gout.

EGGS "À LA GIONO"

One of the specialties of the house. The eggs—from the chicken coop, of course—were served soft boiled, opened on the plate, topped with a bit of coarse salt, crushed pepper, abundantly sprinkled with oil, and served with bread cut into strips.

Terroir writer
(1895–1970)

Very Homemade Vinaigrette

At the Giono house, all salads were sprinkled with olive oil vinaigrette, made following the delicious "rule of four people":

a **miser** for the vinegar

a **sage** for the salt and pepper

a **prodigal** for the oil

and a **madman** for the tossing!

MAMA'S KITCHEN

Giono inherited his taste for good things first from his mother, Pauline, who was from Picardy. He loved to place his lips "on her vanilla cheeks" and remembers the compliments that his friend, the American poet T. S. Eliot, paid to his mother upon trying the pudding she had made them: "The best I have ever had!" the Nobel Prize laureate in literature is said to have exclaimed.

STUFFED CABBAGE

This is one of Jean Giono's favorite dishes, one of those that make you love the cold of winter or gray days.

COOKING TIME: 2 HOURS
SERVES 8

1 large cabbage
3 tablespoons (45 mL) olive oil, plus more for drizzling
7 ounces (200 g) sausage meat or cooked ham
7 ounces (200 g) lightly salted pork belly, diced
1 onion, peeled and finely chopped
Salt and freshly ground black pepper
A few sprigs thyme
1 bay leaf
4 juniper berries
2 or 3 carrots, peeled and chopped
1 stalk celery, chopped
3 cloves garlic, crushed
Scant ½ cup (100 mL) tomato sauce
A few sprigs parsley
2 cups (500 mL) broth, or 1 bouillon cube

Remove the cabbage leaves to reveal the cabbage heart. Discard the large outer leaves, and cut out the ribs from the remaining ones. Chop the heart. Blanch the leaves for 10 minutes in salted water, then place them on a dish towel to drain well.

Meanwhile, prepare the stuffing. In a skillet, warm the 3 tablespoons oil and sauté the sausage meat with half the pork belly, the onion, and the chopped cabbage heart. Season lightly with salt (the stuffing is already salted with the pork belly) and pepper. Add some thyme leaves, crumbled bay leaf, and 2 crushed juniper berries. Spoon this mixture into the center of each of the blanched cabbage leaves, and fold them to form small packages, tying them closed with a piece of kitchen twine.

In an earthenware tian dish or baking dish, pour in a drizzle of olive oil. Add the remaining diced pork belly, the carrots, celery, and garlic. Arrange the stuffed cabbage packages on top. Add the tomato sauce, the 2 remaining juniper berries, and a little chopped parsley. Moisten halfway up with the broth. Cook for about 2 hours at 425°F (220°C), or until the cabbage leaves are lightly browned on top.

Recipe source: La Provence gourmande de Jean Giono, *by Sylvie Giono, Éditions Belin, p. 192.*

Let's Make a Flan

With its crispy crust, thick layer of vanilla cream, golden top, and rich milky flavor, this French pastry offers myriad experiences and a reminder of childhood.

Delphine Le Feuvre

ITS ORIGINS

The British invented the custard tart in the Middle Ages. In France, it wasn't until the reign of Henry IV of England and his coronation in 1399 that the "doucettys," the ancestor of the *tarte au flan* (flan tart) would enter into the language. The flan tart is to French cuisine what *pastel de nata* (an egg tart pastry) is to Portuguese cuisine. In Hong Kong, the variant of the flan is called "dàn tà," or "egg tart."

RULES TO FOLLOW

The crust: use a pâte brisée (flaky pastry dough) without a chemical leavener (baking soda or baking powder) for more flakiness. It should not be rolled out too thinly, otherwise the cream filling may soak through it. Some chefs prebake the dough, while others bake the dough and the flan filling at the same time.

The filling: few ingredients are needed, so choose ones of high quality: farm-fresh eggs, whole and fresh milk, possibly a mixture of milk and cream (35 percent fat), cornstarch, and a vanilla bean.

The cooking: slow, and at medium temperature (around 325°F/170°C), which will give the creamy filling a nice texture and allow the formation of a nice browned bottom crust without burning the filling.

The setting: leave the flan to cool for several hours, or even overnight, for the filling to set. Before slicing it, the tart should be brought to room temperature to make slicing easier!

THE FLAN LEXICON

En faire tout un flan ("to make a whole flan"): an expression for when someone embellishes a story.
C'est du flan ("it's a flan"): this expression refers to the piece of metal from which coins are made, in reference to counterfeit money.
En rester comme deux fonds de flans ("to remain like two rounds of flan"): in reference also to the metal from which coins are made; to be frozen in a state of amazement. The "two rounds of flan" represent amazed eyes.
À la flan ("like a flan"): something badly done, or in a hurry.

THE FLAN
by Philippe Conticini

PREPARATION TIME: 20 MINUTES
RESTING TIME: 1 HOUR
COOKING TIME: 30 MINUTES
SERVES 6

2 vanilla beans
⅔ cup (165 g) + 3 tablespoons plus 1 teaspoon (50 g) low-fat milk (second portion is optional)
¾ cup (165 g) water
1 large (19 g) egg yolk
1 large (50 g) egg
¼ cup (50 g) superfine sugar
2 tablespoons plus 2 teaspoons (25 g) cornstarch
1 sheet (7 oz/200 g) all-butter puff pastry

The custard filling

Split the vanilla beans in half lengthwise and scrape out and reserve their seeds. In a saucepan, bring the ⅔ cup (165 g) of milk, the water, and the empty vanilla bean pods and seeds to a boil. In a bowl, whisk together the egg yolk, egg, and sugar, then whisk in the cornstarch. Remove the empty vanilla bean pods from the saucepan, and pour one-third of the hot liquid over the egg-sugar mixture while whisking vigorously. Pour the mixture back into the saucepan. Cook for 1 minute while whisking vigorously, until thickened. (If you want a fluffier custard, add the 3 tablespoons plus 1 teaspoon (50 g) of low-fat milk while blending the filling in a blender.)

Assembly and cooking

Grease a flan ring measuring 5½ inches (14 cm) in diameter and 1⅓ inches (3.5 cm) high. Cut out a circle from the puff pastry sheet measuring 9½ inches (24 cm) in diameter. Set the flan ring on a parchment paper–lined baking sheet, then line the ring with the dough. Scrape the filling into the ring up to three-fourths from the top of the ring. Place the flan in the freezer for 1 hour. Preheat the oven to 320°F (160°C), and bake the flan for about 30 minutes, or until nice and golden on top.

Variations

La Flognarde: a specialty found in Limousin, Périgord, and Auvergne; a fruity dessert often cooked with apples or plums added to the filling.
Clafoutis: a traditional Limousin recipe, usually made of cherries covered with a custard filling.
Le fion vendéen: a kind of very thick flan, cooked in a high mold typically made of porcelain. Its crust is cooked in boiling water and filled with an egg custard, called *fiounée*.
Far aux pruneaux (Far Breton with prunes) or Far Breton: originally prepared with grapes and apples.
Flan au caramel (flan with caramel): an egg custard cooked in a bain-marie, topped with caramel.
Le flan coco (coconut flan): a recipe from the West Indies made with condensed milk and coconut, which separate into two layers when cooked.

skip to ....
The (Thierry) Far Breton Cake, p. 32

The Poularde

The term *poularde* in French refers to a young chicken that has been castrated and fattened. Here are our three festive ways to prepare this cousin of the capon.

Denise Solier-Gaudry

STUFFED POULARDE

PREPARATION TIME: 45 MINUTES
COOKING TIME: 1 HOUR 30 MINUTES
SERVES 6

1 poularde chicken weighing between 3½ to 4 pounds (1.6 to 1.8 kg)
5 tablespoons (80 g) unsalted butter, softened
3 tablespoons (45 mL) sunflower oil
Scant ¼ cup (50 mL) water
Salt
⅓ cup (100 mL) Madeira or Port
1 cup (250 mL) crème fraîche

Preheat the oven to 400°F (200°C). Stuff the cavity of the chicken with one of three stuffings (recipes follow) of your choice. Using a trussing needle and kitchen twine, carefully close the cavity tightly shut. In a bowl, combine the butter and oil. Using a brush, brush the chicken generously with this mixture. Pour the remaining butter-oil mixture into a baking dish, add the water, and place the chicken in the dish. Season with salt, and bake for about 1 hour and 30 minutes, frequently basting the chicken with the cooking juices. The

chicken is cooked when the juices run clear when it is pierced with a fork.

Remove the chicken from the dish, wrap it in several layers of foil, and let it rest for 15 minutes in the oven with the oven turned off. Meanwhile, deglaze the baking dish with the Madeira, then pour the juice into a saucepan. Add the crème fraîche, and reduce the sauce over medium heat for 5 minutes. Adjust the seasoning, as needed.

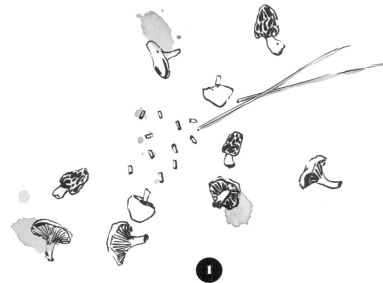

① MUSHROOM STUFFING

10 chives
4 slices bread
⅓ cup (100 mL) milk
10½ ounces (300 g) veal shoulder
1 slice pork belly
14 ounces (400 g) wild mushrooms (morels, chanterelles, horn of plenty, St. George's mushrooms, etc.)
2 tablespoons (30 mL) oil
1 large (50 g) egg
1 large (19 g) egg yolk
Salt and freshly ground black pepper

Wash and chop the chives. Crumble the bread, soak it in the milk, then squeeze it to wring out the milk. Chop the veal and the pork belly together with the soaked bread. Cook the mushrooms in a skillet with the oil until their moisture has evaporated, about 15 minutes. Transfer the mushrooms to a cutting board and roughly chop them. Combine the chopped meat, mushrooms, egg, egg yolk, and chives. Season with salt and pepper.

② CHESTNUT STUFFING

10½ ounces (300 g) chestnuts (from a jar)
4 slices bread
⅓ cup (100 mL) milk
3 shallots
2 tablespoons (30 mL) oil
5 sprigs parsley
1 clove garlic
10½ ounces (300 g) pork rib meat
Salt and freshly ground black pepper
1 large (50 g) egg

Roughly chop the chestnuts. Crumble the bread and soak it in the milk; squeeze it to wring it out, and set it aside. Peel the shallots, slice them, and cook them in a skillet with the oil over low heat for 10 minutes. Wash the parsley and pick the leaves from the stems. Peel the garlic and chop it together with the parsley leaves. Chop the pork meat with the cooked shallots and the drained bread. Season with salt and pepper. Add all the contents to a large bowl, then add the egg, and stir to thoroughly combine.

skip to ....
The Truffle, p.276

③ TRUFFLE AND FOIE GRAS STUFFING

4 sprigs tarragon
8 cups (2 L) chicken broth (from bouillon cubes)
Salt
½ cup (90 g) long-grain rice
10½ ounces (300 g) raw foie gras
1 (¾-oz/20 g) truffle
1 large (50 g) egg
Freshly ground black pepper
Freshly grated nutmeg

Wash and chop the tarragon. Bring the broth to a boil, season with salt, add the rice, and cook for 12 minutes; drain. Cut the foie gras into small cubes. Briefly brush the truffle under running water to clean it, peel it, and slice it into thin slices, then cut it into sticks. In a bowl, combine the rice, foie gras, truffle, tarragon, and egg. Season with pepper and grated nutmeg.

The Alluring Snail!

Preparing this gastropod, a well-known symbol of French gastronomy, requires a little savoir-faire before it lands on your plate.

Marie-Amal Bizalion

ACCORDING TO FASHION

The Burgundy snail was already the preferred snail of ancient Rome and was prepared fattened with milk or bran. In the Middle Ages, the snail replaced meat during Lent. In 1538, cooked snail was very popular in the court via Henry II who loved it, then it suddenly disappeared from mention in culinary writings. "How can we love this disgusting reptile?" cried Cadet de Gassicourt.* In the middle of the nineteenth century, the craze for enjoying snail returned, according to Peter Lund Simmonds:** "Currently, fifty restaurants in Paris serve snails, which are considered a nectar." Today, France consumes 16,000 metric tons per year—the world record.

Cours gastronomique, 1809, p. 205
***The Curiosities of Food*, 1859

Good to Know

To escape the heat, snails disappear into the soil, which gives them an earthy flavor. **In France, it is forbidden to collect them from April 1 to June 30.** It is best to wait until autumn.

A CULINARY TREASURE

Snails are rich in omega-3, high in protein, and low in fat and calories . . .

AN INSIDER'S LANGUAGE

★ ★ ★

A heliculturist is a person who breeds snails. He or she practices heliculture on a **helicultural** farm to raise **Helicidae (snails)**.

Despite some 400 French heliculturists, 95 percent of France's "Burgundy" variety of snails are wild specimens collected in **Poland** or **Hungary**. But it's best to seek out those raised in France, where it can be assured they are always well fed.

THE RECIPE
by *Philippe Héritier**

In spite of the enduring custom, it is useless to make snails suffer by rolling them alive in salt.

PREPARATION TIME: 30 MINUTES
COOKING TIME: 2 HOURS
SERVES 4

48 live large gray (gros-gris) snails
4 cups (1 L) water
1¼ cups (300 mL) white vinegar
1⅓ cups (400 g) salt
For the broth
2 stalks celery, diced
1 onion, peeled and diced
1 fennel bulb, diced
1 leek, cleaned and finely chopped
1 bouquet garni (rosemary, thyme, bay leaf, or other herbs of your choice)
A few sprigs parsley

Blanch the snails for 6 minutes in boiling water. Drain them, then pull them from their shells using a small pick. Using your fingers, separate the firm flesh from the soft black portion (discard this black portion). In a saucepan, stir together the water, vinegar, and salt. Add the snails, bring them to a boil, then lower the heat.

Let simmer for 15 minutes while regularly skimming off any foam that forms on the surface. Drain, transfer the snails to a saucepan of cold water, and add the vegetables and the bouquet garni. Bring to a boil, then lower the heat and simmer for 1 hour and 30 minutes. Skim off any foam that forms on the surface, if necessary. Drain (the cooking liquid can be reserved, reduced, and used as a sauce, if desired).

His snails, raised in the open, are the joy of many Michelin-star chefs such as Jean Sulpice (Maison du père Bise, Talloires) and Laurent Petit (Clos des Sens, Annecy-le-Vieux). Domaine des Orchis, Poisy (Haute-Savoie), 04 50 46 46 06.

THE DIFFERENT VARIETIES

Gros-gris ("large gray")
(Helix aspersa maxima)
Maximum size and weight: 1¾ inches (45 mm), weighing 1 ounce (30 g). It differs from the *petit-gris* ("little gray") by its size and its black margin. Breeders favor it for its ideal size. To prepare them in a delicious way: cook them in broth, then cook them for 20 minutes with a small dice (a *brunoise*) of carrot, celery, and shallot. Add reduced veal stock, and simmer for 30 minutes with garlic and a bouquet garni. Serve with homemade mashed potatoes with roasted hazelnuts.

Petit-gris ("little gray")
(Cornu aspersum)
Maximum size and weight: 1⅓ inches (35 mm), weighing ½ ounce (15 g). A mustard-colored shell with alternating dark stripes, a flared opening, a white margin, and gray body. Common except in the southeast. Nicknamed *cagouille* in Charente, where it's a specialty: sauté 100 living *cagouille* for 3 minutes in hot oil. Add 5¼ ounces (150 g) diced ham, the same quantity of veal forcemeat, 2 onions, a few garlic cloves, parsley, and salt and pepper. Add a few splashes of white wine, and cook for 30 minutes over low heat (test for doneness).

Bourgogne ("Burgundy")
(Helix pomatia)
Maximum size and weight: 2.1 inches (55 mm), weighing 1½ ounces (45 g). Not found in Brittany or Corsica. Light beige to tawny-colored shell, with a cream body. Farming them is rare (if not impossible, as they survive only in the wild). Given its size, you should calculate 2 hours for cooking. This is the snail that is often prepared placed back in its shell with a filling stuffed into the opening with a small pat of garlic butter, then baked at high heat. The stuffing recipe: 10 cloves garlic, 1 shallot, ½ bunch flat-leaf parsley, salt, and pepper. Briefly combine all the ingredients into a coarse mixture, then combine the mixture with 14 tablespoons (200 g) of softened butter.

Limaçon (*Xeropicta derbentina*)
Maximum size and weight: ⅓ inch (10 mm), weighing ⅛ ounce (5 g). The white limaçon colonizes the dry regions of Provence. After 2 days of fasting the snails, place them in a pot of cold water. When they come out of their shells, turn the heat under the pot to low, without stirring: the snail will swell and will not be able to retract back into its shell. Increase the heat to high, and add dried fennel, salt, pepper, bay leaves, thyme, orange peel, and chile pepper. Let simmer for 1 hour, skimming off any foam that forms on the surface. Extract the snails from their shells using a small pick, and enjoy them with *pastaga* (pastis).

3 good breeders

L'Escargotière, Catherine Souvestre. Cooked and frozen petit-gris and gros-gris in jars. Entrammes (Mayenne), 02 43 67 12 29.

Chapeau l'escargot, Steve Troley. Organic certified petit-gris and gros-gris, including a famous terrine with wild garlic (in spring). Tonquedec (Côtes-d'Armor), 06 11 55 53 89.

Escargots Jocelyn Poudevigne. Petit-gris and gros-gris, live or cooked. The frozen snails prepared Burgundy-style are excellent. Mollégès (Bouches-du-Rhône), 04 90 95 41 88.

At the Dairy

Supreme temptation: fromages frais (fresh cheeses) and other dairy specialties are synonymous with France. Whether made from cow's, goat's, or sheep's milk, and whether sweet or savory, these specialty cheeses require a spoon to enjoy them . . .

Véronique Richez-Lerouge

"I myself preferred soft cheese that was pink, the kind in which I was allowed to crush strawberries."
À la recherche du temps perdu
(*In Search of Lost Time*), Marcel Proust

LEXICON

Petit-Suisse (little Swiss cheese)

And yet, it's from Normandy!
Invented around 1850 by Madame Héroult, a farmer in the hamlet of Auchy-en-Bray in the Oise who had a Swiss cowherd working for her. As was custom in Switzerland, he suggested she **add cream** to the fromage frais, which she prepared with rennet and without salt.
The result was a very soft cheese, presented like a small Neufchâtel in a mold, **wrapped in an absorbent paper and sold six at a time**. It was a huge success all the way to Paris. A purveyor in Les Halles, Charles Gervais, partnered with the farmer and developed its production.

Caillebotte cheese
(In French, *caillebotter*, to curdle) This name was give to fromage frais from the region of Aunis. After adding rennet, it was strained in molds or on grating. Smooth, almost opalescent, caillebotte cheese is also called **jonchée vendéenne**.

French yaourt or yoghourt (yogurt)
is **milk fermented** using only thermophilic lactic cultures (*Bulgaricus*, *Lactobacillus*, and *Streptococcus*) in milk. They are live in the finished product, as per the official definition from 1963.

A tour de France of fromage frais

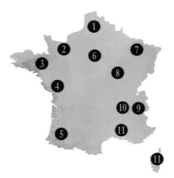

❶ THE NORTH OF FRANCE
In the same region as Maroilles cheese, you'll find **fromage blanc à graisser**, a delicious spread for bread or a gratin. **Fromage blanc ressuyé** is a specialty from the Boulonnais region made by Philippe Olivier, a cheesemaker from Boulogne-sur-Mer. Less common in the area, goat's-milk **Coeur de Chèvre du Pays Boulonnais**, a lovely fromage frais made with the early-spring milk.

❷ NORMANDY
In the Pays de Bray where Neufchâtel cheese and **Petit-Suisse** were invented, there's also **gournay frais (also known as malakoff)**, which is poured into a round, oval, or heart-shaped mold, and served as a dessert with fruit or honey. Less common, the **caudiau** and **coeur de la crème** are enjoyed with crème fleurette and jelly.

❸ BRITTANY
Gros-lait or **Gwell** from the Bretonne Pie Noir (a dairy cattle from Brittany) is a kind of regional yogurt. Made with over thirty different cultures, the cheese is slightly sour and has a smooth texture.

❹ THE VENDÉE AND POITOU
In Nantes, **crémet nantais** is a dessert made with milk curdled with rennet, heated and skimmed with a ladle, then sweetened and poured into a mold and cooled. There's a different version in Angers: the **crémet d'Anjou**, which is made with whipped cream, heavy cream, egg whites beaten to stiff peaks, and poured into a mold and strained. In Poitou-Charentes, the **jonchée niortaise** made from goat's milk dates back to the Middle Ages. It continues to be made today and gets its name from the braided basket rush or rye straw on which the fromage frais is presented. It's made with milk curds that are strained through a traditional cloth called *lirette* in French and flavored with cherry laurel. Molds are long, shaped like a deflated rugby ball. Eaten fresh with fruit liqueur, this sweet and creamy cheese is still made using goat's-milk cheese in Niort. In the region of Aunis, cow's milk is often used; in Île d'Oléron, sheep's milk.

❺ SOUTHWEST FRANCE
In the Gers, everybody knows **Greuilh**, a sheep's-milk Recuite, kneaded by hand, with a drop of Armagnac. In the Pays Basque, they like **gastanberra**, fresh curds with honey, in the Spanish style.

❻ ÎLE-DE-FRANCE
Fontainebleau embodies the sophistication of French dairy specialties. "The famous airy and luscious mousse, its recipe never trademarked, is debated by its makers but not by gourmands," wrote Jean-Paul Géné in the *Magazine du Monde* in 2016. Served in a pot and wrapped in thin muslin cloth, the Fontainebleau is both a cheese and a dessert: 50 percent whipped fromage blanc and 50 percent whipped cream (rarely raw these days) delicately mixed by hand without any sugar.

❼ THE VOSGES
In the land of Munster, the tradition is fromage blanc à la Messine, or **brocotte**, made by cowherds known as *marcaires* in the high pastures of the Vosges. There's also the **bibalakas** (or **bibeleskaes**), the Alsatian relative of cervelle de canut from Lyon, which is a strained fromage blanc with herbs and seasonings, elsewhere known as claqueret. Eaten with baked potatoes and charcuterie, it's simply delicious.

❽ BURGUNDY
Winemakers snack on cone-shaped **claquebitou**, which is a bit like fresh Charolais. Made with partly strained fresh goat curds, it is stored in a pot with pepper, salt, parsley, and mixed herbs. In Bresse, at the Varennes Saint-Sauveur creamery, they still make fromage blanc à la faisselle, which is ladled into molds and is known as La Bressane, according to the original recipe. It's eaten covered in cream.

❾ SAVOIE
In the region of Reblochon cheese, near Thônes and Somoëns, **tomme blanche** is made with cow or milk whey. There's also **sérac**, a French-Swiss cheese made from whey extracted while making *chevrotin* goat's-milk cheese or cow's-milk cheeses. It's poured into square or rectangular wood molds. Once strained, it is removed and chimney smoked. Very fresh and sweet with a note of goat, there's a savory version (salt and pepper) that goes with potatoes, and there's a sweet version served with honey or jam.

❿ RHONE VALLEY
In Ardèche, one will find goat's- or cow's-milk **sarasson**, a cheese made from buttermilk that's similar to blanc battu cheese. Traditionally, this cheese is served plain or seasoned with fresh herbs.

⑩ PROVENCE AND CORSICA
This is brousse country (in French, *brousser* means "to whip, beat"). The **brousse du Rove**, coveted by the finest restaurants in Marseille, and the **brousse de Vésubie** are entirely fresh, with subtle sweet notes. They are sprinkled with orange flower water or made savory with pesto, salt, pepper, and a drop of eau-de-vie. In Corsica, brousse is called locally by the name **brocciu AOP**, which is made with Corsican sheep's-milk whey.

CRÈME FRAÎCHE: A DESSERT'S PERFECT PARTNER

Made from a mix of casein and whey, which float to the surface of milk when left to rest, raw cream comes from separating milk and cream. It's liquid and contains 30 to 40 percent fat. If you're lucky enough to find fresh raw milk, you'll notice that cream separates after two or three days sitting in the refrigerator.

A French specialty, the cream called *fraîche* ("fresh") is fermented slightly using lactic cultures, and, once aged, is thick and slightly sour. If you continue the fermentation process, you'll get what's known as *sour cream*. The more the cream is pasteurized, the more cultures you'll need. Depending on the laws in effect, it's not necessary to indicate on labels whether or not the milk has been pasteurized.

Different forms are available in France: *crème fraîche épaisse* (thick) sold in packages or at a creamery; *crème liquide, semi-liquide,* and *crème fleurette,* all with different fat contents and consistencies.

Crème d'Isigny AOP

is a thick and pasteurized crème fraîche produced exclusively using milk from Bessin and the Cotentin Peninsula. Smooth and rich, it is ripened for sixteen to eighteen hours, as is traditional.

Crème de Bresse AOP

Is a thick or semithick crème fraîche, produced in the Ain, the Saône-et-Loire, and on the edges of the Jura. It is distinguished by a fruity and fresh taste with a sweet note.

FROMAGE BLANC

It has different names in French: *caillé frais, fromage à la crème,* Fontainebleau, *fromage à la pie* ("magpie cheese"), *fromage blanc lissé* or *de campagne* (smooth or country fromage blanc), demi-sel (half-salt), Petit-Suisse, Gros Suisse, caillebotte, frais de brebis, yaourt . . . Traditionally, fermentation is solely lactic. When the milk coagulates (partially skimmed), the curds separate from the whey. The curds are drained through cloth or a strainer. In French, *faisselle* (cheese strainer) is also the name of the process. The piled proteins are either placed in a mold or are stirred and made smooth. The product will then be enriched again with cream, depending on preferences.

Tasting note: sweet and thick, slightly sour, a bit like yogurt. It is particularly flavorful and aromatic in spring if the milk comes from pasture-raised animals.

Culinary preparations: as a dessert, with sugar, with crème fraîche like in southern Burgundy, with honey, fruit or dried fruit, or with chopped onions, salt and pepper, fresh herbs, or garlic like in Lyon. An essential ingredient for chefs and bakers, used in countless savory recipes (quiches, omelets, tarts, mousses, gratins) and sweet ones, it is the backbone of French dairy culture.

skip to
Crème Chantilly: Noblesse Oblige, p. 161

FREEMASONS: KNIGHTS OF THE STOMACH

Renowned for its secret cult, this initiatory order founded three hundred years ago champions the spirit of tolerance, but it also has an irrational love of good food.
Hadrien Gonzales

LE BANQUET: A VERY GOURMAND LODGE

In Paris, there's a lodge affiliated with the Grand Orient called Le Banquet that's essentially made up of restaurant professionals. Why a separate lodge? Among freemasons, *tenues* (meetings) generally take place in the evening, during the week, right at dinnertime: chefs, waiters, and sommeliers therefore cannot attend. Le Banquet generally schedules its meetings on Sunday afternoons at a time of rest.

To note: the Grand Orient Museum in Paris has a menu in its collection that was published in 1922 by a lodge appropriately named "Les Enfants de Rabelais" (The Children of Rabelais).

A SURE SIGN

The title of Meilleur Ouvrier de France (Best Craftsman of France) has been a grail for the profession ever since it was established in 1913. The medal awarded to laureates presents King Solomon holding a compass in his hand, a symbol cherished by the Freemasons. Coincidence?

G.I.T.E.: A TOP-SECRET FOOD GUIDE

"Never mention G.I.T.E. on social media like Facebook or Twitter," warns the cover page. Founded in 1947 in France, the Groupement International de Tourisme et d'Entraide every year publishes a mysterious white book that lists, in fifty-two countries, 2,200 businesses owned by "brothers"—including a large number of hotels and restaurants. If one is a Freemason, going to a brother's establishment can entail a special welcome. Paradoxically, some members display the three circles connected in a triangle on their cars or even their shop windows, like a Michelin Guide plaque.

WHEN JOËL ROBUCHON COMES OUT OF THE CLOSET

A Compagnon du Tour de France, a Meilleur Ouvrier de France, and the most starred chef in the world, Joël Robuchon is alone in openly stating that he is a Freemason. Affiliated with the Grande Loge de France, in 2005 he even authored the preface of book with a rather direct title: *La Cuisine des franc-maçons* (Éditions Derwy). What's more, one wonders if there's a meaning behind the name "L'Atelier" for his restaurants (see French lexicon, below).

French Lexicon for Foodie Apprentices

Agapes (feasts): these meals follow every meeting at a lodge. In France, they're also called "table lodges" and "mastications."

Atelier: table

Baril or barrique (barrel or cask): bottle. As it became established in France, Freemasonry incorporated sometimes very old social behaviors. For example, some of its vocabulary is borrowed from archer guilds and musketeers.

Canon: glass (this word is used in everyday French)

Charge (the canon): fill (the glass)

Ciment (cement): pepper. A word that in this case comes from builders.

Dégrossir (trim): to carve

Drapeau (flag): napkin

"Feu" or "grand feu" (fire or great fire): "drink!"

Glaive (broadsword): knife

Maître de banquet (banquet master): every lodge designates a brother who is in charge of supervising the feasts and the annual banquet.

Mastication: act of eating. The French Masonic dictionary reads: "Masonic mastication is particular in that it must be dignified and elegant, with mouth closed."

Matériaux (materials): dishes

Truelle (trowel): spoon

Tuile (tile): plate

Pierre brute (raw stone): bread

Pioche (pickax): fork

Poudre (powder): drink. Wine is "red powder," water is "white powder," coffee is "black powder," liquor is "strong powder" and eau-de-vie is "intense powder."

Sable (sand): salt

Stalle (stall): chair

Tirer une santé (draw health): drink

skip to
The Club des Cent, p. 240

More Noodles!

In September 1984, the magazine *Cuisine et Vins de France* welcomed Pierre Desproges to its masthead. He was the king of scathing humor and acid wit. For over a year, he cooked up culinary chronicles that were as entertaining as they were irreverent. The title of his column (which can be interpreted in more ways than one): *"More noodles!"*

Estelle Lenartowicz

HISTORY OF AN IMPROBABLE CHRONICLE

Nothing in Pierre Desproges's background suggested that he would one day taunt the conventional bourgeois readership of *Cuisine et Vins de France*. "Subscribers were more likely to be doctors or notaries than rabblerousing disturbers of the peace. You'd typically be reading articles on Michelin-starred restaurants, big cigars, grand cru vintages, and luxury sports cars," says Elisabeth de Meurville, the journalist behind this apparent misalliance. At the time, she was associate editor of the monthly publication, working on a series of celebrity interviews: the subjects' point in common was their love of fine food. A friend quietly suggested that she should talk with humorist Pierre Desproges, who had recently been playing a ridiculously omniscient professor in the TV series *La minute nécessaire de Monsieur Cyclopède*. They became acquainted during an intimate dinner party at the home of the famous chef Guy Savoy. The editor was immediately charmed by Desproges's mischievous wit, while he declared his own passion for wine: "My wine cellar is my life. Well, almost. I'm absolutely devoted to it. I go down there to talk with my wines and caress them with my eyes." By the time coffee was served, she forked over a proposition. "How about cooking up an article for us each month?" "No time—too much work," he replied. But the next day, she was back with an offer he couldn't refuse. "If you agree to write this column, I'll pay you cash [*liquide* in French]—your choice: red wine or white!" There was a burst of laughter on the other end of the line . . . The deal was sealed.

PROFILE OF A GLUTTONOUS GOURMET

On cooking: "I started cooking because I needed to perform manual labor," he explains. "I'm a frustrated leftie and dyslectic as well, so I'm not very handy. Faced with my inability to build library shelves or magazine racks, I started to cook. It's not just a second-best fallback activity. Cooking is an artistic creation. Taste and smell are senses that deserve a full measure of respect." Many of the dishes in his repertoire are based on pasta, seasoned with (among other things) a secret "mélange of meat and herbs" that he developed for his personal interpretation of Bolognese sauce.
On wine: by the end of his life, Desproges's wine cellar housed about

a thousand bottles. It was packed with red Bordeaux (especially Graves), great white Burgundies (premiers crus Chablis and Meursaults), Champagnes, and a few wines from the Loire Valley. His favorite was a Saint-Émilion, Figeac 1971, because it was "as deep as a double-bass player, and longer in the mouth than a Verdi finale," with a "tomato red hue [that] had the flamboyance of an Istanbul sunset."

FRUITS AND VEGETABLES ACCORDING TO DESPROGES

Tomatoes: "Androgynous in its essence, neither completely male or female, the tomato is not a fruit as we're told it is, nor a vegetable as they'd like us to believe. The captivating fascination of this heretical taste experience is enmeshed in perplexing ambiguity—flavors of saline acidity and bitter sweetness that explode in the mouth when you take a bite. Tomatoes deserve respect."
Endives: "The distinctive feature of the endive is its tastelessness. Endives are bland to the point of perverse exuberance. The color resembles nothing, its reflections are indescribable in their non-existence. The taste makes me think of an amnesia victim who has forgotten everything—it's bland as well. . . . An endive lover is easily identifiable: his demeanor is unassuming, there is no fire in his eyes, he is mild-mannered and smiles foolishly while waiting in an interminable line at the unemployment office. . . . He tenderly cherishes banality. He'll go to the polls if the weather's good on voting day, dimly persuaded that it serves some useful purpose."
Asparagus: "They are at their best when eaten with scrambled eggs. Asparagus ennoble white sauces, but do not stand up well to the herbaceously vulgar vinaigrettes. Before the regrettable invention of the refrigerator, they were preserved by cauterizing their stalks in a red-hot pan and stored in charcoal powder to keep them fresh."

ENCORE DES NOUILLES !...

C'est avec l'humilité d'un gastronome approximatif doublé d'un buveur anarchique que j'ose aujourd'hui, chers lecteurs de *Cuisine et Vins de France*, ternir d'une plume profane votre éclatante revue chérie. Cela dit, pour être gueusse, on n'en est pas moins bon vivant, en vertu de quoi il m'arrive parfois d'avoir la fibre olfactive en éveil ou les papilles émoustillées devant ces merveilles du génie humain que sont les vins et les mets de par chez nous. Pire : quand l'appétit m'exacerbe les sens et que l'envie m'en prend, j'ose alors carrément mettre la main à la pâte et confectionner quelques plats dont les moins bien intentionnés de mes amis reconnaissent qu'ils ont mangé pire dans le T.G.V., le vendredi saint. A titre d'exemple, et, encore une fois, toute honte bue, mâchée et digérée, qu'il me soit permis de vous soumettre ici l'une de mes recettes, celle qui aurait pu me rendre célèbre au-delà des frontières naturelles du cocon familial, si elle n'avait été à l'origine d'une poussée d'hépatites B chez les plus rancuniers de mes beaux-frères, oncles et cousins du côté de ma femme, laquelle est originaire de la Vendée, contrée probablement sous-développée sur le plan culinaire, au point que tout plat qui s'écarterait des deux modèles de base, « haricots blancs-crème fraîche » ou « canard challandais », y passerait pour inconsidérément exotique. Cette recette, c'est celle de la cigale melba, un plat que j'ai eu l'occasion d'évoquer sur scène ou à la radio, mais dont j'ai toujours jalousement gardé la recette par devers moi jusqu'à ce jour béni d'aujourd'hui où je vous la livre, à vous, lecteurs de *Cuisine et Vins de France*, qui en êtes seuls dignes.

PIERRE DESPROGES

CIGALE MELBA POUR 6 PERSONNES

Comptez une douzaine de cigales (de La Havane, ce sont les meilleures). Enfoncez-les vivantes dans un teckel que vous aurez préalablement muselé pour éviter les morsures. Jetez le teckel dans un fait-tout avec deux litres d'eau salée. Quand l'eau frémit, le teckel aussi. S'il se sauve, faites-le revenir avec un oignon. A l'aide d'une écumoire, chassez le naturel. Attention : s'il revient au galop, ce n'est pas un teckel, c'est un cheval. En fin de cuisson, passez au chinois, ou au nègre si vous n'avez pas de chinois. Servez très vite, ne m'attendez pas.

"It's very important to **eat well**. Personally, **I've never trusted people who don't appreciate the pleasures of the table**. Because you have to acknowledge, and I'm not exaggerating, that **a lack of gastronomic curiosity and a sense of culinary gloom** often go hand in hand . . . **with a nature that's peevish, belligerent, and puritanical**."

Pierre Desproges, *Les réquisitoires du tribunal des flagrants délires*, Points, 2006.

skip to
Sardine Pâté, p. 39

The Paris-Brest

In 2009, while I was chef of the pastry shop Pâtisserie des Rêves in Paris, I decided to revisit this cake, which had fallen into obscurity. Its secret? An irresistible filling of flowing praline. Try it, and you will see . . .
Philippe Conticini

THE FAMOUS RECIPE

PREPARATION TIME: I HOUR 20 MINUTES
RESTING TIME: I HOUR
COOKING TIME: 50 MINUTES
SERVES 6

For the crumble dough
½ cup (50 g) all-purpose flour
¼ cup minus 1 teaspoon (50 g) turbinado sugar
1 pinch fleur de sel sea salt
2 tablespoons plus 2 teaspoons (40 g) unsalted butter, room temperature

For the pâte à choux (cream puff pastry)
½ cup plus 1 teaspoon (125 g) low-fat milk
½ cup plus 2 teaspoons (125 g) water
8 tablespoons (110 g) cold butter, cut into pieces
1½ cups minus 1 tablespoon (140 g) all-purpose flour
1 level teaspoon (6 g) fine salt
1 heaping teaspoon (6 g) superfine sugar
5 large (250 g) eggs plus 1 additional egg, if needed

For the praline cream
½ cup plus 2 tablespoons (155 g) low-fat milk
2 large (37 g) egg yolks
2 tablespoons plus 1¼ teaspoons (30 g) superfine sugar
1 tablespoon plus 2 teaspoons (15 g) cornstarch
1 sheet (3 g) gelatin, soaked in cold water
3 ounces (80 g) hazelnut praline
5 tablespoons (70 g) unsalted butter

Confectioners' sugar, for dusting
For the praline filling
1 jar store-bought hazelnut spread

Make the crumble dough
In the bowl of a stand mixer fitted with the flat beater, combine the flour, turbinado sugar, and sea salt, then beat in the softened butter. Beat at medium speed until the mixture forms a smooth dough. Spread the dough between two sheets of parchment paper to about ⅒ inch (2 mm) thick. Place the dough in the refrigerator. When chilled, cut out eight circles from the dough measuring 1⅛ inches (3 cm) in diameter using a cookie cutter.

Make the pâte à choux
Place the milk, water, and butter in a saucepan and bring it to a boil. Sift together the flour, salt, and sugar, and add this mixture to the saucepan. Stir the dough over medium heat until the dough is dry and detaches from the sides of the pan, then transfer it to the bowl of a stand mixer fitted with the flat beater. Beat in the eggs one at a time. The dough should be soft and shiny. To check its texture, make a deep trail in the dough using your finger; the trail should close very slowly. If not, add an additional lightly beaten egg, a little at a time. Preheat the oven

to 325°F (170°C). Scrape the dough into a piping bag (or use a spoon). Trace a 6-inch (15 cm) circle onto parchment paper and place the paper on a baking sheet. Pipe (or spoon) eight balls measuring 1½ inches (4 cm) in diameter along the border inside the circle. Start by piping the dough onto the four corners (the opposite points: top and bottom, left and right), and finish with the four points across the diagonal; the balls of dough should connect and form a ring. Arrange the eight circles of crumble dough onto the top of the eight balls of piped dough. Bake the ring for 45 minutes, then allow it to cool to room temperature.

Make the praline cream
In a saucepan, bring the milk to a boil, then remove the pan from the heat. In a bowl, whisk together the egg yolks and sugar until lightened, then whisk in the cornstarch until a smooth paste forms. Add half the hot milk to the bowl while whisking, then pour the entire mixture back into the saucepan. Bring the mixture to a boil for 1 minute, while whisking continuously. When the cream has thickened, remove the pan from the heat. Add the softened gelatin (squeezed of its excess water), the hazelnut praline, then the cold butter, and whisk to combine. Transfer the

mixture to a blender, and blend until the cream is perfectly smooth. Pour the cream into a baking dish so that it spreads out and cools faster. Gently press a piece of plastic wrap onto the surface of the cream to cover it, then place the cream in the refrigerator for 1 hour. Once chilled, transfer the cream to the bowl of a stand mixer fitted with the wire whisk, and beat it at medium speed for 3 minutes.

Make the praline filling
Scrape the hazelnut spread into eight small semispherical silicone molds and place them in the freezer.

Assembly
When the ring of pâte à choux is at room temperature, slice it in half horizontally through the center. Using a pastry bag (or a spoon), fill the eight cavities of the ring with the praline cream. Place the frozen half-spheres of hazelnut spread in the center of the mounds of praline cream, and lightly press them down into the cream to secure them. Place the top half of the ring on top, and dust with confectioners' sugar.

skip to
La Famille Pâte à Choux, p. 120

Salt—Crust for Crust!

After a lot of salt, a little dexterity, and some time in the oven, there is nothing left
to do but to break open the crust . . . cooking in salt crust is a culinary thrill!

Alvina Ledru-Johansson

THE CONCEPT

Seal food inside a salt crust to insulate and cook it.
During cooking, the food inside will release moisture,
causing the crust to harden. Tightly sealed, the food
will gradually cook in its own juices. When it's done,
the result is concentrated flavors, soft textures, and the
preservation of nutrients—without any added fat!

THE BASE

For this method, table salt is set aside. To create a
quality salt crust, choose high-quality coarse salt,
such as from Guérande or Noirmoutier. The natural
moisture of these salts makes them more supple for
snugly sealing in the food.

VARIATIONS

Whether using salt only, or salt mixed with flour,
water, or egg whites, do not skimp on the quantity of
dough or crust that you use. The food to be cooked
should be lying on a bed of coarse salt, then covered
entirely. Estimate 4½ to 6½ pounds (2 to 3 kg) of salt.

When using other ingredients with the salt to make
a crust, place all the ingredients together in the bowl
of a stand mixer, on low speed, and beat until a smooth
dough is formed. Adding aromatic herbs to the dough
is another option. Refrigerate the dough for at least
1 hour before using it.

Vegetables

What crust to use? Salt—and only salt! Root
vegetables are very suitable for this type of cooking
method. Their final texture is unmatched, lying
somewhere between crunchy and melting.
What's more, there is no need to peel them.

— BEETROOT —
by Alain Passard*

SERVES 2

1 white beet weighing 1⅛ pounds (500 g)
4½ pounds (2 kg) coarse salt from Guérande

Bury a washed and unpeeled beet in the salt. Bake
for 1 hour at 325°F (160°C), then let it rest for
30 minutes. Enjoy the warm beet cut into quarters,
served with a demi-sel butter or a dash of
olive oil and a few drops of vinegar.

*Chef at restaurant L'Arpège in Paris, three Michelin stars

Fish

What crust to use? A dough made of salt, flour, and
water. When using a salt-crust dough to cook the fish,
there is no need to scale the fish! The skin will peel off
very easily once cooked. The flesh of the fish will have
an amazing moistness.

— GILT-HEAD SEA BREAM —
by Gaël Orieux*

SERVES 4

For the olive oil ice cubes
⅓ cup (100 mL) fruity olive oil
For the fish
1 gilt-head sea bream
weighing 3½ pounds (1.6 kg),
cleaned and gutted
3½ ounces (100 g) seaweed
1 large (50 g) egg, lightly
beaten
1 tablespoon (15 mL) olive oil
1 large (19 g) egg yolk
For the salt dough
1⅛ pounds (500 g) coarse
gray salt
¾ cup (250 g) fine sea salt
7½ cups (750 g) all-purpose
flour
1½ cups (375 mL) water

The day before, prepare
the olive oil ice cubes.
Divide the oil among
the cavities of an ice tray
and place the tray in the
freezer. The next day,

stuff the cavity of the
fish with the seaweed.
Prepare the salt dough by
mixing all the ingredients
together in the bowl of
a stand mixer. Brush
the fish with the lightly
beaten egg then enclose
it between two layers of
the salt dough. Drizzle
the dough with the oil.
Press to completely seal
the two layers of dough
together. Trim the dough
into the shape of the fish.
Brush the dough with the
egg yolk combined with
a little cold water. Bake
for about 40 minutes at
350°F (180°C). When
serving, place the olive oil
ice cubes directly on the
flesh of the cooked fish.

**Chef of restaurant Auguste
(Paris 7th)*

Beef

What crust to use? A dough made
of salt, egg whites, flour, and water.
The meat displays an ideal
tenderness and juiciness.

— ROAST BEEF —
by Joël Robuchon

SERVES 6

2¼ pounds (1 kg) beef tenderloin
1 tablespoon (15 g) butter
1 tablespoon (15 mL) olive oil
1 sprig thyme
Freshly ground black pepper
2 large (37 g) egg yolks
For the salt dough
1¾ cups (500 g) coarse salt
1 bunch thyme
A few sprigs rosemary
2 large (60 g) egg whites
4 cups (400 g) all-purpose flour

Remove the meat from the refrigerator
2 hours before using it. Prepare the salt
dough by mixing all the ingredients
together in the bowl of a stand mixer.
Brown the beef tenderloin on all sides
in a skillet in the butter and olive oil.
Season it with the thyme and some black
pepper. Encase the tenderloin in the
dough, tightly seal the edges, and brush
the dough with the egg yolks combined
with a little water. Bake for 12 minutes
at 375°F (190°C) for rare. Let stand
20 minutes before serving.

Poultry

What crust to use? A dough made of salt, egg whites,
and flour. After cooking in a salt crust, poultry becomes
more tender. The juice in the flesh remains locked in,
preventing the meat from drying out.

— CAPON —
by Eric Guérin*

SERVES 4

1 capon chicken
For the salt dough
13¼ ounces (375 g) coarse salt
from Guérande
5 cups (500 g) all-purpose flour
6 large (180 g) egg whites
For the watercress
5 large Bintje potatoes
3 bunches watercress
2 tablespoons (30 mL) Dijon
mustard
For the apple-cider broth
4 cups (1 L) chicken broth
2 cups (500 mL) raw apple cider
10 bay leaves
3 tablespoons (50 g) demi-sel butter
Salt and freshly ground black pepper

Prepare the salt dough by
mixing all the ingredients
together in the bowl of a
stand mixer. Bake the capon
wrapped in the salt dough
at 350°F (180°C) for 2 hours
and 30 minutes. Let rest for
30 minutes before breaking

open the dough. Peel and
cook the potatoes and
combine with 2 bunches of
the watercress. Incorporate
the mustard, and set aside
to cool. Heat the broth over
low heat with the cider and
2 of the bay leaves. Add the
remaining bay leaves, and let
steep for 10 minutes. Strain,
and blend with the butter
until smooth. Season with
salt and pepper.

To serve, break open
the salt crust, brush the
capon with the watercress-
mustard sauce, and chop the
remaining watercress and
sprinkle it over the capon.
Serve.

**Chef of La Mare aux oiseaux in
Saint-Joachim (Loire-Atlantique)*

skip to ....
The Truffle, p. 276

Gaston Lenôtre

He's one the greatest names in French pâtisserie. The spirit of this master, who died in 2009, is still alive in the company he founded and nurtured: Lenôtre.
Gilbert Pytel

HAUTE COUTURE PÂTISSERIE

Gaston Lenôtre laid the foundation for modern-day pâtisserie: creative entremets (desserts) that are lighter and made with less sugar. Some have become classics. He focused on high-quality and simple starting ingredients, but neglected neither aesthetics, nor packaging, nor how his customers were welcomed.

Key Dates

1947: first shop opens in Pont-Audemer, near Deauville
1957: first shop opens in Paris, 44, rue d'Auteuil
1998: official food supplier of the FIFA World Cup
2000: Olivier Poussier, the Lenôtre head sommelier, is named "the best sommelier in the world"
2003: Lenôtre takes the helm of the Pavillon Élysée on the Champs-Élysées

Genius of sweets
(1920–2009)

His signature dishes

Feuille d'Automne (Autumn Leaf): a bestseller. Both French meringue and Succès almond meringue with creamy dark chocolate mousse, topped with chocolate curls.
La Bagatelle: Lenôtre's strawberry cake since 1966. Génoise sponge with almonds, vanilla-bourbon mousseline, a mix of two almond pastes, and fresh strawberries.
Summer Fruit Schuss: created in 1968 for the Grenoble Olympic Games: raspberry sablé, fromage blanc mousse, and whipped cream with fruit.

THE EMPIRE

→ Lenôtre owns **fifteen shops in France** (thirteen in Paris and two on the Côte d'Azur) and runs a **twenty-two store franchise in eight countries** (Germany, Spain, Thailand, Saudi Arabia, Kuwait, Morocco, Qatar, and China).
→ In 1968, he founds a 130,000-square-foot (12,000m²) **food facility** in Plaisir (Yvelines).
→ Lenôtre opens a **professional school** that trains more than three thousand interns annually. Forty percent come from abroad.
→ In 1976, Lenôtre takes over **Le Pré Catelan**, where chef Frédéric Anton is awarded three Michelin stars in 2007.

THE PRALINE SUCCÈS OF MAISON LENÔTRE

PREPARATION TIME: 15 MINUTES
RESTING TIME: 1 HOUR
COOKING TIME: 1 HOUR 20 MINUTES
ASSEMBLY TIME: 20 MINUTES
SERVES 8

For the 2 (8-in/20 cm) Succès circles
Batter 1:
5 large (150 g) egg whites
1 tablespoon plus 1¾ teaspoons (20 g) superfine sugar
Batter 2:
¾ cup plus 1 tablespoon plus 1¾ teaspoons (170 g) superfine sugar
¼ cup plus 3 tablespoons plus ½ teaspoon (90 g) confectioners' sugar
¾ cup plus 1 tablespoon (90 g) almond flour
3 tablespoons plus 1 teaspoon (50 mL) milk
2 teaspoons (4 g) confectioners' sugar, for finishing
For the Italian meringue
1 tablespoon plus 1 teaspoon (20 mL) water
¼ cup plus 3 tablespoons plus ½ teaspoon (90 g) superfine sugar
4½ (140 g) egg whites
For the buttercream
⅓ cup plus 2 teaspoons (90 g) whole milk
¼ cup (50 g) superfine sugar
4 large (70 g) egg yolks
18 tablespoons (250 g) unsalted butter, softened

For the decoration
1 cup (100 g) confectioners' sugar
1¾ ounces (50 g) crushed nougatine

Make the Succès circles
(These will keep for up to 15 days in an airtight container.)
Batter 1: Beat the egg whites until stiff peaks form, sprinkling in the sugar halfway through the beating time. Preheat the oven to 300°F (150°C).
Batter 2: In a bowl, combine the superfine and confectioners' sugars, almond flour, and milk. Add a small amount of batter 1 into batter 2, and stir to combine, then add the entire mixture into batter 1. Quickly combine using a spatula, being sure not to overstir and break the mixture. Grease and flour two cold baking sheets or, preferably, line the baking sheets with parchment paper, using a dab of batter placed in the four corners of the pans to adhere the paper to the pans. Draw two circles, each measuring 8 inches (20 cm) in diameter. Pipe a spiral into each circle using a pastry bag fitted with a plain pastry tube measuring ¾ inch (2 cm) in diameter. Sprinkle each piped spiral with 1 teaspoon

(2 g) of the confectioners' sugar. Bake the circles for 1 hour and 20 minutes. Watch them carefully so they do not brown too quickly. Lower the temperature of the oven, if necessary, if they begin to brown too quickly; they should be pale golden when done.
Make the Italian meringue
In a saucepan, heat the water with ¼ cup plus 1 tablespoon plus 1¾ teaspoons (70 g) of the sugar to 244°F (118°C). Beat the egg whites with the remaining sugar. Pour the hot syrup over the beaten egg whites with the mixer running and continue to beat until the egg whites have cooled.
Make the buttercream
In a saucepan, bring the milk and half the sugar to a boil. Whisk the egg yolks with the remaining sugar. Pour the hot milk over the egg yolks while whisking continuously, then pour the entire mixture back into the saucepan, and cook over low heat until thickened; do not let it boil. The custard is ready when it coats the back of a spoon. Transfer the custard to a stand mixer and beat it until it is lukewarm (86°F/30°C). Beat in the butter, then beat in the Italian meringue. Set aside 2 tablespoons of the buttercream for assembly, and add the crushed nougatine to the remaining buttercream; set aside. If prepared in

advance, remove the buttercream from the refrigerator 1 hour before using it.
Assembly
Choose the Succès circle with the more irregular shape to use as the base, and spread 1⅓ pounds (600 g) of the buttercream on top. Place the second circle on top, and press it down lightly. Coat the sides with the buttercream. Cover the top of the cake with the reserved buttercream using a spatula and dust the top with the confectioners' sugar. Refrigerate the cake for 1 hour. Place the cake on a turntable, and coat the sides with the crushed nougatine. Serve chilled.
Storage
The cake will stay moist stored 3 to 4 days in the refrigerator.

skip to
France's Little Pralines, p. 14; Cakes of Yesteryear Rise Once Again, p. 52

Camembert Packages That Tell the History of France

It's often said that a picture is worth a thousand words. This is certainly the lesson taught by Camembert packaging. A French icon since 1888, the cheese has been marketed in boxes that recount French history in living color—and aroma.

Véronique Richez-Lerouge

— VERCINGETORIX —

With his signature horned helmet, Vercingetorix remains a powerful national symbol. The folkloric image of the ancient Gaul with his blond braids has an enduring appeal. Top: a label designed in the 1930s; below: a label from the 1970s.

— CHARLES MARTEL —

Charles Martel, standing strong in the face of the onslaught of an army of gourmands. Label dating from the early 1950s.

— SAINT LOUIS —

Seated beneath his oak tree, the beloved monarch Saint Louis renders justice in the sacred name of Camembert. 1920.

— JOAN OF ARC —

Voices are raised in praise of a Camembert produced in the Ardennes. This rare label celebrates the traditional values of pastoralism. Snackers could munch their cheese while contemplating Joan of Arc amid her cows and sheep. Ca. 1915.

— FRANCIS I —

From a Camembert destined for export in the 1920s: Francis I, the Renaissance monarch who embraced the good things in life.

— 1515 —

The Battle of Marignano. The French knight Chevalier Bayard "without fear and beyond reproach" is mounted on his horse, vaunting the merits of the cheese that lies within. Ca. 1935.

— HENRY VIII AND FRANCIS I —

This scene of the Field of the Cloth of Gold commemorates the meeting between two Renaissance monarchs. Late 1940s.

— RICHELIEU —

The Cardinal de Richelieu and his valiant, heroic, and impulsive musketeers. A producer of Camembert and Pont-l'Evêque asked his printer for "a label that jabs" (and grabs attention), so the printer gave him d'Artagnan. From top to bottom, labels dating from the 1920s, with the last from the 1940s.

— LOUIX XIV —

The drawing shows Louis XIV, an aficionado of good food and Burgundy wine, shedding light on a prosperous nation basking in abundance. A factory appears in the verdant countryside in the distance. 1930s, for a Camembert packaged for the export market.

— 1789 —

Revolution and counterrevolution. Camembert magnanimously aimed to please the conservative Catholic audience in western France just as much as the more urban republican regions in the north and east. Top: Mirabeau's medallion portrait, 1950s; below: Danton in a gilded frame, 1930s.

NAPOLÉON

Camembert pays him homage, appealing to a French clientele, or maybe even an English audience, unfazed by defeat. Top: Napoléon posed as conqueror against the backdrop of a battlefield. 1920s. Below: Napoléon's son, known as "L'Aiglon" ("The Eaglet"), alone with his Camembert. Label designed in the 1930s in celebration of the First Empire.

MARIANNE

All praise to Marianne, the feminine embodiment of the Republic, honored from the time of the Second Empire. A symbol of the nation, her image proliferated on labels beginning around 1900. The appellation "Camembert of the Republic" was copyrighted in 1904. Here we see "Marianne of Picardie." The producers were trying to appeal to an urban audience, particularly a Parisian one, with more progressive—and republican—ideas. Late 1930s.

THE SOWER

A republican symbol created during the Second Empire, the sower was intended to woo a Parisian clientele and disseminate the tidings of her Camembert to a broad audience. Late 1940s, designed by a producer from Picardy.

THE REPUBLIC

A label commemorating the founders of the Republic. 1960s.

BASTILLE DAY

A label honoring the French national holiday on July 14. 1960.

THE GREAT WAR

World War I, which raged from 1914 to 1918, roused sentiments of patriotic fervor. The visibility of the war on Camembert labels corresponded to the growing national popularity of this cheese over the same period. Included in the daily rations distributed to soldiers, millions of these cheeses were produced in the northern half of France.

The Camembert des Françaises honors the women who were recruited to support the home front during the First World War.

The Camembert of the Allies: French, Italian, Russian, and British. 1915.

Le Camembert des Poilus was a call to patriotism, uniting every French household with their heroes in the trenches. 1915.

La Victoire, a feminine allegory of France brandishing a crown of laurel in one hand and a tricolor banner in the other. All the symbols of a victorious France are combined in a depiction with quasi-religious overtones: this is a rendering of "France, Queen of the World."

1940–1945

World War II inspired numerous labels that captured the grim reality of the current situation: militias, ration tickets, GIs . . . Camembert, made everywhere in France, was also tightening its belt in the war effort.

This standard bearer presents a high-fat, wholesome Camembert. Ca. 1942.

Made in the Meuse valley, a Camembert-producing region since World War I. A GI poses with that thoroughly French symbol, a round of Camembert. 1948–1950.

And finally the Cross of Lorraine, symbol of the triumph of the Resistance, displayed here with a thistle and sheaf of wheat. The thistle, Lorraine's symbolic flower, is not routinely associated with Free France's Cross of Lorraine and faithful followers of General de Gaulle. But this Camembert was sold in Colombey-les-Deux-Églises in souvenir shops for the tourists visiting the de Gaulle memorial. 1950s.

SPACE TRAVEL

1969. As mankind launched into the conquest of outer space and science fiction was all the rage, Camembert labels embraced the spirit of the moment, seizing upon kitschy interpretations of flying machines and lunar expeditions.
• Sputnik, Cheese of the Future, produced in the Charentes, aimed for the highest heights.
• Flying Saucer, a pasteurized Camembert from Brittany, aimed to lead snackers into unexplored horizons of gastronomy.
• Le Lem Camembert, produced in the Meuse region, depicts a lunar expedition on its label.

THE MAYOR OF CAMEMBERT

Camembert labels have become such an important medium of communication that the mayor of Camembert gained considerable attention with his golden Marianne longevity-in-office award. 2012.

Milkmaids with Your Snack?

Camembert's distinctive labels, with designs reminiscent of postcards or souvenir postage stamps,
certainly get a lot of credit for the popularity of this cheese.

Véronique Richez-Lerouge

A selection of labels from 1905 to 1958

NO LABELS WITHOUT BOXES

The issue of how best to package and transport cheese arose in the 1880s. Camembert was a particular challenge. It was soft, temperature-sensitive, and easily crushed. The engineer Eugène Ridel is credited with standardizing the packaging of Camembert. He was inspired by boxes made in the Jura region, which began to be used by an exporter in Le Havre in 1890 for transatlantic shipments of Camembert. Working with Georges Leroy, a wood fabricator from Livarot, he perfected the distinctive container that allows each Camembert to be packaged and protected individually. With the advent of modern printing techniques, including mass-produced lithography, offset printing, and the development of photography, the poplar wood Camembert box and its accompanying label launched a new field of creative endeavor. The labels attracted customers with unbridled enthusiasm, vaunting the merits of popular brands. In the process, they became a means of communication between producers and consumers in late nineteenth-century society.

GLAMOUR ON A PLATTER

Women of all walks of life appear on Camembert labels, ranging from the fetching peasant girl to the elegant aristocrat, and the models were posed as if they were haute couture mannequins. The illustrations stirred the sixth sense of appreciative gourmands, who could almost page through Camembert labels as if they were magazines. There's a lot of red, the ultimate warm hue, in these designs, but there's also plenty of blue, green, and yellow, reflecting the full range of colors visible in the natural world. Photography combined with drawings, adding a touch of modernity to the designs.

Tyrosemiophiles: CHEESE LABEL COLLECTORS

The name is a clever semantic construction that combines the ancient Greek τυρός ("turós," "cheese"), σημεῖον ("sēmeîon," "sign," or "distinctive mark"), and φίλος, ("phílos," "friend").

Our thanks to Alain Cruchet and Jean-Pierre Delorme of the Club Tyrosémiophile de France for their assistance in researching this subject.

Ready to Serve

The classic opposition between French service and Russian service is no longer that vivid, but going from one to the other left a lasting mark on French gastronomy.
Loïc Bienassis

SERVICE À LA FRANÇAISE
What's known as "French service" was practiced among the aristocracy during the Middle Ages and the nineteenth century. At the time, a meal was divided into several courses and each one consisted of various dishes, which were brought simultaneously to the table. These dishes were then taken away and replaced by those in the next course.

The number of courses varied and their nature evolved somewhat through the centuries. A supper at the end of the seventeenth century might have consisted of the following:

FIRST COURSE
→ Potages—especially liquid dishes.
→ Appetizers—many kinds.
→ Simmered meats, patés, tourtes (pies) . . .
→ Hors d'oeuvre—generally hot but served in smaller portions than the appetizers.

SECOND COURSE: ROASTS
→ The heart of the meal, consisting of roasted meats on spits or boiled or fried fish.
→ Fowl, game, farm-raised animals, were the typical meats roasted.
→ Side dishes, "salads," purslane, capers, anchovies, cornichons . . .

THIRD COURSE: ENTREMETS
Sweet or savory, very diverse: vegetable dishes, mushrooms, eggs in all styles, giblets, cold pâtés, beignets, creams . . .

FRUIT/DESSERT
At the time, this was the sweet portion of the meal: fruit, creams, jams, pâtes de fruit (fruit paste), dragées, sorbets, macarons . . .

THE FRENCH EAT IN THE RUSSIAN STYLE
In the nineteenth century, service "à la russe" took root and has remained the norm, even if it has evolved: courses are served sequentially and dishes, cut into portions, come one after the other. Service in the Russian and French styles did coexist, with hot dishes served à la russe while cold dishes had pride of place on the table, especially desserts.

IT'S COMPLICATED . . .
In the restaurant world, the expressions *service à la russe* and *service à la française* mean something else entirely than they do for historians!

GAME

Match each number with a letter!

1. Russian service **2. English service** **3. French service** **4. German service** **5. American service**

A. The guest serves himself directly from the dish presented to him.

B. Does not exist.

C. The dish is presented to the left of the guest and is carried in one hand. The server uses a spoon and fork as tongs.

D. The expression is sometimes used to describe plate service. It has been somewhat forgotten but, in fine dining, "plate service," now prevalent, only took root starting in the 1970s. The Troisgros brothers are generally considered to have been the first to promote it in France.

E. Table or cart service. The dish is presented to the guest. Then the meal is plated in the dining room before being served.

Answers: 1E, 2C, 3A, 4B, 5D

Go Suck an Egg

It's hard not to love an egg, there's so much behind its shell. Let's scramble together the ways to cook them.
Marielle Gaudry

A LESSON IN OVOLOGY
What is an eggshell? A porous carapace of calcium carbonate with a thin membrane lining the inside. That membrane, where it separates from the shell at its widest end, forms an air chamber. The larger the air chamber, the more the egg loses freshness. The well-known test to verify that an egg is still good is to plunge it into a bowl of water. A fresh egg will sink to the bottom; after a couple of days, it will stand on end; and an expired egg will float to the surface.

THREE, SIX, NINE?
How long you boil an egg can be summed up by the famous rule of 3-6-9 . . . Before placing them in water, make sure to choose extra-fresh eggs stored at room temperature.
Soft boiled—3 minutes in a saucepan of boiling water. Alternative methods: 1 minute in boiling water, then turn off the heat and leave the eggs in the water for another 3 minutes; or place the eggs in a saucepan, cover them in cold water, and bring to a boil; remove the eggs after 3 minutes.
Coddled—6 minutes in a saucepan of boiling water. Shell and keep in a saucepan of hot, salted water until it is time to serve.
Hard boiled—depending on the size of the egg, 8 to 10 minutes in a saucepan of boiling water. Remove from the stove and cool with water.

"Without admitting that I paradoxically agree that the hard-boiled egg is the hardest kind to make successfully, let us agree that it entails more risk. The clumsy cook who messes up a soft-boiled egg might still obtain a coddled egg. Anyone aiming for a coddled egg might sometimes get a hard-boiled one. But the poor soul who has planned for a hard-boiled egg, but forgets it in the pan for more than eight minutes, will only have the recourse to note that the result is that something Tertullian spoke about, before you know who, which has no name in any language. After the hard-boiled egg, there is nothing. . . ." *Célébration de l'oeuf*, by Maurice Lelong (1962).

> ". . . to cook an egg without a watch, you just have to **recite** *Le Dormeur du Val* three times; **four if you want it coddled.**"
>
> *Les amnésiques n'ont rien vécu d'inoubliable,*
>
> by Hervé Le Tellier (1997)

THE PERFECT EGG?
Cook over low heat at around 149°F (65°C) for 45 minutes. The perfect egg is smooth, with a silky white and a creamy yellow. It hatched in the late 1990s in the laboratory of the physical chemist Hervé This, one of the founders of molecular gastronomy.

TECHNIQUES
Shirred eggs: butter the inside of a ramekin and crack one or two eggs into it, depending on the volume. Bake in a bain-marie for 6 to 8 minutes, then salt and pepper before serving.
Fried eggs: coat a pan with butter, heat, and crack one or two eggs into it. Sprinkle with butter while cooking. Salt and pepper before serving. "Mirror eggs" involve baking in a casserole in the oven. The albumin they contain will form a kind of film over the yolks.
Poached eggs: crack an egg into a ramekin and then carefully slide into a pan of simmering water with white vinegar. Allow the egg to poach for 2 minutes, drain using a slotted spoon, and place in a bowl of cold water. If necessary, you can immerse again in the pan to reheat before serving.

skip to
The Omelet, p. 90

Sole in the Casserole

As Curnonsky said, "sole is the fish most adaptable to different preparations, and the stock made
from its bones and discarded parts is of unparalleled flavor." Let's take a look.

Marie-Laure Fréchet

PORTRAIT OF A FAMILY

An almost perfect oval, with cream-white skin on one side and brown on the other (the one with the eyes), sole is immediately recognizable. And yet the Soleidae family is a big one and includes a large number of flat fish species. Most often, the common sole *Solea solea* (also known as Dover sole or black sole) is the one most used because it is often fished in the English Channel. It's abundant along the European coasts and is related to flounder and lemon sole. It can be fished year-round, with peak season between February and April.

A BIT OF TECHNIQUE: TURBAN OF SOLE

The turban is a way of presenting fish in a ring using a savarin mold. Hot or cold, it's in every French cookbook from the 1950s. To make a turban, clean and fillet three soles. Use the fish to line the buttered mold, overlapping them slightly at an angle. Then fill with fish mousseline. Fold the ends of the fillets over the stuffing. Poach in a warm oven for 25 minutes set in a bain-marie, covered. Let sit for a few minutes after removing from the oven, then unmold and place on a serving dish.

Clean off any juices and foam that has formed on the turban. Glaze with melted butter, to add shimmer. Fill the middle (with vegetables and/or shrimp, for example) and serve with a butter-based sauce.

A QUESTION OF FRENCH VOCABULARY: DRESSING A SOLE

In fact, the French expression is more about undressing because the cooking term involves getting rid of the fish's tail, tail fin, tiny bones, and its white and gray skin before removing the four fillets.

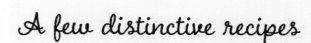

Presenting fillets of sole
They can be left flat, butterflied, stuffed, rolled *en paupiette* . . .

Auguste Escoffier's trick
"To keep your fillets nice and white after cooking, you can shallow poach them, covered, without bringing to a boil. A half cup will suffice for the fillets of one sole."

Tip
After rolling the fillets *en paupiette*, hold in place with a toothpick so that they don't unravel while cooking.

A few distinctive recipes

There are close to two hundred sole recipes in Auguste Escoffier's *Le Guide culinaire*! There's nothing fishy about that.

SOLE MEUNIÈRE, WITH CHANTILLY BUTTER
by Pierre Gagnaire

This sole is fried whole after being lightly dusted with flour, hence the cooking style *meunière*. It is then served with lemon juice and butter, and sprinkled with parsley.

PREPARATION TIME: 15 MINUTES
COOKING TIME: 10 MINUTES
SERVES 2

2 whole soles weighing 1⅛ pounds (500 g) each
12 tablespoons (180 g) unsalted butter
Just over ¾ cup (200 mL) chicken broth
2 tablespoons (10 g) chopped chives
2 tablespoons (10 g) chopped shallots
1 teaspoon (5 mL) lemon juice
Salt and freshly ground black pepper

Cook the fish in a skillet with 7 tablespoons (100 g) of the butter, being very careful not to let the butter brown, as it will be used at the end of the recipe. When the fish is cooked through, carefully lift off the fillets and keep them warm. In the same pan, fry the fish carcasses (the bones and trimmings), then add the broth. Cook until the broth has reduced by one-fourth its original volume; strain, and add the broth to a saucepan. Add the chives, shallots, and lemon juice to the saucepan. Season with salt and pepper. Whisk in the remaining butter, softened, and whisk until the sauce is billowy, like a soft whipped cream. Place the sole fillets in the center of warmed serving plates, accompanied by mashed potatoes. Serve the whipped butter sauce on the side for each guest to pour, as desired, over the fish and potatoes.

SOLE À LA DUGLÉRÉ
by Auguste Escoffier

This dish gets its name from Adolphe Dugléré, an apprentice of chef Antoine Carême who hailed from Bordeaux and was chef of Café Anglais on the Grands Boulevards in Paris at the end of the nineteenth century. The fillets are poached in a fish stock with white wine, and served on a bed of crushed tomatoes, chopped onions, shallots, and parsley. The sauce is made from a reduction of the cooking juices enriched with butter.

PREPARATION TIME: 15 MINUTES
COOKING TIME: 10 MINUTES
SERVES 4
8 medium sole fillets
2 tablespoons (40 g) butter
1 half onion, peeled and chopped
2 shallots, peeled and chopped
2 tomatoes, peeled, seeded, and chopped
1 tablespoon chopped parsley
Scant ½ cup (100 mL) white wine
Salt and freshly ground black pepper
Lemon

Roll up the fillets (secure them, if needed, with toothpicks) and arrange them in a skillet with 2 teaspoons (10 g) of the butter. Add the onion, shallots, tomatoes, parsley, and wine. Season with salt and pepper. Cook for 8 minutes over low heat. Arrange the fillets in a serving dish. Whisk the remaining butter into the sauce until smooth, and add a few drops of lemon juice. Top the fillets with the sauce.

SOLE À LA NORMANDE
by Bernard Vaxelaire*

The recipe is Norman only in name. It was created in 1837 in the kitchen of the Parisian restaurant Au Rocher de Cancale by chef Langlais. "Norman" sole was also inspired by the Norman matelote (stew), a recipe of Antonin Carême (1784–1833).

PREPARATION TIME: 45 MINUTES
COOKING TIME: 30 MINUTES
SERVES 10
3 whole soles weighing 1½ pounds (700 g) each
1⅛ pounds (500 g) small gray shrimp, precooked
1⅛ pounds (500 g) white button mushrooms
1⅔ pounds (750 g) mussels
3 shallots, peeled
½ bottle (375 mL) raw apple cider
Parsley (optional)
2 cups (500 mL) crème fraîche
Salt and freshly ground black pepper

Remove the skin from the fish, and lift off the whole fillets (or have this done by your fishmonger). Cut each fillet in half lengthwise. Peel the shrimp. Cut off and discard the mushroom stems. Briefly rinse the mushroom caps under water, and quarter them. Clean and scrape the mussels. Finely mince 2 of the shallots. Pour 1 cup (250 mL) of the cider into a casserole dish with the minced shallots, and a few sprigs of parsley, if using. Season well with pepper. Bring to a boil over high heat. Add the mussels to the pot, then set the lid on the pot. Stir from time to time by shaking the pot, until the mussels have opened. Turn off the heat, remove the mussels, and strain the cooking liquid into a large skillet.

Chop the remaining shallot and add it to the skillet with 1¼ cups (300 mL) of the crème fraiche. Let simmer for 5 minutes, then add the fillets. Cook for an additional 3 minutes when the liquid begins to simmer again (or remove the fillets as soon as they turn white and the tip of a knife pierces them without resistance).

Remove the fillets, and set them aside on a plate. Add the chopped mushrooms to the skillet. Gently cook them for about 10 minutes. Add any cooking juices from the sole back to the sauce.

Meanwhile, remove the mussels from their shells. Remove the mushrooms from the skillet. Add the remaining crème fraîche and cider to the sauce, and reduce the sauce until it is slightly thickened. Season with salt and pepper. Just before serving, add the fillets, mushrooms, shrimp, and mussels to the sauce, stir, and heat through over low heat without boiling, covered. Serve.

*Former chef of Gourmandises, in Cormeilles (Eure)

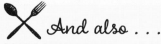

And also . . .

SOLE BONNE FEMME
Sole poached in a fish stock with chopped parsley and chopped shallots. The sauce is enriched with butter or cream.

SOLE AU CHAMPAGNE
Sole fillets poached in Champagne, served with a sauce enriched with cream or butter.

SOLE DIEPPOISE
Fillets poached in a sauce of white wine and fish stock, enriched with a *beurre manié*.

SOLE FLORENTINE
A sole fillet poached then baked au gratin, on a bed of cooked spinach, covered with a Mornay sauce (a cheese béchamel).

SOLE EN GOUJONNETTE
Fillets cut into strips, breaded, then fried. Served with a tartar sauce.

SOLE MORNAY
Sole poached, then baked au gratin with a Mornay sauce (a cheese béchamel).

(butter-flour mixture), with mushrooms, mussels, and shrimp in cream.

Suiting Up

These days, it may be fashionable for a chef to assert his individuality in his personal presentation as well as his dishes, but it was not always thus. Here's a review of the essential contents of a chef's closet.

Hadrien Gonzales

JACKET: the double-breasted jacket has the look of an officer's uniform, and the garment does indeed have deceptive military pretensions. This was no accident; the jacket first appeared in the late nineteenth century when Garlin and Escoffier were theorizing about organizing the kitchen as a "brigade." White became standard for reasons of hygiene. In 1976, Société Bragard, the famed kitchen-wear specialists, introduced the luxurious "Grand Chef" jacket made of Egyptian cotton. That was the same year that Paul Bocuse first decorated his collar with the red, white, and blue insignia of the Best Craftsmen of France. He was also the first to have his name embroidered on the breast of his jacket, a privilege usually reserved for the chef. Around 2000, Joël Robuchon imported a black version of the jacket from Japan. Chef Yves Camdeborde wears a high-collared top with cufflinks.

TOQUE: in 1823, while in the service of George IV, the pastry chef Antonin Carême was struck by a headdress worn by a little girl of the court. "If we swapped these ugly cotton caps that make us look like we're convalescents in a hospital for a light toque, both taste and cleanliness would be enhanced," he announced. In no time, cooks were inserting a cardboard cylinder as a vertical support for their headgear. Paul Bocuse made it an emblem of culinary prestige. In the most conservative brigades, the cooks wear caps that are 6 inches (15 cm) tall, while chefs lay claim to the 9¾-inch (25 cm) versions. These days, cooks foreswear this traditional accessory in favor of berets, head wraps, and baseball caps—or a broad-brimmed Savoyard hat, as sported by Marc Veyrat. At the Plaza Athénée, the brigade goes about its business bareheaded.

APRONS: cooks have never truly invented anything. They share or have shared this item of clothing with blacksmiths, schoolboys, and chambermaids. With or without a bib, looped over the neck or knotted around the waist, always falling below the knees, the apron is usually woven from a mix of cotton and linen with absorbent properties to protect from stains and spatters. The color is white, of course—although in recent years, a slew of rogue cooks (Bertrand Grébaut comes to mind) have reinterpreted the traditional French work wear.

PANTS: only cooking schools still require traditional blue and white houndstooth trousers to be worn by their lowly pupils. In restaurants, they've generally yielded to black polyester pants or jeans. The cuts reflect contemporary style: baggy twenty years ago, slim fit in the last ten years.

NECKERCHIEF: before kitchens were air-conditioned, a linen triangle rolled and knotted around the neck absorbed drops of sweat. In the event of a culinary catastrophe, it could also come in handy as a garrote for the offending cook. Abandoned for a while, the accessory has staged a comeback among trendsetting chefs. Jean-François Piège wears it particularly well, accessorized by Louboutin shoes.

CLOGS: they made their first appearance in the 1980s, inspired by Danish footwear. Bragard introduced these shoes in black or white leather. Clogs don't pinch the toes, they improve blood circulation, and they reduce fatigue. The soles are nonslip, and some models are equipped with a metal tip to protect cooks from falling knives and pans.

SOCKS: no rule on these. Some manufacturers have designed massaging and relaxing models for greater comfort in the kitchen.

Curnonsky

As a writer, journalist, and food critic, Maurice Edmond Sailland, known as Curnonsky, was the "prince of gastronomes" during the interwar period. An ardent champion of *terroir* cuisine, he liked "when things taste like what they are."

Agnès Laurent

Prince of gastronomes
(1872–1956)

AN ORIGINAL

Firstly, a writer: he entered into the world of gastronomy through literature. A young man from Anjou, he moved to Paris and spent time with Alphonse Allais, Courteline, and many others. In 1895, he was a ghostwriter for Willy, Colette's husband, who recognized the role he played in his "best novels." His puns later spiced up his food criticism.

A prince of gastronomes who didn't cook: in his eighth-arrondissement apartment in Paris, where he lived in for more than forty years, he had neither a kitchen nor a dining room. He described himself as "a poor man of letters, simple and debonair, who, in his adult life, has not had a chef, cordon bleu, kitchen, cellar, or dining room." The recipes that appear in the book he published in 1946 are not his, but are rather a selection of recipes he tasted and enjoyed.

A food critic who only had one meal a day: Curnonsky was solid in build. With all the good meals he ate, his 220 pounds (100 kg) quickly became more. At age sixty, he was 337 pounds (126 kg). To get back to a reasonable weight, he decided to only have one real meal a day.

A diverse and princely academician: his times were filled with princes of all kinds; he readily joined in. His main feat was being elected "prince of gastronomes" in 1927. Later, he became the president of the Academy of Gastronomes.

A mysterious death: he died at age eighty-four, on July 22, 1956, under unexplained circumstances. Curnonsky fell into his building's courtyard from his apartment on the fourth floor. Was it suicide? Did he faint? History has favored the latter hypothesis.

Odd nickname

When he was born in Angers in 1872, his surname was Sailland and his first names Maurice Edmond. Curnonsky came later and came from a joke with Alphonse Allais. While they were thinking up a pseudonym, they came up with the idea of choosing a Slavic-sounding one. His friend said, "Why not Sky?" But being a scholarly man, he said it in Latin, which yields: "Cur non Sky?"

HIS 3 KITCHEN MATRIARCHS

Marie Chevalier

Curnonsky's maternal grandparents' cook. This woman from Anjou worked for the family for forty years. "She cooked like a bird sings. . . . She didn't learn about cooking in school or in books. She had it in her from birth and through atavism," he described.

La Mère Blanc

In 1933, he awarded the title "best chef in the world" to La Mère Blanc, who was working in Vonnas in the Ain. Two years later, it was the Gallic capital that was given the honor: he named Lyon the "world capital of gastronomy."

Mélanie Rouat

Curnonsky never stopped singing his praise for this chef in Riec-sur-Bélon, in the Finistère. Awarded two stars, her specialties were lobster in cream sauce, stuffed clams with shallots, and conger eel ragout. He took refuge at her inn during World War II.

RECOGNITION FROM HIS PEERS

Curnonsky did not know how to cook but many recipes bear his name. Great chefs paid him homage.

VEAL MEDAILLIONS CURNONSKY
by Paul Haeberlin
(Auberge de l'Ill – Illhaeusern)

SERVES 4

1 bunch green asparagus
1 shallot, peeled and chopped
3 tablespoons (50 g) butter
1 cup (250 mL) cream
1 (1½-oz/40 g) truffle, julienned, plus its juice
Salt and freshly ground black pepper
4 veal medallions weighing 3½ ounces (100 g) each (cut from the tenderloin)
Flour

Cook the asparagus, then cut off the tips and set them aside; discard the stalks. In a skillet, cook the shallot in the butter, stir in the cream, and cook until the cream is somewhat reduced. Add the truffle to the pan and season with salt and pepper. Season the veal medallions with salt and pepper. Dust them with a little flour, and place them in a separate skillet. Cook for 4 minutes on each side. Arrange the medallions on a serving platter, and set aside and keep warm.

Deglaze the pan with the truffle juice, and stir this liquid into the sauce. Place the asparagus tips on top of the medallions, and spoon the sauce over the top. Serve with corn galettes.

HIS NOTABLE ACCOMPLISHMENTS

La France gastronomique
In 1921, Curnonsky and his colleague Marcel Rouff undertook a massive endeavor: the compilation of a series of guidebooks that would provide information on regional gastronomy and tourist attractions. The concept was driven by the increasing popularity of the automobile. *La France gastronomique* was to number twenty-seven volumes. The first covered the Périgord region, and books on Anjou, Normandy, and Bresse followed. But the series ended, incomplete, in 1930.

L'Académie des gastronomes
The idea emerged in 1927 over a convivial luncheon. Inspired by the model set by the Académie française, forty luminaries would be enthroned, "the most refined palates, the most accomplished connoisseurs and tasters, and the men of letters who have most eloquently written on gastronomy." Each member was paired with a writer and was seated in a chair named after him. When the academy was inaugurated in 1930, Curnonsky became the first president, occupying a chair emblazoned with the illustrious name of Brillat-Savarin.

Cuisine et vins de France
After spending six wartime years with Mélanie Rouat in Brittany, Curnonsky returned to Paris in 1946. He was seventy-four years old. His resources were limited, but he wished to recover his prewar stature. In 1947 he launched the magazine *Cuisine de France*, which became *Cuisine et vins de France* and still exists today.

POACHED POULARDE AND WATERCRESS CURNONSKY
by Claude Deligne (Taillevent)

SERVES 4
1 Bresse poularde (chicken) weighing 4 pounds (1.9 kg)
8 cups (2 L) chicken stock, preferably homemade
2 cups (500 mL) crème fraîche
1 bunch watercress
9 ounces (250 g) carrots
9 ounces (250 g) turnips
5¼ ounces (150 g) string beans, cooked
12 small green asparagus tips, cooked
Chervil sprigs

Truss the chicken and poach it in the stock for 40 minutes. Remove the chicken, and keep it warm, covered with a cloth dampened with chicken stock. Reduce the stock by one-third. Add the crème fraîche, and reduce again to obtain a sauce thick enough to coat a spoon. While the chicken is poaching, clean and blanch the watercress, drain, then blend it in a blender or food processor to a very fine purée. Peel and cut the carrots and turnips into small pieces and cook them in the stock.

Serving
Just before serving, bring the sauce to a boil, add the watercress purée, and strain; remove from the heat. Remove the skin of the chicken, and carve the chicken into eight pieces. Spoon the sauce into the bottom of four large plates and place the chicken pieces in the center, spreading the wings and thighs without coating them in sauce. Cut the string beans into 2-inch (5 cm) long pieces. Arrange the turnips, carrots, asparagus tips, and string beans around the serving plates, alternating them for a good distribution of color. Place three sprigs of chervil on top of the chicken, and place small paper frills on the ends of the drumsticks and wings.

HONOR WHERE HONOR IS DUE . . .
In 2010, French gastronomy was officially included in UNESCO's listing of contributors to the world's Intangible Cultural Heritage. It was less a recognition of culinary achievement than an acknowledgment of the role that eating well plays in French society. The actor Gérard Depardieu, a prominent activist in support of this cause, paid homage to those who had made a major contribution to promoting French cuisine: "Consider the rite of Sunday dinner. We owe this devotion and commitment to men like Curnonsky, the authority of culinary criticism and the prince of gastronomes."

CULINARY REMINISCENCES AND A LEGENDARY CASSOULET
In 1927, Curnonsky was en route from Marseille to Biarritz with three friends. Their mission was to make a halt in Castelnaudary to feast on a cassoulet. A friend had forwarded a letter of introduction to Mère Adolphine, who was famed for cooking "the cassoulet of the gods," but she "had a horror of foreigners, . . . and tourists." At ten o'clock in the morning, Curnonsky presented himself at the lady's abode, but she was slow to respond. She finally opened the door, scrutinized him closely, and bridled when he dared to request a cassoulet for that same evening. "That takes me fourteen or fifteen hours of work . . . You come back here tomorrow . . . Understand? I'll expect you for lunch." Curnonsky recounts what happened next. "After a light hors-d'oeuvre of vegetables, . . . shedding tears of joy that we made no attempt to conceal, we tasted and savored the cassoulet. . . ."
From *Souvenirs littéraires et gastronomiques*

ON THE ART OF TASTING FOIE GRAS
"Fois gras must be tasted in its own time and place . . . I believe and proclaim that one must approach foie gras with an appetite that is fresh and joyful. Sample it as an hors-d'oeuvre at the beginning of the meal . . . Taste it for its own sake (it is definitely worth the effort) at the beginning of the meal, and accompany it with a cool and spirited white wine."
From *Souvenirs littéraires et gastronomiques*

Learn more:
→ *Souvenirs littéraires et gastronomiques*, Curnonsky (Albin Michel). The preface was written by his personal physician, René Chauvelot.

→ *Curnonsky, la saveur d'une époque* (Du Lérot), Philippe Chauvelot. The author is the son of Curnonsky's doctor, who called the writer his "dear uncle." He inherited Curnonsky's literary legacy.

→ *Curnonsky, prince des gastronomes de A à Z*, Jacques Lebeau (L'Ecarlate).

The 4 Types of Cuisine according to Curnonsky

In *L'Infortune du Pot*, Curnonsky distinguishes four categories of French cuisine. He admires and defends all of them, but in his heart he favors the third approach, the *cuisine du terroir* that he himself had come to represent.

Haute cuisine is "one of the jewels of France." "It requires the most select ingredients and the talent of a great chef . . . It is a cuisine for billionaires, but that's no reason to mock or disdain it."

Cuisine bourgeoise is the "triumph of the admirable mistresses of our homes." "In the bosom of a good French family, even the most modest meal expresses the value of the finer things in life."

Regional cuisine is "simply one of the wonders of France." "Each of our thirty-two provinces has its distinctive cuisine, its dishes, and its specialties that are the timeless work of both our home cooks and professionally trained chefs."

"Impromptu, improvisational cuisine" "is concocted with whatever's on hand." "Have you ever tasted a chop or beef steak grilled outdoors over layers of hot coals? It's an incredible experience!"

Dining in Wine Cellars

Take a "wine cellar" and a "dining room" and combine them for a unique dining experience! This new type of restaurant venue is steeped in the concepts of natural wines and simplified cuisine made from artisan products. From the *ville rose* (Toulouse) to Lille to the streets of Paris, here is a list of the top ten *caves à manger* in France!

Gwilherm de Cerval

PARIS
Le Verre volé
The proprietor: Cyril Bordarier
On the plate: Maldon sea salt–smoked herring, wild garlic, bread crumbs, and wild arugula
In the glass: more than 600 labels including the AOC Ventoux white 2016, Domaine de Fondrèche
Address: 67, rue de Lancry, Paris 10th
(01 48 03 17 34)

PARIS
Le Bel Ordinaire
The proprietor: Sébastien Demorand
On the plate: smoked trout, Norwegian bread, cumin yogurt
In the glass: more than 260 labels including the PGI Côtes Catalanes white "Mon P'tit Pithon" 2015, Domaine Olivier Pithon
Address: 54, rue de Paradis, Paris 10th
(01 46 27 46 67)

PARIS
La Cave de Belleville
The proprietors: François Braouezec, Aline Geller, Thomas Perlmutter
On the plate: charcuterie and cheeses
In the glass: more than 650 labels, including the AOC Côte Roannaise red 2015, Domaine Sérol
Address: 51, rue de Belleville, Paris 19th
(01 40 34 12 95)

PARIS
Les Caves de Prague
The proprietor: Thomas Wolfman
On the plate: green asparagus, smoked haddock, and passion fruit
In the glass: more than 350 labels including the AOC Morgon red 2015, Domaine Georges Descombes
Address: 8, rue de Prague, Paris 12th
(01 72 68 07 36)

LILLE
Au Gré du Vin
The proprietors: Patricia and Paul Sirvent
On the plate: charcuterie from Maison Bignalet and green salad
In the glass: more than 600 labels including the AOC Faugères red "Tradition" 2014, Domaine Léon Barral
Address: 20, rue Péterinck, Lille (03 20 55 42 51)

STRASBOURG
Jour de Fête
The proprietor: Frédéric Camdjian
On the plate: leg of lamb confit, roasted carrots, and shiitakes
In the glass: more than 750 labels including the AOC Alsace white "Entre chien et loup" 2015, Domaine Jean-Pierre Rietsch
Address: 6, rue Sainte-Catherine, Strasbourg
(03 88 21 10 10)

TROYES
Aux Crieurs de vin
The proprietors: Jean-Michel Wilmes and Franck Windel
On the plate: farm-raised *pluma de cochon* (pork), cabbage purée, and parsley jus
In the glass: more than 450 labels including the AOC Champagne "Les Vignes de Montgueux," Domaine Lassaigne
Address: 4, place Jean Jaurès, Troyes (03 25 40 01 01)

BEAUNE
La Dilettante
The proprietor: Laurent Brelin
On the plate: organic vegetable salad
In the glass: more than 900 labels including the AOC Côtes du Jura white "Grusse en Billat" 2012, Domaine Jean-François Ganevat
Address: 11, rue du Faubourg Bretonnière, Beaune (03 80 21 48 59)

BIARRITZ
L'Artnoa
The proprietor: Antoine Vignac
On the plate: plate of ham with truffles from Maison Balme
In the glass: more than 450 labels, including the AOC Morgon red 2015, Domaine Marcel Lapierre
Address: 56, rue Gambetta, Biarritz (Pyrénées-Atlantiques) (05 59 24 78 87)

TOULOUSE
Le Tire-Bouchon
The proprietor: Philippe Lagarde
On the plate: pigs' feet, hazelnuts, and pesto with wild garlic
In the glass: more than 600 labels including the PGI Aveyron red "Mauvais Temps" 2015, Domaine Nicolas Carmarans
Address: 23, place Dupuy, Toulouse (Haute-Garonne) (05 61 63 49 01)

WHERE DOES THE "CAVES À MANGER" CONCEPT COME FROM?

This new term refers to a generation of wine merchants who have been serving **food in their cellars** at reasonable prices, and who have a penchant for natural wines. The concept has evolved, creating dining spaces that exist between **the cellar** and **the bistro**, resulting in a new approach to the restaurant experience. Wines in these *caves à manger* are opened with a **corkage fee**. Aux Crieurs de Vin seems to have launched the movement in Troyes at the end of the 1990s, and Le Verre Volé consecrated this new sociogastronomic phenomenon to the Paris scene. Could this be the **end of neighborhood wine shops** and other famous wine stores? Only the future will tell.

Viennoiserie

Viennoiserie is the collective term for the iconic pastries sold in French bakeries.
They are enjoyed for breakfast and snacking throughout the day. Let's review the classics.

Marie-Laure Fréchet

WHAT DO WE MEAN BY "VIENNOISERIE"?

The term *viennoiserie* appeared at the beginning of the twentieth century, initially referring to Viennese breads and croissants introduced by the Austrian August Zang. These were made following the Viennese method, with pastry flour, milk, and yeast (but not butter or layering). Baker's yeast had been developed in Vienna in 1847. He also used "Viennese ovens," which introduced steaming as a cooking method. Today, the category of viennoiserie includes pastries made from dough that is leavened and layered (according to French practice).

❶ *Boule de Berlin*
Brioche dough fried like a beignet, filled with jam or pastry cream and sprinkled with confectioners' sugar. It may have been created by a German pastry maker in the court of the king of Prussia, and shaped in the form of a cannonball in the monarch's honor.

❷ *Brioche à tête*
Brioche cooked in a fluted mold, consisting of a ball of dough as a base topped with a smaller ball or "head," hence its name. It's also called a *brioche parisienne*.

❸ *Chausson napolitain*
Puff pastry turnover, also known as a *chausson italien*, filled with a blend of pastry cream and choux pastry with rum-soaked raisins. The way the dough is sliced into strips is similar to the Neapolitan pastry known as *sfogliatella*, hence its name.

❹ *Chausson aux pommes*
This apple turnover consists of puff pastry in the form of a half-moon filled with cooked apples or apple compote. The technique for making a chausson is described by La Varenne in *Le Pâtissier françois*.

❺ *Chinois*
Brioche dough filled with pastry cream, similar to the *escargot*, a snail-shaped pastry. There are two possibilities regarding its origins: one being from the name referring to the Chinese variety of bitter orange, often used as a confit in the brioche, and the other being from the German *Schneckenkuchen* (cake in the form of a snail).

❻ *Chouquette*
Choux pastry sprinkled with pearl sugar. The technique for making choux pastry was introduced to France around 1540 by the Italian pastry maker Popelini. The dough, which was cooked over a heated stove before being baked, was *à chaud* ("hot").

❼ *Croissant*
Yeast-risen puff pastry in the form of a crescent, the emblem of the classic Parisian bakery. The pastry made its first appearance in this current form around 1920.

❽ *Oranais or lunettes aux apricots*
Bow tie–shaped pastry made from brioche or puff pastry dough filled with pastry cream, with two apricot halves sprinkled with pearl sugar. May have originated in Oran, and been brought back to France by the former colonists known as *pieds-noirs*.

❾ *Pain au chocolat or chocolatine*
Yeast-risen puff pastry rolled around one or two sticks of chocolate.

❿ *Pain au lait*
Small elongated brioche roll, with slashes cut by scissors.

⓫ *Pain aux raisins*
Yeast-risen puff pastry, filled with raisins and pastry cream, rolled into a spiral. Also called a *snail* or *pain russe* ("Russian roll").

⓬ *Pain viennois*
Long roll with a soft, shiny exterior, decorated with long diagonal slashes. It may be topped with chocolate chips.

⓭ *Palmier*
Puff pastry rolled in the shape of a heart, glazed with sugar and then caramelized. The result suggests a palm leaf. It was inspired by the Colonial Exposition held in Paris in 1931.

⓮ *Patte d'ours*
A square of yeast-risen puff pastry filled with pastry cream and scored on one side, suggesting a bear's claw.

⓯ *Sacristain*
A twisted stick of puff pastry, sprinkled with chopped almonds and sugar. Its shape suggests a sacristan's rod.

⓰ *Suisse*
Rectangle of brioche pastry filled with vanilla pastry cream and chocolate chips. Also called a *drop*.

Many thanks to Rodolphe Landemaine for preparing the pastries. www.maisonlandemaine.com

skip to
The Saga of the Croissant, p. 63;
The Tarte au Sucre (Sugar Tart), p. 150

Fries . . .

These little potato sticks provoke heated discussions on both sides of the Franco-Belgian border. The match is on!

Pierre-Brice Lebrun

THE INVENTION

On December 23, 1760, in the Burgundian monastery of Perrecy-les-Forges, the Abbot des Brosses attempted to poison Brother Hilarion with arsenic. The trial records mention "several fried potatoes" and a "white powder" in the brother's bowl. A few years later, the first recipes for fried potatoes were published in Paris.

France 1 : 0 Belgium

Fried potatoes arrived in the kingdom in 1834, with the immigrant Jean-Frédéric Kieffer. He had learned how to prepare them in Paris, and wanted to return home to Bucharest to open a *friterie*. He joined his parents in Liège and set up his stall across from the touring theater site. He was so successful in this location that he decided to stay in Belgium.

THE CUT

Potatoes Pont-Neuf were cut into rounds to be fried in butter, suet, or duck fat. Served in cones, they were being eaten on the banks of the Seine by the time of the Revolution. However, they were relatively expensive. Fried treats did not become democratized until cheaper oil from peanuts produced in the colonies became available.

France 1 : 1 Belgium

The fried potatoes of Jean-Frédéric Kieffer, aka Monsieur Fritz, were a big hit in fairs throughout Belgium. To maximize production, he and his brother decided to cut the potatoes into sticks, deploying the slicing device that Fritz had just invented.

THE COOKING

In France, it's a challenge to find high-quality beef suet, and it's also difficult to find fries cooked the traditional way except for a few holdouts in the North. But it's that twice-cooked method that makes fries so delicious. In France, they usually make do with a single vegetable oil immersion, and all too often the fries are frozen!

France 1 : 2 Belgium

Monsieur Fritz's intent was to precook his fries. He, too, replaced oil with suet, which was less expensive. The secret of the Belgian fry still lies in this alchemy. Students in frites academies are taught: 6 to 7 minutes at 338°F (170°C) in animal fat to cook them, 20 minutes of rest to drain off the fat, then 6 to 7 minutes at 320°F (160°C) in vegetable fat to crisp them up.

THE FLAVOR

Overcooked, badly cooked, and too-quickly-cooked fries are as sullen and miserable as children raised in loveless homes. There remain a few stalwarts in France, who still hold the line against the temptation of dunking a frozen fry into overheated oil. We should respect their principled resistance and lend them our support!

France 2 : 3 Belgium

The two-step cooking process and the use of beef suet give them an inimitable flavor and color. Correctly prepared, a good fry is less greasy than you'd think. Its surface, a deep gold, glistens; its crust crackles as you take a bite, and the savory interior is always succulent and creamy.

ACCOMPANIMENTS

Goes well with steak, andouillettes, the Sunday roast chicken, kebabs, or burgers, and they're rarely eaten unaccompanied. They can be enjoyed by couples, in the company of friends, or just eaten solo . . .

France 2 : 4 Belgium

Fries are eaten on their own with fingers, accompanied by a sauce (some friteries have a lineup of more than fifty options, including the inevitable mayonnaise beloved by purists), preferably served in a paper cone.

THE CULTURE

A few Belgians and Frenchmen from the north have opened friteries here and there all over France. They are true cultural ambassadors of the frite: their courage and determination certainly deserve a point.

France 3 : 5 Belgium

Belgium has five thousand *fritkots* for its ten million or so residents. All Belgians have "their own" friterie, especially on Friday evenings when families treat themselves to a steaming cone with sauce, served alongside croquettes or burgers.

RANKING THE TOP FRITERIES

The interactive website www.les-friteries.com lists the best friteries in France and Belgium. The fries of the Nord-Pas de Calais ranked highest. In 2016, Chez Véronique et Michel in the town of Lens was awarded the distinction of Top French Friterie.

RESULTS

Belgium carries the day. It may not have invented the frite, just as Italy may not have invented pasta or the United States the hamburger, but it has become the frite's native land. Still, France remains the champion of steak frites, thanks to the country's noble varieties of cattle: Charolais and Ferrandaises, Fins Gras du Mézenc, and the Chalosse and Bazas breeds.

The "playfrite" lineup
The frite-stand playlist

Valérie Lemercier – "Goûte Mes Frites" ("Taste My Fries")
Marcel and his Orchestra – "Les Frites" ("The Fries")
Les Blaireaux – "Pom Pom Frites"
Léo Ferré – "Comme à Ostende"
Thomas Dutronc – "Les Frites Bordel"
Yves Montand – "Cornet de Frites"
Stromae – "Moules-Frites" ("Mussels and Fries")
Regg'Lyss – "Mets de l'Huile" ("Pour in the oil")
Las Ketchup – "The Ketchup Song"
Georgette Plana – "Là Où il y a des Frites" ("Where the Fries Are")
Simon Colliez – "Ch'est Toudis des Frites" ("I Told You Fries")
Marcel Amont – "Bleu Blanc Rouge et des Frites"
("Red, White, Blue and Fries")

. . . Frite Stands Rule!

Belgium may claim championship in the frites competition, but France still maintains a bastion of defiant northerners who staunchly resist the influx of mealy frozen fries. Today, there are fewer than five hundred frite stands left in the Nord-Pas-de-Calais region compared to eight thousand a hundred years ago. There is a campaign for their recognition in UNESCO's Intangible Cultural Heritage list.

Marie-Laure Fréchet

TOPOLOGY OF THE FRITE TRUCK

★ The frite stand is an inherent paradox: it is a temporary, movable installation (a former van or mobile home) that has become sedentary. Some have been parked in the same place for over twenty years.

★ Location is paramount. The main square or a major urban artery is ideal. Every local celebration and fair inevitably features friteries. Sports stadiums, too. When there are major matches in northern towns like Lens, soccer fans inhale tons of frites.

★ No friterie would think to exist without giving itself a name. There are two schools of thought when it comes to naming them: a clever name, such as "La Frite à Dorer," ("The Frying Frite") or "La Frite Rit" ("The Laughing Frite"), or simply the proprietor's name, such as "Chez Nono," or "Friterie Nadine."

THE MAKING OF

FIRST COOK IS AT 300°F (150°C)

FRIES COOLING ON THE LEDGE

SECOND COOK IS AT 350°F (180°C)

THE FRIES ARE DRAINED IN A STRAINER

THE FRIES ARE SALTED

A SPLASH OF VINEGAR IS ADDED

AND A CUTE LITTLE FORK!

Sauces
There are well over sixty options. Among the most popular:

Américaine	Mayonnaise
Andalouse	Mustard
Banzaï	Picalili
Bicky	Pita
Burger	Samourai
Ch'ti	Tartare . . .
Hannibal	
Ketchup	

The World's Best Frites
by Suzy Palatin

SERVES 8
8¾ pounds (4 kg) Bintje potatoes

Preparation
Peel, wash, and slice the potatoes into little sticks. Dry them twice with a kitchen towel, then a third time with a paper towel. Immerse them in a first bath of sunflower oil for 7 minutes at 325°F (170°C).

Remove them from the oil, drain them, and let them cool for 20 minutes. Immerse them in a second bath of oil for 7 minutes at 325°F (170°C). Salt, toss, and serve immediately.

WHAT TO SERVE WITH THEM

Frites should be carried back home wrapped in absorbent paper (or better yet, bring your own big bowl for the purpose). Serve them as a main course, perhaps accompanied by a Belgian sausage or the meat sandwich locally known as *un américain.*

THE PERFECT FRITE
★ Potato variety: Bintje
★ Preparation: all self-respecting friteries buy fresh potatoes. They are then washed, cut, and rinsed in water.
★ Proper size: ⅓ by ⅓ inch (10 by 10 mm)
★ Cooking fat: suet (rare in France since the mad cow disease scare) or vegetable oil. Purists insist on horse fat.
★ Cooking time: "It all depends," say frite masters, who have their tricks of the trade . . .

The Art of Drowning Fish

France has 11,467 miles (18,455 km) of coastline, including those of its overseas territories. Before the French Revolution, France's coastal provinces did not speak the same language, so each province had its own local specialties using the surplus of fish and vegetables from their gardens, therefore eliminating the practice of adopting specialties from nearby regions.

Marie-Amal Bizalion

THE FISH SOUP OF TAILLEVENT

Taillevent, whose recipe collection was still an important reference until the middle of the twentieth century, provides an exotic recipe, enriched with spices and noble fish: *"To make serious fish clean and scale fish & then make bread and dip it in a purée of poys and fry sliced onions and put to boil all together ginger cinnamon and small spices and some sour wine & put in some small saffron to color it."* (Roughly, fried fish sprinkled with broth, peas, onions, saffron, ginger, cinnamon, and vinegar.) Manuscript from *Le Viandier*, 145 recipes, ca 1380.

NEVER-FAIL HOMEMADE FISH SOUP

Modified by current chefs with myriad tastes, this dish can be made without much equipment and with little effort. Make it using three or four local species of fish—the least expensive—and, if possible, small crabs. The Marseilles version, a distant cousin of bouillabaisse, is a never-fail recipe: In a lidded pot, cook chopped onions in olive oil with tomatoes, crushed garlic, bay leaf, dry fennel, and orange peel. Let cook gently until softened, then add cleaned and scaled fish while stirring. When the flesh of the fish disintegrates, add water (about 8 cups/2 L for each 2 pounds/1 kg of fish), and season with salt and pepper. Increase the heat to high and cook for 20 minutes. Throw in 2 pinches of saffron, and turn off the heat. Strain the cooking liquid through a cloth-lined colander. Press on the solids with the back of a spoon to release as much of the juices as possible. To fully release all the juices, wrap the flesh in the cloth, put on gloves (the bones are sharp), and twist the cloth with the full energy of a true gourmet.

Scissors, a little water, and there you have it!

In 1963, the brand Maggi invented fish soup from a package. They have been somewhat successful, but no version rivals a homemade one. Powdered fish stock saves time, but then again . . .

MONKFISH BOURRIDE

PREPARATION TIME: 15 MINUTES
COOKING TIME: 55 MINUTES
SERVES 4

For the court-bouillon
1 medium onion, peeled
1 leek, white portion only
2 small carrots
1 stalk celery
2 tablespoons (30 mL) olive oil
1 sprig thyme
1 bay leaf
4 sprigs parsley
1 piece dried fennel
1 orange peel

2¼ pounds (1 kg) monkfish, cut into sections
4 large (75 g) egg yolks
1 small bowl (or jar) aioli sauce

Make the court-bouillon. Chop the onion, leek, and carrots. Cut the celery into pieces. Heat the oil in a large pot, add the vegetables, and cook while stirring, to avoiding browning them. After 10 minutes, add 3⅓ cups (800 mL) of water and the remaining ingredients, and let simmer for 30 minutes.

Turn off the heat, let cool for 15 minutes, then immerse the pieces of monkfish into the court-bouillon. Turn on the heat and let simmer (not boil) for 10 minutes. Remove the fish using a slotted skimmer and set it aside on a plate in a warm place. Strain the court-bouillon through a fine-mesh sieve.

In a heavy-bottom saucepan, combine the egg yolks and half the aioli, and gradually add the court-bouillon with a ladle. Cook over low heat until thickened, but without boiling, and stirring continuously; the consistency should be like a custard and coat a spoon. Remove the pan from the heat. Spoon the sauce on top of the monkfish pieces and add the remaining aioli to a gravy boat.

It is customary to put two slices of toast at the bottom of each plate, topped with a little of the sauce, before placing the fish on top. The bourride can be prepared with other white fish, such as cod, whiting, and Saint-Pierre, just as the Marseillais are accustomed to.

A LITTLE "FRANGLAIS"

All the way from the Vendée coast to North America, fishermen imported their **chaudrée** recipe, which Americans renamed **"chowder."** So the famous **clam chowder** from Boston originated in France!

A WORLD-RECORD SOUP

In 2007, business leaders from Boulogne-sur-Mer created a brotherhood with the single goal of obtaining a world record for the largest *gainée* (chowder), which was achieved in 2008. This chowder is made once each year on the docks in a giant cauldron where they cook 1 metric ton of coastal fish with 2 metric tons of vegetables in 34 gallons (150 L) of cream, and just as much white wine.

The proceeds from the sale of the thousands of plates served are donated to local charities. All this effort for a great cause!

Tip

If your catches of the day are small in size, clean and freeze the small fish as you go along, without forgetting to keep the heads of the best ones. Made into a soup, these little fish are guaranteed to leave you satisfied.

★ ★ ★

skip to
La Bouillabaisse de Marseille, p. 113; In Search of Corsican Soup, p. 95

A tour de France of soups

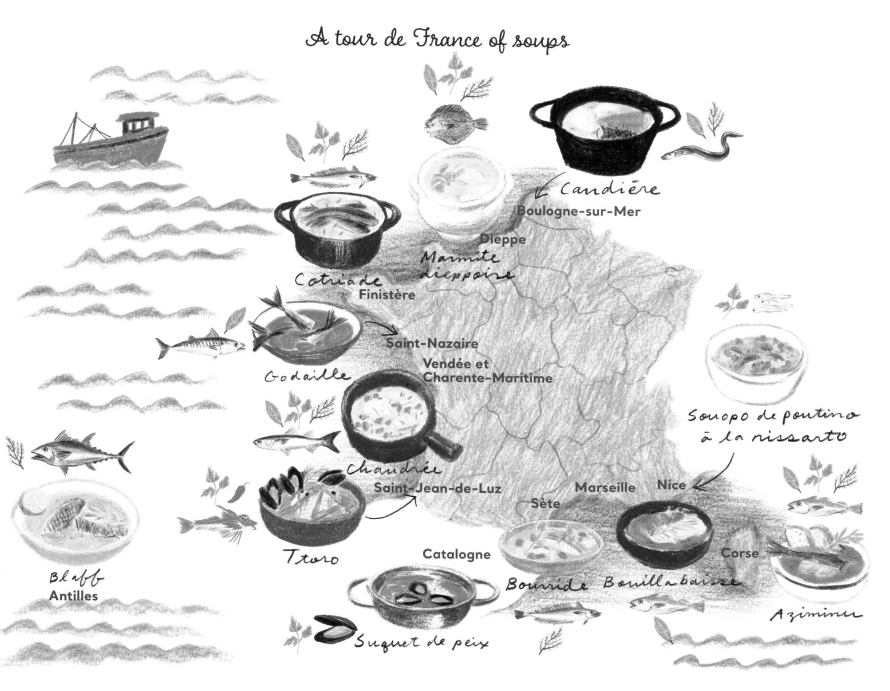

Candière — Boulogne-sur-Mer

Cotriade — Finistère

Marmite dieppoise — Dieppe

Godaille — Saint-Nazaire

Vendée et Charente-Maritime

Chaudrée — Saint-Jean-de-Luz

Ttoro

Suquet de peix — Catalogne

Blaff — Antilles

Bourride — Sète, Marseille

Bouillabaisse

Soupo de poutino à la nissarto — Nice

Aziminu — Corse

Boulogne-sur-Mer
Caudière, caudrée, or gainée
Origin: *caudière*, or *caudrée*: from local dialect for "cauldron," this stew is common in all fishermen's homes, and is a dish made of cooked scrap pieces of seafood. *Gainée* is the share of fish given to sailors by the boss.
Ingredients: conger, sole, turbot, gurnard, mussels, etc., all cooked in white wine with vegetables and cream.

Dieppe
Marmite dieppoise
Origin: created 40 years ago by the restaurant of the same name to honor the best of local fishing.
Ingredients: turbot, monkfish, sole, brill, scallops, etc., in a cider stock, enriched with cream and butter.

Finistère
Cotriade
Origin: from *kaoteriad*, scrap pieces of fish boiled in a *kaoter*, a cauldron filled with seawater. The sailors would eat it sopped with hard bread.
Ingredients: mullet, hake, conger, mackerel, gurnard, mussels, etc., in a rich stock of herbs and vegetables. The broth is ladled over bread, then fish and potatoes are added, and the soup is drizzled with an herbed vinaigrette. The version from Concarneau uses only sardines.

Saint-Nazaire
Godaille
Origin: refers to the leftover pieces distributed to sailors after fishing.
Ingredients: cuttlefish, gurnard, ray, and the indispensable mackerel, in a stew with potatoes and onions. Served with an herbed vinaigrette.

Vendée and Charente-Maritime
Chaudrée or chaudière
Origin: in the local dialect, the word means "cauldron," with many variants. That of Fouras, with cuttlefish and garlic, is the most well known.
Ingredients: young fish, such as ray, mullet, and eel, in a Muscadet bouillon with butter.

Saint-Jean-de-Luz
Ttoro
Origin: during long stays at sea, Basque fishermen treated themselves with grated potatoes added to scraps pulled up from the trawling nets.
Ingredients: gurnard, hake, mussels, and scampi, all cooked separately, sprinkled with stock made with Espelette pepper, hence the name *ttoro*, meaning "as strong as the bull that trounces into the arena."

Catalonia
Suquet de peix
Origin: the name means "fish juice" in Catalan. Potatoes simmered with small fry from the day's catch.
Ingredients: mussels, clams, white-flesh fish, and prawns, in a stock made from potatoes and *picada*, a kind of pesto made with almonds, bread, and saffron.

From Sète to Marseille
Bourride
Origin: from the Provençal *boulido* ("boiled"). Without a doubt the oldest local recipe, without spices or vegetables. Its exact origins are unknown.
Ingredients: only white-flesh fish are used. The broth is enriched with aioli and eggs.

Marseilles
Bouillabaisse
Origin: from Phocaean sailors, 2,600 years ago. At the time, this stew was made with nothing more than water and fish. From the Provençal *boui-abaisso*, meaning "when it boils, lower the fire."
Ingredients: rockfish (scorpion fish, wrasse, etc.) to make the stock. Tender-flesh fish (sea bass, whiting, etc.) for serving. Accompanied by a rouille sauce: a thick, spicy sauce made with garlic and chile.

Nice
Soupo de poutino à la nissarto
Origin: the fishing of sardine and anchovy larvae (fry), called *poutine*, has been practiced for centuries on the coast of Nice. Because of a concern of overfishing since the eighteenth century, the fishing is authorized from January to March only.
Ingredients: poutine, vegetable broth, sometimes vermicelli.

Corse
Aziminu or U ziminu
Origin: a soup made on the boats with fish fry, potatoes, and hard bread.
Ingredients: the same principle and fish are used as in bouillabaisse, with a stock flavored with a splash of pastis. Stale bread is always part of the dish.

West Indies
Blaff
Origin: the term means a spicy court-bouillon. In former times, it was always prepared on-site with fish from a seine: a large net dragged up on the shore.
Ingredients: red snapper, tuna, any ultra-fresh fish, with citrus, cooked in a broth with lime, Jamaican pepper, and chile. Served with rice and bananas. The less-fresh fish are first marinated in lime.

Hare à la Royale

Hare is one of the glories of French gastronomy, with its meltingly tender flesh, thick brown shiny sauce, and intoxicating flavors. This Gothic-Baroque recipe has its obsessive devotees, and its schools of thought. Choose your side!

Valentine Oudard

THE RECIPE
by Julien Dumas (from the Carême school)

PREPARATION TIME:
1 HOUR
RESTING TIME: 8 HOURS
COOKING TIME: 12 HOURS
SERVES 10 TO 12

1 hare weighing 6½ pounds (3 kg)
Scant ¼ cup (50 mL) cognac
Salt and freshly ground black pepper
For the stuffing
5¼ ounces (150 g) bread crumbs
Milk, for soaking the bread crumbs
1 onion
2 teaspoons (10 g) butter
7 ounces (200 g) pork throat

7 ounces (200 g) pork tenderloin
7 ounces (200 g) hare legs
3½ ounces (100 g) truffle peels
7 ounces (200 g) foie gras, diced
Heart, lung, and liver of the hare
2 bunches parsley, chopped
Savory (according to your taste)
1 teaspoon quatre épices spice blend
2½ pounds (1.2 kg) whole duck foie gras (2 lobes)
10½ ounces (300 g) trimmed truffles
For the marinade
2 onions
2 carrots
1 stalk celery

2 gray shallots
2 cloves garlic
8 cups (2 L) red wine (from Languedoc)
2 cups (500 mL) Armagnac
For the sauce
2 tablespoons (25 g) sugar
2 tablespoons (10 g) coriander seeds
2 tablespoons (20 g) juniper berries
Zest of 1 lemon
Zest of 1 orange
For the accompaniment
1⅓ pounds (600 g) tagliatelle pasta
Butter

Prepare the hare
Skin the hare, leaving the head and neck attached. Place a jar in the opening of the belly to collect the blood. Remove the bones from the saddle, one bone at a time, without puncturing the skin of the back. Reserve the bones. Rub the inside of the hare with cognac. Season with very little salt, and season the inner flesh with pepper. Set aside in the refrigerator.

Prepare the stuffing
Place the bread crumbs in a bowl and soak them with some milk. Peel the onion, chop it, and cook it for 5 minutes in a small pan with the butter. Chop the pork throat, tenderloin, meat from the hare legs, truffle peels, foie gras, heart, lungs, and liver. Squeeze the bread to wring out the milk. Add the bread to the chopped meat mixture, then add the cooked onion, parsley, savory, quatre épices spice blend, and 1 tablespoon (15 mL) of the blood. Season with salt and pepper. Stir well to combine, and place the stuffing in the refrigerator. Dip a knife in hot water and cut open both lobes of the foie gras lengthwise. Remove the veins.

Stuff the hare
Place the hare on its back on a work surface. Stuff the rabbit from the chest to its thighs. Place a lobe of foie gras over the entire length of the stuffing. Place the truffles in a line along the inside. Lay the second lobe over the top of the stuffing, covering it. Close the hare by bringing the edges of the belly together and tying it together with a secure overlapping seam, starting with the long edges to the thighs, and sewing it shut

underneath. Tuck the hind and front legs under the hare. Secure them in this position with kitchen twine.

Marinate the hare
Peel the onions, carrots, celery, and shallots. Cut them into dice. Peel the garlic, cut the cloves in half, and remove the germ. Put the garlic in a square piece of cheesecloth. In a skillet, gently cook the onions, shallots, celery, and carrots without letting them brown. Add the garlic pouch, the red wine, and the Armagnac, bring to a boil, then flambé for 5 minutes. When the flames are extinguished, let cool. Marinate the hare for 8 hours in the marinade, refrigerated. Drain the hare, then coat the flesh with the cold marinade. Cook at 350°F (180°C) for 12 hours. Let cool.

Make the sauce
Extract the blood and juices by pressing the carcass. Place them in a saucepan with the cooking juices from the hare, and cook until slightly reduced. Make a caramel by cooking the sugar in a heavy-bottom saucepan. Once the sugar has turned an amber color, add the coriander seeds, juniper berries, and lemon and orange zests. Deglaze the caramel with the reduced juice. Add 2 tablespoons (30 mL) of the hare blood, and heat the sauce, without boiling it, until thickened.

Prepare the accompaniment
Cook the tagliatelle in boiling water for 2 to 3 minutes, drain, and stir in a pat of butter. Julien Dumas serves his hare with celery root tagliatelle, immersed for just a few minutes in boiling water.

What is à la royale?

Where does this name come from? Several theories exist and some are disputed. According to some, Louis XIV, who lost his teeth as he was gaining in years, could no longer eat with a spoon. His chefs therefore created this dish, with its particularly tender flesh in an almost liquid state, to please the king. Others argue that the hare's ears, once cooked, take the form of a crown, which is the source of its "royal" description. Still others claim that the recipe is a modern version of the *lièvre en cabessal* (torchon), which, when presented in this way, is reminiscent of a crown.

The MATCH-Up

Aristide Couteaux
Journalist and senator from the Vienne, nicknamed "Jacquillou" (1835–1906)

Origin: Poitou
Recipe: a hare cooked whole with a compote of garlic and shallots, then the meat shredded (the original recipe mentions 60 shallots, 40 cloves of garlic, and 2 bottles of Chambertin).
How to enjoy it: with a spoon, as it is so tender it nearly disintegrates, almost as melting as a confit or warm rillettes.
Defenders: Joël Robuchon, Paul Bocuse at L'Auberge du Pont de Collonges, Alain Pégouret at Restaurant Laurent, Pascal Barbot at Astrance, and Patrick Tanésy at Tanésy

Antonin Carême
Cook and baker, nicknamed "the cook of kings and the king of cooks" (1784–1833)

Origin: Périgord
Recipe: a hare is boned and wrapped around a stuffing of foie gras and fresh black truffles.
How to enjoy it: sliced. Differentiated by its ability to be cooked as a stew or civet.
Defenders: Auguste Escoffier, Éric Frechon at Le Bristol, Alain Senderens, Julien Dumas at Lucas Carton, Rodolphe Paquin at Le Repaire de Cartouche, Bertrand Guénéron at Au Bascou

A monument of gastronomy, it is one of the rare recipes of French culinary heritage that has produced a veritable war among gourmets.

Lettuces and Chicories

These two vegetable species have become staples to the point of becoming synonymous with the word *salad*. One is sweet, the other bitter. Let's leaf through their traits.

Xavier Mathias

Genealogy of lettuces and chicories

FAMILY	GENUS	SPECIES	SUBSPECIES	COMMON NAME	TYPE	VARIETIES
			capitata	Head lettuce	Batavia	Rouge grenobloise, Pierre bénite, etc.
					Butterhead	Reine de Mai, Merveille des 4 saisons, etc.
		sativa	*crispa*	Cutting lettuce		Feuille de chêne verte, Feuille de chêne rouge, Oreille du diable, Blonde maraîchère, etc.
	Lactuca		*longifolia*	Romaine lettuce	Robust	Sucrine, Craquerelle du midi, etc.
Asteraceae			*angustana*	Asparagus lettuce		Celtuce
		intybus		Wild chicory		Pain de sucre, Witloof, Rouge de Vérone
	Cichorium		*crispum*	Curly endive		Fine de Louviers, etc.
		endivia	*latifolium*	Escarole		Cornet d'Anjou, Cornet de Bordeaux, etc.

> "The endive, as the herbaceous plant of glorified blandness, is the enemy of the man who it keeps from rising above the ordinary, with its middling frenzy, dreams that dim as soon as they are dreamt, and even bicycle clips."
>
> Pierre Desproges, *Dictionnaire superflu à l'usage de l'élite et des biens nantis*, Édition Seuil.

skip to
Let's Talk Salad!, p. 106

CHICORY OR LETTUCE

One is always a bit bitter, the other perfectly sweet. The former comes across as defensive, tempting in vain to ward off a foodie's claws; the other literally melts, almost disintegrates in your mouth, without almost any effort at all. Of the two, which do you think has won more hearts? Of course, lettuce. And yet, there's nothing wrong about trying to bring some sweetness to chicory. Some cooks have even blanched them for a few days before serving. As such, they're deprived of light under an opaque domed lid or sometimes the leaves are folded together so that there cannot be any photosynthesis. What they lose in color, they gain in sweetness. The tinge of bitterness, so subtle, will be a reminder that we are indeed eating chicory.

ANJOU-STYLE CURLY ENDIVE

Nothing is easier than making a complete winter meal: While cooking a few potatoes, wash your chicory, fry up a bit of bacon and slice up a big onion. Crush the potatoes with a fork to make a chunky mash, add the bits of fried bacon and the raw onions. Serve warm over frisée seasoned with a vinaigrette made with cider vinegar.

Tripe on the Table

French gourmets have never resisted treating themselves to tripe, whether it's pork, veal, beef, or sheep stomach. They dry it, smoke it, stuff it—every region has its own approach.

Valentine Oudard

Maocho or maouche

Animal: pig
Terroir: Ardèche
Ingredients: kale, sausage meat, pork belly, lard, onions, shallots, apples, and prunes. The pork stomach is stuffed with the mixture, and then carefully sewn up, wrapped in a towel, and immersed in a bath of simmering water for at least 4 hours.
Variation: "pouytrolle," a dish where the kale and prunes are replaced by Swiss chard or spinach leaves.
Rating the filling: 5/5. Mercifully, it's a one-dish meal. Nice balance of flavors, with a comforting sweet and salty contrast.

Gefilltersäumawe

Animal: pig, calf, or sheep
Terroir: Alsace
Ingredients: the stomach is stuffed with pork loin and jowls, onions, eggs, parsley, marjoram, lard, nutmeg, carrots, leeks, cabbage, and potatoes—nothing more than that!
Variation: the Jewish communities of Alsace have made this tripe dish stuffed with vegetables, onions, chopped parsley, matzo, and ginger a mainstay of their cuisine.
Rating the filling: 5/5. A very robust and well-seasoned dish.

Andouille béarnaise

Animal: pig
Terroir: Béarn
Ingredients: degreased and seasoned tripe dried for several months, traditionally in a barn. It is eaten during the traditional pig slaughtering the following year.
Rating the filling: 3/5. This "wondrous and Pantagruelian sausage" (in the words of food writer Curnonsky) "is absolutely unique, since only one can be made per pig."

Sac d'os

Animal: pig
Terroir: Lozère
Ingredients: the name of this dish—"bag of bones"— says it all. Wasting nothing, peasants kept chops, briskets, spines, and shoulder and breast bones, to which they added the animals' skin, ears, and tails, seasoned with a generous amount of garlic, thyme, and bay leaf. The bundle was preserved in salt or dried and was sometimes incorporated into the famous regional hotpot.
Variations: "pastre" in Aveyron, and "lou schadoche" in Cantal.

Rating the filling: 3/5. That mix of bones and pork rind doesn't look like much, but it sticks to your ribs!

Gandeuillot

Animal: pig
Terroir: Franche-Comté
Ingredients: something in between a sausage and an andouillette. The pig's large intestine is filled with meat and tripe, then sprinkled with kirsch before being smoked over a wood fire. *Gant* ("glove") refers to the shape of the large intestine, which resembles a mitten and "mourns" (French *deuille*) on the stone near the spring where the pig's intestines are cleaned. The word *andouille* has a similar etymology.
Rating the filling: 3/5. This is the ideal meal for cozy winter evenings huddled around the hearth.

Manouls

Animal: lamb
Terroir: Lozère
Ingredients: the stomach is stuffed with sheep tripe and intestines, veal sweetbreads, and salted pork belly. It's all simmered together for 7 hours in a casserole dish, together with onions pierced with cloves, and carrots, a hambone, white wine, and a bouquet garni.
Variations: *trenèls* from Millau, and *pansette* from Gerzat.
Rating the filling: 5/5. Some swear by croissants for breakfast, but they've never ventured into Lozère: in these parts, manouls is served with your morning cup of coffee.

Falette

Animal: lamb
Terroir: Aveyron
Ingredients: Falette refers to lamb tripe, stuffed with sausage meat, diced boiled ham, lean veal, chard leaves, parsley, onions, eggs, and soft bread crumbs soaked in milk.
Rating the filling: 4/5. This lamb dish is very tender, with a good balance between meat and vegetable ingredients.

Lou Piech or Brasse Piech

Animal: calf
Terroirs: Alpes-Maritimes, Nice, and Menton
Ingredients: the "pocket" in the veal breast, with bones and fat removed, is stuffed with chard, rice, eggs, Parmesan, garlic, and chopped parsley. Once the meat is stuffed, two hard-boiled eggs are placed in the center to create attractive slices when the meat is cut into serving portions. The dish is cooked 1 hour in simmering water; halfway through the cooking time, carrots, leeks, potatoes, and a celery stalk are added.
Rating the filling: 4/5. Lou piech is served cold, allowing the diner to enjoy the commingled flavors of meat, chard, and rice.

Tripoux

Animals: calf and lamb
Terroirs: Cantal and Aveyron
Ingredients: lamb tripe cut into 6-inch (15 cm) squares, then sewn together on three sides and filled with tripe, veal sweetbreads, finely diced veal tripe, lard, chopped ham, garlic, and parsley. Sewn shut, the *tripoux* are cooked in a casserole dish with pieces of bacon rind, peeled carrots, onions, and veal feet, all moistened with white wine and vegetable bouillon. The casserole is then tightly sealed and braised for 6 hours.
Rating the filling: 4/5. If you are not yet acquainted with this icon of Auvergnat cuisine, be sure to make your way to Thiézac-en-Carladès in Cantal, where the commune holds an annual celebration of this local specialty at their One Two Tripoux festival.

U Ventru

Animal: pig
Terroir: Corsica
Ingredients: pork stomach stuffed with fresh chopped onion, mint, cabbage, chard leaves, parsley, suet, and blood. The stuffed meat is cooked between 4 and 8 hours depending on its weight. It is served sliced and grilled over a wood fire, accompanied by potatoes.
Rating the filling: 4/5. This substantial tripe dish is very flavorful.

Les petits ventres

Animal: lamb
Terroir: Limoges
Ingredients: the lamb's small stomach is filled with meat from the feet that has been marinated for an hour in a lamb reduction seasoned with herbs. Once cooked, the morsels are wrapped in tripe with a couple of carrots and parsley. This traditional recipe is little known but has given birth to the Brotherhood of Small Stomachs, which holds annual celebrations serving typical regional tripe dishes on the third Friday in October.
Rating the filling: 3/5. Filling your stomach and standing on your own two feet—priceless.

Bibliographic references: *L'Inventaire du patrimoine culinaire de la France*, Auvergne, Albin Michel, 2011; Sylvette Béraud-Williams, *La Cuisine paysanne d'Ardèche*, La Fontaine de Siloë, 2004.

3
USEFUL ADDRESSES FOR TRIPE TREATS

→ **Boucherie Paran,** 20, Grand-Rue, Saint-Alban-sur-Limagnole (Lozère), 04 66 31 50 30. This traditional enterprise still prepares "bags of bones" for loyal clients.

→ **Charcuterie Souchon,** Nasbinals. You can buy those "bags of bones" without making the trek to Lozère. Just contact this charcuterie, which sells them on its website: www.charcuteriedelaubrac.com.

→ **Auberge Chanéac,** Les Sagnes, Sagnes-et-Goudoulet (Ardèche), 04 75 38 80 88. Patronized by true *maocho* aficionados. The Chanéac family has been perpetuating the tradition for several generations. The family-owned inn has a recipe that's become the standard for stuffed pork tripe, the region's iconic dish.

—THE "MAOCHO"—
by Jean-François Chanéac*

PREPARATION TIME: 20 MINUTES
COOKING TIME: 3 HOURS
SERVES 6

4½ pounds (2 kg) cabbage
3 cloves garlic, peeled
3 large onions, peeled
1⅓ pounds (600 g) sausage meat
9 ounces (250 g) bacon
14 ounces (400 g) pork belly, diced
10½ ounces (300 g) prunes
1 pork stomach cleaned, fat and inner lining removed

Finely chop the cabbage, garlic, and onions, and place them in a bowl. Add the sausage meat, bacon, pork belly, and prunes, and stir to thoroughly combine. Stuff the stomach with the stuffing mixture and sew the opening closed with kitchen twine. Wrap the *maocho* in cloth and tie it shut. Immerse the maocho completely in warm water. It should cook slow and gently, for 3 hours. Attention: the water should never boil. Serve with steamed potatoes.

*Chef of Auberge Chanéac in Sagnes-et-Goudoulet (Ardèche).

skip to
The Knives of France's Provinces, p. 196

Made in France

Turn over your casserole, inspect your knives, study your food mill, and check that you see "Fait en France" emblazoned there. France remains the acknowledged leader of artisanal excellence in the production of cooking equipment.
Baptiste Piegay

RACLETTE MAKERS
Bron-Coucke, Orcier - Haute-Savoie - since 1975

BARBECUES
Invicta, Ardennes - since 1924

JAM PANS
Atelier du cuivre, Villedieu-les-Poêles Manche - since 1985

POTS
Sitram, Saint Benoît du Sault Indre, since 1960; **Aubecq,** Auxi le Château Pas-de-Calais, since 1917

CASSEROLES
Le Creuset, Fresnoy-Le-Grand -Aisne, since 1925

CRÊPE MAKERS
Émaillerie Normande, Thury-Harcourt - Calvados, since 1909

ASPARAGUS STEAMERS
Baumalu, Baldenheim - Bas-Rhin, since 1971

BAKING PANS
Mauviel, Villedieu-les-Poêles - Manche, since 1830

FRYERS
SEB, nine locations: Is-sur-Tille - Côte d'or / Tournus - Saône-et-Loire / Lourdes - Hautes-Pyrénées / Mayenne - Mayenne / Vernon - Eure / Saint-Jean de Bournay – Isère. Since 1857 for the establishment of this tinsmithing workshop and 1944 for its relaunch as SEB under the direction of the founder's grandson.

WAFFLE IRONS
Krampouz, Finistère - 1949

GRILLS
Staub, Turckheim - Haut-Rhin / Merville - Nord - since 1974 (business purchased by the German group Zwilling in 2008)

MANDOLINES
De Buyer, Val d'Ajol - Vosges, since 1830

BRIOCHE MOLDS
Gobel, Joué-lès-Tours - Indre-et-Loire, since 1887

VEGETABLE MILLS
Tellier, Argenteuil - Val d'Oise, since 1947

LOAF PANS
Émile Henry, Marcigny Saône-et-Loire, since 1850

PEPPER MILLS
Marlux, Montreuil - Seine-Saint-Denis, since 1875; **Peugeot,** Quingey - Doubs - since 1840

SALAD SPINNERS
Combrichon, Trévoux - Ain since 1945

COOKING RANGES
La Cornue, Saint-Ouen - Val d'Oise, since 1908; **Lacanche** - Côte-d'Or, since 1982

PLANCHA GRILLS
Eno, Deux-Sèvres, since 1909

ROASTING PANS
Matfer Bourgeat, Longny au Perche - Orne, since 1814

TAGINES
Appolia, Languidic - Morbihan, since 1930

SKILLETS
Tefal: Rumilly - Haute-Savoie, since 1956 (acquired by SEB in 1968); **Crafond:** Haut-Rhin, since 1948

CULINARY POTTERY
Nature Utile, Sigoyer - Hautes-Alpes – since 2003

FOOD PROCESSORS
Moulinex, Mayenne - Mayenne / Saint-Lô - Manche - since 1937. Brand reintroduced by SEB in 2001

ROLLER GRILLS
Le Marquier: Saint-Martin-de-Seignanx - Landes, since 1971 - Eure-et-Loir - since 1947

SOUP TUREENS
Revol, Saint-Uze - Drôme, since 1789

SAUTÉ PANS
Cristel (formerly Japy before the bankruptcy and purchase of the company by its employees) – Fesches le Chatel - Doubs - since 1983

Tomatoes

The fruit that's honored as the king of vegetables. The so-called "love apple"
may well blush as we extol its many virtues. Italy's not the only admirer.
Marielle Gaudry

A BIT OF HISTORY AND A FEW KEY DATES

The tomato plant grew wild in the Peruvian Andes as early as the twelfth century. It was subsequently domesticated and cultivated in Mexico.

1521: Hernán Cortés discovered the tomato in Mexico. It was introduced to Spain (1523) and then Italy (1544).

1600: the French agronomist Olivier de Sires, who cultivated tomatoes on his property in Le Pride in the Ardèche region, classified it as an ornamental plant. It was not until the mid-eighteenth century that tomatoes made their way into Provençal kitchens, under the influence of Italian cooking.

1790: during the Festival of Federation, a national holiday, Provençal visitors arriving in the capital clamored for tomatoes in every inn they visited. Les Trios Frères Provençaux and Boeuf à la Mode, two restaurants near the Palais-Royal specializing in the cuisine of the Midi, popularized recipes featuring tomatoes.

STUFFED TOMATOES BY DENISE SOLIER-GAUDRY

Taken from the Provençal recipe for stuffed golden apples, these tomatoes make a good home-cooked dish.

PREPARATION TIME: 30 MINUTES
COOKING TIME: 50 MINUTES
SERVES 6

6 large and round ripe tomatoes
⅓ baguette or 4 slices bread
Just over ¾ cup (200 mL) milk
1 clove garlic
1 shallot
6 sprigs flat-leaf parsley
1⅓ pounds (600 g) leftover meat (from pot-au-feu, chicken, roast pork, etc.), or 14 ounces (400 g) beef and 7 ounces (200 g) pork loin
1 egg
Salt and freshly ground black pepper
⅓ cup plus 1 tablespoon (100 mL) chicken broth
2 tablespoons (30 mL) olive oil

Preheat the oven to 400°F (200°C). Wash the tomatoes and wipe them dry, then slice off the top section. Hollow out the tomatoes using a spoon; reserve the pulp. Season the inside of the tomatoes with salt, then turn them upside down on paper towels to drain. Remove the crust from the bread, cut the bread into pieces, and soak it in the milk. Peel the garlic and shallot. Wash and chop the parsley. Squeeze the excess milk from the bread, then chop it together with the meat; place the mixture in a bowl. Add the egg, garlic, shallot, and parsley, and stir to combine. Season with salt and pepper. Fill the tomatoes with the stuffing, then replace the tops. Arrange the tomatoes in a baking dish. Distribute the reserved pulp around the tomatoes. Pour the broth and the oil into the baking dish around the tomatoes. Bake for 50 minutes.

Tomato purée

6½ pounds (3 kg) ripe and firm tomatoes. Makes 3 (2-cup/500 mL) jars
Good to know: do not remove the skins or salt the tomatoes
Storage: for several months to a year, away from light
A very simple sauce: remove the end from the tomatoes, and cut the tomatoes in half crosswise. Arrange them in two pots, cover them with cold water, and place them over medium heat. Bring to a rolling boil for 5 minutes, then remove the tomatoes, and let them drain. Process them through a food mill. Add the purée to sterilized jars.

Tomato confit

12 ripe and firm tomatoes, to make 24 halves
Good to know: blanch the tomatoes before cooking them. Make an incision crosswise on the bottoms of the tomatoes and immerse them for less than 10 seconds in a pan of boiling water, then immerse them in a large bowl of ice water; set them aside to drain. Remove the stem, then peel off the skins using a knife.
Storage: 1 year in a pantry in a jar of olive oil, protected from light.
Cut the tomatoes in half lengthwise. Seed them. Carefully oil a baking sheet, place the tomatoes in the baking sheet, and sprinkle them with 2 pinches of kosher salt and 2 teaspoons (10 g) of sugar. Crush 6 garlic cloves with the flat side of a knife (or your palm) and distribute them on top of the tomatoes. Add a few sprigs of thyme, and drizzle the tomatoes with olive oil. Bake for 3 hours at 175°F (80°C), turning them over twice during the baking time.

Heirloom French tomatoes

PLATE DE CHÂTEAURENARD: also called "large red," this is a Provençal variety of tomato with a brilliant red color, flat, and fully ripe by mid-June.
ROI-HUMBERT: a small tomato from Provence weighing 1 ounce (30 g), ovoid shape, and used mainly to make sauces.
MARMANDE: bright red, round, flat, and slightly ribbed, this variety appeared in 1863 in Lot-et-Garonne. The town of the same name rolls out the red carpet every year for a tomato festival. This tomato is in process of receiving its Label Rouge (Red Label) certification.

> "The tomato fruit, when ripe, is a beautiful red. It contains a fine pulp, light, and very succulent, and, when cooked in broth or stews, has an elevated tartness and very pleasant taste. It is, as a result, commonly enjoyed in Spain and in France's southern provinces, where it has never been observed to produce ill effects."
>
> *L'ENCYCLOPÉDIE* **BY DIDEROT AND ALEMBERT, FIRST EDITION, 1765**

PROVENÇALE TOMATOES BY DENISE SOLIER-GAUDRY

Originally, in the villages of Provence, tomatoes were prepared confit in the village bakers' ovens. Here is the updated version.

PREPARATION TIME: 20 MINUTES
COOKING TIME: 40 MINUTES
SERVES 4

½ bunch parsley
2 cloves garlic, peeled
6 round tomatoes
Salt and freshly ground black pepper
1 pinch sugar
Bread crumbs
3 tablespoons plus 1 teaspoon (50 mL) olive oil

Preheat the oven to 350°F (180°C). Chop the parsley and garlic. Set aside. Cut the tomatoes lengthwise in half and arrange them side by side in a baking dish. Season the tomatoes with salt and pepper, then sprinkle the sugar over the top. Spread the parsley-garlic mixture and bread crumbs over the tomatoes, then drizzle them with the oil. Bake for about 40 minutes, or until the top is golden brown. Serve immediately.

"Forget" your tomatoes: to make them more concentrated and sweet, you can bake the tomatoes for about 20 minutes, then turn off the oven and "forget" them for several hours, so that they sit in their juices. Prepared in this way, they are a real treat!

TOMATO SAUCE BY JACQUELINE BONCI

Corsica loves tomatoes! One of the best sauces is that of Grandma Bonci in Bastia, using sun-drenched tomatoes from her kitchen garden. Use for pasta.

PREPARATION TIME: 30 MINUTES
COOKING TIME: 1 HOUR
MAKES 1 LARGE JAR OF SAUCE

4½ pounds (2 kg) ripe tomatoes, such as Marmande, Beefsteak, etc.
3 white onions
2 bay leaves
1 pinch nepita (a Corsican herb), optional
1 large pinch salt
1 heaping tablespoon (15 g) sugar
1 tablespoon (15 mL) olive oil
3 cloves garlic, peeled and chopped
4 to 5 sprigs basil, chopped

The first cooking

Place the tomatoes in a deep pot and cover them with water. Peel and slice 2 of the onions and add them to the pot. Add the bay leaves, nepita (if using), the salt, and the sugar. Bring to a roiling boil and cook for 30 minutes, uncovered, to reduce; the red color of the tomatoes should be retained. Let cool. Process the tomatoes and onions together through a food mill after removing the bay leaves; set the purée aside. Reserve the "red" cooking liquid in the pot; it can be used to add to the final sauce if the sauce is too thick.

The second cooking

This second cooking is performed in several steps because the quantity of the purée from the first cooking is too large to complete in one step. Peel and slice the remaining onion. Heat the oil in a saucepan and add the onion slices, and lightly brown them over low heat. Gradually add one-fourth of the tomato purée obtained during the first cooking, and increase the heat to high. Season with salt and pepper. Add garlic and basil. Cover the pan, lower the heat, and let cook for 20 to 30 minutes. The sauce is ready when the oil rises to the top and creates a smooth and shiny surface on top of the sauce, which should be very red in color. Repeat these second cooking steps for the remaining tomato purée.

TOMATO TART BY DENISE SOLIER-GAUDRY

In the 1980s, almost all moms in France made this summer tart. Its simplicity guarantees success . . .

PREPARATION TIME: 10 MINUTES
COOKING TIME: 25 MINUTES
SERVES 6

1 (8-in/20 cm) circle of pâte brisée (flaky pie dough)
1 tablespoon (15 mL) Dijon mustard
2½ ounces (70 g) Emmental cheese, grated
3 fleshy tomatoes, such as Beefsteak
Salt and freshly ground black pepper
1 egg
⅔ cup (150 mL) cream

Preheat the oven to 350°F (180°C). Line a tart pan with the dough. Using a pastry brush, brush the mustard over the bottom of the dough. Sprinkle half the Emmental over the top. Cut the tomatoes into ¹⁄₁₀ inch (2 mm) slices, and arrange them in the pan, barely overlapping. Season them with salt and pepper. In a bowl, whisk together the egg and cream, season with a little salt and pepper, and pour the mixture into the pan. Sprinkle the remaining Emmental on top. Bake for about 25 minutes, or just until browned. Serve warm with an arugula salad.

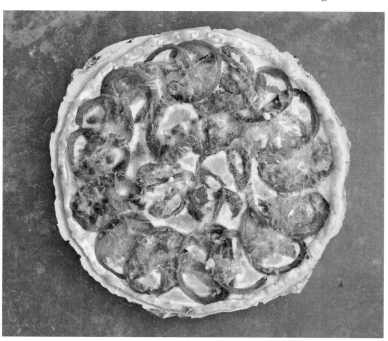

The Quest for Fat

Butter always in the north of France and olive oil always in the south? No, it's not so cut and dry. Different fats are found where they are least expected. Let's take a look (without the calories!).

Frédéric Laly-Baraglioli

THE ERA OF RURAL LIVING (BEFORE 1960)
• A geographical and social predominance of the use of butter.
• A widespread use of animal fats: lard was used in most rural and mountainous areas; duck and goose fat in Alsace and the southwest; and tallow or beef fat in the north.
• The presence of vegetable oils: olive oil was used in the Mediterranean areas (and north, just to the Doubs), walnut oil (used in Anjou, Périgord, Quercy, Isère), and the now-forgotten beech-tree oil, which was widespread but whose use eventually died out in the late 1950s.
• The birth of margarine: an emulsion of beef fat, considered a "butter" for the poor, created in 1869, following a competition created by Napoléon III.

THE ERA OF AGRICULTURE (1960s TO 1990s)
This era represented success and expansion of rapeseed and sunflower oils (new crops grown in France) and peanut oil (with peanuts brought from former French colonies). The movement toward healthier lifestyles, modernism, and productivity gave way to the arrival of these new fats with their neutral taste, replacing traditional vegetable oils, which were unrefined in flavor.

THE ERA OF THE RETURN TO FATS (1990s TO TODAY)
• Lard and tallow—which have almost disappeared—are reserved for more everyday uses (for example, for making French fries).
• Thanks to the recent praise for the use of "good fats" in Mediterranean and French diets, there has been a resurgence in the use of olive oil throughout France and an increased use of duck fat (in theory more than in practice, however).
• There is a diversification of quality vegetable oils in recent years (walnut, hazelnut, pumpkin seed, grapeseed, etc.) and rediscovered forgotten oils such as camelina.
• The use of butter, the champion of all cooking fats, has increased, although margarine's use has stayed steady as well, but with versions based on lighter and cholesterol-lowering vegetable oils.

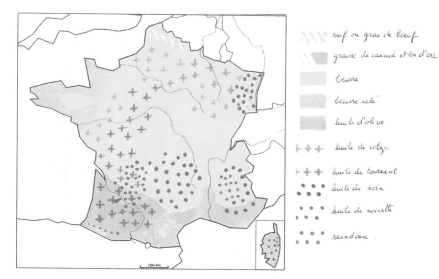

THE FAT SCALE

Vuletta or *bulagna* (Corsica): pure fat of pork cheek grilled (or pork belly from the southwest, the fat only!).
Fat scale: 10/10

The *grat(er)ons* or *rillons* (in Lyon, Tour, or Charente): leftover pork (or duck) meat (rillettes) preserved in fat!
Fat scale: 10/10

Soupe à la graisse ("fat soup") (Cotentin): a soup of potatoes, onions, and vegetables, all enriched with a generous ladle of beef fat.
Fat scale: 9/10

Ortolans (southwest): small passerines (birds) stuffed or larded with bacon, stuffed with foie gras and marrow.
Fat scale: 8/10

Cassoulet (southwest): a superlative blend of fat, and chicken or pork confit.
Fat scale: 7/10

The mashed Ratte potatoes of Joël Robuchon (Paris): 9 ounces (250 g) of butter for every 2 pounds (1 kg) of potatoes (probably more, according to some gourmets).
Fat scale: 7/10

The *kouign-amann* (Brittany): sugar with butter or butter with sugar, all enclosed in a folded bread dough.
Fat scale: 7/10

Cheeses: up to 40 percent fat and protein.
Fat scale: 6/10

The *bugnes* and other sweet beignets: these little deep-fried balls of dough are the stars of Mardi Gras for good reason!
Fat scale: 5/10

Puff Pastry, a Tour de Force

It's all in the technique. Thanks to a rigorous folding process, this dough acquires an incomparable flakiness. It's a must-know technique in the world of pastry, and requires good skill.

Marie-Laure Fréchet

THE ORIGINS OF "FEUILLETAGE"

Of Greco-Byzantine origin, the technique of *feuilletage* (generating flaky layers, also known as "laminating" a dough) has been known since ancient times: layers of fat lie within layers of dough, which is then rolled out. Evidence is available on the existence of puff pastries in France as far back as the Middle Ages, with Rabelais citing them in his *Quart Livre* in 1552.

THE INVENTION OF PÂTE FEUILLTÉE (PUFF PASTRY)

It is unknown who actually invented this dough with its base of butter, which, after multiple folds, separates into "leaves" of flaky layers. It is often attributed to Claude Gellée, known as Lorrain (1600–1682), at one time an apprentice pastry cook before turning to painting. The story goes that he forgot to incorporate the butter into his dough and therefore added it to the dough by folding it in over onto the butter several times.

It is in *Le Pâtissier françois* (1653) that the first mention of the recipe for *feuilletage* through turning and folding is found. La Varenne recommended this dough for making pies and pâtés, which were dishes made only by pastry chefs. The recipe was perfected in the nineteenth century by Antonin Carême, who established, in particular, the number of suggested turns.

THE TECHNIQUE

The artistry of this dough lies in knowing how to incorporate the fat.

The dough is composed of two distinct components:
The *détrempe*: water + flour + salt + butter (optional)
The *fat*: butter or butter + flour (a inversed lamination)

Traditional puff pastry

The butter is wrapped in the *détrempe*, before making five or six simple turns (three-fold) or four double turns (four-fold).
Détrempe: 5 cups (500 g) flour + 1 cup plus 1 tablespoon (250 g) water + 26 tablespoons (375 g) butter + 1⅔ teaspoons (10 g) salt.
beurre de tourage (the roll-in butter): 1⅛ pounds (500 g)

Inverse puff pastry

The *détrempe* is wrapped in the *beurre manié* (butter + flour), before making five turns.
Détrempe: 3½ cups (350 g) flour + ¾ cup (175 g) water + 2½ teaspoons (15 g) salt.
Beurre manié: 2 tablespoons plus 1½ teaspoons (15 g) flour + 28 tablespoons (400 g) butter. This version is lighter and more crumbly than traditional puff pastry.

Puff pastry levée ("leavened")

The *détrempe* contains baker's yeast, milk, fat, or even eggs, depending on its use. It is used for flaky pastries ("viennoiserie"), such as croissants, *pain au chocolat*, or flaky brioche (*brioche feuilletée*). In general, three turns are made.

WHY THE LAYERS?

During baking, the water in the dough turns to steam and tries to escape. It meets resistance in doing so, however, from the layers of butter. The steam then exerts pressure on the layers of dough, causing them to rise and separate, giving the dough a laminated structure.

THE TURNS

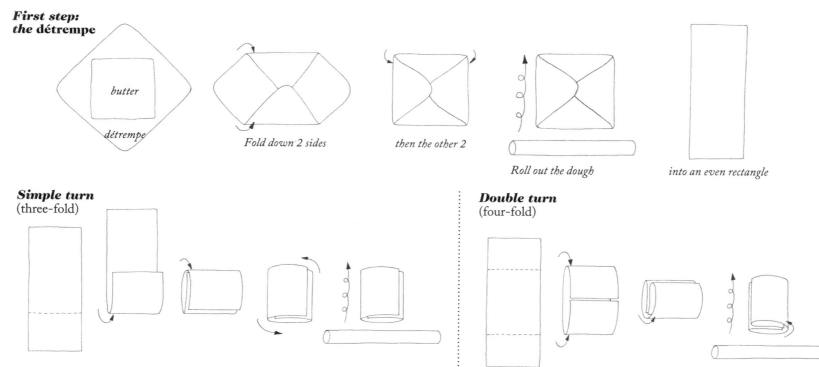

First step: the détrempe

butter

détrempe

Fold down 2 sides   then the other 2   Roll out the dough   into an even rectangle

Simple turn (three-fold)

Double turn (four-fold)

MILLE-FEUILLE

PREPARATION TIME: 45 MINUTES
COOKING TIME: 25 MINUTES
RESTING TIME: 2 HOURS
FOR A MILLE-FEUILLE MEASURING
4 BY 15¾ INCHES (10 BY 40 CM)
14 ounces (400 g) Inverse Puff Pastry
(page 342)
For the pastry cream
2 cups (500 mL) whole milk
1 vanilla bean
6 to 7 large (120 g) egg yolks
¾ cup (150 g) superfine sugar, plus more
for sprinkling
5 tablespoons (50 g) cornstarch
For the white glaze
1 cup (100 g) confectioners' sugar
1 large (30 g) egg white
For the decoration
1¾ ounces (50 g) dark chocolate

Make the pastry cream
In a saucepan, bring the milk to a boil over medium heat with the vanilla bean that has been split lengthwise and scraped of its seeds (add the seeds to the pan). Remove from the heat and let the vanilla infuse for 10 minutes. Remove the vanilla bean pod. Place the egg yolks, sugar, and cornstarch in a large bowl. Whisk vigorously to combine, but do not lighten the mixture. Bring the milk back to a boil. Gradually pour the hot milk through a strainer over the yolk mixture while whisking continuously. Pour the mixture back into the saucepan, and cook over high heat, whisking vigorously until thickened. Remove the pan from the heat. Scrape the pastry cream into a large bowl and press plastic wrap onto the surface to prevent a skin from forming. Set aside in the refrigerator. Roll out the puff pastry dough to a thickness of ¹⁄₁₀ inch (2 mm), and let it rest for 30 minutes in the refrigerator. Cut out three rectangles of dough measuring 4 by 15¾ inches (10 by 40 cm) each. Place the rectangles on a parchment-lined baking sheet. Sprinkle the rectangles with superfine sugar, then cover them with another sheet of parchment paper. Place a rack on top to serve as a weight. Bake for 20 to 25 minutes at 350°F (180°C). Remove the pan from the oven, and let the rectangles cool completely on a rack.

Make the white glaze
Place the confectioners' sugar in a bowl and add the egg white. Whisk until you obtain a smooth and fluid cream.

Assembly
Remove the pastry cream from the refrigerator and whisk it vigorously to smooth it out. Scrape the pastry cream into a pastry bag and pipe rows of pastry cream all the way down the entire length of one of the puff pastry layers to cover the layer completely. Place a second rectangle of puff pastry on top, and repeat by piping rows of pastry cream. Place the last rectangle of puff pastry on top. Carefully pour the white glaze on top (but not over the sides) and smooth it with a spatula. Melt the chocolate and place it in a paper cone (or small disposable pastry bag). Cut the tip of the cone and pipe horizontal lines from left to right (forming close to a "z" pattern). Using a knife, lightly drag the tip perpendicular through the chocolate lines. Refrigerate until ready to serve.

DID YOU KNOW?

The number of leaves in puff pastry can be calculated using the following formula:
Number of butter layers: $b=(n+1)^p$
Number of pastry layers: $f=(b+1)$
where p is the number of turns made, and n is the number of times that the dough is folded.

HOW MANY LAYERS OF PUFF PASTRY ARE IN THE CLASSIC RECIPE?

Answer: if you fold the dough twice to make three layers and make six turns, you'll have $b=(2+1)^6$, or **729 layers of butter** and therefore 730 layers of dough.

The Puff Pastry Family . . .

. . . in savory dishes

Allumette au fromage
Cheese sticks are little strips of puff pastry sprinkled with grated cheese and served with aperitifs.

Bouchée à la reine
An individual pastry sold in charcuteries consisting of a puff pastry crust filled with a blend of veal sweetbreads, chicken breast, and mushrooms bound with a rich cream sauce. It was inspired by Marie Leszczyńska, the wife of Louis XV, who hoped to revive the amorous urges of her unfaithful spouse with an aphrodisiac recipe.

Friand
A pastry sold in charcuteries composed of two pieces of puff pastry filled with sausage meat or a cheese-based filling.

Fleuron
Small cuts of puff pastry, generally crescent shaped, used to garnish a dish.

Soupe VGE
Created by Paul Bocuse in 1975 to honor Valéry Giscard d'Estaing, this soup is based on truffles and foie gras. It is served in a soup bowl with a gratin topping, sealed by a layer of puff pastry that the diner cracks open to reveal the elixir beneath.

Vol-au-vent
Charcuterie pastry attributed to Carême, consisting of a cylindrical puff pastry case, traditionally accompanied by a sauce financière. According to Escoffier, the filling should consist of rooster combs and kidneys, chicken quenelles, mushrooms, truffles, and olives, all bound with a Madeira-based sauce.

. . . in pastry

Arlette
A crunchy, caramelized puff pastry square. It was created by Dalloyau and was named after the employee who wrapped his cookies.

Champigny
A square puff pastry cake filled with apricot preserves.

Chausson aux pommes
A puff pastry turnover filled with cooked apples or compote. A French bakery classic.

Conversation
A mini-tart consisting of a puff pastry base filled with almond pastry cream, covered with a lattice of pastry and royal icing. This pastry was created in the eighteenth century on the occasion of the publication of Mme d'Epinay's book *Les Conversations d'Emilie*.

Dartois
A rectangular pastry consisting of two long strips of puff pastry filled with cream or preserves.

Feuillantine
A flaky petit four with a sugar glaze, baked by the nuns who lived in the Parisian convent of the Feuillantines.

Jalousie
A small cake with a puff pastry lattice that suggests the slats of window blinds known as *jalousies*. Filled with almond cream, currant jelly, or fruit.

Jésuite
A triangle of puff pastry filled with almond pastry cream and covered in royal icing. The icing was formerly dark-colored, causing the pastry to resemble a Jesuit's cap.

Mille-feuille
Puff pastry base filled with pastry cream, first described by La Varenne in the seventeenth century. The top is glazed with sugar or fondant and decorated with a drizzle of melted chocolate.

Mirliton
Mini-tart of puff pastry, filled with almond pastry cream. A specialty of Rouen.

Palmier
Puff pastry covered with sugar, caramelized, and rolled into the shape of a heart, perhaps inspired by the Colonial Exposition held in Paris in 1931.

Pithiviers
A flaky round cake filled with almond pastry cream that takes its name from the town in the Loiret, where it is a local specialty. Its edges are rounded and decoratively scalloped.

Puits d'amour ("fount of love")
A small round cake with a base and crown that form a hollow when baked. It was originally filled with red current jam (hence its name suggesting a "fount of love"), and later with caramelized pastry cream.

Sacristain
A little strip of puff pastry rolled over onto itself, sprinkled with sugar and almonds, evoking the twisted canes carried by sacristans.

Édouard Nignon

Although eclipsed by Auguste Escoffier, he revolutionized cooking via the plate. A champion of bitters, he worked with chicory, gentian, ginger, and more. He opened up his kitchen to the rest of the world, off the beaten track. Within traditional cooking, he also influenced his times with the invention of lobster *à l'armoricaine* and the codification of the *beuchelle à la tourangelle* (panfried kidneys and sweetbread with mushrooms).

Charles Patin O'Coohoon

THE CHEF FROM LA HAUTE

1884: he cooks for the **Baron de Rothschild** at La Maison Dorée on Boulevard des Italiens in Paris.
1890: in Marivaux, **King Leopold II of Belgium** falls in love with his guinea fowl, artichoke hearts, and Mornay sauce.
1892: he takes the helm of the Trianon's kitchen in Vienna, Austria. **Emperor Franz Joseph** relished the *beuchelle*, a dish of kidneys and sweetbread with mushrooms and crème fraîche.
1898: like Auguste Escoffier at the Savoy, he opens Claridge's in London. **Edward VII** is a regular.
1900: he heads the kitchen of the Hermitage in Saint Petersburg. He organizes banquets for **Nicholas II**. Upon the order of the czar, he even opens a French boulangerie.
1908: he purchases the restaurant Larue, Place de la Madeleine, which becomes the most fashionable table in the French capital: **Marcel Proust, Anatole France, Edmond Rostand, Jean Cocteau, Aristide Briand** are all regulars.
1914: he cooks for the heads of Allied States at the Department of Foreign Affairs and becomes **President Woodrow Wilson**'s personal chef.

skip to
La Beuchelle Tourangelle, p. 121

Modern chef and cookbook writer
(1865–1934)

A little-known masterpiece!

In terms of cookbooks, Édouard Nignon is an important figure. A prize that bears his name is awarded to French cookbook writers. He penned three major books of gastronomic literature: *Plaisirs de la table* (1926), *Éloges de la Cuisine Française* (1933), and *L'Heptaméron des gourmets* (1919), his most unique book, practically impossible to find today. It is divided into seven days, each with texts by the likes of Guillaume Apollinaire, Laurent Taihade, and Henri Réginier, and includes menus for lunch and dinner and recipes for proposed dishes. There are memorable texts, for example these lines by Joseph Méry on bouillabaisse that Guillaume Apollinaire recalls in the introduction to the fourth day:

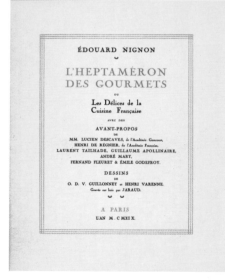

Rockfish from the waters of Syrtes
The Gulf covered in laurel and myrtle
Or before a rock garnished with sprigs of thyme
Their scent arriving at the feast
Then fish feeding rather near the harbor
In the crevices of reefs; the handsome red mullets, the bream
The delicate pagel, the fragrant John Dory
The sea fowl, and the hungry sea bass
Finally the tub gurnard with its bulging eyes.
And others forgotten by ichthyology
Fine fish that Neptune, from the fires of a blazing sky
Picks with a fork and not a trident

EGGPLANT PANINE*

Peel 6 eggplants: on each, cut four grooves lengthwise, not too deep so that the eggplant does not split into quarters. Fill the grooves with thick slices of tomatoes, then wrap each eggplant a few times with string. After, arrange your vegetables in a shallow saucepan and cover them with water; add a wineglass of fine olive oil, the juice of 1 lemon, salt, pepper, and a pinch of paprika. Cook over low heat until there is only oil left. Place the eggplants in an oval dish after removing the string; sprinkle with vinaigrette made using the cooked oil. Season with the juice of 1 lemon, salt, and pepper. Decorate the outer edge of the dish with a crown of stuffed Seville olives and serve over crushed ice.

ASPARAGUS À LA GOULD*

Cook a bunch of nice white asparagus. Strain, sponge dry, and roll them first in melted butter and then in fresh bread crumbs. Roast, sprinkling regularly with melted butter. Serve with a béarnaise sauce.

CRÈME NIGNON*

Pour a 4 cups (1 L) of chicken broth in a saucepan, adding 10 egg yolks diluted with 1¼ cups (300 mL) of heavy cream. Cook as if making a crème anglaise. When the broth is about to coat the spatula, remove from the heat and dilute with 2 cups (250 mL) of fresh mashed peas, cooked *à l'anglaise*. When it comes time to serve this soup, add 1¾ ounces (50 g) of tapioca cooked in chicken broth, then bring the dish to the table before it cools.

*Excerpts from L'Heptaméron des Gourmets *by Édouard Nignon*

The Champignon de Paris

The *Agaricus bisporus* is the most grown mushroom in the world. In France, it is known as the "champignon de Paris" (Paris mushroom), a term that emerged in the nineteenth century. Yet they're rarely farmed in the region of the City of Lights.

Loïc Bienassis

THE *AGARICUS BISPORUS* BECOMES THE "CHAMPIGNON DE PARIS"

Late sixteenth century–early seventeenth century: the technique of growing mushrooms outside is mastered but it does not become widespread until the middle of the seventeenth century. Market farmers understand that the mushrooms popping up in their fertilizer can become a source of revenue.

Circa 1670: Jean-Baptiste de la Quintinie, the director of the royal fruit and vegetable gardens under Louis XIV, grows mushrooms in Versailles.

In the eighteenth century: cellars are used for the first time so as to protect mushrooms from bad weather.

Circa 1810: Chambry, the gardener on rue de la Santé, is said to be the first to have the idea of turning Paris' underground quarries into a business.

First third of the nineteenth century: colonization of Paris' underground, in Passy, probably under today's Palais du Trocadéro in Montrouge.

Starting in the mid-nineteenth century: the quarries of Nanterre, Saint-Denis, Livry, Montesson, Romainville, Noisy-le-Sec, Bagneux, Gentilly, and elsewhere are transformed. In the 1880s, close to three hundred are active.

At the end of the nineteenth century: the Champignon de Paris takes over underground structures in other regions; the Angoumois, the Entre-Deux-Mers, and especially the Val de Loire, its tuffeau stone quarries providing an ideal environment.

HOW ARE MUSHROOMS GROWN?

→ **Darkness,** constant temperature around 55°F (13°C), high humidity (hygrometry of 85 to 95 percent)
→ **Compost:** horse manure, straw, decomposed by fermentation.
→ **Spawn:** mushroom compost (mycelium filaments attached to grains of wheat)
→ **Casing:** a thin layer of crushed lime and mixed peat
→ **Two to three weeks after** casing, mushroom production begins
→ **Harvest by hand,** every day for about six weeks

skip to
Wild Mushrooms, p. 68

STUFFED MUSHROOMS
by Christian Constant and Yves Camdeborde

Recipe from *La cuisine d'Auguste Escoffier* (Michel Lafon)

SERVES 6
About 15 beautiful white button mushrooms
Olive oil
5¼ ounces (150 g) lean bacon cut in small cubes
3 shallots, peeled and finely chopped
Salt and freshly ground black pepper
3 tablespoons (45 mL) tomato sauce
A few springs parsley, chopped
2 teaspoons (14 g) fresh bread crumbs (the soft interior portion)
1 tablespoon (7 g) dried bread crumbs

Preheat the oven to 350°F (180°C). Clean, wash, and dry the mushrooms. Cut off the stems of 12 of the mushrooms. Place the 12 mushrooms caps in a baking dish greased with a little olive oil, curved side down, and bake for 5 minutes. Set aside. Increase the oven temperature to 400°F (200°C). Prepare the stuffing. Chop the remaining mushrooms and the mushroom stems. Heat the bacon pieces in a pan with 2 tablespoons (30 mL) of oil. Add the shallots and chopped mushrooms. Season with salt and pepper, and cook over high heat until the liquid from the mushrooms has completely evaporated.

Add the tomato sauce, parsley, and the fresh bread crumbs. Stir to combine. Fill the baked mushroom caps with this mixture, sprinkle the stuffing with the dried bread crumbs, and drizzle a few drops of oil on top. Bake for 10 to 15 minutes, or until the bread crumbs are golden.

A Gourmet Mushroom

From *Le Cuisinier royal et bourgeois* by Massialot, published in 1691: "The mushroom is of great use in stews: it even makes great dishes of entremets and soups; that's why it's important to always make good stock of them."

French Production

1896
4,000 metric tons
of cultivated mushrooms

In the mid-1960s
40,000 metric tons

Today
110,000 metric tons

Three-fourths are from the Loire Valley, in which the region of Saumur supplies the most; this is far from the 2.3 million metric tons produced in China each year.

There are only 5 mushroom growers in the Île-de-France

They sell only a few tons each year: 3 in the Yvelines (Carrières-sur-Seine, Montesson, Conflans-Sainte-Honorine), and 2 in the Val-d'Oise (Méry-sur-Oise, Saint-Ouen-l'Aumône).

DUXELLES

A name created in the nineteenth century as a tribute to the Marquis d'Uxelles, the employer of La Varenne, the famous author of *Le Cuisinier françois* (1651).

Cut off the dirty stems of 1⅛ pounds (500 g) of mushrooms, and gently rub the caps with a moistened paper towel to remove any leaves or soil. Finely chop the mushrooms. Mince a peeled onion and shallot. Heat 2 tablespoons (30 g) of butter in a skillet. Gently cook the onion and shallot until softened, then add the chopped mushrooms. Season with salt and pepper. Increase the heat to high, and cook until all the moisture has evaporated. Cover, and continue cooking for another 20 minutes over low heat.

The Mothers of Lyon

These ladies were cooks who served up homey cuisine and traditional bourgeois dishes to the diners in their restaurants. Their dedication made an invaluable contribution to Lyon's gastronomic reputation.

Alvina Ledru-Johansson

A FOLK LEGEND

The future "mothers" generally came from rural backgrounds. They left home to try their luck in the city, working for bourgeois family households. Initially employed as domestic factotums, they gradually discovered their talent for cooking. After years of service, they decided to open their own restaurants, featuring local products. Their clients included wealthy industrialists and local politicians at a time when they were not yet regarded as luminaries. Their heirs include Paul Bocuse, Alain Chapel, Jean-Paul Lacombe, Bernard Pacaud, and Georges Blanc, to mention just a few.

The most renowned

MÈRE FILLIOUX

Period: 1865–1925.
Restaurant: a bistro in Lyon's 5th arrondissement. She did the cooking and her husband sold wine.
Signature dishes: Lyonnaise sausages, quenelles au gratin with crayfish butter, artichoke hearts with truffled foie gras, and the legendary poached chicken *demi-deuil* ("half-mourning").
Anecdote: Mère Fillioux (nickname from her real name Françoise Fayolle) would regularly make the rounds of her dining room dressed in a long gown, which earned her the soubriquet of "the Sweeper."

Fillioux, Md de Vins — D. FRÉCHIN, Gendre et Successeur

Téléph. Vaudrey 3-19

73, rue Duquesne LYON

LA MÈRE FILLIOUX — Cliché Lebreton

12 rue royale —— lyon

téléphone : burdeau 15-49

...chez.....
la mère brazier

le bungalow
au col de la luère
téléphone :
35, vaugneray

MÈRE BRAZIER

Period: 1895–1977.
Restaurants: a former grocery shop on the rue Royale. Later, Le Bungalow, a restaurant located about fifteen kilometers away in the Alpine foothills.
Signature dishes: artichoke hearts with foie gras, quenelles financières, lobster Belle Aurore (with brandy cream sauce), Bresse chicken demi-deuil ("half mourning").
Awards: three stars in the 1933 Michelin Guide for her two restaurants.
Succession: her son Gaston, and later her granddaughter Jacotte. Today the chef is Mathieu Viannay.
Anecdote: Mère Brazier served a week in jail for buying provisions on the black market.

MÈRE BLANC

Period: 1883–1949.
Restaurant: the inn that had formerly belonged to her in-laws in Vonnas (Ain), with her husband, a café owner.
Signature dishes: Bresse chicken with cream sauce, crayfish of the Dombes region, crêpes vonnassiennes, made with a potato purée.
Award: two stars in the Michelin Guide and the title of World's Best Cook awarded by the food critic Curnonsky.
Succession: her daughter-in-law Paulette, and subsequently her grandson Georges Blanc, who is today a three-star chef.
Anecdote: Édouard Herriot, mayor of Lyon, adored crêpes vonnassiennes.

The pioneers

MÈRE GUY

Period: eighteenth century, first mention of a "mother."
Restaurant: an open-air dance hall on the banks of the Rhône, which she operated with her husband, a barge owner.
Signature dish: eels stewed in red wine, prepared with fish caught by her husband.
Succession: her two granddaughters took over the establishment fifty years later.

MÈRE BRIGOUSSE

Period: nineteenth century.
Restaurant: a restaurant in the Charpennes quarter of Villeurbanne.
Signature dishes: "tétons de Vénus" (quenelles shaped like women's breasts), chicken in vinegar.
Anecdote: young fellows celebrating their coming of age visited Mère Brigousse to sample a "téton de Vénus."

The forgotten

MÈRE BOURGEOIS

Period: 1870–1937.
Restaurant: Restaurant in Priay, in the department of Ain.
Signature dishes: warm pâté, trout meunière, chicken in cream sauce, floating island custard with pink pralines.
Award: three stars in the 1933 Michelin Guide.
Succession: her daughter, followed by several chefs, the last of whom was Hervé Rodriguez. The restaurant closed permanently in 2010.
Anecdote: she was the first to be recognized by the elite gastronomic organization Club des Cent. Her certificate, which was proudly displayed in the dining room of her restaurant, bore the number 1.

MÈRE BIDAUT

Period: 1908–1996.
Restaurant: La Voûte, a small bistro near Place Bellecour, in Lyon's 2nd arrondissement.
Signature dishes: Lyonnais-style tripe, macaroni gratin, leg of lamb marinated 24 hours and oven roasted with Champagne.
Award: one star in the Michelin Guide.
Succession: Philippe Rabanel, her second son, then chef Christian Têtedoie.
Anecdote: the shopping cart that she took to the food market bore the inscription: "Caution! Weak woman but big mouth." She was well known for her authoritarian and sometimes maniacal conduct.

Elsewhere in France:
→ **Mère Allard** (Marthe Allard) in Paris.
→ **Mère Quinton** in the Auvergne, in Paris, and subsequently in Nice.
→ **Mère Gagnevin** in the Auvergne.
→ **Mère Poulard** in Normandy with her legendary omelets.

skip to
Pâté en Croûte, p. 129

Porcini

Those who have fallen on their knees before a colony of porcini nestled in the moss of a forest clearing—and those who've trooped back from the woods empty-handed under icy rain—can testify to the incredible gift that nature (sometimes) bestows upon us.

Blandine Boyer

Among the hundreds of boletus mushroom species, only 4 have earned the official designation

 Boletus edulis: the star, also called *cèpe de Bordeaux*. When young, its flesh is silky, almost sweet, with the flavor of fresh hazelnuts and a mild anise fragrance. When mature, it becomes more assertive, and when dried its flavor is emphatic, even aggressive.

 Boletus aereus: porcini with black or bronze caps.

 Boletus aestivalis or reticulatus: summer porcini.

 Boletus pinophilus or pinicola: also known as "pinewood king." Grows in coniferous mountain forests.

PREPARING THEM SIMPLY

☞ PREPARING PORCINI

- Sort them as soon as you get home and remove any dubious specimens. Clean them immediately on a dry day, and they're ready to cook.
- Wipe the porcini with a damp cloth. If they're very dirty, or if you see insects or slugs, rinse them for a few seconds in a large bowl of cool water with white vinegar added. Drain them and immediately spread them out in a single layer on a towel. Cook them right away.
- For mature specimens, remove the spongy gills and the skin if it is thick and sticky.
- Store them as briefly as possible, upside down up in the vegetable bin.

RAW
This method is suitable for very fresh caps and young porcini. Slice them very thin in a mandoline and serve them with a bit of fleur de sel, a few drops of lemon juice, and a splash of olive or nut oil. For a chic bistro variation, add young frisée leaves, a poached egg, and bacon.

SAUTÉED
- Slice the porcini and brown over high heat in butter, olive oil, or a combination of the two. Then add parsley and garlic or shallots—it's up to you. Serve as a side dish or use to garnish an omelet. You can also add cream, reduce it slightly, and serve with pasta, veal medallions or steak, filet mignon, chicken, etc.
- Cut them into thick slices (about ¼ in/7 mm), and cook in olive oil in a single layer on both sides, so they're tender in the middle and well browned on the outside. Serve with fleur de sel sea salt and stir in a raw egg yolk.

IN SOUP
Sweat the less comely specimens with shallots in butter, cover with chicken or vegetable stock, and simmer gently. Blend in a little cream. Sprinkle with chervil and perhaps some slivers of raw porcini sliced in a mandoline.

Storing Porcini

PRESERVING
It's best to be careful: mushrooms are naturally nonacidic and therefore vulnerable to botulism. When preserving them, it is essential to cook them at a high temperature with the addition of an acid ingredient. Clean and quarter the porcini and immerse them in boiling salted water. Allow 1 minute of cooking time after the liquid returns to a boil. Refresh them and dry them thoroughly. Then pack them tightly into sterilized containers.
Plain: cover with salted acidulated water (add 1⅔ teaspoons/10 g of salt and 4 tablespoons/60 mL of lemon juice or cider vinegar per 4 cups/1 L). Sterilize for 1½ hours at 230°F to 239°F (110°C to 115°C), in a pot or autoclave. Drain, wipe off, and cook as you would fresh mushrooms.
In oil: cover with mild olive oil (add 1⅔ teaspoons/10 g of salt and 4 tablespoons/60 mL of lemon juice or cider vinegar per 4 cups/1 L). Add unpeeled garlic cloves, peppercorns, and herbs of your choice: oregano, fennel, thyme. Sterilize for 1½ hours at 230°F to 239°F (110°C to 115°C), in a pot or autoclave. Serve as is as a condiment with charcuterie, on pizza, with pasta, etc., and use the oil for cooking. This mixture improves with age. In both cases, if the temperature has not exceeded 212°F (100°C), it's advisable to cook them a second time 48 hours later to assure safety.

FROZEN
As soon as you return home from the woods, clean and slice the porcini or cut them into quarters. Freeze without blanching in freezer bags. Cook without prior defrosting.

DRYING
If preparing them where the weather is warm, spread thinly sliced (about ¹⁄₁₀ inch/2 mm thick) porcini on grilling racks. Set them out in the sun and fresh air, bringing them indoors at night. For colder climates, use a convection oven set at 125°F (50°C) or, preferably, a dehydrator. The dried porcini can be ground to a powder in a coffee mill, for use as seasoning. Be cautious with some commercially grown porcini sold in uneven slices that are uniformly black; they may be infested with worms, or their gills may become sticky when soaked.

PORCINI EN CROÛTE
by Emmanuel Renaut*

SERVES 4

4 beautiful and plump large porcini mushrooms
5¼ ounces (150 g) cooked foie gras
Salt and freshly ground black pepper
9 ounces (250 g) puff pastry
1 egg, for brushing

Clean the mushrooms and dry them. Perform these steps with each mushroom one at a time: cover the mushroom in a little bit of the foie gras to encase it, then season the mushroom with salt and pepper. Enclose the mushroom in a portion of the puff pastry. Lightly beat the egg with a little water and some salt, then lightly brush the dough with this mixture. Set the mushroom aside in the refrigerator. About 15 minutes before serving, bake the mushrooms together at 400°F (210°C) until golden brown.

Chef of Flocons de sel, Megève (Haute-Savoie)

Forgotten French Aperitifs

These aperitifs had faded into obscurity, but they have now been rescued thanks to some of today's innovative bartenders shaking and stirring them once again!

Léo Dezeustre

Spirit	Dubonnet	Lillet	Cap Corse L.N. Mattei	Picon	Byrrh	Noilly Prat	Suze	Grand Marnier	Chartreuse	Absinthe Pernod et fils	Pastis Ricard
Family of spirit	Quinquina	Quinquina	Quinquina	Bitters	Vermouth	Vermouth	Gentian	Liqueur	Liqueur	Anise	Anise
Originally	To fight malaria in the middle of the nineteenth century, chemist Joseph Dubonnet created a remedy based on a mixture of plants, wine, and quinine. In addition to its medicinal properties, this beverage seduces. "Dubo, Dubon, Dubonnet!"	A French aperitif made from white wine and liqueur concocted in 1872 by Raymond and Paul Lillet, Bordeaux wine merchants. There are three versions: rouge, blanc, and rosé.	Invented at the end of the nineteenth century by Louis Napoléon Mattei, a traveler. Its original recipe dates back to 1872, with its name tracing back to that of its region of origin.	In 1837, Gaetan Picon, a young French soldier in Algeria, suffered from a high fever. To treat himself, he created a bitter mixture of oranges and gentian.	The brothers Simon and Pallade Violet, originally shepherds, created this recipe in 1866 based on fortified red wine, plants, and spices. Sold at the time in pharmacies for its healing properties.	Made in 1813 in Marseillan (Hérault), made from white wine aged in oak barrels. After one year, coriander, chamomile, and orange peel are added.	Originating in Switzerland, but becoming naturalized as French in 1885 after the purchase of the recipe by Fernand Moureaux. Composed of 50 percent wild gentian roots.	A fine subtle blend of cognac and oranges. Created in 1880 by Louis-Alexandre Marnier Lapostrolle.	Created near Grenoble in the eighteenth century, eventually produced in Isère by monks and apothecaries.	The name absinthe will always be associated with the famous name Pernod (Henri-Louis). Produced by the Pontarlier distillery, it's made of three plants: green anise, fennel, and wormwood.	Paul Ricard, son of a wine merchant, decided in the late 1920s to produce an aniseed aperitif that was less powerful than absinthe (prohibited by decree in 1915). Pastis, from the Provençal *pastisson* (mixture), was created in 1932.
Did you know?	Queen Elizabeth II claims to enjoy a cocktail of composed gin and this famous French aperitif at the end of each morning.	For several decades, Lillet was the premier wine-based aperitif exported to the United States.	Sixty percent of its sales are in Corsica, making it a truly local product.	Picon arrived in France in 1872, in Marseille, under the name "Amer Picon." It was used by the French army for its therapeutic virtues.	Byrrh, thanks to its recognized medicinal properties, helped to treat the French troops suffering from malaria during the era of French colonization.	An aperitif long forgotten in France, but famous in Martinique, where it is served to celebrate the New Year.	Pablo Picasso, a great fan, decided in 1912 to dedicate a painting soberly titled *Glass and Bottle of Suze*.	Georges Auguste Escoffier made Grand Marnier the key ingredient of his famous crêpe Suzette.	Even today, Chartreuse is produced in the shadows by monks (Rhône-Alpes) who guard the recipe for the elixir, made from 130 different plants.	Although appreciated for its digestive properties, it can cause hallucinations when consumed in large doses!	Contrary to popular belief, the best way to appreciate pastis is to put water in the glass first (4 to 8 times the volume of pastis) then pour in the liquor.
How were they previously enjoyed?	At the beginning of a meal, with or without ice.	Very chilled, between 42°F and 46°F (6°C and 8°C), with a lemon or orange slice.	Throughout the day, served chilled, with ice.	Often diluted with sparkling water or beer.	Generally consumed neat and chilled, at the beginning of a meal.	"European-style," plain, with or without ice.	After 1945, its level of alcohol went from 32 proof to 16 proof. Enjoyed straight up, or over ice.	At the beginning of the meal, with ice, or at the end of the meal served neat.	As an elixir renowned for its medicinal and therapeutic virtues.	Through a very exacting tasting ritual: a sugar cube placed on top of a perforated spoon laid on top of the glass and water allowed to drip through to reduce the liqueur's bitterness.	Popularized by the first paid holiday in France (1936), Pastis Ricard was consumed with cool water before each meal.
How are they enjoyed today?	The Dubonnet has regained a place of prominence among spirits displayed in Parisian bars.	To temper its bitterness, it is often served as a cocktail, especially with grapefruit juice.	In a cocktail, to add vegetal notes and a hint of bitterness.	In cocktails, as a bitter of choice.	Its most popular way is during a festive evening, incorporated into a cocktail.	This is the only vermouth allowed when making a dry martini "American-style."	Just like whiskey + Coke, Suze + Coke has its followers. Suze and tonic remains a safe bet.	Prized for its bitterness.	Enjoyed chilled to lessen the impact of its high alcohol content and to enhance its complexity.	Fashionable because of its reputation and still considered mysterious, some establishments such as Lulu White, in Paris, have chosen to include it in each cocktail.	Younger generations no longer consume pastis. Absinthe has taken over.
Top choice	**The Bentley** (by Harry Craddock) ½ shot Calvados, ½ shot Dubonnet, 2 dashes Peychaud's aromatic bitters	**The Montford** (by Gary Regan) 2 shots Tanqueray London Dry Gin, 1 shot Lillet Blanc, ½ shot Noilly Ambre vermouth, 2 dashes orange bitters	**The Capo Spritz** (by Florie Castellana) 1 tablespoon plus 1 teaspoon (20 mL) simple syrup, 2 tablespoons plus 2 teaspoons (40 mL) Cap Corse Mattei, topped off with a lightly sparkling Muscat	**Oh Cécilie** (by Carl Wrangel) 1½ shots Tanqueray London Dry Gin, ¾ shot Aperol, ¾ shot Martini Rosso red vermouth, ¼ shot Picon, 1 dash Angostura aromatic bitters	**Monet's Moment** (by Erik Lorincz) 1½ shots cognac, 1 shot Byrrh, ⅛ shot absinthe, ¼ shot simple syrup, 1 dash Creole bitters	**Clover Club Cocktail** (by Paul E.Lowe) ¼ shot Noilly Prat dry vermouth, ¼ shot Martini Rosso red vermouth, ¼ shot Monin simple syrup, ½ egg white, 5 raspberries	**La tour Eiffel** (by Gary Regan) 2½ shots Courvoisier VSOP cognac, ½ shot triple sec, ½ shot Suze, 4 drops absinthe	**A1 Cocktail** (by W.J. Tarling) 1½ shots Tanqueray London Dry Gin, 1 shot Grand Marnier, ¼ shot lemon juice, ⅛ shot grenadine	**Le Bijou** (by Harry Johnson) 1½ shots Tanqueray London Dry Gin, ½ shot green Chartreuse, 1½ shots Martini Rosso red vermouth, 4 drops orange bitters, ½ shot chilled water	**L'Ansonia** (by Charles Christopher) 2 shots Dewar's 12-year Scotch whisky, ½ shot Martini Rosso red vermouth, ¼ shot liqueur de Maraschino Luxardo, ⅛ shot absinthe	**Canarie** (popular in the south of France) 1 shot Pastis Ricard, ½ shot Monin Glasco Citron syrup, topped with chilled mineral water

THE MICHELIN GUIDE

1 Only one woman has been awarded three stars in France: Anne-Sophie Pic at the Maison Pic (Valence, Drôme).

€15,800 ($18,400) The 2012 record auction price for a copy of the guide from 1900.

The total number of stars awarded to Joël Robuchon throughout the world in 2016. A record. **31**

2 2 7 The number of starred establishments in Tokyo, the most-starred city in the world, more than Kyoto, Osaka, and Paris.

1933: Twenty-three establishments receive three stars: Le Café de Paris, La Tour d'Argent Lapérouse, Carton, La Mère Brazier (Lyon and Col de la Luère), Le Chapon Fin (Bordeaux), La Réserve (Beaulieu), and La Pyramide (Vienne) among others.

20% The increase in guests to an establishment after being awarded its first star.

€15 ($17.50) What it will cost you for a meal at Tim Ho Wan in Hong Kong, the least expensive starred restaurant in the world.

27% The average price increase for a meal after obtaining a star.

4 The number of chefs that have surrendered their stars: Joël Robuchon in 1996, Alain Senderens in 2005, Alain Westermann in 2006, and Olivier Roellinger in 2008.

240 Annually, the average number of restaurants visited by one of the guide's inspectors.

THE MICHELIN MAN INVESTIGATES

- A team of inspectors was established in the 1930s. Today, there are undoubtedly some thirty for France. The director of the French edition has nevertheless stated about this matter that "the numbers you see everywhere are wrong."
- The inspectors, who are employees of the Michelin Guide, remain anonymous and only introduce themselves after paying for their meal. That's how they end their visit.
- France is divided into some fifteen sectors. Each one is covered by at least two inspectors.
- A table report is written up after the visit.
- The assignment of stars is decided upon during two annual "star sessions," which bring together all inspectors, the editor in chief, and the guide's director.
- All the restaurants in the guide—4,600 for the 2017 edition—were tested at least once. Starred restaurants are "visited" three or four times a year.

And is it a star or macaron (badge)? Ever since the first star was awarded in 1926, the Michelin Man has always given stars. The French term *macaron*, often used so as not to be repetitive, comes from a journalist inspired by the shape published in the red guide.

THE LITTLE RED BOOK

1904 The Michelin Guide steps outside of France with a Belgium edition. By 1911, all of Western Europe is covered. The book serves as a practical guide for motorists.

1956 A red guide for Italy is published. The distribution of stars widens to Europe.

2005 The Michelin Guide ventures outside the Old Continent. A guide for New York is published. Other large American cities follow: San Francisco, Las Vegas, and Chicago.

2007 The Michelin Guide arrives in Asia, with a red guide to Tokyo. Kyoto-Osaka, Hong Kong, and Macau, Singapore, Shanghai, and Seoul follow.

1898 The illustrator O'Galop creates Bidendum (the Michelin Man)

1900 The Michelin Guide for motorists and cyclists is published for the first time. Given to anyone who buys Michelin tires, it provides precious information: a list of mechanics, doctors, hotels, and more . . .

1908 The guide adopts the format still used today. For the first time, hotels are evaluated in terms of their "degree of comfort," which includes the quality of the restaurant.

1920 The guide is no longer offered for free.

1923 The Michelin Guide distinguishes "Recommended hotels and restaurants."

1925 "Recommended restaurants" are indicated by stars. Nevertheless, a finalized ranking system is not established for a few years.

1933 The ranking system we know today is established for all of France:
*** Vaut le voyage (worth the trip)
** Mérite un détour (worth a detour)
* Une bonne table dans la localité (a good restaurant in the area)

THE BEST OF THE

French

WEST INDIES

We're not biased, just clear: the best destination for Caribbean food is, yes, France! It's France in the tropics where eating is like breathing. The culinary repertoire of Martinique and Guadeloupe is a journey in and of itself! Suzy Palatin, the renowned chef originally from Guadeloupe, reveals her favorite family recipes.

François-Régis Gaudry

Do you know your CARIBBEAN FRUIT?

Filling stalls in Pointe-à-Pitre and Fort-de-France, they have names people in mainland France might recognize. But beware, they're not always what you think!

Common name: West Indian raspberry
Botanical name: *Rubus rosifolius* (Rosaceae)
Other names: *framboise marron*, raspberry
Origin: Southeast Asia
Description: similar to its relative in mainland France, large and not as juicy.
Taste: sweet but not as flavorful as the common raspberry.
Use: raw, for jellies, or in punch.
Same family as the fruit found in mainland France? Yes.

Common name: Key lime
Botanical name: *Citrus aurantifolia* (Rutaceae)
Other names: *Lime acide, limettier, lime, ti sitwon, sitwon péyi*
Origin: Tropical Asia
Description: Bright green small fruit, round, smooth and rough, flat on ends, yellow pulp and juicy.
Taste: part sweet, part acidic, rather sour.
Use: Jelly, pastries, punch, sauces, fish seasoning.
Same family as the fruit found in mainland France? Yes.

Common name: spring onion
Botanical name: *Allium fistulosum* (Lilaceae)
Other names: Loignon pèy, chive
Origin: Southeast Asia
Description: probably a local selection stemming from a lily introduced by Westerners. A small, elongated bulb, similar to the scallion: the part outside is green, the part in the ground is white.
Taste: sweet and garlicky, similar to young onions.
Use: all dishes sauces, fish blaffs, bouquet garni (with parsley and thyme). Generally finely chopped.
Same family as the fruit found in mainland France? Yes.

Common name: West Indian cherry
Botanical name: *Malpighia punicifolia*, *M. glabra*, or *M. emarginata* (Malpighiacea)
Other names: Cayenne cherry, Barbados cherry.
Origin: Latin America.
Description: bright red small fruit, round, smooth and rough, flat on ends, yellow pulp and juicy.
Taste: part sweet, part acidic, rather sour.
Use: raw or as juice, compote, gelées, jams, ice cream, cocktails
Same family as the fruit found in mainland France? No.

Common name: West Indian chestnut
Botanical name: *Artocarpus altilis* (Moraceae), from the same family as breadfruit
Other names: *chatenn*.
Origin: Southeast Asia.
Description: oblong seed the size of a chestnut, from a large fruit weighting 3⅓ to 5½ pounds (1.5 to 2.5 kg) with white pulp and covered with soft spikes. Each fruit contains about eighty seeds.
Taste: once extracted from the pulp, the seeds are washed and cooked in salted water. Subtly sweet, similar to the common chestnut.
Use: Christmas turkey stuffing or served as a sauce.
Same family as the fruit found in mainland France? No.

Common name: Tropical apricot
Botanical name: *Mammea americana* (Clusiaceae)
Other names: mamey, mammee, *z'abricot, pyé zabricot*.
Origin: Caribbean.
Description: spherical stone fruit, grayish skin, two to four pits, yellow-orange flesh.
Taste: slightly sour and aromatic, similar to the common apricot.
Use: raw, macerated, in jams, marmalade, fruit paste.
Same family as the fruit found in mainland France? No.

A cuisine of influences

The cuisine of the French West Indies owes its incredible charm and its strong temperament to all the people who have "added their own grain of salt." The islands represent a diverse melting pot of nationalities.

THE ENGLISH COLONISTS
Late eighteenth century

Products	Breadfruit

INDIGENOUS RESIDENTS
(Arawak and Caribbean Indians)
Mesolithic period to seventeenth century

Products	Techniques and recipes
Chile pepper	Smoked meats and game
Allspice	Cassaves (cassava galettes)
Cassava	
Achiote	
Yam	
Avocado	

INDIAN IMMIGRANTS
1854–1885

Products	Techniques and recipes
Turmeric	Colombo (a spicy stew)
Ginger	Masala (spice blends)

THE DUTCH JEWS
(Driven from Brazil by the Portuguese Inquisition in 1654)

Products	Dombrés (dumplings made from flour, a reinterpretation of *knèfes*)

THE SLAVES OF AFRICA
Starting from 1640

Products	
Okra	Congo soup (a soup made by Congolese slaves)
Yam	Fried dishes, such as fritters ("accras," etc.)
Pois d'angole (pigeon peas)	Belélé (a stew of tripe and bananas)
Techniques and recipes	Breadfruit migan (a stew)
Calalou (herb soup)	

THE FRENCH
Late sixteenth century

Products	
Tripe	Octopus daube (a stew)
Lentils	Fish court-bouillon
Cod	Boudin
	Brandade
Techniques and recipes	Baguette
Blancmange (dessert)	Viennoiserie (pastries)
Stuffed crab	Cane sugar
	Rum
	Spatchcocked chicken

THE SPANISH NAVIGATORS
Sixteenth century

Products	
Goat (or "cabri" as wild game)	Pork ("wild boar" as wild game)

PAPA VIVIE'S PIG

Suzy Palatin makes an incredible family dish whose recipe was inherited from her grandfather from Martinique. The essential accompaniment: delicious homemade fries (see page 333).

Preparation time: 15 minutes
Cooking time: 1 hour 45 minutes
Serves 8

For the salt pork
2¼ pounds (1 kg) upper shoulder of pork
2¼ pounds (1 kg) pork spare ribs
2¼ pounds (1 kg) pork loin
3 pork tails
3 lemons
1 onion
4 cloves, for piercing the onion
20 black peppercorns
For the onion vinaigrette
2¼ pounds (1 kg) Paille des Vertus onions
¼ Caribbean red chile pepper
⅔ cup (150 mL) peanut oil
7 tablespoons (105 mL) white vinegar
For the vegetables
4 sweet potatoes
2 cups (500 mL) water

Wash the meats with the lemons: cut the lemons in half and rub them vigorously over the meat, pressing lightly to extract the juice. Rinse the meats thoroughly and, using a small paring knife, scrape the skin off the pork tails.

Arrange all the meats in a large pot, pour in cold water (just enough to cover the meats), then turn the heat to medium. As soon as the water starts to simmer, drain and discard the water.

Repeat this process with the water three times, then place the meat in a casserole dish, pour in just enough water to cover it, and add the onion pierced with the cloves and the peppercorns. Bring to a boil. As soon as the water begins to boil, reduce the heat to low, and cook for 1 hour and 30 minutes. Make the vinaigrette. Peel and finely chop the onions. Place the onions in a bowl and add the chile pepper, peanut oil, vinegar, and two ladles of the simmering broth, and whisk well. Prepare the vegetables. Brush the sweet potatoes under running water, then rinse them well. Cook them in a saucepan of boiling salted water for 20 minutes, or until tender. Peel and cut them in half lengthwise before serving. Arrange the meat on a warm serving platter, and serve with the onion vinaigrette and the cooked sweet potatoes.

MY COD BOKITS

It's a half sandwich, half beignet—this fried bread is a must-have street food from Guadeloupe.

Preparation time: 20 minutes - Cooking time: 30 minutes –
Dough resting time: 2 hours - Serves 6

¾ ounce (20 g) fresh baker's yeast
⅔ cup (150 mL) lukewarm water
3 cups (300 g) all-purpose flour

½ teaspoon (3 g) salt
4 cups (1 L) oil, for frying

Stir together the yeast and warm water, and let stand for 5 to 10 minutes. Sift the flour, add the salt, stir to combine, and make a well in the center. Pour the water-yeast mixture into the well. Knead everything to obtain a soft dough. In a stand mixer fitted with the dough hook, knead the dough at medium speed for 4 to 5 minutes. Let rest for 2 hours. When the dough has doubled in size, roll it to a thickness of ¼ inch (5 mm). Using a cookie cutter or the edge of a drinking glass, cut out disks measuring 3 inches (8 cm) in diameter. Lightly flour a large baking sheet, arrange the dough disks on top, and cover them with a cloth. Let rest for at least 30 minutes.

In a heavy-bottom pot, heat the oil to 325°F (170°C), and immerse the *bokits* for 6 to 7 minutes. When cooked, remove them with a slotted skimmer and thoroughly dab them with paper towels to absorb any excess oil. Split them open, and fill them with flaked cod (see recipe opposite). Bokits are eaten plain, hot, or cold. Fill them with other options such as small pieces of meat, shredded chicken, crumbled tuna, or vegetables, seasoned with a Creole vinaigrette or mayonnaise.

MY CHIQUETAILLE OF COD

Chiquetaille is desalted cod that has been reduced to pieces—whether torn, chopped fine, or shredded— then seasoned. It is a joy when served in Creole salads.

Preparation time: 20 minutes
Poaching time: 15 minutes
Serves 8

1½ pounds (700 g) salted and dried cod
1 bunch flat-leaf parsley
9 ounces (250 g) spring onions
¼ Caribbean red chile pepper
5 cloves garlic
Juice of 2 limes
⅔ cup (150 mL) peanut oil
3 tablespoons (45 mL) white vinegar
Salt

Soak the cod and crumble it according to the method explained in the recipe *Mon Féroce d'Avocat* (opposite). Wash and dry the parsley. Peel the spring onions. Finely chop the parsley, spring onions, and chile. Peel the garlic and press it through a garlic press. Place all the chopped ingredients in a bowl, and add the lime juice, oil, and vinegar. Stir well to combine. Pour this dressing over the cod and stir to combine. Taste, and season with salt, if necessary.

My advice: originally, after desalting, cod was "smoked," that is to say, grilled over a wood fire. You can dry it on all sides in a nonstick skillet. You will get a meatier cod with a nice little toasty flavor.

SEARED PORK

Preparation time: 20 minutes
Cooking time: 50 minutes
Serves 6

2 lemons, halved
1¾ pounds (800 g) pork round
1⅓ pounds (600 g) pork shoulder
6 scallions
1 onion
1 clove garlic
3 sprigs parsley
2 tablespoons (30 mL)
sunflower oil
⅔ cup (150 mL) water
1 sprig thyme
⅛ Caribbean red chile pepper
Salt and freshly ground black
pepper

Squeeze the lemons over the meat on all sides, rinse, then pat the meat dry and cut it into approximately 2¾-inch (7 cm) pieces. Peel the scallions, onion, and garlic; wash the parsley then pat it dry with paper towels. Coarsely chop the onion. Heat the oil in a flameproof casserole dish and cook the pieces of pork over medium heat until browned, adding 1 or 2 tablespoons of water about every 2 minutes. (Do not allow the meat to brown all at once in the oil. Cook it slowly, turning the pieces over occasionally and adding the water; this step will take about 20 minutes.) Add the chopped onion and sauté for another 2 minutes. Tie the parsley, scallions, and thyme together, then add them to the casserole dish along with the chile. Add the water. Bring to a boil, season with salt and pepper, and reduce the heat to medium. Cook for 25 minutes, adding a little water if necessary, or until cooked through. Serve with Creole rice, red rice, or root vegetables.

COLOMBO-SPICE CHICKEN

Preparation time: 20 minutes
Cooking time: 45 minutes
Serves 8 to 10

2 chickens (2½ lb/1.2 kg)
5 limes, halved
2 tablespoons (12 g) Colombo
spice or mild curry powder
1 teaspoon salt
4 large onions
8 cloves garlic

3 tablespoons (45 mL) cooking
oil, plus more for sautéing
3 zucchini
2 tablespoons (12 g) massalé
spice blend or garam masala
10 scallions
4 sprigs parsley
1 West Indies chile or habanero

Rub the chickens with a lime half, then rinse the chickens under cold water and pat them dry. Cut the chickens into pieces and season them with 1 tablespoon of the Colombo spice, the salt, and the juice of 1 lime; set aside to marinate. Peel and dice the onions. Peel the garlic and thinly slice 3 of the cloves. In a flameproof casserole dish, brown the onions and sliced garlic in a drizzle of oil until the onions are translucent. Transfer the onions and garlic to a bowl and set aside. Add the chicken pieces and cook them without letting them brown. Chop the zucchini and add them to the casserole dish, then add the onion-garlic mixture. Add the remaining Colombo spice and the massalé to a small bowl of hot water and stir to combine. Peel the scallions, wash them, then tie them together with the parsley and place them in the casserole dish with ¾ cup plus 1 tablespoon (200 mL) of water. Cook over low heat for 30 minutes (add more water if necessary). Add the whole chile (not cut or opened) to the casserole dish and continue cooking over low heat for 15 minutes. Crush the remaining garlic cloves and whisk them together with the juice of 3 limes and the 3 tablespoons (45 mL) of oil. Add this mixture to the casserole dish and return briefly to a boil. Serve with Creole rice.

COD AND AVOCADO SPREAD

Do not call this a "West Indies" guacamole! Although it is certainly a mashed avocado, it's enriched with cassava flour and cod. And it's fiercely good.

Preparation time: 25 minutes
Cooking time: 10 minutes
Serves 8

10½ ounces (300 g) dried salted
cod
1 large avocado
2 limes, halved
1 bunch scallions, or
4 new onions, or 1 large onion,
peeled and chopped
4 cloves garlic, peeled
¼ Caribbean red chile pepper
3 tablespoons plus 1 teaspoon
(50 mL) peanut oil
3 teaspoons cassava flour

The day before, desalt the cod by leaving it to soak in cold water. Change the water two or three times.

The next day, put the cod in a saucepan of cold water, bring to a simmer, and poach for 10 minutes. Rinse under cold water in a colander. Remove the skin and bones and crumble the flesh, then squeeze it to wring out as much water as possible.

Halve the avocado, remove and discard the pit, then scoop out the flesh and place it in a food processor. Juice the limes into the food processor, then add the cod, scallions, garlic, chile pepper, and oil. Process until you have a smooth, thin paste. Transfer the paste to a bowl and add the cassava flour. Stir to thoroughly combine, taste for seasoning (add salt if necessary), then refrigerate to chill. Serve with slices of bread.

THE CREOLE BUFFET
by Suzy Palatin

The Gastrocrats

The "gastrocrats" are the men and women of pen and fork in France who generate and deconstruct discourse on French cuisine. Food critic Emmanuel Rubin dissects this amusing group.

Emmanuel Rubin

THE HEAVY THINKERS

Claude Lévi-Strauss (1908–2009)
The four volumes of *Mythologiques* (*Le Cru et le Cuit; Du miel aux cendres; L'Origine des manières de table; L'Homme nu*) establish the relationship of foods from an ethno-philosophical perspective, eager to shed light on the question "What is humanity?" A monumental work.
Les Mythologuiqes (Éditions Plon)

Jean-François Revel (1924–2006)
A brilliant and iconoclastic thinker and essayist, Revel in 1979 publishes this scholarly examination of gastronomy from ancient times to present day. The book is a landmark for its then-unprecedented way of understanding this subject through a literary perspective and a lens of sensitivity.
Un festin en paroles (Éditions Texto)

Michel Onfray (1959)
Onfray introduces his works by establishing gastronomy as a field of philosophical reflection in its own right. He developed the idea of a contemporary hedonism and founded the Université Populaire du Goût (the Popular University of Taste), a private university that reestablishes the epicurean way of eating.
La Raison gourmande (Éditions Grasset)

THE FOUNDING FATHERS

Rabelais (about 1494–1553)
Through the genius of his words and through comedy, the humanist Rabelais creates an epic literary monument that taps into the whims of the appetite. Through this work, the terms *Rabelaisian*, *gargantuan*, and *pantagruelian* enter into the French language.
Gargantua (Éditions Gallimard)

Alexandre Balthazar Laurent Grimod de La Reynière (1758–1837)
This adventurous jack-of-all-trades, a lover of pranks and mysticism, first offers a professional culinary viewpoint by chronicling his ideas in the press, before creating a gastronomic guide, tasting committees, and the idea of quality assurance labeling. An essential body of work.
Almanach des gourmands (Éditions Fry Menu)

Jean-Anthelme Brillat-Savarin (1755–1826)
A magistrate and deputy of the Third Estate, Brillat-Savarin writes, two months before his death, the work of a lifetime. An amazing scholarly work, intended as a meditation of transcendent gastronomy. Recipes, reflections, and aphorisms are intertwined through its text.
La Physiologie du goût (*The Physiology of Taste*) (The *Champs* collection, Éditions Flammarion)

THE ECCENTRICS

Maurice Edmond Sailland, known as Curnonsky (1872–1956)
The "prince of gastronomes" served the cause with vivaciousness: books, chronicles, the founder of associations and academies, an AOC lobbyist . . .
La France gastronomique; Les Fines Gueules de France; Souvenirs littéraire et gastronomiques (rare book, first edition)

THE NOTABLES

Edward de Pomiane (1875–1964)
This doctor-researcher at the Pasteur Institute, whose real name is Edouard Pozerski, is passionate about gastronomy and food hygiene. His opuses are prophetic: *Bien manger pour bien vivre*, and *Cuisine en dix minutes*. He is also the pioneer of the culinary radio show.
Radio Cuisine (Éditions Albin Michel)

Marcel Rouff (1877–1936)
Cofounder of L'Académie des gastronomes, this poet and novelist owes his notoriety in the end to the impetuous saga on Dodin-Bouffant, who dedicates himself to the refinements and savory pleasures of gastronomy.
La Vie et la passion de Dodin-Bouffant, gourmet (*The Passionate Epicure*) (Éditions Le Serpent à plumes)

Baron Brisse (1813–1876)
This Provençal pens a daily column in one of the major newspapers of his time, *La Liberté*, gains success, buys the Hotel Scribe, and dies at the table at L'Auberge Gigout Fontenay-aux-Roses.
Les 366 menus (rare book, first edition)

Charles Monselet (1825–1888)
A jack-of-all-trades—playwright, poet, novelist, and journalist—he establishes, above all else, a reputation as an epicurean writer and a pioneer of gastronomic journalism by creating, among others, *Le Gourmet; Lettres gourmandes, manuel de l'homme à table* (rare book, first edition)

Jean-Camille Fulbert-Dumonteil (1831–1912)
Raised in the heart of the Perigord, this dandy half Rastignac, half Bel-Ami embarks on a career writing for the newspaper thanks to his incredible and solid writing ability—the ability to "make poetry from cod."
La France gourmande (rare book, first edition)

James of Coquet (1898–1988)
A successful reporter from the 1930s to 1940s, this winner of the Albert-Londres prize will follow a more peaceful career as a drama and food critic with *Le Figaro Magazine*. His *Propos de table* remains an eloquent jewel of epicurean writing.
Propos de Table (Éditions Albin Michel)

Robert Julien Courtine, known as La Reynière (1910–1998)
Going from the Vichy press during the German occupation of France to the food columns of the newspaper *Le Monde* after World War II, Courtine ("my best collaborator," according to Beuve-Méry) is a quiet force of culinary information during the Glorious Thirty Years.
Un nouveau savoir manger (Éditions Grasset)

Jean Ferniot (1918–2012)

An influential political journalist of Gaullist France and notable man of letters, Ferniot flirts with the epicurean genre in the same way a bourgeois entertains himself with a dancer, managing most notably the magazine *Cuisine & Vins de France*, dear to Curnonsky.
Carnet de croûte (Éd. Robert Laffont)

THE MEDIA STARS

Jean-Pierre Coffe (1938–2016)

An ad man, comedian, and successful restaurateur boosts his ego by breaking into French television on Canal+ (and elsewhere) in the role of a big eater with a love for great food. This role undoubtedly helped (re)-awaken the public's consciousness of the need for good, true, and honest flavors.
Une vie de Coffe (*The Life of Coffe*) (Éditions Stock)

Jean-Luc Petitrenaud (1950–)

This true clown, who spent time at the École du Cirque, is a radio host who also appears on television shows where his endearing quality as a ham helps rejuvenate epicurean interest during the 1990s, thus helping renew the public's interest in good taste.
La France du casse-croûte (Éditions Hachette)

François Simon (1953–)

After spending time with *Presse-Océan*, *Le Matin de Paris*, and *Gault & Millau*, the "masked avenger" critic enters the world of gastronomy with the creation of the *Figaroscope* in 1987. During this time, he fashions his own legendary style and is fastidious about preserving his anonymity.
Comment se faire passer pour un critique gastronomique sans rien y connaître (Éditions Albin Michel)

Périco Légasse (1959–)

First at *L'Événement du jeudi*, then at *Marianne*, but also regularly in front of the cameras in the role of food expert, Périco Légasse has a solid reputation as a militant columnist, enemy of bad food, and extoller of *terroirs*, AOCs, and even the sovereignty of French cuisine.
Dictionnaire impertinent de la gastronomie (Éditions Bourin)

Vincent Ferniot (1960–)

Long before the advent of "foodies," Vincent Ferniot (son of Jean) attempts, with a genuine good nature and a voracious curiosity, to rally the general public's interest in superior products and pleasurable eating.
Trésors du terroir (Éditions Stock)

Julie Andrieu (1974–)

The daughter of actress Nicole Courcel, Julie Andrieu appears on television where, in a feminine and sparkling style, she glamorizes and modernizes the art of television cooking.
Les Carnets de Julie (Éditions Alain Ducasse)

SOURCES OF OTHER GENIUS

Alexandre Dumas (1802–1870)

A writer as much as an epicurean powerhouse, the author of *The Three Musketeers* dedicates a part of his writing acumen to this famous culinary dictionary, published after his death.
Le Grand Dictionnaire de cuisine (*Great Dictionary of Cuisine*) (Éditions Phébus and Éditions Fretin Menu)

Joseph Delteil (1894–1978)

The poet, essayist, and novelist in 1964 pens, alongside his usual work, a small collection of recipes—an enthusiastic, exhilarating, and almost messianic celebration of a cuisine closer to nature.
La Cuisine paléolithique (*Paleolithic Cuisine*) (Éditions Arléa)

Bernard Frank (1929–2006)

This busy dabbler in literature, who gave the label of "Hussards" to Blondin, Deon, Nimier, and Laurent, is also an amazing food columnist. He died at age seventy-seven, utensils in hand, in a Parisian restaurant in the 8th arrondissement.
Portraits et aphorismes (*Portraits and Aphorisms*) (Éditions Le Cherche Midi)

Pierre Desproges (1939–1988)

Less a humorist than a columnist, Desproges understands that the plate is a mirror as much as a refuge for our contemporary manners. His columns are published, for a year, in *Cuisines & Vins de France*.
Encore des nouilles (Éditions Les Échappés)

THE NEW CRITICS

Henri Gault (1929–2000) and Christian Millau (1928–2017)

Legal columnist and political journalist, respectively, Gault and Millau, gourmets by chance, create in the 1960s a veritable editorial and gastronomic machine represented by the guide that carries their namesake, which culminates, in 1971, in the manifesto of Nouvelle Cuisine.
Les guides; Garçon, un brancard! (Éditions Grasset)

Claude Lebey (1923–2017)

It is less his role as a critic with *Paris Match* and *L'Express* than his work as an activist-publisher that places him from the 1980s to 2000s among the great influencers of gastronomy. He earns the attention of chefs, publishes all the great names in Nouvelle Cuisine (from Chapel to Guérard), orchestrates an inventory of culinary heritage, and revives the *bistrotte* in his guides.
L'Inventaire du patrimoine culinaire de la France, 22 volumes (Éditions CNAC-Albin Michel)

Philippe Couderc (1932–)

The 1980s were a decade of demanding food critics and iron palates! A harsh critic (who does not attempt to correct this description) and temporarily at *Minute* and *Nouvel Observateur*, Couderc developed an incredulous and scheming talent.
Les Plats qui on fait la France (Éditions Julliard)

Gilles Pudlowski (1950–)

This very Parisian Frenchman from Lorraine establishes himself from 1980 to 1990 as a baron among food critics. An epicurean, a provocative force in publishing and the press (after a long time at *Point*), and now a blogger.
Les Guides Pudlo (Éditions Michel Lafon), *À quoi sert vraiment un critique gastronomique?* (Éditions Armand Colin)

THE GROUPS

Le Fooding (2000)

A joining of food and feeling, this neologism invented by the journalist Alexandre Cammas in 1999 becomes, the following year, along with Emmanuel Rubin, an *agit-popote* and an incubator of food talent, eager to dispel the "stuffiness" of gastronomy.
Fooding le Dico (Éditions Albin Michel)

Omnivore (2003)

A movement launched by Luc Dubanchet in the wake of *Le Fooding*, a journalist from Europe 1 and Gault & Millau. Centering on the concept of "young cuisine," this group rallies, through publications and festivals, for unhindered cuisine, embodied throughout the world by "creative chefs."
Omnivore Foodbook (biannual review)

skip to ....
Grimod de la Reynière, p. 148

Sautéing Frogs!

The French are not referred to as "frogs" for no reason! A jewel in the crown of French gastronomy, the frog has been a part of Gallic dishes for over ten centuries.
Marie-Amal Bizalion

AN UNCHANGING DISH

The art of preparing frogs has barely changed. In the fourteenth century, according to the recipe of the *Mesnagier de Paris* (1393), one flours the *renoulles* (frogs) before frying them in oil or lard and peppering them.

KEY DATES

In the twelfth century, frogs are not considered meat, and are therefore acceptable for Lent.
Until the 1960s, those consumed in mainland France are sourced from its ponds: the green (*Rana esculenta*) from Dombes and the red (*Rana temporaria*) from between Jura, Ardennes, and Vosges.
Starting in 1970, due to their scarcity and the growth in demand, they are imported alive from Yugoslavia.
On May 6, 1980, a French decree protects French frogs and prohibits their sale (ordinance from June 4, 1980). Live ones start to arrive little by little from Eastern Europe, and frozen ones come from Indonesia at a rate of four thousand tons per year.

THE MAN WITH 100,000 FROGS

In 2010, Patrice François became the first industrial frog rancher in France. Established in Pierrelatte in the Drôme, he raises four tons of *Rana ridibonda* (an excellent green species) per year and hopes to reach twenty tons in a few years—still fewer than what is imported.

BITING THE BITER

"Frog eaters," "froggies": this nickname was given to the French by their English neighbors across the Channel. In 2013, however, a significant deposit of frog-leg bones cooked and eaten at least 8,000 years ago was discovered at Stonehenge—the oldest deposit ever discovered.*
So exactly who is the *froggy*?

*Mark Brown, *The Guardian*, October 16, 2013

WHEELING AND DEALING IN FROGS

How can you be certain of the species imported from Asia once it is cut up and frozen? This is the question that has intrigued two academics.* Their conclusion is enlightening: DNA analysis reveals that 99 percent of frogs sold under the name of *Rana macrodon* are actually *Fejervarya cancrivora*—considerably poorer in quality!

*Anne-Marie Ohler and Violaine Nicolas Colin, theconversation.com, May 25, 2017

FROG LEGS MEUNIÈRE
by Alexandre Gauthier*

In the wake of his father, Roland Gauthier, the chef of this aptly named inn located in the marshes of Pas-de-Calais perpetuates the "frogavore" tradition of the region.

PREPARATION TIME: 50 MINUTES
COOKING TIME: 30 MINUTES
SERVES 6 (AS AN ENTRÉE)

4 lemons
¼ package sandwich bread
3½ ounces (100 g) clarified butter, warmed
2¼ pounds (1 kg) frog legs
Olive oil, for sautéing
18 tablespoons (250 g) salted butter
Unsalted butter, for making browned butter
Fleur de sel sea salt
Freshly ground white pepper

Juice 2 of the lemons and set the juice aside. Remove the rind, white membrane, and seeds from the remaining lemons, then cut the flesh

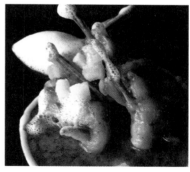

into small dice; set aside. Cut the bread into *brunoise* (small dice) then brown it in a pan in the clarified butter. In a separate hot skillet, brown the frog legs in the oil. Once crisped, add the salted butter and cook until melted and frothy. Add the lemon juice and season with sea salt and white pepper. Arrange the frog legs on plates and top with the diced lemon, the toasted bread pieces, and a drizzle of brown butter (butter melted, cooked until it begins to brown, then whisked).

*Chef of La Grenouillère, Madelaine-sous-Montreuil (Pas-de-Calais)

Traditional French Bread: The Art and the Method

Flour, salt, water: this is the ancient recipe for bread. An everyday food that French baking techniques have managed to bring to its highest form.

Roland Feuillas and Marie-Laure Fréchet

From Ancient Egypt to France: A Brief History of Bread

3000 BC	The Egyptians discover leavened bread by chance, kneading dough with water from the Nile, which is rich in enzymes that create fermentation.
Fifth Century BC	The Greeks invent the hopper mill and make numerous loaves of bread using the yeasts from wine.
AD 1st Century	Pliny the Elder writes that the Gauls add the foam from beer to bread dough and that their bread, considered lighter, is very much appreciated.
AD 6th Century	In France, the mills and ovens belong to the lords, and peasants must pay *banalités* (banality dues) to use them.
Middle Ages	The guild of *tamisiers* or *talmensiers* (flour sifters) appears. Bread is baked at home.
1200	Philippe Auguste authorizes the flour sifters to have their own ovens. They become *panetiers* (official bread bakers for the king).
1250	End of the *banalités* (banality dues). The *panetiers* are now called *boulangers* (because they make rounds of bread).
1790	Abolition of the salt tax. Salt is now used in bread.
1793	Creation of *pain d'équalité* (equality bread)—one bread for all, rich or poor.
1838	The Austrian August Zang sets up a bakery in Paris where Viennese bread is made from yeast.
1857	Louis Pasteur identifies yeast as a microorganism responsible for alcoholic fermentation.
1872	Creation of the first yeast factory in France by Baron Fould-Springer.
1873	Founding of Lesaffre, world leader in the production of commercial yeast.
1903	Invention of the *biscotte* by Charles Heudebert, artisan baker in Nanterre.
1993	The "Bread Decree" outlines the French tradition of bread making.
1997	Jean-Pierre Raffarin establishes the Bread Festival on May 16, Saint-Honoré Day, which celebrates the patron saint of bakers, and regulates the baking profession with certain standards.

MAKING A PREFERMENT (DOUGH STARTER)

To make leavened dough, you have to create a "preferment" (also referred to as the *chef*, *levain*, or *sourdough starter*). Use quality organic flour and spring water.

Day 1: In a clean container, combine 1 ounce (25 g) of high-gluten wheat flour (T80 or higher) or rye flour with 1 ounce (25 g) of warm water. Place a loose-fitting lid on top or cover the jar with plastic wrap poked with holes. Store in a cool place (ideally 77°F/25°C).

Day 2: Add 1¾ ounces (50 g/ ½ cup) of flour and 1¾ ounces (50 g/ 3 tablespoons plus 1 teaspoon) of water to the preparation from day 1 and stir to combine. Cover again and set aside to ferment.

Day 3: Remove half of the mixture from day 2 and discard it. Take the remaining 3½ ounces (100 g) in the jar and stir in 7 ounces (200 g/2 cups) of flour and 7 ounces (200 g/¾ cup plus 1 tablespoon) of water. Cover; let ferment. Repeat this step for 2 to 3 days (being sure to discard half each day) until it begins to bubble and gives off a pleasant sour aroma.

The preferment is ready but needs to be "refreshed" in order to work with it. To do so, mix the preferment with water and flour at a minimum ratio of 1:2:2. For example, if 7 ounces (200 g) of dough is required, you start with 1¾ ounces (50 g) of the preferment, 3½ ounces (100 g/⅓ cup plus 1 tablespoon) of water, and 3½ ounces (100 g/1 cup) of flour, mixed together. Let it ferment for about 4 hours (always covered, but not tightly) before using. It must rise by one-third its original size and have the consistency of a chocolate mousse.

From the refreshed preferment, make the next refreshed preferment for the next batch of bread dough. This preferment can be stored at room temperature if used within 3 days or refrigerated if used within 1 or 2 weeks.

★ Kneading the dough
Kneading permits the mixing of water and flour but it also incorporates air into the dough (about 10 percent of the bread's volume). We start with the *frasage* (mixing of the ingredients), then we start folding the dough. An insufficiently kneaded dough will not have enough body. If it's overkneaded, it will collapse because the network of gluten strands will have relaxed.

★ Proofing
This is the resting period for the dough, during which the yeasts will multiply and aromas will start to develop.

★ Shaping
The dough is divided into smaller dough pieces, then shaped into balls, baguettes, etc.

★ Final proof
This is the second fermentation period before baking the bread.

★ Scoring or slashing
This step is referred to as the "baker's signature." It is through these incisions that water vapor and CO_2 will escape and therefore allow the bread to rise sufficiently in the oven.

● NATURAL BREAD

Leavening is said to be "natural" when the seeding of the dough during fermentation occurs naturally thanks to the yeasts and bacteria present in the air and the flour. Its composition is complex and ensures the aromatic and nutritional richness of naturally leavened bread. In addition, this slow fermentation allows better digestion of the gluten. The bread can also be kept for longer periods without spoiling.

● COMMERCIAL BREAD

In contrast, the commercial bakery uses a single strain of yeast selected for its fermenting power. To reduce the fermentation time (and therefore production time), the bakery often increases the quantities of yeast. However, with today's flours being of lesser quality than they once were, they are no longer sufficient to feed the yeasts. It is therefore necessary to resort to additives, which strengthen the network of gluten and contribute to intolerances to gluten. To compensate for the lack of aromas from baking with added yeasts, the baker adds salt and sometimes starters that are inactivated by heat (the enzymes are dead and no longer involved in the fermentation process).

PREFERMENTS (STARTERS)

The story: this process was probably discovered by chance, after someone left a grain mixture in a warm, humid environment. Housewives, who were the bakers, eventually learned to collect some of their kneaded dough that had risen the day before to start the next batch of dough.

The biology: a preferment (dough starter) is a living symbiotic medium consisting of a wide variety of microorganisms present in the air, in the flour, and on the surfaces of containers. Yeasts, single-cell organisms, breathe and feed like any living thing. In particular, they feed on carbohydrates found in grains. When they deteriorate, yeasts release, among other things, carbon dioxide gas, which causes a dough to rise. Alcohol, lactic acid, and acetic acid are also created. These yeasts are wild and fermentation is therefore spontaneous and slow. They also contain an important bacterial flora that triggers lactic and acetic fermentations and contributes both flavor and nutritional qualities to the bread. Lactic acid bacteria also produce carbon dioxide, which causes the dough to rise.

The practice: it is necessary to depend on experience, and the person who is managing the starter must pay very close attention to atmospheric conditions and to the raw materials used in order to obtain a consistent result. Starters need to be fed regularly to stay alive.

YEASTS

The story: in 1857, Louis Pasteur identified the role of bacteria and yeasts. Subsequently, *Saccharomyces cerevisiae* (literally "beer fungi that uses sugar"), or brewer's yeast, was isolated. It was from certain strains of these brewer's yeasts that commercial yeast was developed. However, this yeast is more unstable, so to better preserve it, it is pressed using a process developed in Austria. The following therefore discusses the Viennese method of bread baking using commercial yeast, as opposed to the French method using wild yeasts.

The biology: commercial yeast is composed of microscopic fungi, *Saccharomyces cerevisiae*, which feed on carbohydrates from flour, therefore releasing carbon dioxide gas. In 1 gram of commercial yeast, there are 10 billion living cells.

The practice: commercial yeast is activated by diluting it in a little warm water or milk and allowing it to bubble for 15 minutes. The fermentation is quite fast. The yeast can be kept cool and freezes well, but dies when cooked to temperatures above 122°F (50°C). Dried yeast is a fresh yeast that has been dehydrated or freeze-dried. It is added directly to the flour in an instant form or diluted in a liquid if it is an active dry yeast.

SOURDOUGH BREAD
Recipe by Roland Feuillas

PREPARATION TIME: 10 MINUTES
RESTING TIME: 14 TO 18 HOURS
COOKING TIME: 40 MINUTES
MAKES 1 LOAF

1½ teaspoons (10 g) unrefined salt
1⅔ cups (400 mL) + 3 tablespoons plus 1 teaspoon (50 mL) spring water
1⅛ pounds (500 g) organic high-gluten flour or T80 flour
5¼ ounces (150 g) refreshed starter (preferment)

In the bowl of a stand mixer fitted with a dough hook, combine, in this order, the salt, the 1⅔ cups (400 mL) of spring water, the flour, and the starter. Knead for 3 minutes on speed 1, then for 3 minutes on speed 2. During the second kneading, add the 3 tablespoons plus 1 teaspoon (50 mL) of water into the mixer bowl in a thin stream. You can also knead the dough for 10 minutes by hand, slowly adding the 3 tablespoons plus 1 teaspoon (50 mL) of water at the end.

When the dough is smooth, fold it onto itself twice, then place it in a pan or bowl. Cover with plastic wrap, poke a few holes in the top with the tip of a knife, and refrigerate for 14 to 18 hours.

When the dough has risen, scrape it from the bowl using a lightly floured bowl scraper and place the dough on a well-floured work surface (ideally of wood).

Fold the dough over onto itself three or four times, without kneading it, while gently punching it down. Place the dough ball in a dough-rising basket or in a large salad bowl covered with a clean, well-floured tea towel.

Let stand at room temperature for 1 to 2 hours.

Meanwhile, preheat the oven to 500°F (260°C). Place a pizza stone or baking sheet inside the oven with a drip tray placed on the rack beneath it. Quickly place the bread in the oven using a pizza peel (or turn the bowl over onto the baking sheet), then pour a glass of water into the drip pan. Quickly close the oven door. After 20 minutes, lower the oven temperature to 425°F (220°C) and continue baking for another 20 minutes.

When the loaf is well browned and the bottom sounds hollow when thumped, take the bread out of the oven and let it cool on a rack.

EQUIVALENTS FOR 1⅛ POUNDS (500 G/5 CUPS) OF FLOUR

Instant dry yeast: 1 packet, or ⅛ ounce (5 g)
Fresh compressed yeast: ½ block, or ¾ ounce (21 g)
Liquid homemade starter: 14 ounces (400 g)
Stiff starter: 10½ ounces (300 g)

skip to
Grains and Flours, p. 370

An Abundance of Brie . . .

Brie de Meaux and Brie de Melun may each have an AOP (*appellation d'origine protégée*), but there are many other Bries as well. Here is a quick overview of Brie in all its forms.

Laurent Seminel

THE MATCH-UP

Brie de Meaux
5¾ to 7 pounds (2.6 to 3.2 kg)
14 to 14½ inches (36 to 37 cm) in diameter
4 to 8 weeks of ripening
45 percent fat in dry matter
2014 production:
6,255 metric tons

Brie de Melun
3⅓ to 4 pounds (1.5 to 1.8 kg)
10½ to 11 inches (27 to 28 cm) in diameter
4 to 12 weeks of ripening
45 percent fat in dry matter
2014 production:
255 metric tons

A ROYAL HISTORY

Pharamond, king of the Franks, consumes cheeses made on the banks of the Marne, east of Paris.
• **Charlemagne** tastes Brie at the priory of Reuil-en-Brie: "I have just discovered one of the best dishes that can be found," he states.
• **Philippe August**e, successor of his father, Louis the Younger, in 1180, offers "galettes of Brie" to his court.
• **Louis XVI**, fleeing the revolutionaries, stops at Varennes to eat. Not wanting to leave the table until he has finished his Brie, he is found and captured.
• **Charles-Maurice de Talleyrand-Périgord** promotes Brie at the Congress of Vienna in 1815. In a European cheese competition that he helps organize, Brie is declared the "prince of cheeses and premier of desserts."

"Three Bries, on round boards, had the melancholy of extinct moons; two, very dry, were in their full stage; the third, in its second quarter, was draining, emptying itself of white cream, spread out in a lake, ravaging its slender board, which one had tried in vain to contain." Emile Zola, *Le Ventre de Paris* (*The Belly of Paris*), 1873.

POTTED BRIE, A FORGOTTEN SPECIALTY

"This same cheese is also served in pots; but it is not sold on the market, and those which we see in this form are brought righteously from Meaux by amateur connoisseurs," writes Grimod de la Reynière.

BRIES
A list of forgotten Bries:
- Brie de Coulommiers, also called "Brie petit moule."
- Brie de Montereau.
- Brie de Nangis.
- Brie de Macqueline.
- Brie de Malhesherbes.
- Brie de Provins.
- Le Noir de Nanteuil (a "superaged" Brie, black and dry, consumed during harvest, hence its nickname "Brie of the Harvest").
- Brie de Melun bleu (dusted with charcoal).
- Somerset Brie: a cheese produced by our friends, the English!

DID YOU KNOW?
"The name 'brioche' comes from a pastry which once had Brie as an ingredient." Alexandre Dumas, *Le Grand dictionnaire de cuisine* (*Great Dictionary of Cuisine*), 1873.

The Kugelhopf

Here, finally unveiled, is the essential *kugelhopf* recipe (in its simplest form).
Pierre Hermé

THE SECRET?
It's the mold. It must be shaped like a turban (with large curved ribs) and made of terra cotta. Metal or silicone molds are forbidden!

PREPARATION TIME: 40 MINUTES
RESTING TIME: OVERNIGHT +
8 HOURS
COOKING TIME: 35 TO 40 MINUTES
MAKES 2 CAKES
2 earthenware kugelhopf molds 6 inches (16 cm) in diameter
5⅛ ounces (145 g) raisins
¼ cup (60 mL) rhum agricole
For the starter
1 cup plus 2½ tablespoons (115 g) all-purpose flour
⅛ ounce (5 g) baker's yeast
⅓ cup (80 mL) milk
For the dough
1 ounce (25 g) baker's yeast
⅓ cup (80 mL) milk
2½ cups (250 g) all-purpose flour
3 pinches salt
¼ cup plus 2 tablespoons (75 g) superfine sugar
2 egg yolks
6 tablespoons (85 g) unsalted butter, slightly softened
1½ ounces (40 g) whole hulled almonds
3 tablespoons plus 1¾ teaspoons (50 g) unsalted butter, melted
Confectioners' sugar, for dusting

The day before
Soak the raisins in the rum.
The next day
Prepare the starter. Combine the flour, yeast, and milk in a large mixing bowl. Cover the bowl with a damp cloth and place it in the refrigerator for 4 to 5 hours, or until small bubbles appear on the surface.
Once the starter is ready
Make the dough. Dilute the yeast in the milk. Place the starter, flour, salt, superfine sugar, egg yolks, and the dissolved yeast in a large bowl. Mix well with your hands or using a wooden spoon until the dough starts to detach easily from the bowl. Add the 6 tablespoons (85 g) of butter in pieces and continue to work the dough until it detaches from the sides of the bowl again. Drain the macerated raisins, and mix them in to the dough. Cover the bowl with a cloth and let rest for about 2 hours at room temperature, or until it doubles in volume. Grease the two molds and place an almond in each indentation at the bottom.

Place the dough onto a floured work surface and divide it into two equal parts. Make two balls by folding the edges in toward the center. Roll each ball on the work surface while pressing it under the palm of your hand in a circular motion. Flour your fingers, take each ball in hand, push your thumb down into the center to form a deep indentation, then stretch the dough out a little and place it in the mold. Let rise at room temperature for about 1 hour 30 minutes. If the room is dry, cover the dough with a damp cloth.

Preheat the oven to 400°F (200°C).

Place both molds in the oven for 35 to 40 minutes, or until golden. Unmold the cakes onto a rack and brush them with the melted butter to keep moist. Let cool, then dust lightly with confectioners' sugar; serve.

If you want to keep the kugelhopf for some time, wrap it in plastic wrap to stay fresh.

Raymond Oliver

As the first television cooking icon, this famous chef of Le Grand Véfour placed regionalism on the Parisian plate.
Charles Patin O'Coohoon

HIS FAMOUS CUSTOMERS

In a short period, all of Paris was visiting Le Grand Véfour:
André Malraux
Jean Giraudoux
Sacha Guitry
Louis Aragon
Elsa Triolet
Marcel Schwob
Jean-Paul Sartre
Simone de Beauvoir
Marcel Pagnol
Juliette Greco
Louis Jouvet
Jean Cocteau
Colette

Signature Dishes

→ **Colette's Coulibiac**
A puff pastry of Russian origin consisting of salmon, egg, and spinach
→ **Jean Cocteau's Pintadeau**
A young guinea hen stuffed with foie gras, cognac, and truffle
→ **Veal Sweetbread with Verjus**
A beautiful serving of sweetbreads accompanied by a verjus sauce
→ **Fish Terrine Taillevent**
A terrine of fish. A tribute to Guillaume Tirel, author of the *Viandier* (circa 1486).

La dynastie Oliver
Louis et Céline Oliver
restaurateurs
↓
Raymond Oliver
chef
Michel Oliver → Stéphanie Oliver
chef   restauratrice
Bruno Oliver → Clémentine Oliver
chef   boulangère
↓
Aleksandre Oliver
pâtissier

Star chef of Le Grand Véfour and the small screen
(1909–1990)

FROM THE GIRONDE TO LE GRAND VÉFOUR

1909
Birth in Langon (Gironde)

1948
Arrival at Le Grand Véfour (Paris 1st)

1953
Earns three stars in the *Michelin Guide*
❀❀❀

1954
Launch of the television show *L'Art et Magie de la cuisine* (*The Art and Magic of Cooking*)

1971
Begins his journey into healthy cooking

1984
Sale of Le Grand Véfour to the Taittinger family

1990
Dies in Paris

SHELLFISH WITH ESPELETTE AND ALMONDS

6 cockles
6 gray clams
6 farm mussels
3 tablespoons plus 1 teaspoon (50 mL) white wine
1 tablespoon (7 g) bread crumbs
1 tablespoon (5 g) chopped almonds
3½ ounces (100 g) coarse salt

For the snail butter
5½ tablespoons (80 g) unsalted butter, melted
1 tablespoon (4 g) chopped parsley
1 tablespoon (4 g) chopped chervil
1 tablespoon (4 g) chopped tarragon
1 tablespoon (10 g) chopped shallot
1 clove garlic, peeled and chopped
1 pinch ground Espelette pepper
1 teaspoon anise liqueur

Prepare the shellfish. Clean the shellfish by soaking them for 30 minutes in salted water. Place them in a saucepan and add the wine. Heat over high heat until the shells open; strain. Remove the upper shell from each shellfish, if desired.

Make the snail butter. Combine the butter, herbs, shallot, garlic, Espelette, and liqueur. Place a bit of this mixture on top of each piece of shellfish. Pour the coarse salt into the bottom of a baking dish and place the shellfish on top. Sprinkle with the bread crumbs and chopped almonds. Preheat the broiler and place the dish under the broiler for 2 to 3 minutes, or just until the bread crumbs are golden.

Excerpt from La cuisine de mon grand-père (My Grandfather's Kitchen) *by Bruno Oliver, Éditions Alternatives*

THE SCHOLAR

Possessing nearly 6,000 works, he owned one of the most important gastronomic libraries in France, compiling gems like a pre-1501 edition of the famous *Viandier de Taillevent*.

A POPULAR TELEVISION CHEF

At the end of 1954, the ORTF, the national public radio and television agency in France, launches a television show devoted to cooking. For 13 years, Raymond Oliver and host Catherine Langeais form a duet full of fantasy, captivating French homes with the show *L'Art et Magie de la Cuisine* (*The Art and Magic of Cooking*). Thanks to this truculent 20-minute program, he stands out as one of the most popular chefs in France and one of the best known abroad. The show becomes a television sensation and lasts for more than 60 years.

. . . ON THE BIG SCREEN . . .

Raymond Oliver's success on television translates equally to the cinema. He plays himself in *Clair de Lune à Maubeuge* by Jean Chérasse (1962). That same year, he appears in Gille Grangier's *Le Gentleman d'Epsom* in a screenplay by Michel Audiard.

. . . AND ON THE RADIO

In the 1950s, the radio drama *Furax* of the duo Pierre Dac and Francis Blanche follows the adventures of clumsy detectives, Black and White, against the actions of the fearsome Edmond Furax. During the second season, Oliver appears as a character in one of the episodes of *Boudin Sacré*.

The French Love Galette des Rois

Enjoying *galette des rois* (kings' cake) during the month of January to mark the Epiphany is one of the most vivacious pastry traditions in France. Every year, French pastry chefs compete based on know-how, creativity, and . . . on cost margin! Here is my favorite recipe.

François-Régis Gaudry

— THE TRADITIONAL GALETTE DES ROIS WITH ALMOND CREAM —
Hugues Pouget*

FIRST, A FEW DEFINITIONS

Galette sèche ("dry" galette): a galette without filling. For those who love puff pastry!

Fabophilie: a habit of collecting the kings' cake charms.

Almond cream: a mixture of butter, almond flour, and sugar.

Frangipane: almond cream with pastry cream added. We prefer the simple almond cream: it's tastier, less oily, and easier to prepare.

THE ESSENTIALS FOR A HOMEMADE RECIPE

The puff pastry

Your puff pastry (*pâte feuilletée*) must be made of pure butter! Ideally, buy your puff pastry at a gourmet grocery, from a good bakery, or from the excellent artisan www.patefeuilleteefrancois.com.

The almonds

Make your own almond flour using whole unskinned organic almonds. Lightly roast them in the oven, then grind them until fine, still in their skins, in a food processor. This almond flour is of better quality and is cheaper than purchased almond flour. I also like to do as Claire Heitzler (the pastry chef of Ladurée) does and add some coarsely crushed almonds into the flour to add some crunch.

Bitter-almond extract

This is the old-school approach to enhancing the almond flavor. For a more subtle almond aroma, a small drizzle of orgeat almond syrup is preferred.

A splash of rum

Traditional almond cream always has a little splash of rum (clear or gold). New-generation pastry chefs opt instead for a recipe without alcohol.

PREPARATION TIME: 20 MINUTES
COOKING TIME: 30 TO 45 MINUTES
MAKES 1 GALETTE APPROXIMATELY 12 INCHES (30 CM) IN DIAMETER (SERVES 8 TO 10)

10½ tablespoons (125 g) unsalted butter, slightly softened
3½ ounces (100 g) demerara sugar
2 whole eggs, cool room temperature
4½ ounces (125 g) almond flour
2 disks pure-butter puff pastry (about 12 in/30 cm in diameter)
1 small charm (or use a bean)
1 egg yolk beaten with 1 tablespoon water or milk, for glazing the dough

Massage the butter with your fingers to obtain a smooth texture, then gradually work in the sugar, then the whole eggs one by one, and finally the almond flour; the mixture should be supple and smooth. On a baking sheet lined with parchment paper, spread out the first puff pastry disk. Using a pastry bag or spoon, spread the almond cream on top of the dough, ensuring the thickness of the cream is even and leaving a ¾- to 1⅛-inch (2 to 3 cm) border around the edge of the dough. Place the charm on top in a random spot, but not in the center!

Moisten the edge of the dough all the way around with a pastry brush dipped in cold water, then place the second puff pastry disk on top. With your fingers, carefully press down the edges to seal the two dough disks together well, but without pressing too hard and forming an excess edge. Use the tip of a knife to score a decorative design on the top. Brush the top of the dough with the egg yolk mixture. Ideally, let the galette chill for several hours in the refrigerator. Preheat the oven to 350°F (180°C) and bake the galette for 30 to 45 minutes, or just until puffed and deep golden. Serve warm.

*Hugo & Victor, 40, boulevard Raspail, Paris 6th; 7, rue Gomboust, Paris 1st

A SWEET POTATO GALETTE?

While browsing the extraordinary *Dictionnaire de la Gourmandise*,* we came across a "sweetened potato frangipane from Spain (the endearing nickname of the sweet potato when it arrived in southern France in the eighteenth century)," from 1839. Our friend Estérelle Payany successfully adapted this recipe. The result is a lighter filling than the original with less butter and more natural sugar!

PREPARATION TIME: 30 MINUTES
COOKING TIME: 1 HOUR
MAKES 1 GALETTE APPROXIMATELY
12 INCHES (30 CM) IN DIAMETER
(SERVES 8 TO 10)

5¼ ounces (150 g) sweet potatoes, washed and unpeeled
4 tablespoons plus ¾ teaspoon (60 g) unsalted butter, slightly softened
¼ cup plus 2 tablespoons (80 g) sugar
1 egg
4¼ ounces (120 g) almond flour
1 splash aged rum
1 pinch fine salt
2 disks pure-butter puff pastry (about 12 in/30 cm in diameter)
1 egg yolk beaten with 1 tablespoon water or milk, for glazing the dough
1 small charm (or use a bean)

Cook the sweet potatoes in a saucepan of boiling water for 15 to 20 minutes. Check for doneness with the tip of a knife. Peel and purée them.

Whisk together the butter and sugar until combined. Whisk in the whole egg, then the almond flour, sweet potato purée, rum,

and salt. Stir just until creamy, but not long enough to incorporate much air. On a baking sheet lined with parchment paper, spread out the first puff pastry disk, then spread the cream on top, leaving a ¾-inch (2 cm) border. Place the charm in a random spot on top of the cream (but not in the center!). Moisten the edge of the dough all the way around with a pastry brush dipped in cold water, then place the second puff pastry disk on top. With your fingers, carefully press down the edges to seal the two dough disks together well, but without pressing too hard and forming an excess edge. Refrigerate for 1 hour. Preheat the oven to 350°F (180°C). Brush the top of the dough with the egg yolk mixture, then use the back of a knife to score a decorative design on the top. Bake for 30 to 45 minutes, or just until puffed and deep golden. Serve warm or cold.

*Annie Perrier-Robert, Robert Laffont, collection Bouquins

A Short History of Serving Kings' Cake

In ancient Rome, the tradition of enjoying *galette des rois* is already a part of the Saturnalia celebration. It is at this time that the custom is created of having the youngest child sit under the table to choose which guest gets which slice of the galette. The *fève* ("charm") used in the cake is a dried bean.

During the Christian era, the galette is associated with the Epiphany, marking the appearance of the Three Wise Men to the baby Jesus. The bean is replaced with a small charm of the baby Jesus.

Is It a Galette or Brioche?

In northern France a *galette*, in the South a *brioche*? It's actually more complicated than this according to Pierre Lacam, author of *Mémorial hitorique et géographique de la pâtisserie* (*The Historical and Geographical Memoir of the Pastry Shop*, 1900): "Paris has its galettes and many variations in all directions, Lyon its yeast-leavened brioche crowns, Reims and Metz, too; Nantes has the *Nantais* and flaky pastry [pâte brisée]; Brittany has leavened doughs made with vanilla sugar; Bordeaux has its *Tortillons de Gapté* and its lemon cakes; Toulouse, its *gâteaux de Limoux*. In general, all of the South has a sweet brioche, even in Lyon, which just goes to show that *Le roi boit*! [Even the King celebrates the Twelfth Night!]"

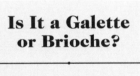
skip to
Puff Pastry, a Tour de Force, p. 342

During the Middle Ages, the Duke Louis II of Bourbon each year designates a poor eight-year-old child as king. He dresses the child in royal clothes, invites him to eat at his table, and offers money for his education.

Under Louis XIV, part of the galette is set aside for the Virgin, then it is distributed to the poor.

During the French Revolution, one serves the "galette of liberty" or "of equality." A crown is added as part of the tradition and the charm takes on a revolutionary look: a porcelain Phrygian cap or a tricorn cap.

In 1975, President Valéry Giscard d'Estaing introduces the tradition of the galettes des rois at the Élysée. But there is no charm hidden under the puff pastry, to ensure that a king is not chosen in the Republic!

Cyril Lignac Invasion

Television programs, bread ovens, and a sugar laboratory! Located in Paris, Cyril Lignac, the Aveyronnais, expands his gourmet adventures. He and his accomplice and pastry chef-chocolatier, Benoît Couvrand, create an amazing duo! Here is proof in three very chocolaty recipes.

François-Régis Gaudry

THE TIGERS

MAKES 10 PIECES

Ingredients
6 tablespoons plus 2 teaspoons (95 g) unsalted butter, plus more for greasing
1¾ cups (175 g) confectioners' sugar
2⅓ ounces (65 g) almond flour
2⅓ ounces/⅔ cup (65 g) pastry flour or T45 flour
½ teaspoon (2 g) baking powder
⅓ teaspoon (2 g) salt
6⅓ ounces (180 g) egg whites (about 6 large eggs)
5¼ ounces (150 g) dark chocolate chips

For the ganache
¾ cup minus 1 teaspoon (170 g) light cream
3⅛ ounces (90 g) dark chocolate
1 ounce (30 g) milk chocolate

Equipment
10 individual kugelhopf molds

Preheat the oven to 350°F (175°C). Melt the butter in a saucepan and cook it until it becomes a nutty brown color. Pour it into a glass bowl to stop the cooking. In a large bowl, combine the sugar, almond and pastry flours, baking powder, and salt. Add the egg whites little by little, then the warm brown butter, and finally the chocolate chips; stir to combine.

Butter the kugelhopf molds. Place 1¾ ounces (50 g) of the dough in each mold. Bake for 15 minutes, or until golden on top. Unmold immediately and let cool.

Meanwhile, make the ganache. In a saucepan, bring the cream to a boil, then pour it into a large bowl over the chocolates. Stir until smooth; let cool.

Place the cakes on a baking sheet lined with parchment paper or a silicone baking mat. When the ganache begins to thicken, pour it into the center of each cake. Let cool and serve.

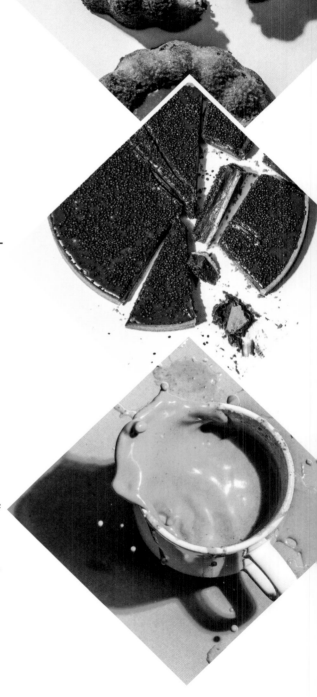

GIANDUJA TART

A decadent and crunchy tart—Cyril Lignac delivers!

SERVES 8

Ingredients
7 tablespoons (100 g) unsalted butter, plus more for greasing
1 ounce (30 g) almond flour
⅔ cup plus 2 teaspoons (70 g) confectioners' sugar
⅛ teaspoon (1 g) fleur de sel sea salt
1 egg
1⅓ cups (165 g) all-purpose flour or T55 flour

For the gianduja ganache
2 tablespoons plus 2 teaspoons (40 g) milk
½ cup plus 1 tablespoon (130 g) light cream
11½ ounces (330 g) gianduja (hazelnut milk chocolate)
Chocolate flakes

Make the pastry crust. Place the butter in a food processor and pulse until a creamy and firm consistency is achieved. Add the almond flour, sugar, and sea salt. Add one-third of the egg, and one-third of the flour and mix well, then repeat with the remaining two-thirds egg and flour. Pulse the mixture to form a ball, then refrigerate it for 1 hour.

Make the ganache. In a saucepan, bring the cream and milk to a boil. Melt the gianduja in a double boiler or in a microwave. Pour the hot cream mixture into the melted gianduja. Stir until blended; finish the emulsion using an immersion blender.

Preheat the oven to 300°F (150°C). Lightly knead the dough. On a floured work surface, roll out the dough to a thickness of ⅒ inch (2.5 mm). Lightly grease a tart pan (or flan ring) and line it with the dough. Bake for 20 minutes, or until golden. Let cool. Pour the ganache into the cooled tart crust and refrigerate for 2 hours to set. Sprinkle with chocolate flakes and serve.

HOT CHOCOLATE

SERVES 8

Ingredients
6⅔ ounces (190 g) milk chocolate
11¼ ounces (320 g) dark chocolate
1 cup minus ½ teaspoon (230 g) light cream
1½ cups (350 g) whole milk
½ vanilla pod, halved lengthwise, seeds scraped out

Place the chocolates in a large bowl. In a saucepan, bring the cream, milk, and vanilla bean pod and seeds to a boil. Remove the vanilla bean pod, then pour the hot cream mixture over the two chocolates. Stir to combine, then transfer the mixture to a blender and blend until smooth. Serve immediately in small mugs.

CHOCOLATERIE CYRIL LIGNAC, GOURMAND CROQUANT, 25, rue Chanzy, Paris 11th; 34, rue du Dragon, Paris 6th

skip to
Intensely Chocolate, p. 139

Roquefort: The Cheese with the Blue Veins

The recognition of a princely cheese—"son of the mountain and the wind" (Curnonsky).

Stéphane Solier

THE STORY OF ROQUEFORT IN NINE DATES

The Legend
A piece of cheese with bread left behind by a shepherd in a cave gives birth to the discovery of "noble mold."

77 AD
Pliny the Elder mentions a cheese from the country of Gabales (Gevaudan), highly esteemed in Rome.

795
Charlemagne discovers a curious moldy cheese at the monastery of Vabres (Aveyron) and learns to appreciate its taste.

1411
Charles VI recognizes the inhabitants of Roqueforts' monopoly on the aging of cheese "as it is practiced from time immemorial in the caves of the village."

1550 and 1666
A judgment of the Parliament of Toulouse punishes merchants selling fake Roquefort.

1782
"Roquefort cheese is without a doubt the premier cheese of Europe" (Diderot and d'Alembert in *L'Encyclopédie* (*The Encyclopedia*).

April 1912
Fifty metric tons of Roquefort are loaded onto and sink with the *Titanic* . . . an obstacle on the road to the cheese's conquest of America!

1925
Becomes France's first AOC cheese.

1996
European recognition with PDO (Protected Designation of Origin)

THE 7 RECENT ROQUEFORT COMPANIES

Ets Carles (1927)
Ets Combes (1923)
Fromageries Occitanes (1994)
Fromageries Papillon (1906)
Ets Gabriel Coulet (1872)
Société des Caves et des Producteurs réunis (1863)
Ets Vernières (1890)

THE REQUIREMENTS OF AOP-REGULATED ROQUEFORT

❀ Raw and whole sheep's milk
❀ Ewes of the Lacaune breed of sheep
❀ Geographical area of production and processing: the "Rayon" (includes six French departments)
❀ Renneting and injection with *Penicillium roqueforti* and lactic ferments
❀ Dry salting (sea salt)
❀ Aging in the caves of Roquefort-sur-Soulzon (Aveyron), in an area 1¼ miles by ¼ mile/2 km by 300 m that is defined by the appellation (the Combalou caves), in the heart of the *fleurine* (natural chimneys allowing remarkable thermal regulation and humidity)
❀ Aging in caves for a minimum of 14 days
❀ Sale possible after 90 days of aging and maturation

ROQUEFORT BY NUMBERS
The second-most-consumed cheese in France, after Comté

16,900 TONS
Annual production in 2014 (down over the last ten years but 74 times more than in 1800!)

769,000
Number of ewes that make up the dairy farm of Ray de Roquefort

32.8 PERCENT
Percentage of fat

5½ TO 6⅓ POUNDS (2.5 TO 2.9 KG)
Weight of a block of Roquefort

7¾ INCHES (20 CM) IN DIAMETER AND 3½ INCHES (9 CM) IN HEIGHT
Dimensions of a block of Roquefort

11
Number of underground levels in the caves where Roquefort is aged

44°F TO 46°F (7°C TO 8°C)
Constant temperature of the Roquefort caves

90 DAYS
Minimum ripening period to acquire the "Roquefort" AOC

90
Number of countries to which Roquefort is exported each year

1,700
Number of people who work every day to produce Roquefort

A CORSICAN ROQUEFORT?
Roquefort producers settled in Corsica (France's île de Beauté) at the end of the nineteenth century, faced with the need to expand the area of milk collection in response to the increased demand for cheese and the varying lactation periods between the Aveyron sheep (February–July) and the Corsican sheep (November–May). Starting in 1899, Roquefort producer Louis Rigal was established in Corsica. He was soon followed by other producers, such as Maison Maria Grimal, Société, and the Solier brothers, all of which made up 5 percent of the Roquefort production starting in 1905.

The number of dairies grew rapidly with the onset of World War I due to the lack of dairy farms on continental Europe. As a consequence, Corsica began to experience, as in the Rayon, the absorption of the small producers by the larger ones.

Even if trading companies admit little Corsican provenance of their milk, Corsica remains today a contributor to the production of Roquefort (with 95 producers and 2,500,000 liters of milk produced in 2010).

skip to ....
The Art of the Accident, p. 66

THE RAYON?
Sheep's milk used to make Roquefort was originally sourced from the Rayon.
• This area was limited for centuries to the surrounding limestone area (Aveyron).
• The area was extended, starting during the second half of the nineteenth century, first to the other regions of Rouergue and the bordering areas (Lozère, Gard, Hérault, Tarn, Aude), then to the Pyrénées and Corsica.

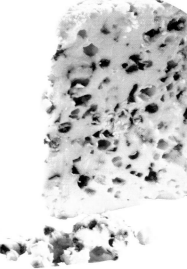

PENICILLIUM ROQUEFORTI

➤ The essential ingredient in the production of Roquefort.

➤ Is a living and natural fungus.

➤ Must be cultivated in France.

➤ Under the effects of the air and moisture of the caves, it develops in the cheese's center, and once established imparts a blue-green color to the cheese.

➤ Each producer of Roquefort uses one or more of the hundreds of identified strains, which give each cheese a distinct flavor and creaminess.

The Other Country for Cod

Salt cod from Portugal? It's an essential part of French culinary heritage! This "fish for the poor," which has now become, due to overfishing, rare and expensive, is worth rediscovering . . .

Frédéric Laly-Baraglioli

Hauts-de-France
· *Cod in salad* with potatoes and beets
· *Cod with Maroilles cheese*

Normandy
· *Normandy-style cod gratin:* potatoes, cream, and mussels

Alsace
· *Cabbage leaves stuffed with cod* and cottage cheese
· *Cod in sauerkraut* (and snails)

Brittany
· *Cod à la brestoise:* with leeks and potatoes
· *Cod à la paimpolaise:* with au gratin potatoes
· *Cod à la dinardaise:* with potato croquettes

Offshore

West Indies
· *Cod fritters*
· *Sliced cod:* in salad with lime, cucumber, garlic, and chile
· *Wild:* with avocado, lemon, and cassava
· *Cod in pastry* (turnovers with scallions and parsley)
· *Cod macadam*

Réunion
· *Cod rougail* or *fleurd'zognons:* with ginger, tomatoes, kaffir lime, garlic, onions, peppers, mango, or green papaya

Saint-Pierre-et-Miquelon
· *Le tiaude* (stew)
· *Cod meatballs* (with potatoes)

Nouvelle-Aquitaine
· *Cod and dill omelette* (Bègles)
· *Aïado Charentais:* with scallions, snails, and olives
· *Perigord cod pie* (with potatoes and walnut oil)

Pays Basque
· *Good-Friday omelet:* with sweet peppers
· *Basquaise:* cod with tomatoes, peppers, and Espelette pepper
· *Zurruputuna:* cod soup, leeks, chile peppers, and potatoes

Occitanie
· *Cod cassoulet* (Tarn)
· *Cod béarnaise,* with white beans and leeks
· *Estofinado* (Aveyron): stockfish, eggs, potatoes, garlic, and walnut oil
· *Cod brandade* (Nîmes)

Provence-Alpes-Côte d'Azur
· *Cod pot-au-feu* or large aïoli, with squid, whelk snails, eggs, and vegetables
· *Cod Raïto:* red wine sauce, onions, olives, and tomatoes
· *Estocaficado:* stockfish stew with tomatoes
· *Nissarda cod:* with tomatoes, bell peppers, and zucchini

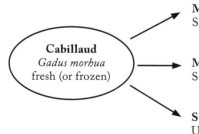

Corsica
· *Cod with Swiss chard,* leeks, and/or raisins
· *Cod beignets*
· *Cod brandade* with brocciu cheese

DESALTING COD

12 TO 24 HOURS BEFORE USING, PLACE THE COD, CUT IN PIECES, SKIN SIDE UP (THE SKIN IS WATERPROOF AND THUS WILL PREVENT DESALTING) **IN A COLANDER** TO AVOID CONTACT WITH THE BOTTOM OF THE WATER CONTAINER, WHERE DEPOSITS OF DISSOLVED SALT WILL COLLECT. PLACE THE COLANDER IN A TUB OF COLD WATER. **CHANGE THE WATER REGULARLY.**

COD—IN THE HEART OF HISTORY AND GEOPOLITICS

From 1500 (probably before): the Basques discover schools of Newfoundland cod and settle there.

From the sixteenth to nineteenth century: cod fishing expands; the French fishermen, known as "Newfoundlanders," or "Icelanders," contribute to the expansion of the ports of Saint-Jean-de-Luz, Bordeaux, Bègles, Paimpol, Dinard, Saint-Brieuc, Saint-Malo, Granville, Fécamp, Dieppe, and Dunkerque . . .

Eighteenth century: Saint-Pierre-et-Miquelon, so-called "dust of the French empire," are preserved to maintain the cod industry.

1988–1992: following the example of the England-Iceland "cod wars," a conflict occurs between France and Canada around the demarcation of fishing zones.

ITS FRENCH NAMES HAVE LOST ITS LATIN ROOTS

Cabillaud *Gadus morhua* fresh (or frozen)

→ **Morue "verte"** Salted, but not dried

→ **Morue or merluche** Salted and dried (using salt)

→ **Stockfish** (literally "stick of fish") Unsalted and air-dried

GOOD FRIDAY FRITELLI DI BACCALÀ
Family recipe by Josette and Madeleine Baraglioli

PREPARATION TIME:
10 MINUTES
COOKING TIME: 10 MINUTES
SERVES 4 TO 6

For the sweet tomato sauce
5 shallots, peeled and chopped
Olive oil, for frying
1 (14 oz/400 g) can tomato sauce
2 to 3 cubes sugar
Salt and freshly ground black pepper
For the beignet batter
1 cup (100 g) all-purpose flour
1 egg
⅓ cup plus 1 tablespoon (100 mL) milk
1¼ teaspoons (5 g) baking powder
1⅛ pounds (500 g) cod, desalted
Freshly ground black pepper

Make the sweet tomato sauce. In a skillet, fry the shallots in a drizzle of olive oil, then add the tomato sauce and sugar cubes; stir to combine. Season with salt and pepper. Reduce to a simmer.

Make the beignet batter. In a bowl, combine the flour, egg, milk, and baking powder. Season with pepper. Remove the skin of the cod. Cut the flesh into 1½-inch (4 cm) squares. Wring the water from the cod by squeezing it hard, then blot it dry with a cloth or paper towel. Dredge the cod in the batter. Add enough olive oil to a heavy-bottom pan for deep frying (about 2 inches/5 cm deep) and heat until hot. Drop the cod pieces in the oil to fry them. Serve with the sweet tomato sauce and a side of rice or boiled potatoes.

BRANDADE OF COD
Denise Solier-Gaudry

PREPARATION TIME:
25 MINUTES
COOKING TIME: 30 MINUTES
SERVES 4

1⅓ pounds (600 g) cod, desalted
2 cloves garlic
⅔ cup (150 mL) olive oil
¾ cup plus 1 tablespoon (200 mL) crème fraîche
Freshly ground black pepper

Place the cod in a pot filled with cold unsalted water and bring it to a boil. As soon as the water is boiling, turn off the heat and let stand for 10 minutes. Drain, let cool, then flake the flesh while removing any skin and bones. Dip the garlic in boiling salted water for 5 minutes, drain, peel, and blend to a fine paste. Pour half of the olive oil into a heavy-bottom casserole dish, warm it, then add the flaked cod. Stir the cod vigorously to obtain a purée. While stirring continuously, pour in the remaining oil without stopping. Add the crème fraîche and garlic purée. Season with pepper; taste to adjust the seasoning as needed. The brandade should have the consistency of a smooth purée. Serve hot.

DID YOU KNOW?

In his last book, *La Vie à bon marché. La Morue* (1929), Escoffier paid tribute to the cod with eighty different preparations.

Why is cod so popular?

Salt cod has long been considered a protein of quality, abundance, and economy. It was *the* fish to consume during lean days of Lent because of the scarcity and cost of fresh fish. Its neutral taste, saltiness, and ability to keep for long periods of time made it adaptable to all kitchens—even those far from the coast!

skip to
Herring—A High-Ranking Fish, p. 50

A Look at Rillettes

Let's give back to Tours what belongs to Tours! Rabelais's beloved "brown jam of pork" originates in the Touraine, even though rillettes from Le Mans are the most popular. Here, we compare them . . .
Marielle Gaudry

WHAT IS RILLETTES?

Originally rillettes was a homemade preparation whose purpose was to preserve meat during the winter months. The dish is achieved by cooking meat pieces for a long time in fat. It is typically made using pork but can also be made of goose, poultry, or rabbit meat. Rillettes was considered "the most succulent treat," according to Balzac, and the mixture was known in the sixteenth century as *rille*, which evokes a piece of meat in strips.

THE DUEL: TOURAINE VERSUS LE MANS

	Tours	Le Mans
Origin	Born in the fifteenth century	Popularized in the nineteenth century with the arrival of the railway and the fast growth of the sandwich
Cooking Method	2⅓-inch (6 cm) pork pieces are cooked, uncovered, for 5½ to 12 hours, sometimes flavored with white wine	1½-inch (4 cm) pork pieces are cooked, sometimes uncovered, for 5 hours, seasoned with salt and pepper only
Appearance/ Texture	Large strips of meat, dry texture, to be eaten with a fork	Strips of meat, soft texture, fattier, spreads like a pâté
Color	Brown	Pinkish gray
Official Organizations	Confrérie des rillettes et rillons de Touraine, founded 1977	Confrérie des chevaliers des rillettes sarthoises, founded 1968
PGI	Protected Geographical Indication (PGI) obtained in 2013	Protected Geographical Indication (PGI) in process
Best Merchants for Purchasing	Hardouin (1936) 50, rue de l'Etang-Vignon 37210 Vouvray	Prunier (1931) 23-25, rue de la Jatterie 72160 Connerré

VARIATIONS

Variants of rillettes are numerous throughout France, and their names within regional boundaries are a little blurred. Due to its accommodating ways for using leftover cuts of meat, rillettes are fattier when made from various scraps of pork, such as the neck or belly. Here are some particular specialties.

***Rillettes comtoises* (Franche-Comté):** a recipe from the 1970s in which pork is smoked according to regional tradition. These rillettes have an unmistakable aroma when spread on bread.

***Grattons lyonnais* (Lyon):** this is the "Lyonnaise cocktail peanut," traditionally served as an appetizer in the form of the crispy pieces, hot or cold, that result from frying the *rigon*, the fatty membrane that surrounds the intestines of the pig.

Basque chichons: also called *graisserons* ("cracklings"). These are Basque rillettes made from pork or duck, often with garlic, depending upon the recipe, and spiced with Espelette pepper.

Grillons périgourdins: unlike those of the neighboring Charente or Limousine, these rillettes call for maceration of the meat as part of their preparation before cooking. They are enhanced with spices such as black pepper, nutmeg, cinnamon, or clove.

skip to
Slices of Sausage, p. 190

A *Tour de France*— The Beignet

Beugner, bugner, bigner . . . no matter the name, everything is fried when it comes to beignets, which remain a traditional sweet at carnivals and festivals.

Marielle Gaudry

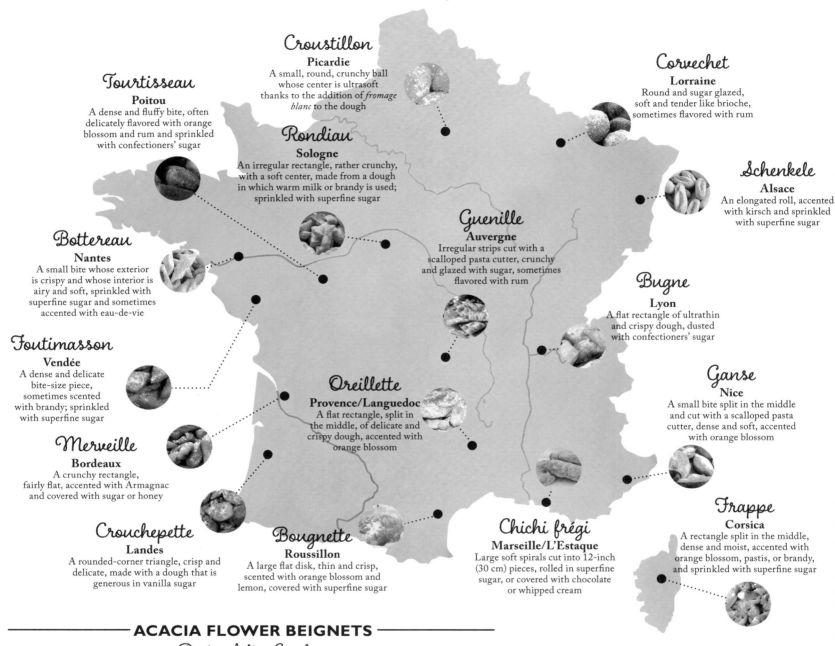

Croustillon
Picardie
A small, round, crunchy ball whose center is ultrasoft thanks to the addition of *fromage blanc* to the dough

Corvechet
Lorraine
Round and sugar glazed, soft and tender like brioche, sometimes flavored with rum

Tourtisseau
Poitou
A dense and fluffy bite, often delicately flavored with orange blossom and rum and sprinkled with confectioners' sugar

Rondiau
Sologne
An irregular rectangle, rather crunchy, with a soft center, made from a dough in which warm milk or brandy is used; sprinkled with superfine sugar

Schenkele
Alsace
An elongated roll, accented with kirsch and sprinkled with superfine sugar

Guenille
Auvergne
Irregular strips cut with a scalloped pasta cutter, crunchy and glazed with sugar, sometimes flavored with rum

Bottereau
Nantes
A small bite whose exterior is crispy and whose interior is airy and soft, sprinkled with superfine sugar and sometimes accented with eau-de-vie

Bugne
Lyon
A flat rectangle of ultrathin and crispy dough, dusted with confectioners' sugar

Foutimasson
Vendée
A dense and delicate bite-size piece, sometimes scented with brandy; sprinkled with superfine sugar

Oreillette
Provence/Languedoc
A flat rectangle, split in the middle, of delicate and crispy dough, accented with orange blossom

Ganse
Nice
A small bite split in the middle and cut with a scalloped pasta cutter, dense and soft, accented with orange blossom

Merveille
Bordeaux
A crunchy rectangle, fairly flat, accented with Armagnac and covered with sugar or honey

Crouchepette
Landes
A rounded-corner triangle, crisp and delicate, made with a dough that is generous in vanilla sugar

Bougnette
Roussillon
A large flat disk, thin and crisp, scented with orange blossom and lemon, covered with superfine sugar

Chichi frégi
Marseille/L'Estaque
Large soft spirals cut into 12-inch (30 cm) pieces, rolled in superfine sugar, or covered with chocolate or whipped cream

Frappe
Corsica
A rectangle split in the middle, dense and moist, accented with orange blossom, pastis, or brandy, and sprinkled with superfine sugar

---

ACACIA FLOWER BEIGNETS
Denise Solier-Gaudry

This recipe is made with acacia flowers, which have a sweetness that is exquisite, but as delicate and fleeting as their season is short (April to May or May to June, depending on the region).

PREPARATION TIME: 15 MINUTES
RESTING TIME: 1 HOUR
MAKES 25 BEIGNETS

1½ cups (150 g) all-purpose flour
1 egg
1 tablespoon (13 g) sugar, plus more for sprinkling
1 tablespoon (15 mL) sunflower oil
1 pinch salt
⅔ cup (150 mL) water
1 egg white
25 fresh acacia flowers
Oil, for frying

Combine all the ingredients (except the egg white, flowers, and oil) by gradually stirring in the water to make a batter. Let it rest for 1 hour. Rinse the flowers gently and use a salad spinner to dry them. Beat the egg white to stiff peaks, then fold it into the batter using a silicone spatula. Heat the oil to 350°F (170°C) in a flameproof heavy casserole dish. Dip each flower into the batter and fry them in batches of four, turning them once while frying. Fry for about 10 seconds only, then remove them using a slotted spoon or skimmer. Place them on paper towels to drain. Sprinkle with sugar and serve immediately.

LYON AND SAINT-ÉTIENNE
BUGNE VERSUS BUGNE

This a specialty of the Duchy of Savoie from the fifteenth century that eventually expanded to the Rhône Alp region.
From Lyon or Saint-Étienne? The *bugne* should be Lyonnaise according to some writings. Rabelais, in his *Pantagruel* in 1532, mentions it in a listing of Lyonnaise specialties, and the name appears on the menu for a dinner of honor organized by the city.
Fluffy or crispy? Although the crisp *bugne* is a more recent evolution of the traditional soft beignet, both cities like to note their differences. In Lyon, it is rather thin and crisp; in Saint-Étienne, it is dense and soft, like brioche.

The Most Popular Television Chefs

The kitchen invades television! A quick tour of our favorite cooking shows from the 1950s to today.

Jérôme Lefort

L'ART ET MAGIE DE LA CUISINE
(THE ART AND MAGIC OF COOKING)
From 1954 to 1966 on RTF Télévision then Channel 1 of the ORTF (the national public radio and television agency in France)
Run time between 15 and 30 minutes
The "recipe": Raymond Oliver, top chef of Le Grand Véfour (three-star Michelin) cooks under the candid eye of a faux housewife: the host Catherine Langeais.
Highlight: the closing song is *Les Oignons* by Sidney Bechet.

LA GRANDE COCOTTE (THE BIG POT)
From 1976 to 1977 on TF1
Run time 25 minutes
The "recipe": a renowned Nouvelle Cuisine chef (such as Bocuse, Guérard, Vergé, Senderens, Lenôtre . . .) prepares a dish with actress Marthe Mercadier in the role of "hostess."
Highlight: the show is coproduced by the journalists Claude Jolly (aka Claude Lebey), future author of the eponymous guide, and Jean Ferniot, father of the journalist and culinary entrepreneur Vincent Ferniot.

LA CUISINE LÉGÈRE (COOKING LIGHT)
From 1977 to 1981 on TF1
Run time 15 minutes
The "recipe": Michel Guérard delivers his cooking tips and tricks to announcer and journalist Anne-Marie Peysson. On the program: joking and laughter and recipes inspired by Nouvelle Cuisine.
Highlight: the show inaugurates the first use of camera "dives," shooting close-ups of the bottom of the pans.

LA VÉRITÉ EST AU FOND DE LA MARMITE
(THE TRUTH LIES AT THE BOTTOM OF A POT)
From 1978 to 1983 on Antenne 2
Run time 30 minutes
The "recipe": dressed appropriately, Michel Oliver presents a homey recipe in a kitchen decorated "American-style" before serving it up at the table with his cooking accomplice (Olivier de Rincquesen, Maurice Favières, Christian Morin).

Highlight: having been at Cours Simon, Michel Oliver views cooking as a theatrical setting. The show's dialogue is written and practiced in advance.

CHÉRI, QU'EST-CE QU'ON
MANGE AUJOURD'HUI?
(HONEY, WHAT ARE WE EATING TODAY?)
From 1987 to 1988 on TF1
Run time 20 minutes
The "recipe:" Francis Vandenhende, chef at La Ferme Saint-Simon in Paris, cooks a bourgeois dish next to Denise Fabre, his on- and off-screen wife. Next is a dish prepared by a child, then in the end a report is presented on the art of the table.
Highlight: cooking, equipment, and ingredients: the show is replete with product advertising.

LA CUISINE DES MOUSQUETAIRES
(THE MUSKETEERS' KITCHEN)
From 1983 to 1997 on FR3 Aquitaine, then France 3
Run time 15 minutes
The "recipe": Marie-Thérèse Ordonez, known as Maïté, presents a rustic recipe in her legendary blunt manner of speaking.
Highlight: Alexandre Dumas's *Le Grand Dictionnaire de Cuisine* (*Great Dictionary of Cuisine*) was the inspiration behind this show and its name!

LES P'TITS SECRETS DE BABETTE
(BABETTE'S LITTLE SECRETS)
1997 on France 3
Run time 3 minutes
The "recipe": with a guest at her side, Élisabeth de Rozières (aka Babette) goes in search of exotic ingredients for her West Indies recipes before making them in the kitchen.
Highlight: it took several years for Babette to popularize an exotic-foods cooking show on French television.

skip to
Raymond Oliver, p. 359

BON APPÉTIT BIEN SÛR!
(BON APPÉTIT, OF COURSE!)
From 2000 to 2009 on France 3
Run time 25 minutes, then 5 minutes starting in 2007
The "recipe": a daily show with Joël Robuchon welcoming new top chefs each week. A report about the guest or a supplier begins each show.
Highlight: this is not Joël Robuchon's first step into television success: from 1996 to 1999, he hosted *Cuisinez comme un grand chef* (*How to Cook Like a Top Chef*) on TF1.

OUI CHEF! (YES CHEF!)
2005 on M6
Run time 2 hours
The "recipe": the first reality television show that invites you to follow, over five episodes, underprivileged young people being trained to work in the future restaurant of Cyril Lignac.
Highlight: when the producers of the show became interested in Cyril Lignac, he was then the chef of La Suite, the Parisian restaurant owned by the Guettas.

TOP CHEF
Since 2010 on M6 and RTL-TVI
Run time 2 hours 20 minutes
The "recipe": faced with a jury of top professionals, twelve to sixteen young chefs compete in incredible culinary challenges to become Top Chef of the Year.
Highlight: the show has launched the careers of many chefs.

LE MEILLEUR PÂTISSIER:
LES PROFESSIONNELS
(THE BEST PASTRY CHEF: THE PROS)
Since 2017 on M6 and RTL-TVI
Run time 2 hours
The "recipe": twelve teams of three professional pastry chefs compete in front of a prestigious panel of chefs to win the title of Best Pastry Chef of the year, participating in high-action challenges.
Highlight: this show is based on another top cooking show called *The Great British Bake Off* airing on the BBC.

Confitures

From a breakfast spread for toast to a dessert topping, pastry filling, and accompaniment on a cheese platter, confiture (jam or preserves) is for all year round! Here is a glimpse of how to serve it properly!

Alvina Ledru-Johansson

A tour de France–jams

Poitou-Charentes
Angelica jam: made from the iconic plant of the Poitou marshes.

Centre-Val de Loire
Chinon wine jam: invented by Claude Fleurisson. For garnishing dishes such as coq au vin, apple tart, or pear poached with wine.
Cotignac
Confectioner of quince jelly.

Lorraine
Red currant jam (seeded with a goose feather): from Bar-le-Duc. Accompanies foie gras and meat.
Mirabelle jam: (from Metz, made with mirabelle plums from Nancy). Accompanies cheeses such as Munster.

Normandy
Confiture de lait (milk jam): Resulting from a mistake made by the chef of the Napoléonic army who left milk, intended for the soldiers, to cook too long.

Pays Basque
Cherry jam from Txassou (a Basque mountain village): Accompanies sheep cheese (*ossau-iraty*) and used as a filling for traditional gâteau Basque.

Chile pepper jam: Accompanies the typical dishes *axoa*, pipérade, and Basque chicken.

Île-de-France
Rose petals jam from Provins: produced by Dominique Gaufillier.

Pays de la Loire
Le pommé: apple jam cooked in cider.

Franche-Comté
Cramaillotte: a jam made from dandelion used as a spread on bread or brioche, or added to yogurt.

Alsace
Dog rose (rosehip) jam or jelly

Provence
Watermelon jam, referred to as *confiture de citres* in Apt and *confiture de mérévilles* in Carpentras.

Corsica
Chestnut, fig, or myrtle jam: served with Corsican cheeses.

Mayotte
Baobab tree jam.

THE SECRET TO SUCCESS
Fruit pectin allows the jams, marmalades, and jellies to "set." Some fruits are considered rich in pectin, such as apples, quince, currants, blackcurrants, raspberries, and citrus fruits. Others have very little, such as pears, cherries, and strawberries.
What's the solution for a lack of pectin? Offset the lack of pectin with jelling sugar, a few pieces of pectin-rich fruit (or use an apple core with seeds, tied in cheesecloth and added during cooking), or a little lemon or apple juice.

WHY USE A COPPER KETTLE?
1. Copper is a fantastic conductor: it absorbs heat quickly and distributes it evenly.
2. Copper facilitates the setting of the jam: copper unites the pectin molecules with the water and fruit.
3. The flared shape of a copper kettle promotes water evaporation.

STERILIZE THE JARS
In order to avoid any health risk or deterioration of the preserves, the jars must be sterilized.
1. Place the jars in a large pot filled with water (they should be completely immersed). Boil them for about ten minutes, then take them out and place them on a clean cloth to dry.
2. Once the jars are filled with the hot preserves, turn them upside down on their lids for a few minutes. The hot air will expand in the jar and, once cooled, will vacuum seal the lid. The jar is now airtight.

FILL THE JARS COMPLETELY
To prevent the pieces of fruit from rising to the top of the jars, fill the jars slowly. The fruits will then be evenly distributed throughout the jam.

IS IT READY?
With each type of fruit, it depends on the quantity, quality, and cooking time. To know if your preserves are ready . . .
The scientific technique: use a thermometer to cook the preserves up to 219°F (104°C). Once this temperature is reached, the mixture can be removed from the heat.
The practical technique: drop a few drops of the preserves onto a small cold plate. If it gels slightly, the preserves are ready to add to the jar!

skip to
Pâte de Fruits, p. 18

DEFINITION

Jam
Fruit (purée and/or pulp) + sugar + water
where the fruit represents at least 35 percent of the total weight

Jam "extra"
Nonconcentrated pulp + sugar
where the fruit represents at least 45 percent of the total weight

Gelée (jelly)
Fruit juice and/or water-based extract + sugar
where the fruit represents at least 35 percent of the total weight

Gelée (jelly) "extra"
Fruit juice and/or water-based extract + sugar
where the fruit represents at least 45 percent of the total weight

Compote
Water + sugar + citrus (pulp, purée, juice, water-based extract, peel)
where the fruits account for at least 20 percent of the total weight, of which ¼ ounce (7.5 g) comes from the endocarp of the fruit

Spring
STRAWBERRIES
from Le Guide Culinaire, by Escoffier

"It's one of the most painstaking preserves to make and can be done in numerous ways. Here is the simplest and fastest."

MAKES 4 JARS

3¾ cups (740 g) granulated sugar
2¼ pounds (1 kg) strawberries, washed, hulled, and cut in half

Put the sugar in a heavy-bottom pot and add just enough water to dampen it, then cook until it starts to simmer. Increase the temperature to between 241°F and 257°F (116°C and 125°C). Skim the foam from the top when it starts to boil. Add the strawberries. Heat for 7 to 8 minutes, or until the water evaporates and the mixture becomes syrupy once again. Strain through a sieve and reserve the strawberries. Continue cooking the syrup over high heat until the indicated temperature reaches between 241°F and 257°F (116°C and 125°C), then add the strawberries back to the syrup and let cook for 5 minutes. Fill the jars with the jam.

Fall
GREEN TOMATOES
from Mamie Raymonde

From the book *Le cuisinier provençal* by Edouard Loubet. "This preserve is a remarkable condiment, recommended for serving with terrine of foie gras or cheese. Our grandmothers made this preserve to keep unripened tomatoes all winter long."

MAKES 12 JARS

6½ pounds (3 kg) green tomatoes
4½ pounds (2 kg) granulated sugar
Zest of 2 oranges

Cut the tomatoes into wedges, then combine them in a bowl with the sugar and orange zest. Set aside to marinate until the tomatoes release their juice. In a large pot, begin cooking the tomatoes over low heat so that they do not stick to the bottom of the pot, then cook at high heat for about 16 minutes, or until cooked down. Stir to combine, then transfer to jars.

Summer
APRICOT KERNEL JAM
from Denise Solier-Gaudry

MAKES 6 JARS

3⅓ pounds (1.5 kg) pitted apricots or about 3½ pounds (1.6 kg) whole apricots
2¼ pounds (1 kg) jelling sugar
15 apricot kernels

Wash and dry the apricots. Pit them then chop the flesh into small pieces. Place the flesh in a large saucepan with the sugar. Stir to combine. Crush the apricot kernels, remove the center almonds, and peel them. Divide them into two piles, then set them aside. Bring the apricot pieces and sugar to a boil, stirring often, then reduce the heat and continue cooking for 8 minutes. One minute before the end of the cooking time, add the apricot almonds. Turn off the heat, skim the top, and pour the preserves into the jars to fill them completely.

Winter
CHRISTMAS JAM
from Christine Ferber

It is in the heart of the vineyards of Alsace that the Queen of Jams prepares her small jars. Her secret? No more than 8.8 pounds (4 kg) of fruit cooked at a time.

MAKES 6 JARS

3⅓ pounds (1.5 kg) quince
6⅓ cups (1.5 L) water
2¼ pounds (1 kg) dried and candied fruits, such as almonds, peanuts, apricots, cherries, apples, or pears
An assortment of spices, such as ginger, cinnamon, nutmeg, or cloves
Juice of 1 orange
1 pinch finely grated orange zest
Juice of 1 unwaxed lemon
1 pinch finely grated lemon zest (from unwaxed lemon)
2¼ pounds (1 kg) granulated sugar

Wipe the quince clean with a cloth. Rinse them, remove their stems, then quarter them. Put the quince in a large pot and cover them with the water. Bring to a boil and simmer over low heat for 1 hour, stirring occasionally. Strain the contents and reserve the juice. Cut the dried fruit into small pieces and add them to quince juice. Add the orange and lemon juice and zests, sugar, and the spices. Bring to a boil while stirring. Skim the top to remove any foam as necessary. Continue cooking over high heat for 5 to 10 minutes, stirring constantly. Let boil for 5 more minutes and transfer to jars.

Organic Growing Booms

Organic farming is gaining ground due to the popularity of organic produce, with seven out of ten French people claiming to consume organic foods regularly. Here we clarify the labeling.

Anne-Laure Pham

Official Governmental Labels

THE *EUROFEUILLE* ORGANIC FARMING LABEL
Year of creation: 2010
Requirements:
- Must include the place of production of the raw materials that make up the product: "EU Agriculture," "non-EU Agriculture," or "EU/non-EU Agriculture."
- The labeled product must contain 100 percent ingredients from organic methods of production, or at least 95 percent organically farmed products in the case of processed food items.
- Mixed farms (organic and conventional) are allowed.
- Quality-control inspections take place twice a year. Current reforms could relax this rule by allowing inspections to be conducted once every two years. Will this relaxing of the rules cause concern?

THE AB LABEL
Year of creation: 1985
Requirements:
- This is an exclusive designation of the French Ministry of Agriculture. Like the European label, this label identifies products that are 100 percent organic or processed food items that contain at least 95 percent organically farmed products.
- Expected to be gradually replaced by the EU label.
- To market products from organic farming, the producer must have been inspected by one of the nine certification bodies approved by Institut national de l'origine et de la qualité (National Institute of Origin and Quality, INAO), such as Ecocert, Agrocert, and Bureau Veritas.
- Inspections occur at least once a year.

The Alternatives

This labeling represents barely 5 percent of the 46,000 organic operators in France. Organic certification is a prerequisite for obtaining them, except for Nature & Progrès.

DEMETER
Year of creation: 1932
Requirements:
Certifies products derived from biodynamics. More than 700 professional members in France, as well as 6,500 others in more than 60 countries abroad.

NATURE & PROGÈS
Year of creation: 1964
Requirements:
Bringing together professionals and consumers, this group promotes agroecology. It describes the European regulation on organic products as limited "to a technical dimension that questions neither the industrialization of organic nor its social and ecological repercussions." Currently there are 1,000 professional members and 1,000 consumer members.

BIO COHÉRENCE
Year of creation: 2010
Requirements:
This label was launched in response to the European organic products regulation, which was considered lax, by an association of consumers, producers, and distributors such as Biocoop, following the 2009 reform of the European environmental regulation on organic farming. It advocates "a progression in the environmental, social, and economic fields." It has nearly 550 members.

skip to
A Parade of Labels, p. 275

Organic Farming in France by the Numbers

32,300 manufacturers; **14,800** other operators (processors, distributors, importers). More than **3.7 million acres** (1.5 million hectares) in agricultural area, or **5.7 percent of the total farming area** of France. The **Occitanie** region contains **7,227** manufacturers, or **20 percent of French organic manufacturers**, followed by Auvergne-Rhône-Alpes and Nouvelle-Aquitaine (4,700 to 4,800 manufacturers). Sales from **all outlets combined**—including food establishments—exceeded **7 billion euros at the end of 2016** compared to 5.76 billion at the end of 2015.

Grains and Flours

—— ◆ ——

Before making bread, you have to consider the grain from which the flour that will be used was made.
Knowing this is the first step in good bread making.
Marie-Laure Fréchet & Roland Feuillas

Grains Used for Bread Flours

These grains are all part of the family Poaceae (grasses). Wheat belongs to the genus *Triticum*.

Einkorn Wheat
(*Triticum monococcum*)

Sometimes incorrectly referred to as "little spelt," but it has little relation to spelt, the cousin of common wheat. It is one of the first grains domesticated by man, but its cultivation was gradually abandoned in France around the Middle Ages. It is rare today. The PGI (Protected Geographical Indication) "little spelt Haute-Provence" was created to protect it. It is rich in proteins, trace elements, and essential amino acids. Poor in gluten, it can, however, be baked, and results in a dense, low-rise bread.

Common Wheat
(*Triticum aestivum*)

This grain is a hybrid of emmer wheat and *aegilop* (from the grass family). It is the primary grain produced in France and in the world, essential in making bread flour. Its main production areas are the Paris Basin, Nord-Pas-de-Calais, le Centre, Poitou-Charentes, and Burgundy. Approximately 12.4 million acres (5 million hectares) of agricultural land are devoted to it (e.g., half of the French grain production farmland). It owes its name to the white and friable starch contained in its grain, unlike durum wheat, which contains a yellow and vitreous material (used for making semolina and pasta). It France it goes by the names *blé tendre* or *froment*.

Spelt
(*Triticum spelta*)

This is a grain in its own right. It is also referred to in France as the "wheat of the Gauls." It is grown mainly in the Paris Basin and Burgundy. It is a grain referred to as "hulled wheat," because it must be hulled. Its yield is low, which explains why it has been abandoned in favor of common wheat. It has excellent nutritional qualities.

Rye
(*Secale cereale*)

In the family of grasses, it is very close to the genus *Triticum*. Rustic and very resistant, it adapts to poor and acidic soils. The Romans disliked its taste and saw its appeal to the barbaric populations that used it as proof of its undesirable quality. Its name in French, *le seigle,* comes from a region of France, Ségala, which extends west of the department of Aveyron, north of Tarn, and northeast of Lot, and where, formerly, only rye grew. A bread-flour grain, it is also used in making *pain d'épices*. Rye can be a carrier of ergot, a disease caused by a fungus that makes the grain toxic and causes what is described as burning pain.

"COUNTRY" WHEAT

In the past, every farmer could grow any variety of wheat and name it as he wished. These were referred to as "country" wheats; that is, types grouped under the generic names of those they resembled. They were called, for example, *Blanc de Flandre, Hâtif de la Saône,* or *Bladette de Bordeaux.* These wheats would be progressively replaced by imported foreign varieties from Spain or Russia, or the first hybrids created by Henry de Vilmorin at the end of the nineteenth century.

To create some organization among these varieties, an official catalog of common wheat was introduced in 1933, accompanied by a sales authorization. As a result, the number of French varieties decreased from 562 to 40 in 1945. Since then, the French have crossed the 250 mark with new hybrid varieties. Ten bread-flour varieties now make up 50 percent of this number, the first being the Rubisko variety. Five seed companies share the market for the French varieties. In the last fifteen years, however, farmers have begun to cultivate ancient varieties, such as the *Rouge Bordeaux, Barbu du Roussillon,* or *Blé Meunier d'Apt* (or *Touselle blanche de Pertuis*).

Other Grains for Other Flours

Maize or Corn (*Zea mays*)
Imported from Mexico to Europe by Christopher Columbus, corn has many varieties and uses. Its flour is used in a mixture or in specialties such as *milla* (a cake from southwest France) and *taloas* (a cake from the Basque country). *Farine de Gaudes* is a grilled corn flour, a specialty of Bresse. Cornstarch is made only from the starch of corn and not the entire grain, as is used to make wheat flour.

Buckwheat
This is a "false" grain since it belongs to the Polygonaceae family, the same as sorrel or rhubarb. These grains are angular in shape and dark in color, hence its name in French, which translates as "black wheat." Imported during the Crusades and popularized by Anne de Bretagne, it was established in Brittany in the fifteenth century. Since 2000, a PGI (Protected Geographical Indication) has identified "buckwheat of Bretagne." It is the essential ingredient of buckwheat pancakes and the cooked dish *kig ha farz*. It does not contain gluten and cannot therefore be used for bread flour.

FLOUR

The French word for flour (*farine*) comes from the Latin *far, farris*, meaning "cultivated wheat, spelt." It is the powder that results from the grinding of the grain seeds.

WHOLE AND INTEGRAL

Flours contain minerals from the bran (the outer shell). When they are heated at 1,652°F (900°C), only the mineral residues in the form of ash remain. The higher the rate of ash or the rate of sifting (T), the higher the flour type number and conversely the less white the flour becomes. For example, heating 1 cup (100 g) of type 55 (T55) flour produces about 0.02 ounce (0.55 g) of mineral ash. The whiter the flour, the more nutrients are lost, as the nutrients are found mainly in the wheat germ and its bran. In contrast, the more "whole" or "complete" the flour is, the richer it is in vitamins and minerals (essentially B and E vitamins).

In France, six types of flour have been approved

Type 45	Type 55	Type 65	Type 80	Type 110	Type 150
White baking flour or "pastry flour" > typically used for making delicate pastries	Common white flour > used for white breads; tart and pizza doughs	White flour > used in making rustic breads (*pain de campagne)* and pizza doughs	Whole wheat or semi-whole wheat flour > used for brown breads	Whole wheat flour > used for whole wheat breads	So-called "integral" flour > used for so-called "bran breads"

Gluten

Gluten is a viscoelastic protein complex consisting of a heterogeneous mixture of gliadins and glutenins associated by covalent (S-S bridge) and noncovalent (hydrogen, ionic) bonds and hydrophobic interactions. It contains proteins (75–85 percent), lipids (5–7 percent), starch (5–10 percent), and water (5–8 percent). It is this assemblage of molecules that earned it its name "gluten," literally "glue" in Latin. Gliadins provide dough with its stretching abilities, viscosity, and plasticity. Glutenins give it its resistance and elasticity. Under the action of yeasts, during fermentation, a release of CO_2 occurs that will be blocked by the glutenic network, which has a rising effect on the dough.

It was the Italian Jacopo Beccari, a professor at the University of Bologna, who discovered it in 1745. By passing a ball of dough under a stream of water, he obtained a sticky and elastic substance, gluten, that separated from the starch.

Gluten is responsible for celiac disease, which requires a strict gluten-free diet. In recent years, a hypersensitivity to gluten has developed. It can be explained by the use of gluten-enriched flours and a technique that shortens the time needed for making bread, consequently not allowing yeasts to predigest the gluten.

MIXES

The composition of a bread made in the "French tradition," according to decree no. 93-1074 from September 13, 1993, authorizes a certain number of "improvers" in addition to the flour, water, salt, preferment, and dried yeasts typically used. These "improvers" have an effect on the fermentation, color of the crumb and crust, and the volume of the rise. Among these are:
→ Bean flour
→ Wheat malt
→ Gluten
→ Soy lecithin
→ Vitamin C
→ Enzymes

These mixtures are created by the millers and delivered ready for use to the bread maker. Some have known brands such as Banette, created by a group of 40 millers; Campaillette, carried by one of the European leaders of the flour mill NutriXo; Baguépi (Soufflet group); or Retrodor (Viron).

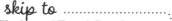

skip to
Traditional French Bread:
The Art and the Method, p. 356

The Degree of Stench!

They reek! They'll stop you in your tracks! Here is a small inventory of French specialties whose odors truly offend.

Delphine Le Feuvre

1. Tripe
A bad experience is guaranteed with any tripe recipe, whether it is cooked Caen-style, as La Ferté-Macé kebabs, or Corsican-style.
On the nose: intestinal—wait, you said intestinal?

2. Cod Liver Oil
Used as a nutritional supplement, it is made from cod liver that is steamed, then pressed and filtered.
On the nose: a fish forgotten in a trashcan.

3. Le Puant de Lille (The Stench of Lille)
The name of this cheese says a lot about its smell.
On the nose: a sneaker locker sitting out in the heat.

4. Le Casgiu Merzu
This Corsican cheese is made by mixing leftovers from tomme cheese, which are left to dry uncovered with the windows open. This allows the flies to arrive and lay their larvae.
On the nose: a rotten cheese with a foul smell, but an aroma always less disgusting than its appearance.

5. The Overcooked Egg
When overcooked, the egg releases a gas originating from a mixture of the iron in the yolk and the sulfur in the white. In addition to the smell, overcooking is noticeable in the grayish layer that separates the white from the yolk when eating a boiled egg.
On the nose: a smell of gases.

6. Le Melet
This term refers to both a small fish caught in Provence and the sauce prepared with it.
On the nose: fish that has spent too much time in the sun.

7. Garlic
This condiment, which serves as a base for Provençal aïoli, has an unpleasant smell only when chopped. The cause is the alliin, one of its components, which turns into allicin and produces the molecules responsible for this strong aroma.
On the nose: bad breath.

8. Munster
This orange and flowing cheese owes its smell to the red bacteria on its washed rind.
On the nose: a Dumpster in a heat wave.

9. Le Maroilles
Its smell is more delicate when cooked—in a tart for example—but the odor of this *ch'ti* (Nord-Pas-de-Calais) cheese really stands out when raw in its rind.
Nose: armpits after three days without a shower.

10. Andouillette
As Édouard Herriot, the former mayor of Lyon, so aptly summed it up: "Politics is like andouillette: it should smell like shit, but not too much."
On the nose: enough said.

11. Cabbage and Other Sulfurous Vegetables (Leek, Cauliflower, etc.)
When cooked, their sulfur compounds release a suffocating odor, hence the need to cook them in a large volume of water.
On the nose: the halls of the Paris subway.

17. Runny Reblochon
This Savoyard cheese, associated with the dish *tartiflette*, grabs the attention of an epicure's nose from its strong odor of hazelnut.
On the nose: a gym after a sports class.

18. Normandy Camembert
Probably the best known stinky French cheese!
On the nose: under its chalky rind, a strong milky smell.

16. L'Époisses
This king of cheeses, according to Brillat-Savarin, has its rind rubbed with marc of Burgundy throughout production.
On the nose: feet that have been wearing shoes too long.

15. Melon
Beware of this fruit when it is too ripe: it produces ethanol!
On the nose: a trashcan in the sun.

14. Le Pont L'évêque
Its musky flavors are due to its six weeks of ripening in Calvados, between Lisieux and Deauville.
On the nose: a rugby locker room.

12. Le Vieux Boulogne
The rind of this Pas-de-Calais cheese is regularly bathed with Saint-Léonard beer while it's aged.
On the nose: socks after a marathon.

13. Le Pissalat en Saumure (Anchovies in Brine)
This very salty sauce is widely consumed in the south of France.
On the nose: rotting seawater.

skip to
Cooking with Feet, p. 209

Whelk Stands Out!

Are whelks boring? When carefully prepared and combined with a little mayo, whelks have a lot to offer!

François-Régis Gaudry

Other names . . .

→ **Chanteur** (Somme)
→ **Calicoco** (Cotentin)
→ **Ran** (Sud-Cotentin, Granville)
→ **Bavoux** (Barfleur)
→ **Torion** (Cancale)
→ **Killog** (Finistère)
→ **Burgaud morchoux** (Vendée)
→ **Murex** (its Mediterranean cousin, with its pointed shell)
→ **Bourgot** (Quebec)
And: **sea snail, *berlot, quanteux, booglu* . . .**

CAN IT BE EATEN?

The black part, which often remains at the bottom of the shell, is questionable. Some people choose to taste it, but they may change their minds: these are its internal organs—the heart, digestive tract, and gills of the animal.

THE WHELKS OF GRANVILLE

The whelk from this area has been protected since February 2017 by a PGI (Protected Geographical Indication). About forty whelk fishermen harvest from 3,000 to 4,000 metric tons per year in the bay of Granville, west of the Cotentin Peninsula in Normandy, where colonies are particularly abundant. The technique used is the trap, a delicate fishing approach that allows the animal to be taken alive without causing it stress.

DID YOU KNOW?

The whelk is a carnivorous necrophagous; it feeds on the fresh corpses of crabs, worms, and bivalve shells.

COOKING THEM AT HOME!

First, you must buy them live at the fish market. Or at the very least, be sure that they are fresh and "cooked the day of" if purchasing them cooked, a claim not always respected at fish stands (beware of the off flavors when tasting them!).

1 Cleaning

Let them soak for at least 20 minutes in cold water. Do not add coarse salt to desalt them, it tends to make them shrivel. Wash them with large quantities of water to rid them of their slime and impurities.

2 Bathing

Place the rinsed whelks in a casserole dish and cover them with plenty of cold water. Put the lid on and turn up the heat. Bring to a simmer and simmer for 12 to 15 minutes, depending on the size.

3 Tenderizing

The secret to tender whelks is to let them cool in their cooking liquid. But if in a hurry, you can settle for whelks rinsed in hot water!

Tasty Variations

The good thing about cooking at home is that you can add a lot of things to the cooking liquid for added flavor.
=> **For a French court-bouillon:** add a bouquet garni and sprig of thyme.
=> **For an Asian court-bouillon with sweet spices (our favorite):** add a peeled onion studded with 2 cloves, a star anise pod, a few peppercorns, a bay leaf, and two pinches of turmeric (your whelks will have a slight orange tint).
=> **For a Thai court-bouillon:** add a stalk of lemongrass cut in half, a sprinkle of chopped fresh ginger, and some kaffir lime leaves.

——— WHELK AND ANDOUILLE DE VIRE TARTINES ———

An amazing marriage of land and sea, this incredible recipe is a signature of Bernard Vaxelaire, a top chef who cooked at Gourmandises in Cormeilles (Eure). His successor, Alexis Osmont, kept this dish on the menu.

MAKES 5 *TARTINES* (TOASTS)
1⅛ pounds (500 g) cooked whelks, shucked and cleaned of their horny operculum and their digestive system
8 slices of andouille de Vire, slightly smoked (about 7 oz/200 g)
1 shallot, peeled and finely chopped
1 bunch mixed herbs (parsley, chives, and chervil), finely chopped
3 tablespoons (40 g) mayonnaise
½ lemon
Freshly ground black pepper
3 tablespoons plus 1 teaspoon (50 mL) olive oil
5 slices rustic bread (not too thick)

Small dice the whelks and the andouille.

In a large bowl, combine the whelks and andouille with the shallot, herbs, mayonnaise, and a squeeze of lemon juice. Season with pepper but do not add salt (the andouille is already salty).

In a skillet, heat the oil and brown the bread slices (on one side). Let cool then spread them generously with the whelk-andouille mixture.

Cut the bread slices into several pieces to enjoy as an appetizer or serve them whole as a starter with a green salad.

skip to ....
Wild Mollusks, p. 84; Mayonnaise, p. 100

Soufflés Are Full of Air!

It's inflated, the soufflé! The soufflé evaporated from the menus of bourgeois cuisine from the 1950s to 1970s. It was, perhaps, too temperamental in an era that had zero tolerance for risk. This is a case for its comeback.

Stéphane Solier

We grew tired of it because . . .

The difficulty in mastering the "inflation": it's a one-shot dish; it's impossible to turn back when something goes wrong!

The tyranny of a dish with "the tawny toque of an African dictator" (Jacques Brunel), who imposes its need for timing!

An old-fashioned reputation: too identifiable with the 1950s and too much a part of "bourgeois" cuisine.

But here we revive it for . . .

Its spectacular and magical character.

Children's love for it.

Its great effect with inexpensive ingredients: egg, butter, flour, a few leftover ingredients for flavor, and a little alcohol.

Its speed of preparation and execution: 30 minutes total!

Very French . . .

The French have always played with bubbles: Champagne, emulsions of all kinds (mousse, mayonnaise, whipped cream), beignets, meringue, puffed pastry . . . and soufflé: everything in French gastronomy seems to flirt with the art of creating clouds!

A FRENCH INVENTION

The origin of the soufflé is attributed to Antoine Beauvilliers: his book *Art du cuisinier* (*The Art of Cooking*), from 1814, included soufflé recipes using pheasant, partridge, woodcock, and chicken. His contemporary Louis-Eustache Ude also published a series of soufflé dessert recipes in *The French Cook* (1813)!

A FRENCH NAME

If the etymology is Latin (*sub-flare*), the substantive participle is born in the French language. During the eighteenth century, the term designates a degree of cooking sugar, and in the nineteenth century, it denotes a sweet or salty preparation. The term is used as is (sometimes with phonetic spellings) in most languages: *cheese soufflé, soufflé de queso, soufflé di formaggio, suflê de chuchu,* and so on.

skip to
Cheeses for Melting, p. 114

CHEESE SOUFFLÉ
by Denise Solier-Gaudry

SERVES 4

3 tablespoons (50 g) unsalted butter, plus more for greasing
1 tablespoon (7 g) bread crumbs
½ cup (50 g) all-purpose flour
1⅓ cups (330 mL) warm milk
Salt and freshly ground black pepper
Fresh nutmeg
4 eggs, separated
3½ ounces (100 g) grated cheese (Comté, Emmental, or Mimolette)

Preheat the oven to 350°F (180°C). Grease a large soufflé dish, then coat the inside with the bread crumbs.

Melt the 3 tablespoons (50 g) of butter in a saucepan. Add the flour and stir well to combine. Add the milk a little at a time while whisking vigorously. Season with salt and pepper and grate in a little nutmeg. Remove the pan from the heat; let cool for 1 to 2 minutes. Stir in the egg yolks one at a time, then add the cheese. Stir to combine. Beat the whites to stiff peaks, then fold them gently into the yolk mixture. Scrape the batter into the prepared dish and bake for 30 to 35 minutes, or until puffed and golden, without opening the door.

A LITERARY PLEBISCITE

The soufflé dominates the menus of French literature. After George Sand, who serves it to her scholarly friends of the Republic, and Alexandre Dumas, who offers no less than eight soufflé recipes in his *Le Grand Dictionnaire de Cuisine* (*Great Dictionary of Cuisine*, 1873), it is André Gide who becomes the champion of its preparation: his son-in-law reports, in his *Guide familier*, about a stay in London in 1924 with "the memory of a certain frozen soufflé topped with honey [that] swelled in his mouth with an unbearable lyricism." The novelist-turned-amateur enthusiast of soufflés, writes about them: "nothing is easier in which to succeed, and yet nothing will fall faster. Yet if not, the light taste is one that you can have with these dishes is incredible" (*Journal*, 1931). The soufflé also delights the taste buds of Proust's heroes. Françoise, the skillful cook in *À la recherche du temps perdu* (*In Search of Lost Time*) was largely inspired by Céleste Albaret, Proust's maid, who has a famous knack for preparing soufflés. And the ambassador, Monsieur de Norpois, "assures him that nowhere does one eat cold beef and soufflés like yours" (*À l'ombre des jeunes filles en fleurs* [*In the Shadow of Young Girls in Flower*], 1919).

The Puffing of a Soufflé According to Hervé This

It would be due to the beaten eggs in which the water bubbles expand? Nay! argues the researcher Hervé This (*Les secrets de la casserole*, 1993; *Révélations gastronomiques*, 1995)!

"The expansion of the water bubbles accounts for only 20 percent. It is, rather, the *rise* of these bubbles, determined to escape, that inflates the mixture. By coagulating, egg white proteins will prevent the bubbles from escaping. We can help keep the bubbles from escaping by forming a crust at the top of the soufflé (using the broiler) and keeping a heat source below it. With this, everything becomes possible: an inflation of over 400 percent; unbeaten egg whites, even a soufflé without eggs, due to its other proteins, such as with a shrimp bisque, will do this as well."

A TRUE DIPLOMAT

The delicacy and magic of a soufflé make it an ideal dish to impress one's guests, and whom better to impress than a head of state! Chef Gérard Idoux (of Le Récamier, Paris) admits how proud he was to have served a sea urchin soufflé in its shell to then chancellor Gerhard Schröder. But the fickleness of the dish made him nervous . . . Danièle Mazet-Delpeuch, who had to serve a zucchini soufflé at the home of President François Mitterrand for his host Gorbachev, thought his end had come when a delay in dinner was announced that required the soufflé to be interrupted while it was cooking!

"An interrupted soufflé never returns! But then, suddenly, a miracle. I can breathe again. The Gods, and skills, saved me."

A FLAWLESS COURSE WITH SIGNATURE FLAVORS ON THE GRANDEST TABLES

Antonin Carême, 1820s: the Rothschild soufflé, with a mixture of candied fruits macerated in Danzig eau-de-vie filled with gold flakes or in fine Champagne, decorated with slices of pineapple and strawberries
Jules Gouffé, 1867: vanilla soufflé
Auguste Escoffier, 1903: whiting soufflé with truffles and hazelnut

AND TODAY:

A salty version

Michel Bras: Vieux Rodez soufflé
Anne-Sophie Pic: soufflé with Mimolette; soufflé with Comté and cumin
Yannick Alléno: eel, beets, and sour onions soufflé; scallop soufflé
Bruno Bangea: tomato soufflé

A sweet version:

Paul Bocuse: Grand Marnier soufflé
Alain Passard: soufflé with avocado and vanilla
Pierre Gagnaire: Tahitian vanilla and South African golden raisins with aged kirsch soufflé
Patrick Bertron: hot soufflé with Cazette de Bourgogne nectar
Christian Constant: Grand Marnier and vanilla soufflé with liquid caramel center
Jérôme Dumant: chocolate, Grand Marnier, and caramel soufflé
Frédéric Simonin: passion fruit soufflé
Jérôme Banctel: chocolate saffron soufflé
Guy Savoy: mirabelle plums soufflé
Bruno Doucet: Grand Marnier soufflé
Jean-François Piège: orange and Grand Marnier soufflé
Marc Veyrat: overripe pear soufflé
Michel Guérard: soufflé with lemon verbena

TO GUARANTEE A SUCCESSFUL SOUFFLÉ, YOU MUST. . .

→ **Use an oven that heats from below** (no rotating heat) and/or a metal mold that conducts heat better from below.
→ **Create a crust on the top of the soufflé** (either by placing it briefly under the broiler or by sprinkling it with sugar or cheese before baking it): the crust, like the fabric of a balloon, will prevent the escape of the air bubbles.
→ **Beat the egg whites very firmly** (and salt is strictly useless in this step!).
→ **Ensure all vegetables and fruits are dried** very well before adding them to the base.
→ **Ensure the oven remains closed until the eggs have set.** After this time, it is possible to open the oven, but only quickly and not too frequently.
→ **Serve your soufflé quickly** to avoid disturbances that will cause it to deflate.

After this, all that remains is for you to enjoy your soufflé while watching it deflate gently—because when a soufflé collapses it is no longer a soufflé!

TO GUARANTEE FAILURE OF A SOUFFLÉ, YOU MUST. . . ✗

→ **Open the door of your oven before the base has time to set,** leave the oven door open for more than 20 seconds, or subject the soufflé dish to a shock. Do these things, and you will inevitably have a collapsed soufflé!

. . . A tip: if this happens to you, know that, when deflated, a soufflé takes on the name of a *mousseline* (Renée Bousquet, Anne Laurent, *Travaux pratiques de techniques culinaires*, Éd. Doin, 2004)! So your mousseline is ready!

Vertiginous Vineyards

The greatest wines are sometimes born on the steepest slopes. And wine growers, such as Richard Virenque, must sometimes double their efforts to work these extreme *terroirs*.
Alexis Goujard

ALSACE

Clos Saint Urbain Rangen de Thann du domaine Zind-Humbrecht 90 percent; 13.6 acres (5.5 hectares); Riesling; volcanic sandstone
We'll paint you a picture: this great vintage is the most southern in Alsace, in Thann, and the most vertiginous in France. The Riesling, Pinot Gris, and Gewurztraminer vines surround the Saint-Urbain white chapel and descend to the Thur River. **Distinctive characteristic:** it exhibits delicate alchemy between a late-ripening terroir and full southern exposure to the sun. **Let's uncork the bottle:** Alsace Grand Cru Rangen de Thann, Clos Saint Urbain Riesling 2013. Bold Riesling with powerful notes of stone and dry grass.

RHÔNE

Maison Rouge du domaine Georges Vernay (Côte-Rôtie) 60 percent; 7.4 acres (3 hectares); Syrah; gneiss rock
We'll paint you a picture: only the archbishops of Vienna had faith enough to climb this little mountain. Then vines were planted at a high density (nearly 10,000 vines/2.4 acres (1 hectare), unveiled by Georges Vernay in 1975. **Distinctive characteristic:** to stay attached to the granitic hillside of the Maison Rouge, Syrah is based on the technique of the stake, where a stake of wood serves as support for the vine. To weed it, you have to dig and pull using string! **Let's uncork the bottle:** Côte-Rôtie, Maison Rouge 2013. Delicately peppery and deep, this wine expresses itself with elegance. An astute palate will be required to appreciate it in fifteen years.

CHAMPAGNE

Clos des Goisses de la maison Philipponnat. 45 percent; 13.6 acres (5.5 hectares); Pinot Noir and Chardonnay; chalk
We'll paint you a picture: this is one of the most popular hillsides of Champagne, an extreme parcel of land isolated in 1935 by Pierre Philipponnat to express the character of this surly terrain in a vintage Champagne. **Distinctive characteristic:** this south-facing hillside offers ripe and vigorous Pinot Noir and Chardonnay grapes. **Let's uncork the bottle:** Champagne Clos des Goisses 2007. This vintage has been aged for ten years: ample and vinous material with a prominent acidity and a generous length.

SOUTHWEST

Virada du domaine Camin-Larredya (Jurançon) 40 percent; 2.4 acres (1 hectare); Gros Manseng, Petit Manseng, Petit Courbu, Camaralet; siliceous clay and sedimentary rock.
We'll paint you a picture: walking on the Larredya path to Jean-Marc Grussaute's small Béarn farm, the Virada takes the shape of a colossal green amphitheater of vineyards that contemplate the Pyrénées. **Distinctive characteristic:** the vines are planted in terraces. The leaves rise to more than 6½ feet (2 m) to capture the sun and breathe the invigorating air of the mountain and the Atlantic breezes. **Let's uncork the bottle:** Jurançon Sec La Virada 2015. Full of salty flavors and exotic fruits, this white wine is propelled in the mouth with a luminous vigor and a finish that is delicately sharp. A great dry white in the land of mellow wine.

LOIRE

Clos de Beaujeu du domaine Gérard Boulay in Chavignol (Sancerre) 70 percent; 1.8 acres (0.75 hectares); Sauvignon Blanc; Kimmeridgian marl
We'll paint you a picture: near the small ridge forming the village of Sancerre, the Clos de Beaujeu, a modest deformation of the original name of the Culs de Beaujeu, rises above the Berrichonne capital of *crottins de chèvre*: Chavignol. **Distinctive characteristic:** here the Sauvignon Blanc is king and blends with the Kimmeridgian marl. A soil of limestone and fossilized oysters—creating great white wines! **Let's uncork the bottle:** Sancerre, Clos de Beaujeu 2015. This Sauvignon needs two years to reveal its rich bouquet of ripe citrus fruits and iodized notes and its long and stimulating finish.

Auguste Escoffier

First chef to have been decorated with the Legion of Honor, considered "the cook of kings and the king of cooks," and above all else to have established the standards of French cuisine.

Charles Patin O'Coohoon

Cook of Kings and King of Cooks
(1846–1935)

3 Escoffier sweet creations

The proportions of the era for these recipes have been respected, but the high concentration of sugar merited a slight adjustment.

Poire Belle Hélène

The origins: in 1864, Escoffier poaches pears in a syrup that he then drapes in warm chocolate sauce and christens "Belle Hélène," in tribute to the eponymous comedic opera of Jacques Offenbach.

The recipe: combine 4¼ cups (1 L) of water, ½ cup (100 g) of sugar, and the juice of a lemon. Bring to a boil and place 6 peeled pears in the liquid to poach them (just until softened). Leave them to cool in the liquid. In a bain-marie, melt 7 ounces (200 g) of dark chocolate, then add ¾ cup plus 1 tablespoon (200 mL) of warm milk; stir until smooth. Accompany the pears with vanilla ice cream and pour the warm chocolate sauce over the top. Serve.

Peach Melba

The origins: at the end of a performance of Wagner's opera *Lohengrin*, Escoffier creates these famous poached peaches that he names in honor of Australian singer Helen Porter Mitchell, better known as Nellie Melba.

The recipe: blanch 6 peaches in boiling water to remove their skins. Pit them, then sprinkle them with sugar. Blend 9 ounces (250 g) of raspberries with ¾ cup (150 g) of superfine sugar. Place the peaches on a bed of vanilla ice cream and spoon the raspberry purée on top. Serve.

Strawberries Sarah Bernhardt

The origins: on the occasion of the first *Dîner d'Épicure* (Epicurean Dinner) to promote the excellence of French cuisine, Escoffier pays homage to the great Sarah Bernhardt with strawberries.

The recipe: sprinkle 2¼ pounds (1 kg) of strawberries with sugar, then drizzle them with 6 small glasses of herb-based liquor (such as green Chartreuse). Make a purée by blending 1⅛ pounds (500 g) of the strawberries with 1¼ cups (250 g) of sugar; whip 3 cups plus 2 tablespoons (750 mL) of cream and fold this into the purée. Make another purée by blending preserved pineapple with 1¼ cups (250 g) of sugar. Place the strawberries on a bed of vanilla ice cream, then spoon the strawberry purée on top. Cover completely with the pineapple purée.

ESCOFFIER'S STANDARDIZATION OF SERVICE

A single prix fixe menu for tourists
The new generation of chefs who overload their menus should beware! Escoffier invented the idea of a single, simplified menu.

Service à la russe
A small revolution. Courses used to be brought to the table all at the same time in a service described as à la française. But with service à la russe, they began to be served in succession as printed on the menu.

The organization of a team
With César Ritz, he standardized life in large kitchens and created ranks among the staff, with the requirement to wear a toque.

IS THE MOON MADE OF CHEESE?

Amused by the controversy over the English disdain for eating frogs and the nickname of *frog eaters* given to the French by the English, Auguste Escoffier constructed a pleasing revenge.

"I promised myself one day during my stay at the Savoy to serve frogs to the English gentlemen. The opportunity arrived. A great ball was to take place in the following days. Many cold dishes, as varied as possible, were on the menu, a series of dishes, so-called for the occasion: *Nymphe à l'Aurore*. The charming and brilliant English society did a great deal of honor to these *Nymphes* without knowing they were delighting in the frog legs they found so despicable."

A sleight of hand: to deceive the English, Escoffier cooked the frogs' legs in a flavored court-bouillon. Once cooled, he wrapped them in a *chaud-froid* sauce with pink paprika. He placed them in a square dish decorated with blanched tarragon leaves and covered them with a thin film of chicken gelée.

Of Vegetables and Men

How do we decide what to include in the category of vegetables? Simple or sophisticated recipes? Sides or main dishes? This diverse category can include them all! Despite vegetables' often ambiguous role on the table, however, their role in the French language is clear, as their many shapes, preparations, and flavors have served as inspiration for expressions and metaphors.

Aurore Vincenti

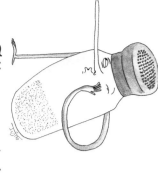

Telling . . . salads?

In French, the term *salade* can mean "lettuce," but it can also represent a mixture that is more than just lettuce. The word *salade* comes from the Latin *sal* (salt), not because a salad should be particularly salty, but in reference to the mixture of herbs, legumes, oil, and seasoning (pepper and salt) that is usually served at the beginning or end of the meal. The French language retains a slang expression for the propensity to tell beautiful and well-constructed stories, often described as "salty," which might also contain a few "untruths" for a little added embellishment. In short, we "season" our stories to our own liking. When you tell stories in this way, you are said to *raconter des salads*.

Do you have the heart of an artichoke?

The artichoke is a seductive vegetable, performing a slow striptease as its leaves are pulled away, one by one. Before revealing its heart, however, it requires a little foreplay. Although its outer leathery petals stand like ramparts, ready to dissuade its attacker, each tantalizes with its own delectable offering to be stripped off with a simple scrape of the teeth. Finally, the artichoke grants access to its tender center, and we are faced with the decision to simply taste it or to completely devour it. An artichoke heart is delicate and, consequently, allows itself to be conquered with ease once it is finally reached. Thus, one who falls in love easily is said to have "the heart of an artichoke" (*le cœur d'artichaut*).

Game over!

If, for you, a bean (*haricot*) is nothing more than a long green or small yellow pod you eat with a pat of butter, you have been fooled. Originally, *haricot* was a mutton stew made with beans, but *haricot* eventually took on the meaning of "bean," while the word itself was derived from the verb *harigoter* or *haricoter*, meaning "to cut to pieces," or "to shred." The origin of the phrase *c'est la fin des haricots* ("there are no more beans") is uncertain, but perhaps it leads us back to that. This expression, dating from the beginning of the twentieth century, comes from the use of the word *haricot* to mean "almost nothing." When you have nothing left, not even *haricots*, then it's truly the end!

With little onions

If I treat you with great love and care, fawn affection upon you with good, simple food, there is a good chance you will come back to me. And whatever I cook *aux petits oignons* ("with little onions") always creates a taste of comfort that makes you want to come back again. It is in these culinary origins that the expression *aux petits oignons* finds its meaning, as early as 1740, of "to treat with loving care." (It's not in this sense, however, that one finds a relation to another slang meaning of *oignon*: "ass." No!) So peeling an onion, chopping it to the point of tears, and making the effort to cook it properly may cause us a fair amount of trouble in the beginning, but the outcome is always good.

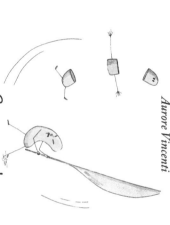

A shallot's race

This expression originates with a slang meaning for the bulb of a shallot that refers to the buttocks, due to its shape. In a *course à l'échalote* (a shallot's race), a person is said to take someone by the seat of the pants and collar and push them forward, forcing them to run. This expression dates back to the 1930s and meant to "pursue," "follow closely on someone's heels," or "hunt." Today it suggests a race for power—something causing stress under pressure—therefore relegating this popular expression to use mostly in relation to politics and the media.

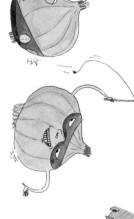

What a turnip!

If you're watching a bad movie, you might say, "What a turnip!" What in the heck did the lowly turnip do to earn such a negative connotation? Perhaps it's due to its relation to the devil's turnip that can be frighteningly hallucinogenic, even lethal. As a consequence, the turnip's reputation was set, and from the end of the thirteenth century, the word has been used to designate something to be avoided or something of very little value. Nowadays, although we like it prepared in all sorts of ways—boiled, roasted, or baked—a "turnip" in the world of cinema does not make for a good Friday night out at the movies!

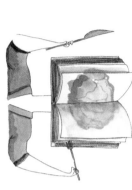

A head of cabbage

The comparison of one's cranium to the shape of certain vegetables was inevitable. The analogy is simple: the spherical shape of the skull recalls that of a head of cabbage or perhaps a crown of broccoli. When in French we say *we have something in the cabbage*, it means we have something "on our mind." The image of layers of leaves superimposed on a core conjures up the idea of man's intelligence: complex layers surrounding our inner thoughts. In the same way, *ciboule* (spring onion) led to the word *ciboulot*, meaning "noggin," because of its many outer layers. We say *pas besoin de se casser le ciboulot* ("no need to rack your brain"). But the comparison between a vegetable and the seat of thought is not always a good one. Ever hear someone say, "He has a pea brain"?

Vegetables and money

There is a very strong link between having something ("in the teeth," which implies "having access to everything") and the expense such a lifestyle entails. *Aller aux épinards* ("going with the spinach") means "rolling up your sleeves"—working hard—to make a living. This expression has nothing to do with the plant itself but from the sound of "pine" (*peen*) in *é-pine* [*peen*]-*ard*. "pine" in French is slang for "penis." The expression therefore has a sexual connotation and was used as early as 1866 regarding prostitution. When one *palper un peu d'oseille* ("holds a little sorrel"), he's stuffing his pockets with a little green—or cash. When money runs out, *on se tourne vers le radis*—"we turn to radishes" (its small size determining its little value). So if *je n'ai plus un radis* ("I have nothing but a radish"), then I have nothing in my pocket.

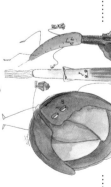

Combining vegetables

Some vegetable names have produced derivatives that the French commonly use. When *on est planté là* ("we are planted there"), we stand, waiting, "planted like a leek" (*planté comme un poireau*)! The expression eventually gave birth to the verb *poireauter* ("to stand around"). The verb *carotter*, from the end of the word *carotte* ("carrot"), also finds its origin in an expression from the end of the seventeenth century, which meant to "live sparingly." The verb *carotter* appeared a little later in the context of a game meaning to "play small," or "play it safe," and later slipped toward the idea of "scamming," but has since become dated. However, its use has been revived in recent years in the language being "cabbage") given to a child or a loved one. Despite its mixed popularity as a food, to be a cabbage is a desirable thing! This word probably comes from the affectionate name *chouchou* (*chou* meaning "to spoil"). And the verb *chouchouter*, which means to "spoil" ...

French Honey

From Corsica to Alsace to Brittany, France is a magnificent country for gathering nectar for making honey, even if the increase in the death of honeybees from the use of chemicals from aggressive agricultural practices is undermining this wonderful heritage. This is a *tour de France* of our best varieties.

Julien Henry

Honey of Paris

Harvest area: Paris
Harvest period: end of July to end of September
Color: amber
Taste: slightly menthol-flavored, reflecting the dominance of linden pollen
Uses: versatile (cooking, flavorings, spread for toast, etc.)
Nota bene: today, bees thrive better in the city than in the country. Now that insecticides are banned in parks and gardens, hives are more productive. Sixty-six to 132 pounds (30 to 60 kg) of honey is harvested on average per hive, compared to 20 in the countryside.

Acacia Honey (Black Locust)

Harvest area: throughout France
Harvest period: May to July
Color: from translucent to pale yellow
Taste: very sweet with vanilla flavors
Uses: ideal for its sweetening power, perfect for green tea as it won't overwhelm the tea's delicate flavor. Frequently used in the kitchen for deglazing.
Nota bene: French production does not meet the demand, so this honey is often imported from Eastern Europe (Hungary, Romania), which has wrongly earned it a bad reputation. These countries' lands have been much more protected from pesticides than those of France for the past 50 years.

Thyme Honey

Harvest area: PACA (Provence-Alpes-Côte d'Azur), Cévennes, and the former Languedoc-Roussillon region
Harvest period: May to June
Color: amber to dark brown
Taste: strong and pungent, with musky notes and a lingering flavor
Uses: as a winter honey it's par excellence, ideal with hot lemon water to fight colds and sore throats.

Bourdain Honey (Black Alder)

Harvest area: Atlantic coast and Massif Central
Harvest period: April to July
Color: dark brown
Taste: balsamic fragrance, light aromas reminiscent of flowers such as violets, pale lilac, and marshmallow
Uses: with fresh dairy products and white cheeses.

Linden Honey

Harvest area: mostly in the North, in Île-de-France and in the mountainous regions (Alps, Pyrénées, Massif Central)
Harvest period: July
Color: white to amber (depending on the presence of honeydew)
Taste: very minty, long finish on the palate
Use: this honey offers the benefits of pollen-producing flowers, making it ideal in soothing herbal teas.

Fir Honey

Harvest area: mainly Vosges, Jura, and Alsace
Harvest period: June to September
Color: dark brown, and can be green, depending on the harvesting area
Taste: sweet and not persistent, with a malty and slightly balsamic taste and a faint evergreen-tree flavor on the finish
Uses: during the winter, ingesting a big spoonful at bedtime; ideal for making *pain d'épices*.
Nota bene: holds an AOC when it comes from the Vosges and a PGI (Protected Geographical Indication) when it is harvested in Alsace.

Sunflower Honey

Harvest area: throughout France, but best known from the Southwest
Harvest period: June to August
Color: yellow
Taste: delicately fruity and aromatic; pleasant and lively on the palate
Use: gloriously creamy. This is honey par excellence as a spread.
Nota bene: second-most-grown oleaginous crop in France, dependent on bees for pollination. Yet it is one of the most highly treated crops to make it phytosanitary, and is often treated with chemicals that are responsible for the death of bees.

White Heather Honey

Harvest area: Provence, ancient Languedoc-Roussillon and Corsica
Harvest period: June to December
Color: light brown
Taste: strong, flavors of licorice with caramel aromas reminiscent of *confiture de lait* (milk jam)
Use: ideal as a spread.

Rapeseed Honey

Harvest area: throughout France—one of the biggest crops of the country
Harvest period: May
Color: amber
Taste: a flavor reminiscent of cabbage and a very discreet aroma
Use: in salty cooking due to its smell.
Nota bene: the cultivation of rapeseed is one of the best examples of aggressive farming that uses harmful pesticides, particularly those detrimental to the health of bees, but paradoxically it is also one of the new "green" energy sources. Beekeepers often find it difficult to maintain this harvest and prefer to call it "spring honey" or "creamy honey." Commercial producers mix it with other varieties, such as *toutes fleurs* ("all-flower") honey.

Chestnut Honey

Harvest area: especially Southwest, Southeast, and Corsica
Harvest period: August to September
Color: brown
Taste: the opposite of acacia on the tasting scale of honey. One of the strongest and most-sought-after honeys. Liquid, with intense aromas, woody flavors, bitter and persistent
Use: ideal in pastry, we love it in ganaches, and especially those by Jacques Genin.

Rosemary Honey

Harvest area: Old Languedoc-Roussillon
Harvest period: May to June
Color: white to slightly amber
Taste: slightly balsamic and very sweet scent, with a long finish
Use: a creamy honey par excellence, at its best on a slice of bread at breakfast.
Nota bene: since Roman times and for a long time thereafter, it was called "honey of Narbonne."

Rhododendron Honey

Harvest area: Mountainous regions (above 4,900 ft/1500 m), mainly Alps and Pyrénées
Harvest period: July to September
Color: white to amber
Taste: light flavor, flowery, vanilla
Use: because of its light flavor, it's ideal for lending slight notes of vanilla to herbal teas.
Nota bene: very rich in trace elements; a powerful restorative.

Buckwheat Honey

Harvest area: Brittany, eastern France
Harvest period: August to September
Color: light brown to black
Taste: a blend of aromas: wood, earth, and toasted grains; subtle, yet pronounced; leaves a certain freshness on the palate
Use: pastry, such as for making *pain d'épices*. One of the few honeys capable of intensifying the flavor of coffee.
Nota bene: the largest producers are China and Canada.

Lavender Honey

Harvest area: Provence, northeast Gard, Alpes-de-Haute-Provence, Hautes-Alpes, Vaucluse, Var, eastern Ardeche, and southern Drôme
Harvest period: July to September
Color: white to amber
Taste: fruity flavors, woody, vegetal and floral aromas
Use: widely used in the manufacture of nougats. Ideal partner for breakfast.
Nota bene: this honey has a PGI (Protected Geographical Indication) and a *Label Rouge* (Red Label) for quality assurance.

Common Heather Honey

Harvest area: mainly southwestern France
Harvest period: June to October
Color: brown to black
Taste: slightly bitter, long in the mouth and with complex aromas; notes of tobacco and licorice, even an animal-like flavor
Use: its powerful flavor and its aromatic complexity make it a privileged partner in the world of gastronomy. The Landemaine bakery in Paris offers a honey sourdough bread of incomparable flavor.
Nota bene: harvest is quite rare because of its complexity. It crystallizes very quickly, even in the beehive frames.

skip to
The Kings of *Pain d'Épices*, p. 121

Buckwheat Honey
Texture:

| Liquid | Creamy | Crystallized | Solid |

Rhododendron Honey
Texture:

| Liquid | Creamy | Crystallized | Solid |

Acacia Honey (Black Locust)
Texture:

| Liquid | Creamy | Crystallized | Solid |

White Heather Honey
Texture:

| Liquid | Creamy | Crystallized | Solid |

Linden Honey
Texture:

| Liquid | Creamy | Crystallized | Solid |

Chestnut Honey
Texture:

| Liquid | Creamy | Crystallized | Solid |

Lavender Honey
Texture:

| Liquid | Creamy | Crystallized | Solid |

Common Heather Honey
Texture:

| Liquid | Creamy | Crystallized | Solid |

Bourdain Honey (Black Alder)
Texture:

| Liquid | Creamy | Crystallized | Solid |

Rapeseed Honey
Texture:

| Liquid | Creamy | Crystallized | Solid |

Fir Honey
Texture:

| Liquid | Creamy | Crystallized | Solid |

Sunflower Honey
Texture:

| Liquid | Creamy | Crystallized | Solid |

Thyme Honey
Texture:

| Liquid | Creamy | Crystallized | Solid |

Rosemary Honey
Texture:

| Liquid | Creamy | Crystallized | Solid |

Honey of Paris
Texture:

| Liquid | Creamy | Crystallized | Solid |

What Is Honeydew?

It is actually the **secretion of insects.** Grasshoppers, aphids, and other mealybugs feed on **the sap** of resin-producing trees (among others), filter it, and release it in the **form of droplets**, especially on the leaves of trees. Attracted by its sweet smell, **bees collect it** before turning it into honey, often very concentrated and rich in **trace elements.** Fir honey is a honeydew, and Corsica is also famous for its honeydew maquis.

Honey from the Islands

CORSICA

Containing rich soils, Corsica, France's île de Beauté, produces honey thanks to an endemic bee, *Apis mellifera mellifera corsica*. It is labeled with the AOP (*appellation d'origine protégée*) "Mele di Corsica." There are six varieties of honey with flavors as complex as they are different.

Spring honey
Harvested beginning in May; sweet and floral. The best years are when its dominant plant is the clementine, giving it a delicate citrus flavor.

Spring maquis honey
Harvested during the spring. Amber, with delicate notes of caramel or cocoa that make it very flavorful. Its dominant plants are, in general, white heather, maritime lavender, and broom.

Autumn maquis honey
Harvested starting in November; amber and very bitter; its dominant plant is the strawberry tree. Highly sought after by pastry chefs and cooks, with flavors of hazelnut and burnt caramel.

Summer maquis honey
Harvested starting in August in the high valleys of the island; a rare honey. Light amber, its dominant plants of thyme and bramble (blackberry) make it fruity and aromatic.

Chestnut honey
Harvested at the end of June in the highlands, powerful and tannic, predominantly from chestnut. It is often considered the best by lovers of strong-flavored honeys. The slight bitterness that emerges at the end on the palate tempers the sweetness and makes the flavor incomparable.

Honeydew of the maquis
Harvested from May to September, amber to dark, malty taste with camphor.

RÉUNION

Full of diversity in its ecological heritage, Réunion has a variety of incredible honeys. The two most common are:

Pink peppercorn honey
The pink berries are the fruits of the false pepper tree, cultivated under the name "pink gold of Réunion." Its honey, which does not crystallize, is amber in color and has slightly spicy flavors. Used especially in cooking, it accounts for about 80 percent of honey production in Réunion.

Lychee honey
Bees love gathering pollen from the flowers of this abundant tree along the coast. Its clear honey with rather coarse crystallization offers unique flavors. There are notes of rose and quince. Some beekeepers consider it one of the best honeys in the world.

WEST INDIES
(GUADELOUPE AND MARTINIQUE)

The French West Indies benefit from a tropical climate, but one that remains tempered by the trade winds. They are diversified and abundant with vegetation, and therefore conducive to the production of honey. There are three main varieties:

Logwood honey
Logwood is a small tree with small flowers in yellow clusters. Its clear and very fragrant honey is the most famous of the West Indies. Some compare it to acacia honey.

Mangrove honey
Characteristic of the two islands, it could be the equivalent of *toutes fleurs* ("all-flower") honey from mainland France. The mangrove is the vegetation found along the coastal and swampy areas of this region.

Ti baume honey
Also known as "Mexican mint," this plant is a perfect aromatic blend of thyme, mint, sage, and oregano. Its amber and dark honey reveals powerful and intense flavors.

GUYANA

Guyana has one of the most preserved forests on the planet. As its production of honey is still quite low, the most common variety is mangrove honey. Often very sweet and with subtle flavors of citrus, it remains a most delicate honey.

Let Them Eat . . . Brioche!*

A Viennese pastry made from leavened and aerated dough containing butter and eggs—
brioche is baked up in all regions of France!

Elvira Masson

4

Brioche de Nanterre
The most classic form: rectangular with eight dough rounds.

4

Brioche de Moulins-la-Marche
Recognizable by its small rounds of dough placed in a round mold.

2

Gochtial
Breton: half bun, half bread, with a brown crust.

4

Pastéchou Brioche
Brioche bread from Finistère enriched with prunes or raisins, shaped like a slipper.

3.5

Brioche aux Griaudes
Also called *pompe aux grattons*. A Bourbonnaise specialty.

10

Gâteau battu (beaten)
Kneaded by hand in Picardy and baked in a tall mold; grooved and cylindrical.

3

Cougnou
"Bread of Jesus" from the north of France.

2

Cramique
A northern brioche made with pearl sugar, raisins, or chocolate chips.

3

Pastis des Landes
Typical of Béarn and Gascony; traditionally served at village festivals and weddings.

2

Tourteau à l'anise
A round brioche "crown" from Villefranche-de-Conflent and its region (Occitanie).

2

Follaert
A specialty of Dunkerque. The shape imitates the dung of Saint Martin's donkey.

1.5

Parisian brioche
A roll made of two balls of different sizes: a smaller top bun (the head) sitting atop a larger bottom bun.

4

Gâteau mollet
100 percent Ardennes. Baked in a tall, fluted mold.

6

Brioche Vosgienne
Stuffed with hazelnuts, raisins, and dried pears.

5

Gâteau Saint-Genix
A Savoyard specialty, garnished with pink praline.

0

Brioche à la tomme fraîche
An Auvergne specialty.

5.5

Brioche tressée de Metz (Braided brioche)
Nicknamed *whété*. A braided brioche.

2

Chinois d'Alsace
A round and swirled brioche, filled with chocolate chip pastry cream.

2.5

Kugelhopf
A gourmet symbol of Alsace; always cooked in a clay mold for authenticity.

8

Pain de Modane
Similar to panettone, flavored with candied melon and filled with frangipane.

3

Bescoin
Brioche from Savoie with saffron and pastis.

7.5

Brioche de Gannat
Of the Auvergne, salty, stuffed with Gruyère cheese both grated and in pieces!

5

Brioche d'Yssingeaux
Very tender and fragrant, with orange blossom.

1

Pogne de Romans
Typical of the Drôme, in the shape of a crown, flavored with orange blossom.

Tour de France— Brioches

5

Brioche de Riom
A specialty served in Auvergne, created in Riom, near Clermont-Ferrand.

1

Brioche de Bourgoin
Originally from the town of Bourgoin-Jallieu, decorated with red and white sugar and garnished with pralines and sugared almonds.

1

Tortillade (Twist)
Also called an anise twist: a brioche roll braided in the shape of a crown.

2.5

Pompe à l'huile provençal
Made with olive oil . . . or butter!

2.5

Gâteau des rois (kings' cake)
Brioche with candied fruits and orange blossom; enjoyed in the south of France for the Epiphany.

5

Tart Tropézienne
Despite what its name suggests, brioche with orange blossom topped with coarse sugar and topped with a hidden half pastry-cream, half whipped-cream filling.

2.5

Cacavellu or Campanile
Corsican Easter cake with aniseed and pastis.

2

Pain de Bonifacio or "Bread of the dead"
A Corsican specialty with raisins and nuts, prepared on the Day of the Dead, November 2.

1

Coque de Béziers
Elongated, with orange blossom and lemon, traditionally tasted at Saint-Aphrodise.

1 → 10

Butter content

skip to
Viennoiserie, p. 331

*Legend attributes this sentence to Marie Antoinette. She would have announced it at the Palace of Versailles before the Parisian people who complained of the increase in the price of bread.

France's Wild Berries

Natural, vitamin-packed, high in flavor—wild berries have always been a precious and natural commodity throughout the French countryside, readily available to anyone. Unfortunately, their use has decreased as populations have moved from rural areas to the cities. Here we give praise to twenty of these small, edible berries.

Denise Solier-Gaudry

LINGONBERRY

Vaccinium vitis-idaea (Ericaceae)

Other names: cowberry, bearberry, mountain cranberry

Small berry the size of a bilberry (its cousin), first white then red and shiny, in clusters at the end of a creeping shrub from 4 to 12 inches (10 to 30 cm). Acidic taste. Often confused with the bearberry (*Arctostaphylos uva-ursi*), which is also edible.

Habitat: embankments, and mountain pastures with acidic soils

Picking season: September and October

Properties: vitamins C and A

Uses: cooked (with game), jelly, compotes, and jams

Apples with lingonberries: peel and bake 4 apples. Meanwhile, cook 7 ounces (200 g) of lingonberries with ¼ cup plus 2 tablespoons (80 g) of granulated sugar for 10 minutes, to make a compote. When the apples are cooked, fill them with the berry mixture. Serve with guinea hen.

STRAWBERRY TREE

Arbutus unedo (Ericaceae)

Other names: Irish strawberry tree, cane apple

A round and very small berry, just ¾ inches (2 cm) in diameter, red when ripe, with starchy flesh containing seeds. It is eaten raw but is better cooked. The shrub grows from 6½ to 10 feet (2 to 3 m) and sometimes up to 33 feet (10 m).

Habitat: Corsican maquis, Provence, Languedoc-Roussillon, Atlantic coast, Brittany

Picking season: September to January

Properties: vitamins, minerals, and antioxidants

Uses: jams, jellies, liqueurs

Strawberry tree compote: sauté 2¼ pounds (1 kg) of arbutus in ⅓ cup plus 1 tablespoon (100 mL) water over medium heat; strain through a chinois then cook for 10 minutes with ¾ cup (150 g) of sugar and the juice of an orange.

COMMON SEA BUCKTHORN

Hippophae ramnoides (Elaeagnaceae)

Other names: seaberry

A "false" drupe containing one seed, ovoid, yellow or orange, shiny, grouped in bundles on branches with an acidulated and astringent flavor. Thorny, bushy shrub with soft branches.

Habitat: dunes of the English Channel, edges of the Rhône and the Rhine. Sea buckthorn is also cultivated in the Savoie and the Southern Alps

Picking season: September and October

Properties: 30 times richer in vitamin C than an orange

Uses: juice, jellies, candies

Sea buckthorn juice: after washing and drying the fruit, process it through a food mill, then strain through a chinois. Combine the juice obtained with the same quantity of orange juice.

SNOWY MESPILUS

Amelanchier ovalis (Rosaceae)

Other names: serviceberry

The size of a pea, pink then blue-black at maturity, it keeps the remains of the calyx at its end. Sweet and aromatic flavor. The plant is a small, rustic tree with soft branches.

Habitat: on scree and in forest undergrowth of eastern France and the Pyrénées

Picking season: July and August

Properties: vitamin C, antioxidants, minerals

Uses: tarts, jams, clafoutis

Snowy mespilus muffins: preheat the oven to 400°F (200°C). Warm ¾ cup plus 1 tablespoon (200 mL) of milk and add ¼ cup plus ¾ teaspoon (60 g) of butter. Whisk in 2 cups minus 2 tablespoons (180 g) of flour, 1 packet of dried active yeast, 1 egg, and 3 tablespoons plus 1¾ teaspoons (45 g) of sugar, and add a handful of snowy mespilus berries. Half fill six silicone muffin cups with the batter and bake for 25 minutes, or until golden.

AZAROLE

Crataegnus azarolus (Rosaceae)

Other names: Mediterranean medlar

A red or yellow cherry-size berry. Tart ribbed flesh with five seeds. A taste of raw apple or cooked plum. The plant measures 10 to 33 feet (3 to 10 m), grows slowly, and fruits after 10 years.

Habitat: Mediterranean climate regions

Picking season: September and October

Properties: vitamins A and C; young leaves and flowers are known to cure sleep disorders and anxiety

Uses: jellies, jams, liqueurs

Caramel-apple azaroles: insert one toothpick into each of twenty azaroles. Make a caramel with 1¼ cups (250 g) of sugar, scant ½ cup (100 mL) of water, the juice of ½ a lemon, and a few drops of red food coloring. Let the caramel rest for 30 seconds, then dip the azaroles in the caramel one at a time. Let any excess caramel drip off, then place them on a sheet of parchment paper.

SERVICE TREE BERRIES

Sorbus domestica (Rosaceae)

Other names: sorb tree, Jerusalem pear, whitty pear

Round or pear-shaped drupe measuring ¾ to 1⅛ inches (2 to 3 cm), yellow, spotted with red. A sharp and astringent flavor that softens and becomes fragrant when overripe. They are ripened on a bed of straw. The plant can reach heights of 66 feet (20 m).

Habitat: native to the Mediterranean regions, where the plant was dispersed by the Romans

Picking season: September

Properties: vitamins A and C

Uses: cider (*le cormé*), eau-de-vie, jams

Applesauce with service tree berries: cook 4 Granny Smith apples (cored) over medium heat with ¼ cup (50 g) of sugar and 3 tablespoons plus 1 teaspoon (50 mL) of water for 20 minutes, or until softened. Add the pulp of 12 overripe service tree berries and stir to combine. Serve as a warm or cold compote.

CORNELIAN CHERRY

Cornus mas (Cornaceae)
Other names: cornelian cherry dogwood, cornejo macho, sorbet
A shiny, oval-shaped drupe measuring ¾ inch (2 cm); green then red, containing a nucleus. Sharp, but pleasant, flavor when ripe. The dogwood is a shrub that can reach a height of 33 to 49 feet (10 to 15 m).
Habitat: east and southeast France, on calcareous soil
Picking season: August and September
Property: vitamin C
Uses: jellies, jams, syrup (has a taste of grenadine)
Preserved cornelian cherries: soak green cornelian cherries in water for 10 days, changing the water daily. After this period, drain, wipe them dry, and place them in a lidded jar. Bring 4¼ cups (1 L) of water and 3 tablespoons (60 g) of salt to a boil for 5 minutes. Let cool, pour the liquid into the jar, and add 2 bay leaves and 2 sprigs of thyme. Close the lid. Set aside for 3 months, then enjoy them like olives!

JUNIPER

Juniperus communis (Cupressaceae)
Other names: common juniper
A blue-purple cone called galbula consisting of coalescing scales that fuse together; three seeds. Juniper is a shrub growing from 3 to 33 feet (1 to 10 m) high, with thorny leaves; bluish-green evergreen.
Habitat: mostly Mediterranean areas
Picking season: from October
Properties: diuretic and digestive properties; essential oil
Uses: infusion, decoction, marinade, sauerkraut flavoring, game, gin
Fried chicken liver with juniper: in a skillet with a drizzle of oil, fry 4 chicken livers, 1 minced shallot, and a quartered tomato for 3 minutes. Season with salt and pepper. Add 6 juniper berries and 1 tablespoon (15 mL) of cognac; stir to combine. Spread on baguette slices and place in a 350°F (180°C) preheated oven for 10 minutes. Serve hot as an appetizer.

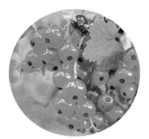

DOG ROSE

Rosa canina (Rosaceae)
Other names: common briar, dog brier
False fruit produced from the swelling of the bract of plants of the genus *Rosa* and filled with seeds (real actual fruit) covered with wiry bristles. Pleasant, tart taste. Thorny shrub with drooping branches 3 to 7 feet (1 to 2 m) long.
Habitat: everywhere: on dry land, hedges, embankments, meadows
Picking season: November, after the first frosts
Properties: diuretic, stimulates immune defenses, vitamin C
Uses: jellies, syrups, herbal teas
Rosehip wine: wash 2¼ pounds (1 kg) of rosehips, dry them, then place them in a large glass jar. Bring 4¼ cups (1 L) of water and 3 cups (600 g) of sugar to a boil for 2 minutes. After cooling, pour this liquid into the jar, then seal it with a piece of plastic wrap and pierce it several times with a toothpick. Set aside for 3 months, stirring occasionally, before filtering and bottling.

WILD STRAWBERRY

Fragaria vesca (Rosaceae)
Other names: woodland strawberry, *fraise des bois*, alpine strawberry
Small, round, or slightly elongated. Fleshy pulp bearing achenes, or "seeds," on its outer surface. Not very sweet but very fragrant. Perennial herb with a height from 4 to 6 inches (10 to 15 cm).
Habitat: everywhere, in the undergrowth, wet slopes, and clearings. Thrives up to 3,200 feet (1000 m) in altitude, except around the Mediterranean
Picking season: according to the climate, from June to August
Properties: vitamin C and trace elements
Uses: used raw on small tarts; sorbets, coulis, jams, liqueurs
 Red fruits salad: combine wild strawberries with other red fruits and berries to make a fruit salad. Combining different types of berries will make the salad more flavorful.

CURRANT

Ribes rubrum (Grossulariaceae)
Other names: garden red currant
Small round berry cluster, translucent, shiny, bright red, with some seeds. Tangy taste. Shrub grows between 3 to 6 feet (1 to 2 m) with erect stems.
Habitat: in the shady undergrowth of the northern half of France
Picking season: July
Properties: vitamin C, minerals, and flavonoids; good for skin and blood circulation

BARBERRY

Berberis vulgaris (Berberidaceae)
Other names: common barberry, European barberry
Small oblong, clustered berries, carmine red, with a very acidic pulp containing three seeds. Thorny shrub from 3 to 13 feet (1 to 4 m).
Habitat: throughout France
Picking season: September and October
Properties: digestive and anticough
Uses: when green, used to season sauces; when dried, used for a bittersweet flavor; jellies, jams, herbal teas
Brown butter and barberry skate: place 3 tablespoons (24 g) of dried barberries in a bowl of water for 15 minutes to rehydrate them; drain. Heat 2 tablespoons plus ¾ teaspoon (60 g) of butter and 2 tablespoons (30 mL) of sunflower oil in a pan and cook 4 skate wings on both sides (10 to 15 min per side). Season with salt and pepper, then add the barberry and continue cooking for 2 minutes, or until the skate wings are cooked through.

RASPBERRY

Rubus idaeus (Rosaceae)
Round or conical, pink to red, each contains one seed and is smaller than the cultivated raspberry. Sweet and fragrant. Raspberry is a thorny shrub growing from 3 to 4 feet (1 to 1.5 m).
Habitat: Alps, Vosges, Massif Central at the edge of forests and in the clearings
Picking season: July to September
Properties: vitamin C and antioxidants
Uses: tarts, sherbets, juices, coulis, vinegar, eau-de-vie
Raspberry jelly: briefly rinse 2¼ pounds (1 kg) of raspberries under cold water. Cook them over medium heat with a scant ½ cup (100 mL) of water for 5 minutes until they have collapsed slightly. Strain them through a chinois. Weigh the collected juice, combine it with the same weight of jelly sugar (with pectin), bring to a boil over medium heat, and boil for 7 minutes. Skim off any foam, pour into sterilized jars, and close the lid. Invert the jars until airtight.

Uses: delicious in jelly, tarts, syrups
 Red currant granita: cook currants in a small saucepan with 3 tablespoons plus 1 teaspoon (50 mL) of water until they are slightly softened and have burst. Weigh the mixture, then measure half this weight in sugar and add it to the currants; stir to combine. Pour this mixture into a container and place it in the freezer, stirring occasionally with a fork to break it up. Serve scooped in a strawberry soup.

SWEET CHERRY

Prunus avium (Rosaceae)
Other names: wild cherry, bird cherry, gean
Dark red drupe with a pit; smaller than a cherry. Sweet and fragrant flesh. The tree can reach 82 to 98 feet (25 to 30 m) high.
Habitat: birds, very fond of these fruits, are responsible for disseminating them throughout the country!
Picking season: June, July, or August, according to the regions
Properties: vitamins, minerals, antioxidants
Uses: Alsacian kirsch, Guignolet, jams, coulis

Cherry clafoutis: preheat the oven to 350°F (180°C). Grease a baking dish. Wash, dry, and chop 1⅛ pounds (500 g) of sweet cherries and place them in the bottom of the baking dish. Whisk together ½ cup (50 g) of flour, ¼ cup (60 g) of sugar, 1¼ cups (300 mL) of milk, and 3 eggs and pour this mixture over the fruit. Bake for 30 to 35 minutes. Five minutes before the end of the cooking time, sprinkle with 2 tablespoons (26 g) of sugar.

BLACKBERRY

Rubus fruticosus (Rosaceae)
Fruit composed of drupoles, each containing a seed; red then turns black and shiny. The bramble is a shrub with long spiny stems. A very fragrant fruit with a sweet and tangy flavor. The blackberry should not be confused with the black mulberry (*Morus nigra*), whose leaves are consumed by silkworms.
Habitat: everywhere, up to 4,900 feet (1500 m) in altitude
Picking season: August to September
Properties: vitamins B and C, antioxidants
Uses: jellies, jams, tarts

Blackberry coulis: thoroughly wash 1⅛ pounds (500 g) of blackberries and place them in a saucepan with scant ½ cup (100 mL) of water. Cook over medium heat until they break down slightly, about 5 minutes. Pass them through a food mill (fine-grind setting), then strain them through a chinois. Combine the juice obtained in the pan with ½ cup (100 g) of sugar and 1/16 ounce (2 g) of agar-agar, bring to a boil for 2 minutes.

MYRTLE

Myrtus communis (Myrtaceae)
Other names: common myrtle, true myrtle
Berries of purple then blue-black, slightly oval, not fleshy, pruinose, with a crown on the end. Very aromatic, with an evergreen-tree and balsamic taste. The myrtle is a shrub with reddish bark, 9 to 16 feet (3 to 5 m) in height.
Habitat: Corsica, Provence, Languedoc-Roussillon
Picking season: September and October
Properties: antiseptic virtues, treats respiratory diseases and insomnia
Uses: condiments, liqueurs

Myrtle liqueur: wash and dry 3 ounces (80 g) of myrtle berries, then place them in a lidded jar covered with 3 cups plus 2 tablespoons (750 mL) of fruit-based alcohol. Let macerate for 2 months. After this time, bring 1 cup (250 mL) of water and ½ cup plus 1 tablespoon (120 g) of sugar to a boil for 5 minutes over medium heat. Cool, then pour the syrup into the jar. Stir to combine before filtering and bottling. Wait at least 1 month before consuming.

BILBERRY

Vaccinum myrtillus (Ericaceae)
Other names: blaeberry, whortleberry, whimberry
Round berry, blue-black at maturity, pruinose. Pleasant taste, slightly acidic. The bilberry tree is a perennial tree 2 feet (50 cm) tall
Habitat: Alps, Massif Central, Vosges, Pyrénées
Picking season: late July to early September
Properties: vitamin C and antioxidants. Heals disorders of vision and memory
Uses: tarts, desserts, jams, liqueurs

Bilberry tart: preheat the oven to 350°F (180°C). Unroll 1 circle of flaky pastry into an 8-inch (20 cm) tart pan and prick the bottom with a fork. Bake for 15 minutes, or until golden. Pour 2 tablespoons (26 g) of superfine sugar over the bottom of the crust and spread 14 ounces (400 g) of bilberries on top. Whisk together 2 tablespoons (30 mL) fresh cream, ⅓ cup plus 1 tablespoon (100 mL) of milk, and 3 tablespoons (39 g) of granulated sugar and pour this mixture over the fruit. Bake for 35 minutes, or just until set.

MEDLAR

Mespilus germanica (Rosaceae)
Other names: common medlar
Berries are round, slightly flattened, ends with an indentation surrounded by a crown; rust color then turns brown, with three pits. Consume only when overripened. Small tree of 10 to 16 feet (3 to 5 m).
Habitat: throughout France
Picking season: October to November. Place the berries on a bed of straw for about 2 weeks
Properties: vitamin A, potassium, tonic
Uses: jams, jellies

Medlar loaf: halve the fruits and remove the pits. Weigh the pulp. Place the pulp in a saucepan with the same weight of coarse sugar and 3 tablespoons plus 1 teaspoon (50 mL) of water. Cook, stirring often. When the mixture detaches from the sides of the pan (after 15 to 20 minutes), pour it into a square baking dish coated with coarse sugar to a thickness of ¾ inch (2 cm). Set aside to dry for a few days. Sprinkle with sugar.

BLACKTHORN

Prunus spinosa (Rosaceae)
Other names: sloe
Drupe ⅓ to ½ inch (1 to 1.5 cm) in size, blue-black, pruinose, tart and astringent, fruit of the blackthorn shrub (a thorny shrub) with brown-gray bark
Habitat: everywhere up to 2,600 feet (800 m) in altitude; in hedges, at the edge of paths
Picking season: August to November
Properties: antioxidants and vitamin C
Uses: jellies, compotes, eau-de-vie, liqueurs such as Patxaran from the Basque Country

Blackthorn liqueur: wash and dry 10½ ounces (300 g) of blackthorn fruit (sloe), then place them in a glass jar with 4¼ cups (1 L) of clear alcohol, seal, and macerate for 1 month, shaking the jar from time to time. Bring 3 cups (600 g) of sugar and ⅓ cup plus 1 tablespoon (100 mL) of water to a boil; let cool, then pour into the jar. After 2 months, filter and transfer to a bottle for use.

ELDERBERRY

Sambucus nigra (Caprifoliaceae)
Other names: European elder, black elderberry
Little black drupes, sweet and soft. Shrub grows from 6½ to 16 feet (2 to 5 m). (When eaten raw, they are toxic.)
Habitat: everywhere well above sea level
Picking season: flowers in May, June; fruits end of August, September
Properties: leaves and flowers are anti-inflammatory and antihistamines. Flowers and fruits treat colds and flu
Uses: lemonade with flowers, jellies, syrups

Elderberry flower beignets: whisk together 2 cups minus 2 tablespoons (180 g) of flour, 1 packet of active dry yeast, 1 tablespoon (13 g) of sugar, 1 tablespoon (15 mL) of sunflower oil, 1 pinch of salt, the juice of 1 orange, 1 egg, and ⅓ cup plus 1 tablespoon (100 mL) of water. Beat 1 egg white to stiff peaks and fold it into the batter. Wash and drain 20 elderberry flowers. In a skillet, heat a drizzle of oil, dredge the flowers in the batter, then brown in the oil. Transfer to a paper towel–lined plate and dust with confectioners' sugar.

Sausages

1 SAUCISSE DE MORTEAU (Franche-Comté): pure pork (fed on the whey of local cows). Flavored with caraway, shallots, cilantro, nutmeg, and wine. Smoked with wood shavings in large pyramidal chimneys. PGI, AOP.

2 SAUCISSE DE MONTBÉLIARD (Franche-Comté): one of the oldest sausages. Meat and pork fat (also high in whey). Flavored with caraway and pepper. Smoked with fir wood or spruce. PGI.

DIOTS DE SAVOIE: popular in Savoie. Shoulder or pork tip defatted, rindless bacon, pork fat, all finely chopped. Seasoned with garlic, salt, pepper, nutmeg, quatre épices, and, according to devotees, red wine.

ATTRIAUX (Haute-Savoie): pork meat and offal (heart, liver, lung, kidney, throat, lean portions), seasoned and wrapped in a casing. A specialty in Thonon.

GANDEUILLOT DU VAL-D'AJOL (Vosges): a mixture of pork meat and tripe wrapped in pork intestines. Excellent cooked and smoked over a wood fire.

3 SAUCISSE DE STRASBOURG or KNACK: pork and beef meat. Seasoned with cumin and other flavor enhancers. The little noise it makes when you bite into it has earned it the nickname "knack," from the sound.

4 METTWURSCHT ALSATIENNE (Alsace): raw, creamy, and smoky, for spreading. Fatty pork and finely chopped beef. Seasoned with paprika, chile, cardamom, and—rum! For spreading on slices of bread.

5 GENDARME DES VOSGES: a rectangular shape. Reddish color. Beef and pork fat. Smoked with beech wood. The two "batons" of sausages attached to each other are reminiscent of the gendarmes (policemen) of the time who dressed in red and who always traveled in pairs—thus the name!

SAUCISSE DE MOU or COURADE (Auvergne): a specialty of Cantal and Rouergue. Lungs, heart, and pork flesh, flavored with red wine. Called "courade," which refers to the guts of pork, or "sausage of cousins" because it's saved for serving to distant cousins rather than closest family members.

SAUCISSE DE POMME DE TERRE (Cantal): potatoes and offal (rind, heart, lean meat, and fat from pork).

6 FIGATELLU (Corsica): a sausage made from liver, spleen, heart, lung tips, pork belly, bard fat, and pork blood. Seasoned with garlic, wine, and some herbs. Eaten fresh, smoked, or dried.

SALCICETTA (Corsican): seasoned only with salt and pepper. Only includes meat and fat scraps that are not used in premium cured meats from the island. Known to be less spicy than figatellu. Presented as a U shape.

7 SAUCISSE DE TOULOUSE: the longest sausage, sold in a coil by the meter. Composed of farm-raised pork.

8 SAUCISSE D'ANDUZE or RAYOLETTE (Cévennes): dry sausage that owes its flavor to the pigs fed with acorns and chestnuts. Comes in two equal parts folded onto themselves and joined by a string.

9 MERGUEZ: chopped beef and mutton. Flavored with cumin, ras el hanout, harissa, and coriander. Its name is from the Berber word *amrguaz*, *am* for "like," and *rguaz* for "man," a reference therefore to the male member!

10 CHIPOLATA: pork meat (lean shoulder meat, fat from the belly). Flavored with paprika. Etymological origin: *cipolla* (onion) in Italian and the Tuscan dish, *cipollata*, a confit of onion, served with pieces of sausage.

CERVELAS: originally pork and brains, hence its name. Composed of beef, lean pork, throat, bard fat, spices, garlic, and onions. Cooked in water with coloring added; its skin turns red when cooked.

11 LUKINKE (Pays Basque): composed of lean meat and fat from pork. Enjoyed dried or as a confit in fat, and stored in earthenware pots.

12 TXISTORRA (Pays Basque): raw meat of pork and beef. Flavored with Espelette pepper, thus its red color. Encased in sheep casings.

The term *saucisse* (sausage) comes from the Old French *saussiche*, a word from the Latin *salsicius*, which means salted minced meat, the adjective *salsus* meaning in Latin "salted." So much fatty deliciousness wrapped up in such a small package! Here are some of France's best examples.

Valentine Oudard

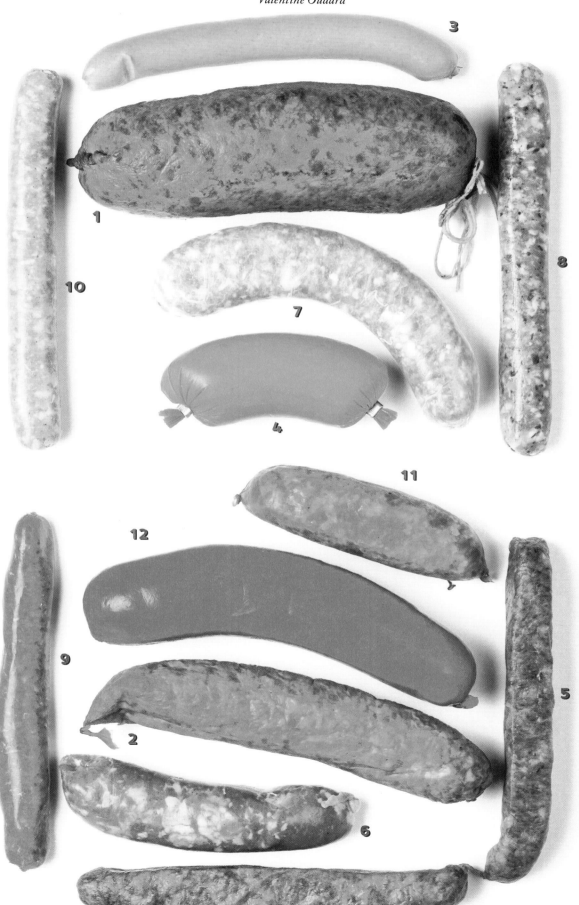

skip to
This Is Boudin!, p. 156

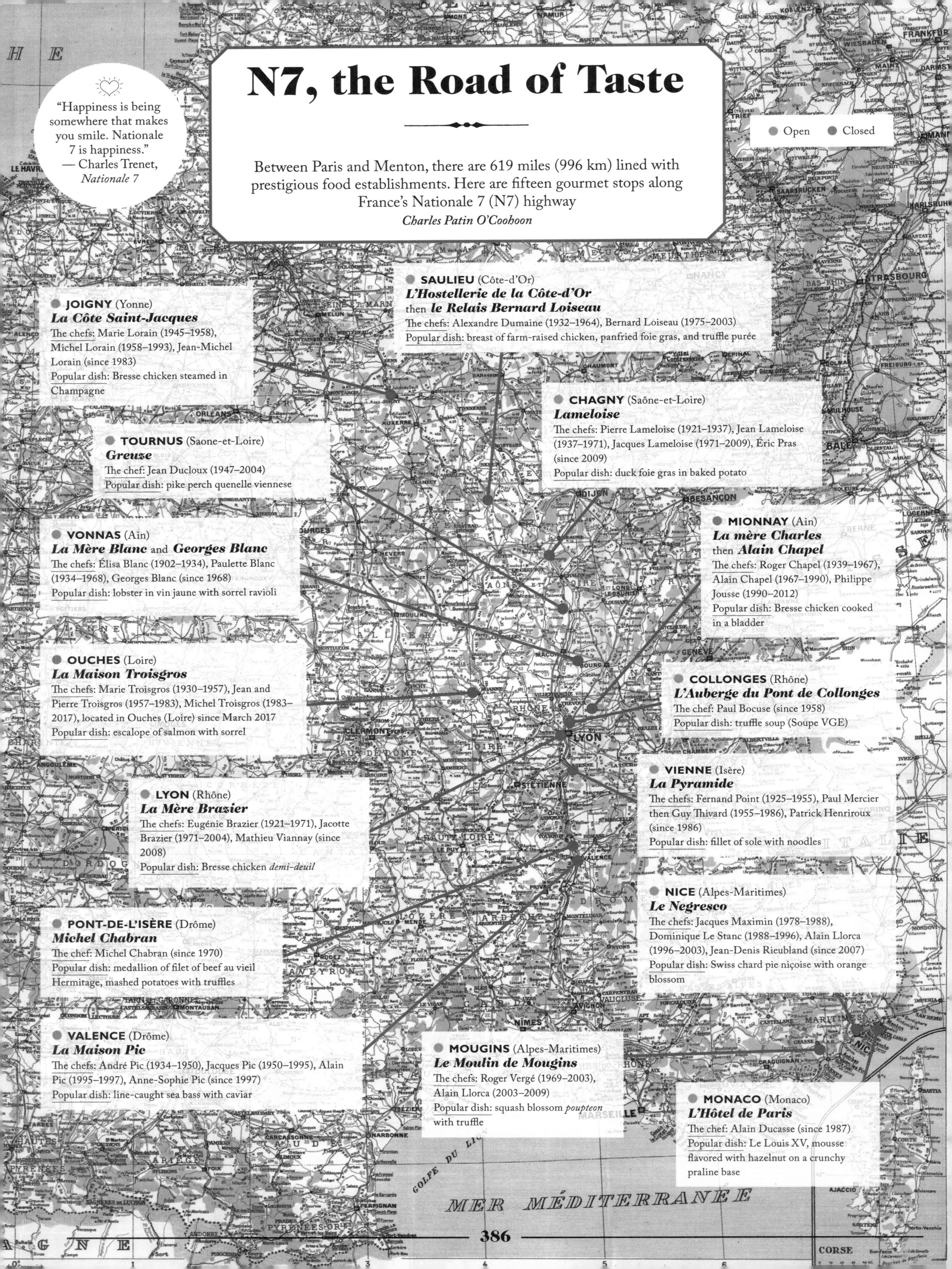

N7, the Road of Taste

Between Paris and Menton, there are 619 miles (996 km) lined with prestigious food establishments. Here are fifteen gourmet stops along France's Nationale 7 (N7) highway

Charles Patin O'Coohoon

"Happiness is being somewhere that makes you smile. Nationale 7 is happiness."
— Charles Trenet, *Nationale 7*

● Open ● Closed

● **JOIGNY** (Yonne)
La Côte Saint-Jacques
The chefs: Marie Lorain (1945–1958), Michel Lorain (1958–1993), Jean-Michel Lorain (since 1983)
Popular dish: Bresse chicken steamed in Champagne

● **TOURNUS** (Saone-et-Loire)
Greuze
The chef: Jean Ducloux (1947–2004)
Popular dish: pike perch quenelle viennese

● **VONNAS** (Ain)
La Mère Blanc and *Georges Blanc*
The chefs: Élisa Blanc (1902–1934), Paulette Blanc (1934–1968), Georges Blanc (since 1968)
Popular dish: lobster in vin jaune with sorrel ravioli

● **OUCHES** (Loire)
La Maison Troisgros
The chefs: Marie Troisgros (1930–1957), Jean and Pierre Troisgros (1957–1983), Michel Troisgros (1983–2017), located in Ouches (Loire) since March 2017
Popular dish: escalope of salmon with sorrel

● **LYON** (Rhône)
La Mère Brazier
The chefs: Eugénie Brazier (1921–1971), Jacotte Brazier (1971–2004), Mathieu Viannay (since 2008)
Popular dish: Bresse chicken *demi-deuil*

● **PONT-DE-L'ISÈRE** (Drôme)
Michel Chabran
The chef: Michel Chabran (since 1970)
Popular dish: medallion of filet of beef au vieil Hermitage, mashed potatoes with truffles

● **VALENCE** (Drôme)
La Maison Pic
The chefs: André Pic (1934–1950), Jacques Pic (1950–1995), Alain Pic (1995–1997), Anne-Sophie Pic (since 1997)
Popular dish: line-caught sea bass with caviar

● **SAULIEU** (Côte-d'Or)
L'Hostellerie de la Côte-d'Or then *le Relais Bernard Loiseau*
The chefs: Alexandre Dumaine (1932–1964), Bernard Loiseau (1975–2003)
Popular dish: breast of farm-raised chicken, panfried foie gras, and truffle purée

● **CHAGNY** (Saône-et-Loire)
Lameloise
The chefs: Pierre Lameloise (1921–1937), Jean Lameloise (1937–1971), Jacques Lameloise (1971–2009), Éric Pras (since 2009)
Popular dish: duck foie gras in baked potato

● **MIONNAY** (Ain)
La mère Charles then *Alain Chapel*
The chefs: Roger Chapel (1939–1967), Alain Chapel (1967–1990), Philippe Jousse (1990–2012)
Popular dish: Bresse chicken cooked in a bladder

● **COLLONGES** (Rhône)
L'Auberge du Pont de Collonges
The chef: Paul Bocuse (since 1958)
Popular dish: truffle soup (Soupe VGE)

● **VIENNE** (Isère)
La Pyramide
The chefs: Fernand Point (1925–1955), Paul Mercier then Guy Thivard (1955–1986), Patrick Henriroux (since 1986)
Popular dish: fillet of sole with noodles

● **NICE** (Alpes-Maritimes)
Le Negresco
The chefs: Jacques Maximin (1978–1988), Dominique Le Stanc (1988–1996), Alain Llorca (1996–2003), Jean-Denis Rieubland (since 2007)
Popular dish: Swiss chard pie niçoise with orange blossom

● **MOUGINS** (Alpes-Maritimes)
Le Moulin de Mougins
The chefs: Roger Vergé (1969–2003), Alain Llorca (2003–2009)
Popular dish: squash blossom *poupteon* with truffle

● **MONACO** (Monaco)
L'Hôtel de Paris
The chef: Alain Ducasse (since 1987)
Popular dish: Le Louis XV, mousse flavored with hazelnut on a crunchy praline base

MER MÉDITERRANÉE

French Movie Chefs

With its wealth of chefs working in major restaurants, brasseries, bistros, and even presidential palaces, French film seems to adore its apron-wearing heroes. Here's a list of winners of the most salivating chefs in the seventh art.

Laurent Delmas

TOP CHEFS ON SCREEN

Kitchens even starred in the very first movies. For example, in 1895, Louis Lumière made *Le Repas de Bébé* (*Baby's Dinner*) in which viewers watch a couple giving their offspring a morning meal. And ever since, French film has continued to give screen life to cooks both invented and real.

BEST CHEF FROM HISTORY

Gérard Depardieu in *Vatel* directed by Roland Joffé (2000).
Role: chef to the Prince of Condé
On-screen appetite level: 8/10
Our review: a perfect role for an actor forever inspired by gastronomy. Depardieu plays Vatel with modesty, impressed perhaps by the final act of the steward and chef who, as we know, took his life when the fish did not arrived on time for a royal dinner.

BEST CHEF IN A MAJOR PARIS RESTAURANT

Jean Gabin in *Nous sommes tous des assassins* (*We Are All Murderers*), directed by Julien Duvivier (1956).
Role: André Chatelin, aka Jean Gabin, owns a restaurant in Paris in the Les Halles neighborhood. They come for his shrimp in Chablis, his fowl terrine, and his coq au vin. And the chef isn't afraid to speak his mind. To an American guest who has asked for a Coke, he answers: "Oh no,

Madame, this is not a pharmacy!"
On-screen appetite level: 9/10
Our review: the movie's title could never apply to the talented André Chatelin.

BEST CHEF IN A REGIONAL RESTAURANT

Arnaudy, the chef in *Cigalon*, directed by Marcel Pagnol (1935).
On-screen appetite level: 8/10
Our review: Cigalon, an irascible chef but an artist at heart, simmers his Provençale *pieds et paquets* for hours on end. He's a master who reviles cannelloni, that "bludgeon of pasta filled with the day's leftovers." Gastronomy is transformed by Pagnol's verve and eloquence: a true feast of words spoken by a marvelous culinary exhibitionist.

BEST LOCAL RESTAURANT OWNER IN PARIS

Michel Aumont, the chef-owner in *Au petit Marguery*, directed by Laurent Bénégui (1995).
On-screen appetite level: 7.5/10
Our review: Hippolyte is the prototype chef of this kind of typically Parisian local establishment. With help from his wife, Joséphine (Stéphane Audran), he treats his clients to classic foie gras, duck, and seasonal morels. If not a monument of gastronomy, it's an homage to pure gourmand conviviality.

BEST "FRENEMEMY" CHEFS FOREVER

Bourvil and Fernandel in *La Cuisine au Beurre* directed by Gilles Grangier (1963).
On-screen appetite level: 6/10
Our review: two chefs work for the same restaurant. One is from Marseille, the other from Normandy. It's a clash of cultures and styles. Butter and cream versus olive oil. No one gets bored in the kitchen or the theater. The movie could have been named "Les Grandes Gueules" (big mouths). In terms of gastronomy, though, let's call it "A lot of noise for nothing!"

BEST BOSS IN A LYON BISTRO

Michel Galabru in *Une semaine de vacances* (*A Week's Vacation*), directed by Bertrand Tavernier (1980).
On-screen appetite level: 9/10
Our review: Michel Galabru could set the standard for a bistro boss in Lyon. Daily specials include gratin of pike quenelles and porcini omelet. And while you wait, a glass of Montrachet. Just what the movie's heroine Nathalie Baye needs to boost her morale.

BEST PERSONAL CHEF

Léon Larive in the *La Règle du Jeu* (*The Rules of the Game*) directed by Jean Renoir (1939)
On-screen appetite level: 10/10
Our review: the cook to the Marquis de la Chesnaye, chef hat on head, officiates in his vast kitchen, which also serves as a dining room for servants. It is there that he reveals the secret behind his potato salad: you have to pour the white wine on fully boiling potatoes. Or how a funny scene contains an indisputable culinary truth. The ultimate.

BEST CHEF TO A HEAD OF STATE

Catherine Frot in the *Les Saveurs du Palais* (*Haute Cuisine*), directed by Christian Vincent (2012).
On-screen appetite level: 8.5/10
Our review: loosely based on the life of Danièle Mazet-Delpeuch, former chef to the President of the French Republic François Mitterand, the film presents the recipe for a tartine with fresh truffles on toasted farmhouse bread with butter. French presidential "simplicity."

skip to ....
Lights, Camera, Action: Eat!, p. 193

What France Owes to Italy . . .

Myriad products and recipes are said to have been invented in Italy during the Renaissance before being introduced on the other side of the Alps by King Henry II's wife. Myth or reality? Let's investigate . . .

Loïc Bienassis

HAUTE CUISINE

Myth: Catherine de Médicis arrived in France around 1533 accompanied by chefs and pastry chefs and played an essential role in inventing French haute cuisine.

Reality: No contemporary of that period mentions the significant influence of Italy. Sixteenth-century French cuisine did not break away from the Middle Ages: spices were still valued, as were bittersweet and sour flavors and bread-based sauces . . .

THE FORK

Myth: Catherine de Médicis introduced the fork to the French court, a sign of superior refinement.

Reality: The Italian aristocracy set forks at their tables as early as the fifteenth century. In France, the use of this utensil was slowly adopted among the elite starting in the sixteenth century.

ARTICHOKES

Myth: Artichokes arrived in France in the sixteenth century with Catherine de Médicis.

Reality: It was indeed via Italy that this vegetable, which was grown in Muslim-Arabic gardens of Spain since the twelfth century, arrived in France four hundred years later.

MACARONS

Myth: Catherine de Médicis gave macarons for the Duke of Joyeuse's wedding in 1581 and that is when the court discovered the sweet.

Reality: Rabelais was the first to use the word *macaron* in French (in 1552). The word has Italian origins, but it has not yet been proven that the cookie does, too. Not one bears the name on the peninsula . . . The first recipes date from the mid-seventeenth century.

PÂTE À CHOUX

Myth: A man by the name of Popelini, who accompanied Catherine de Médicis to France, invented pâte à choux around 1540.

Reality: This Popelini emerged in the early 1890s, written by Pierre Lacam, who seems to have invented him. The first known pâte à choux recipe appeared in the *Nouveau Traité de la Cuisine* by Menon in 1739.

ICE CREAM

Myth: Cosimo Ruggieri, one of Catherine de Médicis's servants, introduced ice cream to Parisians.

Reality: The French and Italians came to make ice cream before—around?—1650. In all likelihood, Italy had made more headway with it . . . .

. . . and Vice Versa

What if there were a bit of France on stovetops across the boot? Here's a short lexicon.

Alessandra Pierini

Il cuoco Piemontese perfezionato a Parigi (1766): this treatise, written by a Piedmontese chef who had learned the secrets of French gastronomy in Paris, introduced northern Italy to *Carciofi* (artichokes) *Tournés*, and *Barigoule*, to mutton thighs à la Périgord and to Ravigote.

From suckling pig to blanquette and pigeon à la bourgeoise, he also shares every cake, feuillantine, and crème caramel. On the table, that meant fricassee, fondue, vegetable *ratatuia*, and much more.

RUSTICO LECCESE

Southern Italy's street food king, this stuffed turnover has unsuspected French origins. Its puff pastry and béchamel are similar to the vol-au-vent, even if the tomato and sweet melted cheese seem typically Italian.

MONSÙ

Neapolitan distortion of the French *monsieur*, this term (pronounced "mon-su") designates the illustrious chefs and cooks who arrived after the Bourbons at the end of the seventeenth century, the stars of Neapolitan gastronomy at the time. In Italian, their recipes were named *ragù, gattò, sciù,* etc. (ragout, cake, cabbage).

MAIONESE

In his book *La scienza in cucina e l'arte di mangiar bene (Science in the Kitchen and the Art of Eating Well*, 1911), Pellegrino Artusi popularized famous French mayonnaise and sang the praises of Sauce Maître d'Hôtel, parsley butter for grilled meat or chops.

BÉCHAMEL

The invention of Louis de Béchamel, Marquis de Nointel, is said to have been inspired by an even older sauce, the *salsa colla*, which was introduced to France by Tuscan chefs after Catherine de Médicis and was called *colle* (glue) in French because it was used to bond together a recipe's ingredients.

RAGÙ

Italianized word with the same root as the French *ragoût*. These recipes have a common denominator, which is chopped meat cooked a special way in a sauce. It derives from the Old French verb *ragoûter*, meaning to rouse taste, appetite.

skip to
The Brits Have It!, p. 132

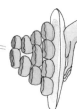

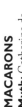

THE LANGUAGE OF BREAD

Because of the leading role it plays in our daily eating routine, bread has inspired a great deal of spoken language. Its symbolism is paradoxical: bread is at once earthy nourishment and heavenly substance; it is mightily democratic and yet underlines class differences.

Aurore Vincenti

Bread is life

This basic food alone symbolizes the fact of being able to eat until no longer hungry. Its very substance stands in for life. The French will say **"to earn one's bread"** (1580) meaning **"to earn one's living."** And if one speaks of **butt bread** in French, it means revenue from prostitution. Without bread, one could die. In French, **to take the bread out of someone's mouth** literally means preventing him from meeting his needs. What's worse, if you **deprive him of the taste of bread**, you're killing him.

Originally, the French expression **"having bread on the breadboard"** meant "being able to live without working." If the bread was already there, you could just take it. It was during World War I that the breadboard and its bread shifted toward work and action.

"If they don't have bread, let them eat cake." That outrageous remark is (falsely) attributed to Marie Antoinette in response to the demands of her starving people. **A symbol of the masses,** bread is at the heart of revolts and major revolutions. When it's used to soak up gravy and is eaten with meals, it tells a lot about social class. For the poorest among us, bread represents **the core of a hardy meal**. It sticks to your bones. It's eaten dry and dipped in soup to soften it. The French word **soupe** originally designated bread that would be sprinkled with broth. Eventually, with a bit of milk, eggs, and sugar, even stale bread isn't lost: it becomes *pain perdu* ("lost bread"—but not really lost!).

In French, **eating your white bread first** means starting off with the most pleasant part. The whiter the flour, the more **refined** it is. So the rich considered white bread to be more prestigious. On the other hand, whole wheat bread and black bread was reserved for the very poor. When one eats one's **black bread** in French, it means starting off with the **hardest part**. But in the 1970s, **that paradigm was turned around**. White bread was seen as having poor nutritional value and so, the darker the bread, the more value it was considered to have.

Bread is soul

With bread symbolizing life, the Jewish and Christian religions have made it **holy**. Bread is a gift from God and becomes the **body of Christ**. The evocation of daily bread in the **Lord's Prayer** refers both to the needs of every day and to the tasks we regularly undertake; it's **our usual lot**, which, in our life, is akin to a routine.

If you want to tell someone who has suffered misfortune, "It serves you right," you might exclaim (in French), "It's holy bread." But the virtue doesn't only apply to mishaps. "It's holy bread" also means "that's excellent" or "that works out well!"

To break bread? Depending on if you sit with the Father or the people, you won't break bread in the same way. . . . The French **casse-croûte** (crust cutter) was originally a tool that served to break **dry and hard bread** crust.

But bread is also . . . about value

What one will do for a **bit of bread** will tend to devalue work and bread itself. The pejorative use postulates that bread is easy food to obtain at a modest price. On the other hand, with the French expression **"it doesn't eat bread,"** bread's value is restored. It means **"it doesn't cost a thing."** In other words, if something eats bread, it'll cost a lot! What's more, if **you don't eat that kind of bread** in French, you're refusing to conform to values that aren't your own. "That kind of bread," although disdained, nevertheless belongs to a value system to which one refuses to subscribe.

Skip to: A *Tour de France* of Breads, p. 158

Did you know?

To have a **good friend** really means **sharing bread with him or her**? The French words *copain* (buddy) and *compagnon* (companion) bring **company and bread together**! They stem from the same Latin **cum** ("with") and **panis** ("pain," French for bread). Friendship is especially a matter of good taste.

You'd like some more bread?

The similarity between the French word **pain** and **poing** ("fist") may have helped form the French slang expression **se prendre un pain** (1864), literally to take a loaf, meaning to get punched. One will note, however, that bread can easily be replaced by **beignet** if instead *on se prend* **une beigne** (you get walloped)!

★

A FEW FRENCH BREAD TERMS FOR BREAD LOVERS

- **Bricheton**
- **Briffe**
- **Briffeton**
- **Brignolet**
- **Tourteau**
- **Boule**
- **Baguette**
- **Flûte**

★

Victor Hugo

His appetite matched his work: monumental! At lunchtime, he would take a seat at restaurants along the Grands Boulevards. In the evening, he would host copious dinners. And at his desk, he liked to feast on "large terrines of cold consommé every two hours."
Estelle Lenartowicz

SHARING

Children: concerned about the plight of little people, starting in March 1862, Hugo opened his home on a regular basis to some forty poor children and served them meat and wine. "The meal will be the same as ours, we shall serve them, they will say as they sit down *Dieu soyez béni* and on rising *Dieu soyez remercié . . .*"
Animals: his unconditional kindness extended even to what was on his plate. He felt compassion for lobsters "ever since he heard them crying in boiling water." One day when he was served mutton, he asked his guests: "What would we do with the poor animals if we did not eat them?"
Jean Valjean's supper: "Meantime Madame Magloire had served up supper; it consisted of soup made of water, oil, bread, and salt, a little pork, a scrap of mutton, a few figs, a green cheese, and a large loaf of rye bread." *Les Misérables* (1862).

A great writer with a great appetite
1802–1885

MORE A GOURMAND THAN A GOURMET

Eating like a horse
According to the literary critic Charles Augustin Sainte-Beuve, "natural history proposes three kinds of big appetites: duck, shark, and Victor Hugo."

Odd culinary habits
Devouring a lobster with its shell or oranges with its peel? No problem for Monsieur Hugo. The writer was also crazy about unlikely combinations: café au lait with a bit of vinegar; a drop of mustard on his Brie . . .

Sweet tooth
His love of sweet food—and wine—was well known.
"When we serve ice cream . . . he has heaps," Richard Lesclide recounts in his *Propos de Table de Victor Hugo* (1885). "He abuses his teeth, which are admirably white. They help him crack walnuts and almonds, despite his childrens' protests. He bites into apples . . . and watching him gnaw sends chills up your spine . . ."

SPATCHCOCKED CHICKEN

This was the favorite dish of the poet. Served in *Les Misérables*, this chicken has the distinction of being presented split open and pressed flat!

PREPARATION & COOKING TIME:
I HOUR
SERVES 4

2 small farm-raised chickens or spring chickens
Cayenne pepper or Espelette pepper
3 tablespoons (50 mL) olive oil infused with:
I clove garlic, minced; 2 chopped rosemary sprigs; and 2 mild chile peppers
For the diable sauce
4 shallots, peeled and minced
4 cloves garlic, crushed, germs removed
2 red chile peppers, seeded and chopped
I tablespoon (20 g) unsalted butter
I tablespoon (20 mL) white wine
⅓ cup plus I tablespoon (100 mL) glace de volaille (chicken glace)
Juice of I lemon
I tablespoon (15 mL) Worcestershire sauce
Salt and freshly ground black pepper
For the red onions
6 red onions, peeled and finely chopped
6 cloves garlic, peeled, germs removed
3 tablespoons (50 mL) grapeseed oil
⅓ ounce (10 g) Szechuan pepper

THE DIABLE SAUCE
In a casserole dish, cook the shallots, garlic, and chiles in the butter. Deglaze the dish with the wine, add the glace de volaille, and let simmer for 15 minutes. Blend using a blender to obtain a smooth and creamy sauce. Add the lemon juice and Worcestershire sauce. Season with salt and pepper.

THE RED ONIONS
Gently cook the onions and garlic in the hot oil until fragrant, but without letting them brown. Add the Szechuan pepper, and cover. Cook until the onions are translucent.

THE CHICKENS
Using scissors, remove the backbone of the chickens and pry the chickens open. Press down to flatten them out, but without pressing too hard to avoid damaging the flesh. Brush the chickens on all sides with the infused oil, and let marinate for 15 minutes.

Insert two long wooden or metal skewers across each wing (through the neck or breastbone) to keep them flat while they cook. Heat the grill and brush it with oil using a cloth. Sear the chickens skin side down for 6 to 8 minutes, then rotate them 90 degrees and sear them for another 7 to 8 minutes. Preheat the oven to 350°F (180°C), turn the chickens over (skin side up), and roast them for 8 minutes, or until cooked through. Brush the chicken after each step

with the infused oil. Let stand for 5 minutes.

SERVING
Quarter the chickens and arrange 2 pieces on each plate with the cooked red onion on the side, or arrange all the pieces in a large serving dish, surrounded by the onions. Warm the sauce and serve it in a gravy boat.

Contemplations gourmandes, by Florian V. Hugo, preface by Alain Ducasse, Éditions Michel Lafon.

The Côte de Boeuf

Carnivores are ravenous for this cut of beef. The *côte de boeuf* (bone-in rib eye) is the upper portion of the animal's rib, covered with meat. Whether cooked in the oven, in a pan, or on the grill, cooking the côte de boeuf requires the cook to follow some very specific principles.

Charles Patin O'Coohoon

COOKING THE CÔTE DE BOEUF

Everything you've always wanted to know about cooking rib steak but were afraid to ask . . .

At what temperature should the steak be before cooking it?
Take it out of the refrigerator right away. It should be allowed to sit at room temperature for at least 3 hours to ensure the center is room temperature before it's cooked.

Should you salt the steak before cooking it?
No. The salt may dry the meat somewhat, causing it to lose some of its juiciness. Salt it only after it's cooked.

Should you pepper the steak before cooking it?
No. When cooked, pepper loses its aromas and becomes bitter. Pepper it only after it's cooked.

Should you coat the steak with fat before cooking it?
Yes. Massage the steak with olive oil for a better crust.

How long should you cook it?
Only a few minutes. For a medium-size steak between 1½ to 2¼ inches (4 to 6 cm) thick, sear it on each side for 7 minutes, then sear the sides for about 30 seconds.

Should you let the steak rest after cooking it?
The resting time is as important as the cooking time, as it allows the meat to relax. Leave the steak to rest under foil for the same amount of time as the cooking time.

How do you test its doneness?
With the touch of a finger. The firmness of the steak depends on the coagulation of its proteins. The firmer the flesh, the more well done it is cooked. When the pressure is soft under your finger, that means the temperature is still rare.

The roasted côte de boeuf
This is not to be confused with Côte-Rôtie, a wine appellation of the Rhône Valley, whose slopes turn brown in the sun. When roasted in the oven, the rib steak is called a *côte rôtie* (roasted rib eye). Before placing it in the oven, the oiled steak is seared over high heat to brown it well on both sides. When cooked on the bone, the dripping fat moistens the meat. The technique appeared in the nineteenth century in the district of La Villette, the location of the slaughterhouses of Paris.

Carving
Because of its size, it is necessary to cut the flesh from the bone, and then cut the meat slightly at an angle in slices approximately ⅓ inch (1 cm) thick.

PAIRINGS WITH CÔTE DE BOEUF THAT WON'T STEER YOU WRONG

WINES
Saint-Émilion
To go with this meaty selection, you need wines with bold tannins and a little age. Tannins tend to dry the palate, and bold dishes call for wines that hold up to their flavors, such as a powerful Bordeaux from the right bank, which is an excellent partner.

A Rhône Syrah
The juiciness of the meat calls for a wine with chewiness and minerality. A Cornas, a Saint-Joseph, or a Côte-Rôti with notes of red fruits and spices will do the job.

THE SAUCES
Troisgros brother's côte de boeuf au fleurie
Cook the steak. Pour the cooking fat into a pan, and cook some chopped shallot in the fat until softened. Deglaze the pan with one-fourth bottle of Fleurie (the red wine of Beaujolais) and whisk a little butter into the sauce. Poach a beef marrow bone, lay it on top of the steak, and spoon the sauce over the top. Cut the meat into 8 slices, parallel to the bone.

Côte de boeuf deglazed with Yves-Marie Le Bourdonnec whiskey
Cook the côte de boeuf in a casserole dish, basting it with about 4½ ounces (125 g) of melted butter. Remove the steak from the casserole dish, and let it rest. Deglaze the casserole with the whiskey and a spoonful of sesame paste, to create a slightly tart jus.

★ ★ ★

THE IMPORTANCE OF AGING
Aging is the process that **improves the quality of the meat** by aging the carcass. Once the cow has been slaughtered, its muscles weaken. The carcass is placed in **a cold room for several days**. The muscle fibers firm up and the muscle becomes rigid (rigor mortis). Under the action of proteolytic enzymes, the collagen disappears, the **meat becomes soft, and the fat seeps into the muscle fibers**. This aging process, whether short or long, releases the flavors and aromas of the meat, and makes it more tender. During this process, the meat can lose up to 60 percent of its weight.

skip to
Bring on the Sauce!, p. 186

Caramel: The Alchemy of Sugar

Heat a bit of sugar and a diverse palette of textures and tastes come into being.
Whether it is used as an ingredient, for decoration, or as candy, everyone melts for caramel.

Marie-Laure Fréchet

HISTORY

Caramel is the origin of candy. At first basic (cook the sugar, spread it over a sheet, and then break it into pieces), it became an art managed by specialists in the seventeenth century. Myriad recipes followed, as did regional specialties, especially in Brittany, Normandy, and northern France. Today, in confectionery, the word *caramel* is exclusively reserved for products made from sugar or honey, milk or milk protein (minimum 1.5 percent), and possibly a fat.

TECHNIQUE

Caramel is the process of heating sugar to its maximum point before burning, until the syrup no longer contains water. It then loses its capacity to sweeten and develops roasted notes that can even be bitter.

Caramel desserts

Crème caramel: a cream made from egg, milk, and sugar and cooked in a mold coated with caramel. It's also known in French as "crème renversée" and "crème aux oeufs."

Milk jam/dulce de leche: a mixture of milk and sugar (10½ ounces to 1⅛ pounds/300 to 500 g per 4 cups/1 L of milk) cooked until thick. It can also be made from sweetened condensed milk.

Crème brûlée: crème made from egg, cream, and sugar. Its top is caramelized. While the recipe resembles Crema Catalana, as early as 1691 it was included in *Le Nouveau Cuisinier royal et bourgeois* by the chef François Massialot. A dessert classic in 1990s restaurants.

Croquembouche: pâte à choux (cream puff dough) balls piled into a cone and bound with spun sugar or caramel. Its glory days were in the nineteenth century, but it's still a dessert staple at French weddings and baptisms.

Tarte Tatin: upside-down apple tart. The apples are caramelized with butter and sugar before being placed in a mold.

Kouign-amann: puff pastry covered with a mixture of butter and sugar. While cooking, the butter and sugar mixture caramelizes and rises to the surface, which gives it a creamy texture on the inside, crusty on the outside.

And also caramels, candies, and chocolates . . .

Praline, Caramel d'Isigny, Carambar, Lutti, Magnificat, Babelutte de Lille, and more

Salted Butter Caramel

The recipe is old and comes from Brittany. It was popularized by the Breton pastry chef, Henri Le Roux, who, in 1977, turned it into a hazelnut candy that was widely successful. Since then, salted butter caramel has become the basis of many desserts. It's often served with rice pudding.

CARAMEL RECIPES

Tips for Success

When it comes to caramel, the less you make, the better the outcome!
→ Use a pan with a thick bottom and high sides.
→ Start dry: just sugar and no water. You could add a bit of glucose.
→ Put away your spatula and whisk: caramel is not stirred. Simply shake the pan if needed.
→ Stay focused: 1 minute away and it can burn.
→ To stop the caramelizing, dip the pan in a bowl of cold water. You could also add a dab of butter or a few drops of lemon.

skip to
La Tarte des Demoiselles Tatin (Tart Tatin), p. 67

Dry

Place ¾ cup (150 g) of granulated sugar into a heavy-bottom saucepan, and place the pan over medium heat. Cook the sugar, without stirring, until it turns light amber in color. Gently swirl the pan so that the sugar browns evenly, tilting the pan by the handle. Immediately remove the pan from the heat when the desired color is achieved.

— ••• —

Liquid

Place 1¼ cups (250 g) of granulated sugar into a very clean heavy-bottom saucepan with 3 tablespoons plus 1 teaspoon (50 mL) of water (and, optionally, 1 teaspoon/5 mL of white vinegar or lemon juice*). Cook without stirring. When the caramel turns an amber color, stop the cooking by dipping the bottom of the pan into cold water. Stir in ⅓ cup plus 1 tablespoon/100 mL of water. Place the pan back over the heat, and cook while slowly stirring to melt any crystalized pieces of caramel and to achieve the desired consistency.

— ••• —

Dairy

Place 1¼ cups (250 g) of granulated sugar in a heavy-bottom saucepan, and cook it until it turns a light amber color. Add 1 cup (250 mL) of milk off the heat, and stir to combine. Place the pan back over low heat. Add 1 cup (250 mL) of crème fraiche, and cook for an additional 1 to 2 minutes, or until thickened.

— ••• —

prevents crystallization of the sugar

Salted butter

Place ½ cup (100 g) of granulated sugar in a heavy-bottom saucepan and moisten it with a few tablespoons of water. Heat, without stirring, over low heat until the sugar turns an amber color. Dip the bottom of the pan in cold water to stop the cooking, then add ⅔ cup (150 mL) of cream to the pan, stirring well. Place the pan over low heat, and add 3 tablespoons (50 g) of salted butter, a little at a time, while stirring.

— ••• —

Nougatine

Lightly grease two sheets of parchment paper with oil. Lightly toast ¾ cup (70 g) of sliced almonds in a dry skillet. Make a dry caramel with 1¼ cups (250 g) of granulated sugar. When the sugar turns amber in color, add the almonds, stir to combine, and pour the caramel onto a sheet of parchment paper. Cover the caramel with the second piece of parchment paper, and roll it out evenly with a rolling pin. Let harden at room temperature.

— ••• —

Milk jam
2 methods

1. Cook a can of sweetened condensed milk for 2 hours and 30 minutes in a bain-marie, or for 1 hour in a pressure cooker. Let cool completely before opening the can.
2. Pour 4 cups (1 L) of whole milk into a heavy-bottom saucepan. Add 2 cups (400 g) of granulated sugar, and 1 split and scraped vanilla bean and its seeds. Bring to a boil, and cook over low heat for 2 hours, stirring regularly until thickened and browned.

— ••• —

CRÈME RENVERSÉE
by Denise Solier-Gaudry

PREPARATION TIME: 25 MINUTES
COOKING TIME: 30 MINUTES
SERVES 4

¾ cup (150 g) superfine sugar
2 cups (250 mL) whole milk
1 vanilla bean
3 large (150 g) eggs
3 large (56 g) egg yolks

Preheat the oven to 350°F (180°C). Prepare the caramel. Place ¼ cup (50 g) of the sugar into a heavy-bottom saucepan, and heat it over high heat without stirring until the sugar turns an amber color. Pour the hot caramel into a cake pan measuring 14 inches (36 cm) in diameter and 4 inches (10 cm) high, or into four ramekins, and swirl the pan to coat the bottom and sides. Heat the milk with the split and scraped vanilla bean and its seeds, then let cool. Whisk together the eggs and egg yolks with the remaining sugar, then slowly pour the hot milk into this mixture, whisking continuously. Strain the custard through a fine-mesh sieve into the pan. Place the pan in a bain-marie and bake for 30 minutes. Let cool to room temperature, cover with plastic wrap, and place the pan in the refrigerator. Invert the pan to unmold the custard just before serving.

CRÈME BRÛLÉE

PREPARATION TIME: 15 MINUTES
RESTING TIME: 1 HOUR
COOKING TIME: 30 MINUTES
SERVES 6

1½ cups (350 mL) milk
1½ cups (350 mL) cream
1 vanilla bean
½ cup (100 g) superfine sugar
8 large (148 g) egg yolks
6 tablespoons (82 g) turbinado sugar

Pour the milk and cream into a saucepan, add the split and scraped vanilla bean and its seeds, and bring to a boil; remove from the heat. Whisk the sugar and egg yolks together in a bowl, and slowly pour in the hot milk, whisking continuously. Strain, and refrigerate for 1 hour. Preheat the oven to 250°F (120°C). Divide the custard into six crème brulée dishes. Place the dishes in a bain-marie, and bake for 25 to 35 minutes, or until the custard is just set. Let cool, then refrigerate. When serving, sprinkle each crème brulée with a spoonful of the turbinado sugar, and caramelize the sugar using a torch.

Stages of Sugar Syrup

	TEMPERATURE	COOKING STAGE	USES
SIMPLE SYRUP	From 212°F to 221°F (100°C to 105°C)	Coats a spoon	Cake glaze, fruit syrups, jams and gelées (jellies), sorbets
SMALL THREAD	From 221°F to 225°F (105°C to 107°C)	A thin thread between two fingers	Candied fruits, gelées (jellies) and fruit mousses
LARGE THREAD	From 225°F to 239°F (107°C to 115°C)	A large stretching thread between two fingers	Candied fruits, glacée chestnuts, buttercream
SOFTBALL	From 239°F to 243°F (115°C to 117°C)	Forms a soft ball in cold water	Parfaits, cold soufflés, Italian meringue
FIRMBALL	From 244°F to 248°F (118°C to 120°C)	Forms a firmer ball in cold water	Soft fondants, soft caramels
HARDBALL	From 257°F to 266°F (125°C to 130°C)	Forms a hard ball in cold water	Firm fondants, soft almond paste, soft caramels
SOFT CRACK	From 275°F to 284°F (135°C to 140°C)	Cracks in cold water	Almond paste, nougat, candies, caramels
HARD CRACK	From 293°F to 302°F (145°C to 150°C)	Breaks into large pieces in cold water	Dry nougats, pulled and blown sugar decoration, spun sugar
LIGHT AMBER	From 311°F to 329°F (155°C to 165°C)	Straw color	Croquembouches, Saint-Honoré, nougatine
AMBER	From 338°F to 356°F (170°C to 180°C)	Dark blond	Crème caramel, coating pans, salted butter caramel
DARK AMBER	From 365°F to 374°F (185°C to 190°C)	Dark and emits a pungent smoke	For color

My Belle Quenelle

To be able to pronounce *quenelle* ("k'nelle") is a good thing. But knowing how to make a quenelle at home is even better!
François-Régis Gaudry

PIKE QUENELLES, SAUCE NANTUA
by Joseph Viola*

SERVES 8

For the panade
1 cup (250 mL) milk
Freshly grated nutmeg
5 tablespoons (70 g) butter
1½ cups plus 1 tablespoon (160 g) all-purpose flour

For the quenelles
1⅛ pounds (500 g) skinless pike fillets, cut into ¾-inch/2 cm cubes and frozen
3 large (90 g) egg whites
5 large (250 g) eggs
1⅔ teaspoons (10 g) salt
1 teaspoon (2 g) ground white pepper
Freshly grated nutmeg
10 tablespoons (125 g) butter, softened

For the sauce Nantua
⅓ cup (100 mL) olive oil
40 live crayfish
3½ ounces (100 g) carrots, small dice
2⅛ ounces (60 g) onions, peeled and chopped
2⅛ ounces (60 g) shallots, peeled and chopped
2 tablespoons (30 mL) tomato paste
3 tablespoons (50 mL) cognac
⅔ cup (150 mL) dry white wine
4 cups (1 L) heavy cream
1 sprig thyme
1 bay leaf
1⅔ teaspoons (10 g) salt
1 teaspoon (2 g) ground white pepper

MAKE THE PANADE (THE DAY BEFORE)
In a saucepan, bring the milk, nutmeg, and butter to a boil; add the flour all at once, stirring vigorously with a spatula, and cook over low heat for 6 to 7 minutes. Scrape the mixture into a bowl and place it in the refrigerator, covered with plastic wrap, overnight.

MAKE THE QUENELLES
In a blender or food processor, blend the frozen pike pieces. Add the panade, stir to combine, then incorporate the egg whites and the eggs, one at a time. Add the salt and white pepper. Add some freshly grated nutmeg, then whisk in the butter until smooth. Pour the mixture into a bowl, cover with plastic wrap, and refrigerate for 6 hours.

POACH THE QUENELLES
Heat a saucepan of salted water to 158°F (70°C). Shape the quenelles using two spoons, and immerse the quenelles in the hot water for 20 minutes. Turn them over and cook them for another 20 minutes. Dunk them in ice water, and refrigerate them overnight.

MAKE THE SAUCE NANTUA
In a cast-iron casserole dish, heat the oil, then cook the crayfish over high heat just until pink. Add the carrots, onions, and shallots, and cook gently, just until softened. Stir in the tomato paste, then add the cognac and ignite it with a long match. Deglaze the pan with the wine, then let cook until somewhat reduced. Add the cream, thyme, and bay leaf. Boil for 2 minutes. Remove the crayfish, pull them apart, and add the heads back to the sauce. Cook for 20 minutes. Strain through a fine-mesh sieve while pressing down on the crayfish heads with the back of a spoon to extract all the juices (the sauce should be thick enough to coat a spoon).

COOK THE QUENELLES
Steam the quenelles for 20 minutes; they should double in size.

SERVING
Place 1 quenelle at the bottom of a soup plate, add the crayfish tails, and coat with the sauce Nantua.

Best Craftsman of France (MOF), at the head of the famous gastronomic bistro Daniel et Denise, with three addresses in Lyon.

Did You Know?
- This is a dish made from pâte à choux (cream puff dough), also called a *panade*.
- This dish from Lyon is probably the ancestor of the Austrian *knödel* (boiled dumplings).

skip to Land and Sea Agreements, p. 117

COOKING WITH BUTTER

If you shake cream long and hard, you'll be rewarded with pure gold.
Here are a few churn-busting butter recipes.

Charles Patin O'Coohoon

The Temperature Is Going Up!

104°F (40°C): temperature for making clarified butter and certain sauces, such as béarnaise.
133°F (56°C): point where milk proteins coagulate. The flavor of butter develops. Beyond this temperature, you can make warm emulsified sauces, as well as beurre blanc.
212°F (100°C): beyond this temperature, food browns too quickly.
329°F (165°C): temperature for beurre noisette.
392°F (200°C): at this point, it's called black butter, and is not used due to health concerns.

Warmed butters

❶ CLARIFIED BUTTER
Butter that is melted with its milk solids removed. It keeps better and can sustain higher cooking temperatures than fresh butter.
How to: cut the butter into small pieces and heat in a pot. Skim off the white impurities that rise to the surface (casein proteins).

❷ BEURRE NOISETTE
Warm foaming butter served on vegetables cooked in water or organ meats such as brains.
How to: heat the butter gently in a pan just until it takes on a golden color and a fragrance of hazelnuts. Watch carefully to prevent it from burning.

Seasoned butters

❸ SALTED BUTTER
A fixture of Breton cuisine. Butter with salt crystals, incomparable in sweet crêpe recipes.
How to: salt was originally added to butter as a preservative. Now 3 percent salt is added at the conclusion of the churning process.

❹ SORREL BUTTER
Butter blended with sorrel purée. It's the ideal accompaniment for omelets and salmon steaks.
How to: purée 1¾ ounces (50 g) of sorrel leaves. Combine the resulting paste with 7 tablespoons (100 g) of butter.

❺ ANCHOVY BUTTER
It became very fashionable in the 1950s, when grilled beef became a popular menu item. Anchovies provide saltiness and enhance flavor.
How to: combine 10½ tablespoons (125 g) of softened butter, 10 anchovy fillets in olive oil, drained, and 1 clove of garlic, peeled, and the germ removed. Serve with rib eye steaks and grilled fillets, letting it melt into the meat.

❻ SNAIL BUTTER
Butter seasoned with garlic and parsley that is pressed into the shell to melt over the snails when they are placed in the oven.
How to: combine 10½ tablespoons (125 g) of softened butter with 4 garlic cloves, half a shallot, finely chopped, and 5 tablespoons (20 g) of minced parsley. Season with salt and pepper.

❼ MAITRE D'HÔTEL BUTTER
A standard in brasseries. Traditionally, the maître d'hôtel would stop by the table to brush grilled meat, fish, or crustaceans with this custom-prepared butter.
How to: combine 10½ tablespoons (125 g) of softened butter and 5 tablespoons (20 g) of chopped parsley. Add the juice of half a lemon, ⅔ teaspoon (4 g) of fine salt, and a pinch of freshly ground pepper.

Cooked butters

❽ BEURRE BLANC
Also known as *beurre nantais*. An emulsion of butter and a reduction based on vinegar and shallots, ideal with fish dishes.
How to: bring 5 chopped shallots in 1 cup (250 mL) of wine vinegar to a simmer, and let it reduce by one-third. Remove from the heat, add 18 tablepoons (250 g) of butter cut into pieces, and whisk vigorously. Season with salt and pepper.

❾ MARCHAND DE VIN BUTTER
A red wine sauce that's a wonderful addition to red meats. Another old-time brasserie classic.
How to: chop up a shallot, add 1¼ cups (300 mL) of red wine, and allow it to reduce by half. Add 1¼ cups (300 mL) of beef bouillon, and reduce again. Blend in 9 tablespoons (150 g) of butter, 4 tablespoons (15 g) of minced parsley, and a dash of lemon juice.

❿ SAGE BUTTER
Marvelous on gnocchi, ravioli, and pasta.
How to: melt 10½ tablespoons (125 g) of butter with a tablespoon (15 mL) of olive oil in a pot. Add a few sage leaves, let them sizzle for a few seconds, and add the zest of a quarter lemon.

LA CRÈME DE LA CRÈME OF BUTTERS

The three French AOP designations.

Beurre de Bresse
This butter is made in the departments of Ain and Saône-et-Loire, on the border of the Jura region. The butter made in Bresse is delicate, with herbal and floral notes and hints of dried fruit, walnuts, and hazelnuts.

Charentes-Poitou
This butter comes from the dairy production of Charente, Charente-Maritime, Deux-Sèvres, Vendée, and Vienne. It's a firm-textured butter with overtones of hazelnuts, ideal for pastry making.

Isigny
This butter is produced in the area around the Baie des Veys, between Bessin and the Cotentin peninsula. This smooth-textured delicacy is the color of a buttercup.

Under the Table at the Élysée Palace

Bernard Vaussion worked for almost forty years for French presidents. Now retired, this cook of great discretion has revealed very rare documents he has kept. Personal and public histories collide.

Hadrien Gonzales

With Valéry Giscard d'Estaing, wishing his staff a happy New Year in January 1980.

With François Mitterand, wishing his staff a happy New Year in January 1982

In March 1985, Mikhail Gorbachev was elected General Secretary of the Communist Party of the Soviet Union, and his wife were welcomed by François Mitterand. It is uncertain if the menu, which consisted of slices of foie gras and Volnay "Clos de Chênes" 1976 complied with the Moscow doctrine. But, after all, perestroika had already begun and the wall would soon fall.

With Nicolas Sarkozy in 2007.

Since the presidency of Nicolas Sarkozy, menu covers are no longer decorated with the French coat of arms—printing costs too much. François Hollande would prohibit truffles and caviar for the same reasons.

Angela Merkel loves to eat at the Élysée Palace. Even though Nicolas Sarkozy eliminated cheese from meals, she would always have a plate brought just for her. Her own chef Ulrich Kerz (in back, here with François Hollande) even came to train with Bernard Vaussion. What exactly sustains the harmony between France and Germany?

For many years, menu covers displayed works of French art. Here Matisse's "Intérieur Jaune et Bleu" ("Interior in Yellow and Blue"), used to decorate the dinner menu served to Queen Elizabeth II on June 9, 1992.

The gâteau de pomme de terre (potato cake) was invented by Marcel Le Servot, chef from 1969 to 1984. Ever since, the recipe has become an Élysée "signature." It is served with meat or fish and can be made with truffles or carrots. Photograph from 2012.

QUICK BIO

1953
Bernard Vaussion is born in Orléans.

1974
Joins the Élysée as a commis chef. Georges Pompidou is still president for a few months. Valéry Giscard d'Estaing follows.

1981
Election of François Mitterand.

1995
Election of Jacques Chirac.

2005
Bernard Vaussion is named executive chef by Jacques Chirac.

2007
Election of Nicolas Sarkozy.

2012
Election of François Hollande.

2013
Bernard Vaussion retires.

THE GÂTEAU DE POMME DE TERRE (POTATO CAKE)

PREPARATION TIME: 45 MINUTES
COOKING TIME: 60 MINUTES
SERVES 6 TO 8

5½ pounds (2.5 kg) medium Charlotte potatoes
Salt and freshly ground black pepper
1 charlotte mold
Butter, for greasing
Gruyère cheese
Parmesan cheese
1 cup (200 g) melted clarified butter

Cut the potatoes into ⅛-inch- (3 mm) thick rounds, and blanch them for 5 minutes in boiling water. Transfer them to a cloth to drain, and season them with salt and pepper. Grease the mold with butter, and arrange a layer of the potato rounds into a crown in the mold by stacking them and slightly overlapping each one. Fill the center hole with potato rounds arranged in the same direction, then sprinkle the layer with some of the Gruyère and Parmesan. Create a second layer of potatoes, stacked in the same way, but overlapping in the opposite direction. Repeat with the center, and a sprinkling of the cheeses. Repeat these steps, creating a total of six or seven layers. Pour the melted clarified butter into the mold over the potato layers, and bake at 350°F (180°C) for 1 hour. Tilt the pan to drain it of excess butter, then unmold the cake onto a serving dish.

Bourgeons de Sapin des Vosges

Nonnette de Remiremont

Bargkass

Soupe à la farine de Gérardmer

Truite des Vosges

Miel de Sapin des Vosges

PETITS CRUS DE FRUITS ROUGES

Memories of the Vosges

The heritage of the Pays de Loire

Brioche VENDÉENNE

Gâteau NANTAIS

Fleur de Sel de Guérande

PORT SALUT (Maine)

Boeuf Fée de Vendée

moule de Bouchot (prince des gastronomes)

CURNONSKY

Soupe de Poisson de l'Île d'Yeu

POMME BÉNÉDICTIN

la Tante Normande (aux pommes)

Les Huîtres

agneau de Pré Salé

caramels d'Isigny

Marie Harel

carotte de CRÉANCES

Specialties of Normandy

Treasures from the Provinces

An (almost exhaustive) inventory of the dishes and foods of France's regions and lands.

Loïc Bienassis

➡ Protected Geographical Indications (PGIs), such as AOPs (*appellations d'origine protégée*), are noted, but they are intentionally not associated to only one region, but instead take into account the entire area of the appellation.

➡ Some products, whose origins are not necessarily associated with a specific region, are included if they have a strong tradition in that region.

➡ Even if a product is known by several names, in general only one name has been listed.

➡ Liberties have been taken to loosely categorize catering trades, such as placing Camargue rice at the farmers' market.

➡ Although many products have gone well beyond the borders of their country of origin, they are listed under the area where they originated, such as the baguette, which is originally Parisian!

➡ Regarding the men and women listed here, they are associated with the places where they express their talents and not to their homeland, so Prosper Montagné, for example, is listed in Carcassonne.

AOP *appellation d'origine protégée*
PGI Protected Geographical Indication
GI Geographical Indication

THE BEST OF THE REGION

AUVERGNE-RHÔNE-ALPES

AB: AUBRAC; AN: ANNECY; AR: ARDÈCHE; AU: AUVERGNE; BE: BEAUJOLAIS; BO: BOURBONNAIS; BR: BRESSE; CA: CANTAL; DA: DAUPHINÉ; DO: DOMBES; DR: DRÔME; FO: FOREZ; GE: PAYS DE GEX; LB: LA DU BOURGET; LN: LYONNAIS; LO: LOIRE; LY: LYON; ML: MONTS DU LYONNAIS; SA: SAVOIE; VE: VELAY; VI: VIVARAIS

AT THE BUTCHER'S

Aubrac
Auvergne pork .... PGI
Black lamb of the Velay
Charolaise of Bourbonnais .... PGI
Chicken of Bourbonnais
Chicken or capon of Cévennes .... PGI
Chicken or capon of the Ardèche .... PGI
Fin Gras de Mézenc: a marbled beef .... AOP
Fleur d'Aubrac (beef of heifer) .... PGI
Guinea fowl of the Ardèche .... PGI
Guinea fowl of the Drôme .... PGI
Kid (young goat) .... DA
Lamb of Bourbonnais .... PGI
Poultry of Auvergne .... PGI
Poultry of Bresse .... AOP
Poultry of the Ain .... PGI
Poultry of the Drôme .... PGI
Poultry of the Forez .... PGI
Poultry of the Velay .... PGI
Salers, a cattle breed
Turkey of Jaligny .... BO
Vedelou, suckling calf .... VE

AT THE FARMER'S

Apples and pears of the Savoie .... PGI
Apples of Auvergne: Canada White Pippin, Canada Gray
Ardèche Chestnut .... AOP
Bell pepper of Ampuis .... LN
Bigarreau cherry of Bessenay .... LN
Bilberry of Ardèche
Black olive of Nyons .... AOP
Blond lentil of Saint-Flour
Blue leek from Solaize .... LY
Cardon of Vaulx-en-Velin .... LY
Chestnut .... CA
Chestnut (dried chestnut) .... AR
Eyrieux Valley peaches .... AR
Garlic from Auvergne
Garlic from the Drôme .... PGI
Grenoble rouge: Batavia lettuce
Le Puy green lentil .... AOP
Pêche de vigne peach of the Lyonnais coast
Ratafia Cherry .... DA
Ratte d'Ardèche: potato
Sweet peas of the Planèze of Saint-Flour
Tournon onion .... AR
Tricastin black truffle
Walnuts .... AOP
Watercress of Saint-Symphorien-d'Ozon .... LN
White Swiss chard of Ampuis .... LN

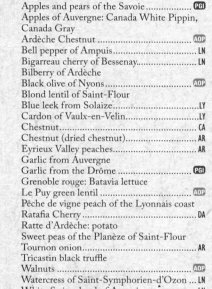

AT THE FISHMONGER'S

Arctic char .... SA, AU
Broad whitefish, Lavaret white fish .... SA
Crayfish
Fried fish of Saône: bleak fish
Fried perch .... LB
Frogs' legs .... DO
Monkfish .... SA
Perch .... SA
Pike and carp .... DO, FO
Trout .... SA

AT THE BAKER'S

Auvergnat bread, round, leavened, topped with a disk, contains rye .... AU
Bescoin: elongated brioche with saffron and anise .... SA
Bourgoin brioche, decorated with bands of sugar, pralines, and candied almonds
Bread of Mondane: brioche with candied fruit, covered with an almond-flour mixture .... SA
Brioche of Gannat, with cheese .... BO
Brioche of Saint-Genix, with pralines .... SA
Brioche with tome: cheesecake made with fresh tome .... AU
Fouace: brioche made from fermented bread dough .... CA
Fougasse with cracklins .... AR
Main ("hand") of Sainte-Agathe: sourdough brioche, flavored with anise or saffron .... SA
Pain tabatière: similar to bread of Mondane, with a kind of flap topping the lower part of the bread .... AU
Pompe aux grattons: in a crown, filled with small pieces of fried pork meat .... BO
Tourte de seigle (a pie with rye flour): yeast-leavened bread .... AU

AT THE CHARCUTIER

Andouille of Charlieu, with chaudin or pork stomach, cut into strips .... BE
Andouillette lyonnaise, with veal caulfat cut in strips
Attriau: a small sausage of caulfat surrounding a mixture of pork and offal .... SA
Boudin: onion, throat, or head meat, milk .... CA
Bressan Boudin: rice and cream
Cabbage sausage, made from pork and cabbage .... FO
Caillette: a ball made from pork and vegetables, in caulfat
Cervelas sausage with truffle and in pistachio/brioche: *sauciesse à cuire* (Lyon), with pork .... LY
Civier de Bressan: head cheese
Diot: fresh minced sausage with pork .... SA
Dry-cured hams: salted, can be smoked .... FO, SA
Farcement: a "cake" made from potatoes, pork belly, prunes, and raisins .... SA
Friton: a kind of pâté made of pork confit .... AU
Goat cheese sausage: dry-cured sausage .... SA
Gratton: grilled trimings of fat and pork .... LN
Grattons/griottons: a kind of rillettes, pieces of pork cooked in the fat of the animal .... AR, DR, LO
Herb boudin: cabbage, leek green, spinach, parsley, chervil, enriched with blood .... FO
Herb sausage: a large sausage for cooking, pork and herbs (cabbage, spinach, Swiss chard) .... AR, DR
Jâmbon d'Auvergne (dry-cured ham) .... PGI
Jambon de l'Ardèche (ham) .... PGI
Jambonnette: pork meat in a cylindrical pocket of sewn rind .... AU
Jésus and Rosette de Lyon, dry pork sausage: the rosette is long; the Jésus is wide and short, oval, with large chopped pieces
Leg of whole goat, salted then dried .... SA
Liogue: cooking sausage; with pork steak, sausage meat, and red wine .... CA
Longeole: raw sausage, made from pork rind and meat .... SA
Lung sausage, made from pigs' lungs, heart, sausage meat. Dried or à cuire .... AU
Murson de la Mure: raw pork sausage .... DA
Pansette de Gerzat: lamb belly stuffed with chopped belly .... AU
Petit pâté chaud de Belley: flaky pastry stuffed with a mixture of veal cushion, and ham and pork throat
Pormonaise: sausage made with smoked cabbage .... SA
Pormonier: sausage made from pork offal and greens (spinach, leeks, Swiss chard) .... SA
Pounti: a pâté made from a mixture of pork and Swiss chard, mixed with a crêpe batter, with whole prunes added .... AU
Roulette du Bugey: pork belly, rolled up, salted, and cooked
Sabardin: sausage made from beef intestines, pork offal, and sausage meat .... FO
Sabodet: sausage or sausage made from pork head and rind, for cooking .... DA
Sac d'os: pork casing filled with bone pieces—ribs, tail, ears—preserved with salt or salted and dried. Should be cooked before eating .... AU
Salted goat: goat meat in brine .... GE
Sauciss de Magland (sausage), smoked and dried pork .... SA
Saucisson and saucisse d'Auvergne (dried, cooked, or raw sausages), made with lean pork .... PGI
Saucisson de l'Ardèche .... PGI
Saucisson de Lyon, very thin dry-cured sausage with bacon
Tourte muroise (a savory pie): different types of doughs; filled with pork and/or marinated veal, mushrooms, olives, onions .... DA
Tripoux: small packets of veal or lamb tripe .... AU

AT THE CHEESE MAKER'S

Abondance .... SA AOP
Arôme de Lyon
Beaufort .... SA AOP
Beurre cru de lactosérum .... AU
Beurre de Bresse .... AOP
Bleu d'Auvergne .... AOP
Bleu de Gex haut Jura/ bleu de Septmoncel .... AOP
Bleu de Laqueuille .... AU
Bleu de Lavaldens .... DA
Bleu de Termignon .... SA
Bleu du Vercors-Sassenage .... DA AOP
Brique du Forez .... FO
Cabécou .... AU
Caillé doux de Saint-Félicien .... AR
Cantal .... AOP
Chambarand .... DA
Chambérat .... BO
Chevrotin .... SA AOP
Crème de Bresse .... AOP
Emmental de Savoie .... PGI
Emmental français est-central .... PGI
Fourme d'Ambert .... AU AOP
Fourme de Montbrison .... AOP
Fourme de Rochefort-Montagne .... AU
Fromage aux artisons .... AU

Fromage (strong): foudjou, tome forte . . .
Gaperon.......................................AU
Grand Murols.......................................AU
Grataron du Beaufortain.......................................SA
Gruyère.......................................SA, DA PGI
Laguiole.......................................CA AOP
Morbier.......................................GE AOP
Persillé de Haute Tarentaise.......................................SA
Persillé des Aravis.......................................SA
Picodon.......................................DE, AR AOP
Raclette de Savoie.......................................PGI
Ramequin du Bugey
Reblochon.......................................SA AOP
Rigotte de Condrieu.......................................AOP
Saint-Marcellin.......................................DA PGI
Saint-Nectaire.......................................AU AOP
Salers.......................................AU AOP
Sarasson.......................................VI, FO
Sérac.......................................SA
Tamié.......................................SA
Thollon.......................................SA
Tome des Bauges.......................................SA AOP
Tome fraîche.......................................AU
Tomme d'Auvergne
Tomme de Belley
Tomme de Savoie.......................................PGI
Tomme grise de chèvre.......................................SA
Vacherin d'Abondance.......................................SA
Vacherin des Bauges.......................................SA

SAVORY DISHES

Aligot: a kind of mashed potato purée with fresh cantal cheese and crème fraîche......CA, AB
Auvergnate cabbage soup: with lamb's quarters (plant *Chenopodium album*), lean and fat bacon, curdled
Auvergnate falette: rolled sheep breast, stuffed with cured ham, salt pork, Swiss chard
Auvergne pouteille: a beef stew with pork feet stewed in red wine
Auvergne rabbit: wild-caught rabbit, with Saint-Pourçain wine
Auvergne soup, made from pork—lean bacon, pork shank, *saucisse à cuire*—cabbage and various vegetables
Baked arctic char, with mushrooms.............SA
Bourbonnaise Gouère: a cheese curd and potato tart
Bourriol: a galette made from buckwheat and wheat flours.......................................AU
Brayaude omelet: potato, Cantal, prosciutto.......................................AU
Bressane eggs: baked, on bread, with cream and Comté
Bugey stuffed veal: veal shoulder stuffed with a preparation of St. George's mushroom sauce, veal, bacon, chicken livers . . .
Caillettes de Chabeuil: preparation in caulfat made from pork, Swiss chard, and spinach.......................................VI, DA
Cantal soup with a Cantal and chicken broth base.......................................AU
Cardoons with marrow: poached marrow; all baked in the oven.......................................LY
Carp stuffed with Dombes stuffing of bread, milk, shallot, garlic, egg, herbs, and carp milt, if available
Cervelle (brain) de canut: fomage frais with salt, pepper, vinegar, oil, shallot, scallions, herbs, garlic, white wine, cream...................LY
Chicken demi-deuil, boiled in chicken broth, with slices of black truffle tucked under the skin.......................................LY
Chicken in cream, in a skillet, topped with a sauce made of cream and eggs...................BR
Chicken in vinegar, in a sauté pan, with vinegar and white wine.......................................LY
Civet de lièvre (rabbit stew): red wine marinade; in a casserole, with the marinade and bacon. Finished with blood, liver, and cream.......................................SA
Co au vin of Chanturgue.......................................AU
Cod auvergne: a sort of mashed potatoes with cod, onions, and potatoes
Cousinat: chestnut soup with bacon...........AU
Crozet: small pasta squares of buckwheat or soft wheat flour.......................................SA
Daube Dauphinoise (beef stew); red wine, bacon, carrots, tomatoes, and onions . . .
Duck à la Duchambais, in a sauce combining vinegar, shallots, crème fraîche, broth, and enriched with duck liver marinated in marc....BO
Farinade: a kind of salty crêpe; grated potatoes are often incorporated.................AU
Fireman's apron: ox tripe dredged in beaten egg, breaded, then panfried or grilled...........LY
Fricassee of caïon: pork marinated in oil, white wine, onions; cooked in a casserole dish with the marinade, red wine, poultry liver, and cream.......................................SA
Frogs' legs à la dauphinoise; prepared with onions, cream, and mushrooms
Frogs' legs Savoyard, cooked in the pan, with onions
Gaudes: cornmeal galettes, mashed............BR
Gratin dauphinois, sliced and baked potatoes in cream; without cheese
Gratin of macaroni lyonnaise: Emmental, Parmesan, crème fraîche
Guinea fowl stuffed with cabbage and Auvergne truffle
Haricots blancs farcis: a stew with sausage meat and chopped veal.......................................AU
Leg of lamb brayaude: combination of garlic cloves, braised in white wine, with carrots and potatoes.......................................AU
Lyonnaise chicken liver cakes: served with a tomato sauce...................LY, BR
Lyonnais salad: curly endive, sheep's feet called "clapotons," chicken livers, boiled eggs, herring fillets
Lyonnaise soup with onion, chicken broth, onions fried in lard
Mourtayrol: a pot-au-feu of fattened hen with saffron.......................................AU
Ox tripe à la lyonnaise, panfried with chopped onions, parsley, and shallots
Patranque auvergnate: stale bread dredged in milk and fresh tome
Pike "au bleu": in a vinegar court-bouillon....LY
Pike quenelles.......................................LY
Polenta: cornmeal.......................................SA
Potato pâté: a savory pie made from potatoes, onions, and parsley.......................BO
Pouytrolle: pork stomach stuffed with vegetables and meat.......................................VI
Râpée de Saint-Étienne: a kind of potato galette
Raviole du Dauphiné: ravioli of Comté and/ or French Emmental cheese, fresh cow's-milk cheese, parsley, fresh eggs.......................PGI
Rissole of Saint-Flour: flaky pastry turnover, Cantal filling.......................................CA
Rissole with meat.......................................DA
Sâlé with Bugey nuts: a bread dough tart filled with sliced onions, crushed walnuts, and sprinkled with walnut oil
Salt pork with Le Puy green lentils............AU
Sanguine: a kind of galette made with chicken blood.......................................AU
Savory salmon pie brivadoise: puff pastry, with St. George's mushrooms.......................BO
Savoyard: large vermicelli (fidés) in a chicken broth with onions
Stuffed cabbage Auvergnat: stuffed with veal, sausage meat, bacon, cooked ham, onion . . .
Stuffed cabbage: stuffed with pork, onion, parsley.......................................AU
Swiss chard voironnaise, with eggs and cheese
Taillerin: flat noodles, made of soft wheat, hard wheat, or buckwheat
Trout with bacon, panfried, in ham fat from Auvergne
Truffade: potatoes, bacon, Cantal, garlic......AU
Tullins soup: with white beans, onions, carrots, leeks.......................................DA
Ubac soup: milk, potatoes, grated cheese, enriched with a veal hock.......................DA
Veal aixoise: veal cushion, in a casserole, with chestnuts and other vegetables...........SA
Vichyssois: thick, with potatoes and leeks, eaten cold
Wine soup: leeks, carrots, onions, turnip in Beaujolais and tapioca.......................LY

DESSERTS AND PASTRIES

Bressane gauffre (waffle), light and thin made of salted water and flour; made in Millard molds or as a flan: a sort of clafoutis, including apples or pears made as a flan.......................AU
Bugne lyonnaise: beignet with or without yeast
Chestnut cake from Forez
Couve crestoise: a round shortbread in a concave shape, with orange peel
Farinette: a very thick crêpe typically enjoyed sweetened.......................................AU
Galette bressane: a brioche pastry, covered with crème fraîche and sugar
Galette de Pérouges: thin and wide galette made from brioche dough, covered with butter and caramelized sugar
Gâteau de Savoie
Pain de courge: a bread made of winter squash.......................................DR
Pâté de la batteuse: a large turnover filled with fruits.......................................FO, ML
Piquenchâgne: a galette made of bread or brioche dough in which pears are inserted whole.......................................BO
Plum-cake Voironnais: quatre-quarts (pound cake) with candied fruit and moistened with rum
Pogne de Romans: a kind of brioche, in the shape of a crown, with orange blossom water
Pompe aux pommes: pâté or a turnover of flaky pastry or puff pastry.......................AU
Quemeaux tart: fromage blanc tart, sweet or savory
Rissole Savoyard: a flaky pastry or puff pastry, stuffed with jam or compote
Suisse de Valence: a shortbread cookie in the shape of a Swiss guard, with candied orange peel
Tarte à l'encalat or tarte de vic: flaky or shortcrust pastry, with a base of milk curd.......................................AU
Tarte à la mie de pain: bottom crust of flaky pastry; a filling made of stale bread, milk, sugar, almond flour.......................LY
Walnut cake: a pastry-covered pie filled with honey, caramel, and crème de noix.......................................DA

VARIOUS

Charroux mustard.......................................AU
Oil of toasted rapeseed.......................................FO, BE
Olive oil of Nyons.......................................DA AOP
Walnut oil.......................................DA

CONFECTIONERY AND SMALL DELICACIES

Bouffette de Mens: two small oval génoises enclosing a layer of sweetened cream.......................................DA
Carré de Salers: small dry cookie
Chambéry chocolate truffle
Chocolat à la Chartreuse (liqueur)
Cloche d'Annecy: chocolates stuffed with hazelnut praline and flavored with Grand Marnier
Cocon de Lyon: yellow almond paste stuffed with praline, orangeat, cocoa butter, and curaçao liqueur
Coeur de Royat: a little heart in white chocolate stuffed with almond paste and candied fruit.......................................AU
Copeau: a twisted cookie, flavored with orange blossom water...................AR, DR
Cornet de Murat: a cone-shaped cookie
Coussin de Lyon: chocolate ganache in an almond paste, all flavored with curaçao
Crème de marrons.......................................AR
Croquant d'Auvergne: a small dry cookie, very hard
Crotte de Marquis: a spherical shell made of milk chocolate, with a chocolate praline interior.......................................BO
Glacéed and candied fruits.......................................AU
Honey of Provence.......................................PGI
Honey of the Cévennes.......................................PGI
Honeys of Savoie: chestnut, mountains of the Ardèche, firs of the Loire, lavender of Drôme Provençale, acacia from Revermont or Vercors
Macaron de Massiac, a macaron with hazelnuts, no almond.......................................AU
Marocain de Vichy: a caramel shell, soft coffee or chocolate center
Marzipan from Aigueperse, similar to a macaron
Nougat de Montélimar: white, tender or hard, with almonds and pistachios
Palet d'or, chocolate decorated with real gold.......................................BO
Pantin d'Annonay: shortbread cookies, covered with a pink icing.......................AR
Pastille de Vichy, a base of salts and mineral waters of Vichy
Pâte de fruits.......................................AU
Pavé de Voiron: a cube composed of a layer of hazelnut praline between two layers of almond praline
Praline d'Aigueperse, brown in color with roasted almonds.......................................AU
Roseau du lac: dark chocolate stick filled with coffee extract.......................................AN
Sucre d'orge de Vichy: round candies, with many flavors
Vérités de Lapalisse: a shell of sugar and a semiliquid interior of various flavors...........BO
Vincuit: a sweet concentrate from pear and apple.......................................BR

DRINKS AND SPIRITS

Antésite: without alcohol, with licorice, to dilute with water.......................................DA
Arquebuse: spirits made from 33 plants: poppy, gentian, mint, etc.......................................DA
Bonal: aperitif with mistelle flavored with yellow gentian and quinaquina...................DA
Chartreuse: herbal liqueur, more than 130 herbs for Grande Chartreuse...............DA
Cherry Rocher: cherry liqueur...................DA
China-china: liqueur with sweet and bitter orange peels, aromatic plants, and spices.......................................DA
Eaux de noix, made from green walnuts macerated in eau-de-vie.......................DA
Génépi: a liqueur based on mugwart.......SA, DA
Liquor of Aiguebelle abbey, based on about 70 different plants: linden, sage, verbena, gentian, etc.......................................R
Liquors of gentian.......................................AU
Marc d'Auvergne: eau-de-vie made from grape marc
Marc of Bugey and Savoie
Mont Corbier: herbal liqueur: hyssop, vulnerary herbs, chamomile.......................SA
Suédois: herbal liqueur, myrrh, aloe, gentian, rhubarb.......................................SA
Verbena: liqueur with verbena.......................AU
Vermouth of Chambéry, plants macerated in dry white wine: absinthe, hyssop, quinaquina . . .
Vins de noix: aperitif made with red wine and green nuts.......................................DA

MEN AND WOMEN (CRITICS, CHEFS, ETC.)

Baraterro, Joseph (1887–1941): Hôtel du Midi, Lamastre
Berchoux, Joseph (1760–1839), author of *La Gastronomie, ou l'homme des champs à table* (1801)
Bernarchon, Maurice (1919–1999), Jean-Jacques (1944–2010), Philippe: Bernachon, pastry chef and chocolatier, Lyon
Besson, René: Charcuterie Bobosse, Lyon
Bidault Léa (1908–1996): La Voûte, Lyon
Bise, Marguerite (1898–1965), François (1928–1984): L'Auberge du Père Bise, Talloires
Blanc, Élisa (1883–1949), Paulette (1910–1992), Georges (born in 1943): today Georges Blanc, Vonnas
Bocuse, Paul (born in 1926): Restaurant Paul Bocuse, Collonges-au-Mont d'Or
Bonnat, Félix (born in 1861), Gaston, Armand, Raymond, and Stéphane: Bonnat chocolatier, Voiron
Bourgeois, Marie (1870–1937): La Mère Bourgeois, Priay
Brazier, Eugénie (1895–1977): La Mère Brazier, Lyon and Col de la Luère
Brillat-Savarin, Jean Anthelme (1755–1826), author of the *Physiologie du goût* (*Physiology of taste*), 1825
Castaing, Paulette (1911–2014): Beau Rivage, Condrieu
Chapel, Alain (1937–1990): Alain Chapel, Mionnay
Fillioux, Françoise (1865–1925): Le Mère Fillioux, Lyon
Giraudet, Henri, founder of Giraudet in 1910 in Bourg-en-Bresse, making the region known as the home of the quenelle
Guy ("Mère Guy"), the first "Mère," second half of the eighteenth century

- Marcon, Régis (born in 1956), Jacques (born in 1978): Régis and Jacques Marcon, Saint-Bonnet-le-Froid
- Mennweg, Albert (1896–1950): Le Filet de Sole, Lyon
- Nandron, Joannès (1909–1963), Gérard (1934–2000): Nandron, Lyon
- Pernollet, Ernest (1918–1995): Hôtel Pernollet, Belley
- Pic, André (1893–1984); Jacques (1932–1992); Anne-Sophie (born in 1969): Pic, now Maison Pic, Valence
- Point, Fernand (1897–1955): La Pyramide, Vienna
- Richard, Renée (1930–2014): Fromagerie Renée Richard, Lyon
- Rochedy, Michel (born in 1936): Le Chabichou, Courchevel
- Roucou, Roger (1921–2012): La Mère Guy, Lyon
- Sibilia, Colette (born 1933): Charcuterie Sibilia, Lyon
- Têtedoie, Christian (born in 1961): Christian Têtedoie, Lyon
- Troisgros, Jean-Baptiste (1898–1974); Jean (1926–1983); Pierre (born in 1928); Michel (born in 1958): Troisgros, Ouches
- Trolliet, Maurice, Alexis: Boucherie Trolliet, Lyon
- Vettard, Antoine (1883–1975): Café Neuf Vettard, Lyon
- Veyrat, Marc (born in 1950): La Maison des bois, Manigod
- Vieira, Serge (born in 1977): Restaurant Serge Vieira, Chaudes-Aigues
- Vignard, Jean (1899–1972): Chez Juliette, Lyon

THE BEST OF THE REGION

BOURGOGNE-FRANCHE-COMTÉ

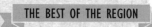

BO: BURGUNDY; FC: FRANCHE-COMTÉ; MO: MORVAN

AT THE BUTCHER'S

- Beef of Charolles .... AOP
- Charolaise (breed of cattle) .... PGI
- Charollais sheep
- Chicken and black capon of Burgundy
- Pork from Franche-Comté .... PGI
- Poultry of Bresse: capon, turkey, poularde (fattened chicken), chicken .... AOP
- Poultry of Burgundy .... PGI
- Poultry of the Charolais .... PGI
- Poultry of the Langres plateau .... PGI

AT THE FARMER'S

- Asparagus of Ruffey .... BO
- Belle fille de Salins: an apple .... FC
- Cassis of Burgundy
- Marmotte cherry .... BO
- Onion of Auxonne .... BO
- Prune of Vitteaux .... BO

AT THE FISHMONGER'S

- Friers of Saône: bleak fish (for frying) .... BO
- Perch
- Pike
- Tench

AT THE BAKER'S

- Bôlon/baulon: barley bread .... FC
- Craquelin: a flaky pastry of leavened dough FC

AT THE CHARCUTIER

- Andouillette of Chablis .... BO
- Andouillette of Clamecy .... MO
- Brési: smoked and dried beef .... FC
- Gandeuillot: smoked pork sausage .... FC
- Ham cooked on the bone, after salting and smoking .... FC
- Ham in wine sediment .... BO
- Hatereau: tripe dumplings .... BO
- Jambon de Luxeuil: ham macerated in red wine, salted with dry salt, lightly smoked .... FC
- Jambon du Morvan: raw, salted and dried
- Jambon fumé du Haut-Doubs (smoked ham)
- Jambon persillé de Bourgogne (Burgandy parsley ham): ham and shoulder salted and cooked, set in a savory jelly with parsley
- Morteau sausage (larger, fattier, smokier than Montbéliard) .... PGI
- Morvandelle pork pie
- Rosette du Morvan: a dry-cured sausage
- Salted and smoked pork meat .... FC
- Saucisse de Foncine, sausage with cabbage, smoked .... FC
- Saucisse de Montbéliard (sausage) .... PGI
- Sausage with cabbage .... FC
- Smoked beef tongue .... FC
- Smoked wild boar and deer .... FC

AT THE CHEESE MAKER'S

- Aisy cendré .... BO
- Beurre de Bresse .... AOP
- Bleu de Gex Haut-Jura/ bleu de Septmoncel .... FC AOP
- Bouton de culotte .... BO
- Brillat-Savarin .... BO
- Cancoillotte .... FC
- Chaource .... BO AOP
- Charolais .... BO AOP
- Chevret du Haut-Jura .... FC
- Cîteaux .... BO
- Claquebitou .... BO
- Comté .... FC
- Crème de Bresse .... AOP
- Emmental français est-central .... PGI
- Emmental grand cru .... FC
- Époisses .... BO AOP
- Gruyère .... FC PGI
- Mâconnais .... BO
- Mamirolle .... FC
- Mont-d'or or vacherin du Haut-Doubs .... FC AOP
- Morbier .... FC AOP
- Pierre-qui-Vire .... BO
- Saint-Florentin .... BO
- Serra: made from whey .... FC
- Soumaintrain .... BO PGI

SAVORY DISHES

- Boeuf à la bourguignonne: red wine, bacon, and onions
- Bourguignonne stew, made from pork, cabbage, and various vegetables
- Bresse chicken with grapes in verjus
- Burgundy snails: butter, shallots, garlic, and parsley
- Cherry soup: as a starter—sour cherries; with butter and sugar .... FC
- Chicken à la vesulienne, stuffed with onions, bacon, chicken offal .... FC
- Comtoise pork stew, with local smoked meats: pork tenderloin, Morteau sausage
- Coq au vin jaune and morels .... FC
- Crapiaux Morvandiaux: A kind of thick crêpe with bacon
- Cratelles (a mushroom) salad: fresh horn of plenty mushrooms, parsley, chives .... FC
- Crayfish in cream .... FC
- Croquettes jurassiennes (Jura): Comté cheese beignets .... FC
- Croûte comtoise: mushrooms in cream on toasted bread, as a gratin .... FC
- Dijon-style rabbit, in mustard
- Entrecôte bareuzai: shallot sauce, forest mushrooms, red wine .... BO
- Frog stock .... FC
- Galette with griaudes: made from the fonds cooked pork fat .... MO
- Gaudes: cornmeal porridge or galettes .... BO, FC
- Gougère: cream puffs with Comté or Gruyère cheese .... BO
- Gratin comtois: Morteau sausage, grated Comté cheese, potatoes
- Hare in Charlotte sauce: sauce made with flour, butter, hare, vinegar, and broth .... FC
- Jaunottes with cream: chanterelles .... FC
- Jura beef tongue, marinated in Jura white wine, braised in the oven .... FC
- Leek gratin with Arbois white wine .... FC
- Lentils in Comté: blond lentils mixed with a preparation of shallots, cream, and Comté cheese .... FC
- Lettuce à la Nivernaise: cooked étouffé, or creamed
- Morteau sausage vigneronne, white wine Arbois, with bacon .... FC
- Morvandelle chicken, in a casserole, with parsley, and Morgan ham
- Morvandelle omelet, with Morvan ham
- Oeufs meurette, eggs poached in a Burgundy sauce
- Ox tripe à la franc-comtoise: with vinegar, cream, and butter
- Peas à la nivernaise, creamed with young legumes: lettuce, small onions
- Pike à la Vesulienne: roasted whole in the oven, with a sauce made of mushrooms and shallots .... FC
- Pochouse: a fish matelote (stew) .... BO
- Quails or thrush, with fresh grapes .... BO
- Salted goat: pickled goat meat .... FC
- Saupiquet des Amognes: panfried Morvan ham with cream sauce and shallots
- Sheeps' tongue à la nivernaise, braised in wine, with bacon and onion
- Soup à la nivernaise: vegetable soup made from mutton broth
- Trout with red wine .... BO
- Tutsche/toutché: galette of brioche dough, salted or sweet .... FC
- Veal cutlets in Comté
- Wild duck with hot sauce: Trousseau red wine sauce in which duck liver can also be incorporated .... FC
- Wine soup, with a meat broth base and Arbois red wine .... FC
- Wine grower's salad: dandelion, lean bacon ... BO

DESSERTS AND PASTRIES

- Cion, a tart of sweetened fromage blanc .... BO
- Dijon Pain d'épices
- Flamusse or flamousse: flan with pumpkin or winter squash .... BO
- Galette de goumeau: a brioche dough topped with a goumeau, a preparation made from eggs and cream .... FC
- Pain aux oeufs: a kind of crème caramel .... FC
- Pain d'épices from Vercel .... FC
- Rigodon: a kind of pudding made from brioches .... BO
- Tapinette: curd tart .... BO
- Tartouillat: a sort of clafoutis .... BO
- Téméraire: fruit cake (apples, hazelnuts, raisins) .... FC

VARIOUS

- Burgundy red wine vinegar
- Burgundy snail
- Burgundy truffle
- Dijon mustard/mustard from Burgundy .... PGI

CONFECTIONERY AND SMALL DELICACIES

- Amande royale: almond-shaped candy (praline, nougatine, and chocolate) .... FC
- Anis de Flavigny: aniseed coated with flavored sugar
- Biscuit de Chablis/Duchy: a cookie used for dipping
- Biscuit de Montbozon, with orange blossom .... FC
- Cassissine de Dijon: black currant paste with a center of black currant liqueur
- Corniotte de Louhans: a flaky pastry in the shape of a tricorne hat, filled with pâte à choux
- Cramaillotte: dandelion flower jelly .... BO
- Donzy croquet, with almonds .... BO
- Dragée of Besançon
- Fir honey from Vosges .... AOP
- Gaufrette mâconnaise: thin rolled waffle
- Gimblette: small cake of pain d'épices with almonds .... BO
- Griotte: Morello cherry in kirsch enrobed in chocolate
- Negus, from Nevers: soft caramel with chocolate or coffee (Abyssinian) in a shell of cooked sugar
- Nonnette: small cake of pain d'épices filled with jam .... BO
- Nougatine de Nevers: nougatine candies coated in colorful royal icing
- Pavé Bisontin Bouteloup: hazelnut almond praline
- Raisiné de Bourgogne:
- Sèche comtoise: a dry cake with a puff pastry base
- Soft caramel .... FC

DRINKS AND SPIRITS

- Anise of Pontarlier, aperitifs
- Aperitifs with gentian .... FC
- Cassis de Dijon
- Cider from Pays d'Othe .... BO
- Crème de framboises .... BO
- Eau-de-vie using marc from Franche-Comté .... GI
- Fine de Bourgogne: wine eau-de-vie .... GI
- Fir tree liqueur .... FC
- Gentian eau-de-vie .... FC
- Kirsch de Fougerolles .... FC GI
- Kirsch de la Marsotte .... FC
- Macvin du Jura: a blend of musts and eau-de-vie from marc from Jura .... AOP
- Marc de Bourgogne: marc eau-de-vie .... GI
- Marc of Jura .... GI
- Prunelle de Bourgogne, liqueur
- Ratafia de Bourgogne
- Ratafia of cider .... BO
- Sloe liqueur .... BO
- Wine eau-de-vie from Franche-Comté .... GI

MEN AND WOMEN (CRITICS, CHEFS, ETC.)

- Burtin, Victor (1877–1937): Hôtel d'Europe and d'Angleterre, Mâcon
- Dumaine, Alexandre (1895–1974): La Côte d'Or, Saulieu
- Frachot, William (born in 1970): Hôstellerie du Chapeau Rouge, Dijon
- Jung, Ernest (1921–2004): Le Chapeau Rouge, Dijon
- Kir, Adrien (the Canon) (1876–1968), mayor of Dijon who popularized the cocktail of his name
- La Varenne (François Pierre de) (1618–1678), cook, author of *Le Cuisinier françois*, 1653
- Lameloise, Jean (born in 1921); Jacques (born in 1947): Lameloise, Chagny
- Loiseau, Bernard (1951–2003): La Côte d'Or, Saulieu
- Menau, Marc (born in 1944): L'Espérance, Saint-Père-sous-Vézelay
- Racouchot, Henry (1883–1954): Les Trois faisans, Dijon
- Rousseau, Pierre (1863–1912), born in Châtillonen-Bazois, chef of the *Titanic*

THE BEST OF THE REGION

BRITTANY

AT THE BUTCHER'S

Coucou de Rennes (hen)
Goose from Sougéal
Poultry of Brittany....................................PGI
Poultry of Janzé ....PGI
Salt-meadow lamb of
Mont-Saint-Michel...............................AOP

AT THE FARMER'S

Armorica Reinette apples
Artichoke camus from Brittany
Breton cabbage
Bricolin: young cabbage sprouts
Carotte de sable of Santec (carrot variety)
Chestnut of Redon
Coco de Paimpol (white beans).................AOP
Endive of Kerlouan
Pink onion of Roscoff...............................AOP
Shallot
Small gray melon of Rennes
Strawberry of Plougastel-Daoulas
Winter cauliflower

AT THE FISHMONGER'S

Abalone
Albacore tuna
Barnacles
Burbot
Clam
Common periwinkle
Conger
Crab
Crayfish
Cuttlefish
Eel
Farmed mussels
Farmed mussels from the bay
of Mont-Saint-Michel ....AOP
Langoustine
Line-caught pollack
Line-caught sea bass
Lobster
Mackerel
Mackerel with white wine
Mullet
Natural white tuna
Oysters from Brittany
Praire clams
Sardine in oil
Sardine of Bolinche
Scallop
Scallop of the Côtes d'Armor....................PGI
Shrimp, common prawn and sand shrimp
Spider crab
Velvet crab

AT THE BAKER'S

Bourgueu: a brioche-style bread
Breton rye bread
Fouesse: a brioche-style bread
Gochtial: bread-brioche
Pain chapeau: tall bread, in the silhouette of a
nun, hence its name
Pain doux (soft bread): brioche-style bread
Pain noir (dark bread), rye
Pain plié: a tall bread that owes its name to
its shape
Pain sucré (sweet bread)
Pastéchou: brioche-style bread with raisins
or prunes

AT THE CHARCUTIER

Andouille of Guémené
Breton bacon: brined pork belly, baked
Breton tripe: bovine tripe, onions, carrots, in a
savory jelly
Pâté Breton, made from pork
Pâté Rennais, made from head and pork offal
Salted fat: pork bard, salt, pepper, and onions

AT THE CHEESE MAKER'S

Breton butter, demi-sel
Fat milk: milk from curd of a slightly viscous
consistency
Fromage de Campénéac
Fromage de Timadeuc
Lait ribot: liquid fermented milk

SAVORY DISHES

Artichokes à la rennaise: in a casserole dish,
with bacon and onions
Bellilois conger pot-au-feu
"Breton" soup with white beans
Breton stews: rennaise—hocks, feet, tails, and
ears of pork; à la quimpéroise—beef, bacon,
smoked sausage . . .
Bricoline soup: young cabbage shoots
Buckwheat and bacon soup
Buckwheat galettes
Chestnut soup from Redon
Cod à la brestoise: baked, with potatoes and
leek sauce
Cod dinardaise: cod croquettes
Cod tongue stew, onions, potatoes
Congre à la Breton: a stew, with conger,
potatoes, onions, and muscadet
Cotriade: Breton bouillabaisse
Godaille lorientaise: a fish soup
Haricots blancs à la bretonne: white kidney
beans from Paimpol cooked in a casserole
with onions and tomatoes
Kig ha farz: Breton stew which includes, in
addition to beef and pork (hock), buckwheat
flour
Kouign patatez: thick potato galette
Leg of salt-meadow lamb à la Bretonne, with
Paimpol kidney beans
Limpet soup
Lobster à l'armoricaine: tomato, tarragon,
shallot, white wine
Lobsters with curry, à la morbihannaise:
butter, onions, cider eau-de-vie, Kari Gosse
(sauce)
Mackerel à la quimpéroise: in a court-bouillon
accompanied by a butter sauce
Miton rennais: panade
Oat mush (oatmeal)
Paimpolaise cod: cod gratin and potatoes
Scallops à la bretonne
Shrimp (gray) in cider
Tripe with leeks in cider, à la vannetaise
Tuna casserole of Cornouaille fishermen:
carrots, peas
Veal kidneys with cider
Velvet crab soup

DESSERTS AND PASTRIES

Far Breton: a kind of custard, now usually
made with prunes
Gâteau Breton: thick cookie with demi-sel
butter
Kouign-amann: puff pastry cake
Pommé rennais
Wheat crêpes

VARIOUS

Buckwheat flour from Brittany.................PGI
Salt or fleur de sel sea salt from Guérande PGI

CONFECTIONERY
AND SMALL DELICACIES

Apple cider jam
Buckwheat honey
Craquelin (first dipped in hot
water then baked)
Crêpe dentelle cookies
Niniche de Quiberon: a thin and cylindrical
lollipop; caramel flavor is the most common
Palet Breton
Patate de Saint-Malo: an almond paste candy,
dusted with cocoa powder

DRINKS AND SPIRITS

Bouchinot: liqueur from infusions of plants
and milk
Brittany cider...PGI
Cider Cornouaille......................................AOP
Cider eau-de-vie from Brittany.................GI
Elixir d'Armorique: herbal liqueur (mint,
génépi)
Mead, chouchen: fermented drink made from
honey diluted in water
Pommeau de Bretagne................................GI

MEN AND WOMEN
(CRITICS, CHEFS, ETC.)

Kéréver, Michel (born in 1934): Hôtellerie du
Lion d'Or, Liffré
Roellinger, Olivier (born in 1955): La Maison
de Bricourt, Cancale

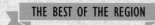

THE BEST OF THE REGION

CENTRE-VAL DE LOIRE

BE: BEAUCE; BY: BERRY; GA: GÂTINAIS; OR: ORLÉANAIS;
SO: SOLOGNE; TO: TOURAINE

AT THE BUTCHER'S

Black turkey of Sologne
Géline (chicken) of Touraine
Goose of Touraine
Mutton of Sologne
Noire du Berry hen
Poultry of Berry...PGI
Poultry of Gâtinais ....PGI
Poultry of the Orléanais ....PGI

AT THE FARMER'S

Countess of Chambord rice bean
Crookneck pumpkin of Berry
Cultivated mushrooms ....TO
Green lentils of Berry ....PGI
Saffron
Truffle

AT THE FISHMONGER'S

Eel
Lamprey
Pike and carp from the waters in Brenne and
Sologne
Shad

AT THE BAKER'S

Fouace de Lerné: a small spicy brioche........TO
Fouée: a flat bread ....TO
Radillat or pain Bénit: galette-style bread
made with butter ....BY

AT THE CHARCUTIER

Andouillette of Jargeau...............................OR
Andouillettes of Vouvray ....TO
Pâté de Chartres: a pâté en croûte with a piece
of foie gras in the center
Pâté de Pâques (Easter pâté):
a pâte en croûte containing an egg...............BY
Rillettes of Tours ....PGI
Rillons: cubes of pork belly cooked in fat .....TO

AT THE CHEESE MAKER'S

(Crottin de) Chavignol..........................BY AOP
Feuille de Dreux
Pithiviers au Foin
Pouligny Saint-Pierre ....BY AOP
Sainte-Maure de Touraine........................AOP
Selles-sur-Cher..................................BY, SO AOP
Valençay..BY, TO AOP

SAVORY DISHES

Beuchelle Tourangelle: sweetbreads and veal
kidneys, mushrooms, and crème fraîche
Citrouillat berrichon: a pastry-covered
pumpkin pie
Freshwater pike perch of Vourillon, baked,
cooked in vouvray, on a bed of oyster
mushrooms and vegetables ....TO
Friture de Loire (fried fish): bleaks, gudgeon,
spirlins, etc.
Matelote of eels (a stew)
Oeufs à la couille d'âne:
poached eggs in a reduced wine sauce ....BY
Potato galette: mashed potatoes
in puff pastry..BY
Potato pâté, in a pastry crust.......................BY
Potatoes Solognotes: potatoes cooked in milk
then baked with cream au gratin
Poulet en barbouille: chicken stew whose
sauce is enriched with blood.......................BY
Rata beauceron: pork belly, onions, potatoes
Sainte-Maure puff pastry of Touraine
Shad with sorrel

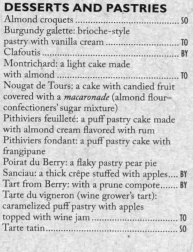

DESSERTS AND PASTRIES

Almond croquets .... SO
Burgundy galette: brioche-style
pastry with vanilla cream .... TO
Clafoutis .... BY
Montrichard: a light cake made
with almond .... TO
Nougat de Tours: a cake with candied fruit
covered with a *macaronade* (almond flour–
confectioners' sugar mixture)
Pithiviers feuilleté: a puff pastry cake made
with almond cream flavored with rum
Pithiviers fondant: a puff pastry cake with
frangipane
Poirat du Berry: a flaky pastry pear pie
Sanciau: a thick crêpe stuffed with apples.... BY
Tart from Berry: with a prune compote....... BY
Tarte du vigneron (wine grower's tart):
caramelized puff pastry with apples
topped with wine jam .... TO
Tarte tatin .... SO

VARIOUS

Orleans vinegar
Pears: dehydrated and flattened .... TO
Walnut oil.. TO

SMALL DELICACIES

Aristocrate: thin caramelized dry cakes
with pieces of almonds .... SO
Casse-museau: small goat-cheese cake .... BY
Cotignac d'Orléans: quince paste
Échaudé de Brenne: a dry cookie .... BY
Forestine: candy filled with praline............. BY
Gâtinais honey
Macaron of Cormery................................... TO
Macaron of Langeais................................. TO
Mentchikoff: Swiss meringue
surrounding a chocolate praline center .... BE
Muscadin: cherry preserved in kirsch
coated with chestnut cream enrobed
in chocolate .... TO
Prasline (or Praline) de Montargis............... GA
Sablé de Nançay (a sablée cookie) .... BY

DRINKS AND SPIRITS

Bernache: fermented grape must .... TO
Pear eau-de-vie from Olivet
Pousse d'épine: an aperitif made with wine
and thorns of blackthorn

MEN AND WOMEN (CRITICS, CHEFS, ETC.)

Bardet, Jean (born in 1941): Jean Bardet
Château Belmont, Tours
Barrier, Charles (1916–2009): Le Nègre;
Charles Barrier, Tours
Dépée, Lucienne-Anne (1906–2006): Auberge
des Templiers, Boismorand
Doreau, Roger (1919–1981): Auberge des
Templiers, Boismorand
Puisais, Jacques (born in 1927), oenologist,
founder of the Institut Français du Goût
(French Institute of Taste) in Tours
Rabelais (1494?–1553), man of letters, author
of *Pantagruel* (1532) and *Gargantua* (1534)

THE BEST OF THE REGION

CORSICA

AT THE BUTCHER'S

Boar
Corsican/Nustrale pork breeds: all Corsican
AOP dry-cured meats are made from this breed
Kid (young goat)
Manzu: young male calf (veal), Corsican breed
Milk-fed lamb, Corsican breed

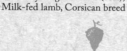

AT THE FARMER'S

Almonds
Arbouse (fruit of the strawberry tree)
Chestnut
Citron
Clementine of Corsica............................... PGI
Fig
Hazelnut of Cervione................................ PGI
Lemon
Mandarin
Orange
Pomegranate
Pomelo.. PGI
Prickly pear

AT THE FISHMONGER'S

Anchovy
Boutargue (Bottarga)
Capon
Common dentex
Eel
Gianchetti
Great spider crab
Mullet
Oyster
Red mullet
Sardine
Sea urchin
Spiny lobster
Trout
Tuna

AT THE BAKER'S

Pan di i morti ("bread of the dead"): brioche
bread with nuts and raisins

AT THE CHARCUTIER

Coppa: dried pork rib meat .... AOP
Ficatellu: liver sausage, fresh or dry
Lonzu: dried pork loin.............................. AOP
Panzetta: pork belly
Pork liver pâté
Prisuttu (prosciutto): dried ham .... AOP
Salamu: dried sausage
Salcicetta: raw sausage
Sangui: boudin—various recipes (onions,
Swiss chard, raisins, pieces of pork brains, etc.)
Vuletta: pork throat

AT THE CHEESE MAKER'S

Bastelicacciu
Brocciu .... AOP
Calinzana
Cuscio
Niolo
Venaco

SAVORY DISHES

Anchoiade: anchovy purée
Artichokes stuffed with brocciu cheese
Aziminu: a kind of Corsican bouillabaisse
Bugliticcia: beignet with sheep's or goat's-milk
fromage frais
Chicken with sage
Cuttlefish or squid with tomato
Fish à l'agliotu: a preparation for different fish
(such as sea bream, mullet, or red pandora)
based in oil, vinegar, garlic, and herbs
Fresh brocciu omelet
Fried eels
Fritele of herbs, beignet
Herb soup from the maquis: potatoes, onions,
beans. Herbs: dandelion, mint, chicory, borage,
sorrel, savory, fennel, wild radish, rosemary,
and myrtle
Kid (young goat) étouffé
Lamb with vinegar bread
Macaroni en pastizzu: a pastry-covered pie
Pestu: stockfish prepared with tomato coulis
and crushed anchovies, tomatoes, peppers,
walnuts, and garlic
Pigeon with olives
Piverunata de Corte: a sauce made with
peppers, tomatoes, and red wine
Pulenda: a Corsican polenta made with
chestnut flour
Rabbit in garlic
Roasted tuna
Sardines stuffed with Swiss chard and brocciu
Sauté of snails: prepared with a cooking stock
from olive oil, onions, anchovies, and tomatoes
Spiny lobster with potatoes
Storzapreti de Bastia: cheese and herb
dumplings
Stuffatu: meat sauce
Summer or autumn minestra: a soup of carrot,
squash, leeks, potatoes, onions, and pork
Tianu of rice with olives, prepared in a tianu, a
glazed earthenware skillet, with ficatelli
Tourte au vert (pastry covered pie with greens)
spinach and/or chard
Wild boar dumplings: wild boar meatballs,
sausage meat, onions, and garlic

DESSERTS AND PASTRIES

Brocciu fritella: a brocciu-filled beignet
Caccavellu: An Easter cake of brioche-style
dough
Castagnacciu: cake made with chestnut flour
Falculella: a sweet cake made with brocciu
Fiadone: a cake made with fresh brocciu
Frappes: beignets
Imbrucciata: a tart with a brocciu filling and
zest of lemon
Inuliata/fugazza: a galette without egg; the
fugazza includes anise or pastis
Migliacciu: salty galette with sheep's or goat's-
milk cheese
Panzarottu: rice beignet
Pastella au brocciu: thin turnover filled with a
brocciu preparation
Salviata: a large dry cake

VARIOUS

Corsican chestnut flour............................. AOP
Olive oil from Corsica .... AOP
Pasta: tagliarini, tagliatelle, lasagna, gnocchi,
ravioli, agnolotis

CONFECTIONERY AND SMALL DELICACIES

Candied citron
Canistrelli: dry cakes made from oil and
white wine
Corsican honey: spring, spring maquis,
honeydew maquis, chestnut, summer maquis,
autumn-winter maquis .... AOP
Fenuchjettu d'Ajaccio: a cookie first
dipped in hot water before baked (échaudé),
containing anise

DRINKS AND SPIRITS

Aqua vita: fruit, marc, arbouse, and hawthorn
eaux-de-vie
Cap Corse: a sweet wine with quinaquina
Cédratine: citron-based liqueur
Fruit wines (orange, cherry, peach, etc.) made
from fruit macerated in wine and eau-de-vie
Muscat of Cap Corse: fortified wine .... AOP
Myrtle liqueur
Pastis Dami
Rappu: lightly fortified wine
Ratafias, fruit eaux-de-vie: clementine, peach,
grape, chestnut, cherry, dried fig . . .

THE BEST OF THE REGION

GRAND EST

AL: ALSACE; AR: ARDENNES; CH: CHAMPAGNE; LO: LORRAINE;
VO: VOSGES

AT THE BUTCHER'S

Lamb of Lorraine and of the Ardennes
Poultry of Alsace .... PGI
Poultry of Champagne .... PGI
Poultry of the Langres plateau.................... PGI
Red turkey of the Ardennes
Vosges cattle

AT THE FARMER'S

Apricot of Nancy
Asparagus of Alsace, Champagne
Bilberry.. AL, LO
Boulette de Bussy: a turnip.......................... CH
Carotte de Colmar à coeur rouge
(carrot variety)
Cornichon .... AL
Green cabbage: Quintal d'Alsace/
sauerkraut cabbage
Lentil of Champagne
Merveille hazelnut of Bollwiller .... AL
Mirabelles plums from Alsace,
Lorraine.. PGI
Onion of Mulhouse
Quetsche .... AL, LO
Rhubarb... CH
Strawberry of Woippy .... LO
Truffle of Champagne, Meusev .... LO
White turnip confit, salted......................... AL

401

AT THE FISHMONGER'S

Carp
Eel ... AL
European crayfish ... LO
Freshwater pike perch
Herring fillet ... AL
Perch: perch fry for frying ... LO
Pike
Rainbow and river (brown) trout
Trout of the Vosges ... LO

AT THE BAKER'S

Braided brioche (zopf) ... AL
Pain Gallu with fruits ... LO
Pain Molzer, mixed flours—wheat, barley, rye ... AL
Pretzel (bretzel) ... AL

AT THE CHARCUTIER

Andouille and andouillette of Troyes ... CH
Andouille of Revin ... AR
Andouille of Val-d'Ajol ... LO
Andouillette of Lorraine
Boudin blanc of Rethel ... AR PGI
Boudin blanc with onion ... AR
Boudin d'Alsace, made with onions and bread dipped in milk
Boudin of Nancy
Cervelas d'Alsace: small cooked sausage made from lean pork meat and pork fat
Cervelas de Troyes: cooked sausage made with beef neck and pork fat
Dry, cured ham and *noix de jambon* (ham pieces) from Ardennes ... PGI
Fromage de cochon (head of pig): head cheese pâté ... LO
Goose foie gras pâté in a pastry crust ... AL
Hure: a cooked sausage ... AL
Hure: a pâté from pork head ... CH
Jambon cru fumé (smoked raw ham) of Alsace
Jambon de Reims (Reims ham): boneless pork shoulder, set in a savory jelly
Jambon fumé cuit (smoked cooked ham) of Lorraine
Kassler: smoked pork ... AL
Pâté champenois: pork meat pie
Pigs' feet à la Sainte-Menehould, with bone, browned in bread crumbs ... CH
Presskopf: pâté of pig offal ... AL
Quenelle of liver ... AL, LO
Quenelle of marrow, beef ... AL, LO
Saucisses and saucissons of Alsace: à cuire, frying, spreading, made from beer, liver, ham, tongue, from trimmings, potatoes, meat, black; *gendarme* (dried, smoked sausage); knack d'Alsace
Saucisses and saucissons of Lorraine: knack (sausage), for spreading, white or peasant style, to fry or grill, from veal liver, ham, blood, saucisse lorraine . . .
Smoked sheep's tongue of Troyes ... CH
Stuffed veal breast ... AL
Suckling pig in savory jelly ... LO

AT THE CHEESE MAKER'S

Bargkas ... VO
Brillat-Savarin ... CH PGI
Carré de l'Est ... LO
Cendré de la Champagne
Chaource ... CH AOP
Crème fraîche fluide (liquid crème fraîche) d'Alsace ... PGI
Emmental grand cru ... CH, LO
Époisses ... CH AOP
Ervy-le-Châtel ... CH
Langres ... CH AOP
Mégin, cancoillotte ... LO
Munster-Géromé ... AL, LO AOP
Soumaintrain ... CH PGI

SAVORY DISHES

Alsatian pasta (with eggs) ... PGI
Alsatian-style sauerkraut, with goose, with salmon
Ardennes-style endives: cooked, wrapped in ham of Ardennes
Ardennes-style pork ribs, stuffed with ham and Gruyère cheese
Asparagus with three sauces: mousseline, mayonnaise, vinaigrette ... AL
Beef stew with beer, à la lorraine
Beer soup: onion, chicken broth, beer ... AL
Bibeleskäs: fromage blanc, often flavored with garlic, herbs, and onions—accompanied by potatoes ... AL
Boar stew, meat marinated in advance—in oil, bacon, carrots, onions, wine, and vinegar ... AR
Boudin omelet, Nancy ... LO
Carp à la juive: carp in a savory jelly ... AL
Carp in blond beer ... LO
Chicken à la champenoise: cooked with bacon and veal's half foot, stuffed with chicken liver and sausage meat
Chique: fromage blanc with shallots, garlic, and herbs ... LO
Coq au vin gris: with smoked bacon, onions, carrots ... LO
Coq au vin of Bouzy ... CH
Dandelion salad in warm meurotte sauce, a warm vinaigrette and potatoes ... LO
Dandelion salad with bacon ... AR
Dumplings with fromage blanc ... AL
Escargot àl'Asacienne (Alsatian-style snails): cooked in a mixture of water and white wine with an herb filling; finished in the oven, with garlic-shallot-parsley butter
Fiouse with fromage blanc: flaky pastry, fromage-based migaine (egg with milk or cream) ... LO
Flambéd tart/flamekueche: cooked in a wood oven; cream filling, fromage blanc, onions, bacon ... AL
Fried carp of Sundgau: thick carp steaks breaded with semolina ... AL
Fried gudgeon of Meuse ... LO
Galette with bacon: dry galette made from bread dough ... CH
Gérardmer flour soup: flour diluted in melted butter and mixed with a hot broth ... VO
Grated raw potato soup, using beef broth or pasta cooking water ... AL
Lorraine stew: pork, white beans, onions, carrots, turnips, and leeks
Matelote (stew) of Metz, with onions
Matelote champenoise: freshwater (river) fish, with natural white wine of Champagne
Meuse-style potatoes: in a casserole, with chopped shallots ... CH
Minced sour liver, red wine, and vinegar ... AL
Mutton neck à la Argonnaise, barded with bacon, breaded ... CH
Omelet lorraine: sour cream, Gruyère, bacon
Omelet with Chaource cheese ... CH
Onion tart: flaky pastry; filling of onions, cream, eggs, and milk ... AL
Ox tripe à la nancéienne, in a casserole dish, with white wine, shallot, Gruyère, crème fraîche
Panfried wild boar chops ... AR
Pike à la champenoise, with white button mushrooms and served with a sauce from its cooking juices and Champagne
Pike in wine jelly ... LO
Pike Meusiens: garlic, onion, sliced carrots, natural white wine of Champagne
Pike with messina sauce: cream, butter, eggs, shallots, parsley, and chervil
Potatoes with roncin (horse): as a baked potato accompanied with fromage blanc ... LO
Pot-au-feu with quenelles of marrow, beef ... AL
Potée boulangère ("baker's stew"), made with several meats: pork loin, beef chuck, mutton shoulder, pork feet, pork tail ... AL
Potée champenoise: various pieces of pork; carrots, turnips, leeks, heart of cabbage
Quiche lorraine
Rabbit in cream with beets, prepared with *vin gris* and smoked bacon; fried beetroot garnish ... LO
Ramequin messin: a kind of cheese soufflé .. LO
Râpés: potato fritters ... LO
Roast sour pork with new potatoes: pork spare rib ... AL
Roasted pork shank with beer ... AL
Saddle of venison à l'Ardennes: bacon, onion, red wine
Salted turnip soup with bacon and pork shoulder, cooked with Riesling ... AL
Sauerkraut salad with boudin noir, consisting of curly lettuce, red cabbage, sauerkraut, and boudin noir ... AL
Savory frog pie: frogs' legs and small pink mushrooms ... LO
Savory Lorraine pie: flaky pastry crust; "Migaine" (egg and milk), pork and veal meat, covered with puff pastry; pâté lorraine: wild boar or rabbit replaces the pork
Savory meat pie: veal and pork meat, white button mushrooms, Alsatian white wine (Riesling) ... AL
Savory pigeon pie: stuffed with pork throat, pigeon liver, veal shoulder ... CH
Soup of vegetables in butter: beans, leeks, carrots, all served whole ... AR
Soup with goose tripe: neck, wing tips, gizzards ... AL
Spätzle: pasta, immersed in boiling water before being dried ... AL
St. Martin roasted goose; stuffing: chicken livers, goose gizzard and liver, goose fat, pork spare rib, veal, salt pork, shallots, green cabbage, chestnuts ... AL
Steamed bread rolls: Dampfnüdle ... AL
Stuffed carp: a filling of panade and white button mushrooms ... AL
Stuffed lamb shoulder à la champenoise: marinated in natural white wine of Champagne, stuffed with chicken liver and sausage meat
Stuffed pork stomach: stuffed with potatoes, onions, shallots, green cabbage, leeks, spare ribs ... AL
Stuffed potatoes with pot-au-feu stew meat ... AL
Toffailles/roïbrageldi: a stew of potatoes étouffé: onions, smoked bacon ... LO
Totelots vinaigrette: small squares of pasta in a vinaigrette dressing, containing crème fraîche ... LO
Tourtelets of Rethel: small savory pies, stuffed with boudin blanc ... AR
Trout in cream ... LO
Trout in Riesling ... AL
Veal ribs, breaded, with mustard, Nancy-style
Venison noisettes/mignonettes in cream: thick-sliced fillet of venison (medallions) ... AR
Vosges trout pâté, in a pastry crust—one varation marinates trout fillets in truffle juice ... LO

DESSERTS AND PASTRIES

Apple strudel: kneaded and stretched dough, apple stuffing, cinnamon, raisins, almonds ... AL
Apple tart à la migaine ... LO
Baba: the original recipe is without rum, but has saffron and dried fruits ... LO
Berewecke: dried and candied fruits, spices, contained in a bread dough ... AL
Bilberry tart ... AL, LO
Braided or twisted brioche, rich in butter ... LO
Fromage blanc beignets ... CH
Fromage blanc tart: flaky pastry bottom crust, fromage blanc ... AL, LO
Galette with sugar, brioche-like ... AR
Gâteau mollet: a kind of light brioche, shaped like a kugelhopf ... AR
Kugelhopf, characterized by its "turban" shape, a raisin dough, with raisins from Malaga ... AL
Linzer tart, with raspberry jam
Maugin tart: flaky pastry, migaine made with fromage blanc and crème fraîche ... LO
Messin-style apple tart: puff pastry, with raisins
Mirabelle plum tart ... LO
Mirabelle plum tôt-fait (a quick pastry) ... LO
Nancy chocolate cake (with butter)/ Metz chocolate cake (with cream)
Pain d'épices ... AL
Quemeu tart: fromage frais tart from Langres ... CH
Quetsche tart, bread dough base
Red plum tart ... CH
Rhubarb tart, Lorraine-style: flaky pastry, with a migaine (egg and milk)
Rhubarb tart ... AL
Saint-Epvre: a cake of vanilla cream with crushed nougatine sandwiched between two macaron disks ... LO
Tantimolles: crêpes rich in eggs ... AR
Tartes with brimbelles: wild bilberries ... LO
Vaute aux cerises: cherry clafoutis ... LO

CONFECTIONERY AND SMALL DELICACIES

Agneau pascal, a cookie in the shape of lamb, decorated with confectioners' sugar ... AL
Bar-le-Duc currant jam, seeded ... LO
Bergamot de Nancy: sugar candy cooked with bergamot essence ... PGI
"Biscuit cochon" of Stenay, a cookie from Reims ... LO
Biscuit rose (a pink cookie) of Reims
Bouchon au marc de Champagne: a chocolate containing marc de Champagne
Boulet de Metz: ganache-almond paste, hazelnut caramel chips, all covered with a layer of dark or milk chocolate
Bourgeon de sapin des Vosges, with essential oil of fir
Caisse de Joinville: small stick of meringue with almonds ... LO
Cheuchon: slices of dried apples ... CH
Chinois/"escargot cake": a large round cake, a sort of assembly of small cakes of leavened dough containing almonds and hazelnuts ... AL
Craqueline: almond paste coated with caramelized sugar ... LO
Croquet de Saint-Mihiel: a cookie with almonds ... LO
Croquignole: a small dry cookie ... CH
Dragée from Verdun
Duchess de Nancy: chocolate praline coated with a royal icing
Gérardmer anise bread, dry cookie ... LO
Gomichon: pâte of apple or pear, baked ... CH
Honeycomb: brioche pastry filled with pastry cream and topped with a mixture of sugar, honey, and almonds ... AL
Macaron of Boulay, pyramid shape ... LO
Macaron of Nancy
Madeleine de Commercy, from Liverdun ... LO
Mannala: a small cake from leavened dough in the shape of a small man ... AL
Marzipan of Reims, similar to a macaron
Mendiant, made with bread, filled with black cherries and various fruits ... AL
Mirabelle jam ... LO
Mirabelle plum confit ... LO
Nonnette de Remiremont, made from fir honey from Vosges
Nonnette of Reims
Pain d'épices of Reims
Red sugar: rock candy in the shape of animals ... AR
Small Christmas cakes: Bredele, with cinnamon, anise, butter, shortbread, iced, almonds, lemon, walnuts, vanilla. Molded, cut, and piped ... AL
Visitandine de Nancy: small almond cake

DRINKS AND SPIRITS

Alsatian eaux-de-vie: wild berries (holly, wild cherry, sloe, bilberry, wild rose, sorb, elderberry, etc.), cherry plum, raspberry, wine lees, quetsche, kirsch (sweet or wild cherry), etc.
Ambroseille: fermented currant juice ... LO
Blond beers from Alsace and Lorraine
Cider of Pays d'Othe ... CH
Kirsch of Fougerolles ... GI
Lorina lemonade ... LO
Lorraine: Mirabelle plum ... AOP
Marc d'Alsace Gewürztraminer (marc eau-de-vie) ... GI
Marc eaux-de-vie from Centre-Est ... GI
Marc of Champagne ... GI
Marc of Lorraine ... GI
Pearlized rhubarb, made with juice from fresh stems of fermented rhubarb
Petits crus des Vosges: a fermented drink made from dandelion or elderberry flowers ... LO
Ratafia, made by adding alcohol to the must of Champagne grapes ... CH
Ruby currant: fermented currant ... CH
Wine eau-de-vie from the Marne, or Fine champenoise ... GI
Wine eaux-de-vie from Centre-Est ... GI

VARIOUS

Alsace mustard, sweet, using white mustard seeds
Champagne honey
Honey of Alsace .... PGI
Horseradish, condiment .... AL
Reims mustard
Reims vinegar
Vosges fir tree honey .... AOP

MEN AND WOMEN (CRITICS, CHEFS, ETC.)

Appert, Nicolas (1749–1841), inventor of airtight food preservation, born in Châlons-sur-Marne
Boyer, Gaston (1913–2000): La Chaumière, Reims
Boyer, Gérard (born in 1941): Les Crayères, Reims
Clause, Jean-Pierre (1757–1827), supposed inventor of foie gras en croûte (foie gras in a pastry crust)
Forest, Louis (known as Nathan Louis) (1872–1933), founder of the Club des Cent, born in Metz
Haeberlin, Paul (1923–2008); Marc (born in 1954): L'Auberge de l'Ill, Strasbourg
Jung, Émile (born in 1941): Au Crocodile, Strasbourg
Klein, Jean-Georges (born in 1950): L'Arnsbourg, Baerenthal; Restaurant of the Villa René Lalique, Wingen-sur-Moder
Lallement, Arnaud (born in 1974): L'Assiette Champenoise, Tinqueux
Pérignon (Dom) (known as Pierre) (1638/1639–1715), legend claims him as the inventor of sparkling Champagne wine
Philippe, Michel (born in 1936): Hostellerie des Bas Rupts, Gérardmer
Westermann, Antoine (born in 1956): Buerehiesel, Strasbourg

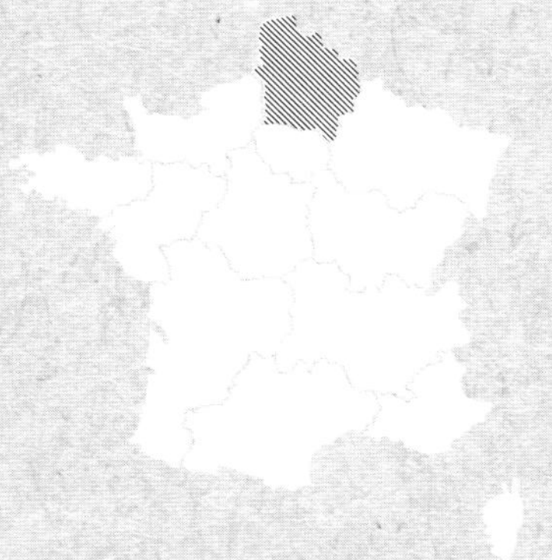

THE BEST OF THE REGION

HAUTS DE FRANCE

FL: FLANDERS; HA: HAINAUT; NO: NORD; NP: NORD-PAS-DE-CALAIS; PA: PAS-DE-CALAIS; PI: PICARDIE; TH: THIÉRACHE

AT THE BUTCHER'S

Belgian Blue-White (breed of cattle)
Poultry of Licques .... PGI
Salt-meadow lamb of the Bay of Somme .... AOP

AT THE FARMER'S

Carrot of Saint-Valéry: carrotte des sables of the Bay of Somme
Endive/chicory
Large green artichoke of Laon
Lingot du Nord: white beans .... PGI
Potatoes of Merville .... NP PGI
Potatoes of Picardie: Aminca, Bellede-Fontenay, Bintje, Caspar, Charlotte, Désirée, Francine, Gipsy, Nicola, Pompadour, Ratte, Roseval, Rosine . . .
Rhubarb
Smoked garlic of Arleux .... PGI
Soissons bean/"Gros jacquot blanc"
Watercress from Bresles

AT THE FISHMONGER'S

Cockle
Eel of Haute-Somme
European pilchard
European plaice
Gray shrimp
Herring: cold-smoked (whole), fresh, lightly smoked, kipper, marinated in vinegar, salted and smoked
Mussels
Red rock mullet

AT THE BAKER'S

Coquille de Noël: brioche bread .... NP
Couquebottrom: a brioche-type bread .... FL
Cramique: a brioche-type bread with raisins
Faluche: round bread, rather flat, slightly cooked .... NP
Picard bread: made of spelt

AT THE CHARCUTIER

Andouille of Aire-sur-la-Lys, and of Cambrai .... NO
Andouillette of Cambrai: veal intestine .... NO
Boudin à la flamande, sweetened: with onions, cream, dried currants, and cinnamon
Duck pâté of Amiens
Lucullus de Valenciennes: slices of beef tongue alternating with foie gras
Pâté d'Abbeville: a pâté made from waterfowl
Pâté picard: a terrine made from pork

AT THE CHEESE MAKER'S

Belval .... FL
Bergues .... FL
Beurre de Cassel .... FL
Boulette d'Avesnes .... HA
Dauphin .... TH
Fromage fort de Béthune: a preparation made from aged cheeses in crocks with spices, white wine, and sometimes alcohol
Gris de Lille
Maroilles/marolles .... AOP
Mimolette vieille .... FL
Mont-des-cats .... FL
Rollot .... PI
Saint-Winoc .... FL
Tomme au foin .... PI

SAVORY DISHES

Andouillette d'Amiens: pork meatballs
Asparagus à la flamande: with a mixture of boiled eggs, melted butter, and parsley
Beef à la picarde, cooked in a casserole, with white wine, onions, and carrots
Beef tongue in hot sauce, with shallots, and vinegar sauce
Beer soup, made with onion, flour, and cream
Bisteu: a pie with a bacon, potato, and onion filling .... PI
Bouffi: cold smoked herring, potatoes cooked in an étouffoir (a sort of damper)
Canard à la picarde: mallard duck cooked in a casserole, with apples
Caqhuse: a simmered stew with pork round steak, with onions .... PI
Carbonade: Beef stew simmered in a beer sauce
Caudière: a fish soup
Coq à la bière (chicken cooked in beer) .... NP
Côtes de veau à la bellovaque: suckling veal cooked in a casserole—with rosés des prés mushrooms, and cream .... PI
Courquinoise: a soup: with conger, crabs, red mullet, mussels, and leeks
Daussades: toasts topped with a preparation made from cream, vinegar, onions, and chopped lettuce .... NP
Eel pâté of the Haute-Somme
Eel with cider, made with yellow eel .... PI
Ficelle picarde: large crêpes stuffed with ham and white button mushrooms and cheese, then baked au gratin
Flamiche aux poireaux: a Flemish leek tart .... PI
Flemish hochepot: a stew with various meats (beef, veal, lamb, pork in various forms)
Fried meatballs with potatoes .... PI
Goyère Maroilles cheese tart
Hénons à la crème: cockles from the Bay of Somme, cooked in cream
Herring à la calaisienne, stuffed fresh herrings, stuffed with onions, mushrooms, and milt
Lapin à l'artésienne: rabbit with hedgehog mushrooms
Macaroni paste in brown sugar .... NP
Mackerel à la boulonnaise, baked, in a preparation of mussels, onions, and mushrooms
Mallard duck with prunes .... PI
Mashed white beans .... PI
Menouille picarde: a dish made with dried beans, bacon, onions, and potatoes
Pike in cider .... PI
Pommes caquettes: potatoes "stuffed" with a mixture of minced garlic, herbs, and crème fraîche .... NP
Potage artésienne, a soupe including pork head, andouille, salt pork, white beans, and cabbage
Potjevlesch terrine: four meats prepared in a savory jelly (veal, rabbit, chicken, and pork) .... FL
Rabbit with prunes and grapes .... NP
Red cabbage à la flamande: "sweet and sour," with apples
Soup hortillonnages: a soup prepared with spring green cabbage, leeks, new potatoes, garden peas in their pods, lettuce, and sorrel .... PI
Spilt pea soup
Welsh: a slice of bread soaked in beer, with a slice of ham, covered with a cheddar cream

DESSERTS AND PASTRIES

Beer and brown sugar tart .... NP
Beignets of Amiens or pets d'âne ("donkey farts"): sweet beignets, made from goat cheese or beef marrow
Craquelin de Boulogne: a sweet puff pastry
Flemish carnival waffle
Galette flamande (Flemish galette), with rum, filled with cream
Galopins: French toast crêpes .... PI
Gâteau battu ("beaten cake"): a rich brioche cake .... PI
Pain crotté: a pain perdu (similar to French toast) .... NP
Rabote/talibur: apple in a flaky crust .... PI
Rhubarb pie .... NP
Stuffed waffle, with light brown sugar .... NO
Tarte à gros bord or au libouli: brioche dough filled with flan, often with prunes .... NP
Tarte à l'badré: a kind of flan .... PI
Tarte à l'coloche: an apple tart .... NP
Tarte à l'oeillette: a kind of sponge cake, with poppy seeds .... PI
Tarte à l'pronée: a dried fruit tart .... PI
Tarte au sucre (sugar tart), brioche .... NP
Waffles made of winter squash .... PI

VARIOUS

Artisan mustard from Picardy, with cider vinegar but also with beer or honey
Pickleweed (*Salicornia*), preserved in vinegar .... PI, PA

CONFECTIONERY AND SMALL DELICACIES

Babelutte de Lille: a caramel candy
Bêtise de Cambrai: a small pillow-shaped candy traditionally flavored with mint, striped with caramelized sugar.
Cacoule: a triangular candy with caramel flavor .... NO
Chique de Bavay: mint-flavored candy .... NO
Linden honey .... PI
Macaron of Amiens, with fruits and honey
Nieulle: a sweet cookie .... NO
Tuile du Beauvaisis: almond tuile cookies, chocolate paste
Vergeoise: beet sugar, blond to brown according to the cooking process

DRINKS AND SPIRITS

Bavaisienne, Blanche de Lille, Ch'Ti, Choulette, Cuvée des Jonquilles, Épi de Facon, Jenlain, Brown Palten of Flanders, Pastor Ale, Brown Pelforth, Brasseur Reserve, Sans-Culottes, Saint-Landelin, Saint-Leonard, Scotch Triumph, Trois Monts . . .
Chicory .... NP
Cider of Thiérache
Colvert beer: Péronne
Genièvre Flanders-Artois .... GI
Northern beer: Angélus, Anosteké,
Perlè: red currant wine
Poiré: pear cider .... NO

MEN AND WOMEN (CRITICS, CHEFS, ETC.)

Dumas, Alexandre (1802–1870), writer, born in Villers-Cotterêts, author of *Le Grand dictionnaire de cuisine*
Gauthier, Roland (born in 1951); Alexandre (born in 1979): La Grenouillère, La Madeleinesous-Montreuil
Parmentier, Antoine (1737–1813), promoter of potato consumption in France
Vatel, François (around 1625–1671), maître d', born in Allaines

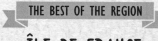

THE BEST OF THE REGION

ÎLE-DE-FRANCE

BR: BRIE; GA: GÂTINAIS; SE: SEINE-ET-MARNE

AT THE BUTCHER'S

Lamb of Île-de-France
Poultry of Gâtinais .... PGI
Poultry of Houdan .... PGI
Rabbit of Gâtinais

AT THE FARMER'S
Asparagus of Argenteuil
Chasselas grape of Thomery
Cherry of Montmorency
Dandelion of Montmagny
Faro apple .... BR
Peach of Montreuil
Peppermint of Milly-la-Forêt
Reine-Claude de Chambourcy (plum)
Watercress of Méréville
White button mushrooms
(Champignon de Paris)

AT THE BAKER'S
Baguette
Croissant
Parisian brioche
Viennese bread

AT THE CHARCUTIER
Boudin noir of Paris
Garlic sausage
Jambon de Paris (slightly salted, cooked
pressed ham)
Parisian-style pork head cheese: pork head,
cooked tongues, in a savory jelly
Pâté de volailles of Houdan, in a pastry crust,
with liver and poultry meat

AT THE CHEESE MAKER'S
Brie de Meaux .... AOP
Brie de Melun .... AOP
Brie de Montereau, de Nangis
Brillat-Savarin .... PGI
Coulommiers
Fontainebleau: fromage frais with beaten
cream added

SAVORY DISHES
Beef cooked in coarse salt
Boeuf ficelle; beef cooked suspended by a
string in vegetable broth
Cauliflower gratin
Eggs with tripe: with béchamel and onions
Frivolities de La Villette: breaded rams' testicles
Gratinée des Halles: an onion soup
Marinated herring fillets with potatoes
Matelote de Bougival: a stew of eels, carp,
gudgeons, and crayfish
Miroton: boiled beef with onions
Navarin, or mutton stew
Peas à la française: peas in butter, with lettuce
and onions
Père Lathuille–style chicken, with artichokes
and potatoes
Potage Argenteuil: a soup with asparagus
Potage Crécy: a soup with carrots
Potage Parisien: a soup with leeks and potatoes
Potage Saint-Germain: a soup with peas
Poularde chicken à la briarde, in cider and
mustard
Purée Musard, with green beans of Arpajon
Rib eye steak in a marchand de vin (a sauce
prepared with red wine and shallots)
Sauce des Halles: a sauce made with bell
pepper, shallot, and red wine vinegar
Veal head in a gribiche sauce: cooked in
a white sauce, the gribiche sauce is served
separately
Veal liver Bercy; Bercy butter: made with
shallots, white wine, butter, and marrow

DESSERTS, CAKES
AND PASTRIES
Amandine: a tartlet with an almond filling
Bourdaloue tart: flaky pastry, half pears
poached in almond syrup

Galette des rois ("kings' cake"): prepared dry
or with a frangipane filling
Manqué: a cake made of eggs, sugar, butter,
and flour
Mocha: a sponge cake with coffee buttercream
Mona Lisa: ganache and coffee buttercream
Niflette: puff pastry tart with pastry cream,
flavored with orange blossom .... SE
Opéra: layers of biscuit sponge cake
Paris-Brest
Puits d'amour ("fount of love"): in former
times, a pastry made of puff pastry in the
shape of a well, today filled with pastry cream
Saint-Honoré: puff pastry, pâte à choux,
Chiboust cream, and caramel
Savarin: usually, and incorrectly, referred to as
a "baba au rhum"

VARIOUS
Meaux mustard, coarse grain
Vinegar of Lagny, made of pure alcohol or
flavored with plant extracts: carrot, mint,
orange, etc.

CONFECTIONERY
AND SMALL DELICACIES
Candied rose petals: jam .... BR
Chouquettes (cream puffs studded with coarse
sugar)
Honey of Gâtinais
"Parisian" macaron/"sandwich": two smooth
macarons cookies with a flavored cream center
Sucre d'orge des religieuses de Moret:
sugar candy made by the nuns of Moret ...... GA

DRINKS AND SPIRITS
Cider of Brie
Clacquesin: liquor from an infusion of
Norway pine resin and plants
Grand Marnier: liqueur made from cognac
and bitter oranges
Noyau de Poissy: liqueur made from cognac
and an infusion of apricot kernels

MEN AND WOMEN
(CRITICS, CHEFS, ETC.)
Alléno, Yannick (born 1968): Pavillon
Ledoyen, Paris
Androuët, Pierre (1915–2005), cheese maker:
Androuet, Paris
Anton, Frédéric (born in 1964): Le Pré
Catelan, Paris
Babinski, Henri Joseph Séverin (aka Ali-Bab)
(1855–1931), author of culinary works, born
in Paris
Beauvilliers, Antoine (1754–1817), opened the
first prominent grand restaurant in Paris
Camdeborde, Yves (born in 1964): Le
Comptoir du Relais, Paris
Carême, Marie-Antoine (known as "Antonin")
(1784–1833), pastry chef and cook, born in Paris
Carton, François Francis (1879–1945): Lucas
Carton, Paris
Delaveyne, Jean (1919–1996): Le Camélia,
Bougival
Demonfaucon, Jean-Baptiste (1882–1956):
Le Georges V, Paris
Ducasse, Alain (born in 1956): Alain Ducasse
at the Plaza Athénée, Paris
Dugléré, Adolphe (1805–1884): Café Anglais,
Paris
Dutournier, Alain (born in 1949): Le Carré
des Feuillants, Paris
Escoffier, Auguste (1846–1935): Ritz, Paris
Frechon, Éric (born in 1963): L'Épicure
(Bristol Hotel), Paris
Gagnaire, Pierre (born in 1950): Pierre
Gagnaire, Paris
Gilbert, Phileas (1857–1942): Bonvalet, Paris
Gouffé, Jules (1807–1877), cook of Napoléon
III, born in Paris

Grimod de la Reynière, Alexandre Balthazar
Laurent (1758–1837), first gastronomic critic,
born in Paris
Guillot, André (1908–1993): Auberge du
Vieux Marly, Marly-le-Roi
Hermé, Pierre (born in 1961), pastry chef:
Pierre Hermé Paris
Ladurée, Louis Ernest (1836–1904), pastry
chef, born in Paris
Lasserre, René (1912–2006): Lasserre, Paris
Le Divellec, Jacques (born in 1932):
Restaurant Le Divellec, Paris
Lenôtre, Gaston (1920–2009): Lenôtre, Plaisir
Lesquer, Christian (born in 1962): Le V, Paris
Marx, Thierry (born in 1962): Sur Mesure by
Thierry Marx (Mandarin Oriental), Paris
Millau, Christian (known as Christian
Dubois-Millot) (1928–2017), French food
critic born in Paris
Montagné, Prosper (1865–1948): Restaurant
Prosper Montagné, Paris
Mourier, Leopold (1862–1923): Le café de
Paris, Le Fouquet's, Paris
Nignon, Édouard (1865–1934): Restaurant
Larue, Paris
Oliver, Raymond (1909–1990): Le Grand
Véfour, Paris
Passard, Alain (born in 1956): L'Arpège, Paris
Piège, Jean-François (born in 1970): Le
Grand Restaurant, Paris
Pomiane, Edouard Alexandre de (known as
Édouard Pozerski) (1875–1964), author of
culinary works, born in Paris
Procopio, Coltelli Francesco (1650/1651–
1727), founder of Café Procope
Robuchon, Joël (born in 1945): L'Atelier
Étoile /Saint-Germain, Paris
Savoy, Guy (born in 1953): Restaurant Guy
Savoy, Paris
Senderens, Alain (1939–2017): Senderens, Paris
Soyer, Alexis (1909–1858), grand French cook
born in Meaux, has spent his entire career in
England
Terrail, André (1877–1954); Claude
(1917–2006); André (born in 1980): La Tour
d'Argent, Paris
Vaudable (Louis) (1902–1983): Maxim's, Paris
Vrinat, André (1903–1990), Jean-Claude
(1936–2008): Le Taillevent, Paris

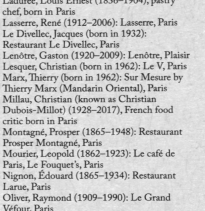

THE BEST OF THE REGION

NORMANDY

AU: PAYS D'AUGE; BR: PAYS DE BRAY; CA: CALVADOS;
CO: COTENTIN; CX: PAYS DE CAUX; MA: MANCHE;
MO: MONT-SAINT-MICHEL; NL: NORMANDY LITTORALE; OR: ORNE

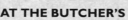

AT THE BUTCHER'S
Cauchois pigeon
Duck of Rouen
Hen of Gournay
Norman breeds of beef, suckling calves
Norman goose
Norman rabbit
Pork of Bayeux
Poultry of Normandy................................. PGI
Salt-meadow lambs of
Mont-Saint-Michel.................................... AOP
Sheeps of the Manche: the Cotentin, the
Avranchin, the Roussin of the Hague

AT THE FARMER'S
Apples of Normandy: Benedictine, Calville
Rouge, Pomme d'Éclat, Reinette of Caux,
Pomme de Revers, etc.
Cabbage of Saint-Saëns
Carrot of Créances
Cauliflower of Val de Saire
Cherries of the Seine Valley
Leek of Carentan
Leek of Créances....................................... PGI
Plums of Jumièges
Poire de fisée (pear) .... BR
Purple radish of Gournay
Turnip of Martot
Watercress of Pays de Caux

AT THE FISHMONGER'S
Abalone
"Blonde de Barfleur" mussel
Blue whiting
Cockle
Common dab
Common seabass
Common sole
Crab
Fresh cod
Gray and pink shrimp
Gray sea bream
Gurnards
Herring, fresh, salted and/or smoked
Lobster
Mackerel
Mussel of Bouchot
Normandy oyster
Nursehound and tope shark
Plaice
Praire clam
Red rock mullet
Salt cod
Scallop
Small poularde clam
Spider crab
Thornback ray
Turbot
Velvet crab
Whelk
Whiting
Yellow pollack

AT THE BAKER'S
Brasillé: salted butter croissant pastry,
rectangular in shape; plain, with apples, or
with raspberries
Brioche moulinoise, round, in clump balls of
dough
Brioche of Vast
Buckwheat bread
Fallue: flat brioche
Pain à soup: round, dried,
to be soaked in the soup .... CO
Pain brié, a very compact bread
Pain plié ("folded bread"), tall,
which owes its name to its shape .... NL

AT THE CHARCUTIER
Andouillette of Rouen
Boudin blanc of Le Havre
Boudin of Coutances: blood, raw onion, fat,
and pork intestine
Boudin of Mortagne-au-Perche, with onion
Cervelas de L'Aigle: dried and smoked sausage
Sang cuit de Cherbourg: pork blood terrine
Saucisson du marin, made with dried
whole pork loin.. CX
Skewered tripe from La Ferté-Macé: pieces of
beef tripe rolled and skewered
Smoked ham of Cotentin
True andouille of Vire, smoked

AT THE CHEESE MAKER'S

Camembert de Normandie ... AOP
Cream of Isigny ... AOP
Isigny butter ... AOP
Livarot ... AOP
Neufchâtel ... BR AOP
Pavé d'Auge
Pont-l'Évêque ... AOP
Trappe of Bricquebec

SAVORY DISHES

Auge valley chicken, cooked in a casserole with mushrooms, calvados, cider, and crème fraîche
Blanquette of leeks with potatoes, in a casserole with cider, onions, and crème fraîche
Braised lettuces, with onions, carrots, and bacon
Brill cauchoise, baked: with chopped shallots and a duxelles of mushrooms, with cider and crème fraîche
Buckwheat bouillie (a porridge), served hot or cold, or can be browned in a pan ... MA
Caen-style tripe: beef tripe, stomach and feet; cooked with vegetables (carrots, celery, leek, and onions) with cider and calvados
Cod of Honfleur, baked: with potatoes and herbs
Coquilles Saint-Jacques à l'avranchaise: scallops filled with minced scallops with cider, garlic, and shallot
Coquilles Saint-Jacques à la honfleuraise: a kind of stew with scallops with cream, calvados, and cider
Demoiselles de Cherbourg à la nage: small lobsters in a court-bouillon made with white wine
Duck à la rouenaise (duck in blood): after the first cooking, the duck carcass is crushed in a press to recover all the blood and used for the sauce; the legs and wings are breaded, the breast is prepared sliced with a sauce made from the blood and liver
Eggs à la fécampoise: stuffed with shrimp and mushrooms
Escalopes de veau à la normande: veal cutlets in cream, with onions, mushrooms, and calvados
Fillets of sole à la normande, sole fillet with mussels, shrimp, and mushrooms; includes a velouté sauce made from sole stock and cooking liquid from mushrooms
Gigot à la normande, stewed with cider; a leg of lamb accompanied by a sauce: cooking juices deglazed with cider, butter, and cream
Mackerel with sorrel: baked wrapped in sorrel leaves
Marmite dieppoise: a soup made from premium fish—monkfish, turbots, brill—and seafood (langoustines, mussels, prawns, scallops)
Matelote of Caudebec: eels with cider (a stew)
Meunier's soup, based on a preparation of chicken breasts and small field (agaric) mushrooms ... OR
Mussels with cream
Normandy braised beef, wrapped in bacon, marinated in cider, calvados, and aromatics; cooked in a casserole in broth and with the marinade, with garlic and onion
Rabbit saddle à la cauchoise, cooked in casserole in a bard of bacon with shallots, butter, crème fraîche, and white wine
Rabbit stuffed à la havraise, cooked in a casserole, stuffed with a pigs' feet; served cold
Roast pork with apples and cider, with calvados and crème fraîche
Rognons de veau à la normande (Norman veal kidneys): with bacon, baby onions, and crème fraîche
Salade cauchoise: with potatoes, celery, ham, cream, and cider vinegar ... OR
Salade verte à la normande, a green salad served with a cream sauce and cider vinegar
Sheeps' feet à la rouennaise
Shrimp à la Cherbourg, in cider
Smoked herrings à la fécampoise: with boiled eggs, covered with béchamel sauce
Soupe aux peis de mai (spring peas): with string beans
Warmed oysters in a Normandy pommeau: with an apple-based sauce, a *pommeau*—a mixture made from apples and calvados—and cream

DESSERTS AND PASTRIES

Baked apples, in honey and cider
Beurré normand: a light cake with apples, calvados, and raisins
Bourdelot or douillon: apple or pear in pastry
Mirliton de Rouen: a tartlet in puff pastry filled with a light almond cream mixture
Pear pâté: a pear pie
Pommes à la grivette: grated apples mixed with curdled milk
Tarte aux pommes d'Yport: a tart filled with apples, sugar, calvados, and crème fraîche
Tarte normande, with apples
Teurgoule: rice pudding with cinnamon

VARIOUS

Cider vinegar
Soup fat/Norman fat: fat of veal kidneys mixed with vegetables (carrot, turnip, onions, etc.) and herbs (thyme, laurel, nutmeg, etc.); solidified, very aromatic, used as a condiment for soup ... MA

CONFECTIONERY AND SMALL DELICACIES

Caramel d'Isigny: made with butter or milk or cream from Isigny, flavored or not
Coques d'or du Mont-Saint-Michel: cooked sugar, flaky pastry with chocolate praline
Mirliton de Pont-Audemer: a cylinder of puff pastry filled with a praline mousse, sealed at both ends with dark chocolate
Raisiné de pomme/Pommé, gelée: with concentrate of unsweetened apple juice added ... CA
Sucre de pomme de Rouen: a stick of cooked sugar with apple flavors
Various sablés normands (shortbread cookies) from Caen, Trouville, Domfrontais . . .

DRINKS AND SPIRITS

Bénédictine: a plant-infused liqueur, spices, and aromatics ... CX
Calvados ... GI
Ciders (from Bessin, Cotentin, Pays de Bray, Perche . . .)
Cotentin cider ... AOP
Domfrontais calvados ... GI
Normandy cider ... PGI
Pays d'Auge calvados ... GI
Pays d'Auge Cambremer cider ... AOP
Pays d'Auge cider ... AOP
Pear eaux-de-vie (Poirés)
Poiré Domfront ... AOP
Pommeau de Normandie: a blend of apple must and calvados ... GI

MEN AND WOMEN (CRITICS, CHEFS, ETC.)

Dorin brothers: Marcel (1887–1967); Lucien (1889–1956): La Couronne, Rouen
Gault, Henri (known as Henri Gaudichon) (1929–2000), food critic
Harel, Marie (1761–1844), legend claims her as the inventor of Camembert cheese
Poulard, Annette (1851–1931): Hostellerie de Mère Poulard, Mont-Saint-Michel
Taillevent (Guillaume Tirel) (1314?–1395), first squire cook of Charles VI

THE BEST OF THE REGION

NOUVELLE AQUITAINE

AG: AGENAIS; BE: BÉARN; BO: BORDEAUX; CH: CHARENTE; CM: CHARENTE-MARITIME; CO: CORRÈZE; CR: CREUSE; DO: DORDOGNE; DS: DEUX-SÈVRES; GA: GASCONGE; GE: GERS; GI: GIRONDE; HV: HAUTE-VIENNE; LA: LANDES; LI: LIMOUSIN; LO: LOT-AND-GARONNE; MA: MARCHE; MP: MARAIS POITEVIN; PB: PAYS BASQUE; PE: PÉRIGORD; PO: POITOU; PY: PYRÉNÉES-ATLANTIQUES; SO: SUD-OUEST

AT THE BUTCHER'S

Blonde d'Aquitaine (cow)
Butchering kid (young goat) ... PO
Capon of Barbezieux ... CH PGI
Capon of the Périgord ... PGI
Chicken of the Périgord ... PGI
Cow of Bazas ... GE, GI, PGI
Cow of Chalosse ... LA
Egg of Marans ... CM
Gray goose of the southwest
Kintoa, Basque pig ... AOP
Lamb of Pauillac ... GI PGI
Lamb of Poitou-Charentes ... PGI
Lamb of the Limousin ... PGI
Lamb of the Périgord ... PGI
Limousine, cattle and sheep breeds; Cul Noir (breed of pig)
Palombe (wood pigeon) ... GI, LA, LG, PY
Parthenaise: a bovine breed ... PO
Pork of the Limousin ... PGI
Pork of the southwest ... PGI
Poularde (chicken) of the Périgord ... PGI
Poultry of Gascony ... PGI
Poultry of the Béarn ... PGI
Poultry of the Landes ... PGI
Poultry of the Val de Sèvres ... PGI
Suckling calf ... BE, DO, LI, PB
Suckling lamb of the Pyrénées ... BE, PB, PGI
Veal of Chalais ... CH
Veal of the Limousin ... PGI
White goose of Poitou

AT THE FARMER'S

Aillet: green garlic shoot ... SO
Apple of Estre ... AOP
Apple of Limousin, golden ...
Artichoke ... PO
Artichoke of Macau ... BO
Asperges des sables des Landes (white asparagus) ... PGI
Beet (crapaudine variety) ... CM
Bilberry ... LI, MA
Bleached chestnut (raw) ... LI, MA
Bricolin/piochon: cabbage ... PO
Chestnut of the Périgord
"Cuisse de Poulet" shallot of Poitou
Espelette pepper ... PB AOP
Fig of Patacaou ... BE
Gesse: leguminous plant ... GA
Haricot-Maïs of the Béarn
Itxassou black cherry ... PB
Kiwifruit of Adour ... PGI
Kohlrabi of Limousin
Large yellow leek of Poitou
Melon of Charentes
Melon of Haut Poitou ... PGI
Melon of Nerac ... BE
Mogette: beans "Pont l'Abbé," "rognon de l'Oise" ... PO
Onion of Niort, light red
Onion of Saint-Turjan, pink, semisweet ... CM
Pear of Marsaneix ... PE
Piment d'Anglet (green chile pepper) ... PB
Piment doux long des Landes (mild chile pepper)
Porcini and bolet mushrooms ... LI, SO
Potato of the Île de Ré, spring, several varieties ... AOP
Prune of Agen ... PGI
Reine-Claude de Vars (plum) ... CO
Reinette clochard apple ... PO
Roussane de Monein (peach) ... BE
Strawberry of Prin ... PO
Strawberry of the Périgord ... PGI
Tomato of Marmande
Truffle ... PE, CO, NORD PO
Walnuts of the Périgord ... AOP

AT THE FISHMONGER'S

Anchovy
Carp
Casseron: very small cuttlefish
Chipiron: small squid
Clam
Cockle
Crayfish
Eel
Eel of the Marais Poitevin
European eel
Lamprey
Langoustine
Mussels of Bouchot ... CM
Oyster Marennes-Oléron ... CM PGI
Oysters of Arcachon
Pibale: young eel
Raiteaux: small skate
Red tuna
Salmon of Ardour
Sardine
Sea scallop
Shad
Shrimp
Wedge sole
White tuna

AT THE BAKER'S

Bordelais gâteau des rois: brioche wreath flavored with orange blossom, topped with candied citron and sugar
Cornue: elongated brioche, ending with two points at one end ... MA, LI
Correzian bread: bread pie
Fouace: brioche bread ... PO
Méture: unleavened corn-based bread ... BE
Pain tourné: a twisted bread ... LI
Sous flamme: a flat white bread slightly cooked ... CH

AT THE CHARÇUTIER

Andouille béarnaise, dried, with pork stomach
Boudin de Poitou: spinach, semolina, onions
Boudin of Béarn: large boudin; in addition to blood, contains chopped offal—head, tongue, heart, throat—pork rind, onion, etc.
Boudin of the Périgord, lean, with pork head and onions
Chestnut boudin ... LI
Easter pâté: pork meat in a pastry crust, or pork and veal, with a hard-boiled egg in the middle ... PO
Fagot charentais: a pork liver meatball in caulfat
Fressure poitevin: a pâté of offal cooked with onions in red wine
Gigourit: a pâté of head meat cooked in wine and onions, enriched with blood ... CH, PO
Giraud: serum of sheep's blood and maybe of calf's blood; cooked in veal casing ... LI
Goose or duck confit ... GRAND SO
Gratton bordelais: a conical-shaped mound of pork pieces—shoulder, loin—cooked in fat
Grenier médocain: pork stomach stuffed with pork stomachs, pork tripe, ham cut into strips, all cooked in a vegetable broth
Grillon charentais, related to rillettes; lean pork cooked in fat

Grillon limousin: minced lean bacon, with pepper and parsley
Gros grillon: pork belly cooked in goose fat..PO
Jambon de Bayonne: salted and dried ham ....PGI
Jambon de Tonneins: cooked ham in crocks or sealed containers........................LO
Jambon du Kintoa .... PB ADP
Meat andouille of Limousin, preserved in brine
Meatball pâté: meatball pie, veal round, pork rib, onion ....CR
Pâté périgourdin: pâté stuffed with foie gras
Pork belly, dried and rolled ....SO
Pork confit: roasts, fillets, cooked and then preserved in fat LI
Pork intestine charentais: pork intestine cooked in fat
Smoked sheeps' tongue: put in a balloon of veal skin, then smoked and cooked
Terrine de Nérac: game pâté stuffed with foie gras ....BE
Tricandille: strips of pork intestine and pork belly cooked in an herbed broth; to consume roasted ....GI
Tripotxa: mutton boudin, including chopped offal and onions..............................PB
Turkey ballottine: turkey meat wrapped around a stuffing of truffle, foie gras, pistachios, bacon fat, beef tongue; all surrounded by a savory jelly....................PE, SO

AT THE CHEESE MAKER'S

Beurre Charentes-Poitou............................ADP
Beurre d'Échiré..PO
Beurre des Charentes....................................ADP
Beurre des Deux Sèvres ....ADP
Bougon ....DS
Cabécou du Périgord
Caillebote/jonchée: fromage frais
Chabichou du Poitou....................................ADP
Corrézon au torchon......................................CO
Couhé-Vérac ....PO
Fromage fumé de Bardos ....PB
Gouzon ....CR
Greuil: caillé de brebis .... BE, PB
Mothais sur feuille..PO
Ossau-Iraty... PB ADP
Pigouille ....DS
Tomme des Pyrénées ....PGI
Trappe d'Échourgnac ....DO

SAVORY DISHES

Axoa: veal stew, with onions, cured country ham, green and red chile peppers
Basque piperade: gently cooked vegetables, to accompany Basque chicken, or as a dish served as a full meal, in which scrambled eggs are incorporated—made with jambon de Bayonne (ham), tomatoes, green bell peppers, onions, and garlic
Basque ttoro: a fish soup, usually using hake or conger and other seafood, with vegetables (potatoes, carrots, onions, tomatoes, etc.)
Beef stew saintongeaise, made in a casserole dish, with carrots, shallots, and bacon
Beef tenderloin with Périgueux sauce (a rich brown sauce with Madeira and truffles)
Beef tenderloin with porcini, roasted in the oven; porcini in a pan with garlic and parsley...LI
Beetroot à la poitevine, sautéed, with sliced yellow onions
Bréjaude: bacon soup—cabbage, leeks, raves, carrots, and potatoes LI
Buckwheat crêpes .... LI, MA
Cabbage stuffed with chestnuts LI
Cagouilles à la charentaise: a preparation with onions, garlic, ham, white wine, and tomato
Cagouilles à la saintongeaise: a preparation with garlic, shallots, parsley, sausage meat, red wine, small onions, garlic, and ham
Cagouilles pot-au-feu, made in a casserole with white wine, onions, carrots, leeks, tomatoes, potatoes; to be eaten with a thin slice of bread drizzled with the strained broth and a vinaigrette
Casseron sautée à la saintongeaise, with garlic and parsley
Chaudrée : a thick fish soup with multiple versions...CM
Chestnut soup: multiple recipes, some based on chicken broth, with onion from Brive LI
Chicken sautéd with porcini, à la limousine, cooked in a casserole dish with garlic and onion; chicken offal and cream are used for the sauce
Chipirons à la luzienne, cooked in a sauce made with tomatoes, onions, and Espelette pepper
Cruchade bordelaise, landaise: a porridge made from cornmeal ground very fine
Cul de bicot rôti à l'ail vert (rump of young goat roasted with green garlic); coated at the end of the cooking time with a panade of sorrel, spring garlic, and white wine
Duck with black cherries, in a casserole........LI
Éclade: mussels cooked over a fire of pine needles..CM
Eel in court-bouillon à la médocaine, with white onions, prunes, and garlic. The sauce is thickened with eel blood.
Eels in parsley, panfried ....PO
Embeurré de chou: green cabbage cooked in boiling water then crushed with butter added
Enchaud périgourdin: pork confit in lard
Entrecôte (rib steak) Bordelaise with shallot sauce, red wine, and beef marrow
Estouffat: a beef stew...SO
Farcedure: a leavened dough, boiled— in soup or stew particularly..............................LI
Foie gras d'oie clouté aux truffes: fresh goose foie gras studded with truffles baked en papillote, accompanied by a sauce made from truffles, onions, and shallots ....PE
Fresh bean soup ....MP
Fricassee of Cul Noir (pork; Basque pig) with chestnuts: pork loin cooked in a casserole, with onions, carrots, blanched chestnuts..LI
Fried small skates..CM
Garbure béarnaise: a stew of roughly chopped vegetables; in Béarn, cabbages and beans are always included; usually with meat, jambon de Bayonne (ham), for example
Garlèche omelet: with roach fish LI
Gigot périgourdin à la couronne d'ail: leg of lamb cooked in a casserole with 60 cloves of garlic, originating from Montbazillac; flambéd with an eau-de-vie before serving
Goose or duck confit: quartered pieces cooked in fat .... PE, LA, SO
Goose or duck foie gras: foie gras terrine recipes, warm foie gras, fresh foie gras with apples or grapes . . . IGP Duck Foie Gras from the southwest (Chalosse, Gascony, Gers, Landes, Périgord, Quercy)
Green mallow soup: uses various herbs and greens, such as Swiss chard, spinach, chicory, etc., and mallow .... BE, PB
Jaud fricassee: rooster flambéd with cognac then cooked in a casserole dish with bacon, onions, mushrooms, and white wine ....CH
Lamprey à la bordelaise, in red wine, jambon de Bayonne (ham), leeks, and garlic. The blood is incorporated into the sauce
Lavignons, sauce of/"Fausses palourde clams": pan sautéd, with white wine, shallots, with parsley and mixture of cream and eggs added at the last moment.......................................CM
Leg of lamb braised with porcini mushrooms in a casserole; with tomatoes, porcini, and minced garlic and parsley..............................LI
Limousine snails: stuffed with a mixture of garlic, parsley, bread crumbs, and butter
Marmitako: tuna stew with potatoes, onions, bell peppers, and tomatoes ....PB
Matahami béarnais, baked: potatoes, pork belly, minced onion and garlic
Milhassou à la corrézienne: grated potato cakes
Mojhettes piates: white beans: in a pan with onions, carrots, and garlic
Mouclade: mussels with white wine, with cream and curry ....CM
Pain de porée: minced leeks with butter and a mixture of cream and egg yolks..........CH
Panfried duck breasts à la chalossaise, peppered
Pâté de pommes de terre: potato pie........ LI, MA
Pâté de porcini: flaky pastry or brioche pie with raw ham, onion, and crème fraîche
Pigeons with herb shoots, topped with a preparation composed of pigeon livers and gizzards, ham, garlic, aromatic herbs, shallots, white button mushrooms, and white wine . . .
Piochons vinaigrette: small "button" green cabbage heads ....PO
Poitevin compote of goose or duck: slow-cooked meats with tomatoes, onions, and white wine
Poitevin farci: a stuffed cabbage; stuffed with greens, herbs, bacon, and eggs
Pommes sarladaises: apples fried in goose fat, with minced garlic and parsley
Porcellous, stuffed cabbage leaves, using a stuffing of pork, veal, lean pork belly, garlic, and bread LI
Porcini à la bordelaise, cooked in a sauté pan, with chopped shallots, bread crumbs, chopped parsley and garlic, and a squeeze of lemon
Porcini stew à la girondine, simmered in a sauce with raw country ham, tomatoes, onions, shallot, garlic, dry white wine, and chicken broth
Porcini with cream à la limousine: cooked in a pan, with shallots
Potato casseroles, sautéed with minced herbs and shallots, topped with cream and egg yolk LI
Potatoes with garlic, cooked in beef broth and garlic then fried with goose fat ....PE
Potée limousine, made with salt pork and an andouille from La Creuse
Poulet au pot Henri IV (chicken in a pot): stuffed with jambon de Bayonne (ham), chicken offal, onion, garlic, and parsley. Cooked in a broth of vegetables, variants exist throughout the southwest
Poulet au pot périgourdine (chicken in a pot Périgord-style), stuffed with sausage meat, chicken offal, bread, chicken blood . . . Cooked in a vegetable broth. Accompanied with a sauce made from egg, walnut oil, white wine vinegar, and shallots
Poulet basquaise (Basque chicken in a pot), cooked in a casserole with jambon de Bayonne (ham), onions, Anglet Espelette peppers, tomatoes, garlic, and regional white wine
Poulet sauce rouilleuse: chicken cooked in a casserole with onions, pork belly, crushed garlic, white wine . . . The blood, liver, and heart of the chicken are used to thicken the sauce and give it its final color ....PE
Poutirous farcis au pain de siegle, baked: stuffed porcini mushrooms. The stuffing is made with rye bread crumbs, egg yolks, shallots, and garlic LI
Primes grâlées au diable: spring potatoes roasted in their pot in a diable sauce, earthenware pot ....CM
Rabbit Chabessal, very slowly cooked in a deep dish, with white wine with a stuffing made from pork and veal LI
Rabbit stew with prunes, marinated in a red wine preparation, with onions, carrots, cloves, Armagnac, oil; cooked in a casserole, with prunes in wine, bacon, onions, and a marinade ....AG
Rabbit with red sauce, cooked in a casserole: containing sauce made with blood and rabbit liver, butter, and onions.......................PO
Ris de veau à la landaise: veal sweetbreads, cooked in a casserole, with mushrooms, white wine, shallots, and carrots
River trout with bacon and walnuts à la corrézienne, sautéed, with minced bacon, walnuts, and chervil
River trout with herbs à la creusoise, in a court-bouillon with herbs and white wine
Rôti de veau fermier aux noix: roast free-range veal with walnuts, cooked in a casserole, with vegetables and chopped nuts
Salmis of pigeon, roasted and topped with a red wine sauce mixed with pigeon hearts and livers, onions, carrots, shallots, ham, and garlic ....SO
Salt cod with beans: flaked cod in white beans, mixed with a sauce made from garlic, leek, and lard.............................BE
Salt cod with potatoes, à la briviste: baked— crumbled cod, slices of potato, and parsley
Salt cod with potatoes: flaked cod, au gratin with potatoes ....PB
Sanguette/sanquette: a small crêpe made from poultry blood, with onion, garlic, shallots, and bread...SO, LI
Sauce aux lumas d'Aunis: a sauces with snails, made in a casserole, cooked in red wine, with onions, garlic, and shallot
Sauce of chicken of Landes, made in a casserole, with raw ham, onions, white wine, tomatoes, and crushed garlic. The liver and the heart of the chicken help bind the sauce
Sautéd pibales (baby eels) with chile pepper sauce, minced garlic, and Espelette pepper ....PB
Sautéd pibales (baby eels) with garlic and parsley...CH
Soupe à l'ouzille (sorrel soup) ....PO
Soupe au giraumon: made with turban squash
Stuffed goose neck: the neck makes a cylinder; the stuffing is made from goose meat, especially offal .... PE, LA, SO
Tench à la poitevin, sautéed; a tench (a fish) soup, with a sauce made from shallots, garlic, parsley, and wine vinegar
Tourin à la tomate: made with tomato, onions, and the fat from a confit.................LA
Tourin blanchi du Périgord: a garlic and onion soup—many variations, such as the béarnaise ouillade (ollada)
Tourin corrézien: a soup of pork belly, bacon, tomatoes, and sorrel
Tourtière de poulet aux salsifis (a chicken pie with salsify)..........................CO
Tourtière poitevine au poulet (a meat pie in flaky pastry); with shallots, sausage meat, and ham
Tripe à l'angoumoise (beef tripe in a baked casserole); with shallot, garlic, carrot, celery, and white wine
Truffles en papillotes, baked, in a thin bard of fat.......................................PE
Veal liver Bordelaise, made in a casserole, liver with garlic and bacon, wrapped in caulfat with shallots and chopped porcini
Veal shank in Pineau, made in a casserole with carrots, leeks, garlic, tomatoes, and Pineau . . .
Vermée charentaise: Eel slices in a red wine court-bouillon, with carrots, onions, and garlic; finished sautéd in a pan with onions, bacon, and some of the strained court-bouillon
Wedge sole meunière...CM

DESSERTS AND PASTRIES

Aréna: a soft almond cake ....HV
Boulaigous limousins: large, thick crêpes
Cassemuseaux: crunchy cookies made with fromage frais, flavored with rum, lemon, or orange blossom ....PO
Chestnut cake, many variations .... LI, MA
Clafoutis, black cherries, with pits .... MA, LI
Crêpes with Périgord anise: infusion of aniseeds incorporated into the dough
Crespet: a large puffed beignet ....BE
Creusois: a soft cake with hazelnuts
Dame blanche ("white lady") du Poitou, floating island: shaped beaten egg whites
Flognarde: clafoutis with or without fruit, such as apples, or pears in particular .... MA, LI
Fromaget (tart)/cheesecake (flaky pastry, batter made from fresh goat cheese) ....PO
Galette de plomb: simple sweet cake made from flour, butter, milk or cream, and eggs...LI
Gâteau à la broche ("spit cake"): a cone-shaped cake, bristling with coarse spines formed by layers of dough added gradually while the cake is turning .... BE, PB
Gâteau basque: a slightly sandy exterior, creamy interior, almond flavored, filled with pastry cream or cherry jam
Gâteau saintongeais: soft, with almonds
Grimolle: a kind of crêpe with apple pieces mixed in the dough ....PO
Jambes de brebis ("legs of sheep") with heather honey: beignets.........................LI
Merveille: a beignet ....SO, CH, PO
Millas: a kind of flan made from cornmeal ....CM
Niniche: fondant au chocolat (a very moist chocolate cake) ....BO
Pastis bourrit: soft brioche-like cake flavored with orange blossom water, rum, and anise...BE, LA
Poitevins honey cakes: honey-based flat cakes
Russe d'Oloron: praline cream sandwiched between two cookies made from almonds, hazelnuts, and meringue ....BE
Tarte à la caillade: a cake made of cheese curds LI
Tourtisseaux de Niort: beignets ....PO
Tourtous corréziens (as their sweet version: a buckwheat crêpe)

VARIOUS

- Bordeaux wine vinegar
- Caviar of Aquitaine
- Goose fat ... SO
- Limousin heather honey
- "Petit Gris" snail, "cagouille" ... CH
- Purple mustard of Brive, made from grape must
- Salies-de-Béarn salt, salt from spring water
- Sea salt from Île de Ré
- Seaweed and pickleweed (*Salicornia*): especially in the form of a condiment, in vinegar ... CM
- Walnut oil ... GA, CM

CONFECTIONERY AND SMALL DELICACIES

- Angélique (Angelica) de Niort: candied, glacéed, in jam, in candies ... PO
- Basque turrón: scented almond paste
- Bayonne chocolate
- Bois-cassé ("broken wood"): flavored caramelized sugar shaped like a wood shard ... CM
- Broyé de Poitou: a dry shortbread galette
- Cannelé: a small cake lightly caramelized on the outside and flavored with rum ... BO
- Cartelin: a dry cake échaudé (first dipped in hot water before baking) ... PO
- Cène d'Eymoutiers: a thin crisp cake, decorated in various motifs ... HV
- Charentais galette (Saintonge): a dry cake made with soft pâte sablé (shortbread dough)
- Chocolates with aged cognac ... CH
- Coq des Rameaux: a shortbread cake in the shape of a rooster, covered with nonpareils ... CR
- Corinette: an elongated madeleine ... CH
- Cornuelle: a triangular cake originally consumed for Palm Sunday; many variations exist ... CH
- Croquant ("crunchy") de Bort, flavored with orange blossom ... CO
- Croquet de Bordeaux, made with almonds
- Délicieux de Jonzac: a cookie, close to a savoiradi (ladyfinger) ... CH
- Douzane: a small braided brioche ... CH
- Duchesse d'Angoulême: a nougatine filled with praline
- Fanchonnette de Bordeaux: a candy filled with pâte de fruit but also chocolate, with almond paste ...
- Gravette de Bordeaux: chocolate flavored with orange, filled with praline or marzipan
- Honeys from Landes, heather
- Honeys from Pays Basque: lime (linden) blossoms, chestnut tree
- Macaron of Lusignan ... PO
- Macaron of Saint-Émilion, small and moist
- Macaron of Saint-Jean-de-Luz, soft, crunchy on the outside ... PB
- Madeleine de Dax: large madeleine flavored with lemon
- Madeleine de Saint-Yrieix: with the aroma of bitter almond ... HV
- Marguerite d'Angoulême: a chocolate shaped like a daisy, flavored with candied orange peel
- Marzipan of Saint-Léonard de Noblat: a small cake with almonds ... HV
- Nougatine du Poitou: sugar cooked with ground almonds, coated with a pink royal icing
- Pine: a dry cake échaudé (first poached in hot water then baked), shaped like a penis ... CM
- Prune of Saint-Léonard-de-Noblat ... HV
- Rousquille d'Oloron: a dry cake flavored with anise and orange blossom, ring-shaped, covered with a white frosting ... BE
- Tortillon: échaudé (first poached in hot water then baked) in the shape of a crown ... AG, PE
- Tourtière: very thin pastry, appearing crumpled, filled with apples or prunes ... SO

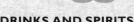

DRINKS AND SPIRITS

- Angelica liqueur of Niort: maceration-distillation in cognac ... PO
- Anisette ... BO
- Armagnac, several AOPs ... AOP
- Basque cider, very lightly sparkling
- Cognac, several appellations ... GI
- Dandelion liqueur ... CH
- Eau/walnut liquor: green walnuts macerated in alcohol then combined with mistelle/eau-de-vie ... LI, PE
- Fine Bordeaux: a wine eau-de-vie ... GI
- Floc de Gascogne rosé or white ... AOP
- Izarra yellow/green: two liqueur recipes; maceration and distillation of plants and spices (cardamom, angelica, etc.)
- Lillet blanc, rosé, rouge: combination of wines and fruit liqueurs ... BO
- Limousin cider
- Pineau des Charentes ... AOP
- Sève, from Limoges: herbal and fruit-based liqueurs: almonds, walnut pits, walnut shells . . .

MEN AND WOMEN (CRITICS, CHEFS, ETC.)

- Boulestin, Marcel (1878–1943), cook, great propagator of French cuisine in the English-speaking world, born in Poitiers
- Briffault, Eugène (1799–1854), journalist, author of *Paris à table* (1846), born in Périgueux
- Coutanceau, Richard (born in 1949): Richard Coutanceau, La Rochelle; Christopher (born in 1978): Christopher Coutanceau, La Rochelle; Grégory (born in 1975): L'Entracte, La Rochelle
- Darroze, Jean (1902–1981): Hostellerie Darroze, Villeneuve-de-Marsan
- Gardillou, Solange (born in 1939); Alain: The Moulin du Roc, Champagnac-de-Belair
- Guérard, Michel (born 1933): Les Prés d'Eugénie, Eugénie-les-Bains
- Ibarboure, Martin (born in 1958) and David (born in 1985): Briketenia, Guéthary; Philippe (born in 1950); Xabi (born in 1982); and Patrice (born in 1986): Les Frères Ibarboure, Bidart
- Lacam, Pierre (1836–1902), pastry chef, author of books, born in Saint-Amand-de-Belvès
- Laporte, Robert (1905–1885); Pierre (1931–2002): Le Café de Paris, Biarritz
- Massialot, François (1660?–1733), cook, author, born in Limoges
- Noël, André (1726–1801), cook for Frederick II of Prussia, born in Périgueux
- Parra, Christian (1939–2015): L'Auberge de la Galupe, Urt
- Soulé, Henri (1903–1966), cook, Le Pavilion in New York, born in Saubrigues
- Violier, Benoît (1971–2016), born in Saintes: Restaurant de l'Hôtel de Ville, Crissier, Switzerland

THE BEST OF THE REGION

OCCITAN

AL: ALBIGEOIS; AR: ARIÈGE; AU: AUDE; AV: AVEYRON; BI: BIGORRE; BL: BAS-LANGUEDOC; CA: CAMARGUE; CE: CÉVENNES; CH: CHALOSSE; CO: COMMINGES; CS: CAUSSES; GA: GARD; GC: GASCOGNE; GE: GERS; HE: HÉRAULT; HG: HAUTE-GARONNE; HL: HAUT-LANGUEDOC; HP: HAUTES-PYRÉNÉES; LA: LANDES; LL: LITTORAL LANGUEDOCIEN; LO: LOZÈRE; LT: LOT; ML: MONTS DE LACAUNE; OC: OCCITANIE; PE: PÉRIGORD; PO: PYRÉNÉES-ORIENTALES; QU: QUERCY; RG: ROUERGUE; RO: ROUSSILLON; SW: SUD-OUEST; TA: TARN; TO: TOULOUSE; TG: TARN-AND-GARONNE

AT THE BUTCHER'S

- Aubrac ... LO, AV
- Barèges-Gavarnie: ovine (sheep) ... HP
- Black chicken of Caussade ... QU
- Black pig of Bigorre ... AOP
- Black turkey of the Gers
- Blonde d'Aquitaine (cow) ... GE, TA, TG
- Bull of Camargue ... AOP
- Capon of the Lauragais
- Cévennes chicken ... PGI
- Fattened poultry of the Piège ... AU
- Gasconne (cow)
- Gray goose of Toulouse
- Heifer of Aubrac ... PGI
- Lamb of Lozère ... PGI
- Lamb of Quercy ... PGI
- Lamb of the Aveyron ... PGI
- Montauban pigeon
- Pork of the southwest ... PGI
- Poultry of Gascony ... PGI
- Poultry of the Gers ... PGI
- Poultry of the Languedoc ... PGI
- Poultry of the Lauragais ... PGI
- Suckling lamb of the Pyrénées ... HP PGI
- Veal from Averyon and Ségala ... PGI
- Vedell of the Catalan Pyrénées: veal ... PGI

AT THE FARMER'S

- Almond
- Artichoke of Roussillon ... PGI
- Asperges des sables (asparagus) ... LL, CA
- Béa du Roussillon: spring potato ... AOP
- Black truffle ... QU
- Black turnip of Pardailhan ... HE
- Bullion beans of Lauragais
- Celery of Elne ... RO
- Chasselas grape of Moissac ... TG AOP
- Cherry of Céret
- Chestnut ... AV, HP
- Chestnut of the Cévennes
- Chickpea of Carlencas ... HE
- Coco de Pamiers (small white bean) ... AR
- Cornichon ... HL
- Curly endive ... RO
- Fig ... BL, HL, RO
- Green asparagus of the Gers ... GE
- Melon of Lectoure ... GE
- Melon of Quercy ... PGI
- Olives (Lucques) from the Languedoc ... AOP
- Olives of Nîmes ... AOP
- Onion of Citou ... AU
- Onion of Trébons, sweet ... HP
- Parsley
- Peach of Roussillon
- Pink garlic of Lautrec ... PGI
- Porcini ... GE, HL
- Purple Garlic of Cadour ... AOP
- Red apricot of Roussillon ... AOP
- Reine-Claude Dorée (Gage tree) ... LT, TG
- Reinette apple of Vigan ... CE
- Respountsous (or Black Bryony); flowering plant in yam family ... AL, RG
- Rice of Carmargue ... PGI
- Rouge de Toulouges: sweet onion ... RO
- Strawberries of Nîmes ... PGI
- Sweet onion of Cévennes ... AOP
- Sweet onion of Lézignan ... HE
- Table grape from Clermont-l'Hérault
- Tarbais bean ... PGI
- Walnuts of Quercy
- Watermelon
- White asparagus of the Midi
- White garlic of Lomagne ... PGI

AT THE FISHMONGER'S

- Anchovies of Collioure ... PGI
- Conger ...
- Eel
- Gray and gilt-head sea bream
- Gray shrimp
- Hake
- Jols: frying fish
- Mackerel
- Mullet
- Mussels of Bouzigues
- Oysters of Bouzigues and Leucate
- Palourde and clovisse clams
- Red tuna
- Sardine
- Scorpionfish and capon
- Sea bass
- Sea snail
- Sole
- Violet (shellfish)
- Wedge clam
- West African goatfish

AT THE BAKER'S

- Aveyron fougasse: brioche
- Biterroise: brioche flavored with orange blossom water ... HE
- Christmas fougasse of Aigues-Mortes: a brioche square, with a strong taste of orange blossom
- Coque aphrodise: a brioche flavored with orange blossom and lemon ... HE
- Coque catalans: a brioche dough topped with various garnishes ... RO
- Coque quercinoise: a brioche fillled with candied fruits
- Fougasse with fritons: leftovers resulting from the manufacturing of lard ... BL
- Limoux cake: brioche in a crown covered with candied fruit ... AU
- Pain à l'anise, brioche ... AL
- Pain de Beaucaire, rectangular, split in two ... GA
- Pain paillasse de Lodève, fermented after kneading ... HE
- Pompe à l'huile, walnut oil or peanut ... AV
- Tourteau à l'anise: a crown of brioche bread with anise ... RO

AT THE CHARCUTIER

- Anduze sausage, dry ... CE
- Boudin Galabar: a large boudin noir with a stuffing made of pork head, offal, and sometimes onion; can be dried ... SO
- Boudin of Aude, contains offal and thyme flower
- Bougnette: a pork meatball in a crêpe ... AL, AR, HE
- Cansalada/sagi: pork fat ... RO
- Coudenat: pork rind sausage ... TA
- Dry ham of Lacaune: whole dried ham from Montagne Noire ... PGI
- Dry sausage with perch, lean pork meat and fat, encasing a perch and dried ... ML, AV
- Embotits: a family of sausages, in casings ... RO
- Fetge: salted and dried pork liver ... AL, AU
- Fricandeau: pork meatball ... AU
- Friton fin: chopped offal cooked in pork fat ... GC, HL
- Friton gros: whole offal, ears, tongues ... AV
- Gambajo: dry ham ... RO
- Jambon noir (black ham) of Bigorre ... AOP
- Juniper pâté, made of pork liver ... LO
- Manoul: a small pouch made of lamb belly containing mutton offal ... LO
- Maôche sausage: Swiss chard and pork ... LO
- Melsat: sausage, particularly with pork offal, bread, and eggs ... TA, AV
- Pâté Catalan, with pork liver
- Sac d'os: pork casing filled with bone pieces—ribs, tail, ears—preserved with salt or salt-dried ... LO
- Saucisson des moissons (sausage): large dry ovoid sausage made from fat and lean pork ... LO
- Sausage in oil, dry, made from lean meat and fat of pork, preserved in the oil ... ML, AV
- Sausage of Lacaune, dried, very lean but including diced fat ... ML, TA
- Sausage of Vallabrègues, dried and smoked, made from beef and pork ... GA
- Stuffed dry leg and ear: stuffed with pork tenderloin and red wine ... LO
- Toulouse sausage, fresh, made from coarsely chopped lean meat
- Trenel: lamb belly stuffed with ham and pork belly ... AV
- Tripous du Rouergue: tripe of veal stuffed with a preparation of tripe and ham

AT THE CHEESE MAKER'S

- Bleu des Causses ... AV, LT, LO AOP
- Cabécou ... QU, RG
- Laguiole ... AV, LO AOP
- Pélardon ... CE, CS AOP
- Peril ... AV, TA, CS
- Rocamadour ... QU AOP
- Roquefort ... AV AOP
- Tome with raw milk from Couserans ... AR

Tome de Barousse .... HP
Tome de Lozère
Tomme des Pyrénées .... PGI

SAVORY DISHES

Aillolis LL
Aligot de l'Aubrac: a very stringy cheese purée, using fresh tome
Azinat: a soup, includes multiple varations: vegetables—green cabbage, carrots, potatoes, etc.—and meat (shank) .... AR
Boles de picolat: meatballs—beef, sausage—stewed with tomato sauce, bacon, ham, olives, onions; served with white beans .... RO
Bourride of monkfish à la sétoise: a soup with leeks, carrots, Swiss chard, and onions
Brandade of Nîmes
Bullinada: a cousin of bouillabaisse: including sea bass, monkfish, scorpionfish, etc., with potatoes and sagi (rancid bacon) .... RO
Camarguaise monkfish civet: monkfish fillets cooked in a sauce made from red wine, shallot, and onion. The sauce is enriched with cuttlefish, goose or duck confit, the pieces cooked in fat .... GE, HG, LT
Cargolada: snails cooked in embers, filled with gently cooked bacon, eaten with bread spread with aioli .... RO
Cassoulet of Castelnaudary, Toulouse, and Carcassonne
Catalan anchovies, with cooked red pepper strips, chopped garlic, and parsley
Escargouillade: snails in a sauce made from ham, onions, shallots, white wine, and garlic .... CO, AR
Estofat: meat marinated in red wine then cooked as an étouffé with various ingredients: bacon, onion, tomato, garlic, potatoes, and fresh mushrooms .... RO
Estofinado rouergat: stockfish rehydrated and crumbled, mixed with mashed potatoes, cream, and garlic
Estoufade de cèpes (porcini) à la gasconne, a slowly stewed dish cooked in a casserole with white wine, ham, and garlic
Estouffat appaméen: Coco de Pamiers (small white beans) cooked in a casserole with raw ham, carrots, bacon, garlic, and tomatoes
Falette d'Espalion: stuffed veal breast, whose recipes vary greatly: made with Swiss chard, ham, bacon, chestnuts, etc., served sliced .... AV
Flèque: potato stew slowly simmered with pork belly, thyme, and bay leaf .... LO
Garbure, multiple recipes: stew of vegetables, roughly chopped; usually includes meat, either goose or duck confit in particular .... GE, BI
Gardiane de taureau, a stew: red wine marinade, onion, garlic, celery, carrots, orange zest, etc. Served with Camargue rice .... CA
Gilt-head sea bream with white wine from the Languedoc, with tomatoes, garlic, shallots, and onions
Goose or duck foie gras recipes: foie gras terrine, warm foie gras (PGI Southwest Duck Foie Gras) .... CH, GC, GE, LA, PE, QU
Goose stew with Cahors wine: pieces of goose marinated in red wine made in a casserole dish with onion, garlic, the marinade, and bacon, incorporating sautéed porcini before serving
Gras-double (ox tripe) à la albigeoise: cooked in vegetable broth then mixed with minced raw ham and enriched with saffron
Llagostada: a lobster civet—yellow onions, garlic, tomato, ham, banyuls . . .
Massacanat de Bigorre: a large omelet filled with veal
Millas; various preparations, sweet and salty, made from cornmeal .... OC
Montpellier butter, a compound butter prepared with watercress, tarragon, parsley, chervil, and spinach, used to accompany fish
Mourtayrol rouergat: a pot-au-feu with cured country ham, beef, cabbage, carrots, and turnips . . .
Ollada: a soup of pork, bacon, potato, cabbage, carrots, leek, and white beans .... RO
Pâtés de Pézenas: a cylinder of dough surrounding minced sheep, sweetened
Porcini mushrooms, fried .... HG
Pork fricassee of Limoux: includes lean meat, liver, kidneys, cured country ham, stewed with white wine, onion, garlic, tomato paste; served with white beans
Poularde à la Toulouse, a stuffing made from poultry offal, Toulouse sausage, garlic; cooked in a casserole dish with white wine, onions, and tomatoes
Poultry pie with salsify .... QU, RG
Pouteille, a stew: beef, pigs' feet, shallots, potatoes, and cooked in wine .... LO
Rabbit in saupiquet: roasted, covered with saupiquet, a spicy sauce with garlic, onion, vinegar, and wine .... RG
Red soup of Sète, made with small fish and small freshwater pond crabs
Rouzole: a meat galette made of ham, rancid bacon, and *ventrèche* (pork belly fillets) .... AR
Squid prepared à la sétoise, stuffed with pork and veal
Stuffed goose neck: the neck is an empty cylinder; the stuffing is made from goose meat, including offal .... GE, HG, LT
Stuffed mussels à la sétoise, stuffed with pork and veal, cooked in a tomato sauce with Noilly Prat vermouth
Thin sardine fillet tarts, with onions and tomatoes .... BL
Tourin: soup made with garlic, goose fat, and sage—various recipes, in Toulouse egg whites are incorporated
Tureau à la Saint-Gilloise: beef fillet marinated in olive oil and herbs, topped with a preparation combining a pepper sauce and a tapenade .... CA
Veal Aillade: a very garlicky stew, with fresh tomatoes or tomato sauce .... GC

DESSERTS, CAKES, AND PASTRIES

Apple Gascon croustade/pastis: a round cake in very thin and "crumpled" puff pastry .... GE, LT
Bras de gitan ("arm of the gypsy"): rolled cake, sponge cake with lemon custard .... RO
Cougnettes: beignets .... LT
Coupetade: stale bread dipped in milk mixed with a flan base; with prunes or dried fruits .... LO
Crème Catalan: milk, eggs, sugar, cornstarch
Fône: flaky pastry, with a "brousse" (cheese) base, a product of the heating of sheep's whey .... AV, TA
Gâteau à la broche ("spit cake"): a cone-shaped cake, bristling with coarse spines formed by layers of dough added gradually while the cake is turning .... AV, HP
Gloria: Savoie cake flavored with lemon and almonds .... AU
Marzipan from Montbazens: made without fat .... AV
Milhassou with pumpkin: a sweet cake made of pumpkin and cornmeal .... HG
Millas: sweet preparations made from cornmeal .... GC, LL
Oreillette (beignets, flavored with lemon or orange blossom) LL
Rissole: flaky pastry, filled, savory or sweet; using prunes in Aveyron
Soleil de Marcillac: a rather dry cake in the shape of the sun, made with almond flour .... AV
Tarte à l'encalat: a crust of flaky pastry, a sweet filling made from the cow's-milk curd .... AV

VARIOUS

Olive oil from Nîmes .... BL AOP
"Petit Gris" snail
Sea salt .... CA, AU
Walnut oil .... HL

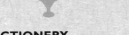

CONFECTIONERY AND SMALL DELICACIES

Alléluia de Castelnaudary ("hallelujah of Castelnaudary"): a dry Berlingot de Cauterets cookie: sugar candy, various flavors .... HP
Berlingot de Pézenas: flavored sugar candy .... HE
Cachou Lajaunie: a paste made from licorice .... TO
Cévennes honey: acacia, heather, calluna, fir tree honeydew .... PGI
Croquant de Cordes: a crunchy almond cake with whole almonds .... TA
Croquant de Mende: a crunchy cookie with almonds .... LO
Croquant Villaret: an crunchy almond cookie with orange blossom, lemon .... GA
Croquignole d'Uzès: a small round crunchy cookie, containing an almond or hazelnut .... GA
Curbelet de Cordes: a dry wafer, very thin, rolled into a cylinder .... TA
Escalette: a thin waffle .... HE
Gimblette d'Albi: a pastry dough first dipped in hot water, then baked, shaped like a ring
Grisette de Montpellier: a small sweet ball made from honey and licorice
Honey of Narbonne, rosemary in particular
Licorice candies .... HE
Minerva/minervette: a glazed slice of brioche .... GA
Navette Albigeoise: a marquise shape in shortbread, decorated with whole almonds
Nougat of Limoux, white .... AU
Pébradou: a crunchy cookie, shaped like a twisted ring, salt and peppered .... AU
Petit jeannot: a small triangular cookie with aniseed .... AL
Prune of Agen
Rousquille: a ring cake covered with confectioners' sugar .... RO
Tourons: soft and hard nougats .... RO
Violette de Toulouse ("violet of Toulouse"): a flower crystallized in sugar

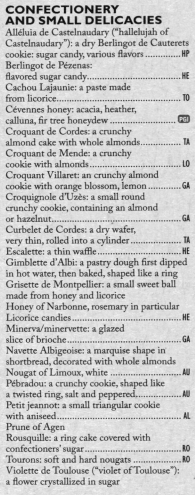

DRINKS AND SPIRITS

Armagnac (several AOP) .... AOP
Byrrh, vermouth .... PO
Cartagena, mistelle .... BL
Cataroise of Béziers, mistelle
Crème de noix .... AU
Fine-Faugères, eau-de-vie of Faugères .... GI
Floc de Gascogne, mistelle .... GE AOP
Gentian of Aubrac
Lemonade of Fontestorbes .... AR
Limonette Milles, lemonade .... PO
Liqueur de noix (walnut liqueur) .... QU, RG
Marc eau-de-vie of the Languedoc .... GI
Micheline: liqueur of plant extracts .... AU
Noilly Prat, vermouth .... HE
Or-Kina, vermouth .... AU
Plum eau-de-vie .... QU
Wine eau-de-vie of the Languedoc

MEN AND WOMEN (CRITICS, CHEFS, ETC.)

Bras, Michel (born in 1946); Sébastien (born in 1971): Michel and Sébastien Bras, Laguiole
Coste Victor (1807–1873), founding father of oyster farming, born in Castries
Daguin, André (born in 1935): Hôtel de France and des Ambassadors, Auch
Dejean, Rene (?–1936): Le Comminges, Saint-Gaudens
Durand, Charles (1756–1854), cook from Nîmes, author of *Le Cuisinier Durand*, one of the first French regional cookbooks
Kayser, Michel (born in 1955): Alexandre, Garons
Vanel, Lucien (1928–2010): Le Restaurant Vanel, Toulouse

THE BEST OF THE REGION

PAYS DE LA LOIRE

AN: ANJOU; LA: LOIRE-ATLANTIQUE; MA: MAINE; SA: SARTHE; VE: VENDÉE; YE: ÎLE D'YEU

AT THE BUTCHER'S

Cow of Maine .... PGI
Cow of Vendée .... PGI
Eggs of Loué .... PGI
Free-range chicken of Loué
Goose of Anjou .... PGI
Maine-Anjou beef .... AOP
Pork of Sarthe .... PGI
Pork of Vendée .... PGI
Poultry of Ancenis .... PGI
Poultry of Challans (duck, capon, black chicken) .... PGI
Poultry of Cholet .... PGI
Poultry of Maine .... PGI
Poultry of Vendée .... PGI

AT THE FARMER'S

Apples, flattened and dried .... AN
Carrot of Nantes
Comice pears .... AN
Cornette d'Anjou (escarole)
Cultivated mushrooms .... AN
Mâche lettuce of Nantes .... PGI
Mogette beans of Vendée .... PGI
Onion of Mazé .... AN
Potato of Noirmoutier
Reinette apple of Mans
Reinette du Mans

AT THE FISHMONGER'S

Clam of Croisic
Eel
European eel (fry)
Farmed mussels
Freshwater pike perch
Lamprey
Oyster of Vendée-Atlantique
Pike
Sardines in oil
Shad
Sole of Sable-d'Olonne

AT THE BAKER'S

Fouace from Nantes: a leavened bread-cake in the shape of a six-pointed star
Fouée d'Anjou: a round hollow loaf
Gâche vendéenne, sweeter than the Vendée brioche and containing cream
Préfou: salty flat bread with garlic butter .... VE
Tourton Nantes: sweet bread with milk
Vendée brioche: sweet and fragrant (eau-de-vie, orange blossom water) .... PGI

AT THE CHARCUTIER

Fressure vendéen: stew of meat and offal
Gogue: vegetable boudin, enriched with blood ... AN, LA
Grillon vendéen: a piece of confit pork belly, in lard
Pâté of "scraps," from pork ... AN, LA
Rillaud d'Anjou: a cube of pork belly cooked in fat
Saucisse with Muscadet (sausage) ... LA
Vendée ham, raw, dry salted

AT THE CHEESE MAKER'S

Caillebotte: fromage frais
Fromage du curé ... LA
Trappe-de-Laval ... MA
Véritable Port-Salut ... MA

SAVORY DISHES

Bardatte: cabbage stuffed with meat of young rabbit ... LA
Bouilleture of the Loire: matelote (stew) of eels
Chouée vendéenne: fresh cabbages with bacon
Cul de veau à la Montsoreau: baked veal rump ... AN
Eel omelet ... LA
Far de Jottes: a stew with Swiss chard and vegetables, baked ... VE
Fish soup of Île d'Yeu
Fricassee of chicken à la angevine: white wine, cultivated mushrooms, fresh cream
Fried sand eel ... VE
Frogs in cream ... VE
Ham knuckle à la nantaise: a pork stew
Lard nantais: braised pork ribs with rinds and offal
Nouzillards (chestnuts) in milk ... AN
Pike (or freshwater pike perch) with beurre blanc
Potironnée: soup made of vendéenne winter squash
Rabbit à la vendéenne, cooked with red wine
Rabbit pâté vendéenne, with veal and ham of Vendée
Roast pork with Reinette apples ... SA
Shad stuffed with sorrel
Soupe aux piochons (green cabbage buds)
Stuffed artichokes à l'angevine: with cultivated mushrooms, cooked in white wine
Tapioca soup (made from chicken broth or beef)
Veal kidneys à la Baugé, shallot, white wine, cultivated mushrooms

DESSERTS AND PASTRIES

Crémet d'Anjou: a preparation made with cream, fromage blanc, and beaten egg whites
Fion: a flan ... VE
Foutimasson: beignets with orange blossom ... VE
Galette de Doue-la-Fontaine: a large cake made from pâte sablée (shortcrust dough) ... AN
Gâteau minute ("instant cake") ... VE
Gâteau nantais: an almond cake from Nantes, flavored with rum
Merisse/Merice/Betchets (small size): a dense cake, sweetened, elongated ... VE
Plum pâté from Angers: a plum tart topped with pastry

VARIOUS

Buckwheat flour from Brittany ... PGI
Salicorne ... LA
Salt of Noirmoutier
Sea salt or fleur de sel sea salt from Guérande ... PGI
Walnut oil ... AN

CONFECTIONERY AND SMALL DELICACIES

Berlingot nantais: cooked sugar with varied aromas
Françoise de Foix/bouché au chocolat: chocolate-coated praline ganache and rum raisins ... LA
Galette de Saint-Guénolé: a dry butter cookie ... LA
Petit mouzillon: a dry cookie ... LA
Quernon d'ardoise, a small square of nougatine covered with blue chocolate ... AN
Rigolette nontaise: a sugar shell, filled with fruit marmalade
Sablé de Sablé (sablé cookies from Sablé-sur-Sarthe, in Sarthe) ... SA

DRINKS AND SPIRITS

Brittany cider ... PGI
Calvados, Calvados Domfrontais ... GI
Cider
Cider and pear eau-de-vie
Cider eau-de-vie from Brittany ... GI
Cider of Normandy ... PGI
Cointreau: sweet and bitter orange liqueur ... AN
Crème de cassis of Anjou
Guignolet: cherry-infused liqueur ... AN
Kamok: coffee liqueur ... VE
Menthe-Pastille ... AN
Normandy pear eau-de-vie ... GI
Poiré Domfront ... AOP
Poiré ... MA
Pommeau de Bretagne ... GI
Pommeau de Normandie ... GI
Pommeau du Maine ... GI

MEN AND WOMEN (CRITICS, CHEFS, ETC.)

Curnonsky (Maurice Edmond Saillant) (1872–1956), food critic born in Angers
Monselet, Charles (1825–1888), gastronomic author born in Nantes

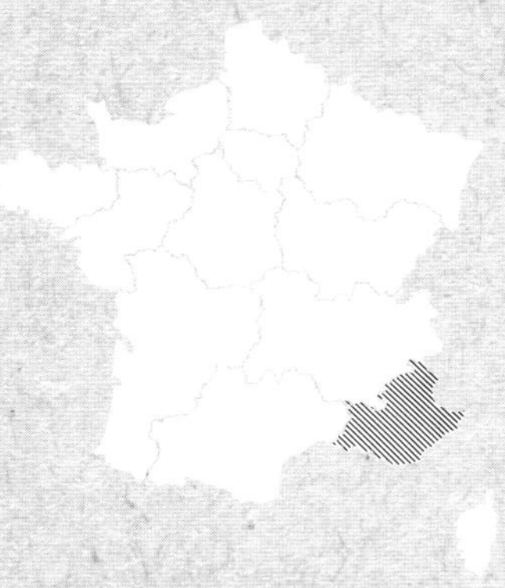

THE BEST OF THE REGION

PROVENCE-ALPES-CÔTE D'AZUR

AL: ALPILLES; AP: ALPES DE HAUTE PROVENCE; CA: CAMARGUE; CV: COMTAT VENAISSIN; DA: DAUPHINÉ; HP: HAUTE PROVENCE; NI: NICE; PN: PAYS NIÇOIS; PR: PROVENCE; VA: VAR

AT THE BUTCHER'S

Bull of Camargue ... AOP
Lamb of Cisteron ... PGI
Suckling goat

AT THE FARMER'S

Apples from the Alps of Haute-Durance ... PGI
Apricot (poman rosé variety)
Asparagus of Lauris
Basil
Black mulberry
Black olives from the Baux-de-Provence valley ... AOP
Black winter truffle
Cardoons
Chestnut of Var, marrouge variety
Chickpea
Curly chicory
Fig of Solliès (black bourjassote) ... AOP
Garlic
Gray fig of Tarascon
Haricot coco rose of Eyragues
Japanese loquat
Kaki muscat of Provence (ornamental tree)
Large green grapes of Ventoux
Lemon of Menton
Long or round zucchini of Nice and zucchini flower
Lucques olives from the Baux-de-Provence valley ... AOP
Melon of Cavaillon (cantaloupe)
Mesclun of Nice: a mix of young shoots for salads, of various species and herbs
Muscat of Ventoux ... AOP
Olives
Olives of Nice ... AOP
Perdrigone plum, of which pistoles are made, dried plums, pitted, flattened
Pointed cabbage of Châteaurenard
Potato from Pertuis
Provençal herbs: thyme, rosemary, oregano, savory, common sage
Purple artichoke of Provence
Quince of Provence
Rice of Camargue ... PGI
Sanguin: mushroom
Scallions: small onion
Snow peas or peas
Strawberries from Carros
Strawberries of Carpentras: strawberry trees with large fruits
Swiss chard of Nice: little chard/poiré (varietals)
Various lettuces
Watermelon

AT THE FISHMONGER'S

Anchovy
Angler
Black sea bass
Boutargue of Martigues
Eel
European seabass
Favouille (small crab)
Fielas or European conger
Gilt-head sea bream
Mullet
Poutine and nonat
Purple sea urchin
Red mullet
Red tuna
Sardine
Scorpionfish and capon
Slipper lobster
Small fish larvae (fry; for frying)
Small rockfish
Squid, cuttlefish and octopus
Violet (shellfish)
Wedge clam

AT THE BAKER'S

Fougasse ... PR
Fougassette: fougasse sweet and scented with orange blossom water ... PR
Pain d'Aix: sourdough bread ... PR
Pompe à l'huile: bread enriched with olive oil ... PR
Tortillade: brioche bread ... PR

AT THE CHARCUTIER

Caillette: pork meatball; Swiss chard or spinach ... VA
Moutounesse: dried lamb meat, salted, sometimes smoked (aka fumeton) ... AP
Saucisson of Arles (dry sausage)

AT THE CHEESE MAKER'S

Banon ... DA, HP AOP
Bleu du Queyras ... DA
Brousse du Rove ... PR
Cachaille: a preparation combining different cheeses with brandy ... PR, PN
Tomme d'Arles
Tomme de Champsaur, de Vésubie, du Queyras ... DA, HP

SAVORY DISHES

Anchoiade, a spread: made of anchovies, garlic, and oil ... PR
Artichokes à la barigoule: small artichokes prepared in a casserole with a preparation of onions, shallots, and carrots ... PR, AL
Avignon mutton stew: shoulder of lamb marinated in a mixture of oil, white wine, onions, carrots, herbs; cooked together in a casserole
Bouillabaisse borgne: with potatoes, leeks, onions, tomatoes, and eggs poached in the soup
Bouillabaisse, made with small rockfish and other fish varieties, scorpionfish and conger in particular; leeks, onions, tomatoes; served with a rouilli sauce ... PR
Chou farci: a large cabbage stuffed with bacon, garlic, cabbage heart, Swiss chard, sausage meat, rice, onion, peas, tomatoes, whole eggs, and herbs ... PR
Cod in raïto: a thick sauce with tomatoes, red wine, olives, and capers ... PR
Cuttlefish in the style of L'Estaque, in a casserole: white cuttlefish, tomato, garlic, and white wine . . .
Esquinado à la Toulonnaise: a preparation made with crab (esquinado), served in the shells: includes onions, capers, garlic, and eggs . . .
European sea bass in salt water, with saussoun: in a court-bouillon with saussoun (a sauce made with anchovies, almonds, fennel, and mint) ... PR
Fritots de pied de'agneau de Barcelonnette: lambs' feet marinated in oil, breaded, then fried ... PR
Gigot of monkfish (prepared as leg of lamb), oven roasted: including peppers, eggplants, zucchini, shallots, and white wine ... PR
Gnocchi: a potato-based dough ... NI
Grand aioli, a large meal for celebrations: aioli with poached cod, hard-boiled eggs, vegetables, such as carrots, cauliflower, potatoes, artichokes, and poivrade (pepper sauce) ... PR
Green pasta with herbs ... PN, AP
Lapin en paquets à la brignolaise (rabbit "packets" Brignole-style): rabbit baked with a preparation made with shallots, tomatoes, bacon, and garlic
Mélets au poivre: a condiment made with small anchovies ... PR
Mussel soup: onions, tomatoes, vermicelli, and saffron ... PR
Pan bagnat: a small round bread filled with a preparation similar to a salade niçoise ... PN
Panisse: a beignet made with chickpea flour ... PR, PN
Pieds et paquets ("feet and packages"): stewed mutton trip and feet ... PR
Pissaladière: a tart made with onions and pissalat (an anchovy condiment) ... PN
Pissalat: A condiment made from *poutine*, or mainly from sardine fry, although for some "authentic" pissalat is made from anchovies macerated in salt ... PN

Polenta: a corn porridge.......... PN
Poulet au pastis (pastis chicken), in a marinade made from pastis, oil, and saffron; cooked in a casserole with the marinade, onions, tomatoes, and potatoes. Served with a sauce of garlic, chile pepper, potato, liver, and oil.......... PR
Provençal beef stew: larded meat marinated in white wine and oil; made in a casserole, and including bacon, tomatoes, olives, small white onions, and garlic . . .
Provençal boar stew, marinated in red wine with oil and vinegar added to the casserole with bacon and the marinade
Provençal tomatoes, baked: half tomatoes topped with garlic, parsley, and bread crumbs
Purslane soup niçoise: potatoes, leek, purslane
Ratatouille niçoise: tomatoes, eggplants, green peppers, onions, zucchini, all cooked separately
Raviole/ravioli: ravioli of squash, baked ravioli, ravioli from Nice (Swiss chard/stew).......... PN
Rougets à la niçoise: panfried then baked with tomato pulp
Salad niçoise: tomatoes, hard-boiled eggs, anchovies, green peppers, white onions, and black olives
Salted squash pie.......... PR
Sarcelle (duck) aux olives, baked; stuffed with bacon, parsley, olives, eau-de-vie.......... PR
Sardines with spinach, stuffed with spinach, anchovy fillets, garlic, and parsley.......... PR
Sea bream oursinado, cooked in a casserole, served with a sea urchin sauce.......... PR
Socca (Nice)/Cade (Toulon): crêpe with chickpea flour
Soupe au pistou, with various vegetables—especially white beans—with pasta; pistou added (basil, garlic, olive oil) in the tureen
Taillerin: thin egg noodels.......... AP
Tapenade.......... PR
Tian Carpentras spinach, baked with a preparation of milk, flour, garlic, and parsley; sprinkled with bread crumbs
Tourton du Champsaur: beignets stuffed with vegetables and cheese, available in a sweet version.......... DA
Trouchia, a kind of baked omelet: Swiss chard, eggs, Parmesan, chervil, and parsley.......... PN

DESSERTS AND PASTRIES

Chichi-frégi: a long beignet rolled in sugar.......... PR
Gâteau des rois ("kings' cake"): a brioche in the shape of a crown with candied fruits on top.......... PR
Oreillette: a beignet.......... PR
Riz aux pignons: rice pudding with pine nuts and candied fruit.......... PN
Saint-Tropez tart: brioche, topped with a mixture of pastry cream and whipped cream
Tian au lait: a kind of flan, with rum and orange blossom water.......... PR
Tourte de bléa: a kind of sweetened pie, with Swiss chard, sweetened, with apples, raisins, and pine nuts.......... PN

VARIOUS

Olive oil from Aix-en-Provence, Haute-Provence, from Baux-de-Provence valley, from Nyons, from Nice.......... AOP
Olive oils
Orange flower water
Salt of Camargue
Spelt flour from Haute-Provence.......... PGI
Spelt from Haute-Provence.......... PGI
Spigol: a seasoning with sweet peppers, turmeric, saffron
Tilleul de Carpentras (silver linden), used in herbal tea infusions

CONFECTIONERY AND SMALL DELICACIES

Berlingot de Carpentras: a hard sugar candy, made from candied fruit syrup
Biscotin d'Aix: a small ball of pâte sablée (shortdough) flavored with orange blossom
Brassadeau: an échaudé (first dipped in hot water then baked), shaped like a ring.......... CV
Brown nougat.......... PR
Calisson d'Aix: marzipan and candied melon
Candied fruits of Apt
Chique (a large hard candy on a stick).......... PR
Citrus jam.......... PN
Croquant: an almond and honey cookie
Honey candy of Allauch: a honey paste ribbon
Honey of Provence: chestnut, heather, lavender.......... PGI
Juniper jam.......... AP
Navette: a dry cookie, long, scented with orange blossom.......... PR
White nougat.......... PR

DRINKS AND SPIRITS

Anise liqueurs: pastis, Pernod.......... PR
Cooked Christmas wine, made into wine after cooking the must.......... PR
Frigolet, herbal liqueurs: thyme, rosemary.......... PR
Génépi liqueur.......... AP
Lérina (green/yellow) (herbal liqueur).......... PR
Oregano du Comtat: liqueur made from marjoram

MEN AND WOMEN (CRITICS, CHEFS, ETC.)

Barale, Hélène (1916–2006): Barale, Nice
Baudoin, Vincent (1899–1993): La Bonne Auberge, Antibes
Brisse, Léon (known as Baron Brisse) (1813–1876), gastronomic author born in Gémenos
Charial, Jean-André (born in 1945): L'Oustau de Baumanière, Baux-de-Provence
Dubois, Urbain (1818–1901), a famous cook, born in Trets
Hiély, André (1903–1971), Pierre (1927–2008): Lucullus, Hely-Lucullus, Avignon
Lalleman, Robert (1897–1984), André (born in 1931), Robert (born in 1966): L'Auberge de Noves, Noves
Maximin, Jacques (born in 1948): Jacques Maximin, Vence
Outhier, Louis (born in 1930): L'Oasis, La Napoule
Passédat, Jean-Paul (born in 1933); Gérald (born in 1960): Le Petit Nice, Marseille
Reboul, Jean-Baptiste (1862–1926), cook, author of *La Cuisinière Provençale*, 1895
Talon, Joseph (1793–1873), native of Vaucluse, generally proclaimed as the inventor of truffle farming
Thuilier, Raymond (1897–1997): L'Oustau de Baumanière, Baux-de-Provence
Vergé, Roger (1930–2015): Le Moulin de Mougins, Mougins

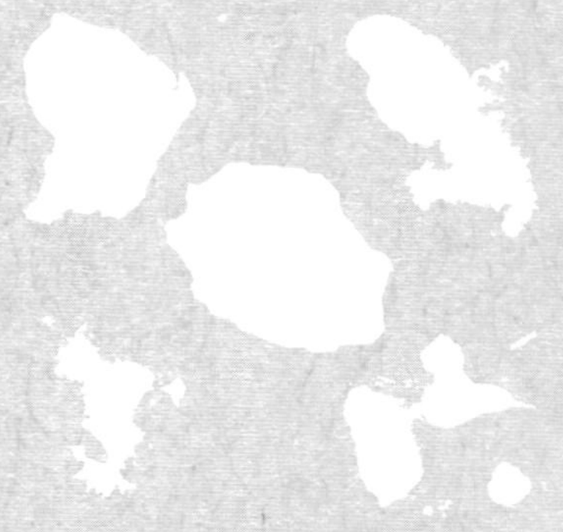

THE BEST OF THE REGION

FRANCE'S OVERSEAS DEPARTMENTS

AN: ANTILLES (WEST INDIES); RE: RÉUNION; GY: GUYANA; GU: GUADELOUPE; MY: MAYOTTE; MA: MARTINIQUE

AT THE BUTCHER'S

Brahman Zebu (cattle).......... AN, GY
Cochon-case (breed of pig).......... GY
Cochon-planche (breed of pig).......... AN
Creole cows of Guadeloupe
Guianese game: agami (bird), agouti (rodent), cabiaï (rodent), cochon-bois (pig), iguana, maraïl (bird), ocko (bird), paca (rodent), collard peccary (mammal), tapir ("maïpouri"), nine-band armadillo, white armadillo
Salted kid (young goat).......... AN, RE
Tangue (rodent).......... RE

AT THE FARMER'S

Achiote: a dye.......... AN, GY
Avocado.......... AN, GY, RE
Bananas: figue-pomme, figue rose, Fressinette, ti-nain, plantain.......... AN, GY, RE
Bè rouj: a spiced lard colored with achiote.......... GU
Bélimbi: a fruit with a very acid taste, used as a condiment.......... AN, GY, RE
Bois d'Inde (West Indian bay tree): an aromatic.......... AN, GY
Bourbon vanilla.......... RE
Breadfruit.......... AN, GY, RE
Brèdes: green leaves from a variety of plants: darling, pumpkin, mafane, taro.......... RE
Caïmite: milk fruit.......... AN, GY
Calou/okra.......... AN, GY
Carambola.......... AN, GY
Caribbean cabbage/malanga/tayove.......... AN, GY
Cashew.......... AN, GY
Cassava.......... GY
Chile peppers: Zoiseau, Z'indien, Lantern, Bonda man Jacques, Sept-bouillons, de Cayenne, Martin.......... AN, GY, RE
Chou de vacoa (cabbage).......... RE
Christophine/chayote/chouchou: a sort of squash.......... AN, GY, RE
Cinnamon.......... AN, GY
Citrus fruits: chadek (grapefruit), Seville oranges, local lemons and limes, kaffir lime, oranges, grapefruit, etc..........AN, GY, RE
Cloves.......... AN, GY, RE
Coconut.......... AN, GY, RE
Coeur de boeuf (beefsteak tomatoes).......... RE
Comou: palm trees whose fruits provide a milk, consumed plain or sweet.......... GY
Cucumbers: long, spicy, for salad, etc.......... AN, GY, RE
Dasheen (taro).......... AN, GY
Eggplant.......... AN, GY, RE
French Guyana spinach
Giant granadilla.......... AN
Ginger.......... AN, GY, RE
Guava.......... AN, GY, MY, RE
Heart of palm.......... AN, GY, RE
Jackfruit/ti Jacque.......... AN, GY, RE
Jamaican honeysuckle.......... AN, RE
Jerusalem artichoke.......... AN
Lentils of Cilaos.......... RE
Lima beans.......... RE
Litchi.......... RE
Local apricots.......... AN, GY
Local cherries/acerola (West Indan cherry).......... AN, GY
Local chestnuts.......... AN, GY
Local Mexican mint, condiment.......... AN, GY
Local onions: chives, as a condiment.......... AN
Longan fruit.......... RE
Mangos: American, Auguste, Bassignac, Bonbon, José, Persinet.......... AN, GY, RE
Maripa: a palm tree whose fruit pulp is eaten.......... GY
Melon of Guadeloupe.......... PGI
Mombin.......... AN, GY
Nutmeg.......... AN, GY, RE
Palm trees
Papaya.......... AN, GY, MY, RE
Passion fruit/maracuja.......... AN, GY, RE
Patawa: a palm tree whose fruits provide a milk, consumed plain or sweet.......... GY
Peppers.......... AN, GY, RE
Pigeon pea.......... AN, GY
Pineapple: Bouteille, Victoria, etc.......... AN, GY, RE
Plum of Chile.......... AN
Plum of Kythira.......... AN, GY
Red dates.......... RE
Rice.......... GY, RE
Rose apple.......... GY
Sapodilla.......... AN, GY
Soursop.......... AN, GY, RE
Spanish lime.......... AN
Sugar apple.......... AN, GY, MY, RE
Surinam cherry/pitanga.......... AN, GY, RE
Sweet potato.......... AN, GY, RE
Tamarin.......... AN
Taro: tuber.......... RE
Turban squash.......... AN, GY
Turmeric.......... AN, GY, RE
Vanilla.......... AN, GY
Wassey: a palm tree whose bud is consumed—the heart of palm—and whose fruit provides a milk consumed plain, sweet, or in sorbet.......... GY
Watermelon.......... AN, GY
Wild cherry/plum-coffee.......... AN
Yams: white, coussecouche, de Noël, purple yam.......... AN, GY, RE
Zambrevattes: leguminous plant.......... RE
Zicaque.......... AN

AT THE FISHMONGER'S

Acoupa weakfish.......... GY
Atipa.......... GY
Balaou.......... AN
Barracuda.......... RE
Bichiques: fry (fish larvae).......... RE
Black mackerel: banana tuna.......... RE
Bourgeois: silk snapper.......... RE
Burgo: mollusk.......... AN
Captaine (Nile fish).......... RE
Carangidae.......... RE
Chadron: sea urchin eggs.......... AN
Chatou/zourite: octopus.......... AN, RE
Chaubette: mollusk.......... AN
Chevaquines: small river shrimp, dried.......... RE
Ciric/chancre: crustacean.......... AN, GY
Clam (palourde).......... AN
Coco.......... GY
Cod.......... AN, RE
Coulan.......... GY
Coulirou.......... AN
Couman couman.......... GY
Coumarou.......... GY
Croupia de mer (black margate).......... GY
Croupia de roche (torroto grunt).......... GY
Flying fish.......... AN
Goret.......... GY
Lambi: mollusk.......... AN
Loubine (common snook).......... GY
Madame Tombée: blubberlip snapper.......... RE
Mahi-mahi.......... AN, RE
Mangrove crab/mantou.......... AN, GY
Mangrove oyster.......... GY
Mullet.......... GY
Palika/tarpon.......... AN, GY
Parassi mullet.......... GY
Passany.......... GY
Patagaye (trahira).......... GY
Petite gueule (Jenny mojarra).......... GY
Pisquette.......... AN
Poisson-coffre (smooth puffer).......... AN
Poussissi.......... GY

Prapra (black acara) ... GY
Red fish, including snapper ... AN, RE
Rumbled ... GY
Sardine ... RE
Sardine from Saint-Laurent ... GY
Shark ... AN, GY, RE
Spiny lobster ... AN, RE
Swordfish ... AN, RE
Thazard (wahoo) ... AN, GY, RE
Titiri (spotted algae-eating goby): fry (fish larvae) ... AN
Torch (kumakuma) ... GY
Tuna: white (albacore), black, yellow (yellowfin), red ... AN, RE
Vieille: grouper ... GY
Wild shrimp from Guyana ... GY
Wolf fish ... GY
Yellow or white machoiran (striped eel catfish) ... GY
Z'habitant/ouassou/camaroon: large shrimp ... AN, RE

AT THE BAKER'S

Bread enriched with lard ... AN
Cassave: cassava cake ... AN, GY
Danquitte: beignet usually filled with chicken or ham ... GU
Flûte: very thin elongated bread, dried and hard ... AN
Macatias: sweet round buns ... RE
Pain au beurre: butter-enriched bread in various forms: braided, twisted crowns ... AN, GY
Pain curcuma-combava-piment (bread): spicy ... RE
Pain frotté: brioche, flavored with vanilla ... RE
Pain massalé épicé: a bread with spices, including coriander, cumin, clove, and turmeric ... RE
Pain natté: leavened bread rich in butter and margarine ... GY
Pomme cannelle: small round brioche, a viennoiserie ... MA
Zakari/Diksiyonnè: rectangular bread with a golden crust pierced with holes, consisting of flaky layers ... AN, GY

AT THE CHARCUTIER

Andouille/Creole andouillette ... RE
Boucané: a preservation process, involving slow smoking meat on a frame over a "boucan" ... AN, GU, RE
Creole boudin (very spicy, varied recipes including oignons-pays [a spring onion from the West Indies], bois d'Inde, clove, etc.) ... AN, GY, RE
Grattons: pork rind confit in oil ... RE
Jambon de Noël: spiced ham, sprinkled with sugar and glacéed ... AN, GY
Salted meat: pork offal—ears, snout—and beef ... AN
Salted pâté: small round pâté, with a spicy stuffing made from pork ... AN

SAVORY DISHES

"Achards": small pickled vegetables—such as young cucumbers, green beans, lemons—macerated in vinegar with peppers and herbs. Variations exist according to the regions; enjoyed as a condiment, eaten as an appetizer, or as a side dish ... AN, GY, MY, RE
Acra/marinade: small spicy beignets consisting of crayfish, peas, salted cod, sea urchin, malanga, giraumon, heart of palm, and eggplant ... AN, GY
Acupa fillets with maracuja (passion fruit) sauce, marinated in juice of local lemons with garlic and oignons-pays (a spring onion from the West Indies), then cooked in the pan with a sauce made with concentrated juice of maracuja (passion fruit) and fresh cream ... GY
Awara broth, a kind of stew: using pulp of the Awara fruit—thick and oily—with salted ham, smoked bacon, salted beef, pork snout, pork tail, salt cod, chile pepper, cabbage, cucumber, spicy cucumber, local spinach, eggplant, small sea crabs, prawns, smoked fish, roast chicken ... GY
Bisque of Tourlourous with small land crabs, puréed, with vegetables, including carrots, onions, oignons-pays (a spring onion from the West Indies), leeks, etc. ... AN
Blaffs: a spicy and herbed court-bouillon, used especially for cooking marinated white fish with the addition of lemon, chile peppers, and herbs. Includes blaff of chadron (sea urchin eggs), croupia, caribbean fish, soudons ... AN, GY
Bonbons piment: small ring-shaped beignets; from a dough made of mashed peas, cumin, ginger, green onions, and green peppers . . .
Bouchons: made from a rice dough surrounding a pork or chicken and green onion stuffing; steamed. These are also eaten as sandwiches with melted cheese, called the "American sandwich bouchon" ... RE
Briani chicken: chicken legs cooked in a pot with yogurt, spices, and herbs such as saffron, cinnamon, cloves, garlic, ginger . . . finished by adding rice and potatoes ... RE
Broth of brèdes: a variety of leaves for cooking placed in a broth with onions and garlic ... RE
Calaouangue: green mango salad with chile pepper, served as an appetizer or as a condiment
Callaloo: a thick soup of crushed leafy vegetables: callaloo (aramanth taro), dasheen (taro), local spinach ... AN, GY
Cari: a generic name for dishes from which curry powder is absent but which generally include onions, garlic, turmeric, local thyme, and tomato, such as chicken cari, tangue (rodent) cari, shrimp, ti' jacque (jackfruit curry), bichiques (fish fry), tuna ... RE
Chadrons tart: a flaky pastry crust; the filling is made from sea urchins, also includes shallots, tomatoes, garlic, and herbs
Chatrou au riz: octopus marinated in lemon juice with local onion and garlic; in a casserole with a marinade and tomatoes. Partially cooked rice is then added at the end ... MA
Chevrettes au lait de coco: a kind of stew with freshwater shrimp, garlic, tomatoes, and onions ... AN, GY
Chiquetaille of cod: grilled, crumbled, mixed cold with onions, oignons-pays (a spring onion from the West Indies), garlic, herbs, chile pepper, lime juice, and oil ... AN
Chop-suey: made from pork, beef, or chicken cut into strips and placed in a marinade made from vermouth, garlic, and nuoc nam, with starch flour; cooked in a wok with various vegetables ... RE
Christophine/chouchou daube: a stew with onions, garlic, and possibly tomato ... AN, RE
Colombos of lamb, goat, pork, chicken, lobster tails/in a casserole; these are preparations incorporating colombo spice powder ... AN, GY
Conch au Gratin, marinated in lime juice and chile pepper; with onions, oignons-pays (a spring onion from the West Indies), garlic, mushrooms—baked in the oven with bread crumbs ... AN
Congo soup: thick and blended, like soup z'habitants, with meat and vegetables ... MA
Crab rice, in a skillet, form a "crème de *chancres* (small sea crabs)" with onions and oignons-pays (a spring onion from the West Indies), mix with rice and the creamy parts of the crabs ... GY
Creole pâté, pâté en croûte: a sweetened pâte sablée (shortbread), pork or chicken meat, turmeric, spices, and lard ... RE
Creole-style red beans: cooked in a large volume of water with bacon, onions, oignons-pays (a spring onion from the West Indies), chile pepper, and garlic
Duck with vanilla: pieces of duck marinated in red wine and vanilla; cooked in a casserole with onion, tomato, garlic, ginger, mushrooms, and a marinade ... RE
Eggplant stew, with bacon, onion, tomatoes ... AN, GY
Fish and meats smoked, marinated, then prepared on the barbecue with aromatic herbs added to the fire: local thyme, split sugarcane, crushed coconut, leaves of bois d'Inde . . . Consumed on its own or integrated with other recipes ... AN, GY, RE
Fricassee of agouti, with thyme, bois d'Inde leaves, pork belly, onion, oignons-pays (a spring onion from the West Indies), garlic, and dry white wine ... GY
Fricassee of brèdes (leafy vegetables), sautéed with onions, garlic, and ginger ... RE
Fricassee of conch in a casserole, with tomatoes, onions, peppers, garlic, and cloves ... AN
Fricassee of z'habitants, with onions, oignons-pays (a spring onion from the West Indies), carrot, tomatoes, garlic, and chile pepper . . .
Fried goldfish, first marinated in lemon juice and garlic ... MA
Fried pisquettes (fish fry, for frying whole) ... AN
Giraumonade: purée of turban squash cooked in a casserole, with onions and garlic ... MA
Gratin of chayotes, mashed with bacon, onion, oignons-pays (a spring onion from the West Indies), bread crumbs dipped in milk, parsley; all sprinkled with bread crumbs and Gruyère ... AN, GY, RE
Gratin of palm tree kale ... GY
Green banana or figue verte/plaintains: used in beignets, mashed, as chips, as fries, in a gratin, in a daube (stew) ... AN, GY, RE
Grilled langouste (spiny lobster) with sauce chien: a sauce made from onion, oignons-pays (a spring onion from the West Indies), garlic, green pepper, herbs, white wine vinegar, and oil ... AN
Grilled snapper with sauce chien (a spicy sauce) ... AN
Grilled stuffed suckling pig, presented whole; multiple preparations, the stuffing is made with giblets and may include onion, oignons-pays (a spring onion from the West Indies), chile pepper, bread crumbs, seeds of the Jamaican pepper, white wine, rum ... AN, GY
Heart of palm salad: heart of palm with oignons-pays (a spring onion from the West Indies), garlic, parsley, oil and vinegar ... MA
Kid (young goat), rooster, chicken masala . . . prepared in a casserole, incorporating masala spice blend
King mackerel in coconut milk: chopped fillets, marinated in lime juice and onions; served in coconut milk . . .
Lambi (conch) boudin: a mix of chopped lambis, oignons-pays (a spring onion from the West Indies), garlic, herbs, chile peppers, bread, and milk ... AN
Lent cari, with wasp larvae
Lime chicken, fricasseed, sautéed, with garlic, herbs, and sprinkled with lemon juice ... AN
Macadam of cod: a stew with onions, oignons-pays (a spring onion from the West Indies), tomatoes, chile pepper, and garlic ... MA
Mataba: cassava leaves slowly cooked in coconut milk ... MY
Matété/matoutou of crab (Touloulous), cooked in a casserole with onions, oignons-pays (a spring onion from the West Indies), rice, tomatoes, garlic, chile pepper, and herbs ... AN
Matoutou of crab: a fricassee of crabs with lemons, bacon, onions, oignons-pays (a spring onion from the West Indies), cassava flour ... MA
Mhogo wa piki: dried cassava meatballs, cooked in coconut milk ... MY
Migan of breadfruit: a stew of pork, onion, oignons-pays (a spring onion from the West Indies), garlic, leaf and seed of Jamaican pepper, parsley, green pepper, and breadfruit ... MA
Morue raccommodée: a kind of cod brandade with potatoes, onion, oignons-pays (a spring onion from the West Indies), chile pepper, and garlic ... MA
Mtsolola: a stew of bananas, breadfruit, and cassava, including fish or meat ... MY
Okra in Creole sauce, cooked in a casserole, with oignons-pays (a spring onion from the West Indies), thyme, parsley, chile pepper; served in a dish with its cooking juices, adding garlic and lemon juice at the end . . .
Okra with tomatoes, cooked in a casserole, with onions ... AN
Ouassous/z'habitants flambéed Creole-style, in a chopped mixture of onions and oignons-pays (a spring onion from the West Indies); with tomatoes and garlic ... AN
Palika rôti-cougnade, marinated in the juice of local lemons, with oignons-pays (a spring onion from the West Indies), and garlic, then grilled; accompanied by a spicy sauce with onions, oignons-pays, garlic, and green chile pepper ... GY
Pâté en pot: a soup of mutton or goat offal—head, tripe, etc.—including many vegetables ... MA
Pilao: chicken or beef in rice, spicy ... MY
Pimentades: a sort of tomato coulis—with chile pepper, oignons-pays (a spring onion from the West Indies), etc.—and creamy: with fish, shellfish, shrimp, atipas, or shark, etc. Sometimes sweetened with coconut milk ... GY
Purée of yam ... AN, GY
Putu-putu, a condiment; spicy sauce ... MY
Red snapper with ginger, court-bouillon of onions, ginger, and lemon accompanied by an enriched sauce made with ginger, tomato, vinegar, and cassava starch ... RE
Réunion legumes: red beans, large Cape peas, lentils, served as sides. These are the main ingredient of various preparations, which can also include onion and garlic
Riz aux pois collés (a rice and pea dish), mixed with vegetables, various combinations exist, with red beans, onions, oignons-pays (a spring onion from the West Indies), pigeon peas ... AN
Romazava: beef, prepared in a casserole with onions, garlic, ginger, tomato, leaves of the Szechuan button ... MY, RE
Rougail salt cod: dried and fried cod, cooked in a sauce made from onions, tomatoes, and chopped chile peppers ... MY, RE
Rougail sausages: smoked and fried sausages, cooked in a sauce made from onions, tomatoes, and green chile peppers ... MY, RE
Samoussa: a triangular beignet stuffed with cheese, meat, or fish ... RE
Sarcives: pork cross-marinated in honey, soy sauce, aniseed, then grilled ... RE
Savory beignets of pumpkin, eggplant, breadfruit, cassava, octopus, lobster, pepper, shrimp, or chicken croquettes ... RE
Scorched pig/stew, in a casserole with onions, oignons-pays (a spring onion from the West Indies), garlic, chile pepper., etc. Served with pigeon peas ... AN
Smoked lime chicken, marinated in lemon juice and garlic; grilled over a fire to which herbs have been added, such as thyme and bois d'Inde, and basting regularly with the marinade ... AN, GY
Soufflé/breadfruit bread, the second is denser than the first ... AN, GY
Soup z'habitants; many variations including meat (pigs' tail, salted beef, etc.) and vegetables (leeks, carrots, turban squash, sweet potatoes, etc.) ... AN
Souskaï of green mangos, macerated in the juice of local lemons, salt, crushed garlic, chile pepper, oil ... MA
Squash soup, with rice, garlic, herbs, and milk ... MA
Stew/fricassee of pork: rib meat cut into small pieces, marinated in oil with onions, oignons-pays (a spring onion from the West Indies), garlic, chile pepper, then all placed in a pot with potatoes ... AN, GY
Stuffed crabs/crab carapace—or mangrove crab in Guyana—crabs stuffed with their flesh and innards, mixed with bread crumbs and herbs ... AN, GY
Stuffed yam: the stuffing is made with beef ... AN
Touffé de titris (small fry): marinated in lime and garlic then stewed with onions, garlic, crushed tomatoes ... MA
Touffé of shark with lime: pieces of shark marinated in lime, garlic, and bois d'Inde; then cooked in a casserole with onion, oignons-pays (a spring onion from the West Indies), tomatoes, and lemon juice . . .
Trovi ya nadzi: bananas in coconut, with meat or fish ... MY
Tuna stew, marinated in the juice of local lemons, onions, and garlic; then cooked in a casserole dish with onion, oignons-pays (a spring onion from the West Indies), tomato, and garlic . . . rum and water are added at the end of the cooking time ... AN
Ubu wa ndrimu: lemon rice soup with seafood ... MY
Warm rice, cooked in oil after cooking in a caisson (shallow poaching liquid), with garlic and chile pepper. Sometimes mixed with leftover meats ... RE
West Indian fish soup: many variations, with rockfish, shellfish, and vegetables (oignons-pays [a spring onion from the West Indies], onions, leeks, garlic, etc.)

White yam fries..AN
Wild-caught cod with avocado/
grilled fresh cod, crumbled, marinated
in water with chile pepper, mixed with
avocado and cassava flour ....AN
Yellow rice, flavored with turmeric ....RE
Zembrocal: rice with smoked foods and
legumes such as beans, zambrevattes,
and lentils, etc. Enriched with garlic,
pepper, chile pepper, or turmeric.................RE

DESSERTS AND PASTRIES

American cake: light and moist, flavored
with vanilla, bitter almond.........................GY
Banana cake, made from banana purée ....AN
Banana, mango, pineapple, or
papaya beignets............................AN, GY, RE
Bananas/pineapples flambéed
in rum .... AN, RE
Bangou: a cream dessert made with
corn milk, coconut milk, and sweetened
condensed milk, and flavored (cinnamon,
nutmeg, or lime) ....GY
Bindingwel: a dense cake, whose
six faces are parallelograms, uses lard ....GY
Breadfruit cake: a sort of dense
flan flavored with rum ....AN, GY
Chaudeau: cream similar to crème
anglaise, flavored with vanilla, lemon,
and cinnamon ....GU
Chemin de fer: a rolled cake, with
vanilla buttercream ....RE
Coconut blancmange: sweet coconut milk,
gelatin leaves ....AN
Coconut cake..RE
Coconut flan, flavored with vanilla ....AN, RE
Cramanioc cake: a kind of
sweet cassava pudding ....GY
Crème de maïs (a corn pudding) .... AN, GY
Creole crème frite: a beignet made
of firm cream and fried ....AN
Creole galette: a galette des rois
("kings' cake") in which coconut
replaces the frangipane .... AN, GY, RE
Creole pâté with papaya confit: the creole
pâté, but the meat is replaced.....................RE
Dizé mélé: a beignet stuffed with
pastry cream...GY
Doconon: a cake made of cornmeal, banana,
and grated coconut, poached in a papillote
made of an arouman leaf.............................AN
Fenyenyetsi: coconut milk rice cake ....MY
Fruit salad: pineapple, banana, pomelo,
mango, guava, carambola, soursop, passion
fruit, purple passion fruit (granadilla),
sapodilla...AN
Gâteau mélélivé ("malicious cake"): combines
sweet potato and coconut ....AN
Gros gâteau ("big cake"), flavored with
lemon and cinnamon; it often includes
a layer of jam, especially coconut ....AN
Gwo syrup cake, made with
various syrups ....GU

Jalousie ("jealousy"): a small pastry made
of puff pastry, covered with jam ....MA
Marzipan: a light cake flavored with lime,
vanilla, cinnamon, orange blossom, lime
mousse, mango, lychee, sapodilla ....RE
Pain de maïs, made from cornmeal..............AN
Pain doux: a sort of génoise (sponge cake),
flavored with vanilla and lime ....AN
Pâté aux fruits (fruit pâtés): banana, coconut,
guava . . .
Pâté cannelle: a rectangular turnover, with
a flaky pastry filled with banana jam and
cinnamon flavor ....MA
Pâté-coco: a coconut tart ....AN
Potin: a small rice cake with pastry cream,
shaped like a small cylinder ....MA
Robinson: pastries stuffed with jam.............MA
Sispa: a galette made from cassava starch;
with coconut and various flavorings, such
as cinnamon or nutmeg ....GY
Sorbets: coconut, lychee, papaya ....AN, GY, RE
Sweet potato cake .... AN, RE
Taro cake, made with puréed taro,
flavored with vanilla ....RE
Ti'son cake: a rich cake, similar to
a quatre-quarts (pound cake), made
from cornmeal ....RE
Toubtoub: dried cassava balls
with coconut ....MY
Tourment d'amour/amour caché: on a base
of flaky pastry; a blend of coconut jam or
plantain—many combined with a pastry
cream—and sponge cake ....AN
Turnovers filled with jam............................GY

VARIOUS

Cane sugar ....AN
Cane vinegar...GU
Cassava/couac flour ....AN, GY
Coffee ....AN, GY
Colombo spice powder: a mixture
of many spices including turmeric,
saffron, coriander seeds, cumin,
mustard, and black pepper ....AN, GY
Conflore/toloman: starch of
the African arrowroot...........................AN, RE
Cornmeal..AN, GY
Cretan dittany starch/arrowroot ....AN, GY, RE
Dakatine: a peanut butter ....RE
Kwabio, condiment: chopped peppers
in salted cassava water ....GY
Massalé powder: a mix of many spices
including coriander, black pepper, cumin,
cardamom, nutmeg, and mustard seed.........RE
Pinda, a peanut paste ....GY
Terrestrial crabs ....AN
Various rougalis (chutney): mango,
tomato, lemon, etc., used as spicy side
sauces; chopped fruits and vegetables,
cooked in oil with chopped onion
and peppers...RE
Zendettes: larvae of insects, fried.................RE

CONFECTIONERY
AND SMALL DELICACIES

Barbados jam (large passion fruit),
limes (whole in syrup), sweet potato,
mango, guava, pineapple, banana,
gingerroot, christophine (chayote) ......AN, GY, RE
Bonbons cravate: a confection in the
shape of a bow tie; thin fried dough ....RE
Bonbons la rouroute: a small round
cake made from arrowroot..........................RE
Bonbons millet: small beignets coated
with sesame seeds ....RE
Bonbons moussache: a pastry in the
shape of a small ball, made from cassava
flour (moussache) ....AN
Candied Tahitian gooseberry (fruit
of the gooseberry tree) ....AN
Chadec glacé: a quarter piece of
chadec (the pomelo), candied ....AN
Coconut flour: coconut powder
cooked with cane sugar........................ AN, GY
Coconut jam: a paste made from
shredded coconut pulp, also used as
an ingredient in pastries.......................AN, GY
Coconut macaron/chikini: a dry galette
made with grated coconut ....AN
Coconut/canned/coconut candies
(small mound of grated coconut
cooked in cane sugar syrup)................AN, GY, RE
Comtesse ("Countess"): a round
shortbread, flavored with bitter
almond and vanilla...................................GY
Cratché/crétque: a piece of coconut
enrobed in caramel .... AN, GY
Doucelette: a chewy coconut milk
confection ....AN
Filibo/pipilit: a soft candy...........................MA
Forest and mangrove honeys ....GY
Glacéed tamarind (tamarind fruit,
glacéed, in syrup) ....AN
Gros kako: a stick of cocoa paste ....AN, GY
Guava jam ....AN, GY
Guava paste: candy, guava purée
cooked and then oven dried........................GU
Honeys ....GU, MA
Lanmou chinois: puff pastry,
sprinkled with sugar ....GY
Lotchio/Lotcho: candy made from
coconut paste, brown in color ....AN, GY
Lychee honey...RE
Pistachio nougat with
roasted peanuts ....AN, GY
Popote de fruit à pain ("breadfruit
tree treat"): the male flower of the
breadfruit tree, candied and crystallized ......AN
Pruneau Désirade (candied
cashew apple)..GU
Ramiquin (a stick of sugar flavored
with mint or anise) ....GY
Sinobol (crushed ice served in a cone
and drizzled with syrup) ....AN

Sorrel gelée (jellied): from
hibiscus flower ....GY
Wang (a powder mixed with
roasted sesame and coconut powder,
sweet or salty) ....GY
Zoa (roasted corn powdered
and sweetened) ....GY

DRINKS AND SPIRITS

Amer: decoction of plant in tafia:
quinquina, bitter liana................................GY
Cachiri: sparkling alcoholic fermented drink
based on cachiri, a cassava
Crème de sapote, made from hazelnuts
and almonds macerated in cane alcohol.......GU
Dodo beer...RE
Large syrup/cane juice/an array of syrups:
concentrated sugarcane juice.......................AN
Mabi: an infusion of bark of mabi wood,
nonalcoholic...MA
Madou: fruit pulp—of cacao and soursop
especially—macerated in sugar water ....GY
Matador syrup: a mixture of
flavored water and cane sugar, an
ingredient in Creole punch..........................GY
Passion fruit juice ....AN
Pineapple beer: a fermented drink
made from pineapple, sparkling...................GY
Plum juice from Kythera ....AN
Red currant syrup, made from the juice of
local current flowers such as
Hibiscus sabdariffa (Roselle) ....AN
Rum and rum-based cocktails:
punch, coconut punch, ti' punch,
love punch, macerated punch,
planter's ....AN, GY, RE
Rum of French overseas departments........[GI]
Rum of French West Indies.....................[GI]
Rum of Guadeloupe.............................[GI]
Rum of Guadeloupe-Marie Galante ....[GI]
Rum of Guyana..................................[GI]
Rum of Martinique ....[GI]
Rum of Réunion..................................[GI]
Shrub: a liqueur made of white rum
and macerations of orange peels,
tangerine, and herbs ....AN
Sorrel syrup: a refreshing decoction
made from the chalices of the flowers
of the sorrel of Guinea, in a sweet and
aromatic water ....GY
Sugar refinery rum from Galion Bay ....[GI]
Tafia: rum made from cane molasses ....GY, RE

TABLE OF SUBJECTS

INDEX

417

French Bibliography and Suggested Readings

COOKBOOKS

- Alleno, Yannick. *Sauces, réflexions d'un cuisinier.* Hachette Cuisine, 2014
- Andrieu, Julie. *Les carnets de Julie.* Alain Ducasse Éditions, 2013
- Anonymous. *Livre fort excellent de cuisine très utile et profitable.* Olivier Arnoullet, Lyon, 1542
- Artusi, Pellegrino. *La science en cuisine et l'art de bien manger* (1911). Actes Sud, 2016
- Audot, Louis-Eustache. *La cuisinière de la campagne et de la ville* (76th ed.; ed. 1898). Hachette Livre BNF, 2012
- Baudic, Jean-Marie. *Il est frais mon poisson.* La Martinière, 2012
- Beauvilliers, Antoine. *L'art du cuisinier* (ed. 1814). Hachette Livre BNF, 2012
- Béraud-Williams, Sylvette. *La Cuisine paysanne d'Ardèche.* La Fontaine de Siloë, 2005
- Bernard, Françoise. *Les recettes faciles.* Paris: Hachette, 1965
- Bousquet, Renée, and Anne Laurent. *Travaux pratiques de techniques culinaires.* Doin, 2004
- Boyer, Blandine. *Banquet gaulois; 70 recettes venues directement de nos ancêtres . . . ou presque!* Larousse, 2016
- Chapel, Alain. *La cuisine, c'est beaucoup plus que des recettes.* Robert Laffont, 1980
- Cochard, Marie. *Les épluchures, tout ce que vous pouvez en faire.* Eyrolles, 2016
- Collection, *Larousse de la cuisinie*
- Collection, *Larousse gastronomique*
- Constant, Christian, and Yves Camdeborde. *La cuisine d'Auguste Escoffier.* Michel Lafon, 2016
- Curnonsky, *À l'infortune du pot. La meilleure cuisine en 300 recettes simples et d'actualité.* Éditions de la Couronne, 1946
- Darenne, Émile, and Émile Duval. *Traité de pâtisserie moderne.* 1909
- Darroze, Hélène. *Mes recettes en fête.* Éditions du Cherche-Midi
- Daveau, Gilles, Bruno Couderc, Danièle Mischlich, and Caroline Rio. *Savez-vous goûter . . . les légumes secs.* Éditions de l'EHESP
- Daveau, Gilles. *Le Manuel de cuisine alternative.* Actes Sud, 2014
- Delteil, Joseph. *La Cuisine paléolithique.* Arléa, 1964
- Derenne, Jean-Philippe. *Cuisiner en tous temps, en tous lieux.* Fayard, 2010
- Desproges, Pierre. *Dictionnaire superflu à l'usage de l'élite et des biens nantis.* Points, 2013
- Douvet, Bruno. *La Régalade des champs.* Éditions de la Martinière, Paris, 2014
- Dubois, Urbain. *La Pâtisserie d'aujourd'hui.* 1894
- *Le Livre de la ménagère, ou Petite encyclopédie de la famille.* Flammarion, 1930
- Ducasse, Alain. *Le Grand livre de cuisine.* Alain Ducasse Éditions, 2009
- Dudemaine, Sophie. *Les cakes de Sophie.* Minerva/La Martinière, 2005
- Durand, Charles. *Le Cuisinier Durand* (ed. 1830). Hachette Livre BNF, 2013
- Emanuelli, Philippe. *Une Initiation à la cuisine du champignon.* Marabout, 2011
- Escoffier, Auguste. *L'Aide-Mémoire culinaire.* Flammarion, 2006
- *La vie à bon marché. La morue.* Flammarion, 1929
- *Le Guide culinaire.* Flammarion, 2009
- *Le riz, l'aliment le meilleur, le plus nutritif, 130 recettes pour l'accommoder.* Menu Fretin, 2016
- *Ma Cuisine.* Syllabaire Éditions, 2017
- Etchebest, Christian, and Éric Ospital. *Tout est bon dans le cochon.* First, 2015
- Ezgulian, Sonia. *Anti-gaspi.* Flammarion, 2017
- Felder, Christophe. *Pâtisserie!.* La Martinière, 2011
- Flouest, Anne, and Jean-Paul Romac. *La cuisine gauloise continue.* Bleu Autour, 2006
- Frechon, Éric. *Éric Frechon.* Solar, 2016
- Frechon, Éric, and Clarisse Ferreres. *Un chef dans ma cuisine.* Solar, 2009
- Giono, Sylvie. *La Provence gourmande de Jean Giono.* Belin, 2013
- Gouffé, Jules. *Le livre de cuisine; comprenant la cuisine de ménage et la grande cuisine* (ed. 1867). Hachette Livre BNF, 2012
- *Le livre de pâtisserie* (ed. 1873). Hachette Livre BNF, 2012
- *Le livre des conserves, ou Recipes pour préparer et conserver les viandes et les poissons* (ed. 1869). Hachette Livre BNF, 2013

- Guérard, Michel. *La Grande Cuisine minceur.* Robert Laffont, 1976
- Hugo, Florian V. *Les Contemplations gourmands.* Michel Lafon, 2011
- Jacquemin, Frédérique. *À table avec Marcel Pagnol.* Agnès Viénot, 2011
- La Chapelle, Vincent. *Le Cuisinier moderne* (ed. 1735). Hachette Livre BNF, 2016
- La Varenne, François-Pierre. *Le cuisiner français; 400 recettes du xviie siècle.* Vendémiaire, 2016
- Lacam, Pierre. *Le Glacier classique et artistique en France et en Italie.* 1893
- *Le Mémorial historique et géographique de la pâtisserie* (ed. 1900). Hachette Livre BNF, 2017
- Lacroix, Muriel, and Pascal Pringarbe. *Les carnets de cuisine de George Sand; 80 recettes à l'épicurienne.* Chêne, 2013
- Larcher, Bertrand. *Breizh Café.* La Martinière, 2014
- Le Caisne, Arthur. *La cuisine, c'est aussi de la chimie.* Hachette Cuisine, 2013
- Lebrun, Pierre-Brice. *Petit traité de la boulette.* Le Sureau, 2009
- *Petit traité de la pomme de terre et de la frite.* Le Sureau, 2016
- Lenôtre, Gaston. *Faites votre pâtisserie comme Lenôtre.* Flammarion, 1975
- Lepage, Isabel. *Les routiers; les meilleures recettes.* Tana, 2017
- Loubet, Édouard. *Le Cuisinier provençal.* Skira, 2015
- Mallet, Jean-François. *Simplissime.* Hachette Cuisine, 2015
- Marfaing, Hélène, Julien Lemarié, Pierre Mollo, and Johanne Vigneau. *Savez-vous goûter . . . les algues?* Éditions de l'EHESP, 2016
- Massialot, François. *La nouvelle instruction pour les confitures, les liqueurs et les fruits.* 1692
- *Le cuisinier royal et bourgeois.* 1691
- Mathiot, Ginette. *Je sais cuisine.* Albin Michel, 1932
- *La Cuisine pour tous.* Albin Michel, 1955
- Maximin, Jacques, and Martine Jolly. *Jacques Maximin cuisine les legumes.* Albin Michel, 1998
- Menon. *La cuisinière bourgeoise.* 1746
- *Les soupers de la cour, ou l'Art de travailler toutes sortes d'alimens pour servir* (ed. 1755). Hachette Livre BNF, 2017
- *Nouveau Traité de la cuisine.* 1739
- Mercier, Louis-Sébastien. *Le tableau de Paris.* La Découverte, 2006
- Mercotte. *Le Meilleur de Mercotte.* Altal, 2016
- Montanay, Jean-Pierre. *Poulpe.* Hachette Cuisine, 2015
- Oliver, Bruno. *La cuisine de mon grand-père.* Alternatives, 2016
- Oliver, Michel. *La cuisine est un jeu d'enfants.* Plon, 1963
- Orieux, Gaël. *Cuisiner la mer; 70 espèces et 90 recettes.* La Martinière, 2016
- Palatin, Suzy. *Cuisine créole, les meilleures recettes.* Hachette Cuisine, 2014
- Pic, Anne-Sophie. *Le Livre blanc d'Anne-Sophie Pic,* Hachette Cuisine, 2012
- Pomiane, Édouard de. *La Cuisine en 10 minutes.* Menu Fretin, 2017
- Reboul, Jean-Baptiste. *La cuisinière provençale* (1897). Tacussel, 2001
- Reynaud, Stéphane. *Cochon & Fils.* Marabout, 2005
- *Terrines.* Marabout, 2009
- Rozières, Babette de. *La cuisine d'Alexandre Dumas par Babette de Rozières.* 2016
- Rubin, Michel. *Le goût de l'agneau; traité de recettes monothéistes, méditerranéennes & moyen-orientales.* Encre d'Orient, 2011
- Simon, François. *Chairs de poule, 200 façons de cuire le poulet.* Agnès Viénot, 2000
- Stromboni, Nicolas. *Du pain, du vin, des oursins.* Marabout, 2016
- This, Hervé. *Les secrets de la casserole.* Belin, 1993
- *Révélations gastronomiques.* Belin, 1995
- Tirel, Guillaume (known as Taillevent). *Le Viandier* (ed. 1892). Hachette Livre BNF, 2012
- Toussaint-Samat, Maguelonne. *La très belle et très exquise histoire des gâteaux et des friandises.* Flammarion, 2004
- Vergé, Roger. *Les légumes, recettes de mon moulin.* Flammarion, 1997
- *Ma Cuisine du soleil.* Robert Laffont, 1999
- Viard, André. *Le cuisinier impérial, ou L'art de faire la cuisine et la pâtisserie* (ed. 1806). Hachette Livre BNF, 2012
- *Le cuisinier royal, ou L'art de faire la cuisine* (ed. 1822). Hachette Livre BNF, 2012
- Vié, Blandine. *Testicules.* L'Épure, 2005
- Viola, Joseph. *La Cuisine canaille.* Hachette Cuisine, 2017
- Violier, Benoît. *La Cuisine du gibier à plumes d'Europe.* Favre, 2015

BOOKS & CULINARY ARTICLES

- Anonymous. *Le Maistre d'Hostel.* 1659
- Anonymous. *Le Mesnagier de Paris* (1393). Le Livre de poche, 1994
- Augereau, Sylvie, and Antoine Gerbelle. *Soif d'aujourd'hui, la compil des vins au naturel.* Tana, 2016
- Baylac, Marie-Hélène. *Dictionnaire Gourmand.* Omnibus, 2014
- Berchoux, Joseph. *La gastronomie, ou L'homme des champs à table* (ed. 1803). Hachette Livre BNF, 2012
- Bertin, François. *Camembert, histoire, gastronomie etétiquettes.* Grand Maison Éditions, 2010
- Blain, Christophe. *En Cuisine avec Alain Passard.* Gallimard, 2015
- Brillat-Savarin, Jean Anthelme. *Physiologie du goût, ou Méditations de gastronomie transcendante.* Champs, Flammarion, 2017
- Brisse, Baron. *Les 366 menus.* 1869
- Buc'hoz, Pierre-Joseph. *L'art alimentaire ou Méthode pour préparer les aliments.* 1787
- Buren, Raymond, Michel Pastoureau, and Jacques Verroust. *Le Cochon. Histoire, symbolique et cuisine du porc.* Sang de la terre, 1987
- Cadet de Gassicourt, Charles-Louis. *Cours gastronomique ou Les diners de Manant-Ville.* 1809
- Carême, Marie-Antoine. *L'art de la cuisine française au xixe siècle.* Menu Fretin, 2015
- Chauvelot, Philippe. *Curnonsky, la saveur d'une époque.* Du Lérot, 2015
- Coffe, Jean-Pierre. *Une vie de Coffe.* Stock, 2015
- Collection, *Fooding, le dico.* Albin Michel, 2004
- Collection, *L'inventaire du Patrimoine culinaire de la France*
- *Alsace.* CNAC, Albin Michel, 1998
- *Auvergne.* CNAC, Albin Michel, 1994, 1998, 2011
- *Bourgogne.* CNAC, Albin Michel, 1993
- *Bretagne.* CNAC, Albin Michel, 1994
- *Languedoc-Roussillon.* CNAC, Albin Michel, 1998
- *Poitou-Charentes.* CNAC, Albin Michel, 1994
- *Rhône-Alpes.* CNAC, Albin Michel, 1995
- Collection. *Les 100 ans du Club des Cent.* Flammarion, 2011
- Coquet, James de. *Propos de table.* Albin Michel, 1984
- Cormier, Jean. *Gueules de chefs.* Éditions du Rocher, 2013
- Corneille, Thomas. *Dictionnaire universel géographique et historique* (ed. 1708). Hachette Livre BNF, 2016
- Couderc, Philippe. *Les plats qui ont fait la France.* Julliard, 1995
- Coulon, Christian. *La table de Montaigne.* Arléa, 2009
- Courtine, Robert Julien. *Un nouveau savoir manger.* Grasset, 1960
- Courty-Siré, Isabelle, Claude Guitard. *Lipp, la brasserie.* Éditions Ramsay, 2006
- Curnonsky, Maurice Edmond Saillant. *Souvenirs littéraires et gastronomiques.* Albin Michel, 1958
- Curnonsky, and Pierre Andrieu. *Les fines gueules de France.* 1935
- Curnonsky, and Marcel Rouff. *La France gastronomique.* 1923
- Curnonsky, and André Saint-Georges. *La table et l'amour, nouveau traité des excitants modernes.* La Clé d'or, 1950
- Delfosse, Claire. *La France fromagère (1850–1990).* La Boutique de l'Histoire Éditions, 2007
- Desgrandchamps, François, and Catherine Donzel. *Cuisine à bord; les plus beaux voyages gastronomiques.* La Martinière, 2011
- Desproges, Pierre. *Encore des nouilles (chroniques culinaires).* Les Échappés, 2014
- Drouard, Alain. "Aperçu historique du costume du cuisinier," *La Revue culinaire.* No. 865, May–June 2010
- Dumas, Alexandre. *Dico Dumas; le grand dictionnaire de cuisine par Alexandre Dumas.* Menu Fretin, 2008
- Dumay, Raymond. *Du silex au barbecue, guide géogastronomique de la France.* Julliard, 1971
- Fantino, Marc. "Le goût du gras; une nouvelle composante gustative," *Revue du Centre de Recherche et d'Information Nutritionnelles.* No. 108, July–August 2008
- Ferniot, Jean. *Carnet de croute.* Robert Laffont, 1980
- Ferniot, Vincent. *Trésors du terroir.* Stock, 1996
- Franck, Bernard. *Portraits et aphorisms.* Le Cherche-Midi, 2001
- Fulbert-Dumonteil, Jean-Camille. *La France gourmande.* 1906
- Fuligni, Bruno. "La Franche mâchonnerie," *Revue 180°C.* No. 4, October 2014
- *Les gastronomes de l'extrême,* Éditions du Trésor, 2015
- Gault, Henri, and Christian Millau. *Garçon, un brancard!* Grasset, 1980

‣Gilliers, Joseph, *Le Cannameliste français* (ed. 1751). Hachette Livre BNF, 2012
‣Gramont, Élisabeth de. *Almanach des bonnes choses de France.* G. Crès, 1920
‣Grimod de la Reynière, Alexandre Balthazar Laurent. *L'almanach des gourmands.* Menu Fretin, 2012
‣*Manuel des amphitryons.* Menu Fretin, 2014
‣*Réflexions philosophiques sur le Plaisir.* Hachette Livre BNF, 2014
‣Gringoire et Saulnier, *Le Répertoire de la cuisine* (1914). Flammarion, 2010
‣Guilbaud, Jean. *Au temps des Halles, marchés et petits métiers.* Sutton, 2007
‣Henryot, Fabienne. *À la table des moines. Ascèse et gourmandise de la Renaissance à la Révolution.* Vuibert, 2015
‣Joignot, Frédéric. "Éloge du gras. Entretien avec le neurobiologiste Jean-Marie Bourrée," fredericjoignot .blogspirit.com
‣Lanarès, Jean-Pierre. *Le Bon Roy Camembert ou l'art populaire dans notre quotidien.* Bréa, 1982
‣Lebeau, Jacques. *Curnonsky, prince des gastronomes, de A à Z.* L'Harmattan, 2014
‣Lebey, Claude. *À Table! La vie intrépide d'un gourmet redoutable.* Albin Michel, 2012
‣Légasse, Périco. *Dictionnaire impertinent de la gastronomie.* François Bourin éditeur, 2012
‣Lelong, Maurice. *Célébration de l'œuf.* Robert Morel, 1962
‣Lesclide, Richard. *Propos de table de Victor Hugo* (ed. 1885). Hachette Livre BNF, 2013
‣Lévi-Strauss, Claude. *Mythologiques.* Plon, 2009
‣Long, Guillaume. *À boire et à manger.* Gallimard, 2012
‣Malouin, Paul-Jacques. *Description et détails des arts du meunier, du vermicellier et du boulenge,* 1767
‣Masui, Kazuko, and Tomoko Yamada. *French Cheeses.* Dorling Kindersley, 1996
‣Mérienne, Patrick. *Atlas des fromages de France.* Ouest France, 2015
‣Mervaud, Christiane. *Voltaire à table.* Desjonqueres, 1998
‣Millau, Christian. *Dictionnaire amoureux de la gastronomie.* Plon, 2008
‣Monselet, Charles. *Lettres gourmandes, manuel de l'home à table*
‣Nignon, Édouard. *L'Heptaméron des gourmets.* Régis Lehoucq editor, 1919
‣*Les plaisirs de la table.* Menu Fretin, 2016
‣*Éloges de la cuisine française.* Menu Fretin, 2014
‣Oliver, Raymond. *Célébration de la nouille.* Robert Morel editor, 1965
‣Onfray, Michel. *La Raison gourmande.* Le Livre de poche, 1997
‣*Le ventre des philosophes.* Livre de poche, 1990
‣Passard, Alain, Catherine Delvaux, and Olivier Ploton. *Le meilleur du potager.* Larousse, 2012
‣Pastoureau, Michel. *Le Cochon. Histoire d'un cousin mal aimé.* Gallimard, 2009
‣Payany, Estérelle. "Le gras, c'est le goût," *Atlas de la France gourmande.* Autrement, 2016
‣Payen, Anselme. *Des substances alimentaires et des moyens de les améliorer, de les conserver et d'en reconnaître les alterations.* Hachette Livre BNF, 2017
‣Pendergrast, Mark. *For God, Country & Coca-Cola: The Definitive History of the Great American Soft Drink and the Company That Makes It.* Basic Books, 1993
‣Perrier-Robert, Annie. *Dictionnaire de la gourmandize.* Robert Laffont, 2012
‣Peters-Desteract, Madeleine. *Pain, bière et toutes bonnes choses . . . L'alimentation dans l'Égypte ancienne.* Éditions du Rocher, 2005
‣Petitrenaud, Jean-Luc. *La France du casse-croûte.* Hachette, 1995
‣Pitte, Jean-Robert. *Gastronomie française. Histoire et géographie d'une passion.* Fayard, 1991
‣Pivot, Bernard. *Dictionnaire amoureux du vin.* Plon, 2006
‣Poilâne, Lionel. *Guide de l'amateur de pain.* Robert Laffont, 1991
‣Pomiane, de, Édouard. *Radio Cuisine.* Menu Fretin, 2016
‣Pudlowski, Gilles. *À quoi sert vraiment un critique gastronomique?* Armand Colin, 2011
‣*Les guides Pudlo,* Michel Lafon
‣Rambourg, Patrick. *À table . . . le menu.* Honoré Champion, 2013
‣*Histoire de la cuisine et de la gastronomie françaises.* Tempus, Perrin, 2010
‣*L'art et la table.* Citadelles & Mazenod, 2016
‣Revel, Jean-François. *Un festin en paroles.* Texto, 2007
‣Rouff, Marcel. *La vie et la passion de Dodin-Bouffant, gourmet.* Sillage, 2010

‣Rousseau, Vanessa. *Le goût du sang.* Armand Colin, 2005
‣Roux, Éric. "Changement de gras!" observatoirecuisinespopulaires.fr
‣Rudder, de, Orlando. *Aux Petits Oignons! Cuisine et nourriture dans les expressions de la langue française.* Larousse, 2006
‣Sarran, Michel. "Le gras, sixième saveur?" leplus.nouvelobs .com, July 31, 2015
‣Schneider, Jean-Baptiste, and Éric Vallier. *Le Canard de Duclair; d'une production locale à un rayonnement Mondial.* Université François Rabelais de Tour, 2012
‣Simmonds, Peter Lund. *The Curiosities of Food.* 1859
‣Simon, François. *Comment se faire passer pour un critique gastronomique sans rien y connaître.* Albin Michel, 2001
‣Staffe, Blanche (known as Baronne Staffe). *Usages du Monde; règles du savoir-vivre dans la société moderne* (ed. 1891). Hachette Livre BNF, 2012
‣Stéfanini, Laurent, under the direction of, *À la table des diplomates.* L'Iconoclaste, 2016
‣Taber, George M. *Le Jugement de Paris; Le jour où les vins californiens surclassèrent les grands crus français.* Éditions Gutenberg, 2008
‣Tendret, Lucien. *La Table au pays de Brillat-Savarin.* Menu Fretin, 2014
‣This, Hervé. "Éloge de la graisse," *Pour la Science.* No. 231, January 1997, p. 13
‣This, Hervé, Tatiana Lissitzky. "Et si vous adoptiez la cuisson au lave-vaisselle?" *Ouest France,* October 21, 2015
‣Ude, Louis-Eustache. *The French Cook.* 1813

———— OTHER SOURCES ————

‣Anonymous, *Il cuoco Piemontese perfezionato a Parigi.* 1766
‣Bazot, Étienne-François. *Manuel du franc-maçon.* 1817
‣Boileau, Étienne. *Les métiers et les corporations de Paris; xiiie siècle. Le livre des métiers.* Hachette Livre BNF, 2012
‣Chevallier, Pierre. *Histoire de la Franc-maçonnerie française.* Fayard, 1974
‣Cuvier, Georges. *Le règne animal distribué d'après son organization.* 1817
‣Delord, Taxile. *Les petits-Paris. Paris-étranger* (ed. 1854). Hachette Livre BNF, 2016
‣Freeman, Frederick. *The History of Cape Cod.* 1858
‣Girard, Xavier. "La soupe des morts," *La pensée de midi.* Actes Sud, number 13, July 2004
‣Jode, Marc de, Monique and Jean-Marc Cara, *Dictionnaire universel de la Franc-Maçonnerie.* Larousse, 2011
‣La Roque, Jean de. *Le Voyage de l'Arabie Heureuse.* 1715
‣Lamothe-Langon, Étienne-Léon de. *Mémoires et souvenirs d'un pair de France.* Hachette Livre BNF, 2016
‣Michel, Adolphe. *Le siège de Paris; 1870–1871.* Hachette Livre BNF, 2012
‣Miot, Henry. *La Gazette des campagnes.* 1870
‣Mistral, Frédéric. *Lou Tresor dou Felibrige, Dictionnaire provençal français.* Éditions des régionalismes, 2014
‣Société d'agriculture, Sciences et Arts, *Revue agricole, industrielle et littéraire du Nord.* 1885, p. 168
‣Nemeitz, Joachim Christoph. *Séjour de Paris pour les voyageurs de condition.* 1718
‣Pérau, Gabriel-Louis. *L'Ordre des Francs-maçons trahi.* 1745
‣Smollett, Tobias. *Voyages à travers la France et l'Italie.* José Corti, 1994
‣Von Kotzebue, August. *Souvenirs de Paris* (ed. 1804). Hachette Livre BNF, 2016

———— LITERATURE ————

‣Apollinaire, *Œuvres poétiques,* "Le repas," La Pléiade, 1956
‣Balzac, Honoré de. *Albert Savarus.* Le Livre de poche, 2015
‣*La Muse du Département, La Comédie humaine.* Volume 4, La Pléiade, 1976
‣*La Peau de Chagrin.* Le Livre de poche, 1972
‣*La Rabouilleuse, La Comédie humaine.* Volume 4, La Pléiade, 1976
‣*Le Cousin Pons.* Le Livre de poche, 1973
‣*Le Lys dans la vallée.* Le Livre de poche, 1972
‣*Le Message, La Comédie humaine.* Volume 2, La Pléiade, 1976
‣*Le Père Goriot.* Le Livre de poche, 2004
‣*Les Employés, La Comédie humaine.* Volume 7, La Pléiade, 1977
‣*Les Illusions perdues.* Le Livre de poche, 2008
‣*Les Petits bourgeois, La Comédie humaine.* Volume 8, La Pléiade, 1978
‣*Physiologie du marriage.* Folio, 1987
‣*Traité des excitants modernes.* Berg International, 2015
‣*Un début dans la vie, La Comédie humaine.* Volume 1, La Pléiade, 1976

‣*Une fille d'Ève, La Comédie humaine.* Volume 2, La Pléiade, 1976
‣Barthes, Roland. *Mythologies.* Points, Seuil, 2014
‣Baudelaire, Charles. *Les Fleurs du Mal,* "L'âme du Vin." Le Livre De Poche, 1972
‣Beauvoir, de, Simone. *Entretiens avec Jean-Paul Sartre.* Folio, 1987
‣Bernanos, George. *La Joie.* Le Castor astral, 2011
‣Blixen, Karen. *Le festin de Babette.* Folio, 2008
‣Buffon, *Histoire naturelle.* Second edition in-12°, volume VI, 1769
‣Cioran, Emil. *De la France.* Carnets de L'Herne, 2009
‣Claudel, Paul. *L'Endormie.* Théâtre, volume I, La Pléiade, 2011
‣Colette, *Colette journaliste; Chroniques et reportages.* Seuil, 2010
‣"La vigne, le vin," *Prisons et Paradis.* Le Livre de poche, 2004
‣*Les vrilles de la vigne.* Le Livre de poche, 1995
‣Deleuze, Gilles. *Abécédaire.* 1988
‣*Dictionnaire de Trévoux.* 1752
‣Diderot, D'Alembert, *Encyclopédie.* 1st edition, 1765
‣Dumas, Alexandre. *Les Trois Mousquetaires.* Le Livre de poche, 2011
‣*Le Vicomte de Bragelonne.* Le Livre de poche, 2010
‣Flaubert, Gustave. *Salammbô.* Folio, 2005
‣Foucault, Michel. *Histoire de la sexualité.* Gallimard, 1997
‣Gide, André. *Journal.* Folio, 2012
‣*Les Nourritures terrestres.* Folio, 1972
‣Giono, Jean. *Colline.* Le Livre de poche, 1967
‣Goscinny, René, and Albert Uderzo. *Astérix en Corse*
‣*Astérix et les Normands*
‣*Le bouclier Arverne*
‣*Le tour de Gaule d'Astérix*
‣Harrison, Jim. *Aventures d'un gourmand vagabond.* Christian Bourgeois, 2002
‣*Dalva.* 10/18, 1991
‣*Entre chien et loup.* 10/18, 1994
‣*Légendes d'automne.* 10/18, 2010
‣Hugo, Victor. *5e agenda de Guernesey,* January 19, 1863
‣*Choses vues.* Le Livre de poche, 2013
‣*Les Misérables.* Le Livre de poche, 1998
‣Jullien, Dominique. "La Cuisine de Georges Perec," *Littérature.* No. 129, 2003, p. 3–14
‣Lambert, Jean. *Gide familier.* Julliard, 1958
‣Le Breton, Auguste. *Razzia sur la chnouf.* Série Noire/ Gallimard 1954
‣Le Tellier, Hervé. *Les Amnésiques n'ont rien vécu d'inoubliable.* Le Castor astral, 1997
‣Maupassant, de, Guy. "Le Vieux," *Contes et Nouvelles.* Volume 1, La Pléiade, 1974
‣*La Parure.* Le Livre de poche, 1995
‣Mirbeau, Octave. *Chroniques du diable.* Belles Lettres, 1995
‣Montaigne, *Essais.* Folio, 2009
‣Pagnol, Marcel. *Judas.* Éditions de Fallois, 2017
‣Perec, George. *La Disparation.* Gallimard, 1989
‣*La Vie mode d'emploi.* Le Livre de poche, 1980
‣*Les Choses.* Pocket, 2006
‣*Penser/Classer.* Points, 2015
‣Platon, *Lois.* GF, Flammarion, 2006
‣Pline l'Ancien, *Histoire naturelle.* Folio, 1999
‣Prévert, Jaques. *Paroles.* Folio, 1976
‣Proust, Marcel. *À la recherche du temps perdu.* La Pléiade, 1987
‣Rabelais, François. *Cinquieme livre.* Points, 1997
‣*Gargantua.* Le Livre de poche, 1994
‣*Pantagruel.* Le Livre de poche, 1979
‣Rey, Alain. *Dictionnaire historique de la langue française.* Le Robert, 2011
‣Richelet, Pierre. *Dictionnaire françois* (ed. 1706). Hachette Livre BNF, 2013
‣Rigolot, François. *Les langages de Rabelais.* Droz, 2000
‣Rimbaud, Arthur. "Les Effarés," *Poésies completes.* Le Livre de poche, 1998
‣Ronsard, de, Pierre. *Odes, Œuvres completes.* La Pléiade, 1993
‣Rousseau, Jean-Jacques. *Émile ou de l'éducation.* GF Flammarion, 2009
‣Saint-Amant, Marc-Antoine Girard de. *Œuvres complètes.* "Le Melon," Hachette Livre BNF, 2012
‣Sévigné, Madame de. *Lettres de l'année 1671.* Folio, 2012
‣Tite-Live [Titus Livy], *Histoire romaine.* GF Flammarion, 1999
‣Verne, Jules. *20 000 lieues sous les mers.* Le Livre de poche, 1976
‣*Michel Strogoff.* Le Livre de poche, 1974
‣Voltaire, *Dictionnaire philosophique.* Hachette Livre BNF, 2013
‣Zola, Émile. *L'Assommoir.* Le Livre de poche, 1971
‣*Le Ventre de Paris.* Le Livre de poche, 1971

Contributors

ANDRIEU, JULIE
Food journalist, host of television and radio food programs

AUGEREAU, SYLVIE
Wine writer, wine grower, columnist for *On Va Déguster* and founder of la Dive Bouteille (a wine-tasting room in Saumur)

BACHÈS, BÉNÉDICTE AND MICHEL
Citrus growers in Eus (Pyrénées-Orientales)

BAUD, NATHALIE
An editorial coordinator, she pours her entire heart into her work, and anticipates and organizes everything. But she also loves food and prides herself on keeping "chef" François-Régis in line!

BAUD, PIERRE
Fig grower in Vaison-la-Romaine (Vaucluse)

BAUD, ROBERT
A scholar, he contributes his efforts to the revival of the regionally renowned ancient vineyard in Le Moutherot (Doubs).

BERGER (LEFORT), JÉRÔME
A gourmet columnist for 15 years who shops the markets, eats out, and cooks at home for his wife

BIENASSIS, LOÏC
Historian, works at the Institut Européen d'Histoire et des Cultures de l'Alimentation (European Institute of Food History), University of Tours

BIZALION, MARIE-AMAL
Raised on olive oil and raw cream between Lebanon, Morocco, and La Creuse, she became a journalist to invade kitchens and faraway countries with *L'Express*, *Le Figaro Magazine*, and others.

BLACK, KÉDA
Whatever you have a craving for, she will be happy to cook it for you. Or she will tell you in her own delicious words how to prepare it yourself.

BOUTIN, ALAIN
Puxisardinophile (collector of sardine cans) and seafood grocer (La Petite Chaloupe, Paris 13th)

BOYER, BLANDINE
This curious and self-taught woman of words, herbs, and plants harvests local products to create natural and instinctively prepared food in the heart of a Cévennes bamboo plantation populated by wild boars.

BRANLARD, JEAN-PAUL
University attorney, lecturer, author, and columnist, specializing in food, culinary, and gastronomy law

BRAS, MICHEL
Chef of Le Suquet in Laguiole (Aveyron); achieved three Michelin stars in 1999

BRUNEL, JACQUES
Journalist on the art of living, ex-food critic for Gault & Millau, and former night owl for *Figaroscope*

BRYS, YANN
Creator of the *tourbillon* (turntable), Best Craftsman of France (MOF) in Pastry 2011

CAMDEBORDE, YVES
One of the leaders of bistronomy (bistro dining), native of southwest France along with his mentor Christian Constant Ardéchoise

CHOUGUI, NADIA
Production manager of *On Va Déguster* on France Inter

COHEN, ALAIN
Fruit and vegetable sourcer at Le Comptoir des Producers

CONSTANT, CHRISTIAN
A proud native of southwest France who, as a trainer of great chefs, regales us with his cooking style, which ranges from rustic to chic

CONTICINI, PHILIPPE
Pastry chef who helped launch Pâtisserie des Rêves pastry shop after creating, among other things, its *verrines*, or desserts in a glass

COURTY, HIPPOLYTE
Founder of L'Arbre à Café who, since 2009, has established a new French "art of the café" based on excellence, biodynamics, and a network of local food suppliers

COUSIN, JILL
A culinary journalist and devotee of the coffee–Roquefort cheese pairing for breakfast, she is always in search of the best baker in France!

DAGUIN, ARNAUD, AND AGNÈS DEVILLE
Friends since childhood and now a loving couple; he a liberated adman and she a food journalist; they sharpened their knives to assist with *Let's Eat France!*

DARROZE, HÉLÈNE
Named best female chef in the world in 2015 and one of the only Michelin-starred female chefs, she divides her time between her restaurants in Paris and London.

DE CERVAL, GWILHERM
Sommelier at Ritz Paris and Le Royal Monceau Raffles Paris; food critic for *Guide Lebey*; wine journalist for *L'Express/L'Express Styles*

DE SAINT-MAURICE, THIBAUT
Professor of philosophy and lover of all foods (especially the lemon tart)

DELMAS, LAURENT
Journalist and film critic on France Inter. The rest of the time, this gourmand is dreaming of all things gastronomic.

DEZEUSTRE, LÉO
Expert in wines and spirits, works at Compagnie des Vins Surnaturels

DORR, GARRY
Connoisseur of fish and seafood, owner of the Le Bar à Huîtres restaurants in Paris

DOUCET, BRUNO
Bistro chef at La Régalade in Paris

DUBOUÉ, JULIEN
Landais chef heading five restaurants in Paris, including A. Noste and its most recent opening to date, Corn'R, dedicated to corn

DUCASSE, ALAIN
This chef from the Landes is at the head of the three-star restaurants the Plaza Athénée (Paris 8th) and Le Louis XV (Monaco).

DUMAS, JULIEN
Chef of Lucas Carton, the gastronomic institution located at Place de la Madeleine (Paris 8th)

DUMOTIER, SÉBASTIEN
Specialist of tarts. There was even once a sign indicating this.

DUPONT, DÉBORAH
Gabber, unconditional gourmet, reader and tester of recipes, and owner of one of the most popular reference cookbook stores in Paris, Librairie Gourmand, creating happy taste buds

EZGULIAN, SONIA
Always cooking up little things that improve everyday life. She directs her culinary ingenuity toward the antiwaste cause.

FERREUX-MAEGHT, ANGÈLE
Angèle has a passion for plants and their benefits. Chef at La Guinguette, she uses plants in all her dishes in her small restaurant—marrying healthy eating with gourmet preparations.

FEUILLAS, ROLAND
Rustic baker in Cucugnan, founder of Maîtres de Mon Moulin

FRACHOT, WILLIAM
Chef since 1999 at the Hostellerie du Chapeau Rouge in Dijon, where he achieved his first and second Michelin star

FRANZO, ÉMILIE
Blogger, author, photographer, and food stylist. With her, there is never a single stray crumb!

FRÉCHET, MARIE-LAURE
Originally from the north of France, and a fierce defender of the northern terroir and its chefs. A culinary journalist, she loves tasting food just as much as she loves writing about it.

FRECHON, ÉRIC
Three-star chef of Épicure, the restaurant at the Hôtel Bristol in Paris

FULIGNI, BRUNO
Lecturer at Sciences Po, he has published thirty books and writes the column "Les archives de la cuisine" in the publication *180°C.*

GAGNAIRE, PIERRE
A cook for 50 years. He considers cooking a (modest) art centered around relationships, sincerity, tenderness, and generosity—giving flavor to life.

GAGNEZ, JÉRÔME
An expert in wines and spirits, founder of *Vers le vin*

GAUDARD, SÉBASTIEN
Head pastry chef on rue des Martyrs (Paris 9th) and a salon de thé in the Tuileries (Paris 1st)

GAUDRY, FRANÇOIS-RÉGIS
The *Let's Eat France!* ringleader

GAUDRY, MARIELLE
An insatiable devourer of food, she suffers from FOMO (Fear of Missing Out) when it comes to the cultural experiences of eating good.

GAUTHIER, ALEXANDRE
Chef at La Grenouillère, near Montreuil-sur-Mer (Pas-de-Calais), a family restaurant he took over in 2003

GENIN, JACQUES
Self-taught fan of cacao. He now focuses solely on confections and chocolates after having worked for a while in pastry.

GERBELLE, ANTOINE
Journalist, editor of TellementenSoif.tv, the first online TV channel covering wine. Author of *Soif d'Aujourd'hui*. Columnist for *On Va Déguster.*

GODART, FLEUR
A promoter of poultry from her family farm and of the wines she loves. She coproduced the comic *Pur Jus* with Justine Saint-Lô.

GONZALES, HADRIEN
Journalist, coordinates the "À table" page of *Le Figaro*. Passionate about culture and the art of living, with a curious mind and a smile on his face, he also writes for *L'Express* and *Paris Worldwide et France.*

GOUJARD, ALEXIS
A backpacker through vineyards for over 10 years who tastes a few thousand wines each year and tells their story in *La Revue du vin de France*. Co-author of *Guide des meilleurs vins de France.*

GRASSER HERMÉ, FRÉDÉRICK E. (KNOWN AS "FEGH")
A citizen of taste with a strong temperament. Makes soft noodles à la Dalí, cooks merguez sausages on the exhaust pipe of a Harley, and makes Coca-Cola chicken . . . just about anything!

GROLET, CÉDRIC
Pastry chef at the Meurice (Paris 1st). Fruits are his trademark.

HENRY, JULIEN
Beekeeper and director of La Maison du Miel in Paris (founded in 1898), he specializes in the selection of honey-making crops for the culinary world.

HERMÉ, PIERRE
An inexhaustible source of gourmandise. Guided simply by his desire to provide pleasure, he has created his own universe of flavors while defying convention.

JEAN-PIERRE, CHRISTIAN
A lover of cherries, which he grows in the basin of Céret (Pyrénées-Orientales)

JÉGU, PIERRICK
Journalist-author, specializing in gastronomy and wine. Collaborator at *L'Express, Saveurs, 180°C, 12°5, Yam, Revue du Vin de France*, etc.

KASPROWICZ, THIERRY
Author of *Guide Kaspro*, the premier food guide of Réunion. He also pens about the riches of the island's soils in the magazine *Mets Plaisirs.*

LALY BARAGLIOLI, FRÉDÉRIC
Gourmand of food, words, and landscapes, enchanted by Corsican and Mediterranean flavors. He loves reading recipes as if they are poems or geographical fables.

LARCHER, BERTRAND
Chef and Breton businessman, he owns several Breizh Cafés in Paris, Cancale, Saint-Malo, and Tokyo.

LAURENT, AGNÈS
Journalist at *L'Express*

LASTRE, YOHAN
Pâté en croute world champion

LE BOURDAT, FABRICE
Pastry chef at Le Blé Sucré (Paris 12th), inventor of the giant madeleine XXL, intended for sharing

LE FEUVRE, DELPHINE
Young journalist, addicted to sweets, American TV, and Instagram. Swears by salted butter.

LEBRUN, PIERRE-BRICE
Belgian by birth. With time spent in Paris and eventually landing in Landes, he writes gourmet books, teaches law, and cares for his hydrangeas.

LEDEUIL, WILLIAM
Chef at Ze Kitchen Galerie and KGB. In 2017 he opened his third location dedicated to pasta and broth: Kitchen Ter(re).

LEDRU-JOHANSSON, ALVINA
Gourmet journalist raised on Swedish meatballs and French cheeses. She holds the CAP and a passion for cooking in one hand, and a curiosity and unforgiving appetite in the other.

LENARTOWICZ, ESTELLE
A culinary journalist and vegan apprentice living among the roofs of Montmartre. She loves pasta, Chablis, and Marcel Proust.

LIGNAC, CYRIL
A multifaceted chef in cooking, pastry, and chocolate, he heads many Parisian establishments.

LONG, GUILLAUME
Comic book author, Sunday cook, and eclectic gourmet. *À boire et à manger* (4 volumes).

LOUBET, ÉDOUARD
Chef at La Bastide de Capelongue (Vaucluse), in the heart of Provence

MARIONNET, PASCAL
Plant cultivator, strawberry grower, and grandson of the inventor of the Mara des Bois strawberry

MARQUES, GEORGES
Possessor of the most beautiful confectionery collection in France, on display in his shop, Le Bonbon au Palais (Paris 5th)

MASSON, ELVIRA
Historical columnist for *On Va Déguster* on France Inter and for the *Très Très Bon* television show on Paris Première

MATHIAS, XAVIER
Organic farmer passionate about diversity and helping spread its benefits. An author and instructor involved in many projects.

MAXIMIN, JACQUES
A great figure of Mediterranean cuisine, he worked on the Riviera before taking the flavors of the sea to his friend Alain Ducasse, at Rech (Paris 17th).

MERCOTTE
Savoyard blogger, combining desserts and judging on the program *Meilleur Pâtissier* (*The Best Pastry Chef*) alongside Cyril Lignac (on M6 France)

MICHALAK, CHRISTOPHE
Pastry chef, formerly at the Plaza Athénée (Paris 8th), who has now opened his own pastry shops

MOILIM, JORDAN
Journalist for *Très Très Bon*. The youngster of the *On Va Déguster* clan: sneakers on his feet, a fork in his pocket, and always a few crumbs in his beard.

ORY, PASCAL
Professor at the Sorbonne, author of *Discours gastronomique français des origines à nos jours et de l'Identité passe à table*. Formerly a food critic; remains a gourmand.

OTTAVI, JEAN-ANTOINE
Gourmet, gourmand, passionate about gastronomy, resident of Corsica

OUDARD, VALENTINE
Gourmet journalist who takes her fork with her into greasy spoons and pastry shops for the program *Très Très Bon*

PALATIN, SUZY
A top-notch cook, fries expert, and cook of West Indian specialties, chocolate cake, and much more

PASSARD, ALAIN
Chef and owner of L'Arpège restaurant (Paris 7th)

PATIN O'COOHOON, CHARLES
Journalist at *L'Express*, editor in chief of *Très Très Bon*. François-Régis Gaudry's dining partner who loves any style of cooking and dining, from wooden spoons to silver cutlery.

PAYANY, ESTÉRELLE
Journalist, critic, author, and gourmet

PHAM, ANNE-LAURE
Food journalist, director of operations at FemininBio, and cookbook writer specializing in craft beer and "green" food

PIC, ANNE-SOPHIE
First female chef to obtain three Michelin stars at Maison Pic in Valence (Drôme)

PIEGAY, BAPTISTE
Editor in chief of *L'Officiel Hommes*. At age 39, he still hasn't identified what his favorite dish is, but that's so much the better.

PIERINI, ALESSANDRA
Italian grocer in love with good products and their history, she travels up and down her country in search of rare finds.

PIERRARD, CAMILLE
Columnist at *Fooding*, Camille is always looking for the best tables, and has cultivated a passion for Saint-Nectaire cheese.

PIERRE, ELISABETH
Independent zythologist, specializing in beer and food pairing, author of *Guide Hachette des Bières et Choisir et acheter sa bière en 7 secondes*

PIÈVE, SÉBASTIEN
Faithful friend and faithful listener-reader of *On Va Déguster*, passionate about the heritage and history of France, a fan of all the culinary riches of France

PRALUS, FRANÇOIS
Holder of the secret of Praluline, invented by his father in Roanne, one of the few artisan chocolatiers to make his own chocolate

PYTEL, GILBERT
Columnist and freelance journalist in love with sweets: cakes, desserts, tarts, chocolates, ice creams, confectionery, cookies, etc.

RAMBOURG, PATRICK
Culinary historian, writer of *L'Art et la table* and *Histoire de la cuisine et de la gastronomie françaises*

RENAUT, EMMANUEL
Originally from Savoie, chef of Flocons de Sel, a three-star restaurant located on the peaks in Megève (Haute-Savoie)

REYNAUD, STÉPHANE
Hailing from a family of butchers and pig farmers, he is an author (of many books), composer (of recipes for Teyssier), and interpreter (in his restaurant in London).

RICHEZ-LEROUGE, VÉRONIQUE
Journalist specializing in dairy products and agricultural matters, she surveys every nook and cranny of the land to safeguard living food heritage.

ROBUCHON, JOËL
The most Michelin-starred chef in the Michelin Guide! Since the early 2000s, he has opened "Ateiler Joël Robuchon" around the world.

ROELLINGER, OLIVIER
Multistar chef, passionate about spices

ROUX, ÉRIC
Journalist, sociologist, and author, expert of popular cuisines

RUBIN, EMMANUEL
A "child of the pan" (his father and mother are restaurateurs), he scribed his first chronicles at age 12, and eventually became a journalist. The cofounder of *Fooding*, he continues to write while eating (and eat while writing) at *Figaro* (a lot) and elsewhere (often).

RUBIN, MICHEL
Author of cookbooks, former president of the Cercle Suédois in Paris

RYON, JÉRÔME
Chef of the restaurant La Barbacane in Carcassonne (Aude)

SAINT-LÔ, JUSTINE
Graduate of the Émile Cohl School and UWE of Bristol. She designs the labels of her brother's wine and coproduces the comic *Pur Jus* with Fleur Godart.

SAMMUT, JULIA
Grocer in Marseille (L'Idéal), a collector of products from the Mediterranean and elsewhere, she is the author of the book *Kalamata, une histoire de famille et de cuisine*.

SAVOY, GUY
At the head of restaurant Guy Savoy (Paris 6th) since 1980, he opened another location in Las Vegas, and three other Parisian establishments.

SÉMINEL, LAURENT
Graphic designer, photographer, and cofounder of *Omnivore* before creating *G'mag* in 2011. He is the founder and director of Éditions Menu Fretin.

SOLIER, STÉPHANE
Cousin of François-Régis Gaudry, associate professor of classic and gourmet literature, and an insatiable lover of Corsican flavors, who has "fallen into the pot" of Italian cuisine

SOLIER-GAUDRY, DENISE
Mother of François-Régis Gaudry as well as a home cook specializing in Corsican peasant cuisine, bourgeois Lyonnais cooking, and everyday cooking

SONTAG, ÉRIC
He was the pastry chef of Crayères in Reims (Marne) for ten years before opening his own shop.

SOUNDIRAM, MINA
Journalist, streetfoodista of *Très Très Bon* on Paris Première, fluent in chicken curry

STROMBONI, NICOLAS
Owner and manager of Chemin des Vignobles, wine cellar and wine bar in Ajaccio

TOLMER, MICHEL
Studied graphic arts and advocates for natural French wines (meaning organic and without chemicals)

TORRE, FÉLIX
Corsican pig breeder

TROCHON, ÉRIC
Chef, culinary advisor, and teacher

TROISGROS, MICHEL
After taking over the family business in Roanne (Loire) after the death of his uncle in 1983, he moved to Ouches (Loire) in 2017.

VANHAMME, ARNAUD
Best Craftsman of France (MOF) fishmonger-oyster seller, he owns a market selling fish and prepared foods (Paris 16th).

VAXELAIRE, BERNARD
Native of the Vosges, chef at Le Bistrot à Deux Têtes (Paris 9th)

VINCENTI, AURORE
A sharp linguist and gourmande

IMAGE CREDITS

Originally published in French as *On Va Déguster La France*
Copyright © Hachette Livre (Marabout), Paris, 2017

Translated from the French by Zachary R. Townsend

Library of Congress Cataloging-in-Publication Data

Names: Gaudry, François-Régis, author.
Title: Let's eat France / François-Régis Gaudry.
Other titles: Pourquoi manger la France? English | François-Régis Gaudry &
    friends present let's eat France
Description: New York : Artisan, a division of Workman Publishing Co., Inc.,
    [2018] | Translation of: Pourquoi manger la France? | Includes index.
Identifiers: LCCN 2018024631 | ISBN 9781579658762 (hardcover : alk. paper)
Subjects: LCSH: Cooking, French. | LCGFT: Cookbooks.
Classification: LCC TX719 .G31513 2018 | DDC 641.5944—dc23
LC record available at https://lccn.loc.gov/2018024631

Book design by Marabout
Cover illustration by Aurore Carric

Published by Artisan
A division of Workman Publishing Co., Inc.
225 Varick Street
New York, NY 10014-4381
artisanbooks.com

Artisan is a registered trademark of Workman Publishing Co., Inc.

Published simultaneously in Canada by Thomas Allen & Son, Limited

Printed in China

First printing, October 2018

10 9 8 7 6 5 4 3 2 1

MARABOUT
s'engage pour l'environnement
en réduisant l'empreinte carbone
de ses livres.
Celle de cet exemplaire est de :
6200 g éq. CO$_2$
Rendez-vous sur
www.marabout-durable.fr

PAPIER À BASE DE
FIBRES CERTIFIÉES